Religions of the World
Second Edition

Religions of the World

Second Edition

A COMPREHENSIVE ENCYCLOPEDIA OF BELIEFS AND PRACTICES

Volume Six: S–Z

J. GORDON MELTON
MARTIN BAUMANN
Editors

TODD M. JOHNSON
World Religious Statistics

DONALD WIEBE
Introduction

ABC-CLIO

Santa Barbara, California • Denver, Colorado • Oxford, England

Library of Congress Cataloging-in-Publication Data

Religions of the world : a comprehensive encyclopedia of beliefs and practices / J. Gordon Melton, Martin Baumann, editors ; Todd M. Johnson, World Religious Statistics ; Donald Wiebe, Introduction. — 2nd ed.
    p. cm.
  Includes bibliographical references and index.
  ISBN 978-1-59884-203-6 — ISBN 978-1-59884-204-3
  1. Religions—Encyclopedias. I. Melton, J. Gordon. II. Baumann, Martin.
  BL80.3.R45 2010
  200.3—dc22   2010029403

ISBN: 978-1-59884-203-6
EISBN: 978-1-59884-204-3

14 13 12 11 10   1 2 3 4 5

This book is also available on the World Wide Web as an eBook.
Visit www.abc-clio.com for details.

ABC-CLIO, LLC
130 Cremona Drive, P.O. Box 1911
Santa Barbara, California 93116-1911

This book is printed on acid-free paper ∞
Manufactured in the United States of America

Contents

A–Z List of Entries

Note: Core essays are indicated with the symbol ◆; country essays are indicated with the symbol ■.

Volume Two

Volume Five

Volume Six

Religions of the World

Second Edition

A COMPREHENSIVE ENCYCLOPEDIA
OF BELIEFS AND PRACTICES

Volume Six: S–Z

S

Sabbatarianism

Within Christianity, Sabbatarianism is the belief that the seventh-day Sabbath of Judaism as a day of worship has not been replaced by first-day or Sunday worship, observed by the great majority of Christians. Jewish law stipulates that from sundown on Friday evening until sundown on Saturday, Jews should be in a state of observing and remembering the Shabbat, the Hebrew term for the Sabbath. Observing the Shabbat is rooted in the book of Genesis in the Hebrew Bible (the Christian Old Testament). The creation story tells of God's activity for six days, followed by a seventh day of rest. This fact is then cited in the Ten Commandments as the reason for the Jewish people to keep the Sabbath, meaning that one remembers God's creation and, like God, observes a day of rest every seven days. Rest is equated with refraining from doing various prohibited activities and engaging in prescribed activities such as worship and study of scripture.

The major prohibited activity, work, was defined and described in some detail by rabbis. It included the preparation of food to be consumed on the Shabbat on the previous day, and a provision to set aside observation of the day if a human life was at stake.

Christianity was born within Judaism. Jesus was a Jew, as were the 12 Apostles. Jesus' teachings include his reflections on Sabbath activity, and as the church grew and non-Jewish membership became dominant and then overwhelming, the designation of the primary day for worship and the nature of Christian observation of the Jewish law, including provisions for rest on the Sabbath, were much debated. Crucial to decision making was an assumption by Christians that Christ's resurrection occurred on a Sunday morning. As a result, the day for weekly worship was Sunday, and the command to keep the Sabbath reinterpreted as now applying to Sunday. As the Julian calendar replaced the Jewish calendar, the beginning of Sunday was at midnight rather than sundown on the previous day.

For those who read the Bible literally and attempted to live by its precepts, the command to keep the Sabbath became a recurring and periodically nagging question. Most accepted the dominant interpretation that Sunday had become the new Sabbath due to the resurrection. However, a minority reached an alternative conclusion.

A new Sabbatarian impulse began, for example, among Anabaptists in 16th-century Europe. Oswald Glait and Andreas Fisher, both former Catholic priests, began to propagate Sabbatarianism around 1528 in Moravia, Silesia, and Bohemia. Glait wrote a booklet on the subject, known today only from the refutation of it by Caspar Schewenckfeld (1487–1581). By mid-century in England, as the Reformation spread, individual believers felt a freedom to ask a variety of questions that arose from their reading of the Bible. The viability of keeping the seventh-day Sabbath, the proper behavior for a Sabbath rest, and the role of government in enforcing the Sabbath came under consideration. Given the heightened authority of the scriptures within Protestantism and the accompanying diminution of church tradition by the Reformers, those who defended the centrality of Sunday were often baffled by the lack of any mention of Sunday worship in the New Testament.

The first Christian congregation organized to keep a seventh-day Sabbath arose in 1617 in London under the leadership of John Trask. It was an independent Baptist church whose Sabbatarianism further called the public's attention to its many departures from the norms of the Church of England. However, the movement started by Trask survived, and by the end of the century some 15 Sabbatarian congregations existed. Meanwhile, Stephen Mumford (ca.1639–1707) traveled to the American colonies and in 1664 joined the Baptist Church in Newport, Rhode Island. Through the rest of the decade he raised the Sabbath question among his brethren but finally became frustrated with their disinterest. In 1671 he opened the first Seventh Day Baptist church in the British American colonies. Others followed Mumford's example in New Jersey and Pennsylvania. The Sabbatarian issue slow gained traction, primarily among Baptists. It had its most unique embodiment in the cloistered communal Ephrata Society formed in rural Pennsylvania by Conrad Beissel (1690–1768), who also led in the spreading of Sabbatarianism among German Pietists in southeastern Pennsylvania. A small German-speaking Seventh Day Baptist work continued into the 20th century, though it never consisted of more than a few congregations.

A national organization for English-speaking Sabbatarian Baptists emerged in 1801 with the formation of the Seventh Day Baptist General Conference. In 1843, a missionary society was formed, and sent its first missionaries into a newly opened China. As the movement spread internationally through the 20th century, a World Federation of Seventh Day Baptist Conferences was formed in 1965. Everywhere it exists, it is a minority movement among Baptists.

The most important development in Sabbatarianism occurred in the 1840s, when Joseph Bates (1792–1872), a Seventh Day Baptist, introduced the practice to the Adventist movement, then reeling in disappointment over Christ's failure to visibly return in 1844. The practice of keeping the Sabbath spread through Adventism and became a matter of extreme controversy through the 1850s and 1860s. Reaction to it divided the movement into three segments. One group rejected the idea and continued to worship on Sunday. One group accepted it and founded the Church of God (Seventh Day). When prophetess Ellen G. White (1827–1915) had a confirmatory revelation about Sabbath observance, the group around her accepted the Sabbath.

Since that time, the Seventh-day Adventist Church has been the major organization spreading Sabbatarianism worldwide.

By the end of the 20th century, the Seventh-day Adventists had spread into more than 200 of the world's countries. From it a number of smaller Sabbatarian Christian groups would emerge. Additional Sabbatarian groups emerged from the Church of God (Seventh Day) including the Worldwide Church of God, which by the 1980s had become the second largest Sabbatarian group in the world. However, in the 1990s, under the leadership of the successors to founder Herbert W. Armstrong (1892–1986), the Worldwide Church repudiated all of Armstrong's unique ideas, including his Sabbatarianism. As a result the church splintered with those continuing to worship on Saturday forming three larger groups—the Living Church of God, the United Church of God, and the Philadelphia Church of God— and a host of smaller groups.

The Church of God (Seventh Day) also nurtures what became known as the Sacred Name movement, which replaced the Greek translations of the Hebrew names of God and Jesus with transliteration of the Hebrew—Yehweh and Yhoshua. By the time of the emergence of the Sacred Name movement, some in the Church of God (Seventh Day) tradition had been exploring the Hebrew feast cycle and had concluded that the obligation to keep those holy days mentioned in the Hebrew Bible were equal to those for keeping the Sabbath. The Sacred Name groups, like the splinter groups of the Worldwide Church of God, continue to keep the Sabbath and observe the Hebrew feast days.

With the multiplication of Sabbath-keeping groups, each facing problems existing in a culture whose legal structures recognized the dominant usage of Sunday as a day of worship, Sabbatarians banded together in 1943 to form the Bible Sabbath Association. It offers smaller Sabbatarian groups, especially independent congregations, support and works to end discrimination against Sabbatarians in the workplace.

J. Gordon Melton

See also: Baptists; Bible Sabbath Association; Church of England; Seventh-day Adventist Church; White, Ellen G.; Worldwide Church of God.

References

Armstrong, Herbert W. *Which Day Is the Christian Sabbath?* Rev. ed. Pasadena, CA: Worldwide Church of God, 1989.

Bacchiocchi, Samuel. *From Sabbath to Sunday: A Historical Investigation of the Rise of Sunday Observance in Early Christianity.* Berrien Springs, MI: Biblical Perspectives, 1977.

Bennett, Todd D. *The Sabbath—Scriptural Truth Concerning the Sabbath and Christian Sunday Observance.* Herkimer, NY: Shema Yisrael Publications, 2005.

Carson, D. A. *From Sabbath to Lord's Day: A Biblical, Historical and Theological Investigation.* Eugene, OR: Wipf & Stock, 2000.

Directory of Sabbath-Observing Groups. Fairview, OK: Bible Sabbath Association, periodically updated.

Sacred Texts

As verbal communication is important for promoting religious doctrines, many religions give attention to the transmission of (sacred) texts in written form. In this way, religions build themselves on the idea of "holy scriptures." One of the earliest occurrences of the term "holy scriptures" can be found in the New Testament (Romans 1:2), when the Apostle Paul refers to the Hebrew prophets and the "holy scriptures." Texts from classical antiquity also refer to "holy words" (Greek: *hieroi logoi*) that can be transmitted in written form. From a historical point of view, the Bible as the "holy scripture" for Christians fostered the idea of "sacred texts" as the center-point for religions. In the study of religions, Friedrich Max Müller (1823–1900) can be seen as the "founding father" of the theoretical importance of the study of sacred texts as core topic for gaining ideas about the origin, purpose, and doctrine of religions. Studying and comparing religions for him depended mainly on the accessibility and translation of sacred texts. For this reason, in 1879 he launched the publication of the Sacred Books of the East series. Texts from the Hindu and Buddhist tradition as well as classical Chinese texts were incorporated in this undertaking, next to these translations of the Zoroastrian textual tradition and the Koran. Because of opposition from Christian theologians, the Bible could not be included in this series. Jewish texts as well as texts from minor or recent religions like the Sikh tradition or the Baha'i Faith are also missing.

The impact of the idea to use sacred books for the study of religions had two consequences: it fostered the idea of a hierarchy of religions with those religions that have "written texts" at the upper end; and it led scholars in religion to concentrate on textual studies and early periods of historical developments of religions as shown by these texts, thus partly neglecting aspects of rituals, practice, and social involvement of religions. Therefore one has to keep in mind that religions in general refer to written tradition, but for some religions the idea of "sacred texts" as exclusive and authoritative texts has only come up in modern times either as a result of the contact with Western scholars and their preconceptions, which are at least indirectly based on the Bible (and the Koran) as a canonical and sacred text, or as a reaction to Christian and Muslim theological conceptions of a "holy book" as the center of religious tradition, in order to identify books within their own traditions as (exclusively) "holy scripture."

Textbooks for the study of religion generally present sections on "sacred texts" for each religion, or some monographic or collective works focus on "sacred books" exclusively, to give an introduction and overview of such texts, for example, books published by Harold Coward, Frederick M. Denny and Rodney L. Taylor, Rein Fernhout, Kenneth Kramer, and Udo Tworuschka. Recently the Verlag für Weltreligionen (Publishing House for World Religions) has started a series of German translations of sacred books of living religions to make them available for a widespread audience to improve religious knowledge.

To give a short overview of the most well-known sacred texts, one can rely on the idea of canonical texts. The Greek word *kanon* means "principle" or "guideline"; thus canonical texts are reckoned as sacred texts that cannot be changed or neglected. In Islam we surely find the most elaborated understanding of canonicity, as the Koran is not only thought to be an earthly copy of the heavenly "mother book" (*umm al-kitab*), but is also the unchangeable word of God. Thus it is the sacred book par excellence, and the concept of a comparable holy book is also applied to other religions, when Islam judges adherents of Judaism, Christianity, and Zoroastrianism as "people of the book" (*ahl al-kitab*). The respective book for Jews is the Hebrew Bible, but regarding sacred texts it is necessary to take into account that Jewish tradition gives importance to both the "written" and "oral" Torah; this makes clear that even if the "oral" Torah can be transmitted in written form in later times, orality is on a par with sacred texts. Regarding both the Hebrew Bible and the Christian Bible (the Old Testament and the New Testament), the decision to regard such texts as sacred scripture within the religious community has been a long historical process, only at the end leading to a normative and absolute holy book, to which further additions or expansions are no longer theologically possible. It is quite possible that the canonization process of the Avesta as a sacred book of the Zoroastrians is dependent on the pattern of the Koran as a holy book for Muslims, as Zoroastrians had to present a copy of a "book" in a dominantly Islamic society to become acknowledged as "people of the book." Worth mentioning is also the case of the Baha'i Faith, whose adherents regard all books published (or theologically: revealed) by Bahá'u'lláh, the founder of that faith, as canonized sacred books that cannot be altered. As these examples make clear, we find sacred texts for monotheistic religions originating in the Middle East. Such texts are compulsory sources of religious doctrine for their believers and all reform or religious change has to be reconcilable with these texts as the basis of the religions.

Turning to the religions of South and East Asia, the situation regarding sacred texts gets more complex, as a concept of canonicity as mentioned above is widely missing. Even if it has become customary in religious studies to speak of the "Pali canon" of Buddhism, this "canon" is less absolute than in the cases mentioned before. The Pali canon offers a "guideline" to Theravada Buddhists, but it is not absolutely compulsory for all Buddhists, as different Buddhist schools or traditions can focus on their own "sacred texts"; a famous example is the so-called Lotus Sutra, which is a highly esteemed text among the Tiantai/Tendai school in Chinese/Japanese Buddhism or among Nichiren

Buddhists, but the sutra is downgraded by the Huayan/Kegon School in Chinese/Japanese Buddhism, which gives the Avatamsaka (or Flower Garland) Sutra the highest rank as sacred text. In Buddhism we observe a wide range of literary texts that can gain different status of sacredness, with the consequence that not all sacred books of the Buddhists are authoritative sources for all Buddhist schools.

We find a similar situation in Hinduism with a traditional differentiation between texts characterized as *sruti* or *smrti*. The first category comprises the Vedic texts (for example, Vedic hymns, Brahmanas, ritual texts, early Upanishads), while epics like the Mahabharata or the Ramayana and the Puranas are only reckoned as *smrti*. While this is true in general, we also find Vaishnavite schools in Hinduism, who also take the Ramayana or the Bhagavadgita as *sruti* or Shaivite Hindus, who view their *agama* texts as *sruti*—that is, preferring these texts as sacred texts by downgrading or even eliminating others.

While both Buddhism and Hinduism thus show a broad context related to sacred texts, the Sikh tradition defines it in a much narrower way; the Adi Granth Sahib is the sacred text for Sikhs, which is both the center of cultic reverence and source of Sikh doctrine, giving canonicity to this text comparable to the relationship of Christianity or Islam to their sacred texts.

To Chinese religions (mainly Daoism and Confucianism), the notion of sacred texts can be applied only in a broad sense, namely, texts that people read with reverence, because these texts are either part of the classical literary heritage of China (Liji, Shiji, Yijing) or they are attributed to masters like Laozi (Daode jing) or Confucius (Lun-yu). Even though both in Daoism and Confucianism there are sets of literary texts labeled a "canon," this does not mean an exclusive authority of these.

To summarize: sacred texts are a wide and diverse category in religions. What they have in common is their relevance for the devotional and spiritual life of the adherents of the respective religion; generally speaking, sacred texts in monotheistic religions are the normative and authoritative source of doctrine and religious law. One additional aspect of sacred texts worth mentioning is the fact that they—despite their diversity—always have been an inspiring source of literary achievements in the given cultures, and also a deposit of ideas that had a considerable influence upon the visual arts in most of the cultures.

Manfred Hutter

See also: Baha'i Faith; Bahá'u'lláh; Confucianism; Confucius; Daoism; Laozi; Nichirenshu; Sikhism/ Sant Mat; Tian Tai/Tendai Buddhism; Zoroastrianism.

References

Coward, Harold. *Sacred Word and Sacred Text: Scripture in World Religions.* Maryknoll, NY: Orbis Books,1988.

Denny, Frederick M., and Rodney L. Taylor, eds. *The Holy Book in Comparative Perspective.* Columbia: University of South Carolina Press, 1985.

Fernhout, Rein. *Canonical Texts. Bearers of Absolute Authority. Bible, Koran, Veda, Tipitaka. A Phenomenological Study.* Amsterdam: Editions Rodopi B.V., 1994.

Girardot, N. J. "Max Müller's Sacred Books and the Nineteenth-Century Production of the Comparative Science of Religion." *History of Religions* 41 (2001–2002): 213–250.

Kramer, Kenneth. *World Scriptures: An Introduction to Comparative Religions.* New York: Paulist Press, 1986.

Tworuschka, Udo, ed. *Heilige Schriften. Eine Einführung.* Frankfurt: Verlag der Weltreligionen, 2008.

Van der Kooij, Arie, and Karel van der Toorn, eds. *Canonization and Decanonization.* Leiden: Brill 1998.

www.verlagderweltreligionen.de

Sahaja Yoga

Sahaja Yoga was founded by Sri Mataji Nirmala Devi (b. 1923). She was the eldest daughter of an Indian barrister and enjoyed an affluent childhood in a Protestant family before marrying a successful diplomat, Sir C. P. Srivastava. In the late 1960s she became a follower of Osho Rajneesh, but left his circle and was highly critical of him thereafter. In 1970, we are told, she became "fully realized," simultaneously enabling others to achieve spiritual "realization" effortlessly. She then began to attract followers herself, initially in India, then in London, where she was based, and in increasing numbers throughout the world. Nine years later she revealed her divine identity as the Adi Shakti (primordial creatrix), and to committed followers she is the Goddess, returned to save the world. Sri Mataji travels widely in order to spread her "global religion." Her movement now claims a presence in 75 countries, each with its own national leader, and has approximately 20,000 converts.

Sahaja Yoga practices combine principles of Tantra with rituals and symbols from other traditions, especially from South Asia, and the majority are performed to banish negativity or to purify. Meditation is described as the raising of the spiritual energy of *kundalini*, usually dormant at the base of the spine, through *chakras*, spiritual centers in the body, which are cleansed of impurities as it passes. When the process is complete, spontaneous union with "The All Pervading Power" is achieved, and individuals experience a cool breeze on the palms of their hands and the tops of their heads. This union is said to cure serious illnesses, to leave practitioners feeling relaxed and balanced, and to lead to increasing sensitivity, to both their own spiritual vibrations and those of others. Sri Mataji's image is felt to be particularly purifying, and members cherish photographs of her surrounded by miraculous light or accompanied by deities. Sahaja Yoga *pujas* involve the worship of Sri Mataji in her different divine aspects.

Sri Mataji promotes arranged marriages between devotees of different nationalities, and these take place, in groups of up to 120 couples, either at international pujas or on the annual India Tour. She advises women to act as the "heart" of their families, and men as the "head," and the vast majority of the leaders in Sahaja Yoga are men. There are two Sahaja Yoga schools, in Rome and Dharamsala, where children of members board. Additionally, the movement runs a number of nongovernmental organizations, including a hospital dedicated to healing according to the principles of Sahaja Yoga. Notwithstanding Sri Mataji's teaching that "truth cannot be owned," her tax-free annual income from Sahaja Yoga activities has been estimated at more than $2 million, and devotees have subsidized the purchase and renovation of a number of properties where she lives, including castles outside Poona, India, and Cabella, Italy, as well as a chateau in France. In the past, concerns have been voiced over her at times authoritarian treatment of her followers and for the welfare of the children in Sahaja Yoga schools.

The international headquarters of the movement is now in the United Kingdom and may be contacted through its Internet site at http://sahajayoga.org.

Judith M. Fox

See also: Rome; Tantrism; Yoga.

References

Coney, Judith. *Sahaja Yoga: Socializing Processes in a South Asian New Religious Movement.* Richmond, UK: Curzon 1999.

Sri Mataji Nirmala Devi. *Meta-Modern Era.* North Wales, PA: Vishwa Nirmala Dharma 1997.

■ Sahara

The Sahara (aka Western Sahara), officially known as Al-Jumhuriyah as-Sahara al-Arabiyah as Dimuqratiyah, or the Sahara Arab Democratic Republic, is a sparsely populated country with approximately 405,000 people as of 2009. Its 103,000 square miles of territory is located on the Atlantic Ocean south of Morocco, most of the land being the westernmost segment of the Sahara desert.

The land was originally populated by Moors, Tubus, and Tuaregs (by the fifth century CE). Several centuries later a number of Yemenites moved into the area and intermarried with the residents, thus producing the dominant Sahrawi people who reside in the country. In the 11th century the first Sahara confederacy emerged, and in future centuries it would be incorporated into the territory of different kingdoms based in neighboring countries.

Arab forces reached the Atlantic coast of North Africa in the first decade of the eighth century, and Islam spread among the people of North Africa over the next few centuries. Here the Kharijite movement that challenged the authority of the Arab caliph was strong. In later centuries, the Sunni Malikite School would come to dominate North Africa, including Sahara and its neighbors.

Spain established a settlement (Dakhla) on the Saharan coast, primarily to protect the far more valuable

Demonstration at a refugee camp in Algeria. Western Sahara's government was forced into exile in Algeria by Morocco in 1991. (Miunicaneurona/Dreamstime.com)

Canary Islands, but in the 1880s began to plan to place the region under Spanish hegemony. Then in 1904, the European powers split Western Africa into four segments, although France (which had established a colony that bounded Sahara on the east and south) was the only other country to show any real interest in the western Sahara. The Sahwari opposed any incursions into their land by Europeans. Through much of the 20th century, Spain, France, and Morocco vied to wrestle control from the Native forces.

After World War II, Spain began to mine phosphate, Sahara's major mineral asset. In the meantime, the United Nations pressed for Saharan self-determination, and Morocco reasserted its claims to the land. In 1975, Spain conceded its interest to Morocco and

SAHARA

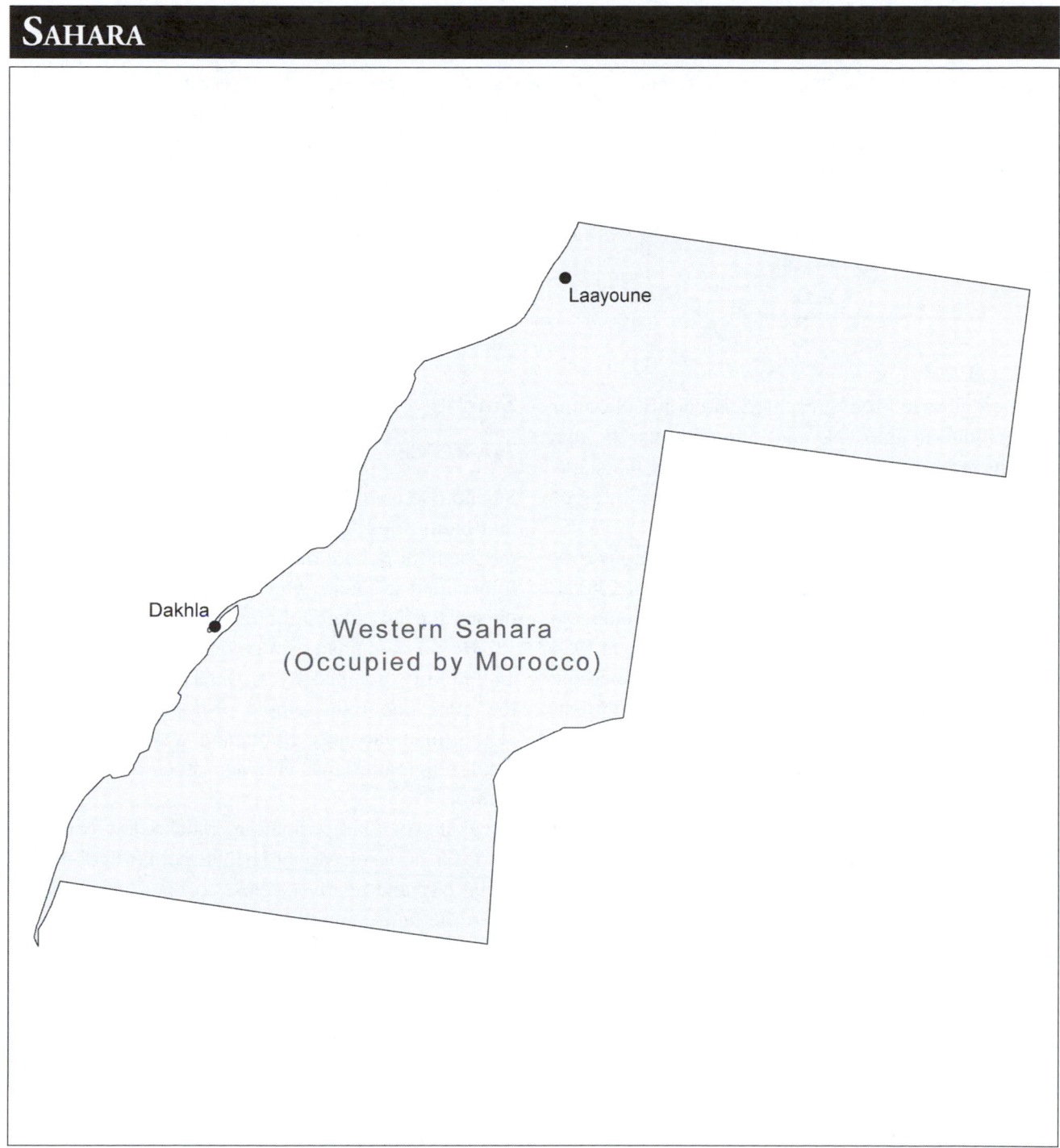

Mauritania, but almost immediately the Sahwari proclaimed the establishment of an independent republic. War with Morocco and Mauritania followed. Although Mauritania pulled out after a few years, the war with Morocco continued through the 1980s. A ceasefire was finally arranged in 1991 that left Morocco in control for all practical purposes; the Saharan Republic's government was forced into exile in Algeria (though recognized by a number of countries).

The Polisario Front, the groups that continued to contest Moroccan sovereignty in Sahara, accepted a UN-negotiated cease-fire. In April 2007, both Morocco

Sahara

Religion	Followers in 1970	Followers in 2010	% of Population	Annual % growth 2000–2010	Followers in 2025	Followers in 2050
Muslims	45,000	527,000	99.4	6.91	770,000	930,000
Agnostics	0	1,600	0.3	7.26	3,500	5,000
Christians	31,600	750	0.1	6.24	800	900
Independents	0	620	0.1	8.78	700	800
Roman Catholics	30,000	130	0.0	−1.37	100	100
Atheists	0	510	0.1	6.88	1,000	1,500
Baha'is	100	240	0.0	6.84	200	300
Total population	**76,700**	**530,000**	**100.0**	**6.91**	**775,000**	**938,000**

and the Polisario Front presented autonomy plans for the territory to the UN, and subsequently the two sides have had face-to-face meetings, but the status of the territory remains very much in doubt as of 2010.

Meanwhile, as Spain asserted its hegemony over Sahara in the 20th century, the Roman Catholic Church began to move beyond its service to the minuscule Spanish expatriate community at Dakhla. Only in 1954 was prefecture designated, the work being delegated to two religious orders, the Oblates of Mary Immaculata and the Salesian Sisters of the Sacred Heart of Jesus. The Catholic presence peaked in the mid-1970s (with 6 parishes), but it has now diminished to fewer than 500 believers.

Protestant presence has been even smaller. The primary attempt to establish a mission was by the Seventh-day Adventist Church, but it did not succeed. There is a small Baha'i Faith community of some 100 members, but virtually the entire citizenry remain Muslim.

J. Gordon Melton

See also: Malikite School of Islam; Roman Catholic Church; Salesians; Seventh-day Adventist Church.

References

Barrett, David, ed. *The Encyclopedia of World Christianity*. 2nd ed. New York: Oxford University Press, 2001.

Hodges, Tony. *Western Sahara: The Roots of a Desert War*. Westport, CT: Lawrence Hill, 1983.

Saicho

767–822 CE

Saicho (Dengyo Daishi), the son of a Chinese family that had settled in Omi, Japan, became a student of the Tian Tai School of Chinese Buddhism, which he transmitted to Japan, where it spread as Tendai Buddhism. Saicho entered the religious life as a child of 11. He was ordained as a novice priest at the age of 14 and fully ordained 4 years later in Nara at Todai-ji, the most important temple of Japanese Buddhism at the time. Japanese Buddhism was still a relative small religion in Japan and very much under imperial control.

Following his ordination, Saicho left Nara and made his home on Mount Hiei, a spot north of the imperial city and relatively close to his family's home. There he built a small hermitage and made a set of vows about his own search for purification and enlightenment. He concentrated his study on several Buddhist sutras, such as the Lotus Sutra and the Perfection of Wisdom Sutra, and the Tian Tai writings attributed to Zhi Yi, which seemed especially to resonate with him. Zhi Yi extolled the virtues of the Lotus Sutra.

In 797, shortly after the imperial court was moved from Nara to Heian (Kyoto), Saicho was asked to serve as the court priest. As a result he was frequently away from Mount Hiei, though his contacts and influence grew in the powerful circle around the court. The emperor's favor was manifest when, in 804, Saicho was sent to China to study and observe Chinese Buddhism. Kukai (774–835), a younger contemporary, accompanied him on the same mission. While in China,

Saicho was exposed to the Vajrayana (esoteric) tradition, but also receiving transmission from Tian Tai masters, who facilitated the accumulation of copies of hundreds of the Tian Tai books. He brought these to Japan. Soon after resettling at Mount Hiei, Saicho set about the process of spreading Tian Tai (which would be called Tendai in Japan) teachings throughout the country. Again his contacts at court benefited him, as he was able to successfully petition for permission to ordain priests. He also enlarged the small hermitage on Mount Hiei, which evolved into Enryaku-ji, the temple that would serve as the headquarters of the new Tendai School.

As his work and importance grew, Saicho engaged in an important debate with a leader of one of the other Buddhist groups based at Nara over the nature of Buddhahood. They argued over whether only some or all beings had the innate potential for enlightenment. Saicho argued for the universal nature of potential enlightenment. The debate would lead to an important decision. In 818, he renounced his Todai-ji ordination (a symbolic break with the Buddhist leadership at Nara), and then petitioned the emperor for the privilege of ordaining Tendai priests separately from the ordination platform at Nara.

Those who sought ordination from him had to undergo a strict regimen he had devised for prospective priests built around 12 years of strict practice at Enryaku-ji. He impressed upon the future Tendai priests that they engaged in spiritual work not just for their own salvation. They had to come to view themselves as similar to bodhisattvas, and understand that in helping others find enlightenment, they would also be helping themselves.

Saicho spread Tendai teachings with the assistance of the close relations he continued to nurture with the imperial court in Kyoto. He argued that Mahayana Buddhism in general, and, of course, Mount Hiei in particular, were "the protector of the nation," an idea that would be periodically revived throughout his life. He eventually used the favor he had developed at court to make his most audacious petition—that he and his students be given separate status as an independent sect. He died in 822 before the emperor ruled on his petition. A favorable response came the following year. Included in the set of decrees made by the emperor, his temple on Mount Hiei was officially named Enryaku-ji.

Edward A. Irons

See also: Kukai (Kobo Daishi); Mahayana Buddhism; Nara; Tian Tai/Tendai Buddhism; Zhi Yi.

References

Groner, Paul. *Saicho: The Establishment of the Japanese Tendai School.* Berkeley, CA: Berkeley Buddhist Studies Series,1984.

Kashiwahara, Yūsen, and Kōyū Sonoda. *Shapers of Japanese Buddhism.* Trans. by Gaynor Sekimori. Tokyo: Kōsei Pub. Co., 1994.

Takeshi, Umehara. "Saicho." In *Buddhist Spirituality: Later China, Korea, Japan, and the Modern World,* edited by Takeuchi Yoshinori, 164–173. New York: Crossroad Publishing, 1999.

Saigoku Kannon Pilgrimage

The Saigoku Kannon Pilgrimage is the most famous pilgrimage in Japan. It is dedicated to Kannon, the bodhisattva of compassion (also known in China as Guan Yin or Avalokitesvara), possibly the most famous and ubiquitous of the Mahayana Buddhist deities. Out of her compassion, she has become a worker of miracles. As in China, sites at which people had miraculous encounters with her would become sites for temples. Each temple of the Saigoku Kannon Pilgrimage is associated with a miracle attributed to Kannon.

According to the Avalokitesvara Sutra, there are 33 specific forms that Kannon may take to save people according to their different conditions in life. The 25th chapter of the Lotus Sutra, one of the more popular Mahayana scriptures, also mentions 33 forms of Kannon. One form Kannon might assume is that of Juuichimen Kannon, depicted with 11 faces/heads to denote a sending out of sweetness and mercy in all directions. Senjyu Kannon, also known as the 1,000-arm Avalokitesvara, symbolizes her ability to embrace Earth and alleviate the suffering of all people. The Bato or Horse-headed Kannon offers protection to cattle and horses. The pilgrimage, which may be made by Buddhists at any time of the year, consists of visits to 33 temples. To make the entire pilgrimage, moving from one temple to the next in order, would involve the individual in a 1,500-mile journey. Most of the temples are in southwest Japan within a day's journey of Kyoto, but will take the pilgrim as far west as the Sea of Japan and eastward to the Pacific Ocean.

The first temple in the sequel is Seigantoji, located near Nagao (some 50 miles south of Osaka). It faces Nachi Falls, the highest in Japan, and is next to the Kumano-Nachi Shrine, a temple of a Japanese syncretistic Buddhist-Shinto sect. The temple possesses a Kannon statue that dates to the seventh century, the time of Buddhism's entrance into Japan, but the main statue is of Nyorin Kannon, one of the different forms assumed by Kannon that the pilgrim will encounter. A Nyorin Kannon that dates to the eighth century is located at Okadera (or Ryugai-ji), the seventh temple of the Kannon Pilgrimage. The second temple is located to the west near Wakayama. After visiting the all temples, the final stop is at Gifu, northeast of Kyoto.

Pilgrims generally carry with them a *nokyocho*, a pilgrim's book with a page for each temple. Each temple has a pilgrim's office that will, for a small fee, inscribe and stamp the book. This will become a record and memento of the pilgrimage. Worshippers will also locate the main Kannon statue at each temple. An act of veneration consists of making a monetary offering, ringing a bell three times acknowledging the Three Jewels of Buddhism—the Buddha, the Dharma (teachings), and the Sangha (community). Many will also light three incense sticks.

The popularity of the Kannon Pilgrimage led to its being copied in other parts of Japan. Through the centuries more than 200 variant duplicate pilgrimages to 33 Kannon temples appeared in every part of Japan, the Bando route that begins at Kamakura being considered the most important after the original Saigoku pilgrimage circuit. It appears to have originated in an encounter with Kannon in a dream of the Emperor Kazan who was told, "I have divided into 33 bodies throughout the 8 provinces of the Bando area, and a pilgrimage to these 33 sites will bring release from suffering." Soon afterward, in 988 CE, the emperor designated Sugimoto-dera in Kamakura as the first temple on the Bando circuit. Centuries later, the Saigoku

and Bando pilgrimages were formally linked to a third circuit, the Chichibu Pilgrimage, which included 34 sites sacred to Kannon. The three pilgrimages together became the Kannon 1000 Circuit.

J. Gordon Melton

See also: Bodhisattva; Kamakura Pilgrimage; Shikoku Pilgrimage; Temples—Buddhist.

References

Mutsu, Iso. *Kamakura: Fact and Legend*. Rutland, VT: Tuttle Publishing, 1995.

Readicker-Henderson, Ed. *The Traveler's Guide to Japanese Pilgrimages*. Trumbull, CT: Weatherhill, 1995.

Schumacher, Mark. A to Z Photo Dictionary/ Japanese Buddhist Statuary. "Kannon." http://www.onmarkproductions.com/html/kannon.shtml.

Statler, Oliver. *Japanese Pilgrimage*. Honolulu: University of Hawaii Press, 1985.

■ St. Helena

St. Helena, the South Atlantic island made famous as the site of Napoleon's exile from 1815 to 1821, is a British Overseas Territory in the mid-Atlantic Ocean. Besides St. Helena proper, the territory includes the island of Ascension and the island group of Tristan da Cunha. Although separated by hundreds of miles of water, the three islands are tied together by their strategic military placement in an area where land is sparse. Together, the islands have 165 square miles of territory. St Helena was uninhabited prior to its discovery by Portuguese sailors in 1502. The British settled St. Helena in 1659, and it has been a British colony ever since. Today (2008) the islands have a total population of 7,600.

Members of the Church of England arrived with the first British settlers, and today the great majority of the islanders are Anglicans. The church, formally established in 1851, is now attached to the Church in the Province of South Africa. There is one diocese, serving St. Helena and Ascension. Tristan de Cunha is under the oversight of the Diocese of Cape Town (South Africa).

St. Helena

Over the course of the 20th century, other Protestant churches and the Roman Catholic Church developed congregations. They include the Baptists, the Seventh-day Adventist Church, the Salvation Army, and Jehovah's Witnesses. Each counts its membership in the low hundreds. The Baptists are affiliated with the Baptist Union of South Africa. The SDAs are attached to the Southern Africa Union Conference.

There is one small group of the Baha'i Faith; on St. Helena, it is the only non-Christian group that has become visible.

J. Gordon Melton

St. Helena

Religion	Followers in 1970	Followers in 2010	% of Population	Annual % growth 2000–2010	Followers in 2025	Followers in 2050
Christians	5,100	6,500	95.7	1.30	7,300	8,000
Anglicans	4,000	4,800	69.9	1.29	5,300	5,800
Protestants	360	520	7.6	−2.33	500	500
Marginals	100	300	4.4	−2.73	450	550
Agnostics	10	230	3.4	7.21	390	500
Baha'is	20	60	0.8	1.65	70	100
Atheists	0	10	0.1	0.00	10	20
Total population	**5,100**	**6,800**	**100.0**	**1.47**	**7,800**	**8,600**

See also: Baptist Union of South Africa; Church in the Province of South Africa; Church of England; Jehovah's Witnesses; Roman Catholic Church; Salvation Army; Seventh-day Adventist Church.

References

Cannan, Edward. *Churches of the South Atlantic Islands, 1502–1991.* Oswestry, UK: Anthony Nelson, 1992.

Royle, Stephen A. *The Company's Island: St. Helena, Company Colonies and the Colonial Endeavour.* London: I. B. Tauris, 2008.

■ St. Kitts-Nevis

St. Kitts-Nevis (more formally, the Federation of Saint Christopher and Nevis) are two of the Windward Islands in the Lesser Antilles on the northeast edge of the Caribbean Sea. They are east of Puerto Rico and west of Antigua. Together the islands have 101 square miles of land and a population of 39,800 (2008).

St. Kitts-Nevis was originally settled by the Carib people, who were first visited by Christopher Columbus in 1493. The Caribs were left alone until Thomas Walker established what was the first English settlement in the Caribbean in 1623. The initial settlement on nearby Nevis was made in 1628. The Caribs were soon eliminated, and slaves from Africa were brought in to work the expanding plantations. For the next century, France and England vied for control of the islands, but they were awarded to England by the Treaty of Versailles of 1793.

In 1816, St. Kitts was included in a single colony that included the Virgin Islands and Anguilla. The Virgin Islands were separated in 1871, and St. Kitts became the center of the remaining colony. After World War II, it was incorporated into the Associate States of the West Indies and developed local autonomy. Anguilla moved to disassociate itself in 1980. Religious freedom is guaranteed in St. Kitts-Nevis.

The Church of England arrived with the first British settlers and for more than 100 years was the only religious organization on the islands. In 1824 the bishop of London handed over control of the parishes to the bishop on Barbados. That same year an archdeaconry of Antigua, which included St. Kitts-Nevis, was established. The archdeaconry became a diocese in 1842 and has since become a diocese of the Church in the Province of the West Indies, headquartered at Nassau, the Bahamas.

Daniel Gottwald and James Birkly, missionaries of the Moravian Church, arrived in 1777 to found the first Protestant mission. They had been invited by John Gardiner, a planter, to evangelize the slaves under his care. They and their successors were soon visiting more than 50 different plantations. When the Methodists arrived in 1787, the two churches cooperated in evangelistic efforts and the building of churches. Methodism was introduced to St. Kitts by Lydia Seaton, formerly a servant who had been converted by Nathaniel Gilbert while living on Antigua. The Reverend Thomas Coke, the associate of Methodist founder John Wesley, visited St. Kitts for the first time in 1787 and later sent Thomas Hammett there to head the work. The Methodists later affiliated with the Methodist Church in the Caribbean

St. Kitts-Nevis

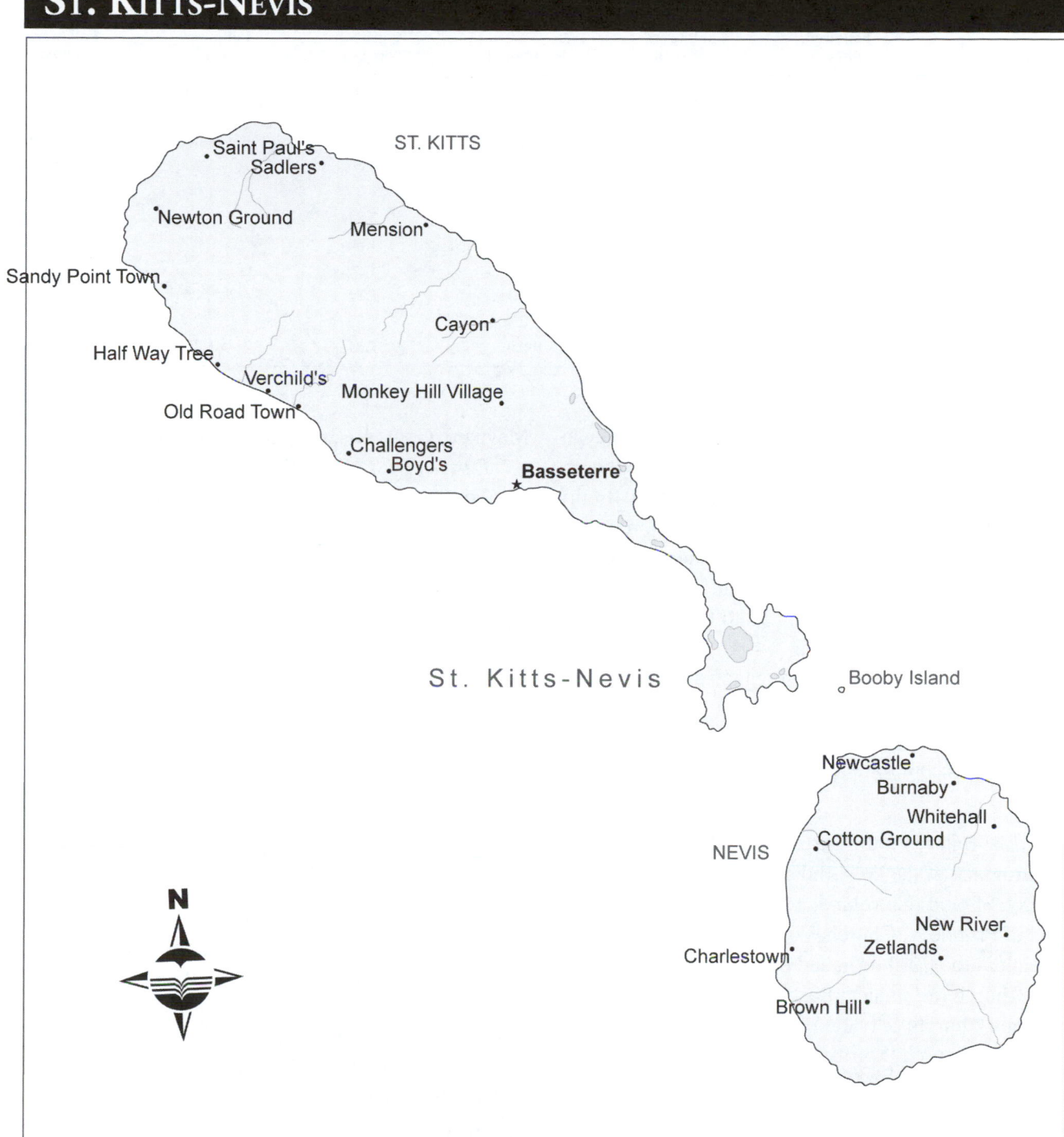

and the Americas and the Moravian work assigned to the Moravian Church in Jamaica. Both churches are now members of the World Council of Churches.

The Roman Catholic Church established work in 1861. It was included in the Diocese of Roseau (Dom-inica) until 1971 and then placed in the Diocese of St. John's (Antigua).

During the 20th century, a variety of churches tar-geted St. Kitts-Nevis for missionary activity, includ-ing the Seventh-day Adventist Church, the Pilgrim

St. Kitts-Nevis

Religion	Followers in 1970	Followers in 2010	% of Population	Annual % growth 2000–2010	Followers in 2025	Followers in 2050
Christians	44,400	49,500	94.5	1.27	57,500	64,600
Protestants	25,900	23,700	45.2	0.06	27,000	29,600
Anglicans	17,500	16,800	32.1	1.04	19,000	21,400
Roman Catholics	4,000	5,100	9.7	0.00	5,900	7,000
Hindus	0	790	1.5	1.30	1,000	1,200
Agnostics	60	850	1.6	3.83	1,400	1,700
Spiritists	0	670	1.3	1.30	800	900
Baha'is	200	260	0.5	1.29	350	450
New religionists	210	150	0.3	1.23	180	200
Muslims	0	140	0.3	1.35	200	300
Total population	**44,900**	**52,400**	**100.0**	**1.31**	**61,400**	**69,300**

Holiness Church (now an integral part of the Wesleyan Church), the Church of God of Prophecy, the Church of God (Cleveland, Tennessee), the Christian Brethren, the Churches of Christ, and the Salvation Army. At the same time a number of indigenous churches such as the Antioch Baptist Church, the Assemblies of the First Born, the Evangelical Faith Church, and the Spiritual Baptists have arisen.

There is little evidence of organized religion apart from Christianity, the most prominent group being the Baha'i Faith. There are also some followers of Islam, Afro-Caribbean religions, and the Rastafarians.

J. Gordon Melton

See also: Baha'i Faith; Christian Brethren; Church in the Province of the West Indies; Church of England; Church of God (Cleveland, Tennessee); Church of God of Prophecy; Churches of Christ; Methodist Church in the Caribbean and the Americas; Moravian Church in Jamaica; Rastafarians; Roman Catholic Church; Salvation Army; Seventh-day Adventist Church; Spiritual Baptists; Wesleyan Church; World Council of Churches.

References

Barrett, David, ed. *The Encyclopedia of World Christianity.* 2nd ed. New York: Oxford University Press, 2001.

Dyde, Brian. *Out of Crowded Vagueness: A History of the Islands of St. Kitts, Nevis and Anguilla.* Northampton, MA: Interlink Publishing Group, 2006.

Maynard, G. O. *A History of the Moravian Church: Eastern West Indies Province.* Port of Spain, Trinidad: Yuille's, 1968.

■ St. Lucia

St. Lucia, one of the Windward Islands of the Lesser Antilles, is located at the western edge of the Caribbean Sea between Martinique and St. Vincent. It was originally valued for the fine harbor at its capital, Castries. It has 238 square miles of territory and a population of 160,000 people, the majority of African descent.

St. Lucia was originally settled by the Arawak people, who around 800 CE were conquered and replaced by the Carib people. The latter group inhabited the island when Christopher Columbus arrived in 1502 and gave it its present name. Both the British and Spanish vied for the island, but neither could defeat the local resistance to their settlement.

Then, in 1660, the French settled on the island, and it became one object in the ongoing British-French conflict over the course of the next century. Finally, in 1814, the British received control as one item in the Treaty of Paris. The British quickly developed the sugarcane industry on a set of plantations built upon slave labor. The present population largely derived from the mixing of the former master/slave population. St. Lucia was incorporated into the Colony of the Windward Islands. It was included in the West Indies Federation

ST. LUCIA

St. Lucia

Religion	Followers in 1970	Followers in 2010	% of Population	Annual % growth 2000–2010	Followers in 2025	Followers in 2050
Christians	102,000	164,000	95.9	1.07	186,000	205,000
Roman Catholics	92,500	124,000	72.5	0.32	135,000	145,000
Protestants	6,500	43,200	25.3	3.38	49,800	54,500
Anglicans	3,000	3,300	1.9	0.00	3,600	4,000
Spiritists	1,500	2,900	1.7	1.09	3,300	3,600
Hindus	0	1,600	0.9	1.09	2,000	2,300
Muslims	0	780	0.5	1.08	1,000	1,300
New religionists	0	650	0.4	1.09	750	850
Baha'is	170	400	0.2	1.12	600	800
Agnostics	0	660	0.4	10.74	1,000	1,600
Atheists	0	60	0.0	1.11	100	200
Total population	**104,000**	**171,000**	**100.0**	**1.09**	**195,000**	**216,000**

View of the fishing town of Soufriere on Saint Lucia, 2009. (Samuel Strickler/Dreamstime.com)

(1959–1962) and received the right of self-government as one of the Federated States of the Antilles in 1967. It became a fully independent country in 1979, though it remains part of the British Commonwealth.

The Roman Catholic Church came to St. Lucia with the French and became fully established in 1719. The Diocese of Castries, initially erected in 1956, was elevated to an archdiocese in 1974. Serving more than 90 percent of the population, it remains by far the largest religious grouping on the island.

Anglicanism entered with the British and claims the largest percentage of the non-Catholic community. The churches were under the Diocese of Barbados prior to the creation of the Diocese of the Windward Islands in 1878. That diocese, headquartered on St. Vincent, is now part of the Church in the Province of the West Indies. The Methodists arrived in St. Lucia in 1809, part of the early expansion of British Methodism through the Caribbean following the American Revolution. The Methodist work is now part of the Methodist Church in the Caribbean and the Americas. In the mid-19th century, the Moravians, who also had been expanding through the Caribbean with a mission devoted to the plantation laborers, arrived. Their work is now incorporated into the Moravian Church, Eastern West Indies Province, headquartered on Antigua. All three churches are now members of the World Council of Churches.

Over the course of the 20th century, a spectrum of churches representative of Evangelical, Holiness, and Pentecostal perspectives arrived on St. Lucia, primarily from the United States. Each has had modest success. Among the more successful have been the Evangelical Church of the West Indies and the United Holy Church of America. The Seventh-day Adventist Church arrived in 1926 and the Jehovah's Witnesses in 1963.

Several movements that have arisen in the Caribbean and subsequently spread through the islands have found their way to St. Lucia. The Rastafarian movement spread from Jamaica in the 1950s and 1960s. In like measure, the Spiritual Baptists have arisen as a popular indigenous church, and the Yoruban religion, also known as Santeria, has gained some degree of popularity. The Baha'i Faith has a small following on St. Lucia.

J. Gordon Melton

See also: Baha'i Faith; Church in the Province of the West Indies; Evangelical Church of the West Indies; Holiness Movement; Jehovah's Witnesses; Methodist Church in the Caribbean and the Americas; Moravian Church, Eastern West Indies Province; Pentecostalism; Rastafarians; Roman Catholic Church; Santeria; Seventh-day Adventist Church; Spiritual Baptists; World Council of Churches; Yoruban Religion/ Spirituality.

References

Gachet, C. *A History of the Roman Catholic Church in St. Lucia*. Port of Spain, Trinidad: Key Caribbean Publications, 1976.

Jesse, C. *Outlines of St. Lucia's History*. Castries: St. Lucia Archeological and Historical Society, 1964.

■ St. Pierre et Miquelon

St. Pierre et Miquelon is an archipelago of eight islands off the southern coast of Newfoundland (Canada), a remnant of French North America. The islands have a combined land area of 93 square miles and a population of 7,000 (2008). The British pushed a claim to the islands through the 1700s, but they relinquished the claim in 1804. The islands were until 1946 a French possession, afterward designated an overseas territory, and since 1975 are an overseas department of France.

The Roman Catholic Church came to the island with its early settlers in 1668. It remains the only Christian church on the islands and claims the great majority of citizens as members. It has been constituted as a vicariate attached to the Episcopal Conference of France. There are some professing Protestants among the residents, but no organized work. There is, however, a spiritual assembly of the Baha'i Faith.

J. Gordon Melton

See also: Baha'i Faith; Roman Catholic Church.

References

Hansen, Bent. *St. Pierre and Miquelon*. Halifax, Nova Scotia: Nimbus Publishing, 1994.

Rannie, W. F. *Saint Pierre and Miquelon*. Beamsville, ON: Rannie, 1963.

St. Pierre et Miquelon

Religion	Followers in 1970	Followers in 2010	% of Population	Annual % growth 2000–2010	Followers in 2025	Followers in 2050
Christians	5,400	6,000	94.5	−0.03	5,900	5,800
Roman Catholics	5,300	5,900	92.7	−0.03	5,700	5,600
Protestants	50	70	1.1	1.61	100	150
Marginals	0	40	0.5	0.00	50	100
Agnostics	40	250	3.9	2.78	350	500
Baha'is	50	90	1.4	0.24	130	200
Muslims	0	10	0.2	2.13	20	40
Total population	**5,500**	**6,400**	**100.0**	**0.07**	**6,400**	**6,500**

St. Pierre et Miquelon

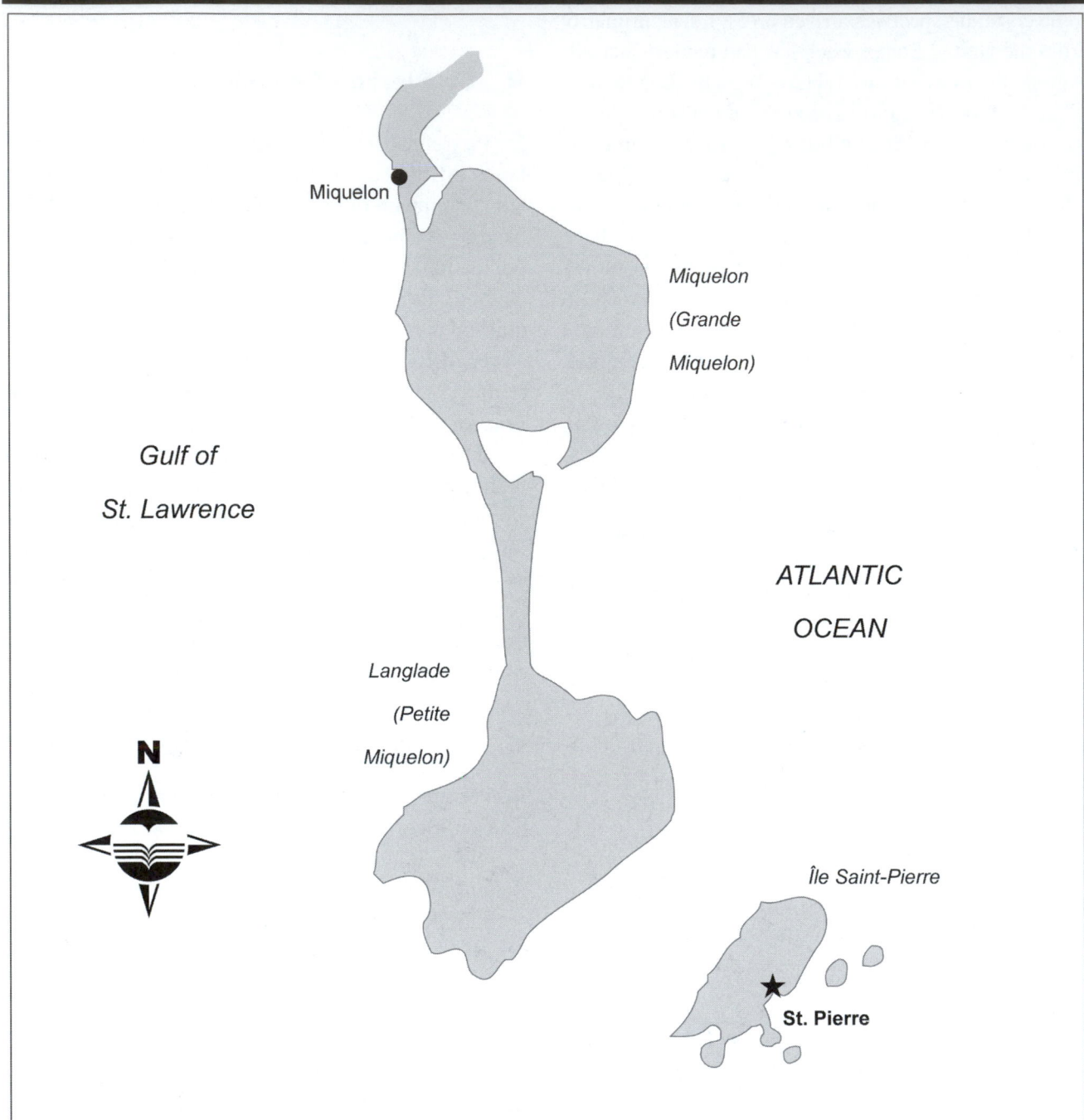

■ St. Vincent

St. Vincent, one of the Windward Islands, is located on the southeastern edge of the Caribbean Sea between St. Lucia and Grenada. Since being granted independence as a member of the British Commonwealth in 1979, its territory of 150 square miles has included not only the main island but also the northern part of the Grenadine Islands immediately to the south. The islands have a combined population of 118,000 (2008).

St. Vincent

Religion	Followers in 1970	Followers in 2010	% of Population	Annual % growth 2000–2010	Followers in 2025	Followers in 2050
Christians	87,700	108,000	88.4	0.47	106,000	83,600
Protestants	17,400	58,000	47.5	1.68	60,000	50,000
Independents	2,600	27,000	22.1	2.66	30,000	27,000
Anglicans	30,000	19,200	15.7	−0.61	19,000	16,000
Hindus	0	4,100	3.4	0.54	5,000	6,000
Agnostics	400	3,200	2.6	3.56	5,000	6,000
Spiritists	1,800	2,200	1.8	0.55	2,300	2,000
Muslims	0	1,900	1.6	0.54	2,500	3,000
Baha'is	600	1,800	1.5	0.54	3,000	4,000
New religionists	0	640	0.5	0.52	700	800
Ethnoreligionists	0	250	0.2	0.51	250	250
Atheists	0	60	0.0	0.39	100	300
Total population	**90,500**	**122,000**	**100.0**	**0.54**	**125,000**	**106,000**

St. Vincent was originally settled by the Arawak people, who were in turn conquered and replaced by the Caribs. These were the people that Christopher Columbus found when he arrived in the area in 1498. The Caribs were left alone until 1783, when England was given hegemony over St. Vincent in a treaty with its European neighbors. They sent a force to defeat the Caribs, who had been joined by some slaves that had escaped from other nearby islands. They were largely defeated and eradicated by 1796. A set of plantations soon emerged, and a large number of Africans arrived to work them.

St. Vincent was incorporated into the Colony of the Windward Islands in 1833. It received some degree of autonomy in 1960 and became a self-governing state in 1969. It became fully independent in 1979. Following the first elections of the new government, members of the Rastafarian movement on Union Island led an armed rebellion that had to be put down by troops brought in from Barbados.

The Church of England came to St. Vincent with the first British settlers. It has remained the largest religious body in St. Vincent, and its largely black membership reflects the island's population. Today, the Diocese of the Windward Islands, a diocese within the Church in the Province of the West Indies, is headquartered on St. Vincent.

Methodism spread through the Caribbean from England in the years immediately after the American Revolution. It reached St. Vincent in 1787, a direct result of the Reverend Thomas Coke's visit to Antigua and the birth of his enthusiasm for missionizing the Caribbean in 1786. The Methodist work is now a part of the Methodist Church in the Caribbean and the Americas.

Through the course of the 20th century, an array of Protestant/Free church bodies have found their way to St. Vincent from both England and the United States. These include Adventism, Holiness, Pentecostal, Baptist, and independent evangelical bodies. The mission of the Pentecostal Assemblies of Canada has grown to become the Pentecostal Church of the West Indies. Among the more interesting bodies is the Christian Pilgrim Church of St. Vincent, an indigenous Christian denomination. The Spiritual Baptists, a movement that has spread through many of the Caribbean Islands, was banned in St. Vincent between 1913 and 1965.

In 1964 the Anglicans, Catholics, Methodists, and the Salvation Army founded the Christian Council of St. Vincent, now known as the Saint Vincent and the Grenadines Christian Council. It is closely related to the World Council of Churches.

The Baha'i Faith has spread on St. Vincent in the years since World War II. At the same time, Yoruban religion, popularly called Santeria, has emerged to visibility among the descendants of Africans. It includes elements brought to the islands from Africa, revitalized by a new influx of those teachings made possible by

St. Vincent

Fancy
Saint Vincent
Wallibou Orange Hill
Chateaubelair Georgetown
Barrouallie
Layou Biabou
Mespotamia
Kingstown Stubbs
Calliaqua

St. Vincent

Bequia
Port Elizabeth
Derrick Petit Nevis Island Bettowia Island
Isla a Quatre
Pigeon Island Baliceaux Island
The Pillories
Dovers
Mustique
Petit Mustique Island
Savan Island
Petit Canouan

Canouan

Mayreau
Union Island Tobago Cays
Ashton
Prune Island
Petit Saint Vincent Island

modern communications. Santeria operates as a semi-secret religion, and the estimate of support is difficult to make.

J. Gordon Melton

See also: Adventism; Church in the Province of the West Indies; Church of England; Holiness Movement; Methodist Church in the Caribbean and the Americas; Pentecostal Assemblies of Canada; Pentecostalism; Rastafarians; Roman Catholic Church; Salvation Army; Santeria; Seventh-day Adventist Church; Spiritual Baptists; World Council of Churches, Yoruban Religion/Spirituality.

References

Fraser, Adrian, and Keith Joseph. *Our Country—St. Vincent and the Grenadines*. Oxford: Macmillan Caribbean, 1993.

Young, V. H. *Becoming West Indian: Culture, Self, and Nation in St. Vincent*. Washington, DC: Smithsonian Institution, 1993.

Saints

The word "saint" is derived from the Latin *sanctus* (Greek: *hagios*), literally meaning "holy." In Christianity it refers to someone who has manifested a holiness of life or someone who has been martyred for the faith, and whom the church believes is now enjoying eternal life with God. In Roman Catholicism, holiness of life is spoken of in terms of "heroic virtue." A saint is someone who has "heroically," or to an exceptional degree, exhibited the supernatural virtues (since they are gifts of God's grace) of faith, hope, and charity and the moral virtues of prudence, justice, fortitude, and temperance.

In its broader meaning, "saint" can be used to corporately designate all the faithful, both the living and the dead, particularly when describing the church as a "communion of saints." The Second Vatican Council uses similar language in describing the church as a "holy nation" in its theology of sainthood (*Dogmatic Constitution on the Church*, no. 50). In such a theology of holiness, the church recognizes that God alone is holy. God calls all persons to a life of holiness with a hope of sharing in eternal divine life. Holiness or sanctity is not something the church bestows on the individual, but is a gift given freely by God that the church subsequently formally recognizes in the individual. All the faithful are called to a life of imitation of these saints, and through a special devotion, or veneration, of such saints can seek their intercessions through prayer since saints enjoy a more perfect relationship, in heaven, with God. A distinction is drawn between the veneration of, or devotion to, saints and the worship that is due to God alone.

History In the early church, the term "saint" was most commonly used to describe those who believed in Christ and who were called to follow him (1 Corinthians 1:2; Romans 1:7). The church pre-eminently recognizes the sanctity of the Apostles of Christ and the Blessed Virgin Mary, the mother of Jesus Christ. The term "saint" was also used to describe those who were martyred for their faith during the persecutions of the first three centuries. The memory of these martyrs, their date of martyrdom, their place of burial, and their relics were venerated in this early period. The term "saint" was later also applied to monastics, who renounced the world and lived lives of asceticism and prayer; to early theologians, who defended and explicated the faith; and to those who were zealous in their preaching of the faith (like missionaries). Miracles were often attributed to such saints.

In its modern usage, canonization refers to the culmination of a process in which someone is declared a saint and is added to the canon, or list, of saints. However, in the early church period the declaration of sainthood could be effected in a number of different ways, the most common being by popular acclamation by the people, or later, by the declaration of a bishop, pope, or synod (or council) of bishops. The synodal process has remained the normal avenue for canonization in the Eastern Orthodox churches. The Roman Catholic tradition gradually developed a more formal process, beginning around the 13th century. Various revisions to the process of canonization followed, with the most recent protocols being announced in 1983. These recent changes were in part occasioned by the demands of modern historical and scientific inquiry.

Indian Catholics walk in a procession, holding a portrait of Sister Alphonsa to celebrate her canonization as a saint, Calcutta, India, October 12, 2008. (AP/Wide World Photos)

Canonization in the Roman Catholic Tradition   In 1983, in the Apostolic Constitution, *The Divine Teacher and Model of Perfection*, Pope John Paul II established new procedures for canonization. There are two phases on the path toward canonization: the diocesan and the Roman. Normally, the process of initiating a case for the canonization of a person is done at a local level by a diocesan bishop, either Roman Catholic or Eastern Catholic, or by the bishop through a request of an individual or group of faithful. The local bishop appoints a postulator, who directs the investigation process at the local diocesan level. In the language of the constitution, those for whom canonization is sought are initially referred to as "venerable servants of God." Local bishops are to inquire about the life of this person, his or her heroic virtues, orthodoxy, or, in certain cases, martyrdom. An examination is also done of any published or unpublished writings (like diaries or letters),

and any living witnesses are interviewed. The bishop is also to submit a declaration that no cult around the postulant has arisen. These reports and eyewitness accounts (the "acts") are then gathered and submitted to the Sacred Congregation for the Causes of Saints, which then initiates the Roman phase of the investigation.

In the *New Laws for the Causes of Saints* (1983), the Congregation distinguished between ancient cases and recent cases, with the major difference being whether or not witnesses can give an oral deposition. Recent cases are normally not brought before the Congregation until at least five years after the death of the person, although the pope may unilaterally expedite this process by dispensing with the waiting period. For the latter case, the two most recent examples under consideration are Mother Teresa (1999, by Pope John Paul II) and Pope John Paul II (2005, by Pope Benedict XVI).

Within this Congregation exists a College of Relators, which is specifically entrusted with studying the cases for canonization and preparing reports (or "positions") of its findings and its reviews of the diocesan reports. This College of Relators can also draw upon consultors, that is, other experts in history, theology, and spirituality. A promoter of the faith oversees this process in its various phases.

Miracles Miracles are seen as divine interventions by God, and thus by extension as confirmations of the sanctity of an individual. The revised constitution makes clear that an inquiry into alleged miracles is conducted separately from the examination of the life of holiness or martyrdom of a servant of God. The Sacred Congregation has a board of medical experts or physicians, who discuss cases of alleged miracles dealing with healing. These experts do not produce a theological judgment that a miracle has occurred, but are only asked whether or not there exists a medical or scientific reason for a miracle or physical cure. No miracles are required for a martyr to be declared a saint.

During this process, relics (such as hair, bone fragments, pieces of clothing) of the servant of God may be collected. The authenticity and preservation of relics is relegated to the Congregation. Relics are used in the church as a means of remembrance and devotion to a particular saint, and are especially kept in places of pilgrimage or as part of an altar.

At the culmination of the entire examination process, the Sacred Congregation, with its member bishops and cardinals, examines the final reports or votes of the relators, expert consultors, physicians, and the promoter of the faith and issues a report to the pope.

There are two distinct levels, the one preceding the other, of the formal recognition of the sanctity of an individual: beatification and canonization. Beatification requires the verification (or "instruction") of one miracle attributed to the servant of God. If authentic, then the pope can declare the person as "Blessed," wherein the church recognizes that this person is a model of heroic virtue. The person is given the title of Blessed, and a limited cult of veneration of this person is permitted at the local level, in a region or in a religious community. The process from beatification to canonization requires the authentication of a second

miracle. Once a second report is submitted and a second miracle verified, the pope can proceed to a declaration of sainthood. This is a definitive declaration by the pope that the saint is enjoying eternal life in God and that a cult of veneration is to be extended to the universal church. Both beatification and canonization normally take place in St. Peter's Basilica in Rome, during a pontifical Mass, and are done solely through a decree of the pope. Those designated with the title saint are assigned a particular feast day, which is commemorated by special prayers in the church's liturgical calendar.

Jaroslav Z. Skira

See also: Eastern Orthodoxy; Francis of Assisi; Helena, Flavia Iulia; Ignatius of Loyola; Mary, Blessed Virgin; Relics; Roman Catholic Church.

Resources:
Cunningham, Lawrence S. *The Meaning of Saints.* San Francisco: Harper & Row, 1980.
Hawley, John Stratton, ed. *Saints and Virtues.* Berkeley: University of California Press, 1987.
Woodward, Kenneth. *Making Saints: How the Catholic Church Determines Who Becomes a Saint, Who Doesn't and Why.* New York: Touchstone/Simon and Schuster, 1996.

Sakyapa

The Sakyapa Order of Tibetan Buddhism has a long history and has produced many renowned scholars and meditators, and Sakya lamas have played leading roles in Tibetan history and politics. Today it is the smallest of the four major traditions of Tibetan Buddhism, but maintains a strong reputation for learning and religious practice. Its major leaders were forced to flee Tibet following the Chinese invasion in the 1950s, and its main center today is in Dehradun, India.

The Order derives its name from Sakya (Gray Earth), the area in central Tibet in which its main monastery is located. Sakya Monastery was founded in 1073 by Konchok Gyelpo (1034–1102) and later became one of the great monastic centers in Tibet after the Sakyapas came to supremacy following Sakya

Pandita's (1182–1251) appointment as regent by Gushri Khan in 1245. This followed a visit by Sakya Pandita to the Mongol court to surrender Tibet to the Mongols. Traditional histories report that the khan was so impressed by Sakya Pandita that he converted to Buddhism, and rather than impose direct Mongol control over Tibet appointed Sakya Pandita to rule in his stead. Sakyapa overlordship continued with Sakya Pandita's successors, but it declined in the late 14th century when Mongol power waned.

The most distinctive Sakyapa meditative practice is called "path and result" (*lamdre*), which is a comprehensive system of practice based on the Hevajra Tantra. Following the Hevajra's doctrine of "the undifferentiability of cyclic existence and nirvana," the lamdre system views the path and its result as being inseparable and mutually implicatory. Path cannot legitimately be distinguished from result because the former leads to the latter. And result subsumes path. From the standpoint of Buddhahood, all dichotomies vanish, and meditators in this system are trained to view all distinctions as merely projections of mind. Mind in turn is said to have an essence of luminosity and emptiness.

An important tenet of the path and result system is the similarity of the "triple appearance" (*nangsum*) and "triple continuum" (*gyüsum*). The first consists of (1) the appearance of phenomena as impure error; (2) the appearance of experience in meditation; and (3) pure appearance. These are said to be fundamentally the same; the only difference lies in how they are perceived. The first refers to how ordinary, unenlightened beings perceive reality, while the second refers to the perceptions of advanced meditators—who have removed some of the mental defilements that cloud the perceptions of ordinary beings. The third aspect is known by buddhas, who have removed all defilements and perceive the true nature of reality.

The triple continuum consists of (1) basis; (2) path; and (3) result. As with the triple vision, the three are said to be undifferentiable. The basis is the two truths (conventional and ultimate truths). The path consists of cultivating method and wisdom. The pure vision is the result and represents the attainment of Buddhahood.

The leadership of the Sakyapa Order is held by male members of the Khon family. According to traditional Sakyapa histories, the Khons were originally adherents of the Nyingmapa Order but split from it when Sherap Tsultrim witnessed a public display of esoteric Tantric rituals at a Nyingmapa monastery and decided that this violated Tantric injunctions concerning secrecy. This attitude continues in the Order today, and Sakyapas tend to be the most secretive of all schools of Tibetan Buddhism, particularly with respect to Tantric teachings and practices. As a possible result of that attitude, Sakyapa is also the smallest of Tibetan Buddhism's four orders (though its literature, philosophical systems, and meditative practices are widely influential). The head of the Order is the "Throne Holder of Sakya" (Sakya Tridzin), who fled to India in the 1950s and founded the Order's current headquarters.

Sakya Centre
187 Rajoour Rd., PO Rajpour
District Dehra Dun
Uttar Pradesh
India

John Powers and J. Gordon Melton

See also: Tibetan Buddhism.

References

Davidson, Ronald. *Tibetan Renaissance: Tantric Buddhism in the Rebirth of Tibetan Culture.* New York: Columbia University Press, 2005.

Deshung, Rinpoche. *The Three Levels of Spiritual Perception.* Boston: Wisdom Publications, 1995.

Gyaltsen, Sakyapa Sonan. *The Clear Mirror: A Traditional Account of Tibet's Golden Age.* Ithaca, NY: Snow Lion Publications, 1996.

Powers, John. *Introduction to Tibetan Buddhism.* 2nd ed. Ithaca, NY: Snow Lion, 2007.

Stearns, Cyrus. *Luminous Lives: The Story of the Early Masters of the Lam 'Bras in Tibet.* Boston: Wisdom Publications, 2002.

Stearns, Cyrus. *Taking the Result as the Path: Core Teachings of the Sakya Tradition.* Boston: Wisdom Publications, 2006.

Salesians

The Salesians, officially the Order of Saint Francis de Sales, is an ordered community of the Roman Catholic Church, founded in 1859 by John Bosco (1815–1888) with an original intention of emphasizing the Christian education of youth. It has both lay and clerical members. It and its various divisions are named for Francis de Sales (1567–1622), a saint of the church, known for his writings on spiritual devotion. Bosco also founded the Salesian Sisters (the Daughters of Mary Help of Christian) with a similar purpose. The Salesian Sisters has grown into one of the largest religious orders for women in the world.

In his 26th year, Bosco befriended an orphan whom he began to instruct in the faith. This relationship led to his founding an oratory in Turin, Italy, that became the motherhouse of his order. The order was formed with recruits from the youth he had been instructing. There were 17 in the original group that constituted the Salesian Order. He received papal approval in 1864 and approval of the constitution of the Order in 1874. Expansion began after official approval, and in 1875 the first missionaries were commissioned. They settled in Argentina. They were led by Giovanni Cagliero, the first Salesian to become a bishop and cardinal.

At the time of Bosco's death, in 1888, the order had spread in Europe to Spain, France, and England, and in South America to Argentina, Uruguay, and Brazil. Growth continued at a spectacular pace through the next century, and the order spread to more than 70 countries. In some cases, they were invited to countries in which Italian communities had emerged where they developed work among both adults and youth.

The Salesian Sisters developed a mirror educational program for girls. Its co-founder with Bosco, Mother Maria Domenica Mazzarello (1837–1881), would later, like Bosco, be canonized. The lay affiliate group, called the Cooperators, focuses its efforts on charitable activities toward youth.

The Salesian Order's work is found around the world. Its more than 2,700 houses are organized into 8 geographical regions and then into provinces. Two provinces serve the western and eastern United States. With more than 20,000 individual members, it is the third largest missionary organization in the world.

Statue of John Bosco, founder of the Salesians, Turin, Italy. (J. Gordon Melton)

Salesian Order
Via della Pisana 1111
CP 9092
I-00163 Roma-Aurelio
Italy
http://www.sdb.org/SDBWEB/index.asp (in Italian)
J. Gordon Melton

See also: Roman Catholic Church.

References

Ceria, Eugene. *The Salesian Society: Foundation, Organization, Expansion.* Paterson, NJ: Salesiana, 1955.

Wirth, Morand. *Don Bosco and the Salesians.* New Rochelle, NY: Don Bosco, 1982.

Salt Lake City

Salt Lake City, Utah, in the western United States, is the spiritual center and site of the international

View of downtown Salt Lake City, Utah, at dusk. (Vlad Turchenko/Dreamstime.com)

administrative offices of the Church of Jesus Christ of Latter-day Saints. The settlement of the Latter-day Saints in the Salt Lake Valley in 1847 was prompted by the assassination of the church's founder and prophet, Joseph Smith, Jr. (1805–1844), in Carthage, Illinois. Smith's death led to a disruption of the Saints' community in Nauvoo, Illinois, and prompted their move to the West, beyond what at the time was the boundary of the United States. The Saints' leadership had become aware of the valley from the early report of explorers.

The development of the city was punctuated by several occurrences. Around July 22, 1847, Orson Pratt (1811–1881), one of the church's apostles, led the advance party of the original group to migrate from Iowa into the valley. They dammed up the most significant source of freshwater, City Creek, and began planting crops. Church president Brigham Young (1801–1877) arrived on July 24 and on the 28th designated the spot between the two branches of the creek where the new temple would be erected. That site would, for the next generation, become the center of the Latter-day Saint community, around which a vibrant commercial urban area developed, spurred by the 1870 completion of the Utah Central Railroad.

As the city grew, it was divided ecclesiastically into what were termed wards (comparable to a Protestant parish), and in each ward a meetinghouse was constructed. Originally, Young designated a 40-acre site as the grounds for the temple (and later to be known as Temple Square). The site was later reduced to 10 acres. The groundbreaking of the temple, which is used for several special events for church members, would be held on February 14, 1853. A decade later, in 1863, the construction of the tabernacle, a large auditorium for important gatherings, including the annual conference of the church's leadership, was begun. It was completed in 1867, but not dedicated until 1875. The temple was not completed and dedicated until 1893.

Already by the 1870s, Temple Square became a site for tourists and visitors to the city; the appointment of an official guide in 1875 signaled the beginning of the use of visits to Temple Square as an occasion to explain the beliefs and practices of the church to non-members. Today, the Square hosts thousands of visitors monthly, and two visitors centers have been placed just inside the Square at the north and south entrances.

Integral to understanding the uniqueness of Salt Lake City is the Latter-day Saint concept of the gathering of Israel. They believed that there would be a

New Jerusalem that would supersede the old Jerusalem, and that it would be on the American continent. That gathering place would ultimately be Independence, Missouri. But the members of the church were and still are locked out of access to the designated temple site in Independence, which is under the control of the small Church of Christ (Temple Lot). One of the purposes of establishing a gathering place was for the erection of a temple and the delivery of temple ordinances to the members. The Salt Lake temple was completed in the 1890s and through the 20th century numerous other temples would be completed. By the middle of the 20th century, the need to gather membership in Salt Lake City had been completed and policy about drawing members to Utah gradually reversed. Members are now encouraged to remain in their home communities and temples have been erected to provide them the ordinances.

In the light of the explosive growth of the church, the uniqueness of Salt Lake City somewhat changed through the last decades of the 20th century. It became the center of the Latter-day Saint West, an area along the Rocky Mountains from Phoenix, Arizona, to Boise, Idaho, in which the Latter-day Saints formed the majority of the religious community and also tended to dominate the political scene. Given the peculiar nature of the American government, it also tended to give the sparsely populated Rocky Mountain states significant political clout in Washington, D.C.

While gradually assimilating into the major currents of American life, Salt Lake City remains peculiarly Latter-day Saint in many ways, with mainstream Catholic, Protestant, and Free churches forming a distinct minority community. Evangelical churches have also made it a center for proselytizing Latter-day Saints, who are viewed as following a different, non-Christian religion, while Latter-day Saints have emphasized their Christian credentials and have sought acceptance within the larger ecumenical scene, with very mixed results. One symbol of its assimilation has been the changing laws concerning the serving of alcoholic beverages in restaurants. The hosting of the Olympics in 2002 became the occasion for ending many of the restrictions that limited the serving of alcohol to restaurants designated as private clubs, and the adoption of laws more consistent with the rest of the country.

Most recently, the Church of Jesus Christ of Latter-day Saints has completed a large new church headquarters building complex just north of Temple Square, which further asserts its role in the city's life while providing more adequate facilities for serving its global membership.

J. Gordon Melton

See also: Church of Jesus Christ of Latter-day Saints; Independence, Missouri; Jerusalem; Smith, Joseph, Jr.; Temples—Church of Jesus Christ of Latter-day Saints.

References
Alexander, Thomas G., and James B. Allen. *Mormons and Gentiles: A History of Salt Lake City*. Boulder, CO: Pruett Publishing Company, 1984.

Huffaker, Kurt A. *Salt Lake City Then and Now*. San Diego, CA: Thunder Bay Press, 2008.

McCormack, John S. *Salt Lake City: The Gathering Place*. Salt Lake City, UT: Signature Books, 2000.

Tullidge, Edward W. *History of Salt Lake City*. Salt Lake City, UT: Star Printing Company, 1886.

Salvadoran Lutheran Synod

Lutheranism emerged in El Salvador only in the middle of the 20th century. In the early 1950s, the newly formed Lutheran World Federation made contact with expatriate German communities in El Salvador. An initial congregation was founded in 1954. The Lutheran Church–Missouri Synod (not associated with the Lutheran World Federation) took the lead in developing a church. The church grew beyond the German community, especially in the 1970s, when congregations arose across the country. The church, however, entered a period of instability following the military coup in 1979 and the division of the country into warring factions through the 1980s. As a result of the existence of armed insurrectionists, death squads, and the resulting deaths of some 50,000 people, some 500,000 people fled to the United States and another quarter of a million to neighboring countries during the early 1980s.

As work related to the Missouri Synod spread through Central America, the various churches were united into the Council of Lutheran Churches in Central America and Panama. Of the several churches, the Salvadoran Church is the largest. In 1972 the church began work among the poor of El Salvador, but as civil unrest increased, they found themselves presented with a situation far beyond their means. In 1983 the president of the synod and the physician in charge of its mobile clinic were arrested and deported. At the next synod meeting, in January 1984, the church, independently of the Missouri Synod, formally applied for membership in the Lutheran World Federation. The Federation had already entered the country with assistance for displaced persons.

By the mid-1980s the synod had only two ordained ministers left, the remainder either having been killed or having fled. The church survived the era of terror through the effort of a group of lay preachers, who remain important to its life. By 2006, the church had recovered and some 17 pastors were serving its 68 congregations and 15,000 members. It is a member of the Lutheran World Federation and the World Council of Churches.

Salvadoran Lutheran Synod
Calle 5 de Noviembre 313
Barrio Sam Miguelito
San Salvador
El Salvador

J. Gordon Melton

See also: Lutheran Church–Missouri Synod; Lutheran World Federation; World Council of Churches.

References

Bachmann, E. Theodore, and Mercia Brenne Bachmann. *Lutheran Churches in the World: A Handbook.* Minneapolis, MN: Augsburg, 1989.

Van Beek, Huibert. *A Handbook of the Churches and Councils: Profiles of Ecumenical Relationships.* Geneva: World Council of Churches, 2006.

Salvation Army

The Salvation Army is an international movement—an evangelical part of the universal Christian Church, with roots in Methodism and the Holiness movement. Its bases its message on the Bible, sees its ministry as motivated by love for God, and accepts a basic mission to preach the gospel of Jesus Christ and meet human needs in his name without discrimination. Although the Army is distinctive in government and practice, its doctrines follow the mainstream of Christian belief and teaching, and its 11 articles of faith emphasize the primacy of scripture, the need for personal salvation, and the possibility of living a Christlike life. The objects of the Army, outlined in the Salvation Army Act of 1980, include "the advancement of Christianity and, pursuant thereto, the advancement of education, the relief of poverty, and other charitable objects beneficial to society or the community of mankind as a whole."

The Salvation Army began as a revivalist mission in East London (United Kingdom), founded in 1865 by William Booth (1829–1912), a former minister in the Methodist New Connexion. The mission adopted the name the Salvation Army in 1878 and is now at work in more than 100 countries, its activities radiating from its International Headquarters in London. The military style of the organization, which promotes mobility and discipline, proved to be an effective stimulus in the Army's fight against evil, and the Army has used to advantage its military features—such as uniforms, flags, and ranks—to identify, inspire, and regulate its endeavors.

In the early 1880s, Salvationists often faced brutal and determined opposition from publicans and brothel keepers who were losing trade and influence. The sight of Salvationists taking the Christian gospel onto the streets, marching with brass bands, uniforms, and banners, often aroused the protesters' anger, and in 1882, some 669 Salvationists were knocked down, kicked, or otherwise assaulted on the streets of Britain alone.

Leadership in the Salvation Army is provided by commissioned officers who are recognized ministers of religion. Full-time officers and employees, as well as soldiers, adherents, and friends who give voluntary service, maintain a wide variety of evangelistic and social programs, under the authority of the General, the Army's international leader, who is elected by a High Council convened for that purpose. The Army also

A World Health Organization official speaks with a Salvation Army member about the condition of the local people and the supplies needed following the December 26, 2004, tsunami that devastated the island of Sumatra in Indonesia. (U.S. Navy)

benefits from the support of many generous donors and friends, including a number who serve on advisory boards. Internationally, there were 16,910 active officers, 9,122 retired officers, 1,109,249 senior soldiers, 181,738 adherents, and 376,905 junior soldiers as of January 1, 2008.

Administratively, the Salvation Army is divided into more than 50 territories and commands, each led by a territorial commander, or officer commanding. Territories are divided into divisions, with a divisional commander leading a team of administrative staff. Each division includes a number of corps and other Salvation Army centers, each with its own commanding officers or managers. Officers from Britain pioneered the Army's work in many countries during the early years, but the aim has always been to develop local leadership and membership; indigenous leaders are now taking increased responsibility in their own countries. The considerable movement of officers between territories is a vital factor in maintaining the Army's internationalism.

The corps is the local Salvation Army center, established both to disseminate the Army's Christian teachings and to serve the needs of the local community. There are currently 14,869 corps throughout the world, where a variety of people meet for worship, fellowship, musical activities, and other events. The corps program will also usually include community activities such as lunch clubs, parent and toddler groups, and advice and counseling services. All are welcome at Salvation Army meetings, which are characterized by lively singing and enthusiastic participation, including spontaneous personal Christian witness and extempore prayer.

Unlike most other Christian denominations, the Salvation Army does not use the sacraments in its worship, not because of opposition to the sacraments, but because Salvationists believe that the sacraments are not essential to becoming a Christian, and that it is possible to live a holy life and receive the grace of God without the use of physical signs and symbols. Salvationists accept a disciplined and compassionate life of high moral standards that include abstinence from alcohol and tobacco. From its earliest days, the Army has accorded equal opportunities to women, every rank and service being open to them. From childhood, young people are encouraged to love and serve God.

Raised as an evangelistic mission, the Salvation Army also spontaneously embarked on schemes to improve the social conditions of the poor, and it has established social service centers, hospitals, clinics, and schools in many parts of the world. Wherever the Army operates, facilities such as thrift stores, eventide homes, hostels, and children's homes have developed to meet local needs, as an expression of practical Christianity. The Army, with other agencies, is also involved widely in providing emergency relief wherever disasters occur, whether through famine, flooding, hurricanes, earthquakes, or war. The Salvation Army was for a time a member of the World Council of Churches but withdrew over the Council's involvement in various intense political issues.

Gordon Taylor

See also: Holiness Movement; Methodism; World Council of Churches.

References

Coutts, Frederick. *No Discharge in this War: A One Volume History of the Salvation Army.* London: Hodder and Stoughton, 1975.

The Salvation Army Act of 1980.

The Salvation Army Year Book. (Published annually.)

Sandall, Robert Arch Wiggins, Frederick Coutts, and Henry Gariepy. *History of the Salvation Army.* 8 vols. London: Thomas Nelson/Hodder and Stoughton, 1949–2000.

Samantabadhara's Birthday

Samantabadhara (also known as the bodhisattva Universal Worthy or in Japan as Fugen-bosatsu and China as Puxian) is one of the primary bodhisattvas in the Mahayana tradition and appears as one of the prime characters in the Avatamsaka or Flower Garland (Adornment) Sutra, along with Guatama Buddha and Manjushri. Toward the end of the sutra, he makes the 10 vows common to the bodhisattva path: to worship and respect all Buddhas; to praise all the Buddhas; to make abundant offerings (that is, give generously); to repent of all karmic hindrances; to rejoice in others' merits and virtue; to request that the dharma wheel continue to be turned (that is, that teaching activity continue); to request the Buddhas to remain in the world; to follow the teachings of the Buddhas at all times; to accommodate and benefit all living beings; to constantly transfer all merits and virtues to benefit all beings.

From these vows, Samantabadhara is often associated with dharma practice, most notably, the effort and focus required to follow one's religious obligations. He is often pictured seated on a white elephant with six tusks and is said to reside on Mount Emei in Sichuan Province, one of the four sacred mountains of Chinese Buddhism, and noted as its patron. Veneration of Samantabadhara/Puxian dates to the third century CE, when Chinese monk Huichi built the Puxian Temple (now known as Wannian Temple) there. Then in 964 the Song Emperor Taizi (927–976) sent a large Buddhist mission of some 300 people under the leadership of a monk named Jiye to India. Upon their return, the emperor authorized Jiye to construct several temples on Mount Emei and to cast a bronze statue, some 62 tons in weight and 28 feet high, of Puxian. The statue now resides in the Wannian Temple.

Samantabadhara has a special role in the groups of the Nichiren tradition who privilege the Lotus Sutra above all Buddhist writings. In the 28th chapter of the Lotus Sutra, he emerges as the protector of its disciples. He tells the Buddha, "if there is someone who accepts and upholds this sutra, I will guard and protect him, free him from decline and harm, see that he attains peace and tranquility, and make certain that no

Statue of Samantabadhara on Mount Emei, China. (Waveone/Dreamstime.com)

See also: Bodhisattva; Mahayana Buddhism; Nichirenshu; Soka Gakkai International.

References

Boheng, Wu, and Cai Zhuozhi. *100 Buddhas in Chinese Buddhism.* Trans. by Mu Xin and Yan Zhi. Singapore: Asiapac Books, 1997.

"Emei Shan." Sacred Destinations. http://www .sacred-destinations.com/china/emei-shan.htm. Accessed May 15, 2009.

The Flower Adornment Sutra. http://www.cttbusa .org/avatamsaka/avatamsaka_contents.asp. Accessed May 15, 2009.

The Seeker's Glossary of Buddhism. New York: Sutra Translation Committee of the United States and Canada, 1998.

The Soka Gakkai Dictionary of Buddhism. Tokyo: Soka Gakkai, 2002.

Vessantara. *Meeting the Buddhas: A Guide to Buddhas, Bodhisattvas, and Tantric Deities.* Birmingham, UK: Windhorse Publications, 1998.

one can spy out and take advantage of his shortcomings." He emphasizes this vow with another: "I now therefore employ my transcendental powers to guard and protect this sutra. And after the Thus Come One [the Buddha] has entered extinction, I will cause it to be widely propagated throughout Jambudvipa [a continent surrounding the mythical mountain Sumeru] and will see that it never comes to an end."

The Universal Worthy Sutra, seen by Nichiren Buddhists as an epilogue to the Lotus Sutra, describes Samantabadhara's beneficence and power, how believers can meditate on him, and the benefit they gain from their meditations.

In the Chinese tradition Samantabadhara's birthday is celebrated on the 21st day of the 2nd month, 2 days after Guan Yin's birthday. Because of Samantabadhara's association with Mount Emei, it is one focus of celebrations.

J. Gordon Melton

Samavesam of Telegu Baptists Churches

The Samavesam of Telegu Baptists Churches is one of two large Baptist groupings in India, the country with more Baptists than any other, apart from the United States. American Baptists initiated work in South India in 1836, the first missionaries finally settling in Nellore in 1840. The first church, and for many years the only center of activity, was founded in Nellore in 1844. A second station was opened in 1866 in Ongole by James E. Clough. It grew rapidly as a number of Madigas, an outcast group, affiliated with the mission. Then in 1876, following a local famine, almost 10,000 joined. As much as possible, Clough encouraged the converts to remain in their former social setting rather than, as occurred elsewhere, to form separate Christian communities. The church subsequently spread among the outcasts in the Telegu-speaking areas through the rest of the century.

Beginning in 1925, there was a measurable movement of caste Hindus into the church, notable in that the evangelists were outcasts. The church also built a strong educational program, providing primary education and technical training that offered a wide range of employment opportunities for the poorer element in Telegu society. Two important institutions for higher education, Madras Christian College and the Women's Christian College of Madras, were also supported, and the first seminary was opened in the 1870s. By 1920, seven hospitals had been built.

After World War II and India's independence, the Telegu mission began the transition to autonomy, a process that took some time and included a period of litigation over church property. Following the transition, the church has continued as an expanding body. In 2006, it reported 844,000 members in 1,214 congregations, approximately two-thirds of all Baptists in South India. The church has taken an ecumenical stance. It is a member of the World Council of Churches, the Baptist World Alliance, and a variety of regional and national ecumenical structures.

Samavesam of Telegu Baptist Churches
C.M.A. Compound, Nellore 524 003
Andhra Pradesh
India

J. Gordon Melton

See also: Baptist World Alliance; World Council of Churches.

References

Clough, John E. *From Darkness to Light: A Story of the Telugu Awakening*. Philadelphia: American Baptist Publication Society, 1882.

Van Beek, Huibert. *A Handbook of the Churches and Councils: Profiles of Ecumenical Relationships*. Geneva: World Council of Churches, 2006.

Wardin, Albert W., ed. *Baptists around the World*. Nashville: Holman, 1995.

■ Samoa

The present state of Samoa (or Western Samoa) consists of those islands of the Samoan archipelago in the South Pacific west of the 171st meridian. Samoa is sandwiched between the nations of Tonga and the Tokelau Islands. The islands together have 1,137 square miles and a population of 217,000 (2008).

The Samoan islands were inhabited by Polynesians by at least 1000 BCE. They were first visited by Europeans (the Dutch) in 1722, but it was almost another century before Europeans began to settle in the islands in any number. After Germany occupied the islands in 1855, merchants concentrated on the lucrative copra business. However, both the British and the Americans continued to express claims for the land, and in 1899 the islands east of meridian 171 were given to the United States. In 1919, following World War I, New Zealand took control of Western Samoa.

After World War II, Western Samoa became a UN trusteeship. In 1962, following a plebiscite on the issue, independence was achieved and a constitutional monarchy in line with traditional social structures in Samoa was established in power. Throughout the 20th century there was significant European/Polynesian intermarriage in Samoa, and a recognizably new group, the Euronesians, have become a measurable part of the population.

Christianity arrived in Samoa at a particularly propitious time, immediately following a popular revolt that had overthrown an unpopular autocratic ruler, Tamafaiga. The first missionary was a Samoan who had found Christianity while among the Methodists in Tonga in 1828. The first churches emerged from his preaching when he returned home. Then in 1830, John Williams, a missionary with the London Missionary Society (LMS), and a team of eight Tahitian teachers visited. The eight remained behind after Williams left. By 1835 there were some 2,000 Christians, and by 1837 some 13,000. By the end of the decade, the overwhelming majority of the islanders had identified with the church, and within a generation the traditional religion had all but disappeared.

In the process of the Christianization of Samoa, the Congregationalists of the LMS and the Methodists, without consulting the Samoans, agreed not to compete with each other in the area; the Methodists agreed to withdraw in favor of the LMS. The Samoans, however, rejected the decision, as the original work in the islands had been Methodist-related. The Samoan Methodists became an independent body. In 1855, the Australian Methodists became autonomous of the

A church in Samoa, where most citizens are Christians. (Martin Krause/Dreamstime.com)

British Methodists and re-established relationships with the Samoans. The Samoan work became first a district and then a conference in the Methodist Church of Australia. It became independent in 1964 as the Methodist Church in Samoa.

At the same time, the work of the LMS prospered and matured into the Congregational Christian Church in Samoa, which became independent of its missionary oversight in 1962. Originally this church covered both Western Samoa and American Samoa, but in 1980 the churches in American Samoa separated to form the Church of Tutuila and Manua, now the Congregational Christian Church of American Samoa. The LMS work also gave birth to an independent congregation in Apia that originated in an English-speaking seamen's church. Although it retains strong relations with the Congregational Christian Church, the small Apia Protestant Church remains an independent body.

These churches contain the majority of Christians in Samoa and form the backbone of the ecumenical community. They are members of the Samoa Council of Churches, and the two larger bodies are members of the World Council of Churches. Historically, both churches have been missionary churches and have supported Samoan missionaries across the South Pacific.

The Roman Catholic Church came to Samoa in 1845 from the Wallis and Futuna Islands. It grew steadily in the face of the Protestant establishment and by the 1960s claimed more than 20 percent of the population. A vicariate that included Samoa and the newer work in the Tokelau Islands was established in 1957. That vicariate was elevated to a diocese in 1966. The present diocese (of Samoa-Apia) was divided in 1982 by the separation of the work in American Samoa and again in 1992 of the work in the Tokelau Islands.

The Church of Jesus Christ of Latter-day Saints arrived in Samoa in 1863 in the person of two missionaries, Kimo Pelia and Samuela Manoa. Their commission to begin work, however, had been made by an excommunicated leader, Walter Murray Gibson, who

Samoa

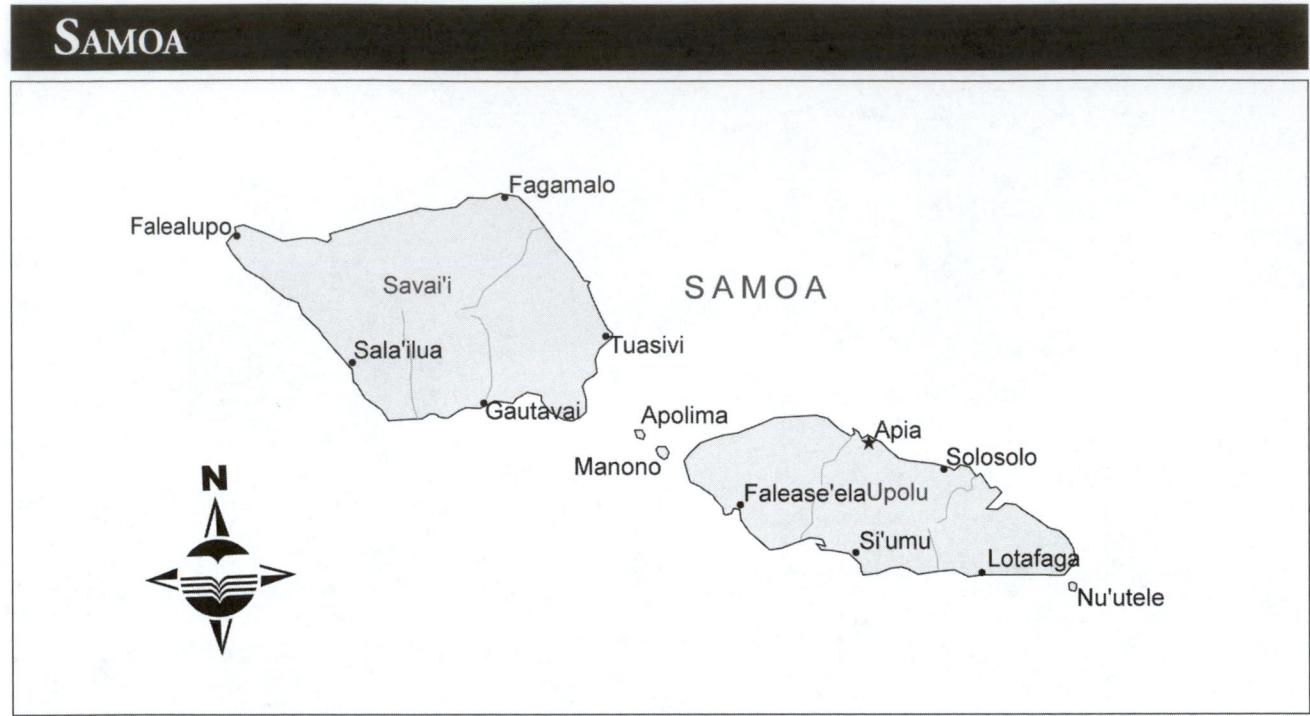

Samoa

Religion	Followers in 1970	Followers in 2010	% of Population	Annual % growth 2000–2010	Followers in 2025	Followers in 2050
Christians	140,000	190,000	98.8	0.69	208,000	211,000
Protestants	82,500	114,000	59.4	0.85	123,000	125,000
Marginals	21,700	70,000	36.5	1.48	76,000	75,000
Roman Catholics	29,800	35,900	18.7	2.43	40,000	40,000
Baha'is	1,800	950	0.5	−0.18	1,000	1,000
Agnostics	0	1,300	0.7	3.88	2,000	3,000
Muslims	0	70	0.0	3.37	100	200
Atheists	0	20	0.0	0.00	50	100
Buddhists	0	20	0.0	0.00	40	60
Chinese folk	0	20	0.0	0.00	40	60
Total population	**142,000**	**192,000**	**100.0**	**0.71**	**211,000**	**215,000**

had built an independent mission in Hawaii. His church lasted into the 1880s, and Gibson went on to become the prime minister of Hawaii. When official missionaries of the church arrived in 1888, Manoa quickly brought the work under their care. The work grew slowly, being somewhat hindered during the years of German control (1899–1914), but it was aided by the publication of the Samoan edition of the Book of Mormon in 1903.

The Mormon work in Samoa was so successful that in 1977 the church announced plans to build a temple (to be used for weddings and other special ceremonies) in Apia. It was finished and dedicated in 1983. By the end of the 1990s the church claimed more than 50,000 members, approximately one-fourth of the country's population.

The other church to reach Samoa in the 19th century was the Seventh-day Adventist Church, which arrived in 1895. It too has experienced steady growth. The Samoa mission was formally organized in 1921 and now exists as part of the Central Pacific Union Mission.

Pentecostalism entered the islands in 1928 through missionaries from the Assemblies of God. It was subsequently joined by the United Pentecostal Church International (a Oneness body), the Church of God of Prophecy, the Church of God (Cleveland, Tennessee), and two indigenous churches, the Makisua Church and the Samoan Full Gospel Church. The Church of the Nazarene, the Christian Brethren, and the Jehovah's Witnesses are also present. Anglicans are represented by several parishes now part of the Diocese of Polynesia of the Anglican Church in Aotearoa, New Zealand, and Polynesia.

The Baha'i Faith, the only major non-Christian community on the island, received a significant boost in 1973 when the king of Samoa announced his conversion. Subsequently, Apia became the location of the world's seventh Baha'i temple.

J. Gordon Melton

See also: Anglican Church in Aotearoa, New Zealand, and Polynesia; Baha'i Faith; Christian Brethren; Church of God (Cleveland, Tennessee); Church of God of Prophecy; Church of Jesus Christ of Latter-day Saints; Church of the Nazarene; Congregational Christian Church in Samoa; Congregational Christian Church of American Samoa; Jehovah's Witnesses; London Missionary Society; Methodist Church in Samoa; Pentecostalism; Roman Catholic Church; Seventh-day Adventist Church; United Pentecostal Church International; World Council of Churches.

References

Franco, R. W. "The History, Role, and Function of the Contemporary Catholic Church in Western Samoa." M.A. thesis, California State University, 1976.

Herman, Bro, and C. Stubel, eds. *Tala O Le Vavau: The Myths, Legends, and Customs of Old Samoa.* Auckland, NZ: Polynesian Press, 1989.

Setu, F. "The Ministry in the Making: A History of the Emergence of the Ministry of the Church in Samoa, 1830–1900." Th.M. thesis, Pacific Theological College, 1988.

Tuimaualuga, L. "The Ministry of the Congregational Christian Church in Samoa in a fa'a-Samoa (Samoan Custom) Framework." B.D. thesis, Pacific Theological Seminary, 1977.

■ San Marino

San Marino is a republic organized in 1866, as the process of Italian unification was rapidly moving forward. According to local mythology, San Marino had existed as an entity since the fourth century CE and is named for a third-century brick mason who moved onto Mount Titano after helping rebuild the walls of Rimini. He later became known as a man of prayer and was canonized. The territory named for him was formally recognized as a separated nation by the pope in 1831. Today it is the smallest republican state in the

San Marino

Religion	Followers in 1970	Followers in 2010	% of Population	Annual % growth 2000–2010	Followers in 2025	Followers in 2050
Christians	18,400	28,900	91.9	2.25	29,700	28,200
Roman Catholics	18,200	27,900	88.5	2.28	28,500	26,800
Marginals	30	300	1.0	0.00	500	800
Agnostics	500	1,700	5.4	3.39	2,200	2,800
Atheists	200	550	1.7	2.34	700	900
Baha'is	70	300	1.0	2.34	500	700
Muslims	0	10	0.0	3.71	30	60
Total population	**19,200**	**31,500**	**100.0**	**2.32**	**33,100**	**32,700**

SAN MARINO

[Map of San Marino showing Serravalle, Acquaviva, Borgo Maggiore, San Marino (capital), and Faetaro]

world, being only 23.6 square miles in area, with a population of 30,000 (2008). It is completely surrounded by Italy and located on Mount Titano, above the Adriatic port city of Rimini. It became well known in the mid-20th century for its elegant postage stamps, which became prized items in collections worldwide.

San Marino is located at the border of two Italian provinces, Romana and Marca, and its Roman Catholic churches are divided between the two dioceses of Rimini and Montefeltro. Roman Catholicism dates to the fifth century, when a Christian hermitage was erected on what is now San Marino.

The only visible dissent from the Roman Catholic Church in San Marino are a small gathering of Jehovah's Witnesses that emerged in the mid-1960s and a single spiritual assembly of the Baha'i Faith.

J. Gordon Melton

See also: Baha'i Faith; Jehovah's Witnesses; Roman Catholic Church.

La Guaita, the main fort built to guard the ancient city-state of San Marino. (Corel)

References

Eccardt, Thomas M. *Secrets of the Seven Smallest States of Europe: Andorra, Liechtenstein, Luxembourg, Malta, Monaco, San Marino, and Vatican City.* New York: Hippocrene Books, 2005.

Leckey, Colin. *Dots on the Map.* London: Grosvenor House Publishing, 2006.

Rossi, G., ed. *A Short History of San Marino.* San Marino: C. N. Packett, 1979. http://www.sanmarinosite.com.

Sanbo Kyodan

The Sanbo Kyodan (Fellowship of the Three Treasures), an international Zen Buddhist organization, was founded on the teachings of Harada Dai'un Sogaku Roshi (1871–1961). Harada did not teach in the traditional Soto Zen style in which he had been ordained as a priest and authorized as a Zen master. He taught both Soto and Rinzai meditation techniques (having also received transmission in the Rinzai tradition); he treated monastics and lay practitioners as equals; and he developed introductory talks for novice monks, rather than leaving them devoid of verbal instruction, as was the way in Soto Zen.

In 1954, Harada's successor, Yasutani Haku'un Ryoko Roshi (1885–1973), formally separated from the Soto lineage in which he had been ordained and founded a new organization, the Sanbo Kyodan, based on Harada's teachings. The Sanbo Kyodan is considered an independent lay stream of Soto Zen that incorporates aspects of Rinzai Zen. Having established the

Sanbo Kyodan in Japan, Yasutani initiated its spread internationally.

Yasutani's successor, Yamada Koun Zenshin Roshi (1907–1989), came to lead the Sanbo Kyodan in 1973. He continued to internationalize the organization, and differentiated the Sanbo Kyodan from the majority of Japanese Zen organizations by dissolving distinctions between monastic and lay practitioners; emphasizing the social dimension of human existence; and continuing to break the traditional sectarian barriers that separated Buddhists and Christians. By the end of Yamada's life, approximately one-quarter of the participants at his *sesshins* were Christians. Kubota Akira Ji'un-ken Roshi (b. 1932) succeeded Yamada as head of the Sanbo Kyodan in 1989.

The majority of Sanbo Kyodan adherents practice the Rinzai Zen meditation method of *koan* practice, although some practice the Soto Zen meditation technique of *shikantaza* (just sitting). A range of activities are available at Sanbo Kyodan centers, including group *zazen* (sitting meditation) periods totaling two hours, half- or full-day periods of Zen practice on weekends, and week-long meditation retreats (sesshins). The student-teacher relationship is essential to practice, and private meetings of the student and the Zen master, called *dokusan*, occur regularly.

At least 40 people have been authorized as Zen masters in the Sanbo Kyodan lineage, most of whom are not Japanese. Robert Aitken, founder of the Diamond Sangha, is one of the best known. Sanbo Kyodan Zen masters are not necessarily Buddhists, and they include ordained members of other religious traditions.

Sanbo Kyodan has more than 40 affiliated centers in Japan, India, the Philippines, Singapore, Australia, Canada, the United States, England, France, Germany, the Netherlands, Spain, and Switzerland. The Sanbo Kyodan has more than 2,500 registered followers in Japan and approximately 3,000 in other countries.

The Secretariat of the Sanbo-Kyodan Society
The Center for Health Care and Public Concern
Kudan-minami 4-8-32
Chiyoda-ku, Tokyo 102-8288
Japan
www.sanbo3a@mbp.nifty.com

Michelle Barker

See also: Diamond Sangha; Meditation; Zen Buddhism.

Reference

Ciolek, T. Mathew. "Harada-Yasutani School of Zen Buddhism." http://www.ciolek.com/WWWVLPages/ZenPages/HaradaYasutani.html. Accessed March 15, 2009.

Sanchi

Sanchi is a small town in central India, near the city of Vidisha in the state of Madhya Pradesh. It is a unique Buddhist site, which though unrelated to an event in either Buddha's life or Buddhist history, became possibly the best preserved center of Buddhist architecture in the country. The village was seemingly selected by the Emperor Ashoka (273–236 BCE) as the ideal site to place a large Buddhist monastery. It was a quiet place suitable for meditation, but close enough to the city of Vidisha, which could support the begging of the monks.

Along with the monastery, Ashoka erected a giant stupa in which he placed some of the relics of the Buddha he had recovered. He also erected a monolithic pillar and seven additional stupas on the Sanchi hilltop. Over the next 150 years, the monastic community would flourish and several dozen additional stupas and religious structures were added to the growing complex. A century after Ashoka, a ruler named Pushyamitra (184–148 BCE), known for his hostility to Buddhism, emerged. Speculation centered upon him as the instigator of the large-scale destruction the stupa undertaken at this time. After his rule ended, the stupa was reconstructed, possibly by his successor, Agnimitra. The stupa was expanded and the dome flattened near the top. The dome now rested on a high circular drum that could be accessed via a double staircase. Access to the dome made it an excellent object for circumambulation, the favored activity relative to a stupa. A second pathway for circling the stupa was created at the foot of the stupa. At a later date, four gateways, each facing one of the cardinal directions were added.

Buddhism declined dramatically in India following the invasion of Muslim forces in the 12th century.

Buddhist stupa on a hill in Sanchi, India. (iStockPhoto.com)

The monastery was abandoned and the site fell into disrepair. Only in 1818 was interest renewed, following its rediscovery by a British officer who wrote a description of it. Unfortunately, the initial reactions to the report were a series of visits by would be archaeologists and treasure hunters who caused much destruction. Finally in 1881 restoration began, culminating in the efforts of Sir John Marshall (1876–1958), who headed the Archaeological Survey of India for many years (1902–1928).

Sanchi was listed as an UNESCO World Heritage Site in 1989.

J. Gordon Melton

See also: Ashoka; Devotion/Devotional Traditions; Monasticism; Relics.

References

Dhavalikar, M. K. *Sanchi.* Monumental Legacy Series. Oxford: Oxford University Press, 2005.

Marshall, John. *A Guide to Sanchi.* Calcutta: Superintendent, Government Printing, 1918.

Mitra, Devala. *Sanchi.* Delhi: Director General, Archaeological Survey of India, 1978.

Sant Mat

See Radhasoami; Sikhism/Sant Mat.

Sant Nirankari Mission

The Sant Nirankari Mandel (or Mission) was founded in 1929 by Baba Buta Singh Ji (1873–1943), who was raised as a Sikh in the Punjab and as a young man found himself on a quest to know God. He also developed a talent for reciting Gurbani (the holy verses from the Adi Granth, the Sikh holy book). His search led him to an encounter with Bhai Sahib Kahan Singh Ji, who taught him a secret of receiving Brahm Gyan, or God Knowledge. Subsequently, Buta Singh began sharing the secret with whosoever showed an interest, the result being that the Sant Nirankari Mission was founded in May 1929. Joining Buta Singh in this effort was Baba Avtar Singh Ji (1900–1969), who would later succeed him as the organization's guru (teacher)/ leader.

After receiving knowledge in a manner that remains confidential among members, they are taught to remember God at all times through repeating "Ik Tu Hi Nirankar" ("Thou Formless One"), from which practice the group receives its name. They also are encouraged to follow five principles: (1) since all assets belong to God, one should not feel proud of their possessions; (2) one should not take pride in one's caste, creed, race, faith, or other similar distinctions, and not hate others on that account; (3) one should not look down on others because of their mode of dress, diet, or living; (4) one should not renounce the worldly life to become a recluse or ascetic; (5) one should not divulge the divine knowledge bestowed by the *satguru* to others without his permission; at the same time, one should not take pride in being enlightened.

The orientation toward the satguru who imparts knowledge relates the Nirankaris to the Radhasoami Sant Mat tradition, which also differs from orthodox Sikhs, who no longer have a living guru and no confidential teachings. Baba Avtar Singh Ji was succeeded by Baba Gurbachan Singh Ji (1930–1980) and the present satguru, Baba Hardev Singh Ji Maharaj (b. 1954). During the 1970s the Nirankaris came into open conflict with the Sikh community, especially those elements who were working for the separation of the Punjab from India. Violent clashes included the attack upon Nirankaris at their worship center, the Baisakhi Samagam, in Amritsar in 1978. When police tried to quell the violence, they opened fire and 18 people were killed. Two years later, Gurbachan Singh was assassinated.

Baba Hardev Singh Ji Maharaj succeeded his father as the new satguru. His leadership has been marked by a number of tours to Nirankari centers across India and around the world. The Sant Nirankari Mandel has its headquarters in Delhi. It established itself there soon after the country became independent, a fact that led to some criticism by the larger Sikh community in the Punjab. There are more than 100 branches of the mission outside India, in 27 countries worldwide (2009).

Sant Nirankari Colony
Delhi-110 009
India
http://www.nirankari.org
http://www.nirankari.net
http://www.nirankari.com

J. Gordon Melton

See also: Sikhism/Sant Mat.

References

Chugh, J. S. *Fifty Years of Spiritual Bliss: Commemorative Souvenir on the Golden Jubilee Nirankari Sant Samagam, November 6–10, 1997.* Delhi: Sant Nirankari Mandal, 1997.

Joshi, Nirmal, and Bhupender Bekal, eds. *Salvation Tours (1995–96).* Delhi: Sant Nirankari Mandal, 1997.

Santeria

Santeria is the common name given to West African, especially Yoruban, religion as it manifested among African residents forcefully brought to the Spanish-controlled islands of the Caribbean during the 18th and 19th centuries. African religion survived in part by adopting a Roman Catholic overlay. Its name derived from the identification of various African deities, the Orishas, with Catholic saints. Practitioners thought of their faith as the Reign of the Orishas (Regla de Ocha). White people, seeing what they considered an undue emphasis on and devotion to the saints, called the religion Santeria. Santeria is also known as La Regla Lucumí (from Lucum, the Yoruba language as it is spoken in Cuba and the United States).

Among the Yoruban and related peoples, the pantheon of divinities is headed by Olorun, the High God. As he is a somewhat remote deity, more attention is directed to the Orisha, who are seen as the creators of the Earth and responsible for planting human life here.

tury did it publicly claim the primacy of its African roots. (It was additionally suppressed during the first decades of the Castro regime in Cuba, though it enjoyed a relaxation of restrictions on religion in the 1990s.) At the same time, while affirming its African heritage, it has retained elements of popular Roman Catholic piety, most noticeably the burning of candles with the saints' pictures on personal altars.

Leadership in Santeria is decentralized. Male leaders (priests) are known as *santeros* (or *babalochas*), and females (priestesses) as *santeras* (or *iyalochas*). There are no schools or seminaries, training being conducted on a tutorial system with a knowledgeable satero/santera. Prior to initiation into the priesthood, individuals enter a period of solitude.

Through the 20th century, with the movement of West Indians to North America, Santeria appeared in many urban centers—its presence being visible in the many botanicas, stores that sell the religious supplies used in the practice of the religion that can be found in Spanish-speaking communities. Also, in North America, in the climate of religious freedom and pluralism, more public centers of the Orisha faith have become public. Possibly the most visible American Santeria center is the Church of Lukumi Babalu Aye, which became the subject of a 1993 Supreme Court case over the church's practice of animal sacrifice, which had been outlawed by the city of Hialeah, a Miami suburb.

The African Theological Archministry, based in South Carolina, has become an important pilgrimage site for African Americans but has increasingly stripped itself of its Santeria past and emerged as a Yoruban religious outpost.

The number of followers of Santeria is unknown, its semi-secret nature, its decentralized organization, and the complex way it mixes with Roman Catholicism making it difficult to make any estimation. It has its strongest centers in Puerto Rico and Cuba, but has a significant following in the United States, especially in Miami, New York City, and Southern California. While it undoubtedly has tens of thousands of adherents in North America, estimates ranging as high as a million remain unsubstantiated. A similar practice is found in Brazil under the name Candomblé and in Haiti as Vodou.

A Santeria priest, or *babalawo*, ministers to a follower in Cuba. (Francoise de Mulder/Corbis)

Among the Orisha are Ogun, the god of metals, and Esu, generally associated with divination. In addition, some ancestors have attained popular status as divine beings, such as Sango (or Chango), and are popularly thought of as identical with the Orisha. In the Santeria system, Sango was identified as Saint Barbara, Babalz Ayi became Saint Lazarus, and Eleggua or Elegba became Saint Anthony (the identification being based upon realms of human life with which the saint was associated). The Orisha are seen as sources of power; they are often approached in ceremonies in which people become possessed with the deity, and their spoken words are seen as communications from that particular deity.

Santeria operated as a clandestine religion during the slave era, and only in the last half of the 20th cen-

Church of Lukumi Babalu Aye
PO Box 22627
Hialeah, FL 33002
http://www.church-of-the-lukumi.org/

African Theological Archministry
Oyotunji African Yoruba Village
Box 51
Shelton, SC 29941
http://www.cultural-expressions.com/oyotunji/
    default.htm

J. Gordon Melton

See also: African Traditional Religions; Candomblé; Devotion/Devotional Traditions; Roman Catholic Church; Saints; Vodou.

References

Adefunmi I, Oba Efuntola Oseijeman Adelabu. *Olorisha: A Guidebook into Yoruba Religion.* Shelton, SC: privately printed, 1982.

Canizares, Paul. *Cuban Santeria: Walking with the Night.* Rochester, VT: Destiny Books, 1999.

De la Torre, Miquel A. *Santeria: The Beliefs and Rituals of a Growing Religion in America.* Grand Rapids, MI: William B. Eerdmans Publishing Company, 2004.

Gonzalez-Wippler, Migene. *Santeria.* New York: Julian, 1973.

Murphy, Joseph. *Santeria: African Spirits in America.* Boston: Beacon, 1992.

Santi Asoka, The

The Santi Asoka is a new "unorthodox" Buddhist movement in Thailand initiated by Bodhirak (b. 1934), a Buddhist monk. It reacts against some wayward practices of Thai Buddhist monks and laity. Also, it attempts to preserve the Thai traditional ways of life and authentic Buddhist life. Vegetarianism is strongly promoted. The establishment of the Santi Asoka is a significant phenomenon of the anti-Sangha movement in Thailand (which includes, for example, the rejection of the Sangha Act of Thailand and the acceptance of ordination of female monks).

The Santi Asoka was founded in 1973. Bodhirak, formerly Rak Rakpong, was a television entertainer and songwriter with some interest in magic and supernaturalism. After his ordination as a Thammayut monk in Wat Asokaram in 1970, he abandoned his supernaturalistic beliefs and practices and received the ordained name of Phra Bodkirak (The Preserver of Enlightenment). His strict observance of the Buddha's doctrine attracted a considerable number of faithful Buddhists who began congregating in Wat Asokaram, his monastic residence. There, he formed a religious group called the Asoka. Since the group was composed of both Thammayut and Mahanikai Buddhists, the abbot was not allowed to stay permanently in the monastery. Bodhirak then had to move to Wat Nongkratum, a Mahanikai monastery, where he was ordained as a Mahanikai monk in 1973. Because of their controversial unorthodoxy in beliefs and practices, their religious propagation was obstructed by the established Thai Buddhist Sangha and self-styled orthodox Buddhists. Bodhirak declared his resignation from the authoritative power of the Sangha administration on August 8, 1975. Bodhirak's challenge to the Sangha led to his disrobing and the end of his monastic status in 1989.

The Santi Asokan Buddhists strictly follow their way of life, which includes adherence to Buddhist precepts and discipline as (they believe) originally taught by the Buddha; they live in the Asokan commune in order to help one another to attain their final goal (the end of suffering, or *nirvana*). The Santi Asokan Buddhists earn their living through sufficient economy and sustainable development. They make and sell many name brand products, including liquid soap, shampoo, and herbal medicine.

The Asokans are differentiated into ascetics (ordained people) and laypeople. Ascetics are composed of the male ordained, the female ordained, and novices. In other words, Asokan ascetics are composed of "monks," "female monks" or nuns, and novices both male and female. The process of ordination is more difficult to follow and to pass than that of other Thai monastic lineages. The Asokan ascetics, unlike other Thai monks and novices, do not shave their eyebrows and follow their own monastic rules and practices. Generally, the Asokans live in strict discipline based on chastity, poverty, and spiritual purification. They are strict vegetarians and abstain from sexual lives.

Their minimal requirement is to adhere to the Buddhist Five Precepts and to work hard in their self-reliant commune.

Formerly, the Asokans rejected the worship of the Buddha images and other traditional symbols of Buddhism. However, since 2004, Bodhirak, their leader, has supported the worship of the Buddhist image constructed in their hermitage and the veneration of the Buddha relics brought by some faithful followers. At present, the Asokans who assert the participation in all socio-political movements have their own political party and openly join in many political movements against the Thai government.

The Asokan community has been the subject of considerable controversy. The Asokans deny the authority and the supremacy of the Sangha Supreme Council, which charged that Bodhirak had transgressed the law by forming hermitages and giving ordination to his disciples. Thus, Bodhirak is accused by other "orthodox" Thai Buddhists of having formed his own teachings and interpretations of Buddha's words regardless of normative meanings of the Theravada canon (the Tripitaka)

The leadership and organization of the Santi Asoka are in the sole hands of Bodhirak. Membership numbers are unknown. The Asokan headquarters is in Bangkok, and there are five additional branches in the country's other provinces. There is no center abroad.

Santi Asoka Monastery
67/30 Soi Tiam Porn
Nawamin Rd., Klong Koom
Bung Koom, Bangkok 10240
Thailand

Pataraporn Sirikanchana

See also: Asceticism; Theravada Buddhism.

References

Bodhirak. *Bodhirak and Religion: The Problem of the Buddhist Messiah (Phee Boon)*. Bangkok: Samakkee Sarn, n.d.

Payutto, P. A. *For the Understanding of Bodhirak's Problems*. Bangkok: Buddha Dharma Foundation, n.d.

Sirikanchana, Pataraporn. "Santi Asoka: Its Rise and Religious Roles in Thai Society." *Journal of Buddhist Studies, Chulalongkorn University* 8, no.1 (January–April 2001): 6–68.

Swearer, Donald K. *The Buddhist World of Southeast Asia*. Albany: State University of New York Press, 1995.

Santo Daime

Santo Daime, one branch of the Ayahuasca movement, is a new religion founded in Brazil at the beginning of the 20th century after Raimundo Irineu Serra was introduced to its use. Ayahuasca is a powerful hallucinogenic brew used by many Native peoples across South America. Over the course of the 20th century it became an integral element in various Brazilian religious movements that, toward the end of the century, spread to North America and Europe. Ayahuasca (or vine of the dead) is also known as *yage* (Colombia) and *caapi* (Brazil). It is prepared from the vine *Banisteriopsis caapi* by boiling vine segments with various other plants. The resulting drink contains several hallucinogenics, including harnilne and/or N,N-dimethyltiyptamine. Archaeological evidence strongly suggests that ayahuasca has been used for centuries. It became known outside Brazil from the description of the experiences of Manuel Villavicencio, published in 1858. Adding to Villavicencio's account were the notes of British explorer Richard Spruce, published in 1908. Then in the 1960s, ayahuasca was rediscovered in the context of the wave of interest in LSD and other hallucinogenics throughout the West. In his 1968 paper "The Sound of Rushing Water," Michael Harder, for example, described his experience with the drug in Ecuador in 1961.

South Americans utilize ayahuasca as a healing substance. They gather, prepare, and consume it with proper ceremony and reverence. In the Upper Amazon, *Banisteriopsis caapi* is mixed with another plant, *Psychotna viridis*, and boiled for a full day and then stored until needed. The drug is believed to connect the individual with the force that ties all things together.

At the beginning of the 20th century, while under the influence of ayahuasca, Raimundo Irineu Serra had a vision of the Virgin Mary who, as Our Lady of Conceição, gave him many new teachings. Out of this experience, he constructed a new religion, Santo Daime, the Religion of the Rainforest. Slowly growing at first, following World War II, it spread across Brazil and then overseas as members have migrated. The appearance of ayahuasca as a sacramental substance by an ethnic religious community has presented legal authorities with a spectrum of problems. At the beginning of 2000, members were arrested in Spain, and the movement has begun an effort to have the drug legalized in the United States and several countries of Western Europe.

Soon after his initial encounter with the Virgin, Mestre Irineu (as the founder is known today) received the text of several new songs that now make up a hymnal for the movement. He also received instructions for three dances, with very simple steps, which were believed to facilitate the flow of divine energy. Additional hymns have been received through the years. As the movement spread to other countries, members received new hymns in languages other than Portuguese, and the movement has accepted these for use during worship.

Santo Daime rituals begin with the separation of the men and women into two groups in the meeting hall. Two lines are formed and the ayahuasca received. As the hymns are sung, some begin dancing. Different songs have different purposes (healing, communicating with spirits, celebration). Additional sips of the sacramental substance are handed out every few hours, and the ceremony may last as long as 8 to 12 hours.

Mestre Irineu was succeeded by Padrinho Sabastiao de Melo, who was in turn succeeded by his son Padrinho Alfredo Gregóno de Melo, the present international leader. A second, smaller group is headed by Padrindo Alfredo's brother, Paulo Roberto de Melo. The larger group was incorporated in Brazil in 1974 as the Eclectic Center of the Universal Flowing Light, the term "Eclectic" referring to the mixing of Christian and traditional beliefs within the church. It is headed by a Spiritual Council and is headquartered at Céu do Mapiá, a community created by Padrinho Sabastiao de Melo. Céu de Mapiá is located in the jungle on the Purus River, a tributary of the Amazon. The branch of the movement led by Paulo Roberto has established centers in Hawaii, California, and the Netherlands.

During the 1990s, the use of ayahuasca spread through North America and Europe and subsequent arrests by drug enforcement officials led to a variety of court cases. In 2006, the U.S. Supreme Court ruled in favor of União do Vegetal, one branch of the larger movement based upon a 1990 decision that had made an exception for the use of psychedelic substances in religious contexts. Earlier, in 2001, a Dutch court had ruled in favor of the Santo Daime Church, saying that it was a bone fide religion and that its use of ayahuasca was not a threat to the public. That same year, Portugal restructured it drug laws and decriminalized most psychedelic substances, including ayahuasca.

Centro Eclético da Fluente Luz Universal
Virgem da Luz
c/o Ricardo Tadeu dos Santos
Rua Arniando Santos
240-Recrejo dos Bandeirantes, 22.790-330
Rio de Janeiro
Brazil
http://www.santodaime.org

J. Gordon Melton

See also: Devotion/Devotional Traditions.

References

Alverga, Alex Polari de. *Forest of Vision: Ayahuasca, Amazonian Spirituality, and the Santo Daime Tradition*. Rochester, VT: Park Street Press, 1999.

Dawson, Andrew. *New Era—New Religions: Religious Transformation in Contemporary Brazil*. Aldershot, UK: Ashgate, 2007.

Metzner, Ralph, ed. *Ayahuasca: Human Consciousness and the Spirits of Nature*. New York: Thunder's Mouth Press. 1999.

■ São Tomé and Príncipe

São Tomé and Príncipe are two islands off Africa in the Atlantic Ocean south of Nigeria. After more than 500 years as a colony of Portugal, they became an independent republic in 1975. Together they have 372 square miles of territory and a population of 206,000 (2008).

São Tomé, Príncipe, and the neighboring islands were among the first colonized by the Portuguese in

The main cathedral in São Tomé, built in the 16th century during Portuguese colonial times. (Inna Moody/Dreamstime.com)

the 15th century. They had a fine port and were an ideal location for the establishment of a processing center where slaves could be brought from the coast of Africa and dispatched to various locations in the Americas.

The islands are now inhabited by the Tongas, the original inhabitants found by the Portuguese, as well as other peoples who came to the island during the days of the slave trade or who arrived after the slave trade was abolished. Although most came from the nearby West African coast, a number derive from the

people of the former Portuguese colonies of Angola and Mozambique.

Although most Africans passed through São Tomé on their way to the Americas, some were brought to work the plantations that were created on the islands. After slavery was officially abolished in 1869, a system of indentured servitude was put in place, eventually leading to revolts and repressive actions by the government. The revolution in 1974 in Portugal set the stage for the independence of São Tomé and Príncipe the following year.

During the years of the slave trade and throughout the 1800s, members of numerous African peoples were brought to the islands; though the Roman Catholic Church was established on the islands in 1534, little attempt was made to convert them. At the beginning of the 20th century, most of the residents of African descent retained their traditional religion. However, intense evangelization efforts were made, and by the 1970s most signs of traditional African religions had disappeared.

In 1534, Pope Paul III (r. 1534–1549) created a diocese for São Tomé and the territory being explored and colonized along the African coast. It was originally attached to the ecclesiastical province of Funchal (Madeira) but later was attached as a suffragan diocese to more established dioceses. Since 1940 it has been attached to Luanda (Angola). The church spread quickly once it turned its attention to the Africans, and by the mid-1970s more than 90 percent of the total population (now some 112,000) had been baptized.

For many years, São Tomé served as the penal colony for Angola. In the 1930s an Angolan who had

São Tomé and Príncipe

Religion	Followers in 1970	Followers in 2010	% of Population	Annual % growth 2000–2010	Followers in 2025	Followers in 2050
Christians	71,600	158,000	95.7	1.67	203,000	273,000
Roman Catholics	62,700	140,000	84.9	1.74	181,000	239,000
Independents	2,000	12,800	7.8	2.01	19,000	29,000
Protestants	1,000	5,900	3.6	8.73	8,000	14,000
Baha'is	50	4,400	2.7	1.72	7,000	12,000
Agnostics	0	2,300	1.4	6.73	5,000	10,000
Ethnoreligionists	2,000	400	0.2	1.67	500	600
Muslims	0	70	0.0	1.73	100	200
Total population	**73,600**	**165,000**	**100.0**	**1.72**	**216,000**	**296,000**

SÃO TOMÉ AND PRÍNCIPE

São Tomé and Príncipe

been exiled to São Tomé, and who also happened to be a Protestant Christian, began a Protestant movement that became the Igreja Evangélica (Evangelical Church). He supplied the first scriptures and hymnbook for his converts by writing down the passages and hymns he had memorized. His effort was assisted by two African Christians sent from Angola, one by the Evangelical Alliance of Angola in 1957 and one by the Evangelical Church of Central Angola in 1960. Today, Protestantism is also represented by the Seventh-day Adventist Church, which arrived in 1938, and the Assemblies of God. There is also a small community of the Baha'i Faith on the islands.

J. Gordon Melton

See also: Assemblies of God; Baha'i Faith; Roman Catholic Church; Seventh-day Adventist Church.

References

Garfield, R. *A History of Sao Tome Island, 1470–1655: The Key to Guinea.* San Francisco: Mellen Research University Press, 1992.

Hodges, T., and M. Newitt. *São Tomé and Príncipe: From Plantation Colony to Microstate.* Boulder, CO: Westview, 1988.

Sapta Darma

Sapta Darma is one of a spectrum of new spiritual movements to arise in Indonesia in the 20th century. The founder of Sapta Darma (the seven teachings) was originally named Hardjosapuro. He lived in Pare, in East Java, and began to experience direct contact with God in December 1952. This came in the form of automatic movements, which became the basis for the spiritual practice. Particularly notable experiences continued for several years and included not only the movements he experienced physically but also reception of teachings (some of which appeared on the wall of his home), changes in his name, and finally of a name for the practice. His name changed first to Brahmono, then to Rodjopandito, and finally to Sri Gotama. Teachings continued to flow through Sri Gotama until his death in December 1964.

As the name of the group suggests, there are seven points to the central teaching; some of them are ethical imperatives, others are statements of ontological conviction. In Sapta Darma, however, focus is on spiritual practice rather than theory or philosophy. Practice in Sapta Darma is called *sujud* (Arabic: surrender). Members experience the same movements experienced spontaneously by the founder. Men sit cross-legged, women with feet tucked under them; all report experiencing an awakening of inner energy originating near the base of the spine. This then moves up the spine, leading to an automatic bow, until the forehead touches the floor.

Women wear a white headdress and robe similar to but not the same as those worn by Muslims. The resonances of Sapta Darma names, practice, and theory with Islamic and Indic teachings are not seen as an indication of influence from them. Followers emphasize that their founder did not receive inspiration from, or even know about, other religious teachings. Sapta Darma holds that its theory of *talirasa* (the rope of feeling) is original. It details the network of energy points in the body related to pathways of life energy and linked to practice of sujud.

Sapta Darma, almost alone among Javanese movements, has argued consistently that it ought to be acknowledged as a "religion." During the Suharto era, that term was reserved for five "world religions." From the 1970s until her death in 1996, Sri Pawenang, who led the Yogyakarta-based organization, was bolder than most Javanists in arguing for legitimacy of its practice. As a lawyer she was able to maintain her argument actively in contexts where others had capitulated. Sapta Darma has been prominent as one of the largest Javanese mystical organizations. It once claimed a membership of around 100,000. It has a stronger village following than most Javanist movements and is also exceptional for having attracted a strong ethnic Balinese following.

J. Gordon Melton

See also: Devotion/Devotional Traditions.

References

Hadiwijono, Harun. *Man in the Present Javanese Mysticism.* Baarn, the Netherlands: Bosch and Keuning N.V., 1967.

Pawenang, Sri. *Wewarah Sapta Darma.* Yogyakarta, n.d.

Sarnath

Sarnath, a town in central west Bihar state, India, has joined Lumbini, Kusinagara, and Bodhgaya as one of the four important sites directly connected to the origins of Buddhism. Here, in around 528 BCE, Gautama Buddha (ca. 563–ca.483 BCE) gave his first presentation concerning what would become known as Buddhism. That initial sermon, entitled Dharmachakra-pravartana, or Turning of the Wheel of Law, focused on the way to end suffering and gain enlightenment, a very basic theme of Buddhist thought. Buddhism really began before Buddha arrived in Sarnath, when he found enlightenment at a place later called Bodhgaya (in central Bihar), as he meditated under a tree. It would be in Sarnath, however, that a following emerged. Many Buddhists consider Sarnath to be the birthplace of their faith. Sarnath is also called Deer Park, the name of the specific place where the first group of Buddhist monks gathered and initiated the *sangha*, the Buddhist monastic community. Sarnath is only a few miles from Benares (also known as Varanasi and Kashi), the Hindu holy city.

In the third century BCE, the Emperor Ashoka converted to Buddhism and subsequently threw his resources behind expanding the monastic life at Sarnath. The local community soon grew to include more than 1,000 monks, and would thrive for a millennium. It began its decline with the establishment of Muslim rule in the area, and it took only a few centuries for everything Buddhist to be destroyed and the sites lost to local memory.

The rediscovery of Sarnath followed the British launching archaeological work in the area in the late 19th century. Archaeologists initially uncovered a spectrum of old Buddhist sites. In the 20th century, the Mahabodhi Society, founded by Sri Lankan activist Anagarika Dharmapala (1864–1933), assumed control

Sarnath is the deer park where Gautama Buddha first taught the dharma and where the Buddhist sangha came into existence through the enlightenment of Kondanna. (Yuliya Kryzhevska/Dreamstime.com)

of the Buddhist ruins. At the beginning of the 1930s, the Society erected a new modern temple at Sarnath, the Mulagandhakuti Vihara, decorated with scenes of the Buddha's life. Its main attraction is a silver casket found in Punjab in 1913. An inscription dated to 79 CE claims that the casket holds relics of the Buddha. After being given to the Society in 1935, it was taken to Sarnath.

As archaeological work in the area continued, the Dharmarajika Stupa built by Ashoka to hold some relics of the Buddha was identified, though the location of the casket that contained the relics was never discovered and no one knows if it still exists. A set of carvings on the stupa have survived and may be seen. The Nulghandhakuti Shrine, an elaborate building used by the Buddha for meditation, was also identified.

J. Gordon Melton

See also: Ashoka; Benares; Bodhi-Gaya; Kusinagara; Lumbini; Maha Bodhi Society; Monasticism; Pilgrimage; Relics; Temples—Buddhist.

References

Majupuria, Trilok Chandra. *Holy Places of Buddhism in Nepal and India: A Guide to Sacred Places in Buddha's Lands.* Columbia, MO: South Asia Books, 1987.

Panabokke, Gunaratne. *History of the Buddhist Sangha in India and Sri Lanka.* Dalugama, Kelaniya, Sri Lanka: Postgraduate Institute of Pali and Buddhist Studies, University of Kelaniya, 1993.

Tulku, Tarthang, ed. *Holy Places of the Buddha.* Vol. 9, *Crystal Mirror.* Berkeley, CA: Dharma Publishing, 1994.

Sarvodaya

Sarvodaya (the awakening of all), which celebrated its 50th anniversary in 2008, with its community empowerment programs that support millions of people in 11,600 villages, is undoubtedly the foremost lay Buddhist movement in Sri Lanka, with a strong and active program for the uplifting of human life both materially and spiritually combined with a proven record of strong commitment to nonviolence, service, and compassionate action. Although its Buddhist roots are explicit in both doctrine and practice, its outlook bears witness to the perspective of its founder and his philosophy of "active social engagement," put into practice in rural Sri Lanka and transcending both ethnic and religious boundaries.

On December 7, 1958, the Lanka Jatika Sarvodaya Sramadana movement was born, with a commitment to the idea that things can be changed for the better. Its single and unique practice was the implementation and the exercise of the idea of the "gift of labor" (*sramadana*). Sarvodaya began implementing its ideal with a two-week social work camp for schoolchildren held in an underdeveloped, neglected, untouchable Candala village named Kantoluva, Bingiriya; its goal was to alleviate poverty and social backwardness among the villagers. On January 1, 1958, Ahangamage Tudor Ariyaratne (b. 1931), the founder of Sarvodaya, had accepted the appointment as a teacher of biology and mathematics at Nalanda College, a prominent Buddhist school founded during the Buddhist revival of the late 19th century. The aim of the grade 10 students' work camp led by Ariyaratne was to provide an opportunity for urban youth to understand rural life and the problems in poor societies in order to enable the students as well as the villagers to see the importance of standing on their own feet.

Although Mahatma Gandhi (1869–1948) had used the term *sarvodaya* to mean the "welfare of all," Ariyaratne reinterpreted it in Sri Lanka as the "awakening of all," in the light of his own reading of the teachings of the Buddha. Ariyaratne believes that the four Sublime Abodes (loving-kindness, compassion, sympathetic joy, and equanimity) and the four Modes of Social Conduct (the absence of desire, hatred, fear, and delusion) taught by the Buddha can help the process of personality awakening. For Ariyaratne, Sarvodaya is an activity of "awakening all" from an individual perspective to a wholesome state that embraces all of humanity. This awakening process works on "spiritual, moral, cultural, social, economic, and political" levels.

One crucial term—sramadana—characterizes Sarvodaya's contribution to social development as a movement inspired by Buddhist ideas of social well-being. Sramadana is the selfless act of sharing one's labor with others. This is an act of charity that Sarvodaya broadly defines as "an act of sharing one's time, thought, effort, and other resources with the community" for the sake of awakening oneself and others. Sarvodaya's interest is in the inculcation of values inspired by Buddhist teachings and these are used as a vehicle for development and social mobility. Sarvodaya seeks to affirm the social dimensions of Buddhism and the way in which Buddhist teachings can be applied to daily contexts in community development settings. Sarvodaya has criticized materiality when the aggressive accumulation of wealth destroys the values of an unsophisticated rural community.

Within the last five decades, Sarvodaya's contribution to community development is extensive: it built 4,300 village roads, constructed 8,000 wells and water systems, provided facilities for 373,322 people to have access to safe drinking water, installed 15,800 toilets, educated 135,000 children, established 7,600 preschools, trained 120,000 members of a youth peace brigade and 200,000 health workers, and is proud to have one million volunteers who are committed to pursue the community development projects.

The Lanka Jatika Sarvodaya Sramadana Sangamaya has an American affiliate, Sarvodaya USA. That organization is dedicated to building a North American community that expresses the holistic community development vision and ideals of Sarvodaya.

In recent years, Sarvodaya has been increasingly attacked both in Sri Lanka and abroad for alleged implementation of urban, bourgeois, middle-class values and ideals among rural people. In the early 1990s, it faced severe political threats, to the point of extinction, from the Sri Lankan government of President Ranasinghe Premadasa (d. 1993). In the last few years, as a non-governmental organization (NGO) heavily dependent on foreign aid, its identity and integrity have been subject to serious criticism and debate.

Nevertheless, the objective of the Sarvodaya movement has been the generation of a "nonviolent revolution toward the creation of a Sarvodaya Social Order that will ensure the total awakening of human personalities." Using Buddhist philosophical insights, the traditional values and aspirations of Sri Lankan culture, and Gandhian ideas, Ariyaratne was able to propose and develop a sustainable, nature-friendly alternative development strategy. In Sarvodaya's five decades of village community development work, four values—truth, nonviolence, self-denial, and charity—dominate the scene and determine its success as a grassroots Buddhist movement.

Lanka Jatika Sarvodaya Sramadana Sangamaya
Damsak Mandira
98 Rawatawatta Rd.
Moratuwa
Sri Lanka
http://www.sarvodayausa.org/

Mahinda Deegalle

See also: Theravada Buddhism.

References

Ariyaratne, A. T. *Collected Works*. 7 vols. Ratmalana, Sri Lanka: Sarvodaya Vishva Lekha, 1978–1999.

Bond, George. *Buddhism at Work: Community Development, Social Empowerment and the Sarvodaya Movement*. Sterling, VA: Kumarian Press, 2006.

Bond, George. "Sarvodaya's Pursuit of Peace." In *Buddhism, Conflict and Violence in Modern Sri Lanka*, edited by Mahinda Deegalle, 226–232. London and New York: Routledge, 2006.

Gombrich, Richard F., and Gananath Obeyesekere. *Buddhism Transformed: Religious Change in Sri Lanka*. Princeton, NJ: Princeton University Press, 1988.

Perera, J., C. Marasinghe, and L. Jayasekera, eds. *A People's Movement under Siege*. Moratuwa, Sri Lanka: Sarvodaya Book Publishing Services, 1992.

Satanism

Satanism refers to the worship of Satan, the Christian devil. While posed as an idea in the Middle Ages, when people accused of being witches were charged with worshipping the devil, self-avowed Satanists do not appear to have arisen prior to the time of Louis XIV. At that time, a group practicing the black Mass (a parody of the central act of worship of the Roman Catholic Church) and the ritual killing of infants was uncovered operating in Louis's court. Satanism, when it has subsequently appeared, has manifested as an attack upon a dominant Christianity and the society it has supported.

Accounts of actual Satanism prior to the 1960s are quite rare. Satanists produced almost no literature, the 1891 volume *La Bas* by French Esotericist Joris Karl Huysmans (1848–1907) being notable by its uniqueness. Each new Satanist group came into existence without reference to prior groups, and each was unable to pass along Satanism to a second generation. Satanism differs from every other religious ideology in that the understanding of what Satanism is and what Satanists do was almost totally the product of the vivid imagination of Christian writers who had never met a Satanist and had had no direct encounter with or information about any actually existing Satanist group. The majority of Satanist groups were created by people who had decided to create something that conformed to a conception about which Christian writers had previously fantasized.

Through the mid-20th century, a variety of cases appeared in which small groups of teenagers assembled in informal Satanic groups, which subsequently became known when they were discovered breaking into churches to steal Communion wafers or vandalizing a graveyard. On occasion the mutilated body of a dog or cat was seen as the remains of a Satanic ritual. Very rarely, murders are tied to Satanism, in most cases Satanism being an excuse for murderous actions that would have been taken in any case.

The perception of Satanism changed significantly in 1968 when Anton Sandor LaVey (1930–1997) announced the formation of the Church of Satan. This unique organization became the subject of much media coverage and even attracted several celebrities. Interest in Satanism, both pro and con, was also stimulated by *Rosemary's Baby*, a 1968 movie about a Satanist cult, and the publication in 1971 of William Blatty's *The Exorcist*. The movie version of Blatty's book (1973) would set off a wave of interest in exorcism, and lead to a fresh set of Christian anti-Satanism texts.

Although various reporters projected exorbitant figures for membership in the Church of Satan, it never had more than a few thousand members, most of whom consisted of people who paid a modest membership fee and received the organization's periodical. By 1974,

however, the core of the Church of Satan had been splintered by a schism among a number of the church's leaders, including Michael Aquino, LaVey's capable assistant. With the exception of the Temple of Set, founded by Aquino, most of the splinters survived only a short time, and interest in Satanism waned significantly.

A new wave of interest in Satanism emerged in the mid-1980s around two phenomena. First, several women, initially Michelle Smith and Loren Stafford, published books describing their reported lives as members of a Satanist group when teenagers. In each case they reported that they had forgotten their involvement and remembered their experience only later during counseling. Although both the Smith and Stafford cases would later be exposed as hoaxes, in a short time additional women came forth with similar stories. Second, a variety of cases appeared in which young children accused adults of having forced them to participate in Satanic rituals as members of ongoing Satanic cults, the most famous case involving multiple accusations directed at the teachers/administrators of a day school in Manhattan Beach, California. The McMartin case lasted for three years and resulted in acquittals of the accused. The turning point in the case came with revelation of the manner in which many of the children had been coached to produce negative testimony.

The second wave of interest in Satanism supplied by the forgotten memory cases and accusations rose as literally hundreds of accusations of Satanic activity were registered during the late 1980s and early 1990s. Government officials and psychological counselors came forward with words of support. The interest passed, however, as a variety of hoaxes and false accusations were uncovered, as the forgotten memories were understood to be cases of what psychologists now call "false memory syndrome," and as no Satanic activity was uncovered that could have been responsible for so many accounts. As in the past, the stories of Satanism in the 1980s proved to be the product of vivid imaginations. While some continue to suggest that a large Satanic movement still exists in North America with ties to Europe, they have been unable to bring forth convincing evidence to back their claims.

What remains of Satanic activity is the spectrum of small groups that have grown out of the Church of

Satan and sporadic, short-lived teenage experiments with the dark side of occultism and malevolent magic. On rare occasions, those experiments, especially when carried out with the use of mood-altering drugs, has led to the death of one or more of the participants.

It should be noted that members of modern neo-Pagan and Wicca groups, because they often describe themselves as witches, are frequently labeled Satanists. This connection between witchcraft and Satanism was made in Europe in the Middle Ages by Christian leaders, many of whom were connected with the Inquisition. From Catholic leaders, the idea passed to Protestant ministers and from them into the popular consciousness. Contemporary neo-Pagans, who have a positive spirituality built around a oneness with nature, have attempted to dispel any association between themselves and Satanism.

J. Gordon Melton

See also: Church of Satan; Roman Catholic Church.

References

Gilmore, Peter H. *The Satanic Scriptures*. Baltimore: Scapegoat Publishing, 2007.

Kelly, Henry Ansgar. *The Devil, Demonology, and Witchcraft*. Garden City, NY: Doubleday, 1974.

Lanning, Kenneth V. *Investigator's Guide to Allegations of "Ritual" Child Abuse*. Quantico, VA: Behavioral Science Unit, National Center for the Analysis of Violent Crime, Federal Bureau of Investigation, FBI Academy, 1992. http://www.geocities.com/Athens/Delphi/4979/lanning.9201.html.

Lewis, James R., and Jesper Aagaard Petersen, eds. *The Encyclopedic Sourcebook of Satanism*. Amherst, NY: Prometheus Press, 2006.

Lyon, Arthur. *Satan Wants You*. London: Rupert Hart-Davies, 1970.

Nathan, Debbie, and Michael Snedeker. *Satan's Silence: Ritual Abuse and the Making of a Modern American Witch Hunt*. New York: Basic Books, 1995.

Richardson, James T., Joel Best, and David G. Bromley, eds. *The Satanism Scare*. Hawthorne, NY: Aldine de Gruyter, 1991.

Smith, Michelle, and Lawrence Pazner. *Michele Remembers*. New York: Congdon and Lattes, 1980.

Stratford, Lauren. *Satan's Underground*. Eugene, OR: Harvest House, 1988.

Sathya Sai Baba Movement

The Sathya Sai Baba movement originated in India but is represented today in 114 countries. The movement has held particular appeal for members of the cosmopolitan elite, who have contributed to its wealth and strength. The nature of this core membership means that the movement constitutes an influential, politically well-connected global network.

According to the organization's website (http://www.sathyasai.org/) there are today more than 1,200 Sathya Sai Baba centers throughout the world. Although the movement is focused upon the Indian guru, Sathya Sai Baba, it claims to be ecumenical in character. Membership of the organization, the website explains, is based upon "a common bond—love of God—and a common goal—spiritual growth." The activities of the centers include study of Sathya Sai Baba's teachings and literature from all world religions, group devotional singing, meditation, and community service. Although the centers charge no official membership fees, many members in fact make donations to their Sathya Sai Baba Centre.

The spiritual leader of the movement, Sathya Sai Baba, is a living Indian guru who was born to a non-Brahmin *kshatriya* family on November 25, 1926, in the village of Puttaparthi in Andhra Pradesh, India. He was named Sathya Narayana Raju. As a child he became renowned for materializing sweets for his friends and for locating things they had lost. At the age of 14 he had a seizure that may have been related to a scorpion bite. Shortly after it he called his family and neighbors to his bedside and declared that he was Sai Baba. In so doing he was claiming to be the reincarnation of the miracle-working Maharashtran saint Sai Baba of Shirdi (ca. 1856–1918). The new Sai Baba, Sathya Sai Baba (Sai Baba of Truth), now claimed to be the second of three Sai Baba incarnations. According to the current Sai Baba, his successor will be born

Indian spiritual guru Sri Sathya Sai Baba, right, blesses his disciples as he arrives on a modified vehicle at an event to celebrate his 78th birthday at Puttaparthy, India. (AP/Wide World Photos)

in 2030 and will be called Prema Sai Baba (Sai Baba of Love).

After his declaration of identity, Sathya Sai Baba began performing miracles and delivering teachings and he soon gathered a following in India. Gradually word spread abroad, and people began flocking to Sai Baba in the hope of being helped by one of his miracles. Devotees' publications describe extraordinary cures, resurrections from the dead, materializations of religious trinkets, mind reading, and astral travel. Sathya Sai Baba's most common miracle, however, is his manifestation of ash known as *vibhuti*, performed by waving his right hand in a circular motion. Usually he gives the ash to devotees, often with instructions to use it medicinally. Above all, it is conviction about Sathya

Sai Baba's paranormal powers that is the hallmark of a devotee.

The movement has great appeal to the cosmopolitan middle classes, particularly among diasporic Indian communities, Europeans, and North Americans. In Puttaparthi various institutions have been established with funds raised by the organization: a school, a college, and a hospital. The global organization is administered pyramidally, structured with regional, national, and local chairmen. A registered center must have a chairman, secretary, and treasurer, and must provide three activities—worship, spiritual education, and charity.

The organization is supported through anonymous donations, and there are no membership fees. The total number of devotees is difficult to estimate since many worship Sathya Sai Baba without registering as members or even attending the centers. Devotees have developed an extensive Internet presence.

The movement follows the style of Hindu *bhakti* devotionalism. It emphasizes the individual's personal commitment to Sathya Sai Baba himself as incarnation of divinity. Love of God is emphasized over scriptural learning or renunciation, and the worshipper is encouraged to transcend desire from within the world. Selfless love and charitable service are promoted over withdrawal from the world. The teachings are ecumenical and stress a single godhead as the essence of all religious traditions. Sathya Sai Baba insists that the true devotee is one who learns to practice his own religion well rather than converting to another.

Sathya Sai Baba education promotes a set of "universal human values" emanating from the Hindu principles of *prema*, *shanti*, *ahimsa*, *sathya*, and *dharma* (love, peace, nonviolence, truth, and duty) but these are said to underlie all religions. The symbol of the Sathya Sai Baba organization is a lotus flower in whose five petals these Sanskrit terms are written. Sathya Sai Baba altars often include a range of godforms from several of the world religions, usually with a picture of Sathya Sai Baba or his feet in the center. Worship is structured along the lines of Hindu *puja* worship and usually includes offerings of flowers to the image of Sathya Sai Baba, chanting of Sanskrit *mantras*, singing of devotional songs (*bhajans*) in Sanskrit and other languages, recitation of prayers, and the offering of burning camphor (*arathi*) to the altar. *Prasad*, or offerings, obligatorily including *vibhuti* are then distributed to the congregation. At some centers individuals will recite personal experiences of miracles to the audience or deliver messages taken from the Sathya Sai Baba literature. The literature used by the movement is not written by Sathya Sai Baba himself but consists of his numerous speeches, written down and published by devotees. Sathya Sai Baba also makes frequent reference to the Bhagavadgita, and even makes unsystematic references to other texts from both Hinduism and other world religions.

The Sathya Sai Baba movement has stimulated considerable controversy. At least one organization in India has launched a crusade against Sathya Sai Baba and other miracle workers. Video films of Sathya Sai Baba performing "faked" materializations have been released and there are publications that offer evidence to debunk some of the devotees' claims of miracle experiences. Stories have also circulated about sexual harassment of boys at the Sathya Sai College, sponsored by the organization and located close to the ashram in Puttaparthi.

Sexual abuse is not the only controversy tainting the godman's reputation. On June 6, 1993, four young male devotees broke into the guru's quarters at night, armed with knives. Their motives are unclear. They were stopped by four of Sathya Sai Baba's attendants. A struggle ensued in which two of the young men were killed and two badly injured. They were then bound with ropes and beaten by others who had heard the commotion. When the police later arrived they shot all four. Investigations were marked by cover-up and the case has never been resolved. Generally, though, the movement has been largely unaffected by the controversies and it continues to attract influential members to its following.

Sathya Sai Baba
Prasanthi Nilayam
Dist. Anantapur
Andhra Pradesh 515134
India
http://www.sathyasai.org/

Alexandra Kent

See also: Devotion/Devotional Traditions.

References

Kasturi, N. *Sathyam, Sivam, Sundaram: The Life Story of Bhagavan Sri Sathya Sai Baba*. 3 vols. Prasanthi Nilayam, India: Sri Sathya Sai Books and Publications Trust, 1973–1975.

Kent, Alexandra. *Divinity and Diversity: A Hindu Revitalization Movement in Malaysia*. Copenhagen: NIAS Press, 2005.

Klass, Morton. *Singing with Sai Baba: The Politics of Revitalization in Trinidad*. Boulder, CO: Westview Press, 1991.

Manual of Sri Sathya Sai Baba Dal and Guidelines for Activities. Bombay: World Council of the Sri Sathya Sai Organizations, 1979.

Sandweiss, S. *Sai Baba: The Holy Man and the Psychiatrist*. New Delhi: M. Gulab Singh and Sons, 1975.

Satmar Hasidism

The Satmar, one of the newer Hasidic communities, has become known as one of the few anti-Zionist groups operating in the Jewish community. Members believe that the present state of Israel is illegitimate and that efforts to set up a Jewish state in Palestine are contrary to Jewish teachings. The group was founded by Rebbe Yoel Teitelbaum (1887–1979), the younger son of the Rebbe for Szigetter Hasidim. Following his father's death, he moved to Satu-Mare (Hungary), where he was eventually named chief rabbi. His charisma and allegiance to tradition brought him a large following. Although he opposed the Zionists, they were the ones who in 1944 saved him from the Holocaust. After living out the war in Switzerland and a visit to Palestine, he came to America in 1947. He set about the task of re-creating a community similar to the one that had existed prior to the war. Many Hungarian Americans flocked to his cause.

Teitelbaum settled in the Williamsburg section of Brooklyn, New York, and soon several hundred families had associated with him. The community adopted the distinctive clothing of the Old World communities and a variety of practices peculiar to ultra-Orthodox life. The establishment of the state of Israel became a problem of major proportion. A few Orthodox had opposed Zionism, a program initiated by liberal and secular Jews, out of a belief that only the Messiah could bring the rebirth of Israel. Although the vast majority of Orthodox groups accommodated to or became avid supporters of Israel, the Satmar continued in their opposition and found support in what it perceived to be the new government's anti-religious policies. The Satmar who resided in Palestine organized rallies against the new state. They also refused to serve in the Israeli army or participate in elections. Following the liberation of Jerusalem in 1967, the late Rabbi Joel Teitelbaum, the Satmar Rebbe, forbade his followers from visiting the Western Wall because it had been regained not by divine miracles but by Israel's army, the military arm of a "regime of heretics."

Teitelbaum was able to rally Orthodox and anti-Zionist Jews, especially those of Hungarian extraction, and the Satmar emerged in Jewish communities in Europe (Belgium, United Kingdom) and South America (Brazil, Argentina, Uruguay). In 1968, Rebbe Yoel had a stroke that hobbled him for the rest of his life. He died in 1979, and after a year of mourning was succeeded by his nephew Rebbe Moshe Teitelbaum (1914–2006).

The Satmar developed a relationship with the Neturei Karta (Guardians of the City), an Israeli-based anti-Zionist group, which placed itself under the Satmar's care and guidance. In 1965, Rabbi Amram Blau, the founder of the Neturei Karta, married a divorced convert to Judaism (formerly a Roman Catholic). As a result, the Satmar forced his ouster from leadership.

Following the death of Rabbi Moshe in 2006, his son Aaron Teitelbaum was declared his successor and installed as the leader of the community at the center in Kiryas Joel. However, his leadership was challenged by his two brothers and his brother-in law. Each of them is in control of a segment of the movement, and as of 2009, there was no sign of reconciliation between the various factions.

There are approximately 100,000 Satmar in the United States (2009), a little more than half of the estimated 200,000 Satmar worldwide. Most live in Brooklyn (70,000), but some have moved to the Satmar community, Kiryas Joel, established in 1974 in Monroe, New York, about an hour outside of Manhattan. Most outside the United States reside in Israel, the United Kingdom, and Belgium.

Satmar Hasidic Community
c/o Congregation Yetev-Lev
12 Garfield Rd
Monroe, NY 10950

J. Gordon Melton

See also: Hasidism; Orthodox Judaism.

References

Mintz, Jerome R. *Hasidic People: A Place in the New World*. Cambridge, MA: Harvard University Press, 1992.

Rubin, Israel. *Satmar: Two Generations in an Urban Island*. New York: Peter Lang, 1997.

Weiss, Maud B., and Michael Neumeister. *The Challenge of Piety: The Satmar Hasidim in New York*. Munich: Gina Kehayoff, 1995.

Winson, Hella. *Unchosen: The Hidden Lives of Hasidic Rebels*. Boston: Beacon Press, 2006.

Satsang Network, The

This loosely organized new religious phenomenon, which appeared in the beginning of the 1990s, reflects several contemporary popular religious trends, mixing different traditions, emphasis on inner experience, and egalitarianism. The network is focused around several dozen Westerners, announced as enlightened or awakened, who travel around the world to give *satsang*, or meetings aimed at helping others to make the transition to enlightenment. Besides the activity of satsang and the core teaching of enlightenment, most of them share reference to one or, more commonly, at least two out of three Indian gurus: Osho (1931–1990), Poonjaji (1910–1997) (with connections to Ramana Maharshi [1879–1950]), and Sri Swami Hans Raj Maharaj in Rishikesh (b. ca. 1925). Another key spiritual master, often referred to, is Sri Nisargadatta Maharaj (1897–1981). The Satsang network has thus come into being at the intersection between several different Indian religious traditions. Another common feature holding the network together is the followers, who often accept several of the Westerners as enlightened teachers and visit satsang given by all of them.

Many of the satsang givers have a history of intense involvement with the Osho movement. After the death of Osho in 1990, several of his disciples started visiting Poonjaji. Vasant (male), from Norway, was the life guard of Osho for several years, before he met Poonjaji in the middle of the 1990s. Arjuna (male), from the United States, and Rahasya (male), from Germany, have similar stories. Thus, the Satsang network could partly be considered a post-Osho development. However, there are also satsang givers without connections to Osho, such as Shantimayi (female, the United States), a disciple of Sri Hans Maharaj with a background in Buddhism, and Gangaji (female, the United States), a disciple of Poonjaji, also with a background in Buddhism. Both of the latter have disciples of their own who in turn are considered enlightened.

The core teaching of the Satsang network is that enlightenment is here for everyone at the present moment. To become enlightened one should just drop all concepts, ideas, and beliefs. A consequence of this teaching is that other ideological traits are downplayed. As in the Osho movement, the world is seen as divine, and there is no need for renunciation. Although no techniques are explicitly recommended to realize enlightenment, sometimes, as in the Osho movement, different kinds of personal growth and therapeutic work are practiced.

Satsang is a traditional activity in the Indian spiritual context, meaning "being together with truth." In the Satsang network, satsang is characterized by active participation of the audience, music, dance, and high spirits. The focus in satsang is on enlightenment and how to drop the thinking that one is not enlightened. The satsang givers clearly occupy a special position in the movement, but at the same time they are conceived of in a much more egalitarian way than Eastern spiritual teachers normally are.

The Satsang network has no central organization, no name, and no membership; it could be considered a conglomeration of several interconnected networks. Some of the satsang givers have their own enterprises or foundations for personal and spiritual development. Some examples include Ganesh Foundation (1750 30th Street, PMB #137, Boulder, CO 80301), Internet site at http://www.shantimayi.com/; the organization of Shantimayi; The Living Essence Foundation (13215 Red Dog Road, Nevada City, CA 95959), Internet site at http://www.livingessence.com/ by Arjuna; Eckhart Teachings (PO Box 93661, Nelson Park RPO, Vancouver, BC, Canada V6E 4L7), Internet site at http://www.eckharttolle.com/, the organization of Eckhart Tolle; and The Gangaji Foundation (2245 Ashland Street, Ashland, OR 97520), Internet site at http://www.gangaji.org/.

The Satsang network is global, satsang givers of different national origin traveling mainly in Europe, the United States, Australia, South America, Japan, and India. Because of the lack of organization, it is difficult to estimate the number of persons engaged. Satsang givers number several dozen, and satsangs must regularly reach several thousand. The level of engagement is, however, often quite low.

Liselotte Frisk

See also: Devotion/Devotional Traditions; Enlightenment.

Reference

Frisk, Liselotte. "The Satsang Network: A Growing Post-Osho Phenomenon." *Nova Religio: The Journal of Alternative and Emergent Religions* 6, no. 1 (2002): 64–85.

■ Saudi Arabia

Saudi Arabia is an Islamic nation whose territory includes most of the Arabian Peninsula. Most of the country's 830,000 square miles of territory is desert, but that desert covers extensive oil deposits. The majority of its 26,000,000 citizens live near the Red Sea or Persian Gulf coasts, though the capital, Riyadh, is in the center of the country. The eastern section of the country, bordering Yemen and Oman, is the most sparsely populated.

The story of the emergence of Saudi Arabia is intimately connected with the rise of Islam. At the time when Muhammad appeared on the stage of history (ca. 570–632 CE), the Arabian Peninsula was home to a variety of groups, many headed by their own sheik and following a traditional polytheistic religion. Around 610, Muhammad began to preach the message he had received from God (later written down in the Koran). He attacked the image worship of his neighbors and called for the destruction of the idols. He also called upon the rich to give assistance to the poor. Muhammad was of the Hashim people, who had risen to dominate Mecca, where a worship center, the Kabah, had been a source of pilgrimage. The Hashimites were in charge of the Kabah, which at the beginning of the seventh century housed hundreds of deity images. One of the commands in the Koran instructed Muhammad and his followers to purify the Kabah.

In 622, Muhammad was invited to Yathib (Medina) to arbitrate the feuds that were dividing its people. Islam is usually dated from that move, called the

Muslim pilgrims in Medina, Saudi Arabia. (Aidar Ayazbayev/Dreamstime.com)

Hegira. Muhammad soon proclaimed the rightness of going to war against Islam's enemies, especially the Meccans, and by 629 he was in command in the city of his birth. He smashed the idols at the Kabah and made it a place of pilgrimage for Muslims.

With the conquest of Mecca, Muhammad emerged as the strongest person on the Arabian Peninsula, and many of the sheikdoms sought an alliance with him. Subsequently, they and their people became Muslims. These alliances both created a new political community and ended much of the fighting between the different groups.

The expansion of Arab power came during the rulership of Umar (634–644): the Arabs moved outward to take control of Syria, Palestine, Egypt, and Persia (Iran). Interestingly, the Arabs were not seafaring people and made no move across the Red Sea to Ethiopia or the Sudan. A hereditary monarchy (the Umayyad Caliphate) would be established in 661 by Mu'awiya I

SAUDI ARABIA

(d. 680). Under him and his successors, the Arab Empire would reach from Morocco and Spain to what is today Pakistan. However, the empire's capital was moved to Damascus, and Arabia proper retained its place primarily as the point of origin of Islam and the site of the *hajj*, the pilgrimage to Mecca required of each Muslim at least once in a lifetime.

Life in Arabia continued at a slow pace oriented on the trade in the cities and the agriculture and sheep-herding in the rural areas. Although nominally a part of successive Muslim empires, the most important being the Abbasid (beginning in 750 CE) and the Ottoman (beginning in the 13th century), many parts of Arabia operated for long periods as semiautonomous regions, of peripheral concern to the rulers of the empire.

Change began to take place with the rise of the Saud family in the 18th century. As the Ottoman Empire was losing its ability to govern so large a territory, the Sauds established the independent Emirate of Najd in the center of the peninsula, with their capital at Riyadh. Forced out of power for a period at the end of the 19th century, they regrouped in Kuwait and reestablished themselves at the end of World War I, with British assistance. In 1926 they moved on Mecca and, following its conquest, Abd al-Aziz ibn Sa'ud, the head of the family, was proclaimed king of Hidjaz and sultan of Nadj. Six years later this kingdom became the modern nation of Saudi Arabia. He adapted the old structures of the land to his rule, assigning the emirs the leadership of districts, and local chiefs and their armies control on the local level. The government continues as an absolute monarchy with no elective political offices.

The rise to power of the Saud family is intimately connected with the Wahhabi movement. Muhammad ibn Walihab (d. 1787) was a Muslim leader who attacked the Ottoman leadership for their lax manner, especially in their observance of the law. He in effect revived the Hanbalite School of Islam, which had largely died out. The Hanbalites had rejected the various methods of expanding the law by using analogy and reason, and felt that the law as handed down in the Koran should be observed as literally as possible. The Saud family found their greatest allies in the Wahhabis, and both of their fortunes rose together. Sunni Islam is the state religion of Saudi Arabia, and the Wahhabi School the dominant form.

The king of Saudi Arabia is considered the spiritual leader of all Muslims. That is recognized in several ways, including his role as guardian of the shrine in Mecca. Each year, following the Aid El Kebir, the Feast of the Sacrifices, he enters the Kaaba, the black cubic shrine at the center of the mosque in Mecca. He washes its interior and changes the black cloth that encloses it. He is the only person allowed to enter the shrine.

A form of Muslim devotion is a common part of Saudi life. The *sharia* (Muslim law) operates throughout the culture (including the school system), and five times daily other matters come to a halt as a brief time is taken for prayer.

Other forms of Orthodox Islam are tolerated in Saudi Arabia. Sunnis of the Shafiite School of Islam are strong in the western part of the country, the region along the Red Sea, and there are pockets of both Hanafite and Malikite believers, especially at al-Hufuf, inland from the Persian Gulf. There are some 60,000 Ismailis at Ahsa, and a small number of Zaydites in the area near the border with Yemen. Through the 10th century, Sufism spread through most of the Islamic Empire, including Arabia, from its main center in Baghdad.

The Muslim establishment in Arabia has several organizations of international importance. In 1963, the Muslim World League was created and remains headquartered in Mecca. It is the Muslim equivalent of the Christian World Council of Churches; it attempts to bring a greater sense of unity to the Muslim world. It also assists Muslims in countries in which they are the minority, and to that end it has opened numerous national offices around the world. The Organization of the Islamic Conference, with headquarters in Jeddah, was established in 1969 during the first Conference of the Muslim World, which was held in Rabat, Morocco. The occasion of its formation was the burning of the al-Aqsa Mosque in Jerusalem. It includes representatives of the majority of nations in which Muslims are the dominant faith, who consult together to promote cooperation and mutual assistance in various fields of interest. Its Triennial Conferences bring together the heads of some 55 nations.

Through the government's Ministry of Education, a number of Muslim institutions of higher learning, which have influence far beyond the border of the country, have been established. Included among these schools are the Faculty of the Sharia and Islamic Studies (Mecca), the Islamic University of Medina, the Higher Institute of Judiciary (Riyadh), and the Islamic Jurisprudence College (Mecca). The annual visitation of pilgrims to Mecca is overseen by the government's Department of Hajj.

According to tradition, Christianity was brought to Arabia by Bartholomew, one of the original 12 Apostles.

Saudi Arabia

Religion	Followers in 1970	Followers in 2010	% of Population	Annual % growth 2000–2010	Followers in 2025	Followers in 2050
Muslims	5,688,000	24,514,000	92.8	2.56	31,882,000	40,911,000
Christians	26,600	1,182,000	4.5	2.60	1,800,000	2,530,000
Roman Catholics	2,600	1,000,000	3.8	2.81	1,500,000	2,100,000
Independents	13,000	77,000	0.3	2.57	140,000	200,000
Orthodox	2,000	51,000	0.2	0.18	70,000	100,000
Hindus	1,000	300,000	1.1	2.56	410,000	550,000
Agnostics	20,000	180,000	0.7	2.56	350,000	500,000
Buddhists	5,000	86,800	0.3	2.56	120,000	160,000
Sikhs	0	51,400	0.2	2.56	80,000	150,000
Ethnoreligionists	0	48,000	0.2	2.56	60,000	75,000
Chinese folk	4,000	24,600	0.1	2.56	34,000	50,000
New religionists	0	15,000	0.1	2.56	35,000	60,000
Atheists	0	8,500	0.0	2.56	18,000	30,000
Baha'is	400	5,400	0.0	2.56	8,000	14,000
Total population	**5,745,000**	**26,416,000**	**100.0**	**2.56**	**34,797,000**	**45,030,000**

Christians did find their way to the peninsula over the next centuries, and by the sixth century a variety of churches could be found. These were completely submerged into Islam from the seventh century. Christianity did not return until the 19th century. The Roman Catholic Church established work at Aden (Yemen) in 1841. A vicariate of Arabia was formed in 1889 and is administered from Abu Dhabi (United Arab Emirates). Work in Dhahran is limited to expatriates, though it has grown in recent years because of the expansion of the oil business.

In 1890, Samuel Zwemer, representing the American Arabian Mission, opened a center in Aden and began an effort to create a Christian presence in the area, but he was never allowed to evangelize in Arabia. During the early 20th century, two churches, one affiliated with the Christian Brethren and one with the Churches of Christ, emerged in Dhahran, but were limited to serving expatriates. Several additional churches have appeared in recent decades, including Unitarian congregations and some small evangelical groups. There are also small numbers of expatriates connected with the Orthodox churches (Greek, Coptic, and Syrian). Officially, all religions other than Islam are prohibited in Saudi Arabia (a fact that became an issue for Americans stationed there during the Gulf War), and attempts at proselytization are dealt with severely by

the authorities. Churches are permitted only as private affairs among noncitizens.

As the presence of Christians is limited to expatriates, so there are small numbers of Buddhists and Hindus from China and India, respectively, and the Baha'i Faith has developed several groups.

J. Gordon Melton

See also: Christian Brethren; Churches of Christ; Hanafite School of Islam; Hanbalite School of Islam; Ismaili Islam; Malikite School of Islam; Muslim World League; Roman Catholic Church; Shafiite School of Islam; Wahhabi Islam; World Council of Churches.

References

Al Saud, T. "Permanence and Change: An Analysis of the Islamic Political Culture of Saudi Arabia with Special Reference to the Royal Family." Ph.D. diss., Claremont Graduate School, 1982.

Al-Yassini, A. *Religion and State in the Kingdom of Saudi Arabia*. Boulder, CO: Westview, 1985.

Alshamsi, Manso. *Islam and Political Reform in Saudi Arabia: The Quest for Political Change and Reform*. New York: Routledge, 2008.

Barrett, David, ed. *The Encyclopedia of World Christianity*. 2nd ed. New York: Oxford University Press, 2001.

Commins, David. *The Wahhabi Mission and Saudi Arabia.* London: I. B. Tauris, 2006.

Delong-Bas, Natana. *Wahhabi Islam: From Revival and Reform to Global Jihad.* New York: Oxford University Press, 2008.

Erlich, Haggai. *Saudi Arabia and Ethiopia: Islam, Christianity, and Politics Entwined.* Boulder, CO: Lynne Rienner Publishers, 2006.

Peters, F. E. *The Hajj: The Muslim Pilgrimage to Mecca and the Holy Places.* Princeton, NJ: Princeton University Press, 1994.

Pullapilly, Cyriac. *Islam in the Contemporary World.* Notre Dame, IN: Cross Roads Books, 1980.

Weston, Mark, and Fowler Wyche, Jr. *Prophets and Princes: Saudi Arabia from Muhammad to the Present.* New York: Wiley, 2008.

Savonarola, Girolamo

1452–1498

The charismatic Italian priest Girolamo Savonarola was one of several Catholic leaders who attempted to institute reform in the church in the generation prior to the Protestant Reformation. He initially rose to an influential position in the Dominican Order and then became a controlling church authority in his native Tuscany. At the height of his power, however, both church and state authorities turned on him.

Savonarola was born in 1452 into a well-to-do family in Ferrara (northern Italy). As young man (1474) he joined the Dominican Order at Bologna. People began to take notice of the young monk as he approached his 30th year as a preacher in Florence. He responded by leaving the city and taking a post as the priest for a convent in Brescia. In 1489 he returned to Florence, where this time his extraordinary oratorical skills found an audience and he became a popular speaker. He spoke eloquently against the sins of his day and the apostasy he saw everywhere around him.

Savonarola's preaching seemed headed for a confrontation with the powerful de Medicis, who ruled the city. Lorenzo, who embodied the Medici wealth, culture, and humanist spirit, however, chose to leave Savonarola alone. A year after Lorenzo passed away (1492), the pope gave his support to Savonarola's being named the vicar general of the Dominican Order in Tuscany (the Italian region of which Florence was the capital), the task being assigned in order to reform the region.

Savonarola concluded that reform was contingent upon a change of regime, and he suggested that Charles VIII (r. 1483–1498) and the French just might be the divinely appointed instrument to carry out the necessary adjustments in the ruling authorities. A short time later, the French overran the city, but their stay was brief. Charles was on his way south to take control of the Kingdom of Naples. After the French departed, Florence was declared a republic, and Savonarola and his followers took control. He named God the controlling force of a new theocracy and instituted a variety of puritanical reforms.

A crisis developed in 1495. Savonarola's followers considered him a prophet, which occasioned his critics charging such claims constituted heresy. When he refused to show up in Rome and respond to the charges in 1497, he was excommunicated. As his situation deteriorated, in 1498, the people threw their support behind some of the Medici's supporters in the city's elections. The new authorities ordered Savonarola not to preach and he found himself denounced publically by a member of the rival Franciscan Order. The public turned against him and his reforms. Arrested on a laundry list of charges, he was tortured and made a variety of confessions. He later withdrew them, but it was too late. He was convicted, and Rome agreed with the verdict. He and two close followers were hung and their bodies burned on May 23, 1498. In spite of what had just happened to them, they maintained their loyalty to the church and the faith right up to their death.

J. Gordon Melton

See also: Roman Catholic Church.

References

Erlanger, Rachel. *The Unarmed Prophet: Savonarola in Florence.* New York: McGraw-Hill, 1988.

Martines, Lauro. *Fire in the City: Savonarola and the Struggle for the Soul of Renaissance Florence.* Oxford: Oxford University Press, 2007.

Olin, John C. *The Catholic Reformation: Savonarola to Ignatius Loyola.* New York: Harper & Row, 1969.

Savonarola, Girolamo. *Selected Writings of Girolamo Savonarola: Religion and Politics, 1490–1498.* Ed. by Donald Beebe, Anne Borelli, and Maria Pastore Passaro. New Haven CT: Yale University Press, 2006.

Savonarola, Girolamo. *The Triumph of the Cross.* Trans. by John Procter. London: Sands and Company, 1901.

Seward, Desmond. *The Burning of the Vanities: Savonarola and the Borgia Pope.* Charleston, SC: The History Press, 2006.

Science and Religion: The Contemporary Scene

Since Charles Darwin's publication of *Origin of Species* in 1859, debates between science and religion that assumed a conflict model turn out on closer inspection to be debates in which rival claims are made for the "correct" meaning to be attached to scientific theories and theological claims. The publication of John Draper's *History of the Conflict between Science and Religion* in 1874 and Andrew Dickenson White's two-volume *A History of the Warfare of Science with Theology in Christendom* is the source of this idea. The "Draper-White Thesis," as it is now known, originated in the view of 18th-century philosophers like David Hume and John Locke that the church was an institution whose ignorance and intolerance had hindered human progress, while science was a force of cultural and intellectual liberation. For the past century this has been the predominant view of the relation between science and religion among laypeople and scientists alike. It brings together a triumphalist view of science and a patronizing view of religion that does not square with the historical facts past and present. While it cannot be denied that in some cases real conflict existed, as in the cases of Galileo and Darwin, the notion of a state of "warfare" between science and religion is simplistic and mostly wrong. The relation between science and religion in the Middle Ages was neither suppression nor support, but a complex mixture of conflict, compromise, understanding, misunderstanding, accommodation, dialogue, alienation, and the going of separate ways. This same pattern continues today, even as the warfare model remains strong in popular understanding and the views of many scientists and conservative Christians.

There are several issues around which a real or imagined conflict revolves. The earliest issues were epistemological: can scientific knowledge be integrated into religion? From the Copernican displacement of the Earth from the center of the solar system to Darwin's theory of evolution, which displaced human beings from the center of the universe, theology was forced into rethinking Christian tradition in light of what the sciences revealed about nature. Epistemological issues remain primary in the contemporary dialogue between science and religion. A second area of contention is methodological and involves the duality between science based on "physical facts" and theology derived from "faith," or between a naturalistic and a religious worldview. Scientific naturalism since Darwin denies the church's right to interfere in the progress of science by introducing theological considerations into scientific debates. Today, among liberal theologians and some evangelicals, any appeal to divine purpose as an explanation of physical processes is rejected as a "god of the gaps" explanation, the assertion of which creates real science-religion conflict that is often heated, as well as incoherent theology. A third area of contention is in the field of ethics. Most recently, the issues have focused on genetic engineering, nuclear power, and medical procedures like birth control and abortion. Past debates focused on such medical procedures as vaccination and anesthesia. In the 18th century, one of the more serious reasons for opposing Darwin was fear that the theory of evolution would lead to the abandonment of ethical constraints in society. With these issues, it is not so much science as its applications that are of major concern. Finally, much of the conflict between science and religion has arisen from issues involving social and political power. This is reflected in conflict between progressive science-based ideologies and conservative and ecclesiastical forces.

These issues are at the forefront of the contemporary academic field of "science and religion," the historical roots of which lie in the 1960s, when scholars began developing constructive methodologies for relating science and religion. Scientist-theologian Ian Barbour is generally regarded as the "founder" of the field with the publication of his *Issues in Science and Religion* in 1971, which was revised in 1990 as *Religion and Science: Historical and Contemporary Issues*. Drawing on the work of Alfred North Whitehead, Thomas Kuhn, Michael Polanyi, Stephen Tomlin, Mary Hesse, Frederick Ferré, and Norwoon Hanson, Barbour's insight was the recognition of the similarities between the methodologies and epistemological structures of science and theology: Both employ metaphors and models in their claims about the world, and both use hypothetical and deductive methods within a revisionist, contextualist, historicist framework. Barbour called this common epistemological framework "critical realism."

Critical realism was pursued in England by physicist-theologian John Polkinghorne and biologist-theologian Arthur Peacocke, who died in 2006. In Germany, Wolfhart Pannenberg brought Karl Popper's understanding of theories as revisable hypotheses into the discussion in his *Theology and the Philosophy of Science* (1976). Nancy Murphy, from the perspective of the philosophy of religion, employed Imre Lakatos's notion of a "scientific research program," which includes a central commitment to a theoretical "hard core," a surrounding belt of ancillary hypotheses, and criteria for choosing between competing research programs. John B. Cobb, Jr., Philip Clayton, Niels Gregersen, Thomas Torrance, and Wentzel van Hyussteen made additional important contributions.

The chief concern of these scholars was to create a methodological framework for dialogue that allows for methodological reductionism (studying wholes in terms of their parts, referred to as "bottom-up causation") as a legitimate method in scientific research while respecting the irreducibility of "top-down" causal processes and properties referred to by theology, philosophy, and other higher-level disciplines. While some postmodernists and anti-realists criticize this approach by pointing to the difficulties that confront realist interpretations of scientific and theological concepts and by questioning the "metanarrative" role of science, critical realism is the predominant view of most scholars participating in the science-religion dialogue.

In numerous ways, the contemporary natural sciences challenge as they reshape theological reflection on the God-nature relationship. In physics, Albert Einstein's theories of special and general relativity challenge our ordinary sense of time's flow and the assumption of a universal present moment. This makes problematic the idea that God experiences and acts in the world in the flowing "now." Just as challenging is the relation between divine action and natural causality. Since Newtonian mechanics pictured nature as a closed machine-like system, divine action was either understood in terms of interventionism or reduced to human subjectivity. But developments within the philosophical interpretation of quantum theory, cosmology, chaos theory, and the neurosciences may provide a foundation for new theories of noninterventionist, objective, special providence. In cosmology, scholars like Robert John Russell, William B. Drees, George Ellis, Ted Peters, Mark Worthing, and William Stoeger focus on the consonance between theological notions of the universe as a creation and features of standard Big Bang theory, including the apparent beginning of the universe at $T = 0$ and the "anthropic principle," quantum indeterminacy, and the odd fact that the physical constants of nature have precisely the values they need for the emergence of life.

In dialogue with evolutionary theory, Arthur Peacocke and process theologians like John B. Cobb, Jr., Ian Barbour, David Griffin, and John Haught have in their distinctive ways written about "theistic evolution," which is the view that what science describes in terms of evolutionary biology can be meaningfully affirmed as God's action in the world. This is not another version of the intelligent design argument because billions of years of natural disaster, suffering, death, and extinction, plus the overall lack of directedness in evolutionary change raises serious challenges to any notion of divine action in nature. Barbour, Peacocke, Cobb, Haught, and Griffin, along with Holms Rolston and Thomas Tracy, center their discussions of theistic evolution on the complex "values" in nature. Evolutionary and ecological thought also plays a central role in Sallie McFague's model of the world as the "body of God" and Rosemary Ruether's discussion of the Gaia hypothesis and God.

Further areas of discussion are how genetics, sociobiology, the neurosciences, and computer science will affect the way we understand the human person. Fruitful theological insights into these issues come from scholars like biologist Francisco Ayala, Ted Peters, Denis Edwards, Anne Forest, Philip Hefner, and Nancy Murphy. Peters also draws together scientific and religious perspectives on ethical issues involving genetic discrimination, gene patenting, cloning, stem cell research, and human freedom. Several of the sciences challenge the notion of redemption, which in Christian tradition focuses on the doctrines of incarnation, Christology, resurrection, and eschatology. The very size and complexity of the universe force us as scientists, persons of faith, or both to look beyond concern for humanity and the Earth to the destiny of the universe as a whole.

Finally, important areas of research are now cutting-edge concerns in contemporary science-religion dialogue. Science itself is recognized as a thoroughly human endeavor open to the investigations of gender analysis. The work of Nancy Howell, Evelyn Fox Keller, and Helen Longino provides a good source for gender analysis of the science-religion dialogue itself. Additional voices from the world's religious traditions are increasingly participating in the science-religion dialogue. These voices include Muslim, Jewish, and Buddhist scholars. Muslims and Jews have always been engaged with the natural sciences, but the participation of Buddhists in this dialogue is a relatively recent phenomenon. The Dalai Lama, B. Alan Wallace, David Galan, and José Cabézon are among the important writers in this field. Generally, Buddhists assert that the natural sciences pose little threat to Buddhism's non-theistic worldview and practice traditions. Indeed, Buddhist dialogue with the biological sciences focuses mainly on the neurosciences because Buddhists tend to claim this branch of the sciences supports Buddhist traditions of meditation. Paul O. Ingram has written about a Buddhist-Christian-Science "trilogue" as part of the focus of the Society for Buddhist-Christian Studies. Other important areas include the history of science, the theological critique of "scientism" and scientific materialism, the relation of science to spirituality, and the roles of philosophy and theology in scientific research programs.

Paul O. Ingram

See also: Science and Religion: History of the Relationship.

References

Ayala, Francisco, ed. *Studies in the Philosophy of Biology: Reduction and Related Problems.* Berkeley: University of California Press, 1974.

Barbour, Ian G. *Religion and Science: Historical and Contemporary Issues.* San Francisco: HarperSan Francisco, 1990.

Birch, Charles, and John B. Cobb, Jr., eds. *The Liberation of Life.* Denton, TX: Environmental Ethics Books, 1990.

Clayton, Philip. *Mind and Emergence: From Quantum to Consciousness.* Oxford: Oxford University Press, 2004.

Cobb, John B., ed. *Back to Darwin: A Richer Account of Evolution.* Grand Rapids, MI: William B. Eerdmans Publishing Company, 2008.

Drees, William B. *Beyond the Big Bang: Quantum Cosmologies and God.* La Salle, IL: Open Court, 1990.

Edwards, Denis. *The God of Evolution: A Trinitarian Theology.* New York: Paulist Press, 1999.

Ellis, George F. R. *Before the Beginning: Cosmology Explained.* New York: Bowerdean, 1993.

Goodenough, Ursala. *The Sacred Depths of Nature.* Oxford: Oxford University Press, 1998.

Haught, John F. *Deeper than Darwin: The Prospect of Religion in the Age of Evolution.* Boulder, CO: Westview Press, 2003.

Haught, John F. *Science and Religion: From Conflict to Conversation.* New York: Paulist Press, 1995.

Hefner, Philip J. *The Human Factor: Evolution, Culture, and Religion.* Minneapolis, MN: Fortress Press, 1993.

Howell, Nancy R. *A Feminist Cosmology: Ecology, Solidarity, and Metaphysics.* New York: Humanity Books, 2000.

Ingram, Paul O. *Buddhist-Christian Dialogue in an Age of Science.* Lanham, MD: Rowman and Littlefield, 2008.

McFague, Sallie. *The Body of God: An Ecological Theology.* Minneapolis, MN: Fortress Press, 1993.

Murphy, Nancy C. *Theology in the Age of Scientific Reasoning.* Ithaca, NY: Cornell University Press, 1990.

Nasr, Seyyid Hossein. *Knowledge of the Sacred.* Albany: State University of New York, 1989.

Nasr, Seyyid Hossein. *Religion and the Order of Nature.* Oxford: Oxford University Press, 1996.

Numrich, Paul D., ed. *The Boundaries of Knowledge in Buddhism, Christianity, and Science.* Göttingen, Germany: Vandenhoeck and Ruprecht, 2008.

Pannenberg, Wolfhart. *Theology and the Philosophy of Science.* Trans. by Francis McDonagh. Philadelphia: Westminster Press, 1976.

Peacocke, Arthur. *Theology for a Scientific Age.* Minneapolis, MN: Fortress Press, 1993.

Peters, Ted. *Playing God? Genetic Determinism and Human Freedom.* New York: Routledge, 1997.

Polkinghorne, John. *Belief in God in an Age of Science.* New Haven, CT: Yale University Press, 1998.

Rolston, Holmes, III. *Science and Religion: A Critical Survey.* Philadelphia: Templeton Foundation Press, 2006.

Ruether, Rosemary Radford. *Gaia and God: An Ecofeminist Theology of Earth Healing.* San Francisco: HarperSan Francisco, 1992.

Ruse, Michael. *The Darwinian Revolution: Science Red in Tooth and Claw.* Chicago: University of Chicago Press, 1999.

Russell, Robert John. *Cosmology from Alpha to Omega: The Creative Mutual Interaction of Theology and Science.* Minneapolis, MN: Fortress Press, 2008.

Torrance, Thomas. *Theological Science.* Oxford: Oxford University Press, 1969.

Wallace, B. Alan, ed. *Buddhism and Science: Breaking New Ground.* New York: Columbia University Press, 2003.

Wallace, B. Alan, ed. *The Hidden Dimensions: The Unification of Physics and Consciousness.* New York: Columbia University Press, 2007.

Van Huyssteen, J. Wentzel. *Theology and the Justification of Faith: Constructing Theories in Systematic Theology.* Grand Rapids, MI: William B. Eerdmans Publishing Company, 1989.

Worthing, Mark W. *God, Creation, and Contemporary Physics.* Minneapolis, MN: Fortress Press, 1996.

Science and Religion: History of the Relationship

Popular generalizations about the relationship between science and religion, whether couched in terms of war or peace, do not stand up to serious historical investigation. There is no such thing as the relationship between science and religion. It is what different individuals and communities have made of it in a wide variety of different historical and cultural contexts. Science as we understand it today began with the Greeks, who designated study of the natural world "natural philosophy." The main recurrent issues discussed among pre-Socratic Greek philosophers were the nature of causality, the role of deities in natural processes, the nature of matter, the nature of the body and the soul, and the place of human beings in the cosmos. In the works of the Greek atomists, and later Lucretius in the first century BCE, a case was made for a naturalistic philosophy in which worlds came into and passed out of existence as the result of the chance collision of atoms. There might be life on other worlds, and natural processes did not depend on the intervention of gods. Other second-century CE thinkers, like the physician Galen, were more responsive to the appearance of what is now called "intelligent design," particularly in anatomical structures. The Epicureans countered that the appearance of design in nature was an illusion and reflected the fact that nature had experimented with every possible combination of organs and limbs, the nonviable combinations having perished long ago. Hipparchos discovered the precession of equinoxes, Archimedes analyzed the lever, Aristarchus of Samos proposed a heliocentric picture of the universe, while Ptolemy's Earth-centered universe dominated European thought until Nicolaus Copernicus in the 16th century. Aristotle set the stage for future developments in biology, physics, and metaphysics, all celebrating human rationality. The relationship between sacred and secular knowledge and the relation between divine power and the natural processes governing the world were important issues faced by early Christian theologians, among whom a diversity of views were held. Although Tertullian (160–220) proclaimed rhetorically, "what has Athens to do with Jerusalem," indicating the independence of Christian theology from Pagan philosophy, Saint Augustine (354–430) focused on the question of whether biblical exegesis should reflect contemporary secular knowledge, concluding that too tight a dependency on scripture could prove embarrassing when the state of knowledge changed. His declaration that science and philosophy should be welcomed handmaids to theology culminated in the Middle Ages with the "two books doctrine," according to which the book of nature reveals God as a creator and the book of scripture reveals God as redeemer.

In both Islamic and Christian cultures the problem of assimilating knowledge of nature was greatly stimulated by different reactions to Aristotle's conception of a world that has existed from eternity. In fact, in Islamic cultures science was practiced on a scale unprecedented in earlier history and played a decisive role in the history of science in medieval Christian Europe. Examples of the continuity of Islamic research traditions include the reform of Ptolemaic astronomy that started in the 11th century; the science of linguistics; the preservations of Greek and Roman learning, particularly the works of Aristotle, in Arabic translations in centers of learning in Baghdad and Spain; mathematics and mathematical geography; engineering and technology; plant biology; and medicine.

The study of nature in Islamic society is based on the Koran's call to study nature as a means of surrendering to God's will, since nature itself models the divine will. Although Islam played a role in defining the position of science in Muslim societies, it did not define the cognitive content of the sciences. For this reason, Islamic discourse on the sciences normally advocated its separateness from religion. As a result, according to Ibn Khaldun (1332–1406) in his *Muqaddima* (*Introduction* [to the science of history]), a concept of value-free or ethically neutral scientific knowledge that is not specific to any one particular culture was developed. In distinction from "religious knowledge," Islamic scholars called the natural sciences "the sciences shared among all the nations." Christian and Jewish theologians eagerly embraced this knowledge as it was transmitted into Europe.

Thomas Aquinas's appropriation of Aristotle's metaphysics in his *Summa Theologica* Christianized Aristotle's natural philosophy by bringing it into critical dialogue with natural theology, meaning conclusions

Page from a 16th-century copy of *Marvels of Things Created and Miraculous Aspects of Things Existing*, by al-Qazwini. (National Library of Medicine)

rationally drawn about God based on the observation of natural processes coupled with exercise of reason. This dialogue is illustrated in Aquinas's treatment of the doctrine of creation, which affirms the continual dependence of all that exists on a transcendent being. Such a world is capable of either the eternalist position of Aristotle or with the conception of a definite beginning in Genesis. Reason alone cannot decide the issue, in which case, the scriptural portrayal of creation in Genesis 1–2 takes precedence as revealed truth. Aquinas also appropriated Aristotle's emphasis on primary or final causation (goals inherent in nature) in governing physical processes because this makes it possible to ask deeper questions about the coordination of the physical processes that constituted the visible world.

Portrait of 16th-century Polish astronomer Nicolaus (Nicholas) Copernicus. Copernicus was the first scientist to publish the idea that the Sun, and not the Earth, was the center of the universe, a finding that dramatically changed both science and religion. (Library of Congress)

For Aquinas, the natural philosophy of Aristotle was incomplete without the postulation of a "Being" who is ultimately responsible for the coordination of these processes, a conclusion that underlies his five arguments for the existence of God. Aquinas's reliance on Aristotle as the philosophical foundation of Christian theology was challenged by the Copernican revolution in astronomy and the Protestant Reformation. Nicolaus Copernicus (1473–1543), who was a cathedral canon in Cracow, Poland, challenged the Ptolemaic worldview that dominated the Latin church, which held that the Earth sits unmoving at the center of the solar system, with the Sun, Moon, and stars revolving around it. Relying on his own empirical observations and mathematical calculations, he argued in *De revolutionibus orbium coelesrium libri sex* (*Six Books on the Revolutions of the Celestial Orbs*) that the Earth rotates on its axis and the other planets of the solar system orbit the Sun. The removal of the Earth from the center of

the Ptolemaic world system seemed heretical to many Catholic theologians because Ptolemy's Sun-centered cosmology seemed to give scientific support for literal readings of the Genesis creation stories, particularly the centrality of the Earth and human beings in God's created order. Martin Luther heard tales of Copernicus's new astronomy, but did not seriously engage it, devoting his energies to the interpretation of scripture, challenging the role of Aristotle in theology, and reforming the church. But one of Luther's reformation colleagues, Andreas Osiander, in 1543, the year Copernicus died, contracted with Copernicus to publish his *De revolutionibus*. Copernicus saw his published book for the first time on his deathbed. For the most part, Copernicus's new cosmology elicited very little theological attention, and certainly no discernible religious excitement, until Galileo Galilei (1564–1642) provided empirical evidence in support of Copernicus's theory through telescopic observations of sunspots, the mountains of the Moon, and the rings and moons of Saturn and the moons of Jupiter. The central issues had to do with interpretations of biblical passages such as Psalm 104:4 and Joshua 10:12–14, which pictured a world with a stable Earth and movements by the Sun and other heavenly bodies around the Earth. The authority of the Bible and the authority of the papacy to interpret the Bible seemed to be at stake, not loyalty to Ptolemy as such. Galileo defended Copernicus against Ptolemy in his *Dilogo sopra i due massimi sistime del mundo* (*Dialogue Concerning the Two Chief Systems of the World*) in 1632. Galileo was condemned by the Inquisition to house arrest for the rest of his life because of his defense of Copernicus's *De revolutionibus*, which was placed on the Index Expurgatorius in 1616. After Galileo, a discourse involving theological elements in the promotion of the sciences and technology began to develop. Francis Bacon (1561–1625) argued that empirically based knowledge when applied for altruistic purposes must have a religious sanction and could even restore human domination over nature, which had been lost at the Fall. Robert Boyle (1627–1691) found evidence of divine craftsmanship in the structures of minuscule creatures revealed by the microscope. Isaac Newton (1642–1727) wrote three scientific works that established the foundations for the mechanical worldview that dominated science until the publication of Albert Einstein's theories of special and general relativity in 1905: *Philosophia naturalis principia mathematica* (1687), *Optics* (1704), and *Arithmetica universalis* (1707). In these works Newton unified the laws of mechanics and the law of gravity by invoking the idea that all bodies everywhere operate with mutual gravitation. On this principle, he ascertained that the forces that keep the planets in their orbits must be reciprocally the inverse squares of their distances from their centers. At the same time, Newton believed that gravitational force could not be explained by reference to the innate properties of matter. In a controversy that took place in the second half of the 18th century, Newton's defender Samuel Clarke (1675–1729) and the German philosopher Gottfried Wilhelm Leibniz (1646–1716) debated the question of how a divine being might act in the world. Clarke argued that the laws of nature defined the way God normally chooses to act, but there was nothing in the laws themselves that prevented other sorts of divine action in the world. By contrast, Leibniz argued that the best of all possible worlds that God created needed no maintenance and emphatically did not require God's actions in the "reformations" of the solar system that Newton thought necessary to keep the laws of motion governing planetary motions from decaying. Newton accepted the doctrine of the passivity of matter and argued that the radical sovereignty of God required the animation of nature to come from God alone and not from matter. Newton exemplified the atomist approach to natural philosophy that dominated natural philosophy in Europe until the mid-19th century. It was part of the business of natural philosophy to discuss the question of God's attributes and relation to the natural world. Because elements of theology were incorporated into natural philosophy, the word "science" did not take on its modern specialized meanings until the mid-19th century. In France, Voltaire (1694–1778) popularized Newton's natural philosophy as part of his attack on the power of the Catholic Church. In Germany, Immanuel Kant (1724–1804) exposed the logical weakness of attempts to argue for a deity on the basis of what is known of natural processes. In Edinburgh, David Hume's (1711–1776) *Dialogues Concerning Natural Religion* exposed the incoherencies of analogies on which the design argument rested. Even if the natural

world did resemble a human artifact, such as a clock or a ship, it did not follow that it was made by only one artificer, and certainly not one whose attributes necessarily coincided with those assumed by Christian interpretations of Genesis 1 and 2. The final separation between theology and science as intellectual disciplines occurred in Charles Darwin's (1809–1882) *Origin of Species*, in which he theorized that all living organisms share common descent. The process driving evolution is natural selection contextualized by environmental factors over great lengths of time, which, because of the work of Gregor Mendel (1822–1884), is known to be rooted in the genetic structure of all living organisms. Darwin's theory of evolution is in direct opposition to the design arguments of William Paley's *Natural Theology* (1803), in which he argued that the design of organisms in the natural world must be accounted for by positing a divine designer, which was the dominant conclusion of natural philosophy before Darwin. But Darwin's theory of evolution is a totally natural explanation of the history of life's origins as well as the evolution of species that does not require God as an explanatory factor. The separation of science from natural philosophy and theology begins with Darwin's theory of evolution. Several aspects of Darwin's theory of evolution challenged the theological assumptions of Christian theology: (1) the nature of biblical authority; (2) the historicity of the Genesis creation narratives; (3) the meaning of Adam's fall from grace; (4) the meaning of Christ's redemptive mission, particularly the meaning of the doctrine of the resurrection; (5) the nature and scope of God's activity in the world; (6) the persuasive force of the argument for design; (7) what it means for human beings to be made in the image of God; and (8) the nature of moral values. Because it was easy to set up a contradiction on each point between ostensibly "scientific" and ostensibly "religious" points of view, Darwin's theory soon came to symbolize the conflict that militant secularists as well as militant fundamentalists still like to swell. On the other hand, more liberal forms of theological reflection have continued to incorporate evolutionary theory into their own specific versions of "evolutionary theology." In other words, while some evangelical and fundamentalist Christians still assert conflict between science and religion, liberal theological traditions have sought to bring Christian faith and practice into dialogue with the natural sciences.

Paul O. Ingram

See also: Luther, Martin; Science and Religion: The Contemporary Scene.

References

Appleman, Philip, ed. *Darwin: Texts, Backgrounds, Contemporary Opinion, Critical Essays.* New York: W. W. Norton and Company, 1979.

Astore, William J. *Observing God: Thomas Dick, Evangelism, and Popular Science in Victorian Britain and America.* Aldershot, UK: Ashgate, 2001.

Blackwell, Richard J. *Galileo, Bellarmine, and the Bible.* Notre Dame, IN: University of Notre Dame Press, 1991.

Bowler, Peter J. *Reconciling Science and Religion.* London: SCM Press, 2001.

Brooke, John Hedley. *Science and Religion: Some Historical Perspectives.* Cambridge: Cambridge University Press, 1991.

Brooke, John Hedley, and Geoffrey Cantor. *Reconstructing Nature: The Engagement of Science and Religion.* New York: Oxford University Press, 1998.

Browne, Janet. *Charles Darwin.* 2 vols. New York: Knopf, 1995.

Eisley. Loren. *Darwin's Century: Evolution and the Men Who Discovered It.* Garden City, NY: Doubleday and Company, 1958.

Ferngren, Gary B. *Science and Religion: A Historical Introduction.* Baltimore: Johns Hopkins University Press, 2002.

Gilbert, James. *Redeeming Culture: American Religion in an Age of Science.* Chicago: University of Chicago Press, 1997.

Grant, Edward. *The Foundations of Modern Science in the Middle Ages: Their Religious, Institutional, and Intellectual Contexts.* Cambridge: Cambridge University Press, 1996.

Heatherington, Norris S., ed. *Cosmology: Historical, Literary, Philosophical, Religious, and Scientific Perspectives.* New York: Garland, 1993.

Lindberg, David C. *The Beginnings of Western Science.* Chicago: University of Chicago Press, 2007.

Lindberg, David C., and Ronald L. Numbers, eds. *God and Nature: Historical Essays on the Encounter Between Christianity and Science.* Berkeley and Los Angeles: University of California Press, 1986.

Lindberg, David C., and Ronald L. Numbers, eds. *When Science and Christianity Meet.* Chicago: University of Chicago Press, 2003.

Russell, Colin A., Hooykaas Reijer, and David Goodman. *The Conflict Thesis and Cosmology.* Milton Keynes, UK: Open University Press 1974.

Sardar, Zaiuddin, ed. *The Touch of Midas: Science, Values, and Environment in Islam and the West.* Manchester, UK: Manchester University Press, 1984.

Thompson, Keith. *Before Darwin: Reconciling God and Nature.* New Haven, CT: Yale University Press, 2005.

Scientology

See Church of Scientology.

Scottish Episcopal Church

During the Reformation of Christianity in the 16th century, Protestants of the Reformed tradition fought with Scotland's rulers, who were Roman Catholics, for control of the country. In 1560 the Scottish Parliament rejected papal authority and reformed the church along Presbyterian lines. A Reformed liturgy was introduced in 1564. The Church of Scotland became a Presbyterian establishment. However, a nominal episcopacy remained in place, protected by some powerful people who adhered to a more Roman approach to Christianity. James IV (who in 1603 also became James I of England) favored the bishops, and as soon as he felt secure on the throne, he began to pick away at the Presbyterians' establishment. In 1610 he secured orders from the Church of England for the Scottish bishops. Two years later he reinstated them in their dioceses and slowly reintroduced other changes.

Charles I (r. 1625–1649) asserted the supremacy of the Crown in Scotland and in 1634 tried to impose

St. Andrew Episcopal Church in Turriff, Aberdeenshire, Scotland. (James Kelly/Dreamstime.com)

a Book of Canons that would bring the Church of Scotland closer to the Church of England. Through the new archbishop of Canterbury, William Laud (1573–1645), he enforced a High-Church approach to worship. In 1637 he imposed a new liturgy on the Scottish church that was like the one used in the Church of England. His attempt to enforce his will on a rebellious nation actually led to his downfall, the establishment of the Commonwealth in England under Oliver Cromwell (1599–1658), and the abolishment of the episcopacy in both England and Scotland. The monarchy was re-established in 1660. Both Charles II (r. 1660–1685) and James II (r. 1685–1688) were Catholics.

In 1661, after Charles II ascended to the throne, Parliament annulled all acts affecting religion passed since 1633 and restored the episcopacy as it had been under Charles I. Four new bishops were appointed for Scotland and consecrated by bishops of the Church of England. The Presbyterians were now disenfranchised. After the Glorious Revolution that brought William II and Mary (r. 1689–1702) to the throne, the religious order changed again. Presbyterians were again placed in charge of the established Church of Scotland, which once again became a Presbyterian Church. It has remained such to this day.

Those who favored the Episcopal order protested. They were especially strong in the more northern part of Scotland. They finally won some toleration in 1712 and, while never reinstated, continue to this day as the Scottish Episcopal Church. Supporters suffered somewhat during the period 1745–1792, when a set of penal laws made it illegal for Episcopalians in Scotland to possess church buildings or to hold public services. Ministers were not allowed to minister to more than five persons at any one time.

The Scottish Episcopal Church is at one with the belief and practice of the Church of England. It would be to this church that former members of the Church of England in the newly formed United States would turn when the British bishops initially refused to consecrate a bishop for the now independent American colonies. In 1874 the Scottish bishops consecrated Samuel Seabury (1729–1796), who had been elected as a bishop by Anglican clergymen in Connecticut. His agreement with the consecrating bishops led to the inclusion of some distinctive elements of the Scottish liturgy into the American liturgy.

After the penal laws were repealed, the church experienced a growth phase and began to acquire buildings, many of which are still in use. In 1982 it modified its form of governance. A general synod composed of three houses (bishops, clergy, and laity) is now the highest legislative body.

The church is led by its primus, one of the bishops who is selected by the House of Bishops. There are currently seven dioceses. The church has experienced some membership losses in the 1990s to the present. In 2006, it reported 44,000 members in 310 parishes. It is a member of the World Council of Churches.

Scottish Episcopal Church
21 Grosvenor Crescent
Edinburgh EH12 5EE
United Kingdom
http://www.scotland.anglican.org/

J. Gordon Melton

See also: Church of England; Church of Scotland; Roman Catholic Church; World Council of Churches.

References

Van Beek, Huibert. *A Handbook of the Churches and Councils: Profiles of Ecumenical Relationships.* Geneva: World Council of Churches, 2006.

Van der Bent, Ans J., ed. *Handbook/Member Churches/World Council of Churches.* Geneva: World Council of Churches, 1985.

Wingate, Andrew, et al., eds. *Anglicanism: A Global Communion.* London: Mowbray, 1998.

Secular Humanism

See Council for Secular Humanism.

Secularization

The spirit and movement of separating public life from religion and faith is known today as secularization. Secularization is the process of drawing something or someone away from a religious orientation or religious loyalty. In this way, secularization, far from being an inevitable or linear consequence of modernity, is a dynamic and changing historical movement, led by individuals and groups who seek to differentiate religion from culture, state, and society. This article is a basic introduction to and historical review of the movement, the theoretical understanding of the process, and the contemporary responses of religion to secularization.

The term "secularization" comes from the Latin *saeculum*, which in the early Christian period meant "era" or "world." Early Christians separated what they called the kingdom of God from the earthly world. The world was thought to be an established space separated from God's province—an idea that modern thinkers suggest facilitated the planting of the "seeds" of secularization within the religion of Christianity. And indeed, the tension between medieval Christendom and empire was a difficult and troubled relationship, with each party pushing back and forth over questions of authority and power. These tensions escalated and eventually provoked the Protestant Reformation of the 16th century. The Reformation created a space where Christians expressed multiple approaches to the world, whether in withdrawal (the Mennonites and Anabaptists); the more neutral arrangement with the state found in the Lutheran communion; or in a form of theocracy as was found in the Reformed tradition, expressed variably in John Calvin's Geneva, the English Puritan Revolution, and the American Boston Puritan Commonwealth of New England.

An elderly Turkish woman holds a national flag during a pro-secularism rally in Istanbul, Turkey, on April 29, 2007. (AP/Wide World Photos)

In the 17th century, secularization took a new and even revolutionary turn with the Enlightenment. Secularists, led by David Hume (1711–1776) in England and Voltaire (1694–1778) in France, sought intentionally to attack Christianity and to remove its power from public life. Intellectual and political leadership advanced the French Revolution (1789), putting forward a universalist vision of reason that would deter and displace religion, unseating the clerics, vanquishing superstition, and bringing forward a secular and, therefore, rational government and culture. The displacement of religious authority was paramount to and motivated by the hope of progress for all humankind. This movement cannot be underestimated; it blossomed into the development of a secularized elite that shaped the po-

litical, cultural, and social structures of modern European nations.

The English and American revolutions of 1642 and 1776 matched the power of the French Revolution in many ways. Some claim that these revolutions generated an equal and perhaps more powerful Anglo-American DNA of modernity, whereby universal reason was mixed with religion; religious liberty partnered with democracy, while Christianity would have no state monopoly. Nevertheless it thrived. After the separation of church and state, primarily expressed in the American experiment, the open cultural and religious markets created not only economic and political liberty but also religious liberty that clerical entrepreneurs would exploit. This experiment in democracy and open religious markets was the engine of the intense American engagement with religion in general and with Christianity in particular.

These were unique trajectories in the Anglo-American and European religious evolutions. European nations have consistently expressed greater secularity; religious membership has declined and the importance of religion in the lives of Europeans has continued to decrease. Some explain this phenomenon as a result of the sponsorship of religion in many European states. The conjecture is that bureaucracies have undercut the motivations of religious leaders. In the United States, because of an open religious market, religions could not depend upon the state but had to make it on their own. Nonetheless, one of the most recent trends in American religious life is the doubling of those who self-identify as claiming no religion, a number that has reached as high as 15 percent of the U.S. population in recent surveys. In general, however, the American experiment in religious freedom has tended to create a much more religious society than its European counterparts.

Theories and Responses to Secularization Max Weber, the German sociologist of the early 20th century, argued that secularization was a function of rationalization. This rationalization of human consciousness created disenchantment—the withdrawal of belief in the divine causality of the universe. That is, moderns (and here he meant Europeans) had lost confidence and belief in invisible agents that would answer prayers or direct human destiny. Emile Durkheim, the French sociologist at the turn of the 20th century, argued that the process of differentiation in modern life separated various spheres of culture and society so that religion no longer impacted or regulated education, social welfare, health, economic behavior, or even family life to the extent that it had in the past. This process undercut the authority of religious figures and their traditions. Religion had become privatized, impacting only the interior lives of individuals rather than shaping their broader public life. This description of the effects of modernity on religion were not so much based on empirical evidence but on prescription, indeed, advocacy for the compartmentalization of religion and its marginalization from culture. The 19th-century French intellectual

Auguste Comte (1798–1857), who coined the term "sociology," posited three stages of humanity: the theological, the metaphysical, and the positive. Comte advocated for a new Religion of Humanity, based on scientific positivism that could and would elevate humanity beyond the earlier more primitive stages of development. Few sociologists took him up on his scientific utopianism but many concurred that religion should be superseded by a more rational science of human morality.

The 20th-century thinking in the sociology of religion was deeply shaped by Peter L. Berger, the Austrian émigré to the United States. In the 1960s, Berger's theory of a passing sacred canopy set the dialogues on secularization in the second half of the 20th century. Berger suggested that the pluralism of modern culture, a result of rationalization and differentiation, undercut the plausibility structures of religious belief and practice. Berger suggested that without a sacred canopy to legitimate religious belief, moderns would turn away from faith and belief in God. Secularization, as a function of modernity, became an established theory to explain secularization in modern religious life. Other theorists, such as Thomas Luckman, suggested that moderns had "an invisible religion," by which they pursued a private orientation of personal purpose and meaning.

In the 1990s, however, scholars such as Jose Casanova, began to question the applicability of secularization theory and whether it was a plausible explanation for modern religious life. Indeed, Casanova argued for the de-privatization of religion, such that religion had once again become a definitive characteristic shaping culture and political life. Some suggested that after the fall of the Iron Curtain, religions were no longer under the coercive force of the Cold War and, therefore, could engage more freely in politics. Others suggested that religion was, in fact, key to many of the recent liberation movements: the fall of the Iron Curtain; the overthrow of apartheid in South Africa; and the American civil rights movement, which was led by African American religious figures. Thus, secularization appears as an inadequate explanation for modern religious life; religion continues to have enormous impact on both private purpose and political actions.

In the contemporary era, three important trends in religion further challenged the inevitability of secularization. First, the rise of religious extremism over the last 20 years presents a challenge to secularization and its core claim that religion and public life are separated in modern life. Religious extremists, in all the major world religions, have used violence to make their points to address social and political grievances. Second, the Southern Hemisphere has witnessed an explosive growth of Charismatic and Pentecostal forms of Christianity in Asia, Latin America, and Africa. David Martin has suggested that global Pentecostalism is the religion best adapted to globalization. It is an egalitarian religion, enabling entrepreneurial agents everywhere to start ministries wherever they live; as a pneumatic and anti-intellectual form of religion, it can adapt to nearly every cultural form, particularly among dispossessed communities that benefit from the promise of healing miracles and the growing emphasis on prosperity; and finally, it is a movement that readily uses modern technology to appeal and communicate its message.

What we have found is that secularization is neither an inevitable nor linear process. There is a formidable array of cultural and intellectual advocates who claims that secularization is a natural result of modernity. But even as intellectuals, like Sam Harris and Christopher Hitchens, and scientists, like Richard Dawkins and Daniel Dennett, describe secularization, they are also its advocates. Evidence shows that, especially in the United States, their campaigns have made a dent in decreasing the percentages of Americans who claim to be Christian; the numbers reflect a decline from 85 percent 20 years ago to 75 percent today. Nonetheless, the spread of cultural pluralism in Western cultures has created a multiplication of open religious markets that allows religious entrepreneurs to communicate their messages and fight for their causes. Today, secularism is very much a live option; the idea that it is more present today than in the past is probably true. But as to its inevitably, we know that far from being a natural conclusion to an inevitable modern process, it is in fact a function of historical, cultural, and political activists who seek to secularize culture and society with mixed results.

James Wellman

See also: Anabaptism; Calvin, John; Globalization; Mennonites; Modernity; Reformed/Presbyterian Tradition.

References

Berger, Peter. *The Sacred Canopy: Elements of a Sociological Theory of Religion.* Garden City, NY: Doubleday, 1969.

Bruce, Steve. *God is Dead: Secularization in the West.* Oxford: Blackwell Publishing, 2002.

Casanova, Jose. *Public Religions in the Modern World.* Chicago: University of Chicago Press, 1994.

Martin, David. *On Secularization: Towards a Revised General Theory.* Aldershot: Ashgate, 2005.

Smith, Christian. *The Secular Revolution: Power, Interests, and Conflict in the Secularization of American Public Life.* Berkeley: University of California Press, 2003.

Swatos, William H., Jr., and Daniel V. A. Olson, eds. *The Secularization Debate.* Lanham, MD: Rowman & Littlefield, 2000.

Wellman, James K., Jr., ed. *Belief and Bloodshed: Religion and Violence across Time and Tradition.* Lanham, MD: Rowman & Littlefield, 2007.

Sedevacantism and Antipopes

In the wake of the Second Vatican Council, several arch-conservative Roman Catholic groups began to adopt a critical attitude toward the hierarchy. The largest of these groups later became the Society (or Fraternity) of Saint Pius X, under the leadership of French archbishop Marcel Lefebvre (1905–1991). Lefebvre, however, never questioned the legitimacy of Pope Paul VI (1897–1978), or that of his successors. Lefebvre's view was that they were leaders of dubious doctrines and actions (thus justifying Lefebvre in promoting what, according to Rome, amounted to a schism), but did not conclude that such wrongdoings should automatically invalidate their papal canonical role. Inside and outside the Society of Saint Pius X, more radical groups emerged, each concluding that, after the Second Vatican Council, the popes had lost their legitimacy as a result of their heretical teachings; this implied that the Holy See of Rome (Latin: *Sedes*) was technically "vacant"—that is, there was no legitimate pope. Hence the name of Sedevacantism was given to the movement, which was vehemently critical of Lefebvre and his Society. The latter, in fact, although critical of the pope, continued to pray for him in its Masses with the ritual formula *una cum Pontifice nostro* (in unity with our pope). Sedevacantists regarded what they called the *una cum* Masses as ipso facto invalid, just as both Sedevacantists and members of the Lefebvre movement regarded Masses celebrated according to post–Second Vatican Council liturgical renewal as invalid.

Sedevacantism was never a well organized movement, consisting as it did of several small groups, often divided on questions of leadership and on the finer points of how non–*una cum* Masses should be celebrated. The very fact that they considered the Holy See to be vacant meant that Sedevacantists by definition could not recognize an international authority, and it kept the movement divided. Some influential centers did emerge, however. Many Sedevacantist leaders were consecrated as bishops in the late 1970s and early 1980s by arch-conservative Vietnamese archbishop Pierre-Martin Ngo-Dhinh Thuc (1897–1984). Those consecrations, not authorized by the Vatican, were, according to Roman Catholic canon law, illicit but not invalid (and they led ultimately to Thuc's excommunication). That meant that Thuc's consecration of the Sedevacantist leaders as bishops was regarded as valid, although they were automatically excommunicated. They were, however, according to Roman Catholic canon law, "real" bishops, with the power to consecrate other bishops in turn and to ordain priests (forthwith excommunicated by virtue of the fact of their ordination by an excommunicated bishop). The question is quite important in Catholic canon law and doctrine, which states that a validly ordained priest (although excommunicated), when pronouncing the words of the consecration in the Mass, really does convert the bread and wine into the Body and Blood of Jesus Christ (something an invalidly ordained priest is not empowered to do). Thus, thanks mostly to Archbishop Thuc (who

died in 1984 fully reconciled with Rome) and to more than 100 "Thuc bishops" ordained directly or indirectly by him, Sedevacantists could rightly claim to have "real" priests and to be able to offer "real" Masses to their followers.

Among those consecrated by Thuc was Father Michel Guérard des Lauriers (1898–1988), who prior to the Second Vatican Council had been a respected Catholic Dominican academic theologian and had joined Lefebvre in 1970 and left him in 1977. Guérard was initially regarded as a leading intellectual light in the international Sedevacantist network. He insisted, however, that he was not technically a Sedevacantist and that his position was slightly different. In his Cassiciacum theory (originally expounded in 1979 in the journal *Les Cahiers de Cassiciacum*), Guérard explained that the Holy See was vacant only "materially"; "formally" Paul VI (as, later, his successors) could still be regarded as pope. Only if a significant number of cardinals and bishops were prepared to start a canonical process against the pope would he cease to be the "real" pope also "formally" (and not only "materially"). Guérard criticized both Lefebvre (who regarded Paul VI as pope both formally and materially) and the Sedevacantist majority (for which Paul VI was not the pope, neither formally nor materially). Guérard's complicated theory succeeded in rallying only one section of the Sedevacantist network around him. The Cassiciacum theory is currently promoted by the Italian-based Mater Boni Consilii Institute and by a number of U.S. groups, in part originating from former Dominican bishop Robert McKenna (b. 1927), who was consecrated bishop by Guérard himself in 1986. Among them are the Saint Dominic Chapel in Highland, Michigan (www.stdominicchapel.com), founded by Robert L. Neville (b. 1972), ordained to the priesthood into the Society of Saint Pius X in 1996, who was consecrated a bishop by McKenna in 2005; and the Most Holy Trinity Seminary, founded in September 1995 and directed by Donald J. Sanborn, also a former member of the Society of Saint Pius X, who in 2002 was also consecrated a bishop by McKenna.

Sedevacantism (not connected with the Cassiciacum theory and regarding the Holy See as vacant in both the formal and the material sense) has its main centers in Mexico, thanks in particular to the activities of a "Thuc bishop," Moisés Carmona-Rivera (1912–1991), who, together with Adolfo Zamora Hernandez (1910–1987, yet another "Thuc bishop"), founded the Union Católico Trento and the Seminar of the Sacred Hearts of Jesus and Mary in Hermosillo (Sonora, Mexico). In the early 1980s, a popular Sedevacantist leader in the United States was Francis Schuckhardt (1937–2006), who in 1967 had founded the Congregation of Mary Immaculate Queen (CMRI, from its Latin name) at Mount Saint Michel near Spokane, Washington, and subsequently broke with Rome in 1970. Schuckhardt, however, was accused of a number of personal wrongdoings and had to leave his own community in 1984; in 1987 he was found in possession of illegal drugs and arrested in California. After his release from jail, he established a semi-clandestine organization known as the Oblates of Mary the Immaculate (not to be confused with the Roman Catholic religious order of the same name). Some former members also claim that Schuckhardt was preparing to declare himself Pope Hadrian VII and had began dressing as a pope (a website by his supporters is available at http://www.bishopschuckardt.com). CMRI survived, however, and even prospered in its post-Schuckhardt phase, with the help of the Mexican Sedevacantists and under the leadership of Bishop Mark Anthony Pivarunas (b. 1958), consecrated by Carmona-Rivera in 1991. In 1993, Pivarunas in turn consecrated as bishop Father Daniel L. Dolan (b. 1951), who converted his parish of St. Gertrude the Great in Cincinnati from a Society of Saint Pius X Mass center to the central point of a network of priests following the Cassiciacum theory extending to several nearby states. Loyal to a "pure" form of Sedevacantism (as opposed to the Cassiciacum theory) is, on the other hand, the Society of St. Pius V, established in New York in 1983 by nine priests who left the Society of Saint Pius X. The majority of them later adopted the Cassiciacum theory and left the Society of St. Pius V, which currently continues its activities under the leadership of Father Clarence Kelly (b. 1941), who was ordained a bishop in 1993 by Mons Alfredo Méndez-Gonzalez (1907–1995), retired bishop of Arecibo, Puerto Rico, at that time a Roman Catholic bishop in good standing.

There may be some 10,000 Sedevacantists throughout the world, with the most important centers in the United States, Mexico, France, Italy, Germany, and the Czech Republic. The small Japanese group Seibo no Mikuni, founded in 1970 by Yukio Nemoto (1925–1988), remains largely isolated because of its peculiar millennial beliefs. Most of them believe that forming a central organization would be tantamount to establishing a schismatic alternative to the Roman Catholic Church. They prefer to remain a network of small groups and see themselves as the only surviving remnant of the one true post–Second Vatican Council Catholic Church. One of their main problems is how to respond to the issue of the future of Catholic authority. By definition, they regard the pope as essential for the church's very survival and infallibility, but, at the same time, they maintain that there is no (legitimate) pope in Rome at present. A large majority of Sedevacantists dismiss as non-canonical, and even ridiculous, the very idea that they could convene a conclave and elect a pope of their own; they prefer to wait for a solution to come directly, and perhaps unpredictably, from God, whose ways, they say, are after all not human ways. A few Sedevacantists, on the other hand, are "conclavist" —that is, they believe a conclave should be called (composed of all, or at least most, Sedevacantist bishops) and a new pope duly elected. Conclavists realize nonetheless that, should a conclave be organized, the majority of the Sedevacantist bishops would refuse to attend it, and that some groups (such as the Italian Association of St. Mary Salus Populi Romani, headquartered in Turin, Italy) regard a conclave as certainly desirable but, at least for the time being, impracticable. Attempts have been made to organize a conclave, however: in 1994, for example, some 20 Sedevacantist bishops from 12 different countries met in Assisi, Italy, and elected as pope a South African priest (and former student at Lefebvre's seminary), Victor Von Pentz (b. 1953), under the name of Linus II. He currently resides in the United Kingdom and maintains but a limited following.

Some conclavists have, on the other hand, joined other alternative popes ("antipopes," according to Roman Catholic theology), who, even before the full development of the Sedevacantist network, had claimed that their role was based both on the alleged heresies of the Second Vatican Council and on mystical visions calling them to the pontificate without the need of any conclave or election. One of the earliest "pretenders" was a French priest, Michel-Auguste-Marie Collin (1905–1974), who claimed to have been called by heaven itself to become Pope Clemens XV during the Second Vatican Council, in 1963. Collin established an alternative Vatican in Clémery, Lorraine, where he also founded a Renewed Church of Christ, known outside France as the Church of the Magnificat. After Collin's death in 1974, his church nearly collapsed entirely, and it is now reduced to a small remnant of what it once was. One of Collin's followers, however, the Québec priest Gaston Tremblay (b. 1928), had already ceased to recognize the French claimant in 1968 and had proclaimed himself Pope Gregory XVII. His movement is called the Apostles of Infinite Love.

Tremblay's main competitor was Clemente Domínguez y Gómez (1946–2005), one of the seers in the alleged Marian apparitions of Palmar de Troya, Spain (1968–1976), and later a "Thuc bishop," consecrated by the Vietnamese archbishop on January 11, 1976. In 1978, Domínguez (in the meantime blinded in a car accident in May 1976) revealed that he had been mystically designated by Jesus Christ as the new pope in a 1976 vision, and his followers confirmed his election as Pope Gregory XVII (the same name adopted by Tremblay in Québec). His Catholic, Apostolic, and Palmarian Church (named after the town of Palmar de Troya) is probably the single largest organization bowing to the authority of an "alternative" pope, with more than 1,000 followers in Spain and several hundreds more internationally. In the 1990s, however, Domínguez was accused of sexual immorality with several nuns of the order he had established in the meantime; in 1997 he admitted his sins and asked for his community's forgiveness. Most followers remained loyal to Domínguez and, after his death in 2005, to his hand-picked successor, former lawyer and "Thuc bishop" Manuel Alonso Corral, who became Pope Peter II. Others, however, have both doubted the sincerity of Domínguez in his apology and questioned his decision to appoint a successor rather than leave this choice to a conclave including the many cardinals he had in the meantime appointed from among his bishops. At the end of 2000, 17 bishops with a couple of hundred followers left the Palmarian Church and formed a splinter movement known as The Tribe.

Other claimants to the role of pope have included Father Gino Frediani (1913–1984), the parish priest of Gavinana (province of Pistoia, Italy), who in 1973 claimed to have been mystically consecrated by Jesus Christ and several Old Testament prophets as Pope Emmanuel I. He gathered several hundred followers; after his death, a hundred have remained active in his New Church of the Holy Heart of Jesus under the leadership of his successor, Father Sergio Melani (who, however, makes no claim to being the new pope). A couple of dozen rival "antipopes" operate in several countries, but none of them have more than a handful of followers. Among them are Father Lucian Pulvermacher (b. 1918), who in 1998 proclaimed himself the new pope under the name Pius XIII (http://www.truecatholic.us); and David Allen Bawden (b. 1959), living in the Kansas countryside, once a seminarian with the Society of Saint Pius X (where he had never been ordained to the priesthood), who on July 16, 1990, was elected by a group of six laypeople (including three women) as Pope Michael.

A special position is nonetheless maintained by William Kamm (b. 1950), a German-born Catholic lay preacher living in Australia and known as "Little Pebble." It is claimed that the Virgin Mary has revealed to Kamm that the post–Second Vatican Council popes, including John Paul II and Benedict XVI, are indeed legitimate (contrary to the Sedevacantist thesis). On the other hand, heaven has designated Kamm as a future pope under the name Peter II. Kamm gathered more than 1,000 followers in several countries, some of them living communally and most of them members of a religious order known as the Order of Saint Charbel (named after the popular Catholic Lebanese saint Charbel Maklouf [1828–1898]). The Australian Catholic bishops, despite his protests, have repeatedly branded Kamm's organization as schismatic and not a legitimate part of the Catholic Church. Their position seemed vindicated when in 2005 and 2007 Kamm was sentenced to two jail terms for sexual relations with two minor girls. Kamm did not deny the relations, but claimed that the Virgin Mary in an apparition had authorized him to take as many as 84 "mystical wives." Kamm is now in jail and will not be eligible for parole before 2013. Many followers have left the Order of Saint Charbel and only a handful remain loyal to Kamm.

Mater Boni Consilii Institute
Località Carbignano 36
10020 Verrua Savoia (Torino)
Italy
http://www.sodalitiumpianum.com

Most Holy Trinity Seminary
1000 Spring Lake Highway
Brooksville FL 34602

St. Gertrude the Great
4900 Rialto Road
West Chester OH 45069
http://www.sgg.org

Our Lady of the Rosary Chapel
15 Pepper Street
Monroe, Connecticut 06468
http://www.rosarychapel.net

Seibo no Mikuni
33-2 Aza Ubasaku Oaza
Matuzuka, Sukagawa-shi
Fukushima 969-04
Japan

Catholic, Apostolic, and Palmarian Church
Abad Gordillo 5
Apartado 4058
41080 Sevilla
Spain

Congregation of Mary Immaculate Queen (CMRI)
Mount St. Michael
8500 N. St. Michael's Road
Spokane, WA 99217-9333
http://www.cmri.org

St. Pius V Church
Eight Pond Place
Oyster Bay Cove, NY 11771
http://www.sspv.net

One Holy Catholic Church Inc. (Pope Michael)
Box 74
Delia KS 66418-0074
www.vaticaninexile.com

Massimo Introvigne and PierLuigi Zoccatelli

See also: Apostles of Infinite Love; Fraternity/Society of Saint Pius X; Roman Catholic Church.

References

Cekada, Anthony. *The Nine vs. Lefebvre: We Resist You to Your Face.* 2008. www.traditionalmass.org/images/articles/NineVLefebvre.pdf.

Cuneo, Michael. *The Smoke of Satan: Conservative and Traditionalist Dissent in Contemporary American Catholicism.* New York: Oxford University Press, 1997.

Delestre, Antoine. *Clemens XV: prêtre lorrain et pape à Clémery.* Metz, France: Serpenois, 1985.

Des Lauriers, Michel Guérard. "Le Siège Apostolique est-il vacant?" *Cahiers de Cassiciacum* 1 (1979).

Historia Sagrada o Santa Biblia Palmariana de Grado Superior según el Magisterio Infalible de la Iglesia. 3 vols. Seville, Spain: Santa Sede Apostolica, 2001.

Le ultime volontà di Dio per la Terra nascoste nei Profeti dell'Antico e del Nuovo Testamento. Gavinana, Italy: Aggeo, 1984.

Paladino, Francesco Maria. *Petrus es tu?* Chateauneuf, France: Delacroix, 1997.

"The Little Pebble": The Last Pope: A Man of Contradiction: Petrus Romanus, Sinner or Saint? Nowra, New South Wales: William Kamm, 1999.

Seicho-No-Ie

Seicho-No-Ie (SNI; House of Life) is one of the older of the many so-called new religious movements (*shinshukyo*) of Japan, emerging (unlike so many of the others) prior to World War II. It is also one of the most successful at recruitment and self-propagation and one of only a relative handful of recently founded Japanese religions to have headquarters in North America, Oceania, Europe, and South America. Indeed, only a little over 40 percent of its 1.8 million followers (SNI's official estimate) are Japanese.

SNI was founded in 1930 by a charismatic individual, Masaharu Taniguchi (1893–1985), who, after many early personal setbacks and disappointments, managed to educate himself by reading a spectrum of Eastern and Western philosophical, psychoanalytic, and spiritual texts. Additionally, his early adult life and thought were especially shaped by his four-year participation in Omoto-kyo, a recently founded faith that practiced healing and taught a Gnostic-like synthesis of monotheism and spiritualism. He also believed himself to have healed his young daughter of a serious illness through affirmations and meditative prayer, and reported at least one mystical experience. On the basis of such experiences and influences, including the writings of Ernest Holmes, founder of the Religious Science movement, Taniguchi launched his religious movement with the publication of a magazine. Two years later he published the first installment of what would evolve into the 40-volume scripture of SNI, *Seimei no Jisso* (*Truth of Life*), more than 16 million copies of which have now been sold.

For anyone familiar with the American New Thought tradition, there is little that appears original in Seicho-No-Ie's doctrine, for metaphysically the extreme idealistic monism of the latter clearly reflected that of the former. Accordingly, Taniguchi taught that: (1) only God and God's manifestation as the spiritual "World of Reality" (*Jisso*) are real; (2) humanity is essentially a part of that world and therefore perfect, though ignorant of that truth; (3) the entire material, phenomenal world is insubstantial and illusory, the product of thought, and therefore malleable by the mind and words; and (4) the proper goal of the religious or spiritual life is to awaken to the truth about one's infinite nature and innate perfection, and thus to realize and manifest such things as wisdom, love, joy, prosperity, and (perhaps above all) health. Taniguchi expressed these convictions in his more than 400 books as an eclectic mixture of Christian and Buddhist language and concepts, slightly tinged with Shintoist beliefs. Although a prolific writer and effective synthesizer and popularizer of existing ideas, he was hardly an original thinker. Indeed, he always insisted that he was merely presenting the essential core of truth common to all the world's religions.

His one unique contribution to the New Thought tradition was in the area of spiritual practice, for it appears that he alone within that movement actually presented a technique by which adherents could access the inner and essential divinity they claim to possess. He proposed a type of daily meditation, *shinsokan*, which involves a kneeling posture, palms pressed together at eye level, the recitation of a sutra, an empowering shout, focused meditation, and some closing affirmations. In addition, he recommended chants and slogans, the most common being expressions of gratitude, which Taniguchi regarded as the most healing mindset of all.

Seicho-No-Ie's organization is patriarchal and centralized. Since Taniguchi's death, it has been under the leadership of his son-in-law and adopted son, Seicho, a strong leader and prolific writer in his own right. The ruling body, the Hombu, operates out of the headquarters, from which it oversees all training events, rallies, seminars, and conferences. Beneath the governing body are regional, prefectural, and local centers. The last of these, called *soai-kai* (mutual love societies), comprise all adult male members plus three affiliate societies for women, youth, and young adults. The soai-kai generally meet monthly for scripture reading, lecture-style teaching, testimonials, and fellowship. Most of this takes place in private homes, though there are a modest number of churches scattered over Japan, as well as two temples in the Nagasaki and Kyoto prefectures.

Ever since its inception, SNI has struggled internally, and occasionally under governmental pressure, over whether it constituted a publishing concern, an organized religion, a spiritual movement, or simply a way of life. In addition, it has experienced some controversy from its ultraconservative political stance, first manifested as an extreme dedication to the emperor in the 1930s and blossoming into outright militarism during World War II. As a result Taniguchi was officially silenced during the American occupation, and the membership declined. After the ban was lifted, he began to promote a renewal of national pride and patriotism. He and the organization also took strong positions against abortion and for education, advocating traditional values, constitutional revision to restore the emperor's sovereignty, and the revival of the use of the national anthem, flag, and holidays.

Seicho-No-Ie spread internationally, initially through the Japanese diaspora, but increasingly via an intentional, though not terribly aggressive, missionary impulse. The official estimate of SNI members mentioned above is probably much more realistic than the 4 to 5 million sometimes claimed by enthusiastic adherents. The Japanese headquarters maintains an Internet site in Japanese and English at http://www.sni.or.jp/. The American headquarters in California sponsors an English-language site at http://www.snitruth.org/.

Seicho-No-Ie Foundation
266, 3-chome, Harajuku
Shibuya-Ku, Tokyo
Japan

Paul Alan Laughlin

See also: Religious Science.

References

Clarke, Peter B., ed. *Japanese New Religions in Global Perspective*. London: Curzon, 2000.

Ellwood, Robert S. *The Eagle and the Rising Sun*: *Americans and the New Religions of Japan*. Philadelphia: Westminster, 1974.

Gottlieb, Nanette, and Mark McLelland, eds. *Japanese Cybercultures*. London and New York: Routledge, 2003.

McFarland, Neill. *The Rush Hour of the Gods*. New York: Macmillan, 1967.

Taniguchi, Masaharu. *Truth of Life*. Tokyo: Seicho-No-Ie Foundation, 1961.

Sekai Kyusei Kyo

Founded in 1935 by Okada Mokichi (1882–1955), a former associate of Omoto (Great Origin), Sekai Kyusei Kyo, or the Church of World Messianity (referred to henceforth simply as Messianity), is concerned primarily with performance of the *johrei* ritual, which consists of the transmission of divine light for the purpose of constructing an earthly paradise. Johrei is administered by a member who, wearing an amulet, or *ohikari*, raises the palm of her or his hand over the recipients, who may or may not be believers, and imparts to them the divine light of healing.

Okada developed a causal theory of illness that linked it to spiritual clouds that could be dispersed not only by the practice of johrei but also by the use of herbal remedies. He was also persuaded that certain kinds of illness are beneficial. For example, the common cold serves to cleanse the body, which would otherwise be rendered dysfunctional by toxic substances. *Shizen noho*, or natural farming, is also a fundamental part of Messianity's teachings and practices.

There are various views among followers as to whether Okada is divine or human. For example, some members, particularly in Brazil, equate him with Jesus; others see him as the Messiah of the present age. Initially Okada proclaimed himself to be the Boddhisatva Kannon, long venerated in Japan as the very essence of compassionate mercy, and later as the Messiah of the New Age. Regardless of whether they regard him as divine or human, all refer to him as Meishu-sama, sama being an honorific such as sir or lord or senhor.

Messianity, as is the case with many other new Japanese religions, is emphatically millenarian and preaches the coming of an earthly paradise resulting from an ever-increasing outpouring of divine light by means of johrei and shizen noho, which is essentially agriculture without the use of toxic chemicals. This approach to agriculture is based on the belief that nature possesses its own intrinsic resources, which are sufficient in themselves to bring forth wholesome crops and plants in abundance.

The movement has an estimated 900,000 members in Japan and is present in many parts of the world. It is particularly strong in Brazil and Thailand, where the membership in both countries is more than 300,000. Messianity is inclusive where belief and practice are concerned. It does not demand of new members who belong to another faith that they abandon it upon joining. The movement has sympathizers and practitioners among some of the Catholic clergy of, for example, Brazil and Bolivia, and in recent times it has attracted some 300 Theravada Buddhist monks in Sri Lanka who now both receive and transmit johrei.

Messianity consists of two main institutions, the Church of World Messianity and the Mokichi Okada Foundation, the former focusing on spiritual matters and the latter on cultural activities including *sangetsu*, or flower arranging and horticulture. Differences between the two branches are becoming increasingly blurred as the leadership attempts to present johrei not as the core practice of the Church of World Messianity as such but as a nondenominational healing ritual that can be effectively administered by any religious or secular institution that has the necessary "faith" in its curative powers. "Faith" here does not mean a belief in a non-empirical, supernatural order, for in the case of johrei the recipient is provided with proof of its beneficial effects before being asked to accept that it has the power to produce them.

Although at present united, Messianity has experienced serious internal divisions, and this has meant the establishment of a number of different branches, each with its own headquarters. Today the main headquarters are at Atami, and the world president is the Reverend Tetsuo Watanabe. Among those who hold the highest positions of spiritual leadership is the grandson of Mokichi Okada, the Reverend Yoichi Okada. The Mokichi Okada Foundation has an extensive Internet site in both English and Japanese at http://www.moa.or.jp/.n.

Sekai Kyusei Kyo
Izunome Kyodan
26-1 Momoyama-cho
Atami, Shizuoka
Japan
http://www.moa-inter.org.jp/ (site for Mokichi Okada
    Foundation)

Peter B. Clarke

See also: Omoto; Shinto.

References

Clarke, Peter B. "Modern Japanese Millenarian Movements: Their Changing Perception of Japan's Global Mission with Special Reference to the Church of World Messianity in Japanese New Religions." In *Japanese New Religions in Global Perspective,* edited by Peter B. Clarke, 129–182. London: Curzon, 2000.

Ellwood, Robert S. *The Eagle and the Rising Sun: Americans and the New Religions of Japan.* Philadelphia: Westminster, 1974.

Foundations of Paradise. Los Angeles: Church of World Messianity, 1984.

Teachings of Meishu-Sama. 2 vols. Atami, Japan: Church of World Messianity, 1967–1968.

Self-Realization Fellowship

The Self-Realization Fellowship (SRF) was founded in 1935 by Paramahansa Yogananda (1893–1952), a Hindu swami (monastic) who first came to the United States in 1920 to lecture to the International Congress of Religious Liberals meeting in Boston and sponsored by the American Unitarian Association. Yogananda was the disciple of Swami Sri Yukteswar (1855–1936), a guru with a concern to reconcile science with the spiritual knowledge of India. Yogananda was college educated and fluent in English. In 1922 he founded a center in Waltham, Massachusetts. In 1924 he embarked on a speaking tour of the United States, attracting large audiences in urban areas. In 1925, Yogananda established his headquarters on an estate on Mount Washington in Los Angeles. He continued lecturing to large crowds. In 1935 his organization, formerly known as the Yogada Satsang Society, was incorporated as the Self-Realization Fellowship. The SRF has a hermitage in Encinitas, a temple in San Diego, and the Church of All Religions in Hollywood, and in 1950 the Lake Shrine complex was dedicated at Pacific Palisades, California.

After Yogananda's death, the SRF was led by James J. Lynn (1892–1955), who after taking *sannyasa* (monastic renunciation) was known as Rajarsi Janakananda. Following his death in 1955, Sri Daya Mata, an American woman, has served as president of the SRF.

Yogananda is the author of the well-known *Autobiography of a Yogi*, first published in 1946 and translated into 18 languages. His account of his meetings with Eastern and Western mystics is intended to demonstrate that spiritual truth is found in all religions. Yogananda is regarded by his devotees as a *premavatar*, an incarnation of divine love. He taught that it is possible to realize the experience of oneself as being one with God through yogic and meditative techniques. The SRF exists to propagate Yogananda's teachings, and it offers a home-study course based on Yogananda's lessons that culminates in initiation into a technique called *kriya yoga*, which the disciple pledges not to reveal. The SRF sponsors a monastic order for men and women and operates a publishing house. SRF altars include images of Krishna and Christ, who are regarded

Shrine of the Self-Realization Fellowship, Encinitas, California. (J. Gordon Melton)

Calcutta). It oversees 90 meditation centers and 21 educational institutions.

Self-Realization Fellowship
3880 San Rafael Ave.
Los Angeles, CA 90065-3298
http://www.yogananda-srf.org/

Catherine Wessinger

See also: Meditation; Yoga.

References

Thomas, Wendell. *Hinduism Invades America*. New York: Beacon Press, 1930.

Wessinger, Catherine. "Hinduism Arrives in America: The Vedanta Movement and the Self-Realization Fellowship." In *America's Alternative Religions*, edited by Timothy Miller, 173–190. Albany: State University of New York Press, 1995.

Yogananda, Swami Paramahansa. *Autobiography of a Yogi*. Los Angeles: Self-Realization Fellowship, 1970.

as the two ultimate sources of SRF doctrines. As of 1992 there were several hundred thousand initiates into SRF kriya yoga with varying levels of commitment to the organization.

Controversies have surrounded leading teachers' splitting away from the SRF and establishing their own organizations. J. Donald Walters, known as Kriyananda, formerly a minister of the Church of All Religions and a vice president of the SRF, separated from the SRF in 1962 to launch his own teaching career. In 1968 he founded Ananda World Brotherhood Village in Nevada City, California. He is a popular speaker on the New Age circuit and offers his own home-study course along with other published materials.

The SRF oversees more than 500 temples and meditation centers now located in 54 countries. In India, SRF is still known as the Yogoda Satsanga Society. It has its national headquarters in Dakshineswar (near

Selwyn, George Augustus

1809–1878

George Augustus Selwyn was the first Anglican bishop of New Zealand. Consecrated as one of the youngest bishops in the Church of England, he reordered the church in his assigned territory and then spent the next quarter of a century pioneering Anglican work throughout Melanesia, where churches retain a primal relationship to the New Zealand diocese to the present. In the process he also pioneered the mobilization of lay leadership in Anglicanism.

Selwyn was born at Hampstead, England, on April 5, 1809. Showing some promise as a student in his youth, his parents sent him to preparatory school at Ealing, and then to Eton College. He completed both his bachelor's degree (with honors, 1831) and master's degree (1834) at St. John's College at Cambridge University. Meanwhile, he decided to enter the ministry and was successively ordained as a deacon (1833) and a priest (1834) in the Church of England. In 1939, he married Sarah Harriet Richardson.

The church initially turned to Selwyn's older brother William in their search for someone both capable and willing to undertake leadership of the emerging Anglican Church in New Zealand, then little known and located halfway around the world. When William turned down the offer, the opportunity to become the first bishop of New Zealand was presented to Selwyn and he accepted. He was still in his 30s when he was consecrated as a bishop in October 1841. Before departing, he stopped at Oxford and Cambridge universities, both of which gave him honorary doctorates in divinity. Selwyn occupied himself on the long voyage by studying Maori, the language of the Native New Zealanders. Once in the islands, he became a fluent speaker and discovered an ability to use his knowledge of Maori in picking up the related languages used on other islands. Also during the voyage he developed a friendship with William Martin (1807–1880), the first chief justice for New Zealand. That relationship would continue for the rest of his life.

Selwyn and his wife arrived in Auckland on May 30, 1842, and took up residence at the Bay of Islands station of the Church Missionary Society (CMS), one of the two missionary agencies overseeing much of the Anglican global missionary program. Over the next years, he traveled widely and encouraged the development of the congregations of his diocese. He also led in the organization of the diocesan synod and the laying out of parish boundaries.

As he began to impose the parish structure on New Zealand, the emergent church assumed authority that for a generation had been in the hands of the CMS. He eventually broke off relationships with the CMS and as a result was forced out of the CMS facilities where he had lived. He moved the headquarters of his diocese to Auckland. At issue in the break with the CMS was his refusal to divide the church's work into two separate divisions, one among the Native people, over which the CMS would retain hegemony, and one that was to work among the European settlers, of which his diocese would consist. He refused to segregate the Maori people, a choice that became evident when the Native students at the College of St John the Evangelist (commonly known as St John's College) shared in all classes and other activities with the European stu-

dents. Selwyn's policy angered many European settlers and clergy who subsequently boycotted the college, but he carried most of the church with him.

In 1857, after more than a decade of work and extensive consultations, Selwyn led a conference that created a Constitution of the Church of the Province of New Zealand. The constitution offered both laity and clergy equal rights in managing the affairs of the church in New Zealand, a most novel idea in its time. In preparation of this act, Selwyn had led in the formation of a second diocese (the Diocese of Christchurch, 1856) and the selection of its first bishop, Henry John Chitty Harper. Two years later, he set up a third diocese based in Wellington, Waiapu, and Nelson. With three dioceses in New Zealand, it was possible to organize a province, and in 1859, Selwyn became its first primate/metropolitan. He presided over the first General Synod meeting in Wellington that same year.

In addition to New Zealand, Selwyn assumed hegemony for the church throughout Melanesia (seemingly assigned to him due to a clerical error back in England). When first imagined, the northern boundary of the New Zealand diocese was designated as the 34th parallel "south" of the equator, however, when the document finally defining the diocese was published, "south" was replaced with "north." Selwyn never questioned the document; he simply acted as if no error had been made. In the 1850s he began to travel among the scattered islands. Among his self-assigned tasks, he sought out capable young people in the congregations and brought them to New Zealand to attend St. John's College. By 1861, he was able to enlarge his province and consecrated John Coleridge Patteson (1827–1871) as the first bishop of Melanesia.

Selwyn proved immensely valuable as a force moving the Anglican cause forward in New Zealand and Melanesia, but in the process made a number of long-term critics. They were finally, in the mid-1860s, able to gain the audience of the church's leadership in England. Thus it was that in 1867, when Selwyn visited his homeland to attend the conference of bishops at Lambeth Palace, he was "asked" to settle in England and become the next bishop of Litchfield. After a brief trip back to the islands, he left for good on October 20, 1868. Chief Justice Martin retired at the same time and also moved to Litchfield, where their friendship continued.

The return to England had significant consequences for the Church of England. Selwyn introduced his idea concerning lay leadership in his new the diocese, and through that act presented it to his episcopal colleagues. He also accepted additional responsibilities for the international church, which led to several trips to North America, where he negotiated the changing relationship between the American and Canadian churches and the archbishop of Canterbury.

Selwyn died at Litchfield, on April 11, 1878, and was buried at Litchfield Cathedral. He was later memorialized in the founding of Selwyn College at Cambridge University (1882) and the naming of the theological college in Dunedin, New Zealand, after him.

J. Gordon Melton

See also: Anglican Church in Aotearoa, New Zealand, and Polynesia; Church Missionary Society; Church of England; Lambeth Palace.

References

Boreham, F. W. *George Augustus Selwyn, D. D. Pioneer Bishop of New Zealand.* London: S.W. Partridge, 1911.

Davidson, Allan K. *Christianity in Aotearoa: A History of Church and Society in New Zealand.* Wellington, New Zealand: Education for Ministry, 1997.

Limbrick, W. E. *Bishop Selwyn in New Zealand 1841–68.* Palmerston North, New Zealand: Dunmore Press, 1983.

Taylor, H. W. *Memoir of the Life and Episcopate of George Augustus Selwyn, D. D. Bishop of New Zealand, 1841–1869; Bishop of Litchfield, 1867–1878.* 2 vols. London: William Wells Gardner 1879.

■ Senegal

Senegal is an African nation on the Atlantic Ocean between Mauritania and Guinea Bissau. It also shares borders with Guinea and Mali. The long, narrow nation of Gambia occupies the Gambia River valley and sits on the Atlantic coast, but is otherwise completely surrounded by Senegal. Senegal's 12,850,000 people, consisting of multiple African peoples, occupy the 74,000 square miles of land.

Senegal has been inhabited since prehistoric times. At the time of European contact, it was home to the Wolof, Fulani (with many subgroups), Serer, and Tukeler, among other peoples. The French colonized the area in the 17th century and took from it many people who were then enslaved in their American colonies. Slavery was abolished in 1848, but France faced continual opposition to its rule through the end of the century. In the 18th century, an Islamic kingdom had been established by Abdel Kader Torodo. In 1776 he adopted the title *almany* (prayer leader) and created a strong theocratic system that proved quite resistant to French control. Senegal obtained its independence in 1960. It had a relatively prosperous two decades under its democratic government, but has been hard hit by the encroaching Sahara desert since the drought of 1983.

Traditional religions remain alive among Senegal's peoples, but they have been steadily replaced over recent centuries by Islam. Less than 10 percent of the population still adhere to the faith earlier identified with their people, the majority residing among the Diola and Serer. Islam first arrived in the area in the 11th century. Some Berber leaders had traveled to Mecca and returned with a young scholar who was given space for a learning center on the Senegal River. An exponent of the Malikite School of Islam, he attracted many followers later known as Almoravids, who developed an army and eventually established a large kingdom that reached to the Mediterranean. In the 12th century, the capital was moved to Marrakesh (Morocco). Today, the West African office of the World Muslim Congress resides in Dakar.

An important aspect of Islam in Senegal involves the prominent Sufi brotherhoods, the first to arrive being the Qadiriyya, said to have been founded by 'Abd al-Qadir al-Jilani, who died drumming; their 300,000 members have become known by the publication and international circulation of some of their drumming music on compact discs. Larger than the Qadiriyya, with some 400,000 members, are the Muridiyya, founded toward the end of the 19th century in Senegal by Sheikh Ahmadou Bamba (ca. 1853–1927). Their name means those who seek after progress on

Street in Saint-Louis, Senegal. The city, founded by the French in 1659 as a slave-trading center, sits near the mouth of the Senegal River. (iStockPhoto.com)

Islam's mystical path. Still larger is the million-member Tijaniyya Sufi Order, who look to Shaykh Ahmad al-Tijani (1737–1815) as their founder. The order has spread throughout West Africa. The orders tend to be exclusivist, an aspect of their life that was opposed by Shaykh Touré and some Muslim intellectual colleagues who founded the Union Culturalle Musulmane in 1953. As the new century begins, more than 85 percent of the Senegalese profess Islam.

Christianity came to Senegal in the 15th century with the arrival of the Portuguese. In the 1480s, a Senegalese chief named Behemoi traveled to Lisbon, where he underwent baptism in 1486. Subsequently, in the 1490s, the first Christian centers were opened in Ziguinchor, just north of the present-day border of Guinea Bissau. Senegal was included in the diocese of Funchal (headquartered on the island of Madeira) in 1514.

Early in the 19th century, the French Catholic Sisters of St. Joseph of Cluny launched a new era of growth for the Roman Catholic Church. The Vicariate of the Senegambia was erected in 1863. In 1955 Dakar was named an archdiocese, and the first African archbishop was consecrated in 1962. Since that time, a push has been made to create a more Africanized priesthood.

Protestantism came to Senegal with members of the Reformed Church of France under the auspices of the Paris Mission. However, few of the missionaries could handle the environment, and most died before any productive work could be established. It was not

SENEGAL

Senegal

Religion	Followers in 1970	Followers in 2010	% of Population	Annual % growth 2000–2010	Followers in 2025	Followers in 2050
Muslims	3,838,000	11,757,000	88.3	2.66	16,168,000	23,035,000
Ethnoreligionists	332,000	810,000	6.1	2.26	820,000	800,000
Christians	230,000	664,000	5.0	2.73	880,000	1,216,000
Roman Catholics	183,000	610,000	4.6	2.42	800,000	1,100,000
Independents	5,100	20,000	0.2	7.23	30,000	45,000
Protestants	4,100	12,300	0.1	3.59	20,000	32,000
Agnostics	0	43,400	0.3	2.64	70,000	110,000
Baha'is	2,400	25,400	0.2	2.64	45,000	70,000
Atheists	0	8,800	0.1	2.64	12,000	20,000
Buddhists	0	1,600	0.0	2.63	2,000	2,500
New religionists	100	1,000	0.0	2.66	1,500	3,000
Total population	**4,402,000**	**13,311,000**	**100.0**	**2.64**	**17,999,000**	**25,257,000**

until 1936 that they were joined by the Worldwide Evangelism Crusade. Since World War II, a variety of Protestant and Free church groups have arrived, all limited by pressure from the Muslim community against proselytizing activities. The most response by the Senegalese has been to the New Apostolic Church (which reports some 10,000 members), the Lutheran Church (of Finnish origin), the Assemblies of God, and the Jehovah's Witnesses. Some of the conservative evangelical churches are associated in the Evangelical Fellowship of Senegal, which is affiliated with the World Evangelical Alliance. There is no Senegal-based church that is a member of the World Council of Churches.

Senegal defines itself as a secular country with freedom of religion, in spite of the Muslim majority. This unusual situation was highlighted by the election of a Catholic to the presidency of the country in 1962. No Hindu or Buddhist groups have been visible in Senegal, though there is a small presence by the Baha'i Faith.

J. Gordon Melton

See also: Assemblies of God; Baha'i Faith; Malikite School of Islam; Muridiyya; New Apostolic Church; Paris Mission; Qadiriyya Sufi Order; Reformed Church of France; Roman Catholic Church; Tijaniyya Sufi Order; World Council of Churches; World Evangelical Alliance; World Muslim Congress.

References

Babou, Cheikh Anta. *Fighting the Greater Jihad: Amadu Bamba and the Founding of the Muridiyya of Senegal, 1853–1913*. Columbus: Ohio University Press, 2007.

Behrman, L. C. *Muslim Brotherhoods and Politics in Senegal*. Cambridge, MA: Harvard University Press, 1970.

Callaway, B., and L. E. Creevey. *The Heritage of Islam: Women, Religion and Politics in West Africa*. Boulder, CO: Lynne Rienner, 1994.

De Dianoux, H. J. "La christianisme au Sénégal." *L'Afrique et l'Asia modernes* 4 (1981): 3–22.

Delcourt, J. *Historie Religieuse du Sénégal*. Dakar: Clairafrique, 1976.

Diouf, Mamadou, and Leichman, Mara A., eds. *New Perspectives on Islam in Senegal: Conversion, Migration, Wealth, Power, and Femininity*. New York: Palgrave Macmillan, 2008.

Mbacke, Khadim. *Sufism and Religious Brotherhoods in Senegal*. Princeton, NJ: Markus Wiener Publishers, 2005.

■ Serbia

The present state of Serbia emerged in 2006 as the remnant of the former Federated Republic of Yugoslavia, which step by step broke apart between 1991 and 2008. The most recent loss of the Province of Kosovo left Serbia with 29,900 square miles of territory and 10,200,000 citizens (2008). Landlocked, Serbia is surrounded by Bosnia and Herzegovina, Bulgaria, Croatia, Hungary, Kosovo, Macedonia, Montenegro, and Romania.

The former Federated Republic of Yugoslavia (FRY) emerged out of World War II and the defeat of the occupying Germans. It broke apart, and Slovenia, Croatia, Bosnia and Herzegovina, and Macedonia declared their independence. The continuing FRY included Serbia and Montenegro. Meanwhile, Serbia's President Slobodan Milosevic (1941–2006) launched a campaign to unite all the ethnic Serbians into a larger Serbia. Through the first decade of the new century, the Federated Republic of Yugoslavia disintegrated. In 2003, the FRY changed its name to Serbia and Montenegro, the name change reflecting a loosening of the federation binding the two republics. Three years later, Montenegro seceded from the federation and subsequently declared itself an independent nation. Serbia responded by declaring itself the successor state to the former union of Serbia and Montenegro and hence the FRY. Continuing hostilities in Kosovo led the province to declare its independence from Serbia in 2008.

In the second century BCE, Rome conquered the eastern coast of the Adriatic Sea and established the province of Illyria over its people. As its territory expanded, it founded a number of cities, including Belgrade. When the Roman Empire was divided into eastern and western regions, the border between the two halves ran through Yugoslavia. Roman control gave way to a variety of invading peoples who moved into the area from the north and west. The last were the Slavs, who eventually dominated the region. The Byzantine Empire moved in to take control of the Slavic population.

Serbia became independent of the Byzantine Empire in the 12th century. Then, in the 14th century, the Turkish Ottoman Empire began its push up the Danube River. Much of Serbia fell to the Turks following the Battle of Kosovo in 1389, and by the end of the century Serbia had disappeared as a political entity. In 1690 the Serbs revolted, and after the revolt was crushed, the Turkish authorities relocated thousands of

Neogothic cathedral of the city of Novi Sad in Serbia at dawn, 2008. (Netfalls/Dreamstime.com)

Albanians to the Kosovo region in the southern part of Serbia.

Turkish authority began to weaken noticeably late in the 18th century. In 1829, Serbia emerged as an autonomous province within the empire, though it was not until 1882 that Serbia became an independent nation. In 1905 neighboring Montenegro became independent. World War I brought an end to the Austro-Hungarian Empire that had gained hegemony over former Ottoman territories north and east of Serbia (Croatia, Slovenia, Bosnia, Herzegovina), and in the 1920s, Yugoslavia was formed as an attempt to assert the unity of the southern Slavic peoples. Not included at first, Slovenia was added after World War II.

Postwar Yugoslavia was seen as a federation of republics, and its many ethnic groups were held together for many years by strongman and dictator Marshall Tito (Josef Broz) (1892–1980). The federation fell apart at the beginning of the 1990s as Slovenia, Croatia, Bosnia and Herzegovina, and Macedonia withdrew and established independent states, though Montenegro remained united with Serbia until 2006.

Serbia inherited a large, heavily armed military from the federation's breakup. Serbian President Slobodan Milosevic launched a campaign to bring those areas of the new independent nations that were dominated by ethnic Serbs back into Serbia. As a result war erupted, first in Croatia, then Bosnia and Herzegovina, and eventually in Kosovo (where a large number of ethnic Albanians resided). Kosovo existed as an autonomous province of Serbia, and Milosevic attempted to end their independent status. To accomplish his goal, Serbian troops attempted to kill or drive out the ethnic Albanian residents. The war was brought to an end only with the intervention of U.S. and European armed forces. Milosevic was subsequently arrested for his role in war crimes committed in Kosovo, but died before his trial could be brought to a conclusion.

In spite of the presence of United Nations troops, violence again erupted in Kosovo in 2004. As new negotiation on the province's future proceeded, at the beginning of 2006, Montenegro seceded from the federation and declared itself an independent nation. Two years later Kosovo declared its fully independent status relative to Serbia.

Christianity had entered Serbia during the Roman period and had become a dominant force by the time the empire withdrew. The various peoples who flowed into the territory in succeeding centuries brought new forms of Paganism, but eventually, by the ninth century, Christianity had reasserted itself. The church came under the authority of the Ecumenical Patriarchate during the years of Byzantine rule, but following the establishment of an independent Serbian nation declared its independence from Constantinople. The break with Constantinople was further emphasized in 1346, when the Serbian archepiscopacy at Pec was elevated into a patriarchate. When the Turkish Ottoman Empire conquered the Balkans in the 14th century, the new authorities suppressed the Serbian Patriarchate and placed the church under the archbishop of Ohrid (Macedonia). The Serbian Patriarchate was not re-established until 1557, but it was again suppressed in 1766 and the Serbian church again placed under the Ecumenical Patriarchate.

The struggle for the re-emergence of Serbian Orthodoxy began in 1832, when some degree of autonomy was granted. However, it would not be until after World War I that a united Serbian Orthodox Church was created (1919) and the following year the Serbian Patriarchate once again allowed to exist. It was not named the official state church, but it enjoyed a number of prerogatives as the church of the ruling elite. Its favored status and financial benefits were dropped by the Marxist government that came to power in 1945.

In 1919 the Macedonian Orthodox Church had been integrated into the Serbian Church, but it became independent in 1967. Meanwhile, the movement of various ethnic peoples during the era of Turkish rule is manifest today in the congregations of the Bulgarian Orthodox Church, the Romanian Orthodox Church, and the Orthodox Autocephalous Church of Albania, still found in Serbia.

Although the Roman Catholic Church was the majority faith in neighboring Croatia, it was very much the minority in Serbia. Nevertheless, it has had a presence through the centuries. In the 16th century, an Eastern-rite Catholic Church developed in Croatia as a Roman counterpart to the Serbian Orthodox Church. From headquarters at the Marcha Monastery, efforts were launched to convert members of the Serbian Church to Roman Catholicism. The church was given its own diocesan bishop in 1777. When the 20th-century nation of Yugoslavia was created, the Diocese of Krizhevci was extended to include all of the country, and it drew members from a variety of predominantly Orthodox ethnic groups (Ukrainians, Serbians, Macedonians, Romanians). Its status as a multinational diocese is presently under consideration. Since the breakup of Yugoslavia, Latin-rite Catholics are under the archbishop of Belgrade (named a metropolitan archbishop in 1986).

Protestants came into Serbia during the 16th century. The autonomous Province of Vojvodina (the northernmost part of Serbia) became the center of Lutheran congregations among Hungarian, Slovak, and German ethnic groups. In the 20th century, two separate churches emerged, the Evangelical Church in the Socialist Republics of Croatia, Bosnia and Herzegovina, and the Autonomous Province of Vojvodina, the primary German-speaking church, and the Slovak Evangelical Church of the Augsburg Confession in Yugoslavia. The former church was at one time a large body, the overwhelming majority of its members being relocated outside Yugoslavia after World War II. The far larger Slovak Church had been connected with the Lutheran Church in Hungary, but it became autonomous in the 1920s following the formation of Yugoslavia.

The Reformed Church also established itself in Vojvodina and Croatia, and like the Lutherans was structurally part of the Reformed Church of Hungary. This church survived through World War I and became autonomous in 1933 as the Reformed Christian Church in Yugoslavia.

Following World War II the German members left, and under the persecution of the Tito regime, many Hungarians returned to Hungary. In the 1990s, the Croatian membership was set apart as an autonomous church. Through the decade, as the wars continued, many Serbians came to Vojvodina, and many Hungarian-speaking people decided to leave. Both the Reformed and Lutheran churches in Vojvodina are

SERBIA

Serbia

Religion	Followers in 1970	Followers in 2010	% of Population	Annual % growth 2000–2010	Followers in 2025	Followers in 2050
Christians	4,621,000	6,329,000	80.7	−0.82	6,866,000	6,876,000
Orthodox	3,848,000	5,406,000	69.0	−0.82	5,854,000	5,820,000
Roman Catholics	546,000	380,000	4.8	−1.31	400,000	420,000
Independents	31,200	120,000	1.5	0.93	200,000	240,000
Agnostics	1,224,000	740,000	9.4	−1.22	400,000	200,000
Muslims	200,000	540,000	6.9	−0.91	500,000	470,000
Atheists	906,000	224,000	2.9	−1.78	90,000	50,000
Jews	7,000	3,000	0.0	−0.91	3,000	3,000
New religionists	1,200	2,000	0.0	−0.90	3,000	5,000
Ethnoreligionists	500	1,600	0.0	−0.91	1,800	2,000
Baha'is	200	1,500	0.0	−0.90	3,000	5,000
Total population	**6,960,000**	**7,841,000**	**100.0**	**−0.91**	**7,867,000**	**7,611,000**

members of the World Council of Churches, and they form the backbone of the Ecumenical Council of Churches in Yugoslavia.

The Baptist Church in Yugoslavia began in 1875 when Heinrich Meyer, the German Baptist leader from Budapest, baptized the first three members of the congregation at Novi Sad. These three people and many of the other early members had been associated with the Nazarenes, a Baptist-like pacifist movement that had previously spread through the region. This original work was primarily among the German-speaking residents of the Yugoslav nations, and it collapsed after World War II. However, in 1898 a second work was initiated among the Slovak-speaking population that developed into a Baptist conference in 1918. Two years later work began among Hungarian Serbians.

In 1924 the Baptist Union of Yugoslavia was formed. It was disrupted by the breakup of the federation in 1990, and Baptist congregations in each of the new countries organized separately. A new Baptist Union of Yugoslavia was organized in 1992. It includes a number of small congregations in Serbia and one in Montenegro. The Methodist Episcopal Church (now a constituent part of the United Methodist Church) began work in Vojvodina in 1898 among German-speaking residents in Bachka. It later spread in the Hungarian-speaking community. These churches were the heart of the Yugoslavia Mission Conference, created in 1922. Methodism grew in spite of its not receiving official recognition by the government. The church

suffered first by a drop in support from the United States during the Great Depression, and then the loss of the majority of its German-speaking members following World War II. It survives as a very small body whose members are part of the United Methodist Church's Macedonia-Serbia Annual Conference, which is part of the larger Central Conference of Central and Southern Europe.

Through the 20th century a variety of Protestant and Free church groups established work in Yugoslavia. The missions begun by both Pentecostals and the Seventh-day Adventist Church have survived and are now among the most substantive churches in the country. The largest Pentecostal church is the Evangelical Church. Several Evangelical sending agencies continue work in the new century that was launched prior to the breakup of the federation, including the Pocket Testament League and Campus Crusade for Christ.

There is a small Jewish community in Yugoslavia centered on Belgrade, which continues a Jewish community in the region that dates to the Roman period. The community that survived the Holocaust is centered on Belgrade, and it includes some 2,000 members. Members are united by the Federation of Jewish Communities of Yugoslavia.

The Muslim community of Yugoslavia was strongest in Kosovo, and Kosovo Muslims, many of Albanian ethnicity, were among the people targeted by Serbian forces during the civil war in the 1990s. Many died, and others were forced to leave the country. The community reorganized in the aftermath of the war, before which they represented between 15 and 20 percent of the population. In breaking with Serbia, Kosovo has left the country with only a miniscule Muslim community in Turkey. The remaining Muslims are primarily Sunnis of the Hanafite School.

Several Eastern religions were established in Yugoslavia as the Marxist regime came to an end. Most prominent among them are two Buddhist groups, the Karma-Kagyupa Tibetan Buddhists and the Kwan Um Zen School. Hinduism is represented by the International Society for Krishna Consciousness. There are also a small number of members of the Baha'i Faith.

As this encyclopedia goes to press, Serbia remains in transition. Many of the church communities are in the process of changing their names to reflect the country's name changes.

J. Gordon Melton

See also: Baha'i Faith; Bulgarian Orthodox Church; Ecumenical Patriarchate/Patriarchate of Constantinople; Hanafite School of Islam; International Society for Krishna Consciousness; Karma-Kagyupa Tibetan Buddhism; Kwan Um School of Zen; Lutheran Church in Hungary; Reformed Christian Church in Yugoslavia; Roman Catholic Church; Romanian Orthodox Church; Serbian Orthodox Church; Slovakia; United Methodist Church; World Council of Churches.

References

Broun, J. "Religion in Yugoslavia: The Background." *America* 165 (November 30, 1991): 414–416.

Cox, John K. *The History of Serbia*. Westport, CT: Greenwood Press, 2002.

Dirizings, Ger. *Religion and the Politics of Identity in Kosovo*. New York: Columbia University Press, 2001.

Flere, S. "Denominational Affiliation in Yugoslavia, 1930–1989." *East European Quarterly* 25 (June 1991): 145–165.

Frid, Z., ed. *Religions in Yugoslavia: Historical Survey, Legal Status, Church in Socialism, Ecumenism, Dialogue between Marxists and Christians, etc.* Zagreb, Croatia: Binoza, 1971.

Norris, H. T. *Islam in the Balkans: Religion and Society between Europe and the Arab World*. Columbia: University of South Carolina Press, 1993.

Perica, Viekoslav. *Balkan Idols: Religion and Nationalism in Yugoslav States*. New York: Oxford University Press, 2002.

Shenk, N. G. "The Social Role of Religion in Contemporary Yugoslavia." Ph.D. diss., Northwestern University, 1987.

Serbian Orthodox Church

The Serbian Orthodox Church traces its roots to the missionary work launched from Constantinople in the second half of the ninth century CE, which produced a Christian Byzantine-Slavonic culture in the region. Serbia became independent of Constantinople toward the end of the 10th century, and its ruler, Steven Nemanja (1168–1196), worked to suppress non-Christian religion in his realm. The first partial ecclesiastical independence of the Serbian land was soon established under the country's first archbishop, Saint Sava (1176–1235). The year 1217 is generally seen as the founding date of the Serbian Orthodox Church. From that time, worship has followed a Serbian liturgy. In 1375 a local patriarchate was established.

This autonomy was gradually suppressed under centuries of Turkish domination that began after the Battle of Kosovo in 1389. Serbia ceased to exist as a separate political entity in 1463. It became the target of both Russia and the Austro-Hungarian Empire toward the end of the 18th century, and while still a part of the Ottoman Empire, it began to re-emerge as a state early in the 19th century. In 1878, as Turkish power waned, the Congress of Berlin recognized Serbia as an independent country.

The restoration of the patriarchal office occurred in 1879, the year after Serbia gained its independence. In the last half of the 20th century, the Serbian Orthodox Church was subject to countless persecutions, first from the Croatian nationalist regime during the years of World War II, and then by the Yugoslavian government that came to power after the war. After the fall of the Communist regime at the beginning of the 1990s

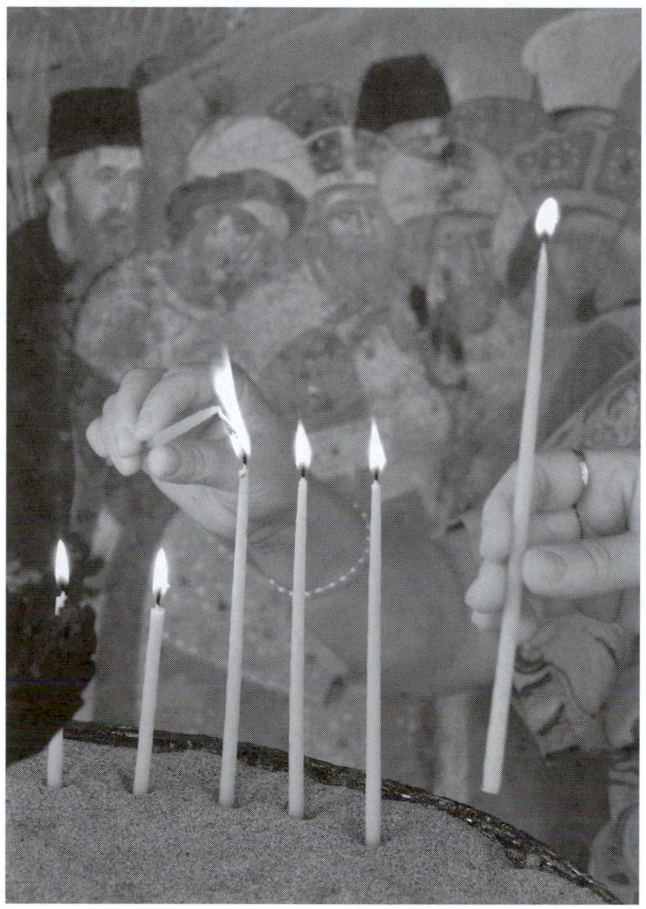

Candles in Serbian Orthodox monastery, Kakovo, Greece. (Zoran Simin/Dreamstime.com)

The church is Eastern Orthodox in belief and practice. A unique aspect of the Serbian church is the Slava, a celebration of the patron saint of a family, which takes the place of the usual Orthodox nameday feast. The patron saint of a family, handed from father to son and never changed, has been traced to the times of the first Serbian Christians; it is an example of enculturation of the Christian faith into an ancient Pagan practice (the veneration of Pagan family idols) that was not suppressed but transformed by Christian piety.

The Serbian Patriarchate has more than 8 million faithful in the former Yugoslavia, with a diaspora all over the Western world (particularly in Germany, North America, and Australia). Dioceses may now be found in Romania, Bosnia, Croatia, France, Germany, Sweden, the United States, Canada, and Australia. The Cathedral of St. Sava in Belgrade is one of the largest church buildings in the Orthodox world. The Serbian Orthodox Church may also be credited with a certain success in evangelizing the Gypsies. The church is, in spite of its criticisms of some forms of ecumenism, a member of the World Council of Churches.

Serbian Church
ul. Kralja Petra Br. 5
PO Box 182
FRY-110 01
Belgrade
Serbia

Andrea Cassinasco

See also: Athos, Mount; Cathedral of St. Sava; World Council of Churches.

References

Spasovoc, Stanimir. *The History of the Serbian Orthodox Church in America and Canada, 1941–1991.* Trans. by Nedeljko Lunich. Belgrade: Printing House of the Serbian Patriarchate, 1998.

Van Beek, Huibert. *A Handbook of the Churches and Councils: Profiles of Ecumenical Relationships.* Geneva: World Council of Churches, 2006.

Velimirovich, Nikolai. *A Treasury of Serbian Orthodox Spirituality: The Serbian People as a Servant of God.* Trans. by Theodore Micka and Steven

and the dissolution of Yugoslavia, the Serbian Orthodox hierarchy did not hesitate to condemn the atrocities committed by members and representatives of its own people. Moreover, the Serbian church, alone among the Orthodox churches in the former Communist countries, has witnessed a complete reconciliation with its members abroad, especially in North America, who had left the patriarchate during the years of Marxist rule.

The Serbian Orthodox Church is noted for a very conservative position within the Orthodox world. Along with the Monastic Republic of Mount Athos, it is the only canonical Orthodox jurisdiction in the Balkan area that did not accept the adoption of the Gregorian calendar. The Serbian Orthodox Patriarchate has also offered the most consistent and articulate criticism of the ecumenical involvement of sister Orthodox jurisdictions.

Scott. Grayslake, IL: Free Serbian Orthodox Diocese of the United States and Canada, 1988.

Serpent Handlers/Signs Following Movement

Serpents have been a source of mystery and great symbolic significance in human cultures for thousands of years, frequently playing a role in religious ritual. Spiritual leaders have handled snakes for a variety of purposes. Handling poisonous serpents as an expression of faith, and as a focal point of worship, emerged only in the early 20th century as the Holiness movement was giving birth to Pentecostalism. Nearly a century later, the taking up of serpents remains among the most enigmatic developments in the chronicling of religious movements.

The practice of handling serpents in worship services probably began in 1908. A few years later the practice was occurring in church services in the Appalachian region of east Tennessee. So too was the practice of drinking poison (usually strychnine). Why did people engage in such seemingly bizarre and dangerous practices? From their perspective the answer was simple: the Bible commanded that believers do so. Mark 16:18 says: "They shall take up serpents; and if they drink anything deadly, it will by no means hurt them."

Passages from sacred texts can go virtually unnoticed for long periods of time and then, seemingly, appear suddenly and become the basis for a schism or a significant movement. Such was the case with these verses about handling snakes and drinking poison.

The enigma surrounding this practice is not so much the fact that a group of people decided to take this verse of scripture literally. Rather, the mystery is the fact that this verse is encased in three additional verses that would become the core of the 20th-century Pentecostal movement (Mark 16:15–18). The first verse is Christ's commandment to preach the gospel to every creature on Earth (usually referred to as the Great Commission). Then, on either side of the verse about serpent handing and drinking poison, is the promise that those who believe in Christ and are baptized will (1) cast out demons; (2) speak with new tongues; and (3) lay hands on the sick and they will recover. The beginning of this scripture reads: "And these signs will follow those who believe."

The nascent Pentecostal movement in Appalachia believed that all five of these "signs" were both the promise of God and a commandment that was to be obeyed. The churches they founded often contain "signs following" in their name. The broader Pentecostal movement readily embraced tongues, healing, and the casting out of demons, but it did not act upon the references to snakes and poison without controversy. In Appalachia, the emerging Pentecostal tradition entertained these controversial ideas for some years before "signs followers" were marginalized.

George Went Hensley was probably the first to take up the practice of handling serpents in religious services; there is little question that he popularized the practice (Kimbrough 2002, 192). But it was A. J. Tomlinson, the leading figure of the issuant Church of God (Cleveland, Tennessee), who popularized and lent a measure of legitimacy to serpent handling. Tomlinson invited Hensley to preach in his church in 1914 and later that year wrote enthusiastically about snake handling in the *Church of God Evangel*. Four years later, Tomlinson asked Hensley to join the denomination, and he accepted.

Serpent handling spread rapidly during the second and third decades of the 20th century, and the Church of God clearly lent legitimacy to this development. In 1928, following a near fatal snakebite, the practice was formally banned in the Church of God. Thereafter, serpent handling would find its niche on the margin of society, where it has remained for the better part of a century. Reports of occasional deaths from snakebite aroused public indignation. During the 1940s the practice was outlawed in Kentucky, Georgia, and Virginia, but that seemed only to reinforce the commitment of the faithful to practice their beliefs.

Although systematic data about how many people participate in serpent handling have never existed, it seems clear that their number has never been very large. Current estimates by scholars who study snake handlers range from about 2,500 down to no more than a few hundred.

For its size, there is probably no other religious movement that has been the subject of more writing and investigation. Journalists and scholars alike have frequently focused on sensationalist themes and characterization of the snake handlers as "bizarre," "exotic," "eccentric," and "grotesque." No small number have found significance in the snake as a phallic symbol. More serious scholarly literature has focused on psychopathology. Appalachia has been viewed as a culture under tremendous stress, and participants in snake handling have been seen as suffering both economic and cultural deprivation.

During the 1990s a group of scholars moved beyond sensationalizing and interpreting serpent handlers' behavior as an indicator of pathology or deprivation. Rather, they found patterns of behavior that are both functional and readily understandable within the context of normal behavior. As with all religions, the faith of the serpent handlers provides communal solidarity (Kimbrough 2002). Their faith gives meaning to their lives as well as spiritual integration (Hood 1998). There is a substantial literature that indicates that serpent handlers are not very different from their community peers (Burton 1993). Finally, contrary to the presumption of most who wrote about snake handlers for most of the 20th century, the new breed of scholars are skeptical about the prospects of this sectarian movement disappearing anytime soon.

Jeffrey K. Hadden

See also: Church of God (Cleveland, Tennessee); Devotion/Devotional Traditions; Holiness Movement; Pentecostalism.

References

Brown, Fred W., and Jeanne McDonald. *The Serpent Handlers*. Winston-Salem, NC: John F. Blair Publishing, 2007.
Burton, Thomas. *Serpent-Handling Believers*. Knoxville: University of Tennessee Press, 1993.
Covington, Dennis. *Salvation on Sand Mountain*. New York: Penguin, 1995.
Hood, Ralph W., Jr. "When the Spirit Maims and Kills: Social Psychological Considerations of the History of Serpent Handling Sects and the Narrative of Handlers." *International Journal for the Psychology of Religion* 8, no. 2 (1998): 71–96.
Kimbrough, David L. *Taking up Serpents*. Athens, GA: Mercer University Press, 2002.

Servetus, Michael

1511–1553

Michael Servetus was a physician and intellectual who became a martyr for Unitarianism. His persecution and execution with the consent of John Calvin entirely on the ground of his having advocated unorthodox religious opinions is seen five centuries later as the major blot on Calvin's otherwise distinguished career.

Servetus was born at Villanova, Spain, and later studied law in France at Toulouse. He developed an interest in theology during his student years, and as early as 1530 expressed his skeptical opinions and doubts about the Trinity to Protestant Reformer Johann Oecolampedius (1482–1531). His publication of his views in a book, *Concerning the Errors of the Trinity*, occasioned his moving first to Lyon, where he assumed a low profile as an editor and proofreader, and then on to Paris, where he studied medicine under a pseudonym. While in Paris he appears to have come to an understanding of the circulation of the blood a century ahead of its formal discovery by William Harvey. He left Paris in 1538, due to conflict over his lecturing on astrology.

Servetus returned to Lyon and then in 1544 was offered a position as the personal physician to the archbishop of Vienna. During these years he operated under several pseudonyms. As Villeneuve, for example, he carried on a confidential correspondence with Calvin. As early as 1546, he sent Calvin the manuscript of his book *Restitution of Christianity*, which was eventually published in 1553. When it was discovered that Servetus had actually authored this later book, he was arrested in Vienna. He escaped, however, and headed for Italy. On his way he stopped in Geneva, where he was recognized and again arrested.

Servetus's own theological reflections were grounded in an awareness that both Muslims and Jews considered the doctrine of the Trinity as an attack on the unity of God. He also turned his attack on the Trinity into a defense of God's unity. He concluded with what had been the major dissenting view on the Trinity, that God was One, that Christ was not divine, and that the Holy Spirit was simply the name of God's power. Pursuing his theological interests in the atmosphere of the Reformation, however, he also concluded, in agreement with some of the Anabaptist themes, that the church (then generally seen as including all people) should be reorganized as a community limited to those who believe and that infant baptism should be replaced with believer's baptism. He developed a rather mystical approach to the Eucharist, believing that believers could partake of divinity and participate in God. Such beliefs were considered heretical by both Protestants and Catholics.

Once arrested, Servetus became the subject of a lengthy trial during which all of his heretical opinions were aired. The court did not miss the fact that his opinions not only attacked Christian orthodoxy, but also supported the opinions of Muslims and Jews. He was condemned and burned at the stake in Geneva on October 27, 1553. Though not directly involved in the proceeding, Calvin is held responsible for Servetus's death considering his power at that time in Geneva.

Servetus did not raise up a community of believers nor did he participate in one, but in more recent years he has been seen as aligned with the Unitarian phase of the Reformation more commonly associated with Socinius. He is also seen as a pre-eminent example of a person persecuted for his beliefs alone, and has been viewed as a martyr for the cause of religious freedom.

J. Gordon Melton

See also: Anabaptism; Astrology; Calvin, John; Socinianism; Unitarian Universalist Association.

References

Bainton, Roland H. *Hunted Heretics.* Boston: Beacon Press, 1953.

Hillar, Marian. *The Case of Michael Servetus 1511–1553: The Turning Point in the Struggle for Freedom of Conscience.* Lewiston, NY: Edwin Mellen Press, 1997.

Hillar, Marian, and Claire S. Allen. *Michael Servetus: Intellectual Giant, Humanist, and Martyr.* Latham, MD: University Press of America, 2002.

Servetus, Michael. *Two Treatises on the Trinity.* Ed. by Earl Morse Wilbur. Cambridge, MA: Harvard University Press, 1932.

Wilbur, Earl Morse, *A History of Unitarianism: Socinianism and Its Antecedents* Cambridge, MA: Harvard University Press, 1945.

Williams, George H. *The Radical Reformation.* Kirksville, MO: Sixteenth Century Journal Publishers, 1992.

Servites, Order of

The Servites, officially the Order of Friars Servants of Mary, was the last of five mendicant orders designated in the Middle Ages. Mendicant orders are forbidden to hold property in common, are not tied to a particular monastic center, and must make their living by either working or begging. Prior to the Servites, the Franciscans, the Dominicans, the Carmelites, and the Hermits of Saint Augustine had been the only groups so organized recognized by church authorities.

The Servites trace their history to seven young men of Florence, Italy, originally related to each other through the cloth trade. While still in their youthful years, these rather prosperous young men began meeting together as a religious society established to honor the Blessed Virgin Mary. As their devotion grew, the seven abandoned their comfortable homes, fine clothes, and possessions and found a dilapidated building outside the city in which to take up residence. People noticed what they were doing and an increasing number began to visit them. Desiring a contemplative life away from much human contact, the group moved again, this time to a nearby mountain, Monte Senario.

The new religious order, which had adopted the Rule of Saint Augustine, evolved as others joined the original seven on Monte Senario. Original recognition was given to the Friar Servants of Mary by the bishop of Florence in the 1240s. Initial actions approving the group were made in Rome in the 1250s. However, controversy swelled around the mendicant orders and the challenge their unpropertied existence exerted. In 1274, a church-wide gathering, the Second Council of Lyons, implemented Canon 13 of the Fourth Lateran Council (1215), which forbad the foundation of any more new religious orders. The bishops at Lyons went further and moved to suppress the half dozen mendicant order that were yet to receive their final approval by the pope. The Servites were on their list. The Council's action was noted by Pope Innocent V, who during his brief reign in 1276 declared the Order suppressed. Fortunately, Pope John XXI, the third pope to take office in 1276, took favorable notice of the Servites. Opinion remained divided for the remainder of the century and only in 1304 did Pope Benedict XI (r. 1303–1304) issue an official approval.

Of the original group that started the Order—Buonfiglio Monaldi, John Buonagiunta Monetti, Bartholomew Amidei, Ricovero Ugguccioni, Benedetto dell' Antello, Gherardino Sostegno, and Alessio Falconieri (d. 1310)—only one lived to celebrate the pope's action. Eventually the group came to be known as the Seven Holy Founders. They were canonized as saints in 1888 and given a common feast day, February 17.

The Servites spread rapidly. By the time the Order was officially approved, it already had centers in Germany, France, and Spain. Through the next century it spread across Europe and even had work in the Philippines and India. It suffered its first major setback in the 16th century in Germany with the rise of Protestantism. From then on it suffered ups and downs as countries changed their attitudes toward Rome. Meanwhile, its largest presence remained in Italy.

The Order was brought to the United States in 1852, when an Austrian priest, Father Antoninus Grundner, began working among the German-speaking Catholics in New York City and Philadelphia. Then in 1870, while in Rome for the First Vatican Council, Bishop Joseph Melcher (1806–1876), of Green Bay, Wisconsin, asked the Servites to begin work in his diocese. That act led to the Order's invitation to Chicago four years later. Chicago soon became the center of the Servites' activity in North America. By the beginning of the 20th century, the work in Europe had become concentrated in Italy and Austria-Hungary, where 36 and 17 of the 62 monasteries were located. There were also monasteries in England (four), Belgium (one), and the United States (four).

The Servites are led by their general, who is elected for a six-year term. Members profess a special devotion to the Virgin Mary that is regularly manifest in the meditation on the Seven Dolors (Sorrows) of Mary, especially on the annual commemoration in honor of the Seven Sorrows on September 15, first granted to the Servites in 1688 and later made a general feast in the church. The Servites also have affiliated an order of cloistered nuns, a third order of secular lay associates, and a lay confraternity of the Seven Dolors.

As the new century begins, Servites are found in almost all the countries of North and South America, across Europe, and in Africa, Asia, and Australia.

UNIFAS (Unio Internationalis Familiæ Servorum)
Segretaria UNIFAS
Sr. Gina Casumaro
Via Giuseppe Luigi Lagrange, 3
00197 ROMA RM
Italy
http://www.servidimaria.org/

J. Gordon Melton

See also: Benedictines; Devotion/Devotional Traditions; Dominicans; Mary, Blessed Virgin; Roman Catholic Church; Saints.

References

Benassi, Vincenzo. *A Short History of the Servite Order*. Rome: General Secretariate for the Servite Missions, 1987.

Do Whatever He Tells You: Reflections and Proposals for Promoting Marian Devotion. Rome: General Curia ISM, 1983.

Ferrazzi, Thomas M. *Servite Anthology: Variety of Subjects*. Chicago: Pro Manuscripto, 1987.

Servite Fathers, comp. *The Servite Manual: Behold Thy Mother, a Collection of Devotions Chiefly in Honor of Our Lady of Sorrows*. Servite Fathers, 1947.

Setsubun

The Japanese adopted a lunar calendar with 12 months each with 2 parts related to the new and full moon, thus giving it 24 segments. The end of each segment and the division marking it from the next segment was termed the Setsubun (or seasonal division). Over time, the term "Setsubun" began to particularly refer to the division at the end of the year and hence immediately before the lunar New Year. The New Year came as winter ended and spring began, which was believed to be the first week of February. Today the Setsubun

Revelers dressed as the devil during the Japanese festival of Setsubun. (Kingyo/Dreamstime.com)

festival is held in Japan on February 3 or 4, the day before the start of spring. The spring Setsubun festival came to be associated with rituals for chasing away evil spirits.

The practices of the spring Setsubun appear to have originated in folk traditions, but over the centuries were adopted by both Shinto and Buddhist temples. By the 13th century, for example, people attempted to drive away evil spirits by mixing the stench of burning dried sardine heads and wood with the noise of drums. This custom survives in the use of fish head shapes as house decorations, the intention being to keep spirits away from the home.

Today, the most common practice of Setsubun is the throwing of roasted soy beans. They may be thrown around one's house or at temples and shrines, or at people. The act of throwing is accompanied by shouts of "Oni wa soto! Fuku wa uchi!" ("Devils out! Happiness in!").

Tied to the tossing of the beans is another custom, eating the number of beans corresponding to one's age. This is particularly a practice of people whose age is a multiple of 12, meaning that the year is the same as the year in which they were born (according to the Chinese zodiac). Local news coverage will feature stories on celebrities at different temples consuming beans. In the home, one person, usually the male head of the household (or a male who is celebrating one of his 12th anniversary birthdays), will put on a demon mask and the other family members will toss soy beans at him as they chant the traditional "Oni wa soto! Fuku wa uchi!"

In a secularized culture such as Japan, variant celebrations of Setsubun are widespread. Disbelief in the existence of evil spirits is widespread and many Buddhists offer demythologized explanations for Setsubun celebrations. At the same time, both Shinto shrines and Buddhist temples will sponsor ritualized bean-tossing events.

J. Gordon Melton

See also: Astrology; Calendars, Religious; New Year's Day; Shinto; Spring Equinox.

References

Carlquist, Helen, and Sherwin Bauer. *Japanese Festivals*. Rutland, VT: Charles E. Tuttle, 1965.

Erskine, William Hugh. *Japanese Festivals and Calendar Lore*. Tokyo: Kyo Bun Kwan. 1933.

Seventh Day Baptist General Conference

Sabbatarianism, the belief that Saturday rather than Sunday is the proper day for Christian worship, arose among Protestants in 17th-century England. They had a basic agreement with Baptists concerning the autonomy of the local church, believer's baptism, and the authority of the Bible as the only source of faith and practice. The latter belief became crucial, inasmuch as in their reading of the scriptures they found no basis for

Sunday worship. As early as 1650, a Sabbath-keeping congregation was founded in London.

In 1664, Stephen Mumford, a Baptist from Tewkesbury, moved to Newport, Rhode Island, and associated with the Baptist church there. Over the next seven years he convinced others of his Sabbatarian ideas, in 1671 establishing the first Seventh Day Baptist church in the American colonies. Those who formed the new church did not condemn those who continued Sunday worship, and they were able to maintain friendly relationships over the years. A second congregation formed in Philadelphia around 1800, and a third in New Jersey five years later. The Philadelphia group influenced some German-speaking Free church believers in the Philadelphia area, who would later create a separate German Seventh Day Baptist Conference.

Through the 18th century, Sabbatarian Baptist congregations spread across the United States. In 1802 representatives of several churches formed the General Conference. A strong emphasis on local autonomy was retained, but the Conference was given the power to carry out special tasks. Publication of Sabbatarian materials was given high priority. A missionary society was formed in 1843, and it opened work in China four years later. It subsequently began work at selected locations around the world, in most cases in response to communications from small groups of Sabbatarians asking for help.

Seventh Day Baptists formed several schools in areas devoid at the time of public education. Three of those schools became colleges. The college at Alfred, New York, became Alfred University, and in 1871 a seminary was located at the school.

In the 1850s some Seventh Day Baptists influenced Ellen G. White and her husband, James White, the founders of the Seventh-day Adventist Church. That church has become the largest Sabbatarian Christian body in the world. Through the 20th century, various groups that have separated from the Seventh-day Adventists have subsequently identified with the Seventh Day Baptists.

The General Conference was ecumenically oriented and became a founding member of the National Council of Churches of Christ in the U.S.A. and the World Council of Churches. However, it withdrew from both of those organizations in the 1970s, as it felt that some of their policies infringed upon congregational autonomy. However, the Conference has remained active in the Baptist World Alliance.

Late in the 20th century, after many years in Plainfield, New Jersey, the headquarters of the General Conference moved to its present location. In 2006 it reported 5,200 members in 96 churches in the United States and Canada. The Conference meets annually and elects a general council that manages its affairs.

Through the 20th century, the General Conference has nurtured Seventh Day Baptist churches in such places as Jamaica, Guyana, Malawi, Ghana, India, Burma (Myanmar), the Philippines, Australia, and New Zealand. Most of those efforts have grown into autonomous conferences. In 1965 the General Conference took the lead in the creation of the World Federation of Seventh Day Baptist Conferences. By 1993, some 17 conferences from around the world were affiliated.

Seventh Day Baptist General Conference
PO Box 1678
Janesville, WI 53547-1678
http://www.seventhdaybaptist.org

J. Gordon Melton

See also: Baptist World Alliance; Baptists; Free Churches; Sabbatarianism; Seventh-day Adventist Church; World Council of Churches.

References

Sanford, Don A. *A Choosing People: The Story of Seventh Day Baptists*. Nashville: Broadman, 1992.

Sanford, Don A. *Conscience Taken Captive: Short History of Seventh Day Baptists*. Janesville, WI: Seventh Day Baptist Historical Society, 1992.

Seventh-day Adventist Church

The Seventh-day Adventists trace their roots to the activity of William Miller (1782–1849), a Baptist preacher and farmer in New York State. Miller, based on his particular interpretation of biblical passages and after several date changes, predicted the second advent of Jesus for October 22, 1844. When the final predication failed to materialize, the Millerites split into several groups led by various charismatic leaders, one of whom was Ellen G. White (nee Harmon, 1827–1915), the primary force behind the Seventh-day Adventists.

Ellen came to the Millerite movement as a teenager and began doing itinerant preaching. After the Great Disappointment, as the failure of Miller's prediction came to be known, she gathered with friends for a prayer session. During this session she had the first of approximately 2,000 visionary experiences. These experiences came to be accepted as authoritative by Seventh-day Adventists. Many of Ellen's visions form the basis of Seventh-day Adventist tenets, or confirmed tenets decided upon by the less spiritually adept members of the group. Today Ellen retains her status as a prophet in the Seventh-day Adventist Church.

Ellen eventually came to advocate the shut door policy, the idea that the October 22 date signified the entry of Jesus into the heavenly sanctuary to begin its cleansing, and that anyone who had not heard and heeded Miller's message was denied salvation. Under the influence of a Millerite preacher named Joseph Bates, Ellen also began to advocate the observance of Saturday Sabbath and a bland vegetarian diet modeled after that of the popular 19th-century health reformer Sylvester Graham (1794–1851). The policies were confirmed during visionary experiences. These two developments are the beginning of what one Seventh-day Adventist scholar refers to as restoration themes: the idea that the return of Jesus depended upon humans returning to proper observance of biblical laws.

In 1845, Ellen married another itinerant Millerite preacher, James White. Together they began earnestly working on spreading the new message. As their married life progressed, some of their stances, again legitimated by Ellen's visions, moderated. For instance, by 1851 the shut door policy became much less strict, admitting children born after 1844 and those who had not outright rejected Miller's message. By 1851 the Whites had two sons. In 1855 the Whites moved to Battle Creek, Michigan. There Ellen's interest in health and diet fully developed. Eventually, Battle Creek became the home to a massive sanitarium run by another influential Seventh-day Adventist, John Harvey Kellogg (1852–1943). Kellogg was also an advocate of dietary reform, and part of the institution's menu was a sort of dried and crumbled bread accompanied by milk and taken as a breakfast food. Kellogg's brother, Will Keith (1860–1951), took this idea and created the Kellogg's Cereal Company.

The Seventh-day Adventists are much like any mainline American Protestant denomination. However, a few unique features should be highlighted. The authority of Ellen G. White's prophecy has already been mentioned, along with observance of the Saturday Sabbath. The Great Controversy is the Adventist idea that all of humanity is now involved in a struggle between Christ and Satan about God's laws and sovereignty. Seventh-day Adventists therefore believe that they are part of a remnant church specifically called to keep the commandments and the faith of Jesus. Seventh-day Adventists teach that Christian behavior includes adequate rest and exercise, avoidance of foods identified as unclean in the Old Testament along with alcohol and tobacco, and a prohibition of "irresponsible" use of drugs and narcotics. The idea that Jesus is now ministering in the heavenly sanctuary is still an official part of Adventist belief. Seventh-day Adventists also still expect the imminent return of Jesus, but set no specific date.

The name Seventh-day Adventist was chosen in 1860; however, the denomination was not officially organized until 1863. Today the denomination is organized into four representative levels: the local churches; local conferences made up of the local churches in a state or territory; the union conference, made up of conferences in a larger territory or group of states; and the General Conference, made up of all the unions in all parts of the world. The General Conference is the highest authority for the church. An elected Executive Committee holds power between sessions of the General Conference. The General Conference is made up of 12 divisions, each with responsibility for a specific geographic area. The divisions represent every major populated area of the world.

Seventh-day Adventists emphasized missionary work from their early years. The first missionary was J. N. Andrews (1829–1883), who traveled to Switzerland in 1874. In 1890 missionary work began in the Pacific islands. The year 1894 saw Seventh-day Adventist missionaries enter Africa and South America, and in 1896 they traveled to Japan. The church now

has established work in 209 countries. Although the website cites publication and distribution of Seventh-day Adventist literature as the prime factor in its worldwide success, Seventh-day Adventists have always made health and education a major part of their missionary efforts.

The church boasts 5,846 schools worldwide, along with 166 hospitals and 371 clinics. The founding of hospitals, clinics, and schools has done much to aid the global spread of Seventh-day Adventism. As reported in 2006, there were 4,820 Seventh-day Adventist churches with a membership of 980,551 in the United States. In 2007, the church reported 64,017 churches and 15,660,347 members worldwide.

Seventh-day Adventist Church
12501 Old Columbia Pike
Silver Spring, MD 20904-6600
http://www.adventist.org

Jeremy Rapport

See also: Adventism; Sabbatarianism; Vegetarianism; White, Ellen G.

References

Damsteegt, P. Gerard. *Foundations of the Seventh-day Adventist Message and Mission.* Grand Rapids, MI: William B. Eerdmans Publishing Company, 1977.

Land, Gary, ed. *Adventism in America: A History.* Grand Rapids, MI: William B. Eerdmans Publishing Company, 1986.

Maxwell, C. Mervyn. *Tell It to the World: The Story of Seventh-day Adventists.* Rev. ed. Mountain View, CA: Pacific Press, 1977.

Numbers, Ronald L. *Prophetess of Health: Ellen G. White and the Origins of Seventh-day Adventist Health Reform.* Rev. ed. Knoxville: University of Tennessee Press, 1992.

Seventh-day Adventist Reform Movements

The Seventh-day Adventist Reform movements are traditionalist splinter groups that separated from the Seventh-day Adventist Church in the 1920s.

A Reform movement emerged within the Seventh-day Adventist Church during World War I, following controversies surrounding conscientious objection. The latter was a position initially advocated by the Adventist Church. Faced with the imminent threat of persecution and of the church's being banned in several countries, however, the leader of the European Division, Louis Richard Conradi (1856–1939), reversed the earlier viewpoint and asked European Adventists to serve in the military forces of their countries (even on the holy day of Saturday). Several young Adventists rejected this decision, however, and decided to defy their governments by going underground. They were supported by roughly 2 percent of German Adventists and by similar percentages in other countries.

The Reform movement originated from local initiatives and initially had no international coordination. The Adventist Church, in order to avoid problems with governments, quickly expelled the Reformists. At the end of the war, the international Adventist leadership tried to heal the division, finally firing Conradi from his position in 1922. Reconciliation, however, proved impossible. In a conference held in Friedensau, Germany, in 1920 and at the General Conference of the Adventist Church of 1922, held in San Francisco, the Reformists' requests were rejected, and separation followed. A Seventh-day Adventist Reform movement was formally incorporated during a conference held in Gotha, Germany, on July 14–20, 1925. A missionary expansion of the newly independent movement followed in the United States, Canada, Argentina, Brazil, Australia, South Africa, and what was then Rhodesia. During World War II, the Reform movement reiterated its conscientious objection position and again underwent persecution. Persecutions also continued after the war in the Communist countries of Eastern Europe.

The Reform movement is today divided into two main branches, as a consequence of a 1951 split. Although the two branches relate different versions of the same events, it seems that at the General Conference of the Reform movement held in Zeist, The Netherlands, in 1951, the main controversial questions were personal rather than doctrinal. Dumitru Nicolici (1896–1981), a Romanian leader who had moved to the United States in 1948, led the branch known as the Seventh-day Adventist Reform movement, while those loyal to the president, Karl (Carlos) Kozel (1890–1989), kept the name International Missionary Society–Seventh-day Adventist Reform movement. Kozel's branch remained strong in Europe, particularly in Germany, while Nicolici's branch drew the majority of members from Australia, Brazil, and the United States. Its leadership later passed from Nicolici to Andrei Lavrik (1902–1976), Clyde Thomas Stewart (1902–1992), and Alfredo C. Sas (b. 1932).

During the 1960s, controversies erupted within the Seventh-day Adventist Reform movement between the United States and the international chapters, but they were satisfactorily resolved in 1967. In the same year, a "peace dialogue" was started between the Seventh-day Adventist Reform movement and the International Missionary Society–Seventh-day Adventist Reform movement. Negotiations for a merger failed at that time, but they were started again in the 1980s and the 1990s with encouraging but non-definitive results. The Seventh-day Adventist Reform movement remains to this date the larger organization, with 27,840 members in 90 countries. The International Missionary Society–Seventh-day Adventist Reform movement has some 15,000 members throughout the world and is headquartered in Germany.

Seventh-day Adventist Reform movement
PO Box 7240
Roanoke, VA 24019-0240
http://www.sdarm.org

International Missionary Society–Seventh-day
    Adventist Reform movement
PO Box 1310
74803 Mosbach/Baden
Germany
http://www.imssdarm.org
        Massimo Introvigne and PierLuigi Zoccatelli

See also: Seventh-day Adventist Church.

References
Balbach, Alfons. *The History of the Seventh Day Adventist Reform Movement*. Roanoke, VA: Seventh Day Adventist Reform Movement, 1999.
Kramer, O. *Rise and Progress of the Reform Movement: My Personal Experience*. Huntington Park, CA: International Missionary Society–Seventh-day Adventist Reform Movement, 1994.
The Principles of Faith of the Seventh-day Adventist Church "Reform Movement" and Her Church By-Laws. Mosbach/Baden, Germany: General Conference Seventh-day Adventist Church Reform Movement, n.d.

■ Seychelles

The islands of the Republic of Seychelles, located in the Indian Ocean northwest of Madagascar, were populated in the 1760s by African slaves under first the French and then the British. The French organized a colony in 1768, but it was replaced by British rule in 1794. In 1903 it was named a British Crown Colony; it was granted self-rule in 1970 and complete independence in 1976. The great majority of the 70,000 residents occupy the largest of the islands, Mahe.

The French established the Roman Catholic Church, which remains the dominant religious force of the land with some 90 percent of residents being baptized members. The Diocese of Victoria (formed in 1890) is attached to the Kenya Episcopal Conference. It operates a string of parochial schools. The first indigenous bishop was named in 1975. There is also an indigenous order of nuns, the Sisters of St. Elizabeth.

The Church of England did not arrive until 1843 and remained the church of the British leadership. Diversity in the religious community was added by the arrival of Indians and Chinese attracted by the strategic position of the islands for trade between eastern Africa and southern Asia. Most Indians were Hindus, but there were also a small number of Muslims, Jains, and Zoroastrians. The Chinese (with a population of less than 100) practice a form of the Buddhist/Daoist amalgam popular in their homeland.

In the 20th century, both the Seventh-day Adventist Church (1929) and the Jehovah's Witnesses (1960) opened work, as did a group of the Baha'i Faith. One evangelical congregation has been formed by the International Christian Fellowship, a British organization. Of more importance, in 1972 the Far East Broadcasting

A beach in the Seychelles. Roman Catholicism is the majority religion in this country. (Banol2007/Dreamstime.com)

Seychelles

Religion	Followers in 1970	Followers in 2010	% of Population	Annual % growth 2000–2010	Followers in 2025	Followers in 2050
Christians	51,500	84,300	96.2	1.02	89,000	92,100
Roman Catholics	46,000	71,100	81.2	0.87	74,400	76,100
Anglicans	3,900	5,400	6.2	0.38	5,700	5,900
Protestants	250	3,600	4.1	3.90	5,000	6,000
Agnostics	230	2,000	2.3	2.99	3,500	5,000
Hindus	310	470	0.5	1.08	600	800
Baha'is	150	380	0.4	1.07	600	1,000
Muslims	170	190	0.2	1.13	250	300
Atheists	0	130	0.1	1.04	200	300
Chinese folk	20	50	0.1	1.36	70	100
Jains	10	40	0.0	1.18	60	80
Zoroastrians	10	30	0.0	1.61	50	50
Total population	**52,400**	**87,600**	**100.0**	**1.06**	**94,300**	**99,700**

SEYCHELLES

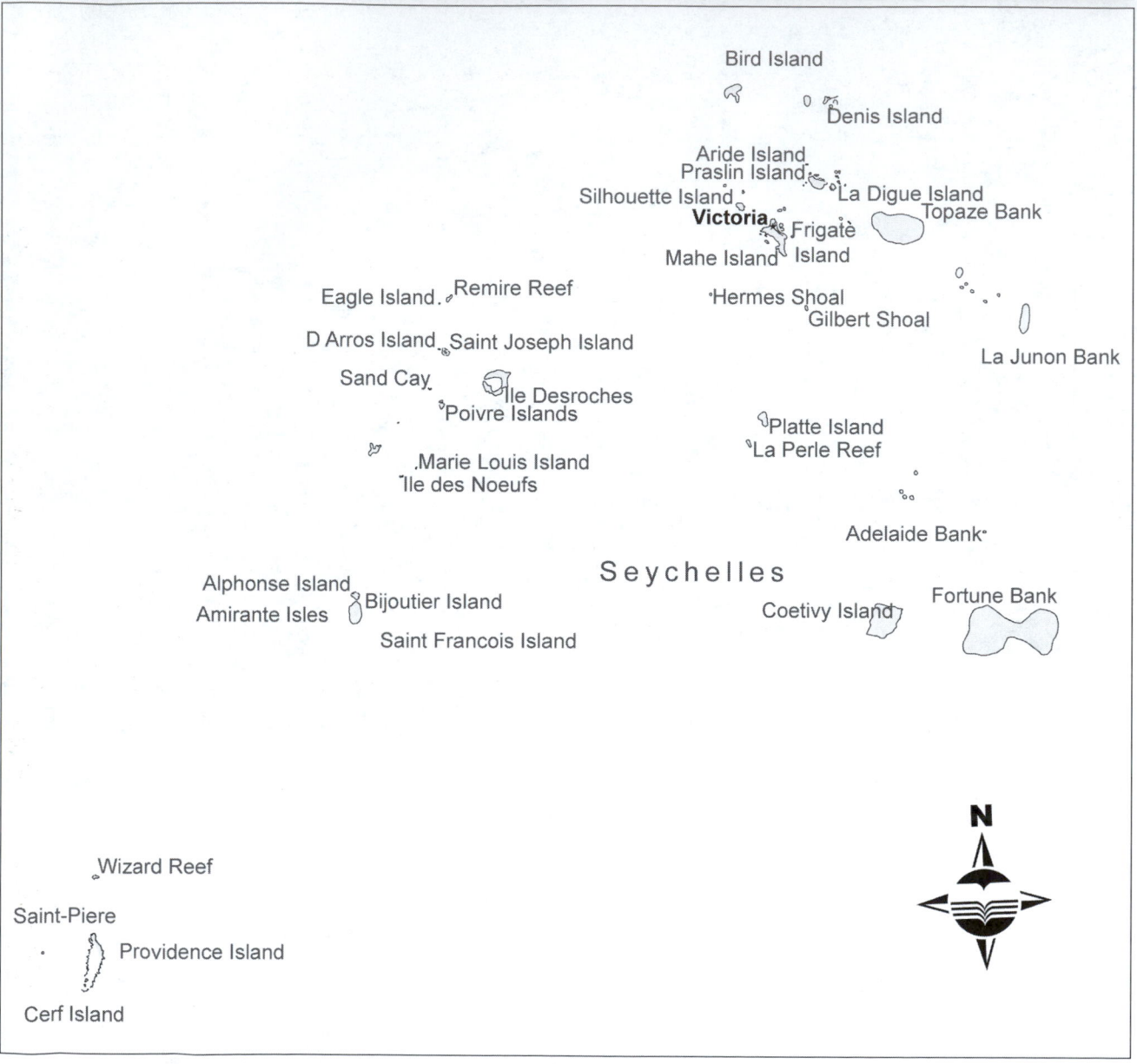

Association established a radio station that targets programming to both Africa and India.

The New Religions have yet to find their way to the Seychelles, in large part because of the out-of-the-way location of the islands.

J. Gordon Melton

See also: Baha'i Faith; Church of England; Jehovah's Witnesses; Roman Catholic Church; Seventh-day Adventist Church.

References

Bradley, J. T. *The History of the Catholic Church in Seychelles*. Victoria, Seychelles: Clarion, 1940.

Metz, Helen Chapin. *Indian Ocean: Five Island Countries*. Washington, DC: U.S. Government Printing Service, 1995.

The Seventh-day Adventist Mission in Seychelles: A Review of Events from Years 1930–1980. Victoria, Seychelles: The Mission, 1981.

Seymour, William J.

1870–1922

African American preacher William Joseph Seymour led the revival at the small mission on Azusa Street in Los Angeles from which modern Pentecostalism emerged and spread globally. Due to racism, for almost a century his role in the founding of the movement was overlooked but has in recent decades been recovered and acknowledged.

Seymour was born on May 2, 1870, in Centerville, Louisiana. Little is known of his life prior to his moving in 1890 to Indianapolis, where he associated with the African Methodist Episcopal Church and then the Holiness movement, as he came to accept the Holiness emphasis on sanctification, an experience of God that allowed believers to be free of outward sin and perfected in love. The Evening Lights Saints also had a strong emphasis on the imminent return of Christ.

While residing in Cincinnati with the Saints, he contracted small pox, which he survived but at the cost of one eye. He also decided to become a minister. He was ordained by the Church of God (Anderson, Indiana). His travels led him in 1903 to Houston, Texas. There, in 1905, he learned of the arrival of Charles Fox Parham. He asked Parham permission to attend the latter's Bible school at which he learned about Parham's approach to the baptism of the Holy Spirit (a staple concern of Holiness people) and the new teachings of the baptism's tie with speaking in tongues, which Parham asserted was the visible evidence of the baptism. The baptism of the Holy Spirit was an empowerment for the sanctified.

Early in 1906, Seymour moved to Los Angeles to pastor a small church. He almost immediately injected the new ideas about the baptism of the Holy Spirit into his sermons. The church's leaders rejected Seymour and the message and proceeded to lock him out of the church primacies. He met together with the few who still wanted to learn about the new teachings in the home of Richard D. and Ruth Asberry on Bonnie Brae Avenue.

On April 9 Jennie Evans Moore (1883–1936) (whom Seymour later married) and Edward Lee began to speak in tongues. Seymour received the experience a few days later on April 12. As news circulated about what had happened, crowds began to gather in front of the small home. New facilities had to be found. They were obtained by renting an old building on Azusa Street (formerly the First African Methodist Episcopal Church of Los Angeles), then being used as livery stable. The building was quickly refurbished with benches and a pulpit made from two boxes. Seymour lived on the second floor.

On April 18, an initial newspaper article presented a negative picture of the gathering on Azusa Street. That same day, however, San Francisco was destroyed by an earthquake. Within a week, thousands of copies of a tract tying the earthquake to the revival were distributed. The earthquake served to more clearly focus the millennial elements of Pentecostal thought, which saw the new outpouring of the Spirit as a sign of the approaching end times. The millennialism gave the movement an urgency that might otherwise not have been present.

Hundreds began to find their way to the small Apostolic Faith Mission, as Seymour called it, borrowing a name Parham had used. Over the next three years, Seymour led three services a day. Most of the leaders of what would become the national and international Pentecostal movement would make the pilgrimage to Los Angeles, where they received the baptism. Those in attendance included African Americans, Mexican Americans, and whites.

Seymour married Moore in 1908. Shortly thereafter, Clara Lund and Florence Crawford (1872–1936), two white women who worked at the mission, took the mailing list and moved to Portland, Oregon, where they founded a rival Apostolic Faith Mission and began issuing a new periodical, *The Apostolic Faith*. Seymour never recovered from the defection, and while he continued to pastor the community that had developed on Azusa Street, he lost touch with the larger movement and was able to work only among African Americans. The larger movement would gradually divide into several segregated congregations, the Pentecostal Assemblies of the World alone able to maintain a working interracial membership.

Meanwhile, in Los Angeles, in 1911 William H. Durham (1873–1912), a white Baptist minister from Chicago, drove a further wedge in the Pentecostal community by his proclamation of the so-called Finished

Work position that limited the baptism and tongues experience to only those who had previously been sanctified. The resulting controversy took a sizable proportion of the Mission's constituency—some 600 believers. Then in 1913, the Mission faced a new controversy. At a camp meeting, several ministers proclaimed the "Jesus Only" message that rejected the traditional doctrine of the Trinity and demanded that Christian baptism be practiced in the name of "Jesus only." Many African American believers found themselves attracted to the "Jesus Only" position.

By 1915, Seymour and the Mission had only a remnant following, but large enough to justify his publication of a church manual, *The Doctrines and Discipline of the Azusa Street Apostolic Faith Mission of Los Angeles*. He assumed the title of bishop and began to travel about the countryside, occasionally in the company of Charles Harrison Mason (1866–1961), the founder of the Church of God in Christ. During these years Seymour founded a number of congregations. While some later joined the Church of God in Christ, some constituted themselves the Apostolic Faith Church (with congregations primarily in Virginia). Seymour's actual role as the leader of these congregations is vague. What is known is that the congregations would associate together in a small denomination, eventually split into several denominations, and more recently come together in the United Fellowship of the Original Azusa Street Mission.

Seymour died of a heart attack on September 18, 1922. His widow succeeded him as head of the Los Angeles congregation and pastored it for several years. A major disruption hit the congregation in 1931, after which its story becomes nebulous. The church building was eventually torn down and no visible remnant of Seymour's work survived in Los Angeles. Jennie Seymour died in 1936.

White Pentecostals wrote often about Azusa Street, but ignored its African American roots and largely wrote Seymour out of the story until the late 20th century. An important step in reclaiming knowledge of Seymour was made by D. J. Nelson, a student of British church historian Walter J. Hollenweger, who in 1981 wrote a dissertation on Seymour at the University of Birmingham (United Kingdom). Since the 1980s, Pentecostal scholars have emphasized Seymour's impor-

tance to the Pentecostal global endeavor. In his preaching, he emphasized the imminent end of this present eon and the need for foreign missions to spread the Pentecostal message. He also exercised a style of leadership that allowed broad participation in the Azusa Street revival by all who attended, including women and non-whites, both of whom would become essential in shaping the course of the movement.

J. Gordon Melton

See also: African Methodist Episcopal Church; Church of God (Anderson, Indiana); Church of God in Christ; Holiness Movement; Parham, Charles Fox; Pentecostal Assemblies of the World; Pentecostalism.

References

Connelly, James T. "William J. Seymour." In *Twentieth-Century Shapers of American Popular Religion*, edited by Charles H. Lippy, 381–387. New York: Greenwood Press, 1989.

Martin, Larry. *The Life and Ministry of William J. Seymour: And a History of the Azusa Street Revival*. Christian Life Books, MO, 1999.

McRobert, Iain. *The Black Roots and White Racism of Early Pentecostalism in the USA*. New York: St. Martin's Press, 1988.

Nelson, Douglas J. "For Such a Time as This: The Story of Bishop William J. Seymour and the Azusa Street Revival: A Search for Pentecostal/Charismatic Roots." Ph.D. diss., University of Birmingham, 1981.

Robeck, Cecil M., Jr. *The Azusa Street Mission and Revival*. Nashville: Thomas Nelson, 2006.

Sanders, Cheryl J. *Saints in Exile: The Holiness-Pentecostal Experience in African American Religion and Culture*. New York: Oxford University Press, 1996.

Sanders, Rufus G. W. *The Seymour Papers: Theological Beginnings of the Modern Pentecostal Faith*. Princeton, NJ: Xlibris, 2008.

Shadhiliyya Sufi Order

The Shadhiliyya Sufi Order is named after Abu al-Hasan al-Shadhili (d. 1258), who is buried at Humaythra near the coast of Egypt's Red Sea. These sufis are found mainly in northern Africa and in Egypt. They have traditionally espoused a nonsectarian view toward Sunni Islamic law schools in order to have a balanced mystical and worldly life. A person's knowledge (*'ilm*) is revealed and understood through one's actions (*'amal*) on earth. The sainthood (*walaya*) in the Shadhiliyya Sufi Order is significantly tied into the experiences of other members in the sufi order. The Shadhili sufis emphasize that each moment is in front of the divine, and there is a constant calling to return to the holy.

The Shadhiliyya Order derives from Abu Madyan Shu'ayb (d. 1198), whose primary disciple, Muhammad 'Alî Ba-'Alawi, contributed to the 'Alawiya Sufi orders in Yemen, South Asia, and Myanmar. Al-Shadhili's famous disciple was Abu-l 'Abbas al-Mursi (d. 1287), whose shrine is in Alexandria, where thousands of sufis still conduct their religious activities publicly.

Leadership of the order has passed to Sidi Shaykh Muhammad Sa'id al-Jamal ar-Rifa'i ash-Shadhdhuli, al-Qutb, al-Gawth, now seen as the "Guide" of the Shadhiliyya Path. He resides on the Mount of Olives in Jerusalem as the imam of the Masjid al-Aqsa (the Dome of the Rock). The Dome of the Rock is related to the tradition of the Night Journey of the Prophet Muhammad, who is believed to have traveled from Mecca to al-Aqsa and from there to heaven. Since 1993 the shaykh has traveled widely, teaching the Shadhiliyya path to all who wish to learn it. The strength of the order is in Algeria, Tunisia, and Morocco.

In North America, the Order may be contacted through the Shadhiliyya Sufi Center in Pope Valley, California. Publications are handled through Sidi Muhammad Press in Napa, California.

Shadhiliyya Sufi Center
PO Box 100
Pope Valley, CA 94567
http://www.suficenter.org/

Shadhiliyya Sufi Order
c/o Sidi Muhammad Press
2656 First St., #413
Napa, CA 94558
http://www.sufimaster.org/tariqa.htm

Qamar-ul Huda

See also: Islam; Sufism.

References

Buckman, David. "The Underground Friends of God and Their Adversaries: A Case Study and Survey of Sufism in Contemporary Yemen." *Update* 39 (1997): 21–24.

Cornell, Vincent. *Realm of the Saint: Power and Authority in Moroccan Sufism.* Austin: University of Texas Press, 1998.

Danner, Mary Ann Koury, trans. *The Key to Salvation: A Sufi Manual of Invocation—Miftah al-Falah.* Cambridge, UK: Islamic Texts Society, 1996.

Ibn al-Sabbagh. *The Mystical Teachings of al-Shadhili.* Trans. by Elmer H. Douglas. Ed. by Ibrahim M. Abu-Rabi. Albany: State University Press of New York, 1993.

Shafiite School of Islam

The Shafiite School of Islam is one of the four *madhhabs* (schools) of jurisprudence deemed orthodox within the world of Sunni Islam. The school traces its origin to the career of one man, Muhammad ibn Idris ibn al-Abbas ibn Uthman ibn Shafi (767–820), a Palestinian raised in Mecca who then widely traveled in the Islamic world. As he began to teach and write, he was presented with the task of synthesizing and reconciling the competing schools of legal interpretation represented by the Hanafite and Traditionalist schools. Toward the end of his life, he dictated his most famous book, *Al-umm*, in which he laid out his own perspective and left behind a record of the differences between the other schools.

Shafi was writing as the process of defining the traditions relative to the Prophet Muhammad and his companions (*hadith*) were being compiled and assessed, and he placed great importance on the authentic traditions, as opposed to the legal consensus of the scholars (*ulama*) that had been reached in the leading centers of Islamic learning—Baghdad and Medina.

Shafiite teachings took root in Persia (Iran) in the ninth century, during the years of the Abbasid Empire, and they remained the most influential school of thought into the 13th century. In addition, Shafi spent his last years in Egypt, and his teachings took root there, becoming the official school during the Ayyubid dynasty (1167–1252) and remaining of continuing importance until the rise of the Fatimid dynasty (which established a non-Sunni Shia Ismaili government). The adoption of the Hanafite School of legal interpretation by the Ottoman Empire, however, pushed the Shafiite School out of the centers of Islamic power in the Middle East. It had become the dominant school among the trading classes and through them was taken to Indonesia (now the most populous predominantly Islamic nation in the world) and to the Muslim communities along the east coast of Africa whose most famous center was Zanzibar.

J. Gordon Melton

See also: Hanafite School of Islam; Islam; Muhammad.

References

Bakhtiar, Laleh, and Kevin Reinhart. *Encyclopedia of Islamic Law: A Compendium of the Major Schools*. Chicago: Kazi Publications, 1996.

Coulson, Noel J. *Conflicts and Tensions in Islamic Jurisprudence*. Chicago: University of Chicago Press, 1969.

Coulson, Noel J. *A History of Islamic Law*. Edinburgh: Edinburgh University Press, 1994.

Hallaq, Wael B. *A History of Islamic Legal Theories: An Introduction to Sunni Usul al-Fiqh*. New York: Cambridge University Press, 1997.

Horrie, Chris, and Peter Chippindale. *What Is Islam?* London: Virgin, 1998.

Schacht, Joseph. *An Introduction to Islamic Law*. Oxford: Oxford University Press, 1964.

Watt, Montgomery. *The Majesty that Was Islam*. New York: Praeger, 1974.

Shah Faisal Mosque

The Shah Faisal Mosque, the largest mosque in the world at the time of its construction, is located near Islamabad, Pakistan. It is the product of the founding of the new nation of Pakistan (1947). As the violence in which the nation was born died out, a proposal for a new national mosque was assembled and a site selected. The proposal was then offered to King Faisal of Saudi Arabia (1906–1975) on the occasion of his 1966 visit to Pakistan. King Faisal reacted favorably to the proposed mosque and offered to support it financially. The Pakistanis reacted to his generosity by naming both the mosque and the main road from the mosque to the city in his honor. They selected Turkish architect Vedat Dalokay to design the new worship center.

A decade later, by the time the cornerstone of the mosque was laid in October 1976, King Faisel had been assassinated. King Khalid, who had succeed to the throne of Saudi Arabia in 1975, attended the ceremonies. Work on the building would continue for another decade and was finally completed in 1988. The resulting complex covers 47.87 acres, while the covered area of the prayer hall encompasses 1.19 acres. It accommodates some 100,000 worshipers in the prayer hall and an additional 200,000 in the grounds just outside the prayer hall at any given time.

The Faisal Mosque remained the largest mosque in the world only a few years. It was superseded in 1993 by the completion of the Hassan II Mosque in Casablanca, Morocco. More recently, two Saudi Arabian mosques, the Al-Masjid al-Har (or Grand Mosque) in Mecca and the Al-Masjid al-Nabawi (or Prophet's Mosque) in Medina, have eclipsed even the Hassan mosque in size.

The Faisal Mosque serves as the national mosque in Pakistan. Among the first uses made of it following its completion was as the site of the funeral of General Muhammad Zia-ul-Haq (1924–1988), who served as the country's president for 11 years (1977–1988) until his assassination. He was subsequently buried in a tomb adjacent to the mosque.

J. Gordon Melton

See also: Mecca; Mosques.

References

Serageldin, Ismail, and James Steele, eds. *Architecture of the Contemporary Mosque*. London: Academy Editions, 1996.

Shaw, Isobel. *Pakistan*. Lincolnwood, UK: Passport Books, 1996.

Shaivism

In the broadest sense, Shaivism refers to ritual and theological traditions that focus on the worship of Shiva or his consort Shakti as the supreme divinity from which the universe emerges and into which it is eventually absorbed. Like Vishnu, Shiva is part of the pantheon of the Rig Veda, where he is known by the name Rudra. From these early references, it is clear that Shiva-Rudra's character is ambigious and paradoxical. Rigvedic poets praised Rudra as the lord of medicine and simultanously asked not to be harmed by his arrows. This aspect of Shiva's personality continues throughout the Puranas, where he encompasses the central paradox of the Hindu tradition, the tension of *dharma* and *moksha*, as he is simultaneously the renouncing, meditating ascetic and the ideal husband and family man to his wife Parvati and his two sons, Ganesha and Karttikeya/Skanda. As Ardharanishvara, the Lord who is half woman, he encompasses and transcends the opposition of sex/gender. As Nataraja, the Lord of the dance enshrined at the great temple at Cidambara located in Cuddalore District of the east-central part of the Tamil Nadu, his dance creates, maintains, and destroys the universe. As he dances *samsara* and *maya* into being, he also is the source of liberation (moksha) for his devotees. The *linga*, the aniconic representation of Shiva, unmistakably expresses Shiva nature as a deity who encompasses and overcomes opposition. The linga, which at one level has sexual significance, symbolizes the creative potentiality of Shiva (his dharmic nature) at the same time as it represents the power of restraint and renoucement (his ascetic dimension). The earliest conceptualization of Shiva as a deity that represents totality is found in the Shvetashvatara Upanishad, where he is identified with *atman*.

Shaisvism developed in the medieval period in two distinct traditions. Puranic Shaivism formed within the context of the *smarta* brahmin householder. Smarta brahmins broadly refers to the living brahmanic tradition that integrates Vedic orthopraxy as elaborated in *smirti* and ritual practices of the Puranic texts, including the performance of Vedic domestic rituals and the observance of *varnashramadharma*, with the ritual practices of puja of the Puranas, which focus on the worship of Shiva using Vedic *mantras*. Non-puranic

Shaiva sadhu (holy man) seeking alms in front of a temple in Pashupatinath, Nepal, 2008. (Zzvet/Dreamstime.com)

Shaivism consisted of primarily exclusive groups that required intitiation (*diksha*) into their ritual traditions and whose aim was primarily to obtain liberation (moksha). These traditions were further classified in Shaiva Tantras into two divisions: path of mantras (*mantramarga*) and the higher path (*atimarga*). Atimarga traditions stressed the search for liberation, while the mantramarga focused on liberation as well as the attainment of supernatural power (*siddhi*) and pleasure (*bhoga*) as part of the initiate's spiritual journey. The atimarga is represented by the Pashupata tradition, the oldest Shaiva group, which is mentioned in the *Mahahbarata* (ca. 500 BCE–500 CE). The mantramarga tradition is found in the numerous *shaiva tantras*, which are connected to a variety of Shaiva ritual traditions.

Shaiva traditions are broadly divided into Shaiva Siddhantas and Shaiva non-Siddhantas or Kapalikas.

The Shaiva Siddhanta tradition that had developed in Tamil Nadu by the 11th century was heavily influenced by devotional poetry composed by the 63 Nayanars (ca. 500–750), Tamil Shaivia saints from all segments of Tamil society whose devotional fervor toward Shiva was expressed through poetry, worship of Shiva, and service to his devotees. Shaiva *bhakti* stresses the emotional dimension over the realization of the non-distinction of self and Lord. The aim of devotion to the Lord is to attain a direct, unmediated relationship with Shiva, in which the devotee became mad with love manifested in the trangression of social norms and personal behavior. The Shaiva Siddhanta is a strictly dualistic system of thought in which there are three distinct ontological categories: Shiva, the supreme lord (*pati*), the self (*pashu*), and the world, which binds (*pasha*) the self. Shiva and the self are eternally distinct, but the self is bound within the cosmos by ignorance (*avidya*), impurity, and *karma* illusion (*maya*), the substratum of the cosmos. The initiate (diksha) can only achieve liberation by means of Shiva's grace channelled through the body of the teacher (*shivaguru*), in whose form (*murti*) Shiva has been established. Through service, worship, and meditation, the soul is purified of the impurities that cover it. Upon liberation, the soul becomes ominiscient and omnipotent like Shiva, but remains eternally distinct from Shiva. Although the Siddhanta path is open to all *varnas*, it is not open to children, women, the old, the mentally ill, or the physically disabled.

Kapalikas or non-Siddhanta Shaivas get their name from the great vow (*mahavrata*) that they undertake. They carry a skull-topped staff (*khatvanga*) and a skull begging bowl in imitation Shiva's great penance for the sin of killing a Brahman (*brahmahatya*). Shiva cut off Brahma's fifth head, after the latter attempted to have sexual relations with his own daughter. As a result, Brahma's skull became permanently stuck to Shiva's hand until he reached Kapalamocana, one of the sacred *tirthas* of Varanasi. These ascetics lived in cremation grounds and engaged in activites that from an orthodox brahmanic perspective are considered to be highly polluting, such as offering blood, meat, and alcohol to fierce deities including Bhairava and Kali.

In Kashmir, the Kaula tradition of Shaivism, which developed during the medieval period, incorporates the cremation-ground asceticism of the Kapalikas into the traditional orthodox life of the householder. The Trika School of Kashmiri Shaivism articulates a complex theology whose aim is the realization of the identity of all manifestations, including the self, with the pure consciousness (*caitanya*) of Shiva. Liberation in the Trika system is achieved throught the realization of the nondistinction of self and Shiva or Kali.

The Pashupata Shaivas, perhaps dating back to the second century CE, aimed at transcending varnashramadharma in order to attain a higher, perfected (*siddha*) stage beyond the fourth Vedic *ashrama* (*sannyasin*). To achieve this goal, the initiate (*sadhaka*), a Brahmin male who had undergone the *upanayana* ceremony, the traditional high-caste initiation, undertook a vow (*vrata*) of spiritual practice (*sadhana*) that progressed in three stages. Initially, the ascetic initiate took on the physical marks of a Pashupata: avoiding bathing in water and instead covering himself in ashes and engaging in the worship of Shiva through dancing, singing, laughter, and repetition of the sacred mantras. During this stage, the sadhaka lived in or in the vicinity of a Shaiva temple. In the second stage, the initiate left all physical signs and markers of his *vrata*, including the temple, and publicly engage in antisocial behaviors, such as acting as if he was crippled, make lewd gestures toward women, and generally acting as if out of his mind. Such behavior was meant to incur the anger of passers-by and the subsequent loss and transfer of their merit to the sadhaka. At the same time, the sadhaka's *papa* (evil) was transferred to the abuser. In the final stage, the initiate completely renounced society and withdrew to an isolated place to meditate on the five sacred mantras and *OM*. Upon completion of third stage, the ascetic became a permanent dweller of the cremation ground and lived on whatever was available as food until his death. Liberation was achieved upon death, when union with Shiva was achieved through Shiva's grace. The Pashupata traditions seems to have died out around the late 15th century, but their doctrines have been preserved in various texts and subcommentaries.

Carlos Lopez

See also: Asceticism; Devotion/Devotional Traditions; Hinduism; Meditation; Tantrism; Temples—Hindu; Women, Status and Role of.

References

Chitgopekar, Nilima. *Encountering Shaivism: The Deity, the Milieu, the Entourage.* New Delhi: Munshiram Manoharlal Publishers Private, 1998.

Dyczkowski, Mark S. G. *Doctrine of Vibration: An Analysis of the Doctrines and Practices Associated with Kashmir Shaivism.* Albany: State University of New York Press, 1987.

Fürlinger, Ernst. *The Touch of Shakti: A Study in Non-dualistic Trika Shaivism of Kashmir.* New Delhi: D. K. Printworld, 2009.

Lorenzen, David N. *The Kapalikas and Kalamukhas: Two Lost Shaiva Sects.* Berkeley: University of California Press, 1972.

O'Flaherty, Wendy Doniger. *Shiva: The Erotic Ascetic.* Oxford: Oxford University Press, 1981.

Shakta Movement

The Shakta movement (Shaktaite, Shaktism, Shakti movement, sometimes without the "h" in the spelling) is one of the major theological dynamics in Hinduism. Its ideology is essentially a supreme Mother-Goddess phenomenon common in many primal religions. The Shakta movement has ties to other Hindu movements, such as Shaivism; it flourished in India under the Maurya, Sunga, and Satavahana dynasties.

Proponents of the Shakta movement are predominantly Hindu with some following in Buddhism. They begin with the assertion that the Ultimate Divinity is female, not male. The male deities are subservient to Shakti (*shakti* is also another term for feminine spiritual energy and is also a separate name for a female Hindu deity). The Devi Mahatmya, a major Shakta text, retells many traditional Hindu myths, but portrays the feminine deities with new superior positions. Most Hindus do not object to the Shakta movement and have even incorporated Shakta teaching into their own belief systems. There are also multiple groups of Shakti followers in Hinduism, some being liberal with others being Shakti exclusive.

Hinduism is currently undergoing a major renaissance worldwide, and the Shakta movement is a part of that renaissance. In addition to the revival of Hindu tradition, a new appreciation for civil and women's rights is also coming into play. The Shakta movement is a direct recipient of these new allowances. More female gurus are being revered by Hindus as reincarnations of holiness and enlightenment, whereas in the past only men were viewed with such reverence. Female deities are being studied and exalted along with, and in some cases even more than, male divinities.

The Kali followers, Shaivites, and the Brahmo Samaj are helping to lead the way for the Shakta movement. Some Hindu holy men, such as Vivekananda (1863–1902), Sri Ramakrishna (1836–1886), and Sri Aurobindo (1872–1950), helped to assist the cause of the Shakta movement. Many women have claimed to be direct reincarnations of Shakti, thus attributing to themselves great reverence. Such women include Sarada Devi, Ramakrishna's wife (1853–1920); Mira Richard, Aurobindo's companion (1878–1973); and the renowned Anandamayi Ma (1896–1982). Despite the fact that these women are all deceased, they all have followings within the Hindu community and in the Shakta movement today. Many Shakta movement Hindus actually have pictures of these women as objects of worship that they revere as much as an icon of Shiva, Durga, or Vishnu.

The Shakta movement has had an effect upon Hinduism and Jainism. Both religions have their own religious orders exclusively for women. Buddhism, in particular, has elevated the status of the feminine divine. Avalokitesvara, the prominent Bodhisattva in Mahayana Buddhism, has been represented in many female forms as well as male forms. Many Buddhist *mudras* (hand gestures) represent union between a deity and his corresponding Shakti. Some Buddhist groups have incorporated Tantrism into their Shakta movements. The sexual aspect of this are seen more in old Tibet and Nepal than in India and Khmer.

Kumar Jairamdas

See also: Brahmo Samaj; Hinduism; Mahayana Buddhism; Tantrism; Yoga.

References

Coburn, Thomas. *Encountering the Goddess: A Translation of the Devi-Mahatmya and a Study of Its Interpretation*. Albany: State University of New York Press, 1991.

Hawley, John, and Donna Wulff. *Devi: Goddesses of India*. Los Angeles: University of California Press, 1996.

Kinsley, David. *Hindu Goddesses*. Los Angeles: University of California Press, 1988.

Vanamali. *Shakti: Realm of the Divine Mother*. Rochester, VT: Inner Traditions, 2008.

Shaktism

In the broadest sense, Shaktism refers to the worship of *shakti*, the primordial feminine power that creates, maintains, and re-absorbs the universe in the form of a personal supreme Goddess, who is understood to encompass all. The supreme Goddess takes many forms, including Amba, Durga, Kali, Lakshmi, Parvati, or Tripurasundari, all of which are understood to be a manifestation of one great Goddess, simply called Devi. Shaktism incorporates various ritual and theological traditions that have developed with one form of the divine feminine as the cultic focus.

A tradition of goddess worship may be traced as far back as the Indus Valley, where the presence of numerous terra-cotta female figurines found at all levels of excavation suggests a general concern for fertility and that the worship of female divinity was a popular feature of Indus religiosity. In the early Vedic texts, female deities are mentioned, but for the most part they play a minor role in the mythology and religious system. The Rig Veda mentions a few goddesses, the most prominent being Ushas (Dawn), to whom 20 hymns are dedicated, and who is vividly described. Other goddesses such as Prithivi (Earth), Ratri (Night), Nirriti (complete annihilation), Shraddha (confident intention), and Vac (sacred speech) represent natural phenomena or abstract or ritual concepts. However, it is clear that nothing akin to the later Hindu cult of a Great Goddess is to be found in the Vedic texts. Goddesses figure more prominently in the Ramayana and Mahabharata, where they appear as consorts of a male deity. Sarasvati, a river that figures prominently in the Rig Veda, is transformed through a series of identifications with the goddess Vac into the goddess of wisdom and the consort of the creator, Brahma. Parvati and Lakshmi are identified as consorts of Shiva and Vishnu, respectively. In the Mahabharata, Arjuna praises Durga, who is identification with the terrifying aspect of Parvati or Uma before the great battle for the explicit purpose of defeating the Kauravas. In Krittivasa's Ramayana (15th century), Rama performs a *puja* to Durga before going to battle with Ravana.

It is in the Puranas that the Goddess attains her prominence in the Hindu tradition. Goddesses are portrayed not simply as active consorts but as independent agents in the cosmic battle between the gods and the demons (*asuras*). The Devi Mahatmya of the Markandeya Purana (fourth century) presents the Devi, who is identical with Durga, as the ultimate source and reality of the universe. The story of the Goddess is told in the context of the central Vedic myth, the battle between the gods and the asuras in three episodes.

The first episode is clearly cosmogonic. At the moment just before the universe has been created, when Vishnu lies asleep on Shesha, who floats on the cosmic waters, Brahma, seated on the lotus that emerges from Vishnu's navel, sees two demons, Madhu and Kaitabha, who have fallen out of Vishnu's ears. As he is being attacked by the two demons, Brahma praises the Goddess as Yoganindra (the cosmic sleep of the yogic state of absorption) to enliven Vishnu by departing from his body, so that he can engage in his *dharma*-supporting activity and defeat the two demons.

The second episode consists of the battle against Mahisha, the buffalo demon, who the gods are unable to defeat. Out of anger at their inability to defeat Mahisha, the gods emit their great brilliance (*tejas*), which coalesces into the shape of a beautiful woman to whom each god respectively gives his weapon, emblem, or ornament. After defeating Mahisha, the gods praise Devi as the supreme protector and savior of the world and ask her to return whenever they remember her.

The third and longest episode takes place in the liminal space between heaven and Earth, the Himalayas, where two demons, Shumbha and Nishumbha, have stolen the three worlds and the gods' share of the sacrifice. As the gods are worshipping Vishnumaya,

Roadside temple dedicated to the goddess Kali in Tiruvannamalai, India. (Aravind Teki/Dreamstime.com)

the Goddess who exists in all beings, Parvati approaches that spot to bathe in the Ganga. Upon being praised, Ambika emerges from Parvati's body and thereupon Parvati became the dark one, Kali. Seeing Ambika on the battlefield, Shumbha sends a marriage proposal to her, which she refuses, saying that she may only marry a man who would defeat her in battle. Shumbha sends the demons Canda and Munda to capture her, but that only triggers Ambika's anger, which is manifests in the form of the goddess Kali. By means of Kali and various other shaktis that manifest on the battlefield as the Seven Mothers (*saptamatrikas*), Ambika defeats the demonic army and finally destroys Shumbha and Nishumbha.

Theologically, the Devi Mahatmya and the slightly later Devi Bhagavata Purana present the Goddess as the supreme source of all divine power, both male and female. In the *matmya* episode, the Goddess as Yoganindra becomes the supreme agent, by whose power Vishnu is able to act and defeat Madhu and Kaitabha. It is the great male god Vishnu who is subject to the power and authority of the Goddess. In the Devi Gita, a section of the Devi Bhagavata Purana, the Goddess is addressed as Female Ruler of the Universe (Bhuvaneshani) and identified as the impersonal *brahman*, which is infinite being, consciousness, and bliss (*sat cid ananda*).

Like Vaishnavism and Shaivism, Goddess traditions have been influenced by tantric rituals and ideologies. Shakta traditions influenced by *tantra* are broadly divided into the "family of the Black Goddess" (Kalikula) and the "family of the auspicious Goddess" (Shrikula).

The Kalikula school stresses the mythological narratives and rituals connected with terrifying (*ghora*) aspects of the Goddess, including Kali, Candi, and Tara. Like other tantric *mantramargas*, the Kalikula's goal is to gain power (*siddha*) through ritual practices that transgress orthodox brahmanic norms and embrace impurity. Texts of the Kalikula tradition conceive of the ferocious Kali, often depicted as standing on Shiva's corpse, as transcending male form and as the light of pure consciousness from which the universe emerged and into which it is reabsorbed. Historically, shakti traditions focused on Kali have been found primarily in North Indian, especially in Assam, Bengal, and Orissa.

The Shrikula traditions emphasize the gentle and motherly aspect of the Goddess, such as Lakshmi, Parvati, and Durga. The Shrividya tradition of South India and Kashmir is the cult of Lilata Tripurasundari ("the beautiful playful Goddess of the three cities"), which falls under the mantramarga focusing on external rituals and their magical effects, as well as the esoteric understanding of the *shricakra*. The shricakra is a sacred diagram formed by five downward-pointing triangles that intersect four upward-pointing triangles, the intersections of which form 43 triangles. The downward-pointing triangles represent Shakti, while the upward-pointing ones represent Shiva. The shricakra is the aniconic representation of the Goddess, which represents the union of Shiva and Shakti and thus the manifestation and contraction of the absolute as sound (*shabda*). The Goddess is supreme and transcendental, whose manifestation is the cosmos. She is the active power that unfolds and contracts the universe during the cosmic cycles.

Shrividya theology conceives of the human body as the gross manifestation of the supreme or causal body. Liberation (*moksha*) is achieved by retracing the manifestations of the supreme body back to its source, the Goddess. As in other tantric systems, this spiritual journey is achieved through the realization of the hierarchical correspondences between the human body and the cosmos. The goal is to incite the goddess Kundalini, the shakti that dwells at the base energy center (*cakra*) of the human body, to unite with Shiva, who is located at the crown of the head.

The theological notion of the Goddess as all encompassing is expressed at the level of practice through the system of "seats of the goddess" (*shaktapithas*) that identify the Goddess with the sacred landscape of India. The mythological foundation of the identity of the mythic landscape of India as the Goddess is found in the story of the dismemberment of Sati, Shiva's first wife. Sati's father, Daksha Prajapati, was celebrating a great sacrifice to which he did not invite Shiva. Outraged and insulted by her father's failure to invite the great god Shiva to his sacrifice, Sati immolates herself in Daksha's sacrificial fire. When Shiva learns that Sati has killed herself, his anger manifests as Virabhadra, who destroys Daksha's sacrifice and kills Daksha. Most versions of the myth then tell about how the sacrifice was reinstituted, with the inclusion of Shiva along with the other gods. However, in some versions, Shiva discovers Sati's body and is overwhelmed by grief and despair. He picks her up and begins to wander throughout the universe with Sati's body in his arms. The gods become concerned that Shiva's grief threatens the stability of the cosmos and the world will deteriorate into chaos. The gods conspire to deprive Shiva of the source of his grief, Sati's body. Vishnu secretly follows Shiva around the universe gradually slicing off bits of her body until Sata's body has disappeared. When Shiva realizes that there is no body, his grief ends, and he returns to the mountains to carry out his ascetic mediation.

The pieces of Sati's body fall to earth and become the sacred seats of the Goddess (*pithas*). The four most important pithas are at Jalandhara in the Punjab, Uddayana in the Swat Valley, Purnagiri in the state of Uttarakhand, and Kamarupa in Assam. In these important places of pilgrimage (*tirtha*), the tongue, nipples, and vulva of the goddess are said to have fallen. The network of pithas serves to sacralize the land and the geography of India. India is understood as the body of the Goddess herself and as being inherently sacred. In this manner, the all-encompassing Goddess becomes localized and accessible to her devotees.

Carlos Lopez

See also: Asceticism; Devotion/Devotional Traditions; India, Hinduism in; Modern Period; Pilgrimage; Shaivism; Tantrism; Vaishnavism; Women, Status and Role of.

References

Apffel-Marglin, Frédérique. *Rhythms of Life: Enacting the World with the Goddesses of*

Orissa. New Delhi: Oxford University Press, 2008.

Brooks, Douglas Renfrew. *Auspicious Wisdom: The Texts and Traditions of Shrividya Shakta Tantrism in South India*. Albany: State University of New York Press, 1992.

Kinsley, David. *Hindu Goddesses: Visions of the Divine Feminine in the Hindu Religious Tradition*. Berkeley: University of California Press, 1988.

Pintchman, Tracy. *Seeking Mahadevi: Constructing the Identities of the Hindu Great Goddess*. Albany: State University of New York, 2001.

Shambhala International

Shambhala International is a reformed version of a Tibetan Buddhist organization initially known as Vajradhatu. Vajradhatu was founded in Boulder, Colorado, by an exiled Tibetan lama of the Kagyu lineage, Chogyam Trungpa Rinpoche (1939–1987), in 1973. Chogyam Trungpa was a flamboyant character who, after giving up his monastic vows, gained a reputation as a bon vivant, though his writings on spiritual themes attracted an audience that reached well beyond his personal following.

A major center was founded in Nova Scotia, Canada, in 1983, where the movement's international headquarters are currently located. The headquarters serve more than 100 Shambhala Centers throughout the world in the United States (79), Canada (21), Europe (38), New Zealand (1), Australia (1), and Japan (1). In the mid-1990s the movement claimed a total paid membership of around 4,500.

Chogyam Trungpa developed an eclectic form of Tibetan Vajrayana Buddhism, incorporating elements drawn from the Japanese Zen tradition, Japanese arts, and Western psychology. He attracted followers among artists and writers such as the poet Allen Ginsberg (1926–1997). Ginsberg was particularly associated with the Naropa Institute, an accredited university that Chogyam Trungpa founded in Boulder in 1974. Its curriculum continues to stress the arts, philosophy, and psychology.

Chogyam Trungpa appointed his American disciple Osel Tendzin (Tom Rich) as his successor, but in 1988 it was revealed that he was HIV-positive and that he had passed the condition on to one of his disciples. The revelations led to serious disruptions within the movement that were eventually to be addressed by the creation of a new leadership under the authority of Chogyam Trungpa's eldest son, Osel Rangdrol Mukpo, in 1991. In 1992 he announced his plans to amalgamate all Vajradhatu activities under the new title of Shambhala International.

Shambhala International began formally in 1976 as Shambhala Training, the secular arm of Vajradhatu. The name is drawn from a Tibetan myth that features a kingdom of enlightened beings ruled by sagacious monarchs. The intention of the training is to create people capable of establishing a society that mirrors the Shambhala kingdom in this world. Although Shambhala International's programs include the teaching of meditation practices and deploy Tibetan Buddhist concepts, Shambhala International presents itself as a secular organization. Participants can adhere to their own religious preferences and do not have to think of themselves as Buddhists. Nevertheless, the movement continues to support contemplative centers such as Gampo Abbey in Nova Scotia and conducts weddings and funerals. At the same time, it promotes education and training programs aimed at business corporations as well as individuals.

All of these activities are intended to contribute to Shambhala International's goal of creating what is described as an "enlightened society." For many members, however, the most significant aspect of their participation remains rooted in their personal practice based on Chogyam Trungpa's eclectic interpretation of Vajrayana Buddhism.

Shambhala International
1084 Tower Rd.
Halifax, Nova Scotia B3H 2Y5
Canada
http://www.shambhala.org/

Sandra Bell

See also: Enlightenment; Karma-Kagyupa, Tibetan Buddhism.

References
Bell, Sandra. "'Crazy Wisdom,' Charisma, and the Transmission of Buddhism in the United States."

Nova Religio: The Journal of Alternative and Emergent Religions 2, no. 1 (1998): 55–75.

Dawson, Lorne, and Lynn Eldershaw. "Shambhala Warriorship: Investigating the Adaptations of Imported New Religious Movements." In *Croyancees et Societes*, edited by Bertrand Ouellet and Richard Bergeron, 199–231. Montreal: Editions Fides, 1998.

Trungpa, Chogyam. *Born in Tibet*. London: George Allen and Unwin, 1966.

Trungpa, Chogyam. *Cutting through Spiritual Materialism*. Berkeley, CA: Shambhala, 1973.

Shan Dao

613–681 CE

Master Shan Dao, though not the founder of the Pure Land Tradition in China, was its great popularizer. He was born in Lin Zi, Shang-tong Province, almost three centuries after Hui-Yuan (334–416) the founder. Shan Dao was but 10 when he became a monk and began his study of the Buddhist sutras. His further study of the Meditation on the Buddha Infinite Life Sutra led him to embrace the Pure Land teachings, which focus upon the calling upon the name of Amitabha Buddha in the faith that Amitabha will carry the believer to the Western Paradise upon his or her earthly death. In 641, at the age of 28, he visited the Pure Land teacher Tao-ch'o at Hsyan-chung-ssu Temple, and was further influenced deeply by Tao-ch'o's lecture on the Meditation on the Buddha Infinite Life Sutra.

Several years later, Shan Dao moved to Ch'ang-an, the capital of China under the Tang dynasty (618–970), and began his life of disseminating the practice of invoking the name of Amitabha Buddha. He authored *The Commentary on the Meditation on the Buddha Infinite Life Sutra*, in which he divided Buddhist practices into two categories. Those practices directed toward Amitabha Buddha were correct and all the rest he considered of a lesser nature. The correct practices he listed as invoking the name of Amitabha, chanting sutras, meditating on the Buddha, worshipping images of Amitabha, and singing the praises of the Buddha, the first of the five being the essential one. Importantly, Shan Dao lifted up the vocal invocation of Amitabha while de-emphasizing the visualization of Amitabha in the Western Paradise that Hui-Yuan had seen as a second practice beside calling upon the name of the Buddha. Though placing visualization practices in a secondary level in his writings, he taught visualization, which Hui-Yaun had advocated, to his followers.

Through his many years, Shan Dao is said to have copied by hand more than 100,000 scrolls of the Amitabha Sutra, the main Purer Land text, and produced some 300 mural paintings on Pure Land themes. A legend grew around him which claimed that while he invoked Amitabha, a ray of bright light poured forth from his mouth.

Honen (1133–1212), who founded Pure Land Buddhism in Japan, was converted to his belief and practice from reading the writings of Shan Dao. Honen came to believe Shan Dao was an incarnation of Amitabha and treated his writings as scripture. Subsequently, Honen's student Shinran (1173–1262) listed Shan Dao as one of the three Chinese Pure Land patriarchs and within his own writings quoted Shan Dao extensively.

J. Gordon Melton

See also: Honen; Pure Land Buddhism; Shinran.

References

"Commentary on the Meditation Sutra." Jodo Shu Research Institute. http://www.jsri.jp/English/Pureland/SUTRAS/kammuryoju-kyo/zendocom.html. Accessed May 15, 2009.

The Seeker's Glossary of Buddhism. New York: Sutra Translation Committee of the United States and Canada, 1998.

Shan Tao, and Julian F. Pas. *Visions of Sukhavati: Shan-Tao's Commentary on the Kuan Wu-Liang Shou-Fo Ching*. Albany: State University of New York Press, 1995.

The Soka Gakkai Dictionary of Buddhism. Tokyo: Soka Gakkai, 2002.

Sharad Purnima

Sharad Purnima is a Hindu harvest festival celebrated on the evening of the full moon of the Hindu lunar month of Ashwin (September–October). The month of

Ashwin comes after the annual rainy season. Its major observances are in rural communities.

The celebration is especially directed to Lakshmi, the goddess of wealth and consort of the god Vishnu, who is said to move around in the night asking, "Who is awake?" To those she finds awake, she bestows gifts of wealth.

The origin of the celebration appears to come from Bihar state, where a story is told of a relatively poor brahmin named Valit who left home in disgust with his wife, who was known for her quarrelsome nature. His leaving was occasioned by her disturbing a ritual honoring Valit's ancestors. On his trip he ran into some young girls who were descendants of Kailiya Nag, the giant venomous snake that Krishna had subdued. Valit began gambling with the girls by the light of the full moon and lost what little money he had with him.

At that moment, however, Lakshmi and Vishnu were passing by. Lakshmi graced Valit with a handsomeness similar to that of the god of love. The girls with whom he had been gambling now fell in love with him and gave him all their riches. He returned home and lived happily ever after.

On the night of Sharad Purnima, Dudha-Pauva, a mixture of parched rice made from the recently harvested crops, soaked in cold milk, will be offered to Chandra, the moon deity, and then passed to gathered devotees. Devotees of Durga think of her as having gone into an extended rest following her nine-day war with Mahishasura. On this night, in Durga temples she will be awakened with music and drumbeats and taken in a torch-lit procession around the temple. Devotees of Krishna look upon this night as the anniversary of Krishna's divine play with Radha and the Gopis (cow girls).

Constance A. Jones

See also: Devotion/Devotional Traditions; Hinduism.

References

Mukuncharandas, Sadhu. *Hindu Festivals (Origin Sentiments & Rituals)*. Amdavad, India: Swaminarayan Aksharpith, 2005.

Pattanak, Devdutt. *Lakshmi: The Goddess of Wealth and Fortune—An Introduction*. Mumbai, India: Vakils Feffer & Simons, 2003.

Shasta, Mount

Mount Shasta is an extinct volcano in northern California's Cascade range, near the Oregon border. It rises more than 14,000 feet above sea level, but possibly more important, it stands some 10,000 feet above the surrounding area. It is physically unconnected to the other mountains in the region, thus rising abruptly amid miles of relatively flat ground that encircles it, giving a spectacular view from most directions

Early on, its became integral to the creation myth of the resident Native Americans of the area, most notably the Modoc and Shasta peoples. They tell of the Great Spirit creating the mountain by cutting a hole in the sky and forming the mountain of ice and snow. The Great Spirit used the mountain to step onto the Earth. He created the forests and the animals that inhabited them (especially the grizzly bear) and commanded the Sun to melt the snow, thus providing water for rivers and streams and the fish that fill them. The Great Spirit resided on the mountain. His daughter fell off the mountain. Grizzly bears raised her, and she subsequently married one of them. Her children were the first humans. Their marriage violated the Great Spirit's authority, for which the grizzly was condemned to walk on four legs and their human children were scattered around the world. The mountain also plays a role in a large number of Native stories.

Native Americans still live in the area and continue rituals oriented on the mountain. Each year, for example, members of the Wintu conduct ritual dances aimed at ensuring the continued flow of several sacred springs.

In the 20th century, European Americans inspired by the mountain began to create their own stories of its significance. As early as 1908, an article in the *Overland Monthly* tied the mountain to Lemuria, the lost continent initially hypothesized in the late 19th century to balance speculation on Atlantis, the ancient lost continent believed to have existed in the Atlantic Ocean. California was seen as a remnant of Lemuria, an idea that would then be picked up and popularized by H. Spencer Lewis (1883–1939), the founder of the Ancient and Mystical Order Rosae Crucis (AMORC) and the author of *Lemuria, the Lost Continent of the Pacific*, a 1931 book that has remained in print to the

Mount Shasta in northern California. (Brian Longmore/Dreamstime.com)

present. As the Lemurian legend evolved, it incorporated the idea of a hollow mountain in which surviving Lemurians continued to reside and from which they occasionally emerged to interact with the current inhabitants of the surface world.

Just weeks before the publication of Lewis's book, Guy Warren Ballard (1878–1939) walked the slopes of the mountain where he met a person whom he later identified as Saint Germain, an ascended master from the Great White Brotherhood, a spiritual fraternity believed by many in the Western Esoteric tradition to guide the destiny of humankind. Saint Germain commissioned Ballard as his official Messenger to herald a coming Golden Age. After leaving Shasta and returning to Chicago, Ballard founded the I AM Religious Activity and the Saint Germain Foundation. Both AMORC and the I AM Religious Activity opened centers in Mount Shasta, the community at the base of the mountain, and to the present the I AM movement sponsors an annual pageant on the life of Christ, as

interpreted by Ballard. The unique perspective offered on Christ was that he did not die at the end of his earthly existence but simply ascended into heaven to assume his place in the heavenly hierarchy. Ballard, and later his wife, Edna Ballard (1886–1971), communicated numerous messages from the hierarchy.

The AMORC and I AM accounts of Mount Shasta were bolstered by the sightings of flying saucers that began in the later 1940s and the subsequent reports of contact with the extraterrestrial beings who reputedly inhabited the saucers. Most contactees, the people claiming such contacts, channeled messages from the Space Brothers in the same way that mediums channeled messages from the spirit world. The most famous of the UFO contactees to be identified with Shasta was Dorothy Martin (1900–1992), who moved to Shasta in the 1960s. She took the religious name Sister Thedra and headed the Association of Sananda and Sanat Kumara. Martin had previously gained some fame when she and her small following became the subject of a classic text of sociology, *When Prophecy Fails* (1956), written by Leon Festinger, Henry W. Riecken, and Stanley Schachter.

With the emergence of the New Age movement in the 1970s, Mount Shasta was designated as a modern sacred site and a power spot, a special place where psychical and spiritual energies were concentrated. The mountain began to attract psychics, channelers, and people engaged in various forms of spiritual healing. An active New Age community appeared and swelled every summer. Peter Caddy (1917–1994), one of the founders of the original New Age community at Findhorn, Scotland, moved to Mount Shasta and founded the Gathering of the Way.

Besides those mentioned above, a variety of new Esoteric organizations have come and gone from Shasta over the years. Among those still to be found there are Ascended Masters Teaching Foundation and the Mount Shasta Trinity Center. A spectrum of groups not headquartered in the town hold annual events there. The round of Esoteric spiritual activities and services are covered by the quarterly *Mount Shasta Magazine*.

J. Gordon Melton

See also: Ancient and Mystical Order Rosae Crucis; I AM Religious Activity; Mountains; New Age Movement; Western Esoteric Tradition.

References

Andrews, Richard. *The Truth behind the Legends of Mount Shasta*. New York: Carlton Press, 1976.

Beckely, Timothy Green. *Mysteries of Mount Shasta: Home of the Underground Dwellers and Ancient Gods*. New Brunswick, NJ: Inner Light/Global Communications, 2008.

Cerve, Wishar S. [H. Spencer Lewis]. *Lemuria: The Lost Continent of the Pacific*. San Jose, CA: Supreme Grand Lodge, AMORC, 1931.

Chaney, Earlyne. *Secrets of Mount Shasta*. Anaheim, CA: Stockton Trade Press, 1953.

Clark, Ella Elizabeth. *Indian Legends of the Pacific Northwest*. Berkeley: University of California Press, 1953.

Holsinger, Rosemary. *Shasta Indian Tales*. Happy Camp, CA: Naturegraph Publishers, Inc., 1982.

Marcus. *Celestial Raise*. Mount Shasta, CA: Association of Sananda and Sanat Kumara, 1986.

Mazariegos, Darla Greb. *Mount Shasta*. Mount Pleasant, SC: Arcadia Publishing, 2007.

Melton, J. Gordon. *New Age Encyclopedia*. Detroit: Gale Research, 1990.

Walton, Bruce, ed. *Mount Shasta: Home of the Ancients*. Mokelume Hill, CA: Health Research, 1985.

Shavuot

Shavuot is a Jewish holiday that celebrates God's giving the Torah (or Law, the first five books of the Hebrew Bible). It is also a spring festival that celebrates the first harvest and with it the ripening of the first fruits. Shavuot is known as the Feast of Weeks or of the First Fruits. Christians have an analogous holiday called Pentecost. Shavuot is a two-day holiday that begins at sundown on the fifth day of the Hebrew month of Sivan (usually May or June on the Common Era calendar). It is one of three pilgrimage holy days in the Jewish calendar, when, in the days prior to the destruction of the temple, Jews would normally travel to Jerusalem for the observance. It appears that the shift of emphasis from the harvest to the remembrance of the giving of the Torah occurred at the time of the Jewish exile in Babylon.

The date of Shavuot is tied to Pesach, which celebrates God's freeing of the Jewish people from their enslavement to the Pharaoh. They traveled into the Sinai desert and on Shavuot God gave them the Law. The people committed themselves as a group to be loyal to God. Shavuot is a national holiday in Israel, which sets aside one day for its observance. Outside Israel, it is generally a two-day celebration, except among Reform Jews, who celebrate only one day. While Pesach and Shavuot acknowledge the Exodus events, their dating was also tied to the harvest cycle in Palestine, which began with the harvesting of the barley around Pesach and ended with the harvesting of wheat around Shavuot. Shavuot was the first opportunity each year to being the *bikkurim* (first fruits) to the temple in Jerusalem. The first fruits would include offerings from the seven main plants grown as crops in the region: wheat, barley, grapes, figs, pomegranates, olives, and dates (Deuteronomy 8:8).

There are no specific rituals commanded for Shavuot, but a variety of practices have emerged over the centuries. The main event is a service at the synagogue in which the receiving of the Torah is re-enacted. It begins with the chanting of a seventh-century prayer, the Akdamut (Introduction), followed by the reading of the account of the events at Mount Sinai. The prayer calls upon the Jewish community to remain loyal to their faith. As the Torah reading concludes, the congregation rises and reaffirms their acceptance of it. An important event on the second day of Shavuot is the reading from the book of Ruth, which tells a story that took place at harvest time. Ruth was a non-Jew who accepted the faith.

In remembrance that at the time of the events at Sinai, the people did not yet know the soon to be observed laws concerning the ritual process for killing animals for food, milk-based foods are the main foods served at meals during Shavuot.

J. Gordon Melton

See also: Judaism; Pesach; Reform Judaism; Sinai, Mount.

References

Eckstein, Yecheil. *What You Should Know About Jews and Judaism.* Waco, TX: Word Books, 1984.

Greenberg, Irving. *The Jewish Way: Living the Holidays.* New York: Jason Aronson, 1998.

Schauss, Hayyim. *The Jewish Festivals: A Guide to Their History and Observance.* New York: Schocken, 1996.

Shemini Atzeret

See Sukkot.

Shia Islam

Over the first centuries of its existence, Islam was divided into two main communities, the Sunni and the Shia. The split emerged slowly in the years after the death in 661 CE of Ali ibn Abi Talib, the son-in-law of Muhammad (ca. 570–632) and husband of Fatimah (ca. 605–633). Some among the Muslims developed a special veneration for the physical family of Muhammad. However, after Ali's death, the caliphate (the political leadership of the Arab Muslim community) passed to the Umayyads (that is, caliphs drawn from the clan of Umayyad).

The Shias came to believe that Ali had been the best qualified to succeed Muhammad, rather than the three people chosen as caliph between the Prophet's death and the designation of Ali in 656 as the fourth caliph. Over time, they came to believe that Muhammad had chosen Ali as his successor. The Shias also came to believe that Islam needed an imam (or guide) as a guardian of Islamic revelation and the bearer of the Prophet's authority. Hence the need for those in the Prophet's family to lead them. Gradually, "those of the Prophet's family" came to be seen as Ali, Fatimah, and their progeny.

One center of the Shias (literally, partisans of Ali) was Kufa in Iraq, where Ali had briefly resided. There, followers claimed al-Husan (d. 669), Ali's son, as the successor. After his death, attention turned to his brother, al-Husayn (d. 680). He eventually came to Kufa to assume the leadership of the Shia community. Al-Husayn died in a failed attempt to overthrow the Umayyads. His defeat briefly focused attention on his half-brother, al-Hanafiyya (d. 700).

During the eighth century, various Shia groups with authority placed in varying lines of descent from Muhammad and Ali came to exist, many extinguishing themselves in political opposition to the caliphate. One group, the Imamiyya, traced its lineage through al-Husayn's surviving son, Ali, better known as Zayn al-Abidin (d. 714), and his son, Muhammad al-Baqir (d. ca. 732). The latter was a jurist of note who more clearly articulated the role of the imam as community guide. He also left the community to his learned son, Ja'far al-Sadiq (d. 765), who worked during the turbulent period that saw the Abbasids overthrow the Umayyad caliphate. The various Shia groups supported the Abbasids, but then became the objects of persecution by the new caliphate. Many in Iraq rallied to the side of al-Sadiq, who went on to develop the idea of a sinless and infallible imam as the authoritative spiritual guide needed by humanity. The imam has the knowledge of the Koran, both its exoteric and esoteric teachings, and obedience is properly due him.

As the majority Shia lineage was developing, one problem of note arose when Zayd b. Ali (d. 740), the son of Zayn al-Abidin, was named the new Shia imam. He, however, soon rejected his role and the idea of a physical lineage of imams. He quickly lost the support of the majority, who quickly gave their allegiance to his brother Muhammad al-Baqir, and soon deleted any mention of Zayd as ever having held the office. Zayd found his support in Yemen and a line of imams, each successor chosen for his demonstrated ability rather than parentage, and continued to lead the community of Zaydites.

Following al-Sadiq were seven additional imams, beginning with Musa al-Kazim (d. 796/797), the younger son of al-Sadiq. During al-Kazim's time of leadership, a dispute developed over whether he or his older brother, Ismail (d. 762), was the rightful imam. Ismail had died prior to his father, and the main body of Shias accepted his younger brother as the seventh imam. Some, however (the followers of Ismaili Islam), looked to Ismail as the proper imam and adopted his descendants as their new imams. The Ismailis have splintered into a number of groups, the largest group being the Nizari Ismailis, led by the Aga Khan and organized around His Highness Prince Aga Khan Shia Imami Ismaili Council, and the Shiah Fatimi Ismaili Tayyibi Dawoodi Bohra. Both groups now have their largest followings in India.

The main body of Shias, continuing to recognize the descendants of Musa al-Kazim, eventually came under the leadership of the 12th imam, Muhammad al-Muntazar (d. ca. 879), who had become imam at the age of four in 873. Within a few days, however, the youthful imam disappeared and was never found. He had no brothers, and to all appearances the lineage had died out. A crisis of authority emerged. The leaders of the community proposed a novel hypothesis. They suggested that al-Muntazar had assumed a concealed presence in the world, invisible to humanity. However, he will appear at some point in the future as the chosen one whom the Koran suggested would appear shortly before the end of the world. There was an early expec-

tation that the appearance would occur at some point in the next century.

To continue leadership in the Shia community, a Council of Twelve, the *ulama*, moved into the vacuum created by al-Muntazar's disappearance. They selected one of their number to possess at any moment the authority once held by the imams in Ali's lineage. The ulama assumed more authority century by century as al-Madhi, the Hidden Imam, failed to manifest.

The Shias grew slowly through the 15th century, but in the wake of the Mongol invasion of Persia (Iran) and the rise of the Safawid dynasty at the beginning of the 16th century, Shia Islam became Persia's state religion. The Safawid ruling family claimed a direct lineage from Musa al-Kazim, and Shia Islam subsequently spread throughout the Safawid Empire, which stretched from India to Syria. At the height of its power, the ulama began to appoint judges, ayatollahs, who formed their own courts and had the power of judgment.

Today the Shias, also known as the Twelvers or Ithna-Ashariyah, are the dominant group in Iran, Yemen, and Azerbaijan, and have a slight majority in Iraq. There is a significant Shia minority in Afghanistan, Pakistan, and Saudi Arabia, while smaller Shia communities exist in the other Middle Eastern states and a number of African countries; through the 20th century, they developed in the West.

In Iran, the ulama remains the chief judicial body for the Shia community and the state. It appoints from among its members a single person to be al-Madhi's representative on Earth. One of these representatives, the Ayatollah Khomeini (1902–1989), became world famous when he was at the focus of the Iranian Revolution in 1979. The worldwide Shia community currently (as of 2010) looks to the spiritual leadership of Ayatollah Ali Khamenei (b. 1939), who resides in Tehran.

The Shia community has given birth to a variety of movements. In Iran and Iraq, for example, the community is divided into two major legal schools, the Usuli and the Akhbari. The smaller group, the Akhbaris, found primarily in the southern parts of the two countries, has the more strict interpretation of the law. The larger Usuli School has the more liberal legal perspective and permits some latitude in the interpretation of the law in reaching legal decisions.

2610 | Shiah Fatimi Ismaili Tayyibi Dawoodi Bohra

In Iran, the hope of the appearance of al-Madhi supplied the base upon which two popular movements developed in the 19th century. The first was led by Sayyid Ali Muhammad Shirazi (1819–1850), known as the Bab, or the Gate. The Babi movement then gave birth (after the Bab's execution by the Persian authorities) to the Baha'i Faith, which looked to Mirza Husayn Ali (1817–1892), known as Bahá'u'lláh, or the Glory of God, as the one predicted by the Bab. Even though the Babi movement remained relatively small and confined to Persia, the Baha'i Faith has become an important global religion that understands itself as fully independent of Islam.

Through the centuries, the Shia community has been the source of numerous dissenting groups, more than 70 of which have been identified. Though small, they continue to exist throughout the entire Muslim world (from North Africa to Indonesia). Like the majority communities, they accept the basics of Islam, but they have varying opinions concerning the specifics of eschatology, generally revolving around their belief about the manifestation of the Hidden Twelfth Imam. Additional distinctive groups have emerged out of the Ismaili community around the same set of issues.

J. Gordon Melton

See also: Ali ibn Abi Talib; Baha'i Faith; Bahá'u'lláh; His Highness Prince Aga Khan Shia Imami Ismaili Council; Ismaili Islam; Muhammad; Shiah Fatimi Ismaili Tayyibi Dawoodi Bohra; Zaydites.

References
Bakhash, Shaul. *The Reign of the Ayatollahs: Iran and the Islamic Revolution.* New York: Basic Books, 1984.
Dadtary, Farhad, and Zulfikar Hirji. *The Ismailis: An Illustrated History.* London: Azimuth Edition/Institute of Ismaili Studies, 2008.
Halm, Heinz. *Shiism.* Trans. by J. Watson. Edinburgh: Edinburgh University Press, 1991.
Khomeini, Ruhollah. *Islamic Government.* New York: Manor, 1979.
Tabataba'i, Sayyid Muhammad Husayn. *Shi'ite Islam.* Trans. and ed. by S. H. Nasr. Albany: State University of New York Press, 1975.
Ul-Amine, Hasan. *Shorter Islamic Shi'ite Encyclopedia.* Beirut: n.p., 1969.
Yann, Richard. *Shi'ite Islam.* Oxford: Blackwell, 1995.

Shiah Fatimi Ismaili Tayyibi Dawoodi Bohra

The Shiah Fatimi Ismaili Tayyibi Dawoodi Bohra are the largest of the several branches of the Bohras, Ismaili Muslims who in the 11th century acknowledged the authority of al-Mustali (caliph in Egypt, 1094–1101) and later al-Tayyib, the infant heir to the caliph's throne who had disappeared in 1130. They believe that al-Tayyib was not killed, as most have concluded, and now exists as the Hidden Imam. The leadership of the community was eventually placed under the care of an administrator, who has the title *al-mutlaq*, who possesses all the authority of an imam, as he acts in the absence of the Hidden Imam. Leadership in the al-Tayyib community had arisen in Yemen after being suppressed in Egypt, but in 1517, when the Ottoman Empire extended its boundaries to include Yemen, it moved to Gujarat, India. It later moved to Surat, north of Mumbai, and more recently to Mumbai (Bombay).

The Bohra community went through a crisis of succession in 1589 when the majority party accepted Daud Burhan al-Din (d. 1612) as the new al-mutlaq. Since that time, the position has remained in the family of Daud (or Dawoodi). It continues under the authority of the current al-mutlaq, His Holiness Dr. Syedna Muhammed Burhanuddin, who is aided by a chief assistant (often the designated heir), the *ma'dhun*, and a second assistant, the *mukasir*. Local leadership is provided by priests known as *shayikhs* or *amils*.

When they reach the age of 15, each Bohra takes an oath of loyalty to the community and its leadership. That oath is renewed annually. The Bohras recognize seven (two more than most Muslims) essential pillars of their faith: *walayah* (devotion to Allah, the Prophets, the imam [al-Tayyib], and the al-mutlaq); *taharah* (purity/cleanliness); *salah* (prayers); *zakah* (religious dues); *sawn* (fasting); the *hajj* (pilgrimage to Mecca); and *jihad* (holy war).

The Shiah Fatimi Ismaili Tayyibi Dawoodi Bohra has a college for the training of amils at Surat. Dawoodi Bohras have approximately one million adherents. The majority reside in India, with smaller communities in Pakistan, other Middle Eastern countries, East Africa (since the 18th century), and the West (since the 1950s). Adherents can be recognized by their appearance. Men have beards and wear white, gold-rimmed caps; women wear a colorful dress, the *rida*.

Shiah Fatimi Ismaili Tayyibi Dawoodi Bohra
c/o Dawat-e-Hadiyah
Administration of the 52nd al-Dai al-Mutlaq
His Holiness Dr. Syedna Muhammed
    Burhanuddin
Mumbai
India
http://www.geocities.com/huzefadiwan/index.htm
http://www.torontojamat.com/

J. Gordon Melton

See also: Ismaili Islam; Shia Islam.

References

Amiji, H. M. "The Bohras of East Africa." *Journal of Religion in Africa* 7 (1975): 27–61.

Daftary, Farhad. *A Short History of the Ismailis.* Princeton, NJ: Marcus Wiener, 1998.

Davoodbhoy, T. A. A. *Faith of the Dawoodi Bohras.* Bombay: Department of Statistics and Information, Dawat-e-Hadiyah, 1992.

Roy, Shibani. *The Dawoodi Bohras: An Anthropological Perspective.* Delhi: B. R. Publishing, 1984.

Shikoku Pilgrimage

The Shikoku Pilgrimage is a pilgrimage primarily associated with Shigon Buddhists of Japan, so named as it occurs on the island of Shikoku, the smallest of the four main islands of Japan. The island is particularly associated with Kukai (774–835) (aka Kobo Daishi), the founder of Shingon Buddhism, who was born and spent much time of his life on Shikoku. During his early life he spent a period as a mountain ascetic, spending his quiet time in Shikoku's more secluded holy places.

The pilgrimage includes visits, in memory of Kukai, to 88 of the islands' hundreds of temples. There are claims that he had visited all of them, but records verify his presence at only a very few. In the days before modern transportation, a pilgrimage would take the pilgrim to every segment of the island and take between 50 and 60 days to complete. Today most people use automobiles, though they still wear the traditional white pilgrim's garb.

Traditionally, the pilgrims begin their trip at Kukai's mausoleum located at the Shingon headquarters on Mount Koya near Wakayama (on the main island of Honshu). While there, the pilgrim seeks Kukai's guidance and assistance. A quick boat trip across the Kii Channel takes pilgrims to Tokushima on the island's northeast shore. Generally, the island was walked around the coast with side trips to visit the mountain temples in the interior.

For those unable to make the entire pilgrimage, the most important sites include Zentsuji, where Kukai was born; Shosanji, the mountain temple, where he is known to have performed various rites and austerities; and Cape Muroto, where he meditated and many believe found his religious awakening.

J. Gordon Melton

See also: Koya, Mount; Kukai (Kobo Daishi); Pilgrimage; Shingon Buddhism.

References

Readicker-Henderson, Edward, ed. *The Traveler's Guide to Japanese Pilgrimages.* Trumbull, CT: Weatherhill, 1995.

Schumacher, Mark. A to Z Photo Dictionary/ Japanese Buddhist Statuary. "Kannon." http://www.onmarkproductions.com/html/kannon.shtml.

Statler, Oliver. *Japanese Pilgrimage.* Honolulu: University of Hawaii Press, 1985.

Shin Buddhism

See Pure Land Buddhism.

Shingon Buddhism

The Shingon (or True Word) sects of Japanese Buddhism look to Kobo Daishi (literally, "great teacher"), born Kukai (774–835), as their founder. Kukai arose out of obscurity as a religious seeker at the beginning of the ninth century CE. In 804, he traveled to China, where he studied esoteric Buddhism with Hui-kuo (746–805). He was ordained in 805 and returned to Japan. He spent the next 30 years propagating Shingon and died at Kongobu-ji Temple on Mount Koya in 835.

As in Tibetan Buddhism, Shingon Buddhism teaches that there are three modes of manifestation (the three bodies) of the Buddha, the Enlightened One: *dharmakaya* (truth body), *sambhogakaya* (enjoyment body), and *nirmanakaya* (manifestation body). The dharmakaya is Buddha as unchanging and eternal existence, which Shingon names the Mahavairovcana Buddha,

the primary object of veneration within the community. Buddha may also manifest as a bodhisattva, such as Amida Buddha of the Pure Land tradition.

The dharmakaya is that aspect of the Buddha that has eternal and unchanging existence. This is the foundation of being of all things in the universe. It is also the underlying foundation of being of the two other bodies of the Buddha. In the Shingon tradition, the dharmakaya Buddha is given the name Mahavairocana. Finally, there is the more limited form that Buddha might take in order to deliver instruction to sentient beings such as humans. Such a form was assumed by the historical Buddha Sakyamuni. The focus on Mahavairocana does not limit the attention that a Shingon believer might give to other Buddhas.

Kukai taught that Mahavairocana Buddha was responsible for generating all life in the cosmos and the universe embodies his teachings. The deeds performed by humans, with their physical bodies, their words, and

Narita-san Shinsho-ji (Narita Mountain New Victory Temple) is one of the greatest temples in the Kanto area around Tokyo in Japan. It belongs to the Shingonshu Buddhist sect and contains a vast complex of buildings and grounds. (Mihai-bogdan Lazar/Dreamstime.com)

their spirituality, are those of the Buddha. Once aware of this fact, humans are able to enter a state of Buddha consciousness and attain enlightenment. Through the use of *mudras* (meaningful signs/gestures made with the hand), vocalizing a *mantra* (mystical sounds/words), or contemplating one of the Buddhas, a person can enter the highest states of Buddha consciousness. These practices can all be found in the fire rituals for which Shingon temples have become known. These teachings are found in the primary sacred texts of Shingon, the Dianichi Sutra (Mahavairocana-sutra) and the Kongo-cho Sutra (Vajrasekhara-sutra).

In the 12th century, the Shingon movement divided into two major branches. Kabukan (1095–1145) revived some neglected aspects of Shingon and mixed it with Pure Land emphases such as the repetition of the Nimbutsu mantra and hope of enlightenment in this life and movement into the Pure Land after death. Kabukan's new doctrine, Shingi, was opposed to the traditional or old doctrine, Kogi. Both branches of Shingon would later divide into a number of sub-branches. Some seven sub-branches of the Kogi and two branches of the Shingi were forced to merge in 1941 as World War II began. Most of these sub-branches as well as new ones would reappear after 1945.

The primary bearer of the Shingon tradition is the Koyasan Shingonshu. It and no less than 16 other branches of Shingon are members of the Japan Buddhist Federation. Koyasan Shingonshu has its headquarters at Kongobu-ji Temple where Kobo Daishi is buried. Besides temples across Japan, Koyasan Shingonshu has temples in the United States (17), of which 13 are in Hawaii (2009), and South America (18). In America, the Shingon Buddhist International Institute has been formed to research and promote Shingon thought.

Koyasan Shingonshu
132, Oaza Kotyasan
Koya-cho
Ito-gun, Wakayama
Japan
http://www.koyasan.org/

Koyasan Shingon Mission North America
342 E. 1st St.
Los Angeles, CA 90012

Shingon Buddhist International Institute
PO Box 3757
Pinedale Station
Fresno, CA 93650-3757
http://www.shingon.org/

J. Gordon Melton

See also: Japan Buddhist Federation; Kukai (Kobo Daishi); Pure Land Buddhism; Tibetan Buddhism.

References

Arai, Abbot Yusei. *Shingon Esoteric Buddhism: A Handbook for Followers.* Fresno, CA: Shingon Buddhist International Institute, 1997.

Buddhist Denominations and School in Japan. Tokyo: Bukkyo Dendo Kyokai, 1984.

Hakeda, Yoshito. *Kukai: Major Works.* New York: Columbia University Press, 1972.

Kiyota, Minoru. *Shingon Buddhism, Theory and Practice.* Los Angeles: Buddhist Books International, 1978.

Light of Buddha. Los Angeles: Koyasan Buddhist Temple, 1968.

Murthy, K. Krishna. *Buddhism in Japan.* Delhi: Sundeep Prakashan, 1989.

Shinnyoen

Shinnyoen, Garden of Absolute Reality, a new religion, or *shin shukyo*, based on the esoteric Shingon School of Buddhism, was founded in several stages by Ito Tomoji (1912–1967) and her husband, Ito Shinjo (1906–1989), beginning in 1936 in the Tachikawa suburb of Tokyo; at that time, it was known as the Risshohaku Association. To ensure legal recognition, the movement was affiliated with a well-established Shingon sect, Shingonshu Daigoha, and in 1948 it became a legal religious organization in its own right, using the name Makoto Kyodan, which it changed to Shinnyoen in 1951. Shinnyoen became a religious juridical entity in 1953.

Prior to founding Shinnyoen, Ito Shinjo studied the science of divination known as Byozeisho and also trained at the Daigo School of Shingon esoteric Buddhism, where he received the title of Great Master

(Acharya); his wife inherited an important spiritual gift referred to as *reino*, or spiritual faculty, from her aunt. Believing themselves to be suitably trained and endowed, they together took on the role of "mediums of salvation" for all who were concerned to know their destiny or have their fortunes told.

The tragedy that struck them as parents when their two sons died from an incurable illness in childhood was to be imbued with deep spiritual significance and value. The death of the two brothers, the holy brothers, or *ryodoji sama*, as they are known, was interpreted to mean that the spiritual path uniting this world and the invisible world had been opened, and the Bakku Baiju, or the great power of salvation, had been unleashed.

Shinnyoen stresses its Buddhist credentials and, by contrast with Agonshu, claims to be new and even unique by being the only religion to base its doctrines on what it claims to be the last teachings of the Buddha, Siddhatta Gotama, the Mahaparinirvana, or Great Nirvana, Sutra. Buddha, according to Shinnyoen, revealed that this sutra contained the essence of all his previous teachings. Like so many other Japanese new religions and new, new religions based on one or another of the Buddhist sutras, Shinnyoen is also eager to stress that the teachings of Mahaparinirvana Sutra are open to all to know and understand, and not the exclusive preserve of a few dedicated Buddhist clerics.

There are several levels of spiritual development in Shinnyoen. There is the lay order of monks, which consists of those who have undergone special training and taken formal vows. In addition, there are the four levels of *daijo*, or Mahayana; of *kangi*, or happiness; of *daigangi*, or great happiness; and of reino, or spiritual faculty. Practice of the faith, service to the movement, and engagement in activity to spread the movement constitute the criteria for a member moving from one stage to another.

Like Tenrikyo, Shinnyoen operates on the basis of a lineage system, in the sense that all new members have what is referred to as a "guiding parent," that is, the person who introduced them to the movement. That person continues to assist the new follower, or "guided child," with understanding of the doctrines and with their practice. The doctrines, or "secrets of Buddhism," are derived in the main from esoteric Buddhism and are revealed to followers by mediums—all followers can with appropriate training eventually become mediums—who are believed to receive support from the members of the founders' family, now existing in the spirit world. Mediums are highly regarded as true disciples of Buddha.

Sesshin, or spiritual guidance, is an important part of Shinnyoen practice and is provided with the help of spiritual mediums, or *reinosha*, who act as mirrors for trainees. Such mediums provide four kinds of spiritual guidance (sesshin), two of which are for the general improvement of members—*kojo* sesshin and *sodan* sesshin—and two of which are for the resolution of specific problems—*sodan* sesshin and *kantei* sesshin. Special meditation sessions known as *eza* are provided for those who aspire to higher levels of enlightenment.

Shinnyoen encourages all followers to carry out the Three Practices, which are *kangi*, or joyous offerings leading to the purification of the mind; *gohoshi*, or service leading to the purification of the body; and *otasuke*, or the purification of speech, which consists essentially of sharing the teachings with others and bringing them to the Buddha.

The movement's present leader is Ito Shinso, called by followers Kyoshu-sama, a daughter of the founders. Today there are an estimated 650,000 Shinnyoen members in Japan, and the movement has established centers in the United States, in several European countries, and in Taiwan, Hong Kong, and Singapore. In all of those countries the following is relatively small: for example, there are no more than 1,000 members in Europe.

Shinnyoen, Garden of Absolute Reality
Grand Temple at 1-2-13 Shibazaki-cho
Tachikawa, Tokyo 190-0023
Japan
http://www.shinnyo-en.or.jp/ (in Japanese)
http://www.sef.org/ (in English)

Peter B. Clarke

See also: Agonshu; Shingon Buddhism; Tenrikyo.

References

Nagai, Michiko. "Magic and Self-Cultivation in a New Religion: The Case of Shinnyoen." *Japanese Journal of Religious Studies* 22, nos. 3–4 (1995): 301–321.

Sakashita, Jay. "Shinnyoen and the Transmission of Japanese New Religions Abroad." Ph.D. diss., University of Stirling, Scotland, 1998.

Shiramizu, Hiroko. "Organizational Mediums: A Case Study of Shinnyoen." *Japanese Journal of Religious Studies* 6, no. 3 (1979): 70–82.

Shinran

1173–1263

Shinran, the son of Hino Arinori, a low-ranking courtier in Japan, was the founder of the Japanese Jodo Shinshu tradition, which grew to be the largest branch of Pure Land Buddhism in Japan. Pure Land Buddhism seeks to facilitate the salvation of its members through the simple practice of calling upon the name of Amitabha Buddha (known as Amida Buddha in Japan).

Little is known about Shinran's life prior to his becoming a monk in 1181. He settled in the Tendai monastic complex on Mount Hiei not far from Kyoto. After 20 years of discipline and study, however, he left Mount Hiei. He expressed disenchantment with the monastic life, but had also been drawn to the teachings of Honen (1133–1212), founder of the Jodo-shu, the first of the Japanese Pure Land sects. Shinran studied with Honen from 1201 to 1207 and became an exponent of his belief that anyone who recites the *nembutsu* (that is, repeats Amida Buddha's name "Namu Amida Butsu") and simultaneously entrusts himself or herself to Amida Buddha's vow of compassion (to save all beings at all times and in all places without any discriminations) would attain rebirth in the Western Paradise (the Pure Land). The Pure Land was not the ultimate goal, but it would be a fitting environment where the devotee would be able fulfill the practices that led to Buddhahood.

Honen proposed that the universality of Amida Buddha's vow did not make distinctions between good and evil persons. He also discounted any necessity for long years of study and practice. His ideas were attacked from all elements in the Buddhist community and various leaders petitioned governmental authorities to censure Honen and stop his nembutsu teachings. This pressure, bolstered by the unfortunate action of two disciples who violated a prohibition that had been put in place in 1207 and converted devotees to the Pure Land teachings, prompted the emperor to action. He banished Honen and seven of his leading disciples, among whom was Shinran, from the capital. Honen, now 76 years old, was sent to Shikoku, while Shinran was exiled to Echigo (present-day Fukui and Toyama prefectures) on the Japan Sea coast. The penalties included the loss of their Tendai ordinations. They were, in the eyes of society, mere laypeople.

Accepting his fate, Shinran assumed the name Fuji'i Yoshizane and married. He and his wife had six children. In 1214, Shinran moved with his family to Hitachi (present-day Ibaraki Prefecture) in the Kanto region, where he quietly but actively began to build a large following, primarily among the farmers and trade persons. He established Pure Land meeting centers, which he termed *dojos*. In 1234 Shinran turned the dojos and their respective congregations to his followers and moved to Kyoto with his family.

Shinran would spend much of his life in Kyoto revising the *Kyagyo shinshu* (the full title in English reads *A Collection of Passages Revealing the True Teaching, Practice and Realization of the Pure Land Way*) and writing a variety of essays. The *Kyagyo shinshu* consists almost wholly of passages drawn from the Chinese Pure Land sutras with short commentaries inserted by Shinran. The finished product articulates the spiritual vision of the several Pure Land sutras. The first and most important, the Larger Pure Land Sutra, lists the 48 vows that Dharmakara undertakes to fulfill his quest to become Amida Buddha and establish a Pure Land with the intent to save all beings. Of these 48 vows, Shinran asserted that the 18th is most crucial. It states, "If I were to become a Buddha, and people, hearing my Name, have faith and joy and recite it for even 10 times, but were not born into my Pureland, may I not gain enlightenment."

Over the course of the development of Pure Land thought, the idea of reciting Amida's name evolved to mean uttering the Amida's name in the form "Namu Amida Butsu"—"I take refuge in the Buddha Amida." Invoking the name of the Buddha is now an integral part of the Pure Land devotee's ritual and spiritual life.

In the place of rigorous spiritual discipline, a traditional theme in Buddhist thought, Shinran advocated the centrality of *shinjin*, true or sincere faith, which he found in the writings of the Seven Patriarchs: Nagarjuna (ca. 150–250) and Vasubandhu (ca. fourth century) of India; Tan Luan (476–ca. 542), Dao Cho (562–645), and Shan Dao (613–681) of China; and his fellow countrymen Genshin (942–1017) and Honen (1133–1212). In asserting that faith is central, and echoing themes that would later emerge in Christian Protestant thought, Shinran assumed that the believer possesses nothing true or absolute. Spiritual release comes when the devotee perceives his or her inadequacies and surrenders to the absolute Other Power (*tariki*) of Amida Buddha. Amida Buddha's compassionate efficacy is the source of salvific power. Even shinjin or faith, the prime condition for birth in the Pure Land, emerges as a gift; and the sincere utterance of the nembutsu is an invocation of gratitude and joy for Amida's compassion.

In 1256 Shinran's wife returned to Echigo with three of their children to oversee property that she had inherited. The youngest daughter, Kakushinni, remained in Kyoto to care for her aging father. Following his death, she established the gravesite and chapel that would evolve into the Honganji, the main temple of the Shin tradition.

Over the next centuries, the Shinshu tradition would become the Buddhist tradition with the largest following in Japan. It finds its main expression in its two main divisions, the Honpa Honwanji and Higashi Hongwanji. Pure Land thinkers argued that it is not possible for the laity to engage in long years of discipline and study required by the other sects, and further, the universal accessibility of enlightenment offerred through the Pure Land teaching more closely approximated the Mahayana ideal of universal salvation. Many Buddhists came to agree.

Edward A. Irons

See also: Honen; Jodo-shinshu; Jodo-shu; Nagarjuna; Pure Land Buddhism; Tian Tai/Tendai Buddhism.

References

Dobbins, James C. *Jodo Shinshu, Shin Buddhism in Medieval Japan.* Bloomington: Indiana University Press, 1989.

Kasahara, Kazuo. *A History of Japanese Religion.* Tokyo: Kosei Publishing Company, 2001.

Matsunaga, Alicia, and Daigan Matsunaga. *Foundation of Japanese Buddhism.* Vol. 2. Los Angeles: Buddhist Books International, 1976.

Nakasone, Ronald Y. *Ethics of Enlightenment: Essays and Sermons in Search of a Buddhist Ethic.* Fremont, CA: Dharma Cloud Publishers, 1990.

Ueda, Yoshifumi, and Dennis Hirota. *Shinran: An Introduction to His Thought.* Kyoto: Honganji International Center, 1989.

◆ Shinto

Shinto (the Divine Way), the traditional religion of Japan, is today represented by a spectrum of religious groups in the land of its birth, the largest segment of the movement being Shrine Shinto, which finds embodiment in the thousands of public shrines that dot the landscape. Shrine Shinto was the state religion of Japan in the decades prior to World War II. Sect Shinto designated the 13 Shinto organizations (Kurozumikyo, Shinto Shuseiha, Izumo Oyashirokyo, Fusokyo, Jikkokyo, Shinshukyo, Shinto Taiseikyo, Ontakekyo, Shintotaikyo, Misogikyo, Shinrikyo, Tenrikyo, and Konkyoko) recognized by the government during that period. In addition, there are more than 100 new Japanese religions, some founded before 1945 and suppressed by the government and others founded after 1945, which draw primarily on Shinto themes.

Early in Japan's history, numerous extended family groups (clans) developed, each of which developed religious practices largely tied to its land. There was no central political structure or unified culture. By the third century CE an agriculturally based religion had become prominent, and over the next centuries Japan would come together as a nation around the prominent Yamato clan (the source of the later imperial family). During this formative period, two of what would become leading Shinto shrines, Ise and Izumo, were created.

Crucial to the creation of a national Shinto religion (which incorporated the many local variations) was the introduction of Confucianism and its emphasis on ethics and social order, the spread of the cosmology that divided the world into ying-yang polarities, and

Shinto temple in Japan. (Corel)

later the arrival of Buddhism. Each challenged the elite elements of Japan to create a uniquely Japanese faith comparable to that of neighboring states. One result was the compilation of the Kojiki (712) and Nihon Shoki (720), the two sacred texts of Shinto that describe the overarching myth out of which the many local cults would operate.

Shinto views the world as alive with divinity. The term *kami* refers to the many deities of heaven and Earth who may include among them some human beings and an array of natural objects (birds, plants, and natural features). Anything above the ordinary or that might awaken a sense of awe or mystery in the human mind may be listed as a kami, including the succession of emperors who have led the country.

Although kami of local significance are acknowledged at different shrines, some kami gained a significance as part of the national myth of Japan's origin. The deities Ame-no-mi-naka-nushi-no-Kami (Kami Master of the Center of Heaven), Taka-mi-musubi-no-Kami (High Sacred Creating Kami), and Kami-masubi (Sacred Creating Kami) are seen as the primordial dei-

ties who were present when nothing but the primal chaos existed. They were responsible for the formation of the Earth and the deities who were later to create Japan and its people.

The High Kami in heaven sent the primal parents—Izanagi (male) and Izanami (female). Their interaction gave birth to numerous islands and other deities. Then Izanami was burned as the fire-god was given birth. She descended into the underworld, where she was trapped after eating of its food. In his attempts to free Izanami, Izanagi bathed in the ocean as a cleansing act. His ablutions also resulted in the appearance of Amaterasu, the goddess who is seen as the ancestress of the Japanese imperial family. While at a festival, another kami held a mirror up for Amaterasu to gaze upon herself. She would later give this mirror to her grandson, who was sent from heaven to establish the Japanese royal lineage. The mirror is now said to be residing hidden in the Ise shrine.

Shinto has an essential communal element, and much of its activity occurs in the many shrines that are found throughout Japan. The shrines, abodes of the kami, are generally located in spots of particular natural beauty or some noteworthy geographical feature. The site itself is marked off with a fence, and the entrance with the distinctive gate (*torii*) to which a sacred rope (*shimenawa*) is attached. At the shrine, the kami are invoked on a cycle that follows the agricultural seasons and that affirms the myth of national origins. Many shrines are located at the foot of a mountain, which has the effect of marking the land of death and renewal (the mountain) from the plains, the land of life and activity. Others may be found at the point where two streams merge.

Common elements in Shinto rituals are the offering of foods, which in turn has had a profound influence on the Japanese diet, and purification, harkening back to the baths taken by Izanagi in his attempts to free his wife from the underworld. Food offerings may be classified by type (animal, vegetable, fish), style of preparation (raw or cooked), mode of offering, or whether it is to be viewed by the deities or eaten by them. Frequently the offered food becomes part of a banquet consumed later by the worshippers.

Purification rites have been developed in response to a variety of life's setbacks, from the sickness and death of a loved one to natural calamities and national disasters. They came to include reactions to forms of ritual impurity (from menstruation to sexual activity) and to symbolize the hope of renewal.

After 538, Shinto developed in dialogue with Buddhism, the latter becoming an increasing part of Japanese life. Shinto and Buddhist temples were often constructed adjacent to each other, and they found a common ground in their esoteric element. Buddhists came to accept Shintoism as a lesser form of itself, and locally, syncretistic Buddhist/Shinto cults developed that centered on specific shrines and local deities. Shugendo became one of the more interesting new religions drawing deeply from both Buddhist and Shinto sources.

Shintoism experienced a revival in the 15th century after many shrines were destroyed in the Onin War (1467–1477). Out of the ashes emerged Yoshida Kanetomo (1435–1511), who dedicated his life to their reconstruction (especially those most associated with his prominent family), the return of Shinto supremacy in the land, and the re-establishment of imperial authority. He recast Shintoism as the original faith and the source of Daoism, Confucianism, and Buddhism. He expounded a new theology built around an exoteric teaching (as found in the Kojiki and Nihon Shoki) and esoteric teachings that he claimed had been revealed by deities to his family (resulting in additional scriptural texts). Kanetomo became the leading figure in Shintoism, and his school would dominate the religion during the next centuries.

The work of Kanetomo and his successors would during the Edo period (1600–1868) lead to a shift in Shinto away from a primary dialogue with Buddhism to one with Confucianism. At the same time a new scholarly movement, called *kokugaku* (national learning), attempted to redefine Japanese tradition and self-identity. Hayashi Razan (1583–1657), who led the new trend, emphasized the immanence of the Absolute as the divine within the inner life of the individual, the divine life expressed in ethical behavior, and, most important for Japan's future, the primary manifestation of divine virtue in the imperial government. During the Edo period, especially in the writings of Yoshikawa Koretari (1616–1694), the deity Kuninotokotachi no Mikoto, identified with the primal chaos, emerged as the central figure in the Shinto pantheon.

The continued development of Shintoism in the 18th century set the stage for major developments in the 19th century. The variety of Shinto groups, later to constitute Sect Shintoism, began to emerge. Most of these new groups were the result of the activity of a creative founder who was also responsible for the composing or receiving by revelation of a distinctive new scripture. These groups were later classified by the major themes they developed. Some emphasized attachment to traditional texts (Kojiki and Nihon Shoki), Confucian ethical principles, or purification rituals. The Fuji and Ontake sects emphasized the longstanding worship at sacred mountains. Spiritual healing, utilizing Shinto rituals, became the center of Tenrikyo and Konkokyo.

A new era for Shinto came in 1868 with the emergence of the Meiji government. The new government brought to the fore a form of Shintoism usually referred to as State Shinto. It combined the thought of Hirata Atsutane (1776–1843) with the cult that had grown up around the imperial family. Atsutane had been an effective propagandist of the return of Japan to imperial rule and the establishment of Shinto as the sole religion of the land. State Shinto propagated the belief in the divinity of the emperor and sanctified Japan's national political policies. It proposed as its idea *saisei itchi*, the unity of religion and government. Students of Atsutane were recruited to head a revived Office of Shinto Worship whose initial mandate was the separation of Shintoism from Buddhism and Christianity. As a result, Shinto shrines were stripped of all Buddhist and Christian symbols, and the imperial palace was denuded of the heretofore dominant Buddhist altars and symbols.

In the 1870s, step by step, the government asserted its authority over the Shinto shrines and leadership. The Agency for Spiritual Guidance was given authority over all Shinto priests and designated their place of appointment. The national rituals to be performed at each shrine were also prescribed. The emperor was declared sacred and inviolable in 1889, and, in 1900, Shinto's special place was re-emphasized by its being placed under the Bureau of Shrines in the Home Ministry, while Buddhism and Christianity were relegated to a separate Bureau of Religion in the Ministry of Education. In the meantime, Sect Shinto had an intermediary position. The sects were treated much like Buddhism and Christianity, being seen as private religious organizations under the jurisdiction of the Bureau of Religion. Most important, they were not allowed to create shrines or to copy shrine architecture in their worship centers, including the use of a torii as a gateway entrance.

Increasingly, Shinto was seen as an arm of the state. In 1911 it ordered all schools (including private religious schools) to take their pupils to shrines for nationally directed ritual events. In 1932 a Catholic school refused to comply with the regulation on grounds of religious freedom. Students at one Catholic school had been asked to visit a shrine particularly associated with Japan's military history. As a result of the protest, the government declared the shrines "nonreligious" sites whose task was to foster national loyalty. Shintoism was thus redefined in such a way as to be compatible with any particular religious affiliation; the inclusion of Shinto ritual into both private and public life became a sign of loyalty as Japan went to war. Amulets from the Ise shrine became ubiquitous.

The loss in World War II affected Shintoism most of all. The coming of religious freedom gave Sect Shinto a new life, and several sects emerged as popular movements whose adherents numbered into the tens of thousands. Then, on December 15, 1945, General Douglas MacArthur (1880–1964) issued the "Shinto Directive," which ordered the separation of State Shinto from the government. Most important, the government was to end its support of the shrines. This mandate was embodied in the Constitution of 1947.

In the late 1940s, State Shinto evolved into what is today known as Shrine (*jinja*) Shinto. The formerly government-supported shrines were reorganized into a private religious corporation, the Association of Shinto Shrines, with which the great majority of shrines affiliated. There were more than 100,000 such shrines in 1945. By the beginning of the 1980s, some 79,000 shrines were maintained as part of the new system of voluntary support. Two seminaries, one at Kokugakuin University in Tokyo and the other at Kogakukan University in Ise, train Shinto priests. The Association represents Shintoism in various interfaith activities, including the World Conference on Religion and Peace. It also accepts women into the priesthood.

In spite of the proliferation of Shinto sects, the Association includes the majority of the 2 to 3 million Japanese who identify themselves as Shintoists, the number of whom is somewhat difficult to assess, as many people carry dual affiliations, a continuing result of Meiji era practices. Support for Shintoism in Japan pales next to that for Buddhism, which now commands the allegiance of more than half the population. The special Shinto of the Imperial House (*koshitsu*) also survives in a variety of practices associated with the emperor and his family, the shrines at the royal palace, and the Grand Shrine at Ise. The most important rite is Niinamesai, the annual offering of the first fruits of the grain harvest, which includes a thanks to the deities for their blessing and a sharing of the food with the deities, especially Amaterasu.

The Grand Shrine at Ise, now a popular tourist attraction, includes two shrines. One is dedicated to Amaterasu and, as the shrine of the legendary ancestress of the emperor, has a special relationship to the imperial family. Traditionally, the emperors would make reports to the goddess at the shrine, which was believed to hold the fabled mirror she had passed to her grandson. A second shrine is dedicated to Toyouke, the goddess of food. Every 20 years, new shrines replicating the old ones are erected. Upon their completion, as part of a ceremony of renewal, the ritual objects in the old shrines are transferred to the new ones, and the old shrines are then completely dismantled.

Shinto, as the religion of the Japanese people, has been largely confined to that country. However, early in the 20th century, it was established among Japanese immigrants in Hawaii. Although largely suppressed during World War II, it slowly revived after the war as questions of the loyalties of Japanese Americans were resolved. Shinto has subsequently appeared, in small numbers, in diaspora communities in Canada and South America.

J. Gordon Melton

See also: Buddhism; Confucianism, Daoism; Ise Shrine, The; Izumo Ôyashirokyô; Konkyoko;

Kurozumikyô; Ontakekyo; State Shinto; Tenrikyo; World Conference on Religion and Peace.

References

Bocking, Brian. *A Popular Dictionary of Shinto*. New York: McGraw-Hill, 1997.

Breen, John, and Mark Teeuwen, eds. *Shinto in History*. Richmond, UK: Curzon, 2000.

Hardacre, Helen. *Shinto and the State, 1868–1988*. Princeton, NJ: Princeton University Press, 1991.

Kasulis, Thomas P. *Shinto: The Way Home*. Honolulu: University of Hawaii Press, 2004.

Nelson, John K. *A Year in the Life of a Shinto Shrine*. Seattle: University of Washington Press, 1996.

Ono, Sokyo. *Shinto: The Kami Way*. Rutland, VT: Charles E. Tuttle, 1967.

Yamakage, Motohisa. *The Essence of Shinto: Japan's Spiritual Heart*. Tokyo: Kodansha International, 2007.

Shri Ram Chandra Mission

The Shri Ram Chandra Mission is one of the several neo-Hindu movements that became popular both in India and in the West in the 20th century.

Shri Ram Chandra ("Lalaji," 1873–1931) was born in Fatehgarh (Uttar Pradesh, India) in 1873. In 1908 he returned to Fatehgarh from Kaimganj, where he had lived for several years, and started tutoring a small number of pupils who accepted him as their spiritual master. In 1914 he established his first regular *satsang*, or group meditation, and from 1929 on he consecrated his whole life to teaching and commenting on the Vedas. He died in 1931. His successor, also called Shri Ram Chandra (1899–1983), although not a relative, was born in Shahjahanpur and was known in the movement as Babuji. In 1945 he incorporated the Shri Ram Chandra Mission (named after his master and not himself). Originally a civil clerk (hence the name Babuji, from the word *babu*, meaning clerk), he decided in 1954 to devote himself full-time to the work of the mission and went on to supervise its worldwide expansion. He died in 1983 and was, in turn, succeeded by Shri Parthasarathi Rajagopalachari, born in Madras-Chennai in 1927 and known in the mission as Chariji.

The mission teaches a system of yoga called *Sahaj Marg*. This is a variety of traditional *Raja yoga* (royal yoga), modified in accordance with modern lifestyles. Although other Raja yoga schools have rather complicated and lengthy trainings, Sahaj Marg is basically simple and includes no secret rituals, names, or mantras. New pupils immediately start meditating with the help of a "preceptor" for 30 minutes (later, when they are more experienced, one hour), simply sitting and focusing their attention on the "Divine Light," which is supposed to be already present in their hearts. The mission recommends another 30 minutes of "purification" at the end of each day, in order to clear the mind of the distractions accumulated throughout the day. A short prayer is also suggested before going to bed. This process is known as the "inner trip," or *yatra*, through a number of spiritual realms moving gradually closer to the Center. During this process, the pupil receives help from the transmission of the master's own energy, a "force without force," or without qualification, also known as *pranahuti*, or the gift of life (after *prana*, life; and *huti*, gift). It is possible to achieve a state of union with the divine at the end of the process, and it is this that is regarded as the ultimate aim of true yoga.

In 1967 the Shri Ram Chandra Mission established the Sahaj Marg Research and Training Institute, with headquarters at Chennai (India) and Lausanne (Switzerland) as an international yoga research center. There are more than 50 ashrams in India, the largest of them in Manapakkam, seven miles from Chennai; there are also two ashrams in the United States, and others in Europe, the largest being in Augerans (France) and Vrads Sande (Denmark).

Shri Ram Chandra Mission (Shahjajnpur U.P.)
Manapakkam
Chennai 600 116
India
http://www.srcm.org

Massimo Introvigne and PierLuigi Zoccatelli

See also: Devotion/Devotional Traditions; Yoga.

References

Chandra, Ram. *Truth Eternal*. Chennai, India: Shri Ram Chandra Mission, 1973.

Complete Works of Ram Chandra. 2 vols. Pacific Grove, CA: Shri Ram Chandra Mission, 1989–1991.

Rajagopalachar, Parthasarathi. *My Master.* Chennai, India: Shri Ram Chandra Mission, 1975.

Shugendo

Shugendo, literally the Way (*do*) of practicing or acquiring (*shu*) magico-religious power (*gen*), is the name given to a broad range of beliefs and practices associated with sacred mountains in Japan. It has no actual founder but grew out of loose organizations of people who entered mountains either temporarily or permanently in order to attain the power of the divine forces (*kami*, *hotoke*) associated with them. Stories of ascetics and esoteric practitioners, such as Shugendo's legendary founder En no Gyoja, share motifs of immurement in mountains, restricted diet or fasting, the recitation of mantras, and contemplation. The growing formalization of mountain practices and the incorporation of regional sacred mountains and their practitioners—particularly under Buddhist auspices—led, by the 13th century, to the emergence of two dominant streams of Shugendo, one affiliated with the shrine-temple complex at Yoshino and the other with that at Kumano. By the 17th century, the main streams were Honzan-ha and Tozan-ha, centered on Yoshino-Kumano and affiliated with Tendai and Shingon, respectively; Haguro-ha in northern Japan; and Hikosan in Kyushu. The former two looked on En no Gyoja as their founder, while Haguro and Hikosan maintained local traditions. Shugendo was banned in 1872 as part of the Meiji government's policy of creating Shinto as a state ideology and suppressing all signs of syncretism. Shugendo was particularly vulnerable, because it had developed as an admixture of Japanese beliefs about mountains and their *kami* (deities), esoteric Buddhist practices and doctrines, shamanistic and mediumistic understandings of the relationship between the human and the divine, and Chinese ritual and divinatory techniques. Shugendo sects mushroomed after freedom of religious association was legalized in the postwar constitution.

The practice most associated with Shugendo is that of the Ten Realms. Mahayana Buddhism postulates Ten Realms of rebirth: hells, hungry spirits, beasts, *ashuras*, human beings, heavenly beings, *shravakas* (disciples of the Buddha), *pratyeka*-buddhas (self-enlightened buddhas), bodhisattvas, and buddhas. Shugendo practice in the mountains incorporates the idea of progressing through these realms of enlightenment, combined with an earlier, shamanistic pattern of death and rebirth. Medieval records suggest that this pattern was once widespread; now, however, it survives only at Hagurosan in Yamagata Prefecture.

The Akinomine (Autumn Peak) of Hagurosan, originally lasting more than a month, has gradually been condensed to the present seven days (August 24–September 1). Practitioners divide their time between making pilgrimages to sacred places in the mountains during the day, to access sacred power, and reciting sutras for two sessions of around two hours every night. Six specific practices associated with the first 6 of the 10 realms are carried out in conjunction with symbolic rituals centering on death and rebirth. The hells are represented by a ritual called *nanban ibushi*, in which pungent smoke is fanned through the hall at the end of the sutra-recitation sessions on the first three nights. The hungry spirits are symbolized by fasting on the first three days; the beasts by complete abstinence from the use of water (other than drinking); the ashuras by Tengu-zumo (wrestling); human beings by repentance (repeated prostrations while reciting the names of the deities and buddhas of the mountain); and heavenly beings by *ennen* (sacred dance), though now Noh chants have been substituted. The underlying theme of death and rebirth is symbolized, sometimes in multiple forms, by an initial funeral service (prior to entering the mountain); conception (throwing a pole up the steps of the temple, the touching of blazing torches together); growth in the womb (ceremonies to "pacify the spirit," altar decorations); and birth (uttering the birth cry on the final day, running down the mountain, jumping over flames).

Shugendo doctrine traditionally has borrowed much from Buddhism and has been concerned with esoteric explanations of the meaning of terminology, ritual, and dress. It does not have scriptures as such. In recent years Shugendo centers have made much of the contribution that Shugendo can make to ecological understanding. Although it is traditionally a male preserve, women shugen are active in all centers, though they are still banned from entering the region around Sanjogatake (Yoshino), the most sacred peak of Kumano-Yoshino Shugendo. Full female participation is a continuing controversy here, though in other centers, such as Hagurosan, women have begun to occupy senior positions formerly restricted to men.

Gaynor Sekimori

See also: Birth; Fuji, Mount; Mahayana Buddhism; Mountains; Pilgrimage; Shingon Buddhism; Tian Tai/Tendai Buddhism; Women, Status and Role of.

References

Earhart, H. Byron. *A Religious Study of the Mount Haguro Sect of Shugendo: An Example of Japanese Mountain Religion.* Tokyo: Sophia University, 1970.

Miyake, Hitoshi. *Shugendo: Essays on the Structure of Japanese Folk Religion.* Ann Arbor: University of Michigan Press, 2001.

Sekimori, Gaynor. "The Akinomine of Haguro Shugendo: A Historical Perspective." *Transactions of the International Conference of Eastern Studies*, no. 40 (1995).

Swanson, Paul L. "Shugendo and the Yoshino-Kumano Pilgrimage: An Example of Mountain Pilgrimage." *Monumenta Nipponica* 36, no. 1 (1981): 55–84.

Tyler, Royall, and Paul L. Swanson, eds. "Shugendo and Mountain Religion in Japan." Special issue of the *Japanese Journal of Religious Studies* 16, nos. 1–2 (June–September 1989).

Shwedagon Pagoda

Shwedagon Pagoda, the most sacred Buddhist site in Myanmar, is a stupa designed to hold Gautama Buddha's relics located in Yangon, Myanmar's capital. The founding of Shwedagon seems to harken back to the beginnings of Yangon itself, which prior to the middle of the 18th century was but a small fishing village named Bagan. The village has probably been inhabited since the sixth century BCE; since the area was then

The Shwedagon Pagoda in Yangon, Myanmar. The pagoda was a Buddhist shrine built to house relics of saints. (Corel)

marshy the Singuttara hill may have been a more inviting location, rising above the surrounding marshy land. Also, it may at that time have been associated with a community of people from Orissa, in India.

According to one story, in the fifth century BCE, just as the land was emerging out of prehistory, two Burmese merchants visited Gautama Buddha at Bodhgaya in India. They found him sitting under the Bodhi tree, just seven weeks after he attained enlightenment. Buddha gave the merchants eight strands of his hair, which the two men brought with them when they returned home. The hairs were subsequently enshrined in a casket on Singuttara hill. Reportedly, there was already a shrine housing relics of three earlier enlightened ones. Over the shrine, a stupa was erected. Other stories relate a visit by Ashoka (ca. 304–232 BCE), the Indian king and staunch supporter of Buddhism, who repaired the shrine.

There is actually no written evidence of Shwedagon and the shrines located there until the 15th century, when an inscription telling of a trip by Burmese monks to Sri Lanka for ordination mentions the hill. The inscription is in both the Mon and Burmese languages.

The present stupa, the centerpiece of the complex, was erected in the 1770s. It rests on a raised platform and reaches some 321.5 feet into the air. It is plated with 53 tons of gold. At the very top of the stupa's spire is the "diamond bud" (*sein-bu*), which holds an orb encrusted with 4,351 diamonds—including one measuring 76 carats. Around its base are four large devotional halls, called *tazaung*, in the center of each of the four sides surrounding the stupa. There are an additional 64 smaller shrines, called *zeidi-yan*, between each of the tazaung. These smaller shrines were added in the early 1900s.

The British turned Yangon into the capital of the country (then called Burma) in 1885. During the British era, which ended in 1948, it was known as Rangoon.

Edward A. Irons

See also: Ashoka; Bodhgaya; Enlightenment; Relics.

References

Aung, Myint, Thaung Wai, and U Kyi Win, eds. *Shwedagon: Symbol of Strength and Serenity*. Yangon, Myanmar: Yangon City Development Committee, 1997.

Moor, Elizabeth, U Win Pe, and Hansjörg Mayer. *Shwedagon: Golden Pagoda of Myanmar*. London: Thames & Hudson, 1999.

U, A. Than. *Shwedagon*. Rangoon: Government of Burma, 1957.

Siddha Yoga

Siddha Yoga is a registered trademark of the SYDA Foundation, which was established in 1974 to support the teaching work of the Hindu monk Swami Muktananda (1908–1982), who considered himself to be a spiritual successor to Nityananda (1897–1961), an ecstatic believed to have magical powers and who spent the later years of his life bathing in the hot springs in Ganeshpuri Village about 50 miles northeast of Mumbai. Each of them attracted a following that included leading members of government and the finance and film industries in India. With considerable help from New Age sages Richard Alpert (Baba Ram Dass) (b. 1931) and Werner Erhard (born John Paul Rosenberg, 1935) and from New Journalism writer Sally Kempton, after 1970 Muktananda was able to extend his own following to affluent and elite sectors of society in Los Angeles, New York, and beyond.

Muktananda described Siddha Yoga as a spiritual path based on grace. It is a devotional movement in which the master or presiding guru is believed to function as a channel of grace for the benefit of the devotee. While spiritual disciplines or practices are strongly recommended to followers, the sine qua non is the presence of the person and the awakening of the inner spirit of the master. Recommended practices include a vegetarian diet, a daily routine that includes singing Hindu religious songs and chanting prescribed traditional texts, donating time and money to service of the guru, and silent meditation. Although this can be done alone at home, attendance at programs periodically scheduled at a local Siddha Yoga mediation center and on special occasions at a more distant gathering place or ashram is encouraged, too. However, with the availability of streaming video and digital recordings, the experience of the guru's presence increasingly is virtual rather than literal.

There is no universally agreed founding date for the movement. It may have had its starting point in Muktananda, who repeatedly said that Nityananda initiated him and ritually installed him as a guru in his own right on August 15, 1961. But before that, as early as 1956, Muktananda had begun to attract followers to his small Gavdevi Ashram, later enlarged and renamed Gurudev Siddha Peeth, just outside Ganeshpuri. Later, in three so-called world tours during the 1970s, he visited Australia, Europe, and the Americas, where he was lionized as "the guru's guru" perhaps due to endorsements by Alpert, Erhard, and others or else the celebrity bestowed by an influential article in *New York* magazine written by Sally Kempton, who soon after became a press agent and editor for the guru. She continued to serve as a very influential member of the movement's small monastic order until her departure from the organization in 2002.

Muktananda's reputation declined in the final years of his life due to allegations of secret sexual activities with young female devotees. Although he made oblique reference to the allegations in an open letter that was distributed before he died, the SYDA Foundation has refrained from making any official response to the reports. The way in which Muktananda arranged for two co-equal successors to assume leadership after his passing was almost as controversial, and within three years produced a schism in which Swami Chidvilasananda (born Malti Shetty in 1955) was successful in retaining the full resources of the Foundation while her younger brother, Swami Nityananda (born Subash Shetty in 1962), carried few followers away when he established his new organization called Shanti Mandir.

Siddha in its Hindu context may mean complete, perfected, or fully realized, and the movement takes it to mean that the sources, methods, and goals affirmed in its devotional theology of grace are indeed perfectly capable of completely transforming the devotee into a liberated being. Nityananda of Ganeshpuri, Swami Muktananda, and Swami Chidvilasananda are represented as illuminating models of the archetype of the Siddha in a personal form and as mediators of an invisible transcendent realm called Siddha Loka, which is functionally similar to the realm of ascended masters found in I AM, Theosophy (Theosophical Society), and similar modern revivals of ancient teachings. Many Siddhas are likely to be alive on the planet at any time, but only a highly evolved being can discern them. By definition each guru in the lineage of masters in the Siddha Yoga movement is such a being. The guru is assumed to be a capable guide for devotees in two basic ways: as an instructor and as a transmitter of enabling power for complete spiritual development.

Siddha Yoga teachings are drawn from many kinds of written and oral sources, mainly Hindu, but without limitation to any single sector of the tradition. They come from texts of the Veda, Advaita Vedanta, Saiva Agama, and Tantra, and give special prominence to Kashmir Saivism and to devotional texts that honor the role of the guru and that praise Hindu goddesses. Siddha Yoga seems to have an open or an emerging canon of scripture that is determined by the presiding guru's assessment of what the devotees need. Devotees, in turn, can practice Siddha Yoga at home, in groups, or by enrolling for fee-based short courses without relinquishing the religion of their birth or family. From a devotee's point of view, the key feature of Siddha Yoga is a relationship to the guru as a spiritual catalyst, expressed through affiliation rather than membership.

Siddha Yoga
PO Box 600
371 Brickman Rd.
South Fallsburg, NY 12747-5313
http://www.siddhayoga.org/

Gene R. Thursby

See also: I AM Religious Activity; Kashmir Saivism; Meditation; Tantrism; Theosophical Society (Adyar); Vegetarianism; Yoga.

References

Altglas, Veronique. "The Global Diffusion and Westernization of Neo-Hindu Movements: Siddha Yoga and Sivananda Centres." *Religions of South Asia* 1, no. 2 (2007): 217–237.

Caldwell, Sarah. "The Heart of the Secret: A Personal and Scholarly Encounter with Shakta Tantrism in Siddha Yoga." *Nova Religio* 5, no. 1 (2001): 9–51.

Pechlis, Karen. "Gurumayi, the Play of Shakti and Guru." In *The Graceful Guru: Hindu Female Gurus in India and the United States*, edited by Karen Pechlis, 219–243. New York: Oxford University Press, 2004.

Williamson, Lola. "The Perfectibility of Perfection: Siddha Yoga as a Global Movement." In *Gurus in America*, edited by Thomas A. Forsthoefel and Cynthia Ann Humes, 147–167. Albany: State University of New York Press, 2005.

■ Sierra Leone

Sierra Leone is an African nation situated on the Atlantic Ocean between Guinea and Liberia. A variety of African peoples, including descendants of people freed

SIERRA LEONE

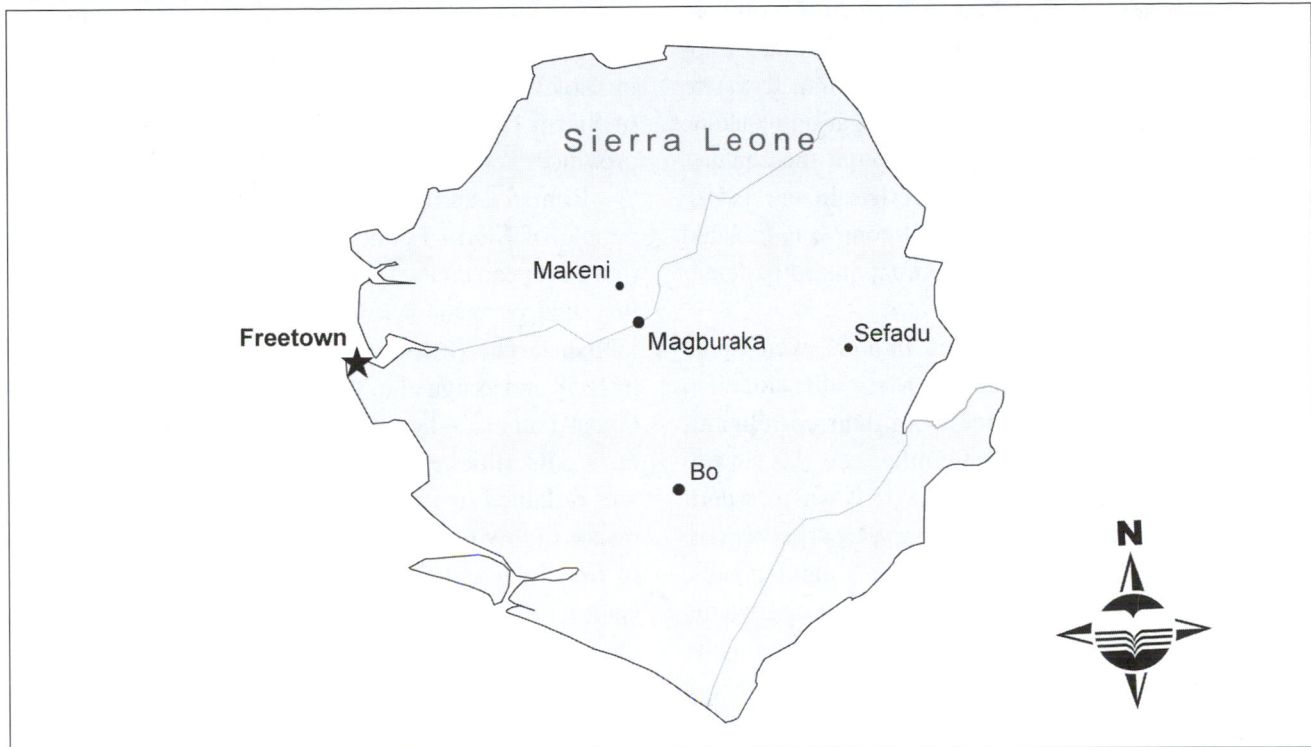

from slavery by the British and deposited at Freetown, make up the present population of 6,300,00 people who inhabit the country's 27,700 square miles of land.

Sierra Leone was originally settled by a spectrum of peoples, the Temne (in the north) and Mende (in the south) being the largest. From the 15th to the beginning of the 19th century, the coast was visited by the Portuguese and other slavers, gathering people to ship to the Americas, but settlements were sporadic.

A new era for Sierra Leone began in the 1780s. British abolitionists purchased a small tract of land for the settlement of repatriated former slaves. The first settlers arrived in 1787, and their numbers grew in 1792 with a group from Nova Scotia. Following the America Revolution, former slaves who had sided with the British on the promise of freedom after the war were relocated to Nova Scotia. Many, uncomfortable with the climate, accepted the offer of British abolitionists for relocation to Africa. The former Nova Scotia residents landed at what in 1792 would become known as Freetown. A third group (the Maroons) would arrive from Jamaica in 1800, and the population would grow

with other former slaves as well. But also, within a generation, the settlement would be co-opted by the British government as its drive to control Africa emerged. The repatriated Africans, known as Creoles, would become a distinct group, identified by their adoption of European ways and their feeling of superiority to the Native peoples.

The small Freetown settlement became the capital of the new colony of Sierra Leone, and the British took control of the inland areas over the course of the 19th century. In 1960, Sierra Leone became an independent state, but in 1971, after several years of instability, it broke ties with England and declared itself a republic. However, poverty, corruption, and unrest have continued to the present and culminated in a decade-long civil war (1991–2001). An unstable condition remains from the war years, and UN peacekeepers continue to monitor the situation.

Among the former slaves who settled in Nova Scotia were Methodists and Baptists. Upon their arrival in Freetown, they founded the first Christian churches. David George (1743–1810) was the leader of the Nova

Scotian Baptists and became the pastor of the Freetown Baptist Church, the first Baptist congregation on the African continent. Prior to the American Revolution, he had formerly been a member of the all-black Baptist church in Silver Bluff, South Carolina. It was to be a generation before a second congregation would be established. The work struggled through the century, aided briefly by the Southern Baptists in the 1850s. The Baptist Convention of Sierra Leone was founded in 1974, but by the end of the century it still had only about 6,000 members.

The Methodists who arrived in 1792 were some 200 strong. After opening the first Methodist church in Africa, they sought assistance from their co-religionists in England, but the British conference was slow to develop a missionary consciousness; it was not until 1811 that they recruited a missionary, George Warren, to assist with the work. He died after only eight months, and his successors quarreled with the congregants and split the work into several factions. In the middle of the century, the United Brethren in Christ (now a constituent of the United Methodist Church) began a separate work, and later in the century the Wesleyan Methodist Connection (now an integral part of the Wesleyan Church) and the African Methodist Episcopal Church assumed support for missionary efforts. At the end of the 20th century, all of these works continued, with the original Methodist Church of Sierra Leone being the largest. It is the only Sierra Leone–based church that is a member of the World Council of Churches.

Men who had been active in creating Freetown were among the founders of the Church Missionary Society (1799). As might be expected, the Church Missionary Society turned its attention to Sierra Leone as one of its first missionary targets. They hoped to convert the Creoles and to use them to missionize the continent. The climate took its toll on the British missionaries, and many died, but along the way they founded two schools that became important in the colony's development, Fourah Bay College (for men) and Annie Walsh Training Institution (for women). As quickly as possible, they trained African priests. A diocese was erected in 1852, thus allowing for the ordination of African clergy without the necessity of their traveling to England. A European held the episcopal chair until the middle of the 20th century.

In 1951, Sierra Leone was one of five Anglican dioceses that merged to form the Church of the Province of West Africa. Moses Scott, the African bishop of Sierra Leone, was the first archbishop of the new province. There are now two dioceses in Sierra Leone.

Roman Catholics made initial efforts to reach the people of Sierra Leone over the centuries since the first European contact, but it was not until the 19th century that permanent missions and churches were established. The vicariate of Sierra Leone was designated in 1858 and assigned to the Lyons Fathers and the Holy Ghost Fathers. The church experienced slow growth during its initial century. The first Sierra Leone priest was ordained in 1939. In 1950, Rome assumed direct responsibility for the work and established the dioceses of Freetown and Bo. In the 20th century, the Roman Catholic Church became the largest religious group in the country.

A variety of Protestant and Free church groups arose in Sierra Leone over the course of the 20th century. As early as 1905, two young women who had been influenced by the Pentecostal revival in Los Angeles began a small mission in Freetown, and then directed work among the Kru people and other groups (Kissi, Limba, Loko) in the extreme eastern part of the country. This work was later assumed by the Assemblies of God. The New Apostolic Church, which began work in the 1960s, has also enjoyed great success.

The original Methodist Church, though not from any desire of its own, became the first of African Initiated Churches, both in Sierra Leone and the whole of the continent. A number of independent churches arose in Sierra Leone during the 20th century, including some from other countries, such as the Church of the Lord, Aladura and those indigenous to Sierra Leon, such as the National Pentecostal Church.

While Christianity entered from the coast, Islam entered from the interior. Sunni Islam of the Malikite School had been established in West Africa in the 11th century. It found a response in the northern and western parts of the country among the Susu, Vai, Bullom, Yalunke, and Temne. During the 20th century, many Mende became Muslim. Unlike some nearby countries,

Sierra Leone

Religion	Followers in 1970	Followers in 2010	% of Population	Annual % growth 2000–2010	Followers in 2025	Followers in 2050
Muslims	1,011,000	2,887,000	46.7	4.32	4,200,000	6,805,000
Ethnoreligionists	1,466,000	2,421,000	39.1	3.84	3,003,000	4,164,000
Christians	218,000	767,000	12.4	5.94	1,232,000	2,151,000
Protestants	97,800	328,000	5.3	1.92	480,000	800,000
Independents	19,000	175,000	2.8	2.23	315,000	600,000
Roman Catholics	47,500	227,000	3.7	22.25	400,000	700,000
Agnostics	0	90,000	1.5	4.32	170,000	350,000
Baha'is	750	14,700	0.2	4.32	25,000	40,000
Hindus	1,400	3,200	0.1	4.32	6,000	8,000
New religionists	100	1,400	0.0	4.31	2,600	5,000
Atheists	0	200	0.0	4.26	500	1,000
Total population	**2,697,000**	**6,185,000**	**100.0**	**4.32**	**8,639,000**	**13,524,000**

such as French-speaking Senegal, the Sufi brotherhoods are not very active in Sierra Leone.

Sierra Leone has been especially responsive to the Ahmadiyya Muslim movement, which many Muslims consider sectarian and even heretical. The Ahmadiyyas began work in 1957 and have found their best response among the Mende people (now comprising 90 percent of the Ahmadiyya membership). The Baha'i Faith has also had considerable response and now reports more than 10,000 members.

The liberal Protestant churches in Sierra Leone are associated together in the Council of Churches in Sierra Leone, which is affiliated with the World Council of Churches. More conservative bodies are associated with the Evangelical Fellowship of Sierra Leone, which is an affiliate of the World Evangelical Alliance. The Interreligious Council of Sierra Leone (IRCSL), a broad-based organization representing the major Christian and Muslim organizations in the country, has been active in the search for peace in the war-torn land.

The violent situation in Sierra Leone during the 1990s has not been conducive to the influx of new religions, and the country's religious pluralism remains confined to the traditional religions of the native people, Islam, and Christianity. There is a small Hindu presence among Indian expatriates and a small group related to the Ancient and Mystical Order Rosae Crucis.

J. Gordon Melton

See also: African Initiated (Independent) Churches; African Methodist Episcopal Church; Ancient and Mystical Order Rosae Crucis; Assemblies of God; Baha'i Faith; Church Missionary Society; Church of the Lord; Church of the Province of West Africa; Holy Ghost Fathers; Malikite School of Islam; Methodist Church of Sierra Leon; New Apostolic Church; Roman Catholic Church; United Methodist Church; Wesleyan Church; World Council of Churches; World Evangelical Alliance.

References

Fisher, H. "The Ahmadiyya in Sierra Leone." *Sierra Leone Bulletin of Religion* 2, no. 1 (1960): 1–10.

Hanciles, Jehu. *Euthanasia of a Mission: African Church Autonomy in a Colonial Context.* Westport, CT: Praeger, 2002.

Olson, G. W. *Church Growth in Sierra Leone: A Study of Church Growth in Africa's Oldest Protestant Mission Field.* Grand Rapids, MI: William B. Eerdmans Publishing Company, 1969.

Sierra Leone Studies Association. *Islam and Trade in Sierra Leone.* Trenton, NJ: Africa World Press, 1997.

Skinner, D. E. "Islam in Sierra Leone during the Nineteenth Century." Ph.D. diss., University of California, 1971.

Sikh Dharma

Sikh Dharma, an outgrowth of—and successor organization to—the Healthy, Happy, Holy Organization, was founded by Yogi Bhajan (1929–2004) in 1969. Bhajan was a well educated Sikh and former customs officer from Delhi, India. He moved to Toronto, Canada, in 1968, where he initially taught hatha yoga classes. From Toronto he moved to Los Angeles in December 1968, and the next year he founded an ashram and the Healthy, Happy, Holy Organization (3HO). People were attracted to 3HO by Bhajan's classes in Kundalini Yoga and Mahan Tantric Yoga, previously a secret practice. Yogi Bhajan's teachings, which initially focused on yoga disciplines, gradually changed to emphasize an increasingly orthodox form of Sikhism, the religion in which Bhajan was raised. This new focus was reflected corporately when 3HO was supplanted by Sikh Dharma. 3HO was retained as Sikh Dharma's educational wing.

Like many of the other Eastern religious groups that took root in the West during the later years of the 1960s counterculture, 3HO initially attracted disaffected young people. As a consequence, individuals associated with Bhajan's Sikh Dharma are usually Westerners rather than Punjabis. (Punjab, a province in northwest India, is the Sikh homeland.) They take formal initiation into the Sikh faith by joining the Khalsa, the Brotherhood of the Pure Ones, a fellowship begun by Guru Gobind Singh. Members of the Khalsa are required to keep the traditional practices introduced by Guru Gobind Singh that became the distinguishing marks of the Sikh community, known popularly as the five k's: *kesh*, long hair, a sign of saintliness; *kangh*, a comb for keeping the hair neat; *kach*, short pants, for quick movement in battle (later interpreted as the admonition to wear underwear, which in South Asia is associated with sexual control); *kara*, a steel bracelet signifying restraint; and *kirpan*, a sword of defense (it later became acceptable for Sikhs to carry a sword symbolically).

3HO Sikhs are vegetarians, usually preferring natural foods. Fish, meat, alcohol, and drugs are prohibited. They also prefer natural methods of healing. Additionally, the traditional religious practices and holidays of Sikhism are observed by 3HO Sikhs. These holidays include Balsakhi Day, the birthday of Khalsa (April); the Martyrdom days of Guru Tegh Bahadur (November) and Guru Arjun Dev (May); and the birthdays of the 10 gurus.

There has been a good deal of controversy with respect to Sikh Dharma's relationship with the older Punjabi Sikh community. American Sikhs criticized Punjabi Sikhs for becoming lax in their discipline, especially in their adherence to the five k's. Additionally, in the 1970s, Sikh leaders in Amritsar took the unprecedented step of giving Bhajan administrative authority over Sikh affairs in the Western Hemisphere, an appointment that carried with it the title Siri Singh Sahib. Some Punjabi Sikhs living in the West were outraged by this appointment. Rather than challenging Amritsar, however, they responded by criticizing Bhajan on such issues as his emphasis on yoga and diet—an emphasis that is not part of traditional Sikhism. Other Sikhs in India echoed this line of criticism. Although these issues were never resolved, Bhajan's emphasis on orthodoxy was supported by Amritsar. New controversies arose following the upheavals that took place in the Punjab in the 1980s, with Bhajan coming under attack from Sikh nationalists for his refusal to support an independent Sikh homeland.

Sikh Dharma centers may be found in more than 20 countries around the world, including Taiwan, Australia, South Africa, Brazil, and many of the European nations.

Sikh Dharma
Rt. 3
Box 11 32D
Espanola, NM 87532

Sikh Dharma International Secretariat
PO Box 351149
Los Angeles, CA 90035
http://www.yogibhajan.com
http://www.3ho.org

James R. Lewis

See also: Guru Gobind Singh's Birthday; Martyrdom of Guru Arjan; Martyrdom of Guru Tegh Bahadur; Meditation; Nanak, Guru; Sikhism/ Sant Mat; Summer Solstice; Vegetarianism; Yoga.

References

Dusenbery, Verne A. "Punjabi Sikhs and Gora Sikhs: Conflicting Assertions of Sikh Identity in North America." In *Sikh History and Religion in the Twentieth Century*, edited by Joseph T. O'Connell, Milton Israel, and Willard G. Oxtoby, 334–355. Columbia, MO: South Asia Books, 1988.

Elsberg, Constance Waeber. *Graceful Women: Gender and Identity in an American Sikh Community*. Knoxville: University of Tennessee Press, 2003.

Jakobsh, Doris. "3HO/Sikh Dharma of the Western Hemisphere: The 'Forgotten' New Religious Movement?" *Religion Compass* 2 (2008).

Khalsa, Kirpal Singh. "New Religious Movements Turn Towards Worldly Success." *Journal for the Scientific Study of Religion* 25 (1986): 233–245.

Khalsa, Shanti Kaur. *The History of the Sikh Dharma of the Western Hemisphere*. Española, NM: Sikh Dharma Publications, 1995.

Laue, Thorsten. *Kundalini Yoga, Yogi Tee und das Wassermannzeitalter. Religionswissenschaftliche Einblicke in die Healthy, Happy, Holy Organization (3HO) des Yogi Bhajan*. Münster, Germany: LIT, 2007.

Tobey, Alan. "The Summer Solstice of the Healthy-Happy-Holy Organization." In *The New Religious Consciousness*, edited by Charles Y. Glock and Robert N. Bellah, 5–30. Berkeley: University of California Press, 1976.

◆ Sikhism/Sant Mat

Sikhism was founded by Guru Nanak (1469–1539) in 16th-century India. Nanak was born into a Hindu family in Punjab, a province in northern India. Although Hindus constituted a majority of the population, in Nanak's time Muslims ruled most of the subcontinent. He took instruction in Hindu lore from a village teacher and also attended a Muslim school. Although certain older interpreters of the Sikh tradition asserted that he was attempting to reconcile Hinduism and Islam by forming a syncretism of the two, the consensus of more recent scholarship is that Nanak saw him-

Sikh men bathing in the holy pool at the Golden Temple of Amritsar in Punjab, India, 2007. (Jeremy Richards/Dreamstime.com)

self as founding a completely new religion superseding both Hinduism and Islam.

Sant Mat, by way of contrast, is a *sampradaya*—a school of religious teaching transmitted through a line of gurus—that, at least traditionally, did not seek to establish itself as a separate religion. The Sant teacher Ramananda, for example, stayed within the Hindu fold, while Kabir, perhaps history's most famous Sant master, remained identified as a Muslim. Although Sant Mat arose in North India during the late Indian Middle Ages, the core meditation technique of the school, Surat Shabd Yoga, or Nad Yoga, appears to be much more ancient.

Sikhism and Sant Mat have been associated with each other for a number of different reasons. These include their common location and period of origin, the many shared themes in their teachings, similar conceptions of the divine, and the fact that the majority of contemporary Sant Mat teachers are Sikhs. Some early 20th-century scholars went so far as to claim that Guru Nanak was actually a student of Kabir—a speculative assertion with no documentable historical basis. Mainstream Sikhs do not practice Surat Shabd Yoga and would adamantly reject any suggestion that Nanak and the other Sikh gurus were part of the Sant Mat tradition. The following discussion will survey first Sikhism and then Sant Mat.

At about the age of 16, Guru Nanak became an accountant in the household of an important Muslim official in the town of Sultanapur. He began to gather a group of followers who bathed together in a river before dawn every day and met in his home in the evening to sing religious songs. One day he failed to return from his morning swim. His friends found his clothes on the banks of the river and dragged the waters in an unsuccessful attempt to recover his body. Three days later, Nanak reappeared. He is said to have stated at the time: "There is neither Hindu nor Muslim, so whose path should I choose? I shall follow God's path. God is neither Hindu nor Muslim and the path which I follow is God."

Later he explained that during the time he was missing he had been carried into God's presence, where he had received a cup of nectar and a message from God to go forth into the world to teach the repetition of the name of God and the practices of charity, meditation, and worship.

Nanak traveled widely to spread his religious message. According to tradition, he made four journeys, visiting Assam in the east, Sri Lanka in the south, Ladakh and Tibet in the north, and Mecca, Medinah, and Baghdad in the west. Nanak's followers began to call themselves *sikhs*, which means students or disciples.

In 1504, India was invaded by a Muslim conqueror from Central Asia. By 1525 the sultan of Delhi had been deposed and the Mogul Empire established in its place. During this time of upheaval, Nanak looked for a place of refuge and stability. He and his family established a religious center at Kartarpur, a village built on land donated by a wealthy member of the new faith.

Nanak stressed that there is but one God. Although he regarded his revelation as transcending both Islam and Hinduism, his teachings also embodied certain traditional South Asian ideas, such as karma, reincarnation, and the transitory nature of the world. He emphasized the unique role of the guru as necessary to lead people to God. He urged his followers to meditate, worship God, and sing devotional hymns.

According to Sikhism, the ultimate purpose of religion is union with God through his indwelling presence in the human soul. Receiving divine grace in this way, human beings are freed from the cycle of birth and rebirth, and then pass beyond death into a realm of infinite and eternal bliss. Nanak's teaching offered a clear and simple path to this goal. By meditating on the divine name, human beings are cleansed of their impurities and enabled to ascend higher and higher until they achieved union with the eternal one. Sikhs hold that suffering in the world arises as a result of humanity's separation from God.

Toward the end of his life, Nanak ensured that his teaching would not die but would survive and become a new religion. He appointed a successor, Lehna, passing over his own two sons, whom he did not regard as suitable. Nanak gave Lehna a new name, Angad, meaning "limb." Lehna would become a "limb" or a part of Nanak. After Guru Nanak's death in 1539, Angad became the second of what would become 10 Sikh gurus. He compiled a hymnal of Guru Nanak's compositions, to which he added his own.

The third guru, Amar Das, served from 1552 to 1574. He dug a well with 84 steps at Goindwal that became a place of pilgrimage and a focus of special rites and festivals. Amar Das nominated his son-in-law Ram Das Sodhi as the fourth guru. Thereafter the guruship remained in the Sodhi family. The fourth guru, Ram Das, began the Golden Temple of Amritsar, the present headquarters of the world Sikh community. He nominated his son Arjan as the fifth guru.

Arjan completed the Golden Temple, which is still Sikhism's central shrine, with four doors on four sides to indicate that it was open to all castes. He also installed the Adi Granth (First Book), the collected writings of Nanak and the other gurus, within it. Arjan was eventually tortured and executed by the Mogul emperor. His martyrdom ended the first phase of Sikhism. Before his imprisonment, Arjan had nominated his son Hargobind as the sixth guru and girded him with two swords, symbolizing spiritual and temporal power. He left instructions that his son should "sit armed upon the throne and maintain an army to the best of his ability."

The sixth guru, Hargobind, established a group of horse and foot soldiers. He was imprisoned by the Mogul emperor for several years, but upon his release he regrouped and fought against the Moguls. The seventh guru was Hargobind's grandson Har Rai. The eighth guru was Har Rai's son Harikrishan, who died as a child. Upon the death of the young eighth guru, the Mogul emperor nominated a successor. The Sikhs, however, acclaimed Tegh Bahadur as their ninth guru. Guru Tegh Bahadur traveled through the Punjab preaching. His popularity prompted the Mogul emperor to have him arrested and beheaded in 1675.

The 10th guru, Gobind Singh, completed the Adi Granth and further militarized the Sikhs by forming the Khalsa, the Community of the Pure. Members of the Khalsa were initiated by a baptism in which they drank and were sprinkled with sweetened water stirred with a sword. They added *Singh* (Lion) to their name and adopted the five *k*'s: *kesh*, long hair, a sign of saintliness; *kangh*, a comb for keeping the hair neat; *kach*, short pants, for quick movement in battle; *kara*, a steel bracelet signifying sternness and restraint; and *kirpan*, a sword of defense. The Khalsa was open to men and women of all castes. Members were admitted only after an initiation ceremony at which they pledged themselves to an austere code of conduct. Each morning they were to bathe at dawn and spend time in meditation. Liquor, tobacco, and narcotics were forbidden. They pledged loyalty to the teachings of the gurus. Sikhs who did not accept baptism into the Khalsa fraternity came to be known as Sahajdhari.

After all four of his sons died in fighting the Moguls, Guru Gobind Singh proclaimed that the line of the gurus would come to an end with himself. After Gobind Singh's death, the Adi Granth—subsequently referred to as the Guru Granth Sahib—was established as the guru, and no further human gurus were allowed. Subsequently, the Guru Granth was installed upon a throne and treated as a living presence in every Sikh temple.

Following Gobind Singh's death, the Khalsa became a military and political power in Punjab. Conflict between the Sikhs and the Mogul Empire continued. In 1799 the Sikhs captured Lahore and made it their capital. The Sikh kingdom of Ranjit Singh dominated the Punjab and other areas of northwest India. This kingdom granted religious freedom to the Hindus and Muslims. During the rule of Maharajah Ranjit Singh, from 1799 to 1839, large numbers of peasants converted to the Khalsa.

During the 19th century, the Sikhs fought against British invaders. The army of Ranjit's successor was defeated in 1849, and the Sikh kingdom was annexed to British India. Partially because the British administration was perceived as being generally fair and evenhanded in Punjab, the Sikhs remained loyal to the British during the Great Mutiny of 1857 and afterward became preferred recruits to the British army. The Sikhs continued to increase in numbers under British rule, largely because of the special favors accorded to the Khalsa in the army and the civil services.

In 1931 leading Sikh authorities and associations in India held a meeting at Amritsar and drew up a document called the *Rehat Maryada* (*Guide to the Sikh Way of Life*) that all Sikhs are expected to follow. In this document, a Sikh is defined as anyone who believes in one God, the 10 gurus and their teaching, and the Guru Granth. Every Sikh is expected to serve the community of the faithful, lead a life of prayer and meditation, and recite or read a prescribed number of hymns each day.

The British withdrew from the Indian subcontinent in 1947. When the British decided to partition the Punjab between the new states of India and Pakistan, the Sikhs were bitterly disappointed. Many places sacred to them, such as the birthplace of Guru Nanak, were in the western section of Punjab, which was given to Pakistan. East Punjab remained in India. Eventually 2.5 million Sikhs were forced to immigrate to East Punjab.

In the Indian census of 1971, the number of Sikhs (both Khalsa and Sahajdhari) was more than 10 million, which was still less than 2 percent of the population of India. About 85 percent of the world's Sikhs live in Punjab, northern India. There are also significant diaspora communities in the United Kingdom and Canada.

There are several Sikh sects. The Udasi, or "detached," are followers of Sri Chand, the ascetic elder son of Guru Nanak. They did not convert to the Khalsa started by Guru Gobind Singh. During the period of Sikh persecution by Mogul rulers, the Udasi took over the management of several Sikh shrines and introduced Hindu icons and rituals into Sikh temples. This met with the disapproval of orthodox Sikhs, who divested the Udasi of their control of the temples in the 1920s. Most Udasi today observe Hindu customs and pay nominal homage to the Adi Granth.

The Nirmala, or "unsullied," are a sect of theologians started by Guru Gobind Singh. The guru had a group of scholars study Sanskrit and the Vedas to be better equipped to interpret the writings of the gurus, which make frequent allusions to Hindu mythology and sacred texts. Nirmala wear white clothes and are vegetarians.

The Namdhari, or "adopters of the name," are a sect founded by Balak Singh, who criticized the rich lifestyle of the Sikh aristocracy and preached the virtues of poverty. He exhorted the Sikhs to practice no ritual except repeating God's name. The Namdhari dress in white handspun cloth, abstain from liquor, and are vegetarians. Their *gurdwaras* are free of ostentation, and their wedding ceremonies are performed in austere simplicity.

The Nihangi, or "crocodiles," are a militant order of Khalsa. They wear blue clothes and always carry weapons. Today they live mostly on alms and are notorious for their addiction to hashish. The Nirankari believe in the succession of gurus continuing after Guru Gobind Singh and pay homage to a living guru. They include persons of all religions without requiring conversion to Sikhism.

If one considers Sant Mat to be a Sikh sect, it is easily the largest. The most prominent contemporary Sant Mat lineage is the Radha Soami (or Radhasoami) movement. The Radha Soami Satsang, Beas is one of a number of movements flowing from the teachings of Param Sant Soami Ji Maharaj (Soami Ji). Soami's successors quarreled and split over succession to leadership of the movement he created. Radha Soami Satsang, Beas developed from the teachings of Baba Jaimal Singh. The successor to Baba Jaimal Singh, Maharaj Sawan Singh, spread the teachings throughout India and, eventually, to the West. Under the leadership of Sawan Singh's grandson, Charan Singh, the Radha Soami Satsang, Beas became the largest of all of the Sant Mat groups in the world.

The notion that God is light and sound is a core doctrine of the Sant Mat tradition. Rather like Western Gnosticism, Sant Mat teaches that the cosmos is a multilevel emanation in which human souls are trapped, and that the spiritual aspirant needs a series of words or names keyed to each of the lower levels in order to move through these levels and reach the divine source. There are five lower levels, for which one therefore requires five words. A sound current (a "river" of vibration; alternately pictured as a ray of light) from the higher levels—an emanation from the high God—flows down through all of the lower levels. A living guru imparts five secret names (the *simram*) to the aspirant at the time of initiation. Contemplating the sound current and the inner light (the visual aspect of the divine sound) with the master's guidance allows the individual to follow the sound back to the source from which it emanated (the Supreme Being), resulting in spiritual liberation. Those who follow the system must live according to a code of behavior that includes vegetarianism, abstinence from alcohol, and high moral character. Two and a half hours per day are to be set aside for meditation.

Radha Soami has also been the source of a number of new religious movements. For example, the father of Maharaj Ji, the current leader of Elan Vital (formerly the Divine Light Mission), was originally a disciple of Sawan Singh. New splinter groups have often arisen out of disputes over who should be the new leader following the death of a guru. One of the more important splinter groups was Kirpal Singh's Ruhani Satsang, which was formed in the wake of the passing of Sawan Singh. Kirpal Singh's followers, in turn, have splintered repeatedly following his death. Kirpal Singh was also one of Paul Twitchell's teachers, and a number of outsiders have pointed out Kirpal Singh as likely the source of ECKANKAR sound current practices. ECKANKAR itself has influenced or given rise to a number of other new spiritual groups.

James R. Lewis

See also: Celebration of the Guru Granth Sahib; ECKANKAR; Elan Vital/Divine Light Mission; Energy; Gnosticism; Golden Temple; Guru Gobind

Singh's Birthday; Martyrdom of Guru Arjan; Martyrdom of Guru Tegh Bahadur; Meditation; Nanak, Guru; Radhasoami; Ruhani Satsang; Sikh Dharma; Vegetarianism.

References

Barrier, N. Gerald, and Verne A. Dusenbery. *The Sikh Diaspora: Migration and the Experience Beyond Punjab.* Delhi: Chanakya, 1989.

Cole, W. Owen. *Popular Dictionary of Sikhism.* Richmond, UK: Curzon, 1990.

Fripp, Peter. *The Mystic Philosophy of Sant Mat.* Punjab, India: Radha Soami Satsang Beas, 1978.

Grewal, J. S. *The Sikhs of the Punjab.* Cambridge: Cambridge University Press, 2008.

Juergensmeyer, Mark. *Radhasoami Reality: The Logic of Modern Faith.* Princeton, NJ: Princeton University Press, 1991.

Lane, David Christopher. *The Radhasoami Tradition: A Critical History of Guru Successorship.* New York: Garland, 1992.

McLeod, William Hewat. *Historical Dictionary of Sikhism.* Methuen, NJ: The Scarecrow Press, 2005.

Nesbitt, Eleanor. *Sikhism: A Very Short Introduction.* Oxford: Oxford University Press, 2005.

Rai, Priya Muhar. *Sikhism and the Sikhs: An Annotated Bibliography.* Westport, CT: Greenwood Press, 1989.

Singh, Harbans. *The Message of Sikhism.* Delhi: Delhi Sikh Gurdwara, 1978.

Singh, Khushwant. *A History of the Sikhs.* New Delhi: Oxford University Press, 1977.

Takhar, Opinderjit Kaur. *Sikh Identity: An Exploration of Groups Among Sikhs.* Aldershot, UK: Ashgate, 2005.

Tatla, Darshan Singh. *Sikhs in North America: An Annotated Bibliography.* Westport, CT: Greenwood Press, 1991.

Silesian Evangelical Church of the Augsburg Confession

The first Lutheran congregations in Silesia began to emerge in the 1620s, and by the middle of the century the Protestant Reformation had celebrated its victory in this region. In 1568 the first rules for worship services in this locality were published, which have been regarded as a legislative ground for the Silesian Evangelical Church of the Augsburg Confession (Slezská církev evangelická augsburského vyznání) up to present time. With the end of the period of the Counter-Reformation and the re-Catholization, Silesia witnessed another growth of Lutheranism after the issuing of the Edict of Toleration by Joseph II. In 1861, following the issuance of the so-called Protestant Edict, the first Lutheran congregations became part of the Evangelical Church of Augsburg and Helvetic Confessions in Austria-Hungary, having formed the so-called Seniorate of Silesia. After the fall of the Austro-Hungarian monarchy and the foundation of an independent Czechoslovak Republic, a self-governing seniorate was founded in Czechoslovakia under the name of the Evangelical Church of the Augsburg Confession in Eastern Silesia. Since 1948, the church has used its present name.

The character of the church is regional and national —it operates in the region of Silesia, and many of its members are of Polish nationality. That is also the reason why, apart from Czech, one of its official languages is Polish.

The church follows the Augsburg Confession of 1530 and the doctrine of Martin Luther. In its religious practice, it keeps the traditions of baptism and the Lord's Supper, while at the same time rejecting the notion of transubstantiation. However, it acknowledges the presence of Christ's Body and Blood in the Sacrament of the Altar during the moment of holy Communion. Its basic forms of liturgy are two Sunday services, carried out in Czech and Polish. Organizationally, it follows a Presbyterian structure. The synod is the highest legislative body.

The church numbers its members at approximately 30,000 (2006). It is a member of the World Council of Churches.

Silesian Evangelical Church of the Augsburg
     Confession/Slezská církev evangelická augsburského vyznání
Na Nivách 7
CZ-737 01 Český Těšín
Czech Republic

Dusan Lužný

See also: Evangelical Church of the Augsburg and Helvetic Confessions in Austria; World Council of Churches.

References

Bachmann, E. Theodore, and Mercia Brenne Bachmann. *Lutheran Churches in the World: A Handbook.* Minneapolis, MN: Augsburg, 1989.

Van Beek, Huibert. *A Handbook of the Churches and Councils: Profiles of Ecumenical Relationships.* Geneva: World Council of Churches, 2006.

Simalungun Protestant Christian Church

The Simalungun Protestant Christian Church (Gereja Kristen Protestan Simalungun) was established in 1961, when the Simalungun-speaking congregations in the Protestant Christian Batak Church (HKBP) requested autonomy so they could develop a ministry especially for their people. Simalungun is a Batak dialect with some similarity to Sanskrit. The people are concentrated in rural Sumatra in a mountainous region near Lake Toba.

The church traces its history to 1903. The first sermon was preached in Simalungun country by Theophilus Pasaribu, an evangelist from among the neighboring Toba people, who accompanied a Rhenish Mission evangelist into the region. G. K. Simon, a missionary who settled in the region, translated portions of the New Testament into the Simalungun language. The mission began just as a feeling of nationalism had arisen in Sumatra, and the church was identified with the Dutch authorities. Growth was slow.

During World War II, the church was able to keep some of its work going because of its knowledge of the Japanese Christian Toyohiko Kagawa, with whom the Japanese occupation forces were familiar.

The HKBP had formed the Simalungun District in 1940, and in 1950 it established a school for the training of Simalungun pastors. The assignment of several of the pastors from the first graduating class away from the Simalungun area first prompted talk of separation of the district.

The new church continued the organization and beliefs of the parent body. It is led by a synod, but congregations have a high level of autonomy. An executive council administers the church's affairs between synod meetings. The church ordained the first female pastors in 1988, and it has a strong cadre of female evangelists.

The church reported 201,000 members in some 600 congregations in 2006. It sponsors the Bethesda Hospital in Sardok Dolok and an educational center at Sondi Raya. It is a member of the Lutheran World Federation and the World Council of Churches.

Simalungun Protestant Christian Church
PO Box 101
21142 Pematangsiantar
North Sumatra
Indonesia

J. Gordon Melton

See also: Lutheran World Federation; Protestant Christian Batak Church; World Council of Churches.

References

Bachmann, E. Theodore, and Mercia Brenne Bachmann. *Lutheran Churches in the World: A Handbook.* Minneapolis, MN: Augsburg, 1989.

Van Beek, Huibert. *A Handbook of the Churches and Councils: Profiles of Ecumenical Relationships.* Geneva: World Council of Churches, 2006.

Simchat Torah

See Sukkot.

Simeon Stylites

The monk Simeon (or Simon) Stylites (ca. 390–459) became one of the most noteworthy characters in Christian history by his adoption of an extreme form of asceticism that church members of the fifth century accepted as a sign of sanctity. He began his adult life in a monastery, which he left after nine years to become a hermit. Ten years later he sat down on a column, the top of which was a mere 40 inches in circumference.

Portrait of Simeon Stylites, a Christian ascetic who took up residence atop a series of pillars in the fifth century CE. (Bettmann/Corbis)

He would remain on that heightened place for two decades. During this time, he gained a reputation as a miracle worker. Many of the rich and powerful came to see him. His status in the church was no better demonstrated than when the Roman Emperor Theodosius II (r. 408–450) visited to seek out his counsel.

Following his death in 459, a large procession formed to take his body to Antioch (Syria). His body was preserved for a time, and as late as 580, Evagrius (ca. 536–ca. 600), who left one of the most important accounts of Simeon in his *Ecclesiastical History*, reported having seen Simeon's head, still considered a most sacred relic.

A variety of stories began to be told about Simeon —that he ate only once a week and not at all during Lent, or that he spent the last year of his life standing on one leg. While most of these stories are now discounted, he did begin a new practice, living on a pillar, which remained popular for several centuries. Among his more well-known successors were a disciple named Daniel (d. 493) and a saint who took Simeon's name (and is generally referred to as Simeon the Younger [d. ca. 596]).

J. Gordon Melton

See also: Asceticism; Relics.

References
Challoner, Richard. *Life of St. Simon Stylites (389–459).* Willets, CA: Eastern Orthodox Books, 1977.

Doran, Robert. *The Lives of Simeon Stylites.* Kalamazoo, MI: Cistercian Publications, 1992.

Evagrius Scholasticus. *The Ecclesiastical History of Evagrius Scholasticus.* Trans. by Michael Whitby. Liverpool, UK: Liverpool University Press, 2000.

Torrey, C., and F. Lent. *The Letters and Life of Simon Stylites.* Maidstone, UK: Oriental Orthodox Library, 2007.

Sinai, Mount

Mount Sinai, also called Mount Horeb, is the place where Moses received the Law from God. In the ancient accounts of the receiving of the Law, Moses and

He would remain on that column located near Aleppo, Syria, for a quarter of a century, dependent upon those who knew of him to bring him food.

Once seated in place, Simeon's fame spread quickly as did his reputation for holiness. Those who observed him understood him to be trying to lift himself above mundane concerns and successfully resisting the downward tug of his human nature. He stayed in place for seven years, on what was a relatively short column. The column was then raised some 65 feet into the air.

Pilgrims on Mount Sinai in Egypt. (Mangojuicy/Dreamstime.com)

the people of Israel are said to have crossed the Red Sea to the Sinai Peninsula. Three months after their departure from Egypt, they arrived at the mountain (Exodus 19:1–2), and the Israelites camped at its base. The description of the location of the mountain in the text of the book of Exodus (and the added material in Deuteronomy) make finding the exact location difficult. That spot was not marked by the Israelites in later centuries, though the prophet Elijah was noted for having retreated to Horeb, the journey described as taking him a long way, that is, the proverbial 40 days and 40 nights (1 Kings 19:8). Post-exilic Israel lost its knowledge of Judaism's birthplace.

The story of Sinai began with Moses, born into slavery in Egypt at some point in the 12th or 13th century BCE. Moses' birth coincided with the Egyptian Pharaoh decreeing that all male Hebrew infants were to be drowned at birth. He was saved when the Pharaoh's daughter found him floating in a basket in the Nile and adopted him. Raised among royalty, he was 40 before learning of his Hebrew heritage. He later killed a cruel Egyptian slave overseer and had to flee into the Sinai in exile. Absorbed into the nomadic society of Sinai, he found himself grazing sheep on the edge of Mount Sinai when he had an extraordinary experience. He saw a bush burning that was not being consumed by the flames (Exodus 3:1–13). God spoke out of the bush and commanded Moses to return to Egypt, mobilize his people, and bring them out of Egypt and back to the mountain.

When the Israelites arrived, Moses climbed the mountain, this time for a lengthy stay—40 days and 40 nights (Exodus 24:16–18). Here he received the two stone tablets upon which God inscribed the Ten Commandments, as well as instructions for the construction of the ark of the covenant that would hold the tablets. Once it was ready, the Israelites departed from Sinai.

While the events of Sinai were told over and over again, the location of Sinai was not a major topic in writings for a number of centuries. Thus in the first century, the Christian Apostle Paul located it in Arabia (Galatians 4:25), and subsequently in his work "Against Apion," the historian Josephus located Sinai as a mountain lying between Egypt and Arabia.

Today, most people when attempting to locate Mount Sinai look to Jebel Musa (or Mountain of Moses), a 7,497-foot-high mountain in the middle of an otherwise mountainous region of the south Sinai Peninsula. It is near the city of Saint Katherine and next to Jebel Katerina (aka Mount St. Catherine, the tallest peak on the peninsula). Other mountains surround Jebel Musa on all sides. The current identification of Jebel Musa with the biblical Mount Sinai seems to date to the third century. Hermits took up home in the mountain's caves and came to the conclusion that their new home was the ancient holy mountain. That claim was and still is unsupported by any archaeological evidence (a characteristic also shared by all the other suggested alternative sites).

Jebel Musa's status as the biblical Mount Sinai was confirmed by Helena, the mother of the Emperor Constantine, who shortly after he had made Christianity the privileged religion of his empire traveled to the Holy Land (330) in search of relics and knowledge of the founding events in the new faith. She designated the site where Moses saw the burning bush and the plant that burned. The shrub plant still grows at the site. Finding confirmation of her choice of Jelel Musa in a dream, Helena had a tower and a small chapel erected there and by the end of the decade monks began to gather around the bush, tower, and chapel. The monks

were subject to raids by the Bedouins who inhabited the region, and in 542 the Byzantine Emperor Justinian I (483–565) built a basilica that replaced Helena's chapel. The basilica, named the Church of Transfiguration, memorialized Jesus' transfiguration in the presence of Moses and Elijah on Mount Tabor (Matthew 17). Around the church he built a large wall that served to protect it and the monks who lived at what now became the Monastery of the Transfiguration.

The Monastery of the Transfiguration is generally called St. Catherine's Monastery after an early Christian martyr, Dorothea of Alexandria (b. 294), who was tortured and beheaded by Emperor Maximus (r. 383–388) after she criticized his Pagan worship. According to the legend that developed around her, her body vanished and was miraculously taken to the peak of Jebel Katerina by a band of angels. Equally miraculous, three centuries later, that is after the wall built by Justinian, monks discovered her body, which remained in an incorrupt state, and carried it to the monastery. Her relics remain at the monastery.

The monastery has the status of an autonomous jurisdiction in the Eastern Orthodox world. Its abbot is an archbishop, and the monastery the only parish of the Orthodox Church of St. Catherine. The archbishop is usually consecrated by the head of the Greek Orthodox Patriarchate of Jerusalem. Traditionally a male enclave, the only door was an elevated opening through which monks and other male believers could enter and leave and food could be brought in. It is also home to some 3,000 ancient manuscripts. Here in 1853, Count Constantin von Tischendorf (1817–1874) discovered the Codex Sinaiticus, the oldest complete copy of the Christian New Testament, dating to the fourth century. The codex also contained two popular early Christian works, the "Epistle of Barnabas" and most of the "Shepherd of Hermas."

Muslims revere Mount Sinai as the place where God handed down his Law. In 623, the prophet Muhammad signed the *Actiname* (Holy Testament), which exempted the monks of St. Catherine's from the usual taxes (*jizya*) and military service required of non-Muslims in Muslim territory. It also provided for Muslims to assist the community as needed. At a later date (some point between 1101 and 1105), the monks permitted a small chapel within the monastery to be transformed into a mosque. It was used regularly for several centuries and then largely abandoned until restored in the early 20th century. It is used occasionally in the present era.

Pilgrimages to Sinai were popular until the era of the Reformation. They remained low in numbers until the 1950s, when the Egyptian government paved roads leading down the western coast of the Sinai Peninsula in order to gain access to the oil fields in the area. They added a dirt road to Jebel Musa, which was paved in the 1980s (following the return of the area to Egyptian control by Israel). Since 1986 regular tourist service to St. Catherine's has been available.

Today's pilgrims are invited to the peak of Jebel Musa, where they can see a small chapel constructed in 1934. It was built over the ruins of an earlier church constructed over the rock that tradition identifies as the very rock from which God carved the Tablets of the Law. A cleft in the rock of the chapel's western wall is identified as the site where Moses hid himself as God's glory passed by (Exodus 33:22). On the way to the top stands a chapel on what is known as Elijah's Basin, identified as the spot where Elijah spent time with God in the cave. Nearby is the spot reputedly where Moses' brother Aaron and 70 elders remained during the time Moses received the Law. Better documented, to the northwest is Jebel Safsaafa, where various Byzantine figures such as Saint Gregory of Sinai (1265–1346) resided. If Jebel Musa is the place where the Law was given, then the Plain of ar-Raaha, at the foot of Jebel Safsaafa would have been the place where the Israelites camped out while in the area.

Pilgrims of both genders are welcomed to St. Catherine's today and a more convenient entrance has replaced the traditional one. In the church, they may view one of the world's finest icon collections. In the library (a modern building erected in the 1930s) they may view the ancient manuscripts and books. The Chapel of the Burning Bush, the most sacred spot in the complex, is found below and behind the altar of the church. The bush itself is protected by a stone wall.

In 2002, St. Catherine's Monastery and the area around it were named as a World Heritage Site by UNESCO. In the immediate surrounding area are a variety of sites that are designated as the places where various events associated with the giving of the Law are said to have occurred. These have all been designated through the centuries since Helena's visit.

The primary site challenging the identification of Jebel Musa as the biblical Mount Sinai is Jabal al Lawz in Saudi Arabia, a site championed by adventurers Robert Cornuke and Howard Blum.

J. Gordon Melton

See also: Constantine the Great; Helena, Flavia Iulia; Monasticism; Moses; Muhammad; Paul.

References

Baddeley, Oriana, and Earleen Brunner, eds. *The Monastery of St Catherine*. London: Thames & Hudson, 1997.

Blum, Howard. *The God of Exodus—The Discovery of the True Mount Sinai*. New York: Simon and Schuster, 1998.

Cornuke, Robert, and David Halbrook. *In Search of the Mountain of God: The Discovery of the Real Mt. Sinai*. Nashville: Broadman & Holman Publishers, 2000.

Manley, Deborah. *Travelling Through Sinai: From the Fourth to the Twenty-First Century*. Cairo: AUC Press, 2007.

Paliouras, Athanasios. *The Monastery of St. Catherine on Mt. Sinai*. St. Catherine's Monastery at Sinai, 1985.

■ Singapore

Singapore, literally the city of the lion, received its name from a vision that came to a visiting prince many centuries ago. It is a large island, some 263 square miles, separated by a narrow causeway from mainland Malaysia. More than 75 percent of its 4,600,000 people are of Chinese heritage.

Singapore was originally inhabited by Malayans, and much of its history has been tied to its northern neighbor. In 1824, Singapore and several adjacent islands were purchased by the British from the sultan of Johore. The British began immediate improvements of the port and brought both Chinese and Indians in to work. Along with the Chinese were significant numbers of Indians, Pakistanis, and Sri Lankans.

A view of Singapore's business district and harbor. The island of Singapore has become an economic hub in Asia due in part to its advantageous location at the tip of the Malay Peninsula. (Corel)

The British incorporated Singapore into a colony called the Straits Settlements. After World War II, the ports of Penang and Melaka, the other major parts of the colony, became part of the Malayan Union, and Singapore became a crown colony. Internal autonomy was granted in 1949. It later became part of the Malayan Federation, but in 1965, under the leadership of Prime Minister Lee Quan Yew, it withdrew and became an independent country within the British Commonwealth. Yew continued to lead the country, now an economic enigma in Southeast Asia, until his retirement in 1991. He was succeeded by Goh Chok Tong.

Although Singapore has been accused of passing a set of laws restrictive of personal freedoms, and even of human rights abuses in the 1980s, the small nation with an extremely diverse religious community has been a model of religious freedom and interfaith harmony and cooperation. The Islamic community is based

upon the original Malayan inhabitants, while the Chinese brought Buddhism and related Chinese religion. The British initiated the Christian community, and there are distinct smaller communities of Sikhs, Hindus, and Jews.

The Muslim community in Singapore is quite diverse. It consists of Malayans, most of whom adhere to the Shafiite School, but with a component of Shias with roots in India and Pakistan and others from China and Indonesia. The government recognizes (in part) the validity of Islamic law (the *sharia*), and the Majlis Ugama Islam (Islamic Religious Council) cooperates with the government in regulating the community according to Muslim rules.

Many of the Chinese in Singapore came from the Chinese community in Malaya, and as such they adhere to Theravada forms of the faith rather than the Mahayana forms that dominated in China. Also, Buddhist missionaries from Thailand have been active in

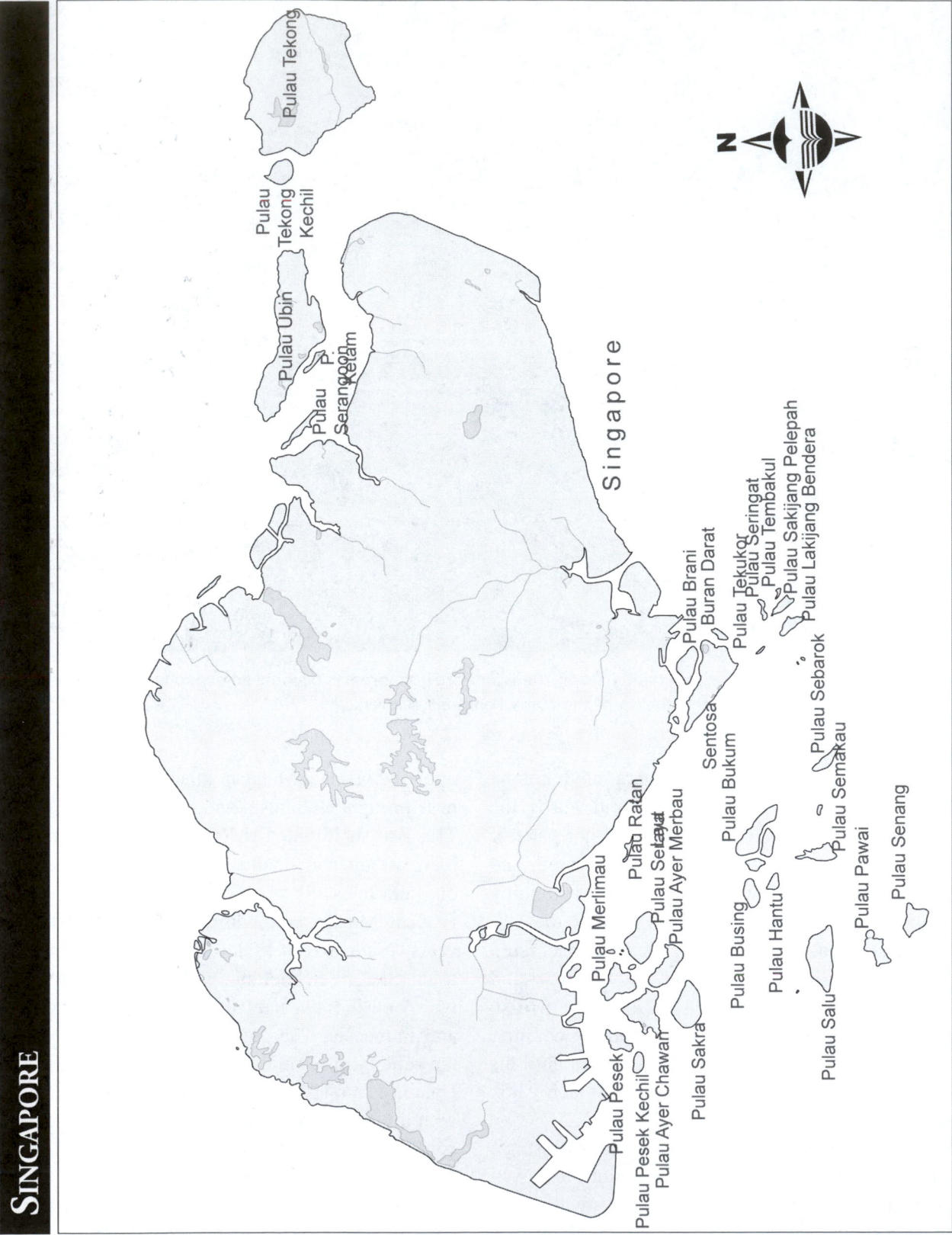

the Chinese community, further strengthening the Theravada base. The primary Buddhist organizations are the Singapore Buddhist Federation and the Singapore Buddhist Sangha Organization. There is also an important regional center of the World Fellowship of Buddhists headquartered at the Buddhist Union.

It is estimated that approximately 30 percent of Singaporeans are Buddhist; another 20 percent are identified as Daoist and followers of Chinese religion, mixing Daoist, Buddhist, and Confucian elements. The boundaries between Buddhism and Daoism, in practice, are at best fuzzy.

Although most Buddhists are of Chinese heritage, a minority of Buddhists with roots in Sri Lanka are found in the Singapore Sinhala Buddhist Association, and both Thais and Tibetans (Kagyu Dharma) have opened centers. The True Buddha School, a Chinese group following Vajrayana (Tibetan) practice, has multiple centers in the country.

Hinduism was brought to Singapore by Indians, primarily Saivites from Tamil, in southern India. They have built a series of temples in the city according to traditional style and standards. The entire community is invited to their major celebrations. Between 3 and 4 percent of Singaporeans are Hindus.

The Jewish community in Singapore traces its beginnings to around 1840. A synagogue, Maghain Aboth, was opened in 1878, but services had previously been held in a private home on a street known today as Synagogue Street. Most Jews were from Baghdad (Iraq), but the population became more diverse over the course of the 20th century. There are now two synagogues serving several hundred Jewish families.

Christianity arrived on the Malayan Peninsula when Catholic priests set up a mission in the wake of the Portuguese conquest in 1511. The Diocese of Melacca (including Singapore and the portion of Malaysia immediately to the north) was established in 1557 and flourished for almost a century. However, the Dutch took over in 1641, and they suppressed Catholicism in favor of the Reformed Church (but made little attempt to convert the indigenous population). Following the British purchase of Singapore, a degree of religious freedom returned, and the Roman Catholic Church entered a growth phase, finding marked response among the Chinese. In 1841 a vicariate covering Singapore

and Malaysia was re-established, and in 1888, Singapore became the seat of a revived Diocese of Malacca. Since 1953, it has been an archdiocese. The Malaysian area was separated from the archdiocese in 1972. In the meantime Singapore became the residence of an apostolic visitor (a representative of the Vatican) charged with coordinating the church's work among the Chinese outside of the People's Republic of China.

In 1814 a representative of the London Missionary Society, a Presbyterian, opened work in education in Singapore but had little success in converting people. In 1846 the missionaries withdrew, but a small church continued under local leadership; soon other Presbyterians (including some Chinese immigrants) arrived. The Presbyterian work, long tied to work across Malaysia, separated from the Malaysian jurisdiction in 1975. The majority of Presbyterian churches in Singapore reorganized as the Presbyterian Church in Singapore and created both an English-speaking and a Chinese-speaking presbytery.

In 1826 the East India Company appointed an Anglican chaplain to serve the Europeans then residing in Singapore. The first Anglican church, St. Andrew's, became the base of missionary activity in 1856 with the arrival of missionaries from the Society for the Propagation of the Gospel in Foreign Parts from England. Work was pursued in several different languages, and by 1909 it had grown to the point that appointment of a bishop seemed appropriate. The Diocese of Singapore was separated from Malaysia in 1970. The present Anglican Diocese of Singapore has charge of work in Thailand, Laos, Cambodia, Vietnam, and Indonesia. It is an integral part of the Council of Churches in East Asia, which includes several extra provincial Anglican dioceses and provides some of the structure of a province. Currently, the bishop of Singapore is also the chairman of the council.

The South India conference of the Methodist Episcopal Church (U.S.A.) expanded their work into Malaysia and Singapore in 1885 and three years later set Malaysia (including Singapore) apart as a separate mission. Work was pursued in four languages (English, Chinese, Tamil, and Malaysian) and spread through Malaysia, Burma, and present-day Indonesia. In 1936 two conferences were created, one for Chinese-speaking members and one for English-speaking. In 1968, three

Singapore

Religion	Followers in 1970	Followers in 2010	% of Population	Annual % growth 2000–2010	Followers in 2025	Followers in 2050
Chinese folk	1,125,000	1,788,000	38.9	1.19	1,771,000	1,516,000
Muslims	373,000	856,000	18.6	1.50	950,000	935,000
Christians	162,000	740,000	16.1	2.30	895,000	963,000
Roman Catholics	80,000	230,000	5.0	2.58	280,000	300,000
Protestants	35,500	209,000	4.6	2.44	270,000	300,000
Independents	15,700	183,000	4.0	1.65	221,000	245,000
Buddhists	200,000	660,000	14.4	1.50	800,000	880,000
Hindus	120,000	226,000	4.9	1.50	252,000	250,000
Agnostics	62,000	215,000	4.7	1.50	300,000	350,000
New religionists	10,200	70,000	1.5	1.50	90,000	82,000
Sikhs	20,000	20,300	0.4	1.50	22,500	20,000
Baha'is	700	6,900	0.2	1.50	10,000	13,000
Atheists	2,000	6,400	0.1	1.50	8,000	12,000
Shintoists	0	1,200	0.0	1.49	2,000	2,000
Ethnoreligionists	0	1,000	0.0	1.50	1,500	2,000
Jews	400	850	0.0	1.50	1,000	1,000
Zoroastrians	150	250	0.0	1.45	300	300
Total population	**2,075,000**	**4,592,000**	**100.0**	**1.50**	**5,104,000**	**5,026,000**

Methodist churches in the United States merged to found the United Methodist Church, and the Singaporean Methodists became part of a new autonomous body, the Malaysia and Singapore Methodist Church. The work that had developed among the Tamil-speaking people was set apart as a Tamil Provisional Conference. In 1976 the Malaysian and Singaporean elements of the church divided, resulting in the present Methodist Church in Singapore, the largest Protestant body in Singapore.

In spite of its diminutive size, Singapore became home to an amazing array of other Christian churches over the course of the 20th century. Many of these were brought to Singapore by and operate within an ethnic expatriate community. Members of the Armenian Apostolic Church (Holy See of Echmiadzin) arrived as early as 1850. A variety of missionary-minded Protestant churches from England and the United States have opened churches, and a spectrum of Chinese indigenous churches have appeared. Among the latter, the True Jesus Church is among the most interesting and successful. Recently, the International Churches of Christ have made Singapore an important base of operations for its expansion throughout southeastern Asia. There are four Lutheran denominations represented in

Singapore, all headquartered in neighboring countries (Malaysia and Indonesia).

The Jehovah's Witnesses, who established work in 1912, were stripped of their legal status by the independent Singaporean government because of their stand against universal military service. They no longer have kingdom halls in Singapore but continue to proselytize on the island from a base across the causeway in Malaysia. The first congregation of the Church of Jesus Christ of Latter-day Saints was opened in 1968. The Singapore Mission is one of eight missions in the Asia Area of the church.

Above and beyond the large Buddhist, Christian, Hindu, and Muslim communities, there is also a Sikh community consisting of Punjabis and a set of spiritual assemblies of the Baha'i Faith. A number of the so-called new religions from Japan, Taiwan, and the United States have attempted to start work, and groups such as the Soka Gakkai International (a Nichiren Buddhist lay movement) and the Ancient and Mystical Order Rosae Crucis can be found. The large number of different groups in Singapore means that the great majority are limited to a small membership.

The government in Singapore encourages religious harmony and supports the activity of the Inter-

Religious Organizations Council. Also, the larger religious communities have established cooperative councils. Among Christians, the National Council of Churches of Singapore, which grew out of the former Council of Churches of Malaysia and Singapore, founded in 1948, is affiliated with the World Council of Churches. Other denominations are members of the Chinese Church Union, the Singapore Council of Christian Churches, and the Association of Bible Believing Churches. The Evangelical Fellowship of Singapore is affiliated with the World Evangelical Alliance, whose international headquarters is split between Singapore and the Philippines.

J. Gordon Melton

See also: Armenian Apostolic Church (Holy See of Echmiadzin); Baha'i Faith; Church of Jesus Christ of Latter-day Saints; International Churches of Christ; Jehovah's Witnesses; London Missionary Society; Roman Catholic Church; Shafiite School of Islam; Society for the Propagation of the Gospel in Foreign Parts; Soka Gakkai International; True Buddha School; True Jesus Church; United Methodist Church; World Council of Churches; World Evangelical Alliance; World Fellowship of Buddhists.

References

Abdullah, T., and S. Siddique, eds. *Islam and Society in Southeast Asia*. Singapore: Institute of Southeast Asian Studies, 1986.

Cheu, Tony Hock, ed. *Chinese Beliefs and Practices in Southeast Asia: Studies on the Chinese Religion in Malaysia, Singapore and Indonesia*. Selangor, Malaysia: Pelanduk Publications, 1999.

Chinese Customs and Festivals in Singapore. Singapore: Singapore Federation of Chinese Clan Associations, 1989.

Clothey, Fred W. *Ritualizing on the Boundaries: Continuity and Innovation in the Tamil Diaspora*. Columbia: University of South Carolina Press, 2006.

Elliott, Alan J. A. *Chinese Spirit-Medium Cults in Singapore*. Darby, PA: Diane Publishing Co., 1990.

Kim, Khoo Kay, Elinah Abdullah, and Wan Meng Hao, eds. *Malays/Muslims in Singapore: Selected Readings in History, 1819–1865*. Selangor, Malaysia: Pelanduk Publications/Singapore: Centre for Research on Islamic and Malay Affairs, 2006.

Kuo, Eddie C. Y. *Religion in Singapore*. Singapore: Census of Population, Monograph #2, 1990.

Mialaret, J. *Hinduism in Singapore: A Guide to the Hindu Temples of Singapore*. Singapore: Donald Moore for Asia Pacific Press, 1969.

Sng, B. E. K. *Church and Society: Singapore Context*. Singapore: Graduates Christian Fellowship, 1989.

Suyadinata, Leo, ed. *Ethnic Chinese in Singapore and Malaysia: A Dialogue Between Tradition and Modernity*. Singapore: Marshall Cavendish Academic, 2002.

Tai, Kao Keng, Dorothy Kao, and Grace Tan. *Singapore Church Directory*. Singapore: Singapore Every Home Crusade (issued annually).

Singapore, Buddhism in

Buddhism in Singapore is made up of migrant populations that arrived during the early 19th and the 20th centuries. When these migrants arrived, they brought along their cultures and reproduced them in a colonial environment. Chinese migrants brought along a syncretic Chinese religious belief system. Chinese religion is a composite mixture of Buddhism, Daoism, and Chinese folk beliefs. There was also a small group of Singhalese migrants during this period that brought Theravada Buddhism into Singapore.

With independence and the formation of the Singapore nation-state in 1965, the syncretic Chinese religion has undergone various changes. Along with a rise in education and social status, many Chinese have started to reassess their religious affiliation. This results in a separation of Buddhism from a syncretic Chinese religious belief system. The 1990 Singapore Census of Population showed that 31 percent of the total population of approximately 3.1 million (approximately 970,000) are Buddhists, and that Buddhist adherence is spread evenly among all age groups.

Today, Buddhism in Singapore can be divided into several types. Mahayana Buddhism includes elements

Buddha Tooth Relic Temple in Singapore. (Ints Vikmanis/Dreamstime.com)

of Daoism and Chinese folk beliefs. It is commonly practiced by the majority of the Singapore Chinese. Theravada Buddhism is practiced primarily by the Singhalese, but there are also a sizable number of Chinese Theravada Buddhists. From the 1980s on, both Tibetan Buddhism and Japanese Buddhism (represented by the Singapore Soka Association) have made their presence known in Singapore. At the same time, Buddhism was also undergoing modernizing changes and secularization. A growing group of Buddhists who called themselves Reformist Buddhists emerged in the 1980s. Reformist Buddhism is a lay movement that does not recognize traditional boundaries and focuses on scriptural teachings and interpretation of the Buddhist texts. The Reformist Buddhists refer to their approach as the Buddhayana tradition.

There are more than 100 Buddhist and Buddhist/Daoist temples in Singapore, with many temples practicing a combination of Buddhist and syncretic Chinese religion. The largest is the Phor Kark See Temple. Among the several Theravada temples, the popular Mangala Vihara Buddhist Temple is representative.

Lay Buddhists have organized several organizations, such as the Cheng Beng Buddhist Temple, the Singapore Buddha Sasana Society, and the Singapore Buddha Yana Organisation. All these Buddhist temples and associations are members of the Singapore Buddhist Federation, an umbrella body that provides leadership for the Buddhist community in Singapore. The Federation was formed in 1949. Since then, it has expanded on its activities to include not only the dissemination of Buddhist teaching but also education, social welfare, and charity work. Today there are six Buddhist clinics, one secondary and two primary schools, and homes for the elderly under its supervision. Apart from these activities, individual temples and lay organizations are also involved in active dissemination of Buddhist knowledge to the public and are involved in welfare and charity work. Some temples house a home for the aged, while others house a home for children with physical disabilities.

The Buddhist Sangha is represented by a large majority of Mahayana monks and nuns, with a small number of Theravada and Tibetan monks. There are also a few monks who do not want to be associated with these traditional Buddhist labels. At present there are more than 100 monks and 50 nuns in Singapore. The Sangha Council of Singapore governs their social and religious behavior.

From the 1990s on, Buddhist organizations in Singapore have taken on the role as a welfare provider and have increasingly become involved in the provision of various types of welfare and social services to the general public. In addition to the provision of education facilities and welfare homes, it has also become involved in the provision of health and medical needs for the general public. One key example is the Ren Ci Hospital and Hospice Care run by the Foo Hai Monastery, which provides free medical care for the poor.

As Buddhism moves into the 21st century, its role as a welfare provider has become fully entrenched within the Singapore society and embraced by the Singapore state and the population at large.

Khun Eng Kuah

See also: Mahayana Buddhism; Theravada Buddhism; Tibetan Buddhism.

References

Kuah, Khun Eng. "Maintaining Ethno-Religious Harmony in Singapore." *Journal of Contemporary Asia* 28, no. 1 (1998): 103–121.

Kuah, Khun Eng. "State and Religion: Buddhism and Nation-Building in Singapore." *Pacific Viewpoint* 32, no. 1 (1991): 24–42.

Kuah-Pearce, Khun Eng. *State, Society and Religious Engineering: Towards a Reformist Buddhism in Singapore.* Singapore. Institute of Southeast Asian Studies, 2009.

Kuo, Eddie C. Y., and Tong Chee Kiong. *Religion in Singapore.* Singapore: Census of Population, 1990.

Ling, T. "Religion." In *Management of Success: The Moulding of Modern Singapore*, edited by K. S. Sandhu and P. Wheatley. Singapore: Institute of Southeast Asian Studies, 1989.

Wee, V. "'Buddhism' in Singapore." In *Singapore: Society in Transition*, edited by R. Hanssan. Kuala Lumpur: Oxford University Press, 1976.

Sivananda Saraswati, Swami

1887–1963

Swami Sivananda Saraswati was one of the most famous of the Indian spiritual teachers of the 20th century. The founder of the Divine Life Mission, an international organization with a number of offshoots, Sivananda was a yoga teacher who authored more than 200 books on various aspects of Hindu thought and practice.

Sivananda (also spelled Shivananda) was born Kuppuswami Iyer, the son of a pious Hindu government official. Desiring to be a doctor, he attended college and then medical school. His father died, however, before he completed his medical training, and as the eldest son, Kuppuswami was forced to leave school to assume his father's duties until his younger siblings were established. He was able to continue his interest in medicine during these years by editing a journal that specialized in preventive medicine and the Indian Ayurvedic approach to wellness. He eventually landed a job as the administrator of a hospital in Malaysia, where he met a wandering holy man who led him into beginning a spiritual search.

Having completed his family responsibilities, he returned to India and began a pilgrimage around the country. Shortly after his arrival in the holy city of Rishikesh, Swami Viswananda Saraswati initiated him into *sannyas* (the renounced life) and gave him his religious name. He took up residence at the Swargashram, on the Ganges River at Rishikesh. He spent his time in meditation and study, and given his background progressed swiftly. In a short time he was giving spiritual guidance to a growing group of disciples to whom he taught bhakti yoga (devotion) and karma yoga. He also opened a medical dispensary to serve the residents of the ashram.

In 1934 he moved across the river from Swartgashram and established his own ashram that included the Ananda Kutir, "abode of bliss," with a dispensary and meditation rooms for silent retreats. Two years later he founded the Divine Life Trust (a legal entity) to facilitate the enlarged vision of spiritualizing all of India. The Divine Life Society began as an auxiliary to the trust. Through the Society Sivananda launched a monthly periodical and then the Forest Academy, where he offered yoga training to his students.

Swami Sivananda never visited the West, but his many students who did come transformed him into one of the most influential people in the Western Hindu community and a major force in the dissemination of yoga throughout the world. Two of his students, Swami Vishnu Devananda (1927–1993) and Swami Satchidananda (1914–2002) founded the Sivananda Vedanta Yoga Centers and Integral Yoga International, respectively, both with multiple centers in the United States and Canada. As early as 1959, Swami Chidananda (b. 1916), who eventually succeeded Sivananda as head of the Divine Life Society, organized the Society in the United States. Another student, Swami Jyotirmayananda (b. 1931), founded the Yoga Research Foundation in 1962. Inspired by him, Swami Sivananda Radha (Sylvia Hillman, 1911–1995) founded the Yosodhara Ashram Society based in Vancouver.

Swami Sivananda died July 14, 1963.

J. Gordon Melton

See also: Devotion/Devotional Traditions; Integral Yoga International; Meditation; Rishikesh; Vedanta Societies; Yoga.

References

Fornaro, Robert John. *Sivananda and the Divine Life Society: A Paradigm of the "Secularism," "Puritanism" and "Cultural Dissimulation" of a Neo-Hindu Religious Society.* Syracuse, NY: Syracuse University Press, 1969.

Krishnananda, Swami. *Swami Shivananda and the Spiritual Renaissance.* Rishikesh, India: Shivanandanagar, 1959.

Life and Works of Swami Sivananda. Freemantle, Western Australia: Fremantle Branch, Divine Life Society, 1985.

Shivananda, Swami. *Sadhana.* Rishikesh, India: Shivanandanagar,1958.

Shivananda, Swami. *Science of Yoga.* 18 vols. Durban, South Africa: Divine Life Society, 1977.

Shivananda, Swami. *Yoga Asanas.* Rishikesh, India: Shivanandanagar, 1969.

Venkateshananda, Swami. *Gurudev Shivananda.* Rishikesh, India: Shivanandanagar, 1961.

■ Slovakia

Slovakia, a relatively new nation, formed in 1993 with the peaceful division of the former Czechoslovakia. Located in Central Europe, the completely landlocked country is surrounded by the Czech Republic, Austria, Hungary, Ukraine, and Poland. Its 5.5 million people reside on its 18,860 square miles of territory.

Slovakia was settled by Slavic tribes during the fifth and sixth centuries CE. Their Pagan religion belonged to the West-Slavic sphere, and it survived until the coming of Christianity in the ninth century. Also, at the beginning of the ninth century, an independent duchy spread through the territory of Slovakia with its center in Nitra. During the reign of the Earl Pribina, in the year 830, the first Christian church was constructed in Slovakia. At the time, Christian influence was conditioned by political loyalty to the German town of Salzburg, and this church was therefore consecrated by Adalram, the archbishop of Salzburg. Nevertheless, the Slavs in Nitra had as yet not converted to the new faith. Despite the work of missionaries from Ireland, Scotland, Germany, and Wallachia, neither inhabitants nor ruling elites converted to the Christian belief.

After the year 833, under the reign of the Earl Mojmir, the territory of Slovakia became part of the first state of the western Slavs named Great Moravia. Aiming to oppose the political expansion of his powerful neighbor, Rastislav, the ruler of Great Moravia, asked the pope to establish an independent church province. The pope refused, and therefore the following year,

Old Castle, Banska Stiavnica, Slovakia. (Richard Semik/
Dreamstime.com)

activities in Great Moravia. Pope Hadrian II subsequently gave the missionaries an audience, sanctified the holy books in the Slavic language, and ordained the first Slavic clerics.

For the first time in Europe, the pope agreed to a liturgy in a national language other than Greek or Latin. Unfortunately, Constantinus died in Rome; thus Methodius returned to the territory of Great Moravia as the first Slavic archbishop. He brought with him a copy of the papal bull *Gloria in altissimis Deo*, which confirmed the use of Slavic liturgy. Soon after his establishment in Great Moravia, Methodius again traveled to Rome in the name of the Earl Kocel. While there he received the resolution establishing the independent church province, the Pannonian see (archprovince), and was named the official papal representative (legatus). The position of Methodius as archbishop and the use of the Slavic liturgy was further reconfirmed by the pope in 880 in the bull *Industriae tuae*, issued on the occasion of Methodius's attestation of the Nicene Creed and of Roman orthodoxy. This act eventually led to the end of the use of the Slavic liturgy in the Byzantine rite in Great Moravia. The Romanization of the Slavic church was intensified by the actions of the German bishop Viching in Nitra, the main enemy of Methodius. After Methodius's death in 885, Viching took the initiative in disbanding his school and dislodging all its pupils. Subsequently, Slovakia naturalized the German clerical hierarchy.

After the battle at Bratislava in 907, which started the period of destruction of Great Moravia by the Magyars, the territory was in total chaos. By the end of the 10th century, the eastern part of Great Moravia (now the majority of the territory of Slovakia) became a duchy of the Hungarian kingdom, while the western part was transformed into the Czech state. The Hungarian earl, Gejza I, accepted Christianity in 997 under the ministrations of Bishop Vojtech of Prague. The Hungarian (Magyar) state organized the political and church administration at Slovakia after the fall of Great Moravia. It continued the orientation toward Western (or Catholic) Christianity, but the process of Christianization of the Hungarian nomads as well as the native Slavic inhabitants proceeded slowly. In the centuries of political chaos, many of the Slavs in the south had

Rastislav, based primarily on a political rationale and the idea of independence, asked the Byzantine emperor Michal III to send Christian teachers. In 863 Michal III sent the missionaries Constantinus (826–869) and Methodius (d. 885) from Thessalonika to Great Moravia. The two mastered the local dialect of the Aegean Slavs and then played an important role in the process of Christianization, especially as related to church administration and the education of clerical elites. They also translated the most important sacral books into the Slavic language and introduced Slavic into the liturgy. When, in 867, Constantinus (or Cyril) and Methodius planned to visit Constantinople, they received an invitation from the pope, who, despite their alignment to Eastern Orthodoxy, wished to control their

SLOVAKIA

been assimilated by the Hungarians, while in the north they sought the security of inaccessible places (such as mountains). Under the new political order, the See of Nitra was re-established by the year 1115. In addition, a new see was created in Jager, though the head of the hierarchy of the Hungarian state was the archbishop in Ösztergom.

Through the Middle Ages, the territory of Slovakia was fixed on Western Roman Catholicism. Many monasteries were established, and the number of holy orders operating in Slovakia increased. Catholicism became part of the national culture until the time of the Protestant Reformation. In the second half of the 16th century, Reformed and Lutheran doctrines were disseminated through Slovakia, and by the beginning of the 17th century some 90 percent of the inhabitants of Slovakia had become Protestants. This fact explains why the subsequent re-Catholization at the instigation of the Habsburg rulers of Hungary in the 17th century was so difficult. Jesuits in Trnava and Bratislava proved very effective. It was the period of repression of local

nobility, confiscations of the properties of Protestant churches, and forced mass conversions to Catholicism throughout the countryside. As a result, Protestantism survived only among the Slovak middle class and in a small number of villages. The development of Slovak culture up to the beginning of the 20th century followed two independent lines, Catholic and Protestant. Only in 1781, as a result of the tolerant policies of Emperor Joseph II, were Protestants granted equal rights with the Catholic majority. Paradoxically, it was from the Protestant, rather than the Catholic, circles that the majority of dominant personalities of Slovak culture of the 19th century arose, including, for example, Ludovít Štúr, the creator of the Slovak literary language. Through the upheavals of the modern world, somehow or other, the majority confession in Slovakia remained Roman Catholicism.

As of 1991, around 60 percent of the citizens belonged to the Roman Catholic Church. Only 8 percent of Slovaks belong to one of the Protestant churches, the largest being the Evangelical Church of the Augsburg

Slovakia

Religion	Followers in 1970	Followers in 2010	% of Population	Annual % growth 2000–2010	Followers in 2025	Followers in 2050
Christians	3,880,000	4,609,000	85.4	0.10	4,684,000	4,218,000
Roman Catholics	3,533,000	4,020,000	74.5	1.61	4,060,000	3,576,000
Protestants	816,000	510,000	9.5	−0.72	550,000	570,000
Orthodox	216,000	51,000	0.9	0.08	50,000	50,000
Agnostics	393,000	603,000	11.2	−0.73	500,000	360,000
Atheists	250,000	180,000	3.3	0.00	120,000	80,000
Jews	4,000	2,500	0.0	0.00	2,500	2,500
Baha'is	0	700	0.0	0.00	1,000	2,000
Muslims	500	550	0.0	0.00	700	1,000
Total population	**4,528,000**	**5,396,000**	**100.0**	**0.00**	**5,308,000**	**4,664,000**

Confession in the Slovak Republic, whose adherents include approximately 6 percent of the population. From the other confessions in Slovakia, only two groups have as much as 1 percent of the population: the Greek Catholic Church (3 percent) and the Reformed Christian Church of Slovakia (Calvinist) (1.5 percent). Among the other churches, the Orthodox Church, with 0.5 percent, also plays an important role in the life of Slovakia. In the year 1977 the pope established the independent province of the Slovak Catholic Church through his bull *Qui divino*.

In spite of it, during the whole atheistic regime (1948–1989), Christianity in Slovakia (Catholic, Protestant, or other) suffered repression. Church life was formally tolerated by the state, but in fact church members were discriminated against in education and social status. Activists were arrested, and, unlike the situation in other Communist regimes, played an important role in the Catholic Church. From its circles came the core of dissidents who organized the resistance and the so-called Tender Revolution (1989) in the Slovakian part of the former Czechoslovakia. After the fall of Czechoslovakia and the formation of independent Slovakia in 1993, Catholicism's influence on the public and cultural life of the country dramatically increased.

Milan Kováč

See also: Evangelical Church of the Augsburg Confession in the Slovak Republic; Greek Catholic Church; Reformed Christian Church in Slovakia; Roman Catholic Church.

References

Dekan, Ján. *Moravia Magna*. Bratislava, Slovakia: Tatran, 1980.

Polácik, Stefan, ed. *Atlas der Religionen, Religiöser Gemeinschaften und Religiosität in der Slowakei.* Bratislava, Slovakia: Chronos, 2000.

Vanco, Martin. "The Beginning of the Great Moravian Empire: Christianization." In *Medieval Rotundas in Slovakia,* edited by Martin Vance. Bratislava, Slovakia: Chronos, 2000.

■ Slovenia

Slovenia, a product of the breakup of the former country of Yugoslavia, lies south of Austria between Italy and Croatia. A largely mountainous country, it has a small outlet on the Adriatic Sea. Its 2 million people reside primarily in the river valleys of its 7,780 square miles of territory.

The Slovenes, a southern Slavic people, settled in what is now the Republic of Slovenia in the seventh century CE. However, in 743 the area was conquered by the Bavarians, and the Slovenes began a long period of subjugation to various Germanic powers. The Slavs who lived north of the Drava River were Germanized, but those to the south were able to retain their identity as Slovenians. Beginning in the 13th century, Austria became the dominant influence in the region. Austrian rule continued throughout the 19th century, except for a brief period during the Napoleonic era.

Churches in Ljubljana, Slovenia's capital. (iStockPhoto.com)

During the late 19th century, Slovenians began to identify with the pan-Slavic movement but had to settle for the union of the Slavic regions of the Austro-Hungarian Empire into an autonomous political area within the empire in 1917. After World War I and the fall of the empire, the region was assigned to Austria. Following World War II, Slovenia became one of the six republics within the Federation of Yugoslavia. It prospered as one of the country's most industrialized area.

In 1990 a move to separate from Yugoslavia became noticeable, and the following year Slovenia declared its independence. That independence was recognized by the countries of Western Europe, and, fortunately, Slovenia was able to stay out of the war in the 1990s that ravaged its former comrades in the other Yugoslavian republics.

The Roman Catholic Church established itself very early among the Slovenian people, and the work of native priests and monks (who constituted the great majority of the Slovenian intelligentsia during the Middle Ages) is credited with the southern Slovenes' retaining their identity as a people. It also separated them from the Orthodox-dominated regions farther south and the Croatian Catholics, who had been heavily influenced by Italian leadership. The church was supported by the Austrian Catholic hierarchy through Slovenia's many centuries under Austrian control, but it suffered under the secularization that occurred in the postwar period (1945–1991). Today the church is led by the archbishop of Ljubljana and the Slovenia Episcopal Conference. They command the loyalty of the majority of the 2 million citizens.

Protestants came into Slovenia as the Reformation spread through German lands in the 16th century. The Lutheran Church suffered losses during the Counter-Reformation, and many Lutherans found refuge in the Prekmuije region, where the church is still strong. It was able to recover somewhat during the period of religious tolerance that began with Joseph II. Lutherans were incorporated into the Hungarian Lutheran Church but emerged as the Evangelical Christian Church in

SLOVENIA

Slovenia after World War II. Today, as the Evangelical Church of the Augsburg Confession in Slovenia, it is the largest Protestant body in Slovenia and a member of the Lutheran World Federation and the European Council of Churches, though it has not joined the World Council of Churches. The large Reformed presence in Hungary spilled over into Slovenia, and, early in the 20th century, some 800 Reformed church members, mostly of Hungarian ethnicity, formed 3 congregations in Slovenia. They became independent in 1921 as the Reformed Church in Yugoslavia. It developed a relationship with the Reformed Christian Church in Yugoslavia. In 1993 the Reformed Christian Church in Slovenia was established, and the Reformed Church of Hungary accepted responsibility for providing pastoral oversight. It currently has a close working relationship with the Slovenian Lutheran Church. Protestants in Slovenia cooperate in the Council of Christian Churches in Slovenia.

The Seventh-day Adventist Church entered the region in 1909, and in 1925 it organized the Croatian-Slovenian Conference (reorganized in 1992). The work is headquartered in Zagreb, Croatia. Baptists came into the area in the person of Martin Hiastan, an agent of the British and Foreign Bible Society in the years prior to World War I. His first convert, Jurij Carter, began holding meetings in his home in 1923. The little church became associated with the Baptist church in Zagreb. It was not until 1938 that there was enough Baptist strength for a Slovenian conference to be organized.

The Italians who occupied Slovenia during World War II closed the Baptist churches and imprisoned some of the Baptist leadership. Following the breakup of Yugoslavia, the four surviving Baptist churches formed the Union of Baptist Churches in Slovenia.

The Church of Jesus Christ of Latter-day Saints had initiated work in Slovenia in 1899 through the efforts of Mischa Markow, a Hungarian who had previously

Slovenia

Religion	Followers in 1970	Followers in 2010	% of Population	Annual % growth 2000–2010	Followers in 2025	Followers in 2050
Christians	1,550,000	1,813,000	90.6	0.14	1,764,000	1,545,000
Roman Catholics	1,477,000	1,622,000	81.1	–0.03	1,569,000	1,369,000
Orthodox	30,200	58,000	2.9	2.09	60,000	65,000
Protestants	35,400	29,000	1.4	1.15	30,000	35,000
Agnostics	69,000	105,000	5.2	0.50	100,000	85,000
Atheists	50,000	45,800	2.3	0.16	40,000	30,000
Muslims	1,000	37,000	1.8	0.16	36,000	33,000
Baha'is	0	350	0.0	0.19	600	900
Jews	100	120	0.0	0.17	120	120
Total population	**1,670,000**	**2,001,000**	**100.0**	**0.16**	**1,941,000**	**1,694,000**

settled in Salt Lake City, Utah. He was banished after only a month of work. His effort was not revived until the 1970s, when the LDS were able to establish themselves as a legal entity in Yugoslavia. The first meetings were held in Ljubljana. In 1993 the first full-time elder from Slovenia arrived in Salt Lake City for training. Jehovah's Witnesses came into Yugoslavia in 1925 and continued to work quietly in the decades after World War II, even though officially banned. They emerged quickly after the breakup of Yugoslavia and can now be found in various locations across Slovenia.

Various religions have come to Slovenia since its independence in 1991. They include the Unification Movement, Sahaja Yoga, and the International Society for Krishna Consciousness. Several Esoteric groups such as the Theosophical Society and the Ordo Templi Orientis had been able to function quietly even earlier. The small Jewish community in Slovenia was ravaged first by the Holocaust and then by the movement of members to Israel. Fewer than 100 remain today.

J. Gordon Melton

See also: Church of Jesus Christ of Latter-day Saints; International Society for Krishna Consciousness; Jehovah's Witnesses; Lutheran World Federation; Ordo Templi Orientis; Roman Catholic Church; Sahaja Yoga; Seventh-day Adventist Church; Theosophical Society (America); Unification Movement; World Council of Churches.

References

Benderly, Jim. *Independent Slovenia: Origins, Movements, Prospects.* New York: Palgrave Macmillan, 1996.

Cox, John K. *Slovenia.* New York: Routledge, 2005.

Flere, S. "Denominational Affiliation in Yugoslavia: 1930–1989." *East European Quarterly* 25 (June 1991): 145–165.

Frid, Z., ed. *Religions in Yugoslavia: Historical Survey, Legal Status, Church in Socialism, Ecumenism, Dialogue between Marxists and Christians, etc.* Zagreb, Croatia: Binoza, 1971.

Ramet, R. "Religion and Nationality in Yugoslavia." In *Religion and Nationalism in Soviet and East European Politics,* edited by R. Ramet. Durham, NC: Duke University Press, 1989.

Smarta Tradition

The Smarta tradition is a living Hindu tradition whose origins can be traced back to the classical age of Hinduism. This tradition was derived from Puranic traditional practices. The Smartas combined the concept of *varnashramadharma* (social organization around castes) with *puja* (worship) to a few select major deities. The Smartas get their name from the sacred *smriti* texts. This class of texts are "things that are remembered," or secret oral teachings passed down from generation to generation. Many teachings are still secrets disclosed only among devout Smartas. As the Smarta size grew smaller and smaller, the teachings were written down for the sake of future preservation. Smarta teaches its adherents that they are the true root of Hinduism.

The Smartas revere and worship five principal deities—Vishnu (preserver god), Shiva (destroyer god), Surya (sun god), Ganesha (remover of obstacles), and Durga (warrior goddess). Smarta puja perpetuates rites from the Vedas (mainly the Rig Veda) and the repetition of many mantras (secret meditative incantations). Smarta worship is more of a solemn duty than a devotional part of life, thus communion with the divine or eternal salvation is rarely the focal point or even an important aspect in Smarta worship rituals.

The Smartas consider themselves a Hindu subgroup, and the predominant Smarta population consists primarily of wealthy Indians. Today, wealthy Hindus tend to practice Smarta-style Hinduism rather than Vaishnava or Saivite styles.

Kumar Jairamdas

See also: Devotion/Devotional Traditions; Hinduism; Meditation.

References

Basham, A. L. *The Origins and Development of Classical Hinduism.* New York: Oxford University Press, 1989.

Eck, Diana. *Darsan: Seeing the Divine Image in India.* 3rd ed. New York: Columbia University Press, 1998.

Smith, Joseph, Jr.

1805–1844

Joseph Smith, Jr., was the founder of the 19th-century Christian restoration movement popularly known as Mormonism, most commonly connected to the Church of Jesus Christ of Latter-day Saints, now based in Salt Lake City. The multi-million-member Church of Jesus Christ of Latter-day Saints is one of the 10 largest religious groups in North America, but it is but one of some 50 groups that also claim Smith as their founder, including the Community of Christ (Independence,

Portrait of Joseph Smith, Jr., founder of the Mormon Church. (Library of Congress)

Missouri) and the polygamy-practicing Fundamentalist Church of Jesus Christ of Latter-day Saints (Colorado City, Arizona).

Smith was born in Sharon, Vermont, on December 23, 1805, but he moved with his family to New York State in 1816, settling in Palmyra, southeast of Rochester. He claimed that he received a divine visitation from God the Father and Jesus in 1820, an episode known as the "First Vision." Smith also said that on September 21, 1823, an angel named Moroni told him of gold plates buried in the hill Cumorah near Palmyra. Smith married Emma Hale (1804–1879) in 1827, the same year that Smith claimed to discover the gold plates. He translated the plates into the Book of Mormon. That work was printed in March 1830, and a new church was founded by Smith on April 6.

Joseph and a small group of followers moved to Ohio in 1831. A mission to Missouri was launched in 1832 but resulted in ongoing persecution, including deadly mob attacks. Smith himself was jailed in Missouri for six months in 1838–1839. After escaping from custody Smith moved the Mormons to Commerce, Illinois. He renamed the city Nauvoo and lived there until his death. Nauvoo prospered and the Latter-day Saints erected a large temple. As the city grew to be the largest in Illinois, Smith became deeply involved in the state's politics, one of several issues leading to the development of heightened hostility against the Mormons both in the county and throughout the state.

In the summer of 1844, dissenting residents of Nauvoo printed a newspaper challenging Smith's leadership. After the press that printed the paper was destroyed, Smith and several compatriots were arrested and taken to the county seat at Carthage. There, Smith and his brother Hyrum were killed by an angry mob on June 27, 1844.

The teachings of the Book of Mormon conform in large measure to classical Christian doctrine, setting aside the issue of its historical integrity. The work purports to tell the history of Jewish groups who immigrated to the Americas before the time of Christ. Smith's own direct revelations appeared first in the Book of Commandments in 1831 and then as the Doctrine and Covenants in 1835. Other revelations were canonized in *The Pearl of Great Price* in 1851, seven years after Smith's death. Smith's most controversial work is probably the Book of Abraham, which was his translation of Egyptian documents that came into his possession in 1835. Smith claimed that the papyri were actually from the ancient patriarch.

By all accounts Smith was a charismatic figure who was able to draw people into his religious vision. He was also maligned for his views and subject to intense criticism, most notably over his later teachings and adoption of polygamy, the latter as early as 1841. Smith advanced novel understandings of salvation, including baptism for the dead, and advocated a plurality of gods as of 1842. The earliest criticisms of him had to do with advocating extra-biblical revelation, his claims of private encounters with God, and the authenticity of the Book of Mormon. Under Smith's successor, Brigham Young (1801–1877), the church he founded went on to advocate the practice of polygamy, leading the national government to act against it, but renounced it, in stages, beginning in 1890. The Church of Jesus Christ of Latter-day Saints spent much of the 20th century attempting to separate itself from the idea.

James A. Beverley

See also: Church of Jesus Christ of Latter-day Saints; Community of Christ; Martyrdom; Polygamy-Practicing Mormons; Salt Lake City; Temples—Church of Jesus Christ of Latter-day Saints.

References

Arrington, Leonard. *The Mormon Experience*. New York: Knopf, 1979.

Brodie, Fawn M. *No Man Knows My History*. New York: Alfred A. Knopf, 1977.

Bushman, Richard. *Rough Stone Rolling*. New York: Knopf, 2005.

Compton, Todd. *In Sacred Loneliness*. Salt Lake City, UT: Signature, 1997.

Huntress, Keith. *Murder of an American Prophet: Events and Prejudices Surrounding the Killing of Joseph and Hyrum Smith, Carthage, Illinois, June 27, 1844*. San Francisco: Chandler, 1960.

Marquardt, Michael. *The Rise of Mormonism: 1816–1844*. Longwood, FL: Xulon Press, 2005.

Shipps, Jan. *Mormonism: The Story of a New Religious Tradition*. Urbana: University of Illinois Press, 1985.

Vogel, Dan. *Joseph Smith: The Making of a Prophet*. Salt Lake City, UT: Signature, 2004.

Society for the Propagation of the Gospel in Foreign Parts

The Society for the Propagation of the Gospel in Foreign Parts (SPG) is the older of the two Anglican missionary organizations that contributed substantially to the spread of the Church of England internationally in the 19th century and led to the formation of numerous Anglican churches that currently exist around the globe. The Society, formed in 1701, originated from a survey of conditions among the settlers in the British

American colonies by Thomas Bray (1656–1730). Early discussions resulted in two goals for the new society: the serving of the religious needs of English settlers far from Britain (primarily in North America and the Caribbean) and the conversion of the Native populations in British colonies.

Although established as an independent body with private funds, it quickly bound itself to the established church, beginning with its royal charter and the convening of its first meeting at Lambeth Palace under the chairmanship of Archbishop Thomas Tenison (1635–1715). Work was confined to North America and the Caribbean during its first century, among the first people commissioned being a teacher for African American children in New York City. However, as the British Empire expanded during the 19th century, the SPG followed. The independence of the American colonies freed resources to be used in other parts of the world.

At the beginning of the 19th century, the SPG was joined by a second Anglican missionary organization, the Church Missionary Society. The latter, a product of the Evangelical Awakening in England in the previous century, was decidedly Low Church in its sympathies, while the SPG had been very much identified with the High-Church wing of Anglicanism.

Work began in India in 1818, and that in Africa and the Middle East soon followed. The SPG extended its concern to Malaysia in the middle of the century, and later in the century opened missions in Japan and Korea.

In the 20th century, the SPG adjusted to the maturing of the missions into the new independent Anglican churches that now constitute the worldwide Anglican Communion. In many areas they continued to support missionary personnel, especially among those churches still struggling for financial independence. However, the change in the missionary thrust in the years after World War II also cost the SPG popular support, and its income suffered accordingly. In 1965 and 1968, the SPG merged with two other organizations, the Universities' Mission in Central Africa and the Cambridge Mission to Delhi, to produce a new organization, the United Society for the Propagation of the Gospel. The United Society continues to support personnel in more than 20 countries and works with more than 50 churches worldwide.

United Society for the Propagation of the Gospel
Partnership House
156 Waterloo Rd.
London SE1 8XA
United Kingdom
http://www.uspg.org.uk/

J. Gordon Melton

See also: Anglican Communion/Anglican Consultative Council; Church Missionary Society; Church of England.

Reference

Dewey, M. *The Messengers: A Concise History of the United Society for the Propagation of the Gospel.* London: Mowbray's, 1975.

Society of Saint Pius X

See Fraternity/Society of Saint Pius X.

Socinianism

Socinianism, an anti-Trinitarian movement that emerged within the larger Protestant Reformation of the 16th century, derives its name from two Italian Reformers, Lelius Socinius (1526–1562) and his nephew, Faustus Socinius (1539–1604), both natives of Siena, Italy. The movement began as a secret society in the Diocese of Venice (which for a period in the 1530s was a haven for Italian Reformers) that met to discuss the doctrine of the Trinity. (Most Christians believe that God is one but expressed in three persons of the Father, Son, and Holy Spirit.) Among the members was Lelius Socinius, a Catholic priest and acquaintance of other Reformers: Heinrich Bullinger, John Calvin, and Philip Melanchthon. When the opposition of the society to Trinitarian belief became known, it was disbanded and its members quietly departed to Poland, where they discovered they were also not welcome. Lelius finally found a haven in Zurich, from where he stayed in contact with a group of non-Trinitarian believers in Krakow. The Polish anti-Trinitarians survived through the years, though suffering some division following Lelius's death in 1562. In 1574 they were able to issue a catechism.

Meanwhile, Giorgio Biandrata (1515–1590), one of the leaders of the Venetian society, had moved to Transylvania (then under Turkish Ottoman control), where he became the court physician to Transylvania's ruler, Hungarian King John Sigismund, who had championed the Transylvanian Diet's adoption (1564) of Calvinism as the state religion. Biandrata proceeded to win the leader of the Reformed (Calvinist) Church, Francis David (1510–1579), to his non-Trinitarian position. David thus became head of a Unitarian church centered in Transylvania.

Meanwhile, Faustus Socinius, who was able to remain behind and unite the Polish Unitarians, was called to Transylvania to assist David, who had been imprisoned for his Unitarian views that denied both the Trinity and that Christ was an entity worthy of worship. The Transylvanian Unitarians also worshiped on the Sabbath. In contrast, Socinius believed that Christ was the Promised Man and the Mediator of creation and thus the author of regeneration. Though he was not God, Socinius believed that Christ was worthy of adoration. David could not accept Socinius's views, and ultimately died in prison.

Meanwhile, the new European focus for Socinianism at Racow, Poland, flourished. Among Faustus's last acts was the drawing up of a new catechism, which was published in Polish the year after his death (1605) and then in Latin four years later. In a relatively protected situation, even as the Catholic Counter-Reformation gained strength in Poland, the Socinians established schools, held synods, and produced numerous pieces of literature from their own printing presses.

With Socinian literature and influence being felt throughout Europe, in 1638 the Catholic authorities called for the banishment of all Unitarians, and on this issue Protestants were in hardy agreement. One by one, the various European countries, even Poland, moved to suppress the movement. Additional animus was attached to them as their theology was examined. Not only did they deny Christ's divinity, they also denied the real presence in the sacraments (especially the Roman Catholic idea of transubstantiation), original sin, hell, and infant baptism. They taught that the Holy Spirit was to be seen not as the third person of the Trinity, but as an operation of God, the power for sanctification.

Socinianism was stamped out in Poland and other Catholic countries by the Counter-Reformation. Protestants in England and Holland, where Socinians briefly emerged, were hardly kinder, though in England, a thin lineage of Socinian thought survived to inspire what would become British Unitarianism in the 18th century.

J. Gordon Melton

See also: Roman Catholic Church; Unitarian Universalist Association.

References

Hillar, Marian. "From the Polish Socinians to the American Constitution." *A Journal from the Radical Reformation. A Testimony to Biblical Unitarianism* 3, no. 2 (1994): 22–57. http://www.socinian.org/polish_socinians.html. Accessed July 15, 2009.

Wilbur, Earl Morse. *A History of Unitarianism.* Vol. 1, *Socinianism and Its Antecedents.* Boston: Beacon Press, 1945.

Williams, George H. *The Polish Brethren: Documentation of the History and Thought of Unitarianism in the Polish-Lithuanian Commonwealth and in the Diaspora, 1601–1685.* Atlanta, GA: Scholars Press, 1980.

Soka Gakkai International

Soka Gakkai is the largest Buddhist sect in Japan. With 8 million members or more, Soka Gakkai members represent at least 6 percent of the Japanese population and 14 percent of Japan's 56 million Buddhists. Another 4 million members worldwide, consisting of Japanese emigrants and sizable numbers of converts, make Soka Gakkai Japan's most successful 20th-century export religion. It has an organized presence in Africa (South Africa), Asia (Hong Kong, India, Japan, Korea, Malaysia, Philippines, Singapore, Sri Lanka, Taiwan, Thailand), Europe (Austria, Denmark, Finland, France, Germany, Hungary, Iceland, Ireland, Italy, Luxembourg, The Netherlands, Norway, Spain, Sweden, Switzerland, the United Kingdom), North America (Canada, the United States), Central America (Costa Rica, Panama, Mexico), Oceania (Australia, New Zea-

Soka Gakkai believers chant prayers to start an evening gathering at a small apartment in Tokyo in 2004. (AP/Wide World Photos)

land), and South America (Argentina, Brazil, Chile, Paraguay, Peru, Uruguay, Venezuela).

Soka Gakkai was founded in Japan in 1930 by an educator, Tsunesaburo Makiguchi (1871–1944), who organized the Soka Kyoiku Gakkai (Value Creation Education Society) in an attempt to give the Japanese educational system a more Humanist focus. Shortly before Japan's entry into World War II, Makiguchi and his protégé, Josei Toda (1900–1958), converted to Nichiren Shoshu Buddhism—a sect that claims to teach the "true Buddhism" as taught by Nichiren (1222–1282). Zealous converts, Makiguchi and Toda were imprisoned on charges of lese majesty for their refusal to cooperate with the Religious Organizations Act (1940), which created a three-religion establishment, centered on State Shinto and designed to promote patriotism and loyalty to the increasingly militarist regime.

Following Makiguchi's death in prison and the end of World War II, Toda, the movement's second president, reorganized Soka Gakkai as a lay association of Nichiren Shoshu. In the chaotic aftermath of the war, Soka Gakkai grew rapidly, mostly among the displaced residents of urban environments. However, Toda's zeal, and the zeal of new converts, attracted public suspicion. New converts sometimes destroyed ancestral altars as an expression of exclusive devotion to their new religion; indeed, they may have been encouraged to do so by the movement's leadership. The practice of *shakubuku*, an aggressive and argumentative means of recruitment, also set the movement at odds with established religions and led to accusations that Soka Gakkai brainwashed its members. Massive rallies and parades sponsored by Soka Gakkai reminded onlookers of the demonstrations of Fascist regimes during World War II. Together, these features gave Soka Gakkai in Japan the image of a dangerous "cult," whose leaders had ulterior and untoward motives.

Daisaku Ikeda (b. 1928), Soka Gakkai's charismatic third president, led the international growth of the movement. Although Ikeda and his successor, Einosuke Akiya, have gone to great lengths to improve the movement's public image, suspicion remains. Soka Gakkai's political involvement through the organ of the Komeito, a political party founded by the Soka Gakkai, and the near godlike reverence that members have for President Ikeda have tended to perpetuate public distrust. Although it has been subject to a generalized suspicion toward Eastern religious movements in the United States, Europe, and South America, the movement's history outside of Japan has been tranquil by comparison to its Japanese history.

Belief and Practice   Nichiren was a 13th-century monk who taught that all individuals contain within themselves the potential for enlightenment and that this potential can be unlocked by exclusive devotion to the Lotus Sutra. The Lotus Sutra is understood to be the most perfect expression of the Buddha's wisdom. By chanting the title of the Lotus Sutra, *Nam-Myoho-Renge-Kyo*, one forms a connection with the ultimate reality that pervades the universe—the karmic law of cause and effect. In common with other followers of Nichiren, Soka Gakkai members chant this phrase, along with portions of the Lotus Sutra and prayers for world peace (collectively called *Gongyo*), in front of a copy of the *Gohonzon*, a mandala originally inscribed by Nichiren that features the title of the Lotus Sutra surrounded by characters representing the 10 realms of consciousness.

The 10 realms refer to 10 basic life conditions, which everyone possesses and experiences—hell, hunger, animality, and belligerence, through tranquility, rapture, learning, and realization, to bodhisattva, and ultimately Buddhahood or enlightenment. These "life conditions" are not understood as external circumstances imposing upon the individual but rather as modes of being. Thus, one's external circumstances are but a reflection of one's inner life condition, and by changing one's way of being in the world, one can improve the external circumstances of one's life.

Soka Gakkai, furthermore, promotes the belief that individual enlightenment is the first step toward world peace. As individuals become enlightened, they can work together to raise awareness of issues of intercultural understanding and tolerance, issues of the environment, and the threat of military technology. As an organization, therefore, Soka Gakkai sponsors a variety of educational, cultural, and political projects and participates in the United Nations as a nongovernmental organization. The organization, for instance, has founded a major university as well as primary and secondary schools in Japan. It also sponsors art museums, a concert association, retreat centers, and research associations, both in Japan and in Europe and America. Every year members submit a peace proposal to the United Nations on behalf of President Ikeda.

The Schism of 1991   For more than 50 years, Soka Gakkai existed as a lay movement affiliated with the Nichiren Shoshu sect. But latent tensions between the Soka Gakkai and the Nichiren Shoshu leadership came to a head in 1990, when the high priest accused Daisaku Ikeda, who remains the movement's primary spiritual figurehead, of slandering Buddhism by asserting that the priests and laity are equal before the Gohonzon. Although a formal apology was issued by the Soka Gakkai leadership, and apparently accepted by the priests, tensions between Soka Gakkai leaders and the priests continued to grow. When the priests raised obligatory fees for funerary and other ritual services, Soka Gakkai leaders objected that the priests had become greedy and authoritarian. In reply, the priests accused Soka Gakkai leaders, primarily Ikeda, of slandering the priesthood. In November 1991, the high priest of Nichiren Shoshu ordered the Soka Gakkai to disband and issued a writ of excommunication for all members who remained affiliated with the Soka Gakkai.

Ironically, in many countries Soka Gakkai seems to have benefited greatly from that split. The schism served to enhance the autonomy of the various national organizations, making it easier for these organizations to adapt to the circumstances in their immediate environments. To fill the gap left by the priests, Soka Gakkai developed roles for voluntary "ministers of ceremony," who now preside over weddings, funerals, and other ritual services.

Although Soka Gakkai's growth worldwide slowed during the 1990s, it remains steady. The organization thus appears to have successfully weathered its developmental challenges, and its future appears secure. Soka Gakkai International has regional and national offices serving the movement worldwide and an extensive Soka Gakkai Internet presence.

Soka Gakkai International Headquarters
Office of Public Relations
15-3 Samon-cho
Shinjuku-ku, Tokyo 160-0017
Japan
http://www.sgi.org
    Phillip E. Hammond and David W. Machacek

See also: Nichiren Shoshu.

References

Eppsteiner, Robert. *The Soka Gakkai International: Religious Roots, Early History, and Contemporary Development.* Cambridge: Soka Gakkai International, 1997.

Hammond, Phillip, and David Machacek. *Soka Gakkai in America: Accommodation and Conversion.* Oxford: Oxford University Press, 1999.

Machacek, David, and Brian Wilson, eds. *Global Citizens: The Soka Gakkai Buddhist Movement in the World.* Oxford: Oxford University Press, 2000.

Metraux, Daniel A. *The International Expansion of a Modern Buddhist Movement: The Soka Gakkai in Southeast Asia and Australia.* Lanham, MD: University Press of America, 2001.

Metraux, Daniel A. *The Lotus and the Maple Leaf.* Lanham, MD: University Press of America, 1996.

Seager, Richard Hughes. *Encountering the Dharma: Daisaku Ikeda, Soka Gakkai, and the Globalization of Buddhist Humanism.* Berkeley: University of California Press, 2006.

Wilson, Brian, and Karel Dobbelaere. *A Time to Chant: The Soka Gakkai Buddhists in Britain.* Oxford: Clarendon Press, 1994.

Solar Temple, Order of the

This defunct movement was founded by a French citizen, Jo Di Mambro (1924–1994). Di Mambro had previously been a member of the Ancient and Mystical Order Rosae Crucis (AMORC) from 1956 to the late 1960s. During that period, he apparently also developed his first contacts with French groups interested in launching a Templar "resurgence." In 1973, Di Mambro became president of a Center of the Preparation of the New Age, and in 1976 he organized a community called the Pyramid. In 1978 he settled with his followers in Geneva, where he created the Golden Way Foundation. This Foundation developed cultural activities attracting outsiders, too, but at the same time it sheltered esoteric rites of Rosicrucian and Templar inspiration for those intensely engaged in the work. A community always remained the core of the various groups led by Di Mambro.

In the early 1980s, a Belgian homeopathic physician, Luc Jouret (1947–1994) joined the group and, being a gifted speaker, became its main propagandist. He soon became well known in the New Age and Esoteric circuit in French-speaking countries. Cultural clubs named Archedia were launched and functioned as an exoteric counterpart to the Esoteric order, then called the International Order of Chivalry, Solar Tradition. However, while hundreds of people sometimes attended Jouret's lectures, the membership of the Order remained more modest, apparently peaking at around 500 members. People forming the core community did not necessarily belong to the order. The name the Order of the Solar Temple is being used here in a generic way, since the movements became famous under that name; there were, however, several simultaneous or successive groups with different names, and reorganizations were frequent.

The ideological sources of the movement were eclectic and reflected many of the ideas common in the occult subculture. However, its message put an unusual emphasis upon imminent apocalyptic turmoils, as a prelude to the passage to new conditions for those people who would manage to survive and become the seeds of the new Solar Race: In case there would not be a sufficient number of people answering the call of

2660 | ■ Solomon Islands

the Temple for staving off global disaster, at least there would be "enough survivors to carry the species toward the evolutionary blueprint intended for mankind." During the 1980s, there was a clear survivalist orientation.

For a number of reasons, including internal dissent, survivalism on this planet was abandoned by Di Mambro and a core group around him from the early 1990s; the mood turned increasingly pessimistic. The leaders of the Solar Temple decided that the only way was a "transit" toward another world. That was accomplished in October 1994. Some left willingly, but a number of members apparently did not realize that their "transit" involved being killed; others, considered traitors, were assassinated, including a couple and their baby child savagely slaughtered in Quebec. Most of the other 50 victims died in Switzerland, including the leaders. In December 1995, 16 members lost their lives in France and, in March 1997, 5 people in Quebec.

Although some people continue to believe in some of its doctrines, the Solar Temple no longer exists as a group. But the impact of the repeated "transits" created an aftershock extending well beyond the Solar Temple: for instance, it contributed to the radicalization of the campaign against "cults" by authorities in countries such as France.

Jean-François Mayer

See also: Ancient and Mystical Order Rosae Crucis; New Age Movement; Western Esoteric Tradition.

References

Delaforge, Gaetan. *The Templar Tradition in the Age of Aquarius*. Putney, VT: Threshold, 1987.

Hall, John R., and Philip D. Schuyler. "The Mystical Apocalypse of the Solar Temple." In *Apocalypse Observed: Religious Movements and Violence in North America, Europe, and Japan*, edited by John R. Hall, 111–148. London: Routledge, 2000.

Lewis, James R., ed. *The Order of the Solar Temple: The Temple of Death*. Aldershot, UK: Ashgate, 2006.

Mayer, Jean-François. "'Our Terrestrial Journey Is Coming to an End': The Last Voyage of the Solar Temple." *Nova Religio: The Journal of Alternative and Emergent Religions* 2, no. 2 (1999): 172–196. http://religioscope.info/article_172.shtml.

■ Solomon Islands

The Solomon Islands are a set of islands northwest of Australia in the South Pacific, the most famous of which is Guadalcanal. Some 581,000 people are scattered among the 10,600 square miles of land. Most of the islands' residents are Melanesians, but minorities from Europe, China, and Polynesia settled there over the course of the last century.

The Solomons have been inhabited by Melanesians for some 4,000 years. Europeans first discovered the islands in 1567, when the Spaniard Alvaro de Mendeña landed. Beginning in the 18th century, slavers raided the islanders and transported captured islanders to Fiji and Australia to work the sugar plantations.

Only after World War I did England move to establish a colony over the Solomons. The Japanese invaded and held the islands until recaptured by Allied forces. Following World War II, the archipelago was divided into two parts. The western half was later annexed to Papua New Guinea. The remaining portion became a British colony until granted independence in 1978. During the 1990s, the country was beset with problems of crime and corruption so severe as to threaten the country's existence. In 2002, an Australian-led multinational force entered the country on a mission to restore order, assist in reorganizing the government, and disarm some local militias that had arisen. Their effort, which continues, has been deemed largely successful.

Traditional religion has survived in the Solomons. The dominant faith at the time the first Christian missionaries arrived was a polytheistic system that recognized a somewhat remote supreme being who went under different names on the different islands. The more operative concept, made famous by anthropological description, is *mana*, the impersonal power that pervades the cosmos at every level. Mana is a comprehensive concept that explains a variety of phenomena, and it

SOLOMON ISLANDS

can be used by religious practitioners to heal and work magic. Following long-term contact with Europeans, a number of new variations of the traditional religion appeared. The best known of these new traditional religions were the "cargo cults" based around the airplanes that brought unfamiliar objects to the islands during and after World War II.

The Roman Catholic Church arrived in the Solomons when Marist priests opened a mission in 1845. It was later abandoned, but by that time the Anglican Church in New Zealand had launched a mission to Melanesians. In 1861, John C. Patterson, designated the missionary bishop for Melanesia, began a decade of leadership ended by his untimely death at the hands of residents of the Santa Cruz Islands. Patterson was succeeded by John Selwyn, who continued Patterson's policy of gathering the most talented among the converts and sending them to New Zealand for formal training. The Anglican work on the Solomons grew as a missionary diocese in the Province of New Zealand.

In 1970 it was set apart as the Church in the Province of Melanesia. It is the largest church in the islands, including some 30 percent of the 320,000 citizens.

Roman Catholics soon re-established work, and by 1897 a prefecture was erected that grew into a vicariate in 1912. In 1916 the islands were divided into two dioceses, one for the western Solomons and one for the southern islands, the latter based on Guadalcanal at the capital, Honiara. Approximately 20 percent of the population are professed Catholics.

Methodists from Australia came to the Solomons in 1902 and brought Native workers from Samoa and Fiji with them. In 1922 the New Zealand Church assumed responsibility for what had grown into a district, but the church was largely destroyed by the Japanese; it was rebuilt, however, in the years immediately after hostilities ended. In 1968 the Methodist Church of the Solomons participated in a merger with the Congregationalists on New Guinea to form the United Church in Papua New Guinea and the Solomon Islands, now

Solomon Islands

Religion	Followers in 1970	Followers in 2010	% of Population	Annual % growth 2000–2010	Followers in 2025	Followers in 2050
Christians	151,000	506,000	95.3	2.58	675,000	917,000
Protestants	46,800	220,000	41.4	2.38	290,000	380,000
Anglicans	50,000	171,000	32.2	2.48	200,000	270,000
Roman Catholics	30,800	105,000	19.8	2.28	150,000	205,000
Ethnoreligionists	9,000	16,500	3.1	2.60	16,000	15,000
Baha'is	400	3,300	0.6	2.75	5,000	8,000
Buddhists	0	1,700	0.3	2.61	2,500	3,600
Agnostics	300	1,500	0.3	3.96	3,500	7,000
Muslims	0	1,700	0.3	9.92	2,400	3,600
Atheists	0	250	0.0	2.82	500	1,000
Total population	**161,000**	**531,000**	**100.0**	**2.60**	**705,000**	**955,000**

divided into the United Church in Papua New Guinea and United Church of the Solomon Islands, separately.

In 1904 the South Seas Evangelical Mission, a faith mission based in Australia, grew out of the older Queensland Kanaka Mission. Its first missionary was Florence S. H. Young. She was followed by 13 members of the family of Dr. Northcote Young, who opened work on Guadalcanal, Malita, and Makira. Their work grew into the South Sea Evangelical Church, which became an independent body in 1963. By 1970 it had 285 congregations affiliated with it.

The older mission churches, including the Roman Catholic Church, formed the ecumenical Solomon Islands Christian Association in 1967. It includes the several churches that are also members of the World Council of Churches, the Anglican and the United churches. The South Seas Island Church has identified with the World Evangelical Alliance and participates in the Evangelical Alliance of Papua New Guinea and the Solomon Islands.

The Seventh-day Adventist Church contributed to the expanding array of churches in the Solomons in 1914. Its very successful mission is now a part of the Western Pacific Union Mission that includes Vanuatu and New Caledonia. Several indigenous churches have arisen over the years, including the Remnant Church and the Christian Fellowship Church. The latter, the largest of such independent churches, was founded in 1959 by Silas Eto in a schism of the Methodist Church on the island of New Georgia.

The various world religions have only begun to discover the South Sea Islands in general and the Solomon Islands in particular. By 1970s there were small groups of Buddhists, Hindus, and Baha'is.

J. Gordon Melton

See also: Church in the Province of Melanesia; Methodist Church; Roman Catholic Church; Seventh-day Adventist Church; United Church in Papua New Guinea; United Church of the Solomon Islands; World Council of Churches; World Evangelical Alliance.

References

Burt, Ben. *Tradition and Christianity: The Colonial Transformation of a Solomon Islands Society.* New York: Routledge, 1994.

Forman, Charles H. *The Island Churches of the South Pacific: Emergence in the Twentieth Century.* Maryknoll, NY: Orbis, 1982.

Laracy, H. *Marist and Melanesians: A History of Catholic Missions in the Solomon Islands.* Canberra: Australian National University Press, 1976.

Naban, J. *The History of the Work of the Anglican Church in the Solomon Islands.* Suva, Fiji: Pacific Theological Seminary, 1976.

O'Brien, Claire. *A Greater than Solomon Here: A Story of Catholic Church in Solomon Islands 1567–1967.* Catholic Church Solomon Islands Trust Board,1995.

Tippett, A. R. *Solomon Islands Christianity: A Study in Growth and Obstruction*. New York: Friendship, 1967.

Worsley, Peter. *The Trumpet Shall Sound: A Study of Cargo Cults in Melanesia*. New York: Schocken, 1968.

■ Somalia

The history of Somalia was given a new and determinative direction by the entrance of Islam in the eighth century. The land had been home to several ethnic groups for a number of centuries, but they were tied together by a common language and culture. They had been producers of incense and had developed trade with the ancient Egyptians and the Roman Empire. Their ancient religion, however, was gradually replaced by Islam, and the people had become thoroughly Islamized by the 13th century.

Following their conversion to Islam, the Somalis founded a new political entity, the state of Ifat. It was able to sever its subservient relationship to Ethiopia, transformed into the sultanate of Adala, and grew prosperous as it began to trade with the Islamic states along the eastern coast of Africa. Adala was brought down, however, in 1541 when Portugal, which had developed an alliance with Ethiopia, attacked and laid waste to Somalia's coastal cities. The Portuguese presence in the area prevented the sultanate's recovery, and Adala was divided into a set of smaller sultanates. By the time the Portuguese were driven from the area in the 17th century, the Ottoman Empire had moved into the region and established its hegemony over northern Somalia while the sultanates in the south sought a relationship with the sultan in Zanzibar.

Europeans reappeared in the area in the 19th century, and French, British, and Italian forces established their countries' presence. The British and Italian area became independent in 1960 and merged to form the present state of Somalia. The French territory is now the country of Djibouti.

A parliamentary government assumed control of the country but failed to perform, and in 1969 a military coup under General Siad Barre occurred. It gained popular support as it moved to correct some of the country's problems, not the least being illiteracy. It brought the country almost to ruin, however, by attempting to lay claim to the Plateau of Ogaden just across the border in Ethiopia. Increasing opposition to the Barre government led to civil war in 1991. The forces of the United Somalian Congress succeeded in driving Barre from power, but then divided into two factions that have since vied for control of the country. In the midst of the struggle, the United Nations and the United States attempted to intervene, unsuccessfully. As of the beginning of the new century, there is as yet no central government in the country.

Islam in Somalia was somewhat reshaped during the years of the Ottoman Empire. That part of the

Somalia

Religion	Followers in 1970	Followers in 2010	% of Population	Annual % growth 2000–2010	Followers in 2025	Followers in 2050
Muslims	2,220,000	5,334,000	98.7	2.88	7,757,000	11,860,000
Christians	4,200	59,200	1.1	1.33	66,200	78,300
Orthodox	200	55,000	1.0	1.36	60,000	70,000
Independents	60	1,000	0.0	0.00	2,000	3,000
Protestants	550	1,100	0.0	1.67	2,000	3,000
Ethnoreligionists	0	7,000	0.1	2.86	9,000	13,000
Agnostics	2,500	2,300	0.0	2.12	6,000	12,000
Hindus	500	2,000	0.0	2.86	4,000	8,000
Baha'is	700	1,400	0.0	2.89	3,000	8,500
Atheists	1,000	800	0.0	2.89	1,400	4,600
Total population	**2,229,000**	**5,407,000**	**100.0**	**2.86**	**7,847,000**	**11,984,000**

SOMALIA

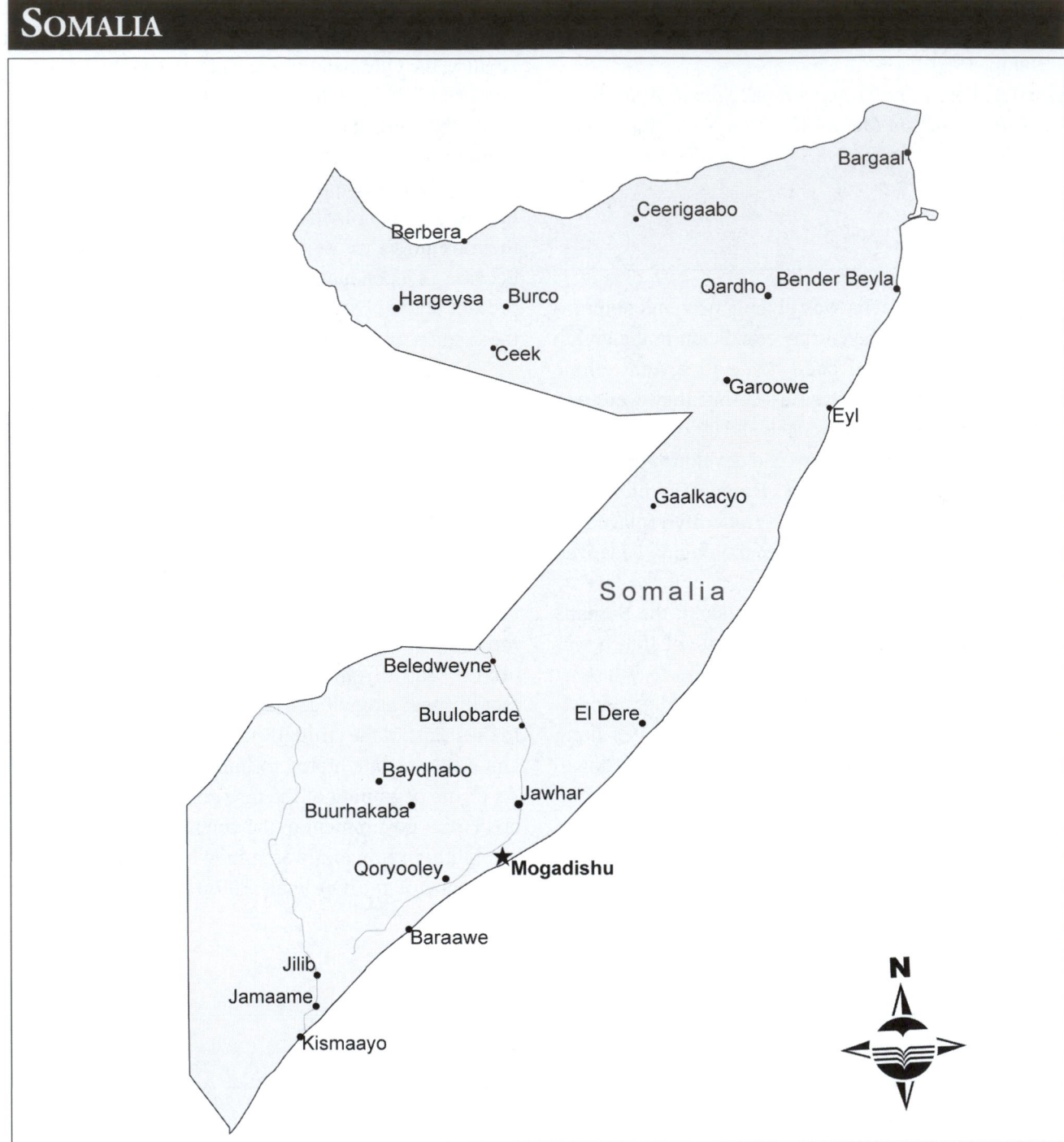

country formerly under Ottoman rule is largely of the Hanafite School, while the part that was related to Zanzibar is primarily of the Shafiite School. There are a small number of Shias, mostly of Pakistani origin. The capital, Mogadishu, has been the site of the East Africa regional office of the World Muslim Congress.

Christianity was introduced into Somalia in 1881 but greatly expanded after the Italians took control of the southern coast, including Mogadishu. However, it has had very little success, even prior to the independent government's prohibition of proselytizing activity, and its several thousand members are still primarily expatriates. In 1972 the government nationalized all of the Catholic church's property. However, in spite of the changes in the church's status and the resultant departure of much of its personnel, a Diocese of Mogadishu was created in 1975.

Lutheran missionaries from the Church of Sweden came to Somalia in 1898. They opened a set of educational and medical facilities and engaged in evangelistic outreach, but they had their greatest success among a group of Bantu-speaking former slaves. The mission was disrupted when Italian authorities expelled the missionaries in 1935. The work was revived after World War II by Mennonites and the Sudan Interior Mission, but it was hurt by the same nationalization of church property that destroyed so much of the Catholic work in 1972. Most Sudan Interior Mission missionaries left soon afterward. By 1976 all foreign missionaries had left the country. Two groups of Somali nationals, one formerly associated with the Mennonites and one with the Sudan Interior Mission, continued to meet after the missionaries left. In the 1980s, a few Mennonites were able to return.

There are also a few Hindus (expatriate Indians) and Baha'is in the country. The Baha'i Faith had some success in the 1970s, and at one point a member of the Barre government was a member. It has had some initial success among the Iranian expatriate community, but in 1975 the Iranians were expelled.

J. Gordon Melton

See also: Baha'i Faith; Church of Sweden; Hanafite School of Islam; Shafiite School of Islam; World Muslim Congress.

References

Bayne, E. A. *A Religious Nationalist in Somalia: A Comment on Modern Nationalism Allied with Islam as a Unifying Dynamic.* New York: American Universities Field Staff, 1966.

Lewis, I. M., ed. *Islam in Tropical Africa.* London: Oxford University Press, 1966.

Miller, F. "Sufi Influences on Somali Society." M.A. thesis, Duquesne University, 1973.

Trimingham, J. S. *The Christian Church and Mission in Ethiopia (including Eritrea and the Somalilands).* London: World Dominion Press, 1950.

Song Shan

In Daoist thought, there were five directions. Along with the north, east, south, and west, the center was also considered an additional direction. This idea is amply illustrated in the concept of the five sacred mountains, which were looked upon as pillars supporting the heavens. Song Shan, in Henan Province, was the Daoist mountain of the center. Song Shan stretches for 40 miles between the cities of Luoyang and Zhengzhou. Luoyang, the ancient capital of China, is the site of the White Horse Temple, the first Buddhist temple in China, built in 68 CE.

The most important Daoist site on Song Shan is Zhongyue Temple at the foot of and on the south side of Taishi Hill. It originated as the Taishi Shrine in the Qin dynasty (220–207 BCE). Emperor Wudi (r. 141–87 BCE) greatly expanded it in 110, and it was largely rebuilt during the Ming dynasty. The current complex was rebuilt following the design of the imperial palace in Beijing during the reign of Manchu Emperor Qianlong (r. 1736–1795) of the Qing dynasty. It is larger (with some 400 structures) and better preserved relative to the similar complexes found on the other four sacred mountains.

While the Daoist history on Song Shan is impressive, the Buddhist presence rivals it. For example, the Songyue Pagoda, a sixth-century pagoda, is the earliest known Chinese brick pagoda. It was constructed in 523 CE adjacent to Songyue Monastery on Mount Song. Even more famous is the legendary Shaolin Temple, near Zhengzhou City. It is to this temple that Bodhidharma, the reputed founder of Chan/Zen Buddhism lived and at which he developed what became a new martial art, kung fu. In 495, he also built the Shaolin Pagoda adjacent to the temple. Today, about 984 feet to the west of the Shaolin Pagoda is the Pagoda Forest, home to some 240 pagodas erected since the days of the Tang dynasty (618–907).

Fawang Temple is a Tang dynasty Buddhist temple located northwest of the town of Dengfeng and at the bottom of Song Shan's Yuzhu Peak. This temple's grounds include a set of Tang Dynasty pagodas, the most prominent being a 131-foot-tall stone tower that enshrines a jade statue of the Buddha given to the temple in 1409 by a member of ruling family of the Ming dynasty (1386–1644) who resided in Luoyang.

Monk at Shaolin Temple of Song Shan, China. (Linqong/Dreamstime.com)

The tallest peak of Song Mountain rises some 4,900 feet above the landscape. In 2008, the mountain and its temples and pagodas were named a United Nations Educational, Scientific and Cultural Organization (UNESCO) World Heritage Site.

J. Gordon Melton

See also: Bodhidharma; Daoism; Heng Shan; Hua Shan; Tai Shan; Temples—Buddhist; Zen Buddhism.

References

Einarsen, John, ed. *The Sacred Mountains of Asia*. Boston: Shambhala, 1995.

Geil, William Edgar. *The Sacred 5 of China*. London: John Murray, 1926.

Hahn, Thomas H. "Daoist Sacred Sites." In *Daoism Handbook*, edited by Livia Kohn, 683–708. Leiden: Brill, 2004.

"Sacred Mountains of China." Places of Peace and Power. http://www.sacredsites.com/asia/china/sacred_mountains.html. Accessed May 15, 2009.

Songgwangsa

Songgwangsa, or Spreading Pine Temple, is a large Son (Zen) Buddhism center founded by the Master Chinul (1158–1210) on Songgwang Mountain in Jeollanam-do Province in the southwest corner of the Republic of (South) Korea. It is designated one of Korea's Three Jewels Temples, each temple representing either the Buddha, the Dharma, or the Sangha. Songgwangsa represents the Sangha, that is, in Korean Buddhism's understanding, the Buddha's followers, both monks/nuns and laity. For this reason, the temple complex has some unique aspects.

By 1190, Master Chinul had begun the mature phase of his career. He had rejected the lax Buddhism of the city (in Seoul) and had moved to Kong Mountain, where he formed a new retreat society based upon his belief that each person was already an enlightened Buddha and what was needed was the recovery of his or her pristine enlightened state. A growing number began to find their way to his small center on Kong Mountain, which soon outgrew its facilities. By around 1197 he had selected the present site in southern Korea, which became the setting for his new temple complex. One legend that has been told over the centuries is that in order to find the right place, he carved a crane out of wood. It flew off and landed when it located the correct place on Songgwang Mountain.

On his journey to take up residence in the new temple, Chinul and his companions made a retreat on Chiri Mountain to consider the direction to be taken with the new community. During this retreat, they experienced a variety of supernatural events that were subsequently interpreted as confirmation that Chinul had realized a final and higher state of enlightenment. Once installed at Songgwang Mountain, Chinul became the dominant voice in the Korean Son community.

Chunil initially built a small hermitage on Mount Chogyesan, but quickly expanded the site to accommodate the growing community. The Masters' Portrait

Hall was reputedly built where the crane bird actually landed. It is this hall that came to represent the followers of the Buddha. It houses a large collection of stele and pagodas containing the ashes of some of the many masters who have lived here, including Master Chinul.

Songgwangsa reached the height of its glory in the 16th century, but through the rest of millennium was largely destroyed on several occasions. On each occasion it was repaired and/or rebuilt, but never to its former completeness. Master Kusan (1901–1983), one of the energetic young teachers to arise in the decades following the end of the Korean War (1950–1953), was able to attract a number of non-Korean students and in 1973 established an International Zen Center at Songgwangsa. He also launched the restoration effort at Songgwangsa, which his successor carried to fruition. Through the last half of the decade, the residents were able to restore the site according to its original plans. From this effort, 14 buildings were reconstructed, most notably the Main Hall, which houses the monastery's three main statues of the three Buddhas—Dipankara, the primordial Buddha; Sakyamuni, the historical Buddha; and Maitreya, the future Buddha.

It is usual for the Main Hall to be the highest building in Korean monastic complexes, but Songgwangsa manifests one of its unique aspects in this regard. Here, the Teaching Hall, the Masters' Portrait Hall, and the residence of the spiritual leader are in the highest positions, due to Songgwangsa being one of the Three Jewels Temples. Of interest, adjacent to the spiritual leader's residence is his assistant's house, a small structure that has survived since the 15th century. It is the oldest building at Songgwangsa and one of the oldest living quarters in Korea.

Songgwangsa currently serves as the head temple for the 21st district of the Chogye Order, the largest of Korea's Buddhist groups.

J. Gordon Melton

See also: Chinul; Chogye Order; Haein-sa Temple; Korean Buddhism; T'ongdo-sa Temple; Zen Buddhism.

References

Buswell, Robert E., Jr. "Songgwang-sa: The Monastery of the Sangha Jewel." *Korean Culture* 10, no. 3 (Fall 1989): 14–22.
Buswell, Robert E., Jr. *Tracing Back the Radiance: Chinul's Korean Way of Zen*. Honolulu: University of Hawaii Press, 1991.
Buswell, Robert E., Jr. *The Zen Monastic Experience*. Princeton, NJ: Princeton University Press, 1993.
Kusan Sousa. *The Way of Korean Zen*. New York: Weatherhill, 1985.

Soto Zen Buddhism

Soto Zen Buddhism is the largest school of Zen in Japan, with more than 17,500 temples at its peak in the 18th century. Today, the school maintains approximately 15,000 temples in Japan. Several hundred affiliated temples exist in Europe and the Americas, transmitted by both Japanese immigrants in the late 19th century and by European and American converts during the 1960s and 1970s.

This school was originally developed in China by Tung-shan Liang-chieh (807–869) and became one of five Chinese Chan (Zen) lineages. It was transmitted to Japan by Dogen Kigen (1200–1253). The Soto Zen School emphasized the practice of "silent illumination" Zen meditation (Japanese: *shikantaza*) and the observance of strict monastic codes as the path to enlightenment. These practices were detailed in Dogen's seminal text, the *Shobogenzo*.

Especially under the influence of the so-called second founder of the Japanese Soto School, Keizan Jokin (1268–1325), the organization also incorporated devotional forms of worship to numerous local deities, adopted esoteric Buddhist rituals, and received patronage from local lords to grow into a major force in Japanese religious life. Its temples offered healing, rain-making, and funerary rituals, among others, that attracted numerous adherents. The sect's head temples of Eiheiji and Sojiji have acted as priestly training centers for the school in Japan.

Soto Zen in the West among Japanese immigrants has served as a repository of Japanese culture and Buddhist ritual, especially funerary and ancestral rites. Among converts, on the other hand, it has focused on the primacy of meditation and its application in daily life, with a particular emphasis on involvement of the laity.

Pagoda of a Japanese Buddhist temple in Kyoto. (Till Scheel/Dreamstime.com)

Eiheiji
Eiheiji-cho
Yoshida-gun, Fukui-ken 910-12
Japan
http://global.sotozen-net.or.jp/eng/

Sojiji
2-1-1 Tsurumi-ku
Yokohama-shi, Kanagawa-ken 230-8686
Japan

Duncan Williams

See also: Dogen; Enlightenment; Meditation; Monasticism; Zen Buddhism.

References

Bielefeldt, Carl. *Dogen's Manuals of Zen Meditation.* Berkeley: University of California Press, 1988.

Bodiford, William. *Soto Zen in Medieval Japan.* Honolulu: University of Hawaii Press, 1993.

LaFleur, William, ed. *Dogen Studies.* Honolulu: University of Hawaii Press, 1985.

Williams, Duncan. *The Other Side of Zen: A Social History of Zen in Tokugawa Japan.* Princeton, NJ: Princeton University Press, 2004.

■ South Africa

South Africa is the southernmost country of the continent of Africa. Off its southern coast, the Atlantic and Indian oceans meet and its coastal cities, especially Cape Town, were for centuries stopping points for ships sailing between Europe and Asia. To the north lie Namibia, Botswana, Zimbabwe, and Mozambique. The country of Lesotho is completely surrounded by South Africa and Swaziland is almost in a similar position. South Africa is now home to more than 49 million people. It encompasses some 471,000 square miles.

European settlement of South Africa began with the arrival of the Dutch in 1652. Settlement radiated from Capt Town over the next centuries. Meanwhile, what would eventually be carved out as the modern country was home to a variety of Native people, including the Khoi and San.

The British seized the area in 1806, prompting many of the Dutch settlers to move inland. Significant population growth followed the discovery of diamonds (1867) and gold (1886). The Boer War (1899–1902) was fought as the Dutch settlers resisted the extension of British hegemony over their settlements. The British won and subsequently set up a coalition white power structure that left the Native population in subjugation. The Union of South Africa was formed in 1910. It evolved into the present Republic of South Africa in 1961. Following the election of the National Party to power in 1948, a system known as apartheid was put in place, which called for the separate development of the races—not just African and European but also the Asians, who would become a significant if minority part of the population. Significant world opposition to apartheid developed through the 1970s and 1980s and eventually led to its destruction. The first elections in the new desegregated South Africa occurred in 1994 and ushered in a black majority government under the African National Congress (ANC), which has since ruled the country, though not without a significant and growing minority opposition. For many years a prisoner due to his anti-apartheid activism, Nelson Mandela became the first African president of the country.

The oldest sign of religion in South Africa comes from Ingwavuma in northern Kwa Zulu/Natal at a place called Border Cave, where there is evidence of Middle Stone Age occupation. Some of the human remains found there show affinities to the later Khoi and San populations of the western parts of South Africa. Particularly fascinating are the remains of the body of a child that had been covered in red clay before burial, which suggests an understanding of a reality that tran-

scends earthly existence. These remains are dated to about 100,000 years ago and are some of the oldest indications of religious activity in the world.

The oldest piece of rock art in southern Africa dates from 27,000 years ago and was recovered from the Apollo 11 Cave in Namibia. Burial remains indicate, however, that people who strongly resemble the contemporary San were present in the southern African region as early as 12,000 years ago. Their famous rock engravings, which are scattered over large parts of South Africa, were numerous up until 2,000 years ago. At that time changes in lifestyle took place, and from that point on the religious activities of the Khoi and San are reasonably well documented.

The culturally distinct Khoi (sometimes referred to as Khoikhoi or Hottentot) and the San (Bushmen) evolved from the same genetic stock, referred to as Khoisan. In prehistoric times they were probably spread over most of the southern African region, but by the time the colonists arrived in the 17th century they were confined to the southwestern parts of the country.

The San were hunter-gatherers who relied on fruits and vegetables of the veldt as well as game for their diet. The movement of game and the sparse rainfall of the region controlled their lives, and they were socially organized into small roving bands that traversed the desert in search of water and food. They recognized the existence of a greater as well as a lesser god. The greater god resided in the eastern sky and the lesser in the western sky. These gods were whimsical and were capable of sending good or bad fortune to people. Of much importance in San mythology is the unpredictable divine trickster figure Kaggen, who could change his appearance at will and who played pranks and upset the normal order of things. The only defense humans had was to intensify the supernatural energy that they possess, called *n/um*. This was accomplished through communal dancing in which the rhythm of the dance would induce an altered state of consciousness in the healer. Through the dance, singing, trance, and fire, the n/um of the dancer-healer was brought to "boil"; it overflowed in sweat and nose bleeding, which in turn repelled evil.

For the San all of nature was invested with a numinous quality, and their attitude toward the world was one of deep reverence and respect. Animals such as the

South African church. (Monkey Business Images/Dreamstime.com)

eland and the mantis manifested divine qualities, and the stars were said to be the eyes of dead ancestors or great hunters. These people lived in a delicate balance with the natural environment, and their only defense against the expansionist activities of the colonists was to retreat from their preferred territory to the Kalahari Desert. Today there are no more than about 50,000, and many live in the neighboring countries of Namibia and Botswana. No common body of beliefs has survived among the small groups.

The Khoi people were nomadic pastoralists who settled mainly in the western Cape and moved only when water and pasture were needed for their animals. They had developed the ability to smelt iron and used it to fabricate weapons and implements. When their pastoral activities encroached on the hunting area of the San, it was the San who were forced to abandon the territory and move farther northward.

The Khoi believed in a cosmic duality of spirit. Tsui/Goab was the benevolent giver of rain and all things good, and Guanab was the evil god who brought misfortune, illness, and death. These gods would, however, sometimes inexplicably go against their own nature and bring about the opposite qualities. Whereas these gods influenced only the communal life, it was the ancestral cultural hero Heitsi-Eibib who was invoked for individual success and healing. There are many stories about his exploits, particularly about his many deaths, which are attested to by his many gravesites, where offerings or stones were left for good luck.

With the arrival of the colonists, the Khoi culture crumbled in the face of superior weapons and missionary efforts to Christianize them. Eventually all Khoi were exterminated or incorporated and absorbed into the various groups in the Cape.

While the Khoi and the San inhabited the arid western parts of the country, the black African peoples, or Bantu-speaking people, inhabited the eastern and central parts of the country. Those parts consisted of rolling grasslands toward the coast as well as a vast inland plateau west of the Drakensberg. Different lifestyles developed among these people, varying with the climate, altitude, and soil. The lush, mountainous eastern parts of the country allowed for small self-sufficient and independent settlements (usually on a ridge), within hailing distance of neighbors. West of the Drakensberg, in the interior, the land is flat and rainfall inconstant. There the people needed larger tracts of land to sustain living, and the population was divided into very large centrally located settlements.

In the early 19th century, violent clashes between the people of different settlements led to the merging of groups into powerful nation-states, complete with their own royal houses. These groups were categorized by early ethnographers as the Nguni-speaking group (Xhosa, Zulu, and Swazi) and the Sotho-Tswana group (Northern Sotho, South Sotho, and Western Sotho or Tswana), the Venda and the Shona.

Although the religious practices of these groups differed notably, the main features show remarkable congruence. All the beliefs and practices are centered on the cardinal belief that there should be harmony between the natural and the spirit worlds. If human beings behaved with due deference toward the ancestors, and in accordance with prescribed social convention, everyone would prosper and flourish. If anyone misbehaved in any way, the harmony would be disturbed and the protection of the ancestors lifted, so that misfortune would strike the offenders.

It is therefore clear that the main element of all the religious practices of the Bantu-speaking people was ancestor veneration. Each homestead had its own ancestors, who were included in the celebrations and decision making of everyday life and were looked to for protection and prosperity. On a larger scale, every tribe or nation also had its own ancestors who were responsible for the welfare of the nation. Specialists in the form of diviners, by virtue of their ability to mediate in the spirit world, were on hand to help seek out the cause of suffering and misfortune and to help restore the order with prescribed sacrifices and purification rituals.

On the whole, scholars of African traditional religion agree that there was a belief in a Supreme Being or Creator who was so powerful and detached that human beings could not approach him. There are, however, also dissenting voices who maintain that this is a Western and Christian interpretation that was thrust upon a discrete religious system.

In South Africa today there are many who still abide by the old ways, and although it is estimated that more than 70 percent of black South Africans profess to be Christians, their Christianity is often more influenced by the traditional religion than African religion is influenced by Christianity. It is safe to say that many of the African Initiated Churches in South Africa today are not only influenced by traditional religion but that they also represent a synthesis of traditional religion and Christianity.

When the Dutch came to South Africa in 1652 they brought Reformed Christianity with them, and all other forms of religion were prohibited. Islam had been brought to the Cape as early as 1658 by slaves who were imported from the East Indies, but it was only in 1804, when the Dutch government granted religious freedom to all people, that they could establish their first mosque. Because Islam did so much to address the social and educational needs of the community, the religion attracted people from all classes and races and became a center of resistance against slavery and social injustice. From 1860 on, Islam was also established in Natal, when Indian laborers were brought to the province. From there it quickly spread to the Transvaal, and today there are an estimated half-million Muslims in South Africa and the number is growing.

The Reformed faith was originally brought to South Africa by members of the Netherlands Reformed Church, but following the British takeover of the Cape Colony, Presbyterians from the British Isles, especially adherents of the Church of Scotland, expanded the Reformed community. Through the 20th century, these several churches splintered and reunited and today exist as more than 15 different denominations, including the Dutch Reformed Church, the Evangelical Presbyterian Church in South Africa, the Presbyterian Church of Southern Africa, the United Congregational Church of Southern Africa, the Uniting Presbyterian Church in Southern Africa, and the Uniting Reformed Church in South Africa. The last named was formed by a merger in 1999. Two years later it selected the Reverend Diane Vorster as the new moderator of its general assembly, the first time a woman has headed a major South African Christian denomination.

SOUTH AFRICA

Over the course of the 19th century, the major Protestant traditions brought to South Africa included the Anglicans (now included in the Church in the Province of South Africa), Methodists (Methodist Church of South Africa), Baptists (Baptist Convention of South Africa), and Moravians (Moravian Church in Southern Africa). Pentecostalism spread to South Africa soon after its establishment in America, the Apostolic Faith Mission of South Africa being its earliest representa-

tive. It has continued as an important segment of the Christian community, and South Africans have participated fully in the Charismatic movement. Several new South African Charismatic churches, such as the International Fellowship of Charismatic Churches, have now become global bodies.

A number of the Protestant churches are members of the South African Council of Churches, which is affiliated with the World Council of Churches. Many

South Africa

Religion	Followers in 1970	Followers in 2010	% of Population	Annual % growth 2000–2010	Followers in 2025	Followers in 2050
Christians	17,181,000	40,260,000	81.7	1.17	42,593,000	44,672,000
Independents	4,616,000	19,050,000	38.7	2.16	20,883,000	21,755,000
Protestants	6,463,000	10,039,000	20.4	0.41	10,100,000	10,680,000
Roman Catholics	1,589,000	3,250,000	6.6	0.52	3,510,000	3,820,000
Ethnoreligionists	4,308,000	4,350,000	8.8	0.32	3,500,000	3,000,000
Agnostics	150,000	1,530,000	3.1	1.47	2,220,000	3,000,000
Muslims	270,000	1,240,000	2.5	1.10	1,600,000	2,000,000
Hindus	433,000	1,175,000	2.4	1.10	1,500,000	1,800,000
Baha'is	15,300	223,000	0.5	1.10	300,000	400,000
Atheists	5,000	170,000	0.3	1.10	215,000	300,000
Buddhists	2,200	158,000	0.3	1.10	180,000	200,000
Jews	120,000	80,000	0.2	–0.05	80,000	80,000
Chinese folk	1,600	33,900	0.1	1.09	36,000	42,000
New religionists	10,000	22,600	0.0	1.09	30,400	40,000
Confucianists	0	20,000	0.0	1.09	25,000	30,000
Sikhs	4,000	11,000	0.0	1.10	14,000	17,000
Spiritists	2,000	3,000	0.0	1.10	4,000	5,000
Jains	0	2,000	0.0	1.10	3,000	4,000
Total population	**22,502,000**	**49,278,000**	**100.0**	**1.09**	**52,300,000**	**55,590,000**

of the more conservative evangelical groups are associated with the Evangelical Alliance of South Africa affiliated with the World Evangelical Alliance.

The first priests of the Roman Catholic Church settled in the Cape in 1805 but were not allowed to begin missionary work until 1820. A vicariate was established in 1837. The first black bishop was consecrated in 1953. The church is currently led by the Episcopal Conference of South Africa.

It was only after 1804, when religious freedom came to the Cape, that practicing Jews came to settle in South Africa. The first synagogue (the Tikvat Israel—Hope of Israel) was established in 1841 in Cape Town. Today about half of the estimated 100,000 Jews in the country live in and around Johannesburg, where they are involved mainly in trade and the professions. Many Jews played leading roles in the struggle for freedom in this country, and today many still continue to make important contributions to public life.

Hinduism, the last of the great world religions that have a major presence in this country, first came to Natal in 1860 with Indian indentured laborers. More laborers as well as many merchants followed soon af-

terward, and today South Africa has a vibrant Indian community of about one million people, 60 percent of whom are Hindus. Most Hindus belong to the Sanathanist, or ritualistic, tradition, but there are also three streams of neo-Hinduism present in South Africa—Arya Samaj, neo-Vedanta (for example, the Ramakrishna Centre and the Divine Life Society), and Hare Krishna (the International Society for Krishna Consciousness).

According to 1991 census figures (the last census that included compulsory questions on religious affiliation), about 67 percent of the population adhered to Christianity (33 percent to various African Initiated Churches, 18 percent to the Reformed family, 11 percent Roman Catholic, 9 percent Methodist, 6 percent Anglican, and 4 percent Lutheran). About 2 percent of the population belonged to Islam, 1.5 percent to Hinduism, and 0.2 percent to Judaism. Approximately 30 percent of the population did not fall into any of these categories, and that probably accounted for adherents of African traditional religion and a nonreligious component. According to the 1996 census (in which questions on religion were optional), only 54 percent of

South Africans followed Christianity, but 34 percent had no religion or did not state one. Some 13 percent stated that they did not belong to any religion. As there was no way of indicating adherence to African traditional religion, one may assume that the 34 percent who claimed no religion or declined to answer the question included a strong component of adherence to African religion. At present there is a strong movement by adherents of African religion to return their religion to its ways and practices prevalent before colonialization, and to imbue it anew with dignity, honor, and acceptability within the South African cultural milieu.

In 1994 the long agonizing chapter of apartheid in the history of this country came to a close when the first democratically elected government took office under the presidency of Nelson Mandela. During the apartheid era many religious leaders in this country were involved in either the promotion of, or the resistance to, the system. Although the names of those who had sought to promote apartheid on biblical grounds will sink into oblivion, others, such as that of Anglican archbishop of Cape Town Desmond Tutu, Nobel Laureate for Peace, will go down in history as powerful and compelling examples of agents for justice and transformation.

H. Christina Steyn

See also: African Initiated (Independent) Churches; African Traditional Religions; Apostolic Faith Mission of South Africa; Arya Samaj; Baptist Union of South Africa; Church in the Province of South Africa; Church of Scotland; Divine Life Society; Dutch Reformed Church; Evangelical Presbyterian Church in South Africa; International Society for Krishna Consciousness; Methodist Church of South Africa; Moravian Church in Southern Africa; Netherlands Reformed Church; Pentecostalism; Roman Catholic Church; United Congregational Church of Southern Africa; Uniting Presbyterian Church in Southern Africa; Uniting Reformed Church in South Africa; World Council of Churches; World Evangelical Alliance.

References

Chidester, David. *Religions of South Africa.* London: Routledge, 1992.

Krüger, J. S. *Along Edges: Religion in South Africa: Bushman, Christian, Buddhist.* Pretoria: Unisa, 1995.

Krüger, J. S., G. J. A. Lubbe, and H. C. Steyn. *The Human Search for Meaning: A Multireligious Introduction to the Religions of Humankind.* Pretoria: Via Afrika, 1966.

Prozesky, Martin, and John De Gruchy. *Living Faiths in South Africa.* New York: St. Martin's, 1995.

Spong, Bernard, and Audrey R. Chapman, eds. *Religion and Reconciliation in South Africa: Voices of Religious Leaders.* West Conshohocken, PA: Templeton Foundation Press, 2003.

Villa-Vicencio, Charles. *The Spirit of Freedom: South African Leaders on Religion and Politics.* Perspectives on South Africa, 52. Berkeley: University of California Press, 1996.

Southern Baptist Convention

The Southern Baptist Convention, the largest Protestant/ Free church body in the United States, was founded in 1845 as a result of a deep controversy within the larger American Baptist fellowship. Baptists, based as they were in the local church, had been slow to organize. In the early 19th century, they formed a set of organizations (societies) designed to assist the congregations in presenting a united voice, publishing religious materials, and expanding through home and foreign missions. Each society had its own rules and membership. The controversy over slavery presented it with the necessity of making some unforeseen decisions.

In the decades following the American Revolution, Baptists spread to every corner of the United States as then constituted. The southern half of the nation had developed around a system of agriculture that depended on slaves, and Baptists had found an opening for missions among the slave population. At the same time, many slave owners and their friends had become Baptists. And American Baptists, even in the South, were aware of the problem raised by the demands for freedom that undergirded the American Revolution, coupled with the ambiguous nature of the Bible's discussion of the subject. The early Christians, most notably the Apostle Paul, had made no direct challenge to the slavery then operative in the Mediterranean Basin.

As the slavery controversy that would lead to the American Civil War (1860–1865) deepened, the Baptists found it increasingly difficult to remain neutral, and the issue continued to be raised in different forms. For example, many southern delegates who supported the American Baptist Home Missionary Society came to believe that a disproportionate number of home missions were being established outside the South. The issue came to a head in 1845, when Georgia delegates proposed a man for appointment as a home missionary. The board turned him down by refusing to act on the matter. Then the Alabama delegates sent an inquiry to the Triennial Convention overseeing foreign missions and asked if slaveholders could be appointed as foreign missionaries. The Convention's reply included a statement that it would not act so as to give the appearance of approving of slavery.

These two actions were enough for some, and in 1845, Baptists in the South met and approved the plan for the formation of the Southern Baptist Convention. Unlike the American Baptists, the Convention would unite all of the missionary functions into a single organization. A foreign mission board and a home mission board were established immediately, and plans were projected for future educational and publications work. Because of the devastation of the American Civil War, plans for further expansion had to be postponed to the end of the century. To avoid too much centralization, the foreign missions board was established in Richmond, Virginia, where it remains to this day. The home missions board was opened in Marion, Alabama, and later moved to Atlanta, Georgia, where it now is located.

After the Civil War, Southern Baptists also passed through a significant controversy that contributed to their unique place in the Baptist world. Advocates of the so-called Landmark position, most notably James R. Graves (1920–1993), argued that Baptist churches are the only true churches in the world, that the true church is a local, visible organization, and that Baptist churches and the kingdom of God are coterminous. Graves insisted that Baptist churches had existed at every age, and hence the contemporary Baptist movement could be traced to the time of Christ (rather than

to the independent movement in 16th-century England). Among the implications of the Landmark position were that Baptists should have no pulpit fellowship (that is, should not exchange ministers to lead worship) with other Protestant groups, and that Baptist congregations should limit Communion to members of Baptist churches. Although the Landmark position was ultimately rejected, it deeply influenced Southern Baptist life into the mid-20th century. It eventually would become the established position of the American Baptist Association.

After the Civil War, slowly, step by step, Southern Baptists built their denominational life. In 1888 the Woman's Missionary Union was created. The Sunday School Board appeared three years later. Several Baptist institutions for higher education existed in the South prior to the Civil War, but as a whole, Baptists were suspicious of colleges and seminaries; it would be the 20th century before the great expansion of Southern Baptists into higher education would occur.

In the new century, concern turned to the increasing problem of coordinating the growing Convention and its boards and agencies. In 1917 the Convention revised its constitution and created an executive committee assigned the task of directing all the work being nurtured by the Convention. The executive committee became the primary agent for carrying out the will of the Convention as expressed in its annual meetings. The committee as it developed included the officers elected by the Convention, a representative from each of the boards, and a representative from each state.

Through the 20th century, the Southern Baptists expanded throughout the United States and became both a national body and the nation's largest Protestant group. With the opening of a church in Vermont in 1964, it finally had churches in all 50 states. Although membership is still concentrated in the South, its greatest expansion in recent decades has occurred outside the South. Through the first decades of the 20th century, Southern Baptists operated under a comity agreement with Northern Baptists to limit competition. However, in 1942 such comity came to an end. Both Northern Baptists (now the American Baptist Churches in the U.S.A.) and Southern Baptists realized that, given the congregational nature of their movements, they could exercise little control over the movements, or the desire for affiliation of local Baptist churches. It was also the case that the two groups were developing distinct theological differences with the Southern group assuming a distinctly more conservative stance.

During its first generation, Southern Baptist missionary activity was concentrated in China and Africa. The expansion of work into Roman Catholic Italy in 1870 signaled the beginning of an era of growth. Through the rest of the century, missions were opened in Mexico, Brazil, and Japan. Through the 20th century, work expanded into more than 90 countries worldwide. In the decades since World War II, the Convention has also faced the problems of the ending of colonialism and the growth of former missions into autonomous churches. In many cases these changes have led to a reorientation of Southern Baptist participation with former mission churches in new partnership relations. However, the commitment to global evangelism remains, and in 2005 the Convention supported 5,100 full-time missionary personnel overseas.

The Convention did not found seminaries, but gradually adopted seminaries founded independently by Southern Baptists. As of 2000 it supported six seminaries in the United States. It also sponsors 52 colleges and universities and provides support for more than 100 colleges and seminaries overseas.

Like Baptists in general, Southern Baptists accept the Bible as their definitive creed, but they have periodically published summaries of the major beliefs that focus their faith. In 1925, in the midst of attacks on the Convention by its most fundamentalist wing, the convention adopted a doctrinal statement called "The Baptist Faith and Message" (revised in 1963). This statement served through most of the 20th century. In the last half of the century, however, Southern Baptists became increasingly embroiled in a controversy between its more conservative evangelical wing and its more moderate wing. This controversy threatened to split the Convention, and in the 1990s several structures, such as the Cooperative Baptist Fellowship and the Alliance of Baptists, were established to consolidate the interests of the moderates, who had become a minority within the Convention. Much of the controversy has swelled around the seminaries, whose professors have continually been the source of liberal theological perspectives. The primary issue has been

biblical authority: conservatives have tended to make affirmation of the inerrancy of the Bible (the belief that the Bible is without error on all matters about which its speaks) a test for holding a leadership position within the Convention. The controversy also led the Southern Baptists to withdraw from the World Baptist Alliance.

The Southern Baptists grew spectacularly through most of the 20th century. That growth was in part due to their decision to follow members from the South who had migrated to other parts of the United States and become a national church. Aggressively evangelistic, Southern Baptists experienced membership increases that steadily pushed it to the front of the Protestant community and eventually ahead of the Methodists to become the largest Protestant church in the United States, second only to the Roman Catholic Church (which has been the largest American Church since the mid-1840s). In 2006 it reported 16,300,000 members in more than 44,000 churches.

Southern Baptist Convention Executive Committee
901 Commerce St., Ste. 750
Nashville, TN 37203

Southern Baptist Foreign Mission Board
PO Box 6767
Richmond, VA 23230

Southern Baptist Home Missions Board
1350 Spring St., NW
Atlanta, GA 30367
http://www.sbcnet.org

J. Gordon Melton

See also: American Baptist Association; American Baptist Churches in the U.S.A.; Baptists; Cooperative Baptist Fellowship.

References

Baker, Robert A., ed. *A Baptist Source Book*. Nashville: Broadman, 1966.

Dockery, David S. *Southern Baptist Consensus and Renewal: A Biblical, Historical, and Theological Proposal*. Nashville: B & H Academic, 2008.

Encyclopedia of Southern Baptists. 4 vols. Nashville: Broadman, 1958–1971.

Fletcher, Jesse C. *The Southern Baptist Convention: A Sesquicentennial History*. Nashville: Broadman, 1994.

Hastings, C. Brownlow. *Introducing Southern Baptists: Their Faith and Their Life*. New York: Paulist, 1981.

Sutton, Jerry. *The Baptist Reformation: The Conservative Resurgence in the Southern Baptist Convention*. Nashville: Broadman & Holman Publishers, 2000.

■ Spain

Spain is located at the southwestern corner of Europe and, together with Portugal, forms the Iberian Peninsula. Part of the Spanish territory, however, is extrapeninsular—namely, the Balearic Islands, the Canary Islands, and the autonomous cities of Ceuta and Melilla, at the northern coast of Africa. The capital city is Madrid, at the center of the peninsula; it is also the largest city in the country and an important economic and industrial center. Politically, Spain is organized as a regional state, not equivalent to but in practice not very dissimilar from a federal state. There are 17 autonomous regions (*comunidades autónomas*) with their respective legislatures and executive powers, as well as with their respective capital cities; to them we should add Ceuta and Melilla, two autonomous cities with a special status and lesser competences than ordinary regions.

The population of Spain is estimated at approximately 46 million, and according to the National Institute of Statistics (www.ine.es) approximately 10 percent are immigrants, especially from Latin America, Eastern Europe, and Northern Africa. There are no official statistics about religion in Spain, but questions about religion or belief are included in the monthly surveys (*barómetros*) performed by the Center of Sociological Research (a public agency: www.cis.es). The figures of the last surveys show that between 75 and 80 percent of Spaniards recognize themselves as Catholic; around 17 to 20 percent declare themselves atheists or agnostics, and less than 2 percent as faithful of other religions.

The official and dominant language is Spanish, which is spoken by the virtual entirety of the native population and legal aliens; there is bilingualism in some regions that possess a historical autochthonous language, especially Catalonia, Pays Basque, Galicia, Balearic Islands, and Valencia. Ethnically Spain has been traditionally quite uniform (white Caucasian, to follow the usual North American terminology), with the exception of a small percentage of Gypsy population, especially abundant in the south, Madrid, and Barcelona, with a total estimated population of 650,000 (data provided by the Spanish Ministry of Education and Culture; http://www.mepsyd.es/politica-social/inclusion-social/poblacion-gitana.html, accessed March 11, 2009). Although white predominance still clearly subsists, the panorama has changed with the increasing immigration coming from Latin America and Africa (especially Morocco), which has introduced a relatively large population of Andean, Afro-American (above all from Dominican Republic), and Arabic ethnic origin; the change is particularly visible in the large cities. Spain is economically a well developed country and possesses a diversified economy in the three sectors (but tourism is definitely a major source of income for the country). The unemployment rate has dramatically increased recently—in March 2009 it got close to 3.5 million, that is, around 15 percent.

Religion in the History of Spain: 1st–15th Centuries
When Christianity began, the Iberian Peninsula was already part of the Roman Empire; with the exception of some northern territories, Spanish people had been deeply Romanized. An old tradition affirmed that the Peninsula was evangelized by Apostle Saint James the Greater (this tradition was the basis for the development of the Way of Saint James, or *Camino de Santiago*, in the Middle Ages). Although historical research has cast serious doubts on the reliability of this tradition, it is certain that conversion to Christianity was a relatively rapid process in Roman Hispania, notwithstanding the persecutions of Christians ordered by different Roman emperors. By the late third century Christianity was deeply rooted in the population and Spain was producing mature theologians.

Since 409 Spain was invaded by different "barbaric" peoples from Central and Northern Europe. By the fall of the Western Roman Empire, in 476, the Visigoths constituted the dominant kingdom in the

Peninsula; Visigoths were a minority in comparison with Hispano-Roman population but they were the rulers of the territory. The kingdom's religion was a matter strongly controlled by the king. In the late sixth century the Visigoths converted from Arianism—a Christian heresy—to Roman Catholicism. The initiative was taken by King Reccared, and the Third Council of Toledo (589) was the instrument for the conversion of Arian bishops and the integration of both ecclesiastical hierarchies. The councils of Toledo, convoked by the king but presided by an archbishop, dealt both with religious and political issues, and were an important means to organize the coexistence between Visigoths and Hispano-Romans. During the seventh century, the Catholic Church gave political cohesion to the Visigothic monarchy and made significant contributions to the Spanish cultural development, with Saint Isidore of Seville as the central figure of that period.

In 711 the Visigothic Kingdom of Spain fell under the Muslims' invasion. The Muslims conquered almost the whole Iberian Peninsula—which they called Al-Andalus—in an astonishingly rapid military campaign. The Islamic rulers substituted for the Christian rulers. In the 750s an Umayyad emirate, independent from Damascus, was established in Cordoba; the golden age of Islam in Spain came when the Cordoba emirate was transformed into a caliphate in 929. From the early eighth century, the Spanish political history is, to a great extent, the history of the struggles between Islamic kingdoms and Christian kingdoms. The latter finally took over the entire Peninsula in the late 15th century; this was the end of the eight-century period called the Reconquest (*Reconquista*). In those centuries, the degrees of religious tolerance, or intolerance, in Christian and Islamic territories, respectively, varied according to political and cultural circumstances. Overt persecution of the faithful of the other religion was not the rule but rather the exception. However, despite some recent idealization of the coexistence of the three monotheistic religions in Islamic territories, there was nothing comparable with a contemporary notion of religious freedom. To be Christian in a territory governed by Muslims (*mozárabe*), and vice versa (*mudéjar*), usually entailed remarkable discrimination with regard to the people's legal and economic status. This fact often stimulated conversions on both sides, although coerced conversion was rare.

On the other hand, there were important settlements of Jewish people in Spain at least since the late first century, after the great diaspora following the destruction of the temple of Jerusalem by Titus in 70 CE. Significantly, the Hebrew name of Spain, Sepharad, gives name to the Jewish branch of Sephardim. Their relationships with the Catholic Church do not seem to have been friendly, as demonstrated by some anti-Jewish provisions of the Council of Iliberis (Granada) in the early fourth century. The Arian period of the Visigothic monarchy opened a period of tolerance and an amelioration of the situation of Jews. However, shortly after the kingdom's conversion to Roman Catholicism in 589, new persecutions and measures against Jews came. During the first period of the Islamic domination in Spain (8th to 11th centuries) Jewish people could live and develop peacefully, particularly in southern Spain.

After the fall of the Caliphate of Cordoba, which disintegrated into *taifas*, or petty kingdoms, at the end of the 1020s, and especially after Northern African peoples (Almoravids and Almohads) took control of the Muslim territories in Spain in the late 11th century, there was a massive immigration of Jewish population to the Christian kingdoms, where they could find better living conditions. Some Jews fled out of Spain, including Maimonides, who was one of the leading philosophical figures of the 12th century. In Christian territories, until the late 15th century, the situation of Jews oscillated between tolerance and persecution. More often than not, they were subject to discriminatory measures, but it was frequent to find Jewish people occupying important positions in the world of culture, finance, and—sometimes—politics, as had happened also in the Cordoba caliphate. They played a central role in the School of Translators of Toledo, which constituted, in the 12th century, a unique environment of intercommunication between Christian, Islamic, and Jewish cultures, and contributed substantially to the rediscovery of ancient Greek philosophy in medieval Europe. However, ecclesiastical pressure determined that, in the long run, anti-Semitic policy prevailed in Spain. The paradox is that the Catholic

Good Friday procession with people in traditional hooded dress, Malaga, Spain. (Thomas Payne/Dreamstime.com)

Church that urged the persecution of Jews was the same church that promoted the mendicant orders; built the magnificent Romanic and Gothic cathedrals, so full of spirituality; and impelled the foundation of the great European universities in the Lower Middle Ages, which paved the way for the Renaissance (Salamanca was one of the first and most significant European universities).

Religion in the History of Spain: 15th–20th Centuries It is usually assumed that the constitution of Spain as a modern state and nation began in the late 15th century. In 1492, Queen Isabella of Castile and King Ferdinand of Aragon, married in 1469, conquered the Nasrid kingdom of Granada, thus making

a unified kingdom of Spain (in reality it was a plurality of kingdoms with a common monarch until the Decree of *Nueva Planta* in 1716). Significantly, Isabella and Ferdinand are known as the "Catholic monarchs" (*reyes Católicos*), because the spreading and strengthening of Catholicism formed one of their main goals in politics, both within the territory of the Spanish Peninsula as well as in the subsequent Spanish expansion in America. With them, the idea that Catholicism was part of the Spanish national identity became firmly established and remained—with manifold consequences and only a few breaks—until the late 20th century.

1492 was also a decisive year because of two other reasons: the first expedition of Christopher Columbus to America, which marked the beginning of the Spanish expansion in the New World and permitted the spreading of Christianity throughout an immense continent; and the expulsion of Spanish Jews, shortly followed by the expulsion of Muslims, in 1502. Jews, like Muslims, had to choose between conversion to Catholicism or exile. This led to a new diaspora of Sephardim Jews (around 200,000 people left the kingdom); some of them immigrated to America, but the largest part spread all over the Mediterranean countries. Most Muslims remained in Spain and converted—sincerely or insincerely—to Catholicism.

For Queen Isabella, like for the Emperor-King Charles I (1516–1556) and his son Philip II (1556–1598), religious unity was an essential element of political unity in Spain. In their foreign policy, as in their domestic policy, they were endeavoring to build a great Catholic empire. This idea led them to fight for the purity of Catholic doctrine in the Iberian Peninsula, to urge an intense and prompt evangelization of indigenous peoples in America, and to fight against the advance of Protestantism in Europe. Indeed, the support of Charles I and Philip II, as well as the contribution of a considerable number of Spanish bishops and theologians, were essential for the development of the Council of Trent.

The main instrument utilized by the Spanish monarchy to guarantee the kingdom's religious unity was the Spanish Inquisition, founded in 1478 by Queen Isabella and King Ferdinand with papal approval. Since the very beginning the institution was controlled almost entirely by the Spanish monarchy, which put the Inquisition in the hands of the Dominican Order. Initially, the Spanish Inquisition's main goal was to discover and punish insincere converts from Judaism (contemptuously called *marranos*) or from Islam. After the Lutheran Reformation, the extirpation of the first Protestant cells in Spain was also a main objective. The Spanish Inquisition was particularly active during the 15th and 16th centuries (although it was abolished only in 1848). It conducted its procedures against heresy often with extreme harshness and sometimes cruelty, although seemingly with no more cruelty than the Anglican and Calvinist institutions. The Spanish Inquisition's procedures always followed the same pattern and were carefully recorded. They frequently ended with an *auto de fe*—a public ceremony, presided over by ecclesiastical and secular authorities, in which humiliated repentant sinners acknowledged their mistakes and pertinacious heretics were severely punished, sometimes publicly burned to death at the stake. The purpose of autos de fe was to show the power of the Inquisition (also called Holy Office) and to deter people from incurring heretical beliefs.

The Inquisition's activity impeded the development of Protestantism in Spain. In the mid-16th century there were Lutheran communities of some significance in Seville and in Valladolid (the former gained a certain momentum among popular classes, the latter involved rather the social and intellectual elites). The nobility of the Kingdom of Navarre received the influence of Calvinism—with some episodes of intolerance toward Catholic practices—especially during the second half of the 16th century. However, the Inquisition repressed steadily and efficiently their activities and proselytism; the autos de fe celebrated in Seville and Valladolid in 1559 were particularly famous and important, but there were many others through the rest of the century. This fact determined that Protestantism was virtually nonexistent in Spain from the late 16th century or the early 17th century until the 19th century.

A similar inquisitorial policy was applied in the vice kingdoms of America. However, we must not forget that the Inquisition was an instrument of the monarchy and was not representative of the Spanish church's attitude as a whole. On the contrary, there were frequent conflicts and tension between the Spanish Inquisition, run by the Dominicans, and the rest of ecclesiastical institutions—including the popes. On the other hand, it was due to the influence of the Catholic Church that the Spanish colonization of America was probably the most humane of all the enterprises of the kind developed by other European kingdoms at that time (the so-called black legend has emphasized the negative aspects of Spanish intervention in the New World; but the fact is that, in comparative terms, no other colonization in history has produced such interracial societies as the ones existing in Latin America). The church was sincerely interested in the evangelization of the new continent. Most of the evangelists were members of religious orders and many of them—like Bartolomé de las Casas—defended vigorously the indigenous peoples' rights. In particular, the "reductions" established by Jesuits reached the very heart of numerous indigenous civilizations and, along with evangelization, performed a cultural and educational work of extraordinary efficiency; indeed, the expulsion of Jesuits from Spanish territories, decreed in 1767 by King Charles III, did a serious harm to the indigenous cause. The School of Salamanca, and particularly Francisco de Vitoria, a Dominican himself, who is considered the founder of international law, provided an important philosophical and theological support for the Indians' rights, and consequently for the spiritual and cultural work of religious orders in America.

The evolution of Christianity in Spain and Spanish America was, therefore, fundamentally Catholic. The religious unity of Spain received an additional impulse in 1609 with the expulsion of *moriscos*, Moors apparently converted to Catholicism but who, in a considerable percentage, had preserved their tradition, culture, and beliefs. Around 400,000 people left the country. This fact, as with the expulsion of Jews in 1492 (and like, probably, the prohibition and persecution of Protestantism), caused irreparable damage to the Spanish economy and culture.

From the late 15th century until 1978, Catholicism was the official religion of the Spanish state, with only two ephemeral interruptions. The Catholic Church was never a state church in the technical sense, but Spain was a confessional state. Through the 19th and 20th centuries, almost all the numerous Spanish constitutions proclaimed Catholicism as the official religion of the country (including the Constitution of 1812, which introduced the principles of liberalism in Spain). The two exceptions were the Constitution of 1869 (derogated in 1876) and the Republican Constitution of 1931 (derogated in 1939).

As in other European Catholic states, Spain's consolidation as a modern state and an absolute monarchy was accompanied by the typical characteristics of regalism. There was a reciprocal support and concession of privileges between church and state. Essentially, the state guaranteed the Catholicism of the country and granted certain economic privileges to the church, which enjoyed an enormous social and cultural influence in the kingdom and in the American territories. In turn, the monarchy obtained political support from the

ecclesiastical authorities and benefited from certain prerogatives on ecclesiastical matters (*iura maiestatica circa sacra*), especially the power to control the appointment of bishops as well as the ecclesiastical laws to be applied in its territory. On the other hand, we must not lose sight that in Spain, until the second half of the 20th century, the ecclesiastical institutions took care, to a great extent, of some assignments that are considered today part of the welfare state's typical competences, in particular education, charity, and hospitals. The cooperation between church and state was materialized in the Concordats of 1717, 1737, 1753, 1851, and 1953.

In the long run the state became the strongest part of this bilateral relationship, as occurred in other European regalist states and in other analogous regimes in Protestant areas. This produced an increasing tension between secular and ecclesiastical authorities. The penetration of Enlightenment ideas in Spain reinforced the position of the monarchy and led to the expulsion of Jesuits under Charles III in 1767 (supported by most Spanish bishops). A similar attitude, together with obvious economic interests, inspired the state's massive confiscation of a great part of the immense ecclesiastical properties in Spain in the 19th century (*desamortización*, or confiscation of mortmain property), which was particularly intense between 1834 and 1855. In addition, ecclesiastical taxes—another important source of income for the Catholic Church—were suppressed in 1841. As a consequence, the church became economically dependent on the state, a fact that modified substantially their relationship in the future.

From the Second Republic to General Franco's Regime The status quo experienced a dramatic change in 1931, when the Second Republic was declared. The 1931 Constitution proclaimed formally the freedom of religion and conscience, but the Constitution itself and the subsequent legislation adopted a markedly hostile regulation of religious institutions, which severely restricted the Catholic Church's freedom without actually creating an environment of freedom for other religious denominations. Hostility replaced cooperation. The dominant sentiment in some Republican governments—particularly at the beginning and at the end of the Republic—was not freedom but rather

SPAIN

revenge, with the explicit intention of terminating the Catholic Church's mighty social and cultural influence on Spanish life. The excessive anti-ecclesiastical reaction led to opposite reactions on the other side. Spanish society became divided in two halves from the religious perspective. This fact seriously disturbed social peace—above all when the radical leftist parties formed the government in 1936—and was one of the main causes of the Civil War (1936–1939). Thus, the effects

of the Second Republic experience were not limited to merely constituting a parenthesis in the Catholic tradition of the Spanish state; the intransigence of the main political forces and their inability to agree on a common project paved the way for a three-year civil war, which led to the dictatorship of General Francisco Franco, who ruled the country until his death in 1975.

Franco's regime returned to the confessional state —in a "hard" version—and was decidedly supported by the Catholic hierarchy until the 1960s. This new age of church-state close collaboration, expressed in the 1953 Concordat with the Holy See, has been often called "National Catholicism," for the identification between nation and religion was again a substantial part of public policies, especially inside the country; of course, Catholicism was not the only element of ideological cohesion in Franco's regime, but religion provided a sort of "historical legitimacy" to the dictator. The natural consequence was intolerance of other religions, stimulated or consented by the Catholic Church, whose official doctrine still proposed the confessional state as the ideal regime; religious non-Catholic worship was permitted only in private. In practice, the effects of this religious intolerance were particularly detrimental for other Christian churches. Spaniards of the Islamic and Jewish religions resided mainly in the Spanish territories in Northern Africa (Protectorado Español de Marruecos), where they enjoyed a specific legal status, more favorable than that of the non-Catholics living in the Peninsula.

The paradox is that the first manifestation of religious tolerance by Franco's regime—the 1967 Law of Religious Freedom—was impelled by the Catholic Church, which had changed some of its basic views on church-state relations in the Second Vatican Council's Declaration *Dignitatis humanae*. In addition, in the late 1960s some influential Spanish bishops were overtly willing to create a new framework for the relationships between the church and Franco's dictatorship, which was noticeably in the latter's final stage. The 1967 law put an end to religious intolerance in Spain and provided real legal status to non-Catholic religious denominations; it was certainly based upon a restrictive notion of religious freedom, but probably no more restrictive—and perhaps less—than the concept of other fundamental rights and public liberties in the Spanish political context of the time.

Present-day Situation: Religion in Spanish Society
From a sociological perspective it is difficult to provide precise numbers, for in Spain there are no official statistics about religion, and the estimations of the adherents to the different religions are based on non-official surveys or on the data provided by the religious denominations. In any event, it is undisputed that the Catholic Church is the religion of the vast majority of the Spanish population. As indicated before, and taking into account the average results of the surveys conducted by the Center for Sociological Research, about 80 percent of the Spanish population recognize themselves as Catholics, while less than 2 percent identify themselves as members of other religions, and 18 percent declare not to have any religion. The Spanish cities of Ceuta and Melilla, located on the coast of Northern Africa, constitute a particular case because of the clearly more visible presence of an Islamic population. In these enclaves a systematic calculation was done in 1986 by the National Institute of Statistics, with the result that the percentage of Muslims was 18 percent in Ceuta and 32 percent in Melilla (12,000 and 17,000 people, respectively—these are small cities); current non-systematic estimations, based on names registered in the city census and in schools, usually provide a percentage of nearly 40 percent of adults and 60 percent of minors. The overall figures about the percentage of Catholics in Spain correspond by and large to other data concerning the religious choices of citizens. Thus, approximately 75 to 80 percent of parents demand Catholic instruction for their children in pre-university schools, and this percentage has been stable in the last years (these data combine the information related to public and private schools; source: Spanish Bishops Conference, www.conferenciaepiscopal.es). The percentage of Catholic marriages, instead, has been experiencing a decline in recent years: from 76 percent of the total number of marriages is Spain in 2000 to 63 percent in 2004, and 55 percent in 2007 (last available data; source: National Institute of Statistics, www.ines.es); data concerning marriage, however, must be interpreted in the light of the indissolubility of Catholic marriage—after a civil divorce, a Catholic cannot remarry before the church unless an ecclesiastical court declares that his or her previous canonical marriage was null and void according to canon law.

The Catholic Church still retains a powerful social influence, although public morals are much less rooted in the Catholic doctrine than in the past. Like in other European countries with a traditional majority church, there is an increasing trend in Spain—even among people who define themselves as Catholic—toward living openly according to ethical rules not entirely coincident with official Catholic morals, and toward a less close relationship with the ecclesiastical establishment. The number of clergymen and members of religious orders has decreased in comparison with the 1960s, but the figures seem stabilized since the mid-1980s (around 20,000 priests and more than 200 ordinations per year). At the same time, there is a remarkable number of charitable institutions and NGOs of Catholic inspiration, with numerous young volunteers.

With regard to the number of faithful of other religions, there is no doubt that religious pluralism has been increasing in Spain in the last decades. However, the numbers provided by sociological surveys do not correspond so closely to the data offered by religious denominations, and this suggests that either some of the latter figures may be somewhat higher than reality, or the surveys are not precise enough, or some people of religions other than Catholic feel reluctant to give true answers in officially conducted surveys. The number of Jews is deemed to be between 30,000 and 40,000. The Evangelical Federation, which is supposed to gather the most significant Protestant communities in Spain, counts 1.2 million members according to their own estimations; many of them are permanent residents that came from other European countries. The Islamic leaders claim that the current Muslim population is close to 1 million, most of them immigrants from Islamic countries. An imprecise, but not insignificant, number of Muslim communities are not integrated into the Islamic Federation that signed a cooperation agreement with the state in 1992, and the same happens with Jewish and Protestant communities. In addition, the Christian Orthodox population has noticeably risen in the last years, especially because of emigration from Eastern European countries with religious Orthodox predominance; Orthodox sources maintain that their faithful in Spain exceed 1 million; in any event, the number of legal immigrants from predominantly Orthodox countries is currently estimated around 700,000 (of which Romanians are, by far, the largest community). Jehovah's Witnesses claim to be 200,000, including active members as well as "sympathizers," and the Mormon Church affirms to have around 40,000 faithful. The number of Buddhists is, according to the Buddhist Spanish Federation, in the range of 60,000.

The Legal Framework of Religion in Spain The current legal and political framework of religion in Spain was designed by the Constitution promulgated in 1978, which transformed the preceding regime into a democratic state that meets entirely the standards of freedom characteristic of Western democracies and international law. In the years that followed, the Spanish state signed the most relevant international documents regarding human rights, including the European Convention of Human Rights. Spanish society, in its largest part, accepted rapidly and enthusiastically the new model of political life. The increasing religious pluralism of society is no longer seen by Spaniards as a negative reality, or as contrary to the Spanish traditional identity, but rather as the normal effect of freedom. Religion has ceased to be, for the first time in centuries, a source of social and political conflicts.

The 1978 Constitution abandoned the traditional confessionality of the state. The constitutional framework of religion is now based upon four fundamental principles: religious freedom, equality, neutrality, and cooperation. The state protects the exercise of freedom of religion and conscience by every individual and group. All citizens are equal before the law and therefore no one can be subjected to discrimination on the ground of his or her religion or beliefs. Neutrality determines that the state has no official religion and is not competent to evaluate the different religious groups according to their doctrines or tenets; it may only judge their social effects. However, there is no strict separation between state and religion; on the contrary, the Constitution provides that "the public authorities shall take into account the beliefs of Spanish society and maintain the consequent relationships of cooperation with the Catholic Church and the other religious denominations."

The constitutional right to religious freedom was developed by a statute enacted in 1980, the Organic Law on Religious Freedom (Ley Orgánica de Libertad Religiosa), which contains the basic legal framework for religious freedom and for the legal status of religious denominations. One of the declared legislative projects of the current government (2009) is the reform of this law, after the experience of almost 30 years, and following an ongoing process of consultation with the main religious denominations operating in Spain.

State cooperation with religious communities has been channeled especially through formal agreements that are aimed at providing a specific legal status for the most significant religions in Spain. Thus, in 1979 the old Concordat was replaced by a set of four agreements with the Holy See that, in fact, altogether constitute a Concordat and are assimilated to international treaties under Spanish law. The purpose of those agreements was to preserve those benefits that the Catholic Church had traditionally enjoyed and were deemed compatible with the new constitutional principles: for example, civil effects of canonical marriage, religious education in public schools as an optional subject for students, but mandatory for the schools, financial support and tax exemptions, protection of the clergy-communicant privilege, religious assistance in the military, and hospitals or penitentiaries. Many of these benefits have been subsequently granted also to some of the main religious minorities in Spain, in particular to those of more historical significance, when the Spanish state signed, in 1992, three agreements of cooperation with the federations, respectively, of evangelical churches, Jewish communities, and Islamic communities (note that these were the very same religions persecuted by the Spanish monarchy five centuries ago). The possibility of such cooperation agreements, until then reserved for the Catholic Church, was opened by the 1980 Organic Law on Religious Freedom.

If we leave aside state cooperation, which is at the moment restricted to religious denominations with a cooperation agreement, all religious groups are recognized the same basic freedom once they have acquired legal identity in Spanish law through registration in the Registry of Religious Entities. The procedure of registration is, in principle, quick and simple. No minimum number of faithful or minimum number of years in Spain is required, just some essential identification data and expression of the "religious purpose" of the applicant group. However, some groups have experienced difficulties being accepted by the Registry as properly religious in nature, and have had to resort to the courts to be granted access to registration. This has occurred in particular with the Unification Church and the Church of Scientology, whose access to registration, denied by the administrative authorities in charge of the Registry, was granted by the courts, respectively,

in 2001 and 2007; these judicial decisions have made the registration procedure even easier than it was before.

Registration as such, however, does not entitle a group to state cooperation, which, as indicated above, is currently restricted to the Catholic Church and to those other religious denomination that, after being recognized by the public authorities as having "well-known roots" in Spain, have reached a formal agreement with the state, that is, the three aforementioned federations of Protestant, Jewish, and Islamic communities. On the other hand, these federations, together with the Catholic Church, represent a high percentage of the Spanish population, and this is one of the reasons why the present state of things is often considered satisfactory, in the sense that—it is said—state cooperation with religion reaches the vast majority of the population. This being true, the problem is that the sociological situation has kept changing over the years, and the percentage of the population represented by religious denominations left out of the agreements system—and therefore out of all state cooperation—has rapidly increased. According to the figures indicated before, if we take together the ever-growing Christian Orthodox community, the Jehovah's Witnesses, the Buddhists, the Latter-day Saints, as well as the Protestant, Jewish, and Muslim communities not integrated into the federations with formal agreement, we observe that there are denominations representing at least a population of 1 million that are totally excluded from state cooperation.

It is undeniable that, viewed in the context of Spanish history, the existing problems are relatively unimportant but, still, we can say that the current Spanish system of relations between state and religion can be perfected. This is, indeed, the opinion of the religious denominations themselves. The Catholic Church sometimes argues that the Spanish state does not fulfill adequately some of its obligations derived from the 1979 Concordat (its contribution to preserve the historical property of ecclesiastical origin, which is immense and precious, or the implementation of the provisions regarding Catholic instruction in public schools). However, the main claims are those relating to the consequences of the constitutional principle of equality. Thus, the Evangelical, Jewish, and Islamic federations

Spain

Religion	Followers in 1970	Followers in 2010	% of Population	Annual % growth 2000–2010	Followers in 2025	Followers in 2050
Christians	33,017,000	40,871,000	90.6	1.32	41,302,000	40,460,000
Roman Catholics	33,596,000	41,630,000	92.3	0.90	41,454,000	40,345,000
Independents	37,100	295,000	0.7	2.35	400,000	450,000
Marginals	40,900	210,000	0.5	0.87	280,000	320,000
Agnostics	605,000	3,050,000	6.8	3.63	3,820,000	4,213,000
Atheists	140,000	490,000	1.1	1.19	550,000	600,000
Muslims	5,000	620,000	1.4	6.95	850,000	1,000,000
Buddhists	0	47,000	0.1	4.19	60,000	75,000
Jews	8,500	15,000	0.0	1.53	15,000	15,000
Baha'is	3,900	14,000	0.0	1.35	25,000	35,000
Sikhs	0	1,400	0.0	1.53	1,800	2,500
Total population	**33,779,000**	**45,108,000**	**100.0**	**1.53**	**46,623,000**	**46,401,000**

that signed the 1992 agreements aspire to obtain a complete equalization with the Catholic Church's legal treatment, particularly with regard to the state's financial support, and also to ameliorate their legal status in other areas such as religious education in public schools, access to public mass media, or religious assistance in military centers, hospitals, and detention centers. Three other significant religious minorities—Mormons, Jehovah's Witnesses, and Buddhists—have recognized "well-known roots" in Spain but do not have the hope of being accepted to a negotiation process leading to a cooperation agreement with the state in the next years; consequently, they claim that the state should, at least, grant them some of the legal and economic benefits already at the disposal of the denominations with a cooperation agreement. Finally, the religious denominations registered in the Registry of Religious Entities argue that they are totally excluded from any possibility of state cooperation and that the effects of the legal personality recognized to a religious denomination do not differ much, in practice, from the legal personality recognized to ordinary associations. These are some of the reasons that have led to the current governmental project (2009) to reform the 1980 Law on Religious Freedom. At this time, the result of this legislative project is still uncertain.

Javier Martínez-Torron

See also: Arius; Jehovah's Witnesses; Roman Catholic Church; Spanish Evangelical Church; Spanish Reformed Episcopal Church.

References

History:

Cuenca Toribio, José Manuel. *Relaciones Iglesia-Estado en la España contemporánea (1833–1985)*. 2nd ed. Madrid: Alhambra, 1989.

Garciá Villoslad, Ricardo, ed. *Historia de la Iglesia en España*. 7 vols. Madrid: Biblioteca de Autores Cristianos, 1979–1982.

Menéndez y Pelayo, Marcelino. *Historia de los Heterodoxos Españoles*. 3 vols. 3rd ed. Madrid: Consejo Superior de Investigaciones Científicas, 1992.

Meyerson, Mark D., and Edward D. English, eds. *Christians, Muslims, and Jews in Medieval and Early Modern Spain: Interaction and Cultural Change*. Notre Dame, IN: University of Notre Dame Press, 1999.

Payne, Stanley G. *Spanish Catholicism: An Historical Overview*. Madison: University of Wisconsin Press, 1984.

Religion in Spain at Present:

Ferreoro, Juan. *State-Religion Relations in Spain: Legal and Constitutional Framework*. In *Legal Aspects of Religious Freedom*. Ljubljana: Office of the Government of the Republic of Slovenia for Religious Communities, 2008.

Ferrer Ortiz, Javier, ed. *Derecho Eclesiástico del Estado español*. 6th ed. Pamplona, Spain: Eunsa, 2007.

Garcimartín Montero, Carmen. "Direct Financing of the Religious Denominations in Spain." *Journal of Church and State* 48, no. 1 (2006): 175–196.

General Directorate of Relations with Religious Denominations (*Dirección General de Relaciones con las Confesiones*), Ministry of Justice, Spain. http://www.mjusticia.es/cs/Satellite?c=OrgPaginaMJ&cid=1213946265540&pagename=Portal_del_ciudadano%2FOrgPaginaMJ%2FTpl_OrgPaginaMJ.

Hera, Alberto de la. "Relations with Religious Minorities: The Spanish Model." *Brigham Young University Law Review* (1998): 387ff.

Lopez Garciá, Bernabé, et al. *Arraigados: minorías religiosas en la Comunidad de Madrid.* Madrid: Icaria 2007.

Mantecón, Joaquín. *Islam in Spain.* In *The Legal Treatment of Islamic Minorities in Europe.* Leuven, Belgium: Peeters, 2004.

Martínez-Torrón, Javier. "Religious Freedom and Democratic Change in Spain." *Brigham Young University Law Review* 777 (2006).

Morán Garciá, Gloria." The Spanish System on Church and State." *Brigham Young University Law Review* 535 (1995).

Oliva, Javier G. "Religious Freedom in Transition: Spain." *Religion, State and Society* 36, no. 3 (2008): 269ff.

Rstruch, Joan, et al. *Las otras religiones: minorías religiosas en Cataluña.* Madrid: Icaria, 2007.

Seglers, Alex. "Religious Education in the Spanish School System." *Journal of Church and State* 46, no. 561 (2004).

Spanish Evangelical Church

The Spanish Evangelical Church derives its doctrinal tenets from the 16th-century Protestant Reformation movement (Martin Luther and John Calvin) and from the Pietist movement of the 19th century (John Wesley). The first Assembly of the Church took place in 1869. It is one of the most ancient Protestant entities located in Spain.

In 1871 the name Spanish Christian Church was adopted. Subsequent to merging with the Congrega-tionalists of the Union Ibero-Evangelists, it adopted the present designation. In 1953 the Methodist Church of Catalonia and Baleares (which had resulted from the activity of the Methodist Episcopal Church, now an integral part of the United Methodist Church) joined the Spanish Evangelical Church. The Spanish Evangelical Church follows the pattern of democratic structure and has a presbyterian-synodal model for administration. The local church or congregation is the basic unit or cell of the Spanish Evangelical Church. Its organization comprises, among others, an elders council for each local church or congregation, a presbytery for each region, and regional synods. Every two years a General Assembly or Synod of the entire church in Spain is held.

Presently, the Spanish Evangelical Church has 58 places of worship (38 churches and 20 missionary centers) in 22 Spanish cities, which gather some 3,000 believers. Local communities meet around the reading and teaching of the Word of God (the Bible) as the central element of the service. The Last Supper and baptism are considered sacraments that help the believer in the expression and comprehension of the spiritual realities of the Christian faith. In addition, the Spanish Evangelical Church celebrates pastoral ordination, confirmation, marriage blessing, and burial as rites of religious significance.

For state legal purposes, the Spanish Evangelical Church is integrated in the Federation of Religious Evangelical Entities of Spain (FEREDE), which signed an Agreement of Cooperation with the Spanish government in 1992. The purpose of that agreement is to facilitate the exercise of religious freedom to the signatory religious entities and to establish mutual cooperation between the state and signatory religious entities.

The Spanish Evangelical Church runs several religious-oriented entities, among them the Seminary SEUT (Seminario Evangélico Unido de Teología), several evangelical schools (El Porvenir and Juan de Valdés), and elders houses in Santa Coloma de Gramanet (Catalonia), Madrid, and Palma de Mallorca.

In 1992 the FEREDE, on behalf of various Christian denominations in which the Spanish Evangelical Church is included, signed an Agreement of Cooperation with the Spanish government. That agreement has helped to ameliorate and regularize the legal status of the Evangelical Church and its sociological reputation after years of subtle misunderstandings and social prejudice.

The church is a member of the World Council of Churches.

Spanish Evangelical Church
Noviciado 5
E-28015 Madrid
Spain

Rafael Palomino

See also: Calvin, John; Luther, Martin; United Methodist Church; Wesley, John; World Council of Churches.

References

De la Hera, Alberto, and Rosa M. Martínez de Codes. *Spanish Legislation on Religious Affairs*. Madrid: Ministerio de Justicia, 1998.

Dirección General de Asuntos Religiosos. *Guía de entidades religiosas de España*. Madrid: Ministerio de Justicia, 2004.

Spanish Evangelical Church. http://www.iee-es.org. Accessed December 1, 2008.

Vidal Regaliza, Daniel. *La Iglesia Evangélica Española*. Madrid: Centro Ecuménico Misioneras de la Unidad, 1976.

Spanish Reformed Episcopal Church

The Spanish Reformed Episcopal Church belongs to the Anglican Communion and preserves the ancient Christian liturgy of the Visigoths and Mozarabs. It is the original Spanish expression inside the Anglican Communion.

The Spanish Reformed Church began in 1868 in Gibraltar, headed by Juan Bautista Cabrera, who was exiled from Spain during the reign of Isabella II, queen of the Spaniards (r. 1833–1868). After Isabella was ousted by the revolution of 1868, Cabrera returned to the country and founded the church in Seville. Between the years 1868 and 1880, the Spanish Reformed Episcopal Church was associated with the wider Protestant movement (Spanish Reformed Church). In 1880, in a synod held in Seville, an autonomous and inde-

pendent Episcopalian Church took shape. Bishop Cabrera was consecrated in 1894 through the cooperation of the Church of Ireland.

The Spanish Reformed Episcopal Church belongs to the worldwide Anglican Communion (since 1979) and to the World Council of Churches. The Spanish Episcopal Church holds a national biennial synod. It has published its official journal, *La Luz*, since 1869.

The Spanish Reformed Episcopal Church runs several religious-oriented entities, including the Seminary SEUT (Seminario Evangélico Unido de Teología), the Ecumenical Centre Villa Adelfos (Castellón), and Agrupación de Mujeres de la Iglesia Catedral del Redentor. The church oversees places of worship in 14 Spanish cities with approximately 1,500 members.

The church is currently led by the Right Reverend Carlos Lopez-Lozano. In 1992 the Federation of Religious Evangelical Entities of Spain, on behalf of various Christian denominations in which the Spanish Reformed Episcopal Church is included, signed an Agreement of Cooperation with the Spanish government that facilitates the development of the church in Spanish society.

Spanish Reformed Episcopal Church
Calle dela Beneficiencia 18
E-28004 Madrid
Spain

Rafael Palomino

See also: Anglican Communion/Anglican Consultative Council; World Council of Churches.

References

Andrés Puchades, Antonio. *La Iglesia Española Reformada Episcopal*. Madrid: Centro Ecuménico Misioneras de la Caridad, 1976.

The Church of England Yearbook. London: Church Publishing House, published annually.

De la Hera, Alberto, and Rosa M. Martínez de Codes. *Spanish Legislation on Religious Affairs*. Madrid: Ministerio de Justicia, 1998.

Dirección General de Asuntos Religiosos. *Guía de entidades religiosas de España*. Madrid: Ministerio de Justicia, 2004.

Spanish Reformed Episcopal Church. http://www.anglicanos.org/. Accessed December 1, 2008.

Spirit Possession

The concept of spirit possession is based on the belief that a human being can be entered by a nonmaterial entity endowed with a distinct identity, intellect, and will; the entity can make use of any and all of the faculties of the person's body. Typically, the entity will speak in its own voice using the vocal apparatus of the possessed person. However, other actions can also be attributed to the entity rather than to the "host." Effects of the phenomenon are received in a variety of ways by human cultures. In general, spirit possession is regarded as pathological, but in the case of deity oracles, possession can be placed at the service of the community.

Oracular possession is reported in a wide spectrum of cultures. The entity in these cases speaks through a medium on a more or less regular basis. Associated phenomena, implying varying degrees of "possession," may include the inspirational influence of deities such as the Muses on the creative arts, or prophetic inspiration, or frenzies and "enthusiasm." The Delphic oracle was a woman, the Pythia, who would sit within the temple of Apollo to be regularly consulted in all matters of importance. Apollo, though not alone among gods speaking through oracles, was particularly esteemed for this phenomenon. He would speak through the medium-oracles of Delphi, Didyma, Claros, and other places, who would go into a trance in order to channel the cryptic messages of the god. During the Persian Wars, for example, the Athenians were advised by the Delphic oracle to seek refuge in their "wooden walls"—which meant that they would be victorious against the Persians at sea with their ships. In the legends of the House of Atreus, the Delphic Oracle revealed that the sacrifice of Iphigenia, child of Agamemnon and Clytemnestra, was required to calm the adverse winds stirred up by Poseidon so that the Argive fleet could attack Troy. In China and in some Indian Tantric lineages, oracles may be channeled by children over whom certain prayers are said; the child goes into a trance and delivers the message of the deity in the manner of a medium. It seems that the phenomenon of child oracles is related to the notion of a child chosen to embody a deity, such as the Kumari in Kathmandu; a child of a high-caste Newari family is chosen

at an early age and only ceases to embody the goddess at the onset of menstruation.

The Tibetan state oracles are an excellent example of deity possession phenomena. There are at least two state oracles currently consulted by the Tibetan government in exile: the well-known Nechung Oracle and the lesser known Ga' Dong Oracle. Both of these oracles are still active at Dharamsala, the seat of the Tibetan government in exile. In each case, a monk is the regular medium or host for the deity. The monk, who wears an elaborate and extremely heavy set of vestments for the occasion, goes into a formal trance as the entity takes over his body. The Nechung Oracle delivers his messages in a very high-pitched, whispering voice; senior monks tape record the messages, which are quite long. In addition, other monks take notes of the messages, which are above all directed to His Holiness the Dalai Lama and are meant to guide official policy. For the benefit of the crowd, the deity disperses blessed barley grains that have been dyed red; these are especially valued for placement in luggage and shipping packages to protect from thieves and customs officials. After about 20 minutes, the trance ceases and the monk, exhausted by the ordeal, is carried out on the shoulders of a group of monks. The Ga' Dong Oracle goes into a trance after the Nechung, in a different location. The Ga' Dong is much more energetic and even wrathful in manifestation. The voice is deeper and more urgent, and the entire performance resembles the sacred dances of such deities as Mahakala. Barley grains dyed a deeper shade of red are dispersed to the crowd. Other auspicious rites accompany the manifestation of the oracles, such as the free distribution of sutra texts printed up by a donor.

Prophetic Possession Being seized or used by a deity is known in the Bible; Jeremiah uses very dramatic and even erotic language to describe the prophetic experience of divine "seduction" (Jeremiah 19:7). However, prophetic possession, similar to that recorded for other ancient cultures, is recorded in several passages of the Bible such as Judges 6:34, 2 Kings 3:15–16, and 1 Samuel 10:5. The Hebrew prophets were more usually allowed to ascend in spirit before the heavenly throne, there to hear the deliberations of the heavenly court in the presence of the God of Israel (1 Kings 22:19–23). The verdict of the court on the people, their

Mateena Shakya, four, locally known as Kumari and considered a living goddess, looks on as she is carried on a palanquin escorted by priests and devotees to attend the horse race festival in Kathmandu, Nepal, March 26, 2009. (AP/Wide World Photos)

rulers, and their times was handed over to the prophet to be delivered to the people regardless of the consequences as a "word of the Lord." Thus ancient Israelite prophecy is typically presented as direct revelation given in a visionary experience rather than possession or frenzy. However, the Deuteronomist redactor of the Hebrew scriptures (Deuteronomy 18:10–11) is most likely the source for those passages that augment the differences between Israelite prophecy and prophecy in the cults of other local deities (1 Kings 18:20–40).

Shamanic possession trances, however, emerge within the repertory of healing performances typical of these "chosen" human beings with access to preternatural entities. The shaman is believed to be able to diagnose and cure illnesses using powers acquired from spirit guides, sometimes in animal form. The shaman (male or female) enters the "other world" in a state of trance (empowered by mind-altering drugs or rhythmic drumming) in order to encounter spirit guides and gain knowledge for the purpose of diagnosis and treatment. As in the case of prophets, the typology resembles inspiration or revelation more than possession. However, at times the shaman's performance is that of an entranced, possessed person being used by deities or spirit guides to deliver a message. One of the more elaborate forms of the descent of a deity into the personality of a sacred reciter is the recitation of the Tibetan Epic of Gesar. In this case, the "deity" is Gesar or Vajrasattva, who descends (*lha bab*) into the body of the "singer of tales" in order to give the reciter the sacred words of the epic. Thus, an entire recital of the multivolume epic can take place over a period of more than a week. I was able to observe a small portion of such a recitation in eastern Tibet in 2000; in that case the chief lama of a remote monastery recited the epic in trance from a small booth equipped with loudspeakers; monks from his monastery performed the epic as a kind of drama, with makeup and elaborate costuming, some of which resembled the vestments of the state oracles. Since the Tibetan belief in reincarnate lamas implies a kind of "possession" of a body by a previously incarnated, enlightened master for a series of lifetimes, we might wish to mention it here as a form of lifelong possession at the service of a particular community.

Healing Practices Connected with Spirit Possession

Obeyesekere (The Medusa's Hair) reports on possession phenomena in Sri Lanka, where marginalized women become mediums for deities that communicate messages to inquirers, particularly about divination and healing. The sign of a possessed person is one or more "dread locks" (*jati*), each of which represents one of the deities that descends into the medium from time to time to deliver messages. The phenomenon of marginalized people becoming mediums for deities is widespread, and seems to follow the ancient pattern of the "chosen one" who begins life as an ordinary or even low person, but by the power of a particular deity is "lifted up" to become an instrument by which the deity influences the lives of others, including more powerful others. There is therefore a strong sociopolitical component to these forms of possession.

Channeling and Mediumship

In every civilization, including modernity, there have been mediums who perform so as to be believed in as channels for a variety of entities. In the United States, a number of mediums claim to be channeling ancient souls who have a message for modern times. Mediumship, particularly with regard to communication with the dead, has found a place in the "mass media" representing the latest expression of Spiritism, which grew in popularity in the United States during the 19th century, when even President and Mrs. Abraham Lincoln hosted séances at the White House during the Civil War years. In Italy, an association of laity with Catholic connections attempts to contact the dead in order to comfort the bereaved. The Institute of Noetic Sciences (IONS) has sponsored scientific research on channeling at its center in Petaluma, California.

Demonic Possession

Demonic possession is reported in most human cultures. Typically, it is the result of a curse or spell, or of mediumship gone awry. Other explanations for demonic possession include the claim that the possessed person is a victim of some previous crime or sin; thus possession is a form of punishment, brought on by the spiritual vulnerability of an impure person. There are also instances of voluntary possession, in which a spiritual aspirant desires to acquire the power to overcome demons through undergoing the trial of possession. However, traditional exorcists in almost all world religions vigorously oppose the practices of mediumship and acquired possession. The reason for this is that demonic entities can interfere with the procedures followed by mediums, and there is no guarantee of a sound result of voluntary possession. As a result, the entities that are said to have been contacted are not in fact the beloved dead or purported "higher powers," but demons imitating other entities. In time, these entities can bring deception, disease, financial ruin, mental confusion, possession, and death. In some instances, powerful demonic entities seem to have captivated the attention of large numbers of persons, only to disappear completely after a certain amount of harm was done. An example seems to have been the "Michael" entity of the 1970s in the New York City area. In Italy, the traditional practice of Christian exorcism has never completely died out and there are still experienced exorcists active within the Catholic Church. Research among these priests suggests that demonic possession is a distinct phenomenon, discernibly different from forms of mental illness.

Possession brings with it violent trance states, undiagnosable physical illnesses, imitations of mental illness, bodily deterioration, family discord, sexual dysfunction, and other destructive phenomena. The typical method for diagnosing possession is to engage in prayer in the presence of the victim; usually a trance state followed by various violent reactions is the response to simple prayers, even without the use of the formal Rite of Exorcism. The tradition insists on a number of criteria such as preternatural knowledge on the part of the demonic entity in order to authorize the use of the Rite of Exorcism. In practice, not all demons know multiple languages, nor do they all practice preternatural knowledge (prophecy or mind reading). It is crucial to have a good diagnostic survey done by an objective mental health specialist because some forms of psychosis also induce trance, changes of the voice, bodily distortions, and the like. The exorcist develops certain intuitive abilities over time that make it possible to detect a demonic presence even in the midst of chaotic performances that mimic other forms of dysfunction. Demonic possession is overcome through the spirituality of the exorcist, spiritual growth on the part of the possessed person, and the proper use of the Rite of Exorcism. The priest-exorcist works under obedience to the bishop or bishops who have appointed him to the task. Usually a network of prayer and spiritual support is necessary. It is also extremely helpful to instruct the victim in Christian doctrine because the victim's cooperation with the process of liberation is indispensable; often the experience of possession and liberation brings about a rapid development of holiness in the victim. Untreated possession, however, can lead to bodily death and spiritual collapse, since the goal of demonic entities is to degrade the human person.

In the case of Hindu and Buddhist exorcists, one notes a considerable body of convergence in diagnosis and methods of liberation with the traditional Christian, Jewish, Egyptian, shamanic, and Babylonian practices, even though the explanatory theological systems are divergent. Buddhists insist on a compassionate approach to the entities, knowing that sooner or later these beings will be reborn in the human condition and will be seeking liberation, whereas the Christian exorcist believes that these entities are eternally damned. Thus, the Christian exorcist is often more violent in the approach to the demons than is actually necessary. With experience, one learns to dominate the entities with prayer, and not to rely on overly dramatic confrontations. A strong, subtle, persistent approach shows greater reliance on divine providence, in harmony with the spiritual teachings of all the great saints.

Anyakayapravesha Anyakayapravesha is the practice of entering a recently deceased body. Hindu and Buddhist Tantric texts speak of the possibility of a spiritually advanced practitioner developing the ability to enter and operate within the body of a recently deceased person. Why would anyone need to do this?

In the Tantric systems, full realization of enlightenment and the acquisition of spiritual skills or powers (*siddhis*) are accomplished by lengthy repetitions of rituals and mantras. Should a practitioner reach the time of death without completing all the recitations, it might imperil the accumulated merits of a lifetime of spiritual discipline. For this reason, a yogin who is aware of imminent death should know how to find the fresh body of a young, healthy person and enter it so as to continue with spiritual practice. Rogue practitioners are said to do this in order to make illicit use of a corpse for sexual activities, theft, and the acquisition of magical powers.

Francis V. Tiso

See also: Exorcism; Modernity; Possession.

References

Balducci, Corrado. *Gli Indemoniati*. Rome: Coletti Editore, 1959.

Eliade, Mircea. *Shamanism: Archaic Techniques of Ecstasy*. Princeton, NJ: Princeton University Press, 1964.

Flint, Valerie, et al. *Witchcraft and Magic in Europe: Ancient Greece and Rome*. London: The Athlone Press, 1999.

Gauccio, Francesco. *Compendium Maleficarum*. Milan, 1635.

Heinze, Ruth Inge. *Trance and Healing in Southeast Asia Today*. Bangkok: White Lotus Publishers, 1988.

Hitchcock, John T., and Rex L. Jones. *Spirit Possession in the Nepal Himalayas*. Warminster, UK: Aris and Phillips, 1976.

Levack, Brian P., ed. *Articles on Witchcraft, Magic and Demonology*. Vol. 9, *Possession and Exorcism*. New York: Garland Publishing, 1992.

Loewe, Michael, and Carmen Blacker, eds. *Oracles and Divination*. Boulder, CO: Shambhala, 1981.

Lord, Albert B. *The Singer of Tales*. Cambridge, MA: Harvard University Press, 1960.

Obeyesekere, Gananath. *Medusa's Hair: An Essay on Personal Symbols and Religious Experience*. Chicago: University of Chicago Press, 1981.

Parke, H. W. *Greek Oracles*. London: Hutchinson, 1967.

Rowland, Christopher. *The Open Heaven: A Study of Apocalyptic in Judaism and Early Christianity*. New York: Crossroad, 1982.

Svoboda, Robert E. *Aghora: At the Left Hand of God*. Albuquerque, NM: Brotherhood of Life Publishers, 1986.

Spiritism

Spiritism is based on the work of Hippolyte Léon Denizard Rivail (1804–1869), who began to explicate his teachings in 1854 under the pseudonym Allan Kardec. Kardec was among the first people attracted to the Spiritualist movement that spread to France in the 1860s. He developed his own teachings from his contact with mediums and published several books. Translated into Portuguese, the books spread his particular form of Spiritualism, which included a belief in reincarnation, an idea anathema to British and American Spiritualists at the time.

In Brazil his concepts were adopted, elaborated, and sometimes reinterpreted by various authors, especially Chico Xavier, currently the most prominent representative of Brazilian Spiritism. He emphasizes, as do some other authors, the religious character of Spiritism. The doctrine of Spiritism centers on the idea of a continuous evolution of the individual soul in various manifestations. Death is considered an intermediate state between two lives in visible material form. Kardec taught that contact can be made with the spiritual world. This explains the important role of mediums in the local centers of Kardecism, which regularly become locations where people seek to communicate with deceased relatives. The worldview of Kardecism contains basic ideas of Christianity and intends to complete or fulfill them. Especially in terms of ethics, Spiritism is clearly Christianity-oriented, which leads Kardecists to engage in a wide range of charitable activities.

The history of institutionalized Kardecism in Brazil began in 1865, with the first official group of Spiritists in Salvador, Bahia. From 1873 on, Rio de Janeiro witnessed a wave of foundations of Spiritist circles and centers. In 1884 the Federação Espírita Brasileira was established as a national umbrella organization of local groups. At the end of the 1880s and in the following decades, umbrella organizations emerged at the state level. As for local centers, there was already a saturation by the 1950s. Official statistics for 1956 counted 2,950 local Brazilian groups, each with an average of 318 members. Kardecism's character as an urban phenomenon that attracts mainly middle-class, more erudite Brazilians has continued to this day.

In the national censuses, which have included Kardecism as a separate religious category since 1940, Spiritists never exceeded 2 percent of the population. In 1991 only 1.12 percent of the population declared themselves Kardecist, and only 3.6 percent of those lived in rural areas. The *Datafolha* study of 1994 confirmed not only the concentration of Spiritism in urban surroundings but also the high level of education of most adherents. According to the survey, 89 percent of Kardecists lived in large or medium-size cities, with concentrations in Sao Paulo and Rio de Janeiro. In each of those two cities, Kardecists made up 8 percent of the population.

The Internet site for the Federação Espírita Brasileira includes the text of Kardec's two primary works, *The Spirit's Book* and *The Medium's Book*. Centers of the Federação can now be found across South America and in Portugal.

Brazilian scholars treat Kardecistic Spiritism as one of several "mediumistic religions." In 1991, some 1,644,354 Brazilians, or 1.12 percent of the population, declared themselves Kardecists, while the *Datafolha* study of 1994 identified 3 percent of the adults entitled to vote as adherents of Kardecistic Spiritism. This number is less surprising if one recalls the campaign of Pentecostal churches against Afro-Brazilian "cults" and the social pressure that led practitioners of Candomblé and Umbanda to associate themselves with the less controversial category of "Spiritism."

Federação Espírita Brasileira, National Headquarters
SGAN 603 Conjunto "F"
Av. L-2 Norte
Brasília, DF
Brazil

Federação Espírita Brasileira, Regional Headquarters
Avenida Passos, 30, downtown
Rio de Janeiro, RJ

Brazil
http://www.febrasil.org.br/

Frank Usarski

See also: Candomblé; Spiritualism; Umbanda.

References

Kardec, Allan. *The Medium's Book.* Trans. by Emma E. Wood. New York: Samuel Weiser, 1970.

Kardec, Allan. *The Spirit's Book.* Trans. by Anna Blackwell. Sao Paulo: Livaria Kardec Editora, 1972.

Spiritual Baptists

The Spiritual Baptists are a rapidly expanding international religious movement with congregations in St. Vincent, Trinidad and Tobago, Grenada, Guyana, Venezuela, London, Amsterdam, Toronto, Los Angeles, and New York City. Like other religions of Caribbean origin, the Spiritual Baptists seem to have started out as a "religion of the oppressed." In recent years, however, congregations in Trinidad have attracted membership among wealthy East Indians, Chinese, and Europeans. Nevertheless, the religion is still overwhelmingly black, with Asians and whites constituting less than 5 percent of the total membership.

The central Spiritual Baptist rite is called "mourning." Spiritual Baptists participate in mourning ceremonies for a variety of reasons: to cure cancer, to see the future, or to communicate with the deceased. For most participants, however, the major reason for participating in the rite is to discover one's "true" rank within an elaborate 23-step church hierarchy. Every Baptist is expected to mourn often, and all Baptists desire to advance within the church hierarchy.

The 1990s ushered in a period of increasing respectability and visibility for the faith. In 1996 a general conference of Spiritual Baptist bishops was held at the Central Bank Auditorium in Port of Spain, Trinidad. Archbishop Murrain's address to the conference called for: (1) building a new cathedral that would include a library for researchers who want to "make a history" of the Spiritual Baptist faith; (2) the establishment of a trade school; and (3) construction of a "Spiritual Baptist Park" that would serve as a pilgrimage site for Spiritual Baptists in the Caribbean and throughout the world. A seminary—the Southland School of Theology—has been established, and a comprehensive Spiritual Baptist minister's manual was published in 1993. In addition, the day of the repeal of the Shouters Prohibition Ordinance (shouters being a derogatory name for the Spiritual Baptists) in 1953 is now a national holiday in Trinidad and Tobago. An African Spiritual Park and meeting hall have been established at Maloney, Trinidad.

In 2007, Spiritual Baptists from throughout the Caribbean gathered in Maloney for the 12th anniversary of Shouter Baptist Liberation Day. Speakers included President George Maxwell Richards, former Prime Minister Basdeo Panday, and Archbishop Barbara Gray-Burke. All praised what they saw as a close and productive relationship between the government and the Spiritual Baptists. But all recognized that there was still work to be done.

Nevertheless, it is difficult to gauge the impact of these changes on rank-and-file believers. Thus far, the impact has been minuscule. Southland School of Theology has few full-time students, the Spiritual Baptist ministers' manual is rarely consulted, and construction has yet to begin on the trade school or the cathedral. The majority of Spiritual Baptist churches in the Caribbean remain small and lack a solid financial base.

The Spiritual Baptists are led by the Council of Elders, which includes individuals (both male and female) who have been consecrated as archbishops. For the average Caribbean church member, things continue very much as before. There has, however, been tremendous church growth outside the Caribbean. Today, the largest and most prosperous Spiritual Baptist churches are located in Great Britain, Canada, and the United States. A number of Caribbean Baptist leaders have become associate pastors of churches in Europe and North America.

Council of Elders Spiritual Baptist Shouters Faith of
    Trinidad and Tobago
2A-2B Saddle Rd.
Maraval
Trinidad and Tobago
West Indies

Stephen D. Glazier

See also: Rastafarians.

References

Duncan, Carol B. *This Spot of Ground: Spiritual Baptists in Toronto.* Waterloo, Canada: Wilfrid Laurier Press, 2008.

Gibbs de Peza, Hazel Ann. *My Faith: Spiritual Baptist Christian.* St. Augustine: The Multimedia Production Centre School of Education/Faculty of Humanities and Education/University of the West Indies, 1999.

Glazier, Stephen D. *Marching the Pilgrims Home: A Study of the Spiritual Baptists of Trinidad.* Salem, WI: Sheffield, 1991.

Gray-Burke, Archbishop Barbara. "A Brochure for Teachers on Spiritual Shouter Religion in Trinidad and Tobago." http://www.n2consulting.com/brochure.html. Accessed December 1, 2001.

Hackshaw, John Milton. *The Origin of the Christian Religion, the Baptist Faith, the Independents, and Spiritual Baptist Churches.* Trinidad, West Indies: Citadel, 2000.

Laitinen, Maarit. *Marching to Zion: Creolisation in Spiritual Baptist Rituals and Cosmology.* Helsinki: Research Series in Anthropology, 2002. http://www.ethesis.helsinki.fi.

Lum, Kenneth Anthony. *Praising His Name in the Dance: Spirit Possession in the Spiritual Baptist Faith and Orisha Work in Trinidad, West Indies.* New York: Harwood, 2000.

Stephens, Patricia. *The Spiritual Baptist Faith: African New World Religious Identity, History, and Testimony.* London: Karnak House, 1998.

Spiritual Christian Evangelical Church

According to an official history of this Oneness Pentecostal denomination, the Iglesia Evangélica Cristiana Espiritual (IECE; Spiritual Christian Evangelical Church) was founded in Tampico, Tamaulipas, Mexico, by an independent Irish missionary, Joseph Stewart (1871–1926), in 1926. Stewart was born on September 9, 1871, the 10th son of Joseph Stewart Sloan and Jane Hall, in the village of Rosedernate, near Cloughmills, County Antrim, Northern Ireland. The family was dedicated to working in agriculture, which was the only means of subsistence in the region.

All the Stewarts were faithful members of a local Presbyterian church but the surprise visit by "two missionaries" to their village in 1893 had a disruptive impact on the family. The missionaries found lodging with the Stewart family and were invited to preach at the Presbyterian church in Clough. The two missionaries are not identified by name or organization, but what they preached and taught is known today as the Oneness Pentecostal doctrine, which was rejected as heresy by the local pastor and most of his church members.

The two missionaries gave a message that the people in this rural Irish congregation were not accustomed to hearing but that greatly impacted Joseph Stewart. The message, in a direct and clear manner, urged the congregation to live a holy life, full of the fear of God, and stated that baptism should be conducted only in the name of Jesus. This message, with a frontal attack on sin, was backed up by alleged manifestations of the Holy Spirit, including the gift of tongues (glossolalia). This deeply moved 22-year-old Stewart, who was "filled with the power of God and had the good fortune to speak in tongues, being sealed by the baptism of heaven" (the baptism in the Holy Spirit). According to the denominational history, Stewart was an energetic young man, very spiritual, and a good singer, and played several musical instruments.

In early 1894, Stewart made a decision to leave his family to go preach the gospel with the message of the "apostolic doctrine" that he had received. First, he joined the Faith Mission of Edinburgh and engaged in missionary work in rural Scotland for a few years before returning home to rest and recuperate for a season. Second, during the period 1897–1903, Stewart served as a missionary with the British-based nondenominational Christian Soldiers Association in Egypt and South Africa, where he ministered to British troops. After he resigned from the Christian Soldiers Association in March 1903, he worked on the family farm in Ireland, which was a blessing because the abundant harvest made it possible for him to carry out his previous plan to go to South America as a missionary. He had been preparing for this by studying Spanish.

Stewart's third missionary adventure took place during the period 1902–1912 in Argentina, where he served with the Christian and Missionary Alliance (CMA), a non-Pentecostal Trinitarian organization of the Holiness tradition. Stewart and David Buchanan soon became friends, and the latter, after coming to an understanding of the Oneness Pentecostal doctrine preached by Stewart, began to experience a radical change as he adopted and supported Stewart's doctrinal position: water baptism (or rebaptism) in the name of Jesus, personal holiness, and the gift of tongues as evidence of the baptism in the Holy Spirit; as well as denouncing fornication, adultery, and all other vices.

During his eight years (1904–1912) of missionary service in Argentina, serious problems began to emerge within the CMA missionary family in Argentina because of the Oneness Pentecostal doctrine preached by Stewart. While most of the CMA missionaries rejected this doctrine, a few accepted it, including Stewart's wife, Genoveva Harrison Stewart, along with David Buchanan, Alberta Bachelor, and two other Irish missionaries whose names are unknown.

When this situation was brought to the attention of CMA officials in New York, it was decided to dismiss those who espoused the Oneness Pentecostal doctrine due to conflicts with the CMA's official doctrinal position. Their dismissal occurred on December 9, 1911. The stated reason for their dismissal was "owing to their difference of conviction on questions relating to Restorationism and the future life" (CMA Annual Report for 1912). Restorationists sought to re-establish, renew, or restore the Christian church on the pattern of primitive Christianity as set forth in the New Testament —specifically regarding the charismatic gifts, such as speaking in tongues, miraculous healing, and prophecy. The CMA stance was both a rejection of Pentecostalism in general and a rejection of the Oneness doctrine in particular.

After they had been dismissed by the CMA, Stewart and his family, and David Buchanan and his wife, left Argentina. The Stewarts went to Northern Ireland and the Buchanans to the United States, where they settled in San Diego, California. After spending some time with his family in Ireland and visiting his wife's parents in Boston, the Stewarts traveled across the country from east to west, arriving in California and settling in Santa Barbara in 1914, where Stewart's fourth missionary adventure began. During that year

and the next, Joseph preached the gospel among Mexican immigrants between Santa Barbara and San Diego with his friend David Buchanan. The turmoil produced by the Mexican Revolution brought tens of thousands of Mexicans to Southern California during the period 1910–1920.

Due to a lack of gainful employment and the economic recession in the United States in 1915, Stewart and his family traveled to Canada, where he ministered with the Christian Workers' Church of Canada (later reorganized under the name of Associated Gospel Churches in 1925) for about three years. In 1919, the Stewarts returned to California, first to Santa Barbara and then to San Diego, where they worked with David Buchanan again as missionaries among the Spanish-speaking population for several years.

However, in February 1923, the U.S. government decided to deport Stewart as an "undesirable alien" and put him on a ship headed to Northern Ireland, while his children remained in the United States under the care of his wife's parents in Indiana. Previously, Stewart's wife became ill with meningitis and died in June 1922. He arrived in Ireland in March 1923, extremely sad and enormously concerned about his children.

During the nine months that he stayed on the family farm, he worked diligently plowing the fields, and once again the land provided him with sufficient income to afford to set out to find his children; this time he headed to Mexico on his fifth missionary adventure. While processing his passport and respective permits to leave the country, he headed to the port of Glasgow, Scotland, where he boarded the British ship *Diplomat* on December 1, 1923, and sailed to the port of Tampico, Tamaulipas, on Mexico's Caribbean coast, where he touched Mexican soil for the first time on January 6, 1924.

Mexican Apostolic church historian Manuel J. Gaxiola (1994) states that Stewart visited several Protestant churches in the port of Tampico after his arrived in 1924, where he met Ireneo Rojas Castillo, who later became president of the IECE after its formal establishment in 1926. Together, Stewart, Rojas, and other leaders established the first of many "spiritual churches" that later became associated with the IECE.

Stewart traveled to other places in northern Mexico between 1924 and 1926, and when he returned to

Tampico in January 1926 he discovered that the first church he helped establish had grown to about 200 members. Later in 1926, some of the small congregations established by Stewart and his associates in northern Mexico were organized under the name Iglesia Evangélica Cristiana Espiritual with headquarters in Tampico. Stewart ordained Juan Carreón Adame for the ministry of elder (Gaxiola 1994, 165) prior to leaving Tampico in 1926 and traveling to the city of Guadalajara, Jalisco, where he became seriously ill and died later that year.

Many of the early converts to Stewart's brand of Oneness Pentecostalism had previously been associated with non-Pentecostal Protestant denominations in northern Mexico. These included Presbyterians, Congregationalists, Baptists, Methodists, Christian Church (Disciples of Christ), and the Friends Church (Quakers); some were converts from Roman Catholicism.

Concurrently with these events, some members of the early Apostolic Faith movement (churches associated with the Apostolic Church of Faith in Jesus Christ of Mexico or its sister denomination in the United States, the Apostolic Assembly of Faith in Jesus Christ) were drawn away by the prophetic witness of two charismatic leaders, known as Saul and Silas, whose real names were Antonio Muñoz and Francisco Flores, respectively, who appeared in northern Mexico in 1924. The bearded and unwashed prophets, with similarities to the biblical John the Baptist, preached a message of repentance and faith, which required people to denounce their old religion and material possessions, and to be rebaptized in the "Name of Jesus." Their "authority" was derived from "special divine revelation" through their own prophecies, dreams, and visions, rather than from the Bible, which was a relatively unknown and unread book in those days in northern Mexico, according to Gaxiola.

The Saul and Silas movement produced a great deal of confusion and dissention within the churches associated with the Apostolic Church of Faith in Jesus Christ in northern Mexico during the decade 1925–1935, which caused some Apostolic pastors and members—including entire congregations—to leave the Apostolic Faith movement.

Such was the case of Felipe Rivas Hernández's (1901–1983) home church in Torreón, Coahuila, where Saul and Silas caused much conflict among Apostolics in 1924–1925. The result was that some Apostolic leaders and church members decided to form another organization in December 1927, known as Consejo Mexicano de la Fe Apostólica (Mexican Council of the Apostolic Faith), under the leadership of Francisco Borrego as pastor general. This group later became affiliated with the IECE with headquarters in Tampico, Tamaulipas, founded by Joseph Stewart in mid-1926.

After the death of Stewart in late 1926, the first pastor general of the IECE was Francisco Borrego of Torreón, followed by Ireneo Rojas Castillo in 1934 and continuing until his death in 1954, according to Gaxiola. In 1993, the president of the IECE was Félix Moreno Hernández, who registered this denomination with the Mexican government's Secretaría de Gobernación under the Department of Religious Associations. As of April 2008, Félix Moreno Hernández was still the president, according to a local press report.

Overall, the IECE is considered to be socially very conservative and apolitical in terms of its religious practices and its relationship with the larger society. Its other-worldly orientation is said to offer its adherents a retreat from the world's problems ("a refuge for the masses") while providing them with a strong sense of community. According to several reliable sources, some of the unique characteristics of this Oneness Pentecostal denomination are as follows.

It only uses the Reina Valera 1602 version of the Spanish Bible as holy scripture.

Members are taught that all the other churches (Protestant, Catholic, or whatever) are erroneous, while the IECE doctrines and practices represent the True Gospel. Members are not allowed to visit or have fellowship with believers of other denominations, although since 1972 there have been a few exceptions to this rule. Its leadership tends to be authoritarian and hostile to other denominations, but the denomination is missionary-minded and seeks to plant new churches where needed, both nationally and internationally.

The traditional Protestant Trinitarian doctrine is rejected as being unbiblical and polytheistic. Believers must be baptized (or rebaptized) in Jesus' name in order to experience True Salvation based on the Oneness doctrine (Acts 2:37–42).

The pastor functions as a type of priest before whom church members have to confess their sins; he is a disciplinarian who is in charge of maintaining proper order and decorum with the congregation; and he has the authority to remove rebellious members from the fellowship of the church (the practice of shunning or excommunication).

Members are prohibited from earning a living from sports activities, which are considered to be worldly pursuits.

Women are prohibited from cutting their hair, using makeup, using jewelry, and wearing slacks; their skirts and dresses must be less than 8 inches above their shoes. Men are prohibited from wearing shorts in public places. Women must cover their heads with a scarf while praying. Women and men must be seated on opposite sides of the sanctuary during religious services.

Not much is known about the historical development of this denomination since 1926, but it has been reported by Gaxiola and other sources that the IECE has experienced several notable organizational splits due to leadership conflicts during the past decades. Nevertheless, the denomination has experienced geographical expansion within Mexico as well to other Latin American countries, as well as membership growth in many of the existing congregations. In 1994, Gaxiola reported that the IECE had an estimated 14,000 baptized church members in Mexico, and that it had expanded its work into the United States, Central America, and South America.

According to a later source (date unknown), there were 362 IECE congregations and 578 missions (*campos de evangelización*) in Mexico, as well as an unknown number of associated churches in other countries: the United States, Argentina, Colombia, Paraguay, El Salvador, Honduras, Nicaragua, Costa Rica, Ecuador, Peru, and the Philippines.

In July 2005, IECE held its 79th Annual Convention in its own installations in San Luís Potosí, Mexico, with the participation of an estimated 18,000 people from many parts of Mexico and several other countries. In the city of San Luis Potosí alone, the work of IECE is organized in 4 districts, with an estimated 3,000 adherents, according to a local press report.

Iglesia Evangélica Cristiana Espiritual
Avenida Carlos Salazar No. 2008 Oeste
Colonia Obrera
Monterrey
Nuevo León, CP 64010
Mexico

Clifton L. Holland

See also: Christian and Missionary Alliance; Pentecostalism.

References

Castillo de La Torre, J. Pablo. "Historia de la Iglesia Evangélica Cristiana Espiritual." http://members.fortunecity.es/castillojp/iece_historia.html. Accessed June 15, 2009. English version translated from Spanish by Linda J. Holland on June 17, 2009, "History of the Spiritual Christian Evangelical Church." San Pedro, Montes de Oca, Costa Rica.

Castillo de La Torre, J. Pablo. "¿Que es la I.E.C.E.?" http://members.fortunecity.es/castillojp/iece_o_que_es.html. Accessed June 15, 2009.

Christian and Missionary Alliance. Annual Report, 1912. http://www.cmalliance.org/resources/archives/downloads/annual-report/1911-1912-annual-report.pdf . Accessed June 15, 2009.

Gaxiola-Gaxiola, Manuel J. *La Serpiente y la Paloma: Historia, Teología y Análisis de la Iglesia Apostólica de la Fe en Cristo Jesús de México (1914–1994)*. 2nd ed. Nacaulpan, Mexico: Libros Pyros, 1994.

Hernández Arroyo, Benjamín, Baltazar Cuevas Hernández, Josué Silva Ibarra, Josué Zamarripa Araujo, and Raúl Castañon Santana, eds. *Historia de la Iglesia Evangélica Cristiana Espiritual*. Monterrey, Mexico: Iglesia Evangélica Cristiana Espiritual (IECE), 1992.

"Las características de la IECE son." http://www.foroekklesia.com/showthread.php?t=45374. Accessed June 15, 2009.

Martínez Saldierna, Hortencia. "Actividades iniciadas desde el jueves atraen a creyentes de otras entidades y extranjeros." *La Jornada*, San Luís Potosí, Mexico (July 25, 2005). http://www

.lajornadasanluis.com.mx/2005/07/25/politica5
.php. Accessed June 15, 2009.

Salmerón Hernández, Angélica. "La iglesia Evangélica Cristiana Espiritual ha adoptado una forma
de vida recatada." *El Mundo de Córdoba*,
Veracruz, México (April 6, 2008). http://www
.elmundodecordoba.com/index.php?command
=show_news&news_id=70398. Accessed June
15, 2009.

Spiritual Churches (Ghana)

The prophet-healing African Initiated Churches (AICs) in Ghana are now popularly known as the "Spirit churches" (Akan: *Sunsum Sore*). Liberian prophet William Wade Harris (Harrist Church) preached in western Ghana for only a few weeks, but his influence remained, particularly in the first Spirit church to be formed there: the Church of William Wade Harris and His Twelve Apostles (later the Church of the Twelve Apostles). Harris's converts, Grace Tani and Kwesi John Nackabah, founded this church in 1918 following Harris's instruction that 12 apostles be appointed in each village to look after his flock. Tani was a traditional priestess when she was converted by Harris and became one of his assistants. When Harris was deported from the Ivory Coast, Tani returned to Ghana, fell ill, and called for Nackabah to pray for her healing. Nackabah was also a diviner until baptized by Harris and given the emblems of authority: a cup for holy water, a calabash with which to beat out evil spirits, a staff cross, and a Bible. Tani, now Madame Harris Grace Tani, remained the spiritual leader of the church, with Nackabah administrative and public leader. This dual arrangement was a convenient method used by several AICs to overcome traditional male resistance to female leadership.

The new church followed the Harrist tradition by emphasizing healing through faith in God and the use of holy water. Similarly, the Bible was placed on people's heads and gourd rattles were used to drive out demons and heal people. Polygyny was permitted, and new members were first ritually purified through washing. The healing was administered in healing gardens (communal dwellings), and the holy water was usually kept in basins under a wooden cross in the gardens. Nackabah died in 1947, to be succeeded as bishop by John Hackman. After the death of Hackman in 1957 and Tani in 1958, schisms occurred, largely along ethnic lines. The church is now divided into several groups, the most prominent being the Nackabah People, the William Wade Harris Twelve Apostles Church, and the Twelve Apostles Church of Ghana.

The most prominent churches in Ghana are the Musama Disco Christo Church, the Twelve Apostles Church, and the African Faith Tabernacle, with about 125,000 affiliates each in 1990. The African Faith Tabernacle was founded by Prophet James Kwame Nkansah in 1919, a movement influenced in doctrine and practices by the form of North American Fundamentalism from which it originated. The prophet Charles Kobla Wovenu, a former Presbyterian government clerk, commenced the Apostolic Revelation Society in 1939, consisting mainly of Ewe, with a holy city at Tadzewu. He left the Presbyterian church in 1945 when he was told to stop praying for healing.

In 1963 the Eden Revival Church (now known as the F'Eden Church) was commenced by a Presbyterian schoolteacher, Charles Yeboa-Korie (b. 1938), when he received visions that he was to become a healer. He used prayer with accompanying liturgical objects such as Bibles, blessed water, handkerchiefs, olive oil, candles, and incense in order to bring healing from sickness and deliverance from demons. Later, modernization and contact with Western Christianity caused the candles and incense to disappear, and Yeboa began to see his church as forming a bridge between the AICs and the "mainline" churches. In 1970, F'Eden was the first AIC to be admitted to the national Ghanaian Christian Council.

Aladura Churches from Nigeria (such as the Christ Apostolic Church, the Cherubim and Seraphim, the Celestial Church of Christ, and the Church of the Lord, Aladura) have come to Ghana and have significant followings. Several of the spiritual churches in Ghana formed an ecumenical cooperative organization in 1962, the Pentecostal Association of Ghana, the name chosen to illustrate the self-identity of the "spiritual churches" of Ghana as "Pentecostal." Another ecumenical organization, called the Council of Independent Churches in Ghana, has also been formed. Observers estimated that in 1996 there were more than 3,000 AICs in Ghana.

Allan H. Anderson

See also: African Initiated (Independent) Churches; Aladura Churches; Celestial Church of Christ; Cherubim and Seraphim/Eternal Sacred Order of the Cherubim and Seraphim; Christ Apostolic Church; Church of the Lord; Harrist Church; Musama Disco Christo Church.

References

Anderson, Allan H. *African Reformation: African Initiated Christianity in the Twentieth Century.* Trenton, NJ: Africa World Press, 2001.

Bakta, G. C. *Prophetism in Ghana: A Study of Some "Spiritual" Churches.* London: SCM, 1962.

Beckman, David M. *Eden Revival: Spiritual Churches in Ghana.* St. Louis, MO: Concordia, 1975.

Consultation with African Instituted Churches, Ogere, Nigeria, 9–14 January 1996. Geneva: World Council of Churches, 1996.

Spiritual Churches (Kenya)

The first African Initiated (Independent) Churches (AICs) to emerge in Kenya were the "spiritual churches" that began among Luo Anglicans around Lake Victoria. The Roho (Spirit) movement commenced in 1912, first as a popular charismatic movement among young people within the Anglican Church. Afterward, its best known founders, Anglican deacon Alfayo Odongo Mango (1884–1934) and his nephew Lawi Obonyo (ca. 1911–1934), began a prophetic ministry around 1933, when several remarkable healings and other miracles were reported.

In spite of the opposition by Anglican authorities, Mango installed new rites of baptism and Communion, and his home became a center to which people came and then fanned out. Mango began to prophesy the end of colonial rule and predicted future development in Kenya. The Roho were accused of acts of violence and banned from the local Anglican church.

Mango, Lawi, and seven of their followers were murdered by a mob of several hundred, as Mango's house was set alight. The Roho thereafter began a vigorous missionary expansion movement called Dini ya Roho (Religion of the Spirit), emphasizing the power of the Spirit and dressing in white robes with red crosses. The Roho churches say that Mango's sacrificial death atoned for their sins and opened heaven to Africans. Mango is prayed to as "our Saviour," and he has inaugurated a new era of the reign of the Holy Spirit in Africa. These churches enjoin monogamy on their leaders, and they are known for their processions through the streets of towns and villages. The Roho movement now has several schisms and has spread to Tanzania.

A Holy Spirit movement among the Abaluyia emerged after a Pentecostal revival in a Friends/Quakers mission in 1927, also called Dini ya Roho. The movement resulted in the Holy Spirit Church of East Africa and the African Church of the Holy Spirit. All these Roho churches do not have sacraments of baptism and Communion, but they do have rituals for purification before church services, before meals, and before entering and leaving houses. In common with other spiritual and prophetic churches, these churches reject the use of medicines; their members wear white robes with a red cross, turbans, and beards and remove shoes during services. Church meetings have ecstatic phenomena, especially prophecy, speaking in tongues, the interpretation of dreams, and healing. One of the most prominent spiritual churches in western Kenya is the African Israel Church, Nineveh.

The Arathi (Prophets), also known as Watu wa Mungu (People of God), or, as now better known, Akurinu, is a spiritual church movement among the Gikuyu of central Kenya. It started in a Pentecostal revival in 1922, when manifestations of the Spirit—including speaking in tongues, prophecy, visions, and other ecstatic phenomena—were present, and in which there was an emphasis on prayer and the confession of sins. Joseph Ng'ang'a received a divine call in 1926 and, after a four-year seclusion, began preaching the downfall of European colonialism. His followers wore long white robes and expected a new golden age for the Gikuyu. When the Spirit came on them they roared and shook violently, a practice that continues today. The movement spread throughout the Gikuyu region, and

Worshippers with the African Israel Church, Nineveh, march through the streets in the Kibera slums February 10, 2008, in Nairobi, Kenya. (Getty Images)

the colonial authorities became increasingly nervous about what they saw as a religious expression of African nationalism. The Akurinu were banned, and Ng'ang'a and five other leaders were arrested.

Later in 1934, Ng'ang'a and two followers were killed by a police contingent. The repression of the movement increased, and many Akurinu were arrested and imprisoned. Others fled to other parts of Kenya, where the movement spread farther, setting up communities and living together wherever they went. Schisms began to appear in 1949, and there are now more than 30 Arathi churches in Kenya, nearly all of which use "Holy Ghost" in their church title. Like the Roho churches, they do not baptize with water but practice a "baptism of the Holy Spirit" by a threefold shaking of hands and laying on of hands. Despite the similarities with the Roho movement, the Akurinu movement was formed with little or no contact with

Western missions or spiritual churches elsewhere. It has consciously attempted to form a radically African type of Christianity, in which the pattern of the mission churches plays no significant role, and that may make the Akurinu churches unique.

Allan H. Anderson

See also: African Church of the Holy Spirit; African Initiated (Independent) Churches; African Israel Church, Nineveh; Friends/Quakers; Pentecostalism.

References

Githieya, Francis K. *The Freedom of the Spirit: African Indigenous Churches in Kenya.* Atlanta, GA: Scholars Press, 1997.

Hoehler-Fatton, Cynthia. *Women of Fire and Spirit: History, Faith and Gender in Roho Religion in Western Kenya.* Oxford: Oxford University Press, 1996.

Rasmussen, Ane Marie Bak. *Modern African Spirituality: The Independent Spirit Churches in East Africa, 1902–1976*. London: British Academic Press, 1996.

Spiritual Healing Church (Botswana)

The Spiritual Healing Church is properly described as a "child" of the independent church movement in South Africa. It was founded by Jacob Mokgwetsi Motswasele (1900–1980), who was born to Israel and Kiole Motswasele in 1900 in Thaba Nchu, South Africa. Motswasele belonged to the Barolong clan and Seleka tribe and was raised a Methodist. As a young man he migrated to Matsiloje, in the Tati District of Botswana, then known as the Bechuanaland Protectorate. There he began to experience religious dreams, which intensified in 1923 when the Prophet Harry Morolong came to Matsiloje from Thaba Nchu, Bloemfontein, South Africa, to lead a revival mission. Prophet Morolong had been inspired by Walter Matitta (1885–1935), founder of the Church of Moshoeshoe in Lesotho. After Morolong's visit, Motswasele and others who continued to gather for prayer experienced the spiritual phenomena of trembling and speaking in tongues.

Between 1930 and 1948, Motswasele was a migrant worker in Johannesburg, South Africa. There he was influenced by Christinah Nku, a prophetess of the St. John's Apostolic Faith Mission, and he became a member of the Bantu Methodist Church. Upon returning to Matsiloje, he began a ministry of prayer and healing. He was seen as a man who possessed many gifts: healing, "sight" (diagnosing illness, interpreting dreams, foretelling the future), preaching, rain-making, and simply having power from God. Around that time he became known as the Prophet Mokaleng. In 1952 he founded the Apostolic United Faith Coloured Church, which after numerous name changes is now known as the Spiritual Healing Church. The first baptism was held April 16, 1953. In 1955 construction on a church building was begun. In 1966, Israel Motswasele (1934–1999) replaced his father, Mokaleng, as head of the Spiritual Healing Church. Mokaleng remained a prophet until his death in 1980. Although Israel was certainly seen as having power from God, his gifts were more administrative.

Forming a new African Initiated Church (AIC) in the 1950s was difficult in the Bechuanaland Protectorate, as both British authorities and local tribal leaders (*dikgosi*) vigorously sought to restrict such "dissident" and "unwelcome" movements. Although most AIC leaders were harassed and persecuted, Mokaleng was allowed to operate in a low-key manner. Perhaps his relative freedom was due to the fact that Matsiloje was in a remote and generally neglected district, and that local subchiefs were not very powerful. By the late 1950s, Mokaleng was allowed to travel, starting "prayer groups" in other areas. By the late 1960s, and with independence in 1966, restrictions against AICs began to loosen. In 1966 a congregation was formed in Gaborone and by 1968 this congregation was allowed to erect a building—the first AIC building in the capital. Although the Spiritual Healing Church has often been viewed as a member of the Apostolic family of AICs from South Africa, when it was allowed to register in 1973, the government requested that the word "Apostolic" be removed from in front of "Spiritual Healing Church."

At least four unique features characterize the Spiritual Healing Church. First, while most AICs are suspicious of other Christian organizations and churches, Israel Motswasele took the bold step of inviting Mennonite workers into the midst of the church in the mid-1970s to provide Bible and leadership training. Second, this church places uncommon emphasis on the presence and appearance of church buildings. Third, as AICs are often differentiated by unique dress codes, the church uniform robes for the Spiritual Healing Church are blue and white, and they are worn by baptized members only. A final unique feature is that while many AICs crumble or stagger because of poor management, the Spiritual Healing Church is recognized as being uncharacteristically well run and organized.

Part of the reason that the Spiritual Healing Church is well run is that beginning in 1966 with Israel Motswasele and his father, Jacob, roles for administration and prophecy have been separated. In 1984 the administrative head became known as the "archbishop." Prophets are chosen by the Holy Spirit, who is free to choose family members to this ministry, such as Israel's brother Joseph. The archbishop is now elected, but charisma and appointment by the predecessor are still very important factors. As with the Methodist Church in Africa, other roles in the church include, in order of increased authority, preachers, deacons, evangelists, and full ministers. Women's voices in the church are increasingly being heard, although women are still permitted to participate only on lower levels of the hierarchy, primarily as deacons. There are quarterly meetings for leaders in each of the district conferences: Gaborone, Mahalapye, Francistown, and Maun.

Despite being well-organized, the Spiritual Healing Church has not been able to avoid splits and secessions. In 1973 a conflict arose between Mokaleng and Matlho Kepaletswe, the latter seceding to form the Revelation Blessed Peace Church. Other splits have been more peaceful, and the following AICs are better described as "daughter churches": St. Faith Holy Church, Saints Gallery Church, St. Philip's Faith Healing Church, and the Lesidi Church.

The Spiritual Healing Church has grown rapidly since the late 1960s, due largely to its healing ministry. The most recent available statistics, from 1990, indicate that there were 26 congregations in Botswana with approximately 16,000 members, and the numbers are undoubtedly higher today. Growth is especially strong in urban areas, where the church attracts young people who have moved to the city to find employment. There is a branch of the Spiritual Healing Church in Namibia, and some church planting efforts have also been under way in South Africa.

Some practices that characterize the Spiritual Healing Church include prohibitions against tobacco, alcohol, and eating pork, nonscaly fish, and animals that are already dead. The Spiritual Healing Church has its own service book, which it published in 1977, and includes litanies for a variety of services. Although the church generally recognizes and takes seriously traditional African spirits, ancestors, and other forces, it has its own way of dealing with those entities and the crises they bestow. Three festivals are especially important in the Spiritual Healing Church. Easter is the highlight of the year, and every third year all congregations gather in Matsiloje for a celebration that lasts four or five days. In the two intervening years, district churches meet together. On January 25, a memorial service is held for the founder, Mokaleng, marking the date of his death. Each August an all-night festival is held to celebrate the Feast of Unleavened Bread.

Although there is a high reverence for the scriptures, because of illiteracy, traditional African approaches to authority, and an overall emphasis on pneumatology, there is little perceived need to expand Bible knowledge beyond the limited number of passages that the present leaders are familiar with and commonly preach upon.

The Spiritual Healing Church has its headquarters at Matsiloje, Botswana.

Andy Brubacher Kaethler

See also: African Initiated (Independent) Churches; Church of Moshoeshoe; Methodism.

References
Amanze, J. N. *Botswana Handbook of Churches*. Gaborone, Botswana: Pula, 1994.
Boschman, Don. "The Conflict between New Religious Movements and the State in the Bechuanaland Protectorate prior to 1945." Th.M. thesis, Harvard Divinity School, 1989.
Friesen, Rachel Hilty. "A History of the Spiritual Healing Church." M.A. thesis, Toronto School of Theology, 1990.
Friesen, Rachel Hilty. "Origins of the Spiritual Healing Church." In *Afro-Christianity at the Grassroots*, edited by G. C. Oosthuizen et al., 37–50. Leiden: Brill, 1994.
Rantsandu, B. "The Conflict between the Spiritual Healing Church and the Authorities before Independence." In *Afro-Christianity at the Grassroots*, edited by G. C. Oosthuizen et al., 51–54. Leiden: Brill, 1994.

Spiritual Human Yoga

Spiritual Human Yoga (SHY) was originally known as Universal (and) Human Energy; today it uses the name of Mankind Enlightenment Love (MEL) as well. It was founded by a Vietnamese émigré, Luong Minh Dang (1942–2007). Data about his biography are controversial. Between 1961 and 1975 he apparently served as an officer in the South Vietnamese navy; after the

Communist takeover, he immigrated to the United States, becoming a U.S. citizen in 1985. He gained rapid recognition as a healer in St. Louis, Missouri, first among Vietnamese immigrants and later outside the Vietnamese community. The movement was established in 1989, and from the United States it expanded into Mexico, Brazil, Western and Eastern Europe, Turkey, Israel, and Thailand.

By 1998 some 10,000 students had reached Level 6, at that time the highest in the movement. According to Dang, his teachings derive from Dasira Narada (1846–1924), a Sri Lankan master on whom information independent of SHY literature is not available. According to SHY, Narada initiated Dang in Vietnam in 1972, and died in Sri Lanka in 1980. SHY teaches that a Universal Energy permeates the universe and (having entered through the *chakras*) flows through the cells of the human body. SHY's techniques claim to enable its followers to control the Universal Energy and to use it for the well-being of humanity in general. SHY students are taught how to direct the Universal Energy toward those who most need it, thus (inter alia) healing the sick. SHY's techniques are introduced as being faster and easier to master than others, such as Reiki, which also involves the flow of a universal energy. Up to Level 5 inclusive, the Universal Energy is transmitted through the practitioner's hands; at higher levels, at which small pyramids are also used to store Energy, transmission is telepathic. Master Dang developed his teaching up to Level 20.

SHY does not have any common religious structures. There are no rituals or rites of passage. Master Dang's teachings, on the other hand, include a spirituality, particularly at Level 4 and higher. This spirituality is eclectic: Dang quoted Franz Anton Mesmer (1734–1815), an early exponent of the Energy so important to the SHY perspective, and Edgar Cayce (1877–1945), whose teachings are spread through the Association for Research and Enlightenment, and he encouraged his students to read *The Grail Message*, written by Abd-ru-shin (Oskar Ernst Bernhardt, 1875–1941), the founder of the Grail movement. Buddha and Jesus are also revered as spiritual masters, although a certain critique of more traditional religions is inherent in SHY teachings, and Dang certainly believed that his regular contact with the Higher Beings allowed him to receive more updated information.

In Europe, Dang became a target of the anti-cult crusade, and he was arrested in Belgium in January 1999. After 65 days of imprisonment, he was released on bail and allowed to leave the country. He was arrested again in October 2005, and then transferred to Switzerland, where he was kept in jail before being released on bail. He was sentenced in absentia in Brussels to four years in jail (half of the term as a suspended sentence), being accused of swindle and teaching illegal medical practices—the exclusive use of which led to the death of a baby.

Although the Belgian accusations concerned mostly finances and controversial healing techniques, the media tended to stress SHY's most apocalyptic elements at the time of the 1999 controversy. In fact, Dang believed that the 21st century would prove to be a great divide in the history of humanity, and he expected crucial events to take place sometime soon. SHY is a millenarian movement in the sense that it anticipates that in the not-too-distant future there will be the advent of a new heaven on Earth, culminating in the final defeat of illness and death itself.

After Master Dang passed away unexpectedly in Australia, where he had settled in 2000, Theresa Thu-Thuy Nguyen (b. 1957), whom he had married in 1998, claimed to take over Master Dang's mission as "the Ambassador and leading instructor of the Universal Energy School," using the global name of Academy of Human Universal Energy and Spirituality (HUESA). But the founder's son, Luong Minh Trung, relocated with his family from Australia back to St. Louis, stating that the Master's soul continued to transfer energy for the higher-level seminars (thus not endorsing the role claimed by Theresa Thu-Thuy Nguyen). Students of Universal Energy are now split between those following either Theresa Thu-Thuy Nguyen or Luong Minh Trung, but some have not taken sides and prefer to wait and see.

Mankind Enlightenment Love (MEL)
4448 Telegraph Road
St. Louis, MO 63129
http://www.mel-hq.com/

Academy of Human Universal Energy and
    Spirituality (HUESA)
6 St. Johns Avenue
Springvale, Victoria 3171
Australia
http://www.huesa.org/
http://www.ue-global.com (independent forum, with
    participants from the different wings of Universal
    Energy)

> *Jean-François Mayer, PierLuigi Zoccatelli,*
> *and Massimo Introvigne*

See also: Association for Research and Enlightenment; Energy; Grail Movement.

References

Mayer, Jean-François. "Healing for the Millennium: Master Dang and Spiritual Human Yoga." *Journal of Millennial Studies* 2, no. 2 (Winter 2000). http://www.mille.org/publications/winter2000/winter2000.html or http://www.bu.edu/mille/publications/winter2000/winter2000.html.

Nguyen, Tri-Thien. *L'Energie Universelle et Humaine: Une méthode naturelle de guérison énergétique.* Romont, Switzerland: Editions Recto-Verseau, 2001.

Spiritualism

Spiritualism is a 19th-century movement that emerged in the United States around the belief that its leaders, called mediums, could contact and speak to the spirits of the deceased. Arising in an atmosphere in which many traditional religious beliefs, especially survival of death, were being questioned, Spiritualism claimed to be able to demonstrate the reality of the survival of death. Crucial to such demonstrations were the mediums, individuals who had the special ability to interact with the spirit world, often while in a trancelike state, and bring meaningful messages to people from deceased relatives and friends.

Spiritualists date their movement from March 31, 1848, when Kate Fox (d. 1892) and her two sisters, Leah and Margaret, began to converse with what they believed was the spirit of a deceased individual who formerly resided in their home. Communication was established through strange rapping noises that they had heard. Once they perceived that the rappings had a rational content, they worked out a code to begin communication.

The interest shown by neighbors in the phenomenon led no lesser a person than newspaper editor Horace Greeley (1811–1872), fabled editor of the influential *New York Tribune,* to investigate and report on it. News reports led others to attempt such communications, and within a few years a wide variety of modes of communication were being reported. Spiritualism spread quickly through the 1850s, and parties at which attempts to communicate with spirits were made became a popular form of entertainment. On a more serious level, books advocating the Spiritualist hypothesis—that humans survive death in a spirit existence and that communication through a medium is possible—were published, lecturers advocated Spiritualism, and mediums gave public demonstrations. A more sophisticated direction to the new movement was offered by Andrew Jackson Davis, a prominent trance medium, who wrote extensively about his spirit contacts and the afterlife that he and other Spiritualists referred to as Summerland.

Spiritualism also drew upon earlier demonstrations of Mesmerism, a movement that grew out of the work of French physician Franz Anton Mesmer (1734–1815), who claimed to have found a subtle force underlying the universe that could be used to produce altered states of consciousness. Mesmerism would lead to the discovery of hypnotism in the 19th century. Spiritualists claimed that mediums could demonstrate "scientifically" the reality of life after death.

Crucial to the development of Spiritualism in the late 19th century was psychical mediumship, the claimed ability of some mediums not just to speak to and relay information from the spirits of the deceased but also to produce an array of phenomena. These, such as the levitation of objects, the materialization of spirits, and photography of the dead, appeared to go far beyond the phenomena discovered by mundane science. By the end of the 19th century, physical phenomena had become the most spectacular claim undergirding belief in Spiritualism.

Medium holds a séance, ca. 1920. In the early 20th century, Spiritualism captured the popular imagination. (Library of Congress)

In the 1880s, a group of scientists and others organized to investigate the claims being made in Spiritualist phenomena and to speculate on the nature of a universe that allowed such phenomena to exist. The investigations of the Society for Psychical Research in Great Britain and similar societies in continental Europe and North America, although initially hopeful, eventually drastically reduced the claims of the kinds of psychic phenomena for which there was some modicum of evidence. Psychical researchers almost completely destroyed the claims of physical phenomena, the great majority of which rested upon fraud. Through the 20th century, parapsychology, a new approach to psychic phenomena centered upon laboratory research, replaced psychical research, which had focused its attention upon the observation of mediums and psychics.

In the United States, the Spiritualist movement was given some structure by the organization of camp meetings, popularly modeled on the camp meetings being perpetuated among evangelical Protestants and associations of spiritualists at the state level. It grew as a secular movement based around the demonstration of phenomena, but it developed a religious dimension as those convinced of the truth of the phenomena began to speculate on the nature of reality in light of the afterlife.

Through the last decades of the 20th century, three factions appeared. One group saw Spiritualism as a secular movement limited to the production of demonstrable phenomena. A second group saw it as a religious group based upon the ongoing contact with the spirits of the deceased (and other spiritual beings such as angels) and the information about the afterlife derived from such contact. This second group was divided over Spiritualism's relation to traditional Christianity. The larger groups saw Spiritualism's differences with Christianity, while a smaller group attempted to interpret Spiritualism as a Christian movement. In the 1890s, the first attempt to organize a national Spiritualist denomination resulted in the 1893 formation of the National Spiritualist Association, later renamed the National Association of Spiritualist Churches.

Spiritualism spread to England in the 1860s and soon thereafter to continental Europe. In England a spectrum of Spiritualist organizations emerged, including the Spiritualist Association of Great Britain and the London Spiritualist Alliance. In the 20th century, the Greater World Christian Spiritualist League and the Church of the White Eagle Lodge joined the community as significant organizations. As it developed in France, Spiritualism found a popular leader in the person of Allan Kardec (1804–1869). From France the movement was exported to South America, where it found particular success in Brazil. Kardec was an advocate of reincarnation, and his teachings, known as Spiritism, were alienated from Christianity. They found expression in the Federação Espírita Brasileira, based in Brazil.

In America, Spiritualism spread through the 1920s, but by mid-century it began to decline under criticism of Spiritualist phenomena and in the face of competition from a growing Esoteric community. Always considered a fringe element in the religious community in America, it became more established in Great Britain, especially after repeal of the archaic Witchcraft Laws in the 1950s that had occasionally been used to charge mediums with fraud. It enjoys its greatest success today in Brazil.

Although the emphasis of Spiritualism was always spirit contact for the purpose of demonstrating life after death, another phenomenon that in the late 20th century came to be known as channeling also had a role in the Spiritualist community. Some individual spiritualists, including many mediums, made contact with what were considered wiser and more evolved spirit beings not particularly connected with the families of those who came to the Spiritualist demonstrations. These evolved beings talked of the nature of the afterlife and expounded on a wide range of philosophical and theological concepts. The teachings of such spiritual beings were later collected and published. Given the widely divergent opinions expressed by the entities who spoke in channeled material, such channelings would occasionally be the basis of new separate movements, such as the Universal Faithists of Kosmon, the Grail Movement, and Universal Life.

In the late 20th century, channeling became an essential element of the emerging New Age movement. As a whole, Spiritualists watched the New Age movement from the sidelines and were noticeably absent for New Age conventions and events. Even though movement called the general public's attention to a variety of spiritual realities usually the central focus of Spiritualism, Spiritualists were not attuned to other New Age emphases, and in the end did not benefit significantly from the New Age's popularity.

Spiritualism now exists in a number of small associations, each with a small number of congregations and one or more camps. Camps in southern states stay open all year, while those farther north tend to be purely summer affairs. The largest association is also the oldest, the National Spiritualist Association of Churches, which has 85 congregations (2008) scattered across the United States.

J. Gordon Melton

See also: Church of the White Eagle Lodge; Grail Movement; National Spiritualist Association of Churches; New Age Movement; Universal Faithists of Kosmon; Universal Life.

References

Buescher, John B. *The Other Side of Salvation: Spiritualism and the Nineteenth-Century Religious Experience.* Boston: Skinner House Books, 2004.

Doyle, Arthur Conan. *The History of Spiritualism.* 2 vols. London: Cassell, 1926.

Gauld, Alan. *Mediumship and Survival: A Century of Investigation.* London: Heineman, 1982.

Kerr, Howard. *Mediums, Spirit Rappers, and Roaring Radicals.* Urbana: University of Illinois Press, 1972.

Leonard, Todd Jay. *Talking to the Other Side: A History of Modern Spiritualism and Mediumship: A Study of the Religion, Science, Philosophy and Mediums that Encompass this American-Made Religion.* New York: iUniverse, 2005.

Melton, J. Gordon. *Encyclopedia of Occultism and Parapsychology.* 5th ed. Detroit, MI: Gale Research, 2001.

Nelson, Geoffrey K. *Spiritualism and Society.* New York: Schocken, 1969.

Owen, Alex. *The Darkened Room: Women, Power, and Spiritualism in Late Victorian England.* Chicago: University of Chicago Press, 2004.

Spring Dragon Festival

The dragon is a ubiquitous symbol throughout China and traditional Chinese lore. The dragon was seen as a positive creature, or more precisely as an auspicious creature, and served as a symbol of the emperor. The basis of the Spring Dragon Festival is the dragon's association with water, as the bringer of rain. The festival is based upon an ancient belief that on the second day of the second lunar month (generally in early March on the Common Era calendar) the dragon raises its head. In agricultural areas, it was hoped that the dragon's action would lead to large barns being full and small ones overflowing.

A popular Daoist legend recounts the coming of Wu Zetian, a Tang dynasty queen to the throne. In his anger, the Jade Emperor ordered the four dragon gods

Chinese young men perform the dragon dance during the Spring Dragon Festival, 2010. (Donkeyru/Dreamstime.com)

to withhold the rain for three years. One dragon took pity and allowed it to rain. The Jade Emperor punished the dragon by hiding him away in a mountain for 1,000 years, or until "golden beans give birth to flowers." The people went searching for the golden beans, which they discovered to be popping corn. When the Jade Emperor saw that the people had in fact met his conditions, he called the dragon back to heaven to oversee the rains for the growing season. Since this time, popped corn is one of the three foods most associated with the festival. In addition to popped corn, Spring Dragon foods include noodles, symbolic of the dragon's lifting his head, and fry cakes, associated with the dragon's gallbladder, the gallbladder being associated with courage.

The Spring Dragon Festival was celebrated in northern China, where the spring rains (monsoon season) tended to start after the second day of the second lunar month.

J. Gordon Melton

See also: Chinese Religions; Daoism; Dragon Boat Festival.

References

Latsch, Marie-Luise. *Traditional Chinese Festivals.* Singapore: Greaham Brash, 1984.

Liming, Wei. *Chinese Festivals: Traditions, Customs, and Rituals.* Hong Kong: China International Press, 2005.

Spring Equinox

The Spring, or Vernal, Equinox was one of four points in the year (the others being the Winter and Summer solstices and the Fall Equinox) discovered and marked by ancient peoples who observed the heavens. At the Winter Solstice, from the viewpoint of an observer in the Northern Hemisphere, the Sun rises at a point farthest to the south and is in the sky the least amount of time. As the days pass, the Sun rises at a point slightly farther north each day and finally reaches a point, 3 months later, around March 21, when it is in the sky for 12 hours and below the horizon for 12 hours. That point is the equinox. Viewed from above Earth, the

equinox is that point where the center of the Sun passes through the plane created by the Earth's equator. Following the Summer Solstice, the Sun will appear to be moving south and again reach a point where the day and night are equal—the Fall Equinox. In the Southern Hemisphere, the Vernal Equinox is September 21.

Both the Spring and Fall Equinox were important dates in the ancient calendars, the latter being the time for the end of harvest festival for a wide variety of peoples in the temperate and northern climate zones. As the modern calendar began to be developed, however, the Spring Solstice assumed a far more important role. First, in the Middle East, as the Zodiac was developed, the Spring Solstice, defined as when the Sun moved from the sign of Pisces into Aries, was the beginning of the year and the moment for the annual adjustment of the calendar. As the Zodiac was passed from nation to nation, the Spring Equinox maintained its importance. It then became crucial to Julius Caesar whose new Roman calendar posited two crucial events —the beginning of the year on January 1 and the Spring Equinox in March. Thus for much of the world, the Spring Equinox became either the beginning point of the year or a major supplement marker and time for celebration. Among the major calendars that begin on the Vernal Equinox is the new Saka calendar adopted by the postcolonial government of India. The calendar begins with New Year's Day on the Vernal (Spring) Equinox, March 21 or 22, on the Common Era calendar. The Baha'i Faith's Bodi calendar also begins on the Spring Equinox (March 21). The last of the Baha'is 19 months, which occurs just prior to the Spring Equinox, is a month of fasting.

In the mid-19th century, Persia (Iran), where the Baha'i Faith originated, extensive use began of the Zodiacal or Borji calendar, which begins the new year on March 21 when the Sun enters the sign of Aries. Each remaining month was begun on the day the Sun entered a new sign. The 12 months had either Arabic or Parsi names. In 1925, the shah of Iran replaced the Borji calendar with an Iranian solar calendar. It also followed the 12 Zodiacal signs but gave them their Persian names. Thus the New Year begins on Farvadin 1 (or March 21 in the Common Era calendar). The years are countered from 622, the year of the Prophet Muhammad's *hegira*.

Farvadin 1–4 (March 21–24) is celebrated as the Iranian New Year.

The Spring Equinox remains an important moment for Western astrology, but has otherwise been a non-entity on the calendars used by Jews, Christians, and Muslims. The major spring festival of the Jews, namely Passover, is calculated on a lunar calendar and thus moves significantly from year to year, as does the Christian Easter celebration.

The primary groups that celebrate the Spring Equinox in the West currently are the closely related neo-Pagans and Wiccans. Both use the modern Common Era calendar and meet for the eight equally spaced dates that include the Summer and Winter solstices, the Spring and Fall equinoxes, and the four dates halfway between them. For Wiccans and Pagans, the Spring Equinox begins the planting season, often for the urbanized, a time to plant flowers or a small garden. It is also seen as a time to plant new seeds symbolically in the sense of planning new projects that will produce results at a later date.

One interesting if obscure religious acknowledgement of the Spring Equinox originates within the Jewish community. The Talmud, the volumes of Jewish law written down in the second century BCE, suggests that an individual should make a special blessing when the Sun reaches its "turning point," that is, the Vernal Equinox. Further, it notes that the Sun returns to this position every 28 years. Writing in the 11th century, the great French rabbi Rashi (1040–1105), who authored a commentary on the Talmud, taught that the Sun, which according to the book of Genesis was created on the fourth day of creation, was placed by God in the sky at the exact position it reaches at the Vernal Equinox. That moment in time every 28 years provides a unique glimpse of the creation and an opportunity to the one who is thus aware to bless the Creator for his work. This blessing, which a person has the opportunity to offer once every generation, is termed the Birkat HaHammah. This event most recently occurred on April 8, 2009.

J. Gordon Melton

See also: Baha'i Faith; Calendars, Religious; Common Era Calendar; Fall Equinox; New Year's Day; Summer Solstice; Wiccan Religion; Winter Solstice.

References

Crowley, Vivianne. *The Principles of Paganism.* London: Thorsons, 1996.

Farrar, Janet, and Stewart Farrar. *A Witches Bible Complete.* New York: Magickal Child, 1984.

Parise, Frank, ed. T*he Book of Calendars.* New York: Facts on File, 1982.

Waskow, Arthur. "Blessing the Sun: Looking Backwards." Birkat HaHammah. http://www .blessthesun.org/tiki-index.php?page=Articles +and+Divrei+Torah. Accessed June 15, 2009.

Sri Aurobindo Ashram

The Sri Aurobindo Ashram (SAA) in Pondicherry (Tamil Nadu, South India) derived from the presence and ideas of Aurobindo Ghose (1872–1950) since 1910 and from the presence and work of the Mother (Mira Richard, 1878–1973) since 1920. Sri Aurobindo was born in Calcutta and educated in Great Britain, and after his return to India in 1893, he was involved with the Indian independence movement. Because of those activities he was jailed for a year in 1908. While in prison he had a religious experience and, according to the records, achieved a state of *samadhi* (deep contemplation) through the practice of yoga. Upon his release, he went to Pondicherry. There he developed a system inspired by the Indian philosophies of Samkhya, yoga, Vedanta, and Tantra, to which he added some integrating elements of Western philosophies. He called his system Integral Yoga.

In November 1926, Aurobindo withdrew to his room in order to intensify his inner work. The whole material and spiritual management of the ashram devolved on the Mother. This was the desire of the disciples, then about 25 in number, who had gathered around Aurobindo to practice yoga under his direction. The ashram members devoted their lives to the ideal of Integral Yoga, the spiritual philosophy and practice of Aurobindo, which was published in a huge number of articles and books. The central idea is that of evolution, directed both at the evolution of nature/matter, society, and individuals toward their spiritual perfection and realization of the divine consciousness, and at the devolution of the spirit in order to manifest the divine in the world and to create a divine life in matter, society, and man. There is no need for asceticism or retreat from the world, and meditation alone is not enough; knowledge as well as determination and power of action and creation are also necessary for spiritual growth.

The organization of the SAA provided various facilities for members to fulfill this ideal, including small-scale industries, trade, sports, education, libraries, and studios for dance, music, painting, and so forth. The core of the SAA is the Sri Aurobindo International Centre of Education, established in 1951 and renamed in 1959. In 1960 the Mother set up the Sri Aurobindo Society (SAS) for the realization of harmony in the world. The SAS was also necessary for managing the SAA, including its funds. SAA enjoys United Nations Educational, Scientific and Cultural Organization (UNESCO) support. In 1968 the international city of Auroville came into existence as a place where the divine could be realized in the physical. People from all over the world and from many parts of India live and work there, engaged in ecology, city planning, education, and culture. The spiritual center of Auroville is a large structure, the Matrimandir. In September 2001, some 1,680 Aurovillians lived in the city, coming mainly from India, France, and Germany.

There have always been controversies among the SAA, SAS, and Auroville over understanding and living the principles and conflicting ideas of individual freedom and self-realization, as well as over the need for social cooperation requiring structure and organization, administration, and leadership. In 1980 the Indian government took over the responsibility of Auroville; the SAA now is run by the SAA Trust.

Striving for the divine consciousness is regarded to be beyond religious, national, or racial boundaries. Although no missionary work is carried out in India or abroad, a number of branches were established in India as well as in France, the United States, Canada, Germany, Spain, Italy, the Netherlands, Sweden, Switzerland, and Great Britain. These branches publish the works of Aurobindo and the Mother and organize seminars and conferences to disseminate the idea of human unity through the practice of Integral Yoga. The SAA and Auroville organize and participate in international projects.

Sri Aurobindo Society
c/o Bureau Central
3 Rangapillai Street
Pondicherry–605001
Tamil Nadu
India
http://www.sriaurobindoashram.org
http://www.auroville.org

Melitta Waligora

See also: Meditation; Yoga.

References

Ghose, Aurobindo. *The Life Divine.* Pondicherry, India: Sri Aurobindo Ashram, 1973.

Ghose, Aurobindo. *Synthesis of Yoga.* Pondicherry, India: Sri Aurobindo Ashram, 1972.

Kluback, W. *Sri Aurobindo Ghose: The Dweller in the Lands of Silence.* New York: Peter Lang, 2001.

McDermott, Robert, ed. *Six Pillars: Introductions to the Major Works of Sri Aurobindo.* Chambersburg, PA: Wilson, 1974.

Minor, Robert N. *The Religious, the Spiritual, and the Secular: Auroville and Secular India.* Albany: State University of New York Press, 1998.

Sri Chinmoy Centre

Sri Chinmoy Centre is an international organization of individuals in more than 60 countries who claim Sri Chinmoy (1931–2007) as their spiritual leader, guide, and exemplar. Centre members aspire to world peace and harmony by means of serving humanity in a variety of ways, especially through offering instruction in meditation and exercise.

Sri Chinmoy was born Chinmoy Kumar Ghose in what is now Bangladesh. He was placed in the ashram of Sri Aurobindo in Pondicherry when he was orphaned at the age of 12 and spent 20 years at the ashram, achieving great states of enlightenment. Sri Chinmoy came to New York City in 1964, where he began organizing a following throughout the United States, including Chicago, Seattle, and Washington, D.C.

Sri Chinmoy advocated a method of guru devotion as the fastest means by which one can attain spiritual

Peace leader Sri Chinmoy plays an *esraj* during an outdoor concert in Jamaica, Queens, a borough of New York City, on August 15, 1997. (AP/Wide World Photos)

progress toward realization of what he called the Supreme (that is, God). Guru devotion requires the guru to formally accept and initiate the disciple, while the disciple must serve the guru, make the guru's needs and desires his or her own, and obey the guru implicitly. By meditating on the guru or on his image—which is the central practice of the group—the disciple is actually serving the Supreme that resides in the guru. Sri Chinmoy called this the path of love, devotion, and surrender, by which the disciple realizes the Supreme through the grace of the guru. Critics, however, claim that this practice led to sexual abuse and intimidation by Sri Chinmoy.

Sri Chinmoy was a lifelong advocate of fitness as a spiritual goal, as well as an accomplished athlete himself. In 1977 he inaugurated a series of marathon and endurance races, and promoted ultra-marathons to publicize the need for world peace. The peace runs raised controversy at times, when American public school children were encouraged by local school boards to participate in races sponsored by a Hindu group. The athletic guru, who played tennis daily well into his seventies, received ridicule for his claim to raise 7,063.75 pounds in a one-arm overhead lift. He said that he performed other miraculous feats, such as lifting entire football teams, elephants, or one-ton pickup trucks on a single platform. Despite such claims, the guru was well respected for his peace efforts by world leaders, with former Soviet President Mikhail Gorbachev and Archbishop Desmond Tutu speaking of his dedication to world peace at the time of the guru's death. Sri Chinmoy conducted twice-weekly prayer and meditation sessions for staff at the United Nations Headquarters in New York for 37 years, and more than 700 UN dignitaries, members of the U.S. Congress, and world religious leaders attended his memorial service. His followers claim that he wrote 1,500 books and 115,000 poems, composed 20,000 songs, created 200,000 paintings, and performed at almost 800 peace concerts around the world.

Although Sri Chinmoy did not charge for his services as guru, a network of "Divine Enterprises" sells numerous items produced by the guru himself, including paintings, books, and tapes and CDs of his flute, *esraj*, and cello playing, as well as his devotional songs. The enterprises include vegetarian restaurants, boutiques, health food stores, printing shops, flower shops, and sporting goods stores. Devotees have continued to promote extreme sports and endurance races after the guru's death and maintain Divine Enterprises around the world.

Sri Chinmoy Centre
PO Box 32433
Jamaica, NY 11432
http://www.peacerun.com/
http://www.peacerun.com/

Rebecca Moore

See also: Devotion/Devotional Traditions; Meditation.

References

Madhuri [Nancy Elizabeth Sands]. *The Life of Sri Chinmoy*. Jamaica, NY: Sri Chinmoy Lighthouse, 1972.

Sri Chinmoy. *The Master and the Disciple: Insights into the Guru-Disciple Relationship.* Jamaica, NY: Aum, 1985.

Sri Chinmoy. *The Wisdom of Sri Chinmoy.* San Diego: Blue Dove, 2000.

http://www.srichinmoy.org/

http://www.srichinmoycentre.org/

■ Sri Lanka

Sri Lanka (until 1972, Ceylon) is a multiethnic, multireligious, and multilingual (Sinhalese, Tamil, and English) country of 21 million people (2009). At a rough estimate, there are 74 percent Sinhalese (low-country and Kandyan) and 18 percent Tamils (both Lankan and Indian). Important minorities are Moors, Malays, and Burghers (of mixed origin: Dutch, British, Ceylonese). On the basis of the 1981 census (total population, 14.8 million), religious populations are as follows: (Theravada) Buddhists, 10.3 million; Hindus, 2.3 million; Christians, 1.1 million; Muslims, 1.1 million; other faiths, 8,300. There is a close association between Buddhism and Sinhalese, and Hinduism and Tamils; Sinhalese, Tamils, and Burghers are Christians (Catholics and diverse Protestant groups); Moors and Malays are Muslims.

Buddhism was transferred to Sri Lanka by Mahinda (son of Aśoka) in the time of King Devanampiya Tissa (ca. 250–210 BCE). The Sinhalese tradition (*Mahavamsa*—that is, *The Great Chronicle*) sees in the events (the rejection of South Indian invaders) of the reign of King Dutthagamani (161–137) a confirmation of an intimate connection between national aspirations and the Buddhist cause, a tendency that revived in history several times. For several reasons, Sri Lanka became important for Theravada Buddhism: in the Alu-Vihara (2 miles from Matale) the Pali canon

Ancient Buddhist temple, Sri Lanka. (Corel)

SRI LANKA

Sri Lanka

Religion	Followers in 1970	Followers in 2010	% of Population	Annual % growth 2000–2010	Followers in 2025	Followers in 2050
Buddhists	8,287,000	13,315,000	68.0	0.39	13,662,000	12,443,000
Hindus	1,970,000	2,550,000	13.0	0.43	2,600,000	2,350,000
Muslims	906,000	1,870,000	9.6	0.43	1,950,000	1,800,000
Christians	1,088,000	1,714,000	8.8	0.75	1,942,000	1,911,000
Roman Catholics	954,000	1,410,000	7.2	0.98	1,600,000	1,550,000
Protestants	65,100	200,000	1.0	2.08	230,000	240,000
Independents	21,200	170,000	0.9	2.92	230,000	250,000
Agnostics	40,000	90,000	0.5	0.43	120,000	140,000
Baha'is	6,700	15,000	0.1	0.39	25,000	35,000
Atheists	16,000	14,000	0.1	0.43	20,000	25,000
Sikhs	25,000	2,800	0.0	−5.19	3,000	3,000
Zoroastrians	1,800	2,400	0.0	0.42	2,400	2,400
Ethnoreligionists	1,000	1,000	0.0	0.43	1,000	1,000
New religionists	0	1,000	0.0	0.41	1,500	3,000
Chinese folk	500	800	0.0	0.42	1,200	1,500
Shintoists	0	160	0.0	0.40	400	500
Total population	**12,342,000**	**19,576,000**	**100.0**	**0.43**	**20,328,000**	**18,715,000**

was written down for the first time (in 80 BCE); in the fifth century CE, the great commentator Buddhaghosa composed highly important works (*Visuddhimagga*) that later became "norma normans" of Theravada Orthodoxy. Different Buddhist schools struggled to gain predominance in Sri Lanka, although only King Parakramabahu I (1153–1186) established the Mahavihara-tradition (of Buddhaghosa) as "orthodox." In this regard Sinhalese Buddhism became standard for all South Asian Buddhism.

In addition to (Hinduistic) influences from India, which distracted Sri Lankan Buddhists for centuries, Muslim traders settled down along the coasts of Sri Lanka (but never became really influential). In the early 16th century the Portuguese started Catholic missionary work in Sri Lanka. Following colonial powers (Dutch, 1640; British, 1798–1956) promoted their preferred religion. In British times the Anglicans (now included in the Church of Sri Lanka, a union of several Protestant churches) and the Methodist Church, Sri Lanka gained ground. But the Roman Catholic Church has continued to be the largest Christian community.

Traditional Buddhism regained strength by the import of new ordination lines from Thailand (Siyam-Nikaya, 1753) and Burma (Amarapura-Nikaya, 1803; Ramaññnna-Nikaya, 1865). These constitute the Ma-

hasangha (established order of monks) up to today. In the late 19th century a "new" Buddhism developed, which is to a certain extent the result of the encounter and confrontation with Protestantism. Scholars call this form either Protestant Buddhism or Buddhist Modernism. A mythic starting point of this development was one of the debates between low-land Buddhists and Anglicans/Methodists in Panadura (1873). Influenced by a publication of this famous debate, the Theosophical Society (through its president Henry S. Olcott) started to assist the "new" Buddhists in their emancipatory struggle. One of the most influential Buddhist figures in recent times, the *anagarika* Dharmapala (1864–1933), founder of the Maha Bodhi Society, worked in that fashion.

Heinz Mürmel

See also: Ashoka; Church of Sri Lanka; Maha Bodhi Society; Methodist Church, Sri Lanka; Roman Catholic Church; Theosophical Society (Adyar).

References

Bartholomeeusz, Tessa J. *In Defense of Dharma: Just-War Ideology in Buddhist Sri Lanka.* London: RoutledgeCurzon, 2002.

Bechert, Heinz. *Buddhismus, Staat und Gesellschaft in den Ländern des Theravada-Buddhismus. Bd.*

1: Allgemeines und Ceylon. Frankfurt: Alfred Metzner Verlag, 1966.

Gombrich, Richard, and Gananth Obeyesekere. *Buddhism Transformed: Religious Change in Sri Lanka.* Princeton, NJ: Princeton University Press, 1988.

Manogaram, Chelvadurai, and Bryan Pfaffenberger, eds. *The Sri Lankan Tamils: Ethnicity and Identity.* Boulder, CO: Westview, 1994.

Peebles, Patrick. *The History of Sri Lanka.* Westport, CT: Greenwood Press, 2006.

Seneviratne, H. L. *The Work of Kings: The New Buddhism in Sri Lanka.* Chicago: University of Chicago Press, 1999.

Smith, Bardwell L., ed. *Religion and Legitimation of Power in Sri Lanka.* Chambersburg, PA: ANIMA, 1978.

Wickremeratne, Ananda. *Buddhism and Ethnicity in Sri Lanka: A Historical Analysis.* Kandy, Sri Lanka: International Centre for Ethnic Studies, 1995.

Sri Lanka, Hinduism in

In Sri Lanka there are two main representations of Hinduism: the Sri Lankan Tamil Hindus, who live mainly in the northern and eastern provinces, and the Indian Tamil Hindus, who live in the central highland on the island, especially in the area around Kandy and Nuwara Eliya. The Indian Tamil Hindus are mostly low-caste people. They came to the island in the 19th century from Tamil Nadu, imported by the British to work on their tea, coffee, and rubber plantations. The Sri Lankan Tamil Hindus are mostly from farming and fishing castes. They trace their roots back to the kingdoms prior to the time when King Elara (king of the *damilas*) was defeated by Dutthagamani (161–137 BCE)—the beginning of a Buddhist era as described in the Sinhalese chronicle Mahavamsa, written in the sixth century CE. The Tamil Hindus count, in all, 1.7 million—or around 8.5 percent of the Sri Lankan population of 21 million (2009). (The remaining Tamils, some 26 percent, are either Muslims or Christians.)

Both groups are mostly Shaivites, with a strong affiliation to the worship of Shakti and Shiva's two sons, Ganesha (Pillaiyar or Vinayakar in Tamil) and Karttikeya (Murugan in Tamil). Both groups practice a similar form of Tamil Shaivism rooted in the Shaiva Siddhanta tradition, a tradition that became vitally important in Tamil Nadu from around the seventh century and that is based on the *smriti* collection Tirumurai and the 28 Agamas considered as being *shruti* texts. The Tirumurai, a collection of 12 books written by the 63 *bhakti* poets called the Nayanmars, presents a strong bhakti devotion to Shiva and his manifestations. The Agamas describe the practice of the religion, including descriptions of how to practice yoga, when to conduct the daily *puja* (worship) and festivals, descriptions of how to install the god statues in the temples according to the four points of the compass, and the like. The Agamas also have an implicit theology with a monistic ontology, in which creation is seen as the radiations of God (Shiva), and in which *mukti*, or release from *samsara* (cycle of rebirth), is described as being identical to God, not as being a part of God. There will always be a distinct difference between Shiva and the devotees.

The combination of this theology and the bhakti-devotion is manifested in the temple worship, where the way of attaining mukti is possible through the *darshanas* (sights) of God, in which Shiva's *arul-shakti* (the energy of grace) will be shown to the devotee who is clean in body and mind.

In spite of these similarities, the two groups do not seem to go to the same temples for puja, even if they live in the same neighborhood (exceptions are pilgrimage sites such as Kataragama or Kathiramam in Tamil—the most important pilgrimage site on the island after the troubles started between Hindus and Buddhists in Jaffna). This is not only an issue of caste; it is also caused by differences in history and worship.

The reformist Arumuga Navalar (1829–1879) plays an especially important role in Sri Lankan Tamil Hinduism. He emphasized the difference between the secular sphere and the religious sphere, a distinction that made him emphasize the religious institution as the basis for the religious life, and as the only place in which one can cope with the limits of human behavior. Here, in the right atmosphere, human desires will be kept under control, because the puja will engage the body, mind, and voice. This distinction has two major

Painted figures on a Hindu temple in Sri Lanka. (Corel)

outcomes visible in the Sri Lankan Tamil Hinduism of today: (1) an awareness of orthopraxis, when it comes to temple worship; and (2) an adjustment of tradition, when it comes to the secular working sphere.

Since the beginning of the 1980s, when the violent conflict between the Sinhalese and the Tamils escalated, Tamils fled the island to South India and the West. There are currently more than 150,000 Tamils in Canada and some 200,000 in Europe living as refugees. Wherever they settle, they have established their temples and socio-cultural institutions to maintain their tradition.

Marianne Qvortrup Fibiger

See also: Reincarnation; Tamil Shaivism; Yoga.

References

Bandage, Asoka. *The Separatist Conflict in Sri Lanka: Terrorism, Ethnicity, Political Economy.* London: Routledge, 2008.

Bartholomeeusz, Tessa J. *In Defense of Dharma: Just-War Ideology in Buddhist Sri Lanka.* London: RoutledgeCurzon, 2002.

Carter, John Ross, ed. *Religiousness in Sri Lanka.* Colombo, Sri Lanka: Marga Institute, 1979.

Dubey, Ravi Kant. *Indo–Sri Lankan Relations: With Special Reference to the Tamil Problem.* New Delhi: Deep and Deep, 1989.

Manogaram, Chelvadurai, and Bryan Pfaffenberger, eds. *The Sri Lankan Tamils: Ethnicity and Identity.* Boulder, CO: Westview, 1994.

"Religions in the History of Yalppanam." *Lanka* 5 (December 1990): 3–223.

State Shinto

Modern State Shinto (Kokka Shinto), the official religion installed in Japan following the Meiji Revolution

(1868), harkened back to the earliest version of government-supported Shinto (seventh century CE) but also included many modern innovations. It evolved through the Meiji period (1868–1912) as a means to supply religious justification for the revival of the emperor's social standing. Just three years after coming to power, the government issued an edict, which directed that shrines were to be used for state ritual, though as yet no official body had been created to oversee Shinto. (The Jingikan, a traditional government office which had been re-established in 1868, oversaw the *kami*, or gods, in general, but not Shinto specifically.) The government also did not want to allocate funds for the upkeep of most shrines—only the most famous ones such as Ise received support. The government's relation to Shinto was vague and conflicted until 1900, when the Jinjakyoku, or Shrine Bureau, was established.

The establishment of the Jinjakyoku as a unit of the Home Ministry indicated the state's new and stronger role relative to Shinto. In preceding decades, yet another bureau, the Bureau for Shrines and Temples (Sajikyoku), had hegemony over both Buddhist temples and Shinto shrines. But beginning in 1900, Shinto was managed by its own bureau, and all other religions were overseen by the newly established the Bureau for Religions (Shukyokyoku). State Shinto became a separate reality.

In 1906, the government moved to ensure funding to Shinto shrines from local government budgets. With funds secured, the national government went on to dictate rules for shrines in a variety of areas, including etiquette and ritual (1907), finance (1908), and rites (1914). In the process authorities promulgated three separate laws prescribing garb and ritual at the main imperial shrine at Ise. As these laws were put in place, the government also emphasized the non-religious functions in which the Shinto shrines engaged. Authorities assumed that visiting the shrines and paying obeisance to both the kami and the emperor was simply each citizen's civic duty. They saw this as a patriotic task transcending any particular religious beliefs, an observation that directly affected Christians and Buddhists, who were expected to perform rituals at the shrines alongside their Shinto neighbors. It was also common for school classes to visit Shinto shrines several times each year. Besides performing these so-called

non-religious functions, the average shrine also continued to perform the variety of traditional religious practices it had always done, such as selling charms and performing funerals.

The Meiji emperor died in 1912 and his widow two years later. The construction of a shrine to honor them was initiated immediately after World War I. The national project to build the shrine had the effect of also highlighting the importance of the local shrines during the post-Meiji or Taisho era (1912–1926); however, at the same time, most shrines were under-funded and neglected by the government. The government acted in a somewhat "opportunistic" manner toward the Shinto shrines. On the one hand, it affirmed their integral role in the perpetuation of a pro-Japanese ideology that included veneration of the imperial family, while on the other hand it neglected their continuing religious functions. Government officials seemed to lack an understanding of the religious sentiments of those citizens who self-identified as Shintoists.

Through the era between the two World Wars, the Japanese Diet increasingly managed the Shinto shrines and deities in a way simply to increase social solidarity in the face of forced changes. Events such as the Kanto earthquake of 1923, new movements like Socialism, and the realities of Japanese life with the ups and downs of economic life kept the Diet under intense pressure through the 1920s. Meanwhile, a rising level of criticism of life at the shrines finally forced the government to establish a Commission for Shrine Research in 1929. The new Commission was charged with investigating the shrines' legal status and economic resources, ranking them, and reviewing their ritual practices. Through the 1930s, the level of criticism did not abate as the government continued to be accused of ignoring the religious issues of shrine life.

In 1940, with the country at war on several fronts, the cabinet moved to set up yet another new bureau, the Office of State for Deity Affairs (Jingiin). The new bureau was not to simply oversee state ritual, but given powers to manage the entire shrine network. The Jingiin assumed responsibility for the Ise shrines, all other shrines, all priests and shrine officials, and ultimately anything regarding "reverence" paid to deities. The government upped its involvement in shrine life by directly assuming the duty of spreading the ideology of State Shinto as an institution. The Home Ministry now took charge of maintaining as well as promoting State Shinto.

The system of state-supported Shinto was among the big losers of World War II. Within months of assuming control of the government, the occupation forces forbid the government to continue any support for the Shinto shrines. They also directly attacked the underlying assumption of the emperor's divinity. He was but a mortal person. The ties between modern Shinto and the Japanese state abruptly ended. The shrines had to reorganize, and today they operate under the umbrella of Shrine Shinto, offering Shinto religion to those who claim it as their personal faith.

Edward A. Irons

See also: Ise Shrine, The; Meiji Jingu; Shinto.

References

Kasahara, Kazuo, ed. *A History of Japanese Religion.* Tokyo: Dosei Publishing, 2001.

Koremaru, Sakamoto. "The Structure of State Shinto: Its Creation, Development and Demise." In *Shinto in History*, edited by John Breen and Mark Teeuwen, 272–294. Richmond, UK: Curzon Press, 2000.

Statues—Buddhist

Buddhism was initiated by Siddhartha Gautama the Buddha (563–483 BCE), and for its first centuries, representations of the Buddha were discouraged. This lack of "pictures" of the Buddha seems to be in line with the early Buddhist scripture called the Digha Nikaya (a collection of discourses by the Buddha included in the Sutta Pitaka), one of the "three baskets" of the Pali canon from which Theravada Buddhism finds it authority. The Digha Nikaya contains sayings in which the Buddha specifically discourages the making of representations of himself after the death of his human body. As Buddhist art, especially sculptures, emerged in the third century BCE, the Buddha tended to be represented by a symbol rather than by a human body.

The Buddha's presence could be suggested by images of the Bodhi tree (*Ficus religiosa*) under which he attained enlightenment, the cushion on which he sat when he attained enlightenment, the stupa representing his passing from this life, or *paranirvana*, his footprint(s) signifying his presence, or the Dharma Wheel representing the first sermon. At times the Buddha is presented as part of a trident, a symbol of the Buddhist's Triple Jewels—Buddha (the teacher), Dharma (the teaching), Sangha (the community)—the essential core of the faith.

It is suggested that sculptors hesitated to portray the Buddha in human form because the qualities of transcendence, purity, and spirituality can be more effectively conveyed symbolically. It was believed by many that having achieved paranirvana, Siddhartha had ceased to exist and since he was not of this world, one could not depict the Buddha's spiritual accomplishments. This condition of non-existence became an obstacle to the artist who wished to present visually the formless and transcendental Buddha.

The development of iconic representation of the Buddha coincided with the rise of Mahayana Buddhism and the popularity of devotionalism built around bodhisattvas that emerged in prominence during the first and second centuries CE. The heroic and sacrificial character of the bodhisattva, the evolved being who vows to save all beings by sharing the merits she or he has accumulated, is an outgrowth of the idealization of the historical Buddha, though some scholars have suggested that it intruded in Mahayana Buddhism from the outside. Importantly, Mahayana ideals differed from Theravada teachings that understood the historical Buddha as an exceptional individual and teacher. With the spread of the new perspective among the population, more readily accessible images of the Buddha were needed to replace the highly abstract notions of enlightenment and presence represented by footprints and other symbols. The development of the Buddha image was one response.

When the first images of the Buddha finally appeared in the first century CE, the artists showed no intention to sculpt either an anatomically correct human Buddha or a historical likeness of Siddhartha Gautama. The idealized images that appeared in Mathura in northern India followed a tradition of presenting the human form composed of a set of 32 major and 80 minor *laksana*, or marks associated with manly beauty and heroic ideals. Thus the Buddha came to possess a smooth and perfectly proportioned body, with every aspect of the image seen as representing an ideal found in nature—ears like mangos, thighs like a gazelle, and limbs like a banyan tree. Long arms allow the Buddha to embrace all beings. The ear lobes recall the nobility who wore heavy ear ornaments. The golden body gives off a wondrous scent. On the palms of his hands and/or the soles of his feet one finds the dharma wheel or Buddhist form of the swastika.

As in Christian art representing Jesus, the image of the Buddha image is often surrounded by a halo and/or aureole (circles of light), symbolic of the Buddha's immeasurable brilliance of truth and wisdom. The Buddha's wisdom is seen in the *ushnisha*, a "bump" or extracranial protrusion.

The carefully constructed Mathuran images contrast sharply with those that appeared about the same time in Gandhara, in what today is Pakistan and Afghanistan. Here the Hellenistic tradition brought by Alexander the Great was still alive and art followed very different standards. Sculptors crafted Buddhist images with anatomical accuracy, spatial depth, and foreshortening. The straight sharply chiseled Apollonian noses, brows, and mustaches capture a "frozen moment." The Gandharan artists also transformed the ushnisha into a topknot or turban and adorned the body with a diaphanous (thin), toga-like robe.

These two early images of the Buddha would over the next centuries merge to create synthesized images and be carried far and wide as Buddhism spread where they would develop into the many schools of Buddhist art that would appear throughout Asia to the present. Over the centuries, especially after the destruction of Buddhism in India following the Muslim invasion of the 11th century, two very different traditions of Buddhist sculpture can be seen in the Theravada and Mahayana lands.

The Mathuran tradition of picturing an idealized Buddha image came to predominate in Theravada lands. It was also the case that, while developing different nationalistic variations, Theravada sculptors in southern Asia limited their work to the portrayal of the historical Buddha and the events related to this life. In visiting a temple in Sri Lanka, Thailand, or Myanmar, one will tend to find the central worship area domi-

nated by a single statue of the historical Buddha carved or molded from costly materials—marble and gold being most evident, but occasionally other precious substances like jade.

In Theravada lands, the Buddha seated in a meditative pose is seen most often, but a standing Buddha is a popular alternative and in Thailand and Myanmar the reclining Buddha is a unique form of representation. In viewing the Buddha, the placement of the hands is most important. The hand positions, termed *mudras*, convey meanings well known throughout the Buddhist world. For example, the sitting Buddha is often shown with his left hand resting in his lap and the right hand over the thigh with the palm facing forward and the fingertips touching the Earth. This form, called the Bhumisparsa mudra, symbolizes the Buddha's renunciation of worldly attachments, a key moral precept for Buddhists. Equally popular, the Buddha will be seen with both hands lying in his lap with both palms facing upward, the Dhyana mudra, symbolizing the disciplined mind seeking enlightenment. The reclining Buddha is usually seen as a representation of the Buddha's state of enlightenment just prior to his *mahanirvana* (death).

This tradition of picturing primarily the historical Buddha is also alive and well in the meditative forms of Mahayana Buddhism—Chan, Son, and Zen—outside of Theravada lands. Meditation halls, if they have any representation of the Buddha at all, will tend to have but a single statue of the historical Buddha.

In sharp contrast to Theravada lands, the artists of the main Mahayana lands, especially those of the Vajrayana and Pure Land traditions, from China and Tibet to Korea and Japan, have sought not only to picture the historical Buddha, but all of the many celestial Buddhas and bodhisattvas and the transcendental lands they inhabit. The Pure Land sutras, for example, describe in exquisite detail the "other world" of the Western Paradise that is reigned over by Amitabha (or Amida) Buddha. Maitreya, the future Buddha, emerged as a popular figure during the Kushan Empire (first–third centuries CE) period, soon to be joined by the likes of Vairocana, the universal Buddha, Bhaisajya-guru, the Medicine Buddha, and Kshitogarbha, Earth repository Buddha. These "other" Buddhas, especially Amitabha, the central figure in Pure Land Buddhism, often assume the central position in Buddhist temples and shrines and will either push the historical Buddha to a subordinate position or even completely replace him. Outside the Buddhist community, especially in material written for consumption by modern tourists, statues of the various male Buddhas and bodhisattvas tend to be confused with images of the historical Buddha.

No figure is more popular than the Bodhisattva Avalokitesvara, who also appears as the female bodhisattva Guan Yin (aka Kwan Yin or Kannon), possibly the most ubiquitous figure throughout the Mahayana world. Guan Yin transcends even the Buddhist context and appears among the Daoist deities of the popular Chinese religions.

Buddhist Mega Statuary These celestial beings and their realms pictured in Mahayana literature have inspired the creation of monumental images and spectacular symbolism. This trend to build mega statues (usually defined as those twice the size of normal humans) was especially noticeable in the 20th century, but appeared quite early. Toward the beginning of the fifth century CE, for example, the 175-foot-tall Vairocana Buddha, the universal monarch, was hewn into a cliff at Bamiyan in Afghanistan This was the statue that was destroyed by the Taliban (along with the smaller but also impressive 120-foot-tall accompanying Buddha) in 2001. In 752 CE a 53-foot-tall seated Vairocana Buddha was cast and erected in the Todai-ji Temple in Nara, Japan. It would become the model for the giant Amida Buddha at Kamakura, Japan, constructed early in the 13th century. Theravada Buddhists did not escape the notion of building mega statues, and impressive representations of the historical Buddha may now be seen across southern Asia.

Mega statues come in all shapes and sizes; most assume a sitting (meditative) or standing position, but statues of the historical Buddha in southern Asian assume the reclining position. The statues may be roughly divided between those of the historical Buddha and those of the other Buddhas and bodhisattvas. The various statues are also distinguished by the material from which they are constructed—stone, wood, concrete, bronze, or steel. Statues made of more mundane material may be covered with valuable metal (most com-

monly gold) and/or jewels. Among the more impressive of the mega statues are the following.

Standing Buddhas The Vairocana statue, in Baniyan, Afghanistan, when destroyed in 2001, was cited as the largest Buddhist statue in the world, though it was actually somewhat smaller than the statue at Leshan, China. It was the biggest for several centuries after it was carved out of the cliff's stone in the fifth century. Plans have been announced to reconstruct it, but the continued war in the region has delayed any action.

Spring Temple Buddha, a copper statue of Vairocana Buddha, in Lushan County, Henan, China, is one of several prominent mega statues that have been erected in the People's Republic of China (and signifying a new more positive attitude of the government toward Buddhism). Erected in 2002, it stands at 420 feet with a 66-foot lotus pedestal. It is the tallest statue in the world. The announcement that the statue was being planned followed the destruction of Baniyan statue and the beginning of the proposed giant statue of Meitreya Buddha by the followers of the Dalai Lama.

The Gautama Buddha statue in Monywa, Sagaing Division, Myanmar, which stands 380 feet on a 44-foot base, is the second-tallest statue in the world and the tallest in southern Asia. It was completed in 2008 and stands behind a 295-foot-long statue of the reclining Buddha.

The Ushiku Daibutsu, a statue of Amida Buddha, is located in Ushiku, Ibaraki Prefecture, Japan. Completed in 1995, it is the third-tallest statue in the world and the largest statue in Japan. Its 394-foot height includes a 33-foot base and 33-foot lotus platform. Visitors inside the statue may take an elevator to the observation floor located 279 feet above the surrounding land.

The Guan Yin statue at Sanya on the island of Hainan, off the coast of China, was completed in 2005. The inaugural service for the 591-foot statue was led by 108 prominent Chinese Buddhist monks. It is now the fourth-tallest statue in the world.

Seated Buddhas The Leshan Giant Buddha of Leshan, Sichuan Province, in the People's Republic of China, depicts Maitreya, the future Buddha. Begun in

Sitting Buddha, Penang, Malaysia. (J. Gordon Melton)

the year 713, it took almost a century to carve out of the hillside. Its scenic location is above the spot where three rivers converge. At 233 feet, it is the largest stone Buddha statue in the world. The fingers on each hand are about 11 feet long.

The Kannon statue, Usami, in Shizaoka Prefecture, Japan, sits outside the Usami Kannon Temple. At 164 feet, it is the tallest sitting Kannon (Guan Yin) statue in the world. It was completed in 1981.

A statue of the historical Buddha at Dickwella, Sri Lanka, on the grounds of the Wewurukannala Temple is the largest Buddha statue in Sri Lanka. At 164 feet it rivals the Kannon statue at Usami.

The statue of Amitabha Buddha on Lantau Island has become one of the symbols of Hong Kong and one of its major tourist attractions. At 85 feet, it is surpassed in size by a number of seated Buddhas, but all are of stone or concrete. The Hong Kong Buddha is now described as the largest seated outdoor bronze Buddha statue in the world.

A similar statue, though made of concrete, of a seated Amitabha is located in Pukuashan, Changhua, Taiwan. It reaches 86 feet in the air and is the largest seated Buddha statue in Taiwan. In 2006, a 236-foot standing Maitreya Buddha was erected at Ermei Township, Hsinchu County, Taiwan, as the centerpiece for the recently opened Maitreya Holy Land.

Reclining Buddhas The largest image of the reclining Buddha exists as a relief carved from the stone at Yiyang County, Jiangxi Province, in the People's Republic of China. As with all reclining Buddhas, it pictures the historical Buddha. The image is 1,365 feet long (and 223 feet high), but is not freestanding.

Reclining Buddha mega statue, Penang, Malaysia. (J. Gordon Melton)

The largest freestanding reclining Buddha is located at Monywa, Myanmar, close to the Kyauktawgyi Pagoda and in front of a recently completed standing mega statue. It is 295 feet in length. Myanmar is home to the five largest reclining Buddha statues, including the largest one located indoors.

The largest reclining Buddha in Thailand is located indoors at Wat Pho in Bangkok. It is 151 feet in length and covered in gold leaf.

The largest Buddha statue in Korea is a statue of the Medicine Buddha located at Donghwasa Temple at Tongilyak-sa. Donghwasa was dedicated to the cause of the reunification of the Korean Peninsula. It rises almost 100 feet into the air, though a third of that height is supplied by its large pedestal. Two pieces of Buddha's bones presented by the government of Myan-

mar rest in the body of the statue, believed to be the largest granite Buddha statue in the world. It is the largest statue of the Medicine Buddha.

Other Mega Statues   The founder of the reformed or Gelugpa School of Tibetan Buddhism, Tsong Khapa, is often honored with statues. The largest is at Gongsa Monastery, Qingha, China. It has been recognized by the *Guinness Book of Records* as the largest indoor gold-plated Buddha statue.

A notable standing Guan Yin statue is located at a temple complex northeast of the Chengde Imperial Palace in Chengde, Hebei Province, China. It is 73 feet tall and is believed to be the highest and largest wood statue in the world. In the Yong-He Gong Temple, the Tibetan temple in Beijing, however, there is a standing Maitreya statue that had been presented by the Dalai Lama to the Emperor Qianlong, the son of Emperor Yongzheng. The entire statue is carved from a rare sandal tree. It is 85 feet in height and 26 feet in diameter, with 26 feet buried under the ground. The *Guinness Book of Records* lists it as the largest wooden statue.

The Maitreya Project Before his death, Lama Thubten Yeshe (1935–1984), the founder of the Foundation for the Preservation of the Mahayana tradition, the primary organization promoting the Gelupga School of Tibetan Buddhism, and supporting the Dalai Lama, expressed the idea of creating a large statue of Maitreya, the future Buddha, in the Himalayan Mountains of northern India. The idea has been carried forward by his successor, Lama Thubten Zopa Rinpoche (b. 1946).

As developed, the project aims at the erection of a 500-foot bronze statue of Maitreya to be built at Kushinagar, Uttar Pradesh, India, where the historical Buddha lived his last days on Earth. The statue, when completed, would become the largest statue in the world. The Maitreya figure would be seated on a throne, and the building constituted as the throne is designed to house several temples, an exhibition hall, a museum, a library, an audio-visual theater, and various hospitality services. It will be surrounded by a landscaped park with places for meditation, fountains, and tranquil pools. The buildings and grounds of the project will contain a remarkable and inspiring collection of sacred art.

As the project will take some time to finance and complete, a portion of the funds being raised is being siphoned off to initiate immediately some of the public services envisioned as an integral part of the overall effort. Those services began with an educational fund that annually provides free education to around 500 students at a project-supported school at Bodhgaya, India.

Edward A. Irons

See also: Bodhisattva; Gelugpa; Guan Yin's Birthday; Kamakura; Kushinagara; Mahayana Buddhism; Mudras; Pure Land Buddhism; Statues—Christian; Theravada Buddhism; Tibetan Buddhism; Tsong Khapa.

References

Fisher, Robert E. *Buddhist Art and Architecture.* New York: Thames and Hudson, 1993.

Saunders, E. Dale. *Mudra, a Study of Symbolic Gestures in Japanese Buddhist Sculpture.* Princeton, NJ: Princeton University Press, 1960.

Sechel, Dietrich. *The Art of Buddhism.* New York: Crown Publishers, 1963.

Tobu Museum of Art, et al. *Buddha the Spread of Buddhist Art in Asia.* Tokyo: NHK, 1998.

Statues—Christian

Christianity emerged into prominence in the fourth century after years of existence as an underground and somewhat clandestine movement. Prior to the various steps taken by Constantine the Great (272–337) to first legalize and then privilege Christianity, art consisted of drawings and paintings at sites used for worship. Beginning in the fourth century art and architecture in the Christian world flourished and developed in various directions, most notably in the construction and decoration of the interior of church buildings. Images of Christian scenes and Christian heroes proliferated. As a cult of saints emerged, questions were raised about the use of images in Christian life and worship, and in the eighth and ninth centuries an intense controversy ensued over the use of what was termed "graven images," strictly forbidden in the Ten Commandments. For two periods (730–787 and 814–842) the emperors of the Byzantine Empire backed the iconoclasts, who condemned the making of any images (either paintings or statues) that intended to represent Jesus or one of the saints.

Those who opposed and finally won over against the iconoclasts argued that the appearance of Jesus overrode the second commandment as he was the visible image of the invisible God. They also contrasted Christian icons and statuary over against idols. The latter picture things/persons who were unreal, while Christian art pictures real persons.

The victory in Constantinople by those opposed to iconoclasm led to the development of a Western Catholic position on sacred images. Church leaders around the Emperor Charlemagne (747–814) had erroneously come to believe that the Byzantines had approved the worship of images. In countering this opinion, they approved the veneration of images as the representation of the reality of the divinity of Christ and sanctity of the saints. More substantively, they rejected the Orthodox position that icons (images of Christ or one of the saints) partook in some degree of the nature of the thing they represented. Catholics understood images (be they icons or statues) to be simply objects made by artists that stimulated the senses of the faithful. They had no inherent spiritual value, but were to be respected solely for what they represented.

In the medieval period, Catholicism and Eastern Orthodoxy began to be distinguished on a variety of issues, but one was the continuance of the use of statuary in Christian worship, both inside and outside of church buildings, in the West. In the East, where the iconoclastic controversy had been focused, the iconoclastic position was reinforced by the conquering Muslims. Once Islam gained political hegemony, icons survived much easier as part of religious life, whereas statues practically disappeared. In the West, Christ was widely represented in statues, as was the holy family and the saints.

The use of statues within the Roman Catholic Church would be called into question by the Protestant Reformation. While Lutherans were less intense on the issues of religious statues, the Reformed movement led by John Calvin (1509–1564) made a point of condemning Rome of idolatry. Calvinists removed all statuary from their churches. Most churches growing from the Reformation have continued the stance against statuary.

Christian Mega Statues The creation of mega statues (usually defined as statues larger than twice normal human size) within the Christian (Catholic) community was a 20th-century phenomenon. Most statuary, even at shrines, tend to be life size or smaller. Through much of the century, the model for the Christian mega statue was the statue of Christ the Redeemer that stands atop Corcovado Mountain 2,300 feet above the city of Rio de Janeiro, Brazil. With its pedestal, it stands 120 feet tall. Its extended arms spans 98 feet. After nine years of work, it was completed in 1931, and until the 1980s

was the largest Christian statue in the world. A chapel is located in its base.

Completed in 1994, the statue of Cristo de la Concordia, a statue of Jesus Christ, located on San Pedro hill in Cochabamba, Bolivia, is now the tallest statue of Christ in the world. It stands 112.2 feet tall and rests on a pedestal that adds an additional 20.5 feet. Its total height of 133 feet makes it larger than Rio's Christ the Redeemer, if only by a few feet.

In recent decades, a third statue entered the scene as a Christina mega statue. Cristo del Otero, located in Palencia, Spain, is a 98-foot statue of Christ designed by Víctorio Macho. It is almost equal in size to the Christ the Redeemer statue, making it the third-tallest statue of Christ in the world.

One Christian mega statue of note is found in Asia. The Cristo Rei (Christ the King) statue located at Dili, the capital of Timore Leste, was the gift of Indonesia's then-president Suharto (1921–2008) in 1995. Timore Leste, then known as East Timor, was a part of Indonesia. In 2002 it became an independent country. The statue depicting Christ with open arms and standing on a globe was located at the end of a peninsula and faces outward toward the rest of Indonesia.

A decade prior to the completion of the Cristo de la Concordia, in 1983, the devotees of the Blessed Virgin Mary in Trujillo, Venezuela, completed a statue in her honor on the hills above the city. At 153 feet, the Virgen de la Paz is now the tallest statue in Latin America and the tallest Christian statue in the world. The statue, designed by Manuel de La Fuente, was placed on a hill above the site where Mary was said to have appeared on occasion and where to this day devotees gather to pray and place flowers (a sign of thanksgiving for favors granted). Visitors to the statue may climb within its hollow interior to points that provide views of the surrounding countryside.

Second only to the Virgen de la Paz is La Virgen de Quito located on the Panecillo, a hill just south of Quito, Ecuador. The Panecillo stands at some 9,840 feet and is visible from the center of the city. The statue is approximately 148-feet, including the 36-foot base upon which it rests. The statue, commissioned in 1976, copies an 18th-century statue in a church in Quito that is unique in that the Virgin is given a set of angel's wings.

The third-largest statue of the Virgin Mary appears to be the one designated as Our Lady of the Rockies located on the continental divide overlooking Butte, Montana. Completed in 1985, it stands 90 feet in height with a base located 8,510 feet above sea level.

Prior to the 20th century, the largest Marian statue overlooked the city of LePuy, France. The bronze statue of the Virgin and child, named *Notre-Dame de France*, was made from 213 Russian cannons taken following the Siege of Sevastopol (1854–1855), a major battle in the Crimean War. It was completed and dedicated in 1860.

Frequently cited among the mega statues of Mary is the one of the Madonna and child in Khaskovo, Bulgaria. In fact, the Khaskovo statue is only 46 feet high, though it rests on a 56-foot platform. The statue was granted a *Guinness Book of Records* certificate, though with the qualifying statement that it is a statue of the Virgin with child. It is the largest Marian statue in the Eastern Orthodox world. It was officially completed and dedicated in 2003.

J. Gordon Melton

See also: Calvin, John; Constantine the Great; Eastern Orthodoxy; Istanbul; Roman Catholic Church; Statues—Buddhist.

References

Christie, Yves, and Velmans Christi. *Art of the Christian World, A.D. 200–1500*. New York: Rizzoli International Publications, 1982.

"In Focus: The World's Largest Religious Statues." http://www.bravenewtraveler.com/2009/04/10/happy-easter-the-worlds-religious-statues-in-photographs/. Accessed March 25, 2009.

McClinton, Catherine Morrison. *Christian Church Art Through the Ages*. New York: Macmillan, 1962.

Steiner, Rudolf

1861–1925

Rudolf Steiner, one of the most impressive of the late 19th- and early 20th-century Western Esoteric scholars, was also the founder of two Esoteric communities, the Anthroposophical Society and the Christian Community.

The Austrian philosopher of religion and writer Rudolf Steiner. (Getty Images)

Steiner was born February 27, 1861, in Kraljevic, Hungary (now Croatia), the son of a railroad worker. His father's job took the family to Pottshach, Austria (1863), then to Neudoerfl, Hungary (1869), and finally to Vienna in the 1870s. At the age of 18 he entered the Technical University in Vienna with the idea of eventually going to work for the railroad like his father. His life, however, now began to move in other directions. He had been a very sensitive child and had had various experiences with a supersensible reality. These experiences exerted considerable influence on Steiner, who gravitated toward studies in the humanities and the arts. He eventually transferred to the University of Vienna, where he was introduced to the work of Johann Wolfgang von Goethe (1749–1832).

In 1883, Steiner was invited to edit the scientific writings for the Kuerschner edition of Goethe's works and write the introduction. He would spend more than a decade on the task, during which time he would become well known for his scholarly accomplishments. In 1888 he was offered a position at the Goethe Archives at Weimar. Between 1890 and 1897 he worked on the Weimar edition of Goethe's works. He completed his doctoral degree in 1891.

While in Weimar, he had time to pursue what would become the dominating concern of his life, bridging the gap between the world of sense experience and the invisible spiritual world. He published his first major exploration of the spiritual life, *The Philosophy of Spiritual Activity*, in 1894, in which he offered his initial reflections on the role of thinking as a spiritual activity and conscience as a moral reality.

In 1897, Steiner moved to Berlin as the editor of a literary magazine. Here, he encountered the newly opened chapter of the Theosophical Society, which soon provided the environment for his future work. He began to lecture for the Society regularly. He also went through an intense period of inner struggle that culminated in a visionary experience of witnessing the crucifixion of Christ on Golgotha. This experience led him to conclude that he had gained a true Esoteric understanding of the meaning of Jesus' mission and Christianity.

Steiner now entered a new phase of his intellectual work and during the first decade of the new century would write a number of books sorting out his Esoteric perspectives. His new approach to Christianity was presented in *Christianity as Mystical Fact* (1901). He followed with *Knowledge of the Higher Worlds and Its Attainment* (1904), *Theosophy* (1904), and *Occult Science: An Outline* (1909).

With some hesitancy, in 1902 he became the head of the German section of the Theosophical Society. He disliked their emphasis on Eastern philosophy, preferring a Western Esoteric approach to the spiritual life. His concerns came forward in 1909, when he publicly disagreed with Annie Besant, the international president of the Society, at one of their conventions. She gave a talk in which she spoke of Buddha's superiority over Christ, while Steiner responded with a talk about Buddha as a precursor of Christ. The following year, Besant announced the formation of the Order of the Star of the East to prepare the way for Jiddu Krishnamurti, whom Besant believed to be the coming World Savior. Steiner refused to promote either the Order or Krishnamurti.

As the Order gained prominence in the program of the Society, Steiner proposed that Anthroposophy be formed as a section within the Society for those who did not wish to follow the Society's Oriental drift. That proved a short-term solution, and the following year he resigned from the Theosophical Society and formed the Anthroposophical Society.

As part of his work with Theosophical Society, Steiner had written and produced several mystery plays. In fact, his second wife was an actress. The break with Theosophy spurred him to design a building in which what he saw as the proper atmosphere for the drama would be present. The infant Anthroposophical Society found the resources to build the proposed structure in Dornach, Switzerland, just as World War I was begun. He named it the Goetheanum.

Steiner spent the war years in relative quiet, but during the decade after the war he vigorously promoted Anthroposophy and laid the ground work for the future application of his work in some prominent areas. In Stuttgart, for example, he opened the first Waldorf School to explore his ideas about education. Society members would subsequently found similar schools wherever the organization spread. In 1922, he responded to some religious leaders within the Society by sanctioning the founding of the Christian Community, which embodied his approach to theology and worship. In 1923–1924 he reformed the Anthroposophical Society and added an Esoteric section for primary explorations in self-development through what he termed spiritual science.

When Steiner died at Dornach on March 30, 1925, the Society was still largely confined to German-speaking Europe. It made its way to the German American community in the mid-1920s and soon spread across Europe. The practical application of his ideas would lead to the formation of structures to practice biodynamic agriculture, Anthroposophical medicine, and the new art of eurythmy.

J. Gordon Melton

See also: Anthroposophical Society; Besant, Annie; Krishnamurti Foundations; Western Esoteric Tradition.

References

Easton, Stewart C. *Rudolf Steiner: Herald of a New Epoch.* Spring Valley, NY: Anthroposophic Press, 1982.

Hemleben, Johannes. *Rudolf Steiner*. East Grinstead, UK: Henry Goulden, 1975.

Shepherd, A. P. *Rudolf Steiner: Scientist of the Invisible*. Rochester, VT: Inner Traditions/Bear & Company, 1987.

Steiner, Rudolf. *Christianity as Mystical Fact*. West Nyack, NY: Rudolf Steiner Publications, 1961.

Steiner, Rudolf. *Cosmic Memory*. West Nyack, NY: Rudolf Steiner Publications, 1959.

Steiner, Rudolf. *The Life, Nature and Cultivation of Anthroposophy*. London: Rudolf Steiner Press, 1963.

Steiner, Rudolf. *Rudolf Steiner: An Autobiography*. Trans. by Rita Stebbing. West Nyack, NY: Rudolf Steiner Publications, 1977.

Welburn, Andrew. *Rudolf Steiner's Philosophy*. Edinburgh: Floris Books, 2004.

Wilkinson, Roy. *Rudolf Steiner: An Introduction to His Spiritual World-View: Anthroposophy*. East Sussex, UK: Temple Lodge, 2001.

Stella Maris Gnostic Church

The Stella Maris Gnostic Church, one of a number of South American Gnostic sect groups, emerged from obscurity in the summer of 1999, when reports circulated that its members had disappeared into the mountains, ready to commit suicide. The story later proved to be a hoax.

Modern Gnosticism emerged in 19th-century Europe as part of the occult milieu. It was then taken to South America early in the 20th century by German teacher Arnoldo Krumm-Heller (1876–1949), who had been given authority to carry the movement to Latin America at a conference in Germany in 1907. At about the same time, he was also consecrated as a bishop in the Gnostic Catholic Church by H. C. Peithman. The Stella Maris Gnostic Church was founded in 1989 by Rodolfo Perez and former members of the Universal Christian Gnostic movement. It is headquartered in Cartagena, Colombia.

In June 1999, the mother of one of the church's members complained about the group and asked the local authorities to assist her in removing her daughter from it. They did not feel it was their responsibility to act. A month later, the group left Cartagena for its annual retreat. The day after the small group (with fewer than 100 members) departed, Colombian papers carried stories that the group had headed for the Sierra Nevada Mountains, where they expected to meet a spaceship that would take them to another world. The Sierra Nevada has been the focus of UFO reports, and many flying saucer buffs believe it to be a place where direct contact with extraterrestrials is possible.

The story was picked up by newspapers internationally and tied to memories of the suicide of the members of the Heaven's Gate group. However, the next day, Perez and several members of the group went on Colombian television to point out their lack of interest in UFOs. They emphasized that they would return home when their retreat was over. The retreat was not taking place in flying saucer country, but San Pedro, Colombia. The media had been routinely informed of the facts concerning the retreat, but the leading Colombian daily, *El Tiempo*, ran the initial story without referring to the facts that they had at hand.

The story of the group press conference was carried by the Colombian media, but no follow-up appeared in the international media for almost a year. In the spring of 2000, however, an obscure British magazine, *Fortean Times*, finally printed the story of the hoax in its May issue. Very quickly, the small church returned to obscurity. A variety of Internet sites have posted the stories from 1999, but the church has not been in the news since.

J. Gordon Melton

See also: Gnostic Catholic Church; Gnosticism.

Reference
Murdie, Alan. "The Stella Maris Cult." *Fortean Times* 133 (May 2000): 66.

Sthanakavasi Jain Tradition

The origins of the Sthanakavasi (literally, hall-dweller) Svetambara Jain tradition can be traced to the Gujarati Jain reformer Lonka Sah, Lunka or Lumpaka (ca. 1415–1489), who protested against the laxity of the contemporary Tapagaccha Murtipujak Svetambara Jain mendicants, because their conduct did not match the prescriptions of the oldest canonical texts. Lonka was the first layman who started a new religious movement within the Jain tradition. Because he copied manuscripts for Jain monks, he had unique access to the Jain scriptures and noticed that the oldest Svetambara scriptures do not mention the practice of merit-making by giving money as religious gifts (*dana*) for the construction of temples, nor the performance of image-worship (*murti-puja*) or similar ostentatious rituals involving the breaking of flowers and other acts of violence. On the contrary, the scriptures prescribed possessionlessness and strict asceticism: nonviolence, self-restraint, and penance. Lonka, therefore, rejected both image-worship and the authority of 14 (or 15) of the 45 canonical texts that contain references to it. He also denounced the legitimacy of the existing image-worshipping monastic orders and started to live as an uninitiated ascetic, following the oldest textual prescriptions himself.

The surviving original sources for Lonka's biography and doctrine are not entirely reliable. But most texts agree that, in contrast to common practice, Lonka accepted alms from all castes but no money, that he did not possess a mouthmask (*mukhavastrika*), a stick (*danda*), or a broom (*rajoharana*), and that he practiced neither image-worship nor the Jain rites of purification (*pratikramana* and *posadha*), which also involved elements of image-worship. Lonka quickly gained a large following among the Jains in Gujarat. Although he did not create a monastic order himself, he laid down instructions for his followers. The original texts were thought to be lost until 1964, when D. D. Malvaniya claimed to have rediscovered them in the L.D. Institute library in Ahmedabad in the form of two anonymously written manuscripts: *Lunka Na Saddahiya Ane Karya Atthavan Bolno* and *Lunka Na Hundi*.

The Lonkagaccha mendicant tradition was formed by Lonka's first disciple, Bhana, who apparently initiated himself and 45 followers of Lonka's doctrine sometime between 1471 and 1476 by accepting the five great vows of the Jain ascetics (*mahavrata*). In the first decades of the 16th century the Lonkagaccha split into several more or less organized regional or revisionist Lonkagaccha groups, most of which comprised lay-ascetics, or *yatis*, who did not accept all of the five

great vows or reverted to image-worship. In the mid-16th century, the Lonka tradition was split into more than 13 independent branches, which further divided into separate subgroups. Until the demise of the Lonkagaccha yatis in the 19th and 20th centuries, only four branches survived: the Lahauri Lonkagaccha (founded ca. 1504); the Nagauri Lonkagaccha (ca. 1528); the Gujarati Lonkagaccha Mota Paks (Varsinha Paks or Kesav Paks) (ca. 1555); and the Gujarati Lonkagaccha Nana Paks (Kumvar Paks) (ca. 1555).

In protest against the renaissance of image-worship and the renewed laxity of conduct of most Lonkagaccha (lay) ascetics, five reformers—the so-called *panca muni*—split off from the Kesav Paks, the Kumvar Paks, and the Ekal Patriya Panth (a lay movement of unknown origin) in the early 16th century and founded the principal Sthanakavasi mendicant traditions, which still exist today. The five traditions share three doctrinal characteristics: (1) rejection of image-worship, (2) strict ascetic conduct in accordance with the prescriptions in the 32 accepted Jain scriptures, and (3) compulsory use of a mouthmask to prevent the swallowing of living beings such as insects and dust. The square white mouthmask is now the principal external feature of all Sthanakavasi mendicants (the Terapanth Svetambara mendicants use a rectangular blue mask). Sthanakavasi laity generally reject material forms of worship (*dravya*) and practice only asceticism (*tapas*) and inner forms of worship (*bhava*), such as meditation (*dhyana*) and study (*svadhyaya*). Instead of images, they venerate the mendicants as living symbols of the Jain ideals.

They also practice *daya dharma*, the religious work of compassionate help (dana) for animals and human beings, in order to accumulate merit (*punya*) and thus to advance on the path of salvation. These three typical forms of ritual practice are known under the titles *guna puja*, *deva guru*, and *dana-daya*. In 1760, Muni Bhikhan, the founder of the Terapanth Svetambara Jain tradition, severed himself from the Dharmadasa Sthanakavasi tradition because he rejected merit-making as such, in favor of a purely salvation-oriented ascetic style of life.

The Sthanakavasi Jain tradition is presently divided into 26 mendicant orders whose origins can be traced to one or more of the five principal reformers (*kriya uddhara*) of the aniconic Jain tradition, although the available sources are inconsistent: (1) Jivaraja has been acknowledged as the initiator of all crucial innovations of the Sthanakavasi tradition, though some sources give priority to Lava. He lived sometime between 1524 and 1641 (probably having been born in Surat) and separated himself from the Kumvar Paks in 1551, 1609, or 1629. Apparently it was he who selected the 32 Svetambara scriptures that are now accepted by all Sthanakavasis (possibly by adding the Vyavaharasutra or the Avasyakasutra or both to Lonka's list, but there is no compelling evidence), and who introduced the mouthmask (*muhapatti*), the *rajoharan*, and other paraphernalia used by present-day Sthanakavasi mendicants. (2) Dharmasimha (1599–1671) severed himself from the Kumvar Paks in 1628, 1635, or 1644 in Dariyapuri in Ahmedabad and founded the Ath Koti (eight class) tradition. He was a scholar and wrote vernacular commentaries (*tabbo*) on the Prakrit Jain scriptures. He introduced a special pratikramana rite for his lay followers and taught that there is no accidental death, because the lifespan of a living being is determined by its own karma. (3) Lava or Lavji Rsi (ca. 1609–1659), the founder of the Dhundhiya (seeker) tradition, also known under the name Rsi Sampraday, was born in Surat and split from the Kesav Paks in 1637, 1648, 1653–1655, or 1657. (4) The founder of the Baistola (22 schools) tradition, Dharmadasa (1645–1703) from Ahmedabad, was originally a member of the Ekal Patriya Panth, but under the influence of Lava and Dharmasimha founded his own tradition in 1660 through self-initiation. (5) Hara, the ancestor of the Sadhumargi tradition (a branch of the extinct Kota Sampradaya), separated himself from the Kumvar Paks in 1668 or 1728.

The name *sthanaka-vasi* (hall-dwellers), though in evidence in a text written in 1630, was not regularly used as a common designation for all five traditions until the unification movement of the early 20th century. Doctrinally, only Dharmasimha's Ath Koti tradition in Gujarat differs significantly from the other four schools, which disagree only on minor points of philosophy and ritual. The Sthanakavasi traditions as a whole nowadays are divided along regional lines between the Gujarati and the non-Gujarati (North Indian) traditions. The non-Gujarati traditions are further sub-divided into those who joined the reformist and centrally organized Sramanasangha, which was founded in 1952 in Sadari in Rajasthan in a merely partially successful attempt to unite all Sthanakavasi groups, and those who remained outside or left the Sramanasangha. Both the Sramanasangha and the independent traditions include mendicant orders that derive from four of the five main Sthanakavasi traditions (the exception is the Ath Koti traditions), which were split into some 33 different organized groups at the beginning of the 20th century. Although they are nominally under the command of one single *acarya* whose consent is essential for all initiations and excommunications (at present, Acarya Dr. Sivmuni), the original 22 founding traditions of the Sramanasangha continue to operate within its framework more or less independently.

Some monastic orders never joined the Sramanasangha, among them all Gujarati Sthanakavasi traditions, the Jnanagaccha of the Dharmadasa Ramratna tradition (founded by Jnanacandra, Ujjain, 1732) and the Nanakgaccha of the Jivaraja tradition (Nanakram, eighteenth century). Because of perpetual discord between the founding traditions, many disappointed senior ascetics left the Sramanasangha again and established their own independent groups: Muni Hagamilal and the modernist Arhat Sangha (Susilkumar, 1926–1994, New Jersey, 1974) of the Jivaraja tradition; the Mayaram Sampradaya (Mayaram, 1854–1912) of the northern Lava tradition; Acarya Nanalal of the Hara Sadhumargi tradition (Hukmicand, early 19th century); and four groups of the Dharmadasa tradition: the Jaymalgaccha (Jaymal, 1708–1796; Rajasthan, 1748 or 1783); the Ratnavams (Ratnacandra, Rajasthan, 1796); the Dharmadasa Sampradaya (Umesmuni, late 20th century); and Upadhyay Amarmuni (1901–1992), the inspirational force behind the modern Virayatan Order, which was founded by Sadhvi Candana in Ragriha, 1974.

None of the Gujarati groups joined the Sramanasangha, which is essentially a Hindi-speaking order. With the exception of the Khambhat Sampradaya (Lava, Ahmedabad, 1648) and the three Ath Koti traditions—the Dariyapuri Ath Koti Sampradaya (Dharmasimha, Ahmedabad, 1628); the Kacch Ath Koti Mota Paks (Krsna, originally Dharmadasa Sampraday, Kacch

1715–1782); and the Kacch Ath Koti Nana Paks (Jasraj, Kacch, 1786)—the majority of the independent Sthanakavasi traditions in Gujarat descend from Mulacandra (1651–1725), one of Dharmadasa's 22 leading monks. Mulacandra's main disciples formed separate local groups after a dispute at a mendicant assembly in 1788 in Limbdi. Not all of the emerging Gujarati Dharmadasa traditions survived, and some of them split further into subgroups labeled great (*mota*) and small (*nana*). The seven principal orders of today are all named after the place of origin that is also their main seat: Limbdi Cha Koti Mota Paks (founded by Ajramar, Limbdi, 1788); Limbdi Cha Koti Nana Paks (Hemcand and Gopal, Limbdi, 1859); Gondal Mota Paks (Dungarsi, Gondal, 1788); Gondal Sanghani (Ganga Svami, Gondal, 1794); Barvada (Mota Kahan, Barvada, 1788); Botad (Jasa, Botad, ca. 1850); and Sayala (Naga, Sayla, 1772–1812). They are not led by an elected administrator cum teacher (acarya), like the independent traditions outside Gujarat, but by the male ascetic with the highest monastic age, or *diksa paryaya*, which may or may not be called acarya. His main decisions have to agree with those of the often hereditary leader (*sanghapati*) of the lay community.

The overall number of Sthanakavasi mendicants is much higher than generally assumed. In 1999 there were 3,223 mendicants, 533 *sadhus*, and 2,690 *sadhvis*—that is, 27.5 percent of all Jain mendicants, distributed in roughly equal proportions among the Sramanasangha (1,096), the 12 Independent traditions (967), and the 13 Gujarati traditions (1,160). The nationwide umbrella organization of the Sthanakavasi laity, the All India Svetambara Sthanakavasi Jain Conference, the motivating force behind the movement toward unity, was founded in 1906 in Morvi in Gujarat, but it split in 1984 into two independent organizations because of the irreconcilable differences in ritual culture and language between Gujarati- and Hindi-speaking Sthanakavasi traditions.

Akhil Bharatvarsiya Svetambara Sthanakavasi Jain
    Conference (Hindi)
Jain Bhavan
12 Sahid Bhagat Singh Marg
New Delhi 101001
India

Akhil Bharatvarsiya Svetambara Sthanakavasi Jain
    Conference (Gujarati)
1 Vijay Vallabh Cauk
Paydhuni
Mumbai 400 002
India

Peter Flügel

See also: Asceticism; Jainism; Monasticism; Terapanth Svetambara Jain Tradition.

References

Flügel, Peter. "Protestantische und Post-Protestantische Jain Reformbewegungen: Zur Geschichte und Organisation der Sthanakavasi I." *Berliner Indologische Studien* 13–14 (2000): 37–103.

Flügel, Peter. "Protestantische und Post-Protestantische Jain Reformbewegungen: Zur Geschichte und Organisation der Sthanakavasi II." *Berliner Indologische Studien* 15–16 (2002).

Hastimal, Acarya. *Jain Dharma Ka Maulik Itihas.* Vol. 4. Jaipur, India: Jain Itihas Samiti, 1987/1995.

Hastimal, Acarya, comp. *Pattavali Prabandh Sangraha.* Ed. by Narendra Bhanawat. Jaipur, India: Jain Itihas Nirman Samiti, 1968.

Jnanasundara, Muni. *Srimad Laumkasah.* Phalodi, India: Sri Jnana Puspamala, 1936.

Malvaniya, D. "Lokasah Aur Unki Vicar-Dhara." In *Gurudev Sri Ratna Muni Smrti-Granth*, edited by Vijay Muni Sastri and Harisankar Sarma, 365–383. Agra, India: Gurudev Smrti Granth Prakasak Samiti, 1964.

Manilal, Muni. *Sri Jaindharmano Pracin Sanksipt Itihas Ane Prabhu Vir Pattavali.* Amadavad, India: Jivanlal Chaganlal Sanghvi, 1934.

Stevenson, Sinclair. *Notes on Modern Jainism, with Special Reference to the Svetambara, Digambara and Sthanakavasi Sects.* New York: Barber Press, 2008.

Stonehenge

The intriguing mysterious prehistoric stone circle known as Stonehenge is one of the world's oldest and most famous holy sites. It is the most outstanding of several prehistoric monuments located in Wiltshire,

View of Stonehenge, Neolithic monument on the Salisbury Plain near modern-day Wiltshire, England. (Corel)

England, including Avebury and Silbury Hill. While much about Stonehenge remains unknown, it is best understood as the culminating product of the stone-building culture that produced these many monuments across the British Isles.

Archaeologists have been able to put together an account of the several distinct stages of Stonehenge's construction. The oldest part of the monument was a large, circular earthwork consisting of a ditch, a bank, and holes dug in the underlying Wiltshire chalk. This initial phase of Stonehenge can be roughly dated to the third millennium BCE. Around 2100 BCE, the builders brought a set of stones from the Preseli Mountains in Wales. Popularly termed the blue stones, some weighed as much as four tons each and were brought to their new home by a route that covering some 250 miles over land and via two rivers. At the site, the builders lifted the 82 stones to an upright position in a semi-circle. At about the same time, the entranceway to the site through the outer earthworks was widened, and two heel stones were located outside the central site.

The largest stones at Stonehenge (weighing up to 50 tons) were brought in from the northern part of Wiltshire possibly a century later. The builders placed them upright in a circle around the blue stones and topped them with lintel pieces. As part of this construction phase, five stones were placed in the center of the site in a horseshoe shape. A final construction phase was completed around 1500 BCE, when the blue stones were rearranged into a circle and horseshoe. At this same time, the Stonehenge Avenue, a pair of ditches and banks tying the site to the nearby River Avon, was constructed. A similar "avenue" also leads from the river to Durrington Walls.

Stonehenge's builders, at every stage, as with the other stone monuments across Great Britain, were a pre-literary people who left no written record of their life and only scant representational artwork. Over the centuries, as the many sites across Great Britain were abandoned, understanding of the use for which they had been built was lost. Later residents in their area raided the sites for building materials. Archaeologists have most recently tried to reconstruct picture of the ancient society that built Stonehenge, while many intrigued by the ancient site have produced a broad range of speculations about its exact purpose.

Stonehenge had been neglect for centuries when, in the 18th century, a few people turned their attention to it and the associated Wiltshire sites. Speculation in the 19th century tended to tie Stonehenge to the ancient Druids, known primarily from the writing of Julius Caesar. However, little real progress in understanding the stones was not made until the latter half of the 20th century, when more systematic archaeological work was concentrated on the megalithic culture. That work pushed the dating of Stonehenge to the Neolithic peoples who inhabited the British Isles prior to the Druids, Romans, and Danish folk, when written documents first appear.

Insights into Stonehenge occurred in the 1960s, when some students of the stones with astronomical knowledge discovered that the placement of some of the stones, including those in the center and the heel stones outside, were arranged in such a way as to indicate the occurrence of different astronomical phenomena, especially the movement of the Sun in the sky between the Summer and Winter solstices. This discovery raised the question of whether the builders had used them to plan planting and harvesting activity and possibly integrated such knowledge into setting dates for religious observances.

The modern neo-Druids who saw Stonehenge as a Druid worship site immediately seized upon the new astronomical speculations and added them to their arguments for continued use of Stonehenge for religious services. For many years, the Druids, with a small number of worshipper-spectators, had been admitted to the site for celebrations at the beginning of the day on the Summer Solstice. The establishment of rights of access for the Druids has been heightened in recent decades.

The most extensive recent work on Stonehenge is being done by the Stonehenge Riverside Project, an archaeological study led by a cadre of scholars from several British universities led by Mike Parker Pearson of Sheffield University. The project has focused upon Stonehenge within the larger context of the other nearby monuments and land features in Wiltshire. The research, with extensive time in the field by the schol-

ars, graduate students, and other interested helpers, began with a suggestion of Ramilisonina, an archaeologist from Madagascar, that Stonehenge was built not for the builders themselves, but their ancestors. Also, he saw the site tied to River Avon via the Avenue, and hence tied to additional monuments upstream (Woodhenge and Durrington Walls), all of which might be part of a funerary and processional route. While still in progress, the project has already gathered some evidence supportive of the hypothesis.

As Stonehenge became a major tourist site, significant damage was done by souvenir hunters, and the site itself is now fenced off. In 1986, Stonehenge was added to the list of World Heritage Sites designated by the United Nations.

J. Gordon Melton

See also: Avebury.

References

Burl, Aubrey. *The Stone Circles of the British Isles*. New Haven, CT: Yale University Press, 1976.

Hawkins, Gerald S., and John B. White. *Stonehenge Decoded*. New York: Barnes & Noble, 1993.

Mohen, Jean-Pierre. *The World of Megaliths*. New York: Facts on File, 1990.

Newham, C. A. *The Astronomical Significance of Stonehenge*. Leeds, UK: John Blackburn, 1972.

Souden, David. *Stonehenge Revealed*. London: Collins & Brown, 1997.

Subud

Subud is an association of men and women from various religions who worship God through a spiritual practice called *latihan*. Although the beliefs related to Subud are infused with religious ideas and terminology, members do not consider that it is a religion or even a teaching. It is described, rather, as "a symbol for the possibility for mankind to follow the right way of living."

Subud was founded in Indonesia around the late 1920s by a Javanese Muslim named Muhammad Subuh Sumohadiwidjojo (1901–1987), whose followers call him "Bapak," an Indonesian term of respect and affection, meaning "father." From the age of about 16,

Muhammad Subuh received a number of spiritual messages. He worked as a bookkeeper and studied with several spiritual masters (*kiai*) before receiving the *latihan kejiwaan*, the spiritual exercise of Subud, as a revelation in 1925. Around 1933 some of Bapak's friends received the latihan, and the practice slowly spread throughout Java. A small group, guided by Bapak, started an organization called Ilmu (esoteric spiritual knowledge) Kasunyatan (emptiness). Subud has been established in the West since the late 1950s, when it attracted the attention of some followers of George I. Gurdjieff (ca. 1866–1949).

The name Subud, introduced by Bapak at the inaugural meeting of a new organization in 1947, is derived from three terms: *susila* (which is translated as "the good character of man in accordance with the Will of Almighty God"); *budhi* (meaning "the force of the inner self within man"); and *dharma* (meaning "surrender, trust and sincerity towards Almighty God"). Taken together, *Susila Budhi Dharma* is understood as: to follow the will of God, or the power of the life force that works both within us and without. Bapak emphasized that Subud has "no holy book, no teaching, no sacred formula. In Subud the members only surrender with patience, trust, and sincerity to Almighty God." Subud is a "process," a "receiving."

The latihan, which is seen as a form of pure worship in which one comes into direct, personal contact with the Grace and Power of God, lasts about half an hour and may be practiced by oneself. However, members are encouraged to attend a group latihan twice a week. It starts by standing with the group (men and women practice separately) with one's eyes closed; some then feel a vibration; most begin to feel a spontaneous impulse to move, dance, cry, laugh, or sing. This is experienced as an inner cleansing and a receiving of divine guidance, which spills over into the participant's everyday life. Practitioners report feeling happier, enjoying improved personal relationships, health, and work experiences. For some, however, the process of purification brings out problems that have to be dealt with—an experience that can be difficult and painful.

Only members may attend the latihan; newcomers have to wait about three months before being invited to join. Then, with the assistance of a "helper," they can be "opened" by partaking in their first latihan.

Members of many different religions, or no religion at all, may practice the latihan. Bapak instructed his followers that there should be no proselytizing or advertising in Subud. He also recommended that there should be no membership fees, although donations are welcomed to cover expenses. Membership of Subud does not entail any special lifestyle or activities beyond practicing the latihan. However, it is believed that the practice can lead to guidance on personal matters, and most members drink little or no alcohol and are unlikely to eat pork.

Worldwide, there are an estimated 10,000 members in some 385 groups in more than 70 countries, with about 2,500 in the United States and 1,000 in the United Kingdom. Although some have left at various periods, numbers have been sustained, with some second-generation members requesting to join when they reach the minimum age of 17. The association has helpers at various levels and is divided into geographical zones that send representatives to international Subud organizations. Throughout the years, several Subud businesses have been established, not all of which have been financially successful. Nonetheless, Subud has sustained various charitable projects under the name of Susila Dharma International, which has UN-affiliated status.

International Subud Committee
839 Arbor St.
Wooster, OH 44691

Eileen Barker

References

Geels, Antoon. *Subud and the Javanese Mystical Tradition*. Richmond, UK: Curzon, 1997.

Lyle, Robert. *Subud*. Kent, UK: Humanus, 1983.

Sullivan, Matthew Barry. *Living Religion in Subud*. London: Subud Publications International, 1990.

Sumohadiwidjojo, Muhammad Subuh. *Susila Budhi Dharma*. Loudwater Farm, Rickmansworth, UK: Subud Publications International, 2001.

Webb, Gisela. "Subud." In *America's Alternative Religions*, edited by Timothy Miller, 267–273. Albany: State University of New York Press, 1995.

■ Sudan

Sudan is a large African country (965,000 square miles) located immediately south of Egypt along the Red Sea. Its western border with Libya and Chad is in the Sahara Desert. To the south, it shares borders with the Central African Republic, the Democratic Republic of the Congo, Uganda, and Kenya, and to the east with Ethiopia and Eritrea. Sudan is home to 40,200,000 people.

Settlement of the lands adjacent to the Upper Nile River and the associated rivers that feed into it occurred in prehistoric times, and as early as 3000 BCE this territory came under the control of Egypt. It was thus not until the eighth century BCE that an independent state, Napata, came into existence. In 730, Napata conquered Egypt, and for several generations its leaders ruled as pharaoh. After the fall of Napata in the seventh century, three states emerged that would continue for the next two millennia. These three states, Nobatia, Dongola, and Alodia, formed important functions in the trade between the Middle East and sub-Saharan Africa.

These states came under Christian influence in the fourth century CE. Then, in the seventh century, Muslim Arabs entered Dongola. In exchange for retaining the territorial integrity of Dongola and Alodia, the two states allowed Islamic proselytizing in the area. Egyptians invaded in the 14th century. Their influence led to the destruction of Dongola and the emergence of new Islamic states. Then in 1820, Egyptian forces under Muhammad Ali, the Albanian who had come to rule Egypt, occupied Khartoum. Over the next year, they unified the several countries and created the modern state of Sudan. As British influence grew in Egypt, further changes were introduced, including the abolishing of slavery.

Foreign rule led to revolution. Muhammad Ahmad raised an army in 1881 that led to British intervention in 1882. The revolt climaxed with the defeat of the British at Khartoum in 1885 and the establishment of an independent government. His victory was short lived, however, and with French assistance, Ahmed's rule was overthrown in 1898.

The independence of Sudan was finally accomplished in 1956, but civil war ensued between the predominantly Arab Muslim north and the African Christian south. The coup d'état by Gaafar al-Nimeiry in 1969 led to the end of the war but did not solve the problems between north and south. In a last attempt to retain power, in 1983 he imposed Islamic law on the whole country. Opposition organized in the south. Over the course of the next two years, a liberation movement in the southern region asserted its autonomy. War developed between the movement's guerrilla army and Sudanese forces. The many different peoples of the south, some Christians and some followers of traditional African religions, have been caught in the middle. The continued warfare in the south of Sudan has been the source of numerous atrocities and much suffering.

Until the fourth century CE, traditional African religions dominated across what is now Sudan. There are more than 570 ethnic groups that have been identified, each at one time having its own religion and dialect. In the fourth century, Orthodox Christianity from Egypt found its way up the Nile. In the fifth century, Orthodoxy split between those who supported the Orthodox statement expounded at the Council of Chalcedon and the Monophysite perspective that dominated in Egypt. Both opinions gained a following in the Sudan. The following century, the Ethiopian Church (which favored the Monophysite position) was introduced from the east and found a following. Much of the initial Christian following was lost to Islam—especially in the former Dongola and Alodia (the northern two-thirds of the present country)—over the next centuries. Variant forms of Islam emerged, some related to changes in the Egyptian leadership, but, as in the Muslim countries to the west, the dominant form had been the Sunni Malikite School.

When Muhammad Ali invaded the country, he attempted to impose a strict Sunni Hanafite interpretation of Islam. This imposition was part of the cause of the revolt under Muhammad Ahmad, proclaimed by his followers to be al-Mahdi, the leader and prophet who, many Muslims believe, will emerge to rescue and unite Islam at some time in the future. After the defeat of al-Mahdi, a legal system that mixed Hanafi and British elements was introduced, and the Malikite School reasserted its dominant role. However, through the 20th century, a very diverse Muslim community arose that

SUDAN

Sudan

Religion	Followers in 1970	Followers in 2010	% of Population	Annual % growth 2000–2010	Followers in 2025	Followers in 2050
Muslims	10,041,000	29,313,000	71.1	2.04	38,840,000	52,220,000
Christians	1,169,000	6,788,000	16.5	2.15	10,174,000	14,855,000
Roman Catholics	690,000	3,700,000	9.0	1.44	5,400,000	7,500,000
Anglicans	300,000	2,350,000	5.7	0.98	3,500,000	5,000,000
Protestants	59,500	1,400,000	3.4	4.80	2,200,000	3,600,000
Ethnoreligionists	3,154,000	4,630,000	11.2	1.95	4,500,000	4,800,000
Agnostics	100,000	425,000	1.0	1.45	650,000	1,000,000
Atheists	30,000	69,000	0.2	2.04	95,000	140,000
Baha'is	500	2,600	0.0	2.04	5,000	10,000
Jews	50	1,700	0.0	2.04	1,700	1,700
Hindus	0	800	0.0	2.06	1,200	1,800
Total population	**14,495,000**	**41,230,000**	**100.0**	**2.04**	**54,267,000**	**73,029,000**

includes numerous large Sufi brotherhoods and the continued followers of al-Mahdi, the Ansars (some 3 million strong). Among the Sufi brotherhoods the Khatimiyya are the largest, but the Qadiiyya, Shadhiliyya, and Tijaniyya are also prominent.

The Ahmadiyya Muslim movement has attempted to spread through Sudan but has been outlawed as heretical. The Baha'i Faith entered Sudan in the 1890s but has not shown much success for over a century of effort.

A small Ethiopian Orthodox community has survived in Sudan, and Greek Christianity survives under the jurisdiction of the Greek Orthodox Patriarchate of Alexandria and All Africa. The Monophysite perspective survives in the Coptic Orthodox Church and the Ethiopian Orthodox Tewahedo Church, both of which have established dioceses in Sudan.

These three churches dominated the Christian community until after the defeat of al-Mahdi by the British in 1898. The next year the Church Missionary Society introduced the Church of England into the Sudan, the first center being at Omduman. In 1901, American Presbyterians from the United Presbyterian Church (now part of the Presbyterian Church [U.S.A.]) entered from their base in Egypt. The Anglican work has matured as the Church of the Province of the Sudan. The Presbyterian mission has resulted in two churches, the Presbyterian Church of the Sudan (in the south) and the Sudan Presbyterian Evangelical Church (earlier ex-

isting as the Sudanese presbytery of the Evangelical Church–Synod of the Nile as its Sudanese presbytery).

A variety of Christian groups attempted to open work in the Sudan through the 20th century, among the most successful being the Sudan United Mission (1913), whose work led to the present Sudanese Church of Christ, the Africa Inland Mission (African Inland Church, 1936), and the Sudan Interior Mission (Sudan Interior Church, 1937). Several African Initiated Churches have arisen, including the Eternal Life Church and the Evangelical Revival Church, both schisms from the Anglicans.

The Roman Catholic Church also entered Sudan following the British victory in 1898. The first Sudanese priest was ordained in 1944, but growth was stymied by the war that followed independence. All of its seminaries and many church buildings were destroyed. However, with the reorganization that occurred at the beginning of the 1970s, including the elevation of the vicariates and prefectures into diocese in 1972, Catholicism has grown into the largest Christian body in the country. It grew from 600,000 members in 1970 to 2.7 million by 1995. As with other Christian churches, its strength is in the southern region. One can only speculate as to the extent of growth had the continuing warfare of the last generation not occurred.

Islam, with 70 percent of the population, and Christianity, with 16 percent, dominate the religious life of the Sudan. Traditional African religions survive among the Didinga, Ingressana, Meban, and a variety of other ethnic groups. They constitute about 1 percent of the population and reside primarily in the south. The liberal Protestant community has joined together to form the Sudan Council of Churches, affiliated with the World Council of Churches. The more conservative churches have combined to form the Sudan Evangelical Christian Association, which is associated with the World Evangelical Alliance.

J. Gordon Melton

See also: African Initiated (Independent) Churches; Ahmadiyya Movement in Islam; Baha'i Faith; Church Missionary Society; Church of England; Coptic Orthodox Church; Ethiopian Orthodox Tewahedo Church; Evangelical Church–Synod of the Nile; Greek Orthodox Patriarchate of Alexandria and All Africa; Hanafite School of Islam; Malikite School of Islam; Presbyterian Church (U.S.A.); Qadiriyya Sufi Order; Roman Catholic Church; Shadhiliyya Sufi Order; Sudan Interior Church; Tijaniyya Sufi Order; World Council of Churches; World Evangelical Alliance.

References

Both, Peter Lam. *South Sudan: Forgotten Tragedy.* Bloomington, IN: 1st Books Library, 2003.

Holt, P. M., and M. W. Daly. *A History of the Sudan: From the Coming of Islam to the Present Day.* London: Longman, 2000.

Hunwick, J. O. *Religion and National Integration in Africa: Islam, Christianity, and Politics in the Sudan and Nigeria.* Evanston, IL: Northwestern University Press, 1992.

Jok, Jok Madat. *Sudan: Race, Religion and Violence.* Oxford: Oneworld Publications, 2007.

Karrir, Ali Salih. *The Sufi Brotherhoods in the Sudan.* Evanston, IL: Northwestern University Press, 1992.

Simone, T. Abdou Maliqalim. *In Whose Image?: Political Islam and Urban Practices in Sudan.* Chicago: University of Chicago Press, 1994.

Vantini, G. *Christianity in the Sudan.* Bologna, Italy: EMI, 1981.

Warburg, Gabriel. *Islam, Sectarianism, and Politics in the Sudan since the Mahdiyya.* Madison: University of Wisconsin Press, 2002.

Werner, Robert, William Anderson, and Andrew Wheeler. *Day of Devastation, Day of Contentment: The History of the Sudanese Church across 2,000 Years.* Nairobi: Paulines Publications Africa, 2000.

Wingate, F. R. *Mahdism and the Egyptian Sudan: Being an Account of the Rise and Progress of Mahdism, and of Subsequent Events in the Sudan to the Present Time.* 2nd ed. London: Cass, 1968.

Sudan Interior Church

The Sudan Interior Church is the product of the missionary activity of the Sudan Interior Mission (SIM), now known as the Society for International Ministries. SIM was founded in 1893 by Canadians Walter Gowans (1868–1894) and Rowland Bingham and American Thomas Kent (d. 1894) as an independent missionary society dedicated to the evangelization of the Sudan, then one of the few countries without a single Christian missionary. The three arrived in Nigeria in December 1893, where Bingham fell ill. The others pressed inward, where Gowans and Kent died early in 1894. Bingham returned to Toronto and organized a support council and began to rebuild the effort. However, the first mission station would not be opened until 1902.

Work began in Nigeria (rather than the Sudan) and spread from Patigi to Bida (1903) and Wushishi (1904), and it became the core of the present Evangelistic Church of West Africa. Prior to its finally reaching the Sudan, work would spread to Niger (1924), Ethiopia (1927), and Upper Volta, now Burkina Faso (1930). The work in the Sudan would actually be a result of the work in Ethiopia, and it began in 1936 after its missionaries were expelled from that country. They had initiated work among the Dinka people.

Work in the Sudan prospered for a generation, but in 1961, three of the four stations were closed by the government. The following year, the Sudan passed the Missionary Societies Act, which placed a number of restrictions on the mission. In 1964 the process of missionary expulsion began, actions that marked the heightening of the civil war that continues in the southern part of the Sudan. Through the 1960s the number of missionaries dropped from 36 (serving at 9 stations) to 5, those last leaving in 1970.

The Sudan Interior Church has emerged as an autonomous body out of the pressure placed on the former mission in the 1960s. The church is a member of the Sudan Council of Churches, which unites the minority Christian community. It is a conservative evangelical body that affirms the major Christian beliefs shared by all Protestants.

In the 1980s the Sudan Interior Mission merged with three other similar missionary agencies that had work in Asia and South America to form SIM. SIM has no international headquarters but operates through national councils that can now be found in a number of countries. In 1980 the Sudan Interior Church and other autonomous churches that grew from the missions founded by the Sudan Interior Mission and the three other agencies now a part of SIM created the Evangel Fellowship, an association of 12 churches. In 1996, the Evangel Fellowship formed the Evangelical Fellowship of Missions Association to coordinate their mutual missionary efforts.

Sudan Interior Church
PO Box 220
Khartoum
Sudan

SIM U.S.A.
PO Box 7900
Charlotte, NC 28241
http://www.sim.org

J. Gordon Melton

See also: Evangelicalism.

References

Bingham, Rowland. *Seven Sevens of Years and a Jubilee: The Story of the Sudan Interior Mission.* Toronto: Evangelical Publishers, 1943.

Fuller, W. H. *Run While the Sun Is Hot.* New York: Sudan Interior Mission, 1967.

Society for International Missions. http://www.sim .org/. Accessed November 15, 2001.

Sufi Movement, The

See International Sufi Movement, The.

Sufi Order in North America, The

The Sufi Order in North America is a branch of the Sufi Order International, a religious organization whose primary aim is to promote the spiritual teachings of Hazrat Inayat Khan (1882–1927) and his son, Pir Vilayat Khan (1916–2004). The Order is not recognized as a traditional Islamic Sufi order because its membership is open to people of all faiths and it does not promote traditional Islam. Most of its members are white, middle-class Westerners, many of whom have been affiliated with the Order since the 1970s. The Order is a prototypical New Age religion, with its eclectic embrace of traditional religious practices, its desire to synthesize science and religion, its expectation of a dawning New Age of spiritual unity, and its interest in both Eastern and Western methods of psychological, physical, and spiritual healing. The group has been one of the most visible transmissions of Sufi spirituality to the West over the past 100 years.

Hazrat Inayat Khan was a renowned Indian musician who became a disciple of Hazrat Abu Hashim Madani, a Sufi master from a branch of the famed Chisti Order in India. Before his death, Madani asked Khan to bring Sufism to the West. Khan arrived in the United States in late 1910. He taught Sufism and performed music on the East and West coasts before traveling to Europe and Russia to organize formal Sufi centers. The seeds of future division were sown at this time, as different disciples (*murids*) were placed in charge of national centers in Europe and North America.

In 1926, Khan named his 11-year-old son, Vilayat, to be his successor as head of the Sufi Order. Following his father's death in 1927, Vilayat studied philosophy, psychology, and music in Paris and Oxford and began intensive meditation training under various Sufi masters in the Middle East and India. He emerged as a legitimate successor to his father's work and reinstated the Order in the United States during the 1960s. His efforts in California were helped by Murshid Samuel Lewis (1896–1971), an eclectic teacher who had received initiation into several Sufi orders during a lifetime of spiritual seeking. Lewis brought his group of students into the Sufi Order in 1968, but some of those students later left the Order in 1977 over disagreements with Vilayat's regulations and formed the Sufi Islamia Ruhaniat Society.

During the late 20th century, Pir Vilayat Khan became an internationally recognized spiritual teacher who gave frequent public lectures and participated in various religious congresses, interfaith dialogues, meditation camps, and New Age expositions in the United States, Western Europe, and India. Pir Vilayat and Pir Zia, his son and successor, were invited to attend the United Nations Peace Summit for world spiritual and religious leaders in 2000.

The Sufi Order International's teachings generally consist of the writings of Hazrat Inayat Khan and their further elaboration by Pir Vilayat and Pir Zia. All three khans teach the essential unity of spiritual ideals across religious traditions. Pir Vilayat sought to establish in his initiates a "stereoscopic consciousness" that cultivates simultaneous awareness of everyday human reality and the most elevated levels of the Divine Being. He emphasized that the realm of ordinary perception both reveals and veils a sublime reality that is unfolding itself within and through human life. The universe is evolving, in other words, toward a Chardin-like Omega point. In books such as *Toward the One* and *Awakening: A Sufi Experience*, Pir Vilayat synthesized prayer, meditation, and breathing methods from different spiritual traditions with traditional Sufi practice in order to foster the disciple's experience of the underlying unity of all things in the Divine Ground. All of Pir Vilayat's teachings were a natural outworking of his father's intention to foster tolerance and mutual understanding between East and West and between the different branches of the Beni Israel traditions.

The teaching work of the Sufi Order International includes seminars and retreats that focus on spiritual healing arts, meditation practices, the spirituality of music, esoteric studies, and universal dances of peace. Although the Sufi Order International is headquartered in France, the Sufi Order in North America is headquartered at the Abode of the Message, a residential Sufi community founded in 1975 in New Lebanon, New York. The former Shaker colony houses Omega Publications and its retailing outlet, Wisdom's Child Bookstore, and Sacred Spirit Music. The Abode hosts an annual program of spiritual retreats, the Healing Arts center, and ongoing classes in *dhikr* (a traditional Sufi chanting practice), dervish whirling, and Universal Worship. This latter liturgy was developed by Inayat Khan and draws on elements of the world's major religions. Teaching centers exist in large cities throughout the United States and Europe, with centers and branch leaders appointed by the president of the order.

On February 4, 2000, Pir Zia Inayat Khan received the teaching mantle of Pir Vilayat in an investiture ceremony at Hazrat Inayat Khan's tomb in Delhi, India. He was also elevated to the presidency of the Sufi Order in North America, although Pir Vilayat remained chairman of the board of directors until his death in 2004. Pir Zia divides his time between the Abode, India, and Europe. He is particularly interested in creating stronger ties with established Sufi orders in the Middle East and Asia and with helping Sufism as a tradition to move in a more universal direction. Pir Zia is committed to his grandfather's vision of building Universal temples that honor all religions. The Order is currently developing an institute designed to promote and implement its vision of a humanity that is tolerant, just, and unified in spirit, if not in the particulars of traditional beliefs and practices. Zia has adopted modern communications media and authors a blog available on the Internet.

Sufi Order International
North American Secretariat
5 Abode Rd.
New Lebanon NY 12125
http://www.sufiorder.org/

Phillip Charles Lucas

See also: Devotion/Devotional Traditions; International Sufi Movement; Meditation; New Age Movement; Sufism.

References

Khan, Pir Vilayat Inayat. *Awakening: A Sufi Experience.* New York: Jeremy P. Tarcher/Putnam, 1999.

Khan, Pir Vilayat Inayat. *The Message in Our Time: The Life and Teaching of the Sufi Master, Pir-o-Murshid Inayat Khan.* San Francisco: Harper & Row, 1978.

Khan, Pir Vilayat Inayat. *Toward the One.* New York: Harper & Row, 1974.

Khan, Pirzade Zia Inayat. *Pearl in Wine.* New York: Omega Publications, 2006.

Sufism

The inner esoteric spiritual dimensions of the Islamic religious tradition is commonly referred to as Sufism (Arabic: *tasawwuf*). Since the time of the Prophet Muhammad, Muslims have contemplated the existence of God and meeting the divine in the hereafter. However, practitioners of tasawwuf, or Sufis, have focused on encountering the divine in the present lifetime. The earliest scholars of the tradition—such as Hasan al-Basri, Rabi'a al-Adawiya, Bayazid Bistami, and Mansur al-Hallaj—had stressed various components of leading an ascetic life and defining technical terms that came with the inner journey (*tariqah*) toward Allah. To access a closeness with God, Sufis developed a wide body of literature that discussed the spiritual experiences of the traveler, especially detailed accounts of consciousness or unconsciousness experienced on the journey.

To earn the intimacy of God, Sufis have relied on learning the direct knowledge of the divine (*al 'ilm al-laduni*) through the rigorous spiritual training by a Sufi shaikh who had already been enlightened by the knowledge of God (*ma'rifa*). According to the classical Sufi scholars, the primary theological premise in Sufism is that Prophet Muhammad was trained by God himself so that the Prophet would embody these inner practices and beliefs and teach his followers. A common private conversation between God and the Prophet, or *hadith qudsi*, stated: "I was a hidden treasure and I loved that I be known, so I created the creation in order to be known." For Sufis, since the moment of creation human beings have been working toward being nearer to God. The human heart has a natural tendency to feel incomplete until it dwells in the presence of God (*hulul*).

For Sufis there is an outer (*zahir*) and inner (*batin*) reading of the world, particularly in the interpretation of the Koran and the customs of the Prophet (*sunnah*). For those who truly desire to understand and experience the inner dimensions of God's speech, Sufis have argued for studying the hidden and inner meanings of the Koran, or *batn al-qur'an*. The realization of God in the journey (*'irfan*) was not exclusively for select human beings, but as the Prophet Muhammad had an intimate dialogue with God in his heavenly ascension (*layla mi'raj wa isra*), Sufis claim this event laid down a mystical paradigm for others to follow. Sufi Muslims begin with the fundamental profession of Islamic faith: "There is no God but God, and Muhammad is the messenger of God." The first part reinforces the oneness of God at all times, while the second part speaks of the Prophet's special status as the messenger of God. For Sufis, Prophet Muhammad is the mystical exemplar and major focus for meditations, veneration, and invocations.

The Sufi tradition rapidly developed manuals as a form of religious learning (*'ilm*) alongside of the normative religious sciences of law and the customs of the Prophet. During the classical period of Sufism, mystical knowledge was understood as superior to the traditional knowledge taught in the colleges. By the early 11th century, Sufi scholars and Muslim intellectuals like Ibn Sina (or Avicenna, d. 1037) incorporated Sufi knowledge (*'irfan*) with metaphysical studies of Greek philosophy into the traditional curriculum. The discrepancies between the mystical path (tariqah) and the education in the colleges (*madrasa*) began to be minimized with Ahmad al-Ghazzali (d. 1111), who advocated a balanced approach to Islamic spirituality and orthopraxy. Mainstream scholars and religious authorities accepted Sufism as Sufis themselves were able to accommodate them with a refined theology that moved beyond personal ecstasy and was based on reason, critical self-reflection, and analysis of the soul's journey.

Sufis organized themselves into orders that were highly structured for the disciples to be trained in the mystical journey. Unlike Christian monastic orders, such as the Franciscans and the Jesuits, Sufi orders did not have to take vows of celibacy, nor were they under the supervision of a central authority like the pope. Each Sufi order was based upon the teachings and authority of the Sufi teacher, who needed to have a lineage to the Prophet Muhammad. The Sufi orders established lodges (*khanaqah*) in which disciples lived and were taught by their respective teachers, but not all disciples lived in the lodges. There was a master-disciple (*pir-murid*) relationship within the orders, and disciples needed to pass initiation in order to be a member. The institution of Sufism meant that it was accessible to anyone who wanted to reach God from the mystical path; it also gave distinct identities to

Whirling dervishes integrate music and dance into their solemn religious rituals. (Corel)

each of the Sufi orders. Sufi disciples were given specific instructions on how to pray with more attention, to bring more love to their lives, to direct their wealth toward the poor, and to learn detailed spiritual exercises for enlightenment.

Sufi orders are found throughout the Muslim world. Among the more prominent Sufi orders to emerge out of Mesopotamia (Iran/Iraq) are the Rifaiyya, Suhrawardiyya, and Qadiiyya. These are among the earliest of the Sufi orders. Rifaiyya was founded in Basra, Iraq, in the 12th century, soon spreading from Iraq into Syria and Egypt. The Suhrawardiyya formally established themselves in the early 12th-century Iraq and spread westward into India. The Qadiriyya Sufis originated in Iran in the 12th century and spread both eastward and westward into India and North Africa.

Sufism continued to grow in popularity in North Africa as the Rifaiyya Order expanded into Syria and then Egypt. Shortly thereafter it spread to Northwest Africa, where it gained the support of the ruling Al-mohad dynasty (1130–1269), whose territory included Morocco, Algeria, Tunisia, and Muslim Spain. The Shadhiliyya developed in the 13th century in Tunisia and continues to flourish in contemporary Algeria, Tunisia, and Morocco.

In Central Asia and Anatolia (equivalent to modern-day Turkey), a number of major Sufi orders emerged between the 12th and 17th centuries in Turkey and Central Asia. The Yasawiyya, originating in Turkestan, led in spreading the movement among the Turkish tribes of Central Asia. Among the important Central Asian orders is Chistiniyya, the foundation of which is generally ascribed to Mu'in al-Din Chishti (ca. 1142–1236), a native of Sijistan. The Order spread into India, where it became that land's largest Sufi order. It split into several factions and has a high profile in the West, through two branches of the work founded by Hazrat Inyat Khan, the Sufi Order International and the International Sufi Movement. Yasawiyya appears also to have given birth to the Bektashi

Sufis, who continue strong in Albania and nearby Balkan countries.

The Mevlevi Sufi Order derives from the experience, work, and writings of Turkish poet/mystic Jalal ud-din Rumi (1207–1273); they are famous as the "whirling dervishes." The order is based on Rumi's place of burial, Konya, Turkey. Along with the other Turkish orders, it was suppressed when the secular government assumed authority in 1925. It declined for several decades but experienced new life in the West at the end of the 20th century. Equally hurt by the formal abolition of Sufi groups in Turkey were the Naqshbandnya; however, they survived through their non-Turkish centers and have enjoyed more success. The Order was founded by Baha al-din Naqshband (d. 1389) near Bukhara in Central Asia, and subsequently it spread from India to Turkey. It flourished under the Ottomans and Mughals, and after a setback in the mid-20th century, it too has found new life in the contemporary West and in Islamic nations.

In the 18th century, the Wahhabi movement attached to Islam many popular practices that had entered through Sufism—including the veneration of saints and pilgrimages to their gravesites, while encouraging a strict adherence to Islamic law. In Africa the spirit of reform contributed to the establishment of several new orders, such as the Tijaniyya, founded in the 1780s by Ahmad al-Tidjani (d. 1815) and, in the same spirit a century later, the Muridiyya. Both have spread across North Africa and western sub-Saharan Africa, and since World War II into the West.

More extreme was the Sanusiyya, founded in Cyrenaica (eastern Libya) in the 1840s by Muhammad b. ali Sanusi (1787–1859). The Sanusiyya rejected all forms of luxury. Like other African orders, it included a strong sense of veneration for the Prophet Muhammad. They were a critical resistance group fighting against French colonial rule, and they took the lead in creating the modern state of Libya. Overthrown in 1969 by Colonel Muammar al-Qadafi, they have been an important element in the opposition to his regime.

http://www.arches.uga.edu/~godlas/Sufism
http://world.std.com/~habib/sufi.html#resources
http://www.sufibooks.com/

Qamar-ul Huda

See also: Bektashi Sufi Order; Chistiniyya Sufi Order; International Sufi Movement; Mevlevi Sufi Order; Muhammad; Qadiriyya Sufi Order; Qadiriyya Rifa'i Sufi Order; Sufi Order in North America, The; Suhrawardiyya Sufi Order; Tijaniyya Sufi Order; Wahhabi Islam.

References

Chittick, William. *The Sufi Path of Knowledge: Ibn 'Arabi's Metaphysics of Imagination.* Albany: State University of New York Press, 1989.

Chittick, William T. *Sufism: A Beginner's Guide.* Oxford: Oneworld Publications, 2007.

Ernst, Carl. *The Shambhala Guide to Sufism: An Essential Introduction to the Philosophy and Practice of the Mystical Tradition of Islam.* Boston: Shambhala, 1997.

Lewisohn, Leonard, ed. *The Legacy of Mediaeval Persian Sufism.* New York: Khaniqah Nimatullah, 1992.

Lings, Martin. *What Is Sufism?* Cambridge: Islamic Texts Society, 1993.

Nasr, Seyyed Hossein. *The Garden of Truth: The Vision and Promise of Sufism, Islam's Mystical Tradition.* New York: HarperOne, 2008.

Rizvi, Syed Athar Abbas. *A History of Sufism in India.* 2 vols. New Delhi: Manoharlal, 1978.

Schimmel, Annemarie. *Mystical Dimensions of Islam.* Chapel Hill: North Carolina Press, 1975.

Trimingham, Spencer. *The Sufi Orders in Islam.* Oxford: Clarendon, 1971.

Suhrawardiyya Sufi Order

The Suhrawardi Sufis were recognized as an important Sufi order with its founder, Shaikh Abu'Najib al-Suhrawardi (d. 1168), the uncle of Abu Hafs 'Umar Suhrawardi (1144–1234). Abu'Najib al-Suhrawardi was originally from the town of Suhraward, which is west of Sultaniyya, in the province of al-Jibal, Iran. Abu'Najib was the rector of the Nizamiyaa Academy and an authority on *hadith* (the sayings of the Prophet Muhammad). He also wrote a famous Sufi treatise on etiquette and Sufi practice.

Equally profound was Shihab al-din Yahya Suhrawardi (1170–1208), a mystic-philosopher who expanded upon the School of Illumination (Hikmat al-Ishraq), which used rational discourse as a basis for experiential wisdom. The Ishraqi School was a coherent and philosophical system of inquiry into knowledge, symbolism, and wisdom.

Later, Shaikh Abu Hafs 'Umar al-Suhrawardi consequently wrote an equally profound Sufi text called the 'Awarif al-Ma'arif (Knowledge of the Spiritually Learned), which is still used in the Sufi world for spiritual lessons. Al-Suhrawardi was designated as the shaikh al-Islam, or supreme Islamic religious authority, under Caliph al-Nasir (1179–1225); he preached the importance of adhering to Islamic law, customs of the Prophet, and the Koran.

The Suhrawardis professed intense studies of law, Koranic studies, philosophy, theology, and the complete adherence to Islamic customs set by the Prophet Muhammad. Knowledge of the divine is attainable through constructive reasoning and contemplation; the mystical way meant living moderately and not being lost in complete poverty or asceticism. The Suhrawardi Sufis can be found in South Asia, Iran, Syria, Central Asia, Europe, and North America.

The Suhrawardi Foundation in Lahore, Pakistan, publishes materials on Sufism and the modern world. The elder Sufis continue the Suhrawardi tradition of mystical studies and practice. The Suhrawardi Foundation of North America holds conferences and poetry meetings to better understand the Sufi journey.

Qamar-ul Huda

See also: Muhammad; Sufism.

References

Huda, Qamar-ul. *Striving for Divine Union: Spiritual Exercises of the Suhrawardi Sufis.* Surrey, UK: Curzon, 2002.

Razavi, Mehdi Amin. *Suhrawardi and the School of Illumination.* Surrey, UK: Curzon, 1997.

Thackston, William. *The Mystical and Visionary Treatises of Shihabuddin Yahya Suhrawardi.* London: Octagon, 1982.

Walbridge, John. *The Leaven of the Ancients: Suhrawardi and the Heritage of the Greeks.* Albany: State University of New York Press, 2000.

Wilson, M. *A Sufi Rule for Novices: Kitab Adab al-Muridin of Abu-Najib al-Suhrawardi.* Cambridge, MA: Harvard University Press, 1973.

Ziai, Hossein. *Knowledge and Illumination: A Study of Suhrawardi's Hikmat al-ishraq.* Atlanta: Scholars Press, 1990.

Sukkot

The Festival of Sukkot, or Booths, is a 7-day holiday period that begins on the 15th day of the month of Tishri, only 5 days after the conclusion of the 10 Days of Awe that begin with Rosh Hashanah and culminate with Yom Kippur. Sukkot represents quite a drastic transition, from the most solemn holy days in the Jewish year to one of the more joyous. Sukkot is immediately followed by two additional holidays, Shemini Atzeret and Simchat Torah.

Sukkot has a double thrust, in that it functions as a harvest festival, but also remembers the 40 years that the Israelites lived a nomadic life in the Sinai desert after leaving Egypt but before they made a home for themselves in the land of Canaan. During this time, believers build a temporary shelter, a booth called a *sukkah* (*sukkot*, pl.), in which they reside, a shelter that recalls the temporary homes in which the Israelites resided during the wandering.

The basic parameters and timing of the holidays are laid out in the Torah, in the book of Leviticus (23:33–44): "And the LORD spoke unto Moses, saying: Speak unto the children of Israel, saying: On the fifteenth day of this seventh month is the feast of tabernacles for seven days unto the LORD. On the first day shall be a holy convocation; ye shall do no manner of servile work. Seven days ye shall bring an offering made by fire unto the LORD; on the eighth day shall be a holy convocation unto you; and ye shall bring an offering made by fire unto the LORD; it is a day of solemn assembly; ye shall do no manner of servile work. These are the appointed seasons of the LORD, which ye shall proclaim to be holy convocations, to bring an offering made by fire unto the LORD, a burnt-offering, and a meal-offering, a sacrifice, and drink-offerings, each on its own day; beside the sabbaths of

Orthodox Jews preparing for Sukkot. (Odelia Cohen/Dreamstime.com)

the LORD, and beside your gifts, and beside all your vows, and beside all your freewill-offerings, which ye give unto the LORD. Howbeit on the fifteenth day of the seventh month, when ye have gathered in the fruits of the land, ye shall keep the feast of the LORD seven days; on the first day shall be a solemn rest, and on the eighth day shall be a solemn rest. And ye shall take you on the first day the fruit of goodly trees, branches of palm-trees, and boughs of thick trees, and willows of the brook, and ye shall rejoice before the LORD your God seven days. And ye shall keep it a feast unto the LORD seven days in the year; it is a statute forever in your generations; ye shall keep it in the seventh month. Ye shall dwell in booths seven days; all that are home-born in Israel shall dwell in booths; that your generations may know that I made the children of Israel to dwell in booths, when I brought them out of the land of Egypt: I am the LORD your God. And Moses declared unto the children of Israel the appointed seasons of the LORD."

The sukkah may be built in one's yard according to particular specifications. It must be large enough to fulfill the requirements for the week's activity and have no less than two and a half walls made of material that will not blow away in a high wind. The roof or covering must be made of something that has grown in the ground; tree branches, corn stalks, or bamboo reeds are often used. The covering materials should generally make the dwelling shady, but are left loose, neither bundled together nor tied down. They allow rain in, and those inside can see the stars. If it is raining, rainproof material may be put over the booth to protect its inner contents, but it must be removed as soon as the rain ceases.

In the modern world, quickly assembled sukkot are available for purchase, or they may be made from scratch. Canvas is often used for the walls. One should spend as much time as possible in the booth during the seven days. The first two days of the festival are treated as Sabbaths, and no work is allowed. Though the Bible calls for one day of rest, due to the problems inherent in observing the Moon (by which the timing of the holiday and getting the word out to people in the countryside was determined), two days would often be observed to make sure the holiday had been observed correctly. Such two-day observance had became a custom among Jews outside Israel, and continued even after later sages fixed the Hebrew calendar for the future based on mathematical calculations.

The first and last (Hoshana Rabbah) days of Sukkot include gatherings at the synagogue, while the five middle days include special prayers that are read by the family within their booth. The first day and the second day of the festival in the lands of the diaspora are treated as Sabbath days of rest. The middle days are less than a Sabbath, but distinct from normal workdays. One may engage in work necessary for getting through the days, including food preparation, but nothing that interferes with the holiday spirit. This time is often treated as a vacation and a time to entertain friends and visit with neighbors, and enjoy festive meals.

Integral to Sukkot is the invitation of symbolic guests to the family booth each day. These spiritual guests, or *ushpizin*, are traditionally seven biblical heroes—Abraham, Isaac, Jacob, Moses, Aaron, Joseph, and David. Among the Hasidic Jewish communities, there are seven Hasidid heroic figures who accompany the seven traditional heroes, and in the contemporary post-feminist world, seven women are also included in the invitations. It is thought that one of the traditional heroes of the faith visits the sukkot each day.

Also integral to the festival are the materials (called the four species) that are held during the Sukkot blessings in synagogue. The four species are an *etrog* (citron), a citrus fruit native to Israel, and three kinds of branches—one palm, two willow, and three myrtle branches—which are bound together and are called the *lulav*. The citron is held in one hand and the lulav in the other. As one repeats the blessing over these, the four species are waved in six directions (north, east, south, and west, and up and down), in acknowledgment that the Almighty is everywhere. Some see the four species as four types of Jews and the Sukkot blessing reminds everyone that all four are important to the community.

Closely associated with Sukkot are two adjacent but quite separate holidays, Shemini Atzeret and Simchat Torah. Because they immediately follow Sukkot, they are often incorrectly thought of as part of Sukkot. Shemini Atzeret is observed on the 22nd day of the month of Tishri, and everywhere but Israel, Simchat Torah is observed the following day. In Israel, Shemini Atzeret and Simchat Torah are observed on the same day, Tishri 22. During the two holidays, one no longer resides in the booths, although outside of Israel, some continue to reside in the sukkah on Shmini Atzeret but not on Simchat Torah. Also the four species are not used on these holidays.

Shemini Atzeret is the "assembly of the eighth day." It is explained as a time for the Jewish people to have a more intimate and exclusive celebration with the Almighty. They think of it as if God has been their host and they the guests through Sukkot. But as the time of visiting comes to an end, God asks the guests to stay an extra day, to extend their time together. The day is observed as a Sabbath, and those observing it do no work.

Simchat Torah is a day for "Rejoicing in the Torah," the first five books of the Hebrew Bible (also known as the Five Books of Moses). Through the year, at synagogue services, one reads through the entire Torah, a few chapters each week. This cycle is completed on Simchat Torah, and on that day, the last chapter of the Torah (in Deuteronomy) is read to be immediately followed by the reading of the first chapter of Genesis. The completion of the cycle is an occasion for rejoicing that occurs as people process around the synagogue carrying Torah scrolls. The service includes spirited singing and dancing in the synagogue with all the Torah scrolls, which are removed from the ark in which they normally rest.

The first day of Sukkot and the joint celebration of Shimin Atzeret and Simchat Torah are official public holidays in Israel. In the days prior to the destruction of the temple and the diaspora of the Jewish people through the Middle East and around the Mediterranean Basin, Sukkot was one of three major holidays (along with Passover and Shavuot, or the Festival of Weeks), during which Jews made a pilgrimage to Jerusalem for the celebration.

Christian Appropriation The Hebrew Bible was incorporated into the Christian Bible as the Old Testament, and is held in high esteem by most Christian denominations. In North America in the 19th century, from their reading of the books of Moses, a new appreciation of the Jewish festival cycle appeared among a small group of Christian denominations, most notably those that had emerged from the disappointed expectation of the Second Coming of Christ announced by William Miller in the 1830s. Initially, some groups adopted the seventh-day Sabbath. In the 20th century, some groups that grew out of the Church of God (Seventh-day) began to follow the Jewish liturgical year, the most notable being the Worldwide Church of God. For these groups, what they termed the Feast of Tabernacles ("tabernacle" being the common translation of sukkot in English-language Bibles) became the most important event of the year. Members of the Worldwide Church of God would save 10 percent of their income to enjoy a week of feasting with fellow church members at campgrounds around North America and increasingly other countries to which the church spread. The money would be spent on fine camping equipment and fine food and given in offerings at the church meetings.

In the 1990s, the Worldwide Church of God went through a radical change of belief and practice that included the abandonment of its belief in the Old Testament festival cycle. It lost most of its members to several splinter groups such as the United Church of God and the Philadelphia Church of God, and an uncounted number of smaller groups, which continue this Christianized version of the Feast of Tabernacles.

Sukkot is also celebrated among the different Messianic Jewish groups that emerged in the 1970s. These groups consider themselves to be Jews who have discovered that Jesus Christ (whom they refer to by his Hebrew name Yashua) to be the Messiah, a claim rejected by all mainstream Jewish groups. Messianic Jews continue as much of Jewish culture, including synagogue ritual, that they find compatible with their Christian faith and reinterpret Jewish holidays as her-

alding Christianity. They also invite Gentile Christians to celebrations as a means of educating them about their Jewish heritage.

J. Gordon Melton

See also: Days of Awe; Hasidism; Judaism; Rosh Hashanah; Worldwide Church of God; Yom Kippur.

References
Eckstein, Yecheil. *What You Should Know About Jews and Judaism.* Waco, TX: Word Books, 1984.
Greenberg, Irving. *The Jewish Way: Living the Holidays.* New York: Jason Aronson, 1998.
Posner, Raphael, Uri Kaploun, and Sherman Cohen, eds. *Jewish Liturgy: Prayer and Synagogue Service through the Ages.* New York: Leon Amiel Publisher/Jerusalem: Keter Publishing House, 1975.
Schauss, Hayyim. *The Jewish Festivals: A Guide to Their History and Observance.* New York: Schocken, 1996.

Sukyo Mahikari

Sukyo Mahikari is a Japanese new religion founded in 1959 by Okada Yoshikazu (1901–1974), a former member of the imperial guard who suffered for many years from physical afflictions and economic misfortunes.

On the night of February 27, 1959, Okada received a vision of God, who called him with the words: "Get up. Change your name to Kotama [Jewel of Light]. Raise your hand. Trials and tribulations are coming." This experience marked the beginning of the movement that was called Sekai Mahikari Bunmei Kyodan. Okada came to be called Sukuinushisama (Lord Savior) and assumed a divine status in the movement as the original mediator of the saving and healing light of God. Between 1959 and 1967, Okada is said to have received a series of 57 revelations that were collected and published for the first time in Japanese in 1969 as the sacred scripture of the movement, called the Goseigen. From the end of the 1960s, Mahikari underwent a rapid growth in Japan, and in the early 1970s the first centers were opened outside of Japan. In 1972 a center was opened in Paris, and from there missionaries spread all over Europe, North and South America, and

Africa. After the founder died in 1974, the movement split. One group continued the original name of the movement and was led by one of the closest disciples of Okada, Sekiguchi Sakae (1909–1994). The other group followed the leadership of the adopted daughter of the founder, Okada Keiju (Sukuinushisama), and took the name Sukyo Mahikari. The latter has become the larger of the two groups and is usually the organization generally associated with the name Mahikari. The exact number of members in the movement is kept a strict secret, but it may be between 500,000 and 1 million. The movement claims about 1,200 centers in 80 countries.

The central focus of the movement is the practice of *okiyome*, which consists of the transmission of divine light through the palm of the hand of an initiate to another person or to any animate or inanimate object in need of purification or protection. This practice was largely inherited from Sekai Kyusei Kyo, another 20th-century Japanese religion of which Okada had previously been a member. At the basis of this practice lies the belief that most afflictions and misfortunes are caused by spirit possession, resulting from negative karmic actions in this or in a past life. It is the forehead that is regarded as the seat of possessing spirits and that is the main focus of the practice of okiyome. The power to transmit the Light resides in an amulet, called the *omitama*, which is formally received at the end of the initiation course and which is surrounded by numerous taboos.

Besides okiyome, which can (and should) be practiced at any time and place, members are also enjoined to participate in monthly rituals, called *mimatsuri*, and in yearly spring and autumn festivals. The latter take place at the central shrine (the Suza) in Takayama, Japan, and members are encouraged to make the pilgrimage to the place of birth of the movement and if possible participate in these events. Since spirit possession is the origin of all evil, another important ritual practice in the movement consists of the worship of ancestors every morning and evening at a private altar in the home.

The teachings of Sukyo Mahikari are transmitted in three initiation courses, each requiring an increasing commitment to the movement. The elementary teachings, which constitute the heart of the movement, focus on the etiology of diseases and misfortunes. Although the emphasis is on the notion of possession, ethical principles (mostly of Confucian origin) are inculcated as a means to avoid spirit possession. The advanced courses focus mostly on sacred history and on the millenaristic and nationalistic beliefs of Mahikari. Within the pantheon of Gods and spirits of Mahikari, one God, called Mioyamotosumahikariomikamisama (or Su-God), is worshipped as the origin of creation and salvation. It is to this God that most prayers are addressed.

Sukyo Mahikari is organized as a theocracy, with the leader, called Oshienushisama, as its absolute authority. The world is organized in different regions (Sidobus) encompassing centers of different sizes, from a small local center called *han*, to a fully developed *dojo*. The movement is supported by an elaborate system of donations: monthly donations to the center, donations for particular projects undertaken by the movement, and donations in thanksgiving for particular blessings or for receiving light at every visit to the dojo.

Sukyo Mahikari
2-596-1 Kamiokamoto-machi
Takayama City
Gifu Prefecture
Japan

Catherine Cornille

See also: Sekai Kyusei Kyo.

References

Cornille, Catherine. "The Phoenix Flies West: The Dynamics of Inculturation of Mahikari in Western Europe." *Japanese Journal for Religious Studies* 18, nos. 2–3 (1991): 265–285.

Davis, Winston. *Dojo: Magic and Exorcism in Modern Japan.* Stanford, CA: Stanford University Press, 1980.

McVeigh, Brian. *Spirits, Selves and Subjectivity in a Japanese New Religion: The Cultural Psychology of Belief in Shukyo Mahikari.* Lewiston, NY: Edwin Mellen Press, 1997.

Tebecis, Andris. *Is the Future in Our Hands? My Experiences with Sukyo Mahikari.* Sandy, UT: Sunrise Press, 2004.

Young, Richard. "Magic and Morality in Modern Japanese Exorcistic Technologies." *Japanese Journal of Religious Studies* 17 (1990): 29–50.

Suleiman I

1494–1566

Suleiman I, known in the West as Suleiman the Magnificent, ruled the Ottoman Empire for almost half a century (1520–1566), during which time it greatly expanded through North Africa, across the Middle East, and into Central Europe. He proved a wise and knowledgeable ruler, whose broad talents manifested in his military prowess, the rewriting of the Ottoman legal system, his attempts to rule with justice and equity, his empire's patronage of the arts, and his own writing of poetry. The Ottoman Empire he built would last for another four centuries and revive the glories of the Islamic Califa originally established in the seventh century.

Suleiman was born in Trabzon, most likely on November 6, 1494, the son of Selim I (ca. 1470–1520) and grandson of Bayezid II (r. 1481–1512), then the sultan of the Ottoman Empire. His grandfather abdicated in favor of his father in 1512. As a child, Suleiman had begun the broad studies that would prepare him to rule. He served as a governor in his father's empire from the age of 17 and became the sultan following his father's untimely death in 1520. Suleiman was but 25 years old.

Once on the throne, Suleiman prepared to move against Belgrade (Serbia), left in Christian hands by Mehmed II (r. 1451–1481), who had turned from interest in Europe after two defeats in 1462 and 1475. Belgrade fell to Suleiman in August 1521. He next moved against Hungary, which was finally defeated in 1526 at the Battle of Mohács. War continued, with the Hapsburgs of Austria forming the front line of defense of Europe. After briefly relinquishing control of Hungary, in 1529, Suleiman retook it and marched on Vienna, the last major obstacle to Western Europe. He was unsuccessful in 1529 and again in 1532, after which, like his grandfather, he turned his attention elsewhere.

The Safavid rule in Persia (Iran) represented the Shia Muslim community over against the Hanafite

Portrait of the Ottoman sultan Suleiman I, also called Suleiman the Magnificent. (Time & Life Pictures/Getty Images)

Sunni Islam that held sway in the Ottoman Empire. A source of tension through the early years of Suleiman's rule, in 1535, Suleiman moved against it and quickly took Bagdad. He would spend the next two decades fighting the Safavid ruler, slowly taking possession of Georgia, Azerbaijan, Iraq, and southern Persia, but unable to finally bring an end to the Safavid rule.

Simultaneously, Suleiman also moved to dominate the waters of the eastern Mediterranean. He placed his navy in the hands of Admiral Khair ad Din, better known as Barbarossa. Suleiman's treaty with Francis I of France and Barbarossa's victory over Spain at the Battle of Preveza secured Ottoman control in the eastern Mediterranean for the remainder of Suleiman's rule.

Suleiman supported France in its 1544 war with Spain, which occasioned Suleiman's consolidation of power across the northern coast of Africa. Barbarossa also led forces against Spain, from whom his combined army and navy forces took Naples.

Suleiman's empire was structured around *shariah*, the law derived from the Koran; however, there was a large body of law that operated in areas not specifically covered by shariah. Through the 1530s, Suleiman collected all the legislation issued by his predecessors who had established the empire. He completely revised the legal system and issued a unified code for the empire. Included in his edicts were statutes raising the status of his Christian subjects. He also expanded the education system built around schools attached to the larger mosques. Suleiman's reforms remained in place through the remaining centuries of Ottoman rule.

Suleiman also left his mark architecturally. He oversaw renovations of the Dome of the Rock and the Kaaba, Islam's most holy site at the mosque in Mecca, and promoted the building of two new major mosques —the Selimiye Mosque in Edime (Turkey) and the Suleymaniye Mosque in Istanbul.

At the end of his life, Suleiman again turned his attention to Hungary, but died in 1566, just two days before his army won the Battle of Szigetvar (Hungary). He was buried in a mausoleum adjacent to the Suleymaniye Mosque, near the tomb of one of his wives, the mother of his son and successor, Selim II (r. 1566–1574).

At the time of Suleiman's death, the Ottoman Empire stretched from Algeria along the coast of North Africa to Eritrea. It included Palestine and much of present-day Saudi Arabia. It extended northward through the Balkans into Hungary and eastward around the Black Sea through the Caucasian Mountains into northern Persia (Iran).

J. Gordon Melton

See also: Istanbul; Mecca; Mosques.

References

Bridge, Anthony. *Suleiman the Magnificent, Scourge of Heaven*. New York: F. Watts, 1983.

Clot, Andre. *Suleiman the Magnificent*. London: Saqi Books, 2004.

Downey, Fairfax Davis. *The Grand Turke, Suleyman the Magnificent, Sultan of the Ottomans*. New York: Minton, Balch & Company, 1929.

Greenblatt, Miriam. *Süleyman the Magnificent and the Ottoman Empire*. New York: Benchmark Books, 2003.

Sulpicians

The Sulpicians, or the Order of Saint Sulpice, is a Roman Catholic organization that resembles a religious order but is in fact a society of apostolic life, an association whose members come together for a specific purpose. It differs from religious orders in that members (especially those in the priesthood) do not take additional vows, and priests remain under the primary jurisdiction of their diocesan bishop rather than the organization. In the Sulpicians, members typically do not join at the beginning of their priesthood career, but after some time serving in the priesthood and gaining experience.

The Sulpicians trace their beginning to France in the 1630s and the work of Jean Jacques Olier (1608–1657). Olier, a well-educated man from a well-to-do family, experienced a miraculous healing of an eye condition. Already headed for the priesthood, he forsook his aristocratic position in favor of service to the poor. He subsequently became involved with a church renewal movement led by people such as Vincent de Paul (1581–1660), later canonized as a saint; theologian Charles de Condren (1588–1641); and Mother Agnes of Jesus (Saint Agnes of Langeac, 1602–1634). Olier saw a need for the development of a sound spiritual life and better educational level among the clergy and to that end in 1641 he established a seminary. Shortly thereafter he was assigned as the parish priest of the Church of St. Sulpice in Paris and he relocated his seminary at the church. The Order of Saint Sulpice began with his inviting several priests to join him and assist in his work.

Olier announced the Society of the Priests of the Seminary of Saint Sulpice to the French bishops, who were informed that the group stood ready to educate and provide spiritual formation (training in the spiritual life) to candidates for the priesthood. They would train the priests and then return them to their home dioceses. This new seminary thus varied from the standard program of diocesan seminaries, which accepted teenagers who had as yet not decided to enter the priesthood. The Sulpicians were now dedicated to their narrow but crucial task, and proved themselves capable. Their work steadily expanded.

As early as 1657 Olier sent four priests to Montreal, then still a miniscule community with an uncertain future. Almost immediately, they assumed leadership of the town and the surrounding countryside and began, along with their religious work, directing settlers arriving in the slowly growing community. They encouraged settlers to create new villages at spots around the city in the hope that they would serve as a first line of defense, the surrounding land being inhabited by hostile Native Canadians. The Canadian work was supplemented by priests who fled France in the wake of the French Revolution (1789–1799). Meanwhile, the work in France suffered greatly, but survived,

In 1790, Bishop John Carroll reached out to the Sulpicians to assist building the church in the United States. In the wake of the American Revolution, he had only 35 priests to serve some 30,000 laypeople in his diocese. The Sulpicians arrived in 1791 to open what was to become St. Mary's Seminary. It was the first institution of higher learning sponsored by Roman Catholics in America. The seminary, relocated to Emmetsburg, Maryland, would later provide a nurturing environment for Sister Elizabeth Seton (1774–1821) as she founded Saint Joseph's Academy and Free School and then her own order, the Sisters of Charity. The order has continued to work at St. Mary's, which during the pontificate of Pope Pius VII was the first American school with a pontifical faculty (with the right to grant degrees in the name of the Holy See).

In the second decade of the 19th century, Mary Elizabeth Lange (1784–1882), an African from Haiti, settled in Baltimore as a refugee. Here she met the Sulpician priest Father James Hector Joubert. Joubert worked with Lange, who had a small inheritance, in the founding of a community of African American women to provide education for African American children. The result was the formation of the first order founded and led by African American women, the Oblate Sisters of Providence.

The work of the Sulpicians is anchored in a spiritual life originally given shape by Charles de Condren, which attempts to integrate attention to the Eucharist, liturgical prayer, meditation, and the daily routine of prayers in the Divine Office with the vow taken by priests to live a life of celibacy, obedience, and simplicity of life. At the various seminaries where the Sulpicians work, they live among the seminarians and attempt to make themselves available for teaching spiritual formation by both instruction and the example of their own lives.

Today, the Sulpicians are organized into three provinces: France, Canada, and the United States. The French provincial house remains in Paris, and the Sulpicians still oversee the parishes of Saint Sulpice and Notre Dame de Pauvres, and members are scattered among various French catholic seminaries. In Canada, the Order operates primarily out of the seminaries in Montreal and Edmonton. In the United States, the Order oversees St. Mary's Seminary in Baltimore, Maryland; St. Patrick's Seminary in Menlo, California; and the Theological College, Washington, D.C., and administers the continuing education programs in spiritual formation through the Center for Continuing Formation at St. Mary's Seminary in Baltimore and the Vatican II Institute at St. Patrick's Seminary in California. Individual Sulpicians are at work in a number of diocesan seminaries and around the world in Brazil, Colombia, Japan, Vietnam, and various French-speaking African nations. There are at present more than 300 priests who are full members of the Order.

J. Gordon Melton

See also: Roman Catholic Church.

References

Hebermann, Charles George. *The Sulpicians in the United States*. Ithaca, NY: Cornell University Library, 2009 (originally published 1916).

Kauffman, Christopher J. *Tradition and Transformation in Catholic Culture: The Priests of Saint Sulpice in the United States from 1791 to the Present*. New York: Macmillan, 1988.

Thompson, Edward Healy. *Life of M. Olier: Founder of the Seminary of St. Sulpice*. London: Burns and Lambert, 1861.

Sumarah

Sumarah is a Javanese word referring to the condition of total surrender. Thus the name Paguyuban Sumarah, for the Indonesian spiritual association, is also a description of its practice. The aim of meditation, termed *sujud* in Indonesia, is to surrender every aspect of personal being so the self functions as a vehicle for God's will. Sumarah is currently an association of about 6,000. The seat of the organization, the Dewan Pimpinan Pusat (DPP), is in Jakarta. Regional centers exist in all major Javanese cities, and in a few regions, notably Madiun, a large number of villagers have joined. Sumarah is not identified with any religion. Although most members are Muslim, there are also Buddhist and Christian followers.

Sumarah is a practice. It has no canon of teachings, no sacred texts, and no sacred sites or buildings. There is no "guru," and the direction of attention in meditation is "inward"; the authority that meditators are meant to attend to is that of the "true teacher" (*guru sejati* or *hakiki*) inside. Nevertheless, guidance (*tuntunan*) within weekly group sessions is a critical vehicle for practice. Guides, termed *pamong*, speak spontaneously through attunement to those participating. All Sumarah members lead normal working and family lives. The aim of practice is not isolation from society but a balance of outer (*lahir*) and inner (*batin*) being in every moment.

The origins of Sumarah lie in the revelatory experiences (*wahyu sumarah*) of Sukinohartono in 1935. Pak Kino, as he was called, was born at the turn of the century near the court city of Yogyakarta. He worked as a court attendant and bank clerk until his death in 1970. After his revelation a circle of friends began to share the practice, so that by 1940 the seeds of an organization had been sown through most of Central and East Java. Those seeds germinated during World War II under Japanese occupation. During the revolutionary struggle of the late 1940s, an influx of many new and younger members gave rise to the need for a formal organization.

Just as Indonesia gained independence, the association crystallized into what is now Paguyuban Sumarah, usually referred to as just Sumarah. From 1950 until 1966 the formal organization was led by Dr. Surono and centered in Yogyakarta. From 1966 until his death in 1997, the most important leader was Arymurthy in Jakarta. Throughout the period since independence, Sumarah has been one of the several dozen most prominent national movements within the sphere of Javanism (*kejawen*, earlier also termed *kebatinan*). Although not one of the largest movements, it has been especially important nationally because its leaders have been simultaneously active in umbrella organizations that represent kebatinan on the national scene.

Although there have been several hundred international practitioners since 1971, there is no international organization.

DPP Paguyuban Sumarah
Yayasan Sukino
Pendopo Sumarah
Gang Setiyaki, Wirobrajan
Yogyakarta
Indonesia

J. Gordon Melton

See also: Islam; Javanism; Meditation; Sufism.

References

Howe, David. "Sumarah: A Study of the Art of Living." Ph.D. diss., University of North Carolina, 1980.

Stang, Paul. "Inner Dimensions of the Indonesian Revolution." In *Autonomous Histories, Particular Truths*, edited by Laurie Sears. Madison: University of Wisconsin/Center for Southeast Asian Studies, 1993.

Stang, Paul. *Politik Perhatian: Rasa dalam Kebudayaan Jawa.* Yogyakarta, Indonesia: Lembaga Kajian Islam dan Sosial, 1998.

Summer Solstice

The longest day of the year, Summer Solstice, along with the related Winter Solstice, was among the earliest astronomical phenomena observed by people observing the sky and relating what they saw to the changing weather and agricultural seasons. In the Northern Hemisphere, if one observes the rising Sun in the

People dance at Stonehenge in southern England, June 20, 2008, in anticipation of the moment when the sun rises over the stones for the Summer Solstice. (AP/Wide World Photos)

spring, it appears to rise a little bit farther north day by day until it reaches a point in the last half of June where the northern drift stops. After what appears to be a pause, it begins to rise bit by bit farther south each day. In the Southern Hemisphere, of course, the drift is exactly opposite. The Summer Solstice is the point at which the drift stops and pauses before starting in the opposite direction. The Summer Solstice, usually June 21 on the Common Era calendar, occurs in the midst of the northern growing season—after planting has been completed but prior to the beginning of the harvest.

Summer Solstice was celebrated in most ancient cultures. However, most of these celebrations were abandoned as the major world religions spread and ab-

sorbed the thousands of indigenous religions. Christianity designated June 24 (the Summer Solstice on the old Julian calendar, and six months prior to Christmas) as the birthday of John the Baptist, who was believed to have been born six months prior to the birth of Jesus. John's birthday, or Midsummer Day, is observed by the Roman Catholic Church, the Eastern Orthodox churches, and a few Protestant churches. Midsummer Day, blending Christian themes and Pagan practices, is celebrated across Europe and is an official holiday in several countries, including Latvia and Estonia.

The last half of the 20th century saw the founding of the neo-Pagan movement, which has as its largest visible segment the Wiccan or Witchcraft movement. This movement was inspired by the ancient Paganism of Northern and Western Europe and posed eight equally positioned holidays that anchored its liturgical year. The Summer Solstice was one of the eight Pagan/Wiccan festivals. For modern neo-Paganism (and accompanying Pagan revivalist movements in Europe), the Summer Solstice has become one of its most important holidays and a time for large outdoor gatherings. As relatively little is known about either the practices or the details of belief of the ancient Pagans, a non-literary people, the new Pagans have been able to pour content into their ritual and practice from a variety of sources, most notably Western Esotericism.

In the 18th century, England saw the founding of two organizations that became precursors of the modern neo-Pagan movement, the Druids. As early as 1649, John Aubrey (1626–1697) suggested that the ancient Druids discovered by Julius Caesar when he came to Briton, oversaw the building of Stonehenge, a view later championed by William Stukeley (1687–1765), who it appears founded the first modern Druid revivalist group in 1717. A more permanent group, the Ancient Order of Druids, was founded in 1781 by Henry Hurle. Over the years, several additional Druid groups were formed and died. By 1955 only one group, the British Circle of the Universal Bond, survived. It claimed to be the true descendant of the 18th-century groups, and thus inherited the right to conduct the Summer Solstice celebrations that had become an annual event at Stonehenge.

The claims of the Druids were caught up in the breakthrough archaeological work on Stonehenge in the 1960s, when some scholars discovered that the placement of some of the stones, including those in the very center and the heel stones far outside, were arranged in such a way as to point to major astronomical occurrences, most notably the apparent movement of the Sun in the sky between the Summer and Winter solstices. This discovery raised questions of how Stonehenge functioned in the ancient agricultural cycle of the British Isles and especially how the knowledge of the solstices and equinoxes were integrated into the religious thinking of British Pagans. Druids and Wiccans immediately seized the new archaeological insights and began using them as foundational information for their practice. The Druids saw it as further confirmation of their claims to use Stonehenge for religious rituals.

As Stonehenge passed into the care and control of the British government, and was fenced off from visitors to prevent further damage, the Druids have been the only outsiders to gain access to the site, each year on the morning of the Summer Solstice, when they ritually greet the rising Sun. Access to Stonehenge was withdrawn in 1985, when revilers and police clashed, but was reinstituted in 2000. In 2009, some 35,000 people showed up for the Summer Solstice celebration.

J. Gordon Melton

See also: Calendars, Religious; Common Era Calendar; Eastern Orthodoxy; Roman Catholic Church; Stonehenge; Wiccan Religion; Winter Solstice.

References

Carr-Gomm, Philip. *The Druid Tradition*. Shaftesbury, UK: Element, 1991.

Crowey, Vivianne. *The Principles of Paganism*. London: Thorsons, 1996.

Farrar, Janet, and Stewart Farrar. *A Witches Bible Complete*. New York: Magickal Child, 1984.

Hawkins, Gerald S., and John B. White. *Stonehenge Decoded*. New York: Barnes & Noble, 1993.

Matthews, John, ed. *The Druid Sourcebook*. London: Blandford, 1887.

Matthews, John, ed. *The Summer Solstice: Celebrating the Journey of the Sun from May Day to Harvest*. Wheaton, IL: Quest Books, 2002.

Sunni Islam

See Islam.

■ Suriname

The South American nation of Suriname (formerly known as Dutch Guiana) is located along the Atlantic Ocean between British Guyana and French Guinea. Its southern border is shared with Brazil. The country includes 62,323 square miles of territory. It is the smallest sovereign state in South America in both area and population. Its 480,000 citizens (2009) have tended to concentrate along the narrow coastal plain rather than the remote interior region. The capital of the Republic of Suriname is Paramaribo (population 240,000), where half of the population resides; it is located in the northern part of the country on the Atlantic coast.

Suriname is famous for the outstanding biodiversity of its pristine Amazonian rainforests in the southern region of the country. The Central Suriname Nature Reserve, noted for its flora and fauna, is the biggest and one of the most popular reserves. The Brownsberg Nature Park overlooks the Brokopondo Reservoir, one of the largest man-made lakes in the world.

Surinam is one of the most ethnically diverse nations in South America. The official language of Suriname is Dutch, but most Surinamers can communicate with one another through the use of the lingua franca, Sranantongo, a local language originally spoken by the Creole population. Other languages spoken are Hindi, Javanese, Chinese (Hakka and Mandarin), English, and other tribal languages of the Amerindians and the Bush Negroes (Maroons).

There is a strong correlation between ethnicity and religious faith in Surinam. Many political parties, including six of the eight governing coalition parties, have strong ethnic ties, and their members tend to adhere to or practice a single faith. For example, within the governing coalition, the majority of members of the mostly ethnic-Creole National Party of Suriname (NPS) are Moravian, members of the mostly ethnic-Indian United Reformed Party are Hindu, and those of the mostly ethnic-Javanese Pertjaja Luhur Party tend to be Muslim. It is also the case that political parties have no requirement that party leaders or members adhere to a particular religion. The nation's president, for example, is both the leader of the NPS and a practicing Roman Catholic.

Based on the 2004 census of population, religious affiliation is distributed as follows: Hindu 27.4 percent, Protestant 25.2 percent (predominantly Moravian), Roman Catholic 22.8 percent, Muslim 19.6 percent, and other religions/none 5 percent. The Constitution provides for freedom of religion, and other laws and policies contributed to the generally free practice of religion. The law at all levels protects this right in full against abuse, by either governmental or private actors.

The Surinamese population is composed of many ethnic and religious groups, each of which has contributed to Surinam's unique cultural heritage. The largest ethnic group is the Hindustani, which makes up 27 percent of the population; it is composed of descendants of contract-laborers from India (1873–1916, about 34,000 arrived in 64 shiploads) and is predominantly Hindu with a minority of Muslims.

The Creoles (also known as Afro-Surinamese), about 18 percent of the population, are the descendants of African slaves (250,000 were imported between 1612 and 1818) and European settlers, mainly of Dutch origin, and reside on the northern coast. They are largely Christian (both Catholic and Protestant) but also practitioners of the Winti religion and/or Myalism-Obeah, which are folk religions of West African origin, similar in some respects to Vodou in Haiti and Santeria in Cuba and Puerto Rico, but are less syncretistic with Christianity. These so-called slave religions were considered subversive in colonial times, because they served as the inspiration and catalyst for revolt against slave owners and colonial authorities in an oppressive slavery system.

The Bush Negroes, or Maroons, about 15 percent of the population, are descendants of run-away African slaves who fled the coastal plantations in the 1660s and took refuge in the dense tropical forests, where they continue to live in relative isolation and preserve their ancient culture and religious traditions. They are grouped in six politically distinct peoples (Aluku-Boni, Kwinti, Matawai, Ndjuka, Saramaka, and Paramaka). The Maroons have an extremely elaborate ritual life that is totally integrated with their matrilineal social organization.

The Javanese, about 15 percent of the population, are descendants of contract-laborers from the Dutch East Indies (about 33,000 between 1890 and 1939) and are predominantly Muslim. Like the Chinese and Hindustanis, most of them left the plantations after their labor contracts ended and started small farms, at a time when the plantations were declining in importance for the nation's economy: the number of sugar plantations decreased from 80 in 1863 to only 4 in 1940.

Amerindians are 3.7 percent of the population, Chinese are 1.8 percent, and the remaining 12.5 percent are of mixed race: all of the ethnic groups described above mixed with descendants of Europeans and Middle Easterners—Dutch, Portuguese (mainly from Madeira), Lebanese, Syrian, and Jewish immigrants.

A large number of faiths, including U.S.-based church groups, have established missionary programs throughout the country since World War II. It is estimated that nearly 90 percent of the U.S. missionaries are affiliated with Baptist church associations. The Inter-Religious Council (IRC) was formed in 1989 in Paramaribo, composed of representatives from various groups, with monthly meetings to discuss and plan ecumenical activities. The IRC is also a member of the Religions for Peace Caribbean Inter-religious Network, which is a coalition of national inter-religious councils and regional religious organizations in the Caribbean region, dedicated to inter-religious cooperation for conflict transformation, peace building, and sustainable development.

Suriname was originally settled around 3000 BCE by the Arawak and later by the Carib Amerindian peoples, who had developed a culture based on hunting, fishing, and gathering by the time that Christopher Columbus (1451–1506) navigated the coastline in 1498. The territory was formally claimed by Spain in 1593, but the first European settlement did not take place until 1616, when the Dutch arrived at the mouths of several rivers between present-day Georgetown, Guyana, and Cayenne, French Guiana. The first Dutch settlement began in 1616 in this region.

In 1667, by the Treaty of Breda that ended the Second Anglo-Dutch War (1665–1667), Suriname became a Dutch colony, at about the same time that the

Dutch colony of New Amsterdam (founded in North America in 1625) was ceded to the English (1664–1674) and was renamed New York City. However, the territory of Suriname was contested by Britain, who claimed settlement rights; in 1651, about 100 Englishmen from Barbados arrived with their slaves to establish a plantation colony, which was the first permanent settlement in the territory.

During the Dutch and English colonial periods, the colonists developed an agricultural economy that produced sugar, coffee, cacao, and cotton on more than 400 plantations. In the beginning, manual labor was provided by Amerindians and after 1640 by African slaves. After the final abolition of slavery by the Dutch in 1863, many former Negro slaves abandoned the plantations and the owners were faced with a shortage of manual labor. Consequently, the Dutch colonial authorities approved the importation of Chinese contract-laborers in 1853, followed by East Indians (from India) as "indentured servants" between 1873 and 1916, and, later, by Javanese from the Dutch East Indies (now, Indonesia) between 1894 and 1939. The contract-laborers had to work for five years to pay plantation owners for the cost of their ship fare to Surinam. After the Chinese, East Indian, and Javanese laborers were free of their contract obligations, they were able to return to their home countries or renew their contracts to work in Surinam for real wages. About one-third of the East Indian laborers returned to India after their initial five-year contract ended. Those who chose to remain in Suriname were given land, a bonus payment from the government, and special loans to assist them in beginning a new life as independent farmers. In 1922, Suriname became part of the Kingdom of the Netherlands; and, in 1927, the contract-labor immigrants became eligible for Dutch citizenship.

By the beginning of the 20th century, Suriname was home to a complex mixture of ethnic groups and religious traditions. These various ethnic groups tended to remain separate, divided both by ethnic tradition and by language. The divisions became important as the country moved toward independence, and they served as an obstacle to the development of a sense of national consciousness that delayed the move from colonial status until 1975.

Following independence, approximately one-third of the population took the opportunity to move to the Netherlands, taking advantage of their Dutch citizenship. After a period of government instability in the 1980s, including several coups, a democratic system was put in place in 1990. It is estimated that around 250,000 people of Surinamese descent currently live in the Netherlands, while thousands more live in the Dutch West Indies, the United States, and countries neighboring Suriname.

The importation of East Indians to Suriname further complicated the nation's social stratification system, in which "whites" (plantation owners and overseers, owners of merchant houses, and administrators), Creoles (in a variety of intermediate occupations), and former Negro slaves (mainly agricultural workers or peasants) formed a hierarchy in that order. The East Indian contract-laborers (mostly lower-class and "untouchables") also were placed at the lowest level of the social order, because they occupied agricultural jobs vacated by freed slaves.

East Indian immigrants in Suriname, called "coolies" by the larger society, tended to maintain their ancient cultural values brought with them from India (mainly from the United Provinces of India, West Bihar, and the Ganges Plains of North India), although they had different linguistic, caste, socio-economic, ecological, cultural, and religious traditions. However, their ethnic identity as Hindustanis was based on a concept of "Mother India," which the East Indian immigrants to Suriname considered the place of origin of their common cultural and religious traditions. Consequently, in Surinam, they formed a new ethnic group within a pluralistic society and developed a new consciousness as "Hindustanis," which enabled them to effectively resist the process of cultural and racial syncretism later. However, all East Indians, whether or not they were born in Suriname, were considered aliens until granted citizenship in 1927.

The historical ethnic division of labor broke down during the 20th century, especially after World War II (1939–1945) and the achievement of independence (1975). New avenues of economic competition have emerged in business, the government bureaucracy, and the professions. However, the stereotypes originally derived from the ethnic division of labor and internalized by the subjugated groups, and the attitudes associated with it, are still prevalent. Nevertheless, the considerable wealth of many East Indians in Suriname today attests to their success in overcoming social discrimination and political alienation and achieving upward social mobility and a higher standard of living than their predecessors. The pressure to maintain traditional marriage and family values is very strong among the Hindustanis, but intermarriage with other ethnic groups has resulted in an erosion of those values.

Language is an important element of ethnic identity. Therefore, the efforts by Suriname's Hindustani community to revive the Hindi (also called Sarnami) language, beginning in the 1950s, were viewed as a conscious attempt to recover its distinctive ethnic heritage. Several religious and cultural organizations have played an important role in this revitalization process.

Christianity Christianity was introduced to Suriname in 1683 with the arrival of several Roman Catholic priests. However, they stayed only for four years. Priests came again in 1786, but again for only a brief stay. Then in 1735, permanent Christian work was launched by the German Moravian Brethren. The Moravian Church in Suriname now includes more than 10 percent of the country's 476,000 people.

The Evangelical Lutheran Church in the Kingdom of the Netherlands and the Reformed Churches of the Netherlands (now the Protestant Church in the Netherlands) established work in 1741 and 1750, respectively, but primarily served the white residents and lost many members after independence in 1975. A variety of other Protestant and Free churches have established work in Surinam, but none have more than a few thousand members each.

The Suriname Committee of Christian Churches dates to 1960. It is affiliated with the World Council of Churches (WCC) and includes the Moravian, Dutch Reformed, Lutheran, and Roman Catholic churches.

After two Catholic priests from the Netherlands settled in the colony in 1817 and established the Prefecture Apostolic of Dutch Guyana-Suriname, the Roman Catholic Church soon had a large following among the general population. The Vicariate Apostolic of Dutch Guiana, with its seat at Paramaribo, was established in 1842 and missionary work was assigned to the Redemptorists (Congregatio Sanctissimi Redemptoris) by the Holy See. In 1842, there were only about 13,300 Roman Catholics in Suriname.

The first bishop of the Diocese of Surinam was consecrated in 1958. In 1950, there were only 5 parishes that were served by 42 religious priests, in addition to 91 male religious and 181 female religious workers. Only five bishops (all Dutch) have headed the Diocese since 1907, and the current leader is Bishop Wilhelmus Adrianus Josephus Maria de Bekker (appointed in 2004).

The Diocese of Surinam is a jurisdiction of the Archdiocese of Port of Spain (Trinidad). Today, about 23 percent of the population is Roman Catholic. In 2004, there were 31 Catholic parishes in Suriname, served by 6 diocesan and 16 religious priests, assisted by 20 male religious and 11 female religious workers. There has been a serious decline in the quality of pastoral care given to the Catholic community as a result of the decline in the number of Catholic priests since the mid-1960s (from 57 priests in 1966 to 22 priests in 2004) and religious workers (from 98 male and 201 female religious in 1966 to 20 male and 11 female religious in 2004).

Traditionally, Catholic religious devotion in Suriname is a sphere of activity dominated by women and children, whereas men were not expected to show much concern about religion. This trend has been strengthened by the role of church-run public schools administered by the Roman Catholic Church in partnership with the government.

Prior to independence in 1975, most of the religious schools in Suriname were operated by the Roman Catholic Church, which provided all the needed funding with the exception of teachers' salaries and a small maintenance stipend that was provided by the government. The government educational system subsidized many of the primary and secondary schools established and managed by religious organizations; these were considered public schools and the teachers were considered public servants. Consequently, the Roman Catholic Church played an important role in the socialization process by providing religious and moral

SURINAME

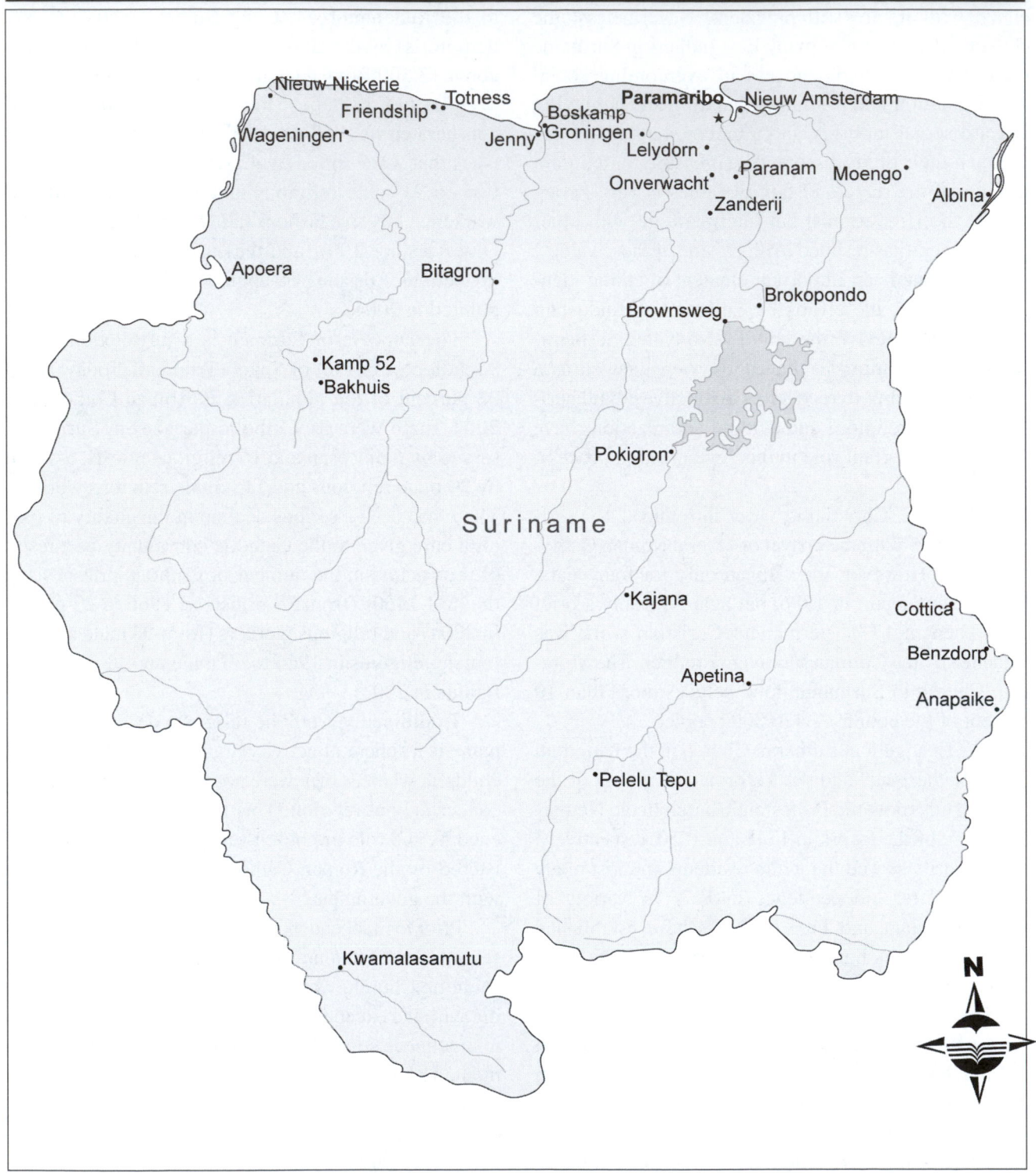

instruction to a diversity of ethnic groups. School attendance is compulsory for all children until 12 years of age.

Particularly influential has been the important role played by the Roman Catholic Church in preparing leaders of the nationalistic movement in the post–World War II period. The influence of Roman Catholic social thought has continued to affect Surinamese political life until the present, mainly through church-run primary and secondary schools.

The Protestant movement in Suriname is composed of about 20 denominations, the oldest of which is the Dutch Reformed Church, founded in 1668, now called the Reformed Church in Suriname. At the beginning it was a church for the Dutch colonists and most church activities took place in Paramaribo and around the various plantations in the countryside. Until the 1850s, Surinam (Dutch Guiana) was a Dutch-speaking state church, with the state paying for pastors and church upkeep, and existed almost exclusively for the elite class. After the 1850s this denomination opened itself to the lower classes and to the African slaves; the latter used a Pidgin English in worship services. The central church building in the capital city still serves as the auditorium of the University of Suriname, and it was there that the first president of the country took the oath of office when Suriname became an independent state in 1975.

The German Moravian Brethren (Unitas Fratrum) arrived in 1735 to conduct missionary work among the Arawak Indians near Saron on the lower Saramacca River. Between 1762 and 1813, they also engaged in missionary work among the Maroons (Saramakas) in the headwaters of the Gran Rio and, after 1830, among African plantation slaves, with whom they previously were prohibited from evangelizing. In 1851, they abandoned their work among the Saramakas due to the unhealthy climate and few conversions; then they turned their attention to another Maroon group, the Ndjukas, who were living near Koffiekamp on Sara Creek in the interior.

The Moravian missionaries received only enough money from the mother church in Germany to take them to their port of departure in Europe and had to work for their ocean passage. After arriving in Suriname, they worked at whatever occupation would pro-

vide their necessary food and clothing: picking coffee, repairing shoes, dressmaking, gardening, and working in construction. These lay missionaries were successful in establishing many local congregations among the lower classes and the slave population. Today, the Moravian Church is the largest Protestant denomination in Suriname in terms of adherents.

The Dutch Evangelical Lutherans arrived in 1741, mainly to serve the small white population of plantation owners, administrative officials, and merchants. The Anglican Church arrived during the British occupation of 1799–1816 to serve English colonists and other international residents. Congregations are now included in the Diocese of Guyana as part of the Church in the Province of the West Indies.

All of the other Protestant groups present today arrived after World War II, mainly from the United States, to serve the general population: Pilgrim Holiness Church (now Wesleyan Church) in 1945; the Seventh-day Adventists, 1945 (increased from 14 to 17 churches between 1997 and 2007; and from 2,677 to 3,616 members); West Indies Mission, 1954 (now WorldTeam); the Assemblies of God, 1959; International Missions, 1961; Independent Faith Mission, 1967 (Baptist); the Southern Baptists, 1971 (United Baptist Church, formed in 1991); Fellowship International Mission, 1972 (independent); the Church of God (Cleveland, Tennessee), 1982; the Church of the Nazarene, 1984; the Mennonite Board of Missions, 1985; the Orthodox Presbyterian Church, 1987; the Christian and Missionary Alliance, 1987; the Church of God of Prophecy, 1992; and the United Pentecostal Church, 2003.

Other Protestant and Free church denominations are also present (founding dates unknown): Evangelical Methodist Church, African Methodist Episcopal Church, Evangelical Congregational Church, Church of Christian Liberty ("reformed fundamentalist"), Association of Baptist Churches, and the Pentecostal Mission Church.

In 2000, according to Brierly (1997), the largest Protestant denominations in Suriname were estimated to be the following: the Moravian Church (46 churches and 29,000 members), the Seventh-day Adventists (18 churches and 3,400 members), the Dutch Reformed Church (6 churches and 3,100 members), the Lutheran

Church (6 churches and 2,050 members), the Evangelical Church of the West Indies (20 churches and 1,600 members), all Pentecostal denominations (18 churches and 1,330 members), and all other Protestant denominations (about 70 churches and 3,770 members). The total Protestant membership in Suriname was estimated to be less than 50,000 among fewer than 200 congregations.

Islam   In the 1890s, the Dutch began the transporting of Javanese (mostly Muslim) to serve as indentured laborers on sugar plantations to replace the freed slaves. By 1940 about 33,000 Javanese immigrants had arrived in Suriname. With the closure of many of the sugar plantations in the middle of the century, the Javanese began to establish themselves as small-scale farmers, as did the Chinese and Hindustanis. Most Javanese preferred to live close together in family units or villages in rural areas, where they could maintain their culture, language, and religious practices.

Islamic mosques in Suriname are led by *maulanas* (Muslim priests), who also function as traditional healers. Most Javanese villages have two mosques, which represent two groups within the Islamic community: the East prayers and the West prayers. The latter also believe in Agama Djawa, in which ghosts and their ancestors play an important role. When important events happen, there is always a sacrificial meal in which only the men take part. The *dukun*, a traditional healer in Javanese communities, serves as a midwife and prepares natural medicines from a variety of herbs, leaves, rhizomes, flowers, and fruits.

Most people of Javanese ancestry in Suriname are Muslims today, and very few have converted to other religions. About 20 percent of the Surinamese population is culturally Javanese and religiously Muslim. The majority of the Javanese are Sunni Muslims of the Shafiite School, whereas there are a small numbers of other Islamic groups. The Ahmadiyya movement in Islam (founded by Mirza Ghulam Hazrat Ahmad [1835–1908] in the 1890s in the Punjab of India), which was declared apostate and non-Muslim by orthodox Muslims in India and Pakistan during the 1980s, has a small following in Suriname, as does the Bazuin of God movement. The World Islamic Call Society, which works to convert the world to Islam (founded in 1972, with headquarters in Tripoli, Libya) has an office in Paramaribo.

Hinduism   About 80 percent of the Hindustani immigrants were Hindus. Some of them eventually returned to India, but those who remained in Suriname and their descendants constitute a "diasporic community" that, in 2004, constituted approximately 27 percent of the total population. However, far fewer claim to be adherents of Hinduism.

Hindus have remained faithful to their ancient traditions, language, and beliefs, which sets them apart in this multicultural society. Hinduism is a family and home religion that is characterized by many rituals and religious festivals, which can be performed at home or in community halls rather than in the Hindu temples. Within their own community, Hindustani music, dance, art, images, and literature are very important for maintaining cultural cohesion.

There are five known Hindu groupings in Surinam today: the Shri Sanatan Dharma Mahasabha (the "eternal religion" of orthodox believers, the majority group); the Arya Samaj (a 19th-century liberal reform movement from North India, known as the "society of nobles," with about 16 percent of the Hindu population, which arrived in Suriname in 1928); the Sri Sathya Sai Baba movement (followers of Sathya Sai Baba); the Transcendental Meditation movement (followers of Maharishi Mahesh Yogi, now organized within the Global Country of World Peace); and the International Society for Krishna Consciousness (ISKCON), followers of A. C. Bhaktivedanta Swami Prabhupada (1896–1977). Although Hinduism is limited largely to the East Indian immigrant population and their descendants in Suriname, where it provides social cohesion, some of the Hindu-based religious groups mentioned above seek to gain followers among the non-Hindu population.

Judaism   The Jewish community dates to the arrival of Sephardic Jews in the mid-1600s, following the Dutch abandonment of their land in Brazil. Presumably some Ashkenazi Jews arrived from England a short time later. A Portuguese Jewish Congregation of Suriname was founded in 1661–1662, and a first synagogue was completed in 1667 at Jodensavanna. The

Suriname

Religion	Followers in 1970	Followers in 2010	% of Population	Annual % growth 2000–2010	Followers in 2025	Followers in 2050
Christians	184,000	232,000	50.0	0.79	238,000	207,000
Roman Catholics	80,000	144,000	31.0	4.45	157,000	145,000
Protestants	74,200	82,500	17.7	0.65	82,000	72,000
Marginals	1,000	5,300	1.1	0.80	8,000	10,000
Hindus	87,000	95,000	20.4	0.72	98,000	86,000
Muslims	50,000	73,500	15.8	0.72	75,000	63,000
Agnostics	3,600	22,900	4.9	0.05	25,000	25,000
Spiritists	11,000	16,500	3.5	0.72	17,100	15,100
Ethnoreligionists	30,000	9,700	2.1	0.72	9,000	8,000
New religionists	100	3,800	0.8	0.72	5,000	6,000
Baha'is	3,000	4,500	1.0	0.73	6,500	7,500
Buddhists	1,000	2,800	0.6	0.72	3,500	3,500
Jains	500	1,300	0.3	0.72	1,500	1,700
Chinese folk	600	1,200	0.3	0.73	1,300	1,200
Jews	650	860	0.2	0.71	900	900
Atheists	0	550	0.1	0.70	700	800
Total population	**372,000**	**465,000**	**100.0**	**0.72**	**482,000**	**426,000**

congregation followed the practice of the Congregation of Amsterdam. Today, there are two synagogues in Paramaribo, both Sephardic, which serve an ethnic community of about 700 people.

Buddhism There are a small number of Chinese, whose ancestors, unlike the East Indians and Javanese, began arriving in Suriname prior to the abolition of slavery; the first shipload of Chinese contract-laborers arrived in 1853. Some of their descendants have retained their Buddhist faith (or folk religions), while others have converted to Christianity.

Other Religious Groups Indigenous religions are practiced by the Amerindian and Afro-descendant Maroon populations. The surviving Amerindian groups (Akuriyo, Arawak, Carib-Kaliña-Galibi, Trío, and Wayana) are concentrated principally in the interior and to a lesser extent in coastal areas. Most Amerindians adhere to traditional animistic beliefs and practices such as magic (white and black, good and evil), witchcraft (*bujeria*), herbal healing (*curanderismo*), and shamanism (the shaman is an intermediary with the spirit world). Those of Amerindian, Creole, or Maroon origin who identify themselves as Christian often simultaneously observe animistic religious traditions.

The Bush Negroes (Maroons) of the interior region practice an animistic religion that has been labeled by anthropologists as the "most African of all religions in the Americas." However, the Maroon religion is similar in some ways to the Winti religion that is practiced by the Creoles.

The Afro-Surinamese Creole population (not to be confused with the Maroons) of the northern coast practices the Winti religion, brought to the Americas by their African ancestors, which developed among the slaves during the colonial period. Winti (meaning "wind") is derived from a traditional African polytheistic belief system of West African origin. It acknowledges many gods and ghosts with each one having their own myths, rites, offerings, taboos, and magical forces.

Myalism and Obeah is reportedly practiced in secret by some Creoles, even among adherents of Christian churches. Myalism is an African-derived belief system (from Central and West Africa) that developed among blacks in the British West Indies during the slavery period. Obeah is the specific practice of "black magic" or witchcraft by priests, known as "obeah-men" or "obeah-women," although most sorcerers are male and most folk healers are female.

After World War I, a new wave of Chinese (largely Buddhist), Lebanese and Syrian (Muslim and Eastern

Orthodox Christians), and Portuguese (mainly Madeira islanders who were Roman Catholic) immigrants arrived in Suriname, as well as Portuguese-speaking migrants (Roman Catholic) from neighboring Brazil. After World War II, several marginal Christian groups arrived: Jehovah's Witnesses (45 churches with 2,317 members in 2007) and the Church of Jesus Christ of Latter-day Saints (Mormons, founded in 1988; 7 churches with 1,057 members in 2008). There are also small groups of Baha'i, the United Ancient Order of Druids (1996–1998, two lodges established), Freemasons (Provincial Grand Master of the Regular Freemasons in Suriname), the Ancient and Mystical Order Rosae Crusis (AMORC), and the Worldwide Extraterrestrial Phoenix Movement of Surinam (which calls itself, "Ambassador of the Golden Age and the Second Coming of Christ to the World").

Brazilian anthropologist Livio Sansone reports that large numbers of Surinamese in the Netherlands (mainly in Amsterdam) have adopted the beliefs, practices, music, and dress of the Rastafarians by contact with Jamaicans. More recently, Rastafarians have established themselves in Suriname.

J. Gordon Melton and Clifton L. Holland

See also: African Methodist Episcopal Church; Ahmad, Mirza Ghulam Hazrat; Ahmadiyya Movement in Islam; Arya Samaj; Assemblies of God; Baha'i Faith; Christian and Missionary Alliance; Church in the Province of the West Indies; Church of God (Cleveland, Tennessee); Church of God of Prophecy; Church of Jesus Christ of Latter-day Saints; Church of the Nazarene; Druidism; Evangelical Church of the West Indies; Freemasonry; Global Country of World Peace; International Society for Krishna Consciousness; Jehovah's Witnesses; Moravian Church in Surinam; Protestant Church in the Netherlands; Rastafarians; Roman Catholic Church; Santeria; Sathya Sai Baba Movement; Seventh-day Adventist Church; Shafiite School of Islam; Southern Baptist Convention; United Pentecostal Church International; Vodou; Wesleyan Church; Witchcraft; World Council of Churches.

References

Brierly, Peter. *World Churches Handbook.* London: Christian Research, 1997.

Catholic-Hierarchy website. "Diocese of Paramaribo." http://www.catholic-hierarchy.org/diocese/dpara.html.

Dryfoot, Arthur Charles. *The Shaping of the West Indian Church, 1492–1962.* Gainesville: University Press of Florida, 1999; published jointly with The Press University of the West Indies in Jamaica.

Fernández Olmos, Margarite, and Lizabeth Paravisini-Gebert, eds. *Sacred Possessions: Vodou, Santería, Obeah and the Caribbean.* New Brunswick, NJ: Rutgers University Press, 1997.

Gautam, Mohan K. "The Construction of the Indian Image in Suriname: Deconstructing Colonial Derogatory Notions and Reconstructing of the Indian Identity." http://www.saxakali.com/indocarib/sojourner7a.htm.

Glazier, Stephen D. *Encyclopedia of African and African-American Religions.* New York: Routledge, 2001.

Hamilton, J. Taylor, and Kenneth G. Hamilton. *History of the Moravian Church: The Renewed Unitas Fratrum, 1722–1957.* Bethlehem, PA: Interprovincial Board of Christian Education, Moravian Church in America, 1967.

Hoefte, Rosemarijn. *In Place of Slavery: A Social History of British Indian and Javanese Laborers in Suriname.* Gainesville: University Press of Florida, 1998.

Hoefte, Rosemarijn, and Peter Meel, eds. *Twentieth Century Suriname: Continuities & Discontinuities in a New World Society.* Kingston, Jamaica: Ian Randle Publishers, 2001.

Horowitz, Michael M., ed. *Peoples and Cultures of the Caribbean: An Anthropological Reader.* Garden City, NY: The Natural History Press, 1971.

Kranenborg, Reender. "Winti: A New Witchcraft Religion in the Netherlands." *Journal of Contemporary Religion* 9, no. 1 (1993): 10–16.

Maynard, G. O. *A History of the Moravian Church: Eastern West Indies Province.* Port of Spain, Trinidad: Yuille's Printerie, 1968.

Orna, Hanan. "A Brief History of East Indians in Suriname," chapter 6 of *Sojourners to Settlers: The Indian Migrants in the Caribbean and the Americas*, by Mahin Gosine and Dhanpaul Narine. http://saxakali.com/indocarib/sojourner6.htm.

Price, Richard, and Sally Price. *Stedman's Suriname: Life in an Eighteenth-Century Slave Society*, an abridged, modernized edition; originally published in 1796. Baltimore: Johns Hopkins University Press, 1992.

The PROLADES-RITA (Religion-In-The-Americas) Database. "Religion in Surinam." http://www.prolades.com/cra/regions/sam/sur/sur-rd.htm.

Sansone, Livio. "Ethnicity and Leisure Time among Surinamese Adolescents and Young Men in Amsterdam." In *Bonoeman, rasta's en andere Surinamers*, edited by Paul Van Gelder, 185–218. Amsterdam: University of Amsterdam Press, 1984.

Stephen, Henri J. M. *Winti Culture: Mysteries, Voodoo and Realities of an Afro-Caribbean Religion in Suriname and The Netherlands*. Amsterdam: the author, 1998.

Suparlan, Parsudi. *The Javanese in Suriname: Ethnicity in an Ethnically Plural Society*. Tempe: Arizona State University Press, 1995.

Taylor, Patrick, ed. *Nation Dance: Religion, Identity and Cultural Difference in the Caribbean*. Bloomington: Indiana University Press, 2001.

U.S. Department of Commerce. *International Religious Freedom Report, 2008*. http://www.state.gov/g/drl/rls/irf/2008/108540.htm.

U.S. Department of State, Bureau of Western Hemispheric Affairs. *Background Note: Suriname* (June 2009). http://www.state.gov/r/pa/ei/bgn/1893.htm.

Van der Berg, C., and P. van der Veer. "Pandits, Power, and Profit: Religious Organization and the Construction of Identity among Surinamese Hindus." *Ethnic and Racial Studies* 9, no. 4 (1986): 514–528.

Van Velzen, M., with U. E. Thoden, Ineka Van Wetering, and W. Van Wetering. *In the Shadow of the Oracle: Religion as Politics in a Suriname Maroon Society*. Long Grove, IL: Waveland Press, 2004.

■ Svalbard and Jan Mayen Islands

Svalbard (literally, cold coast) and the Jan Mayen Islands form an overseas territory of Norway located in the North Sea, north of the European mainland. Together they consist of some 150 islands, with 23,559 square miles of land, most of which is within the four main islands. As of 2008, only 2,165 people live in the largely inhospitable environment sandwiched between the Norwegian Sea and the Arctic Ocean.

These previously uninhabited islands were discovered in 1596 by Jacob Heemskerck, a Dutchman on a whaling expedition. They were claimed by the Dutch until granted to Norway in the Treaty of Spitsbergen (1920). In the meantime, in 1713 the Russians established a presence.

Today the few residents on the islands are mostly engaged in mining or in running various weather and research stations. In the summer there is some tourism.

Svalbard and Jan Mayen Islands

Religion	Followers in 1970	Followers in 2010	% of Population	Annual % growth 2000–2010	Followers in 2025	Followers in 2050
Christians	1,300	2,400	59.8	1.61	2,800	3,600
Protestants	1,000	1,400	33.7	1.28	1,600	2,000
Orthodox	300	880	21.5	2.23	1,000	1,300
Agnostics	400	1,600	38.9	0.05	1,800	2,300
Buddhists	0	60	1.3	0.85	70	100
Total population	**1,700**	**4,100**	**100.0**	**0.98**	**4,700**	**6,000**

SVALBARD AND JAN MAYEN ISLANDS

The only visible religious life on the island is the Church of Norway (Lutheran), which sends chaplains to conduct worship for the people stationed there (most clergy coming on temporary assignment). The territory is assigned to the Roman Catholic Church's Vicariate of North Norway, headquartered at Tromso, but there is little Catholic presence amid the residents and there are no Catholic services.

The islands have been a source of conflict between Norway and both Denmark (with hegemony over Greenland) and Russia.

J. Gordon Melton

A Russian church in Barentsburg, Svalbard. (Dusko Matic/Dreamstime.com)

See also: Church of Norway; Roman Catholic Church.

References

Arlov, T. B. *A Short History of Svalbard*. Polar-hándbok no. 4. Oslo: Norsk Polarinstitutt, 1989.

Dowdeswell, Julian, and Michael Hambrey. *Islands of the Arctic*. New York: Cambridge University Press, 2002.

Lundgre, Stefan, and Olle Carlsson. *Svalbard: The Land Beyond the Northcape*. Arlov: Berlings Grafiska, Sweden, 1997.

Swaminarayan Hinduism

Swaminarayan Hinduism is one of the fastest-growing Hindu groups in the first part of the 21st century. Prosperity in its home state of Gujarat has propelled growth and building of extensive temple and social institutions as part of a Hindu revival; and the growth of non-resident Gujarati populations abroad, especially in the East Africa in the early 20th century and in the United Kingdom, North America, and parts of Europe and Australasia more recently, have created significant transnational networks that are shaping Gujarati ethnic identity and Hindu self-awareness in India and abroad.

Swaminarayan Hinduism began as an early 19th-century reform movement in Gujarat. The founder, Sahajanand Swami (1781–1830), became an important religious teacher and reformer in Gujarat during the period of political disunity and social upheaval that coincided with the imposition of British rule in Gujarat.

Sahajanand Swami attacked three social evils: female infanticide, widow burning, and opium addiction. He opposed the British trade in opium and the pernicious effects of drug addiction on the peasants. He also advocated the protection and social uplift of

Swaminarayan temple, suburban Chicago. (J. Gordon Melton)

women by opposing large dowries, establishing separate precincts in the temples for women, and permitting some celibate women to reside in temple precincts.

Sahajanand Swami preached against the practices of corrupt *sadhus* and lax discipline among householders. The major reform he instituted was a strict discipline for his sadhus, including five primary vows: (1) celibacy and strict separation from women; (2) renunciation of all family ties; (3) avoiding attachment to the objects of the senses; (4) holy poverty; and (5) overcoming ego. Although the sadhus renounced the world, they lived in towns and cities to organize social and religious affairs. Sahajanand Swami established a strict householder discipline that did not require renunciation of the world. His followers took five vows: not to eat meat, not to take intoxicants, not to commit adultery, not to steal, and not to defile oneself or others.

Nonviolence, vegetarianism, and freedom from addictions were stressed. As the group grew, Sahajanand Swami himself soon became the object of veneration. Vaishnava theology teaches that when human plight is great, Vishnu appears to bring true religion and salvation. Krishna was the most prominent deity in Gujarat, and images of Krishna and his consort Radha were placed in Swaminarayan temples, but Sahajanand Swami came to be worshipped as Lord Swaminarayan. The theology of the group presents him as the manifestation of the highest reality, Purushottam; supports worship of his image in temples; and describes his heavenly abode as Akshardham. Swaminarayan established major temples at Vadtal and Ahmedabad and appointed his brothers' sons to be *acharyas* and administrators of two Swaminarayan dioceses that divide all Gujarat and India north and south.

Swaminarayan Hindus accept the Vedas and other basic sacred Hindu scriptures and doctrines, and they preserve four additional texts that are attributed to Swaminarayan's inspiration. The Sikshapatri contains rules for sadhus, householders, women, and acharyas. The Vachanamritam is a collection of philosophical sermons given by Swaminarayan. The Satsangijivan is a five-volume Sanskrit compendium of all the teachings, history, and legends from the life of Swaminarayan. The Lekh is more narrowly focused on regulations about the succession of the acharyas of Ahmedabad and Vadtal.

A major division occurred in 1906 when a sadhu named Swami Yagnapurushdas (1865–1951) split from the Vadtal Temple to establish his own group with a few sadhus and a small number of householders. The doctrine of the Bochasanwasi Akshar Purushottam Swaminarayan Sanstha (BAPS) is that Yagnapurushdas and his successors are the human abode (*askhar*) of Purushottam. The current leader, Narayanswarupdas Swami, popularly known as Pramukh Swami (b. 1921), presides over a rapidly growing institution. The number of BAPS sadhus has risen to 800.

A smaller group was founded by Muktajivandas Swami, a sadhu who left the Ahmedabad Temple in the 1940s and set up a new institution at Maninagar. In 1972 he revealed that he was the personification of the Swaminarayan Gadi, and thereafter he received divine honors. He died in Bolton in 1979 while on tour to visit his disciples in Great Britain.

Gujarati emigrations and rapid modern mobility and communication established Swaminarayan Hinduism as a growing transnational religion. Gujarati workers in British East Africa built temples that are still active in Kenya, Tanzania, and Uganda. After the independence of African countries, many immigrated to Britain. Significant Gujarati immigration to the United States followed liberalization of the immigration laws in 1965. BAPS alone has more than 800 temples and 3,300 centers, including 56 temples in the United States. Two international organizations have been formed by followers of the two original dioceses of Ahmedabad and Vadtal: the International Swaminarayan Satsang Organization (ISSO) and the International Swaminarayan Satsang Mandal (ISSM). Each group is building temples in India and abroad, and BAPS has been especially successful in building large traditional temples and cultural complexes at Gandhinagar and Delhi in India, and abroad in Nairobi, London, Toronto, Chicago, Houston, and Atlanta. BAPS is noted in the *Guinness Book of Records* for the largest Hindu temple and the most temples (713) dedicated by a single person (Pramukh Swami).

Swaminarayan Hinduism continues to be a significant force in the preservation of personal and group identity for many Gujaratis in India and in the contemporary diaspora.

BAPS
Shree Swaminarayan Mandir, Shahibaug
Amdavad-380 004
Gujarat
India
http://www.swaminayayan.org

ISSO and ISSM
Shree Swaminarayan Mandir
2114 Pine St.
Grand Prairie, TX 75050

ISSO and ISSM
Shree Hari House 99B
Cobbold Rd.
Willesden
London NW10 9SL
United Kingdom
http://www.swaminarayan.nu

Raymond B. Williams

See also: Vegetarianism.

References

Dave, H. T. *Life and Philosophy of Shree Swaminarayan*. London: George Allen and Unwin, 1974.

Williams, Raymond Brady. *An Introduction to Swaminarayan Hinduism*. Cambridge: Cambridge University Press, 2001.

Williams, Raymond Brady. *Religions of Immigrants from India and Pakistan: New Threads in the American Tapestry*. Cambridge: Cambridge University Press, 1988.

Williams, Raymond Brady. *Williams on South Asian Religions and Immigration*. Aldershot, UK: Ashgate, 2004.

■ Swaziland

Swaziland, an African kingdom of some 6,642 square miles now ruled by King Mswati III, its absolute monarch, is largely surrounded by South Africa, but shares a short border with Mozambique. Its 1,129,000 citizens are almost all drawn from the various southern African peoples, some very different, who united to oppose Zulu expansion from Natal and the Transvaal. Sobhuza, the head of the Dlamini, who had brought about the union, died in 1839. His son, M'swazi, would rule for the next three decades, during which time the primary force threatening the nation became the Boers. The nation is named after M'swazi.

In 1867, Swaziland, a relatively small land, became a British protectorate and remained administratively separate as Great Britain established its control over all of South Africa. The drive to full independence was accelerated by the break between South Africa and the United Kingdom in 1960. The country was granted internal autonomy in 1967 and full independence the next year. It adopted a parliamentary monarchy, and King Sobhuza II was the first ruler of the independent nation. In 1973 he dissolved Parliament and proclaimed himself the absolute monarch. He instituted a new Constitution that included a legislature consisting of members elected by the public and those appointed by the king. The prime minister and the queen mother both held important leadership responsibilities.

The death of King Sobhuza in 1982 led to a power struggle within the royal family. In 1986, 19-year-old prince Makhosetive assumed the throne as Mswati III, and he continues to lead the country. He has adopted a conservative stance that continues the country's strong ties to South Africa, upon which it is economically dependent.

Traditional religion in Swaziland has revolved around the royal family, and the welfare of the state was seen as a reflection of the king's well-being. He

SWAZILAND

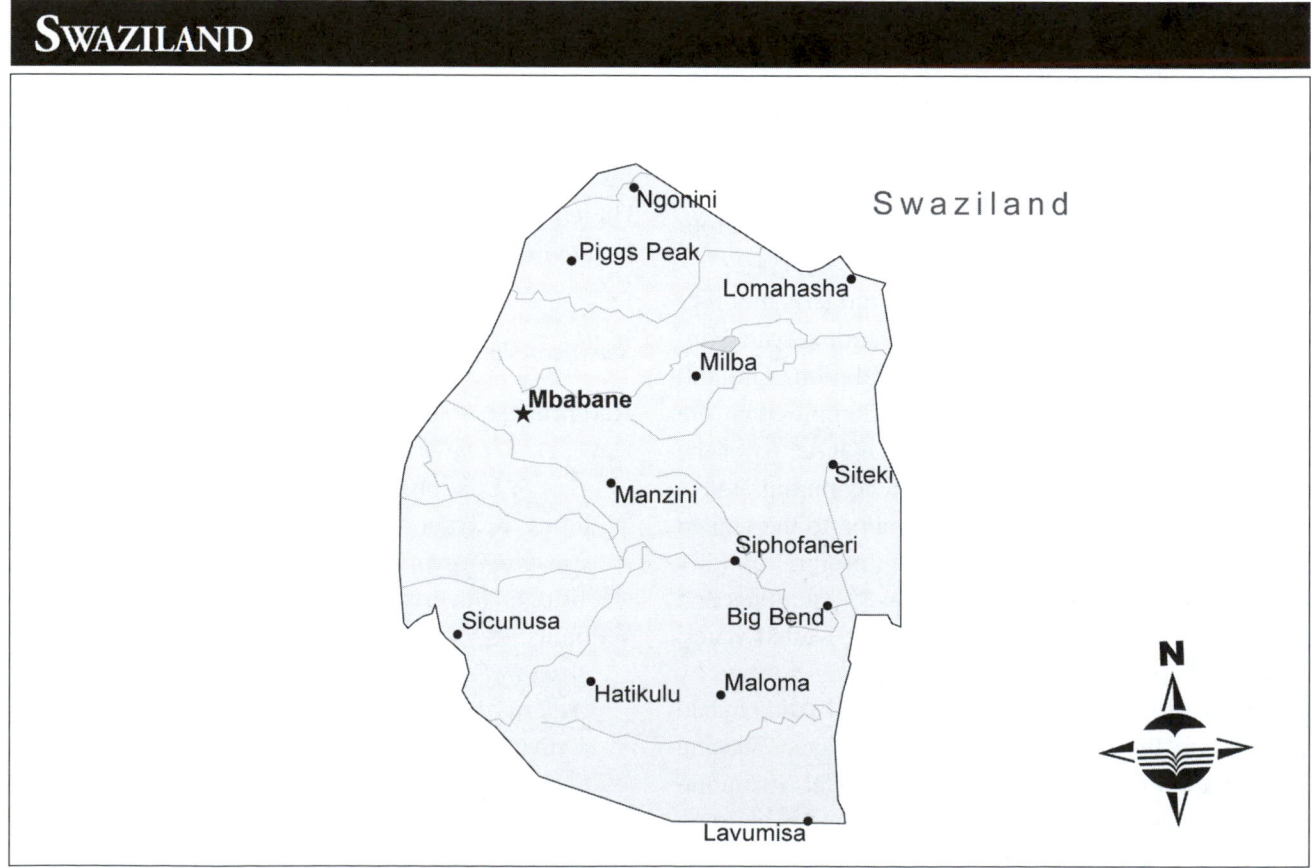

Swaziland

Religion	Followers in 1970	Followers in 2010	% of Population	Annual % growth 2000–2010	Followers in 2025	Followers in 2050
Christians	308,000	1,021,000	88.0	1.42	1,111,000	1,234,000
Independents	86,500	556,000	47.9	1.94	600,000	660,000
Protestants	65,300	120,000	10.3	2.46	150,000	170,000
Roman Catholics	34,000	56,000	4.8	0.70	60,000	70,000
Ethnoreligionists	139,000	110,000	9.5	−0.39	90,000	70,000
Agnostics	0	14,000	1.2	1.22	20,000	27,000
Muslims	300	7,500	0.6	1.22	9,000	12,000
Baha'is	7,000	5,300	0.5	1.22	8,000	12,000
Hindus	0	1,800	0.2	1.23	3,000	4,000
Atheists	0	300	0.0	1.24	600	800
Total population	**454,000**	**1,160,000**	**100.0**	**1.22**	**1,242,000**	**1,360,000**

and his mother were revered as the makers of rain. The royal ancestors are also seen as having an intercessory role with Umlhulumcandi, the First Being. Traditional religionists also have a strong belief in the phenomenon of possession, and possession by spirits, ancestors, and animals is a common part of religious practice. Approximately 10 percent of the people continue in their traditional belief system. That number dropped steadily, however, through the 20th century.

The Swaziland king invited Methodist missionaries from South Africa into his realm in 1825. However, that and several other attempts to evangelize the nation over the next several decades ended in failure. Permanent work really began in 1881 with the arrival of the United Society for the Propagation of the Gospel to build the Church of England. Their work was constituted a diocese of the Church in the Province of South Africa in 1968. In 1887, German Lutherans began work that has matured into a diocese of the Evangelical Lutheran Church in Southern Africa. Methodists made a new beginning in 1895 and finally built a substantial work integrated into the Methodist Church of South Africa.

As the major Protestant churches came into Swaziland from South Africa, so also was the country invaded by African Initiated Churches, originally formed in their larger neighbor. Possibly the first independent church to arrive was the Independent Methodist Church (a schism from the African Methodist Episcopal Church). Between 1906 and 1936, some 20 indigenous groups established work, the largest being branches of the Zionist and Apostolic Churches, the Christian Catholic Holy Spirit Church in Zion, the Christian Apostolic Church in Zion of South Africa, and the Swazi Christian Church in Zion of South Africa.

In 1939 the king of Swaziland attempted to unite all the small independent churches operating in the country into a national church. Although his success was only partial, the United Christian Church of Africa did come into being, and the king is still considered its leader. A cathedral was erected in 1970 and opened in 1979 as the National Swazi Church. It is the site of special Easter services attended by the royal family.

The Roman Catholic Church arrived rather late, when brothers with the Order of the Servants of Mary opened their initial mission in 1913. The work was freed from the Vicariate of Natal in 1923 with the creation of the Prefecture of Swaziland. In 1961 the new suffragan diocese of Swaziland was attached to the diocese of Pretoria. The erection of the diocese was a result of two decades of rapid growth following the end of World War II.

The Swaziland Conference of Churches, which includes not only the older missionary churches but also the Roman Catholic Church, the Seventh-day Adventist Church, and a number of new conservative evangelical churches, was formed in 1965. In 1976 the Roman Catholic, Lutheran, Mennonite, and African Methodist churches founded the Council of Swaziland Council of Churches, which is affiliated with the World Council of Churches. Many of the African Initiated

Churches are united in the League of African Churches in Swaziland, and conservative Evangelicals have established the Association of Evangelicals of Swaziland, affiliated with the World Evangelical Alliance.

Islam and Judaism have made little impact on Swaziland, and there are no visible communities of Buddhists or Hindus. The primary non-Christian community to arise in the 20th century was the Baha'i Faith.

J. Gordon Melton

See also: African Initiated (Independent) Churches; African Methodist Episcopal Church; Baha'i Faith; Church in the Province of South Africa; Church of England; Evangelical Lutheran Church in Southern Africa; Methodist Church of Southern Africa; Roman Catholic Church; Seventh-day Adventist Church; World Council of Churches; World Evangelical Alliance; Zionist and Apostolic Churches.

References

Armitage, F. L. "Abakamoya: People of the Spirit: A Study of the Zionist Movement in Swaziland with Special Reference to the Swazi Christian Church in Zion of South Africa and the Nazareth Branch." Ph.D. diss., University of Aberdeen, 1976.

Booth, Alan R. *Historical Dictionary of Swaziland.* Methuen, NJ: Scarecrow Press, 2000.

Byaruhanga-Akilki, A. B. T. *Religion in Swaziland.* Kwaluseni, Swaziland: University of Botswana, Lesotho, and Swaziland, 1975.

Cazziol, Roger C. *The Swazi Zionists: An Indigenous Religious Movement in Southern Africa.* Kwaluseni: University of Swaziland, 1987.

Kasenene, Peter. *Religion in Swaziland.* Braamfontein, South Africa: Skotaville, 1993.

Ndlovu, H. L. "The Royal Easter Ritual and Political Action in Swaziland." Ph.D. diss., McMaster University, 1993.

Perkins, F. J. "A History of Christian Missions in Swaziland to 1910." Ph.D. diss., University of Witwatersrand, 1974.

Sowazi, Eunice N. *Mingling with the Mud of Humanity: A Celebration of the First Twenty Years of the Council of Swaziland Churches.* Manzini, Swaziland: Ruswanda Publishing Bureau, 1996.

■ Sweden

One of the Scandinavian countries, Sweden is located between Finland and Norway, with its coastline bordering the Baltic Sea and the Gulf of Bothnia to the east. To the southwest, Sweden borders the narrow passage between the Baltic and North seas. The long, narrow country reaches into the Arctic and includes 173,700 square miles of land. In 2009, the population was just over 9 million.

Megalithic monuments, rock-carvings, and grave-mounds bear witness to prehistoric religion during the Stone, the Bronze, and the Iron ages. In one of the earliest written sources about religion in Swedish territory, Adam from Bremen, in a report to his archbishop in 1070, speaks about a Pagan temple in Uppsala, where the gods Thor, Woden, and Frej were worshipped through sacrificial rituals every ninth year. Most probably Sweden shared the Old Norse mythology and cosmology described in the Icelandic literature (the Eddas).

Christian missions began in Sweden in the ninth century. A small congregation was founded in 830 by Ansgar, a Frankish-German monk considered the "Apostle of the North." Through Viking settlements and trading, the impact of Christianity increased. Olof Skötkonung, considered the first king of Sweden, was probably baptized in the year 1000. In 1164, Uppsala was designated as the see of the archbishop. Saint Bridget (Birgitta) of Sweden, known for her visions and revelations and the founding of an order, lived in the 14th century. At the time of the Reformation, in the 16th century, the Church of Sweden switched its allegiance from the Roman Catholic Church to Lutheranism, and now exists as an evangelical Lutheran church. During the following centuries the position of the church as a state church was strengthened, and Swedish citizenship implied church membership. Adopting or giving expression to a faith that was not strictly in accordance with the teachings of the church became a penal offense and could lead to exile.

The religious currents of the 18th century, such as Pietism, also spread in Sweden. Later on, Methodism, the Baptists, the Holiness movement, and other revival movements were brought to the country from England and North America. In Sweden these revival move-

A view across an open field to the historic Gudhem Church and monastery ruins in Sweden, 2009. (Patrik Gunnari/Dreamstime.com)

ments turned into popular movements (*folkrörelser*), in opposition to the Church of Sweden and to a society with a state church system. Moreover, the liberal ideas of the 19th century contributed very significantly to breaking the religious hegemony of the church. During the second part of that century, a number of denominations were acknowledged and given permission to act as Free churches alongside the state church. Also the Church of Jesus Christ of Latter-day Saints was by then established in this country. During the first decades of the 20th century, the Jehovah's Witnesses became noticeable; Pentecostalism had also gained adherents.

Swedish people had to wait until 1952 to obtain full freedom of religion, even the right to reject any religious affiliation whatsoever. Today, however, the once homogeneous country of Sweden has turned into a pluralistic and a multicultural society. This change has been mainly due to labor immigration and the influx of refugees. Sweden has a population of 8.8 mil-

lion, and of those, 12 percent are immigrants. All this has, of course, meant changes in the field of religion. The year 2000 was a memorable year in that the state church system as such was abolished. The full impact of that event on the religious community as a whole still remains to be seen.

Today, 7.4 million Swedes, or 83 percent of the population, are members of the Church of Sweden. In 1975, 10.8 million church attendances for the Sunday-morning service were reported, and among 15-year-olds, 63 percent had been confirmed; in 2000, the corresponding figures had fallen to 6.6 million and 43 percent. On the other hand, during the same period, attendance at music services/concerts (*musikgudstjän-ster*) has increased from 1.4 to 2.4 million people. These data may serve as examples of religious change in Sweden. In 1960, the first ordination of woman priests took place. Today, of those in the ministry, almost one-third are women, two of whom are bishops.

The once rebellious Free church denominations are today well integrated into Swedish society, and they participate in ecumenical work. As far as membership within these denominations is concerned, the trend is one of decline, from 255,500 in 1985 to 216,000 in 1999. The largest is the Pentecostal movement (Pingströrelsen), with 90,000 members. The Pentecostals reach out to immigrants, and meetings, though small, are held not only in the common Western languages but also in Amharic/Tigrinya, Arabic, Persian, and Romany for the Roma (Gypsies). The Mission Covenant Church of Sweden (Svenska Missionsförbundet), having originated from a Low-Church movement, has 67,000 members. It accepts both infant baptism and believer's baptism, and is a member of the World Alliance of Reformed Churches. InterAct (Nybygget), with 28,800 members, is the only denomination that has had a small but distinct membership increase. It was established in 1996 through a union between three Baptist denominations founded in the 19th century. It is a member of the World Evangelical Alliance. Also present are the Baptist Union of Sweden (Svenska Baptistsamfundet); the Swedish Alliance Mission (Svenska Alliansmissionen); the Salvation Army; the Methodist Church; a branch of the U.S.-based United Methodist Church; and the Seventh-day Adventist Church. All these churches are organized in the Swedish Free Church Council (Sveriges Frikyrkosamråd).

The Roman Catholic Church and the Orthodox and Oriental churches in Sweden have some characteristics in common, though their histories differ. They are churches with many immigrants, their growth is strong, and they are primarily found in the big cities. The Catholic Church has 150,000 members, indicating that the membership has more than doubled since 1975. The church is probably the most multicultural organization in Sweden. Apart from the congregations, there are the so-called national groups, the largest being the Polish community (30,000 members) and the Spanish-speakers (20,000 members). Mass is celebrated regularly in Arabic, Croatian, Hungarian, English, French, Gheez, Italian, Portuguese, Slovene, and Vietnamese. The Orthodox and Eastern churches have altogether 100,000 faithful, a figure that has doubled since 1975. The Greek Orthodox Patriarchate of Antioch and All the East is the largest, with 28,000

members. The Serbian Orthodox Church has 23,000 members. Many of the Greek Orthodox Church members, who came to Sweden as labor migrants, have returned to Greece. Then there are the Bulgarian, Estonian, Finnish, Macedonian, Rumanian, Russian, Armenian, Coptic, and Ethiopian Orthodox churches, plus the Apostolic Catholic Assyrian church of the East. There is also a Swedish Orthodox deanery.

Among the Protestant foreign churches, the Estonian Evangelical Lutheran Church is the biggest (12,000 members), followed by the Hungarian Protestant Church (6,000). All churches and denominations mentioned above are members or observers in the Christian Council of Sweden (Sveriges kristna råd).

The Faith Movement (Trosrörelsen) was established in Sweden in the early 1980s, when Ulf Ekman, once a priest in the Church of Sweden but later influenced by the teachings of Pentecostal teacher Kenneth Hagin in Tulsa, Oklahoma, founded a congregation in Uppsala, the Word of Life (Livets Ord). There are now some 40 congregations with 6,000 members affiliated to the Word of Life. In the beginning the growth of the Faith Movement caused conflicts with the surrounding religious society. The Word of Life pursues an extensive missionary work, particularly in the former Soviet Union, where quite a number of congregations and Bible schools have been founded. In recent years India has been at the focus of this kind of activity. The Vineyard also has some propagation in Sweden, with 1,000 members in 10 congregations and house groups. The International Churches of Christ have one congregation in Stockholm, with some 150 members.

Up to the beginning of the 20th century, almost 8,000 Mormons had left for Utah. Today the Church of Jesus Christ of Latter-day Saints in Sweden numbers 8,500, which implies an increase of more than 50 percent since 1975. Almost half of the members belong to congregations in the three big city areas of Stockholm, Malmö, and Gothenburg. In 1985 a temple was built in a suburb of Stockholm. The Jehovah's Witnesses have also increased by more than 50 percent, and there are now 23,500 members or publishers; at the memorial in 1999, some 36,000 individuals were present. In contrast to the Latter-day Saints, their congregations are more evenly distributed throughout the country. To a higher degree than the Pentecostals, the Jehovah's Wit-

SWEDEN

Sweden

Religion	Followers in 1970	Followers in 2010	% of Population	Annual % growth 2000–2010	Followers in 2025	Followers in 2050
Christians	6,022,000	6,101,000	66.0	0.15	5,913,000	5,934,000
Protestants	8,830,000	7,489,000	81.0	−0.96	7,400,000	7,241,000
Orthodox	31,500	132,000	1.4	−0.03	155,000	165,000
Roman Catholics	58,900	152,000	1.6	8.61	180,000	200,000
Agnostics	1,197,000	1,683,000	18.2	1.16	2,158,000	2,542,000
Atheists	799,000	1,095,000	11.8	0.36	1,265,000	1,400,000
Muslims	2,400	250,000	2.7	0.96	380,000	450,000
Buddhists	300	40,000	0.4	0.60	55,000	60,000
New religionists	5,800	16,300	0.2	0.14	18,500	20,000
Jews	15,000	16,000	0.2	0.38	16,000	16,000
Hindus	0	13,500	0.1	3.17	17,000	21,000
Ethnoreligionists	0	9,600	0.1	0.38	10,000	11,000
Baha'is	1,500	6,500	0.1	0.86	8,000	10,000
Confucianists	0	6,000	0.1	0.38	7,000	9,000
Chinese folk	0	4,800	0.1	1.21	6,000	8,000
Spiritists	0	20	0.0	1.09	30	50
Total population	**8,043,000**	**9,242,000**	**100.0**	**0.38**	**9,854,000**	**10,481,000**

nesses have gained adherents among immigrants. Taken together, immigrants make up 10 percent of the members; there is even an Arabic congregation. Denominations like the Liberal Catholic Church, the New Apostolic Church, and the Church of Christ, Scientist may have roughly 2,000 members among them, including adherents of the Swedenborgian movement.

Among the non-Christian world religions, the Jews were given special permission to settle in Sweden, and to practice their religion, as early as the end of the 18th century. Today there may be 16,500 Jews, of whom 8,000 are members of a community, a figure that has been fairly constant. The big waves of immigration in recent years account for the enormous growth of Muslims in Sweden. The number of regular attendants at the different mosques in Sweden can be estimated at 100,000, though the number of immigrants and refugees with Muslim backgrounds ("ethnic" Muslims) may amount to 300,000 or even more. A big mosque, which can accommodate 1,500 people, is located in Stockholm. Other mosques—buildings that have been established and built for the sole purpose of being a mosque—can be found in Malmö, Trollhättan, and Uppsala. In Gothenburg there is a mosque of the Ahmadiyya movement in Islam. The Baha'i Faith, with 900 adherents, is a middle-class

phenomenon consisting of Iranians, but with many Swedish converts as well. The Hindus can be estimated at some 3,000 to 5,000, the International Society for Krishna Consciousness included. The Sikhs number about 800. Further, there are some 8,000 to 10,000 Buddhists in Sweden, among them a number of Western converts, Zen and Tibetan Buddhists in particular.

Of course a number of new religions have established themselves, even in Sweden. There are formations such as the Church of Scientology (in 2000 they were granted permission to conduct marriages), a few adherents of the Raelian movement, and the Church Universal and Triumphant, but also a number of neo-Hindu and neo-Pagan groups, including Wicca and neo-shamanism. Tentatively, the number of regular and active members within these movements may be estimated at 10,000—and some 500 of those hold to the Æsir cult. This figure has not changed very much in recent decades. Closely related to these religions and movements are the large number of loosely organized, New Age–inspired groups. If belief in reincarnation would do as a criterion of susceptibility to these kinds of new religiosity, they may involve some 400,000 individuals (the Hindus and the Buddhists excluded). Finally, Humanisterna (The Humanists), promoting

Humanism as a philosophy of life and affiliated with the International Humanist and Ethical Union, has some 700 members.

A study from 1999 including all religions showed that, during a September weekend, one million people, or 12 percent of the population, took part in a religious event either by attending services or through media religion (or both). That is a result which, when all religions and different faiths are considered, questions the picture of Sweden as a highly secularized country.

Margareta Skog

See also: Ahmadiyya Movement in Islam; Apostolic Catholic Assyrian Church of the East; Church of Jesus Christ of Latter-day Saints; Church of Scientology; Church Universal and Triumphant; Churches of Christ; Eastern Orthodoxy; Estonian Evangelical Lutheran Church; Free Churches; Greek Orthodox Patriarchate of Antioch and All the East; Humanism; International Churches of Christ; International Humanist and Ethical Union; International Society for Krishna Consciousness; Jehovah's Witnesses; Liberal Catholic Church; Mission Covenant Church of Sweden; New Apostolic Church; Pentecostalism; Raelian Movement International; Roman Catholic Church; Salvation Army; Serbian Orthodox Church; Seventh-day Adventist Church; Swedenborgian Movement; United Methodist Church; Wiccan Religion; World Alliance of Reformed Churches; World Evangelical Alliance.

References

Skog, Margareta, ed. *Det religiösa Sverige: Gudstjänst-och andaktsliv under ett veckoslut kring millennieskiftet.* Örebro, Sweden: Libris, 2001.

Tegborg, Lennart, ed. *Sveriges kyrkohistoria.* 8 vols. Stockholm: Verbum, 1998–.

Turville-Petre, E. O. G. *Myth and Religion of the North: The Religion of the Ancient Scandinavia.* London: Weidenfeld and Nicolson, 1964.

Swedenborg, Emanuel

1688–1772

Emanuel Swedenborg, scientist and seer, was a prominent Swedish intellectual and expert in the field of geology and mining, who left his science behind to

Portrait of Emanuel Swedenborg, 18th-century Swedish intellectual. (Library of Congress)

pursue conversations with angels that led to his writing spiritual commentaries on the Bible that revealed what he proposed was the scriptures' deeper spiritual meaning. He later proposed a new vision of the church that became the basis of several ecclesiastical bodies in the years following his death.

Swedenborg was born in Stockholm, Sweden, on January 29, 1688, and was the second son and third child of Jesper Swedberg (1653–1735) and Sara Behm's (1666–1696) nine children. His mother and older brother died in Uppsala in 1696 in an epidemic. His father was a Lutheran priest who was elevated to the position of bishop of Skara in 1702. His mother's family had extensive mining interests. Today Jesper Swedberg is remembered for his hymns and his influence on education, while his mother was known for her sweet disposition and her piety. After his mother's death his father remarried in 1697.

Swedenborg was educated at home until he entered Uppsala University at the age of 11 in 1699. He graduated in 1709 with a focus on the classics. A year later he sailed to London and remained abroad until 1715, absorbing the wealth of information concerning modern science and technology found in England and continental Europe. Prior to returning home to Sweden, he summarized what he had learned, and he wrote down an extensive list of his own inventions: among them were an airplane, a steam engine, and a submarine.

He was a polymath who was initially intrigued with universal quantifiability and science. He founded and published Sweden's first scientific journal, *Daedalus Hyperboreus*, in 1716–1717. He was appointed an assessor on the important and prestigious Board of Mines by King Karl XII (r. 1682–1718), and he served Sweden in that capacity for a quarter of a century, when iron constituted 70 percent of Sweden's exports. He also found time to explore and publish works on cosmology and anatomy during the 1730s and early 1740s; eventually he felt he was called by the Lord to reveal the internal sense of the Bible. He labored in the realm of spirit for 27 years and during that time he wrote and published 18 different titles in Latin, some of them multivolume works. From 1749 until 1768 he published his religious writings anonymously. He claimed authorship of his last four works, including his crowning work of theology, *True Christianity* (1771), which he signed "Emanuel Swedenborg, servant of the Lord Jesus Christ."

He published his eight-volume opus, *Secrets of Heaven*, between 1749 and 1756. This work unveils the inner meaning of Genesis and Exodus through the use of correspondences. According to Swedenborg, the story of creation is the story of human regeneration—a lifelong process that is essential for salvation. The seven days of creation correspond to that inner spiritual process. An individual must move from the state of self love depicted as the void and darkness found in the beginning on the first day, to later states in which living affections and truths are kindled in the human heart, found on the fifth day, represented by the all the living creatures, each created according to their kind; and finally to the creation of a living soul, male and female, that looks to the marriage of wisdom and love, that alone can generate states of useful service to the neighbor and the Lord.

Heaven and Hell, published in 1757, has been and remains his most popular work. It has been continuously available since publication and has been translated into at least 25 languages. It has inspired artists and writers around the world as well as ordinary people. The writers include William Blake (1757–1827), Edgar Allan Poe (1809–1849), Honoré de Balzac (1799–1850), Feodor Dostoevsky (1821–1881), August Strinberg (1849–1912), Howard Pyle (1853–1911), and Jorge Luis Borges (1899–1986). Swedenborg's rich depictions of the spiritual world have satisfied many people seeking knowledge of the afterlife, and his discussion of the nature of life after death has brought comfort to countless people confronting the loss of a loved one.

Reality, according to Swedenborg is both spiritual and natural. The spiritual world is the world of causes, and the natural world is the world of effects. He claimed that he was eyewitness to the long-awaited apocalypse, which took place in the spiritual world in 1757. This event constituted the last judgment, and it re-ordered the spiritual world, thereby increasing freedom in the natural world. From a Swedenborgian perspective, the vast changes that have taken place in the world, both good and evil, can be traced to this spiritual event.

Swedenborg's religious writings gradually became known during his lifetime and generated a range of responses, negative to positive, from philosophers like Immanuel Kant (1724–1804); religious figures like Friedrich C. Oetinger (1702–1782), Johann A. Ernesti (1707–1781), Gabriel A. Beyer (1720–1729), and Thomas Hartley (1708–1784); and ordinary people. Swedenborg felt he was called only to write and publish and never attempted to found a church.

While he was open about discussing his spiritual experiences and his writings with people who were genuinely interested, he never attempted to convince or convert. In *True Christianity* he proclaimed in number 508 that "Now it is permitted to enter with understanding into the mysteries of faith." He died in London on March 29, 1772. A church was founded based on his writings or the "charisma of the book" in England in 1787 by a group of individuals who had never personally known Swedenborg, These writings are the founding teachings of several New Christian religious organizations.

The religious works of Emanuel Swedenborg have also been read by, and perhaps have influenced, to some degree, the founders of several new religious movements: Joseph Smith, Jr. (1805–1844), founder of the Church of Jesus Christ of Latter-day Saints in 1830; Thomas Lake Harris (1823–1906), founder of The Brotherhood of the New Life in 1861; Mary Baker Eddy (1821–1910), founder of Christian Science in 1879; Madame Helena P. Blavatsky (1831–1891), founder of Theosophy in 1875; Rudolf Steiner (1861–1925), founder of Anthroposophy in 1913; the Reverend Sun Myung Moon (b. 1920), founder of the Unification Church in 1954; and Michael Zaharakis, member of The Saint Thomas Christians, who introduced his church to Swedenborg's teachings after which Swedenborg was canonized by the Saint Thomas Christians in 1982.

D. T. Suzuki (1870–1966) is generally credited with bringing Zen Buddhism to the West; what is less known is that he brought Swedenborg's writings to Japan. He translated four of Swedenborg's works into Japanese and in 1913 he wrote a book about Swedenborg in Japanese, convinced that "Swedenborg's theological doctrines greatly resemble Buddhism" (Suzuki 1996, 6). He wrote: "Revolutionary in theology, traveler of heaven and hell, champion of the spiritual world, king of the mystical realm, clairvoyant unique in history, scholar of incomparable vigor, scientist of penetrating intellect, gentleman free of worldly taint: all of these combine to make one Swedenborg" (Suzuki 1996, 3).

Jane Williams-Hogan

See also: Blavatsky, Helena P.; Eddy, Mary Baker; General Church of the New Jerusalem; Moon, Sun Myung; Smith, Joseph, Jr.; Steiner, Rudolf; Swedenborgian Movement; Unification Movement; Zen Buddhism.

References

Acton, Alfred. *The Letters and Memorial of Emanuel Swedenborg*. 2 vols. Bryn Athyn, PA: Swedenborg Scientific Association, 1948.

Rose, Jonathan, Stuart Shotwell, and Marylou Bertucci, eds. *Scribe of Heaven: Swedenborg's Life, Work, and Impact*. West Chester, PA: Swedenborg Foundation. 2005.

Sigstedt, Cyriel O. *The Swedenborg Epic: The Life and Works of Emanuel Swedenborg*. New York: Bookman Associates. 1952.

Suzuki, D. T. *Swedenborg: Buddha of the North*. Trans. by Andrew Bernstein. West Chester, PA: Swedenborg Foundation. 1996.

Williams-Hogan, Jane. "Swedenborgian Traces in Modern Religious Movements Old and New." In *Croyance et societes*, edited by Bertrand Ouellet and Richard Bergeron. Quebec, Canada: Éditions Fides, 1996.

Swedenborgian Church of North America

The Swedenborgian Church of North America, one of several churches to grow out of the teachings of Swedish visionary and theologian Emanuel Swedenborg (1688–1772), was established in Philadelphia, Pennsylvania, in 1817 as the General Convention of the New Jerusalem Church. Boston, Massachusetts, however, has long been the organizational center and spiritual home of the church. At the time of the founding of this organization, there were already 17 different societies in the United States with approximately 360 members. The purpose of the organization was threefold: (1) to lay the foundation for permanent organization and central control of the church; (2) to regularize ordination; and (3) to support missionary efforts. Although the founding generation of this organization theoretically considered an episcopal form of church government, they opted for the more democratic congregational form. It suited the spirit of the times, as well as the previous history of the church.

The Swedenborgian Church of North America has a "congregational" governmental structure. It holds an annual convention in which delegates from the various congregations assemble to conduct the business of the church. These annual meetings have been held since 1817 without interruption. At these meetings decisions are made regarding ordination, the by-laws, and the overall policies of the church. At the meeting, the administrative offices of the church are also filled. The offices are president, vice president, recording secretary, and treasurer. The president is elected for one three-year term and may be elected to serve an addition three years. After serving two terms, he or she is not immediately eligible to run again. The other administrative officers of the church serve for terms of one year and are eligible for re-election without limit. The president and other administrative officers, along with three ministers and six laypersons, form the General Council, which constitutes the governing body of the church. One minister and two laypersons are elected annually to serve terms of three years. The General Council is assisted in its work by Support Units that are specifically focused on functional areas, such as communications, education, ministry support, and so forth. The chairs of the Support Units form the cabinet, which is chaired by the president. There is also a Council of Ministers that oversees the pastoral and theological matters of the church.

The Swedenborgian Church of North America reported in its journal, for the year 2008, that it has a total membership of 1,608, of whom 1,197 are listed as active members. This is almost a 25 percent decrease in active membership since 2000. The journal listed 36 churches, 31 in the United States and 5 in Canada, 59 active ministers, and 7 authorized lay leaders. While the actual membership and the number of active churches have decreased recently, the number of active clergy and lay leaders has increased. There has been a large increase in the number of ministers working as chaplains, and efforts have been made to begin ministries where there have been no previous Swedenborgian churches. Congregations are being established in Silver City, New Mexico, and Lansing, Michigan, and the San Diego church is doing outreach in Mexico. The General Convention highlights ecological and environmental awareness because of their commitment to being good stewards of the world. Many of the members are active in Eco-Justice programs. General Convention Swedenborgian churches are located in the United States, Canada, and Guyana.

In recent years the Swedenborgian Church has attempted to move beyond external criteria for membership and leadership roles in the church. In the case of the ministry, the church developed a "Statement of In-clusiveness," preferring to make decisions regarding ordination based on "the quality of ministry that it believes the individual is capable of providing." Women have been ordained into the ministry since 1975, and there are currently 27 listed on the roll, comprising 46 percent of the ministry. Since 1997 a person's sexual orientation is no longer regarded as an impediment to ordination. In 2004 the denomination selected the first non-clergy, non-male president, Christine Laitner.

There are two patterns of worship in the Swedenborgian Church, traditional and contemporary. The traditional format is similar to Low-Church Episcopal. A liturgy is used with opening responses, chants that are sung, two readings from the Word (Bible) separated by an anthem or solo, a sermon that is extemporaneous or read from a manuscript, pastoral prayer, affirmation of faith, hymns, offertory, and a benediction. Some of the churches that use this format have incorporated children's talks into it.

There are also contemporary services in the Swedenborgian Church. Although they vary greatly, a consistent feature is extensive lay participation. Sacred dance and skits have been incorporated into these services, as well as contemporary music. They also involve sharing on the part of the congregants. There has been some controversy surrounding both of these styles of worship, because the church membership has strong preferences. But there has also been some movement toward a middle position, as societies that favor traditional forms have incorporated some more contemporary aspects in recent years. Both styles of worship require careful thought and planning if they are to be effective.

The Convention theological school, the Swedenborg School of Religion, was closed in 1999, after 135 years as a free-standing school, and the property in Newton, Massachusetts, was sold. Early in 2001 the Swedenborg School of Religion formed a partnership with Pacific School of Religion (PSR) in Berkeley, California. The Swedenborg House of Studies was established that year. It offers an ordination program leading to a master's of divinity degree, as well as a certificate of theological studies in conjunction with PSR. Distance education is a prominent feature of the new program with most of the 10 students, 8 women and 2 men, currently in the ordination track receiving their education at a distance. The library is housed on the PSR campus and is electronically integrated with that of the Graduate Theological Union. This makes the resources of the Swedenborg House of Studies accessible worldwide through an interlibrary database.

The central office of the Swedenborgian Church of North America is located in Massachusetts in a church building designed by the noted architect Ralph Adams Cram. The Wayfarers Chapel in Southern California is the national monument of the Swedenborgian Church to their founder, Emanuel Swedenborg. It is often called the "Glass Church," and it attracts more than a quarter of a million visitors annually. The Swedenborgian Church in San Francisco is more than 100 years old and is a beautiful example of the Arts and Crafts School of architecture.

Swedenborgian Church of North America
11 Highland Ave.
Newtonville, MA 02460

Swedenborg House of Studies
Pacific School of Religion
1798 Scenic Ave.
Berkeley, CA 94709
http://www.swedenborg.org/

Jane Williams-Hogan

See also: General Church of the New Jerusalem; Swedenborg, Emanuel; Swedenborgian Movement.

References

Block, Marguerite Beck. *The New Church in the New World*. New York: Octagon, 1968.

Journal of the Swedenborgian Church, 2008. Newtonville, MA: Swedenborgian Church of North America, 2008.

Swedenborg, Emanuel. *True Christian Religion*. West Chester, PA: Swedenborg Foundation, 1996.

Williams-Hogan, Jane. "Institutional and Communal Response to the Writings of Emanuel Swedenborg in Britain and the United States." In *Scribe of Heaven: Swedenborg's Life, Work, and Impact*. West Chester, PA: Swedenborg Foundation, 2001.

http://www.swedenborg.org/documents/2008Journal _Web.pdf

http://www.swedenborgiancommunity.org/files/ messenger

Swedenborgian Movement

Swedenborgian churches are founded upon the theological writings of Emanuel Swedenborg (1688–1772). Swedenborg was born in Stockholm and died in London. A scientist, philosopher, and civil servant, he published an extensive theological corpus from 1749 to 1771. He stated in *True Christianity* that "the Lord [Jesus Christ] manifested himself before me, his servant, and sent me to this office," in order "to receive the doctrines [of the new Jerusalem] in [my] understanding [and] to publish them by the press." From the time of his call in 1744 until his death, he wrote and published 18 different titles in 30 volumes. All of his theological writings were written in Latin. His first theological work, *Arcana Coelestia* (*Secrets of Heaven*) (1749–1756), was published in eight volumes. It presents the spiritual or internal sense of the biblical books of Genesis and Exodus. Also included in his corpus are works entitled *Heaven and Hell* (1758), *The Last Judgement* (1758), *Revelation Unveiled* (1766), *Divine Providence* (1764), *Love in Marriage* (1768), and *True Christianity* (1771).

Swedenborg called his theology a "new" Christianity. It emphasizes the oneness of God, who is the Lord Jesus Christ; the reality of the spiritual world and how it operates; the spiritual nature of the last judgment, which he claimed took place in 1757; the essential spiritual nature of human beings; the correspondence between the spiritual world and the natural world; human freedom in spiritual things; the marriage of love and wisdom in the Lord; the partnership of faith and charity leading to a life of use; and the sacred nature of marriage.

Swedenborg himself never attempted to found a church based upon the revelation he was given. He saw himself as a spiritual explorer and scribe. There were only a handful of people who claimed allegiance to his teachings at the time of his death, but groups of followers emerged in Sweden and England almost immediately afterward. His followers in Sweden belonged to the elite and well-educated circles of society. In

England they came from more diverse social backgrounds, and a significant number of readers and followers emerged among the artisans in Lancashire. Conflicts with the Crown and the Lutheran Church in Sweden impeded development of a legally organized New Church until 1874. In England, however, a church was organized to promote New Church worship as early as 1787.

There are two well-established Swedenborgian organizations incorporated in the United States. One is called the Swedenborgian Church of North America; the other is the General Church of the New Jerusalem. The Swedenborgian Church, also called the General Convention, is the more liberal of the two organizations. Its church government is democratically organized. It is a member of the National Council of Churches and sees itself as an advocate for liberal political causes in the United States and the world. The Convention advocates group diversity and environmentally aware thinking as part of its spirituality. The General Church is more conservative and does not feel that the church should take stands of political issues, leaving such activism up to the individual. Its church government is hierarchically organized. Although not advocating diversity per se, the membership of the General Church is racially and ethnically the most varied of any Swedenborgian organization worldwide.

The Swedenborgian movement from the beginning has been international in character. In the 18th century readers of Swedenborg's religious writings were found in Sweden, England, Germany, France, and America. Readers formed themselves into groups in Skara, Gothenberg, and Stockholm, Sweden; London, Manchester, and Birmingham, England; Boston, Philadelphia, and Baltimore, the United States; Tübingen, Germany; and Strausborg, France, among other places.

The General Conference of the New Church was first organized in Great Britain in 1787, and by 1815 it had instituted a congregational structure. Church business was to be conducted at an annual conference, which has been held yearly since that time up to the present. In 2004–2005 the General Conference had 741 adult members in 26 societies and 8 circles and 2 overseas societies, one in Mauritius and the other in New Zealand. The membership figure represents a 56 percent decrease over 6 years. These congregations are served by 12 active ministers in the United Kingdom and one in New Zealand. The General Conference has recently opted to ordain women and has begun a dispersed learning program in conjunction with its theological school, the New Church College, Radcliffe, Manchester.

The General Conference was supportive of the development of the New Church in the 19th and early 20th centuries. Today there are independent Swedenborgian New Church organizations in Australia, South Africa, and Nigeria that were at one time closely associated with the General Conference. The developments in South Africa and Nigeria are particularly worthy of mention, because Africans have been particularly responsive to the religious writings of Emanuel Swedenborg. The roots of the New Church of Southern Africa go back to the discovery of a copy of Swedenborg's *True Christian Religion* by David W. Mooki in 1909. He found a copy in a used furniture store, bought it, read it, and decided that its message concerning the one God, the Lord Jesus Christ, was true. He wished to found a church based upon this truth. Certain that there were more books and an organization already in existence somewhere in the world, he converted the members of his African Holy Catholic Church congregation to the teachings of the New Church. He made contact with the British Conference in 1917. As a result, his church became a missionary church of the General Conference. His efforts thrived, and by 1960 the church had 25,000 members, 39 churches, and 114 ministers. They became independent in 1969, under the leadership of David Mooki's son Obed, and took on the name cited above. The New Church of Southern Africa is congregationally organized, and church business is addressed annually in a conference and then supervised by a president for the remainder of the year. Given the strong leadership style of Obed Mooki, his death in 1990 created problems for the organization. A schism that had occurred shortly after Mooki's death had been healed by 2005. In September 2009, a centennial celebration was held.

Currently the church is opening and dedicating one new church building every year, and is looking toward the construction of new administrative center in Orlando, South Africa, adjacent to their theological training college. In 2000 the membership of the New

Church of Southern Africa stood at about 15,000 adult members. They had 41 ministers, 50 evangelists, and more than 80 societies. The resolution of the schism strengthened the church and its church building program indicates a growing membership.

The New Church in West Africa developed in Nigeria within the same time frame as the New Church in South Africa, with a similar story of development. Africanus Mensah bought copies of Swedenborg's religious writings through an advertisement, and upon reading them he became convinced of their truth. He made contact with the General Conference, and his organization was recognized by them in 1939. When Mensah died in 1942, there were approximately 1,000 adult members in 13 societies. The church is congregational in structure, and in 1981 it became an organization independent of the General Conference in the United Kingdom. In 2005 the year book of the General Conference lists two independent Swedenborgian organizations in Nigeria, one headquartered in Ondo State called the New Church in West Africa, and the other found in Akwa Ibom State called the Church of the New Jerusalem in West Africa.

A European Association of the New Church is headquartered in Switzerland. This is an umbrella organization for groups located in France, Germany, Italy, and other countries in Europe. There are also independent Swedenborgian New Church organizations in, among other countries, the Czech Republic, India, Kenya, Korea, the Philippines, Russia, the Ukraine, and Sri Lanka.

General Conference of the New Church
20 Bloomsbury Way
London WC1A 2TH
United Kingdom

New Church of Southern Africa
PO Box 592
Orlando East 1803
Soweto
South Africa

New Church in West Africa
PO Box 22
Owo
Ondo State
Nigeria

Church of the New Jerusalem in West Africa
PO Box 68
Etinan
Akwa Ibom State
Nigeria

European Association of the New Church
Buchholzstrasse 141
CH-8053
Zurich
Switzerland

Jane Williams-Hogan

See also: Church of Sweden; General Church of the New Jerusalem; Swedenborg, Emanuel; Swedenborgian Church of North America.

References

Spaulding, John Howard. *Introduction to Swedenborg's Religious Thought*. New York: Swedenborg Publishing Association, 1977.

Williams-Hogan, Jane. "Institutional and Communal Response to the Writings of Emanuel Swedenborg in Britain and the United States." In *Scribe of Heaven: Swedenborg's Life, Work, and Impact*, edited by Jonathan Rose, Stuart Shotwell, and Mary Lou Bertucci, 245–335. West Chester, PA: Swedenborg Foundation, 2001.

Woofenden, William Ross. *Swedenborg Researcher's Manual*. Bryn Athyn, PA: Swedenborg Scientific Association, 1988.

■ Switzerland

With the advent of the Reformation, the Swiss Confederation became a religiously mixed country. Under the influence of theologians such as Huldrych Zwingli (1484–1531) in Zurich, John Oecolampadius (1482–1531) in Basle, Guillaume Farel (1489–1565) in Neufchatel, and John Calvin (1509–1564) in Geneva, several Swiss cantons turned to Protestantism; others continued their prior alignment to the Roman Catholic Church. One split into two half-cantons, and both religions were tolerated in some territories jointly owned by several cantons. Up to the 19th century, religious fault lines would have lasting consequences for

Old church near Brig, Switzerland. (Corel)

Switzerland also at the political level: there were several internal conflicts related to religious differences.

The next step was the making of the federal state in the 19th century. Liberal political circles, eager to modernize the country, saw the conservative and hierarchical spirit of the Roman Catholic Church as an obstacle, in opposition to democratic aspirations. In addition, while the Protestant churches in Switzerland were cantonal ones, easily controlled by local authorities, the Roman Catholic Church formed a supranational religious organization, and its faithful were obedient to a spiritual power located abroad. This led to several clashes; as a result, a secret, separate alliance (Sonderbund) was concluded by seven Catholic cantons in order to help each other in case of an aggression. This was unacceptable to the other cantons, and a brief military campaign in November 1847 led to the defeat of the Sonderbund.

In 1848 the first federal Constitution was adopted and ushered in Switzerland's modern political system.

Another federal Constitution came into force in 1874, and remained in force (with amendments) until 2000. The 1874 Constitution affirmed the inviolability of freedom of conscience and belief, but some passages showed a clear suspicion toward possible infringements by the Roman Catholic Church. In addition, it was forbidden to create new dioceses in Switzerland without the permission of the federal government, or to establish new convents or religious orders; the Jesuits (seen at that time as the spearhead of Roman Catholicism) were not allowed to operate on Swiss territory. The articles banning the Jesuits and the foundation of new convents or religious orders were taken out of the Constitution in 1973; they had not been enforced for many years. But it was not until 2001 that the obligation to get approval from the federal government for the creation of new dioceses disappeared from the Constitution.

The 19th century also saw the emergence of religious pluralism. There had already been people outside the mainstream previously. At the time of the Reformation, radical trends emerged with the Anabaptists (Zurich, 1525), who were severely persecuted; some managed to survive in isolated places—the Mennonites still exist today. Jews were present too, but it was only during the second half of the 19th century that they came to enjoy equal rights with other residents, including the right to settle at any place in Switzerland. About the same time, additional religious groups appeared in Switzerland. Among Protestants, a number of ministers and laypeople became influenced by revivalist ideas and felt unsatisfied with the control exercised by the civil authorities upon churches in their respective cantons. This gave birth to Free churches in a few cantons, especially the Canton of Vaud, where a number of Protestant ministers, influenced by the ideas of theologian Alexander Vinet (1797–1847), resigned from the state church in protest against political intrusions in church life.

Beside the Free churches, other small, independent Christian communities, now known as the Christian Brethren, emerged at various places, among them the followers of John Nelson Darby (1800–1882), who spent several years in Switzerland (especially in the areas of Geneva and Lausanne). On the Catholic side, groups of Catholic liberals separated from Rome and created the Old Catholic Church in Switzerland after the First Vatican Council. The first Russian Orthodox church in Switzerland was consecrated in 1866. Finally, emergent new religious movements also set foot in Switzerland during that period: representatives of the Church of Jesus Christ of Latter-day Saints reached Switzerland as early as 1850; and the first European converts to the Seventh-day Adventist Church were baptized in 1866.

With the exception of Jews, however, religious pluralism remained confined to the Christian heritage. Inasmuch as Switzerland never did consider itself a country of immigration (although that comes to be increasingly challenged today) and never was a colonial power, extra-European, non-Christian populations were virtually nonexistent in Switzerland until the second half of the 20th century. Especially impressive has been the rapid development of the Muslim community, built upon immigration. According to the national census, which is conducted every 10 years and includes a question on religious affiliation, there were fewer than 3,000 Muslims in Switzerland in 1960, more than 16,000 in 1970, more than 150,000 in 1990, and more than 310,000 in 2000. The Swiss Muslim community consists primarily of Sunnis of the Hanafite School who came to the country from Turkey and the Balkans.

As in other European countries, the increase of the Muslim population led in recent years to some debates. Using one of the resources of the Swiss democratic system (popular initiatives forcing a national vote requesting a change in the federal Constitution, provided the initiative gathers enough citizens' signatures), an alliance of right-wing and evangelical activists managed to collect by the summer of 2008 more than 114,000 signatures asking to introduce a constitutional article banning the building of minarets (of which there are only a handful in Switzerland, none of them used for calling to prayer). Minarets are seen as a physical expression of Islamic power and conquest. In a November 2009 referendum, a constitutional amendment banning the construction of new minarets was approved by 57.5 percent of the participating voters. Only 4 of the 26 Swiss cantons, mostly in the French-speaking part of Switzerland, opposed the initiative.

Orthodox churches have also grown in Switzerland, mostly through immigration, especially from Serbia. According to the 2000 census, they made up 1.81 percent of the population (up from 0.33 percent in 1970). While Greek and Russian parishes had already a stable organization in Switzerland, both the Serbian and the Romanian patriarchates have developed efforts to organize parishes in the country in recent years. Oriental Orthodox (Copts, Ethiopians, Erythreans, Syriacs) have also established parishes, beside the already existing (but small) Armenian community.

Although the Reformed churches had been the largest religious group until the national census of 1960, the Roman Catholic Church took the lead after the 1970 census, on account of a higher birthrate as well as a higher percentage of Roman Catholics among immigrants (who came from Southern Europe: Italians, Spanish, and Portuguese came to work in Switzerland). The difference between the two confessions has increased over the years: in 2000, Roman Catholics constituted 41.82 percent of the Swiss population, while

SWITZERLAND

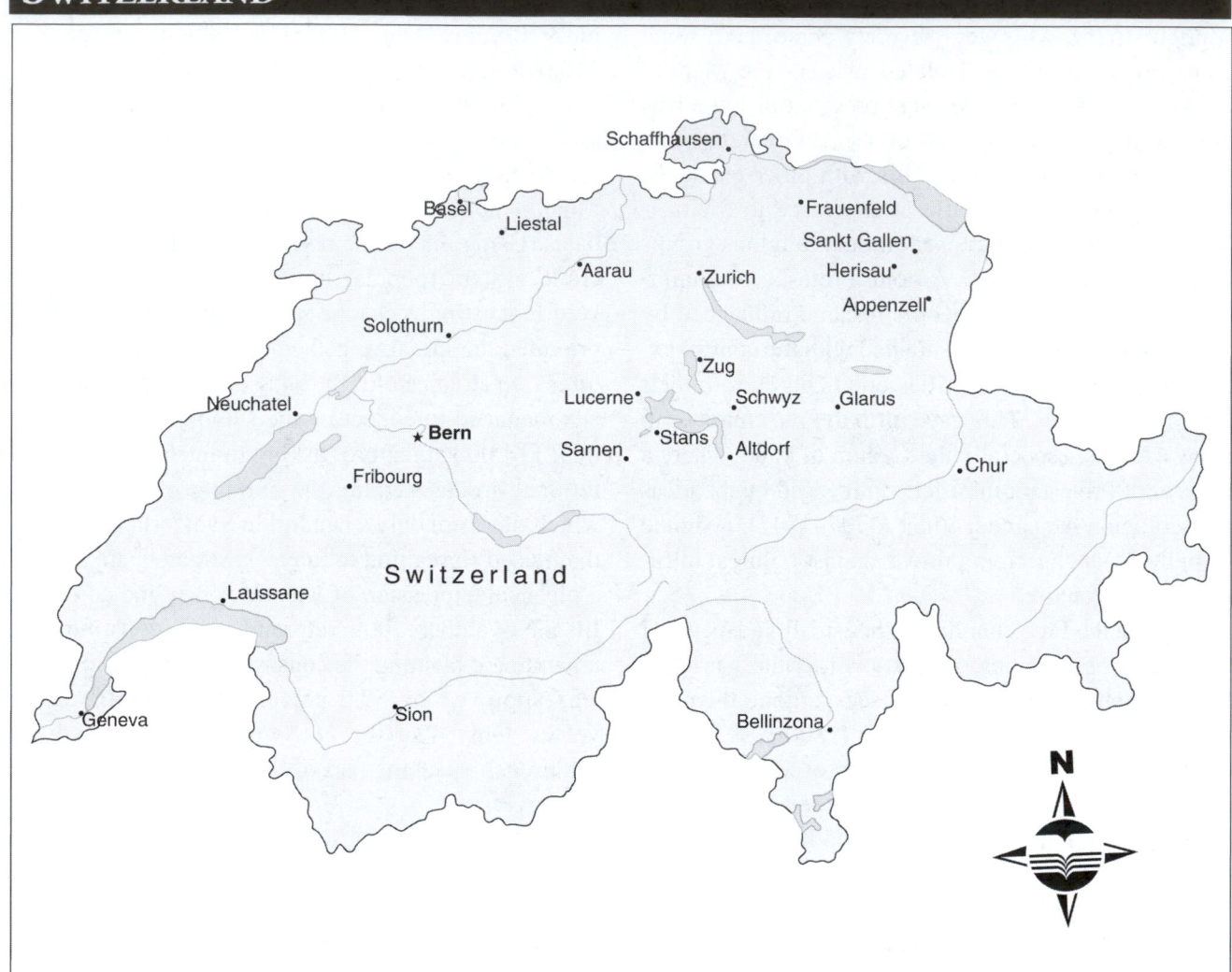

Reformed were down to 33.04 percent (compared with 46.42 percent in 1970). Roman Catholicism, however, is far from being homogeneous. Many Swiss Catholics have imbibed Protestant principles and the democratic spirit; inasmuch as the rules in several cantons give a high level of control to laypeople in church affairs, there are possibilities for pressure. It would be difficult for a bishop on a very conservative line to affirm his authority over all parts of his diocese: in 1997 the bishop of Chur, Wolfgang Haas, had to be transferred by Rome to a newly created archbishopric in Liechtenstein because many parishes in his diocese had gone into open revolt and refused to accept him (or pay their contributions) on account of his conservative views. On the other hand, it was in Switzerland

that the late ultraconservative French archbishop Marcel Lefebvre (1905–1991) came to create the Fraternity/Society of Saint Pius X and a seminary for the training of traditionalist Catholic priests in 1969. Since 1970 the seminary has been located at Ecône, in the Canton of Valais; the Catholic traditionalist movement has found an especially strong local following in that area. It was at Ecône that Archbishop Lefebvre consecrated four bishops in 1988.

There are other important trends in the religious life of Switzerland, which affect the established churches. As in several other Western European countries, the number of those claiming affiliation to one of the mainline churches has been decreasing. The unaffiliated may actually be the fastest growing group on

Switzerland

Religion	Followers in 1970	Followers in 2010	% of Population	Annual % growth 2000–2010	Followers in 2025	Followers in 2050
Christians	6,074,000	6,230,000	82.3	0.11	6,280,000	6,479,000
Roman Catholics	2,861,000	3,282,000	43.4	0.55	3,296,000	3,471,000
Protestants	2,808,000	2,486,000	32.9	−0.52	2,530,000	2,534,000
Independents	95,800	160,000	2.1	1.05	200,000	220,000
Agnostics	46,800	836,000	11.1	2.94	1,113,000	1,332,000
Muslims	16,400	315,000	4.2	0.44	351,000	350,000
Atheists	20,000	110,000	1.5	3.00	150,000	180,000
Buddhists	2,000	26,000	0.3	0.44	32,200	36,000
Hindus	2,000	24,200	0.3	0.44	26,600	28,500
Jews	20,700	18,000	0.2	0.44	16,000	16,000
Baha'is	3,100	4,200	0.1	0.44	5,500	7,500
New religionists	2,000	3,400	0.0	0.44	4,000	5,000
Total population	**6,187,000**	**7,567,000**	**100.0**	**0.44**	**7,978,000**	**8,434,000**

the religious map of Switzerland: from 3.8 percent in 1980, this group had reached 11.11 percent of the population in 2000. In a city like Basle, the percentage of unaffiliated people now constitutes the largest single group in the population, accounting for more than a third of the local population. "Unaffiliated" does not necessarily mean "nonbelieving" or "nonreligious," however; but up to now, it does not seem that minority religions have significantly gained from the weakening of traditional religions, since affiliation to religious groups outside of the historical religions (Catholicism, Protestantism, Orthodoxy, Judaism, and Islam) remained in 1990 less than 3 percent of the population. The largest of those latter groups is the New Apostolic Church, with about 27,000 faithful (down from 37,000 10 years earlier). Non-mainstream Protestants (evangelicals) have progressed and were 1.44 percent in 2000 (up from 0.42 in 1970), not including people of evangelical persuasion still affiliated with the mainstream Reformed churches, which means that the actual percentage of evangelicals in Switzerland is probably double that number. In the 1,500 evangelical congregations in Switzerland (including Methodists, 0.12 percent), 1,200 belong to some 40 different denominations, while 300 are independent.

As everywhere in the world, the Roman Catholic Church in Switzerland is organized into dioceses. Except for the Diocese of Lugano, whose boundaries correspond to those of the Italian-speaking Canton of

Ticino, other dioceses do not strictly correspond to cantonal borders or cover several cantons, although there is in most cantons a cantonal Catholic corporation for administrative purposes. Most of the Reformed churches, on the other hand, are organized along cantonal lines and are regrouped together within the Federation of Swiss Protestant Churches. Despite a significant statistical decline, the established churches still keep a strong position in Switzerland, since they do enjoy an official status. Religious affairs are a prerogative of the cantons; there is no federal agency dealing with those issues. Of the 26 cantons, only 2 have a regime of separation between state and religion, and even in those cases, the formerly established churches still enjoy a special status. This means that, in 24 cantons, people affiliated with the recognized churches (usually the Roman Catholic Church and the canton's Reformed Church, but in some cases also the Jewish community and the Old Catholic Church) will pay church taxes (as in Germany). It is important to understand that the recognition is a cantonal one, not a national one, and it is possible that some cantons will sooner or later choose the way of separation. The fact that only some religious communities enjoy a public law status does not mean that the others are discriminated against or prohibited from operating: there are few problems of religious freedom in Switzerland, where even emergent, fringe groups are usually able to function without any hindrance. In 2000 the federal government clearly rejected a request from a group of members of the federal Parliament asking the federal authorities to introduce a nationwide policy on "cults."

The headquarters of the World Council of Churches, as well as those of the Lutheran World Federation and the World Alliance of Reformed Churches, are located in Geneva. In addition, several movements have established their international headquarters in Switzerland, such as the Anthroposophical Society in Dornach (near Basle) and the Moral Re-Armament (renamed CAUX-Initiatives for Change in August 2001) in Caux (near Montreux).

Jean-François Mayer

See also: Anthroposophical Society; CAUX-Initiatives for Change; Christian Brethren; Fraternity/Society of Saint Pius X; Jesuits; Lutheran World Federation; New Apostolic Church; Old Catholic Church in Switzerland; Roman Catholic Church; Seventh-day Adventist Church; World Alliance of Reformed Churches; World Council of Churches

References

Baumann, Martin, and Jörg Stolz, eds. *Eine Schweiz—viele Religionen*. Bielefeld, Germany: Transcript, 2007.

Bovay, Claude. *L'évolution de l'appartenance religieuse et confessionnelle en Suisse*. Bern: Office Fédéral de la Statistique, 1997.

Bovay, Claude. *Le Paysage religieux en Suisse*. Neuchatel, Switzerland: Office Fédéral de la Statistique, 2004.

Kraus, Dieter. *Schweizerisches Staatskirchenrecht*. Tübingen, Germany: J. C. B. Mohr (Paul Siebeck), 1993.

Mayer, Jean-François. "La liberté religieuse en Suisse." *Conscience et Liberté* 55 (1998): 6–37.

Vischer, Lukas, et al. *Ökumenische Kirchengeschichte der Schweiz*. Freiburg-Basel: Paulusverlag-F. Reinhardt, 1994.

Synagogues

"Synagogue" is a Greek term for the main gathering place in the Jewish community for Sabbath worship, which also serves as a place through the week for study of the scriptures and spiritual fellowship. A variety of names are used for the synagogue including *bet knesset* (house of assembly), *bet tefillah* (house of prayer), and the Yiddish term, *shul* (school). Shul emphasizes the idea of the synagogue as a place of study. Reform Jews also name their synagogue either temple or congregation.

Some trace the synagogue back to the time of Moses; however, the oldest documented synagogue, known from some dedication inscriptions stones, was located in Egypt in the third century BCE. The oldest known synagogue building belonged to the Samaritan sect and is located on the Greek island of Delos. The oldest mainstream Jewish synagogue is found in Jericho and dates between 70 and 50 BCE. That being said, most scholars see what is today called the synagogue as originating in the Babylonian Captivity (586–516 BCE) as assemblies where Jews could perpetuate their faith; after the return to Jerusalem, religious life was reorganized. Ezra and his successors not only revived temple ceremonies, but nurtured Sabbath worship with prayer and readings in gatherings analogous to modern synagogues. Such assemblies were termed *knnesets*. The earliest mention of an assembly in a document comes from Alexandria (Egypt) in the third century BCE. Once the temple in Jerusalem was destroyed in 70 CE by the Romans, the synagogue became the center of Jewish religious life.

The synagogue emerged as simply a place for gathering, but over the centuries attained a level of sanctity. Buildings began to be constructed specifically for the weekly gathering. Where possible, the sanctuary of the synagogue, where the main weekly service is held, is oriented so that worshippers can face Jerusalem. Some prayers are supposed to be said while facing the city.

In the front of the room is the ark, a cabinet that holds the scrolls of the Torah, the five books of Moses (Genesis, Exodus, Leviticus, Numbers, and Deuteronomy), the most holy books of the Hebrew scripture. Inside the doors of the ark is a curtain, the *parokhet*, recalling the curtain that was in the sanctuary of the temple. The parokhet is opened or closed as the service proceeds, depending upon which prayers are being said. A member of the congregation is chosen to open and close the doors and curtain during the Sabbath service, a duty considered an honor. Slightly above the

Jewish synagogue, Old Town Tbilisi, Georgia. (Corel)

ark is the *ner tamid*, the eternal lamp, so placed as to honor an ancient commandment (Exodus 27:20–21) to keep a light burning in the tabernacle that held the ark of the covenant. Many synagogues also have a menorah (an eight-armed candelabrum). The menorah recalls the one in the temple, but has a different number of arms so as not to duplicate it.

Either in the center of the room or in the front, there is a raised dais called the *bimah*. The bimah is used when reading the Torah scrolls and it is often from the bimah that the service is led. Leading the service is the rabbi and, if available, the cantor.

Orthodox synagogues divide the sanctuary into two spaces, one for men and one for women. The sections are separated by a wall or a curtain. The ark, Torah scrolls, and bimah are in the section for the men. Reform synagogues removed the division in the sanctuary.

In the era between the World Wars, American synagogues began to participate in a larger movement called the institutional church. During this time, urban congregations began to develop as community centers and added space for sports activities (most notably a gymnasium) and artistic and cultural programs. In general, synagogues strive to create an aesthetically pleasing environment without appearing ostentatious.

The largest synagogue in the world, seating some 6,000 worshippers, is Belz World Center in Jerusalem, Israel, dedicated in 2000. It serves as the gathering place for the Belzer Hasidim. Another Hasidic group, the Satmar, have built the second largest synagogue as their center in Kiryas Joel, New York. The largest synagogue in Europe, again a Hasidic synagogue, is the Bratzlav Center located in Uman, Ukraine, near the grave of Rabbi Nachman of Bratzlav (1772–1810) and the cemetery where more than 20,000 Jewish victims of the Haidamak massacre of 1768 are buried. There are a variety of synagogues that have become famous due to their outstanding architecture or the history associated with them.

J. Gordon Melton

See also: Hasidism; Moses; Orthodox Judaism; Reform Judaism; Satmar Hasidism.

References

Assis, Yom Tiv. *And I Shall Dwell Among Them: Historic Synagogues of the World*. New York: Aperture, 2005.

Gruber, Samuel D. *Synagogues*. New York: MetroBooks, 1999.

Kee, Howard Clark, and Lynn B. Cohick, eds. *Evolution of the Synagogue*. Harrisburg, PA: Trinity Press, 1999.

Levine, Lee. *The Ancient Synagogue—The First Thousand Years*. New Haven, CT: Yale University Press, 2000.

Levy, Isaac. *The Synagogue: Its History and Function*. Edgware, UK: Vallentine, Mitchell, 1964.

■ Syria

Syria is a Middle Eastern country on the Mediterranean Sea south of Turkey. It also shares borders with Lebanon, Iraq, and Jordan, and a small but very important border with Israel. The Golan Heights, a militarily strategic highland immediate east of the Jordan River, the original border between Israel and Syria, was seized by Israel in 1967 and remains a matter of dispute between the two countries. Syria is now home to 19,748,000 people, plus an additional 40,000 people residing on the Golan Heights. The country includes 70,622 square miles of territory plus the 436 square miles of the occupied territory.

Syria's prehistory begins with the invention of writing, which took place in southern Babylon perhaps around 3000 BCE and evolved into cuneiform script. Israelites and other Semitic peoples had migrated there and settled near Jerusalem around 1400 BCE. The Hebrew Bible tells some of their stories of war, the development of monotheism, and territorial expansion. Boundaries have changed throughout the centuries because Syria was once denoted to be the entire region between the peninsulas of Anatolia and Sinai. A variety of Pagan faiths flourished there, and King Hammurabi is remembered as a noted lawgiver.

As intriguing as it is, Syria's ancient history lies beyond the parameters of this encyclopedia, which begins with the empire of Alexander the Great, dating between 356 and 323 BCE.

The Hellenistic era was a time of change, following the death of Alexander, when the Seleucids, named for Alexander's general Seleucus, controlled the region. After their demise, the Ptolemies of Egypt reigned for 100 years until Antiochus the Great defeated Ptolemy and took over southern Syria. By then Greek culture, the hallmark of those regimes, had cross-fertilized the region. Later, about 31 BCE, Syria was a significant province of the Roman Empire. Roman rule undermined the Syrian social structures and eroded the cohesiveness among indigenous groups. Syria was later divided into two provinces, Syria Coele in the north, with two Roman legions garrisoned there, and Syria Phoenice, which had one.

By the fifth century CE, Syria had been partitioned into five provinces. The city of Antioch was the seat of the governor and the cultural center for developments in art, medicine, law, and philosophy, and, most important, for the development of Christianity. According to Christian tradition, the followers of Jesus were first called Christians at Antioch (Acts 11:26), and Antioch became the center of one of the ancient patriarchates. The actions of the successive patriarchs of Antioch helped shape the doctrinal aspects of the Christian religion.

After the Roman Empire crumbled, Syria became wedged into the Byzantine Empire with Constantinople as headquarters, but during the first half of the seventh century, Syria was one of the first regions incorporated into the Muslim Caliphate. In 633–634, a decisive and vigorous campaign won the territory for the Arabs. In 636, the capital, Damascus, finally surrendered to the new authority. Conversions to Islam followed the Muslim victory, though Christians and Jews were generally treated with tolerance. From 639 to 750, the Umayyad dynasty reigned with Damascus as its capital. When the Arabic Abbasids defeated the Umayyads in 750, they moved the center of power to Baghdad (which in Arabic is known as the city of peace), where for several centuries their caliphate ruled in splendor. The flowering of Islamic culture proceeded, committed to the arts as well as warfare, while

Aleppo, Syria, one of the oldest inhabited cities in the world. (iStockPhoto.com)

providing the infrastructure for the early schools of Islamic jurisprudence.

The Fatimid dynasty, a Shia sect named for the daughter of Mohammad, wrested control from the Abbasids. For a time during the eighth and ninth centuries, the Fatimids dominated much of the Mediterranean areas of northwest Africa. The Church of the Holy Sepulcher, a pivotal Christian holy site, was destroyed in 1010. Their use of mercenaries became their downfall, however. In 1020 their leader Hakim (996–1021) proclaimed that he was a reborn God. Some Syrians accepted his claim, and today they are identified as the Druze. A rival group, the Assassins, in 1130 killed Amir, the last able Fatimid caliph who ruled from Egypt. Consequently, anarchy followed. In 1171 the last of the Fatimid rulers died. A group of ruthless mercenaries dedicated not to religion but power by assassination seized control.

The Assassins, a neo-Ismailite order named for their use of hashish, minimalized religious instruction, fostered murder, and spread terror through the land (1090). For nearly two centuries they operated as professional executioners. The Mongol invasions halted their reign of terror in 1272, when the Syrian stronghold at Masyad was destroyed. A sprinkling of the descendants of the Assassins, known as Ismailis, remain in Syria today. The Aga Khan, based in Bombay, India, is their spiritual leader, with 140,000 adherents scattered throughout India and now dispersed worldwide.

Arabs form the Sunni majority, including the Bedouins (who constitute about 7 percent of the population) and the Kurds (also with 7 percent). Armenians (a small 2 percent) are generally the descendants of early settlers who follow Arab customs or those latecomers who arrived after the persecutions of World War I and maintain their Armenian language and identity.

Today, Syria is a Muslim state. Approximately 85 percent of the population practices Sunni Islam of the Hanafite School. The largest Shia sect, the Alawis, are

Syria

Religion	Followers in 1970	Followers in 2010	% of Population	Annual % growth 2000–2010	Followers in 2025	Followers in 2050
Muslims	5,684,000	19,803,000	92.4	2.73	25,423,000	32,117,000
Christians	621,000	1,174,000	5.5	2.19	1,356,000	1,605,000
Orthodox	414,000	640,000	3.0	0.91	700,000	800,000
Roman Catholics	179,000	465,000	2.2	4.45	550,000	650,000
Protestants	20,900	40,000	0.2	1.02	55,000	70,000
Agnostics	50,000	425,000	2.0	4.46	700,000	1,100,000
Atheists	12,000	25,000	0.1	2.73	40,000	65,000
Jews	4,000	90	0.0	−7.17	90	90
Baha'is	100	180	0.0	2.87	300	500
Zoroastrians	0	40	0.0	2.86	50	60
Total population	**6,371,000**	**21,428,000**	**100.0**	**2.73**	**27,519,000**	**34,887,000**

concentrated near Latakia in the northwest province. The Syrian Alawis are not to be confused with the Alevis of neighboring Turkey. The Syrian Alawis make up about 13 percent of the population. The Druze are a minority, with about 380,000 adherents, though they are a dominant majority in the southwestern province of Suwayda. Ismailis are found in very small numbers near Hama and in Homs. A small number of Twelver Shiites are grouped near Aleppo, and they make up 1 percent of the population. The Yezidi, whose religion combines elements of Islam, Judaism, Nestorian Christianity, Zoroastrianism, and Manicheanism, was founded in the 12th century by Shaikh Adi. It has some 19,000 adherents, most in Djebel Sinjar near Aleppo. The Baha'i Faith, with roots in Iranian Islam, initially tried to missionize Syria in 1892. They were not accepted, and to the present, the Baha'is have only a minuscule presence in Syria.

Judaism has an ancient presence in Syria, much of the Jews' history being recorded in the Jewish Bible (which Christians call the Old Testament). It was swelled by the addition of Jews expelled from Spain and Portugal in the 1490s. During the early 20th century the population was more than 20,000, but given the events since the rise of the state of Israel, only some 4,000 remain.

Prior to the advent of Islam, Syria also had a strong Christian heritage that had initially established itself in the Antiochian Jewish population. The city of Antioch had a large church where the Apostle Paul was headquartered. Antioch became a major spiritual epicenter as its theologians hammered out doctrines pertaining to the nature of Christ. After the Council of Chalcedon in 451, Eastern Orthodoxy predominated. Only in the 16th century did the Roman Catholic Church gain a foothold, when at various times Orthodox Christians found it convenient to form Eastern-rite dioceses in communion with Rome. Among them, the Maronite Catholic Church can be traced to the Crusader Kingdom of Antioch in the 12th century. Between the 16th and 18th centuries, additional Eastern-rite churches developed, most important, the Melkite Catholic Church and the Chaldean Catholic Church.

Christians make up about 8 percent of the inhabitants of Syria. The Greek Orthodox Patriarchate of Antioch and All the East has the largest congregations, which are deeply rooted in an Arab identity. They are Greek in that they follow Byzantine traditions. The Greek Orthodox became the mother church for the Jacobites (Syriac Orthodox Patriarchate of Antioch and All the East) who broke away in the sixth century as a result of the Monophysite controversy concerning the nature of Christ. The patriarch lives in Damascus and maintains friendly relations with other Orthodox congregations, particularly the Russian Orthodox Church (Moscow Patriarchate), who supported the quest for a Syrian to be appointed as patriarch of Aleppo. The Armenian Apostolic Church (Holy See of Echmiadzin) forms the third major Christian community in Syria based near Aleppo, with about 300,000 followers.

Six Roman Catholic groups exist in Syria today. The Melkites, with their main strength in Aleppo, are

SYRIA

a predominant group. Their patriarch, who resides in Damascus, has an extensive jurisdiction that includes Jerusalem (Israel) and Alexandria (Egypt). There is an enclave of Maronites near Aleppo, but their numbers are few, as most reside in neighboring Lebanon. Latin Catholics also live near Aleppo, where their vicar dwells. Aleppo played an important geographical role in the transmission of Christian principles beginning in the 13th century, when Crusaders headquartered there. Chaldeans inhabit eastern Syria near the Iraqi border, with 1,500 people near Aleppo and another 500 near Damascus. The Holy See has a nuncio residing in Damascus serving as liaison with the Syrian government.

Early missionary reports frequently merged activities in Syria and Lebanon. This is because the two countries were, at one time, a single geographical area, until separated by the French Mandate in 1918 for administrative reasons. Initial missionary activity from Western nations centered around Beirut, which is now in Lebanon. Joseph Wolff of the London Jews Society visited Syria in 1822–1823 looking for converts to Christianity from among the Jewish population.

Representatives of the American Board of Commissioners for Foreign Missions arrived in the Middle East and traveled extensively in Palestine and Syria. Missionaries Pliny Fiske and Levi Parsons stirred religious unrest within the Catholic and Orthodox communities while being largely ignored by the Muslim community. The American Board left Syria and Iran in 1870 and turned their work over to the United Presbyterian Church (now the Presbyterian Church [U.S.A.]), which has a medical and educational focus in the Middle East. Aleppo College is an outstanding institution, which is supported by the Armenian Evangelical Union, The National Evangelical Synod of Syria and Lebanon, the American Presbyterians, and the United Church of Christ.

The National Evangelical Synod, founded in 1823, is one of the oldest missionary groups. The National Evangelical Christian Alliance of Syria, established in 1921, has about 1,000 members. The Church of the Nazarene has existed since 1970 and has seven churches. The Diocese of Jerusalem of the Episcopal Church in Jerusalem and the Middle East governs the small Anglican presence of 3,000. In the 1990s, Pentecostal/Charismatic renewal movements spread through the Christian community in Syria, with more than 100,000 people participating. In the wake, new Pentecostal congregations have appeared, but as in earlier generations, converts to this latest form of Christianity have come primarily from previously existing Christian communities within Syria, rather than from Islam.

Islam's place in Syrian society has changed during the past 100 years. Under the rule of the Ottoman Empire (1517–1918) and during the early years of the 20th century, legal scholars (*ulama*) advocated strict adherence to Muslim jurisprudence traditions, three being operative in Syria today. The court systems follow the Hanifite School, while the Shafaiite School is more likely to govern family issues in both Syria and Lebanon. There is a small minority that support the Hanbalite tradition, closely associated with the conservative Wahhabi school identified with the royal family of Saudi Arabia.

Syria has an innovative history associated with its use of the several legal traditions. Syrian religious scholars have tended to study with teachers of each school of jurisprudence, thus yielding a pluralistic approach to the Muslim community. This pluralism has facilitated a level of acceptance of the various Sufi orders and other minority groups. In the early years of the 20th century, the Syrians rejected the ultraconservative Wahhabi movement, partially because of their spirit of judicial tolerance, their allegiance to the system of jurisprudence reflected by the Ottoman Empire, and their history of diversity in beliefs.

However, problems arose in the early 20th century when reformers clashed with Sufi orders. Controversy developed over the Sufi love of visits to shrines and the tombs of saints, which is in direct conflict with Sunni doctrine. Most important, reformers challenged the rules so dear to the Shafiite and Hanafite jurists. The resultant religious instability contributed significantly to the collapse of the Ottoman Empire after World War I. Amir Faysal of the Meccan Hashemite clan briefly seized control of Syria but was ousted by the French in 1916. The League of Nations mandated a French protectorate in 1918. Syria mobilized against Western hegemony, and even the marginalized Druze and Alawi communities combined forces with mainstream Muslims.

In 1949 a new nonreligious civil code based on an Egyptian model was adopted. Four years later, Islam's legal arm recognized a Law of Personal Status that governed family matters for Sunnis, Alawis, and Ismailis. In contrast, the Druze (not considered true Muslims), the Jews, and the Christians each have their own codes of jurisprudence to govern their members.

In 1963 a military coup brought the socialistic Ba'ath Party into power. In 1970, Hafiz al Assad began his three decades as president. Upon his death in 2000, his son Basher Assad succeeded him. Missed by most Western observers, Assad was a member of the minority Alawi community, as is his son. Their rule has given the Alawis a significantly higher profile in Syria, though some Sunnis still reject the idea of a president from what they see as a heretical minority tradition. The Syrian president appoints his cabinet. However, 250 members of the People's Council (the legislature) are elected from cities and rural areas within Syria. The country, except for a brief period during 1974–1975, has been under martial law because of constant warfare coupled with internal dissention. Today, secular and religious ideologies are flashpoints fueling human rights violations for dissident groups.

The rise of the Muslim Brotherhood, initiated in Egypt soon after the end of World War II but allied with the Wahhabi leadership in Saudi Arabia, was a reactionary backlash to the quest for secularism, and because of the furor, the Syrian cabinet established a law that the head of state must be a Muslim. However, ongoing clashes continue with the Brotherhood over the place of religion in affairs of state.

For a brief time, Syria was united with Egypt in the United Arab Republic (1958–1961) and participated in the Arab-Israeli wars of 1967 and 1973. Syrian troops intervened in Lebanon in 1976, fearing an Israeli-backed political takeover. However, Syria did not support Iraq during the Gulf War in 1990–1991, partially because the countries are ruled by rival Ba'ath parties.

The Middle East Council of Churches (affiliated with the World Council of Churches) formed in 1927 near Beirut, and it includes four Syrian-based churches. After the Arab-Israeli wars, the Council has been active in helping with resources for the 340,000 displaced persons, mainly Palestinian refugees, who are stateless. There are another 300,000 people who have been internally displaced throughout the political and religious strife. The World Council of Churches has subsidized much of the work done to help these homeless people, who have a substandard quality of life, maintain their integrity under duress.

J. Gordon Melton

See also: Alevism; American Board of Commissioners for Foreign Missions; Armenian Apostolic Church (Holy See of Echmiadzin); Baha'i Faith; Chaldean Catholic Church; Church of the Nazarene; Druze; Eastern Orthodoxy; Episcopal Church in Jerusalem and the Middle East; Greek Orthodox Patriarchate of Antioch and All the East; Hanafite School of Islam; Hanbalite School of Islam; Ismaili Islam; Maronite Catholic Church; Melkite Catholic Church; Middle East Council of Churches; National Evangelical Synod of Syria and Lebanon; Presbyterian Church (U.S.A.); Roman Catholic Church; Russian Orthodox Church (Moscow Patriarchate); Shafiite School of Islam; Syriac Orthodox Patriarchate of Antioch and All the East; United Church of Christ; Wahhabi Islam; World Council of Churches; Yezidis.

References

Abd-Allah, U. F. *The Islamic Struggle in Syria.* Berkeley, CA: Mizzen, 1983.

Bliss, Frederick. J. *The Religions of Modern Syria and Palestine.* New York: Scribner, 1912.

Fact, M. A. "The Alawis Community of Syria: A New Dominant Force." *Middle Eastern Studies* 20, no. 2 (1984): 133–153.

Haidallah, I. A. *The Legal Status of Non-Moslem Communities in the Near East, and Especially Syria and Lebanon.* Beirut: American University of Beirut, 1965.

Moaddel, Mansoor. *Jordanian Exceptionalism: A Comparative Analysis of State-Religion Relationships in Egypt, Iran, Jordan, and Syria.* New York: Palgrave Macmillan, 2002.

Syriac Orthodox Patriarchate of Antioch and All the East

During the fifth century CE, the Christian church was struck by what was termed the Monophysite controversy, a stage in the Christian movement's development of the orthodox definition of the Trinity and the divinity of Christ. In 451 the Council of Chalcedon promulgated the position that Christ was of one substance with the Father as regards his Godhead and at the same time of one substance with humanity as regards his manhood. The Monophysite position spoke to the nature of Christ and suggested that Jesus' human nature had been taken up and absorbed into his divine nature. They did not ascribe to the Council of Chalcedon, though they did follow the findings of previous councils and use the standard creed promulgated earlier by the Council of Nicaea in 325.

Monophysite exponents led in the formation of several churches that separated from Eastern Orthodoxy and the Roman Catholic Church. Among the last to form was the Syrian church, which is generally dated to the consecration of Jacob Baradeus (500–578) as bishop of Edessa in 542. Edessa was then a major center of the Christian church in its movement into Asia. Bishop Jacob was both a fervent Monophysite and possessed of the favor of Empress Theodosia (of the Byzantine Empire). He was able to use his position to travel through the empire from Turkey to Egypt and eastward to Persia, founding Monophysite congregations. His initial work was continued by his followers until inhibited by the emergence of Islam in the seventh century. They spread the church as far east as India and China.

The church uses a Syriac liturgy and a Syriac translation of the Bible, which has been available since the second century. As the church has spread, other languages have been introduced over the centuries.

The church's history has been marked by several disasters in the modern era. It suffered greatly when the Mongols passed through in the 14th century. It lost many members when the Roman Catholic Church established the Syrian Catholic Church as a Syrian affiliate in the 18th century. At the beginning of the 20th century, many of its members were killed by the Turks. During the 20th century, some reversal of the downward trend was made when it accepted many Orthodox in India under its umbrella, and in 1964 the Syrian patriarch consecrated and re-established the office of the Catholicate of the Orthodox Syrian Church of the East in India.

For many years, beginning in the 13th century, the church had been headquartered at Mardin, Turkey, but it moved to Homs, Syria, in 1933 to escape Turkish violence and then in 1957 relocated to Damascus. In 2000 the church changed its name from Syrian Orthodox to Syriac Orthodox, indicating its use of the Syriac language rather than any ties to the current nation of Syria. The Syriac Orthodox Patriarchate of Antioch and All the East (popularly known as the Syrian Orthodox Church or the Jacobite Church) is now under the leadership of His Holiness Ignatius Zakka I. Ivas, its patriarch. The church has bishops in Iraq, Lebanon, Jerusalem, Turkey, the Netherlands (for parishes in Europe), Sweden (for Scandinavia), the United States, Australia, and Brazil (for South America). The largest number of members associated with the church (14,000,00 in 2006) are in India, where more than 700,000 reside. The church is a member of the World Council of Churches.

Syriac Orthodox Patriarchate of Antioch and All the
    East
PO Box 22260
Bab Tooma
Damascus

Syria
http://www.syrianorthodoxchurch.org/

J. Gordon Melton

See also: Eastern Orthodoxy; Roman Catholic Church; Syrian Catholic Church; Syrian Orthodox Church of Malabar; World Council of Churches.

References

Chaillot, Christine. *The Syrian Orthodox Church of Antioch and All the East: A Brief Introduction to Its Life and Spirituality*. Geneva: Inter-Orthodox Dialogue, 1998.

Orthodoxia. Regensburg, Germany: Osrkirchliches Institut (issued annually).

Ramban, Kadavil Paul. *The Orthodox Syrian Church: Its Religion and Philosophy*. Vadatampady, Puthencruz, India: Pathrose, 1973.

Roberson, Ronald G. *The Eastern Christian Churches—A Brief Survey*. 5th ed. Rome: Edizioni Orientalia Christiana, Pontificio Istituto Orientale, 1995.

Van Beek, Huibert. *A Handbook of the Churches and Councils: Profiles of Ecumenical Relationships*. Geneva: World Council of Churches, 2006.

Van der Bent, Ans J., ed. *Handbook/Member Churches/World Council of Churches*. Geneva: World Council of Churches, 1985.

Syrian Catholic Church

The Syrian Catholic Church emerged in the 17th century out of missionary activity launched by missionaries of the Roman Catholic Church in Aleppo in northwest Syria. At the time, the majority of Christians in the area were affiliated with the Greek Orthodox Patriarchate of Antioch and All the East, the so-called Jacobite Church, which had not affirmed the teachings of the Ecumenical Council held at Ephesus in 431 concerning the nature of Christ. The Council affirmed that Christ had both a human and a divine nature, while the Syrians generally held the Monophysite position that Christ had only a divine nature.

The Catholic mission had spectacular success through the 1650s, and in 1662 a patriarch with Catho-

Iraqi Christians light candles after attending Christmas mass at the Syrian Catholic church in al-Karrada, central Baghdad, December 2007. (AFP/Getty Images)

lic leanings, Andrew Akhidjan, was elected head of the Syrian Orthodox Church. Following his death, however, a split occurred, and the two factions (one pro-Rome and one independent of Rome) each elected a patriarch. However, the authorities of the Ottoman Empire supported the Orthodox faction, and no successor to the Catholic bishop was elected.

Those Syrians who followed the Syrian-Antiochene liturgy and practice but were oriented on the authority of the bishop of Rome continued to exist but found themselves in an increasingly precarious position. In the 18th century, they were forced underground. Then in 1782, the Syrian patriarch declared his allegiance to Rome and fled to Lebanon, where he established Our Lady of Sharfeh Monastery. He began a new line of Syrian Catholic patriarchs. Finally in 1828, the Ottoman government granted recognition to the Syrian Catholic Church. In 1850 the headquarters of the church was moved to Mardin, in southwestern Turkey.

The church expanded during the last half of the 19th century but fell victim to the massacres of Syrians that occurred during World War I. As a result of those massacres, many Catholics fled to Lebanon, and in the 1920s the patriarchate moved to Beirut. Like every patriarch, the current patriarch, Ignatius Joseph III Younan (b. 1944), who took office early in 2009, has added Ignatius to his patriarchal name. There are some 132,000 Syrian Catholics (2008), most residing in Lebanon, Syria, Turkey, Egypt, and Iraq. There are parishes in the Sudan and Israel, and the faithful in North America are organized into Our Lady of Deliverance Syriac Catholic Diocese. The church is active in the Middle East Council of Churches.

The church oversees two religious orders, both named for Ephraem the Syrian, a fourth-century saint-theologian. A publishing house and seminary are located at Our Lady of Sharfeh Monastery. Worship is conducted in Syrian, though most members now speak Arabic.

Syrian Catholic Church
Rue de Danms
BP 116-5087
Beirut
Lebanon

J. Gordon Melton

See also: Greek Orthodox Patriarchate of Antioch and All the East; Middle East Council of Churches; Roman Catholic Church.

References

Liesel, N. *The Eastern Catholic Liturgies: A Study in Words and Pictures.* Westminster, MD: Newman, 1960.

Roberson, Ronald G. *The Eastern Christian Churches: A Brief Survey.* 5th ed. Rome: Edizioni Orientalia Christiana, Pontificio Istituto Orientale, 1995.

Syrian Orthodox Church of Malabar

The year 1653 can be considered the founding of the modern Syrian Orthodox Church of Malabar, while its history leads us to a time period between the first and third centuries CE. The church traces its origins to the Apostle Thomas. As a result of a synod in the year 2000, the church refers to itself as the Syrian Orthodox Church of Malabar; previously it had been the Malankara Jacobite Syriac Orthodox Church.

The Syrian Orthodox Church of Malabar considers itself the church of the Syrian Christians of India, whose presence can be documented from the third century. To support this claim, the church refers to individual documents that suggest that the Syrian Christians of India stood under the jurisdiction of the patriarch of Antioch. But there is more historical evidence that India's Syrian Christians were members of the Apostolic Catholic Church of the East prior to the arrival of the Portuguese. Along with all other jurisdictions of Mar Thoma of India, the church is convinced that its origins can be traced to the presence of the Apostle Thomas in India. After the Portuguese forced the church to unify with the Roman Catholic Church under Menezes at the synod of Diamper in 1599, it took decades until the local Syrian opposition, led by Archidiakon Thoma Parambil (Thomas de Campo), made intensive efforts to acquire a Syrian bishop. But Mar Atallah, the former Syrian-Orthodox archbishop from Damascus, who arrived in 1652, was captured by the Portuguese and taken to Europe. Thereafter the Thomas Christians took an anti-Latin oath, and 12 priests were consecrated by the Archdeacon Thomas (d. 1673) in an emergency ceremony. As a result, a faction of the Indian Thomas Christians came into being, the members of which have since been referred to as the Malankars.

In 1655, Thomas I received help and apostolic succession from the Metropolite Gregorios Abdalgalil of Jerusalem and other bishops of the Syriac Orthodox Patriarchate of Antioch and All the East who traveled to India. As a result of the presence of these bishops, the Syrian Christians took on, under Thomas I, the West-Syrian liturgy and recognized the synod of Ephesus.

Once again, in the middle of the 18th century, problems arose surrounding the consecration of the church's leader, with the transition from Thomas IV to Thomas V and then Thomas VI. However, a delegation from the Syrian Orthodox bishops once again ordained

validly and without conflict Thomas VI, later referred to as Dionysios I the Great (1761–1808).

In 1836 the general assembly of the Malankars strengthened their ties to the Syrian Orthodox Church in order to resist the Anglican Church Missionary Society, which was intent on reforming the Orthodox Syrians. With the synod of Mulanthuruthy in 1876, the Syrian Orthodox patriarch Petros IV (d. 1894) reorganized the Church of the Malankars, for which he had a full mandate. The reform Malankars were excommunicated and left the church (they formed the present-day Mar Thoma Syrian Church of Malabar). But as early as 1911 there was a conflict between the Syrian Orthodox patriarch Abdallah II (1909–1915) and the Metropolitan Dionysios VI. This conflict arose when Abdallah tried to replace the Metropolitan Dionysios VI, who wanted more autonomy, with one of his own hierarchs. But with the help of the former Syrian Orthodox patriarch Abdalmasih II (who was deposed of his office in 1905 by the sultan), the Malankars managed to re-establish the Office of the Maphrian in India, which had been eliminated in the 19th century and had been united with the Office of the Metropolite of Malankara since 1934. As a result, there were two opposing Malankarian Syrian Orthodox jurisdictions: the so-called Catholicos faction and the Patriarch faction. While the autonomists called for Indianization, those loyal to the patriarch sought to preserve old traditions. In 1975 the autonomist Augen I was suspended by the Syrian Orthodox synod in Damascus and was replaced by Katholikos Basileios Paulos II (d. 1996). Since then, the Malankars have once again appeared permanently divided—despite a decision of the Supreme Court of India in 1995 that aimed at unifying the Malankars.

The faith and the liturgical tradition of the Syrian Orthodox Church in India are similar to those of the Syriac Orthodox Church. The church approved the first three ecumenical councils (Nicaea, Constantinople, and Ephesus) and denies the addition of the Filioque clause in the Apostles' Creed. They do not accept the concept of the Immaculate Conception of Mary. The liturgical language of the Syrian Orthodox Church is Syriac.

Membership in the Syrian Orthodox Church is estimated at approximately 650,000 people. The leadership of the church is part of the Syriac Orthodox episcopal synod. The leader is the Malankara Metropolitan and Chatholicose, respectively, and is supported by the Managing Committee of the church, the secretary of the church, and the trustees of the church. The church is divided into ten dioceses.

The Syrian Orthodox Church is also present outside India, primarily in expatriate/diasporic communities in Europe and North America. His Greatness Thomas Mor Themotheios is in charge of dioceses outside of Kerala, and His Greatness Joseph Mor Gregorios is in charge of the United Arab Emirates and European dioceses.

The Syrian Orthodox Church of Malabar has a theological seminary in the state of Kerala at Udayagiri (near Mulanthuruthy). The seminary also functions as a center for the ecumenical activities of the church. In Kerala, ardent theological dialogues are taking place between the Syrian Orthodox Church and the Catholic Church (the foundation being a joint statement presented by Patriarch Yakub III and Pope Paul VI in 1971). As a result a draft resolution was prepared, and both churches have agreed in principle to allow marriages between its members. The Syrian Orthodox Church is also an active member of ecumenical organizations such as the World Council of Churches, the Christian Conference of Asia, and the National Council of Churches in India.

Syrian Orthodox Church
c/o H.G. Thomas Mor Dionysius Metropolitan
Mount Senai Bishop's House
Kothamangalam
Kerala 822101
India

Martin Tamcke

See also: Apostolic Catholic Assyrian Church of the East; Christian Conference of Asia; Roman Catholic Church; Syriac Orthodox Patriarchate of Antioch and All the East; World Council of Churches.

References

Kaniamparampil, Kurian Corepiscopa. *The Syrian Orthodox Church of India and Its Apostolic Faith*. Tiruvalla, India:1989.

Madey, Johannes. "Background and History of the Present Schism in the Malankara Church." *Oriens Christianus* 60 (1976): 95–112.

Paul, Daniel Babu. *The Syrian Orthodox Christians of St. Thomas*. Ernakulam, India: Cochin, 1968.

Philip, E. M. *The Indian Church of St. Thomas*. Kottayam, India: 1951.

Williams, Raymond B. *Christian Pluralism in the United States: The Indian Immigrant Experience*. Cambridge: Cambridge University Press, 1996.

Syro-Malabar Catholic Church

The Syro-Malabar Catholic Church emerged in the 15th century when Portuguese Roman Catholics discovered the Syrian Orthodox Church of Malabar (which now exists in two branches, the Malankara Orthodox Syrian Church and the Mar Thoma Syrian Church of Malabar). The Malabar church traced its origin to the legendary ministry of the Apostle Thomas in the years after the death and resurrection of Jesus. As the Portuguese established their authority in India, Catholic missionaries began to impose a variety of Roman Catholic liturgical changes and practices upon the church. A number of these were formally adopted at a synod in 1599 held at Diamper. Portuguese were appointed as bishops, clerics were required to adopt a celibate existence, and the Inquisition was established to deal with heretics.

Over the next generation opposition to the new order grew, and in 1653, at another synod at Diamper, the majority of the church broke with Rome. They returned to their pre-Catholic practices. Pope Alexander VII subsequently appointed the Carmelites to rectify the problems in India. They arrived a short time later, and over the next decades many of those who had broken with Rome returned. The Carmelites held the leading positions in the church through the 19th century. By the 1680s a Syro-Malabar Catholic Church and a reordered Syrian Orthodox Church of Malabar emerged, and both have continued to the present. The Syro-Malabar church is in full communion with the Roman Catholic Church.

For the next 200 years, the Latin-rite Catholic churches and Syro-Malabar congregations with their heavily Latinized liturgy remained part of the same jurisdiction. Then in 1887, Pope Leo XIII separated the two groups. In 1896 the Vatican erected three vicariates apostolic for the Syro-Malabar Catholic Church and placed indigenous bishops in charge. A fourth diocese was created in 1911. Through the 20th century, these four dioceses grew into five provinces, each headed by an archbishop and each including additional dioceses. As of 2008, there were 26 dioceses, 13 of which are in Kerala. In 1923 the vicariate apostolic of Ernakulam was elevated to an archdiocese, and in 1992 it was named the major archdiocese of Ernakulam-Angamly. The current archbishop, Cardinal Varkey Vithayathil (b. 1927), is the head of the Syro-Malabar Church.

The Syro-Malabar Catholic Church has an estimated four million members. That figure represents the remarkable growth since the 1930s, when there were fewer than half a million members. The church sponsors two major seminaries at Bangalor and Ujjain, and a number of religious orders. The several congregations in the United States and Canada have been organized into the one diocese of the church with jurisdiction outside of India.

As early as 1934, Pope Pius XI authorized a study of the Syro-Malabar liturgy with the aim of possible restoration of its pre-Latinized format. A revised liturgy was finally published in 1957, but it has not proved a popular format in India, where the Latinized liturgy had been used for several centuries.

Syro-Malabar Catholic Church
Major Archbishop's House
PB No. 2580
Kochi, Kerala 682 031
India
http://www.smcim.org/

J. Gordon Melton

See also: Malankara Orthodox Syrian Church; Mar Thoma Syrian Church of Malabar; Roman Catholic Church; Syrian Orthodox Church of Malabar.

References

Hoke, Donald, ed. *The Church in Asia*. Chicago: Moody, 1975.

Moffett, Samuel Hugh. *A History of Christianity in Asia*. Vol. 1, *Beginnings to 1500*. San Francisco: HarperSanFrancisco, 1992.

Neill, S. C. *A History of Christianity in India*. 2 vols. Cambridge: Cambridge University Press, 1984, 1985.

Syro-Malankara Catholic Church

The Syro-Malankara Catholic Church originated in 1926 out of disagreement within the Malankara Orthodox Syrian Church in southern India. The Malankara church traces its beginning to the ministry of the Apostle Thomas, who, it is claimed, came to Kerala soon after the resurrection of Christ and founded several churches prior to his martyrdom. In the 15th century Indian Christians came in contact with the Roman Catholic Church. Missionaries who arrived with the Portuguese began to exert considerable influence over the church, and in 1599, at a synod at Diamper, imposed a variety of practices from the Latin rite on the church. In 1653 the majority of the Indian faithful rejected Roman authority and returned to the Syriac liturgy that they had previously used.

The re-established Orthodox Church then turned to the Greek Orthodox Patriarchate of Antioch and All the East, often called the Jacobite Church, for the episcopal orders lost during their years affiliated with Rome. In the 19th century, the Church of England, which had come to India with British rule, began to exert its influence on the Malabar church. Some suggestions for reform were accepted by parts of the church, leading it to split into two branches, the Mar Thoma Syrian Church of Malabar and the Malankara Orthodox Syrian Church. The Mar Thoma Church accepted the reforms suggested by the Anglicans and has established formal communion with the Church of England.

The Malankara Church continued with its traditional practice and its communion with the Syriac Orthodox Patriarchate of Antioch and All the East. However, in the 1880s, a dispute developed with the patriarch of the Syrian Orthodox Church, who began to assert his ownership of the property of the Malankara Church. That dispute would continue in several phases until the 1950s. In the midst of this controversy, five Malankara bishops opened negotiations with Rome. They asked that their liturgy be retained and that they remain as bishops of their diocese. Originally, on September 30, 1930, two of the five made their profession of the faith. The next day, they were joined by two more of their episcopal colleagues. They and those priests and laypeople received with them constituted the Syro-Malankara Catholic Church, a church in full

communion with the Roman Catholic Church. In 1932, Mar Ivanios visited Rome. He was named archbishop of Trivandrum, and along with his archeparchy, the Eparchy of Tiruvalla was established. The new church drew significant support from the Malankara Church, and by 1960 it claimed more than 68,000 members.

At the time of its founding, the Roman Catholic Church already recognized a Syro-Malabar Catholic Church operating in the same area; however, this church uses a very different liturgy and has a variety of practices adopted from the Portuguese in the 1600s. With minor changes, the Syro-Malankara Catholic Church maintains the Syriac liturgy that had been used prior to the arrival of Europeans in Kerala.

Besides the archeparchy (archdiocese), there are six exarchies (dioceses) in India. The church has 413,000 members (2008). Its current leader is Major Archbishop Isaac Clemmis Thottunka (b. 1959), who took office in 2007. There are scattered congregations across North America, but no diocese.

Syro-Malankara Catholic Church
Archbishop's House
Trivandrum 695 004
Kerala
India
www.malankaracatholicchurch.net

J. Gordon Melton

See also: Church of England; Greek Orthodox Patriarchate of Antioch and All the East; Malankara Orthodox Syrian Church; Mar Thoma Syrian Church of Malabar; Roman Catholic Church; Syrian Orthodox Church of Malabar.

Reference

Roberson, Ronald G. *The Eastern Christian Churches: A Brief Survey.* 5th ed. Rome: Edizioni Orientalia Christiana, Pontificio Istituto Orientale, 1995.

T

Tabernacles, Feast of

See Sukkot.

T'aego Pou

1301–1382

T'aego Pou, to whom most practitioners of Korean Son Buddhism trace their lineage, carried out a reorganization of the Son community a little more than a century after Chinul (1158–1210) had succeeded in reforming it.

T'aego was born in Kwangju, in southern Korea. The religious life was presented to him as a child and he was but 13 when initially ordained as a monk. He attained his first awakening six years later, and, after more than a decade of practice, he attained his deeper enlightenment when he was 37. Several years later he settled at Mount Samgak (near modern-day Seoul) at Chungheungsa Temple, where he built Sosolam Hermitage east of the temple. Here he would complete his first major writing, the *Gailpyeon*, and here he would attract many students. During this time he would also become known as an accomplished poet.

T'aego's visit to China for two years (1346–1348) became a watershed event for him. While in China, he met a spectrum of Buddhist Chan leaders, among them Shi Wu, the patriarch of the Linji Chan School. Shi Wu verified T'aego's awakening and commissioned him to spread the Linji (termed in Korea, Imje, and in Japan, Rinzai) teachings through his homeland. T'aego returned home with the idea that he would remain at Sosolam the rest of his life. Changes in the Korean political situation, however, altered his plans.

Korea entered a tumultuous period as the Chinese Yuan dynasty (1271–1368), which had hegemony over Korea, moved into its last years. In 1351, the Korean king Kongmon (1351–1374) asserted Korea's independence and the next year invited T'aego to his court in the role of the king's teacher. Once established, T'aego used his position to obtain the king's backing for a broad program of uniting the several Son groups into which the Son community was divided into a single organization. Because of his study and authorization from China, his popularity was quite high. In 1356, the king showed his support for the reorganization plan by naming him as the teacher of the nation.

It took a decade to complete the reorganization of the Korean Son centers, after which T'aego retired from public life. Following his death in 1382, he was honored with the title Son Master of Perfect Realization. His relics now reside in a granite stupa on Mount Samgak.

Edward A. Irons

See also: Chinul; Rinzai (Japan), Lin-Chi (China), Imje (Korea), Lam-Te (Vietnam); Zen Buddhism.

References

Cleary, J. C., trans. *T'aego Pou: A Buddha from Korea.* Boston: Shambhala Publications, 1992.

Kim, Jaihiun J., trans. *Poems by Zen Masters.* Seoul, Korea: Hanshin Pub. Co., 1988.

Soeng, Mu. *Thousand Peaks: Korean Zen— Traditions and Teachers.* Cumberland, RI: Primary Point Press, 1991.

Taiwan

See China: Taiwan.

Tai Shan

Tai Shan is one of five sacred mountains in China associated both with ancient Chinese indigenous religion and with Daoism and which have remained sacred sites to the present. Traditional veneration of mountains in China differs somewhat from that in the West, where mountains have been considered places of encounters with the divine (Mount Sinai) or the abode of deities. They have assumed the role of a deity themselves. Of the various mountains considered sacred, Tai Shan is the most sacred of all. The Shu-ching, a classic text of Chinese traditional history, compiled around the fifth century BCE, related the story of pilgrimages of the ruler Shun (2255–2206), who traveled to the four mountains that defined the boundaries of his realm every five years. Of the traditional sacred mountains of China visited by Shun, Tai Shan is the only one mentioned by name.

Through the centuries, the Chinese emperors thought of Tai Shan as the actual son of the Emperor of Heaven, from whom they received their own authority to rule the people, while for the people, the mountain functioned as a point of communication with the god who oversaw the affairs of humans. It stood long before the construction of Tiantan, the Temple of Heaven in Beijing, where annual rituals were carried out to stabilize Chinese prosperity. The mountain was also the home of Taishung fujan, the mountain lord who served as the ruler of souls. Tai Shan was also seen as the residence of the deceased. When the emperor made his visit to the five mountains, Tai Shan would be the first stop. Earthly emperors were required to annually present themselves before the heavenly emperor, validate their right to ruler, and offer a ritual sacrifice.

Many of the ancient emperors are believed to have come to Tai Shan, but the first documented visit occurred in 219 BCE. The Emperor Shih-huang, best known for having built the Great Wall, left a rock carving noting his pilgrimage. Subsequent accounts of imperial visits note the large retinue that would accompany the emperor, including courtiers, soldiers, and the merely curious. On such occasions, the six-mile route from the top to the bottom of the mountain would be packed with people, and over the years they have left evidence of their visits by inscribing poems and passing thoughts on the rock lining the 7,000 steps to the mountain's peak.

Upon reaching the top, pilgrims find two temples dominating the site—the Temple of the Jade Emperor (the Emperor of Heaven), the ruler of this world in traditional Chinese religion, which houses a bronze statue of the deity; and the Bixia, a temple dedicated to the Princess of the Azure Clouds, one of the Jade Emperor's daughters. Women are especially drawn to the Bixia. Women who have had trouble having a child and their mothers yearning for a grandchild make their way to the Bixia to prayer for children and grandchildren. Also, accompanying the image of the Princess are two goddesses known for their miracles, one believed especially attentive to eye ailments and the other to the ailments of children.

On the way up and down the slope, pilgrims will find several smaller temples and a variety of services—inns, eateries, and souvenir ships—established over the centuries to assist the pilgrims (and more recently the many tourists). Numerous additional temples are located in Tai'an and Jinan, the two cities located at the base of the mountain at either end.

For the Daoists, each of the sacred mountains represented a different direction (which coincided with their role of marking the extent of the country). Tai Shan anchors the east, between the cities of Tai'an and Jinan in Shandong Province, between Beijing and Shanghai. The government has taken steps to improve transportation to Tai Shan and has added a cable car for those not up to climbing the 7,000 steps. The government now views the mountain in terms of Chinese history and culture rather than as posing any kind of religious threat. It rises abruptly 5,069 feet above the plains that surround it. In 1987, it was added to the United Nations Educational, Scientific and Cultural Organization's (UNESCO) list of World Heritage Sites.

J. Gordon Melton

See also: Heng Shan; Song Shan; Temples—Buddhist; Tiantan.

References

Baker, Dwight C. *Tai Shan—An Account of the Sacred Eastern Peak of China.* Taipei: Ch'eng Wen, 1971 (originally published 1925).

Einarsen, John, ed. *The Sacred Mountains of Asia*. Boston: Shambhala, 1995.

Hahn, Thomas H. "Daoist Sacred Sites." In *Daoism Handbook*, edited by Livia Kohn, 683–708. Leiden: Brill, 2004.

Mt. Tai Shan Landscape. House of Shandong Province: People's Publishing, 1982.

"Sacred Mountains of China." Places of Peace and Power. http://www.sacredsites.com/asia/china/sacred_mountains.html. Accessed May 15, 2009.

■ Tajikistan

Formed in 1991 as the Soviet Union was dissolved, Tajikistan is a Central Asian country surrounded by Afghanistan, Uzbekistan, Kyrgyzstan, and China. As part of its territory was taken from Uzbekistan early in the 20th century, Uzbeks form a significant minority group in the country. As of 2008, 7,212,000 citizens inhabited the country's 55,250 square miles of land. The Tajiks of Tajikistan are distantly related to the Tajiks who inhabit the Tashkurgan Tajik Autonomous County in northwest China.

The area that composes the modern state of Tajikistan was inhabited by the sixth century BCE, and within its territory several important trading centers for the ancient Central Asian world arose. The land was first overrun by the Persians, and then in the fourth century BCE by Alexander the Great (356–323). In the millennium after Alexander, the region was occupied by various invading armies. In the sixth and seventh centuries CE, Turkish peoples moved onto the land, only a short time before the Arab Muslim Empire incorporated Tajikistan into the caliphate. Islam was introduced at this time and soon became the dominant religion of the people. During the years of the succeeding Tahrid and Samanid kingdoms, the Tajik people emerged as a separate ethnic group (in the ninth and 10th centuries). Their language is a dialect of Persian.

Tajikistan was part of a series of kingdoms through the next centuries, finally falling into a set of fiefdoms in the 17th century. Some of these were subservient to the Bukhara Khanate based in Uzbekistan. Then in the 1860s the Russians moved into Central Asia, and through the 1870s they annexed the northern half of

Entrance to a mosque in Tajikistan. (Radist/Dreamstime.com)

Tajikistan. The Khanate of Bukhara retained some degree of independence, and much of western Tajikistan was reorganized as the Province of Eastern Bukhara.

Soviet power in the region was established in stages, but in 1924 the Autonomous Soviet Socialist Republic of Tajikistan was incorporated into the new Soviet Socialist Republic of Uzbekistan. It was separated from Uzbekistan in 1929 and remained in the Soviet Union until independence in 1991. Following independence old tensions between Tajiks and Russians flared, and many Russians bearing needful skills returned to their homeland.

Through the 1990s the new government faced a somewhat unstable adjustment to post-Communist life, including a civil war led by a former prime minister (1997). The government has been especially concerned

Tajikistan

about conservative Islamic groups, and in 1998 a treaty with Uzbekistan was reached out of common concern about terrorists being trained in Afghanistan. In 1999 the Parliament passed a law banning religious organizations from having a direct relationship with any political party.

The majority of Muslims follow the Sunni Hanafite School. This community came under sharp attack during the Stalinist years, but the attempts to suppress it relaxed in the decades following World War II. Soviet authorities returned control of the community to local leadership, and even placed the imams on government salaries through the Muslim Board of Central Asia (1943). Russian became the language of discourse, and Muslim leaders tried to picture Russian culture as more attractive than the Turkish one that had become popular in the 19th century. Imams for this officially sanctioned Muslim activity were trained at the two seminaries in Uzbekistan.

Besides the Hanafite majority, there is also a visible Wahhabi presence, with their main support being in the Kurdistan region in the southern highlands. The

Tajikistan

Religion	Followers in 1970	Followers in 2010	% of Population	Annual % growth 2000–2010	Followers in 2025	Followers in 2050
Muslims	1,856,000	6,003,000	85.0	1.22	8,208,000	10,249,000
Agnostics	570,000	820,000	11.6	1.14	500,000	300,000
Atheists	421,000	120,000	1.7	1.09	100,000	80,000
Christians	82,500	101,000	1.4	0.60	97,300	97,500
Orthodox	62,200	87,000	1.2	0.31	77,000	68,000
Protestants	20,300	9,500	0.1	1.81	12,000	15,000
Independents	0	2,500	0.0	4.56	5,000	10,000
Ethnoreligionists	0	6,600	0.1	1.20	7,000	8,000
Buddhists	0	5,000	0.1	1.19	8,000	14,000
Baha'is	0	3,200	0.0	1.22	5,000	8,000
Zoroastrians	0	2,400	0.0	1.20	2,400	2,400
Jews	12,000	950	0.0	−0.61	900	900
Total population	**2,942,000**	**7,062,000**	**100.0**	**1.19**	**8,929,000**	**10,760,000**

Wahhabis gained strength from those Muslims opposed to Soviet intervention in neighboring Afghanistan. There is also a Shia community, centered in the Gorno-Badakhshan Autonomous Oblast, and a group of Ismaili, known as Pamiris, that originated in the 10th century and currently reside in the remote Pamir Mountains. There is a popular folk Islam that undergirds all of the various Muslim groups and lends special support to the Naqshbandñya Sufi Brotherhood.

Christianity, in the form of the Russian Orthodox Church (Moscow Patriarchate), was introduced with the arrival of the czar's forces in the 1860s. The church grew as Russians moved to the region both before and after the Soviet era. Today its several parishes have been incorporated into the single diocese that covers Uzbekistan, Turkmenistan, Tajikistan, and Kyrgyzstan. St. Nicholas Cathedral in Dushanbe is the center of the Orthodox community.

In the 1920s, Soviet authorities deported two Baptist pastors and their wives to Dushanbe, Tajikistan's capital. They became the core of the first Protestant church in the region, and through the rest of the decade they were joined by other Baptists who migrated and settled in Dushanbe or nearby. In 1930 the church chose I. Ya. Danilenko as its first minister. A second congregation was formed by the closely related evangelical Christians. The two small groups united in 1936, but the next year authorities closed the church. When it was allowed to reopen in 1944, some 35 members re-

mained. It experienced slow but steady growth through the next half-century, and at the time of independence it had more than 800 members; in addition, other congregations had been formed throughout the country. The church suffered greatly from independence and the civil war that followed. Many of its members (especially the Russians and the German-speaking) chose to leave, and by the middle of the 1990s, only some 350 members could be found.

Besides the Baptists there are small numbers of Lutherans and Pentecostal believers in Tajikistan. The small number of members of the Seventh-day Adventist Church has been incorporated into its Asian-Caucasian Conference, which additionally includes members in five other counties. There is a small Armenian community that adheres to the Armenian Apostolic Church. The attempts to rebuild the Protestant community in the years since independence have met obstacles in the new regulations imposed by the government. The Jehovah's Witnesses have been completely banned (as of 2010).

The Judaic community of Tajikistan is closely related to the one in Uzbekistan. They speak a distinct dialect of Tajik, called Judeo-Tajik. They are found primarily in Dushanbe. Jews may have arrived in the region as early as the sixth century BCE. They were the only people in the region who did not accept Islam in the seventh and eighth centuries CE. Attempts at forced conversion by Muslims in the 17th century led to the existence of secret Jews, not unlike the Marranos of Spain. At the end of the 18th century, a Moroccan rabbi, Joseph Maman (Mamon) Maghribi, settled in Bukhara. He led a revival of Jewish life and introduced the Sephardi prayer rite that replaced the Persian rite previously used in most synagogues.

As early as the 1880s, Jews began to move to Israel, and in the 1970s some 8,000 of the 30,000 Jews believed to be living in Tajikistan and Uzbekistan migrated. By the beginning of the new century, most of Tajikistan's Jews had migrated. In 2008, the government ordered the demolition of the country's last active synagogue as part of a planned renovation of the capital city.

J. Gordon Melton

See also: Armenian Apostolic Church (Holy See of Etchmiadzin); Hanafite School of Islam; Ismaili Islam; Judaism; Naqshbandiya Sufi Order; Russian Orthodox Church (Moscow Patriarchate); Seventhday Adventist Church; Wahhabi Islam.

References

Atkin, M. *Tadjikistan: Nationalism, Religion, and Political Change*. Washington, DC: National Council for Soviet and East European Research, 1992.

Harris, Colette. *Muslim Youth: Tensions and Transitions in Tajikistan*. Boulder, CO: Westview Press, 2006.

Jonson, Lena. *Tajikistan in the New Central Asia: Geopolitics, Great Power Rivalry and Radical Islam*. London: I. B. Tauris, 2006.

Khalid, Adeeb. *Islam after Communism: Religion and Politics in Central Asia*. Berkeley: University of California Press, 2007.

Muriel, A. *The Subtlest Battle: Islam in Soviet Tajikistan*. Philadelphia: Foreign Policy Research Institute, 1989.

Samuels, T. B. "Tajikistan and the Islamic Revival." M.A. thesis, University of Virginia, 1987.

Taliban

The Taliban, the "Students of Islamic Knowledge Movement," the organization that controlled the largest part of Afghanistan as the 21st century began, got its start among youth that were attending *madrasas*, religious schools, which had been set up in Pakistan by Afghan refugees during the 1980s, at which time the Russians occupied much of the country. Most of the southern part of Afghanistan was inhabited by people who were ethnically Pashtuns and speakers of a distinctive language, Pashti. This same ethno-linguistic group was dominant in that part of Pakistan adjacent to Afghanistan. The Pashtuns were traditionally followers of the Hanafite School of Sunni Islam. The new movement among the students, a primary expression of Islamism, placed an extremely conservative interpretation on their tradition, much as the Wahhabis did in Arabia, and found inspiration from the Pakistani-based Jamaat-e-Islam and its founder, Sayyid Abul al-Mawdudi (1903–1979).

By the early 1990s, the Taliban had evolved into a formal organization under the leadership of a council (*ulama*, literally a community of learned men) and the council's leader, Mullah Muhammad Omar. Movement leaders spread through the Pashtun areas of Afghanistan and quickly gained a large following. Formed as a militia, in 1996 the Taliban moved on Kabul, the capital, and quickly took over from the divided ruling elite, who had been drawn from the Uzbek and Tajik ethnic groups whose strength lay in the north (many of whom were either Shia Muslims or secular Marxists). The defeated leaders quickly formed an alliance against the Taliban and remained in control of the northern third of the country. (Through the 1990s, the United Nations and the United States did not recognize the Taliban, considering Afghanistan a land without a government. They recognized instead the government of Shia leader Burhanuddin Rabbani, of the Northern Alliance, as the rightful leader of Afghanistan. Only Pakistan, Saudi Arabia, and the United Arab Emirates recognized the leadership in Kabul.)

Once in control of the capital, Taliban leaders instituted a strict interpretation of Islamic law that included traditional modest dress for women, restrictions on female education, and denying access to male physicians. It also reintroduced various forms of punishment that have largely been banished from the West (flogging, amputation of limbs, and execution by stoning). They moved to end the lawlessness that had come to many parts of the country in the wake of the Rus-

Members of the Taliban pose with AK-47 assault rifles and rocket-propelled grenades in Zabul province, south of Kabul, Afghanistan, October 2006. (AP/Wide World Photos)

sian withdrawal, and found televisions and video cassettes offensive to Islam. Although those actions made the Taliban unpopular in many quarters, it was the destruction of large Buddhist statues, considered by many as art treasures, in March 2001 that brought widespread denouncements from around the world.

In 1996 the leaders of the Taliban invited Osama bin Laden (b. 1957) to re-establish his organization, al-Qaeda, in Afghanistan. Subsequently, al-Qaeda was charged with a series of attacks upon U.S. citizens and property, culminating in the attacks on the United States on September 11, 2001. The Taliban was implicated in these attacks because of its harboring bin Laden in Afghanistan. In October 2001, the United States began military actions in Afghanistan aimed at capturing bin Laden and his associates and destroying al-Qaeda. Sec-

ondarily, the attack has been on the Taliban as an accessory to the terrorism perpetuated by the al-Qaeda network. The attack destroyed the Taliban government but by no means destroyed the organization. It retreated into the rural areas of the country and has continued to put up resistance.

As the attempt to establish a post-Taliban government proceeded, the United States continued to house forces in the country even as it diverted attention to its invasion of Iraq. Hostilities have continued in Afghanistan to the present, with the fortunes of the Taliban alternately waxing and waning. It has also become entrenched in Pakistan, the mountainous area immediate adjacent to the Afghanistan border.

In 2009, the United States moved to reduce its commitments in Iraq and simultaneously began to build its forces in Afghanistan to stop any possibility of a revival of support for the Taliban.

In the 1990s, the Taliban had developed a presence in the United States, but it disappeared following the bombing of the Pentagon and World Trade Center in 2001. By early 2002, their Internet site, http://www.taleban.com, was no longer functioning and no pro-Taliban site remained.

J. Gordon Melton

See also: Hanafite School of Islam; Islam; Islamism; Jamaat-e-Islam; Shia Islam; Statues—Buddhist; Wahhabi Islam.

References

Anderson, Jon Lee, and Thomas Dworzak. *Taliban.* London: Trolley, 2004.

Bick, Barbara. *Walking the Precipice: Witness to the Rise of the Taliban in Afghanistan.* New York: Feminist Press of CUNY, 2009.

Maley, William, ed. *Fundamentalism Reborn? Afghanistan and the Taliban.* New York: New York University Press, 1998.

Matinuddin, Kamal. *The Taliban Phenomenon: Afghanistan, 1994–1997.* Karachi: Oxford University Press, 1999.

Rashid, Ahmed. *Taliban: Militant Islam, Oil and Fundamentalism in Central Asia.* New Haven, CT: Yale University Press, 2001.

Zaidi, Syed Manzar Abbas. *The New Taliban: Emergence and Ideological Sanctions.* Hauppauge, NY: Nova Science Publishers, 2009.

Tamil Shaivism

Tamil Shaivism (or Saivism) refers both to a broad category that may include any type of Shiva-worship in the 2,000 years or more of its existence in the Tamil-language region of southern India, and to a specific system of devotionalism that developed in this region. In the latter case, Tamil Shaivism typically denotes Shaiva Siddhanta, an organized sect that promotes a distinct theology, articulated in Tamil and Sanskrit texts that also inform Shaiva temple rituals today.

Shiva-worship appears in the Tamil literary record from the early centuries CE. In the Purananuru (ca. first–third centuries CE), a king is advised to circumambulate a temple of "the three-eyed god," a common epithet of Shiva. By the fifth century, the Silappadigaram epic shows that Shiva's mythology, iconography, and worship were well known. Beginning from the sixth to ninth centuries, Shiva's popularity spread when devotees called *nayanmar*, "leaders," made pilgrimages to local sacred places and celebrated Shiva's manifestations there. Through accessible Tamil songs, poet-saints like Appar, Sambandhar, Sundarar, and Manikkavachagar promoted *bhakti*, the ecstatic, loving devotion to a personal deity, and helped create an enduring temple-centered religious culture.

This popular devotional movement grew alongside —and soon intertwined with—a school of Shaivism that came to be called Shaiva Siddhanta ("perfected" or "fully concluded"). It apparently originated in northern India sometime before the eighth century CE among monastic communities in what is now Madhya Pradesh. Between the 10th and 13th centuries, monastic lineages spread throughout India. The school emphasized the liberating role of ritual, a dualistic philosophy, and respect for conventional caste and gender distinctions. It also tended both to accept the legitimacy of the Veda and to assert the superiority of Shaiva Siddhanta over it, as stated in texts said to be revealed by Shiva and transmitted in Sanskrit in oral and written forms. The tradition eventually lost its all-India spread, but became and remains the normative form of organized Shaivism in Tamil Nadu.

Shaiva Siddhanta was originally based on 28 primary Agamas, said to be knowledge of Shiva first revealed by the Lord himself and eventually written down; more than 200 subsidiary Agamas exist as well. The earliest of these Sanskrit works are datable to the eighth century CE, but they must have existed in oral or written form for some time before that. These texts focus primarily on rules for ritual worship, doctrinal exegesis, and rites of initiation and funerals; some, not all, add guidelines for correct conduct and yogic practices. Many Agamas also provide information on iconography of divine images, temple architecture, and guidelines for conducting festivals.

The dualist doctrine of Shaiva Siddhanta's Agamas accepts three fundamental and separate realities: Shiva (*pati*), souls (*pashu*), and fetters (*pasha*). Shiva is the ultimate God who is omniscient, omnipotent, and eternally liberated. Souls, too, have most of the same inherent qualities, but, caught in a state of spiritual bondage, they do not realize their true nature. Out of his grace, Shiva creates the universe through the agency of divine beings in order to provide the conditions for souls to find release from the shackles of ignorance, *karma*, and materiality. Ritual plays a crucial role in the soul's spiritual progress. A qualified guru, who acts as Shiva's representative, removes most of the disciple's fetters through the "liberating initiation" (*nirvanadiksha*). The disciple should also ritually worship Shiva every day in order to remove new karmic bonds that he continues to generate after initiation. The ultimate goal is to become like or equal to Shiva.

Later Shaiva Siddhantan texts developed the Agamas's teachings in new ways. Medieval preceptors, first from northern India and later from the Tamil-speaking south, composed Agamic commentaries, doctrinal syntheses, and manuals of ritual instruction, all in Sanskrit. Many of these writings sought to unify the teachings of the Agamas. Then, from the 13th to 14th centuries, philosophical works in Tamil were composed and canonized as the Meykandasastiram, authoritative texts composed by the author Meykandar and later writers. Unlike the Sanskrit works, the texts of this collection heightened the importance of devotion and understood liberation as the merging of the soul into Shiva.

Shaiva Siddhanta's dualist stance has faced serious competition from the non-dualist philosophy of Advaita Vedanta. Although non-dualist ideas appear even in a few Agamas, important thinkers like Aghorashivacharya (12th century) and Umapati Shivacharya (14th century) vigorously defended the fundamental separation of Shiva and souls. But later authors such as Shivagrayogin and the Appayadikshita (both 16th century) helped promote a non-dualist understanding of Shaivism that continues today. The popular Tamil idea that the highest goal for devotees is to "melt" or merge with Shiva also contributed to the shift away from dualism.

Shaiva Siddhantan religious professionals are of two main types, distinguished by caste and function. Male priests of the Adishaiva Brahman subcaste perform the rituals in most Shiva temples for the welfare of the lay public and the state. High-caste, non-Brahman male ascetics residing in monastic institutions compose the other group of professionals. Their lineages were established by the 16th century in the Tanjavur region as centers of Shaiva learning and private religious practice.

Today, Shaiva Siddhanta in India is organized most strongly at the local level. Training schools for priests, temple and monastic administrative structures, and caste and kinship networks provide institutional support, while ascetic leaders and respected priests offer limited leadership. The sect extends membership to the four *varna* social classes, but excludes the lowest castes, for whom social and legal redress began only in the 1940s and remains far from complete. Women may receive initiation as lay members but are barred from priestly and monastic ranks and may not perform ritual worship in the elaborate manner of initiated males.

Outside India, the tradition appears mostly among expatriate Tamil communities, as in Sri Lanka, Malaysia, Singapore, and North America. One exception is the Saiva Siddhanta Church, based in Hawaii. The late Sivaya Subramuniyaswami, a convert of American origin, founded this international organization in 1949. The organization aims to propagate a form of non-dualist Shaiva Siddhanta around the world.

It is not easy to calculate Shaiva Siddhantan membership, let alone that of Tamil Shaivas in general. Although formally initiated practitioners are no doubt few, Shaiva Siddhanta's ritual tradition has exerted great influence because its priests conduct the rites at most Shiva temples in Tamil-speaking Hindu communities. In India notable Siddhantan worship centers include the great temples of Madurai, Tiruvannamalai, and Rameshwaram. Important monastic institutions include Dharmapuram and Tiruvavatuturai.

Ginette Ishimatsu

See also: Asceticism; Hinduism; Pilgrimage; Tirumala/Tirupati; Yoga.

References

Davis, Richard H. *Ritual in an Oscillating Universe: Worshiping Siva in Medieval India*. Princeton, NJ: Princeton University, 1991.

Dunuwila, Rohan A. *Saiva Siddhanta Theology.* Delhi: Motilal Banarsidass, 1985.

Fuller, C. J. *Renewal of the Priesthood: Modernity and Traditionalism in a South Indian Temple.* Princeton, NJ: Princeton University Press, 2003.

Good, Anthony. *Worship and the Ceremonial Economy of a Royal South Indian Temple.* New York: Edwin Mellen, 2004.

Koppedrayer, K. I. "Are *Sudras* Entitled to Ride in the Palanquin?" *Contributions to Indian Sociology* 25, no. 2 (1991): 191–210.

Tantrism

Tantrism is term used by scholars of South Asian religions to describe ritual and theological traditions that aim at spiritual liberation (*moksha*) as well as the attainment of supernatural powers by means of certain ritual practices that will lead to the cosmic reintegration with the deity, who is conceived as identical with supreme power. As such Tantrism does not refer to a particular group or sect, but to a set of elements and influences that are found to varying degrees in Hindu, Buddhist, and Jain textual, theological, and ritual traditions.

The word *tantra* encompasses a group of post-Vedic Sanskrit texts, composed between the eighth and 11th centuries, and associated body of ritual practice that have had significant impact in the development of the Hindu tradition. Tantras belonging to the Shaiva traditions are called Agamas (tradition), while those that those affiliated with Vaishanva traditions are called Samhita. These Tantric traditions probably have had a much longer tradition of transmission and preservation that predates collected and redacted texts in the form in which they are available today. Tantric texts generally present a systematic programmatic search for liberation (moksha) and spiritual power centered on Vishnu, Shiva, or the Goddess as the focus of theological speculation.

It is often difficult to distinguish specific traditions—Vaishanava, Shaiva, or Shakta—in part due to the esoteric nature of these traditions. These traditions of ritual exegesis were restricted to those had been initiated (*diksha*) and became members of the spiritual lineage (*parampara*) of a specific teacher (*guru*). The guru would reveal the teachings only to his students. The trope of secrecy was expressed both in the method of teaching and in the texts, which often state that the Tantra (as a book) should never be recited or even housed among non-initiates. Some Tantras not only claimed to be revelation (*shruti*) and thus intimately linked to the Vedas, but some claimed to surpass the truth revealed in Vedas. Others implicitly acknowledge the status of the Veda as sacred by attributing their ultimate origin to the verbal tradition, which was revealed by Shiva, and as such were the culmination of Vedic revelation.

Taking into account the context of the Tantras as we have them, it is probable that Tantric traditions originated among particularly marginalized ascetic groups, especially those who practiced some form of cremation-ground asceticism. These ascetics, who lived in cremation grounds, were probably mostly members of the lower-caste groups, and their ritual and ascetic practices transgressed the standard Brahmanic orthopraxic concern for ritual purity. These ascetic traditions practiced cremation-ground asceticism, as is noted in the Pali Buddhist sources. However, it is also clear that Tantric texts incorporate various stands of mainstream Vedic thought, especially the system of correlations or identities (*bandhus*) between the cosmic, ritual, and human order of reality. As in the Vedas, Tantric texts understand cosmic processes to have counterparts in the microcosmic plane. Indeed, much of the esoteric speculation in Tantric texts regarding the bipolar, bisexual nature of the Absolute, the creative nature of sound (*shabda*) and word, and the complex mapping of the cosmos unto the human body is based on the type of speculation about the nature of Vedic sacrifice and ritual carried out by orthodox Brahmans of the Vedas. Thus, rather than thinking about Tantric movements as having originated from popular, extra-Vedic contexts, the texts indicate that many Tantric texts were an outgrowth of the same intellectual system of thought as that of the religious specialists of the time, the Brahmans. Tantra does not refer to a particular tradition or ritual system, but rather to a body of practices and concepts that have had an impact on the development of various Hindu traditions and systems of thought. Thus, beyond specific Tantric texts, it is not possible to historically identify traditions or groups that can be classified as exclusively Tantric.

Tantric texts generally address four general topics: doctrine (*vidya*), ritual (*kriya*), yoga, and behavior (*carya*). It is by means of ritual, yoga, and behavior that the Tantric adept (*tantrika* or *sadhaka*) seeks to control his or her body to manipulate the various levels of reality in order to attain liberation. Tantric ritual achieves this goal through the hierarchical identification of an elaborate geography of the body with its cosmic counterparts. By establishing these identities, oppositions are overcome in unity. Tantric practice includes recitation of *mantras* and the construction of complex geometric designs (*mandalas*, *yantras*) used for meditational practice, which require special initiation. The spiritual practices of the left-handed (*vamacara*) Tantras seek to overcome duality by complete immersion into all aspects of the world, which is conceived as completely pervaded by *shakti*. The adept undertakes the *pañcatattva* ritual, in which he or she ritually partakes of the five forbidden truths, the so-called five *m*'s—alcohol (*madya*), meat (*mamsa*), fish (*matysa*), parched grain (*mudra*), and illicit sexual intercourse (*maithuna*). By completely embracing those things and acts that transgress accepted orthopraxy, the adept overcomes the duality of clean and unclean, sacred and profane, and shatters the bondage to the world.

Tantric traditions are monistic, with a focus on a singular essence or godhead that is understood as being polarized into male and female aspects. The female dimension of this singular essence is *shakti*, the energy without which the male god cannot act. It is this feminine aspect of the godhead that is conceived as the active force responsible for the cosmic process of creation.

By the 11th century, Tantric practices and metaphysical doctrines had become popular beyond the restricted circles of cremation-ground ascetics and had spread in Brahmanic circles, especially in Kashmir, where Tantric rituals and philosophic ideas had made their way into courtly circles. In Kashmir as in other areas, Tantric rituals and practices were incorporated not only into the elite circles, but also into the wider householder (*grihastha*) society. Mantras that were originally used to coerce and control supernatural forces and powers were domesticated mantras and identified

as manifestation of the gods. Early Tantric ritual practices, which involved engaging in generally unaccepted, antisocial practices, came to be understood as purely symbolic in nature, only to be used as a tool for meditational practice. Puranic traditions absorbed and re-interpreted many Tantric elements and eventually incorporated them into the corpus of classical Hindu art, practice, and thought.

Carlos Lopez

See also: Asceticism; Meditation; Sacred Texts; Shaivism; Vaishnavism; Yoga.

References

Flood, Gavin D. *The Tantric Body: The Secret Tradition of Hindu Religion*. London and New York: I. B. Tauris, 2006.

Gourdiaan, Teun, and Sanjukta Gupta. *Hindu Tantric and Shakta Literature*. Wiesbaden, Germany: O. Harrassowitz, 1981.

Harper, Katherine Anne, and Robert Brown, eds. *The Roots of Tantra*. Albany: State University of New York Press, 2002.

Padoux, Andre. *Vac: The Concept of the Word in Selected Hindu Tantras*. Albany: State University of New York Press, 1990.

White, David Gordon. *Kiss of Yogini: "Tantric Sex" in Its South Asian Contexts*. Chicago: University of Chicago Press, 2003.

■ Tanzania

Tanzania is an eastern African nation of some 364,898 square miles located on the Indian Ocean between Kenya and Mozambique. The country also shares borders with Uganda, Rwanda, Burundi, the Democratic Republic of the Congo, Zambia, and Malawi. It is home to 40,200,000 people (2008). Most of Tanzania consists of the former British colony of Tanganyika, but in the 1960s the islands of Zanzibar, and the fabled Zanzibar City, joined in the formation of the new nation.

Tanzania's Rift Valley has been inhabited for a million years, and it is the site from which some of the oldest human fossils known have been extracted from rock strata. However, in much more recent times it

A Christian church in Tanzania. (Janis Jansons/Dreamstime.com)

was settled by Bantu people, now divided into more than 120 separate ethnic groupings. Tanzania entered modern history in 695 CE, when Prince Hamza of Oman, the first of a number of losers in various political struggles on the Arabian peninsula, settled on the East African coast. Hamza chose Zanzibar as his new home. He was followed by a group from Mecca who founded Mogadishu (Somalia). Later immigrants founded Mombasa (Kenya) and Beira (Mozambique). The Arabs intermarried with the Zandi, or blacks, creating a new trading culture along the coast that tied East Africa to Arabia and eventually to India and lands farther east.

The Portuguese arrived at the beginning of the 16th century and by the 1520s had taken control of the East African coast. They destroyed the Zandi culture and economic structure. They remained in control until 1688, when the sultan of Oman recaptured Zanzibar, part of a lengthy effort to drive the Portuguese out of the region. The sultan settled in Zanzibar, and his family remained in control into the 18th century. During this time, the slave trade flourished. Toward the end of the century, Zanzibar was lost to rival Arab leaders. The movement of the British into the region in the early 19th century stopped the movement of slaves out of Zanzibar and turned the rulers' attention to the mainland and the development of plantations that absorbed the slaves. Cloves became the new cash crop.

The weakening power of the sultan in the face of European encroachments came to a head in 1884, when a German arrived and annexed land on the mainland. His actions were backed by German warships. In 1886 the European powers gave Tanganyika, Burundi, and Rwanda to Germany, and Zanzibar became a British protectorate in 1890. Following Germany's defeat in World War I, the British took control of Tanganyika. It remained a colony until 1961, when the modern nation of Tanzania was proclaimed.

TANZANIA

The settlers from Oman who developed Zanzibar brought with them the Ibadi Kharijite form of Islam that predominates in Oman. Kharijism is usually distinguished by its lack of allegiance to the Arab caliph and by its belief that leadership in the Muslim community should not be limited to descendants of the Prophet Muhammad. Rather, leaders should be chosen on a merit system. It developed prior to the emergence of the four schools of Sunni Islam and the split between Sunnis and Shias. It places much more emphasis on the Koran in making legal decisions than on the *hadith*, the traditions concerning Muhammad.

The movement of Muslims from other parts of the Arabian peninsula to become an integral part of Zandj culture ensured that the Kharijite sect did not gain control of the culture, which eventually was ruled by the Sunni Shafiite School, the dominant segment of the Tanzanian Muslim community except on Zanzibar

Tanzania

Religion	Followers in 1970	Followers in 2010	% of Population	Annual % growth 2000–2010	Followers in 2025	Followers in 2050
Christians	5,000,000	23,690,000	54.4	2.92	34,625,000	51,666,000
Roman Catholics	2,807,000	12,380,000	28.4	2.75	17,900,000	26,000,000
Protestants	1,068,000	8,450,000	19.4	3.28	12,500,000	17,350,000
Anglicans	386,000	3,350,000	7.7	2.17	5,000,000	7,500,000
Muslims	4,211,000	13,250,000	30.4	2.60	18,200,000	25,700,000
Ethnoreligionists	4,300,000	5,820,000	13.4	1.49	6,000,000	6,000,000
Hindus	21,000	375,000	0.9	2.60	520,000	740,000
Baha'is	41,000	190,000	0.4	2.60	280,000	440,000
Agnostics	18,000	110,000	0.3	2.60	200,000	300,000
Buddhists	0	60,000	0.1	2.60	85,000	115,000
Atheists	3,000	24,000	0.1	2.60	40,000	60,000
Sikhs	3,000	12,800	0.0	2.60	20,000	25,000
Jains	800	10,000	0.0	2.60	18,000	30,000
Jews	100	300	0.0	2.58	400	600
Zoroastrians	100	120	0.0	2.43	150	150
Total population	**13,598,000**	**43,542,000**	**100.0**	**2.60**	**59,989,000**	**85,077,000**

Island. Islam spread dramatically in the period between the two World Wars. In the 20th century, the community was enlarged by a number of Indo-Pakistanis, mostly Shias.

The cosmopolitan nature of modern Dar es Salaam has permitted the diversity of the Muslim community to manifest, and today there are centers of Ismaili, Bohras, and Ithna-Asharis. The Ahmadiyya Muslim movement arrived in 1934, and it now has more than 40 branch centers. Approximately 32 percent of Tanzanian's residents are Muslims.

Christianity originally came to Tanzania in the 16th century with the Portuguese, but its presence was superficial and short lived. Then, in 1860, several priests moved to Zanzibar. The Holy Ghost Fathers arrived three years later and eventually developed their first center at Bagamoyo, founded as a settlement for freed slaves. When the White Fathers arrived in 1878, they used Bagamoyo as their point of departure into the interior. Other orders followed. The dioceses of Dar es Sallam and Tabora (two of the now four archdioceses) were designated in 1887.

Tanzania was part of the famous exploratory travels of David Livingstone, a missionary of the London Missionary Society. His visit to Oxford and Cambridge in 1857 led to the formation of the Universities'

Mission to Central Africa, a High-Church Anglican sending agency, and to the launching of the first mission to Tanzania, in 1860. That same year, the London Missionary Society, which was already at work in Rhodesia (Zambia), pushed northward into Tanzania around Lake Tanganyika. The Church Missionary Society, a Low-Church Anglican sending agency, arrived in 1886. The Anglican work would eventually mature into the Church in the Province of Tanzania.

The German colonial advent into Tanzania led to the arrival of several Lutheran missionary societies, beginning in 1886 with the Berlin Mission at Dar es Salaam. The expanded Lutheran work was turned over to several American churches, including the Augustan Lutherans, after World War I. Eventually, German missionaries were readmitted, but they were forced out again during World War II; American churches (now merged into the Evangelical Lutheran Church in America) and the Church of Sweden filled the vacuum. In 1937 the Federation of Lutheran Churches of Tanzania was created and became a step to the formation of the Evangelical Lutheran Church in Tanzania in 1961. With more than 2 million members each, the Anglican and Lutheran churches are by far the largest churches (other than the Roman Catholic Church) in the country.

Beginning with the African Inland Mission in 1908, a spectrum of churches and missionary sending agencies began work. Among the more successful have been the Church of God (Cleveland, Tennessee), the Moravians, the New Apostolic Church, the Assemblies of God, the Seventh-day Adventist Church, and the Baptist Convention of Tanzania (affiliated with the Southern Baptist Convention). The extensive Pentecostal growth in Tanzania has been aided by the effort begun by Swedish (Pentecostal Churches in Tanzania) and Canadian (Pentecostal Assemblies of Canada) missionaries. In the 1990s, several Korean groups became active in Tanzania, including a mission team from Yoido Full Gospel Church.

In spite of its proximity to Kenya, Tanzania has had relatively fewer indigenous churches formed within its bounds. The larger African Initiated Churches—such as the African Israel Church, Nineveh, and the Legion of Mary—have come into the country from adjacent states.

The larger mission churches formed the Tanganyika Missionary Council, which evolved into the Christian Council of Tanzania, an affiliate of the World Council of Churches. More recently, several of the more conservative missionary agencies formed the Tanzania Evangelical Fellowship, loosely associated with the World Evangelical Alliance.

Within the context set by the two dominant religious communities, Tanzania has become home to a spectrum of religions, many originally brought into the country through the international trading center of Zanzibar. At various times the country was open to immigrants from India, the rest of southern Asia, and the South Pacific. The Hindu community, with approximately 250,000 members, is the largest religious community apart from Christianity and Islam. Most Hindus are Asian Indians. Sikhs and Jains have also come from India. Foguangshan is one form of Buddhism (from Taiwan) that has spread through Tanzania from its anchor in the Chinese community, and Soka Gakkai International is active. The largest of the alternative groups, however, is the Baha'i Faith.

J. Gordon Melton

See also: African Israel Church, Nineveh; Ahmadiyya Movement in Islam; Assemblies of God; Baha'i Faith; Church in the Province of Tanzania; Church Missionary Society; Church of God (Cleveland, Tennessee); Church of Sweden; Evangelical Lutheran Church in America; Evangelical Lutheran Church in Tanzania; Foguangshan; Holy Ghost Fathers; Ibadhi Islam; Legion of Mary; London Missionary Society; New Apostolic Church; Pentecostal Assemblies of Canada; Roman Catholic Church; Seventh-day Adventist Church; Shafiite School of Islam; Soka Gakkai International; Southern Baptist Convention; White Fathers; World Council of Churches; World Evangelical Alliance; Yoido Full Gospel Church.

References

Becker, Felicitas. *Becoming Muslim in Mainland Tanzania, 1890–2000*. New York: Oxford University Press, 2008.

Fiedler, Klaus. *Christianity and African Culture: Conservative German Protestant Missionaries in Tanzania, 1900–1940*. Leiden: Brill Academic Publishers, 1997.

Green, Maia. *Priests, Witches and Power: Popular Christianity after Mission in Southern Tanzania*. Cambridge: Cambridge University Press, 2003.

Ludwig, Frieder. *Church and State in Tanzania: Aspects of Changing in Relationships, 1961–1994*. Leiden: Brill Academic Publishers, 1999.

Mukandala, Rwekaza Sympho. *Justice, Rights and Worship: Religion and Politics in Tanzania*. Dar es Salaam: E & D Ltd., 2006.

Nimtz, August H. *Islam and Politics in East Africa: The Sufi Order in Tanzania*. Minneapolis: University of Minnesota Press, 1980.

Ranger, T. O. *The African Churches of Tanzania*. Nairobi, Kenya: East African Publishing House, 1972.

Stefano, J. A. *Missionary Work in the Church of Tanzania in the Past and Present*. Erlangen, Germany: Evangelical Lutheran Mission Publishing House, 1990.

Von Socard, S. *Islam in Tanzania*. CSIC Papers—Africa, no. 5. Birmingham, UK: Centre for the Study of Islam and Christian-Muslim Relations, 1991.

Wright, M. *German Missionaries in Tanganyika, 1891–1941*. Oxford: Clarendon, 1971.

Taoism

See Daoism.

Taoist Tai Chi Society

The Taoist Tai Chi Society (TTCS), together with its religious affiliate, the Fung Loy Kok Taoist Temple, is perhaps the largest Daoist group in the Western Hemisphere. TTCS was founded in 1970 in Toronto, Canada, and maintains its headquarters there. Centers exist in most Canadian cities, and there are several in the United States, notably in Tallahassee, Florida, and Boulder, Colorado. They have a growing presence in Europe and the Caribbean as well.

Moy Lin-Shin, the founder and spiritual leader, was born in Guangzhou (Canton) in southern China in 1931. He moved to Hong Kong in 1948 to escape the revolution. There he trained at the Yuen Yuen Institute, which was established by Daoist monks from Canton who were part of the Longmen sect of the Quanzhen School of Daoism. Moy immigrated to Canada in 1970, ostensibly to teach martial arts but also as a Daoist missionary. He modified standard Yang-style Tai Chi and coined the term "Daoist Tai Chi."

As Moy's original students left Toronto, Daoist Tai Chi clubs sprang up around Canada and later in the United States. Moy's teachings attracted a graduate student from Hong Kong, Eva Wong, who went on to become the in-house intellectual of the TTCS until her break with Moy in the late 1990s. She has published a series of popular books on Daoism with Shambhala Press.

Today the TTCS has "grown to thousands of classes in over 400 locations on four continents," and there are some 10,000 dues-paying members worldwide. Fung Loy Kok Temple, dedicated in 1981, is the religious arm of the Moy organization. Temple spaces, which vary in size, are located upstairs from or in rooms adjoining the Tai Chi studios.

Fung Loy Kok Taoist Temple "observes the teachings of the three great religions of China: Daoism, Buddhism and Confucianism." They are represented by the central triad of the temple altar as Lu Dongbin, Guanyin (Goon Yam in Cantonese), and the Jade Emperor, respectively.

Today, the Society is registered as a charitable organization and is led by a board of directors. Master Moy retired from his official leadership roles in 1995 and died in 1998. Religious activities are performed by lay members, who, at least in Canadian branches, seem to be divided equally into white Canadians and Cantonese immigrants (mainly elderly women). Chanting is performed in Cantonese, which is transliterated phonetically for the non-Chinese members.

The TTCS also owns and operates an international retreat center an hour's drive north of Toronto. There, ground will soon be broken on a Cultivation Center with architecture inspired by the traditional Daoist monastery. This will be the largest Daoist building outside Asia.

The TTCS raises awareness by emphasizing the health benefits of practicing Tai Chi and the service aspect of belonging to the Society. It runs an old-age home and a soup kitchen. Later, Tai Chi students will be introduced to the chanting practice of Fung Loy Kok. The organization does not emphasize philosophy, mysticism, or "spirituality."

The TTCS remains far better known in Canada (not to mention England, Australia, and Poland) than it is in the United States, in part because they have no presence in the American Daoist centers of New York, Los Angeles, and San Francisco. In 2008, the Society reported centers across Canada and the United States and in 23 countries worldwide.

Taoist Tai Chi Society
134 D'Arcy St.
Toronto, ON M5T 1K3
Canada
http://www.taoist.org/

Elijah Siegler

See also: Daoism; Quanzhen Daoism.

References

Wong, Eva, trans. *Cultivating Stillness: A Taoist Manual for Transforming Body and Mind.* Boston: Shambhala, 1992.
Wong, Eva, trans. *Lieh-Tzu, a Taoist Guide to Practical Living.* Boston: Shambhala, 1995.

Wong, Eva, trans. *Nourishing the Essence of Life: The Outer, Inner, and Secret Teachings of Taoism.* Boston: Shambhala, 2004.

Wong, Eva, trans. *Taoism.* Boston: Shambhala, 1997.

Temples—Baha'i Faith

The Baha'i temple—known as a Mashriqu'l-Adhkar, literally the "Dawning Place of the Praise [of God]"—is one of the institutions conceived by Bahá'u'lláh, the founder of the Baha'i Faith. Mashriqu'l-Adhkar is a term with several meanings, depending on context, and can variously refer to: (1) a gathering of Baha'is engaged in devotion to God, especially at dawn; (2) any building dedicated to such worship (as in Iran and the Transcaspian Territory in Russia, where many Baha'i communities designated ordinary houses in their local communities as Mashriqu'l-Adhkars); (3) the complex of institutions surrounding a central house of worship that Bahá'u'lláh ordained to be at the very heart of every Baha'i community; or (4) the central house of worship itself. The only Baha'i temples that exist at present are continental temples. National and local Baha'i houses of worship will, in successive stages, be built in the future, as circumstances and resources allow.

In the Baha'i book of laws, The Most Holy Book (Kitáb-i Aqdas), Bahá'u'lláh ordained that a temple be raised up in every city, town, and village throughout the world: "O people of the world! Build ye houses of worship throughout the lands in the name of Him Who is the Lord of all religions. Make them as perfect as is possible in the world of being, and adorn them with that which befitteth them, not with images and effigies. Then, with radiance and joy, celebrate therein the praise of your Lord, the Most Compassionate." While it was Bahá'u'lláh who instituted the Baha'i temple, it was 'Abdu'l-Baha (1844–1921)—Bahá'u'lláh's eldest son, interpreter, and successor—who further elaborated on its essential architectural character and social purposes. 'Abdu'l-Baha encouraged Baha'is to establish Mashriqu'l-Adhkars in every "hamlet and city." If not possible due to persecution, then a Mashriqu'l-Adhkar could even be "underground."

Baha'i temple and gardens in Haifa. (Hitmans/Dreamstime .com)

Baha'i temples are not the only places of Baha'i worship. Several occasions for collective worship are ordained in the Baha'i writings, such as morning prayers, Nineteen-Day Feasts, Baha'i Holy Day observances, and devotional meetings, not to mention private worship.

Linking worship to service to humanity, the Baha'i house of worship takes on greater social significance in that it is not just spiritual in character, but is dedicated to medical, charitable, educational, and scientific pursuits as well. 'Abdu'l-Baha wrote that the Baha'i temple "is one of the most vital institutions in the world," for, in its full development, "it is also connected with a hospital, a drug dispensary, a traveller's hospice, a school for orphans, and a university for advanced studies" and "other philanthropic buildings"—such as a home for the aged—open to people of all races, religions, and ethnicities. Thus the Baha'i temple is part of a grand vision of community building and urban planning, universally conceived and locally planned. In the words of Shoghi Effendi, Bahá'u'lláh's grandson and "Guardian" of the Baha'i Faith from 1921 to 1957, each house of worship and its dependencies "shall afford relief to the suffering, sustenance to the poor, shelter to the wayfarer, solace to the bereaved, and education to the ignorant."

Also associated with each Baha'i house of worship —although not part of the temple complex, strictly speaking—is a center for Baha'i administration, known as a Haziratu'l-Quds (an Arabic term meaning "Sacred Fold"), although it is not to be connected to the Baha'i temple as such. An institution complementary to the Mashriqu'l-Adhkar, the Haziratu'l-Quds may consist of a council chamber, secretariat, treasury, publishing trust, archives, library, and assembly hall, and may be situated near the Mashriqu'l-Adhkar, although this is not a requirement, as is already the case in Wilmette, Illinois, where the Mashriqu'l-Adhkar—as the headquarters of the National Spiritual Assembly of the Baha'is of the United States—is located in Wilmette and in nearby Evanston.

The basic design for a Baha'i house of worship is distinctive in that each temple requires three essential elements: (1) a nine-sided, (2) circular shape, (3) surrounded by nine gardens with walkways. In Baha'i thought, the number nine symbolizes completion, perfection, and the unity of religions in their pure form. Nine likewise represents the numerical value of the Arabic word, "Bahá'," from which the words "Bahá'u'lláh" and "Baha'i" (follower of Bahá'u'lláh) are derived. While a dome is not an essential requirement, it has so far been a structural feature of all Baha'i temples, as Shoghi Effendi advised in 1955 that "at this time all Baha'i temples should have a dome." Beyond these essentials, a Baha'i temple is typically designed to be culturally distinctive, often incorporating indigenous architectural influences in the design. Each design is selected for its intrinsic merit, irrespective of whether the architect is Baha'i or not. Two houses of worship—in Frankfurt and Panama—were designed by architects not affiliated with the Baha'i Faith, while other non-affiliated architects have collaborated in perfecting the designs in Ishqabad and Sydney.

The doors of all Baha'i houses of worship are open to people of all religions, races, and nations. No sermons may be preached nor rituals performed. Sermons and rituals, as commonly understood, are not part of Baha'i practice anywhere, and the Baha'i Faith has no clergy. Use of pulpits is expressly forbidden in the Kitáb-i-Aqdas, not just in the temples. No fixed speaker's platforms or altars are allowed, although readers may read sacred scriptures from behind an unadorned, portable lectern. During devotional programs, invited readers—of any faith—recite or chant, in any language, the sacred scriptures of the Baha'i Faith and of other religions. Bahá'u'lláh exhorts parents to teach their children to memorize passages from the Baha'i writings, so that they may chant or recite them in the Mashriqu'l-Adhkar. In the Baha'i house of worship in Wilmette, devotional services are currently held at 12:30 p.m. daily.

Music is regarded as a vital part of worship. Prayers and readings set to music may be sung by choirs or soloists a cappella, as only the human voice, with no accompaniment by musical instruments, may be intoned during worship. This restriction applies only to worship in the Temple Auditorium, not to Baha'i worship generally, which includes music of all kinds. Instruments may be played in the vicinity of the Baha'i temple, however. On November 22, 2000, in New Delhi, India, for instance, the opening ceremony of the international "Colloquium on Science, Religion and Development" featured a concert of classical Indian music performed, with traditional instruments, on the grounds of the Baha'i Lotus Temple in New Delhi, India. In the Wilmette temple, instrumental music has been performed in the meeting room below.

At present, there is a Baha'i house of worship on each continent of the world, with the construction of national and local houses of worship reserved for the future, as resources permit. The resources, or funds, necessary to erect and maintain these institutions comes from the regular or earmarked contributions of Baha'is only. Accepting donations from outside sources is strictly forbidden, as only Baha'is have the privilege of contributing to the Baha'i funds. While each Baha'i temple is administered and maintained by the national Baha'i council (known as a National Spiritual Assembly) of the country in which the temple is located, the ultimate oversight of the continental Baha'i houses of worship is by the international governing

Baha'i council, called the Universal House of Justice, established in 1963. There are now seven Baha'i temples, with a eighth under construction, although the first Baha'i temple, which no longer exists, would bring the number to nine.

The first Baha'i temple was built in Ashgabat (Ashkhabad) in Russia's Transcaspian Territory (now Turkmenistan). It was first planned during the ministry of Bahá'u'lláh. This temple was designed by Ustad 'Alí-Akbar Banna of Yazd, under the direct supervision of 'Abdu'l-Baha, during the former's visit to 'Akká in 1893. Construction began in October 1902. Because Banna was killed during an anti-Baha'i pogrom during his visit to Yazd in 1903, a Russian engineer named Volkov was then hired to oversee the construction, which was completed in 1919. In 1928, the temple was expropriated by the Soviet regime, and was then rented back to the Baha'is for two five-year periods. It was finally converted into an art gallery in 1938. In 1948, the temple was damaged by violent earthquakes and further weakened by the heavy rains in the following years. In 1963, Soviet authorities demolished the remaining edifice and converted the site into a public park.

The second Baha'i house of worship was built near the shore of Lake Michigan in Wilmette, north of Chicago. On May 1, 1912, 'Abdu'l-Baha laid the cornerstone, which remains in a special room beneath the main floor of the temple itself. On that historic occasion, 'Abdu'l-Baha explained that "the original purpose of temples and houses of worship is simply that of unity—places of meeting where various peoples, different races and souls of every capacity may come together in order that love and agreement should be manifest between them . . . that all religions, races and sects may come together within its universal shelter."

The principal architect, Louis J. Bourgeois (French-Canadian), who originated the exterior design in 1919, likened the Wilmette house of worship to a "Great Bell, calling to America." Alfred Shaw of Shaw, Metz, and Dolio, designed the exterior and interior cladding, made of white Portland cement concrete with both clear and white quartz aggregate. The temple was dedicated on May 1, 1953. In 1978, it was added to the National Register of Historic Places and has received prestigious design awards. "This unique edifice," wrote Shoghi Effendi, is "the noblest structure reared in the first Baha'i century, and the symbol and precursor of a future world civilization."

The third Baha'i temple is located in Africa, on Kikaya Hill on the outskirts of Kampala, Uganda. It was designed by Charles Mason Remey, who worked closely with Shoghi Effendi in refining the design. Building commenced in May 1957, and the temple was dedicated on January 15, 1961. Standing at nearly 124.7 feet in height, the temple was the highest structure in East Africa at the time of its construction.

A landmark on the scenic northern coast of Sydney, Australia, the fourth Baha'i temple is located in Ingleside on the Mona Vale Hilltop, in the hills and bushland overlooking the beaches below. Also designed by Remey, excavations began in December 1957, and the completed temple was dedicated on September 16, 1961. Like the Wilmette temple, the Sydney house of worship is distinguished by its innovative use of crushed quartz concrete. The temple is topped by a lantern set in place by a helicopter—an innovation in Australian construction. The temple is often used by aircraft and ships for navigational purposes, since the site of approximately nine hectares is the highest point in the area.

The fifth Baha'i temple was designed and built by Frankfurt architect Teuto Rocholl at Langenhain, in the Taunus Hills near Frankfurt-am-Main, West Germany. Its foundation stone was laid in November 1960 and the temple was dedicated on July 4, 1964, by Rúhíyyih Rabbani—distinguished Hand of the Cause of God (an appointed dignitary whose mission is to promulgate and protect the Baha'i Faith) and wife of the late Shoghi Effendi (d. 1957)—representing the Universal House of Justice. All existing Baha'i temples were dedicated by Rúhíyyih Rabbani, in fact.

The sixth Baha'i temple was built on Cerro Sonsonate, a mountain seven miles north of Panama City, Panama. The cornerstone was laid on October 8, 1967. Designed by English architect Peter Tillotson, construction commenced on December 1, 1969, and the temple was dedicated on April 29, 1972. The temple's parabolic dome is built on the principle of a shell. Adorning the dome's supporting walls are abstract designs, in red marble chips, that evoke the decor of temples of the ancient Americas. Mahogany seats, set on a terrazzo floor, complete the interior space, which seats 550 people.

The seventh Baha'i temple was built in Western Samoa, in the Pacific Ocean, at Tiapapata, in the hills behind Apia. Designed by Hossein Amanat, the foundation stone was laid on January 27, 1979, by His Highness Susuga Malietoa Tanumafili II, Head of State of Samoa—the first ruling head of state in the world to become a Baha'i—and by Hand of the Cause, Rúhíyyih Rabbani, representing the Universal House of Justice. Both dignitaries also were prominent in the dedication of the house of worship on September 1, 1984.

The eighth Baha'i temple, known as the Lotus Temple because of its shape, was built near Nehru Place, at Bahapur, in New Delhi, India. Designed by Fariburz Sahba, a Canadian of Iranian birth, the Lotus Temple was conceived as a lotus that appears to float in a series of nine reflecting pools. There are three rows of nine petals each on the outside of the temple—that is, 27 exterior petals on the outside of the temple—and 2 interior rows of 9 petals, which comprise the interior dome of the Lotus. So there are five rows of nine petals each, representing the sacred names, the "Báb" and "Bahá'"—commemorating the two prophet-founders of the Baha'i Faith. Described by one commentator as having the "the grandeur of a palace and the peace of a monastery," the design of Lotus Temple was originally inspired after Sahba had visited several holy places in India, when he realized that the symbol of the lotus blossom was revered by all the religions of the Indian subcontinent. Construction began on April 21, 1980, and the Lotus Temple was dedicated on December 24, 1986.

The Lotus Temple has enjoyed international renown and critical acclaim, having received prestigious awards from architectural and engineering societies. In 1987, the Lotus Temple received a "Structural Award" from the Institution of Structural Engineers of the United Kingdom (the world's leading professional body for structural engineering) for excellence in structural engineering (excellence, creativity and innovation, sustainability, value, and buildability). In that same year, Sahba was honored with the "First Honor Award— Excellence in Architecture" from the Interfaith Forum on Religion, Art and Architecture Affiliate of the American Institute of Architects. In 1988, Sahba was given the "Paul Waterbury Special Citation for Outdoor Lighting" by the Illuminating Engineering Society of North America for what was described as "the Taj Mahal of the Twentieth Century." In 1990, the American Concrete Institute recognized Sahba with its "Finest Concrete Structure in the World" award.

The ninth Baha'i temple, near Santiago in Chile, is the last of the continental Baha'i temples. Designed by Siamak Hariri of Toronto, Canada, this temple is conceived of as a translucent "temple of light." It will, in the words of the architect, be "both monumental and intimate, subtly structured and ordered yet capable of dissolving in light." This temple is constructed of a dome of glowing, translucent stone, and is notable for its absence of straight lines. The structure is created by nine alabaster (translucent stone) and cast-glass "wings," allowing sunlight to filter through during the day, and emitting a warm glow from the interior lighting at night. Gracefully torqued, these wings wrap around the interior of the dome, creating a nest-like structure. Each wing is made of two delicate skins of semitransparent, subtly gridded alabaster, with a steel structure enclosed in curving glass in between, with its primary structural members intertwining with secondary support members, like the structural veining within a leaf. The primary purpose of the nine surrounding ponds is to reflect the temple.

In its April 2001 message, the Universal House of Justice announced that the completion of the continental houses of worship would pave the way for the next stage of Mashriqu'l-Adhkár development: the construction of national houses of worship, as circumstances permit. Wherever possible, each National Spiritual Assembly has purchased a temple site for its national house of worship. In northeast Tehran, Iran, for instance, a two-square mile parcel of land, named Hadíqa, on the slopes of Mount Alburz, had previously been procured for the eventual construction of the first Baha'i house of worship in the birthplace of the Baha'i Faith. As of 2007, a total of 148 temple sites around the world had been acquired for future national Baha'i houses of worship.

It was Shoghi Effendi who heralded the Baha'i house of worship in Wilmette as "the symbol and precursor of a future world civilization." If their respective charitable, humanitarian, educational, medical, and scientific missions are progressively implemented, then the sacred purpose of the Baha'i houses of worship—continental, national, and local—will have been realized, and the concept of worship transformed into one of service to humanity.

On July 8, 2008, the United Nations Educational, Scientific and Cultural Organization (UNESCO) World Heritage Committee designated two Baha'i shrines in Israel—the Shrine of the Báb on Mount Carmel in Haifa, Israel, and the Shrine of Bahá'u'lláh, located near Old Acre on Israel's northern coast—as World Heritage sites. They were the first modern religious edifices to be added to the UNESCO list. Not only are these Baha'i shrines places of commemoration for the Báb (1819–1850) and Bahá'u'lláh (1817–1892), the prophet-founders of the Baha'i Faith, but each of the eight existing Baha'i houses of worship also attracts international attention as well.

In 2007 the state of Illinois announced that the Baha'i house of worship in Wilmette (north of Chicago) had been popularly voted, in an online poll, as one of the "Seven Wonders" of Illinois. On the other side of the world, in New Delhi, India, the Baha'i Lotus Temple, with more than 4.6 million visitors in 2007, is one of the world's most popular tourist attractions today. All of the houses of worship are open to people of all faiths for prayer and meditation, reflecting the Baha'i belief that the world's great religions have come from the same God in critical moments throughout history, as part of a process called "Progressive Revelation." Beyond their popularity and critical acclaim, Baha'i temples have an added significance, in that each is a nucleus for future institutions not typically associated with places of worship.

According to Shonghi Effendi, the Baha'i house of worship in Wilmette, Illinois, is "the symbol and precursor of a future world civilization." Plans call for associating with each Baha'i temple a university, hospital and pharmacy, school for orphans, and traveler's hospice, among administrative and other ancillary institutions. As part of a grand vision, Baha'i temples—as embryonic multipurpose institutions—not only provide spiritual renewal, but are endowed with scientific, medical, educational, and charitable purposes as well. For now, it is their architectural magnificence that has attracted popular and international attention.

Christopher Buck

See also: Baha'i Faith; Bahá'u'lláh.

References

Badiee, Julie. *An Earthly Paradise: Baha'i Houses of Worship around the World*. Oxford: George Ronald, 1992.

Badiee, Julie, and the editors. "Mashriqu'l-Adhkár." *Baha'i Encyclopedia Project*. http://www.bahai-encyclopedia-project.org. Accessed September 5, 2009.

Baha'u'llah. *The Kitab-i-Aqdas: The Most Holy Book*. Wilmette, IL: Bahai Pub Trust, 1993.

Flint, A. R., D. I. Cooper, and S. Naharoy. "The Structural Design and Construction of Two Baha'i Houses of Worship." *The Structural Engineer* 65, no. 3 (1987).

Rafati, V[ahid] and F[ariburz] Sahba. "Bahai Faith IX. Bahai Temples." In "Bahai Faith Part 2." *Encyclopedia Iranica*, edited by Ehsan Yarshater. http://www.iranica.com/newsite/index.isc?Article=http://www.iranica.com/newsite/articles/unicode/v3f4/v3f4a100.html. Accessed September 4, 2009.

Sahba, Fariburz. "Art and Architecture: A Baha'i Perspective." *Journal of Baha'i Studies* 7, no. 3 (1997): 53–82. http://www.bahai-studies.ca/journal/files/jbs/7.3.Sahba(scanned).pdf. Accessed September 6, 2009.

Vegh, Petr, and Greg Hildebrand. "The New Baha'i Mother Temple for South America: Some Aspects of the Façade Design." 11th Canadian Conference on Building Science and Technology, Banff, Alberta, 2007. http://bricks-and-brome.net/03c11.pdf. Accessed September 6, 2009.

Whitmore, Bruce W. *The Dawning Place: The Building of a Temple, the Forging of the North American Baha'i Community*. Wilmette, IL: Baha'i Publishing Trust, 1984.

Temples—Buddhist

Buddhism emerged initially as a monk-centered faith, whose members itinerated though most of the year. Once they began to settle in one place for the rainy season, temples and monasteries began to emerge.

Early Places of Worship What were the earliest Buddhist gathering places like? Some were located near stupas, a building form that predated the monastery. A stupa (or pagoda) is a structure in which the relics of the Buddha or other holy persons are entombed. Stupas were reportedly built immediately after Gautama Buddha's death, though the oldest structure that has survived dates from a later period, the third century BCE—the Great Stupa at Sanchi, India.

The early gathering places were probably settings for meditation. They often began as simple rooms (often a cave or hut, to house a single monk) and later grew into communal gathering places with multiple single rooms for an emerging monastic community. Along with the first rooms (cells) for monks, the first worship centers, *caityas*, were also simple spaces carved out of rock in caves or simply constructed from available building materials. To this day, many monks choose to model their practice and lifestyle on what they know of the Buddha and his early followers, which includes living close to nature in forests, mountains, and/or caves.

The earliest caityas were in India, and hundreds are known from their presence along the ancient trade routes that followed the Western Ghats, an Indian mountain range stretching from Gujarat to Kerala. These were constructed beginning in the second century BCE. Decoration of the caityas was simple, especially before Buddhist art—paintings and sculptures of the Buddha—began to appear in the third century BCE. Over the centuries, the caityas evolved into separate temples, some serving as the center of monastic complexes, others standing independently and serving a largely lay community.

The caitya at the Karla Caves in Mahashastra, India, was erected in the second century CE. One of the larger of the caityas of the period (125 feet by 46 feet), it was carved out of the hillside and contained an apse at one end where a stupa was placed. The interior featured a central aisle and columns placed to facilitate circumambulation within the space.

Temple Development in East Asia When Buddhism was transmitted to China, some of the early structures followed the design of the rooms for monks and ca-

ityas found in western India. As Buddhism spread and developed a significant lay following, temples were built in and adjacent to villages, towns, and urban centers. This process was spurred by the religion's alignment with ruling authorities, who were often known to dictate the placement of temples.

In China, Buddhism had a creative encounter with Daoism, one manifestation of the encounter being the new temples that were erected in urban areas. These were developed along a north-south axis with an entranceway in the south (following Daoist geomancy). Typically, the visitor initially encountered a stupa/pagoda behind which other buildings would be lined up—most noticeably the Buddha hall (where an image of the Buddha would be kept) and the lecture hall (where people gathered for talks on Buddhism), and residences for the monks.

The oldest Buddhist temple in China is the White Horse Temple originally erected in 68 CE in Luoyang, then the capital of the Eastern Han dynasty under Emperor Ming (28–75 CE). The temple faced south, and one entered through a large gate. After entering the visitor came face to face with the Hall of Heavenly Kings, the Buddhist guardian figures, and the Hall of the Great Buddha. From this original temple, others would grow and spread and as Buddhism was transmitted to Korea and Japan temples would be planted there and then adapted to the local culture. As Buddhism evolved, differences especially in the temple interior would emerge.

In China, Korea, and Japan, temple complexes would be built around three structures—the hall of Buddhas, where statues of the Buddhas and bodhisattvas were kept; the meeting (or lecture) hall, where the community could gather to hear teachings; and the stupa or pagoda, where relics of honored ones, from the Buddha himself to local exemplars of the faith, would be kept. In more modern temples, these structures and their functions could be combined in various ways.

Theravada Temples As the temple evolved in southern Asia (Sri Lanka to Vietnam), the temples of Theravada lands remained relatively simple. Though temples can be architecturally elaborate, built from expensive marbles, and decorated with gold and even expensive

Kiyomizu temple complex in present-day Kyoto, Japan, originally built in the eighth century CE. (iStockPhoto.com)

gems, they remain essentially a simple hall, void of furniture, focused on a single statue of the Buddha. The statue is considered a most sacred object and, in the older and more important temples, may be made of fine marble or precious metal and decorated with jewels.

Theravada temples have various relationships with stupas. They may be part of a stupa complex and on occasion dwarfed by the most prominent stupa. They may have a stupa located in a prominent place on the temple grounds, such as in front of the entrance to the temple, or have a stupa as just another item on the temple grounds.

Mahayana Temples The main hall at Mahayana temples houses the many Buddhas and bodhisattvas that are the objects of devotion and veneration. Typically, three statues will dominate Pure Land temples —Amitabha (or Amida) Buddha, with Guan Yin (aka Avalokitesvara) and Mahasamaprapta—the three main

bodhisattvas that Pure Land devotees invoke. Guan Yin's compassion and Mahasamaprapta's wisdom lead to Amitabha's enlightenment. There are numerous Mahayana bodhisattvas, of course, and different traditions may have temples whose statuary may be centered on other than the most popular three, while the number of temples focused primarily on Guan Yin (aka Kannon or Kwan Yin) are numerous.

As the lecture hall is usually the place for the community to gather to hear talks, the main hall will be for individuals to approach the representations of the bodhisattvas with their requests or for thanksgiving over a request that has been granted. Halls are often long and narrow, with the front entrance placed in the middle of one of the longer walls and the deity figures against the back wall. Such halls are designed so that the visitor who enters is immediately face to face with the central bodhisattvas, and may quickly move to either their right or left to visit the others.

The main hall may also be the center of various worship services and holiday celebrations. In the modern age, especially in the West, the main hall and lecture hall are frequently combined into one building, with enough space added in front of the main altar to accommodate a seated group.

Vajrayana Temples Vajrayana temple complexes generally follow Mahayana examples. The stupa, which may contain the relics of honored lamas, often assumed a prominent place either as a stand-alone building or a prominent site within the main hall or lecture hall. In larger temples of monastic complexes, there may be multiple stupas.

The main hall of a Vajrayana temple will have the most deity figures with multiple Buddhas and bodhisattvas represented. Frequently dominating the temple will be statues of the five dhyani Buddhas. Also representations of the major Vajrayana Buddhas and bodhisattvas will be seen including but not limited to Amitabha (Amida); Manjusri; Avolokitesvara (the male form of Guan Yin); Ksitigarbha (aka Jozo in Japan); Medicine Buddha; Vajrapani; Maitreya; White Tara; and Green Tara. In addition, there will be a variety of additional beings, especially protective figures known as the Dharma Guardians.

In addition to the figures represented in the front wall of the main hall, usually in the form of statues, the other three walls of the hall will be decorated with *thankas*, large paintings on cloth (not unlike icons in Eastern Orthodox churches) that most often picture one, a few, or even a large assembly of Buddhas and bodhisattvas or a mandala, a representation of the Vajrayana universe. The thankas not only make beautiful decorations, but are designed to facilitate meditation on the subject of the painting.

Japanese Vajrayana (or Shingon) temples always provide prominent space, usually on each side of the main altar, for two mandalas, the Womb Realm mandala and the Diamond Realm mandala, both of which picture major aspects of the spiritual realms as presented in Vajrayana teachings. Some Vajrayana ceremonies involve the use of fire and many temples will be equipped with open fire pits where a variety of objects may be burned as offerings during worship gatherings.

As with modern Mahayana temples in general, newer Vajrayana temples, especially in the West, have tended to combine the functions of a main hall for the housing of the deity figures with a lecture hall where the teachings are presented to the assemblies of members.

Temples Today In the land of Buddhism's birth, abandoned temples and Buddhist ruins remain in different parts of the country from the era prior to Buddhism's suppression in India in the 13th century. Some of these have been reactivated in the modern world and new temples have been built and opened, most notably adjacent to the pilgrimage sites associated with the historical Buddha. Across the Buddhist world, multiple temples in each country have become the sites of pilgrimages (and tourists) because of their historical and/or architectural significance, or their housing of Buddhist relics or outstanding art work. The old imperial cities of Nara and Kamakura, in Japan, have become the sites at which a spectrum of the Japanese Buddhist sects established prominent temples.

During the Cultural Revolution in China, especially Tibet, many temples and monasteries were destroyed, though a few notable ones, such as the Potala, in Lhasa, escaped. Beginning in the 1990s, there has been an increasing effort to rebuild those monasteries/temples on sites adjacent to a continuing worshipping community.

In parts of the world, temples are placed according to principles of sacred geography and geomancy. In China, the placement of temples relative to mountain settings, also seen as the earthly abode of various bodhisattvas, has been notable. The most famous mountain temples are those found clustered around the four sacred Buddhist mountains—Emei Shan, Jiu Hua Shan, Putuo Shan, and Wu Tai Shan. In Japan, temples have been clustered along pilgrimage routes.

Buddhist temples also serve as gathering places for the celebration of various Buddhist holidays, Wesak or the Buddha's birthday being the most ubiquitous.

Edward A. Irons

See also: Emei Shan; Mahayana Buddhism; Putuo Shan; Relics; Sanchi; Shingon Buddhism; Statues—

Buddhist; Temples–Hindu; Theravada Buddhism; Wesak; Wu Tai Shan.

References

Akhtar, Malik. *A Survey of Buddhist Temples and Monasteries*. New Delhi: Anmol Publications, 2007.

Dohring, Karl, and Walter E. J. Tips. *Buddhist Temples of Thailand: An Architectonic Introduction*. Bangkok: White Lotus Co. Ltd., 2000.

Goodwin, Janet R. *Alms and Vagabonds: Buddhist Temples and Popular Patronage in Medieval Japan*. Honolulu: University of Hawaii Press, 1994.

Hsing, Fu-chuan. *Taiwanese Buddhism and Buddhist Temples*. Taipei: Pacific Cultural Foundation, 1983.

Kapleau, Philip. *A Pilgrimage to the Buddhist Temples and Caves of China*. Rochester, NY: Zen Center of Rochester, 1983.

Malandra, Geri Hockfield. *Unfolding a Mandala: The Buddhist Cave Temples at Ellora*. Albany: State University of New York Press, 1993.

McCallum, Donald F. *The Four Great Temples: Buddhist Archaeology, Architecture, and Icons of Seventh-Century Japan*. Honolulu: University of Hawaii Press, 2008.

Suhnim, Doh Yurng. *Guide to Korean Buddhist Temples*. Seoul: Jogye Order of Korean Buddhism, 1995.

Temples—Church of Jesus Christ of Latter-day Saints

Within the Church of Jesus Christ of Latter-day Saints, the temple is primarily seen as a place for worship. As the only place where a set of the most sacred rites of the church are performed, however, the temple takes on a special sanctity. The Latter-day Saints temple operates somewhat apart from the normal geographically oriented structure of the church. The basic unit of the church is the ward, comparable to a Protestant congregation or Catholic parish. Each ward has a meeting-house where members gather for weekly worship and is the center of a variety of educational, social, recre-

Temple of the Church of Jesus Christ of Latter-day Saints (widely known as the Mormon Church) in Salt Lake City, Utah. (iStockPhoto.com)

ational, and cultural activities. Each ward is headed by a bishop. Wards will affiliate with up to a dozen neighboring wards to form a stake. Stakes are then grouped into areas, the largest sub-units within the church.

In contrast to the ward, which serves a limited constituency with a large variety of activities, the temple serves a widespread constituency and is used for a small number of rites. Those attending any event at the temple must be baptized and confirmed members in good standing. Males must be ordained into the lower level of the priesthood (termed the Melchizedek priesthood). Prior to attending a temple function, members must also have a meeting with their bishop, who determines whether they are living by the precepts of the church, including the law of tithing. Being assured of a member's worthiness, the bishop issues a temple recommend, a document that allows the person to enter the temple. The interview also prepares the person to participate in the temple ordinances.

The temple is the site of several basic ordinances. Some of these rites have their origin in the Latter-day Saints' understanding of heaven. According to them, the afterlife will find people in one of three levels of glory according to the laws they obeyed on Earth. The great majority of people will go to the Terrestrial Kingdom. This is for good people who did not come to the truth of God and Jesus during their earthly lives. The highest, or Celestial Kingdom, is for those who believe the gospel and follow its basic ordinances of baptism by immersion and receive the Holy Spirit by the laying on of hands (that is, they have become members of the Church of Jesus Christ of Latter-day Saints). Within the Celestial Kingdom, there are also levels. The highest level is for those who fully participated in the temple ceremonies.

The basic ordinance performed in the temples is termed the receiving of one's endowments. In specific rooms in the temple that are decorated with pictures depicting the Latter-day Saints' understanding of the cosmos and creation, members participate in a ritual that includes an explanation of the requirements for living in God's presence in the celestial world. Integral to the ritual is the making and receiving of a set of promises. The reception of one's endowment is believed to empower the Christian to overcome all circumstances in life.

Mormons take marriage very seriously and believe that marital relationships will continue in the life to come. One is initially married for this life, but in the temple couples are sealed together for all eternity. In the 19th century, sealing was intimately tied to teachings about polygamy, but under pressure from the outside world these teachings have been dropped. The Mormon Church, however, does continue to teach that a couple's sealing in the temple is a necessary requirement for entrance into the highest levels of the Celestial Kingdom.

Finally, the Church also believes in the baptism for the dead. Those who founded the Church of Jesus Christ of Latter-day Saints in 1830 saw it as a recovery of the apostolic church. Over the centuries, they believe, the essence of the true church had been lost, and thus people, including Christians, who lived in the period between the apostolic age and the founding of the church would not be eligible for the higher levels of heavenly glory. Thus, in each temple is a large baptismal fount at which baptisms of those who died outside of the church may be conducted by proxy. Periodically, the church has been cited in the news for the baptism of some famous historical character or has had to deal with related controversies, most notably the rejection of such baptisms by the Jewish community.

Church founder Joseph Smith, Jr. (1805–1844), oversaw the erection of the first Latter-day Saints temple in the mid-1830s in Kirkland, Ohio. He also laid the cornerstone for a future temple in Independence, Missouri. After only a brief time, the church had to leave behind both the Kirkland temple and the temple lot in Independence. Then a third temple was constructed in Nauvoo, Illinois, in the mid-1840s, but it had to be abandoned following Joseph Smith's assassination and the relocation of the church to Utah. A permanent temple was constructed in the center of Salt Lake City, and additional temples opened in St. George, Manti, and Logan, Utah.

As the Mormon movement expanded beyond Utah, the first temples were constructed in Arizona, California, and Idaho. It was not until 1955 that a temple was opened outside of the United States, in Bern, Switzerland. The Swiss temple heralded the phenomenal church growth that would take place in the decade after World War II. In 2009, the church completed the 129th temple, and 17 are in various states of construction. In addition, in 2002, a reconstructed Nauvoo temple was rededicated. Temples now exist on every continent.

Upon completion, temples undergo an elaborate consecration ceremony. In recent years, it has been the church's practice to allow people who are not church members to visit and see the inside of a Latter-day Saints temple, which they would not be able to do once it is consecrated. Each temple has a Endowment Room, a Celestial Room, a Bride's Room (to prepare for the sealing ceremony), and a Sealing Room.

The practice of allowing non-members to visit about-to-be-consecrated temples has reduced the level of secrecy surrounding Mormon temples. Much of the secrecy has been taken away by the revelations of former church members who have both published the ritual texts and commented at length on the temple ceremonies. Also, Latter-day Saints scholars have furthered the discussion of temple rituals by exploration of their origin in traditional Freemasonry. Meanwhile, Latter-day Saints authorities have staunchly opposed any revelations concerning the secrets of temple activities.

J. Gordon Melton

See also: Church of Jesus Christ of Latter-day Saints; Temples—Baha'i; Temples—Buddhist; Temples—Hindu.

References

Buerger, David John. *The Mysteries of Godliness: A History of Mormon Temple Worship*. Salt Lake City, UT: Signature Books, 2002.

Cowan, Richard O. *Temples that Dot the Earth*. Salt Lake City, UT: Bookcraft, 1989.

Homer, Michael W. "Similarity of Priesthood in Masonry: The Relationship between Freemasonry and Mormonism." *Dialogue* 27, no. 3 (Fall 1994): 1–113.

"The House of the Lord." Church of Jesus Christ of Latter-day Saints. http://www.lds.org/temples/. Accessed May 15, 2009.

Larsen, Dean L. *Mormon Temples (Setting the Record Straight)*. Brigham City, UT: Brigham Distributing, 2008.

Packer, Boyd K. *The Holy Temple*. Salt Lake City, UT: Bookcraft, 1980

Temples—Hindu

Worship by Hindus is not exclusively congregational and may take place out in nature, inside the home, at a simple roadside shrine, or in a temple. Temple worship may have been an ancient phenomenon in India, but the currently identified remains of temples date back only to about the fifth century of the Common Era. This leaves the unanswered question: where did Hindus (or their predecessors) conduct community or large-scale ritual activities before then? Vedic rituals were performed under the open sky or in temporary enclosures that were dismantled after the ritual was completed. Temples constructed of wood or other impermanent materials may have been in existence before the fifth century, but we have no conclusive record of them. Therefore, the classical Hindu temple, in the form of a large stone building or a complex composed of several buildings, seems to be a medieval and modern phenomenon.

A reliable food supply, population growth and urbanization, and stable governments in local kingdoms in much of the subcontinent of India from the sixth century on made it possible for the prosperous to endow local priests with resources to undertake major construction projects. Records that remain from the medieval period, inscribed on rocks or metal tablets, indicate that royalty and landed nobles made generous donations and that temple wealth was accumulated and redistributed in ways that materially enriched the town and region of major temples. One factor in that circulation of wealth was food. It has a central role in Hindu worship as an acceptable offering to installed images of divine beings. Leftovers from the food prepared for ritual offering was given either freely or in return for a small donation to devotees who visited the temple deity. Endowments of agricultural produce or productive land generated ongoing income for the temple institution and for those who served it. The late Burton Stein analyzed the circulation of resources at the Tirupati temple complex in Andhra Pradesh in southern India, and his report on it has become an influential classic.

In addition to their secondary function as economic centers and engines of prosperity, large Hindu temples are primarily centers of learning, repositories of artistic and cultural artifacts, and sites for ritual activity. Traditional temples may be entered by Hindus at almost any time of the day, perhaps preparing by taking a ritual bath and changing clothes, passing through a gateway, leaving footwear, stepping carefully over a threshold and ringing a bell, and then moving clockwise toward the central shrine room in which the main image of the temple's presiding deity has been installed. Some major temples even today reserve the right to refuse admission to non-Hindus or otherwise unqualified persons, so it is important to investigate local rules and expectations in advance.

Whether passing through a temple individually or as a participant in corporate worship such as a morning or evening *arati* ceremony in which one or more designated participants will slowly wave an oil lamp clockwise in front of an installed image, the key interaction is between the divine being as mediated through

Vishwanath Temple in Khajuraho, India, built in the early 11th century CE. (Shutterstock)

the image and the individual devotee who is privileged to experience the sight, or *darshan*, that manifests the qualities of divine power and grace. As a token of the divine-human encounter, a temple functionary is likely to present the devotee with a portion of the food that has been offered to the deity or else a flower, fruit, or coconut that has been blessed by proximity to the image. This is called *prasad*. Some visitors may eat the edible portion while still at or near the temple site, but others will carry it away to share with family members or acquaintances that were not able to accompany them to the temple.

With emigration from India, Hindus for centuries have been building community centers and temples out-side of India, very early in Southeast Asia and from the last half of the twentieth century in Australia, Europe, and the Americas. Economic opportunities that attract Hindu emigrants to those distant lands also provide the means and motivation to reaffirm their link to the old country and to their traditional religious and cultural identity by making certain that a temple would be built in their new location and that design and construction would be carefully supervised to assure that it conforms to the standards preserved in ancient Hindu manuscripts.

Gene R. Thursby

See also: Hinduism; Temples—Buddhist.

References

Daniélou, Alain. *The Hindu Temple: Deification of Eroticism*. Rochester, VT: Inner Traditions, 2001.

Kurien, Prema A. *A Place at the Multicultural Table: The Development of an American Hinduism.* New Brunswick, NJ: Rutgers University Press, 2007.

Mitchell, George. *The Hindu Temple: An Introduction to Its Meaning and Forms.* Chicago: University of Chicago Press, 1988.

Narayanan, Vasudha. "Alaya." In *The Hindu World*, edited by Sushil Mittal and Gene Thursby, 446–477. New York and London: Routledge, 2004.

Stein, Burton. "The Economic Function of a Medieval South Indian Temple." *Journal of Asian Studies* 19, no.2 (1960): 163–176.

Temples—Jewish

The temple in Jerusalem was the center for many centuries of Jewish religious life. It was here that the priests carried out the designated sacrifices on particular occasions. The Holy of Holies in the temple represented the most important site in the world for Jews and only the high priest was allowed to enter it, and only on Yom Kippur, the Day of Atonement. The First Temple was destroyed by the Babylonians and the Second Temple by the Romans, but its memory has been kept alive in the Jewish liturgy. The only physical remnant of the Second Temple today is the Western Wall, which Jews are now able to pray in front; it has become the custom to leave notes in the chinks in the wall, in the hope that their messages reach God. There were other temples for Jews, in Egypt, and for the Samaritans on Mount Gerizim.

King David had wanted to build a temple but was told by God that having shed blood this would not be appropriate (1 Chronicles 28:3). Solomon constructed it and the effort was obviously huge, since he forced his subjects to work on the building and was obliged in the end to cede 20 towns in the Galilee to repay King Hiram of Tyre (1 Kings 9–11). Prayer, but particularly sacrifice, took place in the building, and it lasted for around 400 years until destroyed by the Babylonians, and then a second temple was built, greatly enlarged by King Herod and destroyed by the Romans in 70 CE. In the First Temple the small area called the Holy of Holies contained the two tablets of the Law given to Moses on Mount Sinai, we are told, but these disappeared with its destruction, and on the Day of Atonement the high priest would enter this room, and only then, to carry out a ritual to atone for the sins of the community as well as for himself and his family. The Bible commanded Jewish men to appear, with a sacrifice, in the temple three times a year—Passover, Shavuot, and Sukkot—which came to be called the Pilgrim festivals accordingly.

During the Muslim occupation of Jerusalem two mosques were built on the site of the temple and only the Western Wall remains, being widely regarded as connected to the original building. Many Jews regard walking on the original temple site to be forbidden since it might involve trespassing on the Holy of Holies, which is strictly forbidden. Some Muslims deny the existence of any temples in Jerusalem in order to try to weaken the Jewish claim on the site, and have even suggested that the *kotel*, the Western Wall, is really part of the al-Aqsa mosque and should be known as the Buraq wall, since Muhammad tethered his mount al-Buraq there while ascending through the heavens on his night journey. On the other hand, the reference in the Koran to a *masjid* (17:7) in what is taken to be Jerusalem at a time before there were any mosques suggests that the most plausible translation is sanctuary or temple. It is also referred to in the account of Suleiman ordering the jinn to build it (34:13) and of course in the night journey of the Prophet from Mecca to what is presumably taken to be Jerusalem (17:1).

Orthodox Jews pray three times a day for the restoration of the temple, and the ceremonies that took place there are still much discussed and remembered today. It is worth pointing out though that just as in the Koran there is no direct reference to Jerusalem in the Torah, and this left scope for other groups of Jews or those closely linked with the Jews like the Samaritans to prioritize other locations such as Mount Gerizim. There was also a temple at Leontopolis about 200 BCE, north of modern Cairo, and the second is the Temple of Elephantine dating to 300 years earlier, to about 500 BCE, in Upper Egypt close to Aswan. They seem

Wailing Wall in old Jerusalem, Israel. (PhotoDisc, Inc.)

to have been set up by Jewish soldiers who were working as mercenaries in the area.

The capture of the Old City of Jerusalem in 1967 allowed Jews once again to pray at the Western Wall, and this has become a popular venue. The plaza in front of the wall is now hotly contested by different Jewish groups, some disapproving of women mixing with men or of particular variations in traditional Jewish religious services. Although a majority of Jews in Israel are secular, there is a reluctance to relinquish Jerusalem to a Palestinian state partially due to the strong attachment by most Jews to what remains of the temple and the idea that this should remain as part of the capital of the state of Israel.

The destruction of the Second Temple encouraged the creation of synagogues as houses of prayer, although there had surely been such institutions in existence even while the temple existed. In contemporary America many Reform Jews call their houses of worship temples.

Oliver Leaman

See also: Gerizim, Mount; Jerusalem; Muhammad; Orthodox Judaism; Passover; Reform Judaism; Shavuot; Sinai, Mount; Sukkot; Yom Kippur.

References

Albright, William F. *Archaeology and the Religion of Israel*. Louisville, KY: Fons Vitae, 2006.

Coogan, Michael D., ed. *The Oxford History of the Biblical World*. Oxford: Oxford University Press, 1998.

Kenyon, Kathleen M. *Digging up Jerusalem*. London: Benn, 1974.

Tenri City

Tenri City, the official headquarters of the Japanese new religion called Tenrikyo, is located about 10 miles from the old Buddhist center of Nara. As it has grown, it has incorporated into itself the small village of Shoyashiki, where, on October 26, 1838, the religion's founder, Nakayama Miki (1798–1887), first began to speak about the revelations she had been experiencing (and would continue to experience over the next half century). One element of the revelations concerned a plot of land near the village she been shown upon which was the Jiba, which she was told was the center of the universe. On this land, she saw to the erection of Oyasato, the Parental House, the residing place of Tenri-O-no-Mikoto, God the Parent, who created the universe. From this location, God awaits humanity's return.

As Nakayama's teachings spread, and believers found their way to Shoyashiki, new buildings arose and eventually a city emerged. The movement was eventually recognized by the government and survived the Meiji era (1868–1912) as a part of sectarian Shinto.

In the main temple at Tenri City, believers gather to re-enact the creation story as related by Nakayama in a musical dance-rite called *mi-kagura-uta*. This ritual is performed with the expectation that the present world can be transformed and humans can move from the present social order into the Joyous Life World. In the center of the main temple is the *kanrondai*, a sacred pillar-like structure that marks the exact place of Nakayama's revelation about the origins of human creation.

Following World War II, with the arrival of religious freedoms, Tenrikyo separated from the other Shinto groups. It began a process of reviewing and purifying its teachings to clean out any distortion introduced from the years of close association with the sectarian Shinto groups. In the next decades the movement expanded rapidly. Followers took the opportunity offered by the time of relative success to construct a university, an orphanage, a hospital, a museum, a library, and a publishing house, all at Tenri City.

Among the many buildings at Tenri City, Nakayama (also known as Oyasama) is believed to continue to live and work at one called the Foundress's Sanctuary. Their belief in her continued presence is heralded by their preparation of three meals and hot baths for her every day. Priests, rotating shifts every half-hour, guard the door of the sanctuary as part of their duties, which also include performing rituals of "perpetual veneration."

The city is visited by many annually, and all who come to the city are seen as "returning to Jiba." To mark their pilgrimage, they are given an amulet. It contains a small piece of clothing formerly worn by Oyasama. When they get back home, believers can present this amulet as proof of their "return." It is also worn as a protective device.

J. Gordon Melton

See also: Devotion/Devotional Traditions; Pilgrimage.

References

The Doctrine of Tenrikyo. Tenri City, Japan: Tenrikyo Church Headquarters, 1995.

Ellwood, Robert S., Jr. *Tenrikyo: A Pilgrimage Faith*. Tenri City, Japan: Oyasato Research Institute, 1982.

Straelen, Henry Van. *The Religion of Divine Wisdom, Japan's Most Powerful Religious Movement*. Kyoto, Japan: Veritas Shoin, 1957.

The Teachings and History of Tenrikyo. Tenri City, Japan: Tenrikyo Overseas Mission Department, 1986.

Tenrikyo

One of the very first of what have come to be known as Japan's new religions, or *shin shukyo*, Tenrikyo (Religion of Heavenly Wisdom) was founded in 1838 by Nakayama Miki (1798–1887), a farmer's wife with shamanistic attributes from a village close to Tenri City, which is situated in the Yamato basin only a short distance from the historic city of Nara. In 1838, Tenri-O-no-Mikoto (God of Heavenly Reason), also known as Oyagami (God the Parent), is believed to have taken possession of Nakayama Miki, also called Oyasama (Worthy Parent), for the purpose of revealing to her his divine plan and her role therein, and to bestow upon her the gift of healing.

Nakayama Miki's mission was to consist of delivering people from suffering in preparation for the coming of a perfect divine kingdom (*kanrondai sekai*) in which human beings would enjoy the joyous and blissful life (*yoki-gurashi*) in union with Tenri-O-no-Mikoto. On becoming the shrine of Tenri-O-no-Mikoto,

Nakayama Miki was also provided by this same deity with a plot of ground known as the *jiba*, believed to be the place of origin of the human race and its spiritual home (*oyasato*). On this land stands the principal place of worship (Shinden) at the center of which is the *kanrondai*, or sacred pillar. Both the Shinden and the Kyosoden, the sanctuary of the foundress, are centers of pilgrimage. It is believed that Nakayama Miki continues to dwell in the Kyosoden, where she is attended to as if still physically present by devotees who dust and clean her bedroom, prepare her food, and look after her every need.

As in the case of other Japanese new religions founded by women, Nakayama Miki was greatly helped by a dedicated male disciple in the person of Iburi Izo, a poor carpenter whose wife she had healed of childbirth fever. Iburi Izo displayed his gratitude for this cure by dedicating himself to *hinokishin*, or volunteer work for the church, including the construction of a model of the first kanrondai in 1873 and a sanctuary for Tenri-O-no-Mikoto. Iburi Izo became the joint leader of Tenrikyo on the death of Nakayama Miki in 1887, and in his capacity as *honseki*, or oracle, he spoke through the spirit of the foundress to God. His pronouncements were written down and came to constitute a set of sacred writings known as the Osashizu. These supplement the two most important sacred scriptures, the Ofudesaki (Tip of the Divine Writing-pen), transmitted by God to Nakayama Miki, a transmission that was not completed until 1882, and the divinely inspired Mikagura-uta, or poems that are used as the text of Tenrikyo's worship.

The major Tenrikyo sacred ritual, the dance of creation, the *kagura tsutome*, takes place around the kanrondai and is performed by dancers in masks led by the head of the church, known as the *shimbashira*, a descendant of the foundress. The masks represent figures in the cosmogonic myth developed by Tenrikyo. This dance, performed on the 26th of each month, is believed to hasten the fulfillment of God's plans and is given as the main reason for Tenrikyo's existence. On the day prior to the performance, the Shinbashira "ordains" (in a brief ceremony known as the honseki) those who have completed the course of *besseki* lectures (the nine lectures required for initiation) and the *shuyoka* course (three months' intensive training) and

taken the besseki vow. They are given by the Shinbashira the sacred grant of *osazuke*, or healing, and these graduates, or *yobuku* (literally timbers), are now empowered to perform healing rites using a particular form of hand gesture known as *teodori*, or hand dance, the gesture used in Tenrikyo worship.

The major festival for members from all over the world is the birthday of the foundress, celebrated at the Oyasato, or headquarters, on April 18. Other important services include the Tai-sai, or great services, held on January 26 and October 26. There are memorial services for the dead on March 27 and September 27, as well as a monthly service, the Tsukinami-sai. Three times a month there is the popular sacramental rite of *obiya yurushi*, or easy childbirth, which involves the consecration of white rice that is then placed on the Kanrodai during the *obiya tsutome* service in which the creation is ritually re-enacted.

Regarded as a dissident religious movement, Tenrikyo suffered increasing government probes and harassment, and the foundress, while proud of her country, was critical and at times even scornful of its ruling elite—as were other female founders of Japanese sects, including Deguchi Nao (of Omoto). Nakayama Miki was frequently interrogated, and she was imprisoned on 17 occasions for, among other things, blasphemy and obstructing the public highways by performing elaborate ritual dances at the corners of the village. The movement's fortunes changed, however, and in 1908 it was recognized as one of the 13 Sect Shinto organizations, autonomous organizations authorized by the government between 1868 and 1945.

In 1947, Tenrikyo, believing that its teachings had become distorted by State Shinto, launched the campaign for the Restoration of the Original Teachings (Fukugen). In 1970 it withdrew from the Association of Shinto Sects and had itself placed in the category of "Other Religions." It is one of the largest movements in that group, with a membership of more than one million in Japan. Tenrikyo is also present in many countries outside Japan, including Korea, Taiwan, India, Nepal, the Democratic Republic of the Congo, the United States, France, and Great Britain, but in every case with the exception of Korea it has remained numerically small.

Tenrikyo operates a number of important cultural and educational institutions, including Tenri University, founded in 1925, and the very valuable Tenri Library and Tenri Sankokan Museum. It has also established a publishing house and a hospital. In the latter both spiritual and scientific methods of healing are used.

The structure and organization of Tenrikyo, while formally bureaucratic, is essentially based on the principle of the *ie*, or family system; the *honbuin*, or central administration, consists of descendants of the families of Nakayama Miki and Iburi Izo, or of families very close to theirs. The headquarters are in Tenri City (near Nara), Japan, and are known as Oyasato, or Village of the Parent.

http://www.tenrikyo.or.jp/

Peter B. Clarke

See also: Omoto; Possession; Shinto; State Shinto; Tenri City.

References

Clarke, Peter B. *A Bibliography of Japanese New Religions*. Eastbourne, UK: Japan Library, 1999.

Elwood, Robert S., Jr. *Tenrikyo: A Pilgrimage Faith*. Tenri City, Japan: Oyasato Research Institute, 1982.

Ofudesaki: Tip of the Writing-Brush. Tenri City, Japan: Tenrikyo Church Headquarters, 1971.

Oyasato Research Institute, Tenri University. *The Theological Perspectives of Tenrikyo*. Tenri City, Japan: Tenri University Press, 1986.

Tensho Kotai Jingukyo

Tensho Kotai Jingukyo, the Religion of the Mighty God of Heaven (Tensho refers here to the sun goddess, Amaterasu), was founded in July 1945 by a farmer's wife, Sayo Kitamura (1900–1967), from the village of Hizumi in Yamaguchi Prefecture in the western part of Honshu. Sayo Kitamura, after one of a series of possessions by Tensho, became a living goddess, or *ikigami*, in July 1945. She proceeded to inform her listeners that global catastrophe was imminent. She also announced that the Kami Tensho, who had taken complete possession of her whole being, had commanded her to perform a dance as a means of restoring harmony and peace at that very moment, when the present order of the world was about to collapse into complete anarchy and chaos. From that point, observers referred to the new movement as the Dancing Religion (Odori Shukyo). The dance is also important in securing release from evil spirits and in bringing relief where there is misfortune. In the thinking of the Dancing Religion, as in numerous other Japanese religions (for example, Agonshu), ancestral spirits are seen as bringing suffering to their descendants and the living generally when they themselves have not been redeemed.

A charismatic leader who broke innumerable conventions in relation to style of dress, use of language, and customary forms of greeting, among other things, Sayo Kitamura, known to her followers as Ogamisama (Great God), preached continuously of impending calamity and, in particular, of the devastation that awaited the world on account of the development and use of the atomic bomb. There would, however, emerge in the course of time a new world order in which peace and happiness would reign unchallenged, and this would be brought about by spiritual means, by fulfilling the commands of the absolute deity Tensho Kotai Jingu.

The main teaching of the movement is that misfortune and unhappiness are the result of desires and attachments, and that the only way out of this unhealthful and harmful condition is through prayer that leads to the state of non-ego, or *muga*. The main practice is the ecstasy dance, or *muga-no-mai*, the dance of selflessness. A prayer known as *oinori* is said by members prior to starting this dancing ritual, and it ends with the recitation of the formula *na myo ho ren ge kyo*, a phrase that is regarded as untranslatable and whose meaning and power to transform and purify are in the sounds. This formula and improvised songs (*muga-no-uta*) are sung continuously, each time with ever-increasing intensity and volume as the dance gets underway.

It is believed that the dance bestows on participants the gift of divine insight into the innermost secrets of the universe. Followers believe, further, that this dance will give them spiritual control over the world and purify the souls of all human beings. It is also thought that once they have achieved this high emotional state, followers' prayers gain the power to redeem all evil spirits, including those that might be in possession of the living. A form of speaking in tongues during this selfless dance is not unknown, the different languages heard being those of souls who have entered the participants' bodies to express their gratitude for having been saved.

Other practices include mutual soul polishing meetings known variably, depending on their form, content, and size as *tomomigaki*, *migaki-no-kai*, and *komigakai*.

The movement's headquarters, or *honbu*—regarded as the spiritual home of the people of the world—is located in the village of Tabuse in Yamaguchi Prefecture, close to the village where the founder was born and reared. The present spiritual head is Himigamisama, her granddaughter, the daughter of her son, known as Wakagamisama. The latter performs the role of administrative head of the movement.

Overseas branches exist in the United States, the largest center being in Hawaii, where the active membership is less than 1,000.

Peter B. Clarke

See also: Agonshu; Shinto.

References

Clarke, Peter B. "Modern Japanese Millenarian Movements." In *Japanese New Religions in Global Perspective*, edited by Peter B. Clarke, 129–182. Richmond, UK: Curzon, 2000.

Hamrin, Tima. "Illness and Salvation in Tensho Kotai Jingukyo." In *Japanese New Religions in Global Perspective*, edited by Peter B. Clarke, 240–257. Richmond, UK: Curzon, 2000.

Nishiyama, Shigeru, and Fujii Takashi. "The Propagation and Spread of Tensho Kotai Jingukyo within Japanese American Society on Hawaii Island." In *New Religions: Contemporary Papers in Japanese Religions*, edited by Inoue Nabutaka, 125–161. Tokyo: Kokugakuin University, 1991. http://www.kokugakuin.ac.jp/ijcc/wp/cpjr/newreligions/nishiyama.html. Accessed April 15, 2009.

The Prophet of Tabuse. Tabuse, Japan: Tensho Kotai Jingukyo, 1954.

Terapanth Svetambara Jain Tradition

The Terapanth Svetambara tradition of Jainism was founded by Muni Bhikhan (1726–1803), who was later called Acarya Bhiksu. Bhikhan was born in India in the village of Kantaliya near Jodhpur. His parents were Bisa Osvals of the Sankleca *gotra* and followed the Murtipujak Jain tradition. After the death of his wife, Bhikhan renounced the world and became initiated into the itinerant mendicant order of Acarya Raghunath (1706 or 1708–1790) of the Dhanna Dharmadasa Sthanakavasi tradition in 1751. However, on June 28, 1760, he split from the "lax" Sthanakavasis with four other monks and founded his own mendicant order in Kelva near Rajsamand. In the beginning, his group had only 13 male members, and his opponents scorned it as the path of the 13, or *terah panth*. Bhiksu later paraphrased terah panth as *tera panth*, or your path, and interpreted the number 13 in terms of the principal rules of conduct for Jain ascetics—the 5 great vows, or *mahavratas*; the 3 restraints, or *guptis*; and the 5 comportments, or *samitis*—which he attempted to follow by the letter.

The cause of the schism was a disagreement over a technical point of Jain karma theory. The Jain canonical scriptures teach that the soul can be liberated from its karmic fetters only through the renunciation of all violence—that is, all action. The Dharmadasa Sthanakavasis, like most extant Jain traditions, also propagate compassion, or *anukampa*, as a religious value and emphasize the positive karmic consequences of charity (*dana-daya*) and the protection of life (*jiva daya*). In contrast, Bhiksu argued that because ultimately both bad karma (*papa*) and good karma (*punya*) obstruct the liberation of the soul, a salvation seeker must avoid both. Because he privileged this perspective, he regarded acts of compassion performed for the purpose of accumulating punya even as sinful (papa). The most concise discussion of this issue from the Terapanth point of view can be found in Bhiksu's treatise *Anukampa Ri Caupai*, written in 1787 in the local Marvari language. Bhiksu distinguishes there (and elsewhere) between relative or worldly compassion (*laukik daya*) and absolute or religious compassion (*lokottara* or *dharma daya*)—that is, absolute nonviolence. He argues that although material acts of charity are positive from the social point of view (*vyavahara naya*), they are negative from the religious point of view (*niscaya naya*). In his conception, punya can be gained only as a side effect of acts of renunciation, not independently through acts of material help or other "mixed" actions. His criticism of the laxity of the Sthanakavasi mendicants and other Jain traditions is directed against their non-recognition of the difference between religion and worldly morality.

The terminology of Acarya Bhiksu's teaching of absolute renunciation is influenced not only by the writings of the Digambara Acarya Kundakunda (ca. second to third centuries CE) and the Digambara commentaries of Umasvati's *Tattvartha-sutra* (ca. third to fifth centuries CE) but also by the *tabbas*, or vernacular commentaries, of the Acarya Dharmasinha (1599–1671), the founder of the Dariyapuri Sthanakavasi tradition. Dharmasinha also taught the futility of compassionate help and nonintervention on the grounds that from the absolute point of view the moment of death of every living being is predetermined by its life-span (*ayusya*) karma, even if the causes of death appear to be accidental, and therefore preventable, from a conventional point of view. For other Sthanakavasis the name Terapanth indicates that Acarya Bhiksu's views are akin to those of the proponents of the image-worshipping lay movement of the Digambara Terapantha (which should otherwise not be confused with the aniconic Svetambara Terapanth Order), whose adherents also claim to practice Jainism from an absolute perspective—or *niscaya naya*. The denial of the necessity of the practical point for a non-omniscient living being is, for them, a form of *ekanta-vada* (theoretical absolutism) that contradicts the "Jain theory" of *anekanta-vada* (non-absolutism).

Although the principal outlook of the Terapanth has not changed during its 240-year history, its forms of application and its institutions have changed. To prevent schisms and laxity, Acarya Bhiksu made the rule that there should be only one *acarya*, or teacher cum group leader, and that he should be chosen by his predecessor. On that basis, the fourth acarya, Jitmal (Jayacarya) (1803–1881), created an elaborate institutional framework for the growing monastic order from 1852 on. The ninth acarya, Tulsi (1914–1997), ruled the order from 1934. He modernized the Terapanth and turned it from a world-negating mendicant order into a world-transforming religious movement by emphasizing the significance of education, worldly morality, and social reform. In 1949 he created the "nonreligious"

anuvrat, or small-vow, movement for the implementation of nonviolence and morality in social life. In 1952 he abolished the dogma of non-accidental death and later promoted "worldly" charity for his educational projects. The communal goodwill movement in 1954 was followed in 1960 by the *naya mod*, or new turn, initiative that sought to eradicate "outdated" social customs among the Terapanth laity, such as rituals, casteism, and female *purdha*. In 1970 the Jain Visva Bharati was opened and gained the status of a "deemed to be University" in 1971. It is located in Ladnun, the birthplace of Acarya Tulsi, and functions today as the physical center of the Terapanth, though all important decisions are taken by the permanently itinerant acarya. In 1980, Acarya Tulsi introduced a new category of novices, the *saman(i)s*, who are permitted to use public transport and to travel abroad on missionary tours. For many Jains living outside India, the samans and samanis are the only Jain mendicants they can meet. The present leader of the Terapanth is Acarya Mahaprajna (b. 1920), who was inaugurated in 1994. Mahaprajna contributed greatly to the Terapanth edition of the canonical scriptures, or *agama* (1974–), and the publication of the Terapanth literature in Rajasthani. Under the impression of the success of Goenka's *vipassana* classes in Rajasthan, he introduced a Jain version of insight meditation, *preksa dhyana*, in 1975. And in 1980 he introduced the science of living program, *jnana vijnana*, a step-by-step guide for a nonviolent way of life for children and adults, intended for schools and universities in particular. The chosen successor of Mahaprajna is Yuvacarya Mahasraman (b. 1962).

At present, the Terapanth has about 250,000 followers all over India (including non-Jain members of the *anuvrata* movement); several thousand in Nepal, the United Kingdom, and the United States; and a few families in many commercial centers around the world. Most Terapanth lay followers belong to the traditional business families of the Osval castes. Because of the influence of the missionary tours of the samans and samanis, the influence of the Terapanth is currently spreading worldwide, though primarily among expatriate Jains. The principal religious practices of the Terapanthis are fasting, meditation, and study. Because image-worship is rejected, laypeople venerate the mendicants of the Terapanth order as symbols of Jain ideals.

Jain Vishva Bharati
Ladnun-341 306
Rajasthan
India

Peter Flügel

See also: Jainism; Meditation

References

Budhmal, Muni. *Terapanth Ka Itihas. Pratham Khand: Terapanth Ke Pratham Car Acarya.* 4th rev. ed. Calcutta: Jain Svetambar Terapanth Mahasabha Prakasan, 1964, 1995.

Flügel, Peter. "The Ritual Circle of the Terapanth Svetambara Jains." *Bulletin D'Etudes Indiennes* 13 (1995–1996): 117–176.

Mahaprajna, Yuvacarya. *Preksha Dhyana: Theory and Practice.* 2nd rev. ed. Ed. by Muni Mahendra Kumar. Ladnun, India: Tulsi Adhyatma Nidam, 1992.

Nathmal, Muni [Acarya Mahaprajna]. *Acharya Bhiksu: The Man and His Philosophy.* Translation of *Bhiksu Vicar Darsan* by N. Sahal. Curu, India: Adars Sahity Sangh Prakasan, 1959, 1968.

Tulsi, Acarya. *Anuvrat: A Shield against Immorality.* Ladnun, India: Jain Vishva Bharati, 1989.

Tulsi, Acarya, ed. *Bhiksu-Granth Ratnakar. Khand 1–2. Sanghrahakarta: Muni Cauthmal. Prabhandh Sampadak: Sricand Rampuriya.* Calcutta: Jain Svetambara Terapanth Mahasabha, 1960–1961.

Tulsi, Acarya, and Yuvacarya Mahaprajna, comps. *Terapanth: Maryada Aur Vyavastha. Sampadak: Muni Madhukar.* Jayacarya Series Vol. 9. Ladnum, India: Jain Visva Bharati, 1983.

Thai Forest Monks

The second half of the 19th century in Thailand witnessed an efflorescence of ascetic forest-dwelling monks dedicated to the practice of meditation. These monks led an eremitic life—sometimes alone, sometimes in small groups. They were heirs to a classical division within the Theravada *sangha* (monastic order) between forest dwellers (Pali: *araññavasi*) and town dwellers (Pali: *gamavasi*). This division correlates loosely with a further categorization of monks into those who devote themselves to meditation (Pali: *vipassanadhura*) and those whose vocation is more inclined toward studying texts (Pali: *ganthadhura*).

Austere activities undertaken in addition to the monks' rules (Pali: *vinaya*) came to be associated with the path of meditation. Thirteen in number, these practices are known as *dhutanga*, and they include the practice of sleeping in forests or cemeteries. In Thailand monks who follow all or some of the dhutanga practices are known as *thudong* monks.

Scholars propose that the revitalization of the thudong tradition can be regarded as a reaction to 19th-century ecclesiastical reforms and the emergence of a new monastic fraternity (Pali: *nikaya*), the Thammayut, promoted by the royal monk and eventual monarch, Mongkut (1851–1868). The Thammayut reformers engineered a more standardized and bureaucratic form of state Buddhism, commensurate with moves toward the consolidation and modernization of the state.

Many of the most noted of the thudong monks of the revival were to be found in the northeast region of the country, especially those who belonged to the lineage of the meditation teacher Phra Ajaan Man Phuurithatto (1870–1949). Man was universally acknowledged as an especially holy monk who achieved the highest level of spiritual attainment (Pali: *arahant*). Narratives of Man's life and those of other venerated forest monks became popular and are nowadays printed for distribution as gifts at funerals.

The forest monks served as teachers, healers, and community leaders to the villagers who supported them. From the outset the wandering monks established temporary hermitages during the rainy season. Under pressure from the centralized authority of the ecclesiastical hierarchy, and with the encouragement of local patronage, the hermitages gave way to permanent monasteries whose members continued the thudong tradition by undertaking pilgrimages.

Most recently, organized tours have become popular among prosperous urban folk who seek to acquire religious merit through offering requisites to the forest monks, who are regarded as particularly pure and so unusually productive of merit. The funerals of forest meditation masters have attracted huge crowds, including high-ranking members of the Thai royal family. Such attention has, however, done little to safeguard the independence of forest monks, who are often in conflict with officials of the Forest Department. In 1987 the Thai Sangha Council ordered all monks, except those living in designated monasteries, to leave the forests. Furthermore, forested areas are shrinking. Decades of land clearance and logging have wiped out up to 80 percent of Thailand's forests. Monks from forest monasteries are active in a struggle to conserve what remains.

One famous forest monk and disciple of Ajaan Man was Ajaan Chah. Ajaan Chah (1924–1993) established an international monastery, Wat Pah Nanachat, as a center for the increasing numbers of Buddhists from Europe, Australia, and America who traveled to Thailand to ordain as monks. In 1977 he visited Britain and founded what came to be known as the British Forest Sangha. A branch monastery was established in the 1990s in northern California named Abhayagiri Buddhist Monastery; similarly, branch monasteries exist in Switzerland, Italy, New Zealand, and Australia.

Wat Pah Nanachat
Bahn, Bung Wai
Amper Warin
Ubon Rajathani 34310
Thailand

Sandra Bell

See also: Meditation; Monasticism; Theravada Buddhism.

References

Chah, Ajahn. *Reflections*. Ed. by Dharmma Garden. Taipei, Taiwan: Corporate Body of the Buddha Educational Foundation, 2007.

Cummings, Joe. *Thai Meditation Temples of Thailand: A Guide*. Bangkok: Wayfarer Books/ Trasvin Publications, 1990.

Rajavaramuni, Phra. *Thai Buddhism in the Buddhist World*. North Hollywood, CA: Wat Thai of Los Angeles, 1984.

Tambiah, Stanley J. *The Buddhist Saints of the Forest and the Cult of Amulets*. Cambridge: Cambridge University Press, 1984.

Taylor, J. J. *Forest Monks and the Nation-State: An Anthropological and Historical Study in Northeastern Thailand*. Singapore: Institute of Southeast Asian Studies, 1993.

Tiyavanich, Kamala. *Forest Recollections: Wandering Monks in Twentieth-Century Thailand*. Honolulu: University of Hawaii Press, 1997.

■ Thailand

Thailand is a Southeast Asian country sandwiched between Burma to the west and Laos and Cambodia to the east. The southernmost part of the country is a peninsula that lies between the Andaman Sea and the Gulf of Thailand. On the southernmost part of the peninsula lies the country of Malaysia. Thailand has some 66 million people (2009) residing on its 198,000 square miles of territory.

The most prominent religion in Thailand is, and for many centuries has been, Buddhism. Individual Thai people may take Buddhism very differently, that is, as an intellectual religion, a normative religion, a popular religion, a doctrinal religion, or an engaged religion. No matter what type of Buddhism, as long as it is harmful neither to an individual nor to the public, it is supported by the people and by the government. All Thai Buddhism that complies with the policy of the Thai government, the Sangha Act of 1962, and that is administrated by the Sangda Supreme Council, is considered orthodox Buddhism and, according to the Thai Constitution, is supported by the government.

Some Buddhist movements, for example, the Santi Asoka, are self-governed, reject the authority of the Sangha Supreme Council, and establish their own ways of life and religious practices. They are considered unorthodox and gain no governmental support. In contrast to the Santi Asoka, another influential reformist Buddhist group, the Dhammakaya Foundation, submits itself to the Thai Sangha, and thus is protected by some of its elders. Thailand is also the home of the international headquarters of the World Fellowship of Buddhists, which has its main offices in Bangkok.

According to Basic Religious Data for the year 2007, there were 55,480,000 Buddhists. Thai Buddhism is predominantly Theravada, and thus it places

Wat Phra Singh Temple in Chiang Mai, Thailand. (William Casey/Dreamstime.com)

a great deal of emphasis upon the support of the monastic order. Monks cannot work to earn their living. They are supported by laypeople and the government. In 1998 there were 265,791 Buddhist monks and 97,875 Buddhist novices. In 1999 there were 31,111 Buddhist monasteries throughout the country. Food is donated to monks during their alms rounds, or they are invited to lead a ceremony. That is held to yield more merit to the doer than donating to "ordinary people," as monks are considered holy.

Apart from Buddhism, other religions in Thailand supported by the government are Islam, Christianity, Hinduism, and Sikhism. These religions are subject to the Department of Religious Affairs and under Thai law. Following the Thai Constitution, all religions whose beliefs and practices are harmful neither to an individual, society, nor the Thai nation are allowed to spread throughout the country. Thais are free to profess any religion. Besides, the Thai king, though himself a Buddhist, is the Great Upholder of All Faiths. On the king's birthday each year, leaders of all major religions in Thailand (Buddhism, Islam, Christianity,

Hinduism, and Sikhism) express their well-wishes to the king on television.

According to statistics from each religious center there are approximately a million Muslims, 496,898 Christians, and 30,000 religious followers of Hinduism and Sikhism. There are also religious followers of other minor traditions, such as the Baha'i Faith and Confucianism. They are, however, unable to gain support from the Thai government because of their small number of members.

The Islamic community in Thailand is Sunnite (of the Shafiite School) led by the *chula-raja-montri* (chief imam) whose office is in Bangkok. The Islamic law is used in Muslim courts in four major provinces in southern Thailand, where a number of Malay people reside.

Christianity in Thailand represents two basic groupings: Catholic and Protestant. In 1998 there were about 2,200 Christian clergy. In 1999 there were about 1,500 Protestant churches and 700 Catholic churches in Thailand. All were supported financially by the Thai government. The Protestant community was pioneered by Dutch and British missionaries, the latter represent-

THAILAND

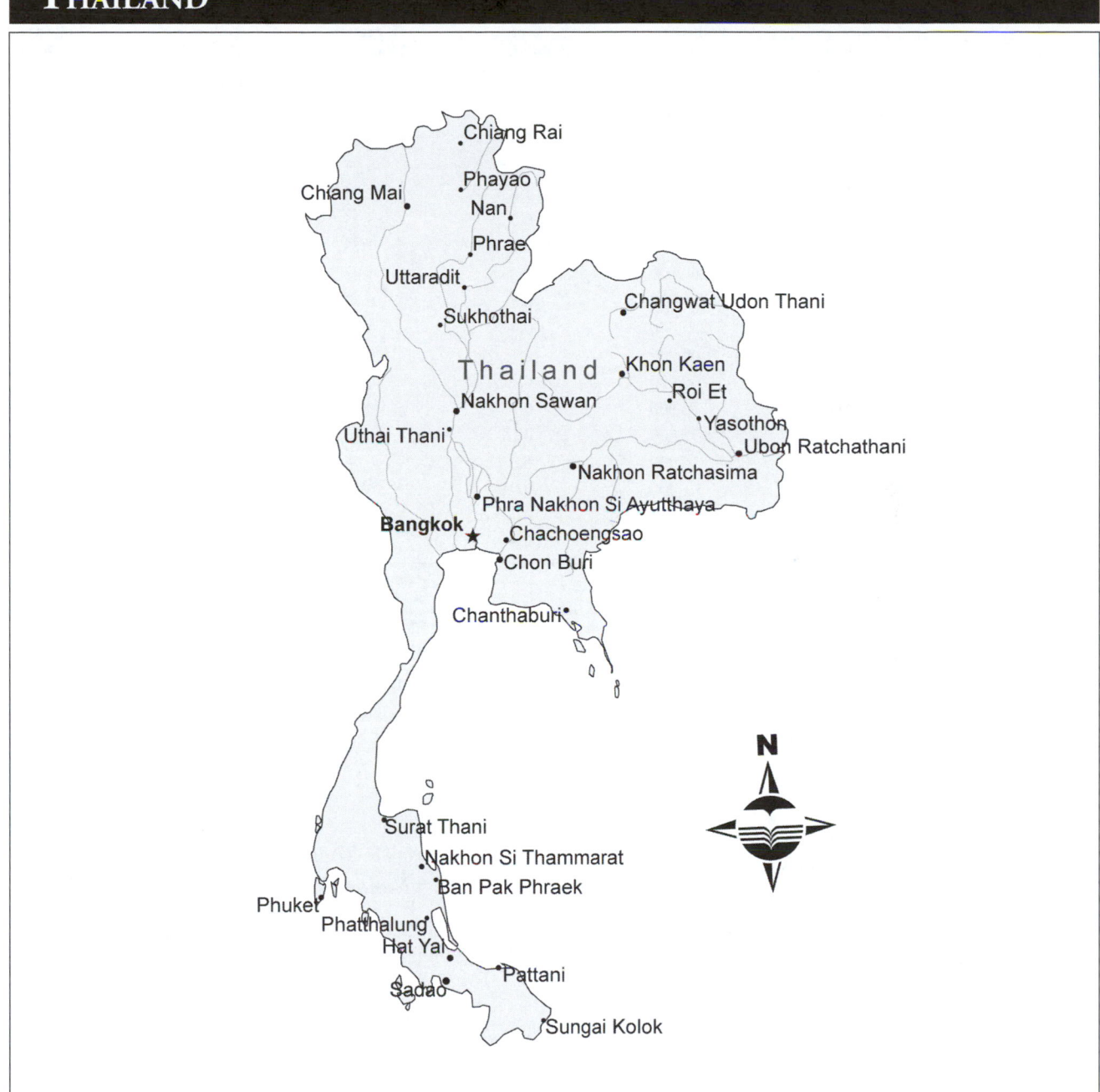

ing the London Missionary Society. They were soon joined by Americans from the American Board of Commissioners for Foreign Missions. A number of the Protestant church groups (Baptists, Presbyterians, Christian Churches [Disciples of Christ], and Lutherans) united in 1934 to form the Church of Christ in Thailand, currently the largest Protestant body. Since World War II, significant growth has been shown by the New Apostolic Church and the indigenous Thai Ezra Churches, the latter a movement that began in northeast Thailand in the early 1980s and by the end of the century had claimed more than 100,000 members.

Christianity has found its support primarily among Vietnamese, Chinese, Karen, and Montagnard ethnic

Thailand

Religion	Followers in 1970	Followers in 2010	% of Population	Annual % growth 2000–2010	Followers in 2025	Followers in 2050
Buddhists	34,405,000	56,497,000	86.8	0.75	59,057,000	57,108,000
Muslims	1,392,000	4,115,000	6.3	0.76	4,500,000	4,700,000
Ethnoreligionists	250,000	1,500,000	2.3	0.45	1,550,000	1,500,000
Agnostics	80,000	1,150,000	1.8	0.77	1,500,000	1,700,000
Christians	372,000	849,000	1.3	1.75	1,025,000	1,112,000
Roman Catholics	154,000	340,000	0.5	3.34	390,000	420,000
Independents	137,000	270,000	0.4	1.75	350,000	400,000
Protestants	78,900	260,000	0.4	1.83	320,000	350,000
Chinese folk	640,000	555,000	0.9	0.76	600,000	600,000
Confucianists	0	235,000	0.4	0.76	265,000	275,000
Hindus	60,000	60,000	0.1	0.76	60,000	60,000
Baha'is	6,400	60,000	0.1	0.76	90,000	120,000
Sikhs	10,000	55,000	0.1	0.76	85,000	100,000
Atheists	30,000	33,000	0.1	0.80	40,000	50,000
New religionists	1,600	16,000	0.0	0.76	30,000	50,000
Shintoists	0	400	0.0	0.76	700	1,200
Jews	70	90	0.0	0.72	100	100
Total population	**37,247,000**	**65,125,000**	**100.0**	**0.76**	**68,803,000**	**67,376,000**

groups residing in China, and to only a small degree among the Thai proper.

Hinduism or Brahmanism plays significant roles in the Thai Royal Court and popular traditions. For most Thais the king is semi-divine. Although he himself is a Buddhist, his power is held to be supported by deities, in both Buddhist and Hindu traditions. All auspicious royal ceremonies, such as the First Ploughing Ceremony, the Royal Inauguration, and the Golden Jubilee of the Royal Enthronement, are partly performed by Brahmins (Hindu priests). Moreover, as Indian civilization with Hinduism has pervaded Thai society since the old days, many Thais believe that their lives are predestined by a Hindu God, especially God Brahma. Although most Thais are Buddhists, they nevertheless believe in the supernatural power of deities.

Sikhism is confined to some Thais of Indian blood living particularly in downtown Bangkok. Confucianism prevails among Thais whose ancestors are Chinese. The Thai people have refrained from waging wars against one another based upon their religions.

Pataraporn Sirikanchana

See also: American Board of Commissioners for Foreign Missions; Baha'i Faith; Christian Church (Disciples of Christ); Church of Christ in Thailand; Confucianism; London Missionary Society; Monasticism; New Apostolic Church; Shafiite School of Islam; Theravada Buddhism; World Fellowship of Buddhists.

References

Keyes, Charles F. *Thailand: Buddhist Kingdom to Modern Nation-State*. Boulder, CO: Westview, 1987.

Sirikanchana, Pataraporn. *Kwam Roo Phuen Than Thang Sasana*. 3rd ed. Bangkok: Thammasat University Press, 1997.

Smith, A. G. "A History of Church Growth in Thailand: An Interpretive Analysis, 1816–1980." Ph.D. diss., Fuller Theological Seminary, 1980.

Thai Department of Religious Affairs. *Yearbook of Basic Religious Data*. Bangkok: Government Printing Office, 2000.

Thelema

Thelema is a magical teaching enunciated by English ceremonial magician Aleister Crowley (1875–1947).

Crowley's Thelemic cult of sex magick (Crowley's unique spelling) derives specifically from a transformative spiritual event that occurred during his visit to Cairo in 1904. Crowley would come to believe that the revelatory communication itself emanated from the ancient Egyptian gods, via an entity named Aiwass (or Aiwaz) whom Crowley believed to be a messenger from Horus. Crowley's personal revelation would also come to acquire a quasi-biblical orientation for it led him to regard himself henceforth as the Beast 666 referred to in the book of Revelation—an association possibly related to his unhappy Plymouth Brethren (now Christian Brethren) upbringing as a child. Following his revelation from Aiwass, Crowley's life and career as a ceremonial magician would subsequently focus on the ongoing personal quest to find the ideal Whore of Babalon (Crowley's variant spelling) or Scarlet Woman, with whom to enact the philosophy of Thelema, or magical will. According to the doctrine of Thelema, Crowley's sex-magick encounters with his Scarlet Women—there would be many more than one throughout his magical career—were sacramental acts confirming Crowley's role as Lord of the New Aeon.

On March 17, 1904, Crowley performed a magical ceremony in his apartment in Cairo, invoking the Egyptian deity Thoth, god of wisdom. Crowley's wife, Rose, who had accompanied him on his trip to Egypt, appeared to be in a dazed, mediumistic state of mind and, the following day, while in a similar state of drowsiness, she announced that Horus was waiting for her husband. Crowley was not expecting such a statement from his wife but according to his diary she subsequently led him to the nearby Boulak Museum, which he had not previously visited. Rose then pointed to a statue of Horus, or Ra-Hoor-Khuit, and Crowley was intrigued to discover that the exhibit was numbered 666, the number of the Great Beast in the Book of Revelation.

On March 20, 1904, Crowley received a mediumistic communication through Rose stating that "the Equinox of the Gods had come" and he arranged for an assistant curator at the Boulak Museum to make notes on the inscriptions from Stele 666. Rose continued to fall into a passive, introspective state of mind and advised her husband that precisely at noon on April 8, 9, and 10 he should enter the room where the transcrip-

tions had been made and for exactly an hour on each of these three days he should write down any impressions received. The resulting communications, allegedly dictated by a semi-invisible Egyptian entity named Aiwass—said to be a messenger of Horus—resulted in a document that Crowley later titled *Liber Al vel Legis* (*The Book of the Law*).

The pronouncements contained in *Liber Al vel Legis* became a turning point in Crowley's magical career. Crowley was specifically commanded by Aiwass to put aside the Kabbalistic ceremonial magic he had learned in the Hermetic Order of the Golden Dawn and was instructed to pursue the magic of sexual partnership—acts of "love under Will"—with his Scarlet Woman. *Liber Al vel Legis* was also completely dismissive of earlier religious traditions that had preceded the 1904 revelation. "With my Hawk's head," proclaims Ra-Hoor-Khuit (Horus) in stanzas III: 51–54, "I peck at the eyes of Jesus as he hangs upon the Cross. I flap my wings in the face of Mohammed and blind him. With my claws I tear out the flesh of the Indian and the Buddhist, Mongol and Din. Bahlasti! Ompedha! I spit on your crapulous creeds."

Liber Al vel Legis summons the Scarlet Woman to "raise herself in pride!" and calls for uninhibited sexual freedom. Accordingly, Crowley came to believe that the so-called Great Work—sacred union, or the attainment of Absolute Consciousness—would be achieved through the sexual union of the Great Beast with the Whore of Babalon: "The Beast, as the embodiment of the Logos (which is Thelema, Will) symbolically and actually incarnates his Word each time a sacramental act of sexual congress occurs, i.e., each time love is made under Will." A review of Crowley's subsequent career shows that he would spend much of his life from this time on seeking lovers and concubines who could act as his Divine Whore. While he would be frustrated in his numerous attempts to find a suitable and enduring partner, there were many who filled the role temporarily.

Liber Al vel Legis also contained instructions relating to ceremonial offerings associated with sacramental sex magick, specifically in the preparation of what later came to be known as "cakes of light." The magical ingredients were derived from sexual congress itself: semen from the male, gluten from the woman's vagina, and preferably fresh menstrual blood, as specified in stanza 24 of Book III of *Liber Al vel Legis*. These ingredients were then consumed by participants as a ritual offering to Ra-Hoor-Khuit.

Nevill Drury

See also: Christian Brethren; Crowley, Aleister; Hermetic Order of the Golden Dawn.

References

Crowley, Aleister. *The Confessions of Aleister Crowley*. Ed. by John Symonds and Kenneth Grant. New York: Hill and Wang, 1970.

Crowley, Aleister. *Liber Al vel Legis*. In *The Magical Record of the Beast 666*, edited by John Symonds and Kenneth Grant. London: Duckworth, 1972.

Crowley, Aleister. *Magick in Theory and Practice*. Paris: the author, 1929. Reprinted in various editions.

Sutin, L. *Do What Thou Wilt: A Life of Aleister Crowley*. New York: St. Martin's Press, 2000.

Theology

From a historical perspective it can be said that in general every religion has been characterized by a theology. At the same time however, it is necessary to affirm that the theologies associated with their corresponding religions are quite varied, since, throughout the centuries, there has been an important development of the concept of theology to reach the currently accepted understanding.

The term is from a Greek root, *theologia*. It is possible to schematically divide the history of the concept, beginning from the elements of *theos* and *logos* that compose it, in light of the importance they have assumed throughout time. Three phases can be distinguished in this schema: (1) the origin related to natural religions; (2) the philosophical elaboration of the concept; (3) the development tied to revealed religion.

The context in which the first theology was born is that of natural polytheistic Greek religion, presumably circa the sixth century BCE. It was characterized by a recourse to myth, that is, to narrations, themselves common to the various archaic religions, through which poets, such as Orpheus, Homer, and Hesiod, expressed the ancient traditions about the gods of Olympus in written word. They theologized, in the sense that they spoke of gods, that is, of the forces that rule nature and the origin of the world, while providing an essential instruction for life. In this period, logos was understood in a largely human sense, as the word that transmits ancient secrets. The word of the poet at once transmitted traditions and praised the divinities (*theoi*), personifying the cosmic forces. Greek theology arose as a history of gods and the world. It is thus a theology understood at once as theogony and cosmonogy, in the expressive form of narration. The divinities and the world are presented as indissolubly united in a common submission to Fate and necessity. Hesiod is a classic example of this first form of theology, which has as starting point mystery and the experience, at times dramatic, that man has of it.

Beginning with the fifth century BCE, philosophical reflection, which in its origin has an essentially religious nature, adopts the term in question. Plato and Aristotle transformed the meaning of theos, moving from mythological polytheism to ontology. These philosophers reacted before the Sophistic criticism, which denied the value of myth, and thus forced the foundations of Greek society into crisis. The strategy consisted of distinguishing the form from the content of myth, in order to show the value of their hidden meaning. This meaning is accessible to reason and universal, because it is based in the Good and the Beautiful. In this perspective, theos is understood in the singular, and identified with the First Principle and with Being itself. Logos thus is primarily understood as reason, that is, as the capacity that man has to understand the order of the cosmos, apprehending the eternal and immutable laws that unite the world and the realm of the divinity. In a certain manner, this theology is tied to a conception of the relationship of the world and God as a continuous ontological ladder that man can climb through his thought, rising from the sensible realm to that of the divine. This ladder leads the goods of this world, and life in particular, back to their source. Nevertheless, at the same time this unitary conception implies a dimension of necessity. From the experience of mystery there is a movement to rational reflection on it, often marked by an excessive trust in man's capacities, or better, in the capacities of the philosopher.

Thus, among the texts that have reached us, Plato (*Republic*, 378.e.7–379.b.1) will be the first who, as far as we know, employed the term "theology." Aristotle will then divide philosophy into three types, mathematics, physics, and theology, according to the relationship with matter and movement of the studied causes (*Metaphysics*, 1026.a.18–21; 123). In this sense, he identifies theology and metaphysics. Thus it can be said of theology that: "It was the people of the Greeks, the founders of philosophy and science, who contributed to the intellectual life of mankind this new form of rational approach to the superhuman world" (Jaeger 1947, 46).

It is in the Hebrew world that theology for the first time assumes the meaning that is actually attributed to it, no longer founded on a generical experience of mystery or in the reflection that comes from this, but on the particular form of experience that is itself revelation of mystery. In this context, God is seen as absolutely distinct and separated from the world. It is this radical separation that awakens the absolute wonder of the Hebrew who encounters God who speaks to him. This is an encounter between he who can be neither seen nor named and man. It is an encounter that is configured as pure gift and that man survives only through the strength that God communicates to him.

This allows Philo, for example, to reinterpret theos in reference to the unique transcendent God. Logos is still understood in a literal sense, as the word of God who speaks and reveals himself. The concept of theology is close to that of prophecy, where the divine element is preponderant: the principal movement is that from God to man. For example, in commenting on the revelation of the name of God, Philo designates Moses as *Theologian* (*De vita Moysis*, 115, 1–2). Philo's choice to use terminology from, as has been seen, the philosophical domain to speak of YHWH will have profound consequences.

In a properly Christian context, Clement of Alexandria opposes the theology of the poets, the followers of myth, and the true theology of philosophers, who in their search for Logos acquired many elements of truth (*Stromata*, 1, 22, 150, 4, 2). In this manner Christianity is placed in continuity with Greek philosophical research. Christ is presented as the true master and identified with the unique transcendent Theos, who not only initiates a covenant with his people, but even becomes incarnate to take the faults of his sons upon himself.

In his reflection, Origen will specify the fundamental difference between the theology of natural religions and that founded in revelation through the confusion that characterizes the first, between the world and its Creator. He will thus explicate what will become the fundamental characteristic of theologia after the third century, that is, the reference to the Trinity, which is identified with the Theos, which is one of its composing terms. This theology is possible only because it is Christ himself who speaks of the Father and reveals the one and triune God (*Contra Celsum*, 2, 71, 5–7). In this sense Jesus is the unique true Theologian. For this reason the Logos that is an element of the term "theologia" is no longer presented as only a human word, nor only as a word of God addressed to men, but is essentially the divine Word, that is, the Word who is God, the second Person of the Trinity, who becomes incarnate for the salvation of man. Word and Reason are now at the *interior* of God, and *are* God. Thus, the proper act of the theologian becomes the recognition of the divinity of the Father, of the Son, and of the Holy Spirit, itself configured as praise and religious worship.

Based on Origen's work, theologia will become a technical term in the debates with the Arians of the fourth century. It will assume a signification of divine immanence—that is, it will indicate God in himself, in his Unity and in his Trinity. The domain of being will thus be distinguished from that of activity, in particular from the actions and events tied to the suffering of Christ in his humanity. For the Cappadocian fathers in particular, theologia will be understood as a direct reference to the mystery of God who is Father from all eternity, in that he has a Son that he eternally engenders in his Spirit.

At the conclusion of this historical outline, it is important to note that in the patristic passage to Theos understood as the one and triune God, the transcendence of the mystery imbues the logos that is a component of theologia with two significations: on one hand it refers, as noted, to the divine Logos, but on the other hand it also implicates human reason, to whom revelation is given. The mystery remains mystery, since man cannot penetrate it because it is transcendent, but revelation permits a knowledge of something, specifically, the gift of God. This reference to mystery must be remembered while considering the historical development that led the term to have the signification of "doctrine about God," which is the most common meaning today.

At the end of the patristic period, the medievals will attempt to build a holistic vision of the world upon the richness of the tradition received from the first Christian thinkers. As the medievals referenced their writings and their authority, there was a risk involved in moving from the level of the being of the mystery to that of its representation. These authors in fact aspired to a representation of *every* element of the life of man ordered toward God, on the model of the cathedral, or of the *summa*. They thus strove for a synthesis that could offer, at a glance, the position of every aspect of man's life in reference to its center, that is, his Creator. In this process however, the attention moved toward representation, and thus losing the sense of mystery and forgetting the primary character of revelation and gift in reference to that which reason can attain and comprehend. Thomas Aquinas's criticisms of Anselm of Canterbury or Richard of Saint Victor are to be read in this sense. Thomas auspiciously left his *Summa* unfinished at the end of his life, due precisely to the (mystical) perception of the abyss between the representation and the mystery of God.

With nominalism, the confusion between the levels of language and reality was further aggravated. The birth of modernity pushed theology to define itself ever more in a doctrinal sense, modeling itself on philosophy. This is in contrast to the development of the first centuries of the Christian era, when it was philosophy that was transformed by the thought that arose from the experience of God who revealed himself. The project of the illuminationist encyclopedia and the requirement from the religious side to situate itself dialectically in reference to it also contributed to the movement in this direction.

In correction, the 20th century in the Western world was marked by a return to a theology tied to mystery and life, as well as to the sources: biblical, liturgical, and patristic. The theologies that accentuate action or theologies "of the genitive" are situated in this tendency. Theologies "of action" unite religion and life in such a way as to configure the world according to the will of God: Liberation Theology and Feminist Theology are two examples. Theologies "of the genitive" arise from the need to read the various aspects of human reality in a religious sense, for example, the theology of the body, that of work, and that of history.

Looking at the various contemporary religions, the three phases of the formation of the term "theology" can be useful to understand in what sense it is used to speak of Hinduism (the chapter "Hindu Theology and Philosophy" in Flood 1996), or Buddhism (Jackson and Makransky 1999). One can definitely observe a tendency to indicate the doctrinal dimension of various religions with the term "theology," which leads some to recommend a metatheology (Hiebert 1994, Bosch 1991), analogous to how metaphysics is understood in relation to physics. This proposal, developed in the framework of the missionary movement, aims to take into account the different contexts in which each theology is developed. At the same time, a greater attention to the history of how theology has been situated in its development from the religious mystery is to be recommended. The analysis of René Girard is a good example, as he does a properly "theological" work according to the original sense of the term, using literary analysis and critical study of the history of religion.

Giulio Maspero

See also: Arius; God, Existence of; Moses.

References

Batiffol, Pierre. "Theologia, Theologi." *Ethology* 5 (1928): 205–222.

Bosch, Donald. *Transforming Mission: Paradigm Shifts in Theology of Mission*. Maryknoll, NY: Orbis Books, 1991.

Flood, Gavin D. *An Introduction to Hinduism*. Cambridge: Cambridge University Press, 1996.

Hiebert, Paul. G. *Anthropological Reflection on Missiological Issues*. Grand Rapids, MI: Baker Academic, 1994.

Jackson, R., and John Makransky, eds. *Buddhist Theology*. London: Routledge Curzon, 1999.

Jaeger, Werner. *Humanism and Theology*. Milwaukee WI: Marquette University Press, 1943.

Jaeger, Werner. *The Theology of the Early Greek Philosophers*. Oxford: Oxford University Press, 1947.

Kattenbusch, Ferdinand. "Die Entstehung Einer Christlichen Theologie. Zur Geschichte der Ausdrücke: Theologia, Theologein, Theologos." *Zeitschrift für Theologie und Kirche* 11 (1930): 161–205.

Smith, W. Cantwell. *Towards A World Theology: Faith and the Comparative History of Religion*. Philadelphia: Westminster Press, 1981.

Stietencron, H. Von. "Theology." In *The Brill Dictionary of Religion*, edited by K. Von Stuckrad, 1879–1889. Leiden: Brill, 2006.

Williams, J. G., ed. *The Girard Reader*. New York: Crossroad/Herder, 2000.

Theosophical Society (Adyar)

The Theosophical Society (Adyar) is an international organization whose main purpose is to promote primarily the oeuvre of Helena Petrovna Blavatsky (1831–1891) and secondarily those among its members who adhere to her teachings. This body of work and perspective serve as the bases of the three objects of the Society: (1) to form a nucleus of the Universal Brotherhood of Humanity, without distinction of race, creed, sex, caste, or color; (2) to encourage the study of comparative religion, philosophy, and science; and (3) to investigate unexplained laws of nature and the power latent in man.

The impact of the Theosophical Society (Adyar) prior to its numerous fissures beginning in 1895 and of those Theosophical societies that arose in the years following that have retained their loyalty to the Blavatsky canon—examples being the Theosophical Society (America), the United Lodge of Theosophists, and the now defunct Theosophical Society in America, with headquarters in New York City—has been profound. Rather than discussing the impact of the Theosophical Society, it would be more accurate to assert the direct impact of Blavatsky on the Theosophical Society (Adyar) and other Theosophical societies and then to argue the impact on movements and associations not directly connected to or descended from the original Theosophical Society. Many teachings within non-Theosophical organizations that share a similar worldview that may be termed Western Esoteric arose either directly from Blavatsky's writings or indirectly through the propaganda of numerous societies that emphasize her teachings, most notably the New Age.

It must also be stated, however, that as important as Blavatsky's contributions were, there were two important disciples of her teachings who helped to popularize what was often an obtuse teaching set forth by Blavatsky. A. P. Sinnett (1840–1921) was an early admirer when Blavatsky arrived in India from New York in 1879; Charles Webster Leadbeater (1854–1934) was a close colleague of the leading propagandist of the early Theosophical Society and later its president. Annie Besant (1847–1933) and Leadbeater made lasting contributions to the Society and the cause of Theosophy, but not, in the opinion of some, always in a positive manner. Sinnett is perhaps most responsible for creating the perception, through his book *Esoteric Buddhism* (1883), that modern Theosophy is predominantly derived from Hindu and Buddhist esotericism. Although Blavatsky writes extensively of this form of esotericism, she also included in her writings other forms of esotericism, such as Jewish Kabbalah. Leadbeater helped to popularize the formidable and often opaque explanations of Blavatsky. It is very likely that newcomers to Theosophical teachings were introduced through Leadbeater's books.

The Theosophical Society, with international headquarters in Adyar (Chennai), India, was founded in New York City in 1875 by a number of individuals, the most important of whom were Henry Steel Olcott (1832–1907) and Blavatsky. Olcott became the first president of the Society (1875–1907), helping in its spread and organization and popularizing its teachings. Blavatsky was responsible for the restatement, according to the Theosophical interpretation, of those teachings that became synonymous with the teachings of the Theosophical Society. Most of the teachings are contained in her two most important works, *Isis Unveiled* and *The Secret Doctrine*. Blavatsky retains special standing for most Theosophists because of her status as disciple, or *chela*, of highly evolved beings—Masters or Mahatmas—who dwelled in an "Occult Brotherhood" and who were the ultimate source of the teachings known as the Ancient Wisdom, the Secret Doctrine, the Wisdom Religion, or Theosophy. This Wisdom existed from the dawn of humanity—a *prisca theologia* or *philosophia perennis*—and was preserved and transmitted through the ages by great teachers and initiates (Pythagoras, Buddha, Krishna, Jesus, Zoroaster, Plato, Porphyry, Proclus, and Patañjali). Furthermore, it was conserved, however imperfectly, in the various religious traditions (Hinduism, Buddhism, Christianity, Judaism, Islam, and Zoroastrianism) and their sacred scriptures (the Veda, the Upanishads, the Bhagavad Gita, the Puranas, the Hebrew and Christian scriptures, the Zohar, the Buddhist canon, and the Avesta), all of which purported to disclose, in the words of Blavatsky, "the 'deepest depths' of the Divine Nature, and show . . . the *real tie which binds all things together.*"

Because of this conviction, the original objects of the Society as stated in its by-laws of 1875 were "to collect and diffuse a knowledge of the laws which govern the universe." Nonetheless, the comparative study of religion and philosophy was not its only aim. There is enough evidence to suggest that the Ancient Wisdom was to be practiced. Indeed, the very word first employed by Blavatsky to refer to this Wisdom was "Magic"—a term that was synonymous with the post-1870s popularization of "Theosophy" as defined and elaborated by her in her later writing career—and which suggests both a combination of practice and understanding. For this reason, members of the Theosophical Society at various periods in its history placed greater emphasis on striving to arouse one's latent powers rather than merely investigating the laws of nature from a theoretical perspective. This was especially true in the early years of the Society to the early 1880s and during the presidency of Annie Besant (r. 1907–1933). One type of training that more advanced members sought to achieve in the early years of the Society was astral projection, or the out-of-body experience.

Since there is no official dogma recognized by the Society, Theosophists possess a diversity of views according to their understanding of Theosophy. One position that is universally accepted, however, is the "Brotherhood of Humanity," the first of the three objects of the Society quoted above. In addition to these objects, the body of teachings generally associated with the Society has been articulated by Blavatsky, especially in her greatest work, *The Secret Doctrine*. Among the teachings are: (1) the notion that religions have both exoteric and esoteric elements, with the Ancient Wisdom or Wisdom Religion (Theosophy) synonymous with the esoteric body of wisdom, taught and preserved by initiates in all the great religions and philosophies; (2) the recognition of the diversity and universality of sources containing the Ancient Wisdom, thereby including not only elements of Western Esotericism—neo-Platonism, Christian Kabbalah, Hermetism, and Hermeticism—but also Eastern components, notably Hindu and Buddhist philosophies; in brief an "Eclectic Theosophy" as opposed to the theosophy of Western Esotericism; (3) the three propositions contained in the introduction of *The Secret Doctrine*: (a) the existence of an infinite and unknowable Absolute, (b) the cyclic nature of the universe and all it comprises, and (c) the identity of the soul with the Universal Soul (of the Absolute) and the need for all souls to progress through the cycle of reincarnation to realize this identity.

As is evident in many movements, disagreements over teachings and authority have led to the formation of new organizations that arose out of the original Theosophical Society. The Hermetic Society was founded in 1884 due to the disagreement with the Orientalist flavor of Sinnett's version of Theosophy as presented in his *Esoteric Theosophy*. In the same vein, the conflict arising over authority led to the 1895 separation of the American Section of the Theosophical Society under William Quan Judge (1851–1896), one of the original founders. Today, the Judge Society continues under the name the Theosophical Society (Pasadena). Furthermore, two controversies severely damaged the reputation of the Theosophical Society and its leaders. The first was the Hodgson Report of 1885, written on behalf of the Society for Psychical Research, which charged Blavatsky with fraud for claiming that her Masters or Mahatmas actually wrote letters to her and to others within the Society. The second surrounded the controversy of the coming World Teacher (Maitreya or the Christ) who would overshadow the body and personality of Jiddu Krishnamurti, the latter expected to serve as the Vehicle for the Teacher. Krishnamurti (1896–1986) spent 20 years preparing for this role, until 1929, when he abdicated his role as Vehicle and abandoned the Theosophical Society, to the great distress of many of its founders. These two episodes severely damaged the reputation of the Society and led to a decline in its membership rolls. From that period to the present, the Society never recovered the notoriety that it enjoyed prior to Krishnamurti's quitting the Society.

In the ensuing years, the Society has maintained a relatively low profile, but has made contributions to the intellectual world by maintaining a research library at its headquarters in Adyar that contains more than 20,000 palm-leaf manuscripts and more than 250,000 volumes, with a focus on Orientalia. It also maintains the Theosophical Publishing House in Adyar and Wheaton, Illinois, the home of the Theosophical Society in America. The Society also performs work for the welfare of poor and disadvantaged children through the Olcott Memorial School and Olcott Memorial High School, which offers free education to its students.

The Theosophical Society (Adyar) continues as the largest of Theosophical organizations with an approximate membership of 30,000 spread over 60 countries, with India and the United States possessing the most members (12,852 and 4,676, respectively).

The contributions and influence of Theosophical teachings to alternative esoterically based movements are numerous. Among these contributions are the following:

1. The Masters or Mahatmas, highly evolved beings such as Koot Hoomi and Morya, neither "Spirits" nor "some other kind of supernatural beings" according to Blavatsky in her *Key to Theosophy*, are men of great learning, especially pertaining to the Ancient Wisdom. These Masters constituted a Brotherhood according to Sinnett, and later the "Great White Brotherhood" according to Leadbeater. The notion of a Master did not originate with Blavatsky or modern Theosophy. It is a concept found in ancient religions such as Christianity and Judaism (angels), Buddhism (*bodhisattvas*), and early modern Esoteric movements such as Rosicrucianism and its later offshoots. It is likely, however, that Blavatsky's Theosophy influenced later organizations such as the Agni Yoga Society, the I AM Religious Activity of the Ballards, the Church Universal and Triumphant, individuals such as Baird T. Spalding and Frederick Oliver, the amanuensis of Phylos the Tibetan, and most certainly Alice A. Bailey's Djwhal Khul.

2. Reincarnation was popularized through the publications of Theosophical literature. Although Blavatsky did not place great emphasis on the concept prior to the 1880s, it was given an important role in Sinnett's *Esoteric Buddhism*, serving as part of a grand scheme of spiritual evolution. Furthermore, reincarnation was viewed in much the same way as that contained in Allan Kardec's (1804–1869) *Le Livre des Esprits*: the soul progressively improves with no regression into lower forms such as animals.

3. Theosophists have contributed much to the popularization of the teaching of karma in the West. From the *Mahatma Letters*, Sinnett's *Occult World* (1881) and *Esoteric Buddhism*, Blavatsky's writings beginning in the 1880s, the Society's co-founder William Q. Judge's articles and *Ocean of Theosophy*, the numerous publications of Annie Besant and C. W. Leadbeater, and innumerable Theosophists who followed, it is almost impossible to avoid its mention in any segment of Theosophical literature. It was the Theosophists who introduced the phrase "law of karma" according to Australian scholar Eric J. Sharpe in his *Universal Gita*, and indeed it does appear in the writings of Blavatsky, W. Q. Judge, C. W. Leadbeater, and Annie Besant.

Although karma is associated with the individual, other forms of karma were introduced or at least popularized. National, racial, and family karma was discussed by Blavatsky in a late article ("Forlorn Hope," 1890) and by Judge in his *Ocean of Theosophy* and more recently as the "karma of a planet" by G. Farthing in his *Deity Cosmos & Man*. One cannot argue that karma derived from Hindu and Buddhist teachings, but such notions as national, racial, and family karma is not likely to be located in either religion.

4. Theosophical teachings have had an impact on the arts and literature. In art, it is certain that Wassily Kandinsky (1866–1944) was influenced by Theosophical ideas, especially concepts of color and of the higher world. Especially influential were Leadbeater's *Man Visible and Invisible* and Annie Besant and Leadbeater's *Thought-Forms*. Other artists include Piet Mondrian (1872–1944), Paul Klee (1879–1940), and the artists of the Transcendental Painting Group (founded in 1938) consisting of Raymond Jonson (1891–1982), Agnes Pelton (1881–1961), and Lawren Harris (1885–1970). Dutch architect, engraver, illustrator, and designer K. P. C. de Bazel (1869–1923), architect J. L. M. Lauweriks (1864–1932), and H. J. M. Walenkamp (1871–1933) actually joined the Theosophical Society in Amsterdam in 1894.

In the field of music, two composers who had direct contact with Theosophical teachings were Jean Sibelius (1865–1957) and Alexander Scriabin (1870–1915). Notable examples in literature include William Butler Yeats (1865–1939), George W. Russell (1867–1935), and Talbot Mundy (1879–1940). Finally, the author of the Oz works, Lyman Frank Baum (1856–1919), was a Theosophist who adopted many ideas from the genre.

To conclude, although the Theosophical Society consisted of relatively few members (never more than 50,000, usually under 30,000 members), with membership spread over 60 countries, its impact in these areas was significant.

James A. Santucci

See also: Bailey, Alice Ann; Besant, Annie; Blavatsky, Helena P.; Church Universal and Triumphant; I AM Religious Activity; Krishnamurti Foundations; Reincarnation; Spiritism; Theosophical Society (America).

References

Blavatsky, Helena Petrovna. *The Secret Doctrine.* 2 vols. in 1. Los Angeles: Theosophy Company, 1974. (A facsimile of the original 1888 edition.)

Gomes, Michael. *The Dawning of the Theosophical Movement.* Wheaton, IL: Theosophical Publishing House [Quest Books], 1987.

The Mahatma Letters to A.P. Sinnett from the Mahatmas M. & K.H. 2nd ed. Transcribed, compiled, and with an introduction by A. T. Barker. London: Rider and Company, 1948 (originally published in 1923).

Olcott, Henry Steel. *Old Diary Leaves.* 6 vols. Adyar, India: Theosophical Publishing House, 1900–1941.

Santucci, James. *La Società Teosofica.* Torin, Italy: Elledici, 1999.

Theosophical Society (America)

The Theosophical Society (America) is also called the Theosophical Society (Pasadena) or simply the Pasadena tradition of Theosophy. It is one of several Theosophical societies. The first Theosophical Society began in 1875 in New York City under the leadership of Helena P. Blavatsky (1831–1891) and Henry Steel Olcott (1832–1907) as an organization that would investigate Spiritualist phenomena and other occult practices and ideas as well as the world's religions. Blavatsky and Olcott left the United States for India in 1878. For several years the Society foundered; then, in 1883, William Quan Judge (1851–1896), one of the original members of the Society, began to recruit members and hold public meetings. He published a magazine, *The Path*, beginning in 1886. In that year he dissolved a Board of Control established by Olcott to govern Theosophists in the United States and created an American Section of the worldwide Theosophical Society that Judge himself headed as general secretary.

Judge was a charismatic leader, personally inspiring many middle-class Americans interested in Esoteric matters and disillusioned with Christianity. His published work conveyed Theosophical teachings in a popular, accessible style. His skills as an organizer, manager, and communicator contributed significantly to the rapid expansion of Theosophical work in the 1880s and 1890s. By the time of his death in 1896,

Theosophical lodges could be found in most major, and many smaller, American cities, and membership numbered in the thousands. Theosophy was a household word, appearing in numerous discussions of religion and culture in the popular print media. It also was targeted by Christian clergy. Many who joined the Theosophical Society were spurned by their friends and families in much the same way that adherents of new religions in the 1960s and later were ostracized by loved ones.

When Blavatsky died in 1891, Judge became the head of the Esoteric School of Theosophy, an elite group composed of individuals thoroughly committed to Theosophical principles. Later he suggested that he and Annie Besant (1847–1933), head of the European Section after Blavatsky's death, share leadership of the Esoteric School. For the next few years controversy ensued, as Besant first sided with Judge, then opposed him. This series of events, often referred to in Theosophical history as the Judge case, remains a controversial chapter in the evolution and development of the movement. As a result of continued attacks on Judge, in 1895 the American Section, while recognizing Olcott as president-founder, declared its autonomy, electing Judge president-for-life of the Theosophical Society in America. Olcott withdrew the branch charters and revoked the membership of those in the United States, Europe, and elsewhere who followed Judge, thus splitting the worldwide Theosophical movement in two.

The next year Judge died and was succeeded by Katherine Tingley (1847–1929). This succession was marked by controversy. Some members of Judge's inner circle accused her of manipulating events and people to make it appear that Judge gave his blessing to her leadership, while other leaders supported her without reservation. She remained a controversial figure, among Theosophists and in the public eye, throughout her tenure. Her name frequently appeared in newspaper articles associated with various legal battles, the earliest major one involving a libel suit that she brought against the owner of the largest Los Angeles newspaper. Within the Society, she inspired members to focus on philanthropic and educational activities, expanding an agenda that emerged in nascent form during Judge's final years.

In 1898, Tingley was named leader and official head of the Theosophical Society, and the organization was renamed the Universal Brotherhood and Theosophical Society (UB and TS). The UB and TS sponsored various reform efforts aimed at improving the Society and individuals through its affiliate, the International Brotherhood League (IBL). Women joined in significant numbers after Tingley became the leader, and much of the IBL's work dealt with issues traditionally associated with women, especially raising and educating children. Under Tingley, a home for orphans and unwed mothers opened in Buffalo, New York, medical assistance was provided for soldiers returning from Cuba following the Spanish-American War, and war relief was provided to the poor and homeless in the Cuban city of Santiago de Cuba.

In 1900 Tingley led an exodus of Theosophists to Point Loma, located on the peninsula west of San Diego, California. Three years earlier, in 1897, at the end of a worldwide tour, she laid the cornerstone of the School for the Revival of the Lost Mysteries of Antiquity there. At Point Loma, Theosophists constructed numerous dwellings and educated young children. They also operated three schools in Cuba patterned after the style of education, called Raja Yoga, which evolved at Point Loma. Educational efforts were the focus of community life at Point Loma, based on the Theosophical conviction that they lived in the dawning of a new era in cosmic history. They believed that reincarnated souls entering the world as newborns were exceptionally amenable to spiritual and moral training. Tingley also worked for the abolition of capital punishment, for prison reform, and for international peace. She emphasized music, the arts, and drama, building the first open-air Greek theater in the United States in 1901.

Theosophists believe that humanity reincarnated many times, according to grand cosmic cycles of ascent and decline that last for millions of years. The progress of waves of life-forms or souls is watched over and helped by the Masters, or advanced beings. Masters supposedly gave Blavatsky the teachings she passed along to other Theosophists, including those found in her magnum opus, *The Secret Doctrine* (1888), and numerous other publications. Point Loma Theosophists read and adhered to Blavatsky's teachings, often filtered through the published writings of Judge and Tingley. The published works of those latter two leaders did not depart substantially from Blavatsky, but recast her teachings in an idiom and vocabulary more accessible to American readers.

Point Loma Theosophists, however, departed from Theosophists elsewhere in their belief that the earthly succession of leaders following Blavatsky was through Judge rather than Besant. They linked the validity of Theosophical teachings to this succession, the Masters supposedly granting each earthly leader in this succession credibility and authority, and sometimes working in and through those leaders in a bicameral relationship in which the personality of the leader was melded with the esoteric power and wisdom of the Master. That was the case with Judge, and later with Tingley's successor, Gottfried de Purucker (1879–1942), a self-taught polymath who devoted many years of study to Theosophy, ancient languages, mythology, and comparative religion.

During his tenure as leader, Purucker lectured on numerous occasions, and his lectures were later transcribed and published. The result was "technical Theosophy," a complex body of teachings based on those of Blavatsky, Judge, and Tingley, but using the teachings of Purucker's predecessors as points of departure for deep and creative reflection. He led the Point Loma Theosophists through the lean years of the Depression, returning their foci to those of Judge: printing and distributing Theosophical literature and encouraging growth among local lodges. He also initiated the Fraternization movement, encouraging contact with various Theosophical organizations and the renewal of brotherly feeling among Theosophists everywhere. Near the end of his administration, during World War II, Purucker moved their headquarters from Point Loma to Covina, California, near Los Angeles.

No clear successor could be agreed upon after Purucker's death, and a Cabinet governed for three years. In 1945, Colonel Arthur L. Conger (1872–1951), a retired officer in the U.S. Army, became the leader. Many lifelong Theosophists did not agree with Conger's selection and left the Society. Most networked informally, although one group found a semblance of an organizational center in Point Loma Publications, Inc., founded in 1971 by Iverson Harris, Jr. (d. 1979)

and W. Emmett Small (1903–2001). Conger expanded the Theosophical Society's publishing program and emphasized local public work, particularly in postwar Europe. Shortly before his death he began moving the headquarters to Pasadena, California. He was succeeded as head of the Theosophical Society (Pasadena) by James Long (1898–1971) in 1951. Long oversaw moving the headquarters, library, and archives of the Theosophical Society to their present location in Altadena, California. Long emphasized living Theosophical teachings and expressing the Theosophical philosophy simply in each person's own words. He founded *Sunrise* magazine in 1951 as a bridge between Theosophy and the public.

Long was succeeded in 1971 by Grace F. Knoche (1909–2006), a Raja Yoga student from birth. The current leader is Randell C. Grubb. The Theosophical Society (Pasadena) includes sections in the United States, Australia, the Czech Republic, Finland, Germany, Austria, the Netherlands (the largest section outside the United States), Nigeria, and South Africa. At their headquarters facility in Altadena, staff members publish Theosophical classics through the Theosophical University Press and hold regular meetings for members as well as inquirers at their library. Such meetings, usually discussions of Theosophical writings by Blavatsky and others, constitute the rituals practiced by most Pasadena-affiliated Theosophists.

In this Theosophical tradition, Theosophy is a matter of inward transformation through mental and spiritual discipline. Meditative practices that alter mind and body, such as hatha yoga, are suspect. So Theosophists in the Pasadena tradition emphasize moral refinement and advance in daily living, coupled with deepening understanding of Theosophical principles through the diligent study of texts. In recent years the Pasadena Society participated in efforts to find common ground among all Theosophical movements, especially the United Lodge of Theosophists and the International Theosophical Society, headquartered in India. Annual conferences for Theosophists from all Theosophical organizations began in 1994 in Brookings, Oregon, and are held annually. At these conferences, speakers address current issues in science, culture, and society as these relate to Theosophy. Participants seek ways to find unity among various Theosophical traditions, perspectives, and groups. Finally, efforts have been made to heal the divisions within the Pasadena Theosophical tradition, although Point Loma Publications and others who left the Theosophical Society (Pasadena) in the 1940s are not likely to return.

Theosophical Society
PO Box C
Pasadena, CA 91109–7107
http://www.theosociety.org/
W. Michael Ashcraft and J. Gordon Melton

See also: Besant, Annie; Blavatsky, Helena P.; Theosophical Society (Adyar); United Lodge of Theosophists.

References

Ashcraft, W. Michael. *The Dawn of the New Cycle: Point Loma Theosophists and American Culture.* Knoxville: University of Tennessee Press, 2002.

Greenwalt, Emmett A. *California Utopia: Point Loma: 1897–1942.* Rev. ed. San Diego: Point Loma Publications, Inc., 1978.

International Theosophy Conferences, Inc. http://www.theosconf.org.

Judge, William Quan. *The Ocean of Theosophy.* Covina, CA: Theosophical University Press, 1948.

Point Loma Publications. http://www.wisdom traditions.com.

Purucker, Gottfried de. *Fountain-Source of Occultism.* Pasadena, CA: Theosophical University Press, 1974.

Ryan, Charles J. *H. P. Blavatsky and the Theosophical Movement.* 2nd and rev. ed. Pasadena, CA: Theosophical University Press, 1975.

Tingley, Katherine. *Theosophy: The Path of the Mystic.* 3rd and rev. ed. Pasadena, CA: Theosophical University Press, 1977.

Theravada Buddhism

Theravada Buddhism is the designation for the various Buddhist traditions prevalent in South and Southeast Asia. Theravada, or Southern, Buddhism, with its local cultural variations and specific ordination lineages is the dominant religious tradition in Sri Lanka (69 per-

cent of the population), Burma/Myanmar (85 percent), Thailand (94 percent), Cambodia (88 percent), and Laos (58 percent). With the global spread of Buddhism in the 20th century, substantial numbers of migrants from these countries have come to live in North America and Europe. Alongside, Western converts have taken up Theravada meditational practices and the study of canonical texts.

The Theravada tradition is the only surviving tradition of some 30 different schools of early Buddhism. Translatable as the "sayings or doctrine of the elders," the school claims to be nearest to the original word and teaching of the historical Buddha (sixth–fifth century BCE). The precursor of the Theravada School had been the Sthaviravada (Sanskrit: doctrine of the elders), which split with the majority fraction of the Mahasanghikas in North India in the fourth century BCE. A century later, the Indian-Sanskrit Sthaviravada came to Ceylon and became the Theravada. Some five centuries after Buddha's death, the teachings were written down in Pali on palm leaves. The numerous texts were collected in three baskets. From that stems the designation of *Tipitaka* (three baskets)—that is, the text collections of the Vinaya Pitaka (basket of monastic discipline), Sutta Pitaka (doctrinal teachings), and Abhidhamma Pitaka (philosophical investigations). These voluminous collections form the canon of the Theravada tradition. There also exist commentaries to the canon and ancillary literature, especially the Visuddhimagga (The Path to Purity), composed by the Ceylonese monk Buddhagosha in the early fifth century CE.

The focal point of Theravada tradition is constituted by the order of monks (*bhikkhu sangha*). Although originally there also existed an order of nuns (*bhikkhuni sangha*), that order dissolved later as the line of nuns' ordination broke. The monk represents the Theravada ideal of a person's nonattachment to worldly relations and affairs, concentrating on practicing the Buddhist path of renunciation in order to extinguish one's delusion, hatred, and greed. The main task of a monk is to live up to that ideal, to hand on the Buddhist teachings and practices, and to instruct the lay Buddhist followers. The laity supports the sangha (monks' order), donating food, shelter, and clothing. A clear hierarchy of religious virtuosi and lay followers is basic to the Theravada.

Although Theravada tradition can be considered outspokenly conservative regarding doctrinal interpretation and forms of life, it has unmistakably changed in the course of time. Following the period of early Buddhism, during the period of traditional Theravada (late third century BCE to the 18th century CE), the sangha established close relations with the ruling powers. Strongly supported by feudal kings, the monasteries became wealthy landlords. In religious terms, monks became preoccupied with conducting ceremonies of chanting *pirit* or *paritta* (texts designed to improve a layperson's material and physical state; however, also of importance to the sangha itself) and presiding at funerals. Considered as "fields to gain spiritual merit," monks functioned mainly as ceremonial priests. This role, its form and content, was strongly criticized, much as in the period of reformist or modern Theravada (19th and 20th centuries), when urban monks and educated middle-class lay Buddhists interpreted Buddhism as scientific, modern, and universal. Confronted by imperial power, Western concepts, and missionary Christianity, this English-educated elite stressed rationalist elements in the Buddhist teachings. They devalued the "cultic" and "ritualistic" practices and emphasized a scripturalist approach to achieving *nibbana* (extinction, liberation; Sanskrit: *nirvana*). Although this modern, or "Protestant," Theravada Buddhism has remained a minority—the vast majority of both monks and laypeople continuing to hold to traditional Theravada concepts—it is this modernized version of Theravada Buddhism that is considered representative of Theravada Buddhism as a whole. An important element of the reinterpretation of Theravada Buddhism is a revival of meditation practices. Practices such as *vipassana* (penetrative seeing) and *satipatthana* meditation (application of mindfulness) have gained a growing interest in South Asia and in the West, in particular.

Martin Baumann

See also: Mahayana Buddhism; Meditation; Monasticism; Sacred Texts.

References

Bechert, Heinz. *Buddhismus, Staat und Gesellschaft in den Ländern des Theravada-Buddhismus.* 3 vols. Frankfurt am Main, Germany: Schriften des Instituts für Asienkunde and Wiesbaden, Harrassowitz, 1966–1973. Rpt.: Göttingen, Germany: Seminar für Indologie und Buddhismuskunde, vol. 1, 1988; vol. 2, 2000.

Bond, George D. *The Buddhist Revival in Sri Lanka: Religious Tradition, Reinterpretation and Response.* Columbia: University of South Carolina Press, 1988.

The Books of the Pali Canon. Oxford: Pali Text Society, 1881–.

Cadge, Wendy. *Heartwood: The First Generation of Theravada Buddhism in America.* Chicago: University of Chicago Press, 2004.

Gombrich, Richard. *Theravada Buddhism: A Social History from Ancient Benares to Modern Colombo.* London: Routledge, 1988.

Gombrich, Richard, and Gananath Obeyesekere. *Buddhism Transformed: Religious Change in Sri Lanka.* Princeton, NJ: Princeton University Press, 1988.

Numrich, Paul David. *Old Wisdom in the New World: Americanization in Two Immigrant Theravada Buddhist Temples.* Knoxville: University of Tennessee Press, 1996.

Thomas Aquinas

ca. 1224–1274

Thomas Aquinas was a member of the Dominican Order who emerged in the 13th century as a prominent theologian best known for his use of Aristotelian philosophy as a framework for doing Christian theology and the thoroughness of his theological inquiry. He lived and taught at Paris, Naples, and Rome and wrote the *Summa Theologiae*, which has come to be seen as the foremost theological work of the Middle Ages. He would later be named a Doctor of the Church, a title bestowed on a very few theological writers who have been designated a saint and who in addition have written theological works from which the whole church has derived great advantage. Doctors of the Church are seen as people who have integrated outstanding intellectual accomplishments with noteworthy sanctity.

Thomas was born around 1224 as the youngest son of Landulfo d'Aquino, who sent Thomas to live among the monks at the prominent Benedictine abbey of Monte Casino with the expectation that he would rise to the position of abbot. He studied theology and philosophy at the University of Naples, recently established by his uncle Frederick II, the king of Sicily (r. 1296–1337). Thomas rejected his parents' plans and at the age of 19 he left the Benedictines for the recently founded Dominican Order. While taking the traditional monastic vows of poverty, chastity, and obedience, the friars of the Dominican Order rejected the more internal focus of the Benedictines and offered a more outward focus on community service. It was organized as a preaching order and the friars were trained in vernacular languages (rather than exclusively emphasizing Latin). Rather than earning their living on the monastery's property, usually in agricultural pursuits, Dominican friars survived from the gifts of those who supported their work.

Thomas's family was horrified by his decision, and they kidnapped him and attempted to lure him back to his father's plan. He resisted the enticements and would later write against those who attempted to force young men to leave the new orders (that would also include the Franciscans and Augustinians). He ultimately escaped his kidnappers, and his superiors sent him to study theology at the Dominican priory in Paris. In 1248, he moved on to Cologne, where for a brief period he became the student of his fellow Dominican Albertus Magnus (1193–1280).

Thomas's education occurred just as the lost works of Aristotle were being introduced into the educational curriculum of Western institutions of higher learning following their rediscovery in the Middle East by the Crusaders. Prior to this time, almost all theology in the West was based on Platonic philosophy.

Upon his return to Paris, he completed his bachelor's degree in scripture and lectured on the Bible and the *Sentences*, written by Peter Lombard (ca.1105–ca.1164), the primary theological textbook of the era. He also began to pen commentaries on the major works of Aristotle, study tools on Aristotle being as yet nonexistent. He soon received his master's of theology degree and began work on his first major theological text, the *Summa contra gentiles* (*Summa against the Gentiles*), an apologetic treatise aimed at missionaries who were evangelizing non-Christians. Thomas

was primarily concerned for his Christian brothers working among Spanish Muslims. Thomas used his knowledge of Aristotle and the several prominent Muslims whose works were circulating in the West (most notably Averroes and Avicenna) to attack the overreliance on reason they demonstrated. He observed that the truth that was, in fact, found in Islam was mixed with much falsehood. He also wrote in defense of the Dominicans and their lifestyle from those who attacked the Order.

In 1259 Thomas began a decade of teaching at various Dominican sites in Italy. During this time he wrote the liturgy for Corpus Christi, the Roman Catholic festival honoring the Eucharist, and compiled the *Catena aurea* (*Golden Chain*), a set of biblical commentaries by the early church fathers. He also began the work on his monumental magnum opus, the *Summa Theologiae*, which would consume most of his energy until 1273.

Upon his return to Paris in 1268, he continued his most active intellectual life. He argued with the more extreme Aristotelians; he wrote commentaries on the New Testament books of Matthew and John; he commented on Dionysius the Areopagite's *Divine Names*; he penned works on the Christian creed, the Lord's Prayer and the Hail Mary prayer; and he composed hymns and delivered sermons.

His life was radically altered on December 6, 1273. That day, while celebrating the Mass, he had an intense mystical vision. He would afterward observe, "Everything I have written seems like straw in comparison with what I have seen and what has been revealed to me." He stopped his writing, and essentially left the *Summa Theologiae* unfinished. He died four months later, on March 7, 1274, while journeying to the Church Council that was about to convene in Lyon. He was buried at the Dominican church in Toulouse, France.

Thomas's Thought   Thomas's great work, the *Summa Theologiae*, is constructed around a series of topical theological questions, beginning with the status of theology as a science (in the Aristotelian sense of that word). Parts 1–3 discuss the existence and triune nature of God, creation, how all beings move toward God as an end, and the incarnation of Christ that provides the means by which creatures move toward God (Part 3). In Part 1.2, Thomas discussed the beatific vision of God in terms of human destiny (his own intellectual career culminating in such a vision). He covered the Christian life in Part 2.2, where he expounds upon the theological virtues (faith, hope, and charity), the cardinal virtues (prudence, justice, courage, and temperance), and the charisms or gifts of the Spirit. He also discusses the relative merits of the contemplative versus the active patterns for living one's life. In Part 3, Thomas covered Christology, the understanding of Jesus Christ and his salvific work and the sacramental life.

The *Summa* ended abruptly after Part 3. Following Thomas's death, his secretary Reginaldo de Piperno attempted to complete it by using material from Thomas's other writings, most notably his commentary of the *Sentences* of Peter Lombard, even though they had been written some 30 years previously. Most modern editions of the *Summa* omit the supplement.

Thomas in Context   Though it would take some time to see it, Thomas essentially moved Christian theology away from its domination by Platonic (and neo-Platonic) philosophy. He did so by mastering the intellectual stream and gently moving it into the Aristotelian camp rather than attempting a harsh break with the past. He emphasized his alignment with all that had preceded him and moved forward into an emerging work that would value science, technology, and urban life.

At the same time, Thomas made a crucially important shift in Christian thinking. Plato had pointed beyond the ultimately unreal world of the manifest world observed by the senses to the superior reality of the realm of ideas. Christian Platonists tended to subordinate time, space, and the physical world to an eternal spiritual realm. Disciplines of study, which allow us to master the social and physical, are devalued relative to theology. Thomas's theology gave an enlarged place for the empirical arts and sciences (law, medicine, natural science, architecture, and engineering), and a new level of legitimacy. Following Aristotle's lead, Thomas provided a place for empirical observation as a proper, natural, and necessary human endeavor.

Thomas's theology also supplied the church with a new philosophical language. Since the end of the centuries of persecution and its quick emergence as the dominant religion of the Roman Empire in the fourth century, the Christian church's major thinkers had relied on Platonic thought forms. Plato had provided the background for the discussions at the Ecumenical councils at which the basic statements of Christian orthodoxy had been hammered out and from which the Nicene and Chalcedonian creeds promulgated. As Thomas turned to the subject of Christology, he aligned himself fully with the church councils and ancient creeds, while presenting a new emphasis on God's action. In Christ, God entered the world not only to save humanity from sin, but to lift it up to the divine. Also, in entering the world, God reasserts the primal creative pronouncement that the created world is good—further basis for the legitimacy of the human arts and sciences.

The last section of the *Summa* that Thomas completed dealt with the sacraments. Catholicism is a sacramental religion, and the sacraments are given for the redemption from sin, and also, as Thomas emphasizes, as tools to assist the individual believer on his or her pilgrimage toward sanctification (holiness). In the process of writing about the sacraments, Thomas would also offer an explanation of the essential action that took place in the Eucharist when the elements of bread and wine were transformed into the Body and Blood of Christ. Drawing on the philosophical distinction between an object's essence or substance and its particular attributes (appearance, texture, taste, color, smell) observed by the five senses, he suggested that in the Mass, the essence/substance of the bread and wine became the body and blood of Christ while the attributes remained unchanged. This change became known as transubstantiation.

Thomas Aquinas Today   Thomas's views were not immediately accepted in his own day, though he found strong support. Just five years after Thomas's death, the general chapter of the Dominicans pronounced penalties against any of their number who would speak irreverently of Thomas or his writings, and subsequent chapter gatherings expressly required the brethren to follow his teachings. In the church's seminaries, the *Summa* gradually replaced Lombard's *Sentences* as the primary textbook for theology, especially after his canonization by Pope John XXII (r. 1316–1334) in 1323 ended any remaining open opposition.

Thomas's thought took an upward trajectory at the Council of Trent, called in large part to deal with the growth of Protestantism. The Council relied heavily on Thomas in its deliberation and the *Catechism of the Council of Trent* (1545–1563), prepared for the use of parish priests, can be seen as essentially a summary statement of his theology. In 1567, Pope Pius V named him a Doctor of the Church, after which the *Summa Theologiae* came to replace Lombard's *Sentences* as the chief text for teachings theology in Catholic seminaries.

By the 19th century, the use of Thomas's writings had declined, but a revival occurred during the pontificate of Pope Pius IX (r. 1846–1878), who presided over the First Vatican Council (1870–1871). Then in one of his first actions after becoming pope, his successor, Pope Leo XIII (r. 1878–1903), called for a continuance of the revived interest in his 1879 encyclical *Aeterni Patris*. He recommended the study of Thomas by all Catholic theological students throughout the world, though not to the exclusion of others. Leo also led in the formation of the Leonine Commission, which produced new critical editions of many of Thomas's works.

The centrality of Thomas's place in the theology of the Catholic Church was challenged by the Second Vatican Council and many believed his period of dominance had ended. He has, however, shown a significant resiliency and continues to remain a key force in Catholic theological discourse.

J. Gordon Melton

See also: Augustinians; Benedictines; Dominicans; Franciscans; Roman Catholic Church; Theology.

References

The *Summa Theologiae* is available on the Internet at http://www.newadvent.org/summa and a printed version is the Blackfriar's edition (London, 1964–1981); the complete edition of Thomas's works is the Leonine edition (Rome, 1882–).

Chenu, Marie-Dominique. *Toward Understanding St. Thomas*. Chicago: Regnery, 1964.

Copleston, Frederick C. *Aquinas*. Harmondsworth, UK: Penguin, 1955.

Gilson, Etienne. *The Christian Philosophy of St. Thomas*. New York: Random House, 1964.

Pieper, Joseph. *Guide to Thomas Aquinas*. New York: Pantheon, 1962.

Selman, Francis. *Aquinas 101: A Basic Introduction to the Thought of Saint Thomas Aquinas*. Orleans, MA: Christian Classics, 2007.

Torrell, Jean-Pierre. *Saint Thomas Aquinas: The Person and His Work*. Washington, DC: Catholic University of America Press, 2005.

Weisheipl, James. *Friar Thomas d'Aquino*. Washington, DC: Catholic University of America Press, 1983.

Three-Self Principles

The three-self principles, guidelines that became a goal of Christian missions across denominational lines in the late 19th century, suggested that missions should strive to become self-governing, self-supporting, and self-propagating. The goal of making mission fields in Africa and Asia especially free of support from Europe and North America and under the guidance and administration of local leaders was a major step in the transformation and indigenization of missions in the 20th century.

The three-self ideal was originally articulated by three prominent Protestant missionaries—Henry Venn (1796–1873), Rufus Anderson (1796–1880), and John L. Nevius (1829–1893). For more than 30 years, Venn served as the honorary secretary of the Church Missionary Society (1841–1872). He hammered out his views in the context of the mid-19th-century emergence of the High-Church wing of Anglicanism. He saw missionary activity as an extremely indigenous concern, the goal of which was the raising up of Native churches that would be "self-governing, self-supporting, and self extending." His ideas opposed the establishment of missionary dioceses, headed by a bishop, prior to the actual development of a local following. He argued that foreign missionaries should quickly turn over control of missions to local leadership.

Operating as an executive for the American Board of Commissioners for Foreign Missions in Boston, Rufus Anderson arrived at essentially the same ideas as Venn. Anderson argued for a focused and purposeful missionary program whose only goal was the creation of a scriptural, self-propagating Christianity. Missionaries were to seek the conversion of the lost, organize them into churches, train a competent local ministry, and lead the congregations to a stage where they become self-propagating. Any other purposes of missionary activity were superfluous and even distracting. By the end of the 1860s, he was clearly articulating the three-self principles.

John Nevius was a Presbyterian missionary who further developed the three-self idea while working in China and Korea. He believed the key to making the three-self principles work was teaching converts to become a witness for Christ among their neighbors and co-workers. The building of local leaders meant that churches were not dependent on foreign funds for their survival and growth.

Churches were often reluctant to give over control of their missions to local leaders—for a variety of reason. However, the basic thrust of the three-self principles took on additional important by the middle of the 20th century with the changes brought by World War II, the subsequent establishment of the United Nations, and the end of colonialism. During the war, churches were forced into self-sufficiency and most demonstrated their readiness for self-governance. After the war, the end to colonization was frequently accompanied with a transformation of missions into autonomous churches.

As a philosophy, the three-self principles survived most visibly in China. The post-revolutionary government expelled all of the foreign missionaries in 1950 and forced the Protestant churches to merge into a single body. At the first National Christian Conference, held in 1954, the government forced the organization of the Chinese Protestant Three-Self Patriotic movement in China. Ostensibly formed to break the Chinese churches' reliance on foreign money, influence, and leadership, the movement became the instrument for training leaders in patriotism (support of the Chinese government) and to facilitate communication between the government and the Christian community. In 1966, as the Cultural Revolution began, and the government attempted to destroy the church, the Three-Self movement was disbanded. It was reorganized in 1980 and has since become an organization to articulate new government policies regarding religion. On a more positive note, it has been an effective organization in creating an image that the contemporary Chinese Protestant church is an indigenous body and no longer a branch of a foreign institution.

J. Gordon Melton

See also: American Board of Commissioners for Foreign Missions; Chinese Protestant Three-Self Patriotic Movement/China Christian Council; Church Missionary Society.

References

Anderson, Gerald H, ed. *Mission Legacies: Biographical Dictionary of Christian Missions.* Grand Rapids, MI: William B. Eerdmans Publishing Company, 1998.

Anderson, Rufus. *Foreign Missions: Their Relations and Claims.* New York: Charles Scribner and Co., 1869.

Nevius, John L. "Historical Review of Missionary Methods—Past and Present—in China, and How Far Satisfactory." In *Records of the General Conference of the Protestant Missionaries of China. Held at Shanghai, May 7–20, 1890,* 171–176. Shanghai: American Presbyterian Mission Press, 1890.

Nevius, John L. *The Planting and Development of Missionary Churches.* New York: Student Volunteer Movement for Foreign Missions, 1899.

Sunquist, Scott W., ed. *A Dictionary of Asian Christianity.* Grand Rapids, MI: William B. Eerdmans Publishing Company, 2001.

Wickeri, Philip L. *Seeking Common Ground: Protestant Christianity, the Three-Self Movement and China's United Front.* Maryknoll, NY: Orbis Books, 1988.

Tian Dao

Tian Dao (Yiguandao) is arguably the most significant Chinese religious response to modernity to result from that period of extended turmoil, the 20th century. Tian Dao temples and congregations spread rapidly throughout urban China in the 1930s and 1940s, only to be effectively eliminated after the founding of the People's Republic of China in 1949. Some leaders managed to leave China, however, and new networks took root in Taiwan, Southeast Asia, Hong Kong, and other areas of Chinese migration.

Tian Dao owes its initial success to Zhang Tianran (1889–1947), from Jining, Shandong Province, in eastern China, and a senior leader in what was then a minor Daoist group known since the late 1800s as Yiguandao, the Way of Pervading Unity. (Members abandoned the term Yiguandao in the late 1940s and now universally refer to themselves as Tian Dao, the Way of Heaven, or Zhenli Tiandao, the Heavenly Way of True Principle.) After assuming leadership in 1930, Zhang initiated reforms that made Yiguandao more attractive to prospective new members. For example, he allowed meat eating, although vegetarianism remained the preferred goal. Members were no longer required to maintain celibacy. Lengthy rituals were simplified. Most important, new emphasis was given to proselytization.

Yiguandao emerged as a way for common people to fulfill both obligations to family and the traditional realm of deities, and also maintain a strong sense of community in uncertain times. Temple networks spread throughout urban China, but particularly in such rapidly industrializing cities as Tianjin and Shanghai. Missionaries established new temples and moved to incorporate existing temple networks and other associations under Zhang's leadership.

Tian Dao experienced a growth phase during World War II. During the Japanese occupation (1937–1945), a puppet Chinese government was set up under Wang Jingwei in Nanjing. Zhang and many of his lieutenants enjoyed free passage throughout much of the occupied areas and had close ties with leaders in the Wang Jingwei government. With the end of the war those ties became a liability, and Tian Dao leaders quickly cultivated new connections with the Nationalist government that briefly reoccupied the cities before the Nationalists' final defeat in 1949. Zhang died in 1947. By cooperating with the regimes in control of urban China, Tian Dao had bet on two losing sides in succession. Unsurprisingly, the incoming Communist regime lost no time in suppressing Tian Dao along with similar groups in the anti-superstition campaigns of the 1950s. Although Zhang's third wife, Sun Yuehui, managed to leave China and settle in Taiwan, the group was essentially leaderless; it could have disintegrated as quickly as it had grown.

In exile, Tian Dao reinvented itself and spread the hard way: from the ground up. Those leaders who had managed to leave mainland China in 1949 settled in Taiwan, Hong Kong, and, in a few cases, in Southeast Asia. Pioneers in Taiwan began to recruit new members and establish home temples despite having few sources of outside funding. Some leaders combined business with their religious efforts.

Recalling Tian Dao's support of the Wang Jingwei regime during the war, the Taiwan government now also suspected Tian Dao of harboring Communist spies, and saw its beliefs as a rival ideology. Tian Dao was actively suppressed by the police in several campaigns between 1963, when it was outlawed, and 1987, when it was finally legalized. Spies infiltrated meetings, and several leaders were arrested and sent to prison. Despite the harassment, Tian Dao flourished in Taiwan and grew to become the largest organized religious group there. It allied itself with local entrepreneurship, and as Taiwan underwent an economic boom between the 1960s and the 1980s, Tian Dao leaders recruited factory owners and workers alike. It provided a sense of community for displaced workers moving into industrial zones, and it actively promoted adult education in the Chinese classics and Buddhist sutras.

By the 1980s most of the Tian Dao temples were generally grouped into eight major sublineages, the largest being the Wen Hua, Bao Guang, Ji Chu, and Xing Yi. The first three of these traced their establishment to pre-1949 mother temples in Shanghai, the fourth to a temple lineage in northeast China. According to a 1981 survey, each of these sublineages had hundreds of subsidiary temples; the total temple count went from approximately 600 in 1981 to 1,200 in 1991. Since the 1980s, Tian Dao groups have spread around Southeast Asia, China, Europe, and America. A reasonable estimate of worldwide membership today is between 5 and 10 million. That number is impossible to confirm, however, since sublineages do not always cooperate, and many temples make no distinction between people initiated yet inactive and those who, once initiated, continue as active members.

Within Tian Dao, proselytization is a means by which members may gain merit that can then be transferred to family members. A member who recruits 100 initiates can request a rite whereby the soul of a deceased relative, such as a parent, can be promoted, or pulled up (chaoba), into heaven. The opportunity to make amends for past non-filial acts, and save one's parents, exerts a strong pull on Tian Dao members. Initiation in Tian Dao ensures an individual's own entry into heaven and release from the endless cycle of rebirth in which all humans are trapped. To reflect this significance, each new initiate is given a small passport recording date and temple name; entry to heaven is barred without this passport. Misspelled names or dates on the passport will, it is believed, similarly block one's entry.

Tian Dao ritual performances involve the assembly gathering before the altar and following two ritual assistants and a presider; all three are usually dressed in formal ritual robes (liyi). Core rituals in Tian Dao practice include the lighting of the incense, the presentation of offerings, and the invitation of deities to the altar. Rituals include the performing of repetitive koushou, bows and salutes, to each of the various deities in the pantheon; Tian Dao is most familiar among people in Taiwan as a bowing religion. Tian Dao congregations also regularly attend communal meals—invariably vegetarian—and lectures. The lectures are the prime means of transferring Tian Dao doctrine.

Tian Dao's extensive pantheon of deities is centered on Ancient Mother veneration. Worship of the Ancient Mother (Lao Mu, also called Wusheng Laomu, the Unborn Ancient Mother) formed in the mid-Ming dynasty (1368–1644) and spread especially throughout the region south of the Yangtze River area. Lao Mu is believed to have created her human children, only to have them lose their way because of the enticements of materiality. In a grand gesture of compassion, she orders Maitreya to return to Earth to save these lost souls and allow them to enter heaven and sit at her side.

The Ancient Mother is said to be present in the flame generated by an oil lamp placed in the center of the altar. Effigies of additional major deities are arrayed behind this light, usually including a smiling, seated Maitreya Buddha in the center; a Guan Yin bodhisattva, the popular deity of compassion and childbirth, to Maitreya's left; Ji Gong Huofo (living Buddha), a popular deity based on a monk from the Song dynasty (960–1279), on Maitreya's left; and, on either ends of the altar, images of Lyu Chunyang and Guang Gong, two popular Chinese deities based on legendary figures. In addition, ceramic figurines or black-and-white photographs of the founder, Zhang Tianran, and, in many temples, his third wife, Sun Yuehui, are sometimes placed at the far ends of these main altars.

Tian Dao groups put little relative emphasis on textual sources. Tian Dao teachings borrow a limited palette of ideas and terms from such Buddhist, Daoist, and Confucian sources as the Maitreya Sutra, the Heart Sutra, the Dao De Jing, and the Analects. Also, spirit writing remains common in Hong Kong, Taiwan, and Southeast Asian Chinese communities. Tian Dao practice involves writing on a sand-filled tray by a team of three selected members, often teenage girls. One of the team, said to be under the direct influence of a deity, writes Chinese glyphs in the sand with a stylus as the second member smoothes the sand with a squeegee and recites what is written. The third team member then records this with pen and paper.

Tian Dao today exists as one of many well-organized international religious groups active in Chinese culture. An umbrella organization, the Tian Dao General Assembly, was established in Taiwan in 1987, but only some 70 percent of Taiwan-based groups belong. Tian Dao groups tend to view other subsects with suspicion.

Today Tian Dao faces two paths into the future. It can redefine and reorient itself as an international movement relevant to people of all backgrounds, or it can focus instead on regaining its previous prominence as a significant movement in China. Either way, Tian Dao is likely to continue as a force among world religions. There are numerous Tian Dao sites in Chinese on the Internet. An English-language periodical, *Golden Voice of Maitreya*, is available.

Tian Dao
12th Fl.
No. 31, Ming-Sheng E. Rd.
Sec. 3, Taipei
Taiwan

Edward A. Irons

See also: Ancestors; Vegetarianism.

References

Introduction to Dao. Taipei: Tsu Kwang, n.d.

Jordan, David D., and Daniel L. Overmyer. *The Flying Phoenix: Aspects of Chinese Sectarianism in Taiwan*. Princeton, NJ: Princeton University Press, 1986.

Song Guanyu. *Tiandao Chuan Deng—Yiguan yu Xiandai Shehui*. Taipei: San Yang, 1996.

Song Guanyu. *Tiandao Gouchen: Yiguandao Diaocha Baogao*. Taipei: privately printed, 1983.

Tian Tai/Tendai Buddhism

Tian Tai (T'ien-t'ai), one of the more important schools of Chinese Buddhism, developed as a recognizable way of doing Buddhism within the larger Chinese Buddhist community in the early Tang dynasty (618–907). As it emerged into a distinctive school of Buddhism, it became known for its ability to synthesize variant strands of thought into an overarching system or philosophy of phenomena. Tian Tai was thus an early Chinese reaction to the many varieties of Buddhist doctrine that had been transmitted to China from India by that time.

Tian Tai Buddhism received its name from the Tian Tai Mountains in eastern Zhejiang, China, a place of rolling if not dramatic mountain ranges and many rivers. The area is filled with spiritual significance. One mountain is the site of one of the 10 Daoist caves, and reputedly the area is the location where the popular Chinese deity figure Ji Gong (or Duke Ji) was born. And here, the founder of Tian Tai, Zhi Yi (538–597), built the Baoguo Si (Temple of Protecting the Nation), an idea that came to him in a dream. He was later able to receive support for his project from the Sui emperor, his main sponsor. This temple continues to function to this day.

Zhi Yi moved to Tian Tai for the last years of his life, where he concentrated on writing and teaching. All of his thoughts were recorded by his disciple Guan Ding.

Tian Tai was just coming into its own when a Japanese priest, Saicho, sent to study in China by his emperor, arrived. He studied for a year at Mount Tian T'ai and returned with a number of Tian Tai texts. The founding of the Tendai (as Tian Tai was known in Japan) School he established at Mount Hiei not far from Kyoto is marked by the emperor's agreeing to allow two priests trained by Saicho to be formally ordained each years. At this time, the emperor had control of all of Japanese Buddhism, and keeping ordination in the former imperial city of Nara and limiting the number of newly ordained priests was one means of exercising that control.

Saicho, later known by the honorific title Dengyo Daishi, continued the Tian Tai perspective that classified the spectrum of Buddhist sutras and approaches to Buddhism on a four-fold scale: the Hinayana teachings; the teachings common to all Mahayana Buddhism; the teachings unique to Mahayana as opposed to Hinayana; and the perfect teachings, as contained in the Lotus Sutra. He antagonized the Buddhist leadership at Nara by suggesting that they basically taught Hinayana Buddhism.

Saicho saw the Lotus Sutra as above all other Buddhist sutras and texts. Based on his appropriation of the sutra, Saicho began to advocate the idea that all beings had the potential for full Buddhahood. This idea contrasted starkly with the view of the Buddhist leadership at Nara, who generally believed that only some people were able to arrive at enlightenment while only a few could reach complete Buddhahood. This basic disagreement served as the foundation for Saicho's several petitions to the emperor that step by step established the independence of the Tendai community from the Nara officials.

Saicho's belief that all partook of Buddha nature also led the Tendai to show great respect toward the spectrum of the Buddhas and bodhisattvas of the larger world of Mahayana Buddhism. Tendai temples came

Enryaku-ji Temple of Mount Hiei, Kyoto, Japan. (Paskee/Dreamstime.com)

to be distinctive by their tendency to include a large number of bodhisattva images. It also led to an essential teaching that all believers should seek self-perfection and act for the benefit of others (that is, manifest the bodhisattva ideal) in their outward life.

In China, Saicho had studied esoteric Buddhism, though he focused on the Lotus Sutra upon his return to Japan. Tendai was open to esotericism and that aspect of its thought and practice would be developed by two of Saicho's disciples, Ennin (794–864) and Annen (ca. 841–ca. 901). Ennin went to China in 838 and began nine years of studying esoteric practices. Along the way, he encountered meditation upon and invocation of the bodhisattva Amitabha (known as Amida in Japan). The addition of the veneration of Amida Buddha at Mount Hiei would later become a major source of Pure Land Buddhism, which turned the veneration of Amida into its focal activity.

Ennin also studied the secret meditations and rituals relative to the Vairocana Buddha as represented in two mandalas, the Diamond Realm mandala and the Womb Realm mandala. In the end, Ennin tended to favor the esoteric teachings above those related to the Lotus Sutra, though it was left to Annen to clearly state the revised perspective. He would come to see mandalas pictorially: presenting the spiritual world coupled with proper actions relative to them invited the believer to partake of the spiritual realm.

With the rise of Amida veneration and esotericism within Tendai, several sub-groupings emerged throughout the Tendai leadership, each following a variant lineage of practice. In later centuries, these lineages led to the formation of the separate Tendai sects of which there are more than 20 in contemporary Japan.

The year 966 was a landmark for the Tendai community. A fire destroyed Enryaku-ji, the Tendai headquarters temple complex on Mount Hiei. The abbot Ryogen (912–985) had to step forward to raise the funds for the reconstruction. As the funds were collected, he also used the opportunity of a new beginning to place a renewed emphasis on education. Ryogen is remembered most for initiating an era of Tendai learning and expansion.

Of the 20 divisions of the Tendai community, the largest is the one that still controls the headquarters at Mount Hiei. Its many associated temples across Japan are divided into 25 districts. It co-sponsors Taisho University (in cooperation with the Jodo-Shu and Shingon Buddhism). It has some 600,000 adherents in Japan, and a small but growing number of centers outside of the country.

Edward A. Irons

See also: Jodo-shu; Kukai (Kobo Daishi); Mahayana Buddhism; Meditation; Nara; Pure Land Buddhism; Shingon Buddhism; Zhi Yi.

References

Buddhist Denominations and Schools in Japan. Tokyo: Bukkto Dendo Kyokai, 1984.

Groner, Paul. *Ryogen and Mount Hiei: Japanese Tendai in the Tenth Century.* Honolulu: University of Hawaii Press, 2002.

Groner, Paul. *Saicho: The Establishment of the Japanese Tendai School.* Berkeley, CA: Berkeley Buddhist Studies Series, 1984.

Kasahara, Kazuo. *A History of Japanese Religion.* Tokyo: Kosei Publishing Company, 2001.

Kashiwahara, Yūsen, and Kōyū Sonoda. *Shapers of Japanese Buddhism.* Trans. by Gaynor Sekimori. Tokyo: Kōsei Pub. Co., 1994.

Pruden, Leo M., and Paul L. Swanson, trans. *The Essentials of the Vinaya Tradition: The Collected Teachings of the Tendai Lotus School.* Berkeley, CA: Numata Center for Buddhist Translation & Research, 1996.

Saso, Michael R. *Tantric Art and Meditation: The Tendai Tradition.* Honolulu: Tendai Educational Foundation, 1990.

Swanson, Paul L. *Foundations of T'ien-T'ai Philosophy: The Flowering of the Two Truths Theory in Chinese Buddhism.* Fremont, CA: Asian Humanities Press, 1995.

Takeshi, Umehara. "Saicho." In *Buddhist Spirituality: Later China, Korea, Japan, and the Modern World,* edited by Takeuchi Yoshinori, James W. Heisig, Paul L. Swanson, and Joseph S.

O'Leary, 164–173. New York: Crossroad Publishing, 1999.

Tiantan

Tiantan, the Temple of Heaven, is the largest temple complex in China. Though today it is no longer used as a worship center, it stands as a major reminder of the traditional Chinese (pre-Buddhist) religion that was a force in the land into the early 20th century. Tiantan was the primary site at which the emperor made the annual thanksgiving for past prosperity and pleaded for an abundant harvest for the next year, a process that climaxed in December at the Winter Solstice.

The first major part of the complex was erected to the southeast of central Beijing. It was begun in 1410 by Emperor Yongle (r. 1403–1424), who had also constructed the Forbidden City. Yongle's finished work was known for the next century as the Temple of Heaven and Earth. Then, in 1530, the Emperor Jiajing (r. 1522–1567) built a separate Temple of Earth on the northern edge of the city, as part of a major building program in Beijing. His work also included greatly expanding the facilities at Tiantan. When completed, the entire complex covered 675 acres. Integrated into the overall structure were numerous squares, representing Earth, which were always located at a lower level than the round structures symbolic of heaven.

Tiantan consisted of three main parts laid out along a north-south axis. The entrance was at the Western Gate, and on ceremonial occasions the emperor would make his first stop near there at the Zhaigong, the Fasting Palace. The emperor initiated the annual winter ceremony with three days of fasting during which time he partook of no meat or wine, refrained from sexual activity, and handled no official matters that had to do with criminal cases. He also took periodic ritual baths.

Fasting and purification completed, the emperor would next move to the far north of the complex. This area was originally dominated by the Dasidian or Big Worship Hall. This building was later (1538) replaced with the Qiniandian or Big Enjoyment Hall. Today this part of the complex also includes the Huangqiandian or Heavenly Emperor Hall and the large circular

Temple of Heaven, Beijing, China. (J. Gordon Melton)

Qigutan or Altar of Prayer for a Rich Crop. Inside the Huangqiandian, at an altar table, the emperor stopped to burn incense.

A thoroughfare called the Danbi Bridge connects the Qiniandian in the north to the rest of the Tiantan complex in the south. Separate pathways along the thoroughfare were laid out for the Heavenly Emperor, the emperor, and the courtiers who attended the annual ceremonies. Immediately across the bridge stands the Imperial Vault of Heaven, and inside this circular building the emperor could find the memorial tablets for the Heavenly Emperor and his own ancestors. On the Winter Solstice, the emperor started the day in this hall, during which time he read prayers and invited those memorialized to participate in the upcoming ceremonies.

The Heaven-Worshipping Altar, a large circular structure at the southern end of the complex, was completed in 1530. From that time forward, the main event of the ritual year would occur within it. A large outdoor structure, it was precisely constructed utilizing multiples of nine in its measurements and decorations. Its structure proclaimed the belief that the Heavenly Emperor resided in the ninth tier of heaven. The human emperor, who represented the Heavenly Emperor to the people, came here on the Winter Solstice, and the main ceremonies occurred in and around this altar. The ceremonies were focused on the emperor's report to the Heavenly Emperor on the past year's abundance and his intercession for the country as a whole with prayers for a new year of prosperity and peace.

Accompanying the several main buildings are a number of lesser structures, including side halls at the Qiniandian where the Sun, Moon, stars, wind, clouds, thunder, and rain were worshipped, and the Butcher Pavilion where the sacrificial animals killed during the ceremonies were actually killed. On the edge of the Danbi Bridge there is a platform where the emperor changed into clothes especially provided for his participation in the sacrifice of the animals.

The worship of Tian (heaven) did not, of course, begin with the construction of Tiantan in the 15th century. It had been carried out for many centuries with growing elaborateness. And the Winter Solstice was but one of many ceremonies acknowledging heaven on behalf of the nation. The emperor would, for example, come to the Heaven-Worshipping Altar to pray for rain each year at the Summer Solstice.

Today, the very secularized government of the People's Republic of China recognizes the historical importance of the ceremonies that took place at Tiantan and considers the key buildings to be among the most important architectural treasures of the country. They are prized, among other reasons, for both their beauty and architectural innovation.

Edward A. Irons

See also: Chinese Religions.

References

Naquin, Susan. *Peking: Temples and City Life, 1400–1900*. Berkeley: University of California Press, 2000.

Tiantan—Temple of Heaven. Beijing: China Esperanto Press, 1998.

Tibet in Western Religious Imagination

The image of Tibet and of Tibetan Buddhism in Western literature has over time undergone profound transformations. Not infrequently, 19th- and early 20th-century writing saw Tibet as a thoroughly backward country, whose superstitious population was dominated by ignorant priests and monks. This was the opinion voiced by Francis Younghusband (1863–1942), who conquered Lhasa in 1903–1904, and by Sven Hedin (1865–1952), who traveled through the closed land around the turn of the 20th century. Scholarly ideals prevalent at that time saw Buddhism as a religion that had once existed in a pure form, but had become increasingly corrupt. "Lamaism" was often singled out as a particularly degenerate form of the Buddhist tradition. The then influential work of British explorer L. Austine Wadell (1854–1938) thus presented the religion of Tibet in terms of the "strange cults and creeds" that had infiltrated original Buddhism.

Most Western present-day conceptions of Tibet are, of course, the very opposite. A number of writers from the late 19th century up to our own time have contributed to presenting Tibet in a sympathetic light, as a land of mystery, and as a source of a profound spirituality that Westerners can tap into. Rudyard Kipling, for instance, crafted a thoroughly positive portrait of a Tibetan lama in his widely read novel *Kim*, published in 1899–1900. Tibet was presented as a land of mystery in a variety of literary genres, including travelogues (Alexandra David-Néel's *Voyage d'une parisienne à Lhasa*, published in 1927; Lama Anagarika Govinda's *The Way of the White Clouds*, 1956), utopian novels (James Hilton's 1933 novel *Lost Horizon* with its description of the utopian valley of Shangri-La), and fictional autobiographies with occult themes (Cyril Henry Hoskin's 1956 best-seller *The Third Eye*, written under his assumed Tibetan name Lobsang Rampa).

If the above genres present Tibet as a land to be read about, other authors, typically representing various currents of Western Esotericism, explored a partly imaginary Tibet for the wisdom that its most enlightened inhabitants might impart to an audience of spiritual seekers. The founding figure of the Theosophical Society, Helena P. Blavatsky (1831–1891), played a significant role by suggesting that the superior spiritual insights that she was able to relay originally came from the trans-Himalayan realm and from her journeys there. Although Blavatsky's writings drew on many other sources of inspiration than Tibet, later authors in the Theosophical tradition gave Tibet a more central role. Walter Evans-Wentz (1878–1965) produced a Theosophically inspired commentary on a translation of the *Tibetan Book of the Dead*, a work that has continued to be in print up to the present day. Alice Bailey

(1880–1949) wrote a large corpus of Theosophical works that she suggested had been telepathically received from a Tibetan spiritual master by the name of Djwal Khul.

Carl Gustav Jung (1875–1961) represents a different stream of Western Esoteric approaches to Tibetan religion. He wrote, inter alia, a psychological interpretation of the *Tibetan Book of the Dead* and commentaries on Tibetan religious art. Some followers of Jung, such as Radmila Moacanin (*Jung's Psychology and Tibetan Buddhism*, 1983), have expanded significantly on the themes mentioned by Jung, and on the similarities that they perceive between Tibetan Buddhism and Jungian psychology.

Among the many other (and often quite radical) reinterpretations of Tibetan religion, mention can be made of UFO contactee George Adamski's occultist movement *Royal Order of Tibet*; Timothy Leary's psychedelic retelling of the *Tibetan Book of the Dead*, published in 1964; Chris Kilham's book *The Five Tibetans* (1994), which introduced a set of five yoga exercises of purported Tibetan origin into the New Age milieu; and James Redfield's New Age novel *The Secret of Shambhala* (1999).

Such literary depictions and Esoteric appropriations certainly continue to flourish also in the present day, but have in recent decades, especially due to the Chinese takeover and the ensuing diaspora situation, been complemented by other types of publications and other channels of information. The scholarly output on Tibetan Buddhism, once a mere trickle, has grown to massive proportions. Tibetan teachers have since around 1970 established schools in Western countries, attracting converts. Some, such as Chogyam Trungpa (1939–1987), became internationally famous—and controversial—representatives of Tibetan Buddhism in the West. A few North American and European converts into these traditions, such as the Dane Ole Nydahl (b. 1941), have in turn begun to establish themselves as Western lamas.

Whereas formally converting to Buddhism is a step taken by few, large audiences in the West have a less committed but thoroughly sympathetic view of Tibet and its religious heritage. This positive interest has in particular focused on the charismatic figure of the 14th Dalai Lama. A person who embodies many distinct roles, he is prized for his global, ecumenical outlook; for his interest in finding a common interface between Buddhism and modern science; for his function in the ongoing conflicts with China; and for his image as a trans-confessional spiritual leader. He is the author of numerous books, some of which have achieved best-seller status. The fact that the Dalai Lama has become an icon of popular culture can also be gauged by the fact that Martin Scorcese's 1997 film portraying his life, *Kundün*, was distributed by Walt Disney Productions.

At present, Westerners interested in Tibet thus have options as diverse as perusing scholarly or more popular literature on the topic, joining a Tibetan Buddhist group, reading Jungian or Theosophical interpretations of Tibetan religion, or—in characteristic New Age fashion—creating their own individual amalgam of these and other sources.

Olav Hammer

See also: Bailey, Alice Ann; Blavatsky, Helena P.; China: Tibet; Tibetan Buddhism; UFO Religions.

References

Bishop, Peter. *Dreams of Power: Tibetan Buddhism and the Western Imagination*. London: Athlone, 1993.

Bishop, Peter. *The Myth of Shangri-La: Tibet, Travel Writing and the Western Creation of Sacred Landscape*. Berkeley: University of California Press, 1989.

Dodin, Thierry, and Heinz Räther. *Imagining Tibet: Perceptions, Projections and Fantasies*. Boston: Wisdom Publications, 2001.

Lopez, Donald S. *Prisoners of Shangri-La: Tibetan Buddhism and the West*. Chicago: University of Chicago Press, 1998.

Tibetan Buddhism

Following its initial introduction in the seventh century CE, Buddhism became the dominant religion in the Tibetan cultural area—which includes the central provinces of Ü and Tsang (now composing the "Tibet Autonomous Region" of the People's Republic of China), the eastern provinces of Kham and Amdo, Mongolia, Bhutan, parts of Russia, and several republics of the

Three prayer wheels and Buddhist pilgrims, Sakya Monastery, Tibet. (Corel)

former Soviet Union, as well as large areas of northern India and Nepal. Traditional histories trace the beginning of the "first dissemination" (*chidar*) of Buddhism to the reign of King Songtsen Gampo (ca. 618–650).

Royal patronage continued during the reign of King Trisong Detsen (ca. 740–798), who together with the Indian scholar-monk Santaraksita and the Tantric master Padmasambhava founded the first Buddhist monastery at Samye in 775. The two Indian masters represent competing paradigms of Buddhism, both of which became influential in Tibet: a monastic and clerical stream that emphasized cenobitic monasticism; and lineages often centered on charismatic lay Tantrics. The former was transmitted mainly from north Indian monastic universities such as Nalanda, while the latter was centered in Bihar and Bengal and generally existed well apart from the monastic establishments.

The early Tibetan dynasty came to an end with the assassination of King Relbachen (r. 815–836), whose death was followed by a brief persecution of Bud-

dhism. This marked the end of the "first dissemination." The "second dissemination" (*ngadar*) began with the arrival in Tibet of AtiŸa in 1042.

Following the ascension of the fifth Dalai Lama, Ngawang Losang Gyatso (1617–1682), to power in the 17th century with the backing of Mongol troops, Tibet was ruled by successive Dalai Lamas (who are believed by Tibetan Buddhists to be physical manifestations of the Buddha Avalokiteshvara). This ended with the Chinese invasion and annexation of Tibet in the 1950s, which began a period of widespread persecution of Buddhism and resulted in the destruction of thousands of monasteries. In 1959 the 14th Dalai Lama, Tenzin Gyatso (b. 1935), fled to India, where he subsequently formed a government-in-exile in Dharamsala. Hundreds of thousands of Tibetans have since followed him into exile.

Many of the monasteries that were destroyed by the Chinese in Tibet have been rebuilt in exile, and today tens of thousands of monks and nuns continue to

Main temple at Yong-He-Gong Lamasary in Beijing, China. (J. Gordon Melton)

study the traditional monastic curricula. In Tibet, however, the Chinese government is deeply suspicious of monastics because many have been at the forefront of anti-Chinese agitations. As a result, the number of monks and nuns is severely restricted, and many are forced to spend several hours each day in "patriotic re-education classes," in which they are taught Marxist dogma. Many monasteries have Chinese secret police in residence, and little time is allowed for study of traditional Buddhist curricula.

There are four main orders in Tibetan Buddhism: Nyingmapa, Sakyapa, Kagyupa, and Gelukpa. Nyingmapa means Old Order; it is so named because it relies on older translations of Buddhist texts, and it traces itself back to Padmasambhava. The latter three are collectively called New Orders (*Sarma*) because they rely on translations prepared during the second dissemina-

tion. All four orders have both scholastic and Tantric traditions, but they differ in the relative emphasis they place on study or meditative practice. In addition, each bases itself on particular Tantric texts and traces itself to particular lineages.

John Powers

See also: Gelugpa; Kagyupa Tibetan Buddhism; Karma-Kagyupa Tibetan, Buddhism; Meditation; Monasticism; Nyingma Tibetan Buddhism; Padmasambhava; Sakyapa; Tantrism.

References

Coleman, Graham, comp. and ed. *A Handbook of Tibetan Culture*. Boston: Shambhala, 1994.

Gyatso, Tenzin (Dalai Lama XIV). *The World of Tibetan Buddhism*. London: Wisdom, 1995.

Powers, John. *Introduction to Tibetan Buddhism.* Ithaca, NY: Snow Lion, 1995.

Samuel, Geoffrey. *Civilized Shamans: Buddhism in Tibetan Societies.* Washington, DC: Smithsonian Institution Press, 1993.

Shakya, Tsering. *The Dragon in the Land of Snows: A History of Modern Tibet since 1947.* New York: Columbia University Press, 1999.

Tibetan Nyingma Institute

The Tibetan Nyingma Institute was founded in Berkeley, California, in the early 1970s by Tarthang Tulku Rinpoche (b. 1935). Tarthang Tulku was one of the first Tibetans to teach in the United States and arrived in 1969 from India with his French Egyptian wife, Nazli. The following year he founded Dharma Publishing, which is perhaps the first dedicated Tibetan Buddhist publishing house in the West. Over the past 40 years it has launched many books on Tibetan art, teaching, and practice.

Shortly after his arrival Tarthang Tulku and his students purchased a large fraternity house near the University of California in Berkeley and converted it into a major place of teaching and practice, thus laying the foundation for the Tibetan Nyingma Institute. In 1975 the organization broke ground for their rural retreat center, Odiyan. Tarthang Tulku's success in establishing a solid institutional base was remarkable. While Buddhism was not unknown in the West, even in the 1960s and 1970s, it lacked dedicated communities and teaching facilities (other than some serving the Japanese American community). For a Tibetan refugee who was only a decade out of Tibet, the establishment of a significant and enduring Dharma center was an important accomplishment.

Tarthang Tulku was raised in eastern Tibet (Kham) and moved to India in 1959 following the Chinese takeover. His father was a Nyingmapa lama and astrologer, and he had received teachings in all four principal Tibetan Buddhist schools while in Tibet. As a young man in Tibet, Tarthang Tulku's principal teacher was Dzongsar Khyentse, Chokyi Lodro (1893–1959). After arriving in India, he taught at the Sanskrit University in Varanasi (Benares) and reprinted Tibetan texts. In Berkeley Tarthang Tulku emphasized meditation practice, the recitation of the mantra of Padmasambhava, *Om Ah Hum Benza Guru Pema Siddhi Hum*, and lived the life of a *ngags-pa* (householder-yogi or lama—a dedicated religious practitioner who resides not in a monastery but in a family situation). He took on the pioneering work of articulating the sophisticated insights of the Tibetan path into modern language and modern life. His writing is characterized by an applied approach to Buddhist spirituality. Books such as *Gesture of Balance*, *Skillful Means*, and *Time, Space and Knowledge* introduced a meditation format that engages with the ordinary world. His work *Kum-Nye Relaxation* was a fresh approach to Tibetan yoga. Dharma Publishing continues to produce translations of Tibetan classics and has reprinted the entire Tibetan Buddhist canon, the *bKa'-'gyur* (the spoken word of the Buddha) and *bsTan-'gyur* (the authoritative commentaries [Kanjur and Tanjur]), as well as thousands of other texts.

Through the late 20th century, Tarthang Tulku's work led to the founding of centers around the world, the principal ones being in California, the Netherlands, Germany, and Brazil, though there are numerous smaller centers throughout the world. He also established the Tibetan Aid Project (TAP), which supports traditional monastic life in India, Nepal, and Bhutan and the rebuilding of monasteries in Tibet. TAP also funds the free distribution of Buddhist texts and important ceremonies conducted by all four principal traditions of Tibetan Buddhism.

Tibetan Nyingma Institute
1815 Highland Place
Berkeley CA 94709
http://www.nyingmainstitute.com/index.htm

Dharma Publishing
35788 Hauser Bridge Rd.
Cazadero, CA 95421
http://www.dharmapublishing.com/p-25-Home.aspx

Tibetan Aid Project
2425 Hillside Ave.
Berkeley, CA 94704
http://www.tibetanaidproject.org/

Diana Cousens

See also: Meditation; Nyingma Tibetan Buddhism; Padmasambhava; Tibetan Buddhism.

References

Crystal Mirror. Vols. 1–4. Emeryville, CA: Dharma Publishing, 1971–1977.

Fields, Rick. *How the Swans Came to the Lake.* 3rd ed. Boston: Shambhala, 1992.

Nyingma Edition of the Tibetan Buddhist Canon, Kanjur and Tanjur. 128 vols. Emeryville, CA: Dharma Publishing, 1981.

Tarthang Tulku. *Kum-Nye Relaxation.* Emeryville, CA: Dharma Publishing, 1978.

Tarthang Tulku. *Skillful Means.* Emeryville, CA: Dharma Publishing, 1978.

Tijaniyya Sufi Order

The Tijaniyya is a Muslim brotherhood or Sufi order (Arabic: *tariqa*) named after its founder, Ahmad b. Mahammad al-Tijani (1737–1815). The sources—the most important being Jawahir al-ma'ani by 'Ali Harazim Barada, a disciple of al-Tijani—allow us to establish 1782 as the year when the Tijaniyya was established in the Algerian desert. In 1798, Ahmad al-Tijani moved to the city of Fez (Morocco), where he spent the rest of his life. By the time of his death, the new Sufi order had already reached areas such as Mauritania to the south and Tunisia to the east.

During the 19th century, the Tijaniyya expanded farther in sub-Saharan Africa: the areas of present-day Senegal, Guinea, Mali, and northern Nigeria came to be included within the sphere of influence of the Tijaniyya. A key figure of this development was al-Hajj 'Umar b. Sa'id Tal (d. 1864), who, in the 1850s, launched a *jihad* against the "Pagan" Bamana rulers and later against the French, who had attempted to include the West African hinterland in their colonial state. Although the military activities of al-Hajj 'Umar earned the Tijaniyya the reputation of being anti-colonial in Africa south of the Sahara, the contrary was the case in its original homeland: the leaders of the order at 'Ain Madi and Temasin (Algeria) were on good terms with the French rulers, and there is evidence that they gave their support to French missions

that were to explore the northern and central Sahara. When Morocco became a French protectorate in 1912, the colonial administration tried to use the Tijaniyya to increase its acceptance among the local Muslim population.

The 19th century saw the continuation of the rapid spread of the Tijaniyya in sub-Saharan Africa. However, after the final military defeat (1890–1893) of the Tijani state established by al-Hajj 'Umar against the French colonial army, a new generation of Tijani leaders emerged who worked for the spread of their Sufi order by peaceful means. With regard to the French presence, these leaders followed the "accommodationist" approach of their Northern African counterparts. Some prominent Tijanis, such as the Senegalese shaykh al-Hajj Malik Sy (1855–1922) or Seydou Nourou Tal (ca. 1880–1980, a grandson of al-Hajj 'Umar), became close allies of the French administration. The only significant exception to the new approach was Shaykh Hamallah from Nioro du Sahel (present-day Mali), the founder of a distinctive branch of the Tijaniyya whose followers clashed repeatedly with French forces. Hamallah died in exile in Montluçon (France) in 1940, and his movement continues to exist in some regions of Mali, Burkina Faso, and the Ivory Coast.

Among the most visible figures of the Tijaniyya in the 20th century were Ibrahim Niasse (d. 1975) from Senegal, Muhammad al-Hafiz b. 'Abd al-Latif (d. 1978) from Cairo, and Ahmad Skiraj (d. 1944) from Morocco. Niasse established a movement known as Jama'at al-fayda (Congregation of the Spiritual Overflowing) within the Tijaniyya in the 1930s. In the following decades, the fayda movement expanded rapidly in West Africa and even reached such distant areas as Darfur (Republic of Sudan). When Niasse died in 1975, the number of his followers was estimated at 20 to 30 million. The proselytizing activities of Muhammad al-Hafiz were concentrated on the Anglo-Egyptian Sudan (and later the Republic of Sudan). In addition, he acquired the reputation of being the most distinguished defender of Tijaniyya doctrine, together with Ahmad Skiraj. Both scholars published numerous books and pamphlets with the purpose of explaining the mystical teachings of Ahmad al-Tijani to a larger audience. For more than 25 years Muhammad al-Hafiz edited the Cairo-based journal *Tariq al-haqq* (*The Way of the Truth*), which dealt not only with Tijani doctrine but also with a wide range of issues such as the exegesis of the Koran, legal opinions (*fatwas*), the history of Islam, and current debates within the Muslim world.

Right from the outset, the Tijaniyya became the target of strong criticism by other Sufis and non-Sufi Muslims. According to Jawahir al-ma'ani, Ahmad al-Tijani—who had been affiliated with several Sufi orders before—founded his own brotherhood after a personal encounter with the Prophet Muhammad (d. 632). Moreover, al-Tijani claimed to be in permanent communication with the Prophet and justified his teachings by pointing to what the Prophet told him during those meetings. However, the authenticity of the alleged sayings of the Prophet was contested by non-Tijanis. Although Sufis usually accepted the possibility of meeting the Prophet even after his death, other Muslims denied such a possibility completely. Controversial statements made by al-Tijani concerned his claim to be the "seal of the saints" (*khatm al-awliya'*), the notion that one recitation of a short prayer formula known as *salat al-fatih* was equivalent to 6,000 recitations of the whole Koran, or the prohibition against visiting any Sufi *shaykh* who is not affiliated to the Tijaniyya, to mention but a few examples. Al-Tijani is even quoted as having said, "Whoever sees me on a Monday or on a Friday will surely enter paradise and will not be punished."

Not surprisingly, such tenets were unacceptable to many non-Tijani Sufis and non-Sufi Muslims. Tijani doctrines have thus been at the root of countless controversies since the Order's foundation. Compared with other Sufi orders, the Tijaniyya is distinguished by its exclusiveness, its outspoken sense of superiority to other orders, and the high degree of confidence of salvation among the followers, because Ahmad al-Tijani gave them the guarantee that they will enter paradise on the Day of Judgment, provided that they comply with the Order's rules. Apart from the severe opposition evoked by such teachings, the Tijaniyya also managed to gain staunch support, particularly among Muslims in West Africa. Membership in this Sufi order always transcended adherence to particular social status groups. Tijani doctrine seems to be attractive to both scholars and the illiterate, nobles and former slaves, peasants and the emerging Muslim urban middle class,

the rich and the poor. Every member is supposed to perform daily recitations, some being on an individual basis (*awrad*, sing. *wird*), while the *wazifa* (duty) and the Friday *dhikr* have to be performed in a group.

At the top of the Order's hierarchy is the eldest living male descendant of Ahmad al-Tijani. The present head is Sidi 'Abd al-Jabbar from 'Ain Madi (Algeria). Generally, all descendants of the Order's founder are considered to be the highest authorities within the Tijaniyya. But other shaykhs can also occupy a high position in the hierarchy when they are granted the title *khalifa*. Below the khalifa is the so-called *muqaddam*, who is allowed to initiate others into the recitation practices of the brotherhood. The Tijaniyya is nowadays the most influential Sufi order in West Africa. Its main areas of influence are Senegal and northern Nigeria, followed by countries such as Mauritania, Gambia, Ghana, Mali, Niger, and Cameroon. The Order also has a significant presence in some regions of Guinea, Burkina Faso, the Ivory Coast, Togo, Benin, and Sierra Leone. More to the east, important Tijaniyya communities can be found in Chad, the western and central regions of the Sudan, and in some regions of Ethiopia. As for North Africa, it seems that the influence of the Tijaniyya has declined over the course of the 20th century. However, the Order is still active in parts of Morocco, Algeria, Tunisia, and Egypt. Since the first half of the 20th century, the Order has also managed to make inroads into Southeast Asia (Indonesia, Malaysia). This expansion was possible primarily through the contacts established in Mecca by Tijani leaders from West Africa and Egypt with pilgrims from Southeast Asia. Tijaniyya centers also exist in Albania, and there seem to be small communities in Turkey, Lebanon, Syria, and even in Iran. In a more recent development, the Tijaniyya Order has started to recruit members among North American Muslims. The proselytizing activities in the United States are coordinated by Shaykh Hasan Cissé from Kaolack, Senegal, a disciple of the above-mentioned Ibrahim Niasse.

As there is no statistical data available, it is impossible to provide the number of followers of the Tijaniyya. For West Africa—nowadays the Tijaniyya heartlands—estimates run as high as 60 million. However, the number of 20 million followers worldwide seems to be more realistic, and the number of those who participate in the Order's rituals on a regular basis is certainly much lower.

At present, the most active centers of the Tijaniyya include Fez (Morocco), where the shrine of al-Tijani is located; Tivaouane and Kaolack (Senegal); Nioro du Sahel (Mali); Kano and Maiduguri (Nigeria); and Kiota (Niger), to mention but a few.

Tijaniyya
Son Excellence Sidi 'Abd al-Jabbar
Khalife des Tijaniyya
'Ain Madi
Cercle de Laghouat
Algeria
http://www.geocities.com/Athens/9189
http://www.crosswinds.net/~tijanicissesa
http://home.earthlink.net/~halimcisse/index.html

Ruediger Seesemann

See also: Muhammad; Sufism.

References

Abun-Nasr, Jamil M. *The Tijaniyya: A Sufi Order in the Modern World*. London: Oxford University Press, 1965.

al-Sa'ih, Muhammad al-'Arabi. *Bughyat al-mustafid li-sharh munyat al-murid*. Cairo: Mustafa al-Babi al-Halabi, 1959.

Barada, 'Ali Harazim. *Jawahir al-ma'ani wa-bulûgh al-amani fi fayd Sayyidi Abi l-'Abbas al-Tijani.* Parts 1–2. Beirut: Dar al-Fikr, 1963.

Brenner, Louis. *West African Sufi: The Religious Heritage and Spiritual Search of Cerno Bokar Saalif Taal*. Berkeley: University of California Press, 1984.

Hunwick, John O. "An Introduction to the Tijani Path: Being an Annotated Translation of the Chapter Headings of the Kitab ar-rimah of al-Hajj 'Umar." *Islam et sociétés au Sud du Sahara* 6 (1992): 17–32.

Robinson, David. *The Holy War of Umar Tal: The Western Sudan in the Mid-Nineteenth Century*. Oxford: Clarendon, 1985.

Robinson, David, and Jean-Louis Triaud, eds. *La Tijaniyya: Une confrérie musulmane à la conquête de l'Afrique*. Paris: Karthala, 2000.

■ Timor Leste

The eastern half of the island of Timor, once part of the nation of Indonesia, became a separate nation in 2002, following a referendum in which more than 70 percent of the people voted for independence. The western portion of Timor remains part of Indonesia. The island is located north of Australia from which it is separated by the Timor Sea. Timor Leste's (East Timor's) 5,790 square miles of territory is home to some 1,109,000 people (2008).

When the Dutch took control of most of Indonesia, the Portuguese retained control of the eastern half of Timor and colonial rule continued into the 1970s. After the Portuguese revolution of 1974, the government moved to allow East Timor to determine its own future. The transition was handled poorly, however,

East Timor farm village high in the mountains. (iStockPhoto.com)

TIMOR LESTE

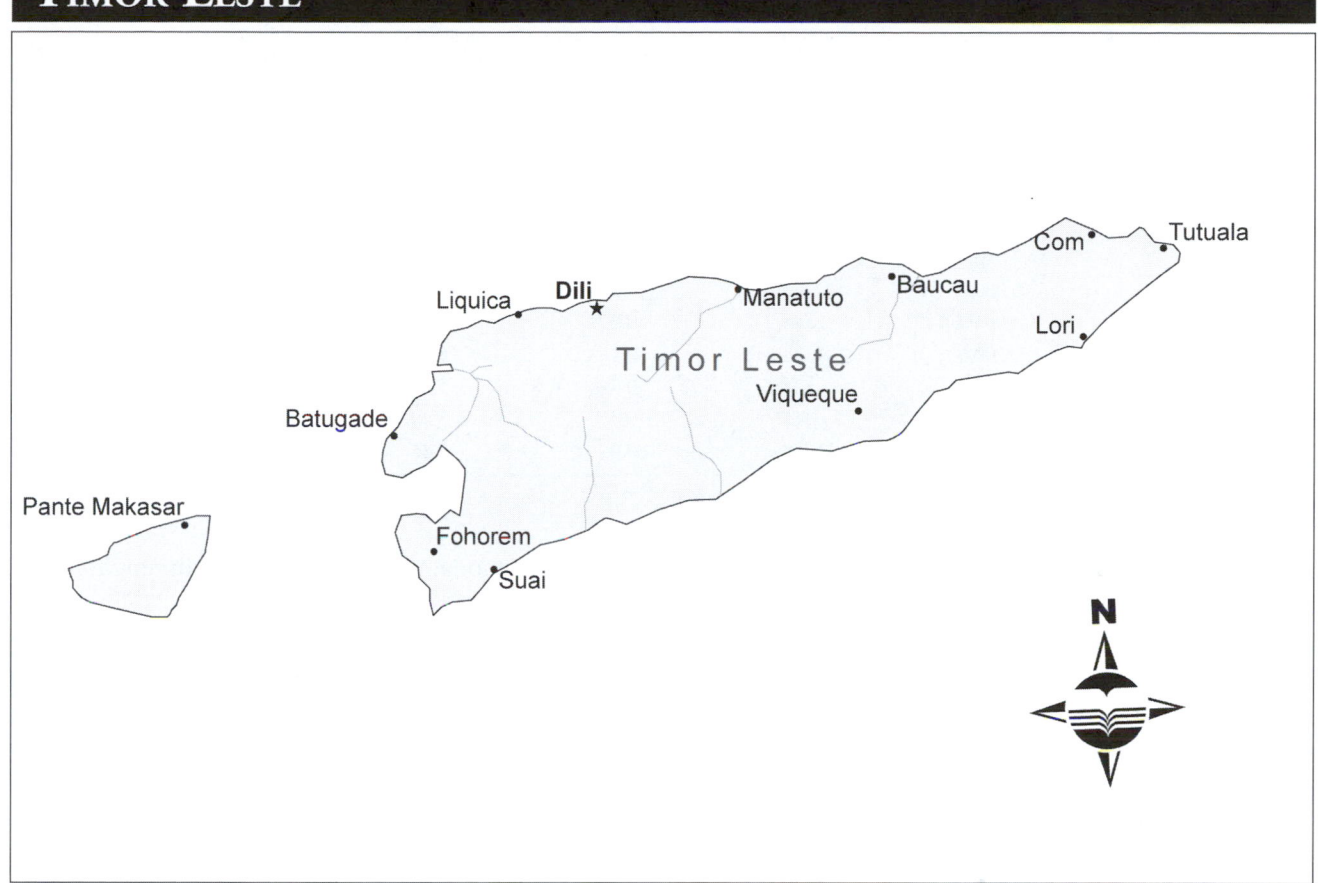

and facing a civil war, the Portuguese administration suddenly abandoned the island in October 1975. One group seeking immediate independence, the Frente Revolucionaria de Timor Leste Independente, or FRETILIN, seized the capital, Dili.

At that point, Indonesia sent troops into Timor Leste, and the civil war reached a climax in December 1975, when a coalition of groups opposed to FRETILIN captured the capital. They formed a provisional government and moved to incorporate the island into Indonesia. The president of Indonesia designated East Timor as an Indonesian province in July 1976. In the meantime, the FRETILIN forces retreated into the mountainous interior and conducted a guerrilla war that continued into the late 1990s. The United Nations called for the Indonesians to withdraw.

Indonesia finally changed its policy on East Timor in 1989. However, the 1990s became a time of increased violence, and it was only with the change of govern-

ments in Indonesia (and the resignation of long-time President Suharto) that a move to respond to East Timor's aspiration for independence occurred. In the meantime, in 1996 the Nobel Peace Prize was awarded to Timorese liberation activists Jose Ramos-Horta (b. 1948) and Catholic bishop Carlos Ximenes. In 1999 the United Nations oversaw a referendum on Indonesia's autonomy proposal. After the great majority voted for independence, the United Nations oversaw the transition and the first elections in 2001. Candidates associated with FRETILIN won the majority of seats in the new legislature.

Timor Leste is home to a vast array of Native peoples, all of whom developed their own particular culture and religion. There are a dozen ethnic groups in East Timor. One important group, the Tetum, contributed their language as a common language in the capital city during the days of Portuguese rule. Tetum subsequently spread throughout East Timor, and today

Timor Leste

Religion	Followers in 1970	Followers in 2010	% of Population	Annual % growth 2000–2010	Followers in 2025	Followers in 2050
Christians	210,000	1,077,000	84.8	5.90	1,776,000	3,134,000
Roman Catholics	207,000	1,035,000	81.4	5.87	1,683,000	2,954,000
Protestants	22,000	53,000	4.2	3.57	104,000	192,000
Ethnoreligionists	384,000	134,000	10.6	2.38	134,000	150,000
Muslims	1,000	47,900	3.8	5.45	80,000	140,000
Agnostics	0	4,900	0.4	5.45	9,000	17,500
Buddhists	6,000	2,400	0.2	5.46	4,000	7,500
Chinese folk	3,000	2,000	0.2	5.45	3,600	7,000
Baha'is	200	1,200	0.1	5.47	2,500	4,000
New religionists	0	600	0.0	5.46	1,000	1,600
Hindus	0	400	0.0	5.40	600	800
Total population	**604,000**	**1,271,000**	**100.0**	**5.45**	**2,011,000**	**3,462,000**

it is spoken by about 60 percent of the residents. Common to many of the groups was the belief in a Lord of the Upper World, various lesser spirits, and, what is very important, ancestral figures. Different religious functionaries (diviners or medicine men) worked to discern the cause of any misfortunes and treated illness (which was believed to be caused by sorcery or the displeasure of spirits). Ancestor worship was focused at the different ceremonies marking the lifecycle. The traditional religions have largely been replaced by Roman Catholicism.

The Roman Catholic Church came to Timor with the Portuguese in 1511. The Dominicans took the lead in evangelizing the people and had an early success when the island's principal ruler was converted in 1561. However, with the coming of the Dutch, the work of the Dominicans was largely disrupted. In 1816 the Oblates of Mary Immaculate reorganized the weakened Catholic community. The work was placed under the Diocese of Macao, but a bishop, the suffragan to Goa, India, was placed in Dili in 1940.

Since the end of World War II, the Catholic Church has made rapid progress in converting most of the island. Membership went from 66,000 in 1956 to more than 700,000 by 1996. It now includes more than 90 percent of the population. It was the case, however, that during the 1980s, Indonesian law required everyone to be aligned with a "monotheistic" religion. Traditional Timorese religions did have legal status, but Catholicism had absorbed various traditional practices and accommodated to traditional indigenous belief systems.

Timor is one of only two Asian countries with a Catholic majority (the other being the Philippines). Much of that growth has been attributed to the church's ability to operate with some degree of independence during the 1980s as the people struggled for independence. The church was attached to Gao rather than aligned with the rest of Indonesian Catholicism, and its bishop took actions that directly opposed Indonesian authority and identified with the people.

Although the country is dominated by Catholicism, there is a small Protestant presence, the Assemblies of God having the largest following. Also, Muslim traders have brought Islam (of the Sunni Shafiite School) to Timor Leste, primarily in the coastal towns. With rapid growth during the years of Indonesian rule, Islam now counts the allegiance of some 3 percent of the population. There are several Baha'i Faith spiritual assemblies and a marginal number of Buddhists of Chinese extraction.

J. Gordon Melton

See also: Assemblies of God; Baha'i Faith; Roman Catholic Church; Shafiite School of Islam.

References

East Timor: A Christian Reflection/Timor Oriental: Une reflecxion Chriéntienne. London: Catholic Institute for International Relations, 1987.

Gunn, Geoffrey C. *East Timor and the UN: The Case for Intervention*. Trenton, NJ: Red Sea Press, 1997.

Smythe, Eric. *The Heaviest Blow: The Catholic Church and the East Timor Issue*. Münster, Germany: Lit Verlag, 2004.

Webb, R. A. F. "The People of the Book: Christians and Muslims in Indonesia: A Brief Survey of Nusa Tenggara Timur." *Indonesia Circle* 35 (1984): 59–69.

Tirumala/Tirupati

Tirupati is a town approximately 85 miles northwest of the Indian city of Chennai (formerly known as Madras) on a plain in the state of Andra Pradesh. Few Westerners have heard of it or of the Tirumala Mountains, though together these places constitute the most frequented pilgrimage site in the world, more frequently visited than Jerusalem, Rome, or Mecca. The mountain range is seen by many as Adishesha, the divine serpent upon which the Hindu deity Vishnu reclines, with its seven peaks making up the serpent's seven heads. Tirupati lies at the foot of the seventh peak, upon which the main temple of the region stands at an elevation of about 2,000 feet.

According to Hindu mythology, Vishnu's mate, Lakshmi, left his side to incarnate on Earth as Princess Padmavati. Vishnu took human form as Venkateshvara and came to Earth to search for her. Her earthly father agreed to allow his daughter to marry Venkateshvara after the god provided proof that he was a man of great wealth.

Today, pilgrims are attracted to three major sites: Sri Venkateshvara's temple on Tirumala, one of the seven peaks; the shrine of Padmavati, located at Tiruchanur about three miles south of Tirupati; and the shrine of Govindaraja in the town of Tirupati. The present Venkateshvara temple dates to the ninth century CE, but it did not emerge as a major center for pilgrimages until the 15th-century Vijayanagara dynasty. The main statue of Sri Venkateshvara (also popularly called Balaji) is believed to have been found at the site (rather than carved by human hands) and the temple later constructed around it. References to the statue date to

the first century CE and an original structure protecting the statue may have been built around that time. In 966 CE, King Saktivitarikata presented a silver image of Venkateshvara to the temple. The sage Ramanuja (1077–1157) visited the site in the 11th century and did much to increase the worship there and build up the town of Tirupati.

The main tower of the temple was built in 1260 CE. The eight-foot statue of Venkateshvara is considered a most sacred object, and it is not known even of what material it is made—stone or wood. Ramanuja is credited with settling the dispute over who the statue actually represents by declaring it an incarnation of Vishnu. He is also believed to have fixed the symbol of Lakshmi to its chest. Since this time the common markings of a Vaishnava ascetic, vertical lines on the nose and forehead, are periodically applied to the statue.

Pilgrims to Tirumala believe that they can attain *mukti* (bliss) by worshipping Sri Venkateshvara. Because of the story of Venkateshvara's search for his mate, the temple is popular with couples about to be married. Worship is primarily done by circumambulation.

Sri Venkateshvara's temple is reportedly now the richest temple in the world. It is the home of a significant collection of rare and precious ornaments and receives many gifts from people who attribute their healing or good fortune to Lord Balaji. Some 331 pounds of pure gold was used to cover the granite canopy over the most holy part of the main temple.

The temple to Venkateshvara is by no means the only noteworthy temple in the area. The Govindaraja temple in Tirupati is dedicated to Krishna, another incarnation of Vishnu. It contains an older shrine to Govindaraja (who is seen in a reclining position) that dates to the ninth century and a new shrine erected by Ramanuja in the 11th. The main temple dedicated to Padmavati is located about three miles from Tirupati at Tiruccanur. Like Venketeshvara, she is shown with four hands, two of which hold lotus flowers and two of which are positioned in *mudras* that depict her granting of favors and her offering of protection to those who come to see her.

The primary annual festival at Tirupati recalls the story of Padmavati's marriage to Venkateshvara. Her statute is removed from the temple in Tiruccanur and carried on an elephant to the main temple on the mountain. As it arrives, Venkateshvara is thought to come out to greet her (his statue not being moved from its permanent resting place).

In 1933 the administrative affairs of the temples in the Tirupati area were turned over to an autonomous body established by the government in Chennai: the Tirumala-Tirupati Devasthanam (TTD) Committee. Meanwhile, since 1965, tens of thousands of South Indians have moved to North America. Here they have built several replicas of the Sri Venkateshvara temple, most notably in Pittsburgh, Pennsylvania; Bridgewater, New Jersey; Cary, North Carolina; Aurora, Illinois; and Agoura, California. There is also a large Sri Venkateshvara temple in Tividale (West Midlands), England.

Constance A. Jones

See also: Jerusalem; Mecca; Rome/Vatican City; Vaishnavism.

References

Chetty, P. M. Muniswamy. *Tirumala-Tirupathi: Sri Venkateswara's Story and Mahatyam.*

Harshananda, Swami. *Hindu Pilgrimage Centres.* Bangalore: Ramakrishna Math, 2005.

Krishna, Nandith. *Balaji, Venkateshwara, Lord of Tirumala-Tirupati—An Introduction.* Mumbai: Vakils Feffer & Simons, 2000.

Rao, Velcheru Narayana, and David Shulman. *God on the Hill: Temple Poems from Tirupati.* New York: Oxford University Press, 2005.

Sitapati, Pidatala. *Sri Venkateswara: The Lord of the Seven Hills—Tirupati.* Mumbai: BVB, 2001.

Smith, H. Daniel, and M. Narsimhachary. *Handbook of Hindu Gods, Goddesses, and Saints.* New Delhi: Sundeep Prakashan, 1997.

Tocoist Church/Church of Our Lord Jesus Christ in the World

In northern Angola, several movements associated with the Kimbanguist Church movements started after the prophet's arrest in 1921. The first significant African Initiated Church began there under the prophet and former Baptist teacher and choirmaster Simbo Toco (1918–1984): the Church of Our Lord Jesus Christ in the World, also known as the "Red Star" after the church's symbol. This movement started in 1949 in the western Congo in a decisive Pentecost of its own, with trembling and speaking in tongues. Toco was arrested by Belgian officials and handed over to the Portuguese government at the Angolan border in 1950, together with 82 Angolan followers. The movement was severely repressed, but it had 10,000 adherents by 1965 and had become multiethnic, thanks to the Portuguese practice of exiling Tocoists to distant provinces. Toco himself was exiled to various parts of Angola and eventually in 1963 to the islands of the Azores, where he worked as a lighthouse keeper until 1974. During the Angolan civil war, Toco, who then lived in Luanda, was in a precarious position because of his origins in an area that supported an antigovernment party.

A leadership struggle in the church followed Toco's death in 1984, and the government did not include the Tocoist Church in its list of 12 recognized churches. The dispute was resolved in 1988 when Luzaisso Antonio Lutango was elected leader of the church and the government lifted its suspension of the church's activities. There were many remarkable similarities between the careers of Simbo Toco and Simon Kimbangu, besides their first names. Like Kimbanguism, the church requires monogamy and forbids pork and alcohol. Tocoist members must wear white in worship, and they are thought to regard Toco as the second member of the Trinity.

The headquarters of the church is in Luanda, Angola.

Allan H. Anderson

See also: African Initiated (Independent) Churches; Kimbanguist Church.

References

Estermann, Carlos. "O tocomsmo como fensmeno religioso." *Garcia de Orta* 13, no. 3 (1965); 325–342.

Grenfell, F. James. "Simbo Toco: An Angolan Prophet." *Journal of Religion in Africa* 28, no. 2 (1998): 210–226.

■ Togo

Modern Togo originated as a small West African country on the Gulf of Guinea sandwiched between the Gold Coast (Ghana) and Dahomey (Benin). It is bordered on the north by Burkina Faso. Its 21,000 square miles of territory is home to its 6,500,000 residents (2007).

The area has been the home of the Ewe, a people related to the Ashanti (of Ghana) and the Ibo and Yoruba (of Nigeria). The Kabye and Mina are also among the more important of the more than a dozen peoples who reside in the country. Through the mid-19th century, the land was a semiautonomous region, ruled by several African chiefs, that became a buffer between the British Gold Coast and French Benin. Then in 1884, at a conference of European powers, Germany asserted its rights to a share in Central Africa. This land was then given to Germany, which named it Togoland. The German commissioner for West Africa, Gustav Nachtigal, signed a treaty with several of the more powerful Togo chiefs.

German control of the area was short lived. During World War I, Britain and France closed the gap between their territories. In 1957 that part of Togo under British control was annexed and merged with the Gold Coast to create modern Ghana. However, the French part remained a separate territory that finally attained independence in 1960. It is that former part of Togo under French control that constitutes the present state. Independence was followed by a period of national unrest that included political assassination and several coups. The 1967 coup brought in Etienne Eyadema, who has remained in power ever since, in spite of periods of strong protest and an abysmal human rights record. He has regularly been re-elected as the leader of the only legal political party.

Traditional African religions remain strong in Togo, claiming the allegiance of as much as half of the population. Among the Ewe, the Supreme Deity is named Mawu. Mawu is feminine, thought of as mother, creator, judge, and law-giver, and temples managed by priests may be found throughout Ewe country, where sacrifices are made to her regularly.

Although the Portuguese had worked the coast of the Gulf of Guinea gathering slaves, and had visited

In Togo, West Africa, the Salinkrang village of the Dagomba tribe maintains this animist fetish to ensure prosperity. (iStockPhoto.com)

the coast of Togo from the 16th into the 19th century, it was not until 1871 that the Roman Catholic Church established its first mission, at Agouyé. A second station was opened in 1886, established by the Society of African Missions, a French order from Lyon. Togo became a prefecture in 1892 and a vicariate in 1924. German Catholic priests were active during the days of German rule, but they were forced to leave in 1918. Priests from the Society of African Missions took their place. The ordination of the first Togo priest signaled the beginning of the indigenization process. The Diocese of Lomé was erected in 1955. The Roman Catholic Church is now the largest Christian body in Togo.

As early as 1847, the North German Missionary Society, which drew much of its support from the Pietist element in the Lutheran churches of northern Germany, sent missionaries into Togo to work among the Ewe people. At the time that the missionaries were

TOGO

expelled in 1918, the mission had been divided, with part in British territory and part in French territory. In 1922 the mission constituted itself as the Evangelical Ewe Church. It developed a congregational polity with a general synod that met triennially. Through the 1920s the United Free Church of Scotland sent in personnel to assist the congregation in British territory, and the Paris Mission did likewise for the remaining congregations. Increasingly, in spite of efforts to prevent it, the church divided. The church in French territory began a theological school in 1929.

In 1955 the United Church of Christ (through its United Church Board of World Ministries) added its support to the church and expanded its work to include the Kabye people in the northern reaches of the country. Then in 1959, the church in French territory became an autonomous body as the Evangelical Church of Togo (Église Evangélique du Togo). The following year, the North German Missionary Society returned, and the Evangelical Church was able to further expand. At the time that Togo became an independent country, the Evangelical Church was already the largest Protes-

Togo

Religion	Followers in 1970	Followers in 2010	% of Population	Annual % growth 2000–2010	Followers in 2025	Followers in 2050
Christians	590,000	3,245,000	45.6	3.26	5,099,000	7,805,000
Roman Catholics	428,000	1,660,000	23.3	2.11	2,737,000	4,080,000
Protestants	66,700	800,000	11.2	4.45	1,322,000	2,195,000
Independents	33,300	155,000	2.2	2.69	250,000	500,000
Ethnoreligionists	1,256,000	2,435,000	34.2	2.37	2,389,000	2,499,000
Muslims	289,000	1,385,000	19.4	3.13	2,342,000	3,600,000
Baha'is	2,100	36,000	0.5	2.92	56,000	80,000
Agnostics	500	16,000	0.2	2.92	30,000	50,000
New religionists	600	3,500	0.0	2.92	5,000	8,000
Atheists	0	1,900	0.0	2.92	4,000	8,000
Total population	**2,138,000**	**7,122,000**	**100.0**	**2.92**	**9,925,000**	**14,050,000**

tant church, and it has remained so. Its present name, the Evangelical Presbyterian Church of Togo, reflects its replacement of the congregational polity it had at its beginning with a presbyterial organization.

As early as 1843, Thomas Birch Freeman, the missionary of the British Methodists (now the Methodist Church in Great Britain), visited Togo. He met with the chief in Anécho and gained his friendship. More important, he gained permission to locate a preaching point and a school in Anécho, from which Methodism was able to begin its spread along the coast communities inhabited by the Mina people. The church has maintained its strength among the Mina people and has been largely unable to transcend that base.

The Assemblies of God, the Pentecostal church from the United States, began work in Togo in 1937 and expanded to the northern part of the country in 1940. In the years after World War II, the church expanded rapidly and soon surpassed the Methodists as the third largest religious group in Togo. Various other American-based Free Churches also came to Togo: the Seventh-day Adventist Church and the Jehovah's Witnesses. However, by far the largest number of churches contributing to the growing pluralistic environment of the country either came from other nearby countries, especially Ghana, or, in a few cases, originated within Togo.

Among the African Initiated Churches founded by Togo believers is Église du Christ, founded by an Ewe pastor in 1962, and the Ordre Sacre de Deliverance (Sacred Order of Deliverance), founded among the Ewe

in 1968. Ghana has contributed a number of groups, such as the Église de la Guerison Divine du Togo (the Divine Healer's Church of Togo), which came to Togo around 1960, and the Sociéte de la Croix Blanche. Nigeria contributed the Church of the Lord, Aladura, and Benin the Heavenly Christianity Church.

Islam of the Sunni Malikite School was introduced into Togo in the 18th century. The first mosque was built in 1820 at Sokodé and found its major support among several of the peoples living in the extreme northern part of the country. In 1973 the Muslims organized the Muslim Union of Togo, which has struggled to block the development of the Sufi brotherhoods and the Ahmadiyya Muslim movement, the Pakistani revivalist movement that opened work in 1960 and that some consider heretical; the Baha'i Faith first appeared in 1955. Muslims now constitute some 15 percent of the population.

J. Gordon Melton

See also: Ahmadiyya Movement in Islam; Assemblies of God; Baha'i Faith; Church of the Lord; Evangelical Church of Togo; Evangelical Presbyterian Church of Togo; Jehovah's Witnesses; Malikite School of Islam; Methodist Church; Paris Mission; Roman Catholic Church; Seventh-day Adventist Church; United Church of Christ; United Free Church of Scotland.

References

Delval, R. *Les musulmans au Togo*. Paris: Publications Orientalistes de France, 1980.

Religeuses au Togo. Lomé, Togo: Archevêché de Lomé, 1991.

Sossah, K. *Panorama sociologique des sects religieuses au Togo: Etude et documents.* Lomé, Togo: Institut National de la Recherche Scientifique, 1976.

■ Tokelau Islands

The Tokelau Islands consist of three South Pacific atolls with a total land area of less than 4 square miles located between Kiribati and Samoa, with a total population of approximately 1,400 people (2008).

The islands have been inhabited for several thousand years by Polynesians who had their first contact with Europeans in 1765. Explorer John Byron found the islands to possess little to interest his government. Only in 1877 did Great Britain move to name the islands a British protectorate. In 1916 they were formally annexed and incorporated in the Gilbert Islands and Ellice Islands colony. Administration was transferred to New Zealand in 1925.

The present name of the islands appeared in 1946, and New Zealand assumed full sovereignty in 1958. However, in the post–World War II decades, the United States also claimed hegemony over the islands, which claim it did not drop until 1980. From 1960 to 1972, New Zealand encouraged immigration of Tokelau Islanders to New Zealand, but in 1972 reversed that policy for one of supporting the retention of cultural life and traditions. Since the 1980s, the United Nations has monitored the ongoing desires of the residents concerning their relationship to New Zealand, but they have continued to enjoy their semiautonomous state. New Zealand has placed its Tokelau Affairs Office on Samoa.

The London Missionary Society, which had been operating in the South Pacific for a half-century, finally sent a missionary to Tokelau in 1861. The early missionaries were extremely aggressive toward the traditional religion, and by the late 20th century it had all but disappeared. Approximately 70 percent of the residents are members of the Congregational Christian Church in Samoa, created in 1962 and based in Western Samoa.

The Roman Catholic Church established work immediately after World War II in 1946. That work was attached to the vicariate headquartered in Samoa in 1955 and eventually grew into the Diocese of Apia (Western Samoa) in 1966 (now the Diocese of Samoa-Apia). It was separated from the diocese as an independent mission in 1992. The only other religious activity in the islands is a small Baha'i Faith community.

J. Gordon Melton

See also: Baha'i Faith; Congregational Christian Church in Samoa; London Missionary Society; Roman Catholic Church.

References

Boardman, D. W. "Religion as a Factor in the Adjustment of Immigrants: Tokelau Island Community in the Wellingston Area." *Social Compass* 26, no. 1 (1979): 73–85.

Hooper, A., and J. Huntsman, trans. *Matagi Tokelau: History and Traditions of Tokelau.* Apia, Western Samoa: Office of Tokelau Affairs, Institute of Pacific Studies, University of the South Pacific, 1991.

Tokelau Islands

Religion	Followers in 1970	Followers in 2010	% of Population	Annual % growth 2000–2010	Followers in 2025	Followers in 2050
Christians	1,500	1,300	93.6	−1.69	1,300	1,200
Protestants	1,000	1,000	71.4	−0.20	980	960
Roman Catholics	400	500	35.7	−0.40	550	530
Marginals	0	20	1.8	0.00	30	80
Baha'is	60	70	5.0	−1.56	100	140
Agnostics	0	20	1.4	14.87	40	60
Total population	**1,600**	**1,400**	**100.0**	**−1.58**	**1,400**	**1,400**

TOKELAU ISLANDS

ATAFU

Atafu ★
Village

*SOUTH PACIFIC
OCEAN*

NUKUNONU

Nukunonu ★
Village

FAKAOFO

Fakaofo ★

N

Thomas, Allan. *New Song and Dance from the Central Pacific: Creating and Performing the Fatele of Tokelau in the Islands and in New Zealand.* Hillsdale, NY: Pendragon Press, 1996.

Turner, George. *Samoa: A Hundred Years Ago and Long Before. Together with Notes on the Cults and Customs of Twenty-three Other Islands in the Pacific.* Chestnut Hill, MA: Adamant Media Corporation, 2005.

■ Tonga

Tonga, whose name means "south," is an island archipelago of 169 islands in the far South Pacific between Fiji and American Samoa. A total of 289 square miles of land are available for its 119,000 residents (2008). The islands are unique in that their local governance was never lost and today the islands retain the only monarchy in the South Pacific.

Tonga was settled more than a millennium ago by Polynesians who arrived from those two island groups. The islanders developed a complex social system headed by the Tui Tonga (ruler), later replaced by local leaders (divided among religious and secular leaders) on the main islands. The Dutch explorer Jakob Lemaire visited Tonga as early as 1616, but it was Captain James Cook who in the 18th century gave them their early name among Westerners, the Friendly Islands.

In the mid-19th century, a civil war broke out. A young leader, Taufa'ahau Tupouin, was victorious and unified the islands under his rule, which lasted until 1893. An admirer of British ways, he called himself George I and introduced a parliamentary system of governance. The British established a protectorate over Tonga in 1890 but did not disturb the local system of government. In 1918 the youthful great granddaughter of George I was crowned Queen Salote. Tonga was never transformed into a colony, and in 1970 it became independent of British oversight under King Taufa'ahau, who continues as head of state.

Missionaries from the London Missionary Society attempted to evangelize Tonga in 1797, but they withdrew after three of their number were killed in 1799. They were succeeded by Australian Methodist Walter Lowery, who arrived in 1822. The work bore little fruit until the mid-1830s, but it suddenly spread rapidly over

Elder Liki from Utah reads religious writings to villagers in Ha'alaufuli Village on April 19, 2007, in the Vava'u island group of Tonga. These visits are part of his two-year proselytizing and missionary work in Tonga for the Church of Jesus Christ of Latter-day Saints. (Getty Images)

TONGA

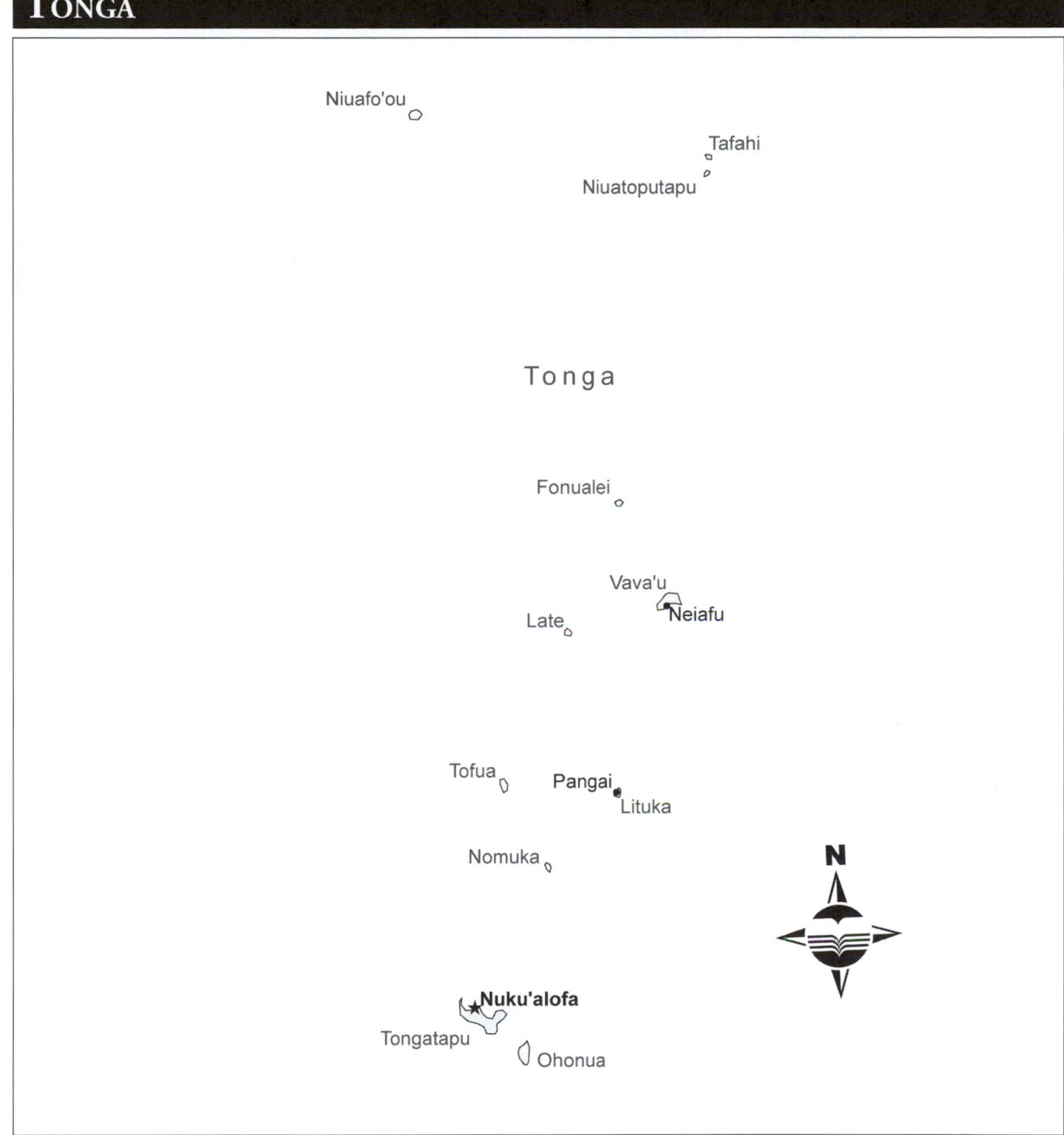

Niuafo'ou

Tafahi
Niuatoputapu

Tonga

Fonualei

Vava'u
Neiafu
Late

Tofua
Pangai
Lituka

Nomuka

N

Nuku'alofa
Tongatapu
Ohonua

the island of Vava'u in 1834 and then spread through the archipelago. King George I, who finally unified the islands, was a Methodist, and in the decade after he established his rule the great majority of the islanders converted. The older Polynesian religion was virtually wiped out.

George I also became the source of the first schism within the Christian community. He developed issues with the Australian Methodists and with the aid of Reverend Shirley W. Baker (1836–1903), a British Methodist and local head of the Australian mission, he established the independent Wesleyan Free Church

Tonga

Religion	Followers in 1970	Followers in 2010	% of Population	Annual % growth 2000–2010	Followers in 2025	Followers in 2050
Christians	97,200	97,400	95.5	0.20	105,000	114,000
Marginals	16,000	55,000	53.9	1.51	58,000	60,000
Protestants	38,700	45,500	44.6	0.24	45,000	45,000
Independents	14,300	21,700	21.3	0.79	25,000	28,000
Baha'is	1,100	3,800	3.8	1.37	6,000	8,000
Agnostics	0	500	0.5	5.46	800	1,000
Buddhists	0	120	0.1	0.17	180	250
Hindus	30	100	0.1	0.20	150	200
Atheists	0	10	0.0	0.00	10	20
Ethnoreligionists	0	10	0.0	0.00	10	20
Total population	**98,300**	**102,000**	**100.0**	**0.26**	**112,000**	**123,000**

and ordered his subjects to join it. The two bodies remained bitter rivals until 1924, when, under a new ruler, a plan of union was worked out. The majority of the Free church, the larger body at this time, united to form the Free Wesleyan Church of Tonga. However, some 6,000 members refused to join the union and continued as the Free Church of Tonga. The Free Church of Tonga has subsequently experienced two schisms, with members leaving in 1929 to form the Church of Tonga and in 1962 to form the Church of the Red Coats. Through these four churches, the Methodists remain the majority church grouping on Tonga, though they declined proportionately as the population has grown and new missionary groups arose in the last half of the 20th century.

The second church to establish itself on Tonga was the Roman Catholic Church. After several unsuccessful attempts, dating back to 1837, to create a mission, Catholic work began in earnest following an 1855 treaty between Tonga and France proclaiming religious freedom as the law of the land. The church grew to the point that a vicariate was erected in 1937 and a diocese in 1976. The first indigenous priest was ordained in 1933. The bishop resides in Nuku'alofa, the capital.

Anglicans arrived fairly late in Tonga (1902) but had little success. Anglican work is part of the Diocese of Polynesia within what is now known as the Anglican Church in Aotearoa, New Zealand, and Polynesia. Somewhat earlier (1895), the Seventh-day Adventist Church began its mission on Tonga, which was formally organized as the Tonga Mission in 1921, a year before the creation of the church's South Pacific Division.

The Assemblies of God entered in the 1930s but did not experience real success until 1966, when they held a Good News Crusade to which hundreds responded. Like the Assemblies of God, the Jehovah's Witnesses arrived in Tonga in the 1930s and experienced a heightened growth in the 1960s, though they have not been as successful in gaining members. More successful than either has been the Church of Jesus Christ of Latter-day Saints, which entered Tonga in 1891. It grew rapidly after World War II, the publication of the Tongan edition of the Book of Mormon in 1946 being a significant factor. Beginning with 2,400 members, by the end of the century the church reported more than 40,000 members in a population of approximately 120,000. It is the second largest religious body on Tonga.

Tonga remains one of the most thoroughly Christianized of the South Pacific countries, which has meant that few newer evangelical churches entered through the last decades of the 20th century, and that the community of people who follow other faiths is small. There is a small Baha'i Faith community, as well as a group of immigrants from India who continue to worship as Hindus.

J. Gordon Melton

See also: Anglican Church in Aotearoa, New Zealand, and Polynesia; Assemblies of God; Baha'i Faith; Church of Jesus Christ of Latter-day Saints;

Jehovah's Witnesses; London Missionary Society; Roman Catholic Church; Seventh-day Adventist Church.

References

Forman, Charles H. *The Island Churches of the South Pacific: Emergence in the Twentieth Century.* Maryknoll, NY: Orbis, 1982.

Harris, D. P. "Missionaries in the Last Kingdom." M.A. thesis, Harvard University, 1989.

Rutherford, Noel. *Shirley Baker and the King of Tonga.* Honolulu: University of Hawaii Press, 1996.

Swain, Tony, and Garry Trompf. *The Religions of Oceania.* London: Routledge, 1995.

Tippett, A. R. *People Movements in Southern Polynesia: Studies in the Dynamics of Church-Planting and Growth in Tahiti, New Zealand, Tonga and Samoa.* Chicago: Moody, 1971.

T'ongdo-sa Temple

T'ongdo-sa, or Pass into Enlightenment, Temple is the largest Buddhist temple in the republic of (South) Korea. Built to house relics of the Buddha, it emerged through the centuries as one of the Three Jewels Temple, each temple emphasizing one of the Buddhist central loyalties to the Buddha, the Dharma and the Shangha. T'ongdo-sa represents the Buddha.

Tongdo-sa dates to 646 CE, during the in the reign of Queen Sondok (r. 634–647), the queen of Silla, one of the two southern Korean kingdoms during the era before the three Korean kingdoms were unified (668). Among her policies, Queen Sondok worked to strengthen Silla's ties to China and one means to doing that was to send monks to study. Among those she sent to China early in her reign was Chajang, a young monk of noble birth and obvious skill. Sondok's father had on several occasions tried to convince him to join his court. Chajang spent a decade in China and before leaving, according to the legends about him, he brought relics of the Buddha he received from the bodhisattva Manjurshi on his return from China.

Chajang initially built a small hermitage on Yongjuk-san Mountain that became his headquarters for the erection of T'ongdo-sa. The completed complex had several unique features. First, the entrance was by a bridge that led one into a forest of pine trees, symbolic of the purification the visitor should be undergoing as he or she steps into sacred space.

The primary structure at the temple was the Main Hall. An aesthetically pleasing building, its ceiling, for example, is decorated with chrysanthemums, but that is not its central feature. The central feature is not what is present so much as what is absent. There is no representation of the Buddha to be seen. Instead of the statue, there is only a window looking out to a bell-shaped stupa, which one reaches by a set of stairs that lead to the platform upon which it rests. The stairs lead to the entrance gate, decorated with dragons, clouds, and two protector guardians. Four protective deities stand at the corners of the platform. The stupa enshrines the relics of the Buddha that Master Chajang brought from China, including Buddha's bones, teeth, 100 relic stones, and a robe. As the stupa houses the relics, there is no need for a mere statue in the Main Hall. The original Main Hall, along with all but one of the more than 100 additional buildings, was destroyed during the Japanese invasion of the peninsula at the end of the 1590s, but it and the Great Hall of Light were quickly rebuilt. They are the two oldest structures at T'ongdo-sa Temple, and have been designated a national treasure by the Korean government.

Among the many buildings now making up T'ongdo-sa are its museum, the memorial shrine to Chajang built in 1727, and the Great Hall of Light, dedicated to Vairocana Buddha, originally built in the 15th century. Vairocana Buddha is usually identified with Dharmakaya, the primordial Buddha, the same Buddha installed in the great Buddha hall at Nara, Japan. Other Buddhas and bodhisattva are honored in the other buildings in the complex.

Today, T'ongdo-sa consists of some 35 buildings and pagodas. Outside the Main Hall, next to the stupa, is a place where the Chogye Order conducts its ordination ceremonies. T'ongdo-sa is located in Yangsan, South Kyongsang Province.

J. Gordon Melton

See also: Chajang; Haein-sa Temple; Korean Buddhism; Songgwangsa.

References

Mohan, Pankaj N. "Wŏn'gwang and Chajang in the Formation of Early Silla Buddhism." In *Religions of Korea in Practice*, edited by Robert Buswell, Jr., 51–64. Princeton, NJ: Princeton University Press, 2007.

T'ongdo-sa: The Temple Without a Buddha Statue." Buddhapia. http://eng.buddhapia.com/_Service/_ContentView/ETC_CONTENT_2.ASP?pk=0000766182&sub_pk=&clss_cd=0002154278&top_menu_cd=0000000750&menu_cd=&menu_code=0000008786. Accessed May 15, 2009.

Toraja Church

The people of the Toraja region of the central highlands of Sulawesi, one of the larger Indonesian islands, resisted incursions into their territory by the Dutch government, Muslims, and Christians. However, in 1906 the Dutch established their authority in the area, and in 1912 the Reformed Church began a mission that in 1913 resulted in the first baptisms. That same year, the Gereformeerde Zendiingsbond, a very conservative Calvinist missionary society based in Holland, assumed responsibility for the mission. The church grew quickly, and through the 1930s a planned development toward independence was put into place. In 1941 the first congregation was declared independent of the mission and called its pastor. There were approximately 15,000 people affiliated with the mission at that point.

The church's plans were interrupted by the Japanese invasion of Indonesia. However, in 1947 an independent Toraja Church with a presbyterian polity was constituted. Then, as Indonesia moved toward independence, an Islamic revolt developed across Sulawesi. Many Muslims opposed the new government and fought a guerrilla war into the 1960s. The revolt forced many Torajans to choose between Christianity and Islam. By the time the revolt had ended, more than 70 percent of the Toraja people had joined the church. The church also founded congregations in other parts of Sulawesi and on Kalimantan and Java, where Torajans had immigrated.

Through the 1970s, the church gave considerable time to rethinking its relationship to the local culture, toward which it had developed a positive stance. One result was a new confession of faith adopted in 1981. In 1988, women were accepted into the ordained ministry. Although retaining a cordial relationship to the founding mission, the church has asserted its independence and joined both the World Alliance of Reformed Churches and the World Council of Churches.

In 2005, the church reported 350,000 members in 891 congregations. It sponsors two hospitals, an orphanage, and a rural training center for female leaders.

Toraja Church (GT)
Jalan Jenderal Ahmad Yani 45
Rantepao—Tana Toraja 91831
Sulawesi Selatan
Indonesia

J. Gordon Melton

See also: World Alliance of Reformed Churches; World Council of Churches.

References

Bauswein, Jean-Jacques, and Lukas Vischner, eds. *The Reformed Family Worldwide: A Survey of Reformed Churches, Theological Schools, and International Organizations*. Grand Rapids, MI: William B. Eerdmans Publishing Company, 1999.

Van Beek, Huibert. *A Handbook of the Churches and Councils: Profiles of Ecumenical Relationships*. Geneva: World Council of Churches, 2006.

Toronto Airport Christian Fellowship

The Toronto Airport Christian Fellowship (TACF) is the church base for a famous Charismatic renewal movement known as the "Toronto Blessing" that began on January 20, 1994. TACF, founded by John and Carol Arnott, a husband-wife team, was originally a part of the California-based Association of Vineyard Churches, founded by John Wimber (1934–1996). TACF separated from the Vineyard in late 1995–early 1996 after serious disagreements over aspects of the renewal connected with the Toronto church.

The Blessing renewal began under the ministry of Randy Clark, a Vineyard pastor from St. Louis, who was holding a revival campaign at the former Toronto Airport Vineyard in early 1994. Clark outlined his own experience of spiritual awakening through the work of evangelist Rodney Howard-Browne, a Pentecostal evangelist from South Africa, who now heads Revival Ministries International in Tampa, Florida. Howard-Browne gained fame through manifestations of "holy laughter" that characterized his revival meetings.

The initial campaign in Toronto continued after Clark returned to St. Louis. The Blessing gained international attention as news spread throughout the Charismatic and Pentecostal Christian world about a supernatural "Holy Ghost" revival in Toronto. By the summer and fall of 1994 thousands were flocking to Toronto for the meetings held six nights every week. *Toronto Life* magazine billed the "Blessing" the top tourist attraction of 1994. Visitors continued to come to Toronto by the thousands from every part of the globe throughout 1995 and early 1996. Since then TACF has given more focus to special conferences and traveling to various countries to export the renewal around the world.

From the outset of the renewal, evangelical Christian critics like Hank Hanegraaff, author of *Counterfeit Revival*, accused TACF leaders of using hypnotism and psychological control to manipulate the crowds into frenzied bouts of laughter, shaking, rolling on the floor, moaning, groaning, crying, and falling down (known as being "slain in the Spirit"). What drew particular concern from Vineyard leader John Wimber were episodes of people acting or sounding like animals during the worship services, though this was not a common occurrence.

In early 1996, TACF formed Partners in Harvest, a nondenominational organization that seeks to unite Charismatic ministries and churches influenced by the revival. There are now more than 100 participating churches from the United States, Canada, and a dozen other countries, including South Africa, Norway, Israel, Brazil, and Australia. There is also a looser affiliation of church groups known as Friends in Harvest who unite in common passion for renewal in the Holy Spirit.

TACF became the target of fresh criticism in 1999 following reports that God was filling people's cavities with real gold during worship services. TACF released a video about the alleged miracles called "Go for the Gold" and their website featured pictures from people who claimed that God had performed dental work on them. Attendance increased as reports circulated about the supernatural claims. The focus on dental miracles diminished after investigation by TACF leaders proved that some of the cases involved routine dental work.

TACF leaders were involved in further controversy in 2008 over the ministry of Todd Bentley, a Pentecostal revivalist from British Columbia, Canada. Bentley had been a visiting speaker at TACF. On April 2, 2008, Bentley started a five-night speaking engagement at Ignited Church in Lakeland, Florida. The campaign was prolonged and by mid-May 10,000 people were attending every night. The revival became known as the "Florida Outpouring" and was featured nightly on God TV. Bentley was interviewed by major print and TV media and he received endorsements from John and Carol Arnott and other Charismatic/Pentecostal leaders.

Bentley was also attacked over his appearance, teachings, and wild behavior and some major Pentecostal leaders, including J. Lee Grady, editor of the prominent *Charisma* magazine, expressed concerns. In August 2008 it was announced that Bentley and his wife were separating and that he was involved with a female staff member. Bentley resigned from the ministry and the revival meetings ended shortly after. He has since remarried, but as of 2009 is receiving spiritual counseling from a colleague.

Apart from the unusual spiritual manifestations, the Toronto Airport Christian Fellowship adopts a doctrinal framework consistent with evangelical Christian norms. The church views God in a Trinitarian perspective and adopts a high view of scripture. TACF continues to have enormous worldwide outreach through its media portal (Revive TV), renewal magazine, international conferences, and school of ministry. The church has been visited by several million people since 1994 and maintains links with some of the most prominent leaders in the Charismatic and Pentecostal world, including televangelist Benny Hinn.

John and Carol Arnott have become well-known figures in the international Charismatic and Pentecostal communities. TACF is now led locally by Steve and Sandra Long, who oversee the main airport site and nine other campuses in greater Toronto.

Toronto Airport Christian Fellowship
272 Attwell Drive
Toronto, ON M9W 6M3
Canada
http://www.tacf.org

James A. Beverley

See also: Charismatic Movement; Pentecostalism.

References

Arnott, John. *The Father's Blessing.* Lake Mary, FL: Creation House, 1995.

Beverley, James A. *Holy Laughter and the Toronto Blessing.* Grand Rapids, MI: Zondervan, 1995.

Hanegraaff, Hank. *Counterfeit Revival.* Dallas, TX: Word, 1997.

Paloma, Margaret. *Main Street Mystics: The Toronto Blessing and Reviving Pentecostalism.* Lanham, MO: Alta Mira Press, 2003.

Traditional Anglican Communion

The Traditional Anglican Communion is an international ecumenical body of conservative churches in the Anglican tradition. In the mid-1970s a significant conservative reaction developed in the Episcopal Church in the United States, occasioned by the ordination of the first female priests and the authorization of a new Prayer Book. Several new jurisdictions were established in the United States that became catalysts for Anglicans in various Anglican churches worldwide to leave those churches in fellowship with the archbishop of Canterbury and to form independent dioceses. In the 1980s such churches emerged in Canada, Australia, New Zealand, and the United Kingdom.

In 1992 the Anglican Catholic Church, the Anglican Catholic Church of Canada, and the Anglican Catholic Church of Australia, including their member dioceses in New Zealand, Hong Kong, and Latin America, formed the Traditional Anglican Communion. Subsequently, the Traditional Anglican Church was formed in England, and it affiliated. As the Communion was being formed, in 1991, the American Episcopal Church merged with the Anglican Catholic Church to form the Anglican Church in America. Some bishops rejected the merger and continue as the Original Province of the Anglican Catholic Church. The bishops of the Original Province had signed the original concordant establishing the Traditional Anglican Communion, but have since withdrawn their support for it. The bishops of the Anglican Church in America continue their support of the Communion.

Additional members included the Church of Ireland (Traditional Rite), the Anglican Church in America, and the Anglican Church of Southern Africa (Traditional Rite), the Anglican Church of India, the Orthodox Church of Pakistan, the Church of Umzi Wase Tiyopiya (South Africa), the Traditional Anglican Church–England, the Church of Torres Strait, the Continuing Anglican Church in Zambia, and the Nippon Kirisuto Sei Ko Kai (Japan). The United Anglican Church was a member for a period but has since withdrawn.

The Traditional Catholic Communion is a minuscule relative to the Church of England and its affiliates, but has assembled a communion of some half million members worldwide. Most of the churches that resulted from the schisms that began in 1976 have chosen not to affiliate with it, but it does represent a growing alternative for those unsettled by the ongoing changes within the larger Anglican world.

In 2002, Archbishop John Hepworth of the Anglican Catholic Church in Australia succeeded Louis Falk as the primate of the Traditional Anglican Communion. Falk, who leads the Anglican Church in America, had been the driving force in the merger of the Anglican Catholic Church and the American Episcopal Church and in the formation of the Traditional Anglican Communion. The Communion formed the International Anglican Fellowship as its missionary arm and charged it with the task of raising money for those churches around the world that were finding it difficult to survive in their effort to maintain traditional faith and worship.

Traditional Anglican Communion
PO Box 746
Blackwood
South Australia 5051
Australia
http://www.acahome.org/

J. Gordon Melton

See also: Church of England; Episcopal Church.

Transcendental Meditation

See Global Country of World Peace.

■ Trinidad and Tobago

The religious plurality of Trinidad and Tobago's 1.3 million people stems from its colonial history and ethnic diversity, making the land a "rainbow nation." During colonial times (1498–1962), the indigenous Arawak population was wiped out by the Spanish. In the late 18th century, French settlers were invited to set up plantations to grow sugar and cocoa. The settlers brought with them Roman Catholicism and slaves from West Africa. The Roman Catholic Church since then has represented Trinidad's religious norm, despite the British takeover in 1802 and the introduction of the Church of England and other Christian denominations later. Anglicans in the Diocese of Trinidad and Tobago were incorporated into the Church of the Province of the West Indies in 1883.

The religious traditions of the West Africans became blended into Catholic African syncretic cults, such as the Shango/Orisha and Spiritual Baptists ("Shouters," with Protestant elements). With the British abolition of slavery in 1834, the need for cheap plantation laborers was fulfilled through indentured workers from India. From 1845 to 1917, more than 140,000 Indians from various regions and religious backgrounds were brought to Trinidad. The diversity of Hindu ritual practices and doctrinal beliefs became standardized during the 19th and early 20th centuries into a homogenized and Brahman (priestly) monopolized "Caribbean Hinduism." The religion aspired to acquire a more respected place in Trinidadian society; thus Hindu folk traditions were purged and marginalized and "official" Hindu worship aligned to Christian patterns. Nevertheless, certain healing practices, evil-eye ceremonies, sorcery, and divination rituals persisted. Interestingly, those practices cut across the generally highly segmented, exclusive, and stratified population of Trinidad and Tobago (the latter having been administratively joined with Trinidad in 1889), that being especially so in the working-class population.

Indians and Africans also brought with them Islamic traditions. Among the Indian segment, Muslims constituted some 12 to 16 percent. As with the African peoples, Indians were subjected to Christian missionary programs, the Presbyterian Church of Canada being most active in attempting to convert the so-called heathen brothers and sisters. Proselytization efforts among Indian Muslims more or less failed. However, among the Indian people, evangelists from

Trinidad and Tobago

Religion	Followers in 1970	Followers in 2010	% of Population	Annual % growth 2000–2010	Followers in 2025	Followers in 2050
Christians	672,000	844,000	62.6	0.23	850,000	786,000
Roman Catholics	363,000	385,000	28.6	−0.06	350,000	275,000
Protestants	119,000	280,000	20.8	1.18	315,000	320,000
Anglicans	150,000	80,000	5.9	−1.14	80,000	70,000
Hindus	220,000	328,000	24.3	0.66	340,000	320,000
Muslims	60,200	97,000	7.2	0.35	104,000	100,000
Agnostics	1,000	31,000	2.3	0.58	50,000	60,000
Spiritists	4,000	19,500	1.4	0.35	21,000	20,000
Baha'is	6,000	16,200	1.2	0.35	22,000	25,000
Chinese folk	4,000	5,200	0.4	0.35	5,200	4,800
Buddhists	2,000	4,100	0.3	0.35	5,000	6,000
New religionists	1,000	1,800	0.1	0.35	2,000	2,000
Jews	300	640	0.0	0.33	700	700
Atheists	0	570	0.0	0.36	700	800
Total population	**971,000**	**1,348,000**	**100.0**	**0.35**	**1,401,000**	**1,325,000**

TRINIDAD AND TOBAGO

Trinidad and Tobago

Charlotteville
Tobago
Roxborough
Plymouth   Moriah
Scarborough
Canaan

Toco
Maracas
Maraval
Saint Joseph
Port-of-Spain   Arima
Arouca
Guaico
Sangre Grande
Chaguanas Trinidad
Tabaquite
San Fernando   Tableland   Rio Claro
Brighton La Brea   Princes Town   Pierreville
Debe
Point Fortin   Penal   Guayaguayare
Siparia   Basse Terre
Fullarton   Moruga
San Francique

N

the Presbyterian Church in Trinidad, and later the Roman Catholic Church, the Anglicans, the Seventh-day Adventist Church, and, most recently, several Pentecostal churches, count some 22.2 percent as members. Thus Hindu and Muslim traditions remain the religious backbone of Trinidad and Tobago's Indian population.

Afro-Trinidadians and Indo-Trinidadians, each with about 40 percent of the population, form the two largest segments. The 2000 census specifies that some 50 percent of Trinidad and Tobago's population regarded themselves as belonging to one of the Christian denominations (having lost since 1990 significantly), whereas 22.5 percent were Hindu, 10 percent were Jewish, 5.8 percent were Muslim, and 5.4 Spiritual or Shouter Baptists (traditional Caribbean with African roots). Among the Christian traditions, Roman Catholicism remained strongest, with 26 percent, followed by Anglicanism (7.8 percent), rapidly growing Pentecostal (6.8 percent), Seventh-day Adventism (4 percent), and Presbyterianism (3.3 percent). Many of the older Christian churches are members of the Christian Council of Trinidad and Tobago, which is in turn affiliated with the World Council of Churches. A strong inroad at the expense of Anglicanism and Roman Catholicism has been made by evangelical and Pentecostal groups since the 1970s. Although the public domain had long been dominated by Christian traditions, since the 1990s a more balanced representation of non-Christian faiths has come to the fore.

Martin Baumann

See also: Church in the Province of the West Indies; Church of England; Presbyterian Church in Canada; Presbyterian Church in Trinidad; Seventh-day Adventist Church; Spiritual Baptists; World Council of Churches.

References

Brereton, Bridget. *A History of Modern Trinidad 1783–1962.* Port of Spain, Trinidad: Heinemann, 1981.

Henry, Frances. *Reclaiming African Religions in Trinidad: The Socio-Political Legitimation of the Orisha and Spiritual Baptist Faiths.* University Press of the West Indies, 2003.

Houk, James T. *Spirits, Blood, and Drums: The Orisha Religion in Trinidad.* Philadelphia: Temple University Press, 1995.

Maynard, G. O. *A History of the Moravian Church: Eastern West Indies Province.* Port of Spain, Trinidad: Yuille's Printerie, 1968.

Simpson, G. E. *Religious Cults of the Caribbean.* 3rd ed. Rio Pedras, Puerto Rico: Institute of Caribbean Studies, University of Puerto Rico, 1980.

Vertovec, Steven. *Hindu Trinidad.* London: Macmillan, 1992.

Yelvington, Kevin A., ed. *Trinidad Ethnicity.* London: Macmillan, 1993.

Trinidad and Tobago, Hinduism in

The Hindu population in Trinidad and Tobago is significant for being the largest community of Hindus in the Caribbean region. They support more than 200 temples on an island about the size of the state of Delaware in the United States. Like other communities of South Asian origin in the region, they have drawn largely on northern Indian ritual traditions to form their contemporary, Caribbean Hindu practice of this ancient faith system.

Indians from South Asia, often in the Caribbean referred to as East Indians, migrated to Trinidad as indentured labor for cane and cacao estates between 1845 and 1917. What began as a system to meet an acute labor shortage in the wake of slave emancipation was maintained as a system that depressed local wages, thus dramatically increasing the total number of immigrants (more than 145,000). The vast majority of laborers were Hindu (87 percent) and came from the middle Gangetic Plain, although a relatively small number were recruited from the Madras Presidency. Despite the hardships and difficulties they found in Trinidad, many Indians remained, and, according to the 2000 census, they now compose 40 percent of the total population. Indians of the Hindu faith currently represent 56 percent of the Indian population and 23 percent of the total population—or approximately a quarter of a million adherents. The majority of migrants were lower caste, although those reputed to have "soft hands" (that is, Brahmins) also migrated in substantial numbers.

Hindu immigrants carried with them religious practices, many of which have been synthesized and transformed by the migration experience and socio-cultural milieu of colonial Trinidad. Caste distinctions have become muted, though not fully ignored in Trinidad today. Also, the majority of Hindus subscribe to their own ritual orthodoxy (that is essentially, but not exclusively, a Vaishnavaite, Puranic, *bhakti*, and congregational-centered amalgam of practices) as defined by the Sanatan Dharma Maha Sabha—the strongest Hindu

Children from Hindu schools throughout Trinidad take part in the Sanatan Dharma Maha Sabha 24th annual children's *phagwa* celebration at the Tunapuna Hindu School on March 7, 2004. *Phagwa* is the festival that signifies the beginning of spring on the Hindu calendar. (AP/Wide World Photos)

organization on the island. In addition, adherents of the Divine Life Society, the Sahya Sai Baba Movement, Vishwanath Parishad, Arya Samaj, and others can be found. One of the clearest examples of a Trinidadian Hindu culture can be seen in their temple architecture.

Hindu temple architecture in Trinidad has its clearest roots in the small priest-owned temples of the central Gangetic Plain during the middle of the 19th century. Essentially, Hindu migrants first depended on holy books, plants, and small statues of the deities (*murtis*) that they brought with them. Since folk deities are generally propitiated under trees throughout India, it is safe to assume that Hindus in Trinidad also continued that practice from the earliest time. Eventually, home shrines gave way to specially constructed traditional-style temples in the house yard or garden. The earliest known temples in Trinidad were erected by the 1860s and were mainly of bamboo wattle and daub construction with a thatch roof. By the 1880s more substantial structures were established in "clay

brick" and stone. These traditional temples can still be found in Trinidad's landscape and are relatively small (about 100 square feet) with a pyramidal or rounded dome (*sikhara*) enshrining the deities.

During the 1920s a new type of temple was introduced called the *koutia*. This is derived from a Bhojpuri Hindi term (*kutia*) that indicates a hut or simple hermitage. The architectural form derives from the Bhojpur region (central Gangetic Plain) of India, where the koutia's significance lies in housing the person who takes care of the temple (*pujari*). In Trinidad, the koutia took on the function of an assembly hall (*mandapa*) when it was added to a traditional temple. Throughout the 1920s and 1930s itinerant swamis (invited from India) traveled from village to village. The koutia was ostensibly built to house them temporarily and as a meeting place in which to sing *bhajans* or read scripture after they left. Villages without a temple also built koutias to attract a swami's visit. Afterward, villagers could use the koutia as a temple with the simple installation of a deity's image. Eventually it became a temple in and of itself, though it is difficult to determine exactly when and where this first took place. Koutias are rectangular, rather than square, and have a flat, shed roof or low-angled gable roof. They rarely have sikharas, except in a few cases in which a dome was added to the front porch of the structure for decorative purposes. By this time, many different deities (primarily Sanskritic) might be installed in the same temple, thus making it possible to worship Mahadeva and Krishna in the same place. In this way, villagers need not travel to different locations to worship a specific deity.

The koutia temple evolved into the Trinidadian temple by the 1950s. The addition of a dome where the deities were enshrined successfully merged the traditional form with the koutia. Thus, the Trinidadian form is also rectangular, with a raised platform and dome at one end, and the rest of the structure extending away from it with space to seat several hundred people in the larger versions. Trinidadian temples always have a sikhara and an assembly hall attached to the domed area. Today it is common to see Trinidadian temples, Koutia temples, and traditional temples with or without a koutia attached. Often on Sundays a community-based ritual called *satsang* is held. *Puja* is performed, scripture is read and interpreted, and bhajans are sung by the group. In addition, yearly events called *yagnas* are held. This is a seven- to nine-day affair sponsored by a family or a village. In all cases, whether through temple architecture or congregational ritual, a very strong sense of Trinidadian Hindu identity is created and maintained.

Carolyn V. Prorok and J. Gordon Melton

See also: Arya Samaj; Divine Life Society; Sathya Sai Baba Movement; Vaishnavism.

References

Khan, A. *Callaloo Nation: Metaphors of Race and Religious Identity among South Asians in Trinidad.* Durham, NC: Duke University Press, 2004.

Laurence, K. O. *A Question of Labour: Indentured Immigration into Trinidad and British Guiana, 1875–1917.* London: James Currey, 1994.

Prorok, C. V. "Evolution of the Hindu Temple in Trinidad." *Caribbean Geography* 3, no. 3 (1991): 73–93.

Prorok, C. V. "Hindu Temples in Trinidad: A Cultural Geography of Religious Structures and Ethnic Identity." Ph.D. diss., Louisiana State University, 1988.

Vertovec, S. *Hindu Trinidad: Religion, Ethnicity and Socio-Economic Change.* London: Macmillan Caribbean, 1992.

True (Old Calendar) Orthodox Church of Greece

The True Orthodox Church of Greece was organized as a reaction to the adoption in 1924 of the New or Gregorian calendar by the Orthodox Church of Greece. In spite of pockets of opposition to the change, no priest rejected it until an extraordinary event, the appearance of a cross in the sky on September 14–15, 1925, the day celebrated as the Feast of the Elevation of the Holy Cross according to the Old, or Julian, calendar. As a result of that event, two priests announced their adherence to the Old calendar. However, it was the monks from Mount Athos who provided the strongest opposition to the New calendar and who took the

lead in founding Old calendar churches. By 1934 there were some 800 such churches, in all parts of Greece.

As of the mid-1930s, no bishop had appeared in support of the Old Calendarists, but in 1935 three bishops left the Church of Greece and adhered to what had become known as the True Orthodox Church of Greece. They immediately consecrated four additional bishops, though two of the three original bishops then returned to the state church. Metropolitan Chrysostomos of Florina emerged as the leader of the True Church.

In 1937, Metropolitan Chrysostomos made a statement that while the state church had erred in adopting the New calendar, it had not lost the supernatural presence of God, and its sacraments were still valid. His statements were rejected by two of his bishops, both of whom formed separate factions, though most of their supporters returned to Chrysostomos's jurisdiction by 1950. At the same time, however, the state church launched a systematic, repressive effort that included an attack upon Old calendar priests, who were deprived of their clerical clothing and often beaten and shaved. Chrysostomos was sent into exile for a year in 1951. Released in 1952, he now was the only bishop left, and he died in 1955 without an episcopal successor. Orders for a new bishop were finally obtained in 1960 from the Russian Orthodox Church Outside of Russia.

Archbishop Akakios headed the church from 1960 until his death in 1963. He was succeeded by Archbishop Auxentios. New controversy developed in 1974, when Archbishop Auxentios suggested, contrary to Metropolitan Chrysostomos, that the state church's sacraments were without grace. In response, two of the bishops adhering to Chrysostomos's more favorable moderate view consecrated a set of new bishops. Those who accepted Auxentios's position also consecrated more bishops, and two separate synods came into existence. Each synod itself split into two factions, leaving the Old calendar movement divided into at least five factions (including the group that had originally separated from Metropolitan Chrysostomos in the 1930s). Two of these factions merged, leaving the four factions (each with its separate synod) that exist today.

Three of the factions believe that grace has been removed from the sacraments of the state-supported

Orthodox Church of Greece. Of those, the largest is led by Metropolitan Chrysostomos II. The moderate faction, which believed that the state church retained grace in its sacraments, eventually looked to Metropolitan Cyprian of Oropos and Fili as its leader. That branch of the Old calendar movement has been able to garner the support of the Old Rite Orthodox Church of Romania and the Old Calendar Church in Bulgaria. This faction is second in size to that led by Metropolitan Chrysostomos II, and in 1994 it entered into full communion with the Russian Orthodox Church Outside of Russia. This branch is now known as the Old Calendar Orthodox Church of Greece, Holy Synod in Resistance. It has the largest American following of the several branches, its American diocese being based in the St. Gregory Palamas monastery in Etna, California.

In spite of the existence of the various factions, the members and clergy of the True Orthodox Church consider themselves as one body united by their disagreement with the stance of the Church of Greece regarding the calendar, and by their general opposition to the participation of the state church in various ecumenical endeavors. They claim some 200,000 adherents, about 120 parishes, and a number of monastic communities. Their churches have no electric lights or pews. Associated parishes are found in Australia and Canada. Each of the four factions also has congregations as well as a diocesan structure based in the United States.

Old Calendar Orthodox Church of Greece, Holy
    Synod in Resistance
c/o Holy Monastery of St. Cyprian
PO Box 46006
133 10 Ano Liosia
Greece

J. Gordon Melton

See also: Old Rite Romanian Orthodox Church; Orthodox Church of Greece; Russian Orthodox Church Outside of Russia.

References

Chrysostomos, Archimandrite, with Hieromonk Ambrosios and Hieromonk Auxentios. *The Old Calendar Church of Greece.* Etna, CA: Center for Traditionalist Orthodox Studies, 1986.

Cyprian of Oropos and Fili, Metropolitan. *The Heresy of Ecumenism and the Patristic Stand of the Orthodox.* Etna, CA: Center for Traditional Orthodox Studies, 1998. http://www.synodin resistance.org/Publications_en/EBookB-4.pdf.

True Buddha School

The True Buddha School is a Vajrayana Buddhist organization founded by Master Sheng-Yen Lu (b. 1945), who was born and raised in Taiwan. As a young man he attended the military college and after graduating spent 10 years in the Taiwanese army as an officer. Just as he was beginning his army career, he had a spiritual awakening at a Daoist temple that led to his being able to travel into spiritual worlds, receive messages from the host of both Daoist and Buddhist deities, especially Guan Yin, and become psychically aware. Along with his work in the army, he became an avid student of religion.

Through the years of his army career, he had numerous spiritual encounters that, along with his studies, led to his becoming an Enlightened Master. He also founded a Daoist temple in 1975 and began to build a following. Many who found their way to him did so from his many popular books (some 200 titles by 2008). Lu also found himself on a spiritual pilgrimage that took him from Daoism to Pure Land Buddhism to Vajrayana Buddhism. He would eventually inherit a Gelugpa Tibetan Buddhist lineage that passed through the Venerable Gon Zhu, a Mongolian lama who became the first Vajrayana teacher to settle in Taiwan. After completing his army service, Lu began for the first time to allow his followers to formally take refuge in the Buddha, Dharma, and Sangha through him. Today, the True Buddha School offers standard Tibetan Buddhist teachings but also continues some of Daoist and Pure Land teachings and practice reflective of Lu's early spiritual pilgrimage.

In 1982, Lu moved to Washington state, in the United States, and built a large temple in suburban Seattle. Two years later he was able to announce his enlightenment and he formally reorganized his following as the True Buddha School. Within a short time he had named the first masters (teachers) and chartered the first chapters. His followers consider him a Living Buddha: an emanation of the White Padmakumara (later revealed to be Amitabha Buddha). Master Sheng-Yen had traveled spiritually to the Pure Land, where he realized that he is an emanation of Padmakumara incarnated in the present as a human being in order to assist the liberation of sentient beings.

The True Buddha School teaches a form of Gelugpa Buddhism that begins for members in their taking refuge in the Three Gems of Buddhism—the Buddha, the Dharma, and the Sangha (that is, Buddha, Truth, and Fellowship)—and additionally in the guru, their teacher. Members are taught a form of Buddhist practice that includes a daily cultivation through the recitation of Buddhist sutras, the calling upon the name of Amitabha Buddha (as in Pure Land Buddhism), and visualization of their receiving empowerment from the pantheon of Buddhist deities. This practice is believed to lead individuals to Buddhahood (enlightenment).

Those seeking to follow the Dharma are advised to seek initiation from a true guru (Master Sheng-Yen). To take refuge in the Living Buddha and become a student of the True Buddha School, one may come to the school's headquarters, now located in the state of Washington in the United States, and receive direct Initiation Empowerment, or one can, on the 1st or 15th of any lunar month, at 7:00 a.m., recite the Fourfold Refuge Mantra ("Namo Guru bei, namo Buddha ye, namo Dharma ye, namo Sangha ye") while prostrating oneself. On those same days each month, Master Sheng-Yen Lu performs a ceremony of "Remote Initiation Empowerment." One may also go to a True Buddha School center and receive initiation. Those who receive initiation are instructed in the daily practice that is expected of a True Buddha School member.

The True Buddha School has become a global institution with more than 300 local chapters and some 30 major temples in more than 20 countries, from Japan to Australia, Brazil, and the United Kingdom, most found in Southeast Asia—Taiwan, Malaysia, and Indonesia. In Indonesia, the movement has made contact with a number of villages in central Java that have practiced Vajrayana Buddhism for many centuries. Leadership is vested in a hierarchy of monks and nuns and volunteer workers. Heading the leadership are the masters, most of whom (all but a few named in the early years of the movement) are monks or nuns.

Temples are locally owned, and they and the many chapters associate with the larger movement by recognizing Grand Master Lu as their guru. International coordination is provided by the True Buddha Foundation, which is headed by a board of masters elected by their peers. Twice annually in the spring and fall, large international gatherings are held at the main temple in suburban Seattle.

The True Buddha School is one of a half dozen new Buddhist groups to emerge in Taiwan in the last generation, but is unique in adopting a Vajrayana perspective—a fact that has set it in opposition to some of the Taiwanese-based Chan and Pure Land organizations. Some five million people have taken refuge in Grand Master Lu, though only a minority of those have gone on to become active members of the school and attendees at one of its centers.

True Buddha School
17012 NE 40th Ct.
Redmond, WA 98052
http://www.tbsn.org/

J. Gordon Melton

See also: Enlightenment; Pure Land Buddhism; Tantrism; Tibetan Buddhism.

References

Lu Sheng-Yen. *A Complete and Detailed Exposition on the True Buddha Tantric Dharma*. Trans. by Janny Chow. Union City, CA: Purple Lotus Society of USA, 1996.

Lu Sheng-Yen. *The Inner World of the Lake*. Trans. by Janny Chow. San Bruno, CA: Amitabha, 1992.

Lu Sheng-Yen. *Introduction to True Buddha School*. 2d ed. Trans. by Yuan Zheng Tang. Singapore: Yuan Zheng Tang, 1993.

Lu Sheng-Yen. *An Overview of the Buddhadharma*. Trans. by Janny Chow. Union City, CA: Purple Lotus Society of USA, 1996.

Melton, J. Gordon. The Affirmation of Charismatic Authority: The Case of the True Buddha School." *The Australian Religious Studies Review* 20, no. 3 (Summer, 2007): 286–302.

Tam Wai-lun. "Integration of the Magical and Cultivational Discourses: A Study of the New Religious Movement Called the True Buddha School." *Monumenta Serica* 49 (2001): 141–169.

Tam Wai-lun. "Re-examining the True Buddha School: A 'New Religion' or a New 'Buddhist Movement'?" *Australian Religion Studies Journal* 20, no. 3 (Summer 2007): 303–316.

True Jesus Church

The True Jesus Church was an early product of the introduction of Pentecostalism into China. Among the pioneers was Alfred Goodrich Garr, Jr. (1874–1944), and his wife, Lillian Anderson Garr, who had received the baptism of the Holy Spirit in Los Angeles in 1906 and soon afterward left for China believing that Lillian spoke Chinese when speaking in tongues. They arrived in Hong Kong in October 1907 and were soon disappointed to discover that Lillian could not speak a word of Chinese. The disconfirmation of his wife's xenoglossia led Garr to conclude that tongues speaking was primarily (if not exclusively) for self-edification, an idea he left behind in China when the couple soon returned to the United States. Pentecostalism subsequently spread from Hong Kong to other Chinese cities.

Among the first people to find their way to the early community of Pentecostals in Shanghai was Lin-Shen Chang (b. 1863), a Presbyterian deacon, who in 1909 began a quest for the baptism of the Holy Spirit. After associating with the fledgling Pentecostal community for several weeks, he returned to his hometown, Tienjin, where on December 21, 1909, he was baptized with the Holy Spirit and spoke in tongues. At about this same time, he reported that God had also revealed to him the importance of observing the seventh-day Sabbath.

Several years later, Paul Wei (aka Wei Enbo, d. 1919), an adherent of the mission begun by the London Missionary Society (British Congregationalists) in Beijing, became seriously ill and found his health through the prayer and the laying on of hands at the local Pentecostal fellowship. Subsequently, like Chang, while praying at his home, he also received the baptism of the Holy Spirit and spoke in tongues. The experience led him to found a house church. At a later date, while engaged in a period of fasting, Wei received an additional revelation about water baptism—it should be in the name of Jesus Christ, "head bowed in the living water." After his revelation, Wei began preaching services under the name International Reformed Jesus True Church. In 1917, the name was shortened to simply True Jesus Church.

In 1918 Lin-Shen Chang (b. 1863) made his way to the True Jesus Church, where he met and convinced Wei that the church should observe the seventh-day Sabbath. Wei, Chang, and another early co-worker, Barnabas Chang (or Zhang Banaba, 1882–ca. 1960), founded the True Jesus Church. Barnabas Chang had been converted by Lin-Shen Chang in 1912 and later ordained by Paul Wei in 1919. Paul Wei died in 1919, only a year after the True Jesus Church was constituted, and Barnabas Chang defected from the movement in 1929 and created a rival organization in Hong Kong.

The True Jesus Church emerged as a unique body within the larger Pentecostal movement—Sabbatarian and non-Trinitarian. But as the church developed, other unique elements were incorporated into its life. Like most Protestant groups, it accepted the two ordinances of baptism and the Lord's Supper, but also included the third ordinance of foot washing. It also taught that the act of baptism, done in response to God's command, cleanses the believer of his or her sin, a position known as baptismal regeneration, which is still taught in some Baptist and Restoration church groups. The truth of the regenerating power of baptism was confirmed to the True Jesus Church leaders by the many accounts of healing miracles that occurred to people as they were baptized.

The proper mode of baptism is full immersion while the believer's head is bowed. The True Jesus Church makes room for infant baptism, citing as biblical justification the Hebrew practice of circumcision on the eighth day after birth (baptism taking the place of circumcision for Christians) and Jesus welcoming the children (Matthew 13). Communion is closed, and only those who have been baptized can receive the Lord's Supper, or holy Communion.

Congregation of the True Jesus Church, East Malaysia. (J. Gordon Melton)

The True Jesus Church practice of speaking in tongues is unique within the larger Pentecostal movement. In most Pentecostal churches, only one person will speak in tongues at any one time, and only a few people will speak in tongues during any given worship service. In stark contrast, in the True Jesus Church, speaking in tongues usually occurs as a group act, with all engaging in prayer at the same time (as long as 15 to 20 minutes or more). To the True Jesus Church, prayer in tongues is directed to God and does not need interpretation. Since, following Garr's lead, the primary function of tongues is self-edification, and no interpretation follows, there is no need to limit those who speak.

The True Jesus Church message spread rapidly. From the Chinese mainland the movement found its way to Taiwan (1927), throughout Southeast Asia (1927), and to Hawaii (1930). Headquarters of the church moved first to Nanjing (1926), and then to Shanghai (1927).

The True Jesus Church was one of the largest Christian denominations in China at the time of the Chinese Revolution and the establishment of the People's Republic of China in 1949. In the 1950s, communication between members inside and outside of China became difficult and the church was suppressed during the Cultural Revolution. In the 1980s, it began to make a comeback, as a fellowship within the Chinese Protestant Three-Self Patriotic Movement (the main Protestant church body within China). Today it reports an estimated one million adherents.

Members outside of China established headquarters in Taiwan and continued to operate throughout the

Chinese diaspora. Gradually, the leadership accepted the fact that it might be some time before contact was reestablished with their brothers and sisters within China. In 1975, delegates to the church's World Conference in Taiwan created the International Assembly of the True Jesus Church. In 1985 leaders relocated the principal office of the International Assembly to Los Angeles, California. Subsequently, four evangelical centers have been established for America, Europe, Northeast Asia, and Southeast Asia.

The True Jesus Church sees itself as the restored Apostolic Church of the End Time that has received the divine revelation of Truth through the Holy Spirit. That Truth has been confirmed through various signs and miracles. The name is also assigned spiritual meaning: God is "True" (John 3:33, 17:3; 1 Thessalonians 1:9) and "Jesus" designated himself the "Truth" (John 14:6), or the "true Vine" (John 15:1). The author of the Gospel of John called him the "true Light" (John 1:9). God called and established the "Church" (Acts 15:14–18). It is believed that the church should bear God's name—that is "Jesus" (Matthew 1:21; John 17:11, 26). The True Jesus Church thus exalts the name of God and considers itself the Christ.

The church's doctrinal position is quite similar to the non-Trinitarian, Apostolic, or "Jesus Only" perspective. It teaches that the reception of the Holy Spirit is necessary for entering the kingdom of God, and that speaking in tongues is the sign of that reception.

In 2008 the church reported 1.5 million members residing in 48 countries, the majority of those being in China. The church had 23 congregations in the United States and 5 in Canada.

True Jesus Church
314 S. Brookhurst St., #104
Anaheim, CA 92804
http://www.tjc.org

J. Gordon Melton

See also: Chinese Protestant Three-Self Patriotic Movement/China Christian Council; London Missionary Society; Pentecostalism; Sabbatarianism.

References

The Five Biblical Doctrines. Garden Grove, CA: Words of Life Publishing House, 1995.

Liu, Garland. "The Role of the True Jesus Church in the Communal Development of the Chinese People in Elgin, Scotland." In *The Last Half Century of Chinese Overseas*, edited by Elizabeth Sinn, 425–446. Aberdeen, Hong Kong: Hong Kong University Press, 1998.

Return to the True Church. Garden Grove, CA: Words of Life Publishing House, 1995.

Rubenstein, Murray. "Evangelical Spring: The Origin of the True Jesus Church on Taiwan, 1925–1926." *Society for Pentecostal Studies Annual Papers* (1986).

Speaking in Tongues: A Biblical Perspective. Garden Grove, CA: Words of Life Publishing House, 1996.

Yang, John. *Essential Biblical Doctrine*. Garden Grove, CA: Word of Life Publishing House, 1997.

Tsong Khapa

1357–1419

Tsong Khapa was a reformer credited with revitalizing the philosophical, ritual, and meditative practice of Buddhism and recognized as the founder of the Gelugpa School of Tibetan Buddhism. The Gelugpa School is the dominant school in Tibetan Buddhism and the one to which the Dalai Lama belongs. Tsong Khapa, however, is recognized by all schools and sects of Tibetan Buddhism as one of the foremost exemplars in their shared history. He is known to devotees as "Je Rinpoche" (Precious Master), and is regarded as an enlightened being.

Tsong Khapa was born in the Amdo Province of eastern Tibet in 1357, but according to his traditional spiritual biography, his life story begins long before his birth. According to his hagiography, in a previous life, Tsong Khapa lived in the time of Gautama Buddha (563–483 BCE), the founder of Buddhism. As a boy, he offered a crystal rosary to the Buddha, who gave him a conch shell in return and prophesied that in a future life he would be a great teacher born in Tibet named Losang Drakpa—the name given to Tsong Khapa when he took his novice monastic vows at seven years of age. Further, it was reported that Tsong Khapa's birth was heralded by the auspicious dreams of his mother and father. Followers acknowledge him as the emanation of two divine personages, the Bodhisattvas of Compassion and Wisdom—Avalokitesvara (aka Guan Yin) and Manjusri.

As a young monk, Tsong Khapa assumed a broad approach to Buddhism and studied under the best teachers of his day from the several different lineages. He was ordained as a child by the fourth Karmapa of the Karma Kagyu School and his main teacher was the master, Rendawa, of the Sakya School. In the end, his own study and mature understanding led him to establish a new school of Buddhism in Tibet, the Gelug, which means "System of Virtue." He established the center of his reformed movement at Ganden Monastery near Lhasa. Ganden is the Tibetan name for the heavenly realm in which Maitreya (the Buddha of the future) resides as he waits for the right moment to take birth.

Tsong Khapa rose to prominence in his day because of his profound understanding of Buddhist teachings, his skill in debate, and his accomplishments in meditation practice. He completed a number of long retreats lasting for four and five years at a time. On one such retreat he is said to have prepared himself by doing three and a half million prostrations. The stone floor with grooves worn into it where he performed the prostrations has survived to the present and still inspires Gelugpa followers as they undertake their practice. Of Tsong Khapa's writings, the most important are *The Golden Rosary of the Good Explanations*, a commentary on the Perfection of Wisdom sutras; *The Great Exposition of Secret Mantra (Ngakrim Chenmo)*; and the work that forms the foundation practice of the Gelugpa School, *The Great Exposition of the Stages of the Path (Lamrim Chenmo)*. Tsong Khapa focused his reformation on the restoration of pure monastic discipline and the reconciliation of the Tantric practices, which includes esoteric sexual practices, with monastic vows.

Four great deeds mark Tsong Khapa's life: (1) the restoration of a Maitreya statue in Lhasa carried out at the end of a four-year retreat in which he and eight disciples received a vision of Maitreya; (2) a clear and profound teaching on the rules of the monastic discipline; (3) the offering of a golden crown to a statue of Gautama Buddha in Lhasa when he inaugurated the Monlam Great Prayer Festival that begins the Tibetan New Year; and (4) the building of the great hall of Ganden Monastery.

Tsong Khapa died at the age of 62 in his bedroom, now known as Tri Thok Khang, one of the Buddha halls at Ganden Monastery. That room still houses some of Tsong Kapa's clothing. It is said that he died sitting in meditation and that his body appeared to his disciples as a body of rainbow light. Subsequently, his body was placed in the nearby Holy Stupa Hall in a silver pagoda. Eventually the 13th Dalai Lama covered the pagoda with gold.

Edward A. Irons

See also: Gelugpa; Guan Yin's Birthday; Meditation; Tantrism; Tibetan Buddhism.

References
Hopkins, Jeffrey. *Tsong-Kha-Pa's Final Exposition of Wisdom*. Ithaca, NY: Snow Lion Publications, 2008.
Powers, John. *Introduction to Tibetan Buddhism*. Ithaca, NY: Snow Lion Publications, 1995.
Thurman, Robert A. F., ed. *The Life and Teachings of Tsong Khapa*. Dharamsala, India: Library of Tibetan Works and Archives, 1982.

■ Tunisia

Tunisia, a North African county on the Mediterranean Sea, lies between Libya and Algeria. Its 63,200 square miles of territory offer a varied geographic landscape from a mountainous northeast, to the desert south, to the lengthy coast line. It is home to some 10,400,000 people (2008).

Tunisia was originally the home of the Berbers; later it became the base from which a series of very different cultures reached out through the Mediterranean Basin. The ancient city of Carthage (located not far from modem Tunis) was established by the Phoenicians around 800 BCE. It became the center of a sizable empire that eventually fell to Rome. In 146 BCE, Rome razed the city. The Vandals overran the Romans in 439 CE. They were in turn driven out by the expanding Byzantine Empire in 533. Finally, in 670, the

Great Mosque of Kairouan, Tunisia. (Evgeniapp/Dreamstime.com)

Arabs moved across North Africa, bringing with them Islam.

Tunisia was incorporated into the Almohad Empire based in Morocco in the 12th century. As that empire fell apart, the Berbers reasserted themselves, and Tunisia subsequently remained independent until the coming of the Ottomans in the 16th century. After centuries of control by various Muslim forces, Tunisia was invaded by the French, who in 1882 overran Tunisia and made it a protectorate. French control of the area was acknowledged by Britain in return for their loss of a role in the Suez Canal.

As early as 1925, Tunisians organized to demand independence. Only after three years of armed conflict (1952–1955) did France relent and in 1956 recognize Tunisia's autonomy. A year later a republic was proclaimed and a president representing the Destur Party elected. Tunisia was transformed into a Socialist state until financial problems forced a more open economy.

The country has since moved toward a more democratized, secularized, and Westernized position.

Islam is both the dominant and official religion of the country. The great majority of the population follow the Sunni Malikite School. The legal structure of the country demands that the president be a Muslim, and it prevents attempts at proselytization by representatives of other religions.

Although most believers follow the Malikite School, there is a significant number of Kharjites on the island of Djerba. In the 1980s a strong fundamentalist movement emerged to oppose the further Westernization and secularization of the country. Included in the critique of the country was a protest of the un-Islamic role assumed by women and the immorality of tourists who flocked to the country's Mediterranean beaches. In 1992, Tunisia's president, Zina El Abidene, denounced the fundamentalists to a gathering of Arab government ministers in Tunis.

TUNISIA

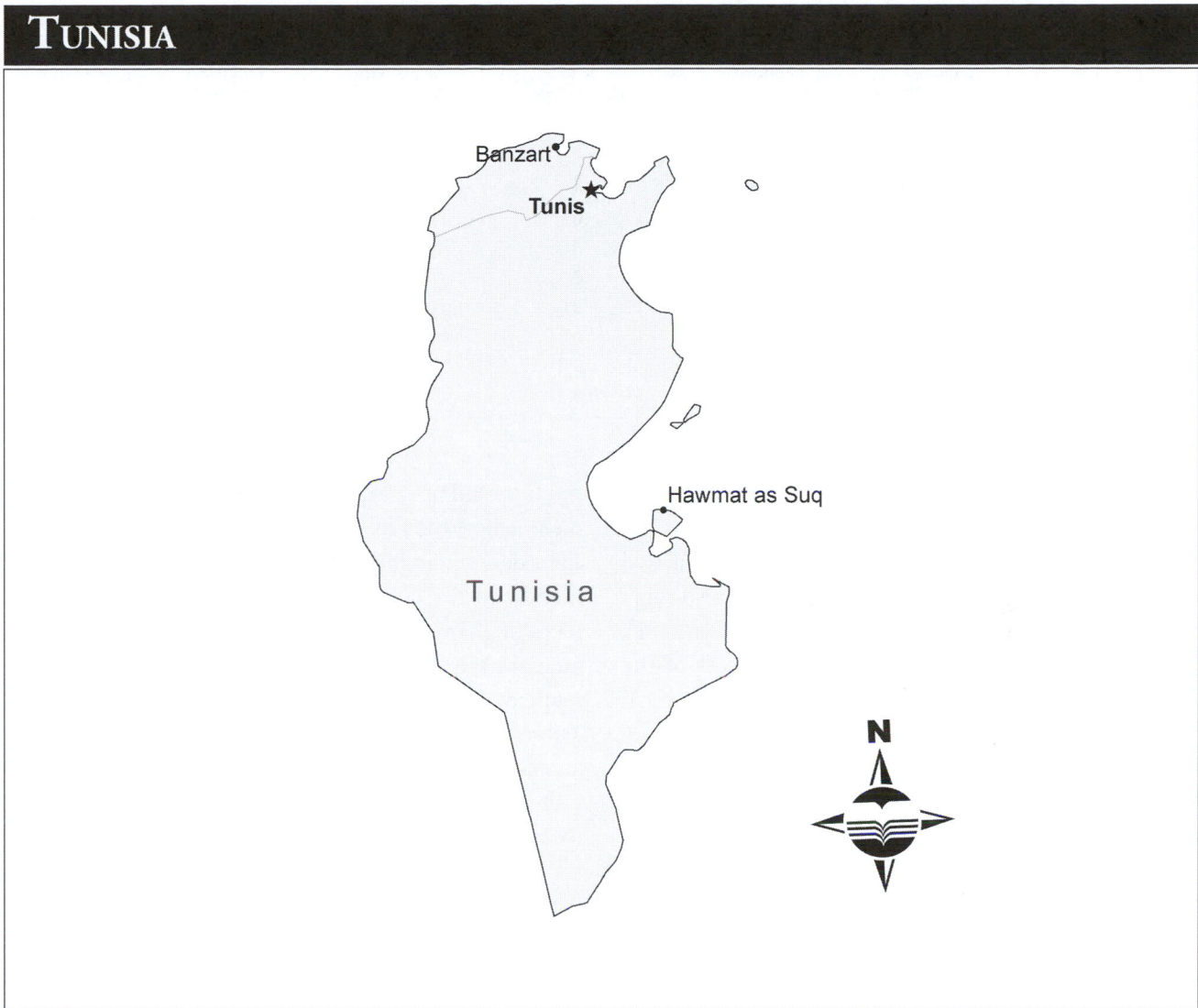

Before the arrival of Islam, Tunisia had been the home of a vital Christian community. It was there at the beginning of the fourth century that the Donatist controversy erupted over the role of those who had betrayed their faith during times of persecution. The Donatists rejected the appointment of such people to positions of leadership. They argued that the efficacy of the sacraments depends upon the purity of the priest who delivers them. In reaction to Donatism, Augustine, the bishop of Hippo (354–430), developed arguments for the use of state power to suppress heretical ideas. An episcopal structure existed in Tunisia until at least the 11th century.

The Roman Catholic Church attempted to re-establish itself in Tunisia at various times but did not build a real following until the 19th century, and that among expatriates. In 1843 a prefecture was erected, and a new archbishop of Carthage was named in 1884. The church grew through the first half of the 20th century, primarily among the French and others who had moved to the country. In like measure, following independence, with the emigration of most Europeans who had lived there, the church suffered considerably. In 1957 the church turned over 65 of its 70 church buildings to the state. Today the church is led by a bishop who resides in Tunis.

Tunisia

Religion	Followers in 1970	Followers in 2010	% of Population	Annual % growth 2000–2010	Followers in 2025	Followers in 2050
Muslims	5,077,000	10,604,000	99.4	1.11	12,090,000	13,062,000
Christians	33,400	29,300	0.3	−0.59	28,900	30,500
Roman Catholics	25,000	19,500	0.2	−1.89	17,000	16,000
Independents	7,100	8,100	0.1	3.02	10,000	12,000
Protestants	630	700	0.0	2.31	900	1,500
Agnostics	3,000	22,000	0.2	1.06	40,000	70,000
Atheists	1,000	3,500	0.0	1.03	5,000	7,000
Baha'is	400	2,200	0.0	1.10	4,000	6,000
Jews	12,000	2,500	0.0	−1.00	2,500	2,500
Total population	**5,127,000**	**10,664,000**	**100.0**	**1.11**	**12,170,000**	**13,178,000**

Anglicans entered Tunisia in 1829 with a mission directed toward the Jewish community, which at the time was 100,000 strong. The mission opened two schools for Jewish children that soon were also serving the Muslim community. Today the work continues under the direction of the Diocese of Egypt of the Episcopal Church in Jerusalem and the Middle East. In 1881 the North African Mission began work in Tunis, and over the next decades it expanded to seven centers. Its work was significantly disrupted by World War II, and most of its centers were closed. In 1962 the mission started a popular Bible-study correspondence course that enrolled some 20,000 people before the government became aware of it and forced its withdrawal in 1964. Subsequently, the mission moved its work to France. The same year that the Mission began, the Reformed Church of France began its work serving French Protestants in Tunisia. The Reformed Church in Tunisia still maintains one congregation of 100 members in Tunis.

During the years of French rule, the Seventh-day Adventist Church (1905), Methodists (1908, from America), and Pentecostals from the Church of God (Cleveland, Tennessee) (1911) established work. A short time later the Greek and Russian Orthodox churches organized a parish for their members who had moved to Tunis to work.

Jews had resided in Carthage prior to the coming of the Christians, and their community survived the changing of governments through the years. In 1881 they had been granted equal rights with the Muslim community, and they had been promised that those rights would be guaranteed by the independent government established in 1957. When they were not, many Jews decided to leave. Over the next decade, the population of the community dropped from 100,000 to 25,000. Many moved to France, others moved to Israel. As the century came to an end, only 3,000 remained. They were found in Tunis, Sfax, and Sousse. There is also a group of Jews on Jerba Island, where an ancient synagogue, El Ghriba, is located. The community is headed by the Grand Rabbinate of Tunisia, located in Tunis.

Like other North African countries with an established Muslim faith, Tunisia has proved unattractive to the many new religions that arose through the 20th century. There are, however, a small number of Baha'is.

J. Gordon Melton

See also: Baha'i Faith; Church of God (Cleveland, Tennessee); Episcopal Church in Jerusalem and the Middle East; Malikite School of Islam; Reformed Church of France; Roman Catholic Church; Seventh-day Adventist Church.

References

Clancy-Smith, Julia A. *Rebel and Saint: Muslim Notables, Populist Protest, Colonial Encounters (Algeria and Tunisia, 1800–1904)*. Berkeley: University of California Press, 1997.

Cooley, J. K. *Baal, Christ and Mohammed: Religion and Revolution in North Africa*. New York: Holt, Rinehart and Winston, 1965.

De Sainte-Marie. *La Tunisie chrétienne*. Lyon, France: Bureaux des Missions Catholiques, 1878.

Fluehr-Lobban, C. *Islamic Society in Practice*. Gainesville: University Press of Florida, 1994.

Perkins, Kenneth. *A History of Modern Tunisia*. Cambridge: Cambridge University Press, 2004.

Shahin, E. E. A. *The Restitution of Islam: A Comparative Study of the Islamic Movements in Contemporary Tunisia and Morocco*. Baltimore: Johns Hopkins University, 1990.

Udovitch, A. *Last Arab Jews: The Communities of Jerba, Tunisia*. London: Routledge, 1986.

■ Turkey

Turkey, known in ancient times as Asia Minor, is technically an Asian country with a small part of its land west of the Bosporus Strait in Europe. It lies south of the Black Sea and north of the Mediterranean Sea. To the east it borders Syria, Iraq, Iran, Armenia, and Georgia. The European portion of the country borders Greece and Bulgaria. Modern Turkey includes 301,400 square miles of territory, which is home to 75,200,000 residents (2007). Kurds, who make up about 20 percent of the country's citizens, form the largest minority group within the dominant Turkish population.

Asia Minor has been home to civilizations reaching back to Pagan times and Anatolia (modern-day Turkey) remains the homeland of numerous cultures, mostly of mixed ethnic origin. Theories indicate a link between Sumerians, Hittites, and Turks because they spoke agglutinative languages and are believed to have come into southern Mesopotamia more than 6,000 years ago from Central Asia. Western culture associates Turkey with the Troy of Homer's *Iliad* and *Odyssey*, as well as tales of the fabled kings Midas (725–696 BCE) and Croesus (560–547). By the sixth century, Turkey was home to the philosophies of Thales, Anaximander, and Anaximenes, who were natives of Miletus. Before Athens emerged, Hellenic culture flourished in Anatolia until the invasion of Cyrus the Great (550–530), who drove the culture to Athens. The conquests of Alexander the Great (334) helped revive Hellenic thought through the Middle East, and during the Roman era, Anatolia had enormous libraries that rivalled Alexandria's in Egypt. The last Anatolian king bequeathed his kingdom to Rome (133), which estab-

Rooftops and minarets of Istanbul, Turkey. (PhotoDisc, Inc.)

lished a capital at Ephesus from which it ruled fairly peacefully for six centuries.

Turkey played a key role in the development of Christianity. Its foremost proponent was Paul, a Jew from Tarsus. He trekked the excellent Roman road system to spread the new religion. His first journey took him to Antioch, Perga, Iconium, Derbe, Attalia, and other cities in Anatolia. His Epistle to the Galatians, the ninth book of the Christian New Testament, was addressed to people of the Galatian region, where descendants of the Gauls (Celts) had pioneered the interior. He took three missionary trips (recorded in the book of Acts) and ran into difficulty in Ephesus, where silversmiths engaged in creating statues of Diana/Cybele/Astarte felt that he threatened their livelihoods. Other figures, such as John the Apostle, were reported

to have taken Mary, the mother of Jesus, to Ephesus, where a small chapel to her celebrates Mass on August 15, which is believed to be her Ascension Day. The author of the biblical book of Revelation, writing from the Isle of Patmos off the Turkish coast, addressed his words to the seven churches of Asia, all in Anatolia: Ephesus, Izmir, Pergamum, Sardis, Philadelphia, Laodicea, and Thyatira.

The Ecumenical Council of Nicaea of 325 CE proved a major milestone in developing Christian doctrine. Five years later, the Emperor Constantine dedicated the city of Byzantium as a new Rome. He was a deathbed convert to Christianity, and his new holy city, Constantinople, would be the seat of the Roman Empire. Eventually, the metropolitan of Constantinople would be given a higher status than those in other Mediterranean cities (Jerusalem, Antioch, Alexandria, and Rome), thus foreshadowing the Great Schism of 1054, when the Roman Catholic Church and Eastern Orthodoxy split. While the barbarians across the Mediterranean were laying siege and weakening Rome, Constantinople thrived. Emperor Justinian (527–565) reconquered the Balkans, Italy, Anatolia, Egypt, and North Africa, while embellishing the architectural structures of the Byzantine Empire. The Church of Holy Wisdom, or St. Sophia, in Constantinople became the most highly acclaimed church in Christendom, unrivaled for 1,000 years.

By the late 13th century, Byzantine rule had declined in power. Within 50 years of the Prophet Muhammad's death, a new religion founded in Saudi Arabia, Islam (submission to God's will), had conquered all of Anatolia and threatened the walls of Constantinople (669–678). Muhammad, the prophet of this new religion, died, and was succeeded by caliphs (deputies) whose job was to oversee the welfare of Islam. Two great dynasties emerged: the Umayyads (661–750), based in Damascus, and the Abbasids (750–1100), who ruled from Baghdad. Both challenged the Christians of Byzantium.

For a brief time the Great Seljuk Turkish Empire (1037–1109), based in Persia, hammered away at Anatolia. In 1071, Seljuk armies defeated the Byzantine force at Manzikert and captured their emperor. They subsequently took most of Turkey and established a capital near Nicaea. They ruled what are now Iran, Iraq, and Turkey, developed beautiful architectural designs, and produced the noted poet Omar Kayyam (d. 1123). Celaleddin Rumi (1207–1273), or "Mevlana," founder of the Mevlana Whirling Dervish order of Sufis, made the century's outstanding contribution to religious poetry and mysticism.

Byzantine culture was weakened by the assertion of Islam. However, the fatal blow to its glory occurred from fellow Christians during the Fourth Crusade (1202–1204). A disheveled European Christian army invaded and plundered Constantinople, doing irreparable damage. While the Byzantines were attempting to recover, legions of Turks running before the Mongols took over areas of the Marmara and Aegean coasts. Under Sultan Suleiman the Magnificent (1520–1566), these Turks finally conquered Constantinople (1453) and made it the capital of their new Ottoman Empire. Suleiman also initiated efforts to incorporate Europe in the Ottoman Empire. After overrunning the Balkans, his successors were finally turned back at Vienna in 1529. As they conquered new territories, the Ottoman sultans placed the non-Muslim religious leadership of each community (including the Orthodox patriarch in Constantinople and the chief rabbi) in political positions responsible directly to the sultan.

During the early 19th century, subject peoples revolted against Ottoman rule. In 1832, the Kingdom of Greece was formed as the Romanians, Bulgarians, Armenians, Arabs, and Albanians successfully agitated for their freedom. European powers watched as the debilitated empire began to come apart. France and England stood ready to occupy and annex the Ottoman territories, using religion as the excuse: to protect Catholic, Protestant, or Orthodox subjects from the Islamic Turks.

The empire sided with Germany in World War I and lost. The last blow to the weakened dynasty was dealt when Greek armies invaded Turkey and the Turkish War for Independence (1920–1922) began. Turks repelled the invading armies under General Mustafa Kemal (1881–1938). The charismatic Kemal took control as the empire collapsed. He abolished both the sultanate and the Islamic caliphate. Treaties from World War I were renegotiated. As a result, 1.5 million Greeks in Turkey returned to Greece, and Turks in Greece were brought back to Anatolia. Earlier turmoil

(1915–1917) had seen 600,000 Armenians and Chaldeans massacred before they could leave the country. Now the survivors emigrated rapidly, and the number of Christians in Turkey dropped drastically.

Kemal established a republic in 1923, and a secular Constitution was adopted in 1924. The new republic abandoned Islam as the state religion and ordered the abolishment of all mystical orders. Both the wearing of the fez and the practice of polygamy were also outlawed. A new Latin alphabet was designed, and Persian and Arabic words purged from the Turkish language. The Gregorian calendar replaced both the Muslim lunar and the older Julian calendars. In 1930, Constantinople was renamed Istanbul. In 1934, the government granted women the right to vote. By then, Kemal had adopted the name Ataturk, or Father Turk. He ruled by fiat through the Republican People's Party until his death on November 10, 1938.

Turkey remained neutral during World War II. Years of postwar turmoil finally led the military to intercede in 1980 to stabilize the situation. Two major trajectories have continued to clash in modern Turkey: the secular understanding of Ataturk and continuing Islamic ideals that look to the union of religion and state. These tensions remain as a modern Turkish state supplanted the traditional religiously ruled empire. These tensions were heightened following the introduction of Western global and technical cultures. Modern Turkey exists between modernity and traditionalism.

Republican secularists abandoned the Islamic world and condemned the practices in the popular folk religion deemed superstitious or unscientific. Authorities also removed economic, political, and social roles from mosques. Religion was limited to personal choice instead of imposed by government mandate. Traditionalists viewed these actions, especially the change to the Western calendar, as an immediate danger to the supremacy of Islam. On a social level, cooperation and integration have not occurred between secularists and non-secularists, leaving Turkey straddling two worlds and thus offering the appearance of cultural instability.

Since Ottoman times, Sunni Islam, of the Hanafite School, has been the religion of the Turkish people, and it continues to be the most noticed and supported religious practice. Hanafite precepts remain the unifying factor in a strident cultural identity. Concurrently, paradoxical practices of folk Islam include fortune telling, astrology, divination, manipulation of spirits, sorcery, the wearing of amulets such as the Mediterranean eye, the circumcision of boys, and praying at the tombs of saints. Despite these deviations from the orthodox, Muslims acknowledge the primacy of an enduring piety in orthodoxy. It is paradoxical that even as Turkish secularism attempts to divorce religion and government, the Department of Religious Affairs (Diyanet) promotes Sunni Islam. About 15 percent of the population are Shia Muslims, considered heterodox by the Sunni majority, as are the small group of Yezidis near Diyarbakir.

Islam is not systematically organized in the manner of Western churches. There are no membership lists or formal bodies to petition for membership. Everyone born into a Muslim family is considered a Muslim unless they deny it. Turks carry national identity cards, and 99 percent of them state Islam as their religion. Secularists rarely change them. An inner sense of belonging is the criterion for inclusiveness. Turks normally do not ask about personal religious beliefs. Male circumcision is non-canonical, but it is ritually practiced with boys between the ages of 7 and 12.

A major factor in the social, ethnic, and political turmoil in Turkey is the question of what to do about the Kurds who live in eastern Turkey and in the mountains bordering Iraq. Kurdish populations wish to maintain their language, social customs, and mores. The official position of Turkey for some years was that these people are mountain Turks and that they should abide by the rules and laws of Turkey. Genocide and mass migration to Europe have caused their numbers to dwindle. The Kurds are primarily Sunnite, but many are Shias of the Alevi tradition. Turkey has no accurate statistics on these minority religious and ethnic groups who do not subscribe to mainstream Turkish tradition. There are also small numbers of Tahtacis and Ahl-el-Hak who are separatist groups but usually pass for Muslim.

Islam is widely manifest in the form of folk piety. For example, Turks generally keep their Korans in high places, as they are believed to provide protection against evil thoughts. Some time ago it was believed that to carry a small Koran would also ward off bullets.

Today, those who carry them do so above the waist. Many write and then sew verses from the Koran into their clothing for spiritual healing. Reciting a verse before bedtime may protect the home from burglars, and before traveling is considered a good omen. Children recite verses to protect them when alone or finding themselves in atypical situations.

There are pious expressions peppered throughout Turkish speech patterns. *Inshallah* means "if Allah wills" and can be used in the positive as a salutation or departure term, or when negativity is present. *Mashallah* praises Allah and means "O, what Allah has willed" and is used consistently in daily life. The *besmele*—"I begin in the name of Allah, the most merciful, the most compassionate"—is normative for canonical prayer and is used before any day-to-day activities. Every call to prayer starts with the *tekbir* phrase *Allahu Akbar:* "It is Allah who is magnificent." The expression *Ya Allah*—"O, Allah"—is used when changing position from something passive to active. Today, some secularists attempt to strip the Turkish language of religious connotations, while others consider greetings such as *aley kum selam*—"May the peace, health, and security of Allah be with you"—to be normative for verbal interchange.

Prayer beads are widely used, especially with Sufi groups. Other groups use them also as "worship using the fingers." The repetitive verses calling on Allah, *zikir*, find confirmation that each prayer has been recited 33 times. Some people carry beads to handle when worried, and that cultural routine is not religious but comforting in a secular way.

Some people wear the blue "evil-eye" bead or attach it to Turkish belongings. At times, the Mashallah, which means "O, what Allah has willed," accompanies it. The bead is a form of folk religion that wards off the evil eye. Some people are thought to have the propensity to gaze at others and inadvertently harm them, although they themselves are well-meaning people. Villagers cover the faces of beautiful babies, or tie sacks around the udders of milk cows when outdoors to protect the production of milk from the evil eye. This evil-eye figure predates Islam and the immigration of Turkish-speaking peoples in the Middle East.

Where folk traditions predominate, one also finds shamans. The shaman, or *hodja*, is believed to be gifted with metaphysical powers. When Islam is used as the format for divining procedures, the hodja is called a Muslim shaman. People for whom contemporary medicine and psychology have failed frequently turn to the hodjas.

The idea of receiving knowledge about a certain circumstance through dreaming is believed to have been taught by Muhammad. There are Muslims who live by their dreams and perform acts of ablution as preparation for dreaming, because ritual impurity negates the authenticity of the dreamer. Ataturk took severe action against hodjas and mediums, sometimes jailing them. Today, folk practices are common, and there are many secularized people who take horoscopes, evil eye beads, and the work of hodjas quite seriously.

At the beginning of World War I, Christians made up about 20 percent of the Turkish population. In 1914 the Roman Catholics had 4 archdioceses and 16 dioceses. The shuffling of populations, emigrations, and especially the mass execution of Armenians significantly reduced the Christian presence. The majority of Christians are Orthodox, though they are scattered in different jurisdictions. The see of the Ecumenical Patriarchate is in Istanbul. He has status and prestige but is without power to intervene in Turkish matters. He has few followers in Turkey proper, his status coming from his far-flung international jurisdiction, which includes the Greek Orthodox in all of the non-Orthodox countries of Europe, the Greek islands of the Aegean Sea, Mount Athos, Crete, and the Americas.

The Greek Orthodox Patriarchate of Antioch and All the East has five congregations in Turkey; the Bulgarian Orthodox Church has two churches and an exarch in Istanbul; the Russian Orthodox Church (Moscow Patriarchate) has a congregation in Istanbul; and the Serbian Orthodox Church has a small membership in the country. Non-Chalcedon Oriental Orthodox are separated into two distinct communities, the Armenian Apostolic Church (Holy See of Echmiadzin) and the Syriac Orthodox Patriarchate of Antioch and All the East (Syro-Jacobite). Together they make up the bulk of the Christian population in Turkey, about 225,000 people. There is also a minuscule Turkish Orthodox Church, the result of a largely unsuccessful attempt to create an indigenous national Orthodoxy separate from the Ecumenical Patriarchate.

Turkey

Religion	Followers in 1970	Followers in 2010	% of Population	Annual % growth 2000–2010	Followers in 2025	Followers in 2050
Muslims	35,747,000	75,670,000	97.4	1.38	86,919,000	95,727,000
Agnostics	30,000	1,500,000	1.9	1.42	2,000,000	2,500,000
Christians	290,000	214,000	0.3	0.28	222,000	224,000
Orthodox	222,000	115,000	0.1	−0.89	100,000	90,000
Roman Catholics	26,500	31,000	0.0	−0.30	26,000	22,000
Anglicans	2,000	22,000	0.0	0.00	22,000	22,000
New religionists	64,000	136,000	0.2	1.37	160,000	177,000
Atheists	10,000	68,000	0.1	1.52	100,000	115,000
Buddhists	5,000	40,000	0.1	1.37	60,000	80,000
Jews	37,000	24,000	0.0	1.37	24,000	24,000
Baha'is	3,700	24,000	0.0	1.38	35,000	55,000
Chinese folk	5,000	14,000	0.0	1.37	22,000	24,000
Ethnoreligionists	15,000	12,600	0.0	1.37	15,000	20,000
Total population	**36,207,000**	**77,703,000**	**100.0**	**1.37**	**89,557,000**	**98,946,000**

The Roman Catholic Church has diocese representing its several rites—Latin, Armenian, Chaldean, Syrian, and Byzantine. Most Latin Catholics live near Istanbul, Izmir, and Ankara. Most of the Chaldeans are clustered near the Iraqi border. Small numbers of Catholics of the Byzantine rite are divided between Rome and the patriarchal vicariate of Istanbul. There are about 28,000 Catholics in Turkey.

A new wave of Protestant Christian missionary work began with the arrival of William Goodall of the American Board of Commissioners for Foreign Missions in Istanbul in 1831. However, most Turkish converts came not from Islam but from the older Christian populations. The Church Missionary Society, the Basel Mission, and the Society for the Propagation of the Gospel in Foreign Parts had abandoned Istanbul by the 1870s on account of an inhospitable environment for religious conversion. Later the American Baptists, the Christian Church (Disciples of Christ), the Church of the Brethren, British Quakers, and the London Jews Society retired from missionizing indigenous Turks. In 1970 the United Church had 84 missionaries in Turkey attempting to help the people without proselytizing. Most of the missionaries are based in Istanbul. The American Academy for Girls has about 18 missionaries assigned to the American College at Izmir. The British and Foreign Bible Society were responsible for translations of Scripture into Turkish. The American Congregationalists established Roberts College, north of Istanbul, in 1871; in 1961 it was given over to the Turkish government, renamed Bosphorus University, and today is a premier institution of higher education and flagship for the Turkish university system.

German Lutherans and British Anglicans (under the Church of England's Diocese of Europe) have parishes in Ankara, Izmir, and Ankara. They have a very small presence of 2,000 people. They serve expatriates, the U.S. military, and diplomatic communities. Turks do not have memberships in these groups. Various Protestant and Free Church groups opened missions in Turkey through the 20th century. However, their success has been marginal.

An indigenous Jewish population of 35,000, most of them Sephardic Jews, live near Istanbul. There has been a Jewish community in Turkey since ancient times, though its makeup was changed by the addition of a number of Jews who were expelled from Spain and Portugal at the end of the 15th century. Their numbers have dwindled since 1948, when many decided to immigrate to Israel. Unity for the Jewish community is provided by the Great Rabbi, who resides in Istanbul.

The number of spiritual assemblies of the Baha'i Faith has expanded rapidly through the 1990s, and Baha'is now number about 1,000. There is a small Buddhist presence, but Islam remains the majority religion, with more than 85 percent of the population; those who profess no religion approach 10 percent. Little shift in these numbers is expected in the near future.

Gail M. Harley

See also: American Board of Commissioners for Foreign Missions; Armenian Apostolic Church (Holy See of Echmiadzin); Baha'i Faith; Basel Mission; Bulgarian Orthodox Church; Christian Church (Disciples of Christ); Church Missionary Society; Church of England; Church of the Brethren; Ecumenical Patriarchate/Patriarchate of Constantinople; Greek Orthodox Patriarchate of Antioch and All the East; Hanafite School of Islam; Roman Catholic Church; Russian Orthodox Church (Moscow Patriarchate); Serbian Orthodox Church; Society for the Propagation of the Gospel in Foreign Parts; Syriac Orthodox Patriarchate of Antioch and All the East; Yezidis.

References

Atasoy, Yildiz. *Turkey, Islamists and Democracy: Transition and Globalisation in a Muslim State.* London: I. B. Tauris, 2005.

Caqaptay, Soner. *Islam, Secularism and Nationalism in Modern Turkey: Who Is a Turk?* London: Routledge, 2006.

Frazee, C. A. *Catholics and Sultans: The Church and the Ottoman Empire, 1453–1923.* Cambridge: Cambridge University Press, 1983.

Garnett, L. M. J. *Mysticism and Magic in Turkey.* New York: Charles Scribner's Sons, 1912.

Howe, Marvine. *Turkey Today: A Nation Divided Over Islam's Revival.* New York: Basic Books, 2000.

Tapper, R., ed. *Islam in Modern Turkey: Religion, Politics and Literature in a Secular State.* London: St. Martin's, 1994.

Tepe, Sultan. *Beyond Sacred and Secular: Politics of Religion in Israel and Turkey.* Stanford, CA: Stanford University Press, 2008.

■ Turkmenistan

Turkmenistan, a central Asian republic on the Caspian Sea between Iran and Kazakhstan, is also bordered by Afghanistan and Uzbekistan. A relative lowland, compared to its southern neighbors, much of the country's 188,500 square miles of land is a sandy desert. It is home to 5,200,000 citizens.

Since ancient times, Turkmenistan has been a reward of numerous conquering states, from Alexander the Great to the Arabs. Modern Turkmens are a relatively later product of the mixing of the Oguz Turks with several of the groups that had moved into the region. That mixing occurred in the 11th through the 15th centuries.

Turkmenistan

Religion	Followers in 1970	Followers in 2010	% of Population	Annual % growth 2000–2010	Followers in 2025	Followers in 2050
Muslims	1,304,000	4,575,000	88.6	1.48	5,703,000	6,536,000
Agnostics	444,000	436,000	8.4	1.18	235,000	118,000
Christians	117,000	79,400	1.5	0.44	67,100	63,100
Orthodox	108,000	64,000	1.2	0.38	46,000	34,000
Marginals	0	5,600	0.1	1.55	8,000	12,000
Independents	0	4,000	0.1	−0.26	6,000	8,000
Atheists	320,000	66,000	1.3	1.01	55,000	52,000
Jews	3,000	3,000	0.1	1.43	3,000	3,000
Baha'is	0	1,200	0.0	1.44	2,000	4,000
Ethnoreligionists	0	860	0.0	1.43	1,000	1,200
Buddhists	0	740	0.0	1.44	900	1,200
New religionists	200	670	0.0	1.42	850	1,000
Total population	**2,189,000**	**5,163,000**	**100.0**	**1.43**	**6,068,000**	**6,780,000**

Mosque in Ashkhabad, Turkmenistan. (Olga Buiacova/Dreamstime.com)

In the 19th century, Turkmenia was conquered by Russia and was incorporated into Bukhara and Khuva, two Russian protectorates. Resistance to Russian domination was fierce, and only in 1881 was all the country pacified. In spite of efforts to break with Russia at the time of the revolution, Turkmenistan was incorporated into the Soviet Union, and the Soviet Socialist Republic of Turkmenistan was created in 1924. The republic actually brought some political unity that had often been denied as parts of the country changed hands and fell under various regimes over the centuries.

Turkmenistan finally emerged as an independent country in 1991. It was the least democratic of the governments of the former Soviet republics, existing under the leadership of strongman Saparmurat Niyasov until his death in 2006. It has since moved toward a more democratic structure. In 1994 the government created the Council on Religious Affairs to provide oversight of the religious (primarily Muslim) community.

Islam came to Turkmenia in the 650s, when the Arab caliphate expanded into Central Asia under Uthman (644–656) and remained a part of the subsequent Umayyad and Abbasid caliphates. The Mongols invaded early in the 13th century, and over the next 100 years they were converted to Islam. Suppressed through the Soviet years, the Islamic community was revived in the 1980s and has done well under the independent government established in the 1990s. From four mosques operating in the country in 1987, several hundred opened during the 1990s.

Beginning in the mid-1990s, the government took steps to ensure that Muslim organizations did not become centers of political protest. It began by taking control of the Muslim schools for clergy training, blocked efforts to form an Islamic political party, and restricted the printing and distribution of religious literature. The government was especially attentive to any suggestion that an Islamic government should re-

TURKMENISTAN

Bekdash

Gyzylgaya

Turkmenbashi

Turkmenistan

Yerbent

Gumdag
Gyzylarbat

Ashgabat

Esenguly

Gowurdak
Kerki

Bayramaly

Tejen

Saragt

Gushgy

N

place the present secular one. In 2000, Niyasov order the burning of 4,000 copies of the Koran, copies that the government had paid to have printed, ostensibly because of the inaccuracy of the translation, but following the translator's having made some public criticisms of Niyasov's un-Islamic activities.

A small Christian presence was established in Turkmenistan during the years of Russian dominance, and a Russian Orthodox Church (Moscow Patriarchate) presence remains. It is part of the single diocese that covers Uzbekistan, Turkmenistan, Tadzhikistan,

and Kyrgyzstan. There are a number of Armenians who reside in Turkmenistan, and they have organized the Armenian Apostolic Church (Holy See of Echmiadzin). Protestants entered the country in the 1890s when I. K. Saval'ev, a Baptist, moved from Vladikavkas (Russia) and F. S. Ovsyannikov, a Mennonite, moved from Samatria Province to Ashkhabad. Two years later the two established a village, Kuropatkinsky, some 12 miles from Ashkhabad, where the first church was erected. Later a church was opened in Ashkhabad. This church became the target of Soviet authorities in the 1930s. The Baptist movement remains small in Turkmenistan, there being only three congregations in the 1990s. These congregations have joined with the Union of Evangelical Christian-Baptists of Central Asia, an association founded in 1992 that also includes the churches in Uzbekistan and Tajikistan.

The secular government maintains hegemony over religion in the country. Groups must register before holding meetings and are subject to periodic raids by officials to check upon compliance with the laws. A spectrum of groups that have surfaced since the county's independence, including the Jehovah's Witnesses, have been unable to obtain such registration.

J. Gordon Melton

See also: Armenian Apostolic Church (Holy See of Echmiadzin); Jehovah's Witnesses; Russian Orthodox Church (Moscow Patriarchate).

References

Blackwell, Carole. *Tradition and Society in Turkmenistan: Gender, Oral Culture and Song.* London: RoutledgeCurzon, 2001.

Edgar, Adrienne Lynn. *Tribal Nation: The Making of Soviet Turkmenistan.* Princeton, NJ: Princeton University Press, 2004.

Hayit, B. *Islam and Turkestan under Russian Rule.* Istanbul: privately printed, 1987.

Khalid, Adeeb. *Islam after Communism: Religion and Politics in Central Asia.* Berkeley: University of California Press, 2007.

Wingate, Reginald. *The Steep Ascent: The Story of the Christian Church in Turkestan.* London: British and Foreign Bible Society, n.d.

■ Turks and Caicos Islands

The Turks and Caicos Islands are two Caribbean island chains located north of Haiti and southeast of the Bahamas. Though separated by some distance, they were earlier a part of Britain's Jamaica colony. Together the islands include a mere 166 square miles of land that serve as home to their 22,400 residents.

The islands were originally inhabited by the Arawak people, and there is research to suggest that it was on one of these islands that Columbus first touched the soil of the New World in 1492. The islands did not face European colonization until 1678, when the British moved in. During the next century the islands faced a common history of the destruction of the Arawak society, the importation of slaves to work plantations, and battles with the French and Spanish. British dominion was firmly established by 1787. Rule was administered from the Bahamas until 1848. Then, in 1874, the islands became a dependency of Jamaica until 1962, after which they again became a separate British colony. They became autonomous by steps, with direct involvement of the British government ending in 1988. The islands remain in the British Commonwealth.

The traditional religion of the Arawak people was destroyed with the people in the 18th century. Christianity entered the islands as the Church of England followed British settlement. It was established in the middle of the 18th century and now claims approximately 20 percent of the islands' relatively small population. The churches are included in the Church in the Province of the West Indies.

Turks and Caicos Islands

Religion	Followers in 1970	Followers in 2010	% of Population	Annual % growth 2000–2010	Followers in 2025	Followers in 2050
Christians	5,600	24,100	92.1	5.20	26,700	28,000
Protestants	3,800	11,000	42.0	3.24	12,100	13,000
Independents	450	3,700	14.1	−1.96	4,700	4,500
Anglicans	1,100	2,400	9.2	2.38	3,500	3,800
Agnostics	0	1,200	4.7	8.17	2,000	2,500
Spiritists	0	680	2.6	5.34	920	1,000
Baha'is	30	160	0.6	5.42	250	400
Atheists	0	10	0.0	4.56	60	80
Total population	**5,600**	**26,200**	**100.0**	**5.33**	**29,900**	**32,000**

TURKS AND CAICOS ISLANDS

Turks and Caicos Islands

West Caicos

Providenciales
Blue Hills
The Bight
Five Cays

French Cay

West Sand Spit

North Caicos
Whitby
Kew
Bottle Creek
Conch Bar
Bambarra
Lorimers
Middle Caicos

Caicos Islands

East Caicos

South Caicos
Cockburn Harbour
Six Hill Cays
Long Cay

Fish Cay

Ambergris Cays

Seal Cays

Bush Cays

Grand Turk Island

Grand Turk

Balfour Town
Cotton Cay
East Cay
Salt Cay

Turks Islands

Big Sand Cay

Endymion Rock

N

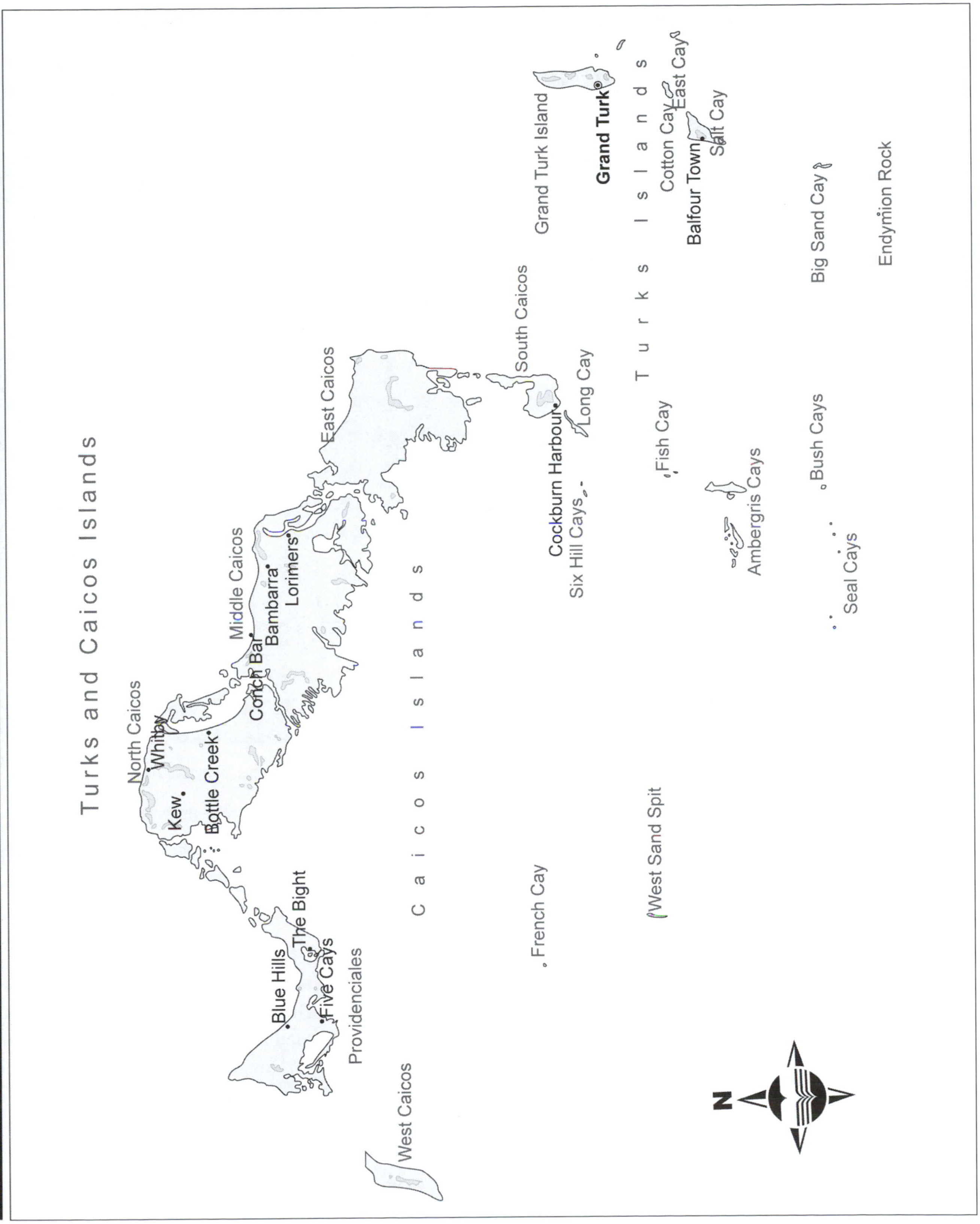

The historic first cathedral in Turks and Caicos situated on Grand Turk Island. (Ramunas Bruzas/Dreamstime.com)

Baptists have had the most success, their work having originated from the British Baptist Union's missionary activity in Jamaica. Baptists from the Jamaica Baptist Union came to Turks and Caicos in the middle of the 19th century. They soon outstripped the Methodists, now the second largest group in the islands, who had come in 1800 as part of the last stages of their spread through the islands that began in 1787. Their work was later incorporated in the Methodist Church in the Caribbean and the Americas.

Through the 20th century, a spectrum of Protestant/Free churches came to the islands (Baptist Bible Fellowship International, Church of God of Prophecy, and the Seventh-day Adventist Church). The Church of God in Christ, an African American Pentecostal church, has established a small presence, as have the enthusi-astic Spiritual Baptists. The Roman Catholic Church has a minimal presence.

J. Gordon Melton

See also: Baptist Bible Fellowship International; Church in the Province of the West Indies; Church of God in Christ; Church of God of Prophecy; Jamaica Baptist Union; Methodist Church in the Caribbean and the Americas; Roman Catholic Church; Seventh-day Adventist Church; Spiritual Baptists.

References

Barrett, David, ed. *The Encyclopedia of World Christianity.* 2nd ed. New York: Oxford University Press, 2001.

Kennedy, Cynthia. "The Other White Gold: Salt, Slaves, the Turks and Caicos Islands, and British

Colonialism." *The Historian* 69, no. 2 (June 22, 2008): 215–216.

Sadler, H. E. *Turks Island Landfall: A History of the Turks and Caicos Islands.* N.p.: the author, 1997.

Smith, Hosay. *A History of Turks and Caicos Islands.* Hamilton, Bermuda: the author, 1968.

■ Tuvalu

Tuvalu is a South Sea island republic located between Fiji and Kiribati. Though it covers a massive area of ocean, the total land area of this the fourth smallest country of the world's nations is but nine square miles. It is home to 12,200 people (2008), most of Polynesian ancestry.

Tuvalu was settled by Polynesians several thousand years ago, most likely by migration from Tonga and Samoa. The Tuvaluans first came into contact with Europeans as early as the 16th century, and at some point they were named the Ellice Islands. However, between 1850 and 1875 they were targeted by slavers, and the majority of the islands' residents were taken to Peru and Chile to work in the mines. The slave trade was stopped only upon effective settlement by the British and the establishment of a Christian mission. In 1892 the British established a protectorate over the islands, and in 1915 incorporated them into the new colony of the Gilbert (now Kiribati) and Ellice Islands.

The islands began the process of independence with a referendum in 1974. Independence became a fact in 1978. A parliamentary system modeled on the United Kingdom was installed. The new nation retained close ties to England.

The London Missionary Society launched a very successful mission in Samoa, and in 1861 Samoan missionaries arrived in the Ellice Islands. They were joined by J. S. White, an LMS missionary in 1870. Over the next three decades, the 3,000 island residents were converted to Congregational Christianity. As a result, the traditional religion (already severely weakened by the losses to the slave trade) disappeared. This work matured into the Church of Tuvalu, which retains the allegiance of more than 90 percent of the islands' residents.

The only other churches operating in the islands are the Seventh-day Adventist Church, which began work in the 1950s in the Gilbert Islands, and the Roman Catholic Church. The Catholic Church had been prevented from operating in the islands until 1964, but today it has several congregations. There is also a small Baha'i Faith presence in Tuvalu.

J. Gordon Melton

See also: Baha'i Faith; Church of Tuvalu; London Missionary Society; Roman Catholic Church; Seventh-day Adventist Church.

References

Chambers, Keith, and Anne Chambers. *Unity of Heart: Culture and Change in a Polynesian Atoll Society.* Long Grove, IL: Waveland Press, 2001.

Tuvalu

Religion	Followers in 1970	Followers in 2010	% of Population	Annual % growth 2000–2010	Followers in 2025	Followers in 2050
Christians	7,200	10,100	94.2	0.44	10,600	10,800
Protestants	7,100	9,500	88.9	–0.11	9,800	9,900
Marginals	20	300	2.8	5.64	450	500
Independents	0	220	2.1	4.56	250	300
Agnostics	0	320	3.0	2.60	400	550
Baha'is	100	230	2.1	0.57	300	400
Atheists	0	40	0.4	0.51	70	90
Buddhists	0	20	0.1	1.61	30	40
Muslims	0	10	0.1	0.00	20	30
Total population	**7,300**	**10,700**	**100.0**	**0.50**	**11,400**	**11,900**

Tuvalu

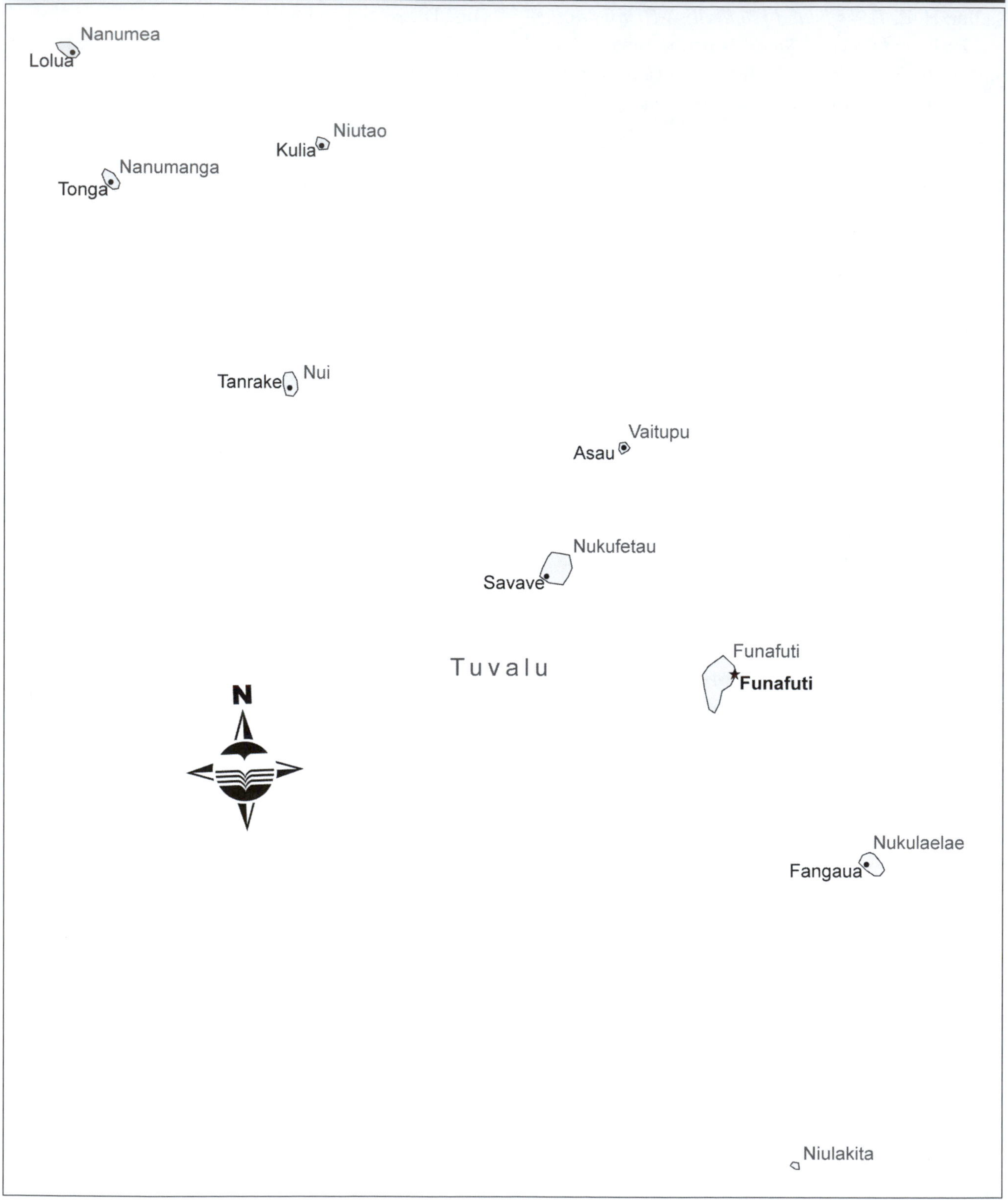

Nanumea
Lolua

Niutao
Kulia

Nanumanga
Tonga

Nui
Tanrake

Vaitupu
Asau

Nukufetau
Savave

T u v a l u

Funafuti
★ **Funafuti**

N

Nukulaelae
Fangaua

Niulakita

Forman, Charles H. *The Island Churches of the South Pacific: Emergence in the Twentieth Century.* Maryknoll, NY: Orbis, 1982.

Kofe, L. *The Tuvalu Church: A Socio-historical Survey of Its Development towards an Indigenous Church.* B.D. project, Pacific Theological College, 1976.

Laracy, Hugh. *Tuvalu: A History.* Suva, Fiji: University of the South Pacific, 1983.

Twelve Tribes

The Twelve Tribes started out as a Christian communal fellowship that emerged from the Jesus People Revival in 1972 under the leadership of Elbert Eugene ("Gene") Spriggs, whom community members consider an apostle, and his wife, Marsha. Through the years the community has evolved into a Hebrew "tribe." It has often changed its name to reflect these developments. It has been known as The Vine Christian Community Church, the Northeast Kingdom Community Church, and the Messianic Communities.

Members of the Twelve Tribes adopt Hebrew names and consider themselves as part of the Commonwealth of Israel forming in the last days, bound together by the New Covenant in the Messiah's Blood (Ephesians 2:12). The communities have evolved a distinct culture around their craftsmanship and handiwork. They also have evolved their own devotional music and dance forms.

Spriggs, the son of a factory quiller and scoutmaster, was born in Chattanooga, Tennessee, and grew up in the Methodist Church. In 1971 he became involved in the Jesus Movement through Marineth Chapel and Center Theater in Glendale, California. Returning to Tennessee, he and his wife opened their residence in East Ridge, a suburb of Chattanooga, and attracted a variety of young spiritual seekers. As a group formed, they copied the early Christian pattern of sharing all things in common (Acts 2:37–47). The group also opened the Yellow Deli, a health food bakery and sandwich restaurant. They prepared whole-grain bread, which symbolized the Gospel of Jesus—the real spiritual food in contrast to the lifeless "White Bread Jesus" found in mainline churches. Eventually they rejected conventional religion and began developing their own worship, gathering on Friday evenings to welcome the Sabbath and on Saturday to break bread and celebrate the Messiah's resurrection.

They made contact with a Christian fellowship in Island Pond, Vermont, that wished to emulate their communal life, and in 1979 the group sold their property and moved north. In Chattanooga the households had been centralized, but in Island Pond they formed independent communes, each household specializing in its own cottage industry. Many members left after the first winter, but the group opened up the Common Sense Restaurant and attracted new members.

The Twelve Tribes accept the basic affirmation of traditional Christianity, but also include various theological innovations concerning communal living, marriage, and eschatology. They also have been influenced by the Sacred Name movement and have adopted the Hebrew designation for Jesus (Yahshua). As their theology has developed, more has been discerned concerning the community's role in the last days, their relationship to Yahshua, and levels of salvation after Judgment. The communities define themselves as the lost and scattered tribes of the ancient Jews undergoing restoration in preparation for eternal life. They believe that their community is undergoing a process of purification as the "pure and Spotless Bride" awaiting her Bridegroom, and that it will probably take three generations to be ready for the Second Coming. By increasing their ranks through conversions and childbearing, they are "raising up a people" in preparation for the Jubilee horn that heralds the return of Yahshua. The group condemns abortion and homosexuality and supports monogamy, premarital chastity, and home schooling.

Since relocating in Island Pond the group has also developed an elaborate ritual life. Public "gatherings" are held on Friday and Saturday night (the Jewish Sabbath and the eve of the First Day) that feature circle dancing, devotional songs, spontaneous speaking, and stories for the children. The public is also invited to their weddings, which dramatize the community's millenarian expectations: the Bride, representing the Community, prepares herself for the call of the groom, her "King."

Some 1,500 people are involved with the movement, of whom roughly half are children. There are

14 associated communities in the United States and additional communities in Argentina, Brazil, France, Germany, Spain, Australia, New Zealand, the United Kingdom, and Canada. The majority of members still reside in New England, mainly in Vermont or in the Boston area. In 1993 the community in Island Pond, Vermont, numbered 15 households. By 1994 it had shrunk to five, as families moved to Bellows Falls, Rutland, and Burlington in Vermont, as well as to Rhode Island and Hyannis, Massachusetts, in order to set up new communities.

Each local community is "covered" by a council of male elders (one from each household). Under the elders is an informal hierarchy of teachers, deacons, deaconesses, and shepherds. Women wear head scarves "in church" or at the "gatherings" and meetings to demonstrate their submission to their husbands and the male elders, who, in turn, are "covered" by "Our Master." The Spriggs, childless and with no fixed abode, travel among the communities offering counsel and inspiration. Evangelism is carried on by contact with individuals whom they meet through their businesses and the distribution of their periodical, *The Twelve Tribes Freepaper.*

The Twelve Tribes have been attacked by anti-cultists ever since the founding of communes in Chattanooga, but they experienced a new level of conflict beginning in 1984 with accusations of child abuse in the community. In that year the Vermont State Police, armed with a court order and accompanied by 50 Social Services workers, raided the Island Pond community homes and took 112 children into custody. Several days later a district judge ruled that the search warrant issued by the state was unconstitutional, and all the children were returned to their parents. Child custody disputes and investigations by Social Services continue, however, partly because of the influence of the anti-cult movement and several former members.

The group's commitment to their biblically based disciplinary practices is the primary focus of concern. Parents are instructed to discipline children who do not obey upon "first command" with a thin, flexible "reed-like" rod (as mentioned in Proverbs 23:13) so as to inflict pain but not injury. No evidence has been produced to substantiate the accusations of child abuse against the group, though these have been repeated for years.

Since the raid the group has attempted to cooperate with state authorities and has made efforts to reach out to neighbors in trying to foster better understanding. On June 25, 1994, the church held a 10-year anniversary celebration "to commemorate [our] deliverance from the 1984 Island Pond Raid." Many of those 112 children, now in their teens and twenties, shared their traumatic memories of the raid, again denied allegations of abuse, and declared their allegiance toward their parents and their community.

Twelve Tribes
2243 Dorchester Ave.
Lower Mills, MA 12124
http://www.TwelveTribes.com

Susan Palmer

See also: Communalism; Homosexuality; Messianic Judaism.

References
Nori, Don. "Persecution at Island Pond." *Charisma* 10, no. 4 (November 1984).
Palmer, Susan J. *Moon Sisters, Krishna Mothers, Rajneesh Lovers: Women's Roles in New Religions.* Syracuse, NY: University of Syracuse Press, 1996.
Swantko, Jean A. *An Issue of Control: Conflict between the Church in Island Pond and State Government.* Palenville, NY: privately printed, 1998.

U

UFO Religions

The term "UFO Religions" refers to a group of extremely diverse, predominantly but not exclusively small Western, religious groups with one thing in common: they have a distinctly religious understanding of what may be broadly termed "the myth of the flying saucer," and the accompanying legends of human intercourse with extraterrestrial beings.

In essence little can be said about these religions that does not apply to most religions in general. Religious leadership, rituals, sacred texts, myths, social structures, and the like are typologically no different from what we find in most spiritual groups outside society's larger religious tradition(s). Sometimes the UFO aspect appears simply as an attachment to well-known religious representations—for instance, when UFOs are considered vehicles of Theosophical Masters from Venus who, in traditional Theosophy, live in Tibet and do not use that kind of transportation. In general, the UFO perspective forms a part of syncretic belief systems.

No UFO cult predates the flying saucer rumors that hit the public imagination around the beginning of the Cold War in the summer of 1947. As it appears, the strange aerial objects that were allegedly seen by more and more people could not be explained to everyone's satisfaction. At a certain point it was suggested that they were spaceships from other worlds, and soon the first "contactee," George Adamski (1891–1965), who claimed to have met with space people in the Californian desert, met his audience. He was soon to be followed by numerous major and minor UFO prophets, each with his (and occasionally her) special message from beings from other planets.

It is debatable whether the general belief in extraterrestrial visitation should be considered a religious idea. However, it is quite obvious that this belief very often takes the shape of genuine religious faith. It is therefore appropriate to distinguish between the broader public imagination and the beliefs expressed in the actual UFO religions.

UFO religions are directly inspired by dominant features of the modern, technologically advanced world. Science, technology, space travel, fears of atomic war, computers, pollution of the natural world, and the like are among the themes incorporated, and thus dealt with, in religious UFO narratives. The occupants of the UFOs are understood to be super-human beings, bringers of all good to people on Earth. The UFO cults are distinctively modern in the sense that they interpret typical aspects of the modern world into their religious apparatus.

UFO religions are usually inspired by ideology perpetuated through the Theosophical Society, and most leaders of such groups are known to have been engaged in different kinds of modern spirituality prior to their UFO-related work. Well-known examples are George King (1919–1997), who founded the Aetherius Society in 1954; Ruth (1900–1993) and Ernest Norman (1904–1971), who headed Unarius (established 1954); Charles Boyd Benzel, the original founder of Mark Age (1960); George Van Tassel (1910–1970), who founded the Ministry of Universal Wisdom; and on the fringe of what may be termed religious UFO groups, George Adamski, who built up the International Get Acquainted Program (IGAP) in 1958.

The basic idea in these groups is the need for humans on Earth to grow spiritually and eventually to align with peoples from other worlds who are already

A car encouraging people to welcome extraterrestrial beings and topped with a model spacecraft sits on property near Jamul, California, October 15, 2000. The property was purchased by the Unarius Academy of Science to serve as a future landing site for "space brothers" from other planets. (Getty Images)

united in a Cosmic Brotherhood. The leader(s) of the group will usually claim to be in personal contact with the space people or higher beings, either man to man (being to being) or by means of telepathy. Other groups, though, have quite a different heritage. The Raelian movement, for instance, draws heavily on Jewish-Christian traditions, claiming that what the Bible recollects in fact is the story of how a group of extraterrestrials some 22,000 years ago created life on Earth by means of hyperadvanced biotechnology. The leader of the group, Rael (born Claude Vorilhon in France in 1945), who was allegedly approached by the extraterrestrials in 1973, is identified as a prophet and a messiah succeeding the biblical characters. Another UFO cult, Heaven's Gate, which met its sad destruction in a collective suicide in San Diego in 1997, had developed its own rare belief system urging believ-

ers to aim at "The Evolutionary Level Above Human" (TELAH).

In all, some 25 different UFO religions may be active today. Further, a line of other religions have incorporated beliefs in UFOs into their theologies. Certain evangelical groups, for instance, believe UFOs to represent Satanic forces, while other Christian groups, such as The Family International, believe them to be associated with angels. UFO-like notions are also found in the Church of Scientology's belief system. Finally, of course, religious interpretations of the UFO-narrative are important to the New Age movement.

Mikael Rothstein

See also: Church of Scientology; Family International, The; New Age Movement; Raelian Movement, International; Unarius.

References

Clarke, David, and Andy Roberts. *Phantoms of the Sky: UFOs—A Modern Myth*. London: Robert Hale, 1990.

Evans, Hilary. *From Other Worlds: The Truth behind Aliens, Abductions, UFOs and the Paranormal*. London: Carlton, 1998.

Lewis, James R., ed. *The Encyclopedic Sourcebook of UFO Religions*. Amherst, NY: Prometheus Books, 2003.

Lewis, James R., ed. *The Gods Have Landed: New Religions from Other Worlds*. New York: State University of New York Press, 1995.

Partridge, Christopher. *UFO Religions*. London: Routledge, 2003.

Reece, Gregory L. *UFO Religion: Inside Flying Saucer Cults and Culture*. London: I. B. Tauris, 2007.

■ Uganda

Uganda, a Central African nation, is completely land-locked, but its southern border sits on Lake Victoria and its western border is partially formed by several of the large lakes of the Rift Valley. It is otherwise surrounded by Kenya, Tanzania, Rwanda, the Democratic Republic of the Congo, and Sudan. Its territory includes 77,000 square miles of land. Its 31,400,000 people are among the most ethnically diverse of the African nations south of the Sahara, representing a number of distinct African peoples. Because of the many languages spoken by the various groups, English has become the common language for government and business.

Inhabited for millennia, Uganda emerges on the historical stage in the 10th century CE with evidence of an urban civilization. In the 13th century the area was invaded by Bacwezi people, who subdued the resident Bantu people. After settling in, they created a number of fortresses that protected their cattle, the key to their wealth and power. Through succeeding centuries, some of the groups of the region were oriented eastward toward Zanzibar and others northward through the Nile Valley to Sudan and Egypt. In the 17th century, Islam began to spread into Uganda.

The national mosque in Kampala, Uganda. (iStockPhoto.com)

The history of the region was changed by the movement through the area of David Livingstone (1813–1873), the fabled missionary of the London Missionary Society. Out of communication with the West for some years, in 1870 he became the object of a highly publicized search by reporter Henry Stanley (1841–1904). Upon his return to England, Stanley denounced the spread of Islam farther south, and he occasioned the sending of missionaries. In 1888 the Imperial British East Africa Company set up a trading enterprise.

British influence in the area was solidified in 1886, when it received European recognition for the establishment of a protectorate, formally put in place in 1893. British control lasted until 1962, when independent Uganda came into being. The land reform program of the new government met opposition from the

Uganda

Religion	Followers in 1970	Followers in 2010	% of Population	Annual % growth 2000–2010	Followers in 2025	Followers in 2050
Christians	6,425,000	28,923,000	85.0	3.22	46,114,000	79,526,000
Roman Catholics	3,395,000	13,700,000	40.2	2.95	21,900,000	38,285,000
Anglicans	1,291,000	12,100,000	35.5	3.51	19,500,000	33,702,000
Protestants	111,000	1,800,000	5.3	3.82	2,900,000	5,000,000
Muslims	588,000	3,857,000	11.3	3.61	6,250,000	10,900,000
Ethnoreligionists	2,130,000	743,000	2.2	1.95	700,000	700,000
Hindus	65,000	275,000	0.8	3.23	465,000	850,000
Agnostics	1,000	130,000	0.4	3.23	250,000	500,000
Baha'is	226,000	92,000	0.3	3.23	200,000	400,000
Atheists	0	12,100	0.0	3.23	20,000	40,000
Jews	500	3,200	0.0	3.23	5,000	8,000
Jains	1,000	3,000	0.0	3.24	5,000	8,000
Sikhs	5,700	1,500	0.0	3.24	2,000	3,000
Total population	**9,442,000**	**34,040,000**	**100.0**	**3.23**	**54,011,000**	**92,935,000**

40,000 Indian expatriates in the country who controlled much of the commercial activity. Following the coup that brought Idi Amin (ca. 1924–2003) to power in 1971, many of the Indians were expelled from the country. Amin's bloody regime was ended when he prompted war with neighboring Tanzania by attempting to annex some of their territory. Unfortunately, the regime of his successor, Milton Obote (1925–2005, r. 1980–1985), was almost as bloody.

The return of economic and political stability in the 1980s was hindered by a guerrilla-led civil war that ended only after a coup at the end of 1985. After seizing power, Yoweri Museveni (b. ca. 1944) attempted to re-create an orderly situation in a country that was heavily in debt and is still beset with poverty. He has stood for election on several occasions. Prior to the 2006 elections, he abolished provisions in the country's laws concerning term limits.

Traditional religions are still practiced in Uganda, but they now can count less than 5 percent of the people among their adherents. Among the groups that have retained a sizable percentage of traditionalists are the Ganda, the largest group in the country. The Ganda have a sophisticated theology that poses the existence of a pantheon of deities headed by a Supreme Being (Katonda) and his family, including Nalwanga (wife), Wanga (grandfather), Mususi (father), and Kibuka (brother). The many deities that surround Katonda

serve as intermediaries between him and human beings, and each is given charge over an aspect of the cosmos of importance to human life (from childbirth to hunting).

The meaningful push of Islam into Uganda began in the mid-19th century. It flowed in from the north (Sudan) and east (Tanzania). Inadvertently, the British encouraged Islam by their use of Muslims as bureaucrats and translators. The community was expanded by the inclusion of Muslims among the Indians who assumed responsibility for developing Uganda's commercial life. Indian Muslims brought Shia Islam, especially in its Ismaili, Ithna-Ashari, and Bohra forms.

The Ahmadiyya Muslim movement arrived in 1921. Considered heretical, it nevertheless attempted to evangelize the Ugandan public, with some response. However, in the middle of the century it divided into three factions that have yet to reunite.

During his 1875 visit to Africa, Henry Stanley met a Ugandan ruler, Kabaka Mutesa I, who requested Christian missionaries to assist him in throwing back the encroachments of Islam, a distorted tale if not an outright fabrication. The Church Missionary Society's first missionaries arrived in 1877. They found Dallington Maftaa, an African preacher commissioned by Livingstone. All of the team, except its leader Alexander MacKay (1849–1890), died within their first two years. Mackay continued to work alone, and his stead-

UGANDA

fastness eventually paid off with converts and additional missionaries, who arrived in the 1890s. The Bible Churchmen's Missionary Society bolstered the CMS's efforts in 1921.

The Anglican work became the largest in the country, not counting that of the Roman Catholics, and it is structured today as the Church of the Province of Uganda, set aside as an independent province in 1961. In 1965 the province elected Erica Sabiti as its primate, the first African to assume such a post. The African Inland Mission had added its strength to the small Anglican community in Uganda in 1918. It worked closely with the Church of England, and eventually its missions/churches were integrated into the new province as its West Nile Diocese.

The Roman Catholic Church was introduced into Uganda in 1879. The brothers of the White Fathers found their way to the court of Kabaka Mutesa. Their subsequent missionary endeavor had an immediate impact. By 1912 there were more than 136,000 members,

and the church now has more than 7 million members. The first Ugandan priest was ordained in 1911, and the first bishop in 1939. In 1969 the church was encouraged by the visit of Pope Paul VI, whose talk emphasized the need to develop a truly African Christianity. Today the Catholic Church numbers in excess of 9 million, more than 40 percent of the country's population.

The development of Christianity in Uganda has been marred by a number of horrendous events, beginning with the persecution of Muslims in 1875 and 1876 in which some 70 Muslim leaders were killed. In 1885 and 1886, between 200 and 300 Anglican and Catholic Christians were killed (an event marked by the Church of the Martyrs at Namugongo, erected by the Catholic Church). Most recently, in 2000, the Catholic Church was embarrassed when a group of former members who had formed a new organization, the Movement for the Restoration of the Ten Commandments, committed a mass murder/suicide in the rural village of Kanungu. Some 780 died (including a number of members who had been murdered at other locations). The group was built around messages received by its leaders from the Virgin Mary.

Pentecostalism was introduced into Uganda in 1935 by the Pentecostal Assemblies of Canada. Their mission (now known as the Pentecostal Assemblies of God) spread; other Pentecostal churches established missions, and new Uganda Pentecostal bodies (such as the Church of the Redeemed) were created. Several hundred African Initiated Churches now are active in Uganda, including the Charismatic Church of Uganda (founded by former Anglicans), the African Israel Church, Nineveh (from Kenya), and the Society of the One Almighty God.

The MRTC incident brought to light several obscure Ugandan apocalyptic and millenarian movements heretofore known only locally. For example, the Holy Spirit movement led by Alice Lakwena (1966–2007) had engaged the government in a war that lasted more than a decade (from 1985 to 1996). Lakwena eventually fled Uganda and spent her last years in exile in Kenya. The Lord's Resistance Army, led by Joseph Kony (b. 1962), a distant relative of Lakwena's, is closely related to a rival group founded by Lakwena's father, Severino Lukoya. In the light of problems encountered among these groups, the government has moved to suppress what it perceives as prophetic movements: most recently, in 1999, the World Message Last Warning Church, founded by Wilson Bushara. Bushara reorganized his group in 2002 and has since sought dialogue and recognition by the government.

Apart from these smaller and more controversial groups, more traditional Christian bodies have entered Uganda and garnered a significant response, including the New Apostolic Church, the Seventh-day Adventist Church, and the Church of God (Anderson, Indiana). There is also an Orthodox presence that originated in a schism among the Anglicans in the 1920s, now under the Greek Orthodox Patriarchate of Alexandria and All Africa. The Orthodox Church joined with the Anglicans and Catholics to found the Uganda Joint Christian Council in 1963. It is now affiliated with the World Council of Churches. More conservative churches have formed the Uganda Association of Evangels, loosely associated with the World Evangelical Alliance.

Hinduism was brought to Uganda by the Indian businessmen who settled in Africa throughout the 20th century. They have built temples in Kampala and, though suppressed during the years of Idi Amin, have returned in strength and have spread throughout the country. There are close to a million adherents following a spectrum of Hindu forms. There are a very small number of Jains and Sikhs.

The Baha'i Faith has had some of its greatest African response in Uganda. It had formed more than 1,500 spiritual assemblies, and Kampala was chosen as the site of its first African temple. However, Amin banned the movement, and the subsequent years of civil war and unrest almost destroyed it. Less than 100 spiritual assemblies were active through the 1990s. The movement has begun a rebuilding process in the new century.

Among the more interesting of Uganda's newer religious movements is the Abayudaya, a group who has practiced Judaism since 1919, when their leader, Semei Kakungulu (d. 1928), after his study and consideration of the Torah, began to observe the Mosaic law, including circumcision. In the intervening years, Western and Israeli Jews have visited Uganda and offered Kakungulu and his followers information on contemporary Judaism. The 500 Abayudaya survived Idi Amin's conversion to Islam and anti-Semitism, and today they reside in four villages outside Mbale, Uganda.

J. Gordon Melton

See also: African Initiated (Independent) Churches; African Israel Church, Nineveh; Ahmadiyya Movement in Islam; Baha'i Faith; Church Missionary Society; Church of England; Church of God (Anderson, Indiana); Church of the Province of Uganda; Greek Orthodox Patriarchate of Alexandria and All Africa; Ismaili Islam; London Missionary Society; Movement for the Restoration of the Ten Commandments, The; New Apostolic Church; Pentecostal Assemblies of Canada; Roman Catholic Church; Seventh-day Adventist Church; Shiah Fatimi Ismaili Tayyibi Dawoodi Bohra; World Council of Churches; World Evangelical Alliance.

References

Abidi, S. A. H., ed. *The Role of Religious Organizations in the Development of Uganda.* Kampala,

Uganda: Foundation for African Development, 1991.

Anderson, W. B., ed. *Christianity in Contemporary Africa: Uganda*. Kampala, Uganda: Department of Religious Studies and Philosophy, Makerere University, 1973.

Behrend, Heike. *Alice Lakwena and Holy Spirits: War in Northern Uganda 1985–97*. Athens: Ohio University Press, 2000.

Hofer, Katharina. *Implications of a Global Religious Movement for Local Political Spheres: Evangelicalism in Kenya and Uganda*. Baden/Baden, Germany: Nomos Publishers, 2006.

King, N. Q., A. Kasozi, and A. Oded. *Islam and the Confluence of Religions in Uganda, 1840–1966*. Tallahassee, FL: American Academy of Religion, 1973.

Knighton, Ben. *The Vitality of Karamojong Religion: Dying Tradition or Living Faith?* Aldershot, UK: Ashgate, 2005.

Langlands, B. W. *Studies on the Geography of Religion in Uganda*. Kampala, Uganda: Department of Geography, Makerere University, 1967.

Rutiba, E. T. *Religions in Uganda, 1960–1990*. Kampala, Uganda: Department of Religious Studies, Faculty of Arts, Makerere University, 1993.

Taylor, John V. *The Growth of the Church in Uganda: An Attempt at Understanding*. London: SCM, 1958.

Uisang

625–702 CE

Master Uisang Sunim is a major figure in the transmission to Korea of Hwaom Buddhism (the Korean version of Chinese Hua Yan Buddhism, also known in Japan as Kegon Buddhism). Hua Yan Buddhism is often called the Flower Garland School for its emphasis on the teachings of the Avatamsaka, or Flower Garland Sutra, in which the bodhisattva Manjusri is a primary object of worship. Hwaom Buddhism would become important on the Korean peninsula just as the three kingdoms of Silla, Koguryo, and Paekche were being brought together into the United Kingdom of Silla (660).

Uisang initially emerges out of obscurity as the companion of Wanhyo (617–686). In 650, the pair left to travel from Koguryo (the northern Korean kingdom) to China to study, but were mistaken as spies and arrested at the border. Eleven years later, they made a second attempt, this time planning to sail from a port city in Paekche. As the story goes, on their way to study with a famous monk, they were caught in a rain storm. Taking refuge in an underground shelter for the night, they discovered on awakening that they were in an old tomb. Before the rain ceased, Wanhyo had an intense spiritual experience that led to enlightenment, of sorts, in which he concluded from it that within the correct state of consciousness, a person experiences no difference between a temple sanctuary and a tomb. The experience led to his eventual abandonment of his monk's status and spending the rest of his life spreading Buddhism among the masses.

Uisang traveled on to China, where he would reside for the next decade, the most important part of his time being spent in study with Zhiyan (or Chih-yen, 602–668), the second patriarch of the Hua Yan School. He returned home, according to one source, because he became privy to a plot of the Chinese to launch a surprise attack on his homeland, which had just gone through a lengthy period of warfare that united the peninsula into the former kingdom of Silla (668). Beginning in 671, Uisang gathered many disciples around him, and even influenced his former companion Wanhyo, who adopted Hwaom perspectives to argue for the uniting of the different Korean Buddhist schools. Receiving the patronage of Silla's King Munmu, Uisang would establish the headquarters for Hwaom Buddhists at Pusok Temple, originally constructed in 676.

Uisang would spend the rest of his life establishing Hwaom Buddhism across Korea. He would have three decades to make it the most important school of Korean Buddhism, which it would remain until the 12th century. The Hwaom School emphasized a doctrine of the interpenetrability of all of the phenomena of the universe. All phenomena arise from the original One Mind, or Buddha Nature. He gave popular expression of this doctrine in his book, *Ocean Seal of Hwaeom Buddhism*, "In one is all, in all is one, one is identical to all, all is identical to one." Uisang is now also viewed as the founder of the Korean Buddhist philosophy.

Edward A. Irons

See also: Bodhisattva; Enlightenment; Korean Buddhism; Monasticism.

References

Chung, Sae Hyang. "The Silla Priests Uisang and Wanhyo." *Korean Culture* 3, no. 4 (December 1982): 36–43.

Ishii Kosei. "The Synthesis of Huayan and Chan in Uisang's School." In *Korean Buddhism in East Asian Perspective*, edited by Geumgang Center for Buddhist Studies, 265–267. Seoul: Jimoondang, 2007.

The Korean Buddhist Research Institute, ed. *Buddhist Thought in Korea.* Seoul: Dongguk University Press, 1994.

Lee, Peter H. "Fa-tsang and Ŭisang." *Journal of the American Oriental Society* 82 (1962): 56–62.

McBride, Richard D., II. *Domesticating the Dharma: Buddhist Cults and the Hwaom Synthesis in Silla Korea.* Honolulu: University of Hawaii Press, 2007.

■ Ukraine

During the pre-Christian period, in what is now Ukraine, various forms of Paganism dominated among the Slavic and non-Slavic tribes that inhabited the region. Animism and belief in a goddess-mother was the main faith of the Cimmerians (ninth to seventh centuries BCE); the gods Tabi, Papa, and Api were the primary deities in the pantheon of the Scythians (seventh to third centuries BCE); the cult of the Sun, fire, and the Great Goddess Astarta was deeply extended among Sarmatians (second century BCE to fourth century CE); and a belief in ghosts and a variety of natural and social forces was characteristic of the faith among the Goths and the Gunnys (third to fifth centuries CE).

The distinctive Paganism of the local Slavic population had developed on its own basis but in close interaction with non-Slavic influences. A few dozens of gods and innumerable ghosts had formed the polytheistic system of Eastern European Slavs, in which Perun

Saint Andrew's Church in Kiev, Ukraine. (Rashevskaya/ Dreamstime.com)

(the god of lightning and rain), Dazhboh (the god of the Sun), and Svaroh (the god of heaven and fire) headed the pantheon. Before the adoption of Christianity, Slavic polytheism appeared to be making a smooth transformation into henotheism with the most intensive worship directed toward Perun.

The first attempt to evangelize the Kyivan Rus' was realized in 866 (or one or two years later) during the time of princes Ascold and Dir. Although this event did not leave any serious effects in the religious history of Ukraine, it was the first direct meeting with Byzantine Christianity (though previously the Kyivan Rus' had had sporadic acquaintances with other Christian branches—Aryanism, Armenian Monophysitism, Manicheanism, and even Nestorianism).

The official conversion of Eastern European Slavic tribes to Christianity started after the mass baptizing

Ukraine

Religion	Followers in 1970	Followers in 2010	% of Population	Annual % growth 2000–2010	Followers in 2025	Followers in 2050
Christians	28,400,000	37,991,000	84.1	–0.14	36,102,000	28,927,000
Orthodox	25,191,000	31,562,000	69.9	–0.81	29,844,000	23,288,000
Roman Catholics	1,667,000	4,630,000	10.3	1.41	4,100,000	3,500,000
Independents	1,102,000	1,200,000	2.7	2.72	1,400,000	1,500,000
Agnostics	10,558,000	4,904,000	10.9	–3.10	2,431,000	1,086,000
Atheists	7,536,000	1,100,000	2.4	–6.83	300,000	100,000
Muslims	250,000	960,000	2.1	–0.80	840,000	650,000
Jews	572,000	175,000	0.4	–4.33	160,000	120,000
Buddhists	0	20,000	0.0	0.17	25,000	30,000
Sikhs	0	8,200	0.0	0.37	8,500	9,000
Ethnoreligionists	0	6,400	0.0	–0.81	6,000	6,000
Hindus	0	5,000	0.0	0.37	6,000	7,000
Baha'is	0	250	0.0	–0.75	600	800
New religionists	0	120	0.0	–0.74	200	300
Total population	**47,317,000**	**45,170,000**	**100.0**	**–0.81**	**39,879,000**	**30,937,000**

of Kyivans in 988 under Great Prince Volodymyr (980–1015), who was later canonized and became one of the most popular local saints. As the conversion resulted from the efforts of priests from Constantinople, subsequent church history flowed out of the context of Eastern Christianity in general and the Byzantine tradition in particular. Since that time Eastern Orthodoxy has been the main spiritual institution in Ukraine. Its history can be divided into three main periods. For seven centuries (988–1686), the Kyivan metropolis was under the Ecumenical Patriarchate in Constantinople; in 1696 it was incorporated into the Russian Orthodox Church (Moscow Patriarchate). In 1918 it began a period of struggle for independence from the Moscow Patriarchate.

During the first centuries following the official conversion of the Kyivan Rus', although influences of Paganism had remained strong, Orthodoxy extended through all the land. The Orthodox Church became an obligatory and official institution in the country. It promoted the development of writing, education, law, architecture, social and political life, the strengthening of family values, and the transformation of interpersonal relations. It also started its own monastic tradition. The Kyiv-Cave monastery from the second part of the 11th century is the most famous monastic center from that time.

Following the Mongol invasion, for a time (1240–1458) the Kyivan metropolitans did not have a permanent place of residence. They transferred the actual place of their see to the northern part of the country (Vladimir, Suzdal, and, finally, Moscow), while keeping their old title—Metropolitan of Kyiv [Kiev] and All Rus'. As a result, the bishops moved to create a new identity (separate from the Kyivan heritage) of a northern-Rus' national self-image, centered on Moscow. At the same time, there was an aspiration to keep all the privileges of the Kyivan church in the southern (Ukrainian) part of the former Kyivan Rus'.

The Moscow metropolis declared its autocephaly from Kiev in 1458, and 10 years later it announced its complete separation. It still existed as an independent body when, in 1596, a number of its clergy, including bishops, signed the Brest Union by which a number of them moved into the Roman Catholic Church. Many of the Orthodox and the Eastern-rite Catholics were forced into the Russian Orthodox Church beginning in 1686. Moscow and Kiev were reunited, but this time the Moscow Patriarchate was in control. Over the next centuries, the Ukrainian church lost many of its unique ecclesiastical features.

Through the 20th century, the Ukrainian Orthodox Church alternated between two quite opposite positions, first as a jurisdiction within the Moscow Patriarchate,

2926 | ■ Ukraine

which took the form of an exarchate (1921–1942, 1945–1990), and then as a formally autonomous church (1918–1921, 1942–1944, 1990–2001). Following the Russian Revolution, Ukrainian leaders began an attempt to exist as an autonomous jurisdiction, though as yet unrecognized by other canonical Orthodox communities (1919–1934, 1942–1944, 1989–2001).

Although the Ukrainian Orthodox Church remains the dominant religious body, relatively strong influences from other Christian churches are also experienced in Ukraine. The Roman Catholic Church's mission to Ukraine began late in the first millennium CE. As early as 960, King Otton I established a mission to Kyiv under the leadership of the monk Adalbert as the first "bishop of Rus'." A permanent presence by the Roman Catholic Church started in the 12th century with the settlement of the Dominicans. New Episcopal sees (including Lviv, Lutsk, and Kamjanets-Podilskyj), which continue to exist, were established in the western Ukraine after successful Polish and Hungarian conquests in the 13th century. Later, especially during the period when Ukraine was a part of the Polish-Lithuanian state, some conversions into the Latin-rite Roman Catholic Church were recorded, though Catholicism has primarily remained a religion of the national identity of Polish, Slovak, and Hungarian minorities in the country. As the new century begins, there are 7 Roman Catholic dioceses with 807 parishes and 50 monasteries in Ukraine. The head of the church, Archbishop Marjan Javorky of Lviv, was nominated as a cardinal in January 2001.

The second branch of the Catholic Church in Ukraine is the Ukrainian Greek-Catholic Church, established in 1596 following the Brest Union, in which five of the seven Ukrainian Orthodox bishops accepted papal supremacy and the teachings of the Roman Catholic Church. They were allowed to preserve the Orthodox liturgy and rite. The new church was tolerated and even supported when Ukraine was part of the Polish-Lithuanian (until the end of the 18th century), Austrian-Hungarian (1772–1914), or Polish (1920–1939) states. But it was declared an anti-national institution and was opposed by the Cossacks (the main national force in the 17th and 18th centuries); later it was completely prohibited in that part of Ukraine that became part of the Russian Empire in the 18th century,

and subsequently in the Soviet Union after World War II. In 1946 all seven bishops and hundreds of monks and priests were imprisoned, and all parishes were converted to the Russian Orthodox Church. The Ukrainian Greek-Catholic Church continued to function outside Ukraine, and it finally restored its activity in Ukraine after 1989. In the 1990s it became the second religious body in Ukraine according to number of parishes (3,317). These are now organized into nine dioceses and three exarchates. There are, additionally, 17 dioceses and exarchates of the church around the world.

A Mukachiv Greek-Catholic diocese (established after the separate Uzhhorod Union with Rome in 1646) functions in Ukraine autonomously from other structures of the church. It is ruled directly by the Vatican and in close relationship with the Ruthenian Catholic Church, which was established in the United States by Ukrainians and Ruthenians from the Carpathian region. The visit to Ukraine by Pope John Paul II in June 2001 was an extremely important event for both branches of the Catholic Church.

Unlike Orthodoxy and Catholicism, Protestantism has never been really influential in Ukrainian society, in spite of two periods of closer acquaintance with Protestant ideas and even some planting of Protestant denominations. In the 16th and 17th centuries, classical Protestantism appeared in Ukraine in the form of Calvinism (the Reformed Church), Anti-Trinitarianism, and Socinianism. Some 200 Protestant congregations appeared in Galicia, Volyn, and central Ukraine, but owing to strong opposition to Protestantism from the Cossacks and official state prohibitions, Protestantism had almost completely disappeared by the beginning of the 18th century.

In the middle of the 19th century, the Baptists moved into the southern and central regions of Ukraine under the influence of German colonists. Over the next decades, approximately 5 percent of the Ukrainian population became members of the Baptist Church. At the same time, lesser numbers of Adventist, Pentecostal, and Jehovah's Witnesses congregations (the latter in western Ukraine) arose during the first half of the 20th century and continue to exist.

Protestantism today has become increasingly important in Ukraine, with almost 50 Protestant denomi-

UKRAINE

nations combining to include 27 percent of existing religious communities (approximately 6,800 organizations). In several regions, the number of Protestant congregations is larger than the number of parishes of more traditional churches. Judging by the number of adherents, the Baptist Church of Ukraine is currently the largest Baptist body in Europe.

Ukraine has also traditionally been home to adherents of non-Christian religions. Judaism was established in the 10th century, and extensive immigration of Western European Jews through Poland took place in the 15th and 16th centuries. They established 79 towns scattered through the country. Then, in the 18th century, Ukraine became the motherland of one of the most influential Jewish movements of modern times, Hasidism. Its founder, Baal Shem-Tov (Besht) (1698–1760), was born in Ukrainian Galicia and spent most of his life in the region near the Carpathian Mountains and in the town of Medzhybizh. Other famous Hasidic thinkers—Josef Koen, Levi Itshak, and Hershon Kurtover—as well as founders of the scientific study of Judaism—Solomon Pappoport and Nahman Krohmal—have worked in Ukraine.

The Jewish community also suffered much through the years. Three hundred local Jewish communities with their inhabitants were annihilated during the Ukrainian war for independence under the leadership of Bohdan Hmelnytskyj in the mid-17th century. Many additional Jews were killed during anti-Jewish pogroms at the beginning of the 20th century. However, the Holocaust during World War II became the most significant tragedy, with 98 percent of the Jewish population being systematically annihilated. Today, following mass emigration in the 1970s and 1990s, fewer than a half-million Jews remain in Ukraine. They have created 230 communities (including Hasidic and Reform synagogues) and several dozen Jewish organizations.

The continuous history of the Muslim community starts in the 11th century, when Kyivan princes invited Muslims into the country for war service. As a result small Islamic communities were created in various cities, though the most intensive spread of Islam was on the Crimean peninsula, where the local Tatar population accepted Islam in the 14th century under Khan Uzbek. From 1475 to 1774, a Crimean-Tatar Islamic state was under the protection of the Ottoman Empire. Attacks on Ukrainian Christians set the Cossacks in permanent opposition to Crimean Tatars. From the time of the incorporation of Crimea into the Russian Empire in 1783 until the Revolution of 1917, Islam continued its development without major conflict with other religions, but it was seriously disrupted in the 1930s by the atheistic policies of the Soviet Union. It completely disappeared after Stalin's deportation of all Crimean Tatars from their ethnic motherlands in 1944. Crimean Tatars began returning to the Crimea in the 1980s, and through the 1990s Islamic traditions have started to revive in Crimea and all of Ukraine. Four hundred Moslem communities (305 of which are in the Crimea) exist now in Ukraine under the supervision of three separate spiritual centers.

Armenian colonies have existed since the fourth century in Crimea and along the northern coast of the Black Sea. Additional Armenians moved to Ukraine (mostly to Galicia and Volyn) during intensive migration in the 11th, 13th, and 14th centuries. In 1365 the head of the Armenian Apostolic Church (Holy See of Echmiadzin) appointed a bishop for Ukrainian Armenians with the see in Lviv. In 1630 this bishop (Michael Torosovych) signed the union with Rome and started the Lviv archbishopric of the Armenian Catholic Church. All the institutions of both churches were destroyed in 1945, however, during the post-Communist period; some 16 communities of the Armenian Apos-

tolic Church and one of the Armenian Catholic Church have restored their activity.

Crimea particularly and Ukraine in general have been among the most famous centers of development of the Karaites, the Jewish group that rejects the Talmud and recognizes only the authority of the Torah. Ukrainian believers have added some Pagan practices and become a new religion, without direct correlation to other Karaist branches in the world. Karaites have been in Crimea since at least the eighth century; in the 13th century, they created new settlements in several cities of western Ukraine. In the late 19th century, Crimea was the world center of Karaism. Fully prohibited during the Soviet time, Karaites have opened eight communities in the post-Soviet era.

Reflecting a trend in the religious world internationally, Ukraine became a place of intensive growth of New Religious Movements (NRMs) through the 1990s. Although there are many NRMs of all types, they do not have a large number of followers. Among newly arrived Christian groups are the Church of Jesus Christ of Latter-day Saints, the New Apostolic Church, the Salvation Army, the Churches of Christ, the Swedenborgian movement, and many Charismatic groups (some 300 congregations). There is one group with Eastern Christian roots—the Church of Transfigurative God's Mother, a Russian Marian Church.

Eastern religions are represented by the International Society for Krishna Consciousness, neo-Buddhists (including several Tibetan Buddhist communities), adherents of Sri Chinmoy, Transcendental Meditation, Sahaja Yoga, and many other small groups. Several groups that seek a universal synthesis of religions include the Unification movement, the Baha'i Faith, and the specifically Ukrainian Great White Brotherhood. Leaders of the brotherhood became known far beyond Ukraine when they predicted the end of the world for November 1993, at which time they also attempted to occupy and worship in the most famous Christian sanctuary of Ukraine—Sophia Cathedral (dating from 1037) in Kyiv.

As in many European nations, the past decade has seen a revival of neo-Paganism, which in Ukraine has included a search for Old Slavic roots. There are two major representatives in the country, the Native Faith, which focuses upon the mainly monotheist idea of

Dazhboh, and the Native Ukrainian National Faith, which accepts polytheism.

There are a wide range of Western Esoteric groups, including the Theosophical Society (as founded by Helena Blavatsky, who was born in Ukraine) and the Brotherhood of Holy Grail. American representatives of the tradition now active in Ukraine include the Church of Scientology, the Church of Christ, Scientist, and Religious Science (Science of Mind).

Although the number of communities of new religions is relatively high, Ukraine still remains a country in which traditional religious priorities and affiliations prevail. According to the most recent sociological surveys, 61 percent of the population define themselves as Orthodox, 8 percent as Greek Catholic, 2 percent as Roman Catholic, 3 percent as Protestant, and only 1 percent as adherents of an NRM; meanwhile, 25 percent are atheists or do not relate to any religious group.

Andrij Yurash

See also: Adventism; Armenian Apostolic Church (Holy See of Echmiadzin); Armenian Catholic Church; Baptists; Church of Christ, Scientist; Church of Jesus Christ of Latter-day Saints; Church of Scientology; Churches of Christ; Eastern Orthodoxy; Ecumenical Patriarchate/Patriarchate of Constantinople; Great White Brotherhood; International Society for Krishna Consciousness; Jehovah's Witnesses; Karaites; New Apostolic Church; Pentecostalism; Religious Science; Roman Catholic Church; Russian Orthodox Church (Moscow Patriarchate); Ruthenian Catholic Church; Sahaja Yoga; Salvation Army; Sri Chinmoy Centres; Swedenborgian Movement; Theosophical Society; Ukrainian Catholic Church; Unification Movement.

References

Baltaden, S. K. *Seeking God: The Recovery of Religious Identity in Orthodox Russia, Ukraine, and Georgia.* DeKalb: Northern Illinois University Press, 1993.

Blazejowskyj, Dmytro. *Hierarchy of the Kyivan Church (861–1990).* Rome: Univ. Cath. Ucr. Clementis Papae, 1990.

Himka, John Paul, and Andriy Zayarnyuk, eds. *Letters from Heaven: Popular Religion in Russia and Ukraine.* Toronto: University of Toronto Press, 2006.

Kolodny, A. M. *Religion and Church in the Democratic Ukraine.* Kiev, 2000.

Millennium of Christianity in Ukraine: A Symposium. Ottawa, Canada: Saint Paul University, 1987.

Mueller, Alfred. *In the Name of God: Rhetoric, Religion, and Identity in Post-Soviet Ukraine.* Bloomington, IN: AuthorHouse, 2004.

Sorokowski, A., ed. *A Century of Christian Culture in Ukraine.* London: Ukrainian Millennium Committee in Great Britain, 1988.

Ukrainian Orthodox Calendar. South Bound Brook, NJ: Ukrainian Orthodox Church of the U.S.A., issued annually.

Ukraine, Eastern Orthodoxy in

As a unique phenomenon of Eastern Christianity, Ukrainian Orthodoxy (UO) has been shaped by many, sometimes controversial, influences. From the time of the baptism of the Kyivan Rus' (988 CE) until the end of the 17th century, it developed in interaction with the Ecumenical Patriarchate in Constantinople, and since the middle of the 17th century, it has been in close communication with the Moscow Patriarchate (that is, the Russian Orthodox Church [Moscow Patriarchate]). During its entire existence, contact with Western Christianity has been very important for its identity. And finally there are many features that testify to the distinctive character of the church's tradition, such as some Pagan traces, unique local practices, specific combinations of saints, openings to different traditions, unique canonical law, the experience of conducting local councils, its own monasticism, and numerous Western adoptions. The church has been a point at which Constantinople Orthodox, Western Roman, and Russian Orthodox traditions converge.

In spite of its diverse past, any actual pluralism in the UO was suppressed while Ukraine was a part of the Russian Empire (1654–1917), and especially after the UO was subordinated to the Moscow Patriarchate (from 1686). The first attempts to establish liberal values in the society after the Russian revolutions in 1905 and February 1917 caused strong demands from

Ukrainian clergy and adherents to separate the Ukrainian church from the Russian one. Prior to 1919, the separation movement had expressed only a general desire to translate all of the church's books and liturgy into Ukrainian. After publishing a decree of the government of the Ukrainian People's Republic (an independent state in 1917–1920) about autocephaly of the UO (January 1, 1919), the exponents of separation divided into two ideological directions that with variations and some changes have existed until the present. One group argued for full separation from Moscow and the creation of an independent autocephalous church, while the other favored the preservation of the organizational connection with the Russian Orthodox Church (ROC) in the form of an exarchate or autonomous church.

In March 1919 the supporters of autocephaly founded the first parishes that declared their full independence from their former religious center, and in October 1921 they conducted an All-Ukrainian Council in which the creation of the Ukrainian Autocephalous Orthodox Church (UAOC) was announced and its hierarchy consecrated. This new church was not recognized by any traditional Orthodox church, as none of the then-current Orthodox bishops took part in the ordinations. In spite of canonical law, a new bishop for the UAOC was consecrated from among and by parish priests (only the Russian Living Church faction of the Russian Orthodox Church recognized the UAOC, in 1923). The UAOC was most active in central, and to some extent northern and southern, Ukraine, where until the end of the 1920s almost 3,000 parishes were within its jurisdiction. In 1929, Stalin had initiated suppression of the UAOC, which he accused of nationalism. Twenty-six of its bishops and thousands of its priests and active members were arrested and killed in the concentration camps. By 1934 all of the institutions of the UAOC were destroyed.

The UAOC revived in February 1942, following the German occupation of Ukraine, when three former bishops of the Orthodox Church of Poland (OCP) declared the second birthing of the UAOC and ordained new bishops (who were from the canonical point of view quite legitimate). In 1944, before the Soviet army reoccupied Ukrainian territory, the hierarchy of the UAOC, the majority of its priests, and hundreds of thousands of adherents left Ukraine and established the church's institutions in diaspora (until 1949 in Western Europe and, after 1950, mainly in the United States, Canada, and additionally in Australia and South America).

Responding to demands of the Ukrainian clergy concerning more independence for UO, in 1918 the ROC had agreed to proclaim the autonomy of the Orthodox Church in Ukraine. However, practically speaking, that independence was never realized. In 1921 the Moscow patriarch Tikhon appointed an exarch to Ukraine, which in effect converted the autonomous church into an exarchate.

Before 1917 the ROC had had 11,753 churches in Ukraine: during the 1920s some 3,000 of those recognized the jurisdiction of the UAOC; some 2,000 (after 1920) found themselves in Polish territory and became a part of the OCP; and fewer than 7,000 churches remained under the authority of the ROC. Initially, parishes of the ROC dominated in the eastern and southern Ukrainian regions, but its infrastructure was almost completely destroyed by the middle of the 1930s as a result of the Soviet state's antireligious policy: fewer than 100 churches remained open. The church in connection with the ROC renewed its structure during World War II, and in 1942 it announced its return to its previous autonomous status, which was transformed again into an exarchate in 1944 when the Soviet Union restored its control over Ukrainian territory. The majority of the bishops of the Autonomous Church left Ukraine.

From 1944 until 1989 the Ukrainian exarchate of the ROC was the only Orthodox religious structure that was permitted by the Communist regime. Immediately after World War II, it brought together 21 dioceses with more than 7,000 parishes. All of the parishes of those churches that were then prohibited in the Soviet Union were included in the ROC's Ukrainian exarchate, including the parishes of the former UAOC, the OCP (in the territories that moved back to the Soviet Union), and the Ukrainian Catholic Church. The number of parishes was further decreased, to 15 dioceses and approximately 5,000 parishes, at the beginning of the 1960s as a result of Khrushchev's antireligious campaign.

The monopoly of the ROC over Orthodoxy in Ukraine was demolished after the beginning of liberal changes in the Soviet Union. In 1989 the third revival of the UAOC in Ukraine was proclaimed by a group of

Orthodox clergy in Galicia. The priest Volodymyr Yarema from L'viv was its ideological leader, and Bishop Ioan Bodnarchuk, formerly with the ROC, led the new movement. The revival of the autocephalous church was strongly opposed by the ROC in general, and especially by Metropolitan Filaret, the head of the Ukrainian exarchate of the ROC, which included at that time almost 70 percent of all Orthodox parishes in the country (approximately 5,000 out of fewer than 7,000).

In the early 1990s, three separate church structures appeared in Ukraine. The Ukrainian Orthodox Church under the jurisdiction of the Moscow Patriarchate (UOC MP) represents a pro-Russian direction in the Ukrainian Orthodoxy. It was created in January 1990 from the former Ukrainian exarchate of the ROC. After the declaration of Ukraine's independence (August 1991), Metropolitan Filaret signed a request to the ROC requesting autocephaly. The ROC deemed the request inexpedient. Two other bishops did not agree with that decision and joined Filaret in creating the Ukrainian Orthodox Church of Patriarchate (UOC KP). Volodymyr Sabodan became the new Ukrainian metropolitan of the UOC MP. In 1996 the UOC MP officially refused the idea of its granting autocephaly in Ukraine.

Parishes of the UOC MP now prevail in most sections of the country. It is the largest religious body in Ukraine (with 36 dioceses) according to the number of religious organizations (9,246 in total), monasteries (122, with 3,519 monks and nuns), brotherhoods (24), and clergy (7,507); its headquarters and main cathedral are on the territory of the most ancient and famous Ukrainian monastery, the Kyiv-Cave Lavra.

The strictly autocephalous direction within UO is represented by two churches—the UOC KP and the UAOC. Neither structure is recognized by any autocephalous Orthodox Church, owing to the strong opposition of the ROC. After 1998 the Ecumenical Patriarchate manifested special interest in UO. Patriarch Bartholomew I has proposed a way to unify the several Orthodox branches and grant autocephaly to the unified UOC.

The Ukrainian Orthodox Church of Kyivan Patriarchate was founded in June 1992 with an eye toward the unification of the whole of the UAOC (which had existed in Ukraine from 1989) and smaller parts of the UOC MP, which, under Metropolitan Filaret, had not agreed with the refusal of the ROC to give autocephaly for UO. It was founded by Patriarch Mstyslav Skrypnyk, who was at the same time the head of the UOC in the United States. The UOC KP is now led by patriarchs Filaret and Denysenko. It includes under its jurisdiction 30 dioceses in Ukraine and 6 dioceses abroad (Russia, Germany, France, Greece, and the United States). It has 16 seminaries and academies, 22 monasteries, 10 brotherhoods, and 18 missions. The main cathedral of the UOC KP is the Church of Saint Volodymyr in Kyiv.

The third Orthodox body, the Ukrainian Autocephalous Orthodox Church (UAOC), was created in 1993 by the small group of former UOC KP clergy, which until June 1992 had been in the UAOC that had existed from 1989 to June 1992. These clergy disagreed with the leadership of the UOC KP of Metropolitan Filaret. The charismatic leader of this group, Volodymyr Yarema, was ordained as a bishop in 1993 and subsequently elected the patriarch of this new UAOC. He was succeeded in September 2000 by the present metropolitan, Mephodij Kudriakov. The UAOC has 11 dioceses, 1,015 religious organizations, 1 monastery, and 6 seminaries. More than 90 percent of its parishes are located in Galicia, though its headquarters have been stationed in Kyiv.

In addition to the three large churches, a variety of smaller Orthodox communities, most with ethnically Russian roots, are also present, including the two branches of the Old Believers Russian Orthodox Church, one with clergy (58 religious organizations) and one without (12 religious organizations). Also visible are the Russian Orthodox Church Outside of Russia (7 religious organizations), the Russian True Orthodox Church (35 organizations), the Apocalyptic Orthodox Church (4 organizations), the Greek Orthodox Church (2 organizations), the Innocentian Church (1 organization), and several independent parishes (4 organizations).

After the intensive movement of Ukrainians through the 20th century, Ukrainian Orthodox structures were established abroad: in America, the Ukrainian Orthodox Church of the U.S.A. was founded in 1924; it now has 3 dioceses and 95 parishes. It was unrecognized until 1995 but has since been in communion with the Ecumenical Patriarchate. The Ukrainian Orthodox Church in Canada, founded in 1918, has 3 dioceses and 260 parishes. Also unrecognized for many years, in 1990 it came into communion with the Ecumenical Patriarchate. There are also separate dioceses in Western Europe, Australia, and South America. Orthodox communities of Ukrainians have also created structures in Romania (the Ukrainian decanate of the Romanian Orthodox Church) and Poland (several dioceses of the OCP in which Ukrainians are in the majority). An independent and informative Internet site devoted to Ukrainian Orthodoxy can be found.

Sociological data show that 61 percent of the Ukrainian population recognize themselves as adherents of Orthodoxy; however, only 35 percent (57 percent of Orthodox believers) are sure concerning their concrete church affiliation (indicative that many people see Orthodoxy more as an abstract historical tradition than as their actual religious practice). The UOC MP, which unites 37 percent of the all-Ukrainian religious organizations (70 percent from the Orthodox organizations), is supported by 12 percent of the population; the UOC KP, which unites 12 percent from the general number of communities (22 percent among Orthodox churches), has 22 percent of the adherents among the all-Ukrainian population; the UAOC (representing 4 percent of all-Ukrainian organizations and 8 percent of Orthodox ones) has 1 percent of the supporters. These figures show that the real jurisdictional priorities of the population do not coincide with existing church infrastructures. They also indicate that the thrust toward an autocephalous structure has significantly stronger support in the society than the pro-Russian position. The likelihood of a unified autocephalous church that will be recognized by the other Orthodox patriarchates is high.

Ukrainian Orthodox Church of Kyivan Patriarchate
Church of Saint Volodymyr in Kyiv
36 Pushkina St.
Kyiv
Ukraine
http://www.ukrainian-orthodoxy.org/index.asp

Ukrainian Autocephalous Orthodox Church
1 Entrance
8-A Triokhsviatytel's'ka St.
Kyiv
Ukraine

Andrij Yurash

See also: Ecumenical Patriarchate/Patriarchate of Constantinople; Orthodox Church of Poland; Romanian Orthodox Church; Russian Orthodox Church (Moscow Patriarchate); Russian Orthodox Church Outside of Russia; Ukrainian Catholic Church.

References
Baltaden, S. K. *Seeking God: The Recovery of Religious Identity in Orthodox Russia, Ukraine, and Georgia.* DeKalb: Northern Illinois University Press, 1993.
Pavlshyn, M., ed. *One Thousand Years of Christianity in Ukraine: Papers from a Symposium at the Australian National University, Canberra, 15 August 1987.* Melbourne: Department of Slavic Languages/Monash University, 1988.
Ukrainian Orthodox Calendar. South Bound Brook, NJ: Ukrainian Orthodox Church of the U.S.A., issued annually.
Zinkewych, O., and A. Sorokowski, eds. *A Thousand Years of Christianity in Ukraine: An Encyclopedic Chronology.* New York: Smoloskypb Publishers and the National Committee to Commemorate the Millennium in Ukraine, 1988.

Ukrainian Catholic Church

Christianity came to what is now Ukraine at the end of the first millennium CE, and following the division between the Roman Catholic Church and Eastern Orthodoxy in 1054, the Ukrainians adhered to the latter. The church in Ukraine was under the jurisdiction of the Ecumenical Patriarchate residing in Constantinople. In the 14th century, Lithuania, a Roman Catholic nation, invaded the region, and much of the national and ethnic identity of the Ukrainians was developed in opposition to the imposed Lithuanian authority.

In 1439 the Orthodox metropolitan of Kiev, Isidore, attended the Council of Florence, a gathering of the bishops of the Roman Catholic Church, and agreed to the union of the Ukrainian Orthodox with the Roman Catholics. Many Ukrainians accepted the union, but many rejected it and remained Orthodox in faith. Then in 1569, following the union of Lithuania and Poland,

Interior of a Ukrainian Greek Catholic church in Nadvirna, Ukraine. (Chernetskiy/Dreamstime.com)

control of the region passed to Poland. Catholic leaders made a new effort to unite Catholic and Orthodox structures as a means of stopping the growth of Protestantism.

In this context, a number of Orthodox began to see a union with Rome as a means of saving their church from absorption into the Latin-rite Roman Church, which was expanding rapidly. Thus in 1596, at a gathering of Orthodox bishops, a new union of Ukrainian Orthodoxy with Rome was proclaimed. Over the next century the majority of Ukrainians accepted it. It survived until the 19th century, when Russia expanded its control in the region. Russian authorities suppressed the Roman Catholic Church and incorporated both the Ukrainian Catholic Church and the Ukrainian Orthodox Church into the Russian Orthodox Church (Moscow Patriarchate). The Ukrainian Catholic Church survived in Galicia, western Ukraine, which had by this time come under Austrian control.

The Ukrainian Catholic Church flourished during the early 20th century under the brilliant leadership of Andrew Sheptyckyj. Beginning in the late 19th century, Ukrainians had started to migrate worldwide, and Catholic parishes began to emerge in the United States, Canada, South America, Australia, and Western Europe. These parishes played an important part in keeping Ukrainian identity alive during the years after World War II, when the Soviet Union annexed Galicia, Poland deported most Ukrainians in Poland to the Soviet Union, and the Soviet government suppressed the Ukrainian Catholic Church. All of the bishops were arrested, and all but one died in prison. Believers were forced to choose between the Russian Orthodox Church and the Latin-rite Roman Catholic Church, though in fact the Ukrainian Catholic Church survived as an underground church.

Only with the weakening of the Soviet Union at the end of the 1980s was a distinctive Ukrainian Catholic

Church re-established, when in 1989 a new bishop of Przemysl was named. In 1991, Cardinal Myroslav Lubachivsky (1931–2000) was able to move into his residence in Lviv. By the end of the year seminaries were established at Lviv, and Ivano-Frankivsk and religious orders were revived. In 2000, Cardinal Lubomyr Husar succeeded Cardinal Lubachivsky as head of the church.

In 2001, Pope John Paul II (r. 1978–2005) visited Lviv. While there he beatified 28 Ukrainian Greek Catholics, 26 of whom had died during Soviet persecutions. Soon afterward, in 2005 Cardinal Husar moved the headquarters of the archdiocese from Lviv to Kiev, the capital of Ukraine, and his title was changed to Major Archbishop of Kiev and Halych. Headquarters of the church will be in the Patriarchal Cathedral of the Resurrection of Christ in Kiev, which remains under construction as of 2010.

Meanwhile the church in diaspora continued on. There are five dioceses in Canada and four in the United States. There are also dioceses in Australia, Brazil, and Argentina. Apostolic exarchates have been appointed for France, Germany, and the United Kingdom. Ukrainian Catholic seminaries are located in Washington, D.C.; Stamford, Connecticut; Ottawa, Ontario; and Curitaba, Brazil. There is a Ukrainian college in Rome. There were a reported 4,224,000 members worldwide in 2008, making the Ukrainian church the largest of the several Eastern Catholic churches.

J. Gordon Melton

See also: Eastern Orthodoxy; Roman Catholic Church; Russian Orthodox Church (Moscow Patriarchate).

References

Dyrud, Keith P. *The Quest for the Rusyn Soul: The Politics of Religion and Culture in Eastern Europe and in America, 1890–World War I.* Philadelphia: Balch Institute, 1992.

Himka, John-Paul. *The Greek Catholic Church and Ukrainian Society in Austrian Galicia.* Cambridge, MA: Ukrainian Studies Fund, Harvard University, 1986.

Kuzio, Taras. *Ukraine: Perestroika to Independence.* London: Palgrave Macmillan, 2000.

Liesel, N. *The Eastern Catholic Liturgies: A Study in Words and Pictures.* Westminster, MD: Newman, 1960.

Sianchuk, John. *Blessed Bishop Nicholas Charnetsky, C.Ss.R., and Companions: Modern Martyrs of the Ukrainian Catholic Church.* Liguori, MO: Liguori Publications, 2002.

Ullam-bana

Ullam-bana is a Chinese festival celebrated in China, Korea, Japan, and throughout the Chinese diaspora. Though most developed in China, Ullam-bana originated in India, where it was tied to the rainy season. Indian monsoon retreats traditionally lasted from the 16th day of the 4th lunar month to the 15th day of the 7th month. Buddhist monks ceased their largely wandering life and generally spent the time in company with others. For the monk, the time allowed for growth and regeneration, but popular speculation suggested that the travel restrictions actually provided protection for newly arisen life forms who might be harmed by traveling monks. Ullam-bana derived from the last day of the retreat period, traditionally referred to as the Buddha Happiness Day, as the monks would have made progress in their cultivation (practice) from their retreat.

Ullam-bana was transferred to China quite early—the first recorded instance dating to 538 CE, when it was noted that the Emperor Liang carried out a fast on the 15th day of the 7th month. Over time the festival was also conflated with the Daoist Zhong Yuan festival of the 15th day of the 7th month, in which officials in the lower realms forgive sins. The combined version of the Daoist and Buddhist celebration meant that the seventh month was the time when the gates of hell would be opened and the suffering ghosts could wander freely in the realm of humans. The souls of those trapped in the underworld, whose descendants have made no offerings for them, would be free to cross the boundaries where the underworld and the visible world meet. These souls are known as *pretas* (the "hungry ghosts" seen in many Hong Kong "vampire" movies) and if unchecked may cause a variety of mischief and evil. Thus Ullam-bana also came to be known as the Festival of Hungry Ghosts, and the entire month as the "ghost month."

For the Buddhist, the observance of Ullam-bana derives its content from the Ullam-bana Sutra, a Mahayana text, which tells the story of the *arhat* (enlightened person) Maudgalyayana (or Mulian). Mulian discovered that his deceased mother was trapped in a realm of pain and suffering most characterized by an inability to eat. He made his way to the netherworld in hopes of ameliorating her situation, but all his efforts proved futile. Finally, he appealed directly to the Buddha, who informed him that by himself he could do nothing to relieve his mother's suffering. The Buddha told Mulian that he had to make offerings of various items to the *sangha* (the monks and nuns), and then join them in prayers for his mother's liberation from hell. His action would affect his mother, but also be advantageous for all of his other deceased relatives.

Ullam-bana marks the day on which Mulian performed what the Buddha had told him to do. On this day, the Buddhist faithful will offer prayers for the souls of their ancestors going back seven generations, but focus especially on deceased parents. They will also visit local temples with offerings for the monks and nuns. The prayers and offerings of the day are believed to alleviate the suffering of ancestors and shorten the time before they are able to enter the heavenly realms. At the same time, those who follow traditional Chinese religion (and there is not a strict line demarking them from Buddhists) may burn spirit money for their ancestors to use in their present spirit life, and will attempt to appease the hungry ghosts by offering them food, drink, and entertainment, and use the occasion to also imbibe of the same.

In Japan Ullam-bana is known as Obon and celebrated on the same day, though with slightly different emphases.

J. Gordon Melton

See also: Ancestors.

References

Kaulbach, B., and B. Proksch. *Arts and Culture in Taiwan.* Taipei: Southern Materials Center, 1984.

Latsch, Marie-Luise. *Traditional Chinese Festivals.* Singapore: Greaham Brash, 1984.

Liming, Wei. *Chinese Festivals: Traditions, Customs, and Rituals.* Hong Kong: China International Press, 2005.

Robinson, Richard H., and Willard L. Johnson. *The Buddhist Religion: A Historical Introduction.* Belmont, CA: Wadsworth Publishing Company, 1997.

Stepanchuk, Carol, and Charles Wong. *Mooncakes and Hungry Ghosts: Festivals of China.* San Francisco, CA: China Books & Periodicals, 1992.

Thompson, Laurence G. *Chinese Religion.* Belmont, CA: Wadsworth Publishing Company, 1996.

Umbanda

Umbanda, a Brazilian-based religion closely related to Candomblé, integrated Afro-Brazilian and kardecistic-spiritistic doctrines and practices, along with various indigenous elements. With its desire to magically manipulate the empirical world according to the sorrows and necessities of its adherents, Umbanda has remained loyal to the Afro-Brazilian tradition. At the same time it has excluded blood sacrifice, and, compared with Candomblé, initiation into Umbanda is considerably less costly, in terms of both money and preparation time. Like Spiritism, Umbanda focuses on an altruistic morality and charity.

As an institutionalized religion, Umbanda emerged in the 1930s, when a far-reaching process of urbanization and industrialization began, and the political context supported the ideological integration of a new society. Hence Brazilian scholars of religion point out that the consolidation of Umbanda reflects the search by a still disintegrated population for a national identity, capable of harmonizing internal contradictions, including racial tensions. Umbanda established itself on a larger scale in the 1950s, especially in Rio de Janeiro, Porto Alegre, and Sao Paulo. Until today the urban character remains a key element. As the *Datafolha* survey showed, 69 percent of all Umbanda members in 1991 were inhabitants of major Brazilian cities, and 56 percent were white.

People prepare offerings to Yemanja, the Goddess of the Sea of the Afro-American religion Umbanda, on February 2, 2010, at a beach in Montevideo, Uruguay. (Getty Images)

Brazilian scholars subsume both Umbanda and Candomblé in the category of "mediumistic religions." The 1991 census treated Candomblé and Umbanda as a statistical unit, with 648,463 members (0.44 percent of the total population). According to the 1994 *Datafolha* study, about 1 percent of Brazil's adult population were associated with Candomblé, and 1 percent with Umbanda, a figure also in high tension with the results of the last national census that counted 416,930 "Umbandistas" (0.28 percent of the population). The Federação Nacional de Tradição e Cultura Afro-Brasileira projected a very different picture, with an estimate that 70 million Brazilians are participants in either Candomblé or Umbanda. Among several Umbanda organizations is the Initiatic Order of the Divine Cross, an Umbanda temple established in 1970 by the medium F. Rivas Neto.

Initiatic Order of the Divine Cross
Rua Chebl Massud, 157
Bairro Água Funda
São Paulo
Brazil

http://www.umbanda.org/conce_e.htm
http://www.jornalumbandahoje.com.br/

Frank Usarski

See also: Candomblé; Spiritism.

References

Bastide, Roger. *The African Religions of Brazil: Toward a Sociology of the Interpenetration of Civilizations.* Trans. by Helen Sebba. Baltimore: Johns Hopkins University Press, 2007.

Brown, Diana DeGroat. *Umbanda: Religion and Politics in Urban Brazil.* New York: Columbia University Press, 1994.

Hess, David J. *Samba in the Night: Spiritism in Brazil.* New York: Colombia University Press, 1994.

Unarius

Unarius, one of several religions to emerge out of the claims of contact with advanced beings from outer space, emerged out of the spiritualist work of Ernest Norman (1904–1971) and his wife, Ruth Norman (1900–1993). Unarians believe that the Normans have been reincarnated a number of times, on occasion together. For example, Ernest appeared as the Egyptian pharaoh Amenhotep, and Ruth as the pharaoh's mother. Most important, Ernest is believed to have been Jesus and Ruth his betrothed. Ruth was also believed to have been the woman who sat as a model for Leonardo da Vinci's *Mona Lisa.* Unarius is seen as the return of Jesus and the renewal of his work, which was so abruptly stopped by his untimely death.

Unarius ("universal articulate interdimensional understanding of science") was organized in 1954, and during its early years it was built around the channeling of Ernest Norman, who claimed contact with beings on a variety of planets. Following his death in 1971, Ruth emerged as a channel and over the next 20 years produced a number of texts. She also produced a basic set of lesson materials, which became the curriculum for new Unarius members. These lessons, "The Psychology of Consciousness" and "Self-Mastery, the Infinite Concept of Cosmic Creation," concentrate on bringing forth the latent potentials in each individual.

The original materials channeled from beings on the planets Venus, Mars, Hermes, Eros, Orion, and Muse related information on life in other worlds, their advanced science, and, most important, information on spiritual development and healing. Healing may occur utilizing energy directed from the great intelligences on other worlds.

Building on her husband's earlier works, Ruth Norman offered an integrated picture of the many planets that she asserted were combined into an Intergalactic Federation. These advanced planets contacted Ruth and invited Earth into the confederation through her. A joining occurred in 1973, with Ruth (spiritual name, Ioshanna) as the principal contact. Since that time, Earth has been seen as progressing so that in the future it can become a full member of the confederation.

Following Ruth Norman's death, Unarius was led by Charles Spiegel (1921–1999). It is currently led by a board of senior students. Members are scattered across North America and study groups operate in Mexico, Austria, and Nigeria (2009).

In 1988, on the occasion of the release of the film directed by Martin Scorsese, *The Last Temptation of Christ*, Ruth Norman issued a claim that she was the reincarnation of the biblical character Mary of Bethany, the sister of Lazarus. She authored a book, *The Bridge to Heaven: My 2,000-Year Psychic Memory as Mary of Bethany—13th Disciple to Jesus of Nazareth*, in which she suggested that Mary of Bethany was the betrothed of Jesus of Nazareth, and was later identified with Mary Magdalene (a prostitute) by Jesus' disciples. In the middle of the first decade of the new century, as Dan Brown's novel *The Da Vinci Code* became a best-seller, Unarius's current leadership reasserted Norman's claim.

Unarius
143 S. Magnolia
El Cajon, CA 92022
http://www.unarius.org/

J. Gordon Melton

See also: Reincarnation; UFO Religions.

References

Ioshanna [Ruth Norman]. *A Space Woman Speaks from Outer Space*. El Cajon, CA: Unarius, n.d.

Norman, Ernest L. *The Voice of Venus*. Santa Barbara, CA: Unarius–Science of Life, 1956.
Pathway to Light: An Introduction to the Unarius Science of Life. El Cajon, CA: Unarius Academy of Science, 1995.
The Universal Hierarchy. *A Pictorial Tour of Unarius*. El Cajon, CA: Unarius Educational Foundation, 1982.

◆ Unbelief

The term "unbelief," as used in this encyclopedia, refers directly to the modern community of people and organizations who advocate those philosophical/ideological positions that do not include a belief in God, either in the singular or plural, and have no use for various supernatural realities, often seen as the essence of religion, including prayer, miracles (in the sense of divine intervention in the natural order), revelation, or life after death. Such philosophical positions go under a variety of names—atheism, humanism, agnosticism, Freethought, rationalism, secularism, and so forth.

Through the centuries, numerous individuals, and even religious groups, have espoused positions that formally could be called unbelief. In the ancient West, unbelief has been ascribed to those philosophers who challenged various supernatural assumptions commonly held within Greek society, such as the belief in demonic inspiration and divination. In the East, Jainism and Theravada Buddhism developed extensive religious systems without the need of positing a God as a focus of worship.

However, modern unbelief does not encompass every form taken by alternatives to theism and polytheism; rather, it refers to the critical approach taken to Western Christianity that emerged in post-Reformation Europe in which unbelief was unbelief in Christian theism (and to a lesser extent, Judaism). Attacks upon the belief in God as irrational and lacking evidential support began to be made in the 18th century, but a foundation for these attacks had been laid by the events of the previous centuries.

At the beginning of the 16th century, Western Europe was united religiously by the Roman Catholic

Church. Although its power varied considerably from country to country, the challenges to its hegemony were relatively localized and were dealt with by the power of the state. However, the attack on the church's power that began with Martin Luther (1483–1546) in the second decade of the new century would by the end of the century remake the religious map of Europe significantly. Different countries would emerge with Lutheran, Reformed-Presbyterian, or Anglican establishments in power, and additional space would be provided for Mennonites, Socinians (non-Trinitarians), and various small mystical groups such as the Schwenfelders.

Relative to the time, the champion of unbelief was Michael Servetus (1511–1553), the Spanish physician who wrote a book comparing the Christian Trinity to the three-headed hound of hell. For this and other opinions expressed in his 1553 work on the restitution of Christianity, he was first imprisoned by the Inquisition. Escaping, he fled to Geneva, where Reformed Church leader John Calvin (1509–1564) saw to his arrest and execution. Although Lutherans, Calvinists, and Anglicans had challenged a set of Roman Catholic beliefs, they did not disagree concerning the doctrine of God (and that unanimity would quickly push the Socinians from their brief ascendancy in Poland).

Protestantism, while still operating within an orthodox Christian world, did begin the process of criticism of popular supernaturalism that had become institutionalized in Roman Catholicism. It challenged the nature of the Eucharist, the central Christian sacrament, and offered alternatives to the Roman Catholic doctrine of transubstantiation, which holds that the bread and the wine once consecrated are transformed in substance into that of the Body and Blood of Christ (although their appearance remains unchanged). Protestants also challenged the use of numerous relics and the doctrine of purgatory (and the accompanying system of rewards and punishments associated with it).

A next step, the challenge to some of the pervasive views shared by both Protestant and Roman Catholic Christians alike, emerged in the 17th century. Deism affirmed the existence of God but generally denied its miraculous or supernatural elements. Such belief generally saw Jesus as a great moral teacher but denied that as the Christ he was the second person of a Triune God. Deism was often seen as a natural or reasonable religion (as opposed to revealed religion). According to its initial advocate, Edward Herbert, Lord Cherbury (1583–1648), Deism focused on five affirmations: the existence of a supreme being; the need for worship; piety and virtue as the primary forms of worship (rather than prayer and ritual); the need to repent of shortcomings; and a set of rewards and punishments awaiting individuals in the afterlife. The Deist worldview undercut belief in God's activity in the world, apart from maintaining the system through natural law and the validity of prayer.

Deism became popular among the educated elite as science developed. Although affirming the existence of God, it supplied a worldview that did not interfere with scientific experimentation and investigation, and a theology that did not answer scientific questions in a way that blocked further inquiry. Deism tended to adopt the view of God as the watchmaker who created the world, wound it up, and left it to run according to natural laws. Deism also included an anticlerical element, and many Deists attacked the church and the authority of its priests and ministers in secular matters, and publicized immoral acts attributed to church leaders in centuries past.

While arising in the 17th century, Deism became a significant movement in the 18th century. British Deist leaders included Lord Shaftsbury (1621–1683), Alexander Pope (1688–1744), Anthony Collins (1676–1729), and Thomas Woolston (1669–1732). In France, Voltaire emerged as the leading Deist spokesperson and used his literary abilities to attack religion in general and the Roman Catholic Church in particular. In the British American colonies, Deism emerged as the faith of the most prominent revolutionaries—Thomas Jefferson, Benjamin Franklin, Thomas Paine, John Adams, and George Washington.

Atheism As Deism was gathering a wide following, a next step was taken away from the dominant religious sentiments in Western society with the development of perspectives that dispensed with the notion of a deity as an ultimate point of reference. Because of the need to establish itself within a society in which the overwhelming majority profess theism, the nontheistic perspective struggled to find space to exist in

Portrait of Voltaire, French Enlightenment-era author and philosopher famous for his crusades against social injustice and religious intolerance. (Library of Congress)

reference to the larger community; it was commonly perceived as a negative position, simply a denial of God and religion. To the contrary, atheists have generally insisted that their position is not so much a denial of God as the development of a perspective on life after having found no convincing evidence that something called God exists, and of creating a lifestyle in which God is unnecessary either as a moral authority or an object of worship.

Atheism thus includes a variety of belief systems that lack any belief in a God or in multiple gods. Some go even further and say that the very term "God" has no meaning to them. The assertion of such a perspective has put atheists at odds with the mainstream of religious thought as it has existed in the West since the 17th century. Although hinted at in earlier works, atheism was first openly asserted in the modern West in 1772 in a book by Paul Henri Holbach (1723–1789), *The System of Nature*, though his position had been implied in several earlier texts in which he criticized the church and Christian theology.

As atheism developed, it did so under a variety of names, each indicating a major theme and a slightly different emphasis in thought—Freethought, rationalism, secularism, and Humanism being the most popular. The concept of Freethought developed in the 18th century to describe systems of dissent from specific religious propositions. As science was emerging as a relatively secular endeavor, Freethought insisted that science be free from various theological debates and conclusions, and be allowed to develop its own vocabulary and methodology as it pursued its investigation of the world—that scientists be freed to follow the paths opened by the logic of their thoughts. Inasmuch as scientific conclusions offered dissenting views on what most considered religious issues, from the sanctity of the human body to the age of the universe, Freethought became identified with non-Christian views and eventually with atheism.

Rationalism refers to any one of several philosophical positions characterized by the elevation of reason to the level of a dominating metaphysical or epistemological principle. In one sense, rationalism has a significant philosophical history, as the philosophical school begun by René Descartes (1596—1650). In the more popular sense, however, rationalism refers to a position adopted by many unbelievers suggesting that religious beliefs and practices be subjected to a rational examination and accepted or rejected on the same basis as one would accept or reject other matters. In examining religions, rationalists tended to reject theological supernaturalism and practices such as worship and prayer, which they tended to condemned as "irrational"—that is, contrary to reason as they used it.

Secularism is a perspective on the world that begins with the division of the world into two realms, the sacred and the secular—that is, the realm of the divine and the religious, and those aspects of life that may be considered apart from either. As originally proposed in the mid-19th century, secularism had a special concern for ethics and the development of ethical systems apart from theology. Secularism thus came to mean the practical process of improving humans and society without reference to religion or religious institutions. Secularism has also taken on special connotations with regard to the single issue of the separation of church and state, in its more absolutist sense—namely that not only should government not interfere with religion, but that religious ideas should not be injected into governmental processes.

Humanism, a term that covers a variety of philosophical perspectives, arose anew in the early 20th century as a renewed attempt to build a human-centered worldview and ethic that by implication rejected supernatural understandings of the operation of the universe and an ethic based upon pragmatic human values and love.

France has been particularly important in the development of unbelief. The term "atheism" was coined in France, where it was often used in conjunction with the term "libertine" (freed man). The latter term came to be used almost exclusively for sexually liberated individuals, but originally it included those who were intellectually and theologically free. Deism flowered in France in the 18th century, Voltaire (1694–1778) emerging as its champion. Denis Diderot (1713–1784) was possibly the first true French atheist.

The revolution in France, as in the American colonies, was led by Deists, but because of the power exercised by the Catholic Church included a strong element of anticlericalism. Atheism was present in post-revolutionary France and produced some outstanding lights, such as pioneer sociologist August Comte (1798–1857), but it found its major expression over the next century in various anti-Catholic events, including the secularizing of the schools in the 1880s. Church and state were separated in 1905. French Freemasonry also created a non-theistic form of its esoteric teachings. In the 20th century, atheism has found expression in various Freethought groups (La Libre Pensée being the largest national organization), and atheists have taken to promoting the national policy against minority religions.

In the last half of the 19th century, throughout the Western world, people who identified themselves as atheists, freethinkers, rationalists, secularists, or Humanists began to create organizations and movements to support their various tendencies, now grouped under the umbrella of unbelief. Among the earliest and most important of the 19th-century organizations were the First Society of Free Enquirers (founded by Abner

Kneeland [1774–1844] in Boston in 1834); the Bund freier religiöser Gemeinden Deutschlands (founded in Germany in 1859); and the National Secular Society (founded by Charles Bradlaugh [1833–1891] in England in 1866).

The Issue of Marxism   In the West, unbelief has generally distinguished itself from what was arguably the most successful non-theistic system to arise in the modern world, Marxism. Marxism has been tied in the public consciousness with totalitarian governments in the Soviet Union and post-revolutionary China.

The philosophy of Karl Marx (1818–1883) was much more anticlerical than atheistic, and he felt that most religion (as experienced in the state-aligned religions of the 19th century) was, as expressed in his most famous quotation, the "opiate of the people": it lulled people into accepting their exploited status in the lower levels of the social order and acquiescing to rule by the few. He had positive views of some Christian movements, but he argued that both Judaism and Christianity were expressions of stages in human development that had to be surpassed if progress were to occur. Marx felt that religions are a human product that, like other human ideologies, reflect the social systems that perpetuate them.

Marx's economic critique of history took form primarily in political parties that went on to participate in the governmental systems of different countries. The atheism that was implicit in his thought became operationalized in the Communist Party. However, it was largely assumed in the 20th century that to be a Communist was to be an atheist, and the support for atheism and the resultant disparagement of religion became embedded in the national policies of those countries in which Marxism became the ruling philosophy—the Soviet Union, the People's Republic of China, North Korea, Vietnam, and the countries of Eastern Europe. Albania was the only country, however, that formally (in 1967) proclaimed itself an atheist nation and acted on that proposition by outlawing all forms of religion, closing all of its churches and mosques, and imprisoning many of the clergy. Only in 1991 was freedom of religion restored.

In the Soviet Union atheism became institutionalized in a succession of organizations: the League of

Karl Marx, the 19th-century German philosopher and socialist revolutionary who founded modern communism. (Library of Congress)

the Godless, the League of the Militant Godless, and the Institute of Scientific Atheism (which continues into the post-Soviet era). Initially the Soviets focused upon efforts to marginalize religion and end the institutional authority of the church. The formation of the League of the Godless, however, represented the emergence of active promotion of atheism through the press, social institutions, and specialized organizations. Through succeeding decades religious policy periodically shifted its emphases between the promotion of atheism and the forceful suppression of religion.

In China, the critique of what were seen as various systems of exploitation reached out to include religion. Chinese policy led initially to the cutting of the ties between religious groups and any foreign leadership, especially in the case of Christianity, the complete reorganization of the various religious communities into five approved religious organizations, and the imposition of an ideology that was more aligned to the new Marxist Maoist government. While this reorganization

was occurring, many government leaders, representing the Chinese community, argued that religion and Marxism were incompatible. Chinese Communist antagonism toward religion reached its zenith during the period of the Cultural Revolution (1966–1976). Since that time a much more accommodationist policy has been adopted, though government attacks on religion have continued.

As the new century begins, religion in China survives, and an official policy of freedom of religious belief has been written into the law. It is also the case that the Chinese Communist Party is officially atheist and that membership in the party and belief in religion are considered mutually exclusive. In between those people who are members of officially accepted religions and the party is a mass of unofficial religious activity that is still subject to periodic suppression by the atheist government. It remains the strong belief in those countries still ruled by Marxism that religion and belief in God will eventually pass away. In the world, the spread of Marxism accounts for the great majority of unbelief, which includes some 55 percent of the North Koreans, 42 percent of the Chinese, 31 percent of the Czechs, and 27 percent of the Russians.

Modern Western Unbelief Through the 20th century, as Marxism rose and then faced the crisis of the fall of the Soviet Union, non-Marxist forms of unbelief emerged as a popular movement that competed for the support of the public with religious groups. Groups professing non-theistic philosophies supported many values commonly offered by religious groups, including answers to the three main religious questions: Where did we come from? Why are we here? Where are we going? Answers to these questions were given without reference to God or the supernatural. Atheist groups also offered moral systems devoid of supernatural authorities and communal fellowship in their various local gatherings, national and international conventions, and even ritual life.

Non-Marxist atheism as a positive philosophy, as opposed to simple irreligion or concern with ultimate questions, enjoyed its greatest response in Europe and European outposts in North America, South Africa, Australia, and New Zealand. It has not fared well in South America, although it found some support in

India, where a movement critical of Hinduism attacked many of the supernatural powers ascribed to various Indian spiritual teachers. As early as 1875, the Hindu Freethought Union appeared in Madras. It survived for two decades. Through the 20th century a succession of Indian organizations appeared, the most successful being the Indian Rationalist Association, founded in 1960.

In the West, organized atheism has proceeded country by country. In the United States, popular leadership was provided by organizations such as the National Liberal League, the Freethinkers of America (Joseph Lewis), the American Association for the Advancement of Atheism, the American Humanist Association, American Atheists (Madalyn Murray O'Hair), and the Council for Secular Humanism (Paul Kurtz). Similarly, across Europe a number of national rationalist, humanist, Freethought, and atheist groups have been organized.

As early as 1880, the International Federation of Freethinkers (since 1936 the World Union of Freethinkers) was organized. The more substantive International Humanist and Ethical Union was formed in 1952. It now includes member groups from around the world. A specifically Jewish form of unbelief emerged in the 1960s and eventually gave birth to the International Federation of Secular Humanistic Jews.

Although the different communities of unbelief have generally reached a consensus on the issues of God and the supernatural, they have disagreed on the issue of religion. Humanists, in particular, have expressed positive approaches to religion and have developed (or continued) religious structures that they feel contribute to ameliorating the human condition or provide a ritual dramatization of the important events of the life cycle—birth, coming of age, marriage, death. Secular Judaism perpetuates synagogue life under the leadership of rabbis. The American Humanist Association "ordains" celebrants (Humanist ministers) who lead celebration services (analogous to Protestant worship services). Operating in a somewhat different context, the Norwegian Humanist organization Human-Etisk Forbund, one of the largest in Europe, has worked for a secular alternative to Christian confirmation (through which most Norwegian youths have traditionally passed). As the new century begins, these "civil" confirmations are celebrated annually in some 90 locations throughout Norway with some 4,000 young people, approximately 10 percent of the relevant age group, taking part.

In response, many atheist and Freethought groups eschew any form of religious activity. They see themselves as over against religion rather than providing a non-theistic or non-supernatural alternative to it. The Council for Secular Humanism is among those groups opposed to associating unbelief in any way with religion.

In the first decade of the new millennium, neo-atheism, a new aggressive atheism, made its appearance in the wake of a rising belief in creationism as a pseudo-scientific hypothesis challenging the teaching of evolutionary biology in the public schools in America. The leading voice of the new movement, which differs from older non-Marxist forms of atheism more by its aggressive attempts to proselytize for atheism than any content in its stance, is Richard Dawkins, (b. 1941), a professor of biology at Oxford University. He has been joined by writers such as Sam Harris and Christopher Hitchens (b. 1949), who lecture widely on evolution and atheism.

During the 1990s, a small cadre of scholars had also proposed a new argument that they felt both challenged current Darwinian approaches to understanding biology while avoiding the issues of religion inherent in creationism. The new position, called intelligent design, appeared to be a way to overcome issues of separation of church and state, especially after several school districts had installed intelligent design in their school's curriculum. Such actions were challenged almost immediately and the case in Dover, Pennsylvania, proved decisive. In the 2005 court decision *Kitzmiller v. Dover Area School District*, the judge ruled that the religious nature of intelligent design was readily apparent to any objective observer. The intelligent design movement, which had become an early target of neo-atheists, largely collapsed after the court ruling.

While atheists accepted the collapse of intelligent design as a victory, the forces mounted against it were far broader than the relatively small atheist or unbelief community. In the United States, at about the same time, they faced a major crisis when in 2004 British philosopher Antony Flew (b. 1923), a prominent atheist through the 20th century, announced that he had become a theist.

Pseudoscience   Increasingly associated with unbelief is the crusade against pseudoscience. A pseudoscience is a set of related ideas based on theories put forth as scientific but which upon examination lack any scientific base. The ideas may be based on an inadequate methodology, false or fraudulent information, or supernatural claims. During the 19th century, occult and Esoteric claims revived, claiming to have scientific support from movements like mesmerism, and then as science expanded, found confirmation in a variety of scientific findings.

At the end of the 20th century, a variety of people examined and debunked the claims of Spiritualist mediums to contact the dead and produce various physical phenomena. As claims of paranormal phenomena proliferated in the years after World War II, including the obvious popularity of astrology, some humanists, led by Paul Kurtz, then a leader in the American Humanist Association, took the lead in the founding of the Committee for the Scientific Investigation of the Claims of the Paranormal (CSICOP), since 2006 known as the Committee for Skeptical Inquiry.

The leadership of the Committee saw the rise of interest in the paranormal, psychic phenomena, alternative forms of healing, UFOs, and related phenomena as dangerous to society and representative of a general decline in critical thinking. The Committee promoted the development of a "skeptical" movement designed to debunk what it saw as pseudoscience, gave rise to local affiliated chapters across North America, and led to the formation of several like organizations, such as the Los Angeles–based Skeptical Society. It also became the model for several similar organizations now found in more than 30 countries around the world. The Committee now nurtures an International Network of Skeptical Organizations with affiliated chapters in some 41 countries (2009) and a regional organization for Europe.

Agnosticism   Arising along with atheism was a slightly different position of unbelief, agnosticism. The term was coined by Thomas Henry Huxley (1825–1895) in 1869 to indicate a methodology of refusing to assert knowledge about things that are not demonstrated or even demonstrable. Huxley's position, as later expanded and popularized, has identified agnosticism as the position that God or the origin of the universe is unknowable, and hence it is best to refrain from opinions on the subject.

The agnostic position has generally assumed a certain methodology in looking at the world and coming to conclusions about matters that could be labeled as "true." Most have found in scientific methodology the way to truth, and hence they rely primarily on reason and the empirical method as the proper way of knowing the universe. Belief in a deity (and many related theological realities) pushes the individual beyond the confines of scientific methodology. Hence, for the person who assumes such a methodology, discourse on God and divine realities is beyond the realm of knowledge. The agnostic chooses to withhold judgment on such matters.

European Council of Skeptical Organizations
Postfach 1222, D-64374
Rossdorf
Germany

J. Gordon Melton

See also: Agnosticism; American Atheists; Atheism; Calvin, John; Council for Secular Humanism; Human-Etisk Forbund i Norge; Humanism; International Federation of Secular Humanistic Jews; International Humanist and Ethical Union; Jainism; Luther, Martin; Roman Catholic Church; Theravada Buddhism.

References

Angeles, Peter A., ed. *Critiques of God: Making the Case against Belief in God.* Amherst, NY: Prometheus, 1997.

Dawkins, Richard. *The God Delusion*. Boston: Houghton Mifflin Harcourt, 2006.

Flynn, Tom, ed. *The New Encyclopedia of Unbelief*. Amherst, NY: Prometheus Books, 2007.

Harris, Sam. *The End of Faith: Religion, Terror, and the Future of Reason*. New York: W. W. Norton, 2005.

Hitchens, Christopher. *God Is Not Great: How Religion Poisons Everything*. Toronto: McClelland & Stewart, 2007.

Howlett, Duncan. *The Critical Way in Religion.* Buffalo, NY: Prometheus, 1980.

Husband, William B. *Godless Communists, Atheism and Society in Soviet Russia, 1917–1932.* DeKalb: Northern Illinois University, 2000.

Johnson, B. C. *The Atheist Debater's Handbook.* Buffalo, NY: Prometheus, 1982.

Kurtz, Paul, ed. *The Humanist Alternative.* Buffalo, NY: Prometheus, 1973.

Lamont, Corliss. *Humanism as a Philosophy.* New York: Philosophical Library, 1949.

Larue, Gerald A. *Freethought across the Centuries: Toward a New Age of Enlightenment.* Amherst, NY: American Humanist Press, 1996.

O'Hair, Madalyn Murray. *Atheist Primer: Did You Know All the Gods Came from the Same Place?* Austin, TX: American Atheist Press, 1978.

Robertson, J. M. *A History of Freethought, Ancient and Modern to the Period of the French Revolution.* 2 vols. London: Watts and Co., 1936.

Shermer, Michael. *Why People Believe Weird Things.* New York: W. H. Freeman and Company, 1997.

Smart, J. J. C., and J. J. Haldane. *Atheism and Theism.* Oxford: Blackwell Publishers, 1997.

Smith, George H. *Atheism: The Case against God.* Amherst, NY: Prometheus, 1989.

Stein, Gordon, ed. *The Encyclopedia of Unbelief.* 2 vols. Buffalo, NY: Prometheus, 1985.

Thrower, James. *Western Atheism: A Short History.* Amherst, NY: Prometheus Books, 1999.

Unification Movement

The Unification Movement (UM) refers to the messianic religious and social movement led by the Reverend Sun Myung Moon (b. 1920). It consists of a complex network of religious, media, industrial, commercial, cultural, and educational enterprises worldwide. Many of these organizations, such as *The Washington Times* and the University of Bridgeport, function independently and include only a few individuals who accept the messianic teachings of the movement. Nevertheless, all of these entities are in one way or another identified with Rev. Moon.

The Unification Church (UC)—formally, the Holy Spirit Association for the Unification of World Christianity (HSA-UWC)—stands at the center of the movement. It was founded May 1, 1954, in Seoul, Korea, but was not legally recognized by the government of the Republic of (South) Korea until 1963. Highly conversionistic, the UC sent its first missionaries to Japan and the United States in 1958 and 1959. The movement was largely dormant in the United States during the 1960s and had only 300 or so members in 1971. However, there was more dynamism in Japan, and in the early 1970s, Rev. Moon decided to concentrate the resources of the movement in America. He conducted a series of evangelistic tours that substantively increased the church's membership and visibility. By 1974, UM sources claimed that members in the United States had increased tenfold to 3,000. The movement filled New York's Madison Square Garden for a highly publicized speech by Rev. Moon on "The New Future of Christianity" in late 1974. He later spoke to large audiences at New York's Yankee Stadium (1975) and the Washington Monument (1976).

In 1975 the church sent out missionaries to 120 nations but still focused much of its activity in the United States. With the close of the evangelistic campaigns, the UM proliferated a variety of nonprofit and business organizations that extended well beyond the confines of the church. By the early 1970s, Rev. Moon had initiated an International Conference on the Unity of the Sciences (ICUS) that brought together numerous scientific luminaries annually. The movement also funded the Professors World Peace Academy (PWPA), which in 1992 gained a controlling interest in the University of Bridgeport in Connecticut. The movement operated Sung Hwa, later Sun Moon, University, in Korea, as well as the Little Angels Arts School. It also established the Bolshoi Ballet Academy in Washington, D.C. The Unification Theological Seminary (ca. 1975) served as the base for a broad-ranging ecumenical program, and during the mid-1970s the movement established its first two metropolitan daily newspapers, *Sekai Nippo* (1975) in Tokyo and *The News World* (1976) in New York City. The movement expended millions in founding *The Washington Times* (1983), which became its flagship media enterprise. In 1989 it

Newly wed couples raise their hands in cheering during a mass wedding, January 23, 1996, in Manila, Philippines. The ceremony was initiated by Rev. Sun Myung Moon, founder of the South Korean Unification Movement. (AP/Wide World Photos)

established a major daily, *Segye Ilbo*, in Korea, and in 1996 it set up *Tiempos Del Mundo*, a Latin American hemispheric daily, in Buenos Aires. The movement's business operations in Korea—including its major holding, Tong-il Industries—were reported to have net assets worth nearly $200 million. The movement focused on maritime ventures in the United States, purchasing shipbuilding yards and fish-processing plants in Norfolk, Virginia; Bayou La Batre, Alabama; Gloucester, Massachusetts; and Kodiak, Alaska, during the late 1970s and 1980s.

Apart from these undertakings, the UM was known for its fervent anti-Communist activities. It set up chapters and training centers for "Victory Over Communism" in Korea and strenuously opposed Marxist advances on Japanese college campuses during the late 1960s and early 1970s. It funded Radio of Free Asia and the Freedom Leadership Foundation (FLF)

in the United States during the same period. In 1973–1974, Rev. Moon initiated a highly publicized National Prayer and Fast for the Watergate Crisis (NPFWC) in support of President Richard Nixon, and he circulated an "Answer to Watergate" in most of the nation's major newspapers. During the 1980s the movement attempted to arm the West ideologically through various organizational affiliates, most notably CAUSA (Confédération des Associations pour l'Unification des Sociétés Américaines), which sponsored high-tech multimedia conferences for conservative leaders and clergy throughout the Americas. *The Washington Times* played an important role and was reportedly the newspaper of choice in the Reagan White House. At the same time, the movement took advantage of perestroika by assiduously cultivating contacts in the Communist world. Rev. Moon invited Soviet journalists to participate in annual World Media Conferences and, importantly, invested heavily in mainland China. These initiatives and others gained Rev. Moon private audiences with Soviet premier Mikhail Gorbachev (1990) and North Korean premier Kim Il Sung (1991).

With the collapse of the Eastern Bloc and Soviet Communism, the UM entered what it regarded as an era of messianic fulfillment, or what Rev. Moon termed the "Completed Testament Age." The movement established innumerable Federations for World Peace and conducted high-profile sisterhood ceremonies between women from formerly enemy nations and peoples. However, the true gateways to the Completed Testament Age were massive International Holy Weddings over which Rev. and Mrs. Moon officiated in 1992, 1995, 1997, 1998, 1999, and 2000. The UM already had conducted record-breaking weddings for 1,800 couples (1975), 2,075 and 6,000 couples (1982), and 6,500 couples (1989). During the 1990s these numbers soared into the hundreds of thousands and even hundreds of millions as members under the auspices of the Family Federation for World Peace and Unification (FFWPU) campaigned worldwide to rededicate marriages and distributed holy wine, holy grape juice, and eventually holy candy on a mass basis. In addition to the globalization of the Blessing, the UM embarked upon an effort to reclaim a "restored and purified" Garden of Eden in the South American outback, acquiring vast tracts of land primarily in the Brazilian state of Mato Grosso do Sol after 1995.

All of these efforts were animated by the conviction that Rev. and Mrs. Moon are "the True Parents of all humanity . . . the Savior, the Lord of the Second Advent, the Messiah," a declaration that Rev. Moon made publicly in 1992. This declaration brought to completion a series of experiences, which began on Easter morning, 1935, when Rev. Moon was praying alone on a mountaintop. Rev. Moon received what he understood to be "a special mission from Heaven through Jesus." Afterward, according to his testimony, he "spent years searching precisely how to bring salvation to humankind." In 1952 he completed a handwritten version of *Wolli Wonbon* (*Original Text of the Principle*). This was followed by *Wolli Haesul* (*Explanation of the Principle*, 1957) and *Wolli Kangron* (*Exposition of the Principle*, 1966), which has served as the movement's definitive theological and holy text.

The latter was translated into English as *Divine Principle* (1973) or *Exposition of the Divine Principle* (1996), and Unificationists regard it as "the new expression of God's truth" that unlocks the secrets of the Bible. It contains chapters on the creation, the Fall, the consummation of human history, the advent of the Messiah, resurrection, predestination, Christology, and an elaborate account of dispensational history, which concludes that the messiah was born as a Korean between 1917 and 1930. The text interprets the human fall in sexual terms and maintains that the crucifixion of Jesus was not God's original will but the result of human ignorance and disbelief. After 1996, Rev. Moon instituted Hoon Dok Hae (gathering for reading and learning), utilizing passages from his many volumes of sermons. Some consider Hoon Dok Hae to have displaced the Principle. Others view it as a complementary and more universal expression of the "Completed Testament Word." In 2004, a new authoritative set of Rev. Moon's words, known as the Cheon Seong Gyeong (Heavenly Scripture), was prepared that ran to more than 2,000 pages.

The UM has not been subject to the apocalyptic configurations that have afflicted and destroyed other movements. Nevertheless, the broad scope and duration of negative reactions accompanying its emergence rendered it one of the most controversial new religious movements of the latter 20th century. The Communist regime in North Korea jailed Rev. Moon in 1948 for, among other things, "bringing disorder to society." The South Korean government jailed him for draft evasion in 1955, and unsubstantiated rumors of church sex orgies swirled in Korean society. During the 1960s, Japanese media referred to the UM as "the religion that makes parents weep," and in 1971 the practice of kidnapping and deprogramming began. During the 1970s, in the United States, the movement was widely regarded as a brainwashing cult that exploited members, known as "moonies," and that practiced "heavenly deception." Alternatively, the UM was depicted as a subversive group abridging the separation of church and state and influencing U.S. policy in behalf of the South Korean government. During the 1980s, the U.S. government jailed Rev. Moon on charges of tax evasion, and during the 1990s there were exposés and allegations leveled against Rev. Moon's family. During the first decade of the new century, controversy erupted over Roman Catholic Archbishop Emmanuel Milingo's participation in a Unification-sponsored "International Marriage Blessing of Religious Leaders" in 2001. Additional irritants were the movement's call for Christian clergy to remove crosses from their churches in 2003 and a "coronation" of Rev. and Mrs. Moon as King and Queen of Peace at the U.S. Dirksen Senate Office building in 2004. Similar patterns of response have been prevalent elsewhere, notably in Europe, the Commonwealth of Independent States (CIS), Southeast Asia, and Latin America. Still, in the United States and many countries, the Unification Church has gained acceptance as a bona fide religion; related movement components operate as legal entities, and it has been able to extend constitutional protections to members.

The UM's organizational structure is charismatic, with Rev. Moon exercising authority over the movement's direction and major operations. Immediate supervision is delegated to trusted elders, mainly Koreans and some Japanese, who form a spiritual hierarchy extending from senior to new members. The Unification Church has incorporated numerous national churches and maintains missions in more than 100 nations. However, leadership is often rotated and membership dispersed to forestall premature institutionalization. The literally hundreds of UM-related nonprofit and commercial organizations have led some to describe the UM as a religious multinational. For many years, the Unification Church maintained a World Mission Center in midtown Manhattan. However, the UM's international headquarters generally have been wherever Rev. Moon resides. During the 1970s and 1980s, that was Irvington, New York. During the 1990s, he resided for substantial periods in South America and South Korea. The movement has constructed a substantial religious shrine north of Seoul at Chungpyung Lake Training Center, where Rev. Moon frequently went for prayer and meditation. The site, which includes a "heavenly palace" with seating for several thousand as well as sacred trees and healing springs, is understood to be the meeting place of heaven and Earth.

Reliable membership totals are difficult to ascertain. During the 1970s, both the movement and its critics exaggerated its size, claiming between 2 and 3 million adherents worldwide. During the 1980s observers tended to downplay the movement's numbers, given a leveling off of conversions in the West. However, this was compensated by growth elsewhere. The number of marriage ceremony participants is the most reliable indicator of UM membership totals. Since 1960 Rev. Moon has "blessed" approximately 100,000 church couples, suggesting an adult UM membership population approaching 200,000. The UM would appear poised to build on these totals, given the favorable age, sex, and geographical distribution of its members and its encouragement of large families.

Unification Church in America
4 W. 43rd St.
New York, NY 10036
http://www.unification.org/
http://www.ettl.co.at/uc/europe/ (in Europe)
http://www.ettl.co.at/uc/index.htm (multilanguage)
Michael L. Mickler

References

Barker, Eileen. *The Making of a Moonie: Choice or Brainwashing?* London: Blackwell, 1984.

Chryssides, George. *The Advent of Sun Myung Moon.* New York: St. Martin's, 1991.

Introvigne, Massimo. *The Unification Church.* Salt Lake City, UT: Signature Books, 2000.

Mickler, Michael L., and Michael Inglis. *Forty Years in America: An Intimate History of the Unification Movement, 1959–1999.* New York: HSA-UWC, 2000.

Sontag, Fredrick. *Sun Myung Moon and the Unification Church.* Nashville: Abingdon, 1977.

Unified Buddhist Church

The Unified Buddhist Church (UBC) of Vietnam is important for two related but distinct reasons. First, during the war in Vietnam, it was from 1964 to 1975 the vehicle of the Buddhist antiwar movement, a highly activist, pacifist movement with widespread popularity in South Vietnam and sufficient power to bring down several South Vietnamese governments. Second,

Vietnamese Buddhist monks in a procession for a Great Chanting Ceremony at Vinh Nghiem Pagoda in Ho Chi Minh City, southern Vietnam, March 16, 2007. (AP/Wide World Photos)

from 1969 to the present it has been the institutional home of the Vietnamese Buddhist monk Thich Nhat Hanh, himself an important leader of the Buddhist antiwar movement in Vietnam, one of the most important leaders of the socially and politically activist Engaged Buddhism movement, and one of the most popular Buddhist teachers in the West today.

Shortly before the founding of the UBC, the South Vietnamese government of Ngo Dinh Diem had been favoring the Catholic Church and repressing Buddhism. The UBC was founded in South Vietnam in January 1964 in order to create a unified (Theravada and Mahayana) Buddhist church through the merging of the various Buddhist sects of South Vietnam. At the time, it represented 80 percent of the population of South Vietnam. The UBC was founded in order to protect Buddhist interests, to encourage Buddhist engagement with Vietnamese society, and to work for

peace. It quickly became the voice of the Buddhist "Third Way" or "Struggle Movement" that was trying to end the war in that country. As such, it many times brought thousands of monks, nuns, and laypeople into the streets to demonstrate for peace and free elections and played a key role in bringing down several pro-war governments. In addition to its antiwar work, the UBC engaged in many actions for relief, healing, and reconstruction. They evacuated villagers caught in the crossfire; reconstructed villages destroyed in battle; arranged care for war orphans; helped develop rural villages with new agricultural methods, basic medicine, and sanitation; and helped prevent bloodshed as the war ended and the government changed hands.

In 1966 a splinter group opposed to the politics of the UBC broke off from the main body; the South Vietnamese government then removed legal recognition from the UBC and transferred it to the splinter group. Thereafter the UBC lacked legal standing in South Vietnam, though it continued its activities. The Ky and Thieu governments of South Vietnam and the postwar government of Vietnam severely suppressed the UBC and imprisoned many of its activists.

The Venerable Thich Nhat Hanh (b. 1926) re-established the UBC in France in 1969 as the Eglise Bouddhique Unifiee; present affiliates of the UBC stem from that re-establishment and recognize Thich Nhat Hanh as their spiritual teacher. In 2005 the government of Vietnam for the first time allowed Nhat Hanh to return to Vietnam and to teach openly.

Thich Nhat Hanh entered Tu Hieu monastery in Hue (central Vietnam) at age 16 and was ordained into the Lam Te (Lin-chi, Rinzai) Zen sect. His studies included both Mahayana and Theravada traditions, emphasizing mindfulness, *gatha* (short verses), and *koan*. Later he studied religion in the United States at Princeton University and lectured on religion at Columbia University.

Returning to Vietnam in 1964, Nhat Hanh, together with others, founded Van Hanh University in Saigon and the School of Youth for Social Service, one of the primary vehicles of Engaged Buddhism during the war in Vietnam and the main training center for Buddhist peace activists. In 1965 Nhat Hanh founded the Tiep Hien Order (the Order of Interbeing), a new branch of the Lam Te School and another manifestation of Engaged Buddhism; the Order consists of laypersons as well as monks and nuns and consists of those who have taken the Order's 14 precepts.

During the years of the Vietnam War, Nhat Hanh was one of the primary theoreticians and spokespersons of the Struggle movement, the Buddhist effort to bring peace to Vietnam while siding with neither North nor South. After his 1966 international speaking tour to publicize the Vietnamese Buddhist perspective he was banned from returning to Vietnam, whereupon he made his headquarters in France. In 1967 Nhat Hanh was nominated for the Nobel Peace Prize by Martin Luther King, Jr., whom he had convinced to publicly repudiate the war. Nhat Hanh led the Buddhist delegation to the Paris Peace Talks on behalf of the UBC; while the delegation was not seated at the talks, they advocated for the Buddhist pro-peace perspective.

Since the war, Nhat Hanh has traveled the world leading workshops and retreats emphasizing mindfulness (cultivating awareness in the present moment) and the nonviolent engagement of Buddhism with society's problems. For Nhat Hanh, to practice Buddhism is to cultivate love and understanding, which will naturally be expressed in all aspects of life. Nhat Hanh's approach is typified in the title of his most famous book, *Being Peace*: one must be peace in order to make peace. His five Mindfulness Trainings are his socially engaged version of the Buddhist five lay precepts—for example, not only does one do no harm oneself, but one also finds ways to prevent others from causing harm, that is, one tries to prevent one's government from going to war. He has published some 85 books of both poetry and prose, more than 40 of these in English.

Today the headquarters of the Unified Buddhist Church, and of Thich Nhat Hanh's community of practitioners, is in Plum Village, France. In Vietnam, Tu Hieu Temple and Bat Nha Monastery are affiliated with Thich Nhat Hanh and the UBC. In the United States, two monasteries with residential monks and nuns belong to this lineage. There are home- and community-based practice groups in most countries of Western Europe, plus Argentina, Australia, Bermuda, Brazil, Canada, China, the Dominican Republic, Guatemala, India, Israel, Japan, Malaysia, Mexico, Netherland Antilles, New Zealand, Poland, Puerto Rico, Russia, South Africa, Thailand, the United States, and Vietnam. This loose-knit lay organization is called the Community of Mindful Living. These all recognize Thich Nhat Hanh as their spiritual teacher. Parallax Press is the publishing division of the UBC and publishes materials on Engaged Buddhism.

Nhat Hanh considers as his students the monks and nuns whom he has ordained and those laypersons who have taken the 14 Precepts of the Order of Interbeing or the five Mindfulness Trainings from him. Nhat Hanh himself does not encourage Westerners to convert to Buddhism; he encourages them, if they are Christians, to "be good Christians"; if Jews, to "be good Jews." He does encourage everyone to take the five Mindfulness Trainings, in an ecumenical spirit, as guides for mindful living. He sees no reason why members of other religions should not engage in Buddhist practices such as mindfulness meditation.

Plum Village
New Hamlet
13 Martineau
33580 Dieulivol
France
www.plumvillage.org

Sallie B. King

See also: Meditation.

References

Forest, James H. *The Unified Buddhist Church of Vietnam: Fifteen Years for Reconciliation.* Hof van Sonoy, Netherlands: International Fellowship of Reconciliation, 1978.

Hunt-Perry, Patricia, and Lyn Fine. "All Buddhism Is Engaged: Thich Nhat Hanh and the Order of Interbeing." In *Engaged Buddhism in the West*, edited by Christopher S. Queen, 35–66. Boston: Wisdom Publications, 2000.

King, Sallie B. "Thich Nhat Hanh and the Unified Buddhist Church: Nondualism in Action." In *Engaged Buddhism: Buddhist Liberation Movements in Asia*, edited by Christopher S. Queen and Sallie B. King, 321–363. Albany, NY: State University of New York Press, 1996.

Nhat Hanh, Thich. *Being Peace.* Berkeley, CA: Parallax Press, 1987.

Nhat Hanh, Thich. *Vietnam: Lotus in a Sea of Fire.* New York: Hill and Wang, 1967.

Union d'Églises Baptistes Françaises au Canada

The Union d'Églises Baptistes Françaises au Canada unites French-speaking Baptists in eastern Canada, being one of the oldest Protestant bodies in a predominantly Roman Catholic area. It is a covenanting partner in Canadian Baptist Ministries.

The Union's roots are in the Grand Ligne Mission that was founded as a school by Mademoiselle Feller (1800–1868) with Louis Roussy (1815–1883) in 1835. In 1849 it became Baptist and by 1855 there were 20 preaching points and more than 3,000 converts. After Feller's death in 1868, nine churches organized as the Union des Églises Baptistes de Langue Françaises while remaining part of the Grande Ligne Mission.

At the beginning of the 20th century there were several thousand members in the churches in the Ottawa-Montreal area and as far east as Nova Scotia and as far west as Manitoba. Against the rising French nationalism, however, the mission was seen as a tool of the English. By 1960, when the Quiet Revolution flourished in Quebec, the decline was clear, with only one in nine of the pastors being French Canadian.

Union d'Églises Baptistes Françaises au Canada received a federal charter in 1966. Reverend Maurice Boillat (1925–1986), a Swiss-born pastor, became the first full-time general secretary who broke down barriers between the Union and the Quebecois culture. It developed headquarters in Montreal; a radio and television studio; a Bible College; and, in 1982, the Centre d'Etudes Theologiques Evangeliques (1994, à Faculté de théologie évangélique).

In 1970 it became the fourth body in the Baptist Federation of Canada with 8 churches and 398 members. It now has 32 churches and preaching stations and 1,300 members in Quebec and New Brunswick that provide both inspiration and completion to Canadian Baptist Ministries.

Union d'Églises Baptistes Françaises au Canada
2285 Papineau
Montreal, Quebec H2K 4J5
Canada
http://www.unionbaptiste.com/

Robert S. Wilson

See also: Baptists; Canadian Baptist Ministries; Roman Catholic Church.

References

Bentall, Shirley. *From Sea to Sea: The Canadian Baptist Federation; 1944–1994.* Mississauga, ON: Canadian Baptist Federation, 1994.

Grant, John Webster. *The Church in the Canadian Experience.* Vancouver, BC: Regent College, 1998.

Priestley, David. "Introduction." In *Memory and Hope: Strands of Canadian Baptist History.* Waterloo, ON: Wilfred Laurier University Press, 1996.

Renfree, Harry. *Heritage and Horizon: The Baptist Story in Canada*. Mississauga, ON: Canadian Baptist Federation, 1988.

Wilson, Robert S. "History of Canadian Baptists." In *Baptist History Celebration, 2007: A Symposium on our History, Theology, and Hymnology*. Springfield, MO: Particular Baptist Press, 2008.

Wilson, Robert S. "Patterns in Canadian Baptist Life." Global Baptist History. Paper presented at the Second International Conference on Baptist Studies, Wake Forest University, July 19–22, 2000.

Zeman, Jarold K., ed. *Baptists in Canada: Search for Identity Amidst Diversity*. Burlington, ON: G. R. Welsh, 1980.

Zeman, Jarold K., ed. *Costly Vision: The Baptist Pilgrimage in Canada*. Burlington, ON: G. R. Welsh, 1988.

Union of Baptist Churches of Cameroon

The Union of Baptist Churches of Cameroon (Union des Églises Baptistes du Cameroun) traces its history to the British Baptist Missionary Association, which begin work in West Africa utilizing converts from among the recently freed Africans residing on Jamaica. In 1843, 42 Jamaicans and 4 European couples established a mission station on Fernando Po (now Bioko), an island off the coast of Cameroon. In 1845, Joseph Merrick, a Jamaican, moved to West Cameroon and began learning the language of the Usubu people. One of the Europeans, Alfred Saker, moved to Cameroon Town (now Duala), where he founded the first Baptist church in Cameroon in 1849.

The Baptist work grew slowly until 1884, when Germany assumed authority in Cameroon. The Baptists turned their work over to the Basel Mission, a Swiss missionary society that drew support primarily from Reformed churches in Germany and Austria. The new workers agreed to respect the Baptist faith of the converts, but many did not like the manner of the Basel missionaries or their introduction of non-Baptist practices such as infant baptism. Those who retained their Baptist distinctives rejected the Basel leadership and turned to German Baptists in Germany and the United States for support. Baptist missionaries arrived to assume control of the mission, and in 1898 they formed the Mission Society of German Baptists.

The German missionaries were expelled during World War I, and the work of the Mission Society was largely turned over to the Paris Mission (of the Reformed Church of France), which agreed to respect the Baptist beliefs and practices. This Mission continued to develop with the assistance of the Paris missionaries, and in 1952 it reorganized as the Union of Baptist Churches of Cameroon. The Union became fully autonomous in 1957.

In 2005, the Union reported 75,000 members in 360 congregations. The Union is a member of the World Council of Churches and the Baptist World Alliance.

Union of Baptist Churches
BP 6007
New Bell, Douala
Cameroon

J. Gordon Melton

See also: Baptist World Alliance; Basel Mission; Paris Mission; Reformed Church of France; World Council of Churches.

References

Allégret, E. *La Mission du Cameroun*. Paris: Evangelical Missionary Society, 1924.

Kwast, Lloyd E. *The Discipling of West Cameroon: A Study of Baptist Growth*. Grand Rapids, MI: William B. Eerdmans Publishing Company, 1971.

Van Beek, Huibert. *A Handbook of the Churches and Councils: Profiles of Ecumenical Relationships*. Geneva: World Council of Churches, 2006.

Wardin, Albert W., ed. *Baptists around the World*. Nashville: Holman, 1995.

Union of Evangelical Christians—Baptists of Russia

The Union of Evangelical Christians—Baptists of Russia, founded in 1979, is the largest organization of Baptist Christians in Russia. The Union also carries the tradition of Baptists in the country, a tradition that has a severely broken organizational presence because of the periodic repression of religion in Russia. In the last decade, with the relative religious freedom of post-Soviet life, Russian Baptists have become known for their allegiance to traditional Baptist standards, including the pious life expected of present members and the testimony of repentance and faith of new members prior to their baptism by immersion.

The Baptist entrance into what was then the Russian Empire had at least three different points of origin. First, in 1855, a man named Plonus, a tailor, moved from Memel (then in Germany but today in Lithuania) to St. Petersburg, where he distributed Christian tracts and gathered a small circle of believers. Three years later, Gottfried Alf (1831–1858), a German Lutheran residing in Poland, was baptized and went on to found Baptist churches in Poland and Ukraine. The German-led Baptist movement spread throughout the empire from the Transcaucasus to Siberia. In some cases, German-speaking communities in various parts of Russia served as the originating point from which Baptist perspectives were disseminated to the surrounding communities.

Toleration was granted to Baptists in those areas in which Lutheranism was the dominant religion, but such toleration was not granted in predominantly Orthodox areas. In Ukraine and Russia proper, the abandoning of the Russian Orthodox Church was not permitted. In spite of this obstacle, in 1887 the German Baptists in the Russian Empire founded the Union of Baptist Churches of Russia and formally separated from the Baptist Union of Germany (now the Union of Evangelical Free Church Congregations [Baptist]).

A second Baptist movement began in Ukraine in the 1860s with the spread of Ukrainian Bibles and literature. One Ukrainian, Efim Tsymbal, raised in the Orthodox Church, received a believer's baptism from a group of Mennonite Brethren living in Ukraine and went on to launch a Baptist movement among the Ukrainian citizenry. He and two evangelists he discovered and baptized, Ivan Ryaboshapka (1831–1900) and Mikhail Ratushni (1830–ca. 1915), found an opening among the Stundists, followers of a movement who gathered for an hour (*Stunde*) of devotion every day. In Ukraine, most Stundists became Baptists.

A movement similar to that in Ukraine began in 1862 in Georgia when Martin Kalweit (1833–1918)

baptized Nikita I. Voronin (1840–1905). This movement drew considerable strength from the Molokans, a Protestant-like group that had rejected the sacramentalism of the Russian Orthodox Church. The new Baptist movement soon spread throughout the Caucasus and in the early 1880s ran into Ukraine. The two groups formed a single united front in 1884 with the founding of the Russian Baptist Union.

In 1874, Lord Radstock, a member of the Church of England with leanings toward the Plymouth Brethren (now the Christian Brethren) teachings of John Nelson Darby, began to preach in St. Petersburg. His work attracted Colonel Vasilii A. Pashkov (1831–1902), who would lend his name to the movement that resulted from Radstock's effort. The movement spread as a spiritual revival among Orthodox believers and was thus able to grow to some extent free of government interference. It survived until 1905 and the granting of religious toleration, and then it went public with the founding of two congregations in St. Petersburg. They called themselves Evangelical Christians. After a brief association with the Russian Baptist Union, Pashkov and the Evangelical Christians separated and in 1909 formed the All-Russian Union of Evangelical Christians.

The Russian Revolution brought significant change, beginning with a period of rapid growth only to be followed by decades of persecution and restriction. By the end of the 1930s, most churches were closed and many pastors and other church leaders arrested on various charges. Finally, in 1944 the government allowed/forced the Baptists and Evangelical Christians to form the All Union Council of Evangelical Christians—Baptists, which was to be the single organization for all Protestants who accepted adult believer's baptism. The Union would eventually become home to Pentecostals and the Mennonite Brethren.

In the years after World War II, the All Union Council was allowed some freedom. It published a periodical; in 1955 it participated in the meeting of the Baptist World Alliance; and in 1962 it was accepted into the World Council of Churches. Then in 1960, during the presidency of Nikita Khrushchev, the Union was forced to sign a letter of instruction to its member congregations limiting evangelism. That letter led to a schism, with the new group taking the name Council of Churches of Evangelical Christians—Baptists. The Council, popularly known as Reform Baptists, accused the Union of cooperating too closely with the state.

Some relief came in 1988 with the reforms that began under Mikhail Gorbachev, but a reunion between the two groups has not been worked out. Then in 1992, a significant change occurred in the wake of the fall of the Soviet Union and the emergence of the Commonwealth of Independent States. The All Union Council of Evangelical Christians—Baptists gave way to the Euro-Asiatic Federation of Unions of Evangelical Christians—Baptists uniting Baptists in 10 independent Baptist Unions. The bulk of the membership remained in the Union of Evangelical Christians—Baptists of Russia, which in the 1990s reported 79,000 members in more than 1,000 churches. The Pentecostal members, always in an uneasy position in the Union, left and organized separately in 1989.

The Union's new five-story headquarters building also houses the headquarters of the federation and the Moscow Baptist Seminary. The Union cooperates in the issuance of the federation's two periodicals. The Union has launched a vast evangelism effort throughout the country and has nurtured the formation of Sunday schools with each of its congregations. In 2008 the Union reported 80,000 members in 1,309 congregations. The Union has withdrawn from the World Council of Churches, but continues its membership in the Baptist World Alliance.

Union of Evangelical Christians—Baptists of Russia
International PO Box 171
Moscow
Russia
http://www.baptist.org.ru/ (in Russian)

J. Gordon Melton

See also: Baptist World Alliance; Christian Brethren; Darby, John Nelson; Union of Evangelical Free Church Congregations (Baptist); World Council of Churches.

References

Sawatsky, Walter. *Soviet Evangelicals since World War II*. Kitchener, ON: Herald, 1981.

Steeves, Paul. *The Russian Baptist Union, 1917–1935*. Lawrence: University of Kansas, 1976.

Wardin, Albert W., Jr. *Evangelical Sectarians in the Russian Empire and USSR: A Bibliographical Guide*. Metuchen, NJ: Scarecrow, 1995.

Union of Evangelical Christians—Baptists of Ukraine

The Baptist Church originated in Ukraine with the movement of Germans who happened to be Baptists into the territory. They formed two churches, in Horczik and Soroczin, in 1864. Simultaneously, other tendencies toward the Baptist position appeared among others of German background in the country, including Mennonites and those independent Pietists called Stundists. The government and the Orthodox Church allowed little room for religious deviance, and persecution began. However, in 1884, a Russian Baptist Union was formed.

Ukrainian Baptists formed an All Ukrainian Baptist Union in 1918, following the Russian Revolution. They were allowed to exist and met regularly through the 1920s. In 1926 they began a periodical to further spread their message. The relative freedom of the 1920s gave way to a period of persecution and repression of the 1930s. They were forced into the All Union Council of Evangelical Christians—Baptists in 1944 but maintained some autonomy through the retention of their own senior presbyter and other presbyters for different sections of the church in the region.

In 1992 the Ukrainian Baptists formed an independent union, though one that retains fraternal relations with similar organizations in Russian and other countries formerly a part of the Soviet Union. Three years earlier they once again had been able to begin a periodical. The Ukrainian Baptists, with more than 142,000 members in its 2,419 congregations, now claim more than half of all the Baptists that once resided in the Soviet Union.

The Union is a member of both the Baptist World Alliance and the Euro-Asiatic Federation of Unions of Evangelical Christians—Baptists.

Union of Evangelical Christians—Baptists of Ukraine
3-a Tolstoi St.

252004 Kiev 4
Ukraine

J. Gordon Melton

See also: Baptist World Alliance; Union of Evangelical Christians—Baptists of Russia.

References
Tolbet, Robert G. *Venture of Faith*. Philadelphia: Judson, 1955.
Wardin, Albert W., ed. *Baptists around the World*. Nashville: Holman, 1995.

Union of Evangelical Free Church Congregations (Baptist)

The Union of Evangelical Free Church Congregations (Baptist), or Bund Evangelisch-Freikirchlicher Gemei-nden, continues the thrust of the Baptist movement in Germany that originated in the 1830s. German-born Johann Gerhard Oncken (1800–1884) grew up in Scotland, where he encountered some evangelical Christians and experienced a personal conversion. In 1823 he returned to Germany to distribute Bibles and Christian literature. Along the way, his own Bible study convinced him of the truth of the Baptist belief that limits baptism to adult believers. The story of his change of belief was eventually called to the attention of American Baptists then still in the early stages of their organization. One of their leaders, Barnas Sears, traveled to Germany in 1833 and contacted Oncken. The following year he baptized Oncken and seven others, who then formed the first Baptist Church in Germany, in Hamburg. This church would become the mother church not only for German Baptists but also for much of Europe. In 1835 Oncken was appointed as a missionary

Georg Jansen, right, leader of the youth of the Free Evangelical Church baptizes Julian Kruse in the water, Muenster, Germany, 2008. (AP/Wide World Photos)

for the American Baptist Triennial Convention (now the American Baptist Churches in the U.S.A.).

The Baptists suffered persecution in their early years, but in 1842 their response to a fire that swept Hamburg gained them the respect of the city. Then legal changes in 1848 and 1850 provided some greater degree of religious freedom. In 1848, Oncken founded a periodical, *Das Missionblatt*. He also began to hold regular classes for ministerial students that grew into the Baptist seminary in 1880. He traveled widely and brought together the groups that became the nucleus around which Baptist churches emerged throughout German-speaking Europe.

Oncken attracted a number of talented assistants, among them Julius Wilhelm Köbner and Gottfried Wilhelm Lehmann. Köbner, the son of a Danish rabbi, established the first Baptist churches in Denmark, and Lehmann led in the organization of German Baptists. In 1848, Lehmann called together representatives of the churches in Germany and created the first association. That led to the formation the next year of the Union of Associated Churches of Baptized Christians in Germany and Denmark.

In the 1870s, Baptists had to struggle to assert their freedom from Oncken who, as the patriarch of the movement, had increasingly wanted to see the many churches in Germany as mere branches of the Hamburg church. The German union was threatened but survived through the end of Oncken's career. The movement continued to grow through the 1930s. In 1936 the Baptist Union accepted the Elim Congregations, a Pentecostal fellowship, into membership, and in 1940 the Baptists merged with the Plymouth Brethren to form the Union of Evangelical Free Church Congregations.

The Union was hard hit by the war; it lost many members and leaders. Half of their buildings, including the seminary and printing facilities in Hamburg, were destroyed. Following the war, the country was divided. For a while the Union held together, but in 1970 the East Germans withdrew and formed a separate union. Meanwhile, the Pentecostals and some of the Brethren congregations withdrew from the Union, and the term "Baptist" was added to the Union's name. Then, in 1991, after the reunification of Germany, the East and West German congregations were reintegrated into a single union.

In 1974 the Baptists of German-speaking Europe came together to create a confession of faith—"An Account of Our Faith"—finally accepted in 1977. The confession affirms the basics of the Reformed faith, the belief in baptism by immersion for adult believers, and the nature of the Christian life.

In 2008 the Union reported 85,000 members in 845 churches. Besides the seminary in Hamburg, many German-speaking Baptists attend the seminary in Rüschlikon, Switzerland. The Union is a member of the Baptist World Alliance.

Union of Evangelical Free Church Congregations
 (Baptist)
Friedberger Str. 101
Postfach 1262
61282 Bad Homberg v.d.H
Germany

J. Gordon Melton

See also: American Baptist Churches in the U.S.A.; Baptist World Alliance; Baptists.

References
Balders, Günter, ed. *Ein Herr, ein Glaube, eine Taufe.* Wuppertal/Kassel, Germany: Oncken, 1984, 1989.
Der bund Evangelisch-Freikirchlicher Gemeinden in Deutschland. Wuppertal/Kassel, Germany: Oncken, 1992.
McBeth, H. Leon. *The Baptist Heritage: Four Centuries of the Baptist Witness.* Nashville: Broadman, 1987.
Rushbrooke, J. H. *The Baptist Movement in the Continent of Europe.* London: Kingsgate, 1923.

Union of Indonesian Baptist Churches

The Union of Indonesian Baptist Churches (Gebungan Gereja Baptis Indonesia) began with the closing of China to foreign religious leadership in 1949. In 1951 three former China missionaries arrived in Jakarta, the capital of the newly independent country of Indonesia. They were assisted by Ais Pormes, an Indonesian trained in Australia and the United States, who soon became pastor of a growing Baptist church in Jakarta.

Growth of the church was slow, though a Baptist presence was built during the next 15 years through the formation of a seminary, a publishing house, and a hospital on Java, with support from the Foreign Mission Board of the Southern Baptist Convention. Thus the mission was in place when, following an attempted government coup in 1965, there was a sudden move to Christianity that the missionaries could only describe as phenomenal. The Union was established in 1971.

During subsequent years, Baptists connected with the Union established work on Sumatra, Bali, and several of the other Indonesian islands. It established a hospital on Sumatra and pursued a rural development program. Korean and Japanese Baptists also added their resources to the expansion of the church.

In 2008, the Union reported more than 47,000 members in 222 churches. It is a member of the Baptist World Alliance.

Union of Indonesian Baptist Churches
PO Box 2474
Jakarta 10001
Indonesia

J. Gordon Melton

See also: Baptist World Alliance; Baptists; Southern Baptist Convention.

References

Nance, John Irvin. "A History of the Indonesian Baptist Mission: 1950–1960." M.A. thesis, Baylor University, 1969.
Wardin, Albert W., ed. *Baptists around the World.* Nashville: Holman, 1995.

Union of Messianic Congregations

See Messianic Jews/Jews for Jesus.

Union of the Armenian Evangelical Churches in the Near East

The Union of the Armenian Evangelical Churches in the Near East began as a reform movement within the Armenian Apostolic Church (See of the Great House of Cilicia) but was established as an independent Protestant community in Istanbul in 1846. It grew through the 19th century to include more than 60,000 members scattered throughout the Ottoman Empire. However, during World War I, the Turks turned on the Armenians and massacred more than two million of them. That event and the subsequent movement of Armenians out of the Turkish-controlled territory decimated the Union.

In the 1920s, the Union reorganized in Lebanon and Syria. Today (2005) it includes some 25 congregations with approximately 9,500 members. It is organized as a union of organized churches who elect a committee of 12 members that carry on the work of the Union. It is related through the Supreme Council of the Evangelical Community in Syria and Lebanon with the National Evangelical Union of Lebanon and the National Evangelical Synod of Syria and Lebanon. Together the three churches support the Near East School of Theology in Beirut.

The Union sponsors Haigazian University College and cooperates with the Armenian Apostolic Church in co-sponsoring a hospital and two nursing homes. It is a member of the Middle East Council of Churches and the World Council of Churches.

Union of the Armenian Evangelical Churches in the
    Near East
PO Box 11–377
Ibrahim Pasha Mar Mikhael
Beirut
Lebanon

J. Gordon Melton

See also: Armenian Apostolic Church (See of the Great House of Cilicia); Middle East Council of Churches; National Evangelical Synod of Syria and Lebanon; World Council of Churches.

References

Bauswein, Jean-Jacques, and Lukas Vischner, eds. *The Reformed Family Worldwide: A Survey of Reformed Churches, Theological Schools, and International Organizations.* Grand Rapids, MI: William B. Eerdmans Publishing Company, 1999.
Chopourian, G. H. *The Armenian Evangelical Reformation: Causes and Effects.* New York:

Armenian Missionary Association of America, 1972.

Van Beek, Huibert. *A Handbook of the Churches and Councils: Profiles of Ecumenical Relationships.* Geneva: World Council of Churches, 2006.

Union of Welsh Independents

Wales, a separate country with a separate language, was united with England in 1536. English became the official language, and as Henry VIII began the Reformation, English replaced Latin as the official language of worship for the church in Wales (Anglican). Although many adopted English as their primary language, voices continually arose requesting worship in Welsh, and in 1588 a Welsh edition of the Bible was finally published.

As a whole, the dissenting traditions (Presbyterians, Congregationalists, and so forth) had less problems with the Welsh language, though dissent in Wales carried the same social disapproval and legal restrictions as it did in England. Independency experienced a revival in Wales as a result of the Evangelical Awakening in the middle of the 18th century, and numerous informal religious societies emerged across the land. Many supported the London Missionary Society (formed in 1795) and joined with the Congregational Union of England and Wales (formed in 1832).

The Union of Welsh Independents (Undeb yr Annibynwyr Cymraeg) formed among Congregationalists in Wales in 1872. It continued the tradition of the Puritan movement of the 17th century but has emphasized the preservation of Welsh culture and language. Within that concern, the Union has participated in various ecumenical endeavors and was early in accepting women into ministerial orders (1925).

In the 1990s the Union reported more than 31,000 members in its 490 congregations. It is a member of the World Council of Churches and the World Alliance of Reformed Churches. It also joins in the conferences sponsored by the International Congregational Fellowship.

Union of Welsh Independents
11 St. Helen Rd.

Abertawe—Swansea
Wales SA1 4AL
United Kingdom

J. Gordon Melton

See also: Church in Wales; International Congregational Fellowship; World Alliance of Reformed Churches; World Council of Churches.

References

Bauswein, Jean-Jacques, and Lukas Vischner, eds. *The Reformed Family Worldwide: A Survey of Reformed Churches, Theological Schools, and International Organizations.* Grand Rapids, MI: William B. Eerdmans Publishing Company, 1999.

Van Beek, Huibert. *A Handbook of the Churches and Councils: Profiles of Ecumenical Relationships.* Geneva: World Council of Churches, 2006.

Van der Bent, Ans J., ed. *Handbook/Member Churches/World Council of Churches.* Geneva: World Council of Churches, 1985.

Unitarian Universalist Association

The Unitarian Universalist Association (UUA) is the primary carrier of the several strains of the liberal religious tradition that developed in 19th-century America in dissent from the orthodox Christian faith. Since the time of the Protestant Reformation, teachers have appeared who advocated non-Trinitarian approaches to theology. However, in the United States a new challenge appeared among the Congregational Churches (now an integral part of the United Church of Christ) in the person of Joseph Priestly. Response to his preaching in the 1790s led to the founding of the first Unitarian churches. Then in 1819, William Ellery Channing (1780–1842) preached a famous sermon that became a catalyst for the formation of a Unitarian movement. In this sermon he called for an emphasis on the oneness of God and the role of Christ as a moral exemplar. The American Unitarian Association was founded in 1825, and the Congregational churches were called upon to choose between the Trinitarian and Unitarian positions.

Even earlier, in the 1760s, John Murray (1741–1815) had been expelled from the London Tabernacle founded by George Whitefield (1714–1770) because of his belief that hell was not the destiny of unbelievers and his preaching that eventually all would be saved. He moved to the American colonies and then became an itinerant preacher. By the time of the American Revolution the first Universalist congregations had begun to appear. These churches came together in 1786 to issue the Articles of Association for Universalist Churches. The association was short-lived, but Murray was succeeded by Hosea Ballou (1771–1852), who accomplished a more permanent organization in 1790.

The Universalist Church of America and the American Unitarian Association grew up side by side through the 19th and 20th centuries. Although they saw themselves as the more liberal wing of the Protestant churches, many felt that they were far more than just another Christian sect. They felt that in denying the Trinity and the doctrine of hell, both groups had placed themselves beyond the boundaries of the faith. Neither group was invited to participate in ecumenical organizations.

The Unitarian Association and Universalist Church merged in 1961 to form the Unitarian Universalist Association. Although the Association acknowledges its roots in Christianity, in the decades since the merger it has steadily moved away from those roots in the acceptance of a broad spectrum of religious perspectives within its membership. Not only are Humanism and other non-theist perspectives acceptable but, in addition, Eastern religious systems have taken root among the members. Possibly the most interesting of recent developments has been the growth of neo-Pagan Witchcraft (or Wicca) in the Association, which has been given structure through the Covenant of Unitarian Universalist Pagans (CUUPs). Christian Unitarians continue to exist as one caucus among many.

The Association is organized congregationally. Congregational representatives gather annually for a national meeting. In 2000 the Association reported 155,000 members in North America. In the new century, the Association has reported spectacular growth (reporting more than 200,000 members as of 2008), much of it seen as the largely New England–based

church has become a national denomination in the United States and spread across Canada. It currently has 1,041 congregations (2008) worldwide.

American Unitarianism was exported by missionaries to India and Japan in the 19th century. As a result of its work in India, the Unitarians became aware of the Brahmo Samaj and the similarity of their beliefs. Eventually the Unitarians withdrew from India and have continued their fraternal ties to the Brahmo Samaj. Through the 20th century, the Association developed followings among expatriate communities in Europe. Universalists, meanwhile, developed a missionary program in Japan.

Unitarians also became aware of their Reformation roots in the teachings of Fausto Socinius (1539–1604), who had great success in spreading non-Trinitarian beliefs in Poland, and Francis David (d. 1579), who propagated Unitarian beliefs in Romania. Their work continues in the Unitarian Church in Romania, with whom the American Association developed a fraternal relationship. In 1995, American Unitarians led in the formation of the International Council of Unitarian and Universalists, to nurture those of a similar persuasion around the world. Through the 19th century some cooperative activity had been carried out through the International Association for Religious Freedom.

Unitarian Universalist Association
25 Beacon St.
Boston, MA 02108
http://www.uua.org/

J. Gordon Melton

See also: Brahmo Samaj; International Association for Religious Freedom; International Council of Unitarians and Universalists; United Church of Christ; Wiccan Religion.

References

Alstrom, Sydney E., and Jonathan S. Carey. *An American Reformation*. Middletown, CT: Wesleyan University Press, 1985.

Mendelsohn, Jack. *Being Liberal in an Illiberal Age: Why I Am a Unitarian Universalist*. Boston: Skinner House Books, 2004.

Miller, Russell E. *The Larger Hope*. 2 vols. Boston: Unitarian Universalist Association, 1979, 1985.

Sinkford, William. *Unitarian Universalist Pocket Guide*. Boston: Skinner House Books, 2004.

Tapp, Robert B. *Religion among the Unitarian Universalists*. New York: Seminar, 1973.

Vetter, Herbert. *Notable American Unitarians 1936–1961*. Cambridge, MA: Herbert F. Vetter, 2007.

Wilbur, Earl Morse. *A History of Universalism*. Cambridge, MA: Harvard University Press, 1946.

■ United Arab Emirates

The United Arab Emirates (UAE) is an Arabian country that lies along the southern coast of the Persian Gulf between Saudi Arabia and Oman. A part of the country reaches eastward to the Gulf of Oman and divides Oman into two geographically separate areas. To the northwest along the Gulf Coast lie Qatar and Bahrain. UAE exists as a federation of seven emirates, including Sharjah, Ajman, Umm al-Qaiwain, Ras al-Khaimah, Fujairah, and most notably Abu Dhabi and Dubai. It occupies some 32,300 square miles, the southern four-fifths of which is desert. The great majority of the country's 4,600,000 people reside along its lengthy coast.

The area was little populated until it became the home of pirates who attacked traders moving between Mesopotamia and India. It was not until the 19th century, when the British moved into the area in strength,

that the piracy was controlled. Under continuing British influence, the various local rulers in the region (called emirs) were brought together in a truce (1835) and then as a British protectorate (1892).

Oil exploration and production began in the region in 1958; it flourished, especially around Abu Dhabi. In 1971 the British withdrew, and seven emirates (of which Dubai and Abu Dhabi are the most powerful) united to form the present United Arab Emirates. Bahrain and Qatar, which also had the opportunity to join the union, decided to remain independent nations. The UAE is one of the top oil-producing countries in the world at present.

The United Arab Emirates is a very conservative Arab country. The area converted to Islam in the seventh century CE, and at one point what is now the UAE was the center of the Carmathians, a dissident Muslim movement. The sheikdom at the heart of the movement grew powerful, to the point of conquering Mecca. The fall of the sheikdom led the surviving residents to turn to piracy as a means of livelihood. More recently, the UAE has become a country of hundreds of thousands of immigrants from other Muslim countries, attracted by jobs in the oil fields. The population of the country went from around 360,000 in 1975 to 1.5 million in the mid-1990s. Immigrants have brought a spectrum of Sunni Islamic schools to the area. As in Arabia and Oman, there are substantial numbers of Wahhabis, and immigrants have established mosques

United Arab Emirates

Religion	Followers in 1970	Followers in 2010	% of Population	Annual % growth 2000–2010	Followers in 2025	Followers in 2050
Muslims	208,000	3,591,000	75.9	4.80	4,638,000	6,237,000
Christians	13,600	597,000	12.6	4.80	852,000	1,167,000
Roman Catholics	2,400	463,000	9.8	5.60	670,000	920,000
Orthodox	5,700	62,000	1.3	1.42	70,000	90,000
Independents	520	26,000	0.5	2.92	45,000	70,000
Hindus	1,000	320,000	6.8	4.80	450,000	650,000
Buddhists	0	95,000	2.0	4.80	130,000	180,000
Baha'is	1,000	60,000	1.3	4.80	90,000	130,000
Agnostics	1,500	48,000	1.0	4.80	75,000	110,000
Sikhs	0	11,500	0.2	4.80	18,000	25,000
Atheists	0	7,200	0.2	4.80	12,000	17,000
New religionists	0	2,400	0.1	4.79	3,500	5,000
Total population	**225,000**	**4,732,000**	**100.0**	**4.80**	**6,268,000**	**8,521,000**

UNITED ARAB EMIRATES

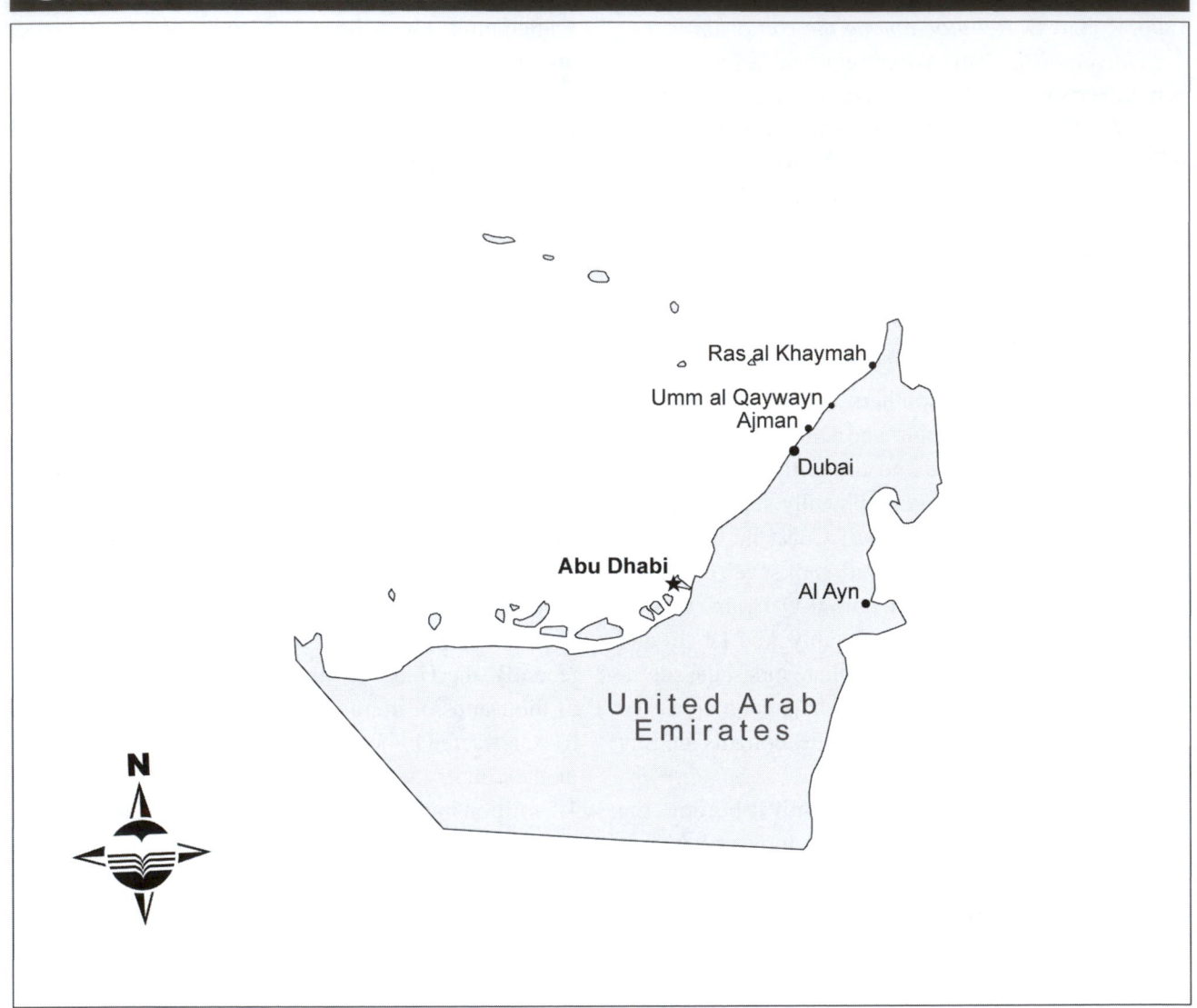

of the Hanbalite, Shafiite, and Malikite schools. There are also Shias from Pakistan, India, and Bangladesh.

The UAE understands itself to be an Islamic state and has made that a matter of law. Since 1975 all proselytizing has been outlawed, and those who violate the law are fined or imprisoned. The primary Christian evangelization effort is through international radio broadcasts.

Christianity attempted to build work in the area in the 19th century but had little success. As early as 1841 a Roman Catholic priest of the Servites traveled through the region. In 1889 the vicariate of Arabia was erected at Aden. South Yemen expelled the vicariate,

which relocated to Abu Dhabi. In the 1970s the vicariate had 11 parishes and 15 chapels, 2 of which were in the UAE. Both parishes were founded in the 1960s and serve expatriates. Additional vicariate worship centers are presently located in Bahrain, Oman, Qatar, and Yemen.

Protestantism entered the area in 1890 in the person of Samuel M. Zwemer (1867–1952) of the Reformed Church in America; Zwemer eventually settled in Bahrain. The Church of England established work once the British acquired some hegemony in the Gulf. Parishes in the region emerged only in the 1960s and were limited to expatriates from the British Isles. The

Sheikh Zayed Mosque in Abu Dhabi, United Arab Emirates. (Orhan Çam/Dreamstime.com)

primary Anglican parish, St. Andrew's Church in Abu Dhabi, is now attached to the Diocese of Cyprus and the Gulf, a diocese within the Episcopal Church in Jerusalem and the Middle East. Other Protestant/Free church groups with work include the Christian Brethren, The Evangelical Alliance Mission (TEAM), and the Reformed Presbyterian Church, Evangelical Synod. The small work of the Seventh-day Adventist Church is attached to the Gulf Section in the Middle East Union Mission. Also, members of various Orthodox churches have relocated to the UAE.

There are a small number of expatriate Hindus in the UAE, and a set of assemblies of the Baha'i Faith.

J. Gordon Melton

See also: Baha'i Faith; Christian Brethren; Church of England; Episcopal Church in Jerusalem and the Middle East; Hanbalite School of Islam; Malikite School of Islam; Reformed Church in America; Seventh-day Adventist Church; Shafiite School of Islam; Wahhabi Islam; Zwemer, Samuel Marinus.

References

Fenelon, K. G. *The United Arab Emirates: An Economic and Social Survey.* London: Longman, 1976.

Horner, N. A. "Present-day Christianity in the Gulf States of the Arabian Peninsula." *Occasional Bulletin of Missionary Research* 2 (April 1978): 53–63.

Hurriez, Sayyid. *Folklore and Folklife in the United Arab Emirates.* London: RoutledgeCurzon, 2002.

Vine, P., and P. Casey. *United Arab Emirates: Profile of a Country's Heritage and Modern Development.* London: Immel, 1992.

United Baptist Church (Mozambique)

The United Baptist Church (Igera Uaiao Baptista) of Mozambique dates its beginning to a mission established by the Church of Scotland in 1913 at Mihecani, Mozambique. During the 1930s support for the mission dried up, and it was turned over to the Nyassa Mission, which also had trouble with sustaining support. In 1939 the work was transferred to the South Africa General Mission (now known as the Africa Evangelical Fellowship). The South Africa General Mission was closed by the government in 1959, at a time when the missionaries were out of the country on furlough. They were refused re-entry, and the Free Baptist Union of Sweden assumed oversight.

The Free Baptist Union had originally come into Mozambique from South Africa in 1921, when it had assumed responsibility for another independent mission. It had established further missions in the southern part of the country by the time it accepted responsibility for the Mihecani mission in the north. The Africa Evangelical Fellowship was able to return to Mozambique in 1985.

The work progressed until 1975, when it began to suffer from the repression of the Marxist regime. During the next seven years, churches were closed, missionary personnel imprisoned, and religious activities severely limited. The United Baptist Church, formally organized in 1968, began a period of spectacular growth, however, following the change of governments in the early 1980s, and by the end of the 20th century it had reported more than 200,000 members. In 1998 the Africa Evangelical Mission merged into the SIM (the Society for International Ministries, originally the Sudan Interior Mission).

The United Baptist Church supports a seminary at Mihecani. The church is a member of the Christian Council of Mozambique, which in turn is affiliated with the World Council of Churches. The church also has a relationship with the United Baptist Church in Zimbabwe, which also grew out of the work of the Africa Evangelical Fellowship.

United Baptist Church
c/o SIM Southern Africa
PO Box 30027
Tokai
Cape Town 7966
South Africa

J. Gordon Melton

See also: Church of Scotland; World Council of Churches.

References

Hansson, Eric, and Barbro Wennbergs, ed. *Mission genom hundra dr*. Tidaholm, Sweden: Fribaptist-samfundets Förlag, 1991.

SIM. http://www.sim.org/index.php/country/MZ. Accessed December 29, 2008.

Thompson, Phyllis. *Life out of Death in Mozambique*. London: Hodder and Stoughton, 1989.

United Board for World Ministries

See American Board of Commissioners for Foreign Missions.

United Church in Jamaica and the Cayman Islands

The United Church in Jamaica and the Cayman Islands dates to the first notice of Presbyterians who were among the Protestants that gathered for worship at Hampden Trelawn, Jamaica. However, organized missionary activity did not start until representatives of the Scottish Missionary Society arrived in Jamaica at the beginning of the 19th century. They quickly extended their activity to Grand Cayman, also the home to some Scottish settlers. Along with establishing worship services, they began schools for the children of Africans. In the 1830s they joined the forces demanding the end to slavery in Jamaica, and following abolition in 1838 they actively participated in evangelical activity among the freedmen. They had already founded the Jamaica Presbytery and the Presbyterian Academy (to train ministers) by 1836. As early as 1846, some graduates of the academy were sent to Calabar, thus initiating what became the Presbyterian Church of Nigeria. They also began a mission among East Indians residing in Jamaica that led to the sending of missionaries to Rajputana in northwest India

The London Missionary Society, representing British Congregationalists, arrived in 1834. The Congregational Union of Jamaica was formed in 1977, but because of continuing financial problems in the land, they remained dependent on the Congregational Union of England and the International Congregational Council.

In 1965 the Congregational Union of Jamaica and the Presbyterian Church of Jamaica merged to form the United Church in Jamaica and the Cayman Islands. In 2005 it reported 60,000 members. It is a member of the Jamaica Council of Churches, the World Alliance of Reformed Churches, and the World Council of Churches.

United Church in Jamaica and the Cayman Islands
PO Box 359
12 Carlton Crescent
Kingston 10
Jamaica

J. Gordon Melton

See also: London Missionary Society; Presbyterian Church of Nigeria; World Alliance of Reformed Churches; World Council of Churches.

References

Bauswein, Jean-Jacques, and Lukas Vischner, eds. *The Reformed Family Worldwide: A Survey of Reformed Churches, Theological Schools, and International Organizations*. Grand Rapids, MI: William B. Eerdmans Publishing Company, 1999.

Van Beek, Huibert. *A Handbook of the Churches and Councils: Profiles of Ecumenical Relationships*. Geneva: World Council of Churches, 2006.

Van der Bent, Ans J., ed. *Handbook/Member Churches/World Council of Churches*. Geneva: World Council of Churches, 1985.

United Church in Papua New Guinea

The London Missionary Society (LMS) joined the effort to bring Christianity to the residents of Papua New Guinea in 1871, and missionaries established stations along the coast. They were joined by Methodists from Australia, who opened work on the Bismarck Archipelago in 1875 and the islands to the south and east of the main island. Their primary effort was among the Dobu people. The work grew slowly but steadily with relatively few incidents, the most memorable being the killing of one LMS missionary and 11 of his converts in 1901.

After World War II, it became increasingly evident that the church should be prepared to become autonomous. Thus in 1963 the LMS helped to form the Congregational Church in Papua New Guinea. Then in 1968 the Congregationalists and Methodists, along with two congregations attached to the United Church of North Australia, merged to create the United Church of Papua New Guinea and the Solomon Islands. At the time of the United Church's formation, the leadership was already largely indigenous, and the transition of authority was smooth. In 1996 the congregations in the Solomon Islands separated to become the United Church in the Solomon Islands.

In the mid-1990s the United Church in Papua New Guinea reported 600,000 members in 2,600 congregations. The church has a congregational polity and an assembly as its highest legislative body. Work continues in the different languages spoken among Papua New Guinea's residents. It cooperates with several other churches in sponsoring the Theological Seminary at Rabaul. It is a member of the World Council of Churches and cooperates with the Council for World Mission.

United Church in Papua New Guinea
PO Box 1401
United Church Assembly Office
Port Moresby
Papua New Guinea

J. Gordon Melton

See also: London Missionary Society; World Council of Churches.

References

Bauswein, Jean-Jacques, and Lukas Vischner, eds. *The Reformed Family Worldwide: A Survey of Reformed Churches, Theological Schools, and International Organizations*. Grand Rapids, MI:

William B. Eerdmans Publishing Company, 1999.

Forman, Charles H. *The Island Churches of the South Pacific: Emergence in the Twentieth Century.* Maryknoll, NY: Orbis, 1982.

Van Beek, Huibert. *A Handbook of the Churches and Councils: Profiles of Ecumenical Relationships.* Geneva: World Council of Churches, 2006.

United Church of Canada

The United Church of Canada has been since its founding the largest Protestant denomination in Canada. A leader in ecumenical activity both nationally and internationally, it was a charter member of both the Canadian Council of Churches in 1944 and the World Council of Churches in 1948. It has retained membership in the World Alliance of Reformed Churches and the World Methodist Council.

The United Church of Canada was created in 1925 by bringing together the Methodist Church (Canada, Newfoundland, and Bermuda), the Congregational Union of Canada, all but a third of the Presbyterian Church in Canada, and a number of local congregations that had been operating as union churches. The hope of the founders that this union would be the first of more to follow has gone largely unrealized. The celebration of the union with the Evangelical United Brethren was quickly followed by disappointment when discussions with the Anglicans to create the Church of Christ in Canada were terminated in 1975.

The denomination's articles of faith were adopted in 1925 as part of the Basis of Union. A "Statement of Faith" was approved in 1940, and what is referred to as the "New Creed" has been in use since 1968. Responding to calls for a new confession of faith that would honor the church's theological diversity and acknowledge its place in a pluralistic world, a statement called "Song of Faith" was prepared and approved when presented to the General Council in 2006. The United Church's receptivity to biblical criticism and its progressive theological orientation have also been evident in educational projects, notably the "New Curriculum" introduced in the 1960s.

Metropolitan United Church, Toronto, Canada. (Ferenz/Dreamstime.com)

The worship practices of the uniting congregations were shaped initially by *The Hymnary* (1930) and *The Book of Common Order* (1932). A new *Service Book* was published in 1969. *The Hymn Book*, published jointly with the Anglican Church of Canada in 1971, was followed a generation later by *Voices United* in 1996, a work that has received a more enthusiastic reception than its predecessor. *More Voices* was published in 2007 as a supplement featuring contemporary and ecumenical music from Canada and around the world. The *United Church Observer* is a denominational publication that since 1986 has been independently incorporated and sets its own editorial policies.

Some of the major events in the denomination's history are intertwined with its controversies. Church union was accomplished only after a long and bitter round of negotiations, drawn out over a period of nearly three decades. After a congregational vote was held in each Presbyterian congregation to determine whether it would join the new church, about a third continued as the Presbyterian Church in Canada. Since then the church has regularly taken positions on political and social issues viewed at the time as risky or controversial. It was the first denomination in Canada to ordain women (Lydia Gruchy, in 1936) and has since elected women to other prominent positions. In 1980, Lois Wilson became the first woman to serve as moderator. Some decisions, such as its positions on remarriage of divorced persons in the early 1960s and ordination of gay and lesbian persons in 1988, generated controversy at the time but have been adopted with less fanfare by others. It continues to study, issue statements, and make efforts to influence governments and other agencies responsible for shaping policy on such issues as abortion, capital punishment, racial equality, land use, refugees, poverty, and same-sex marriage. It is currently grappling with the financial and moral implications of its involvement in helping the federal government to operate residential schools for Native Canadians.

The United Church of Canada is organized at four levels: local congregations or pastoral charges; district presbyteries that exercise oversight of pastoral charges in their jurisdiction; regional conferences that meet annually; and the national General Council, which meets on a biennial or triennial basis. The denomination relates to 12 theological school programs, 4 education and retreat centers, and 6 liberal arts colleges and universities. The educational work of the denomination is also carried on in congregations through organizations for children, youth, and gender-specific associations for adults such as the United Church Women, renamed Women of the United Church of Canada in 2000.

The United Church of Canada operates primarily in Canada, although a few Methodist congregations in Bermuda relate to the Maritime Conference. The churches that merged in 1925 had established missions in such places as Angola, China, India, Japan, Korea, and Trinidad. That work continued and at first expanded after union. The denomination now works under the direction and at the request of indigenous ecumenical partners to provide funds and personnel for projects.

Its development has followed a trajectory similar to mainstream churches in the United States over the same period: it suffered a decline in membership and financial resources during the Depression years; experienced a postwar revival of religious interest; and has recently seen lower rates of membership and participation, reporting the first loss of membership in 1966. It reports (2007) the number of confirmed members as 545,462 and 1,463,128 under pastoral care, while the most recent census data (2001) indicate that 2,839,125 Canadians consider themselves affiliated with the denomination.

United Church of Canada
3250 Bloor Street W.
Etobicoke
Toronto
http://www.united-church.ca

Phyllis D. Airhart

See also: Presbyterian Church in Canada; World Alliance of Reformed Churches; World Council of Churches; World Methodist Council.

References

Chambers, Steven. *This Is Your Church: A Guide to the Beliefs, Practices and Positions of the United Church of Canada*. 3rd ed. Toronto: United Church Publishing House, 1993.

Grant, John Webster. *The Canadian Experience of Church Union*. London: Lutterworth, 1967.

White, Peter Gordon, ed. *Voices and Visions: Sixty-five Years of the United Church of Canada*. Toronto: United Church Publishing House, 1990.

United Church of Christ

The United Church of Christ (UCC), founded in 1957, continues and combines several Reformed Church traditions from Europe in the United States. One of these traditions, that of the Congregational churches, was also responsible for a significant part of the worldwide spread of Protestantism in the 19th century through its vast missionary program.

Worshippers leave the Trinity United Church of Christ following services on June 1, 2008, in Chicago, Illinois. (Getty Images)

The Congregational churches originated with the British Puritans, who came to the American colonies in 1620. Possessed of a Reformed theology, once in the colonies they adopted a congregational form of church governance. Unlike the Pilgrims who had preceded them and settled at Plymouth, Massachusetts, the Congregationalists were not separatists. They held to the autonomy of the local congregation, but that congregation was intimately tied to the township government of the community in which it was located. Heresy and actions opposed to church order were punishable by the town authorities, and harsh treatment would be handed out to the likes of Roger Williams (ca. 1603–1683), a minister expelled from Massachusetts who would later found the Baptist Church in neighboring Rhode Island, and the Quakers (members of the Society of Friends). The Congregational establishment in Massachusetts would continue through the

American Revolution but eventually be lost as state governments conformed to the policy of separation of church and state in the new United States.

At the beginning of the 19th century, the Congregationalist churches assumed a leading role in the emerging world missionary movement pioneered by the Moravian, Methodist, and Baptist churches in the previous century. Representatives of the churches formed the American Board of Commissioners for Foreign Missions (ABCFM) and began an aggressive program of recruiting and sending missionaries to Hawaii and the South Pacific, then to Africa and Asia. The ABCFM became one of the major instruments for turning Protestantism into a global movement through the century.

The Congregationalists were also oriented toward learning and education, and as such they were the founders of many of America's finest institutions of higher learning, such as Harvard and Yale universities. They also became the battleground in which new theological currents could emerge and be tested. Thus, in the 19th century, Unitarianism would arise and split the church. A number of congregations would eventually leave to form the American Unitarian Association (now an integral part of the Unitarian Universalist Association). In the 20th century, prominent ministers would become leading exponents of liberal Protestant perspectives, and the Congregationalists would take the lead in the modern ecumenical movement. Their attachment to the ecumenical ideal would lead them into a series of church mergers.

The Christian Churches originated in the revivals that swept the new United States in the decades following the American Revolution. The founders were attached to two basic ideas. First, they advocated an extreme form of democratic church government based in the local church; they were suspicious of leadership beyond and above the local church. The most prominent of the several groups that created the Christian Churches were the Republican Methodists, led by James O'Kelly. O'Kelly had been a prominent minister in the Methodist Episcopal Church (now an integral part of the United Methodist Church), but he had rejected the episcopal governance of the church that placed authority to assign ministers in the hands of a bishop. The Christians also challenged the division of the church into various sectarian groupings and felt that the followers of Christ should be known simply as "Christians."

In 1931 the National Council of the Congregational Churches and the Christian Churches united to form the General Council of the Congregational-Christian Churches.

At the time of the Protestant Reformation, while most German Protestants adhered to Lutheranism, there was a significant minority who preferred the Reformed Church. Following the founding of the colony of Pennsylvania, many members of the German Reformed Church accepted William Penn's offer to move to the new land where they would be allowed to worship as they pleased. It is estimated that as many as 15,000 were in America at the time of the Revolution. As early as 1725, a schoolteacher who had begun to lead worship services was ordained by the Dutch Reformed Church (now the Reformed Church in America); sub-

sequently, the German churches developed a close relationship with the stronger Dutch Church. In several stages, the German Reformed Church organized as part of the Dutch Reformed Church. It finally became independent in 1793.

The German Reformed Church founded its foreign mission board in 1838. For the next 28 years it worked through the American Board of Commissioners for Foreign Missions, but after 1866 it began to develop independent work.

The Evangelical Synod of North America had its origins in Prussia, where in 1817 the ruler had created the Church of the Prussian Union by encouraging the merger of the Lutheran and Reformed churches in his realm. The church was seen as a bulwark against rationalism and pietism, and personal spirituality was emphasized. Significant attention was given to foreign missions as manifest in support for several missionary societies, most prominently the Basel Mission Society. Beginning in 1833, the Society sent more than 280 missionaries to the United States to work among German Americans. In 1840, under the leadership of Joseph A. Rieger (1811–1869) and George Wendelin Wall (1811–1867), a group of ministers met in St. Louis, Missouri, to form the German Evangelical Church Society of the West.

The Society (after 1866, the Synod) was a loosely organized body designed to serve the congregations. It encouraged the use of the several catechisms that had been developed in Germany that combined Lutheran and Reformed elements. Shortly after the Society formed in St. Louis, two similar organizations arose, in the Northwest and Northeast. In 1872 these three synods merged to form the German Evangelical Synod of North America (the word "German" being dropped in 1927). Like its German counterpart, the Synod developed a strong missionary program both at home among Native Americans and abroad. Additionally, it gave support to higher education and medical facilities.

In 1934 the Evangelical Synod and the Reformed Church united to form the Evangelical and Reformed Church. A short time later, the new church initiated talks with the General Council of the Congregational-Christian Churches. That merger was consummated in 1957, occurring at the height of ecumenical enthusiasm in the United States; it was seen as a model for other churches to follow. It also gave hope to those who wished to see a U.S. version of a united Protestant church that would bring together not only the church making up the United Church of Christ but also various Methodist, Episcopal, Presbyterian, and other churches.

The United Church is organized congregationally with denominational affairs placed in the hands of the General Synod. As with most Protestant churches, relationships with a number of mission churches were reoriented into partnership relations with new independent ecclesiastical bodies. The fabled American Board united with the mission board of the Evangelical and Reformed Church as the United Church Board of World Ministries.

In 2006 the church reported 1,218,541 members in 5,452 churches. The UCC has a strong commitment to ecumenical relations and is a prominent member of the World Council of Churches and the World Alliance of Reformed Churches. It is also one of the most liberal of church bodies and has shown leadership in the ordination both of women and professed homosexuals. Its ministers and lay leaders have been prominent in a range of social causes, from peace to race relations. The church maintains an extensive program of higher education that includes support for a number of colleges and seminaries.

The church continues support for many of the churches that originated as missions of the UCC's several constituent groups. It has a special partnership relationship to the Christian Church (Disciples of Christ), the Evangelical Church in Germany, the Pentecostal Church of Chile, the United Church of Christ in the Philippines, and the Presbyterian Church in the Republic of Korea.

United Church of Christ
700 Prospect Ave., E.
Cleveland, OH 44115–1100

J. Gordon Melton

See also: American Board of Commissioners for Foreign Missions; Christian Church (Disciples of Christ); Evangelical Church in Germany; Friends/Quakers; Pentecostal Church of Chile; Presbyterian Church in the Republic of Korea; Reformed Church in America; Unitarian Universalist Association; United Church of Christ in the Philippines; United Methodist Church; World Alliance of Reformed Churches; World Council of Churches.

References

Gunneman, Louis H., and Charles Shelby Ro. *The Shaping of the United Church of Christ*. Cleveland, OH: United Church Press, 1999.

Johnson, Daniel L., and Charles E. Hambrick-Stowe, eds. *Theology and Identity: Traditions, Movements, and Polity in the United Church of Christ*. Cleveland, OH: United Church Press, 2008.

Paeth, Scott R. *Who Do You Say That I Am?: Christology and Identity in the United Church of Christ*. Cleveland, OH: United Church Press, 2008.

Youngs, J. William T. *The Congregationalists*. Westport, CT: Greenwood, 1998.

United Church of Christ–Congregational in the Marshall Islands

The United Church of Christ–Congregational in the Marshall Islands began with the arrival in 1857 of missionaries, both U.S. and Hawaiian, connected with the American Board of Commissioners for Foreign Missions (ABCFM). As the work grew, in 1865 the administration of the Micronesian Mission was placed in the hands of the Congregational Church of Hawaii's Board of Missions. The work was immensely assisted by the Hawaiian leadership, who developed indigenous leadership and used local leaders to extend the work to new islands. Although some of the American Board's missionaries were Presbyterian, Congregationalism dominated, and the Marshall Islands work developed a Congregational polity.

The work continued under the guidance of the American Board until 1957, when the Congregational Christian Churches in the United States merged with the Evangelical and Reformed Church to create the United Church of Christ. At that time the American Board was superseded by the United Church Board of World Ministries. This change also signaled the beginning of a process of maturing of the Micronesian mission.

In 1979 a referendum was held through Micronesia (then a UN trust assigned to the United States). Although the Caroline and the Marianas Islands voted to become the Federated States of Micronesia, the Marshalls voted to remain in the trust relationship with the United States. They became a separate entity and were granted local autonomy. In 1986 they became a Free Associated State with a continuing special relationship to the United States. In 1990 the Marshall Islands were admitted to the United Nations.

As the country was moving toward independence, so the mission moved toward becoming independent as the United Church of Christ–Congregational in the Marshall Islands. It adopted the polity and theological perspective of the United Church of Christ.

In 2005, the United Church reported 40,225 members (out of a population of 59,000). It is the largest Protestant church in the country and a member of the World Council of Churches. It also retains a relationship with the other churches that have grown out of the ABCFM's Micronesian Mission and participates with them in the United Church of Micronesia.

United Church of Christ–Congregational in the
    Marshall Islands
PO Box 75
Majuro
Marshall Islands 96960

J. Gordon Melton

See also: American Board of Commissioners for Foreign Missions; United Church of Christ; World Council of Churches.

References

Bauswein, Jean-Jacques, and Lukas Vischner, eds. *The Reformed Family Worldwide: A Survey of Reformed Churches, Theological Schools, and International Organizations*. Grand Rapids, MI: William B. Eerdmans Publishing Company, 1999.

Van Beek, Huibert. *A Handbook of the Churches and Councils: Profiles of Ecumenical Relationships*. Geneva: World Council of Churches, 2006.

United Church of Christ in Japan

In 1940 the Japanese ordered all Protestant churches united into a single body, the United Church of Japan, generally called the Kyodan. Most churches complied, and the few who refused to join lost any legal standing. The majority of those who affiliated with the Kyodan remained together when the government changed following World War II, and the church remains the largest Protestant body in the country.

Protestantism entered Japan in 1859 after the Townsend Harris Treaty had cleared the legal hurdles to its presence. Missionaries of the Episcopal Church, John Liggins and Channing M. Williams, were the first to arrive, in May 1859. James C. Hepburn, representing the Presbyterian Board of Foreign Missions, arrived in the fall. He pioneered the work of Bible translation. Then in November, Samuel R. Brown and Guido F. Verback of the Dutch Reformed Church (now the Reformed Church in America) landed. All except Verback had been reassigned from China. Although the treaty had allowed their entrance, the government restricted their activities to Yokohama and Nagasaki, and largely confined them to operating schools and clinics. Attempts to evangelize in conventional ways were considered an offense.

The first convert was baptized in 1864, but the first church was not organized until 1872 in Yokohama. A second church was opened in 1873 in Tokyo. The missionaries also took steps to organize their work without reference to their respective denominations. However, they had to deal with the arrival of additional missionaries representing other churches. The Church Missionary Society (of the Church of England) sent people in 1869, and the first American Baptist missionary came in 1872. Then in 1873, the government removed the restrictions, and the number of missionaries and the groups they represented rose sharply, among them being the Methodists.

The translation of the New Testament was completed and published in 1880. The Old Testament was completed seven years later. With the new Bibles and the legal restrictions gone, the churches entered a growth phase. By this time Japanese leadership had arisen who began to create an indigenous presentation of the faith. By the end of the 1880s, the number of missionaries had almost doubled (from 145 to 383). Then in 1890, the government issued a document declaring its rejection of Christian beliefs and defining Japanese personhood in terms of Shintoism. This document was to be read with great ceremony in all the schools on all public holidays. This action explains the difficulty that met many members of the independent evangelical missionary agencies as they began to enter the country around the turn of the century.

The spirit of cooperation that was present in most of the missionary groups led to a union of the mission of the Presbyterian Church in the U.S.A., the Church of Scotland, and the Dutch Reformed Church in 1877 as the United Church of Christ in Japan (the word "United" was dropped in 1890). In 1887 the three Anglican missionary thrusts from England and America came together as the Japan Episcopal Church. In 1907 the two American and one Canadian Methodist groups united as the Japan Methodist Church. Several of the Baptist groups came together in 1957 as the Japan Baptist Union. Lutheranism entered Japan in 1892 with the opening of work at Saga on the island of Kyushu. Subsequently several churches and a spectrum of Lutheran missionary societies started missions.

In 1913, following the visit of U.S. missionary executive John R. Mott (1865–1955), many of the missions joined together in a "Cooperative Campaign of Evangelism." A new growth spurt followed but finally ground to a halt as Japan geared up philosophically and militarily for World War II. During the 1930s pressure was put upon Christians to engage in shrine attendance, during which time one was expected to bow before a picture of the emperor. The churches rejected the attempt to have Shintoism redefined as nonreligious.

Then in 1939, the Religious Bodies Law was passed that ordered all Protestant Christians to come together in a single organization, or Kyodan. Among the churches that refused to come together in the Kyodan were the Salvation Army, the Anglicans, the Seventh-day Adventist Church, and the Holiness Church. Some 32 groups affiliated with the Kyodan. During the war, missionaries and Christian leaders were suspect. The Holiness Church suffered the most, with 250 of its pastors arrested.

After the war, the U.S. government imposed U.S.-style freedom of religion on Japan, and General Douglas MacArthur made a personal plea for 1,000 missionaries to come to the newly opened land. Those denominations whose missions had come together in the Kyodan sent more than 400 missionaries. However, the many evangelical churches and independent sending agencies sent even more. Most of the churches forced into the United Church of Christ in Japan remained. By the beginning of the 1980s, they had some 200,000 members in 12,600 congregations. Although growth was slight in the last decades of the 20th century, it remains the largest Protestant church in the country.

In 2005, the church reported 195,851 members. The church is a member of the World Council of Churches. The United Church has issued its own ecumenical statement of faith. It is organized congregationally, with a general assembly as its highest legislative body. Its congregations across the country are organized into 16 districts.

United Church of Christ in Japan
Room 31
Japan Christian Center
3-18 Nishi-Waseda
2-chome, Shinjuku-ku
Tokyo 169
Japan

J. Gordon Melton

See also: Church Missionary Society; Church of England; Church of Scotland; Reformed Church in America; Salvation Army; Seventh-day Adventist Church; World Council of Churches.

References

Bauswein, Jean-Jacques, and Lukas Vischner, eds. *The Reformed Family Worldwide: A Survey of Reformed Churches, Theological Schools, and International Organizations.* Grand Rapids, MI: William B. Eerdmans Publishing Company, 1999.

Van Beek, Huibert. *A Handbook of the Churches and Councils: Profiles of Ecumenical Relationships.* Geneva: World Council of Churches, 2006.

Van der Bent, Ans J., ed. *Handbook/Member Churches/World Council of Churches*. Geneva: World Council of Churches, 1985.

United Church of Christ in the Philippines

The United Church of Christ in the Philippines was founded in 1941 and combined the missionary history of the Presbyterians, Congregationalists, Methodists, United Brethren, and Disciples of Christ. The Presbyterian Church in the U.S.A. (now a constituent part of the Presbyterian Church [U.S.A.]) was the first church to launch a missionary thrust in the Philippines following the Spanish-American War and the U.S. annexation of the islands at the end of the 19th century. Dr. James B. Rodgers (1865–1944) arrived in April 1899. He was quickly followed by James Thobum (1832–1922), a missionary bishop for the Methodist Episcopal Church (now a constituent part of the United Methodist Church), who left the Reverend Nicolas Zamora in charge of work until a group of U.S. women landed at Manila the following year. In 1901 the Reverend Homer C. Stuntz arrived as the superintendent.

The Presbyterians founded the first Protestant college, Silliman University, in 1901, and the two churches cooperated in the founding of Union Theological Seminary in 1907. Both churches also faced the religious side of the desire of the Filipinos for self-rule. In 1907, Nicolas Zamora, the first Filipino ordained as a Protestant minister, led a group of Methodists to form the independent Evangelical Methodist Church in the Philippine Islands. A short time later, the Presbyterians lost a group who formed the United Evangelical Church of Christ. And even later the Methodists had a second split that led to the founding of the Philippine Methodist Church.

The Women's Missionary Association of the Church of the United Brethren (now a constituent part of the United Methodist Church) voted to begin missionary activity in the Philippines at its 1901 meeting. The first missionaries, Sanford B. Kurtz and Edwin S. Eby, landed in the islands later that year. They settled on Luzon in the northwest. The Christian Church (Disciples of Christ) missionaries also arrived in 1901 and also established their initial station on the northern part of Luzon, at Laoag. Both missions grew steadily until the beginning of World War II. The American Board of Commissioners for Foreign Missions, which already had a work in the South Pacific, having worked out a comity agreement with the other churches, began work on Mindanao in 1902. The Reverend R. F. Black and his wife settled at Davao and began work among the rather diverse population of Roman Catholics, Muslims, and followers of indigenous religions.

Soon after the first Protestant missions had been launched, an effort to cut competition and duplication of efforts had occurred. As the missions became established, some began to project the vision of a united Protestant church. A first step in that direction occurred in 1929, when the Presbyterians and Congregationalists merged their work into the United Evangelical Church in the Philippines. In 1943 the United Brethren and the Christian Church (Disciples of Christ) merged to form the Evangelical Church in the Philippines. The Evangelical Church and the United Evangelical Church then came together in 1948 with the Philippine Methodist Church and several small independent churches to form the United Church of Christ in the Philippines. Of course, in the midst of this process, the churches experienced the years of Japanese occupation during World War II and the resulting complete disruption of Christian life throughout the islands.

The United Church adopted a new confession of faith reflective of its varied past and the Reformed theological tradition that now dominates its life. It has also become known for its advocacy of justice issues within the country, especially concerning issues of human rights. The church manages a system of secondary schools, several colleges and universities, and four hospitals. It is a member of the World Council of Churches, the World Methodist Council, the Reformed Ecumenical Council, and the World Alliance of Reformed Churches. It was a charter member of the Philippine Federation of Christian Churches. The church reported 950,000 members in the 1990s.

United Church of Christ in the Philippines
PO Box 718
C.P.O., EDSA
Quezon City, Ermita Manila

Quezon City 1099
Philippines

J. Gordon Melton

See also: American Board of Commissioners for Foreign Missions; Christian Church (Disciples of Christ); Evangelical Methodist Church in the Philippine Islands; Presbyterian Church (U.S.A.); Reformed Ecumenical Council; United Methodist Church; World Alliance of Reformed Churches; World Council of Churches; World Methodist Council.

References

Aoanan, Melanio de Guardia. *Ecumenical and Prophetic: The Witness of the United Church of Christ in the Philippines*. Chicago: Claretian Publications, 1998.

Bauswein, Jean-Jacques, and Lukas Vischner, eds. *The Reformed Family Worldwide: A Survey of Reformed Churches, Theological Schools, and International Organizations*. Grand Rapids, MI: William B. Eerdmans Publishing Company, 1999.

Rodgers, James B. *Forty Years in the Philippines: A History of the Philippine Mission of the Presbyterian Church in the United States of America 1899–1939*. New York: The Board of Foreign Missions of the Presbyterian Church in the United States of America, 1940.

Van Beek, Huibert. *A Handbook of the Churches and Councils: Profiles of Ecumenical Relationships*. Geneva: World Council of Churches, 2006.

United Church of Christ in Zimbabwe

The United Church of Christ in Zimbabwe began with the arrival of Congregationalist missionaries representing the American Board of Commissioners for Foreign Missions into the eastern part of Zimbabwe in 1893. The initial stations were set up in Chikore and at Mount Silinda. The mission experienced steady growth through the next century, and in 1973 it became independent.

The church has a congregational polity, with its synod being the highest legislative body. It ordained females to the ministry from the beginning of its existence as an independent church. It is an ecumenically oriented church and holds membership in the World Council of Churches and the World Alliance of Reformed Churches, as well as being a founding member of the Zimbabwe Council of Churches.

In 2005 the church reported 30,000 members. It co-sponsors the United Theological College and the Rusitu Bible Institute.

United Church of Christ in Zimbabwe
30/32 Second Street, Park Town
PO Box CY 2785, Causeway
Harare
Zimbabwe

J. Gordon Melton

See also: American Board of Commissioners for Foreign Missions; World Alliance of Reformed Churches; World Council of Churches.

References

Bauswein, Jean-Jacques, and Lukas Vischner, eds. *The Reformed Family Worldwide: A Survey of Reformed Churches, Theological Schools, and International Organizations*. Grand Rapids, MI: William B. Eerdmans Publishing Company, 1999.

Van Beek, Huibert. *A Handbook of the Churches and Councils: Profiles of Ecumenical Relationships*. Geneva: World Council of Churches, 2006.

United Church of God, an International Association

The United Church of God, an International Association, is by far the largest of the more than 400 offshoots of the Worldwide Church of God (WCOG) formed since the death of WCOG founder Herbert W. Armstrong (1892–1986).

Following the Christmas Eve 1994 sermon by Armstrong's successor as pastor general, Joseph W. Tkach, in which he announced that the WCOG had abandoned the founder's teachings and had moved firmly toward an evangelical Protestant theological perspective, many ministers left Worldwide, taking their congregations with them. In 1995 some 150 elders convened to form "a collaborative organisation" with an avowedly more collegiate form of governance than had been traditional in Worldwide, or than was found in the two previous large breakaways, the Philadelphia Church of God (1989) and the Global Church of God (1992). Many individual congregations that had left the WCOG before the mass exodus that resulted in United, joined the newly formed United Church of God.

In its teachings and practices, the United Church of God is the most moderate of the major offshoots from Worldwide. Although it holds to Armstrong's teachings, it has deliberately re-examined all of them to "prove the truth," rather than accepting them "on faith." This has led to a softening of some attitudes, though the major teachings still follow those formerly held by the Worldwide Church of God: Sabbatarian and millenarian, with a belief in the literal rule of Christ on Earth, a watch on world events that presage the end times, and conservative morality.

The name "United" has proven to be a little embarrassing for the church. A number of individual churches that joined because of what they perceived to be United's "hands-off" attitude to governance have since seceded in protest over decisions by the church's headquarters, particularly over centralized imposition of ministers on churches.

A major split occurred within the United Church in early 1998, when the council of elders removed the church's president, David Hulme, from his post. Hulme left and founded the Church of God, an International Community. A considerable number of individual ministers and congregations within United, including most of those in Britain, followed him. The Church of God, a International Community publishes a quarterly magazine, *Vision*, which is very different in style and content from the magazines of all the other offshoots from WCOG. It claims 2,500 members.

The United Church of God remains the largest of the offshoots in the "Worldwide family," with more members than the next five largest churches taken together. Initially it had between 15,000 and 17,000 members, and in 2008 claimed just over 20,000 in attendance at the annual Feast of Tabernacles, though the actual membership is probably a little less than that. It has congregations in more than 50 countries. With its leadership by an elected council of elders rather than by one man, as in most of the other offshoots, it has avoided both the benefits and the problems associated with strong charismatic leadership, including the inevitable and often difficult issue of succession. In that sense it has become denominationalized quite successfully.

As well as the usual selection of books and booklets the United Church of God publishes a magazine, *Good News*, and has a cable TV program, *Beyond Today*.

United Church of God
PO Box 541027
Cincinnati, OH 45254-1027
www.ucg.org
www.gnmagazine.org
www.beyondtoday.tv

Church of God, an International Community
476 S. Marengo Avenue
Pasadena
CA 91101
www.church-of-god.org
www.vision.org

David V. Barrett

See also: Living Church of God; Philadelphia Church of God; Sabbatarianism; Worldwide Church of God.

References
Barrett, David V. *The New Believers*. London: Cassell, 2001.
Church of God News. Pasadena, CA.
The Journal: News of the Churches of God. Big Sandy, TX: JMC.
Tkach, Joseph. *Transformed by Truth.* Sisters, OR: Multnomah, 1997.

United Church of the Solomon Islands

The United Church of the Solomon Islands began as a missionary effort of Australian Methodists. John Goldie (1870–1954) arrived in the Western Solomons Province in 1902 and established a base at Munda Point on New Georgia. He was assisted by missionaries

Solomon Islanders attend the Wesley United Church service, 2006. (AP/Wide World Photos)

from the Methodist churches in Fiji and Samoa. In 1913, with additional assistance from New Zealand Methodists, the work moved to Bouganville, formerly under German control.

In 1955 the British began to relocate a number of people from the Gilbert Islands to Wagina in the Western Solomons. Many of those people had been members of the mission of the London Missionary Society (Congregationalist) (LMS). The LMS worked out an agreement with the Methodists to receive these people into the Methodist Church.

In 1968 the Methodist Church in the Solomons merged with the Methodists in Papua New Guinea and the Papua Ekalesia (the independent church that developed from the LMS mission in Papua) to form the United Church of Papua New Guinea and the Solomon Islands. Then in 1978 the Solomon Islands became an independent nation. In the 1980s, secessionists on Bouganville demanded independence from Papua New Guinea. This disruption created a communication problem between important segments of the church, and in 1996 the Solomon Islands and Papua New Guinea segments of the church decided to go their separate ways.

The United Church of the Solomon Islands reported 50,000 members in 2005. It is a cooperating partner with the Council on World Mission and a member of the World Alliance of Reformed Churches and the World Council of Churches. Leslie Boseto, a former bishop of the church, was elected president of the World Council of Churches in 1992.

United Church of the Solomon Islands
PO Box 82
Kokeqolo, Munda Western Province
Solomon Islands

J. Gordon Melton

See also: London Missionary Society; World Alliance of Reformed Churches; World Council of Churches.

References

Bauswein, Jean-Jacques, and Lukas Vischner, eds. *The Reformed Family Worldwide: A Survey of Reformed Churches, Theological Schools, and International Organizations*. Grand Rapids, MI: William B. Eerdmans Publishing Company, 1999.

Forman, Charles H. *The Island Churches of the South Pacific: Emergence in the Twentieth Century*. Maryknoll, NY: Orbis, 1982.

Van Beek, Huibert. *A Handbook of the Churches and Councils: Profiles of Ecumenical Relationships*. Geneva: World Council of Churches, 2006.

United Church of Zambia

The United Church of Zambia (UCZ) has brought together a variety of Christian missions formed in the late 19th and early 20th centuries. The oldest strain of UCZ history can be traced to 1885 and the entrance of a group of missionaries led by François Coillard of the Paris Mission (associated with the Reformed Church of France). They had support from Lesotho. Their beginning was inauspicious, as they were arrested and maltreated soon after their arrival in what is now Zambia (formerly Northern Rhodesia). However, they persevered with their work, initially among the Lozi people, and in 1964 the work grew into the independent Evangelical Church of Barotseland.

The London Missionary Society (LMS) started work in 1883 in the northern part of the country at Niamkolo, among the Lungu people. They were soon joined by Presbyterians.

In 1894 a missionary from the Church of Scotland, Alexander Dewar, and a Christian from Tonga, John Banda, came into Rhodesia from Malawi and established themselves at Mwenzo, not far from the border with Tanzania. Their work was supplemented through the early 20th century by teams of students from Malawi who made trips into Zambia to evangelize the population. Among these students was David J. Kuanda, the father of Kenneth D. Kuanda, who would lead the country in the years immediately after Zambia's independence. In 1894 the Primitive Methodists (now a constituent part of the Methodist Church [U.K.]) opened a mission in central Zambia among the Ila people.

In the 1920s, the rich copper deposits in the country began to be mined, and several churches opened a mission station at Copperbelt, a community that arose near the mines. In the 1930s those missions (including centers of the LMS and the Presbyterians) came together as the United Missions of the Copperbelt. This united mission became a catalyst for the LMS and Presbyterians to unite across the country in 1945 as the Church of Central Africa Presbyterian (General Synod) in Rhodesia. In 1958 they were joined by another group of missions in the Copperbelt that had formed the Central Free Church Council to create the United Church of Central Africa in Rhodesia.

In the 1960s, Northern Rhodesia moved toward independence as Zambia, a move that culminated in 1965. That same year the United Church of Central Africa merged with the Methodists and the Church of Barotseland to form the United Church of Zambia. It included members from seven different Zambian peoples.

In 2005, the United Church reported 3 million members in 1,060 congregations. The church sponsors a hospital, several secondary schools, and a farm college. The church has a presbyterian organization with a synod as the highest legislative body. It follows a Reformed theological perspective but acknowledges only the Apostles' Creed and the Nicene Creed as its doctrinal standards. The church is ecumenically active and has affiliated with the World Council of Churches and the World Alliance of Reformed Churches. It also cooperates with the Council for World Mission.

United Church of Zambia
PO Box 50122
15101 Ridgeway
Lusaka
Zambia

J. Gordon Melton

See also: Church of Central Africa Presbyterian (General Synod); Church of Scotland; London Missionary Society; Paris Mission; Reformed Church of France; World Alliance of Reformed Churches; World Council of Churches.

References

Bauswein, Jean-Jacques, and Lukas Vischner, eds. *The Reformed Family Worldwide: A Survey of Reformed Churches, Theological Schools, and International Organizations.* Grand Rapids, MI: William B. Eerdmans Publishing Company, 1999.

Van Beek, Huibert. *A Handbook of the Churches and Councils: Profiles of Ecumenical Relationships.* Geneva: World Council of Churches, 2006.

Van der Bent, Ans J., ed. *Handbook/Member Churches/World Council of Churches.* Geneva: World Council of Churches, 1985.

United Congregational Church of Southern Africa

Johannes van der Kamp came to the Cape of Good Hope as a missionary representing the London Missionary Society (LMS) in 1799. His goal was to open a mission among the Bantu-speaking people of the region. A missionary station was founded at Kuruman, and the first congregations at Graaff-Reinet (1801) and Bethelsdorp (1802). With the assistance of other missionaries, the most famous being David Livingstone and Robert Moffat, the work spread across the colony. In the meantime the British took control, and British settlers began to flood into the Cape. Among them were some of Congregational background who also began to form new churches.

In 1854 the LMS withdrew from the Cape in order to pursue opportunities in the interior of Africa. In 1859 the LMS churches and those of independent origin united to form the Evangelical Voluntary Union. The Union became the Congregational Union of Africa in 1877.

Alongside the British Congregationalists, Americans came to the Cape in 1835. Missionaries representing the American Board of Commissioners for Foreign Missions initiated work among the Zulu people in Natal and then moved into Mozambique to work among the Batswa people. The mission grew to become the Bantu Congregational Church. In 1967 the Congregational Union and the Bantu Church united to form the United Congregational Church of Southern Africa. By this time its work had moved beyond South Africa and Mozambique to Namibia, Botswana, and Zimbabwe.

In 2005 the United Church reported 450,000 members. It is a member of the World Alliance of Reformed Churches and the World Council of Churches. In 1972 the South African Association of the Disciples of Christ merged into the United Church.

United Congregational Church of Southern Africa
PO Box 96014
150 Caroline St.
Brixton, Johannesburg 2019
South Africa

J. Gordon Melton

See also: American Board of Commissioners for Foreign Missions; London Missionary Society; World Alliance of Reformed Churches; World Council of Churches.

References

Bauswein, Jean-Jacques, and Lukas Vischner, eds. *The Reformed Family Worldwide: A Survey of Reformed Churches, Theological Schools, and International Organizations.* Grand Rapids, MI: William B. Eerdmans Publishing Company, 1999.

Van Beek, Huibert. *A Handbook of the Churches and Councils: Profiles of Ecumenical Relationships.* Geneva: World Council of Churches, 2006.

Van der Bent, Ans J., ed. *Handbook/Member Churches/World Council of Churches.* Geneva: World Council of Churches, 1985.

Wing, Joseph. *As One People: Commemorating the Tenth Anniversary of the United Congregational Church of Southern Africa, 1967–1977.* Johannesburg: United Congregational Church of South Africa, 1977.

United Evangelical Church–Anglican Communion of Angola

See Anglican Diocese in Angola.

United Evangelical Lutheran Church

The United Evangelical Lutheran Church (UELC) traces its origin to the early 20th century and the work in Argentina of the Augustana Lutheran Church. The Augustana Lutheran Church had been formed by Swedish Americans who participated in the various mergers that led in the 1980s to the present Evangelical Lutheran Church in America. During the second decade of the 20th century, however, one of the Augustana ministers became the pastor of the Swedish Lutheran congregation in Buenos Aires. While there, Emil Cedar began work in Spanish, including the translation of literature. Following the formation of the UELC, one of the steps in the American merger process, the new church assumed responsibility for the Buenos Aires congregation and sent Edward H. Mueller (d. 1923) to head the work. During the brief five years of his ministry, he founded four additional congregations.

In 1948 the Argentine congregations formed a synod and were formally received into the UELC as an associate synod. In 1951 it joined the Lutheran World Federation (LWF). LWF membership also served as a catalyst, calling attention to the variety of war refugees that had found their way to Argentina, especially from Eastern Europe and the Baltic states. In cooperation with the LWF it assisted refugees from Hungary, Slovakia, Latvia, and Estonia to form congregations. In 1953 the UELC became an autonomous body. It then engaged in a process of assisting their new members to adjust to their new home.

The UELC is headed by its president and the synod, its highest legislative body. It has a membership of approximately 11,000 members. The church sponsors a system of parochial schools and supports the Instituto Superior Evangélicos de Estudios Teologicos, an interdenominational seminary for the training of ministers. It is ecumenically active and a member of the World Council of Churches. Women have been admitted to the ministry since 1981.

United Evangelical Lutheran Church
Marcos Sastre 2891
1417 Buenos Aires
Argentina

J. Gordon Melton

See also: Evangelical Lutheran Church in America; Lutheran World Federation; World Council of Churches.

References

Bachmann, E. Theodore, and Mercia Brenne Bachmann. *Lutheran Churches in the World: A Handbook*. Minneapolis, MN: Augsburg, 1989.
Van Beek, Huibert. *A Handbook of the Churches and Councils: Profiles of Ecumenical Relationships*. Geneva: World Council of Churches, 2006.

United Evangelical Lutheran Church in India

Functioning as both a denomination and an ecumenical body, the United Evangelical Lutheran Church in India (UELCI) was founded in 1926 as the Federation of Evangelical Lutheran Churches. It embodies the major thrust of Lutheran missions in India that began in 1706, when Bartholomaus Ziegenbalg (1682–1719) and Heinrich Plutschau (1677–1752) arrived from Denmark as representatives of the Danish-Halle mission with the support of the Church of Denmark and the Danish king. They settled Tanquebar (a Danish colony) and quickly learned Tamil. Before the end of the decade, Ziegenbalg had produced a Tamil translation of the Christian New Testament, and along the way a Tamil grammar and dictionary. Their work would set a pattern frequently followed by pioneering Protestant missionaries worldwide of concentrating on reducing languages to writing and producing translations of the Bible.

The work of making the most substantive gains in spreading Lutheranism is generally credited to Christian Freidrich Schwartz (1817–1870), who dominated the mission in the late 18th century. The 50,000 converts would become the core of what would later be known as the Tamil Evangelical Lutheran Church.

The early 19th century was a time in which the British limited missionary access to India, and interest among European Lutherans was at its lowest. However, at the end of the 1830s, British authorities developed a new attitude, and Lutherans launched a new wave of missionary activity.

In 1840 the German Leipzig Mission began work in Tamil that was later passed to the Swedish Lutherans. In the 1870s this work was assumed under the new missionary society directly sponsored by the Church of Sweden. The mission would later mature as the Tamil Evangelical Lutheran Church. In 1842, Father C. F. Heyer (1793–1873) arrived in Madras as a representative of the Ministerium of Pennsylvania (now a constituent part of the Evangelical Lutheran Church in America) and the very first foreign missionary commissioned by any American Lutheran body. The North German Missionary Society at Bremen sent missionaries two years later, but their work was absorbed by the Americans in 1850. The American work would mature at the Andhra Evangelical Lutheran Church, one of the largest Christian bodies in India.

Subsequently, missionaries would arrive from the Gossner Mission (1844), the Danish Missionary Society (1963), the Hermannsburg Mission (1865), the Swedish Evangelical Mission (1877), and the Schleswig-Holstein Evangelical Lutheran Mission headquartered in Breklum, Germany (1882). From these efforts no fewer than 10 Lutheran churches serving different language groups and different parts of the country would emerge.

In 1926, in part because of encouragement from the Lutheran World Convention held in 1923, the various Lutheran churches in India formed the Federation of Evangelical Lutheran Churches in India. It developed support for the All-India Theological College and Research Institute in 1953, a major symbol of the hoped-for Lutheran unity. More recently, the churches have expanded their level of trust and the closeness of their fellowship by reorganizing the Federation in 1975 as the Lutheran Churches in India and in the 1980s dropping the plural "Churches" for the singular "Church." Over the years the UELCI has assumed more denominational functions, not the least of which is its serving as the representative body holding the membership of the member churches with the World Council of Churches. Interestingly, the church is not a member of (though it cooperates with) the Lutheran World Federation (LWF). Most of the member churches of the UELCI are members of the LWF.

The UELCI represents more than 1,500,000 church members worshipping in 3,000 congregations (2005).

Churches represented in the UELCI include the Andhra Evangelical Lutheran Church, Arcot Lutheran Church, Evangelical Lutheran Church in Madhya Pradesh, Gossner Evangelical Lutheran Church in Chotanagpur and Assam, Good Samaritan Evangelical Lutheran Church, India Evangelical Lutheran Church, Jeypore Evangelical Lutheran Church, Northern Evangelical Lutheran Church, South Andhra Evangelical Lutheran Church, and Tamil Evangelical Lutheran Church.

United Evangelical Lutheran Church in India
Gurukul Campus
94 Purasawalkam High Rd.
Kilpauk 600 010 Chennai
Tamil Nadu
India

J. Gordon Melton

See also: Andhra Evangelical Lutheran Church; Church of Sweden; Evangelical Lutheran Church in America; Evangelical Lutheran Church in Denmark; Lutheran World Federation; World Council of Churches.

References

Bachmann, E. Theodore, and Mercia Brenne Bachmann. *Lutheran Churches in the World: A Handbook*. Minneapolis, MN: Augsburg, 1989.

Directory—Handbuch. Geneva: Lutheran World Federation, issued annually.

Van Beek, Huibert. *A Handbook of the Churches and Councils: Profiles of Ecumenical Relationships*. Geneva: World Council of Churches, 2006.

United Evangelical Mission

See Rhenish Mission.

United Free Church of Scotland

The United Free Church of Scotland continues the tradition of the Free Church of Scotland (now a constituent part of the Church of Scotland). In 1900 the Free Church merged with another splinter group from the Church of Scotland, the United Presbyterian Church, to form the United Free Church of Scotland. In 1929

The signing of the Act of Separation and the Deed of Demission during the first General Assembly of the Free Church of Scotland at Tanfield in Edinburgh, May 23, 1843. From the painting by D. O. Hill, RSA. (Getty Images)

the United Free Church of Scotland merged into the Church of Scotland. However, a minority segment of the United Church did not concur with the merger and decided to continue under their previous name and administration.

The church has continued to advocate freedom from state control and support. It has also argued for religious equality, which led to its early openness to women in the ordained ministry. Doctrinally it is like the Church of Scotland, that not being at issue in the debates that led to the church's formation.

The highest legislative body in the church is its General Assembly. The church is a relatively small body, with only 4,400 members, but it carries on an active world ministry in Cambodia and, in cooperation with the United Congregational Church of Southern Africa, in Botswana. It is a member of the World Council of Churches and the World Alliance of Reformed Churches.

United Free Church of Scotland
11 Newton Pl.
Glasgow G3 7PR

United Kingdom
http://www.ufcos.org.uk/

J. Gordon Melton

See also: Church of Scotland; United Congregational Church of Southern Africa; World Alliance of Reformed Churches; World Council of Churches.

References

Bauswein, Jean-Jacques, and Lukas Vischner, eds. *The Reformed Family Worldwide: A Survey of Reformed Churches, Theological Schools, and International Organizations*. Grand Rapids, MI: William B. Eerdmans Publishing Company, 1999.

Van Beek, Huibert. *A Handbook of the Churches and Councils: Profiles of Ecumenical Relationships*. Geneva: World Council of Churches, 2006.

■ United Kingdom

The United Kingdom of Great Britain and Northern Ireland (UK) is separated from continental Europe by the North Sea and the English Channel, being at the closest point 21 miles north of the French coast. It consists of four countries: England, Scotland, and Wales (which make up Great Britain) and the six counties of Northern Ireland, which remained part of the UK when Ireland became independent in 1922. The history, especially the religious history, of each of these countries is inextricably bound with that of the others, and yet, at the same time, a story in its own right. While London is the English and UK capital, Edinburgh is the capital city of Scotland, Cardiff of Wales, and Belfast of Northern Ireland.

By mid-2007, the resident population of the UK was estimated at 60,975,000 (England 51,092,000; Scotland 5,144,000; Wales 2,980,000; Northern Ireland 1,759,000). Although English is spoken throughout the UK, Wales has two official languages, English and Welsh (Cymraeg, which is taught in most schools and in which over a fifth of the Welsh population are fluent). Other Celtic languages, such as Scots, Irish, Manx Gaelic, and Cornish, are still spoken in parts of the UK and are, to a greater or lesser degree, officially recognized as minority languages. There are also numerous immigrant languages spoken, more than a million British Asians (2.1 percent of the population) speaking Punjabi, for example. According to the 2001 national census, 92.1 percent of the UK population was white, the rest being largely black Caribbean and Africans and Asians. In response to an optional question in the British part of the census, 71.8 percent said they were Christian (Anglican, Roman Catholic, Presbyterian, Methodist); 2.8 percent Muslim; 1.0 percent Hindu; 0.6 percent Sikh; 0.5 percent Jewish; 0.3 percent Buddhist; 0.3 percent "any other religion"; 5.4 percent "no religion"; and 7.8 percent did not respond. As the result of a media campaign, 0.7 percent (390,000) said they were Jedi, making it the fourth largest reported religion). In Northern Ireland, which had a different census question, 53 percent stated they were Protestant (mainly Presbyterian and Church of Ireland) and 44 percent Catholic, with 3 percent being "other" or "none."

The United Kingdom is a constitutional monarchy with Queen Elizabeth II (b. 1926) as head of state, as well as being head of the British Commonwealth, supreme governor of the Church of England, and "De-

fender of the Faith." In 1973 the UK joined the European Economic Community, and it was a founding member of the European Union in 1992. It is a member of the G8 and the North Atlantic Treaty Organization (NATO), and it has a permanent seat on the United Nations Security Council. The UK does not have a codified Constitution, but a legal system consisting of statutes passed (and revocable) by Acts of Parliament, case law, and international treaties. Although there is a devolved Parliament in Scotland and devolved assemblies in Northern Ireland and Wales, the ultimate legislative authority of the UK is the Westminster Parliament, consisting of an elected House of Commons and a House of Lords, which consists of hereditary and appointed life peers, including 26 "Lords Spiritual" (the 2 archbishops and 24 senior bishops of the Church of England).

There are two Established Churches in the UK: the Anglican Church of England and the Presbyterian Church of Scotland, to which both privileges and restrictions apply, with the question of disestablishment under constant review. Unlike many other European countries, there is no legal definition or official registration of religions. Those who wish to do so may apply for charitable status, which can confer certain financial and status benefits. There have been a few restrictions placed upon some of the newer religions and their adherents (mainly, though not exclusively, with regard to immigration), but generally speaking the only laws that control members of any non-Established religion are those that apply to any other citizens of the country.

Because Britain was more affected than Southern Europe by the Ice Ages, fewer evidences of the early culture remain than is the case in what are now southern France and Spain. It is, however, assumed that there would have been similarities in a belief in an afterlife: a shallow grave found in Wales containing a young man buried with bracelets of ivory and covered with red ochre is estimated to date from roughly 25,000 BCE (shortly before the last great period of glaciation), making it the oldest recorded British burial. The earliest evidence of religion in Britain is archaeological, going back to at least the fourth millennium BCE. Some elaborate tombs, and monuments such as Stonehenge (begun between 3100 and 2100 BCE

United Kingdom

Religion	Followers in 1970	Followers in 2010	% of Population	Annual % growth 2000–2010	Followers in 2025	Followers in 2050
Christians	49,325,000	49,325,000	80.2	0.24	49,528,000	50,192,000
Anglicans	29,059,000	25,900,000	42.1	0.07	25,000,000	25,000,000
Roman Catholics	5,516,000	5,600,000	9.1	–0.47	5,600,000	5,600,000
Protestants	7,713,000	4,200,000	6.8	–0.89	4,200,000	4,200,000
Agnostics	4,400,000	7,820,000	12.7	1.51	10,179,000	11,750,000
Muslims	635,000	1,680,000	2.7	0.92	2,300,000	2,850,000
Atheists	300,000	880,000	1.4	1.47	1,100,000	1,400,000
Hindus	220,000	639,000	1.0	2.11	680,000	850,000
Sikhs	200,000	420,000	0.7	3.83	575,000	750,000
Jews	450,000	280,000	0.5	0.07	275,000	250,000
Buddhists	30,000	195,000	0.3	0.45	250,000	300,000
Spiritists	20,000	75,000	0.1	0.46	85,000	100,000
New religionists	50,000	66,500	0.1	0.42	78,500	85,000
Chinese folk	15,000	60,600	0.1	0.46	45,000	52,000
Baha'is	13,600	36,000	0.1	0.46	40,000	60,000
Ethnoreligionists	0	17,400	0.0	0.46	18,000	20,000
Jains	4,000	18,000	0.0	1.96	30,000	50,000
Zoroastrians	0	4,800	0.0	0.46	6,000	8,000
Total population	**55,663,000**	**61,517,000**	**100.0**	**0.46**	**65,190,000**	**68,717,000**

and believed to have been used for ceremonial purposes), suggest that gods and divine powers played an important role in the Neolithic and Bronze ages.

The oldest surviving mythologies tell of successive invasions from Ireland. Later, trade with the Gallic Celts resulted in a pagan Celtic culture becoming well established in the southeast of England by the fourth century BCE. By the time of the Roman invasion in 55 BCE, the Druids were in a position of considerable power and were suppressed by the Romans for political rather than religious reasons. There is disagreement about how Romanized British Paganism became, but many of the local deities became fused with, or at least were joined by, the gods and goddesses of Rome. Isis and other Egyptian gods also made their way to Britain, which was still a Pagan country in the late Roman period.

Pockets of Christianity are thought to have been introduced to Britain in the second century, but it seems unlikely that it existed in any substantial form much before the middle of the third century. Saint Ninian (ca. 360–432), the first known Christian missionary in Scotland, built a stone church at Whithorn in 379. Other missionaries (often by way of Ireland)

contributed to the establishment of the Celtic Church in the fifth century, with a number of the early monasteries, such as Iona and Lindisfarne, remaining places of pilgrimage to this day. In 597, Saint Augustine (d. 604/605)—not to be confused with Saint Augustine of Hippo—was sent to Britain by Pope Gregory I (ca. 540–604) and became the first archbishop of Canterbury after the conversion of King Ethelbert of Kent (d. 616). During the next centuries, the Celtic Church was gradually absorbed into the mainstream of Western Christianity based in Rome.

After the Norman Conquest of 1066, Roman canon law (the chief agent of papal control in the Western church) became increasingly powerful (and corrupt), provoking the Reformer John Wyclif (1330–1384) to condemn practices such as the selling of indulgences. His followers, known as the Lollards, were suppressed after an unsuccessful uprising in 1414 but are seen as the precursors to the Reformation in the 16th century, by which time England's King Henry VIII (1491–1547) could muster sufficient support to break away from Rome over the question of the dissolution of his marriage to the first of his six wives, Catherine of Aragon (1485–1536), and proclaim himself head of the Church

Allegorical illustration regarding the breaking of ties between England and Rome. (Hulton Archive/Getty Images)

of England in 1534. Henry's daughter, Mary Tudor, attempted during her reign (1553–1558) to restore Catholicism but merely succeeded in fanning the flames of the Reformation. One of the first actions of Mary's half-sister, Queen Elizabeth I (1533–1603), was to secure a Protestant future for England, and since 1559 the Church of England has been "by law established."

The Church in Wales had been legally part of the Church of England when it was still part of the Roman Church, and thus it found itself established as a Protestant church. It became disestablished in 1920. Despite Elizabeth I's officially reforming the church of Ireland, most Irish Christians remained loyal to Rome. In 1869 the statutory union between the Anglican churches of Ireland and England was dissolved, and the Church of Ireland ceased to be established by law. There has never been an established church for Northern Ireland.

Once established, the Church of England was opposed not only by Roman Catholics but also by Protestants who wanted to purify the church even further. Some of these Puritans worked for reform within the Anglican Church, others formed small separatist movements, later known as the English Independent or Congregationalist movement. The Separatist Puritans led by Robert Browne (ca. 1550–1633) found a more tolerant reception in the Netherlands, and the Pilgrim Fathers emigrated from Leiden, via Plymouth, to New England in 1620 under the leadership of John Robinson (ca. 1576–1625).

Scotland's Reformation owes much to the persistence of the Calvinist John Knox (1505–1572), with the Reformed Church of Scotland becoming established along Presbyterian lines in 1560. Subsequent pressure from Stuart kings to make the church episcopal came to a head in 1638 when the Covenanters, revolting against Charles I's attempt to introduce the Scottish Prayer Book of 1637, became embroiled in the Civil Wars (1642–1646; 1648–1651) that were fought between the Royalist Cavaliers and the Puritan Roundheads, led by Oliver Cromwell (1599–1658).

The UK has survived a continuing history of religious dissent. The early English Baptists had settled in London in the first half of the 17th century; in 1650 the name "Quaker" was applied to George Fox (1624–1691) and his followers, who were later known as the Society of Friends. With the turbulence of the Civil Wars, there was a mushrooming of relatively short-lived millennial movements (such as the Ranters, the Levellers, and the Fifth Monarchy Men). Around the 1730s, a surge of revivalism (the Awakening) was witnessed in Wales, England, and, slightly later, in Scotland—it was in 1738 that John Wesley (1703–1799), the Anglican priest who was to found the Methodist movement, experienced a profound spiritual conversion that reinforced his evangelical fervor. In 1843, 474 Disruption Dissenters, constituting nearly a third of the ministry of the Church of Scotland, seceded to form the Free Church of Scotland. The 19th century also saw the arrival of a number of new sects, some of which (such as the Plymouth Brethren [Exclusive] and the Salvation Army) were homegrown; others (such as the Seventh-day Adventist Church, the Church of Christ, Scientist, the Church of Jesus Christ of Latter-day Saints, and the Jehovah's Witnesses) came from the United States of America. Toward the end of the century, one or two other movements, such as Madame Blavatsky's Theosophical Society, began to introduce ideas from the

East to sections of upper-middle-class England. The National Secular Society was founded by Charles Bradlaugh in 1866, and the British Humanist Association appeared in 1928; but Britain has not experienced the virulent anticlericalism found in some other parts of Europe.

The early 20th century witnessed the arrival of several Pentecostal sects from the United States (by way of Norway), followed by the further appearance of "foreign" religions. Successive waves of migrants (particularly West Indians in the 1950s and people of Asian origin from the 1960s onward) changed not only the ethnic but also the religious composition of England. By the 2001 census, Indians were the largest minority group (1.8 percent), followed by Pakistanis (1.3 percent), those of mixed ethnic backgrounds (1.2 percent), black Caribbeans (1 percent), black Africans (0.8 percent), Bangladeshis (0.5 percent), "other Asian" (0.4 percent), Chinese (0.4 percent), "black other" (0.2 percent), and "other" (0.4 percent). While the major denominations were undergoing a steady decline in church attendance and membership, there was a growth (which by no means compensated for the loss in the traditional churches) in Charismatic and Pentecostal Christianity, especially among Afro-Caribbeans who found themselves unwelcome in predominantly white churches. Sunni, Shia, and Ahmadiyya mosques, Hindu and Buddhist temples, Sikh *gurdwaras*, and a few Shinto shrines have become increasingly visible as part of the UK landscape. The distribution of the minority ethnic groups has, however, been very uneven. In England, they made up 9 percent of the total population compared with only 2 percent in both Scotland and Wales and less than 1 percent in Northern Ireland. They have, moreover, tended to concentrate in the large urban centers. Nearly half (45 percent) of the total minority ethnic population (and well over half the black and Bangladeshi populations) live in the London region, where they comprise 29 percent of all residents, with the second largest proportion (13 percent) of the minority ethnic population being found in the West Midlands.

A further development has been the emergence of both indigenous and imported new religions, which became increasingly visible from the late 1960s. Among those originating in the United Kingdom were the Aeth-erius Society, the School of Economic Science, the Emin, the Jesus Army, and the Findhorn Foundation in the north of Scotland, which is visited by New Age seekers from around the world. By 2009, Inform (a government-supported organization providing information about alternative religions) had records on well over 1,000 different groups in the UK—as well as a number of anti-cult and counter-cult movements that had been set up to warn the population about the perceived theological and practical dangers of heresies and alien religions.

A law decreeing the burning of heretics remained in force in England until 1676, although the last persons burned at the stake for heresy in England were two Anti-Trinitarians in 1612. In Scotland an 18-year-old student, charged with denying the Trinity, was hanged at Edinburgh as late as 1697. Witches had been burned or, more frequently, hanged in Britain from the time of the Middle Ages, but the witch hunts reached a peak in the 17th century. The last witchcraft trial in England was held in 1712 (1722 in Scotland).

In 1689 the Act of Toleration had granted freedom of worship to Nonconformists or Free Churches (that is, Protestants refusing to conform to the doctrines or authority of the Established Church), who were then allowed their own ministers and places of worship—subject to their taking an oath of allegiance to the Crown. However, the act did not apply to Roman Catholics or Unitarians, who remained subject to civil and religious constraints until the 19th century. Furthermore, the earlier Test Acts, barring anyone who was not a member of the Established Church from holding public office, remained in force until the second half of the 19th century—religious tests for academics in the universities of Oxford, Cambridge, and Durham were abolished in 1871. The Roman Catholic hierarchy was eventually restored in England and Wales in 1850 (giving rise to a "no popery" furor over "Papal Aggression")—but not until 1878 in Scotland. Ironically, although discrimination on grounds of sex or race became illegal in the 1970s, Northern Ireland was the only part of the UK in which discrimination on religious grounds was an offense until the introduction of the Human Rights Act in October 2000 allowed cases concerning rights given under the European Convention of Human Rights to be dealt with in British courts.

UNITED KINGDOM

So far as British Jewry is concerned, a small community had settled in England after the Norman Conquest, was expelled by Edward I (1239–1307), and then was readmitted during Cromwell's Protectorate (1653–1659). Confessing Jews were sufficiently integrated into British society to be admitted to Parliament in 1858—Disraeli had converted to Christianity 10 years before he entered Parliament in 1837, but although Lionel de Rothschild had been elected a member for the City of London from 1847, he had been unable to submit to the required Christian oaths and had not been permitted to take up his seat. Although making a notable contribution to British society, even the influx of Jewish refugees exiled by the Russian pogroms in 1881, and those fleeing from Nazi persecution in Central and Eastern Europe during the first half of the 20th century, have never resulted in the community's becoming statistically very significant, this being due partly to a high rate of intermarriage. On a few isolated occasions outbreaks of anti-Semitism have hit parts of Britain: anti-Semitic riots occurred, for example, in the Welsh valleys in 1911 and in several large English towns in 1947.

While, generally speaking, Britain has enjoyed a relatively peaceful coexistence among its many religious communities during the past century, there have been some serious clashes, the most critical of which have been in Northern Ireland, where tensions have existed between the Protestant majority, which has enjoyed relative economic and political advantage, and the Catholic minority, which has wanted to be reunited with the rest of Ireland. The conflict erupted into violence in 1968, and well over 3,000 "troubles-related deaths" resulted from terrorist activities by paramilitary organizations such as the Irish Republican Army, the Ulster Defence Association, and the Ulster Volunteer Force. After a series of short-lived cease-fires throughout the mid-1990s, a fragile peace agreement was eventually brokered in 1998. This has resulted in a generally nonviolent situation in the six counties, despite occasional eruptions by small schismatic groups.

In England, toward the latter part of the 20th century, several tense (including a few violent) situations have developed in relation to the diversity of beliefs and practices associated with ethnic minorities, one of these being triggered by the placing of a *fatwa* upon Salman Rushdie (b. 1947) in 1989 after the publication and public burnings of his book *Satanic Verses*. A rumbling Islamophobia was fanned by the destruction of the World Trade Center in New York in 2001, and became even more pronounced when four British Islamist suicide bombers killed 52 commuters and injured hundreds more on London's transport system on July 7, 2005. Despite various measures being taken by the government and moderate religious leaders of all faiths to defuse the situation, there remains at the end of the first decade of the 21st century considerable distrust between sections of the religious communities.

While in the earlier part of the 20th century the Church of England was referred to as the Conservative party at prayer, from around the 1960s it appeared to become less compliant to the establishment (with a small "e"), both theologically and politically. The publication of *Honest to God* in 1963 by the Bishop of Woolwich, John Robinson (1919–1983), the introduction of the Anglican Alternative Service Book in 1980, and a series of provocative statements by David Jenkins (b. 1925), who was the bishop of Durham from 1984 to 1994, all led to acute anxiety among traditionalists about the undermining not merely of the Established Church but also of the very fabric of British society. Tensions between church and state—as represented, respectively, by then Archbishop of Canterbury Robert Runcie (1925–2000) and Prime Minister Margaret Thatcher (b. 1925)—were exacerbated when Runcie commissioned a report on urban poverty (published as *Faith in the City* in 1985) and insisted on praying not only for the British but also for the relatives of Argentines who died in the 1982 Falklands War. The final crunch for some Anglicans came when, in 1992, the General Synod agreed to the ordination of women to the ministry, and then Bishop of London Graham Leonard (b. 1921) led a small exodus of clergy into the Roman Catholic Church. Yet further tensions have erupted over various incidents involving homosexuality among the clergy.

Another development in the 21st century has been associated with the biologist Richard Dawkins, who, through a television series and a best-selling book, *The God Delusion*, has presented a militant atheism to the British public. This has resulted, on the one hand, in a strong reaction from theologians such as Alister

McGrath, and, on the other hand, in the establishment of the Richard Dawkins Foundation for Reason and Science along with a revivalism in organizations such as the British Humanist Association, resulting in such high-profile campaigns as the Atheist Bus Advertisements, with posters on buses throughout Great Britain proclaiming *There's probably no God. Now stop worrying and enjoy your life* in response to the *Jesus said: . . .* ads running on London buses in June 2008.

It is difficult to give an accurate statistical analysis of trends in the religiosity of the UK. This is partly due to the fact that not only does the wording of survey questions vary over time, but the understanding of what each question means to respondents also varies. It is not unusual for apparently contradictory results to emerge; for example, while 72 percent of the population claims to be Christian, several polls have found less than half the UK population saying that they believe in God. However, a slightly more penetrating question has revealed that while 23 percent believed in a God with whom one can have a personal relationship, 38 percent believed in God as something within each person, rather than out there, 16 percent believed in an impersonal spirit or life force, another 16 percent said they do not really know what to believe, and only 9 percent said they did not believe in any kind of God, spirit, or life force. Roughly a third of Britons claim to pray at least once a week, believe that Jesus was both man and God, and think that their religious beliefs have a great deal of influence on their daily life.

If such concepts as "religious disposition" and "Christian community" are used, the UK is still predominantly (roughly two-thirds) Christian—but hardly fervently so, with only a third of the population calling themselves religious (and just 6 percent saying they are "very religious"), while nearly half claimed that they were "not religious." One survey (on religious and moral pluralism) found that 45 percent of Britons said they had no religious affiliation, but there were fewer people (26 percent) who were formally members of a religious group than there were those who, while not formally a member of any religious group, nonetheless *felt* that they were a member. Allegiance to (although not necessarily membership of) religious organizations in the UK as a whole has been estimated as follows: Anglican (43 percent); Roman Catholic (10

percent); Presbyterian (4 percent); Methodist (2 percent); other Trinitarian (4 percent); non-Trinitarian (2.2 percent); Muslim (2.4 percent); Sikh (1 percent); Hindu (0.8 percent); Jewish (0.5 percent); "other" (0.7 percent); and "non-religious" (29 percent). So far as formal membership in Britain is concerned, just over 1.5 million persons are Anglicans, with 1.7 million Roman Catholics, 1 million Presbyterians (including the United Reformed Church in the United Kingdom, which was an amalgamation in 1972 of Congregationalists and English Presbyterians), 0.5 million Methodists, 0.25 million Baptists, and a further 0.5 million belonging to various Independent churches. It should, however, be pointed out that these membership numbers can be misleading, as some religions (such as the Roman Catholic Church) include children, while others include only those who have undergone adult baptism.

Data concerning attendance at a place of worship have also produced a mixture of results. Except in Northern Ireland, involvement in institutional religion is closely related to age, and those over 50 account for well over half the adult church attendance. There is also a noteworthy difference between the countries in self-reported church attendance, the rate in Northern Ireland being roughly twice that in Scotland, which in turn is roughly twice that in England, with Wales having dropped from a rate similar to Scotland's to one similar to England's over the latter quarter of the 20th century. One national survey by Tearfund in 2007 found that 10 percent of the UK adult population went to church at least weekly, 15 percent at least monthly, 26 percent at least yearly, whilst 59 percent never or practically never went to church. Other surveys have put the weekly attendance figure as low as 6.3 percent.

Whatever the actual rate, there is no doubt that, despite short-term variations, Sunday attendance at the traditional churches has fallen dramatically over the past decades. There are, however, commentators who suggest that while institutional religiosity is on the decline, what is sometimes referred to as "the new spirituality" is on the increase, and more than a third (13 percent of whom had denied being "religious") report that they have a spiritual life. As the result of a study of the English town Kendal, Heelas and Woodhead concluded that, while congregational life is undoubtedly declining and is likely to decline still further over the next 40 or so years (possibly down to 3 percent—or less—of the British population), the evidence does not support the claim that a spiritual revolution has overtaken traditional religion. While they found that "holistic activity" in Britain had certainly increased (especially among middle-aged women) to just under a million participants during a typical week, it had by no means caught up with the congregational activity of just over 4.5 million church goers on a typical Sunday. They did contend, however, that the evidence supports the "subjectivization thesis"—that contemporary British culture promotes a shift from one's life being governed by external obligations and objective roles (such as the dutiful wife or successful businessman) to a life that is lived by reference to one's own experiences, which are as much relational as individualistic.

Throughout the centuries the land that now comprises the United Kingdom has undergone many changes as new religions have been introduced and more established religions have undergone numerous changes. It can be plausibly argued that the UK will witness an increasing religious diversification over the foreseeable future. This is likely to be closely, though not entirely, associated with ethnic distinctions. It is also likely that demographic changes, such as differential fertility rates and the influx of new members of the European Community (such as Catholics from Poland), will affect the relative distribution of the different religions. The extent to which such changes will be seen to enrich and the extent to which they will be seen to threaten the United Kingdom, and the outcome of such perceptions, remains to be seen.

Eileen Barker

See also: Augustine of Hippo; Church in Wales; Church of Christ, Scientist; Church of England; Church of Ireland; Church of Jesus Christ of Latter-day Saints; Church of Scotland; Elizabeth I; Free Churches; Friends/Quakers; Jehovah's Witnesses; Roman Catholic Church; Salvation Army; Seventh-day Adventist Church; United Reformed Church of the United Kingdom; Theosophical Society (America); Wesley, John.

References

Badham, Paul. *Religion, State, and Society in Modern Britain*. Lewiston, NY: Edwin Mellen, 1989.

Bebbington, D. W. *Evangelicalism in Modern Britain: A History from the 1730s to the 1980s*. London: Unwin Hyman, 1989.

Brierley, Peter. *UK Christian Handbook: Religious Trends 7. British Religion in the 21st Century: What the Statistics Indicate*. London: Christian Research, 2007.

Brierley, Peter, and Heather Wraight, eds. *UK Christian Handbook*. London: Christian Research, issued annually.

Brown, Callum. *The Death of Christian Britain: Understanding Secularisation 1800–2000*. London: Routledge, 2001.

Bruce, Steve. *Religion in Modern Britain*. Oxford: Oxford University Press, 1995.

Burghart, Richard. *Hinduism in Great Britain: The Perpetration of Religion in an Alien Cultural Milieu*. London: Tavistock, 1987.

Davie, Grace. *Religion in Britain since 1945*. Oxford: Blackwell, 1994.

Davies, Charles Maurice. *Heterodox London: or, Phases of Free Thought in the Metropolis*. 2 vols. London: Tinsley Brothers, 1874.

Davies, Douglas, Charles Watkins, and Michael Winter. *Church and Religion in Rural England*. Edinburgh: T & T Clark, 1991.

Dawkins, Richard. *The God Delusion*. Boston: Houghton Mifflin, 2006.

Forster, Roger, ed. *Ten New Churches*. Harrow, UK: British Church Growth Association/MARC Europe, 1986.

Gay, John D. *The Geography of Religion in England*. London: Duckworth, 1971.

Gilley, Sheridan, and W. J. Sheils, eds. *A History of Religion in Britain: Practice and Belief from Pre-Roman Times to the Present*. Oxford: Blackwell, 1994.

Green, Miranda J., ed. *The Celtic World*. London: Routledge, 1995.

Heelas, Paul, Linda Woodhead, Benjamin Seel, Bronislaw Szerszynski, and Karin Tusting. *The Spiritual Revolution: Why Religion Is Giving Way to Spirituality*. Oxford: Blackwell, 2004.

Hornsby-Smith, Michael P. *Catholics in England 1950–2000: Historical and Sociological Perspectives*. London: Cassell, 1999.

Hutton, Ronald. *The Pagan Religions of the Ancient British Isles: Their Nature and Legacy*. Oxford: Blackwell, 1991.

Matthews, Ronald. *English Messiahs: Studies of Six English Religious Pretenders, 1656–1927*. London: Methuen, 1936.

McGrath, Alister, with Joanna Collicutt McGrath. *The Dawkins Delusion: Atheist Fundamentalism and the Denial of the Divine*. London: SPCK, 2007.

McLeod, Hugh. *Religion and the Working Class in Nineteenth Century Britain*. Basingstoke, UK: Macmillan, 1984.

Oliver, Ian P. *Buddhism in Britain*. London: Rider, 1979.

Reynolds, Arthur. *English Sects: An Historical Handbook*. London: Mowbray, 1921.

Smith, Warren Sylvester. *The London Heretics, 1870–1914*. New York: Dodd, Mead, 1968.

Thomas, Keith. *Religion and the Decline of Magic*. Harmondsworth, UK: Penguin, 1973.

Thomas, Terence, ed. *The British: Their Religious Beliefs and Practices 1800–1986*. London: Routledge, 1988.

Weller, Paul, ed. *Religions in the UK: A Multi-Faith Directory*. Derby, UK: University of Derby/ Inter Faith Network for the United Kingdom, 1993.

United Lodge of Theosophists

The United Lodge of Theosophists grew out of the challenge to the Theosophical movement posed by Robert Crosbie (1948–1919). Crosbie was a longtime Theosophist who rejected what he saw as organizational distractions and formalities, especially the polemics that occurred in the 1890s with the changes of leadership following the death of the co-founder of the Theosophical Society (Adyar), Madame Helena Blavatsky. The American lodges had separated under William Q. Judge. Through the first decade of the 20th century, rivalries in the Theosophical movement were focused in the personalities of Annie Besant, who headed the international movement from India, and Katherine Tingley, who headed the American Society.

In forming the United Lodge, Crosbie posed the vision of a nonsectarian Theosophical grouping. It would be loyal to the founders of Theosophy but not show preference for any individual opinions. The United Lodge was formed in 1909 without a constitution, by-laws, or officers. Members, called associates, sign a statement of sympathy with the "Declaration," and any one of them may found an independent associated lodge.

The United Lodge teaches that there is but one life, a spirit/consciousness that is constantly evolving toward a greater understanding and realization. This evolution proceeds along a course that is native to humanity. The mind is the place of realization and growth, and humans are in a continuous process of growth and development.

The United Lodge has a primary periodical, *Theosophy*, published in Los Angeles, and *The Theosophical Movement*, published in Bombay, India. Seven affiliated lodges are scattered across the United States, and there are 16 others in Europe and India (2009).

United Lodge
245 W. 33rd St.
Los Angeles, CA 90007
http://ult.org

J. Gordon Melton

See also: Besant, Annie; Blavatsky, Helena P.; Theosophical Society (Adyar).

References

Crosbie, Robert. *The Friendly Philosopher*. Los Angeles: Theosophy Company, 1934.

The Theosophical Movement, 1875–1950. Los Angeles: Cunningham Press, 1951.

The United Lodge of Theosophists, Its Mission and Its Future. Los Angeles: Theosophy Company, n.d.

United Methodist Church

The United Methodist Church is the primary body continuing the Wesleyan Methodist tradition in the United States. It is, as of the beginning of the 21st century, the third largest religious body in the country.

Hennepin Avenue United Methodist Church in Minneapolis. (Aliaksandr Nikitsin/Dreamstime.com)

The crises experienced by John Wesley (1703–1791) during his brief work as an Anglican minister in the colony of Georgia (1735–1738) led to the founding of Methodism as a revivalist movement within the Church of England soon after his return to England. By the 1760s, Methodists had joined the migration of other British citizens to the American colonies. Early groups emerged in northern Virginia, Baltimore (Maryland), Wilmington (Delaware), Philadelphia, and New York City. Wesley sent unordained preachers to guide the work. As with the Anglicans, the American Revolution proved a turning point for the movement. All but one of the preachers returned to England, and the remaining Methodists, with John Wesley's consent and guidance, decided to reorganize as an independent denomination.

To facilitate the establishment of the American church, in 1784, Wesley sent the Reverend Thomas Coke (1747–1814), whom he had appointed super-intendent, to America to establish the church. At a conference during the Christmas season of that year, the Methodist Episcopal Church (MEC) was founded. Francis Asbury (1745–1816), the one preacher who had not returned to England, was elected the church's first bishop. He would lead the church for the next 40 years. The church's basic organization was the conference of ministers who met annually under the bishop. At the end of the annual gathering, the bishop announced their pastoral assignment for the coming year. With the bishop assigning ministers to their work, a national strategy for evangelizing the country could be developed. Wesley also edited the Church of England's Thirty-nine Articles of Religion and presented Twenty-five Articles, which the Methodist Episcopal Church accepted as its doctrinal statement. After the war the church grew significantly, and by the 1830s it had become the largest religious organization in America.

In the first decades of the church, it faced and resolved several issues that had led to schisms. As the church grew, many African Americans, especially in the non-slave states in the North, became members. However, African American members were segregated in worship and not welcomed into the ordained ministry. Beginning in the 1790s, a set of schisms occurred among the African American members that led to several new denominations being established, most notably the African Methodist Episcopal Church and African Methodist Episcopal Zion Church. At about the same time, a number of German-speaking immigrants in the new nation were affected by the Methodist revivals. However, Asbury decided that Germans had no future in America, and he declined to set up German-speaking parishes. This led to the establishment of several new "Methodist" denominations, the Evangelical Association (after 1922 the Evangelical Church) and the United Brethren in Christ. In 1830 the Methodist Episcopal Church experienced the first of several schisms, by ministers and congregations who founded the Methodist Protestant Church (MPC). The church had no bishops and allowed congregations a voice in hiring their minister and lay members a role in the national church leadership.

The most significant break occurred in 1844, when the General Conference of the Methodist Episcopal Church (MEC) voted to divide, slavery and the nature of episcopal leadership being the prime issues. The southern conferences reorganized as the Methodist Episcopal Church, South (MECS). At the time of the split, the Roman Catholic Church replaced the Methodist Episcopal Church as the largest religious body in the United States, though both the MEC and MECS continued to grow through the rest of the century.

Not only did Methodism spread across the United States, but by the middle of the 19th century it had fully joined the world missions movement that the British Methodists had helped to initiate. The several Methodist churches sent missionaries to all parts of the globe, and the scope of foreign work increased as more countries were opened to the missionary enterprise.

In the 20th century, the various branches of Methodism began a process of reversing the fragmentation of the previous century. In 1939 the MEC, MECS, and MPC united to form the Methodist Church (1939–1968). In 1946 the Evangelical Church and the United Brethren merged to form the Evangelical United Brethren. In 1968 the Evangelical United Brethren and the Methodist Church united to form the United Methodist Church.

The United Methodist Church does not have a central headquarters, though the headquarters of its Council on Ministries serves some of those functions. Additional offices of its national boards and agencies are located in Nashville, Tennessee (the headquarters of the former MECS); Washington, D.C.; and Evanston, Illinois. The highest legislative body in the church is the General Conference, which meets quadrennially. In the United States the church is divided geographically into five jurisdictions, and each jurisdiction into conferences. Jurisdictional conferences meet quadrennially, during which time elections are held to fill any vacancies in the episcopacy, and bishops receive their assignments for the next four years. Bishops preside over one or two annual conferences and appoint the ministers to their parish assignments. Conferences outside the United States are grouped into seven central conferences that function much as jurisdictional conferences, at which bishops are elected.

At the time of the formation of the United Methodist Churches, the constituent bodies were already participating in the international move to grant autonomous status to foreign churches that had resulted from earlier missionary endeavors. In 1968 a number of the former mission churches took the occasion of the formation of the new church in the United States to assume their autonomous status. Most of these churches have continued a fraternal relationship with the United Methodist Church through the World Methodist Council. The United Methodist Church is also a member of the World Council of Churches. Since the 1990s, the United Methodist Church has been in active conversations with representatives of the African Methodist Episcopal Church, the African Methodist Episcopal Zion Church, the Christian Methodist Episcopal Church, and the Union American Methodist Episcopal Church, looking toward greater alignment and cooperation and possible union.

In 2006 the church reported 7,995,456 members. It supports a massive program of higher education, social service agencies, and medical facilities, both in the United States and abroad.

United Methodist Church
Council on Ministries
601 W. Riverside Ave.
Dayton, OH 45406

J. Gordon Melton

See also: African Methodist Episcopal Church; African Methodist Episcopal Zion Church; Christian Methodist Episcopal Church; Church of England; Roman Catholic Church; Wesley, John; World Council of Churches; World Methodist Council.

References

The Book of Discipline. Nashville: United Methodist Publishing House, 2004.

Frank, Thomas Edward. *Polity, Practice, and the Mission of the United Methodist Church.* Nashville: Abingdon Press, 2006.

Jones, Scott J. *United Methodist Doctrine: The Extreme Center.* Nashville: Abingdon Press, 2002.

McEllhenney, John G., ed. *United Methodism in America: A Compact History.* Nashville: Abingdon Press, 1992.

Richey, Russell E., Kenneth E. Rowe, and Jean Miller Schmidt. *The Methodist Experience in America: A Sourcebook.* Nashville: Abingdon Press, 2000.

Tuell, Jack M. *The Organization of the United Methodist Church, 2005–2008 Edition.* Nashville: Abingdon Press, 2005.

Yrigoyen, Charles, Jr., and Susan E. Warrick, eds. *Historical Dictionary of Methodism.* 2nd ed. Lanham, MD: Scarecrow Press, 2005.

United Methodist Church in Ivory Coast

The United Methodist Church in Ivory Coast (formerly the Protestant Methodist Church in Côte d'Ivoire) dates to the arrival in 1924 of a Wesleyan Methodist missionary, Jon Platt, from Dahomey (Ghana) and Togo, where the Wesleyans (now the Methodist Church in Great Britain) had established work as early as 1842. It is the case that prior to that time, beginning in the first decade of the century, African prophet William Wade Harris (1865–1929), a former Methodist, had established his church in Côte d'Ivoire and neighboring countries. He had predicted the arrival of white missionaries, and many saw in the Methodists the fulfillment of his prophecy.

As the Wesleyans' work in Côte d'Ivoire developed, it was an integral part of the work in Dahomey and Togo. In 1947 it had grown to the point that it was detached from work in the neighboring countries and organized as a district directly attached to the British Methodist Conference. The work in Côte d'Ivoire was given independent status in 1963, and the reorganization was completed the following year. At that time, the first indigenous leader, Samson Nandjui, was selected as the mission's chairman.

In 2001, the Methodists in Côte d'Ivoire, while remaining autonomous, affiliated with the United Methodist Church and changed their name to the United Methodist Church in Ivory Coast.

Although Methodism has become a national movement, with a membership and constituency of approximately one million (2005), the major centers are in the capital, Abidjan, and in Dabou, where the church opened a hospital in 1968. Ministerial education is supported through the Protestant University of West Africa (formerly the School of Protestant Theology), located in Porto-Novo in Benin, and the Protestant faculty of Yaoundé and the Center for Evangelical Literature, both located in Yaoundé, Cameroon. The church is a member of the World Council of Churches and the World Methodist Council. It has formed a structure to handle issues of Christian-Muslim relations.

Protestant Methodist Church in Côte d'Ivoire
41 Boulevard de la République
B.P. 12
Abidjan, 01
Côte d'Ivoire

J. Gordon Melton

See also: World Council of Churches; World Methodist Council.

References

Harmon, Nolan B. *Encyclopedia of World Methodism.* 2 vols. Nashville: United Methodist Publishing House, 1974.

Van Beek, Huibert. *A Handbook of the Churches and Councils: Profiles of Ecumenical Relationships.* Geneva: World Council of Churches, 2006.

World Methodist Council, Handbook of Information, 2002–2006. Lake Junaluska, NC: World Methodist Council, 2006.

United Pentecostal Church International

The United Pentecostal Church International (UPCI), the largest Oneness Pentecostal organization, traces its beginning to the founding of the New Testament church on the Day of Pentecost (Acts 2). It affirms the experience, doctrine, and practice of the Apostles. It emerged within the modern Pentecostal movement with the activity of Charles F. Parham (1873–1929) and his distinctive message concerning the baptism of the Holy Spirit with the initial evidence of speaking in tongues. The ministry of William J. Seymour (1870–1922), a onetime student of Parham's and also a Holiness minister, was equally significant for the founding of the movement. His Azusa Street Mission in Los Angeles, California, was the site of a three-year revival (1906–1909) that resulted in the worldwide spread of Pentecostalism.

The Pentecostal movement experienced a division in 1910, when William Durham (1873–1912), a Baptist pastor in Chicago, dissented on the doctrine of sanctification. A second division occurred when ministers such as Canadian Baptist Frank J. Ewart (1876–1947), Glenn A. Cook (1867–1948), African American pastor G. T. Haywood (1880–1931), and Iranian immigrant Andrew D. Urshan (1884–1967) started baptizing "in the name of the Lord Jesus Christ" instead of with the Trinitarian formula.

On April 15, 1914, Ewart and Cook rebaptized each other in Jesus' name—the decisive act that launched Oneness Pentecostalism as a distinct movement. Soon, they and many other ministers began rebaptizing people, and they adopted a non-Trinitarian explanation of the Godhead. Many members of the Assemblies of God (AG), which had formed in 1914, embraced this teaching, including two prominent ministers, Howard A. Goss and E. N. Bell. Then in 1916, the AG adopted

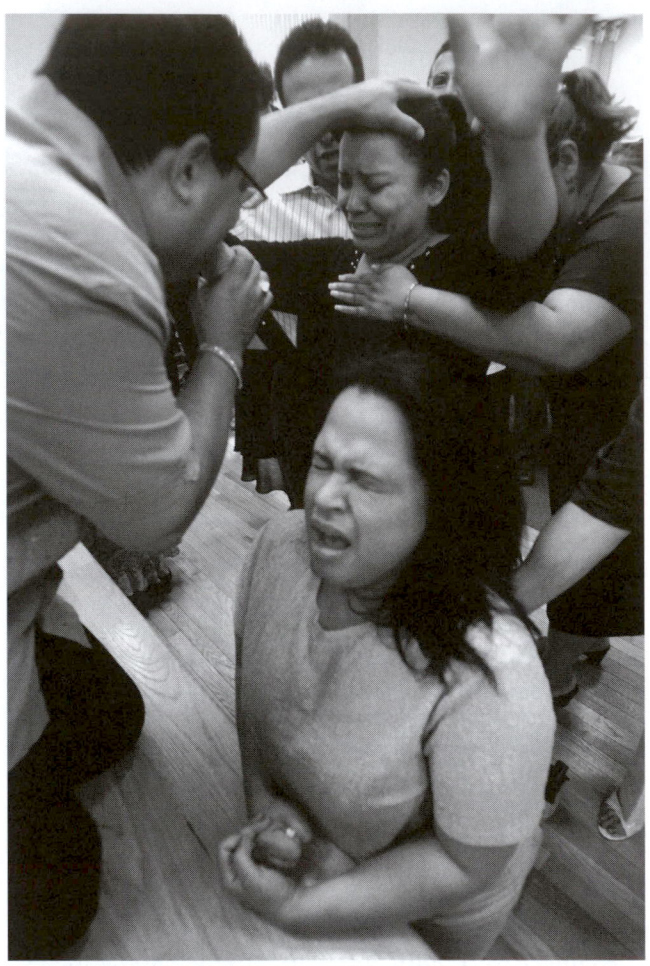

Pentecostal reverend Isaias Mercado prays with parishioners during the Spanish-language service at the La Casa del Carpintero (the Carpenter's House), in Chicago, July 29, 2007. (AP/Wide World Photos)

a Trinitarian statement of faith, forcing the Oneness ministers to withdraw. Some 156 of 585 ministers left the Assemblies.

In 1917 leading Oneness ministers organized the General Assembly of Apostolic Assemblies. In 1918 it merged with a small pre-existing group called the Pentecostal Assemblies of the World (PAW), which had embraced the Oneness message. The uniquely organized PAW was forced to hold all of its conferences in the North, on account of segregationist regulations in the South. As a result, few of the southern ministers could participate fully, and in 1924 most of the whites withdrew from the PAW. They formed three regional organizations, two of which soon merged. The desire for inter-racial unity was so strong, however, that in

1931 the merged group joined with the PAW again, creating the Pentecostal Assemblies of Jesus Christ. Initially its governing board was required to be 50 percent black, but later its racial composition was adjusted to be the same as that of the ministry. Again, the pressures of society worked against this new effort. By 1938 most of the blacks had left and returned to the PAW, which a few ministers had kept alive.

At this point, there were two relatively large, predominately white Oneness Pentecostal organizations —the Pentecostal Church, Incorporated, and the Pentecostal Assemblies of Jesus Christ. On September 25, 1945, these two groups merged in St. Louis, Missouri, forming the United Pentecostal Church. In 1972 the word "International" was added to the official name. The first general superintendent was Howard Goss, who served from 1945 to 1951. Following him were Arthur T. Morgan (1952–1967), Oliver F. Fauss (1967, interim), Stanley W. Chambers (1968–1977), and Nathaniel A. Urshan (1978–). In 1946 a Canadian Oneness group, the Full Gospel Pentecostal Church, joined the new organization.

The UPCI shares many key beliefs with other conservative Protestants, including the existence of one true God; the creation of the universe by God; the inspiration, authority, and infallibility of the Bible; the existence of angels, the devil, and demons; the fall and sinfulness of humanity; the incarnation (Jesus Christ is God manifested in the flesh, the Son of God, and born of a virgin); the atonement (the substitutionary death, burial, and resurrection of Jesus Christ); salvation by grace through faith in Jesus Christ; water baptism; the New Testament church as the people of God; the priesthood of all believers; the rapture of the church; the premillennial Second Coming of Jesus Christ to Earth; the millennial kingdom of Jesus Christ; the last judgment; eternal punishment for the unrighteous; and eternal life for the righteous. The UPCI observes the Lord's Supper and practices foot washing as an ordinance.

Like all other Pentecostal groups, the UPCI teaches the baptism of the Holy Spirit with the initial sign of tongues; miraculous, spiritual gifts for today; and divine healing. In addition, the UPCI embraces three important Oneness Pentecostal distinctives. First, it affirms the Oneness view of the Godhead. God is absolutely and indivisibly one (Deuteronomy 6:4), and in Jesus Christ dwells all the fullness of the Godhead bodily (Colossians 2:9). In order to redeem fallen humanity, God has revealed himself as the Father (in parental relationship to humanity), in the Son (in human flesh), and as the Holy Spirit (in spiritual action) (see Malachi 2:10; Luke 1:35; Genesis 1:2.) These three titles identify manifestations of the one God, not three distinct persons or centers of consciousness in the Godhead. Jesus is fully God and fully man.

Second, the church affirms the plan of salvation according to Acts 2:38. In the new covenant, the application of God's grace and the expression of saving faith come as humans repent of sins, are baptized in the name of Jesus Christ for the remission of sins, and receive the gift of the Holy Spirit (Acts 2:38). Following the pattern of the Apostolic church, water baptism should be administered by immersion in the name of Jesus Christ, for Jesus is the only name given for salvation (Acts 4:12).

Third, the church affirms the necessity of holiness of life. The UPCI teaches that sanctification is a process that begins at the new birth. Citing Hebrews 12:14 and other scriptural passages, the UPCI Articles of Faith emphasize the need for holiness both inwardly (attitudes and thoughts) and outwardly (behavior and dress).

UPCI church services are characterized by demonstrative, spontaneous worship. Important elements of public worship are preaching, singing, testifying, and praying. Evangelistic services typically end with an altar call, extended prayer by the congregation, and the laying on of hands.

The basic form of church government is congregational. The local body controls its own affairs, and the pastor is the leader under Christ. There is a strong district and national organization for the sake of ministerial standards, fellowship, and world evangelism. The organization is governed by its annual general conference. When the conference is not in session, the highest governing body is the Board of General Presbyters. The general board consists of the general superintendent, the general secretary-treasurer, two assistant general superintendents, six divisional directors, the district superintendents, and the regional executive presbyters. A global council, composed of representatives from around the world, coordinates the international efforts of the various national bodies affiliated with the UPCI. The UPCI ordains both men and women. It recognizes women as evangelists, missionaries, and pastors, but it reserves the top executive offices for men.

The work of the church is organized into the following divisions: church administration, editorial, education, foreign missions, Harvestime (radio), home missions (United States and Canada), ladies ministries, Sunday school, youth, and publishing.

The organization owns the Pentecostal Publishing House, which prints materials under the imprints Word Aflame Press and World Aflame Publications. Among the institutions operated or endorsed by the church are the World Network of Prayer, Harvestime radio ministry, the Urshan Graduate School of Theology, 7 Bible colleges in North America and 80 overseas, the Historical Center, Tupelo Children's Mansion (an orphanage), Lighthouse Ranch for Boys (a rehabilitation center), Spirit of Freedom (a ministry to alcohol and drug abusers), and Compassion Services International (a relief agency). The official periodical is the *Pentecostal Herald*.

In 2008, the UPCI reported 4,358 churches (excluding daughter works) in the United States and Canada, and 28,351 in 175 other countries. It reports a total worldwide constituency membership of more than 4 million of which 1 million is in North America. The UPCI is the only Oneness organization to have a large missions program in all areas of the world, with high concentrations of adherents in Louisiana; Mizoram, India; Ethiopia; and New Brunswick, Canada.

United Pentecostal Church International
World Evangelism Center
8855 Dunn Rd.
Hazelwood, MO 63042-2299
http://www.upci.org

David K. Bernard

See also: Assemblies of God; Parham, Charles Fox; Pentecostalism; Seymour, William J.

References

Bernard, David K. *The Apostolic Life*. Hazelwood, MO: Word Aflame, 2006.

Bernard, David K. *A History of Christian Doctrine.* Vol. 3, *The Twentieth Century*. Hazelwood, MO: Word Aflame, 1999.

Clanton, Arthur L., and Charles E. Clanton. *United We Stand*. Hazelwood, MO: Word Aflame, 1995.

Foster, Fred. *Their Story: 20th Century Pentecostals*. Rev. ed. Hazelwood, MO: Word Aflame, 1981.

Hall, J. L., and David K. Bernard, eds. *Doctrines of the Bible*. Hazelwood, MO: Word Aflame, 1990.

United Presbyterian Church of Brazil

The United Presbyterian Church of Brazil began in the 1970s when the more theologically liberal and socially active leaders in the Presbyterian Church in Brazil were alienated by some of the more conservative and anti-ecumenical policies instituted by the church. In 1972 a number of the ministers and laypeople left to form a separate church that in 1973 became the United Presbyterian Church. They found that some ministers and churches of like mind had previously left the Independent Presbyterian Church and formed the National Federation of Presbyterian Churches. The two groups made common cause, and in 1978 they merged to form the United Presbyterian Church of Brazil.

Although it is a relatively small body on the Brazilian landscape, the United Presbyterian Church has become well known for its protests of social injustice and its activities on behalf of the poor. Its theological statements include not only several of the historic Reformed statements of faith but also two more recent documents, the Barmen Confession, adopted by German Christians in protest against Nazism, and the Confession of 1967, originally promulgated by American Presbyterians (now united in the Presbyterian Church [U.S.A.]). In the 1990s the church reported 4,762 members. Its 51 congregation are organized into 8 presbyteries.

The church is ecumenically active at the national and regional levels. Internationally, it is a member of the World Council of Churches and the World Alliance of Reformed Churches.

United Presbyterian Church
CP 01-2 12, Av. Princesa Isabel
Salas 1210-1211
290 10-260 Victoria, ES
Brazil

J. Gordon Melton

See also: Presbyterian Church in Brazil; Presbyterian Church (U.S.A.); World Alliance of Reformed Churches; World Council of Churches.

References

Bauswein, Jean-Jacques, and Lukas Vischner, eds. *The Reformed Family Worldwide: A Survey of Reformed Churches, Theological Schools, and International Organizations.* Grand Rapids, MI: William B. Eerdmans Publishing Company, 1999.

Van Beek, Huibert. *A Handbook of the Churches and Councils: Profiles of Ecumenical Relationships.* Geneva: World Council of Churches, 2006.

United Protestant Church of Belgium

The United Protestant Church of Belgium continues the movement of the 16th-century Reformation into the area now known as the Low Countries. As in the Netherlands, the Reformed Church found support in Belgium, but as a result of the settlement of the struggle for control over the Low Countries in the Treaty of Utrecht (1713), Belgium continued as a predominantly Roman Catholic region. Those Reformed churches that survived were organized under either the Reformed Church in the Netherlands or the Reformed Church of France. There were some 40 Protestant congregations in the land as World War I began in 1914.

Following the war, the Methodist Episcopal Church, South (now a constituent part of the United Methodist Church) began a relief movement in Belgium that also led to the formation of congregations. In 1922 a Methodist Belgian mission was formally initiated, and a school, orphanage, and hospital opened. The Belgian annual conference was created in 1930. The growth of the church through the 1930s was accompanied by a general growth in Protestantism. Through the 1930s, more than 200 Protestant congregations of all types were formed.

Protestants suffered greatly during World War II. The Methodist Church lost much of its property, and many of its leaders were arrested. After the war, American Methodists launched an eight-year rebuilding program. Integral to the program was the erection of a new theological school in Brussels. In 1952 the Belgium Conference was incorporated into the Central and Southern European Central Conference, whose bishop resided in Zurich.

Through the 1960s, various parts of Belgian Protestantism began to look toward organic union. In 1963 the Methodists united with the Evangelical Protestant Church (a work supported by Swiss Protestants) to form the Protestant Church of Belgium. Then in 1978, the Belgian congregations of the Reformed Churches in the Netherlands and the Belgian Christian Missionary Church united with the Protestant Church of Belgium to form the United Protestant Church.

In 2005, the United Protestant Church reported 50,000 members. Although it is a relatively small body, the church has responsibility for teaching Protestantism in the public schools, and it administers a chaplaincy program in the prisons and hospitals. It is a member of the World Council of Churches, the World Alliance of Reformed Churches, and the World Methodist Council.

United Protestant Church
5 rue de Champ-de-Mars
B-1050 Brussels
Belgium

J. Gordon Melton

See also: Reformed Church of France; Reformed Churches in the Netherlands; United Methodist Church; World Alliance of Reformed Churches; World Council of Churches; World Methodist Council.

References

Bauswein, Jean-Jacques, and Lukas Vischner, eds. *The Reformed Family Worldwide: A Survey of Reformed Churches, Theological Schools, and International Organizations.* Grand Rapids, MI:

William B. Eerdmans Publishing Company, 1999.

Van Beek, Huibert. *A Handbook of the Churches and Councils: Profiles of Ecumenical Relationships.* Geneva: World Council of Churches, 2006.

Van der Bent, Ans J., ed. *Handbook/Member Churches/World Council of Churches.* Geneva: World Council of Churches, 1985.

United Protestant Church of Netherlands Antilles

The Netherlands Antilles include six islands, three of which are off the coast of Venezuela (Curacao, Bonaire, and Aruba) and three across the Caribbean, east of the Virgin Islands (St. Maarten, Saba, and St. Eustatius). The Netherlands Reformed Church was introduced as early as 1635, primarily through chaplains that accompanied the employees of the Dutch Indies Company, but it had little influence until after the dissolving of the Dutch Indies Company (1791) and the Napoleonic era. The church had tried to convert the original inhabitants of the islands, but with virtually no success, and there was little interest in converting the African laborers until slavery was abolished in 1863. The Roman Catholicism of the original settlers continues as the dominant religious force.

The Dutch language died out on St. Maarten, Saba, and St. Eustatius, and with it the Dutch Reformed Church, whose members were absorbed into the Methodist and Anglican churches. However, in 1825, King William I, the ruler of Holland, decreed the formation of a United Protestant Church in his Caribbean possessions. This church brought together the members of the Netherlands Reformed Church with the minority of members of what is now the Evangelical Lutheran Church in the Kingdom of the Netherlands. Three units of this church have survived, the churches on Curacao, Aruba, and Bonaire. At the time of their formation, each of these churches was quite small (the one on Bonaire, for example, having a total of 71 members).

The most successful of the churches was on Curacao. It was serviced by ministers from Holland, some of whom made periodic trips to Aruba. It grew several congregations, but lost some strength in 1931 when a group of members left to found the Reformed Churches in the Netherlands (Liberated) in Curacao. In churches where no minister was available, lay readers delivered sermons from texts approved by the Netherlands Reformed Churches. The first minister was permanently stationed on Aruba in 1858. It was not until 1947 that a second minister was assigned. There are now three congregations.

Bonaire's congregation was not organized until the 1840s. The minister also took a different course and began to baptize the children of the African residents. The island's second congregation was organized in 1934.

The United Protestant Church has seven congregations on the three islands (though the churches on Aruba have a more independent status), and in 2005 reported 5,000 members. It is a member of the World Council of Churches. Services are held in Dutch, English, and Papiamento (a new language composed of elements of Spanish, Portuguese, Dutch, and English that predominates among the population). Although it is relatively small, the church provides the main Protestant presence on the three islands.

United Protestant Church of Netherlands Antilles
Fortkerk
Fort Amsterdam
Willemstad
Curacao

J. Gordon Melton

See also: Reformed Churches of the Netherlands; World Council of Churches.

References

Bauswein, Jean-Jacques, and Lukas Vischner, eds. *The Reformed Family Worldwide: A Survey of Reformed Churches, Theological Schools, and International Organizations.* Grand Rapids, MI: William B. Eerdmans Publishing Company, 1999.

Van der Bent, Ans J., ed. *Handbook/Member Churches/World Council of Churches.* Geneva: World Council of Churches, 1985.

United Reformed Church of the United Kingdom

The United Reformed Church, formed in 1972, is the primary vehicle carrying the 17th-century Puritan movement in England. In Scotland, Presbyterianism gained the ascendancy in 1560, with Parliament's acceptance of the Scots Confession. With the establishment of the Church of England under Elizabeth I (1533–1603), who assumed the throne in 1558, those who followed the reformed ideas espoused by John Calvin (1509–1564) in Geneva, and who hoped eventually to further reform the church along Presbyterian lines, emerged as one wing of the Puritan movement. Puritans sought to purify the church further, and they fell along a range of opinions.

The Puritans had their opportunity in the 1640s, when they gained control of Parliament. In 1643 the Westminster Assembly of Divines met to advise Parliament, and in the process they drew up the Westminster Confession of Faith and the Westminster Catechism. More than any other, these documents define British Presbyterianism. Presbyterianism had always to contend not only with the Church of England but also with Independents (Congregationalists) and Baptists. Although Presbyterians wished to take control from bishops and place it in the hands of church elders (presbyters), the Congregationalists and Baptists opted for authority in the hands of the congregations.

The Puritans reigned supreme during the brief period of the Commonwealth (1643–1660), but with the Restoration of the monarchy in 1660, the episcopally led Church of England returned to power. The various Puritan groupings were forced to organize as dissenting churches. Legal restrictions tended to decrease support, though there was some relief with the Toleration Act of 1689. Beginning in the 1740s, England experienced what was known as the Evangelical Awakening, a national revival that had as its main product the Wesleyan Methodist movement. However, both Presbyterians and Congregationalists experienced new life, and one wing of the Methodists remained loyal to a Calvinist theological perspective. It would organize as the Calvinist Methodist Connexion.

Toward the end of the 18th century, dissenting Puritan groups began to take on new organizational expressions. As early as 1783 the presbytery of Northumberland brought Presbyterians in the north of England together. The Presbyterian Church in England was formed in 1836, following the movement of a number of Scots south. The Scottish expatriates also formed the English Synod of the United Presbyterian Church (a Scottish body) in 1863. In 1876, these two groups united to form the Presbyterian Church of England.

Congregationalism in England had taken definite form in 1649 with the issuance of the Savoy Declaration of Faith and Order, which accepted the Reformed theology that underlay the Westminster Confession but opted for congregational church polity. Congregationalists took on new responsibilities with the formation in 1795 of the London Missionary Society, which would send missionaries and Congregationalism around the world. The Society preceded the formation of the Congregational Union of England and Wales in 1832.

The Congregational Union and Presbyterian Church became leading forces in the shaping of Protestantism as a worldwide phenomenon in the 19th century and assumed leadership roles in the ecumenical movement that led to the consolidation of so many churches in the 20th century. The Congregational Union (renamed the Congregational Church of England and Wales in 1966) merged with the Presbyterian Church of England to form the United Presbyterian Church in 1972.

In the meantime, in 1833, Peyton Wyth had brought to England the ideas of radical Presbyterian minister Alexander Campbell (1788–1866), whose work in the United States had led to the formation of a new revivalistic movement that would later lead to the formation of several new denominations, such as the Churches of Christ and the Christian Church (Disciples of Christ). Wyth led in the formation of the new British group called the Churches of Christ. Over the first century it formed some 200 congregations.

In the mid-1970s, the majority of the Association of the Churches of Christ voted to join with the new United Reformed Church, but not by the two-thirds majority needed to effect a merger. Hence, in 1979 the Association dissolved, and two new associations formed. One of these combined in 1980 with the United

Church. The other continues as the Churches of Christ. The merger led to a name change, the United Reformed Church of England and Wales becoming the United Reformed Church of the United Kingdom.

The United Reformed Church's 85,000 members (2005) are grouped into 11 regional synods in England, with an addition synod in both Scotland and Wales. With the addition of the Churches of Christ congregations, the church now has a few congregations in Scotland. The former London Missionary Society has been reorganized by merger with the various other missionary societies operating in the Presbyterian and Congregational world, and in 1977 it completed a thorough theoretical realignment that now envisions its work as a partnership arrangement with churches worldwide. It has re-emerged as the Council for World Mission.

In 1972 the United Church published a new Confession of Faith, which it saw as a contemporary restatement of the Reformed theological tradition. That confession reflects the church's participation in contemporary theological dialogue. The church is a leading member of the World Alliance of Reformed Churches and also is affiliated with the World Council of Churches. The church retains special relationship to the 30 partnership churches associated with the Council for World Mission.

On April 1, 2000, the Scottish Congregational Church brought some 50 congregation into the United Reformed Church and reorganized as its Scottish synod. Congregationalism had come to Scotland at the end of the 18th century with the appearance of the two laymen Robert (1764–1842) and James Haldane (1768–1851), who began to advocate the cause of world mission within the Church of Scotland. The church was slow to respond, and in reaction the brothers began to form independent churches that would support a missionary program. The Reverend Greville Ewing (1787–1841) came to their aid and began classes for the training of ministers in 1799. He was the major voice calling the congregations to form the Congregational Union in 1812.

Although it was small, the church would have an important role in world missions. Among its members would be the immortal David Livingstone (1813–1873), who pioneered Christian missions in central Africa. It cooperated with the London Missionary Society formed by the British Congregationalists.

In 1897 the Congregational Union merged with the Evangelical Union. This latter union had arisen as a protest against the Calvinist emphases in one of the splinters of the Church of Scotland, the Synod of the United Secession. The leader of the Union was a follower of Arminian theology (similar to that espoused by the Methodists). The Union after 1897 was a decidedly more eclectic body. It had an evangelical piety, emphasized social programs, and developed a liberal theology relative to the predominant Presbyterian/Reformed theology that dominated Scotland early in the 20th century. The Union was always a non-creedal church. The Union was a pioneer in ecumenism, partially a product of their missionary work.

Congregationalism in Scotland had emerged around three separate structures: the Congregational Union, the Scottish Congregational College (founded in 1811 in Edinburgh), and the Congregational Women's Union. Each of these functions as an independent organization. In the 1990s, supporters of each responded to a plan to link the three organizations more closely into what was termed a "voluntary church." This move to give a more coordinated and united existence to the Congregational community met with widespread support, and in 1993 the three entities united as the Scottish Congregational Church.

United Reformed Church of the United Kingdom
86 Tavistock Pl.
London WC1H 9RT
United Kingdom

J. Gordon Melton

See also: Calvin, John; Christian Church (Disciples of Christ); Church of England; Church of Scotland; Churches of Christ; Elizabeth I; London Missionary Society; World Alliance of Reformed Churches; World Council of Churches.

References

Bauswein, Jean-Jacques, and Lukas Vischner, eds. *The Reformed Family Worldwide: A Survey of Reformed Churches, Theological Schools, and*

International Organizations. Grand Rapids, MI: William B. Eerdmans Publishing Company, 1999.

Cornick, David. *Under God's Good Hand: History of the Traditions Which Have Come Together in the United Reformed Church in the United Kingdom*. London: United Reformed Church, 1998.

Lewis, Tracey. *From Streams to Oceans: Celebrating 25 Years in the United Reformed Church*. London: United Reformed Church, 1997.

United Reformed Church Yearbook. London: United Reformed Church, published annually.

Van der Bent, Ans J., ed. *Handbook/Member Churches/World Council of Churches*. Geneva: World Council of Churches, 1985.

United Religions Initiative

The United Religions Initiative (URI) was conceived in the mid-1990s by the Right Reverend William E. Swing, the Episcopal bishop of San Francisco. His vision pictured a global interfaith community that could work toward ending religiously motivated violence and replacing such violence with structure based on healing, peace, and justice. Over the next five years the ideals of that vision were spread internationally, and, beginning in 1996, a series of annual Global Summit conferences were convened in San Francisco.

Among the first actions of those who identified with the Initiative was the sponsoring of a 72 Hours of Peace program that began on December 31, 1999. The conferences also considered and initiated some 40 projects in countries around the world that attracted the attention of prominent religious leaders such as Desmond Tutu of South Africa and the Dalai Lama. These initial efforts led to the organization of a variety of local groups (termed "cooperating circles") in different countries, an interim Global Council, and a formal inaugurating conference held in Pittsburgh, Pennsylvania, in June 2000. At the opening of the conference on June 26, people from 39 religious traditions and 44 countries signed the charter and formally established the United Religions Initiative.

It is the task of the URI to promote enduring daily interfaith cooperation that will in turn lead to its ultimate goal of ending violence caused by religious conflict, and lead to a culture characterized by peace, justice, and healing. The first task of the cooperating circles on the various continents of the world was to elect representatives who would form the first Global Council. At the time of its founding, some 75 cooperating circles had been recognized. Although the URI is a new interfaith organization, it has made cooperation with other interfaith groups part of its standard operating format. Peace building remains in the forefront of the Initiative's concerns, and it has published a 300-page guide to the subject available for downloading from its website.

The URI is organized around hundreds of local cooperating circles that act locally on the global vision of the URI. The circles in each region elect trustees who sit on the Global Council, the international decision- and policy-making body whose task is to assist the circles in realizing the vision and values of the URI's preamble, purpose, and principles. The Council also oversees the staff, which includes an executive director, people in charge of various program divisions, and regional coordinators.

The Initiative now includes an unnumbered community of people dedicated to interfaith cooperation and activism, the more active core being organized into 398 Cooperation Circles in 67 countries and representing more than 100 religious groups, spiritual expressions, and indigenous traditions.

United Religions Initiative
PO Box 29242
San Francisco, CA 94129-0242
http://www.uri.org/

J. Gordon Melton

See also: Episcopal Church.

References

Swing, William E. *The Coming United Religions*. Grand Rapids, MI: Conexus Press, 1998.

United Religions Initiative. http://www.united religions.org/newsite/index.htm. Accessed August 15, 2001.

United Society for the Propagation of the Gospel

See Society for the Propagation of the Gospel in Foreign Parts.

United Society of Believers in Christ's Second Appearing

The United Society of Believers in Christ's Second Appearing (Shakers) is a Christian sectarian community of English origins with a distinctive theology and lifestyle, a community that has existed for more than two and a half centuries. The fortunes of the United Society of Believers in Christ's Second Appearing have included times of remarkable success as well as periods of violent persecution. Although only a handful of Shakers remain today at one location in America, Shakerism continues to attract a wide variety of followers who find the history, the religious perspective, and the material culture of the community attractive.

The Shakers, known initially as "Shaker Quakers" because they trembled or shook when in ecstasy, first coalesced in England in the 1740s around two tailors, James and Jane Wardley. Leadership of the small group of religious enthusiasts later passed on to Ann Lee Standerin (1736–1784), an uneducated charismatic and visionary who participated in public demonstrations against the established churches. In 1774 Ann Lee (as she came to be known) led a handful of followers to America, where they eventually took up residence in New York near Albany. These English immigrants were accused of being British sympathizers during the Revolutionary War, and some, including Lee, were imprisoned for a time. The Shakers emerged on the religious scene in 1780, when they began to attract American converts. Lee, known to her followers as Mother Ann, traveled throughout eastern New York and New England on a missionary journey. The sites

An emotional meeting of the Shakers, a utopian community in New York state founded by Anne Lee in 1774. (Library of Congress)

where she was successful in attracting followers often subsequently became the locations of Shaker villages. Lee was regarded by her followers as a gifted prophet, a miracle worker, and their spiritual parent.

Following Lee's death, successive leaders, known as "the ministry," gathered believers into separate communities where life was organized around several fundamental principles, including celibacy, communal property, acceptance of the ministry's authority, organization of new "families," and separation from the "world" outside the villages. Between 1784 and 1826 20 Shaker villages were established, located from Maine in the East to Kentucky in the West. The Shakers reached their numerical height in the 1840s, when approximately 4,500 believers inhabited the scattered villages. The Society's strenuous work ethic resulted in economic success in both agriculture and light manufacturing.

Among distinctive Shaker beliefs are the concept of God as involving both a male and a female aspect (Father and Mother), the association of sin with lust and sexual relations, the identification of Ann Lee with the Christ Spirit (Ann the Beloved Daughter of God parallel with Jesus the Beloved Son of God), and the possibility of Christian perfection. Worship within the community included physical exercises, such as dances and marches, as well as song, testimony, and exhortation. The years following 1837 witnessed a wave of spiritualistic activity in the Society during which time abundant "spiritual gifts" and messages were received by Shaker "instruments," or mediums.

Following the Civil War the Society experienced steady numerical and economic decline. In particular, it failed to recruit and successfully retain male members. The Believers divided over the best strategy to follow in these circumstances, some arguing for accommodation to modern American life, others resisting it in the name of tradition. Villages were closed, resources consolidated or sold off, and by the 1980s only two villages remained in New England, each with a mere handful of Believers. In the year 2000 seven Shakers resided in the last village, Sabbathday Lake, Maine, a site founded in 1794. By 2008 the number of Shakers in Maine had declined to three. Despite the declining numbers, the contemporary Shakers exhibit a measure of confidence about the future. They are surrounded by a large circle of friends, spiritual colleagues, and patrons who admire the believers' religious values, their distinctive culture, and the material objects associated with their history.

Stephen J. Stein

References

Burks, Jean M., ed. *Shaker Design: Out of this World*. New Haven, CT: Yale University Press, 2008.

Duffield, Holley Gene. *Historical Dictionary of the Shakers*. Lanham, MD: Scarecrow Press, 2000.

Kirk, John T. *The Shaker World: Art, Life, Belief*. New York: Harry N. Abrams, 1997.

Stein, Stephen J. *The Shaker Experience in America: A History of the United Society of Believers*. New Haven, CT: Yale University Press, 1992.

Whitson, Robley Edward, ed. *The Shakers: Two Centuries of Spiritual Reflection*. New York: Paulist Press, 1983.

■ United States of America

The United States is the centermost of the three large countries that dominate North America. It lies between Canada and Mexico. The United States is a federal republic made up of 48 contiguous states, 2 additional states, Alaska and Hawaii (in the north Pacific), and the District of Columbia. The country's 3,790,000 square miles make it the world's third largest country in land area. As of 2008, its population in excess of 305,000,000 makes it the third largest country in population (behind only China and India). Included in the population count are an estimated 11 million undocumented residents.

The original inhabitants of what is now the United States of America arrived at least 30,000 years ago from Asia, most likely over a land bridge now submerged beneath the Bering Straits. They spread across the continent, and by the 15th century CE some 500 different groupings, now usually referred to as nations, arose. Some groups were small, occupying a relatively confined niche. Others adopted a nomadic lifestyle that saw them roaming over a large territory and living off the land. In still other climes, a settled agricultural life

United States of America

Religion	Followers in 1970	Followers in 2010	% of Population	Annual % growth 2000–2010	Followers in 2025	Followers in 2050
Christians	190,970,000	257,311,000	81.8	0.85	277,162,000	301,962,000
Independents	34,702,000	72,700,000	23.1	0.94	84,000,000	100,000,000
Roman Catholics	48,305,000	70,550,000	22.4	1.52	80,000,000	90,000,000
Protestants	58,568,000	58,000,000	18.4	−0.15	60,000,000	60,000,000
Agnostics	10,270,000	36,738,000	11.7	2.35	51,150,000	66,400,000
Jews	6,700,000	5,220,000	1.7	−0.31	5,000,000	5,000,000
Muslims	800,000	5,150,000	1.6	1.90	7,000,000	10,000,000
Buddhists	200,000	3,300,000	1.0	2.25	6,000,000	8,000,000
New religionists	560,000	1,600,000	0.5	1.31	2,000,000	2,600,000
Ethnoreligionists	70,000	1,450,000	0.5	1.30	1,350,000	1,500,000
Hindus	100,000	1,445,000	0.5	1.57	2,100,000	3,000,000
Atheists	200,000	1,250,000	0.4	0.31	1,500,000	1,800,000
Baha'is	138,000	500,000	0.2	2.52	750,000	1,000,000
Sikhs	10,000	300,000	0.1	2.43	400,000	500,000
Spiritists	0	158,000	0.1	1.03	175,000	200,000
Chinese folk	90,000	92,000	0.0	1.53	120,000	150,000
Jains	3,000	85,000	0.0	1.42	120,000	180,000
Shintoists	0	62,200	0.0	1.03	70,000	85,000
Zoroastrians	0	17,500	0.0	1.03	18,000	18,000
Daoists	0	12,400	0.0	1.03	15,000	20,000
Total population	**210,111,000**	**314,692,000**	**100.0**	**1.03**	**354,930,000**	**402,415,000**

developed. Possibly the largest single settlement was at Cahokia, Illinois, where a city with upward of 40,000 inhabitants once existed.

Each nation had its own religion that was exclusive to it, though they often resembled those of bordering nations. Across the continent, religious life and ritual expressions varied widely but were related intimately to the land, its animal inhabitants, and the climate. Religion and the secular order were intertwined, and while religious functionaries—shamans, magicians, healers—were present, they often shared spiritual authority with the chiefs. Once the Europeans arrived, the Native peoples began to absorb insights from Christianity, and it often became difficult to distinguish those elements that had been absorbed from those that had been originally present.

The first Europeans to discover North America and possibly land in American territory were the Vikings, but significant contact began early in the 16th century as the Spanish expanded northward from their original settlements in the Caribbean. Initial settlements were in Florida and New Mexico, but later expanded to include the Southwest from Texas to California. Meanwhile, the French expanded up the St. Lawrence River into the Great Lakes region and southward through the Mississippi Valley to New Orleans. Relatively late, with the landing of the settlers in Massachusetts and Virginia at the beginning of the 17th century, the British began to make their all-important settlement of the Atlantic seacoast. Both Dutch and Swedish settlements would be established amid the British colonies, but these eventually gave way to British control.

The arrival of the Europeans would lead to the establishment of most of the state churches. Roman Catholicism was planted in the Spanish and French colonies, the Church of England in most of the British colonies. The congregation of the Church of Sweden (Lutheran) in Delaware and of the Reformed Church of the Netherlands in New York and New Jersey continued under British rule. More important for the future of the land, however, were the colonies formed by various groups of religious dissenters. Congregationalists, losers in the power struggle between the Puritans and

Anglicans in 17th-century England, colonized Massachusetts in 1620. They wished to establish a land in which the Congregationalists were the state church, and they proved most intolerant of other dissenters. Earlier, a small group of the most radical Puritans had settled at Plymouth, Massachusetts. These Pilgrims shared the Reformed faith of the Congregationalists but dissented on the idea of establishing a state church.

The intolerance of the Puritans would lead to the banishment of one of their ministers, Roger Williams, who would settle in Rhode Island, where he would found the first Baptist church in the colonies and create a state that allowed broad religious liberties. Farther south, a member of the Society of Friends created a colony in which the beleaguered sectarian groups from across Europe were welcome. Not only did the Quakers make Philadelphia their home, but Mennonites, Brethren, and members of several mystical groups made their way to Pennsylvania. Finally, Roman Catholics from England, where Catholicism was feared by both Puritans and Anglicans, settled and attempted to establish a colony in which religious freedom reigned. The colony would eventually be taken over by Anglicans from neighboring Virginia and the period of religious freedom curtailed.

The changes brought by the War for American Independence (1776–1781) led to a dramatic change in the religious community. In the new nation, two churches existed in strength, the Congregationalists in New England and Anglicanism in the southern colonies. Anglicanism was identified with the defeated British regime, and few south of New England would tolerate a Congregational establishment. Leading figures in the Revolution—Thomas Jefferson, George Washington, and Benjamin Franklin included—were both pragmatic politicians and Deists. The most liberal religious thinkers of their day, they opted for an experiment in creating a country without a state church. They left the option for a state church up to the individual states, and Massachusetts kept its establishment into the early 19th century. Soon all of the states wrote an anti-establishment clause into their constitutions.

At the time of the founding of the United States, most of the several hundred Native American nations remained intact, though some had been destroyed by disease and war brought by the Europeans. A few of the Native Americans had become the objects of attempts by Christians to convert them, the most successful mission being established by the Roman Catholics in Maryland. Through the 19th century, a variety of churches would open missions among Native Americans; however, their efforts would be continually undermined by their identification with the U.S. government, whose policy of war, breaking treaties, and removal of Native Americans to less attractive lands in the West continued to sour the possibilities for full participation of Native peoples in American life.

The other factor determining the uniqueness of the new nation was the introduction of slavery into the southern colonies and the adoption of a set of laws inhibiting the integration of African Americans into the other colonies. Following the American Revolution, slavery expanded in the South, and anti-black legislation was adopted by most free states. The country fought a Civil War in the 19th century (1860–1865) that resulted in the ending of slavery but did not deal with many of the special laws related to African Americans, including a set of laws adopted in the southern states at the end of the century. Continued unrest because of the legal restrictions on African Americans (and by the middle of the 20th century on other minority groups) led to the passing of broad civil rights legislation in the 1960s.

When George Washington, the first president of the United States, was inaugurated in 1789, there were, apart from the Native American religions, some 17 religious groups, 16 Christian denominations, and a set of Jewish synagogues. The country defined its borders as extending to the Mississippi River, and expansion of settlements into the land of the Native Americans to the west began immediately. In the early decades, the Anglicans, reorganized as the Protestant Episcopal Church in the U.S.A. (now the Episcopal Church), tended to dominate the political scene, and most of the country's early presidents were drawn from its ranks. The Congregationalists, soon allied with Presbyterians who moved to the United States in large numbers following the Restoration of the monarchy in England in 1660, dominated in education and were responsible for the founding of many of the nation's most respected universities, including Harvard, Yale, and Princeton. As a result, the churches of the Reformed tradition also tended to produce the majority of the nation's leading theologians.

As the nation expanded westward, the Baptist Church, the Methodist Episcopal Church, and the Roman Catholic Church were the winners. The Baptists and Methodists, in numbers both minuscule at the time of the American Revolution, moved onto the frontier and experienced great success with evangelizing the largely irreligious settlers. They developed the use of revivals and camp meetings that would evolve and continue to be widely used into the 20th century. By the 1830s the Methodists had become the largest church in the nation. Through the 19th century, the Baptists would eclipse the Methodists, though they would divide into a number of separate denominations.

In the 1840s the Methodists divided into the Methodist Episcopal Church and the Methodist Episcopal Church, South. That act left the Roman Catholics, who were able to remain undivided by the issues fast moving the country to civil war, the largest single church in America. It has remained so to the present. The church grew both by evangelizing the public and as a result of the steady stream of Roman Catholic immigrants. It also grew as Roman Catholic believers residing in the former French and Spanish colonies were added to the nation.

Through the 19th century, to some extent because of the continued immigration from Europe, the number of religious groups multiplied decade by decade. Without a controlling state church, religious debates were often resolved by one side departing to found a new church. Innovation led to new religions, and through the century the Church of Jesus Christ of Latter-day Saints, the Spiritualist movement, the Theosophical Society, the Church of Christ, Scientist, and the New Thought movement would emerge and become established on the religious landscape. The Latter-day Saints would pioneer the settlement of the Rocky Mountain states, and they remain the majority body in Utah and the surrounding region. By the end of the 19th century, there were more than 300 Christian denominations.

One of the most important movements in American religion in the 19th century was launched by the predicted return of Christ in 1843–1844 by William Miller, a Baptist lay preacher. When his prophecy failed, the movement built around him splintered. New dates would be set and doctrinal divergences would emerge. Out of the pieces of a failed movement would come two of the most successful 20th-century religious groups, the Seventh-day Adventist Church and the Jehovah's Witnesses. It would also produce the Worldwide Church of God, which, after a successful half-century, splintered when the main body dropped its unique doctrines and converted to an orthodox Christian position.

Jews had been present in the American colonies, the first synagogues having been built in New York and Rhode Island by immigrants from Brazil who had fled when the Portuguese recaptured Recife from the Dutch in the 1650s. By the time of the American Revolution, there was a modest string of synagogues from Savannah in the South to New England. The Jewish community expanded greatly in the early 19th century, especially through immigration from Germany. In America it would experience a division that also swept through much of the community worldwide. In the West, Jewish leaders would begin to advocate reform and call for the dropping of much of the ritual and legal tradition in favor of an approach that favored the essential ethical and spiritual core of the faith. In response, those who rejected the Reform platform would organize as Orthodox Jews. The arrival of several million Eastern European Jews in the country at the end of the century would not only greatly enlarge the Jewish community but also lead to the emergence of still another perspective, which would take form as Conservative Judaism, in the space between the Orthodox and Reform factions.

With the end of slavery, African Americans were free to develop their own religious institutions. The first African American churches had been formed soon after the American Revolution by Methodists in Philadelphia, New York, and several other northern cities. Two groups emerged as large national bodies in the late 19th century, the African Methodist Episcopal Church and the African Methodist Episcopal Zion Church. After the Civil War, the scattered Baptist churches began to organize nationally, and by the end of the century they had formed the National Baptist Convention,

San Miguel Catholic Church, Santa Fe, New Mexico. Built about 1610, it is the oldest church structure in the United States. (J. Gordon Melton)

U.S.A. Out of that original organization two other national bodies, the National Baptist Convention of America and the Progressive National Baptist Convention, have been formed.

The introduction of so many divisions within the religious community ensured that not one religious organization would dominate; however, many Protestants saw themselves as the leading religious force in the country, and during the last half of the 19th century they joined Protestants worldwide in seeking means to overcome their disunity. Their efforts resulted in the formation of the Federal Council of Churches, which included among its membership most of the older and larger denominations. It also promoted the merger of its closely related member bodies, and major unions

took place within the Lutheran, Presbyterian/Reformed, and Methodist family of denominations.

Although one group of churchmen looked to the development of a united Protestantism, another group became concerned about the changes in church life—especially the theological changes—that had occurred in the larger denominations as a result of the attempt by many church leaders to respond to the social and intellectual challenges of contemporary culture. Conservatives accused the Modernists of rejecting the fundamentals of the faith, including the authority of the Bible, the Trinity, the deity of Christ, and the doctrine of creation. That concern would be focused in the 1920s in the arguments over the biblical account of creation, which the fundamentalists insisted should be taken

United States of America

Augusta
Montpelier
Concord
Albany
Boston
Providence
Rochester
Buffalo
Hartford
New York
Trenton
Philadelphia
Wilmington
Harrisburg
Cleveland
Pittsburgh
Annapolis
Washington D. C.
Baltimore
Norfolk
Richmond
Charleston
Frankfort
Raleigh
Greensboro
Charlotte
Columbia
Jacksonville
West Palm Beach
Miami
Orlando
Tampa
Lansing
Detroit
Ann Arbor
Columbus
Dayton
Cincinnati
Louisville
Nashville
Atlanta
Montgomery
Tallahassee
Memphis
Birmingham
Jackson
Milwaukee
Madison
Chicago
Ames
Indianapolis
Springfield
St. Louis
Kansas City
Little Rock
Baton Rouge
New Orleans
Minneapolis
St. Paul
Des Moines
Omaha
Lincoln
Topeka
Jefferson City
Dallas
Bismarck
Pierre
Cheyenne
Oklahoma City
Austin
San Antonio
Houston
United States of America
Santa Fe
Boulder
Denver
Helena
Spokane
Boise
Salt Lake City
Phoenix
Honolulu
Fairbanks
Juneau
Anchorage
Seattle
Olympia
Vancouver
Portland
Salem
Carson City
Sacramento
San Francisco
Los Angeles
San Diego

N

literally. The Fundamentalist-Modernist controversy split the Protestant community into three factions, which have remained to the present.

The largest group, which retained control of most of the larger denominations, was the Modernists, who saw the need to develop the tradition within the contemporary context. The evangelicals wished to engage culture, but without giving up on what they saw as the essentials of the faith. The Fundamentalist core not only wanted to remain true to the essentials of the faith but also to separate from all association with Modernists, and even from other conservatives who associated with Modernists. These three groups eventually organized their own ecumenical bodies: the National Council of Churches of Christ in the U.S.A., the National Association of Evangelicals, and the American Council of Churches, the World Evangelical Alliance, and the International Council of Christian Churches.

The process of merging closely related churches that became noticeable during the decades of the Federal Council of Churches continued under the aegis of the National Council. During the late 20th century, a number of the largest churches presently existing in America were formed by new unions resulting in the formation of the United Church of Christ (1957), the Council of Churches (1968), the Presbyterian Church (U.S.A.) (1983), and the Evangelical Lutheran Church in America (1988). The largest Baptist churches, the Southern Baptist Convention and the American Baptist Churches in the U.S.A., had drifted to opposite ends of the theological perspective and have not seriously considered merger.

As the Protestant community was reorganizing itself in new structures, and the Roman Catholic Church was feeling its way into becoming an American church, another change was occurring in American religion, the emergence of communities of the world's religions. In 1893, Chicago had hosted the Parliament of the World's Religions, out of which the first Hindu and Muslim organizations would be founded in America. Chinese Buddhist temples had first emerged on the West Coast during the Gold Rush that began in 1849, but Buddhist organizations, especially Japanese Zen and Shin groups, now began to proliferate. A steady growth would be halted in 1924, when a new federal act stopped immigration from Asia and most countries outside of Western Europe.

The laws preventing immigration from Asia and the Middle East were revised in 1965, and a sudden rush of immigration from India, Japan, Korea, and other parts of the world led to the sudden influx of Buddhists, Hindus, and Muslims. Their numbers were additionally swelled by the arrival of teachers and missionaries who began to build new religious movements that would go on to become global religious organizations. Such groups as the International Society for Krishna Consciousness, the Unification Movement, Soka Gakkai International, the Transcendental Meditation movement (World Plan Executive Council), and the Divine Light Mission (now Elan Vital) entered the country at this time. At the same time the African American community became particularly open to Islam, and they now constitute a significant portion of its American membership.

As the Asian religions were spreading, a number of new home-grown movements also began a growth phase, primarily among young adults in the larger urban complexes. These included the Children of God (a communal group now known as The Family International), the Church of Scientology, The Way International, and the Church Universal and Triumphant. These were either variations on Christianity or representatives of Western Esotericism. The sudden proliferation of new and unfamiliar groups led to a reaction by both the older, more conservative churches, which saw the United States as a Christian nation, and the parents of the youthful converts to many of the more high-demand religions. Their concerns fell on deaf ears until the suicide/murder deaths in 1978 of 900 members of the Peoples Temple. Although that group did not fit the profile of the new religious movements in most respects, the deaths led to the expansion of an anti-cult crusade built around the practice of deprogramming, which included the detention of members of new religions by their parents and by people hired to convince the young person to renounce the new faith. That practice ended only in 1995, after a young man who had been kidnapped and detained won a large judgment against the major organization promoting deprogramming, the Cult Awareness Network.

Among the groups that have taken their place in the religious leadership of the post–World War II religious scene have been the Eastern Orthodox churches. These emerged in the 19th century as non–English speaking groups, the largest being from Russia (the Orthodox Church in America) and Greece (the Greek Orthodox Archdiocese [under the jurisdiction of the Ecumenical Patriarchate]). Americanizing through the 20th century, they found common cause in the plight of their mother churches, especially those living under Communist or Islamic governments, and most recently have become significant voices in the National Council of Churches and the World Council of Churches. Like several groups whose patriarchs came under the control of a Marxist government, the Orthodox Church in America (formerly the Russian Orthodox Church) withdrew its administrative connection with the Moscow patriarchate.

As the wealthiest if not the largest Christian country in the world, the United States has contributed immeasurably to the spread of Protestantism, which carried it around the world in the 19th century. Beginning with the American Board of Commissioners for Foreign Missions, most denominations large and small established mission boards and sent missionaries around the world. Out of their efforts have come thousands of new churches (many described elsewhere in this volume). In the 20th century, the missionary effort was bolstered by the Pentecostal movement, which not only grew into an important new segment of the American religious scene but also was among the most missionary-minded of movements. Within a decade of the seminal event in its origin, the revival at the mission in Los Angeles in 1906, it had founded missions on every continent and gone on to become a force in most countries of the world. Its largest representatives in the United States include the Church of God in Christ, the Assemblies of God, the Church of God (Cleveland, Tennessee), and the Church of God of Prophecy. A new wave of interest in Pentecostalism among members of the older Protestant bodies brought hundreds of thousands of new adherents into the movement, many of whom formed a host of new Charismatic denominations.

Through the first decade of the 21st century, more than 2,500 distinct religious communities had emerged in the United States. They represented the spectrum of the world's religions, though the majority were Christians. About half of the population belongs to the more than 1,000 Protestant churches. Slightly more than 20 percent are Roman Catholic, and the Roman Catholic Church is the single largest religious body in America. It is followed by the Southern Baptist Convention, the United Methodist Church, the Presbyterian Church (U.S.A.), the Church of God in Christ, the Evangelical Lutheran Church in America, the Episcopal Church, and the United Church of Christ. There are some 25 additional groups, including the 3 large Jewish congregational associations, which report a million or more members, and some 75 groups, most Christian denominations, with at least 100,000 members. The rest are spread through the many other religions. There is a small but vocal atheist/humanist community, but less than 10 percent of the public count themselves as unbelievers or irreligious.

Hardest to define are the many groups that have grown out of the Western Esoteric tradition. Making up some 3 to 4 percent of the population, the Esoteric and metaphysical community consists of several hundred mostly small religious groups; only a very few (for example, the Church of Christ, Scientist, the Unity School of Christianity) have as many as 100,000 members.

J. Gordon Melton

See also: African Methodist Episcopal Church; African Methodist Episcopal Zion Church; American Baptist Churches in the U.S.A.; American Board of Commissioners for Foreign Missions; Assemblies of God; Christian Brethren; Church of Christ, Scientist; Church of England; Church of God (Cleveland, Tennessee); Church of God in Christ; Church of God of Prophecy; Church of Jesus Christ of Latter-day Saints; Church of Scientology; Church Universal and Triumphant; Ecumenical Patriarchate/Patriarchate of Constantinople; Elan Vital/Divine Light Mission; Episcopal Church; Evangelical Lutheran Church in America; Family International, The; International Council of Christian Churches; International Society for Krishna Consciousness; Jehovah's Witnesses; National Baptist Convention of America; National Baptist Convention, U.S.A.; Orthodox Church in America; Presbyterian Church (U.S.A.); Progressive

National Baptist Convention of America; Roman Catholic Church; Seventh-day Adventist Church; Soka Gakkai International; Southern Baptist Convention; Theosophical Society (America); Unification Movement; United Church of Christ; Unity School of Christianity; Way International, The; World Council of Churches; World Evangelical Alliance; Worldwide Church of God.

References

Albanese, Catherine. *American Religion and Religions*. 4th ed. Belmont, CA: Wadsworth, 2006.

Albanese, Catherine. *A Republic of Mind and Spirit: A Cultural History of American Metaphysical Religion*. New Haven, CT: Yale University Press, 2008.

Butler, Jon, Grant Wacker, and Randall Balmer. *Religion in American Life: A Short History*. New York: Oxford University Press, 2007.

Carroll, Brett E. *The Routledge Historical Atlas of Religion in America*. New York: Routledge, 2000.

Flynn, Tom, ed. *The New Encyclopedia of Unbelief*. Amherst, NY: Prometheus Books, 2007.

Gill, Sam D. *Native American Religions: An Introduction*. Belmont, CA: Wadsworth, 1982.

Hall, Robert L. *An Archeology of the Soul: American Indian Belief and Ritual*. Urbana: University of Illinois Press, 1997.

Hudson, Winthrop S. *Religion in America*. 6th ed. New York: Charles Scribner's Sons, 1998.

Marty, Martin E. *Pilgrims in Their Own Land*. Boston: Little, Brown, 1984.

Melton, J. Gordon. *American Religion: An Illustrated History*. Santa Barbara, CA: ABC-CLIO, 2000.

Melton, J. Gordon, with James A. Beverley. *Melton's Encyclopedia of American Religion*. Detroit: Gale/Cengate Learning, 2009.

Murphy, Larry G., Jr., J. Gordon Melton, and Gary L. Ward, eds. *Encyclopedia of African American Religion*. New York: Garland, 1993.

Nimer, Mohamed. *The North American Muslim Resource Guide*. New York: Routledge, 2002.

Williams, Peter W. *America's Religions: From Their Origins to the Twenty-first Century*. Urbana: University of Illinois Press, 2002.

Uniting Church in Australia

The Uniting Church in Australia was formed in 1977 by the merger of the Methodist, Presbyterian, and Congregational churches. The new church became the third largest religious body in Australia, behind the Roman Catholic Church and the Anglican Church of Australia, a position it retains to the present.

Methodism began in Australia with the arrival of Samuel Leigh, a minister appointed by the Wesleyan Conference in Great Britain. His presence in Sydney was a symbol of the intention of the Conference to create a presence throughout the South Pacific. As other ministers arrived the work grew, and in 1855 the Australasian Conference was organized. In 1873 further growth (including the development of missions in several of the South Pacific islands) led to favorable reaction to a plan to divide the churches into several conferences, to be united by a general conference that would meet triennially. In 1974 the New South Wales and Queensland Conference, the Victoria and Tasmania Conference, the South and West Australia Conference, and the New Zealand Conference were established. Missions in Tonga, Fiji, and the other islands were attached to the New South Wales and Queensland Conference.

Through the 19th century, several smaller Methodist churches had been founded, but in 1902 they merged with the larger Wesleyan group to form the Methodist Church of Australasia. New Zealand was set apart as an independent church in 1913.

The first Presbyterian minister arrived in Australia in 1923, but by that time the first Presbyterian settlers, who had arrived in 1802, had built a church (1809) in Ebenezer. John Dunsmore Lang settled in Sydney and organized the Scots Church. As the work grew, in 1840 the Synod of Australia in Connection with the Established Church of Scotland was created. Almost immediately this church found itself playing out the same debates that split the Church of Scotland, and in 1846 a group separated to form the Free Presbyterian Church of Victoria. In addition, at about this same time, other Presbyterians from Great Britain began to establish work in Australia.

Through the last half of the 19th century, a desire to unite all of the Presbyterians manifested in a series

Uniting church in Brisbane, Australia. (Dannywaters/Dreamstime.com)

of mergers at the state level. Finally a national assembly met in 1901 to form the Presbyterian Church of Australia.

The Congregationalist Church of Australia grew out of the London Missionary Society (LMS), which had selected the South Pacific as its first area for concentrated missionary activity. W. T. Cook, an LMS missionary, settled in Sydney in 1809. Additional churches would be founded by other missionaries across the subcontinent, with particular strength in Melbourne and Sydney.

Initial negotiations looking toward a merger of the three churches occurred in the second decade of the 20th century. At the time it was finally consummated in 1977, the Methodists represented about 60 percent of the merged body, the Presbyterians another 30 percent, and the Congregationalists around 10 percent.

One-third of the members of the Presbyterian Church declined to enter the merger, and they continue today as the Presbyterian Church of Australia. Dissenting elements in the Congregationalist Church formed the Congregationalist Federation of Australia.

Congregations of the Uniting Church in Australia are organized into seven synods, all in Australia proper, all of the former missions in the islands having matured into independent churches in their own right. The National Assembly is the highest legislative body for the church. In the late 1990s, the church reported 1,380,000 members.

The church is ecumenically active and holds membership in the World Methodist Council, the World Alliance of Reformed Churches, and the World Council of Churches.

Uniting Church in Australia
222 Pitt St.
PO Box A2266
Sydney South, NSW 1235
Australia
http://www.uca.org.au/

J. Gordon Melton

See also: Anglican Church of Australia; London Missionary Society; Presbyterian Church of Australia; Roman Catholic Church; World Alliance of Reformed Churches; World Council of Churches; World Methodist Council.

References

Bentley, Peter, and Philip J. Hughes. *A Yearbook of Australian Religious Organizations.* Kew, Australia: Christian Research Association, 1997.

Humphreys, Robert, and Rowland Ward. *Religious Bodies in Australia: A Comprehensive Guide.* Wantima, Australia: New Melbourne Press, 1995.

Uniting Presbyterian Church in Southern Africa

The Uniting Presbyterian Church in Southern Africa was formed in 2000 by the merger of the Presbyterian

Church of Southern Africa and the Reformed Presbyterian Church of Southern Africa. The Presbyterian Church of Southern Africa traces its beginnings to a Calvinist Society formed among Scottish soldiers in South Africa in 1806. The work progressed, but units split off to affiliate with the Congregationalists. However, in 1924, a specifically Presbyterian effort went forward, connected with the United Presbyterian Church (now a constituent part of the Church of Scotland), with newly arrived settlers from Scotland as the heart of the congregation. An initial church building, St. Andrew's Church in Cape Town, opened its doors in 1828, and subsequently congregations were opened in British settlements across the land. The church spread to Zimbabwe in 1896 and shortly thereafter to Zambia.

The various congregations were organized as the Presbyterian Church in 1897. By the end of the 20th century, approximately two-thirds of its 90,000 members were white. The remainder were Native Africans, and a few were of Indian extraction.

The Reformed Presbyterian Church in Southern Africa, formerly the Bantu Presbyterian Church, was the product of missionary activity among Native Africans by different Scottish churches. It became an independent body in 1923. Its primary strength was in Natal and the region around the Cape of Good Hope. It brought some 50,000 members into the new Uniting Church.

The church is a member of the World Council of Churches and the World Alliance of Reformed Churches. The Presbyterian Church of Southern Africa had opened the ordained ministry to women in the 1970s. In 2001 the Uniting Church elected the Reverend Diane Vorsteras as moderator of its General Assembly, the first time a woman has headed a major South African Christian denomination.

Uniting Presbyterian Church in Southern Africa
Joseph Wing Centre
150 Caroline St.
PO Box 96188
Brixton
Johannesburg 2019
http://www.presbyterian.org.za

J. Gordon Melton

See also: Church of Scotland; World Alliance of Reformed Churches; World Council of Churches.

Reference

Bauswein, Jean-Jacques, and Lukas Vischner, eds. *The Reformed Family Worldwide: A Survey of Reformed Churches, Theological Schools, and International Organizations.* Grand Rapids, MI: William B. Eerdmans Publishing Company, 1999.

Uniting Reformed Church in South Africa

One of two large churches claiming the Dutch Reformed heritage within South Africa, the Uniting Church is the result of the spread of the Reformed Church within the nonwhite population of South Africa. As early as 1859 a mission began in Burgersdorp and Middleburg in the northeast corner of the Cape. Then five years later, Henru Gonin began a mission among the Kgatla people residing near Saulspoort. That same year, another missionary began work in Zoutpansberg at Kranspoort in the Transvaal. In the 1870s work spread to the Orange Free State.

As the work spread, synods were established successively in the Orange Free states (1910), Transvaal (1932), the Cape (1951), and Natal (1952). The General Synod of what was known as the Dutch Reformed Church (South Africa) was organized in 1963. The church had developed primarily among the Sozho and Nguni peoples.

In the meantime, in 1881, the Dutch Reformed Church formalized its basic segregationist stance by setting apart its nonwhite congregations into the Dutch Reformed Mission Church in South Africa. It began with four ministers, two elders, and a seminary donated by the parent body. This church grew into a large body that would become a member of the World Alliance of Reformed Churches (WARC). In 1982, as racial turmoil in South Africa was growing, the WARC passed a declaration condemning apartheid and labeling the theological defense of the practice a heresy. As a result of this statement, the Dutch Reformed Mission

Church wrote, and in 1986 adopted, a new confession of faith, the Belhar Confession, which was placed beside the traditional Reformed statements as a standard document (much as the Barmen Confession directed at the Nazi situation was adopted by the Confessing Church in Germany).

The adoption of the Belhar statement led to the development of a plan to reunite all of the Reformed churches in South Africa. This process culminated in the 1994 union of the Dutch Reformed Mission Church and the Dutch Reformed Church in Africa as the Uniting Reformed Church in South Africa. The new church has reported 1,200,000 members.

The Uniting Church is headed by its general synod. A multiethnic church, there are 11 official languages spoken within it. It is a member of both the WARC and the World Council of Churches.

Uniting Reformed Church in South Africa
Private Bag 1
Belhar 7507
South Africa
http://www.vgksa.org.za/

J. Gordon Melton

See also: Dutch Reformed Church; World Alliance of Reformed Churches; World Council of Churches.

Reference

Bauswein, Jean-Jacques, and Lukas Vischner, eds. *The Reformed Family Worldwide: A Survey of Reformed Churches, Theological Schools, and International Organizations.* Grand Rapids, MI: William B. Eerdmans Publishing Company, 1999.

Unity School of Christianity/Association of Unity Churches

Unity began in Kansas City, Missouri, in 1889, when its co-founders, Myrtle (1845–1931) and Charles (1854–1948) Fillmore, dedicated their lives to the study and teaching of what they referred to as "practical Christianity." The catalyst to its founding was Myrtle Fillmore, whose recovery (from tuberculosis) was precipitated by a lecture on mental healing in 1886. Its earliest expressions were a periodical, *Modern Thought,* later renamed *Unity,* and a prayer ministry, the Society for Silent Help, later renamed Silent Unity. Silent Unity, with a little over 2 million contacts annually (ca. 2000), continues to be a primary focus of the Unity School, and its round-the-clock prayer ministry is well known throughout the entire New Thought movement.

Originally established as a ministry of healing and publication, by the early 20th century Unity had assumed a sectarian character. Institutionalization began in 1903 with the incorporation of the Unity Society of Practical Christianity, which evolved into the Unity School of Christianity, the movement's best known organization. Over the latter half of the 20th century, Unity progressively reduced its once extensive periodical outreach, with the pocket-size daily devotional magazine, *The Daily Word* (1.3 million subscribers), its most representative periodical today. In the 1990s it discontinued publication of *Wee Wisdom* (begun in 1893), which had been the longest continually published children's magazine in the world. *Unity* magazine, which was recently changed from a monthly to a bimonthly cycle, has 23,000 subscribers. Unity School appears to remain strongly committed to book publishing, with the works of Charles and Myrtle Fillmore and numerous other authors continuing to be printed and distributed.

Unity School is located at Unity Village, Missouri, just outside Kansas City. The village is an impressive complex made up of many large buildings constructed in a generic Mediterranean style, an expansive array of fountains spanned by a "bridge of faith," ornate landscaping, and walking paths, all dominated by a massive tower, 150 feet in height. The complex is the spiritual center of the Unity movement and serves primarily as a religious education and retreat center. It houses all Unity School operations, including Silent Unity, and functions as a shrine and pilgrimage destination for the more devout of Unity followers. The school is directed by a self-perpetuating board of directors. Its current president and CEO, Charlotte Shelton, is the second leader in the 117-year history of Unity to not be a part of the founding Filmore family. The last member of the Filmore family to lead Unity was Connie Filmore Bazzy, the founders' great-granddaughter. Under the direction of Shelton, the current leadership is developing the Unity Institute with the goal of establishing an accredited center of higher learning.

Unity's second major branch is the Association of Unity Churches (AUC), founded in 1966. The Association is independent of Unity School and serves as the ecclesiastical arm of the movement. Under the leadership of a president and CEO (James Trapp), who is appointed by a board of trustees, AUC ordains and supervises ministers, sanctions churches, and coordinates expansion activities. Members of the board of trustees are elected by representatives from member churches at annual conferences. Membership statistics are not available, but increases in the number of ministries in recent years suggest steady growth. As of 2008 there were 969 active ministers and 1,047 licensed teachers serving in 939 ministries (of which 87 are Alternative ministries) and 48 affiliated study groups in 51 countries. Most notable is Unity's strong presence in Africa, especially Nigeria, where there are 63 affiliated groups.

Unity does not publish membership statistics, but increases in the number of churches indicates sustained growth over the past several decades. Total membership in Unity churches is most likely in the 100,000 range, although the number of participants is probably much higher.

Unity is the largest movement in the New Thought family and distinctive among New Thought groups in its Christian self-affirmation. It uses the Bible as a primary text, recognizing it as a "divine book of life" that "bears witness" to the word of God. Unity was once the trendsetter in the revitalization of allegorical Bible interpretation, but it has done little to advance this type of study since the 1960s. The allegorical method, called "metaphysical" interpretation in Christian Science and New Thought, approaches the text as a symbolic document, in which persons, places, and things represent elements in consciousness. Charles Fillmore's exhaustive lexicon, *Metaphysical Bible Dictionary* (1931), represents the fullest expression of this distinctive New Thought method of exegesis. In addition to the Bible, Unity's other primary religious text is H. Emilie Cady's *Lessons in Truth*, first published in 1894.

Like other early New Thought groups, Unity emerged in the context of Christian Science (as embodied in the Church of Christ, Scientist), through the work of the independent Christian Science teacher Emma Curtis Hopkins (1849–1925), a former protégé of Mary Baker Eddy (1821–1910). The Fillmores were students of Hopkins, receiving their ordination from her in 1891, and the theology of the movement shows her influence. Unity is, thus, best considered a reaction against traditional Christian Science, rather than a further extension of Eddy's system. Mental healing (or "prayer treatment"), once a prominent feature of Unity, seems to be less of a focus in the movement today, with mainstream pastoral counseling and alternative healing methods having equal or greater popularity in many churches.

As part of the New Thought movement, Unity is an expression of popular religious idealism; as such it affirms that the basis of reality is mental (not material) and that mental states determine material conditions. Characteristic of New Thought as a whole, Unity recognizes that God is Mind. Unity is non-doctrinal, although several foundational teachings are notable: (1) the absolute goodness of God and the unreality of evil; (2) the innate divinity of humanity; (3) the omnipotently causative nature of consciousness; (4) freedom of individuals in matter of belief. Unity accepts Christian doctrine, idealistically interpreted, as normative. Unity's distinctive symbol is a winged globe.

Unity School
1901 NW Blue Parkway
Unity Village, MO 64065-0001
http://www.unityworldhq.org

Association of Unity Churches
401 SW Oldham Parkway, Ste. 210
Lee's Summit, MO 64081
http://www.unity.org

Dell deChant and Natalie Hobbs

See also: Church of Christ, Scientist.

References

Albanese, Catherine L. *A Republic of Mind and Spirit.* New Haven, CT: Yale University Press, 2007.

Bach, Marcus. *The Unity Way.* Unity Village, MO: Unity Books, 1982.

Braden, Charles. *Spirits in Rebellion: The Rise and Development of New Thought.* Dallas, TX: SMU Press, 1963.

Cady, H. Emilie. *Lessons in Truth*. Unity Village, MO: Unity Books, 1975.

deChant, Dell. "New Thought." In *World Religions in America*, edited by Jacob Neusner. 4th ed. Louisville, KY: Westminster John Knox. 2009.

Freeman, James Dillet. *The Story of Unity*. Unity Village, MO: Unity Books, 1978.

Mosley, Glenn R. *New Thought, Ancient Wisdom: The History and Future of the New Thought Movement*. Philadelphia: Templeton Foundation, 2006.

Vahle, Neal. *The Spiritual Journey of Charles Fillmore: Discovering the Power Within*. West Conchohochen, PA: Templeton Foundation Press, 2008.

Universal Church of the Kingdom of God

The Universal Church of the Kingdom of God (Igreja Universal do Reino de Deus [IURD]) is a large (possibly the largest) Brazilian Pentecostal body that became controversial and a target of the anti-cult movement in the 1990s and 2000s in several European countries.

In July 1977, Edir Macedo, a Brazilian governmental employee who had subsequently joined a number of Pentecostal denominations, felt called to devote his life to full-time evangelism. With the help of four friends, he bought a former funeral home in Aboliçâo (in Greater Rio de Janeiro) and converted it into a chapel. In the first years, Macedo did not attract more than 100 followers, but success ultimately came through the medium of radio. He first bought 10 minutes' broadcasting time from both Rádio Metropolitana in Rio de Janeiro and Rádio Cacique in Sao Paulo, both popular commercial networks. The ensuing success enabled him to establish his own radio channels, followed by daily newspapers and TV networks. In 1990 he was able to purchase the popular TV Record network, thus becoming the owner of a media empire extending from Brazil to Africa and Europe. Paralleling the media growth, Macedo's church, known as the Universal Church of the Kingdom of God (IURD), drew more than 6 million members with 2,000 places of worship in 46 countries. Its largest constituency outside Brazil is in South Africa.

IURD roots are in Brazilian Pentecostalism in general, although several themes come from the Faith Movement and from popular Brazilian religiosity. It insists on demonization (against which it offers exorcisms), with demons being held responsible for most illnesses, unhappiness, and poverty. Macedo's theology has been called "post-Pentecostal" by Brazilian scholars, and it exhibits a strong degree of anti-Catholicism. In October 1995, Sérgio Von Helder, the IURD bishop of Sao Paulo, kicked a statue of the Virgin Mary during a TV show, and caused a national outcry. Macedo made an official apology to the Roman Catholic Church, but the incident had already added fuel to the fire of the controversy. IURD's TV network, TV Record, is the main rival of the powerful Brazilian network TV Globo, which has emerged as Macedo's most vocal critic. Accused of tax evasion, Macedo spent several days in jail, although he subsequently won most of his court cases.

IURD's worship style is quite noisy, and the calls for money offerings, which are often repeated several times during the same service, have elicited further criticism. IURD neither builds nor uses chapels or churches. It normally purchases movie theaters (including the historic One Million Dollar Theater in Hollywood) and converts them into chapels. In Europe, especially, local residents have complained that movie theaters are being converted into centers for what has been called a "Brazilian cult." In Porto, Portugal, for instance, mass protest led to the cancellation of a deal between IURD and the owners of a large movie theater. In Paris, as part of the current French anti-cult crusade, it was the city's own mayor who led the protest. All this, however, has not stopped the phenomenal growth of Macedo's church. Some Brazilian scholars have also noticed a gradual "Protestantization" of the church, and a cautious dialogue has been started with other Pentecostals and evangelical Protestants.

http://www.igrejauniversal.org.br/

Massimo Introvigne and PierLuigi Zoccatelli

See also: Pentecostalism; Roman Catholic Church.

References

Macedo, E. *Aliança com Deus*. Rio de Janeiro: Editora Gráfica Universal, 1993.

Macedo, E. *Apocalipse hoje*. 3rd ed. Rio de Janeiro: Editora Gráfica Universal, 1990.

Followers and supporters of the Universal Church of the Kingdom of God raise their arms in prayer as they march down a Rio de Janeiro street, January 6, 1995, protesting the government's investigation of fraud charges against the church. (AP/Wide World Photos)

Macedo, E. *Vida com abundância*. Rio de Janeiro: Editora Gráfica Universal, 1990.

Ruuth, Anders. *Igreja Universal do Reino de Deus: Gudsrikets Universella Kyrka, en brasiliansk kyrkobildning*. Stockholm: Almqvist and Wiksell, 1995.

Universal Faithists of Kosmon

The Universal Faithists of Kosmon are dedicated to the teachings of Oahspe, an alternative Bible channeled by Dr. John Ballou Newbrough (1828–1891). Newbrough, a New York City dentist and Spiritualist medium, rose before dawn every morning for 50 weeks during 1881, and through the process of automatic writing he produced Oahspe. The book was published in 1882. Oahspe tells the history of humanity's life on Earth from the viewpoint of "highly evolved intelligent beings," and it adapts spiritual truths for the "New Kosmon Age."

Oahspe (according to the book itself, a compound word from the ancient Panic language meaning Earth, *O*; sky, *AH*; and spirit, *SPE*) claims "to teach HOW TO ATTAIN TO HEAR THE CREATOR'S VOICE, and to see HIS HEAVENS, in full consciousness, whilst still living on the earth." The creator, Jehovih, sent nine demigods to rule over periods of the Earth's history. These periods provide the structure of Oahspe. The history of humanity and religion involve the attempts of 11 prophets—including Zarathustra the Persian, the first prophet to give written revelations; Chine of

China; Eawahtah of North America; and Joshu (Jesus) —to teach truth to humanity. Oahspe teaches that we are now in the Kosmon Era, in which Jehovih's kingdom will be established on Earth, bringing peace and prosperity to all.

Among the first events associated with Oahspe was the founding of a commune in New Mexico to care for orphans, the Shalam Colony. Newbrough had met a wealthy Quaker named Andrew Howland. Howland eventually purchased nearly 1,500 acres of land in the Mesilla Valley, and there the Shalam Colony began. Howland poured money into the colony, and for a short time it apparently flourished. However, a combination of drought, financial difficulties, the death of Newbrough in 1891, and floods proved to be too much, and Howland left the colony in 1901. He finally sold the property in 1907. Despite these difficulties, small groups of people known as Faithists persisted in their devotion to Oahspe, and the book has managed to stay in print ever since.

A notable development on the international front is the work of Faithists in Britain to keep in print a book of ritual and liturgy, *The Kosmon Church Service Book*, for followers of Oahspe. The book details liturgies for weddings, baptisms, and funerals, in addition to the forms for regular worship. The British Faithists also offer ministerial training. Other groups of Faithists are found in Canada, Holland, Australia, New Zealand, Nigeria, and Ghana, in addition to the United States and Britain.

Networks of the faithful seem to be mostly informal, and the Internet and email have emerged as the primary means of communication among Oahspe enthusiasts. The total number of adherents among the various groups is not known. The Universal Faithist of Kosmon website has disappeared and contact is primarily through several Yahoo groups: http://groups.yahoo.com/group/faithist society and http://groups.yahoo.com/group/ufkchurch. Surveying the few remaining Oahspe sites on the Internet as of 2009 indicates that as many as a dozen may be active. Besides the several versions of Oahspe that are currently in print, several Internet sites have the full text of Oahspe available for downloading.

Universal Faithists of Kosmon
c/o C. Vostek, Secretary

3439 Grand Valley Canal Rd.
Clifton, CO 81520
http://OahspeResources.mccooknet.com
http://www.angelfire.com/in2/oahspe3/oindex.html
(text of Oahspe)

Jeremy Rapport

References
Horst, Laura. *A Condensed Version of Oahspe.* Amherst, WI: Palmer, 1977.
Oahspe: A New Bible. Los Angeles: Kosmon, 1942.
Simundson, Daniel Nathan. "John Ballou Newbrough and the Oahspe Bible." Ph.D. diss., University of New Mexico, 1972.
Wentworth, Jim. *Giants in the Earth: The Amazing Story of Ray Palmer, Oahspe and the Shaver Mystery.* Amherst, WI: Palmer Publications, 1973.

Universal Fellowship of Metropolitan Community Churches

The Universal Fellowship of Metropolitan Community Churches is the only intercontinental religious community especially designed to serve the gay/lesbian/bisexual/transgender (GLBT) community that emerged in the last decades of the 20th century. The fellowship began out of the experiences of Troy Perry, a former pastor in the Church of God of Prophecy, a prominent Pentecostal denomination. Perry discovered his homosexuality as a young man, but he repressed it and became a husband and father and a Pentecostal minister in Southern California. However, in the mid-1960s, his homosexuality became public; he was forced to resign his ministry, and his marriage ended in divorce.

Having accepted his homosexuality, Perry was still a Christian with a call to the ministry. In 1968, with the support of a few friends, he placed an advertisement in *The Advocate*, then the most popular periodical within the lesbian and gay community in Los Angeles, inviting people to worship with him in his living room, which served as the first Metropolitan Community Church. From this point on, the church experienced what to many was surprising growth, as

Members of the Metropolitan Community Church of Los Angeles wave to the crowd while carrying a large rainbow flag as they make their way down Santa Monica Blvd., June 22, 1997, in West Hollywood, California. Thousands of people lined the parade route to celebrate the closing day of the Christopher Street West Los Angeles Gay and Lesbian Pride Festival. (AP/Wide World Photos)

laypeople who no longer felt at home in the church of their childhood adhered to the new congregation. The church then spread to other cities, as clergy whose homosexuality had become public left their denominations and aligned with the Metropolitan Community Church. Perry began the church as a Pentecostal congregation, but as other ministers with different backgrounds joined him, the fellowship took on a more ecumenical stance. As the church gained the trust and support of the gay community, it gained a new level of visibility, especially after the publication of Perry's autobiography in 1987.

Although the fellowship generally acknowledges the central affirmations of Christianity, the keystone of its theology is God's love and acceptance of all people, especially those who have a minority self-identification as gay, lesbian, bisexual, or transgender. Almost from the beginning, the church has blessed the union of gay and lesbian couples who are living in a long-term committed relationship, analogous to traditional marriage. Just as mainline Protestants have reinterpreted as cultural accretions the biblical statements seeming to approve slavery and the subjection

of women, so the Metropolitan Community churches treat the biblical anti-homosexual passages as expressions of human, not divine, judgment.

The emergence of the Metropolitan Church has followed the rise of a visible gay community in most urban centers in the West. The history of the developing GLBT community has been marked by resistance, and the church's congregational buildings have on several occasions been targets of antigay forces, who burned them. The church was also hit by the AIDS epidemic, and in 1985 it launched a special ministry to people with AIDS. A major component of this ministry has involved alerting other churches to the seriousness of the problem.

Through the 1990s the church became a global fellowship, currently organized into 7 regions, and the more than 300 congregations are now found in 24 countries around the world. After many years of leading the church, Troy Perry formally retired as moderator in 2005. Reverend Nancy Wilson was elected as the new (and current) moderator. Soon afterward, the church moved its headquarters from Los Angeles to Texas.

The issue of acceptance has been a constant part of the church's existence. It applied for membership in the National Council of Churches in the U.S.A. (1992), but was refused both membership and observer status, though it has been admitted to several councils of churches at the state level. It was granted observer status by the World Council of Churches in 1991. More recently (2002), it was authorized to provide chaplains for the various facilities of the U.S. Veterans Administration. Members have yet to be considered for slots among the chaplains of the armed services.

Universal Fellowship of Metropolitan Community
Churches
PO Box 1374
Abilene, TX 79604
http://www.ufmcc.com/

J. Gordon Melton

See also: Church of God of Prophecy; Homosexuality.

References

Eastman, Donald. *Not a Sin, Not a Sickness: What the Bible Does and Does Not Say.* Los Angeles: UFMCC, 1990.

Perry, Troy. *Don't Be Afraid Anymore.* New York: St. Martin's Press, 1992.

Perry, Troy, with Thomas L. P. Swicegood. *The Lord Is My Shepherd and He Knows I'm Gay.* New York: Bantam Books, 1978.

Perry, Troy, and Thomas L. P. Swicegood, eds. *Profiles in Gay and Lesbian Courage.* New York: St. Martin's Press, 1992.

Troy Perry: Pastor and Prophet. Los Angeles: Metropolitan Community Churches, 2005.

Wilcox, Melissa M. "Of Markets and Missions: The Early History of the Universal Fellowship of Metropolitan Community Churches." *Religion and American Culture* 11 (Winter 2001): 83–108.

Wilson, Nancy L. *Our Story Too: Lesbians and Gay Men in the Bible.* Los Angeles: UFMCC, 1992.

Universal Great Brotherhood

The Universal Great Brotherhood (UGB) was founded in Venezuela in 1948 by Serge Raynaud de la Ferriere (1916–1962) and his student, Jose Manuel Estrada (1900–1982). De la Ferriere developed an interest in Esotericism as a young man. Among his early experiences, he traveled to Egypt, where he underwent a mystical initiation as the "Sublime Crowned Cophto and Great Priest Khediviar." He also was active in the Theosophical Society in both England and France. At one point he had an encounter with a being known as Master Sun Wu King, who gave him his mission to present the initiatic principles to the public. He founded the Universal Great Brotherhood as World War II was drawing to a close and spent the postwar years traveling and establishing UGB centers.

At one point his travels took him to Venezuela, where he met Estrada, who had for almost a decade been proclaiming the imminent coming of an avatar (an incarnation of God) and who had gathered a group to await his arrival. Estrada identified de la Ferriere as that avatar and became his disciple. In 1948 the pair reopened the Great Universal Brotherhood as a new public organization. Two years later de la Ferriere retired to spend the rest of his life engaged in Esoteric work. Estrada became the director general and began to build the organization internationally.

The Brotherhood is an initiatic association designed to assist the transition of society into a new age (the Aquarian Age). This new age will be born in the Western Hemisphere. To facilitate the coming new age, the Brotherhood carries on a two-part program. It offers various programs for the general public of preinitiates. It sponsors healthcare services; advocates vegetarianism; and teaches yoga, astrology, martial arts, and meditation. It invites people to a program of mystical initiation, in which initiates become parts of ashrams that are seen as centers of physical and spiritual mastery and people learn to live in harmony with natural law. Members form a nucleus of those who work for harmony and world peace, and the ashrams become training grounds for the commissioning of missionaries who will go out in the world to spread the word of the coming new age.

The Brotherhood has spread to most of the Spanish-speaking countries of South and Central America and beyond to the United States, Canada, Japan, Australia, Europe, and Israel. The UGB has been named as an associated nongovernmental organization by the

United Nations. In 1962, leadership of the Brotherhood passed to Jose Manuel Estrada, and following his death in 1982 the order has evolved into a more decentralized network of students of Serge Raynaud and Estrada who now function as gurus (teachers) including Guru Pedro Enciso, Guru Juan Victor Mejias, Guru Carlos Elias Michan, and Guru Domingo Dias Porta.

Universal Great Brotherhood
Box Postcard 3987
Caracas 1010-A
Venezuela
http://www.maestre.org/english.htm
http://www.aquarius-studiesenter.no/e/ugbnorway
.html (Norwegian center, in English)

J. Gordon Melton

See also: Astrology; Meditation; Theosophical Society (America); Vegetarianism; Yoga.

References
Biography, the Sublime Master, Sat Guru Dr. Serge Raymaud de la Ferriere. St. Louis, MO: Educational Publications of the I.E.S., 1976.
Montero-Campion, Anita. *My Guru from South America: Sat Arhat Dr. Jose Manuel Estrada.* St. Louis, MO: privately printed, 1976.

Universal Life

Universal Life (Universelles Leben) is a German new religious movement that claims to re-enact the original Christianity of the Apostles in the modern world, on the basis of the Ten Commandments and Jesus' Sermon on the Mount. Members are persuaded that the Holy Spirit is speaking again, through a new prophet, Gabriele Wittek, who was born in 1933 near Augsburg, Germany, and raised as a traditional Roman Catholic. In 1970 her mother's death precipitated in her a spiritual crisis of some impact. Later, we are told, Wittek's deceased mother started to appear to her daughter, until on January 6, 1975, Gabriele began to hear the "internal word." Within this "word" she received instructions from "Brother Emmanuel" and Christ himself. They asked her to spread their teachings (increasingly at odds with Wittek's early Catholi-

cism), at first to small groups and then in large meetings in Europe's main cities, the first being held in Nürnberg on January 22, 1977. In 1976 her followers founded the Heimholungswerk Jesu Christi (Homebringing Mission of Jesus Christ), which in 1984 was renamed Universal Life.

Wittek teaches what she calls an "internal way," rooted in the idea of the soul's pre-existence in the spiritual world. Based on karma, the soul should experience several incarnations, until it becomes purified and able to escape the wheel of reincarnation. In Wittek's universalist theology, mainline Christian notions of eternal punishment and hell are also rejected. Because of their pride, the original souls fell outside the divine realm, thus generating the material world. In order to remind the souls of their divine origin, the Son of God incarnated as Jesus of Nazareth, and will soon become incarnate again. According to Wittek, all these teachings were originally included in the Bible, but they have been corrupted by the churches throughout the centuries, thus making it necessary for the Holy Spirit to speak again in our time through Universal Life.

Some 700 members of Universal Life live communally near Würzburg, Germany, in a large community complex including a school, two hospitals, retirement homes, as well as manufacturing and agricultural facilities. This community is regarded as the first seed of Christ's future kingdom of peace on Earth. Several thousand members, however, do not live in the Würzburg community but regularly visit some 80 centers throughout Germany, other parts of Europe, and the world. Universal Life also owns several radio networks worldwide.

Universelles Leben
Postfach 5643
97066 Würzburg
Germany
http://www.universelles-leben.org

Massimo Introvigne and PierLuigi Zoccatelli

See also: Reincarnation.

References
Healing by Faith—The Holistic Healing. Guilford, CT: The Word, 2000.

This Is My Word, Alpha and Omega: The Gospel of Jesus—A Christ-Revelation which the World Does Not Know. 2nd English ed. Guilford, CT: The Word, 2001.

The Word. Guilford, CT: The Word, 2001.

Universal Soul

Universal Soul is an Italian new religious movement headquartered in Leinì, near Turin, Piedmont. Its founder was Roberto Casarin, born in Turin on April 9, 1963. As a young man, Casarin was a pious Roman Catholic who became well known for his mystical visions and for his gift of healing. Thousands of Catholics congregated in Turin to hear Casarin pray the Rosary, in the hope of being healed by the young visionary. The local Catholic hierarchy, on the other hand, was quite hostile to his success, culminating in the declaration by Anastasio Alberto Cardinal Ballestrero (1913–1998), archbishop of Turin, on June 15, 1982, that Casarin's meetings would henceforth be banned. They continued, nonetheless, and on February 26, 1984, an independent organization was founded known as Associazione Cristo nell'Uomo—Centro di Elevazione Spirituale (Christ in Man Association—Center for Spiritual Elevation).

Casarin's teachings evolved toward the idea of a "God for all people," with a critical view of organized religion as a divisive and controversial factor. From 1985 on it became evident that Casarin's was an independent religious movement, with no remaining links with the Roman Catholic Church. Some of the most active members of Casarin's association later created Comunità Impegno (Community Engagement), which in turn led to the establishment of the Church of the New Jerusalem in 1989. The final separation of the movement from the Catholic Church was confirmed by a declaration published on March 21, 1990, by Ballestrero's successor as archbishop of Turin, Giovanni Cardinal Saldarini. Catholic critics, as well as a former priest of the Church of the New Jerusalem turned vocal opponent, provoked a media campaign against Casarin, centering inter alia on his teachings on sexual ethics, including his tolerance of homosexuality. In fact, these themes play no particularly important role in Casarin's preaching and writings. In 1996, in order to prevent confusion with other movements with similar names, the Church of the New Jerusalem changed its name to Anima Universale—Movimento di Unione Spirituale (Universal Soul—Movement for Spiritual Union), a name also regarded as conveying the essence of the movement's teachings.

As the new century began, Casarin developed a quite eclectic approach. He asserts that humans have forgotten their divine origin and are living under the veil of material illusion. Universal Soul's rituals remind humans of their true divine nature, thereby developing their love toward God and to all their fellow human beings, as well as developing their spiritual awareness. Rituals include baptisms, weddings, funerals, collective meditations and prayers, "rituals of the elements," and "celebrations of mantras." The rituals are led by the priests and priestesses of the Universal Soul, known as Ramias, all of whom are full-time members living communally in the Universal Soul Centers. A particular feature of the Universal Soul is its ability to raise substantial funds for charitable activities, which are then given to humanitarian groups and Third World charities (mostly Roman Catholic, in Africa and India) that are not associated with Casarin's movement. This massive humanitarian effort has received some grudging acknowledgment even by some of the movement's critics. From the original centers, all located in the Italian region of Piedmont, the movement spread to the Venetian area and to the Province of Ancona in central Italy. The construction of a temple in Poggiana di Riese Pio X (in the Italian province of Treviso, Venetian region) generated, in 1999 and 2000, new controversies. The local Catholic Church and some local politicians opposed the construction, calling the movement a "cult." The conflict between the Universal Soul and the Roman Catholic Church appears, at times, paradoxical. Without always acknowledging it, in fact, Casarin and his Roman Catholic critics seem to agree on the one essential issue—that Universal Soul is a new religious experience and not part of Roman Catholicism.

Universal Soul
Via Enrico Mattei 60
10060 Leinì (Torino)

Italy

http://www.animauniversale.it

Massimo Introvigne and PierLuigi Zoccatelli

See also: Roman Catholic Church.

References

Casarin, Roberto. *Ascoltando il Maestro. Insegnamenti di Swami Roberto.* 2 vols. Leinì (Turin): Anima Universale, 2003 and 2007.

Casarin, Roberto. *In questa parte di Eternità Dio si fa tempo per me. Preghiamo insieme.* Turin: CAST, 1997.

Casarin, Roberto. *La Missione dell'Uno. Unione Energetica d'Amore.* Turin: CAST, 1999.

Conti, Paolo. *Un personaggio scomodo. Roberto Casarin. Intervista ad un Maestro della Nuova Era.* Volpago (Treviso): Tipografia Volpaghese, 1994.

Roldán, Verónica. *La Chiesa Anima Universale di Roberto Casarin.* Leumann (Turin): ElleDiCi, 2000.

Zoccatelli, Pier Luigi. "Symbols in the Church of Universal Soul." Paper presented at the 14th International Conference of the Center for Studies on New Religions (CESNUR), Riga (Latvia), August 29–31, 2000. http://www.cesnur.org/conferences/riga2000/plz.htm. Accessed March 1, 2009.

URANTIA Foundation, The

The URANTIA Foundation exists to promote *The URANTIA Book*, a work believed to have been received from an advanced group of beings known as the Orvonton Commission in order to clear up confusion about the nature of God, divinity, and deity on Urantia, the beings' name for Earth. The book claims to tell an "alternate" history of Christianity, the Earth, and the universe. *The URANTIA Book* is divided into four major parts: Part I, "The Central and Superuniverses," describes the nature of the ultimate God and the organization of the universe. Part II, "The Local Universe," describes the immediate vicinity of our planet, Urantia. The history of Urantia, the Earth, is the subject of Part III, and Part IV retells the story of Jesus. Jesus'

real name is Michael. He was born on August 21 in the year 7 BCE, was well educated, and became a skilled carpenter. He conducted a ministry around the Mediterranean for three years beginning in 27 CE and was then crucified and resurrected. According to the Foundation's website, the book's message is that "all human beings are one family, the sons and daughters of one God, the Universal Father." *The URANTIA Book* also reveals "new concepts of Man's ever-ascending adventure of finding the Universal Father in our friendly and carefully administered universe."

According to the Foundation's own account, the origins of *The URANTIA Book* lie in the early 20th century, when a Chicago physician, William S. Sadler (1875–1969), announced that he was the head of the Contact Commission. The Contact Commission transcribed the contents of the book and then presented them to the Forum, a group meeting at Sadler's house that critiqued the papers and presented questions to be answered. The final text of *The URANTIA Book* incorporates the answers to the questions of the Forum. The group that made up the Forum became the core of believers committed to bringing *The URANTIA Book* to all humans. The URANTIA Foundation, a nonprofit, educational foundation operating under a Declaration of Trust, was established in 1950 to be the custodian of the book and to help spread its teachings. The first printing of *The Urantia Book* appeared in 1955.

Fully staffed offices affiliated with the Foundation can be found in Canada, Australia, Finland, Chile, France, England, and Russia. Smaller offices may be found in 18 other countries, including Argentina, Brazil, Belgium, Colombia, Ecuador, Greece, Korea, Mexico, Senegal, and Venezuela. According to *The URANTIA Book*, "The religious challenge of this age is to those farseeing and forward-looking men and women of spiritual insight who will dare to construct a new and appealing philosophy of living out of the enlarged and exquisitely integrated modern concepts of cosmic truth, universal beauty, and divine goodness." The various Foundation offices help to foster this goal in many ways, including facilitating local study groups. The study groups are the primary means of disseminating the teachings of *The URANTIA Book*.

In addition to the 400,000 paperback copies of the book in circulation, the URANTIA Foundation has made extensive use of the Internet. The Foundation's website is large and very well organized. *The URANTIA Book* is available online through the Foundation's website. The Foundation operates an Internet correspondence school, and it is putting a great deal of work into further translations of *The URANTIA Book*. Currently (2009) French, Finnish, Spanish, Russian, Dutch, Korean, Lithuanian, Portuguese, and German versions of the book exist, with further translations into Arabic, Bulgarian, Chinese, Croatian, Estonian, Farsi, Indonesian, Italian, Lithuanian, Polish, Romanian, and Swedish in the process of completion.

An important milestone in the Foundation's work was reached in 2006, when the international copyright to the original English text of *The URANTIA Book* (published in 1955), though not the copyrights of the book in languages other than English, expired. Following that event, the Trustees of the Urantia Foundation have moved to delete the 1955 copyright notice from the English text of *The URANTIA Book* on the Foundation's website, and it will not appear on future published editions.

The URANTIA Foundation
533 Diversey Parkway
Chicago, IL 60614
http://www.urantia.org

Jeremy Rapport

References

Gardner, Martin. *Urantia: The Great Cult Mystery*. New York: Prometheus Books, 1995.

Moyer, Ernest P. *The Birth of a Divine Revelation: The Origin of the URANTIA Papers*. Hanover, PA: Moyer Publishing, 2000. http://www.world-destiny.org/birth/cvrF.pdf. Accessed April 24, 2009.

Sadler, William S. "A History of the URANTIA Movement." http://www.urantia.org/pub/ahotum.html. Accessed April 24, 2009.

The URANTIA Book. Chicago: URANTIA Foundation, 1955.

The URANTIA Book Concordance. Chicago: URANTIA Foundation, 1993.

Ursulines

The Ursulines, officially the Order of Saint Ursula, one of the more important orders that assisted the spread of the Roman Catholic Church in the modern world, was founded at Brescia, Italy, in 1535, by Angela Merici (1474–1540), with an initial purpose of providing education for young girls. Saint Ursula, considered the patroness of education, was chosen as the protecting saint. Angela began with 28 associates as an informal company, and the members continued to live at home. A primitive rule was accepted by the pope in 1544. Then in the 1580s, Charles Borromeo, the bishop of Milan, requested a change in the rule: that the members of the company begin to live in a community and accept a vow of poverty. That rule change was accepted in 1585.

The new rule was first adopted by the sisters in France, where the group experienced its greatest response. In 1612 the community in Paris was recognized as being in a monastic state. By the end of the century, there were 350 Ursuline monastic communities in France with 9,000 residents. They remained strong in France even with the disturbances of the French Revolution.

The Order began to expand internationally from its bases in Paris and Bordeaux. In 1639, Marie of the Incarnation and two other sisters became the first Ursulines in the Western Hemisphere when they landed in Quebec and opened a convent and school for girls. A second beginning was made in New Orleans in 1727, from which the Order spread to Cuba and Texas. From this beginning convent schools were opened at various locations in the United States and around the world in Indonesia, Brazil, India, the Belgian Congo, and Australia. In the meantime, the Order had found its way across Europe, where they pioneered female education in many areas.

Angela Merici was canonized in 1807. Her feast day was added to the church's calendar of saints in 1861. The usual date would have been her death day, January 27. That day was, however, already designated as the feast day of Saint John Chrysostom. Saint Angela was assigned May 31. Then in 1955, Pope Pius XI (r. 1939–1958) designated May 31 as the new feast

Sister Teresita Rivet, of the Order of St. Ursula, helps Lauren Songy, five, with her French counting lesson in New Orleans, 2006. (AP/Wide World Photos)

day for the Blessed Virgin Mary, Queen. Saint Angela's day was moved to June 1. Finally in 1969, it was moved to her death date, January 27, by Pope Paul VI (r. 1963–1978).

The loosely organized Ursulines underwent a significant reorganization in 1900, when Pope Leo XIII (r. 1879–1903) unified the work under a new corporation headed by a superior general. The new corporate title was the Roman Union of the Order of Saint Ursula. The motherhouse was established in Rome. The Order was divided into national provinces. The prioress general and the other international officers are elected at the meeting of the general chapter, held in Rome every six years.

There are more than 200 houses (convents) in more than 25 countries. The more than 7,000 sisters oversee not only primary and secondary schools for girls but also several colleges for women.

There are also a variety of smaller groups that are known as Ursulines, which either did not participate in the formation of the Roman Union or have been organized apart from it. Among these are the Ursuline Union of Eastern Canada, which originated with Sister Marie of the Incarnation and the original Ursuline convent in North America. They are organized in a fashion similar to that of the Roman Union, but did not affiliate with it. Their superior general resides in Quebec. The Ursulines of Belgium began in 1831 at Tildonk and spread across the country in the middle of the 19th century. During the last half of the century, the groups spread to England, the Netherlands, South Africa, and Indonesia. An American house opened in New York in 1924. Headquarters are now at Haecht, Belgium. Work in South Africa and Indonesia has been replaced with centers more recently established in the Democratic Republic of the Congo and India.

Order of St. Ursula
Via Nomentana 236
I-00162 Roma
Italy

J. Gordon Melton

See also: Roman Catholic Church; Saints.

References

Aron, Marguerite. *Les Ursulines*. Paris: Grasset, Les grands ordres monastiques et instituts religieux, 1937.

Caraman, Philip. *St. Angela: The Life of Angela Merici, Foundress of the Ursulines*. London: Longman, 1963.

Clark, Emily. *Masterless Mistresses: The New Orleans Ursulines and the Development of a New World Society, 1727–1834*. Chapel Hill: University of North Carolina Press, 2007.

Kane, Harnett T. *The Ursulines, Nuns of Adventure: The Story of the New Orleans Community*. New York: Farrar, Straus, 1959.

Mazzonis, Querciolo. *Spirituality, Gender, and the Self in Renaissance Italy: Angela Merici and the Company of St. Ursula (1474–1540)*. Washington, DC: Catholic University of America Press, 2007.

■ Uruguay

The Oriental Republic of Uruguay is located on the Atlantic Coast of South America, at the mouth of the Río de la Plata, between Argentina and Brazil. This small country only has 68,039 square miles of land with a population of approximately 3.4 million (2008). The terrain of Uruguay is similar to that of the Argentina pampas, where raising livestock (cattle and sheep) is the principal activity. A continuing problem is that, in reality, there are two Uruguays, not one. One is the Montevideo metro area, with about one-third of the population and with most of the services and privileges of civilization. The other Uruguay is the back country where life is rough and hard, and where the public services are meager and distant.

The inhabitants of Uruguay are predominantly white (about 88 percent) and largely of European origin, mostly Spanish and Italian, but some are descended from Portuguese, English, or other European nationalities. Mestizos (mixed white and Amerindian) represent about 8 percent of the population, and mulattoes and blacks about 4 percent. The indigenous Charrúa were virtually wiped out early in the Spanish colonial era.

Originally identified as a Roman Catholic country, the church and state have been separate since 1919, and the 1966 Constitution guarantees freedom of religion to all inhabitants. The number of Catholic adherents in Uruguay has declined noticeably since 1900. Today, Uruguay is considered the second most secularized nation in Latin America, after the Socialist Republic of Cuba.

According to the 2006 National Housing Survey conducted by the Uruguayan National Institute of Statistics, only 47.1 percent of the population identified themselves as Roman Catholic, while 40.4 percent professed no religious faith whatsoever; the latter includes those who "believe in God but without religion" (23.2 percent) and those claiming to be atheist or agnostic (17.2 percent). Only 11.1 percent identified as "non-Catholic Christians" (includes Eastern Orthodox, Protestant, and others); 0.6 percent as followers of Umbanda or other Afro-Brazilian religions; 0.3 percent as Jewish; and 0.4 percent as adherents of "other religions." However, it should be noted that most prac-

Uruguay

Religion	Followers in 1970	Followers in 2010	% of Population	Annual % growth 2000–2010	Followers in 2025	Followers in 2050
Christians	1,903,000	2,155,000	63.9	−0.08	2,138,000	2,117,000
Roman Catholics	2,115,000	2,300,000	68.2	−0.72	2,218,000	2,117,000
Marginals	24,600	120,000	3.6	1.66	150,000	180,000
Protestants	57,100	110,000	3.3	2.35	140,000	180,000
Agnostics	791,000	950,000	28.2	0.35	1,100,000	1,180,000
Atheists	57,000	213,000	6.3	0.05	250,000	280,000
Jews	52,000	41,000	1.2	0.05	41,000	41,000
Baha'is	3,400	7,500	0.2	0.04	10,000	11,500
Spiritists	1,500	4,700	0.1	0.04	5,500	6,300
New religionists	500	2,000	0.1	0.04	3,000	3,500
Muslims	300	530	0.0	0.04	800	1,000
Buddhists	0	70	0.0	0.00	100	150
Ethnoreligionists	0	40	0.0	0.00	60	100
Total population	**2,808,000**	**3,374,000**	**100.0**	**0.05**	**3,548,000**	**3,641,000**

titioners of Afro-Brazilian religions also self-identify as Roman Catholics due to the syncretistic nature of "popular Catholicism."

According to Latinobarómetro (a public opinion polling organization based in Santiago, Chile), the evangelical proportion of the Uruguayan population increased from 6.8 percent in 1996 to 9.4 percent in 2006.

Archaeological evidence points to the habitation of the eastern shore of the Uruguay River, which marks the boundary between modern Argentina and Uruguay, for at least 10,000 years. Modern history, however, begins in 1527, when Capitan Sebastián Gaboto (or Caboto, ca. 1484–1557) and his Spanish crew sailed up the Uruguay River. At that time, three Amerindian groups—the Charrúa, the Chanaes, and the Guaraní—dominated the area. The Spanish arrived in the territory of present-day Uruguay in 1516, but the Amerindians' fierce resistance to conquest, combined with the absence of gold and silver, limited settlement in the region during the 16th and 17th centuries.

The Spanish paid little attention to this region until, in 1603, the governor of Asunción (Paraguay) introduced cattle into what proved to be good pasture land. The addition of cattle and horses to the native habitat proved a major step in its transformation—cattle, in particular, drove out other mammals and the conversion of the natural habitat to grazing land altered the

local flora. The Spanish founded their first permanent Spanish settlement in Uruguayan territory in 1624 at Soriano on the Río Negro, while the Portuguese founded their first settlement at Colonia del Sacramento in 1680.

Increased Portuguese settlement on the lower coast of South America led the Spanish to assert their hegemony over the area. In 1724, Spanish authorities founded a military fortress at the entrance of the Río de la Plata, where the city of Montevideo now exists, and the territory of Uruguay was incorporated into the Viceroyalty of Peru. In 1776, the Spanish created the Viceroyalty of Río de la Plata, which included the territory now comprising Argentina, Uruguay, Paraguay, and Bolivia.

The decision to create a fourth viceroyalty was a result both of the Spanish Crown's desire to decentralize the rule of his Spanish-American empire and of a recognition that the area south of Brazil required greater military defenses in view of Portuguese encroachments along the northern shore of the Río de la Plata. Spain also wanted to curtail contraband trade between Portuguese ports in Brazil and the Spanish port of Buenos Aires in Argentina.

In 1811, José Gervasio Artigas (1764–1850), who became Uruguay's national hero, launched a successful revolt against Spain, defeating Spanish forces on May 18 in the Battle of Las Piedras. Addressing the 1813 Constitutional Convention, Artigas stated that he openly favored religious liberty for all. In 1814, Artigas formed the Federal League of which he was declared Protector. However, Uruguay did not win its final independence until 1828, following a three-way armed struggle between Spain, Argentina, and Brazil for control of its territory, called the Eastern Province. The nation's first Constitution was adopted on July 18, 1830. During the remainder of the 19th century, Uruguay experienced a series of elected and appointed presidents; interventions and conflicts with neighboring states; political and economic fluctuations; and large inflows of immigrants, mostly from Europe.

Uruguay's political landscape was divided between two parties, the Conservative Blancos (wore white armbands) and the Liberal Colorados (wore red armbands). The Colorados were led by José Fructuoso Rivera (1789–ca. 1854), the nation's first president (r. 1830–1834, and again 1839–1843), who represented the business interests of Montevideo; the Blancos were headed by Manuel Oribe (1792–1857, president between 1835 and 1838), who looked after the agricultural interests of the countryside and promoted protectionism. The Uruguayan parties became associated with warring political factions in neighboring Argentina. The Colorados favored the exiled Liberal Argentine Unitarios, many of whom had taken refuge in Montevideo, while Oribe was a close friend of the Conservative Argentine ruler, Juan Manuel de Rosas.

In 1838, President Oribe was forced to resign by former President Rivera, but Oribe organized a rebel army and began a civil war, called La Guerra Grande, in 1839 that lasted until 1852. After a nine-year siege of Montevideo, Oribe was defeated in 1852 with help from Brazil and Argentine rebels who opposed Oribe's principal supporter, Manuel de Rosas in Argentina. Rosas was a conservative politician who governed Argentina's Buenos Aires Province from 1829 to 1832, and again from 1835 to 1852. Rosas was one of the first famous *caudillos* (strongmen) in Latin America. During his rule, he united Argentina, provided an efficient government, and strengthened the economy.

The economy greatly improved after the La Guerra Grande, due to livestock raising and export. Between 1860 and 1868, the number of sheep in the country rose from 3 to 17 million, because of improved methods of husbandry introduced by European immigrants.

Montevideo became a major economic center for the Río de la Plata region. Thanks to its natural harbor, Montevideo became a major port for the trans-shipment of goods to and from Argentina, Brazil, and Paraguay.

Economic development accelerated during the latter part of the 19th century as increasing numbers of immigrants established businesses and bought land in Uruguay. Partly through their efforts, sheep were introduced to graze together with cattle, ranches were fenced, and pedigreed bulls and rams were imported to improve the quality of livestock. Earnings from the export of wool (which became the leading export in 1884), hides, and dried beef encouraged the British to invest in railroad construction and in the modernization of Montevideo, notably in its public utilities and transportation system, which encouraged additional immigration.

The Liberal Colorado Party, representing both Liberal and Social Democratic traditions, is responsible for developing Uruguay as a welfare state financed by cattle export revenues; it has governed the nation during most of its history since independence. Its roots are in the port city of Montevideo, the new immigrants of Italian origin, and the backing of foreign commercial interests. The Conservative National Party (Blancos), later affiliated with the Christian Democrat movement, represents the interests of the nation's large agricultural producers, the Catholic clergy, and commercial interests.

José Batlle y Ordoñez (1856–1929) of the Colorado Party governed as president from 1903 to 1907 and again from 1911 to 1915. He is credited with creating the modern Uruguayan state and redistributing much of the land previously controlled by a small group of large landowners. His leadership coincided with a period of economic prosperity, and the immigration of a large number of Europeans led to the spread of democratic values. He and his newspaper, *El Día*, were frankly anticlerical, and Batlle was responsible for severing the ties between church and state in 1916, and for banning clerics from controlling public schools. As a result, the active Catholic sector of the population is small and the majority of the people seem quite indifferent to religion.

The nation's economic growth slowed between 1955 and 1961 because Uruguay consumed 87 percent of its national income, which left a scant 13 percent for investment in the nation's infrastructure. The public payrolls were overloaded by the mid-1960s: government agencies and state-owned corporations were burdened with one-fourth of the country's jobs and under constant pressure from labor unions and politicians to multiply jobs without regard to efficiency. By the late 1960s, Uruguay began experiencing serious economic problems, which included inflation, mass unemployment, and a sudden drop in the workers' standard of living, partly because of a decrease in demand in the world market for agricultural products.

President Jorge Pacheco Areco (r. 1967–1972) of the Colorado Party, upon assuming office, immediately implemented price and wage freezes in an attempt to control inflation, and enforced a state of emergency in June 1968 due to growing student militancy and labor unrest. Constitutional safeguards were repealed during his term in office, and the government allegedly used torture during interrogations, brutally repressed demonstrations, and imprisoned political dissidents.

In response to the constitutional crisis and human rights abuses by the government, and increasing inflation and corruption in the business sector, a group of students formed the Tupamaro revolutionary movement, also known as the Movimiento de Liberación Nacional (MLN)—National Liberation Movement—and instituted a campaign of urban guerrilla warfare. The Tupamaros kidnapped and later released several foreign nationals, robbed banks and distributed food and money in poor neighborhoods, freed political prisoners, attacked public security forces, and assassinated police officials. Their efforts succeeded in first embarrassing, and then destabilizing, the government, which responded by imposing modified martial law during a period of civil war, from June 1968 to March 1969.

The U.S.-trained police force and the Uruguayan military unleashed a bloody campaign of mass arrests and selected disappearances (as part of Operation Condor), which diminished the strength of the guerrilla movement. The use of torture by security forces was particularly effective, and by 1972 the MLN's principal leaders had been arrested and imprisoned under terrible conditions for the next 12 years.

In 1971, a truce was declared between the government and the Tupamaros, which led to a relatively quiet atmosphere for the November 1971 national elections, in which Pacheco wanted to run for a second term but was prohibited from doing so by the Constitution. A referendum was held to change the Constitution to allow for re-election, but it was defeated. Consequently, Juan María Bordaberry became the Colorado Party's candidate and won the election for the presidential term 1972–1976.

However, in 1973, President Bordaberry dissolved the General Assembly and began ruling by decree as a military-sponsored dictator until disagreements with the military leadership led to his deposition before his original term of office had expired. During the period 1973–1981, several civilian political leaders participated in the civilian-military administration before General Gregorio Conrado Álvarez took over the reins of government and ruled from 1981 to 1985. Free elections were finally allowed in 1984, and the new democratic government began a process of recovering from a troubled political climate and a negative economic situation.

Meanwhile, many opposition parties began to unite, drawing support from the two traditional parties—the Colorado Party and National Party—and created a new coalition, named the Frente Amplio (Broad Front). After democracy was restored to Uruguay in 1985, the Tupamaros returned to public life as part of a political party, the Movement of Popular Participation (Movimiento de Participación Popular [MPP]).

Today, the MPP comprises the largest single segment of the ruling left-wing Frente Amplio coalition. Between March 1985 and March 2005, there was a democratic transition of power. The national election of 2004 brought the Frente Amplio—a broad coalition of Socialists, former Tupamaros, Communists, and Social Democrats, among others—to power, with majorities in both houses of parliament, under the leadership of President Tabaré Vázquez (2005 to date), who won by an absolute majority.

Roman Catholic Church Christianity was introduced into Uruguay in 1616 with the arrival of two Roman Catholic religious orders, the Franciscans and the Jesuits. The Jesuits took the lead in missionizing the Native population, and Uruguay became a primary region for the development of "communal villages"

Uruguay

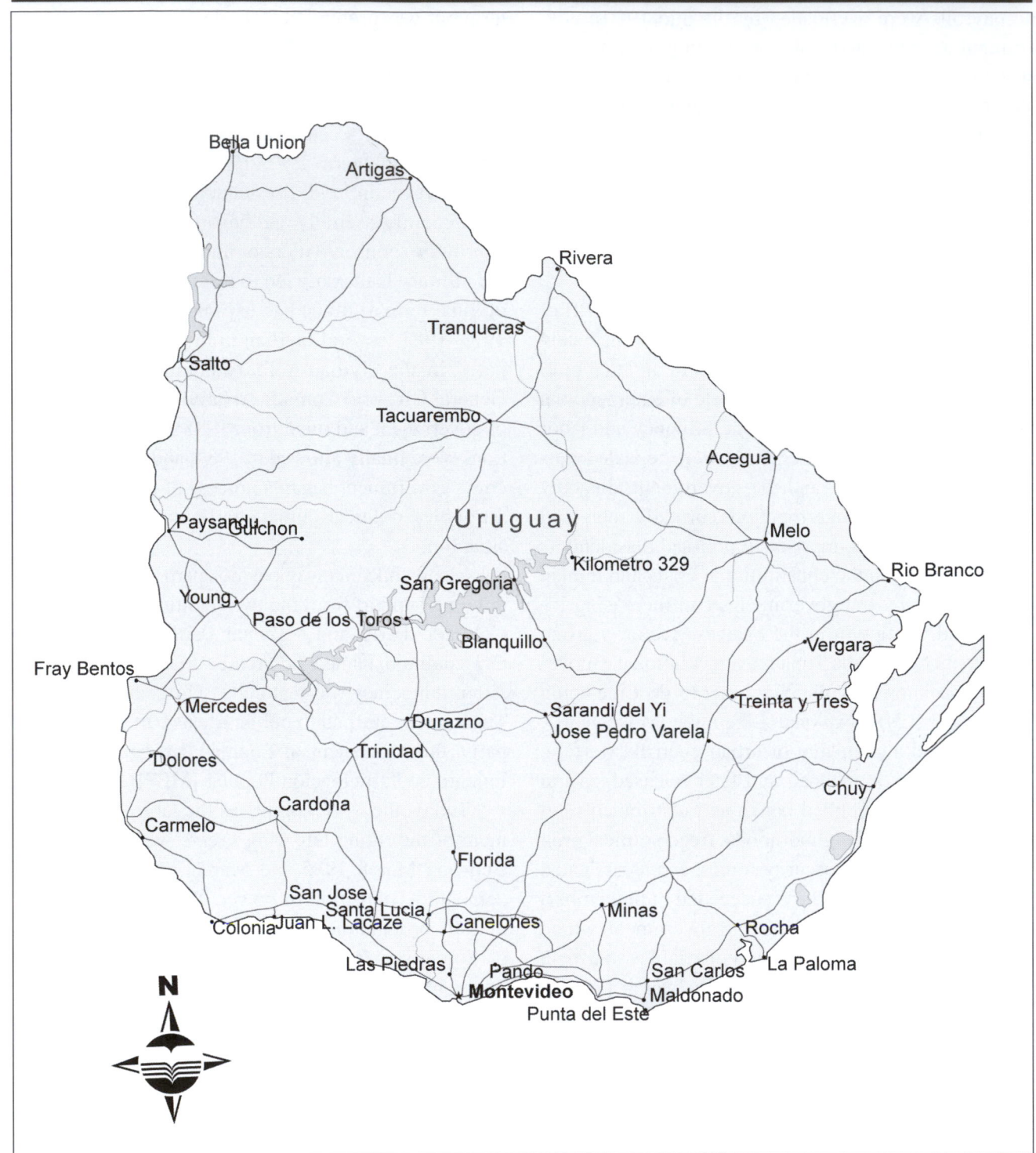

(*reducciones*) into which their converts were relocated. The mission system thrived until 1767, when the Jesuits were expelled by the pope, as part of an international disaster that befell that religious order. The communal villages largely disappeared during the next decade after being taken over by the civil government and other religious orders.

In the meantime, the Roman Catholic Diocese of Buenos Aires (established in 1620) extended its hegemony to the small colonial city of Montevideo in 1726. The Vicariate Apostolic of Montevideo was established in 1830 and upgraded to the Diocese of Montevideo in 1878; it was elevated to archdiocesan status in 1897.

The Uruguayan Catholic Church was greatly affected by large-scale immigration from Europe that began in the 19th century and gave the country its unique character today, with 94.6 percent of the population being of European extraction. Although the immigrants were largely from Catholic countries, many were nominal believers or irreligious, which helps explain the highest percentage of nonreligious persons in the country today.

According to the Reverend Miguel Ángel Pastorino, director of Uruguay's Service for Study and Advice on Sects and New Religious Groups and a member of the Roman Catholic Bishops' National Commission of Ecumenism and Interreligious Dialogue, "in Uruguay there are many nominal Christians, because 54 percent say they are Catholic, but only 2.3 percent attend Mass; and of those who attend Mass, not all are committed to the faith of the Church and its mission." The growth of Protestant denominations and other non-Catholic religious groups in Latin America is due to the "pastoral vacuum" that the Catholic Church has suffered in recent decades, together with its own internal conflicts.

Several diverse tensions arose within the Uruguayan Catholic Church in Uruguay during the 1960s and following years, resulting from challenges posed by the Latin American Bishops Conference in Medellín (Colombia) in 1968, Latin American Liberation Theology, and the Catholic Charismatic Renewal. These new movements polarized Catholic bishops, parish priests, religious workers, and the laity into various factions: traditionalists, who wanted the church to remain as it was prior to the reforms approved by the Second Vatican Council (late 1960s); reformers, who supported the church's modern stance; progressives, who sought to implement the new vision for "a preferential option for the poor" through social and political action aimed at transforming Uruguayan society and establishing social justice through peaceful democratic means; radicals, who adopted Marxist ideology and advocated violent revolution by the people as a means of overthrowing the oligarchy and creating a Socialist state that would serve the marginalized masses; and charismatic agents (priests, nuns, and lay members) who sought to transform the spiritual and communal life of Catholics by means of the power and gifts of the Holy Spirit (including the "baptism of the Holy Spirit and speaking in tongues").

Since the mid-1960s, the Uruguayan Catholic Church—influenced greatly by papal calls for a refocus of attention on the needs of the urban poor—has directed significant resources toward assisting the lower classes and empowering the laity in the church. However, only about half the national population identifies as Roman Catholic today, and weekly church attendance is reported to be very low.

Since 1950, overall, there has been a serious decline in available pastoral services, especially in the nation's largest urban area, the Archdiocese of Montevideo, where the average priest was responsible for twice as many parishioners in 2004 (1:3,483) as compared to 1950 (1:1,709). Between 1950 and 2004, the number of priests (diocesan and religious) in the archdiocese declined from 547 to 244. During this same period, the number of Catholic adherents declined from about 70 percent of the population in the Archdiocese in 1950 to about 63 percent in 2004.

In the midst of this general decline in Catholic demographics, a renewal movement occurred that revitalized the faith of many Catholics and made their lives more meaningful. Diocesan priest Julio César Elizaga (b. 1929) was a pioneer in the Catholic Renewal Movement (CRM) in Uruguay, and one of the few priests in the country who was authorized by the Vatican to conduct exorcisms. In addition, the Reverend Juan Carlos Ortiz, who was a pastor with the Assemblies of God in Buenos Aires, played an important role in the early development of the CRM in Argentina and Uruguay, along with the Trappist monks, during the late 1960s and early 1970s.

According to a 1969–1970 study by CLAR (Confederación Latinoamericana de Religiosos), there were 693 members of male religious orders in Uruguay, of which 64 percent were native-born, 3.3 percent were born in other Latin American countries, and 32.7 percent were born in other countries. Regarding the 1,592 members of female religious orders in Uruguay at that time, 43.4 percent were native-born, 22.6 percent were born in other Latin American countries, and 33.4 percent were born elsewhere. This study revealed that Uruguay had a very high number of native-born male religious workers compared to other Latin American countries; only Colombia, Ecuador, and Mexico had a higher percentage, with 82.1, 76.4, and 87.1 percent, respectively.

In 2004, the Uruguayan Catholic Church reported 10 dioceses with 228 parishes, which were served by 215 secular priests and 271 religious priests (486 total), assisted by 63 permanent deacons and 398 male religious and 1,281 female religious workers. The Archdiocese of Montevideo is led by Monsignor Nicolás Cotugno Fanizzi, S.D.B., appointed in December 1998.

Nuestra Señora de los Treinta y Tres is the patron of Uruguay, whose annual festival is celebrated on the second Sunday of November at the Santuario Nacional de Nuestra Señora de los Treinta y Tres in the city of Florida, Department of Florida, located in the center of the nation. The small image of the Assumption of the Virgin Mary (only 14 inches tall) was first noted in 1779 in a Jesuit mission in the town of Pintado; the image was later moved to the town of Florida and dedicated to 33 heroes of the Uruguayan Independence movement who appealed to the statue of the Virgin Mary for assistance in time of crisis.

The Protestant Movement The first Protestant churches in Uruguay were formed early in the 19th century. American Methodists (now the United Methodist Church) made their initial probe of Uruguay in 1835, and missionary work was established in Montevideo in 1839. Methodist work was closed in 1842 because of the civil war then raging (1839–1852), and it was not until 1870 that a permanent work was re-

established. The affiliated churches became the independent Evangelical Methodist Church of Uruguay in 1969. Early Methodist success in Uruguay is attributed to the missionary labors of Dr. Thomas B. Wood (1844–1922) and to the conversion of a young Italian immigrant, Francisco G. Penzotti (1851–1925), who went on to become a prominent evangelist across the continent and an agent of the American Bible Society.

The Evangelical Church of the River Plate dates to 1840 with the arrival of German Lutheran and Reformed immigrants in Argentina, Paraguay, and Uruguay. Later, they were joined by others from Switzerland, Austria, Hungary, Russia, Brazil, and Romania. Many had in common the German language, and in 1899, they created the German Evangelical Synod of the River Plate, as part of the Evangelical Church in Germany (EKD), with which it became officially affiliated in 1934. In 1965, the synod approved a new constitution and was renamed the Evangelical Church of the River Plate (IERP), and it became independent of the EKD. About 70 percent of the IERP members live in Argentina, the others in Uruguay and Paraguay. Twenty-two Lutheran, Reformed, and United regional churches (*Landeskirchen*) form the Evangelical Church in Germany (Evangelische Kirche in Deutschland [EKD]).

Members of the Waldensian Church (followers of Peter Waldo, a pre-Reformation French schismatic leader in the 12th century) were among the immigrants from Italy who began to arrive in 1856, but it was not until 1877 that an ordained pastor was assigned to provide clerical leadership. Although, today, this is the fifth largest Protestant denomination in the country, many of its congregations continue to be served by lay leadership. New immigrants also began to establish colonies in the Argentine provinces of Santa Fe and Entre Ríos, and at the beginning of the 20th century the Waldensians in Uruguay began to expand their work into the Argentina provinces of Buenos Aires and Las Pampas. In 1895, the Waldensian congregations in the Río de la Plata region began to hold annual conferences, but it was not until 1934 that a formal denominational structure was organized in both countries as the Federation of Waldensian Evangelical Churches of the River Plate. Until 1965, the Federation was an integral part of the Italian Waldensian Church, but in

A wood altar with a statue of Jesus crucified inside of Montevideo Cathedral, Uruguay. (Alexandre Fagundes De Fagundes/Dreamstime.com)

that year it held its own synod for the first time. Over time other Reformed immigrants from Europe arrived in Uruguay and helped strengthen the membership of the Waldensian Church in the Río de la Plata region.

The first Anglican missionaries arrived in 1866 to serve British immigrants and later established the Anglican Church of Uruguay, which is now part of the Anglican Province of the Southern Cone (established in 1981, encompassing Bolivia, Chile, Paraguay, Uruguay, and Argentina). Arriving later in the century were the Christian Brethren (1882) and the Salvation Army (1890) from England, and the Seventh-day Adventist Church (1895) from the United States.

The relative freedom of religion throughout the 20th century was conducive to the establishment of a variety of Protestant and Free Church denominations in Uruguay, mostly from the United States, which includes the following: the Southern Baptist Foreign Mission Board (1911), Lutheran Church–Missouri Synod (1936), Evangelical Church of Uruguay (founded by the Fred Dabold family in 1946), Church of the Nazarene (1948), United Lutheran Church in America (1948), Mennonite Brethren Church (1948), Worldwide Evangelization Crusade (1950), Mennonite Brethren Missions and Services (1950), Augustana Lutheran Synod (1952), independent Christian Churches and Churches of Christ (1952), Mennonite Board of Missions (1954; Uruguayan Mennonite Conference established in 1956), Armenian Missionary Association of America (1954; founded in Worcester, MA, in 1918), Church of God of Prophecy (1957), Baptist Bible Fellowship International (1958), the Christian and Missionary Alliance (1960), Freewill Baptist Association (1961), Baptist World Mission (1968), Christian Church (Disciples of Christ) (1970), Gospel Mission of South America (1970), Church of God (Anderson, Indiana, 1984), and the Baptist General Conference (1991).

Uruguayan Pentecostalism began with the arrival of U.S. missionaries from the United Pentecostal Church in 1930, followed by the Swedish Assemblies of God in 1938, the U.S. Assemblies of God in 1944, the Church of God (Cleveland, Tennessee) in 1945, and the Church of God of Prophecy in 1957. During the 1980s, about 70 Pentecostal denominations existed in Uruguay and their total membership surpassed that of all the non-Pentecostal denominations. As in Brazil and Argentina, Uruguayan Pentecostals have engaged in spiritual warfare against Afro-Brazilian religious cults, which are considered to be Satanic. In addition, the more traditional Pentecostal denominations have opposed the arrival in the 1980s of Brazilian missionaries of the God is Love Pentecostal Church and the Universal Church of the Kingdom of God, which are considered to be contaminated with Afro-Brazilian Spiritism.

Between 1948 and 1951, about 1,200 Mennonites from West Prussia and Poland arrived in Uruguay as refugees after World War II, and had been living in displaced persons camps in Denmark. The Mennonite Central Committee in the United States helped make arrangements for them to be relocated in Uruguay, at first housed in old army barracks and vacant warehouses in Paysandú and Arapey. Being eager to work and earn their own livelihood, individuals and small groups immediately took whatever work they could find, from skilled laborers and factory workers to farm hands and domestic servants. The first permanent agricultural settlement was begun in April 1950 on a 2,900-acre ranch at El Ombu, located about 180 miles northwest of Montevideo, near the small town of Young. The El Ombu ranch was divided into 75 homesteads of varying sizes. The farmers immediately organized an agricultural cooperative and began to develop the land and improve their housing conditions.

By the end of 1955, two additional agricultural colonies had been established: the second was a 4,500-acre ranch located near Tres Bocas, now known as the Gartental settlement; and the third was named Delta and established on 3,600 acres of land in San José Department, about 60 miles northwest of Montevideo. The cooperative practices of the German-speaking Mennonite colonies were a modern adaptation of the historical Mennonite Brotherhood economic principles of mutual aid. These practices made it possible for the colonies to survive economically, whereas individual efforts would not have been successful. There are at least four Mennonite church associations in Uruguay: the Council of Mennonite Brethren Congregations in Uruguay, which was organized among Polish immigrants in 1948 aboard ship before reaching Uruguay; the Conference of Mennonite Churches in Uruguay was established in the mid-1950s, which is affiliated with the General Conference Mennonite Church in North America and with the Union of German Mennonite Congregations in Germany; also, the Mennonite Church U.S.A. established a mission in Montevideo in 1954 to serve the larger community. In addition, the Mennonite Central Committee has maintained a service center in Montevideo since 1948 as a coordinating agency between Mennonites in Uruguay and those in North America. The Mennonite Biblical Seminary was established in Montevideo in 1956 as a bilingual institution (German and Spanish), with the support of North American Mennonite mission boards. The seminary was replaced in 1974 with the Mennonite Study and Retreat Center in Montevideo to facilitate leadership training.

According to Brierly (1997), in 2000, the largest Protestant denominations in the country were the following: the U.S.-based Assemblies of God (with an estimated membership of 10,200), the Seventh-day Adventist Church (8,020), the Baptist Convention (4,500), the Swedish Assemblies of God (4,320), the Waldensian Church (3,200), the Evangelical Church of the River Plate (2,050), the Evangelical Pentecostal Church (from Chile, 1,790), and the Christian and Missionary Alliance (1,397).

About a dozen Uruguayan Protestant denominations have united in the Federation of Evangelical Churches of Uruguay, which is affiliated with the World Council of Churches (WCC). It grew out of the Uruguay Committee of the Confederation of Evangelical Churches of the River Plate, originally founded in 1939. The more conservative evangelical churches have come together in the Christian Association of Evangelical Churches in the Republic of Uruguay, which is affiliated with the Latin American Confraternity of Evangelicals (CONELA) and the World Evangelical Alliance (WEF).

Historically, the Protestant population of Uruguay has been the smallest of the Southern Cone countries, and one of the reasons for this can be found in the long secular tradition of the country. According to the 1908 census, 61.2 percent of the total population was Roman Catholic; 37.2 percent described themselves as atheistic, agnostic, or evolutionist; and only 1.6 percent considered themselves Protestant. In the 1980 national census, Catholics were 59.5 percent, Protestants were 1.9 percent, followers of other religions were 3.6 percent, and those who declared themselves to be "not religious" were 35 percent. In the 2006 census, only 47.1 percent identified as Roman Catholic; 40.4 percent professed no religious faith whatsoever; 11.1 percent identified as "non-Catholic Christians," which includes Eastern Orthodox, Protestant, and marginal Christian groups); and only 1.3 percent were adherents of "other religions."

Other Christian Groups There are several Eastern Orthodox jurisdictions in Uruguay. Immigrants from Greece, Russia, Ukraine, and Armenia have established their several branches of the Orthodox Church. The

Greeks are part of the Greek Orthodox Archdiocese of North and South America under the Ecumenical Patriarchate; the Russians with the Russian Orthodox Church (Patriarchate of Moscow) and with the Russian Orthodox Church Abroad, Diocese of South America and Buenos Aires; the Ukrainians with the Ukrainian Autocephalous Orthodox Church of North and South America and the Diaspora (under Archbishop Odon of Manizales, Eparch of All Latin America, Spain, and Portugal and his superior, Metropolitan Mefodiy of Kyiv and All-Ukraine); and the Armenians are affiliated with the Armenian Apostolic Church (Holy See of Echmiadzin, Armenia).

Several U.S.-based non-Protestant religious bodies are present as well, the largest of which are the Church of Jesus Christ of Latter-day Saints (arrived in 1944 and reported 90,292 members and 162 congregations in 2007) and the Jehovah's Witnesses (with 156 congregations and 10,951 members in 2005). Also present are controversial quasi-Protestant bodies, such as Growing in Grace Ministries International (followers of Miami-based Apostle José Luis de Jesus), the People of God (founded in Paraguay in 1963), the Universal Church of the Kingdom of God, and the God is Love Church (from Brazil). The Seicho-No-Ie, founded in Uruguay in 1978, is a Japanese New Thought group.

The New Apostolic Church International is difficult to classify, but it arrived in South America around 1920 when a number of New Apostolic families from Europe settled near the mouth of the Rio de la Plata in Argentina and Uruguay. This religious group was originally named the Catholic Apostolic Church and was founded in England in 1830; it has roots in Presbyterian, Congregational, and Anglican theology and church polity. It is a pre-Pentecostal body that believes in and practices the charismatic gifts of healing, prophecy, and speaking in tongues. Today, its international headquarters are located in Zurich, Switzerland. According to Brierly (1997), this church body had an estimated 19,300 members in 2000.

Additional Religious Groups Jewish immigration to Uruguay began early in the 10th century and peaked in the 1920s and 1930s, when some 10,000 Jews fled the Nazis. With continued immigration after World War II, some 40,000 Jews eventually came to reside in the country. There are three significant groupings of Sephardic, Hungarian, and German background, which are organized into the Comunidad Israelita Sefardi, Comunidad Israelita Húngara, and the Communidad Israelita. The Israelite Central Committee of Uruguay in Montevideo provides some unity to the Jewish community, which today is estimated at 25,000. According to local Jewish leaders, since 2002 the number of Jews has declined due to emigration.

The Muslim population lives primarily near the border with Brazil, with an estimated 300 to 400 Muslims in the country, but the majority were reported to be minimally active in religious activities. Although there are no mosques in Uruguay, there are two Islamic centers, in Canelones and Montevideo. Also, Subud, a Sufi-related movement founded in Indonesia in the 1920s by Muhammad Subuh Sumohadiwidjojo, has been present in Uruguay since 1958. The small Baha'i community is concentrated primarily in Montevideo.

In April 2006, approximately 850 families practiced Buddhism in Uruguay, some of whom were affiliated with the Diamond Way and Karma-Kagyupa Buddhist organizations.

There is a small Asian-Indian community in Uruguay but most Hindu-related groups are composed of non-Asian Indians, including the International Society for Krishna Consciousness (ISKON), the International Sri Sathya Sai Baba Organization, the Shivapremananda Ashram of the Divine Society (also known as Centro Sivananda Yoga Vedanta), and Transcendental Meditation (known as TM, and organized as the Global Country of World Peace).

The Afro-Brazilian religions of Umbanda, Quimbanda, and Batuque began to appear in the 1940s near the Uruguay-Brazil border and later in Montevideo. Local centers of these religions, such as Templo Afro-umbandista Ile Oxalá Oxalufâ Pâe Dario de Oxala, have spread rapidly, primarily among Brazilian immigrants and Uruguayans of African descent. These Afro-Brazilian religions had approximately 5,000 adherents in Uruguay in 2000. The Afro-Umbandista Federation of Uruguay (Federación Afroumbandista del Uruguay [FAUDU]) was founded in 1994 in Montevideo.

Afro-Uruguayan is the term used to refer to Uruguayans of African ancestry; today, they are primarily located in Montevideo. Also present in Uruguay is Candomblé, another variation of Afro-Brazilian religions associated with the Orixás; for example, the Ketu-Orthodox Apostolic Church (Ilé Oxossi Ataré Oni-Alaketu) is located in Soriano, Cardona Province.

Other small religions include a few in the Western Esoteric tradition, such as: Freemasonry (Logía Masónica del Gran Oriente de Uruguay, founded in 1856 in Montevideo), the Ancient and Mystical Order Rosae Crucis (AMORC), the Grand Universal Fraternity (founded in Venezuela), the Universal Gnostic Movement (1977), the Wiccan Community of Uruguay, the Pagan Society of Uruguay, and the Satanist Church (founded in 2006 by "Hermano Andrex" in Minas, Lavalleja Department).

Several Western Esoteric organizations were founded in Uruguay between 1896 and 1925: the Center of Occult Sciences (1896–1897), the Theosophical and Occult Center (1896), the Occult Lodge (1905), and Rama Hiranya (1905). Interest in Theosophy was kindled in Montevideo by Annie Mennie Gowland, an English resident of Buenos Aires, who made periodic visits to Uruguay, where she offered conferences on the subject and disseminated Theosophical principles, which led to the formal establishment of the Theosophical Society in Uruguay in January 1925, under the authorization of its international founder, Mrs. Annie Besant.

The Psychic-Spiritualist–New Age groups include the Uruguayan Spiritist Federation, the Uruguayan Spiritist Center, the Church of Scientology, Ishaya Techniques, the Silvan Method, and the Unification Church. The latter is formally known as the Holy Spirit Association for the Unification of World Christianity and was founded by the Reverend Sun Myung Moon in Korea in 1954. This group is very active and has major property holdings in Uruguay, including a daily newspaper. Since 1980, Uruguay has become a major center for the dissemination of Unification Church literature throughout Latin America.

The New Acropolis Cultural Center was founded by Jorge Ángel Livraga and his wife, Ada Albrecht, in Buenos Aires, Argentina, in 1957. A break-away group of this organization was founded by Ada Albrecht

after she left Livraga and moved to Uruguay, where she established Hastinapura Uruguay (literally, "city named after the elephants") in 1981. Both of groups are considered post-Theosophical movement organizations.

Also, present in Uruguay is a 30-hectare estate, called Casa Redención (Redemption House) or the Planetary Center of La Aurora, which was founded by Elisabeth César (known by her followers as "Shimani") during the 2000s near La Aurora, and the Shrine of Padre Pío de Pietrelcina (built in 1987) in the Department of Paysandú, located on the southern bank of the Río Daymán about 16 miles from the city of Salto. The region is well known for alleged sightings of flying saucers and extraterrestrials. Shimani is a disciple of the famous Brazilian mystic José Hipolito Trigueirinho Netto (b. 1931), who has authored dozen of books such as *Esoteric Dictionary* (1999) and *Calling Humanity* (2002).

Padre Pío was a Roman Catholic Capuchin Franciscan priest, born as Francesco Forgione in southern Italy in 1887, who is an alleged mystic and miracle worker, venerated worldwide for the stigmata he claimed to have received from an angel; the "stigmata" were open wounds in his hands that reportedly bled for 50 years, from 1918 until he died in 1968.

In July 2005, according to the Reverend Miguel Ángel Pastorino, director of Uruguay's Service for Study and Advice on Sects and New Religious Groups and a member of the Roman Catholic Bishops' National Commission of Ecumenism and Interreligious Dialogue: "Not only is there [in Uruguay] an exodus to different Gnostic and esoteric proposals, Afro-American cults, para-Christian sects, spiritualism, and 'flying saucer' sects [those who believe in UFOs], but there is also a silent turn to religious indifference, a product of the advanced secularization of our large cities."

Clifton L. Holland

See also: Ancient and Mystical Order Rosae Crucis; Anglican Province of the Southern Cone of America; Armenian Apostolic Church (Holy See of Echmiadzin); Assemblies of God; Baptist Bible Fellowship International; Besant, Annie; Christian and Missionary Alliance; Christian Brethren; Christian Church (Disciples of Christ); Christian Churches and

Churches of Christ; Church of God (Anderson, Indiana); Church of God (Cleveland, Tennessee); Church of God of Prophecy; Church of Jesus Christ of Latter-day Saints; Church of Scientology; Church of the Nazarene; Diamond Way Buddhism; Ecumenical Patriarchate/Patriarchate of Constantinople; Evangelical Church in Germany; Evangelical Church of the River Plate; Franciscans; Freemasonry; Global Country of World Peace; International Society for Krishna Consciousness; Jehovah's Witnesses; Jesuits; Karma-Kagyupa, Tibetan Buddhism; Lutheran Church–Missouri Synod; Mary, Blessed Virgin; Mennonite Church, U.S.A.; Moon, Sun Myung; New Apostolic Church; Pentecostalism; People of God; Roman Catholic Church; Russian Orthodox Church Outside of Russia; Salvation Army; Sathya Sai Baba Movement; Seicho-No-Ie; Seventh-day Adventist Church; Theosophical Society (America); United Methodist Church; Umbanda; Unification Movement; Universal Church of the Kingdom of God; Waldensian Church; Wiccan Religion; World Council of Churches; World Evangelical Alliance.

References

Bazzano, Daniel, et al. *Breve visión de la historia de la iglesia en el Uruguay.* Montevideo: OBSUR Librería San Pablo, 1993.

Brierly, Peter. *World Churches Handbook.* London: Christian Research, 1997.

Burgess, Stanley M., ed. "Uruguay." In *The International Dictionary of Pentecostal and Charismatic Movements,* 277–278. Grand Rapids, MI: Zondervan, 2001–2002.

Catholic Hierarchy website. http://www.catholic hierarchy.org/diocese/dmovi.html.

Dieros, Pablo Alberto. *Historia del Cristianismo en América Latina.* Buenos Aires, Argentina: Fraternidad Teológica Latinoamericana, 1992.

Fretz, J. Winfield, and Milka Rindzinski. "Uruguay." In *Global Anabaptist Mennonite Encyclopedia Online.* Undated 1990. http://www.gameo.org/encyclopedia/contents/U76.html.

Geymonat, Roger, ed. *Las religiones en el Uruguay.* Montevideo: Ediciones La Gotera, 2004.

Herring, Hubert, and Helen Baldwin Herring. *A History of Latin America, from the Beginnings to the Present.* 3rd ed. New York: Alfred A. Knopf, 1968.

Holland, Clifton L. "A Chronology of Protestant Beginnings in Uruguay: 1838–2004." http://www.prolades.com/cra/regions/sam/ury/uruguay-chron.pdf.

Holland, Clifton L. *Toward a Classification System of Religious Groups in the Americas by Major Traditions and Family Types.* San José, Costa Rica: PROLADES, 2008. http://www.prolades.com/cra/clas-eng.pdf.

Lapadjián, Pedro. *Huellas de una iglesia: La Iglesia Evangélica y su desarrollo en Uruguay.* Montevideo: Ediciones Trilce, 1994. http://books.google.es/books?id=_VFdS1E0aI0C.

Monti, Daniel P. *Presencia del Protestantismo en el Río de La Plata Durante el Siglo XIX.* Buenos Aires, Argentina: Editorial La Aurora, 1969.

Oro, Ari Pedro, and Pablo Semán. "Pentecostalism in Uruguay." "Pentecostalism in the Southern Cone Countries: Overview and Perspectives." *International Sociology* 15, no. 4 (December 2000): 605–627.

PROLADES-RITA (Religion-In-The-Americas) database. "Religion in Uruguay." http://www.prolades.com/cra/regions/sam/ury/ury-rd.htm.

Red Iberoamericana de Estudio de las Sectas. "La Iglesia Católica de Uruguay alerta sobre la secta Shimani, un grupo platillista." *Boletín Electrónico Info-RIES.* August 12, 2009. http://info-ries.blogspot.com/2009/08/boletin-info-ries-n-145.html.

Secretariado General de la CLAR. *Estudio sociográfico de los religiosos y las religiosas en América Latina.* Bogota, Colombia: Secretariado General de la CLAR (Confederación Latinoamericana de Religiosos), 1971.

U.S. Department of State. *International Religious Freedom Report 2007: Uruguay.* http://www.state.gov/g/drl/rls/irf/2007/90270.htm.

Weber, Linda J., and Dotsy Welliver, eds. *Mission Handbook of U.S. and Canadian Christian Ministries Overseas (2007–2009).* Wheaton, IL: Evangelism and Missions Information Service, 2007.

Your Catholic Voice website. "Miguel Pastorino on the State of Religion in Latin America." July 8, 2005. http://yourcatholicvoice.com/insight .php?article=2338.

■ Uzbekistan

Uzbekistan is a landlocked Central Asian country surrounded by Afghanistan, Kazakhstan, Turkmenistan, Tajikistan, and Kyrgyzstan. Much of the 173,000 square miles of territory is desert with mountains rising in the east. The population is 27,000,000 (2008).

The Uzbek people trace their lineage to a Turkish people in Siberia. These people settled in what is now central Kazakhstan. Meanwhile, in the seventh and eighth centuries CE, in what is now Uzbekistan, a Turkish khanate was created. However, the khanate was quickly replaced by Arab rule, which came to Central Asia along with the subsequent spread of Islam. A prosperous Islamic civilization developed in the next centuries as Buchara, Samarkand, and Urgenc became important centers for trade and education. This era of prosperity was cut short by the invasion of the Mongols early in the 13th century.

In the 15th century, the Uzbek people residing in Kazakhstan gained a new level of unity, and in the 16th century they moved into present-day Uzbekistan; in 1512 the Khanate of Kiva came into existence. Subsequently, several other Uzbek khanates were created, and a set of rival states emerged.

The Russians developed plans for the region late in the 19th century. In 1860 Russian forces entered the area and seven years later created the province of Turkistan, with its capital at Tashkent. Over the next two centuries, the Russians succeeded in reconciling the different khanates to their presence in the region. There was some attempt to create an independent Uzbek government after the fall of the czar, but forces of the new Soviet government crushed that effort. In 1924, Central Asia was reorganized along ethnic lines, and an entity closely resembling the present nation of Uzbekistan was designated as the Soviet Socialist Republic of Uzbekistan. What is now Tajikistan was originally part of Uzbekistan, but separated in 1929.

Uzbekistan was placed in a difficult position during the Gorbachev era, at the end of the 1980s. The government opposed Russian attempts to invade Afghanistan, and a hostile climate led to attacks upon Russian expatriates residing in the region. Uzbekistan moved quickly to separate from Russia in 1991 and form an independent nation. That new government is a democracy, but only in a limited sense. Parties in opposition to the present administration have not been

Uzbekistan

Religion	Followers in 1970	Followers in 2010	% of Population	Annual % growth 2000–2010	Followers in 2025	Followers in 2050
Muslims	6,003,000	24,328,000	85.1	2.29	30,476,000	35,466,000
Agnostics	3,000,000	3,104,000	10.9	−2.37	2,500,000	2,000,000
Atheists	2,022,000	623,000	2.2	−1.20	450,000	300,000
Christians	872,000	371,000	1.3	0.28	378,000	428,000
Orthodox	833,000	240,000	0.8	−0.53	200,000	200,000
Independents	26,000	80,000	0.3	2.76	100,000	120,000
Protestants	7,400	40,000	0.1	0.39	60,000	80,000
Jews	66,000	50,000	0.2	−0.85	45,000	40,000
Ethnoreligionists	0	56,400	0.2	1.47	50,000	55,000
Buddhists	10,000	44,300	0.2	1.47	60,000	90,000
Zoroastrians	0	1,000	0.0	1.47	1,000	1,000
Baha'is	0	900	0.0	1.48	2,000	4,000
Hindus	0	800	0.0	1.47	1,200	1,500
New religionists	40	140	0.0	1.35	200	300
Total population	**11,973,000**	**28,580,000**	**100.0**	**1.47**	**33,963,000**	**38,386,000**

UZBEKISTAN

allowed to form, and there are imposed limitations on free speech and association.

Two laws regulating religious liberty were passed in 1998. The Law on Freedom of Conscience and Religious Organizations, while granting a spectrum of freedoms, restricts religious rights that conflict with national security, prohibits proselytizing, bans religious subjects in school curriculums, prohibits the private teaching of religious principles, forbids the wearing of religious clothing in public by anyone other than clerics, and requires religious groups to obtain a license to publish or distribute materials. The law also requires that all religious groups and congregations register. To register, a group must have at least 100 Uzbek citizen members. The second law revised the criminal and civil codes and provided punishments for a spectrum of activities, such as organizing a banned religious group, persuading others to join such a group, and drawing minors into a religious organization without the permission of their parents.

Like much of Central Asia, Uzbekistan is dominated by Sunni Muslims of the Hanafite School. In 1843 the Russians created the Muslim Spiritual Board of Central Asia, with headquarters at Tashkent, whose authority reached out to neighboring countries. All imams had to register with the board, and it controlled

The great Registan Square in the heart of Samarkand. (Corel)

the two seminaries for the training of religious leaders. In the brief period of lessening Russian authority, an Islamic revitalization movement, Jahid, attempted to reform what they saw as the corrupt leadership and tie Islam more closely to the religion's center in the Middle East. The movement founded a number of new schools that emphasized traditional values and taught classical Arabic as a means of reintroducing the Koran. As the movement gained a high profile, however, the Russians suppressed it.

During the years of Soviet rule, Islam was suppressed by a government openly hostile to religion. However, late in the 20th century, a new revitalization movement appeared, emphasizing Islamic morals and calling people's attention to the *sharia* (Islamic law). Some 80 mosques remained open during the Soviet era, and a reported 4,000 were opened soon after the country gained independence. As economic conditions dipped in the 1990s, during which time the country was making the transition to a market economy, many were drawn to new conservative Muslim movements, especially the Wahhabi movement, which has been generously supported by Saudi Arabia. At the same time, Turkish spokespersons have been supportive of a pan-Turkish approach to Central Asia. The new government operates as a secular state but has granted special status to the Islamic leadership. It both supports and exercises control over the Islamic community through the Spiritual Directorate for Muslims (the Muftiate).

The new 1998 law demanding registration of religious organizations appears to have been largely directed at exercising some control over Muslims worshipping at independent mosques. Since the law went into effect, 1,831 religious congregations and organizations, 1,664 of which were Muslim, have been registered. However, an additional 335 applications were denied, of which 323 were from Muslim groups.

Although the Sunni Muslims dominate religious life, by 2000 the Government's Committee on Religious Affairs had registered some 167 minority religious groups (congregations), including 32 of the Russian Orthodox Church (Moscow Patriarchate), 23 Baptist, 26 Pentecostal or Full Gospel, 10 of the Seventh-day Adventist Church, 47 Korean Christian, 8 Jewish synagogues, 5 of the Baha'i Faith, 2 kingdom halls of the Jehovah's Witnesses, and 2 temples of the International Society for Krishna Consciousness. Regular news reports continue as the struggle of different groups to register or recover a lost registration continue. Among the groups not registered as of 2000 was the Roman Catholic Church, though its registration was pending.

Christianity essentially entered Uzbekistan in the 19th century, with the coming of the Russians. It operates primarily within the continuing community of Russians (some 10 percent of the population), and its parishes are now part of the single diocese that covers Uzbekistan, Turkmenistan, Tajikistan, and Kyrgyzstan.

Baptists from Siberia and central Russia settled near Tashkent in 1898 and began to hold prayer meetings in their homes. The first congregation was established adjacent to the Russian fort at Tashkent and included soldiers among those in attendance. Later in the decade, German Baptists moved into the area. The Tashkent church was closed in 1932 and did not reopen until 1944. During its first decade after World War II, it grew from 65 to more than 1,300 members. During the last decades of the Soviet era, a number of Koreans moved into the country, among whom were some Baptists. By the end of the 20th century, there were more than 20 Baptist churches, the largest number of which were associated with the Union of Evangelical Christian-Baptists of Central Asia, an association founded in 1992 that also includes the churches in Turkmenistan and Tajikistan.

Seventh-day Adventist work includes the Asian-Caucasian Conference, which also takes in Armenia, Azerbaijan, Georgia, Turkmenistan, and Tajikistan.

The Jewish community of Uzbekistan traces its history to the fifth century CE, when exiles from Persia arrived seeking a greater degree of religious freedom. The present communities in Samarkand and Buchara have persisted through the many government changes over the centuries. In the 19th century, Jews from Russia moved to Uzbekistan and settled in Tashkent. Besides the concentration of Jews in the three main cities, there are also Jews scattered throughout the country. During the Soviet era, the Jews of Uzbekistan had a relatively easier time than their fellow believers in other parts of the Soviet Union; however,

they are now threatened by the new laws that demand religious leaders be Uzbekistan citizens.

Uzbekistan has been the source of numerous reports of religious suppression by the state, most reports coming from the Christian community, but Jews and even Muslims have not been exempt, while Jehovah's Witnesses have been especially singled out for attention.

J. Gordon Melton

See also: Baha'i Faith; Hanafite School of Islam; International Society for Krishna Consciousness; Jehovah's Witnesses; Roman Catholic Church; Russian Orthodox Church (Moscow Patriarchate); Seventh-day Adventist Church.

References

Allworth, Edward A. *The Modern Uzbeks*. Stanford, CA: Hoover Institution Press, 1990.

Kalter, Johannes, and Margareta Pavaloi. *Uzbekistan: Heirs to the Silk Road*. London: Thames & Hudson, 2003.

Melvin, Niel J. *Uzbekistan: Transition to Authoritarianism on the Silk Road*. New York: Routledge, 2000.

Muslims of the Soviet East. English ed. Tashkent, Uzbekistan: Muslim Religious Board of Central Asia and Kazakhstan, 1968–?

Rand, Robert. *Tamerlane's Children: Dispatches from Contemporary Uzbekistan*. London: Oneworld Publications, 2006.

Vaishnavism

Vaishnavism is a major sectarian tradition within Hinduism that is focused on the worship of Vishnu in his various forms and incarnations (*avataras*) as the highest manifestation of the divine. The rise of theistic traditions of Hinduism can be traced to earliest Upanishads, such as the Isha and Shvetasvatara, which conceive of a personal supreme deity as the creator of the world and as the ultimate source of liberation (*moksha*). In the Vedas, Vishnu is a minor deity, as can be deduced from the limited number of hymns dedicated to him. He is frequently mentioned in the context of his friendship with Indra in many of the latter's heroic battles against demonic forces, including Vritra. The most important act for which Vishnu is praised in the Rig Veda is as the wide striding one, whose three strides measure out and encompass the Earth, intermediate space, sky, and beyond.

The Bhagavata tradition, the earliest historical manifestation of Vaishnavism, is attested in several inscriptions from the second century to the first century BCE, which indicate that this religious cult was associated with Narayana, Vasudeva, and Samkarshana. During the Gupta period (ca. 320–550 CE), the term *bhagavata* appears in epigraphic materials as part of epithets of Gupta monarchs and rulers, such as *paramabhagavata* ("supreme bhagavata") and *mahabhagavata* ("great bhagavata"). Their primary scripture was the Bhagavata Purana.

The connection of Vishnu to various avataras is found as early as the Mahabharata, where Krishna is identified as Vishnu. In the Bhagavad Gita, we find the earliest expression of avatara doctrine, as Krishna states that when world order (*dharma*) declines and chaos threatens the world, he creates himself to reestablish it. In the Epics and Puranas, Vishnu has numerous avataras, but by the eighth century, a common list of 10 avataras (*dashavataras*) is found in nearly all Vaishnava *puranas*: Matsya (fish), Kurma (tortoise), Varaha (boar), Narasimha (Man-lion), Vamana (Dwarf), Parashurama (Rama with the axe), Rama, Krishna, the Buddha, and Kalki, the messianic avatara who will appear to usher in the end of the Kali Yuga. By far, the most popular avataras of Vishnu are Rama and Krishna, who have become the focal point of major Vaishnava *sampradayas* (lineages).

Vaishnavism is the result of the amalgamation of four main textual and theological currents that crystallized into a textual corpus that has come to characterize the various Vaishnava sampradayas: Bhagavatas, Pancaratra, Vaikhanasa, and Alvars. In addition to the puranic corpus focused on Vishnu and his various avataras, the 12 Alvar, Tamil saint-poets, who composed devotional poetry from the sixth to the ninth centuries, greatly influence the theological vision of Vishnu as transcendent and formless, who also manifests as the consecrated image (*arca*) in the temple. The early Alvars extol the mystical union with Mayon (Krishna), which can be attained only through meditation and temple worship (*puja*).

The Pancaratra tradition associated with the worship of Narayana is another stream of Vaishnavism, which can be traced to sections of the Mahabharata and perhaps as early as the Shatapatha Brahmana. The Pancaratra presents a theology of emanation (*vyuha*) in which Narayana, sometimes called Vasudeva, manifests in four forms: Krishna-Vasudeva (the supreme soul beyond qualities), Samkarshana (the soul and knower of the field), Pradyumna (the mind of all beings, into

Standing Vishnu statue with eight arms under an umbrella at Angkor Wat temple, Angkor, Cambodia. (Otmar Winterleitner/Dreamstime.com)

which all beings disappear at the time of dissolution), and Aniruddha (the ego, agent, effect, and cause from whom all sentient and insentient beings come into existence).

The Vaikhanasa tradition is a Vedic *shakha* (a subschool of Taittariya tradition of the Yajur Veda) that is closely associated with Vaishnavism. Their Vedic ritual (*shrauta*) *sutras* and *smarta* sutras (ca. fourth to eighth centuries) reveal a strong devotional and meditational focus on Vishnu/Narayana as part of their ritual practices. Vaikhanasa smarta sutras describe the ritual of the installation of the sacred image, which is accompanied by recitation of two mantras—*om namo narayana* and *om namo bhagavate vasudevaya*—as well as the invocation of the four aspects of Vishnu

(*purusha* [spirit], *satya* [truth], *acyuta* [imperishable], and *aniruddha* [self-willed]).

The several streams under the umbrella of Vaishnavism consist of various ritual and meditational practices as well as different philosophical or theological perspectives, Historically, the Hindu tradition has recognized four Vaishnava sampradayas—Sri Vaishnavas of Tamil Nadu; the Gaudiya Vaishnavas located primarily in Bengal, Orissa, and Mathura; the Nimavats; and the Pushti Marga founded respectively by Ramanuja (11th century), Madhva (11th century), Nimbarka (13th century) and Vallabha (15th to 16th centuries).

Sri Vaishnava tradition of South India is a synthesis of the northern Indian Pancaratra and puranic tradition with the southern India tradition of the Alvars creating a theological vision in which Vishnu, as the transcendent cause and sustaining power of the universe, is the focus of emotional devotion. Liberation (moksha) from the cycle of birth, death, and rebirth (*samsara*) and *karma* is understood as the loving relationship between the individual soul and the god in Vaikuntha, Vishnu's heaven. Liberation, which is attained at death, is achieved through the cultivation of attachment to Vishnu and the simultaneous detachment from the world through devotional practices, including puja, and service (*seva*) to god. Total self-surrender (*praptti*) and abandonment to Vishnu's saving grace also lead to liberation. Sri Vaishnava tradition has split into the Vatakalai (northern) and Tenkali (southern) branches, which disagree, for example, on their understanding of the nature of caste distinction and how strictly they are to be regarded.

Gaudiya Vaishnavism is the form of devotion to Vishnu that developed in the traditional region of Bengal (Gaudiya), including the modern-day region of Mathura and Vrindavan. Theologically, Gaudiya Vaishnavas share much with Sri Vaishnavas, but differ in the form and expression of devotional practice. The inspirational exemplar for Gaudiya Vaishnavas is Vishvambhar Mishra (1476–1533), who would come to be known as Sri Krishna Caitanya, the name given to him upon taking initiation into renunciation. According to the tradition, Caitanya is believed to be the divine as Krishna and Radha in inseparable embrace. As such, Caitanya is often depicted as Krishna and Radha in one body, half-male and half-female. It is the language of devotion developed by Gaudiya Vaishnavas that distinguishes them from other Vaishnava groups. Gaudiyas elaborate essential Vaishanava doctrines using the terminology of Sanskrit poetics, in which aesthetic experience (*rasa*) takes priority. In the 16th century, Rupa Goswami systematized the devotional passion of the devotee for Krishna into five lasting feelings or moods of the divine (*sthayibhavas*): the feeling of tranquility (*shanti*), the love experienced by the servile devotee (*dasya*), the love experienced by a friend (*sakhya*), the love experienced by a parent (*vatsalya*), and the erotic mood of love (*shringara*). Each of these aesthetic moods aims to discover the kind of love that matches the devotee's emotional aptitudes. In each *bhava*, the distance between devotee and Krishna as object of devotion is progressively broken down until the highest most intimate experience of the divine is reached. In shringara, the devotee experiences love for Krishna through the joy of union, the anguish of separation (*viraha*), and the ecstasy of love in re-union with god as expressed by Radha, Krishna's consort, in Jayadeva's famous 10th-century poem the Gita Govinda. The Gaudiya devotee attains liberation through the constant, ecstatic experience of the divine love-play between Radha and Krishna attained by repeatedly reciting the names of Krishna (*namajapa*), remembering (*smarana*) and savoring the deeds of Krishna as narrated in the Bhagavata Purana, performing puja to the temple *murti* or to the sacred *tulsi* (basil) plant, living in the company of *sadhus*, and living in Mathura, the land of Krishna.

Vaishnavism in its multiple manifestations is very much alive in the contemporary world. It has been transported as the Hindu community has dispersed around the globe and numerous Vaishnava temples have been built outside India. Furthermore, a variety of more recent Hindu movements grounded in the Vaishnava theology and practice have become international organizations, including the International Society for Krishna Consciousness (ISKCON) and the several divisions of the Swaminarayan International.

Carlos Lopez

See also: Devotion/Devotional Traditions; Gaudiya Math; International Society for Krishna Consciousness; Meditation; Reincarnation; Swaminarayan Hinduism.

References

Bryant, Edwin. F. *A Sourcebook on Krishna*. Oxford: Oxford University Press, 2007.

Carman, John B. *The Theology of Ramanuja: An Essay on Interreligious Understanding*. New Haven: Yale University Press, 1974.

Gonda, Jan. *Aspects of Early Vaishnavism*. Utrecht: N. V. A. Oosthoek's Uitgevers Mij, 1954.

Haberman, David. *Journey through the Twelve Forests: An Encounter with Krishna*. New York: Oxford University Press, 1994.

Narayana, Vasudha. *The Way and the Goal: Expressions of Devotion in the Early Sri Vaishnava Tradition*. Washington, DC, and Cambridge: Institute for Vaishnava Studies and Center for the Study of World Religions, Harvard University, 1987.

Williams, Raymond Brady. *An Introduction to Swaminarayan Hinduism*. Cambridge and New York: Cambridge University Press, 2001.

■ Vanuatu

Vanuatu is a relatively new South Pacific island country located off the northeast coast of Australia, between Tuvalu and Kanaky. The more than 80 islands that compose the country have but 4,710 square miles of land. Its 215,000 citizens (2008) are primarily Melanesians.

The islands were originally settled, possibly as early as 1400 BCE, by Melanesians probably migrating there from present-day Indonesia. Those who resided on the islands had their first contact with Europeans when the Spanish explorer Pedro Fernandez de Quiros visited in 1605. Captain James Cook mapped the islands and named them New Hebrides for the Hebrides Islands in Scotland. They were known by that name through the mid-20th century.

Lacking most of the natural resources desired by Europeans, the islands became a major source of slave laborers as the French and British moved into the area. The continuance of the slave trade long after it had been outlawed caused an intense dislike of Europeans among the Vanuatuans, who often took out their anger on missionaries.

Vanuatu

Religion	Followers in 1970	Followers in 2010	% of Population	Annual % growth 2000–2010	Followers in 2025	Followers in 2050
Christians	78,600	230,000	94.4	2.55	309,000	431,000
Protestants	37,000	155,000	64.0	3.29	212,000	295,000
Roman Catholics	13,200	35,800	14.7	2.27	45,000	57,000
Anglicans	10,000	36,000	14.8	2.21	44,000	55,000
Ethnoreligionists	7,000	8,400	3.5	2.57	10,000	10,000
Baha'is	100	2,800	1.2	2.56	5,000	7,000
Agnostics	200	1,500	0.6	6.31	3,000	4,500
Buddhists	70	480	0.2	2.55	700	1,100
Atheists	0	150	0.1	2.52	300	500
New religionists	0	120	0.0	2.65	100	200
Total population	**86,000**	**243,000**	**100.0**	**2.57**	**328,000**	**454,000**

British and French vied for control of the islands through the 19th century, but at the beginning of the 20th century they worked out an agreement to govern the islands jointly. An independence movement developed in the 1970s and gained the overwhelming support of the people by the end of the decade. Overcoming various efforts to subvert it, Vanuatu gained its freedom in 1980.

The indigenous religion, popularly called Custom, survived in strength through World War II. It was especially strong on the islands of Tanan and Aniwa, with a significant presence also on Santo and Vao. It should be noted that there were almost 20 languages spoken in the islands, and a similar number of variations on the indigenous religion existed. Following World War II, the New Hebrides were the site of the original and primary manifestation of what became known as cargo cults. These groups, of which at least eight were identified, recognized a mythical figure called John Frum as the founder and expected him to return to the islands, bringing the same material abundance that islanders saw come out of the cargo planes that brought supplies for troops in the early 1940s. Remnants of the Cargo Cults can still be found, though, like the traditional religions, they have been opposed by the Christian community.

The introduction of Christianity into Vanuatu began with John Williams and James Harris of the London Missionary Society (LMS) and several Samoan Christian teachers who visited Tanan and Erromanga in 1839.

Leaving the Samoans on Tanna, Williams and Harris left for Erromanga, where both were killed soon after they landed. Other missionaries returned the following year and, finding their Samoan brethren safe, began a new work on Aneityum. Their work was hindered by several outbreaks of disease, which the islanders blamed upon the missionaries. The missionaries suffered the most from the continued taking of islanders into slavery, and more missionaries were killed in the New Hebrides than anywhere else in the South Pacific.

The work of the LMS was absorbed into the Presbyterian mission to the islands that began in 1848 with the arrival of Nova Scotian John Geddie. The Reformed Presbyterian Church of Scotland became the major force in Vanuatu with the arrival of John G. Paton, one of the more famous of the missionaries in the South Sea Islands. He had his first success on Aniwa, which became nominally Christian in the 1860s. The Presbyterian Church of New Zealand added their support in 1869, and eventually Presbyterians from Canada and Australia added their support. In 1948 the Presbyterian work was united and reorganized as the independent Presbyterian Church of Vanuatu. It now includes approximately one-third of Vanuatu's citizens.

Part of the significant work of the Presbyterians was the translation of the Bible into the indigenous languages. Thanks primarily to the two Gordon brothers from Scotland, the scriptures had been translated into the four main languages by 1870. By 1901 the Bible had been published in 21 languages.

VANUATU

The Roman Catholic Church established an initial presence in the New Hebrides in 1839, when a missionary arrived on Erromanga; however, their major push did not begin until 1887, as the British and French began to work out their cooperative arrangement for the islands. Over the next decades, the church had great success, especially on the islands of Vao, Atchin, and Wala. A prefecture was established in 1901 and a vicariate three years later. The Diocese of Port Vila was erected in 1966.

Bishop George A. Selwyn of the Anglican Church of Australia, with the cooperation of his colleagues in New Zealand, initiated missionary work in the northern New Hebrides in 1848. They limited their work to the northern islands in order to avoid head-on competition with the Presbyterians. For the first century of its existence, the mission actually was manned and guided by New Zealand Anglicans. Then in 1975, the Church in the Province of Melanesia was established as an independent entity, and Vanuatu became a diocese in the province, which is headquartered in the Solomon Islands.

The Churches of Christ (Non-Instrumental), a free church with Baptist roots, began work in the New Hebrides in 1903 after its representatives had been deported from Kanaky. Their work took hold on Aiba, and they subsequently built a substantial following on Pentecost and Maewo. More recent arrivals include the Apostolic Church (from Australia), the Seventh-day Adventist Church (1912), and the Jehovah's Witnesses (1933).

With the continuation of the traditional religions of the New Hebrides, it is not surprising to find a variety of indigenous churches. The interaction of Christians with the cargo cults has led to several new Christian congregations. The Voice of Daniel was formed by Daniel Tambe, a former Anglican priest on Pentecost Island, as the result of a vision he had in the early 1930s. The Free church derives from a schism within the Evangelical Church in New Caledonia and the Loyalty Islands, imported from Kanaky.

Anglicans, Roman Catholics, and Presbyterians came together in 1967 to form the New Hebrides Christian Council, with the Adventists and Apostolics as observer members. That Council evolved into the Vanuatu Christian Council, now affiliated with the World Council of Churches.

There are only a few religious groups that exist apart from the larger Christian community. The Baha'i Faith began building their work in the 1960s, and Buddhism has been brought to the islands by immigrants from Vietnam.

J. Gordon Melton

See also: Anglican Church of Australia; Baha'i Faith; Church in the Province of Melanesia; Churches of Christ; Evangelical Church in New Caledonia and the Loyalty Islands; Jehovah's Witnesses; London Missionary Society; Presbyterian Church of Vanuatu; Roman Catholic Church; Seventh-day Adventist Church; World Council of Churches.

References

Forman, Charles H. *The Island Churches of the South Pacific: Emergence in the Twentieth Century*. Maryknoll, NY: Orbis, 1982.

Prior, Randall, ed. *Gospel and Culture in Vanuatu*. 5 vols. Hindmarsh, South Australia: ATF Press, 2007.

Rice, Edward. *John Frum He Come: A Polemical Work About a Black Tragedy*. Garden City, NY: Doubleday & Company, 1974.

Trompf, G. W. *Cargo Cults and Millenarian Movements: Transoceanic Comparisons of New Religious Movements*. Berlin: Mouton De Gruyter, 1990.

Trompf, G. W. *Melanesian Religion*. Cambridge: Cambridge University Press, 1991.

Vedanta Societies

The Vedanta Societies are the products of the missionary outreach of swamis (Hindu monastics) in the order inspired by the Indian saint Ramakrishna Paramahansa (1836–1886), considered an *avatar,* an incarnation of God. Ramakrishna's mystical experiences are regarded as proving that there is truth in all of the world's religions, and this continues to be an emphasis of the Vedanta movement. Vedanta means "end of the Vedas," and it refers to the later Vedic texts, the Upanishads, and the philosophical schools based on those texts. The basic Vedantic doctrine is that reality is non-dual and unitary, and that we are all part of the one divine reality. Vedanta was introduced to the United States in 1893, when Swami Vivekananda (1863–1902) spoke at the World Parliament of Religions held in Chicago in conjunction with the Columbian Exposition. His presentation of Hindu thought to the American public was so well received that he remained until 1896 to give lectures in the Midwestern and Eastern United States and in Europe, to instruct students, and to inspire the founding of the first Vedanta Society, in New York City in 1896. Vivekananda returned to the United States in 1899–1900 to lecture in California.

Additional swamis in the Ramakrishna Order came to the United States and founded Vedanta Societies in major cities. Abhedananda (1866–1939) was based in New York City and taught in the United States from 1897 to 1921. Trigunatita led the San Francisco Vedanta Society, which built the first Hindu temple in America in 1906. Paramananda (1885–1940) arrived in 1906 and established centers in Boston and Los Angeles, and lectured all over the United States. In 1923 he founded a spiritual community, Ananda Ashrama, at La Crescenta, California. Prabhavananda (1914–1976) founded a center in Portland, and he established an influential Vedanta Society in Hollywood in 1930. This center grew to become the Vedanta Society of Southern California, with several monasteries, a convent, and the well-known Vedanta Press. In the late 1930s, the British writers Gerald Heard (1889–1971), Aldous Huxley (1894–1963), and Christopher Isherwood (1904–1986) became Prabhavananda's disciples. Nikhilananda (1895–1973) founded a center in Manhattan in 1933 and was a prolific writer and speaker;

A statue of Swami Vivekananda, one of the most influential spiritual leaders of the philosophies of Vedanta and Yoga. He was the chief disciple of Ramakrishna Paramahamsa and the founder of Ramakrishna Math and Ramakrishna Mission. (Nilesh Bhange/Dreamstime.com)

his disciples included Joseph Campbell, the comparative mythologist.

The Vedanta Societies continue to be headed by male Indian swamis, although they have trained American swamis as well as women monastics. The original Vedanta Societies in the United States remain under the spiritual (though not the administrative) authority of the Ramakrishna Order, headquartered in India, and are now part of a worldwide fellowship of autonomous Vedanta Centers. The Ramakrishna Math and Mission oversees a number of centers and institutions across the country. Centers within the United States may be found in New York City, Berkeley, San Francisco, Sacramento, Hollywood, Chicago, Boston, St. Louis, Portland, Providence, and Seattle. The Vedanta center of

Southern California maintains an extensive Internet site at http://www.vedanta.org/, which includes a worldwide directory of Vedanta Societies.

Controversies have arisen over keeping talented swamis obedient to the Ramakrishna Order in India and on how women should relate to the male Indian monastic order. From 1910, Swami Abhedananda lectured independently of the control of the Ramakrishna Order, and when he returned to India he founded a separate organization. When Swami Paramananda died in 1940, his disciples, who included a number of monastic women, decided that his niece, Gayatri Devi, should succeed him as leader, instead of accepting a new swami from India. In 1941 the Ramakrishna Order decided that the centers founded by Paramananda were no longer its affiliates. In the early years, the Indian swamis had to cope with American racism and prejudice against their Hindu religion. Today, the Vedanta Societies have succeeded in being accepted in interfaith interactions in their respective areas.

Ramakrishna Math and Mission
PO Belur Math
District Howrah 711 202
West Bengal
India

Catherine Wessinger

See also: Hinduism; Monasticism.

References

Burke, Marie Louise. *Swami Vivekananda: His Second Visit to the West: New Discoveries.* Calcutta: Advaita Ashrama, 1978.

Burke, Marie Louise. *Swami Vivekananda in America: New Discoveries.* 2 vols. Calcutta: Advaita Ashrama, 1958.

Jackson, Carl T. *The Oriental Religions and American Thought: Nineteenth-Century Explorations.* Westport, CT: Greenwood, 1981.

Jackson, Carl T. "The Swami in America: A History of the Ramakrishna Movement in the United States, 1893–1960." Ph.D. diss., University of California, 1964.

Wessinger, Catherine. "Hinduism Arrives in America: The Vedanta Movement and the Self-Realization Fellowship." In *America's Alternative Religions,* edited by Timothy Miller, 173–190. Albany: State University of New York Press, 1995.

Vegetarianism

The term "vegetarianism" refers to a spectrum of diet regimens that significantly cut back or altogether eliminate the use of any animal products from one's diet. Veganism refers to a diet that does not use any animal products in the diet, while most vegetarians will ingest foods such as eggs, milk, and cheese, that is, animal products that do not require the death of the animal from which they are taken. Popular variant vegetarian diets include the several programs emphasizing raw food and the Macrobiotics diet.

Vegetarianism appears to have first gained a following among the Jains, who had developed a doctrine of *ahimsa*, or harmlessness, by which they meant non-killing. By around 800 BCE, Jains were teaching that the killing of any animal life and even some forms of plant life accumulates *karma* (consequences), which must be neutralized before one can escape the rounds of reincarnation (*samsara*). As this idea developed, within Jain circles, monks developed the practices of sweeping their pathway with a broom to prevent the inadvertent killing of any insects or other small creatures and wearing a mask to prevent their being inhaled. Some abandoned agriculture as it required the harm or death of animals in the process of raising crops.

The Jains' concept of ahimsa penetrated Buddhism, but Buddhists generally avoided some of the more extreme expressions of it. Buddhist monasteries consumed a vegetarian diet, but the average Buddhist monk might accept meat when offered to him as he begged for food. The Vinaya, the guidebook for Buddhist monastic life, did not forbid meat, the only exception being an admonition to refrain from partaking from animals specifically killed to feed the monks. A strict vegetarianism arose primarily among the monks of East Asia. Wesak, the Buddha's birthday, was a time for feasting often with vegetarian meals donated to the monks, and communal vegetarian meals for laypeople.

In Japan, moves toward adopting an ethical system based on ahimsa made some penetration of the culture during the Nara era (eighth century CE), as Buddhism moved into the country from China. The adoption of nonviolent ideas included the development of a Japanese vegetarian diet, but both the ahimsa perspective and the diet were soon abandoned as the government moved to co-opt Buddhism for its own ends.

From Jainism and Buddhism, vegetarianism seeped into the larger Hindu community. Jains attacked certain Hindu practices such as animal sacrifice and the consuming of meat. By the beginning of the first millennium BCE, those in the Brahmin class, which included most priests and many cultural influentials, adopted the idea of ahimsa and as a corollary adopted a vegetarian diet. One step in this direction was to make an exception that allowed the eating of meat from animals that had been sacrificed. This exception was made after defining the death of animals in sacrificial ritual as not *himsa,* or killing.

With the exception of animal sacrifice, which has to a large extent been abandoned in India, the ancient practices of vegetarianism have continued to the present, and even expanded. Animal sacrifice was an integral part of Vedic religion, but in the modern era moves were made to replace it in the light of intense criticism from the West. In 1950, animal sacrifice in Hindu temples was outlawed in the state of Madras in southern India. By this time new rituals had been developed to replace the sacrificial procedures. The primary place where it now continues is in Bengal among worshippers of the dark goddess Kali.

One group, the followers of Tantrics, opposed vegetarianism and integrated the consumption of meat into their rituals, which attempted to reach the divine through the world rather than by withdrawal. The monks (*sanyassins*) had developed an elaborate process of withdrawing from the world—worldly possessions, society, family connections, and the like—which in some cases mixed with the idea of ahimsa and produced a commitment to vegetarianism. Vegetarianism also began to be identified as a step toward spiritual purity and hence the proper attitude of a Brahmin. Finally, one began to see the phenomenon of a whole caste adopting the practice as a means of moving up in the overall social structure.

Vegetarianism was not prominent in the West until the modern age. While one finds the prohibition of certain foods (such as pork), the major Western religious traditions had no problem with eating meat or other animal products. What anti-meat dietary prohibitions emerged were based on the reputed "impurity" of the forbidden foods. Prohibitions primarily centered on pork products and some forms of seafood. The Jewish prohibitions were rejected by the early Christians and the issue became a characteristic separating the two communities. The Islamic community, however, picked up and continued the Jewish prohibitions and Islamic dietary rules generally follow Jewish kosher practice. The rise of vegetarianism in the West appears to have been a result of the influx of ideals from the East that began with the British move into India and China, new sectarian Christian impulses, and the rise of new "scientific" schools of health as predecessors to modern medicine.

The first vegetarian organization in the West was the small Bible Christian Church founded by the Reverend William Cowherd in 1809 in Salford, England. Cowherd, a former Anglican clergyman, had come to believe that abstinence from meat was necessary if a person was to progress spiritually. In 1817, with 41 church members, Cowherd moved to Philadelphia, thus becoming the fountainhead of future vegetarian practice on both sides of the Atlantic. Though a relatively small body, it is noted as influencing a number of reformers who chose to deal with issue of diet. Directly influenced by the church was Sylvester Graham (1794–1851) who invented the still popular graham cracker and lectured widely on the vegetarian diet he had developed. The first secular vegetarian organization was the Vegetarian Society founded in 1847 in Manchester. The American Vegetarian Society was founded three years later. Its first president was William Alcott (1798–1859), a disciple of Graham's perspective. Graham himself became the vice president. They were joined in their endeavor by some of the leaders of the water cure movement, Joel Shew, Russell Trall, and William Metcalfe. Though always a small minority movement, vegetarianism had spread through Europe to the point that a still-existing International Vegetarian Union could be formed in 1908.

At the beginning of the 19th century, vegetarianism was tied to a new issue that would become increasingly important, the protection of the rights of animals and the crusade to end all forms of animal cruelty. The first organization dedicated to these goals, the Millennial Guild, appeared in 1912.

The Christian sectarian support of vegetarianism and the new scientific approaches to diet reform came together in the Seventh-day Adventist Church. Church founder and Prophetess Ellen G. White was interested in health reform, the subject of a number of her prophetic messages. She found cutting-edge support in the form of the Kellogg brothers, John Harvey (1852–1943) and Will Keith. In 1875, John Kellogg became the superintendent of the Western Health Reform Institute supported by the fledgling church in Battle Creek,

Michigan, and three years later opened the famous sanatorium where he was able to develop the new diet he proposed built around cereals and other vegetarian food. The brothers went on to found the company that still bears their name, though the company has long since abandoned their founder's health priorities.

Theosophy became a major force injecting Eastern ideas into the West, and vegetarianism became one of its themes. Annie Besant (1847–1933), who succeeded Henry S. Olcott (1832–1907) as the president of the Theosophical Society, became a vegetarian and used the Society effectively to urge diet change on the members and spread vegetarian ideals beyond its boundaries. She argued that mass slaughter of animals for food demeaned humanity and picked up Cowherd's basic notion that vegetarianism was a prerequisite for spiritual progress. As the Society splintered, the vegetarian perspective was carried into many of the more than 100 new Theosophically inspired organizations like the Liberal Catholic Church and the Rosicrucian Fellowship.

In the United Kingdom the cause of the animals would be picked up by the Spiritualist movement, which gave its backing to organizations like the Anti-Vivisection League, a precursor to contemporary organizations like PETA (People for the Ethical Treatment of Animals). Support for the Indian teaching of ahimsa and the vegan philosophy it espoused was given by the American Vegan Society founded in New Jersey in 1960. Founder H. Jay Dinshah (1933–2000), an Indian American, lifted the banner for ahimsa, which he termed "dynamic harmlessness." Vegetarianism had waned in North America and most had not grasped the connection between it and the nonviolent approach of the highly respected Mahatma Gandhi (1869–1948). Dinshah argued for a comprehensive vegan lifestyle that excluded from one's diet all animals (meat, fish, fowl) and animal products (milk, eggs, honey, and so forth) as well as animal by-products in such things as shoes, clothing, and toiletries.

Dinshah was but one of the people to emerge in the 1970s to espouse vegetarianism and to found a large socially relevant movement that welcomed critiques of the majority society in Europe and America —the New Age movement. The movement provided a vehicle for small movements like the Vegans to reach far larger audiences than they otherwise could ever hope to influence, and they formed a natural alliance with emergent coalitions built around concerns for organic foods without additives; alternative and holistic approaches to health; and the overuse of animals for medical and scientific experimentation.

Contemporaneously with Dinshah, Ann Wigmore of the Hippocrates Health Institute emerged as the great champion of the raw food movement. Possibly no one had the impact of George Ahsawa and Michio Kushi, who became the champions of the Macrobiotic diet. Built on the same principles as Asian martial arts and healing techniques like acupuncture, the Macrobiotic diet started with a selection of cereal grains, of which unpolished brown rice was the most important, and advocated an inexpensive humane and healthy alternative to meat-centered diets. Macrobiotics found a popular audience, as it emphasized a more positive approach to rebuilding a tasty and comprehensive diet, and went far beyond what was often seen as simply abandoning meat in one's diet.

The New Age movement in Europe and America revealed the existence of a number of groups in which vegetarianism predominated, from the Unity School of Christianity to numerous Esoteric groups and many of the new Eastern groups that flooded the West after America changed its immigration laws in 1965. Vegetarianism remains very much a minority practice in the West, but has grown to the point that vegetarian restaurants are now found in almost all large cities and non-vegetarian restaurants go out of their way to have vegetarian options on their menus. While an increasing number accept vegetarianism as a way of life based on scientific and social ethical concern (and even a dislike of the taste of meat), religious ideas remain the foundation of its growth.

American Vegan Society
56 Dinshah Lane
PO Box 369
Malaga, NJ 08328-0908
http://www.americanvegan.org

Hippocrates Health Institute
1443 Palmdale Court
West Palm Beach, FL 33411

J. Gordon Melton

See also: Besant, Annie; Blavatsky, Helena P.; Jainism; New Age Movement; Seventh-day Adventist Church; Theosophical Society (America); Unity School of Christianity; White, Ellen G.

References

Besant, Annie. *Vegetarianism in the Light of Theosophy*. London: Theosophical Publishing Society, 1984.

Bodhipaksa. *Vegetarianism*. Living a Buddhist Life Series. Cambridge: Windhorse Publications, 2004.

Bollee, William. *The History of Vegetarianism and Cow-Veneration in India*. London: Routledge, 2009.

Dinshah, Freya. *The Vegan Kitchen*. Malaga, NJ: American Vegan Society, 1970.

Dinshah, H. Jay. *Out of the Jungle*. Malaga, NJ: American Vegan Society, 1995.

Lappe, Frances Moore. *Diet for a Small Planet*. New York: Ballantine Books, 1971.

Numbers, Ronald L. *Prophetess of Health*. New York: Harper & Row, 1976.

Stuart, Tristram. *The Bloodless Revolution: A Cultural History of Vegetarianism: From 1600 to Modern Times*. New York: W.W. Norton, 2008.

■ Venezuela

Venezuela is located in northeastern South America on the Caribbean Sea between Colombia to the west and Guyana to the east. Its southern border, which reaches into the Amazon River basin, is shared with Brazil. Geographically, Venezuela is a land of vivid contrasts, with four major divisions: the Maracaibo lowlands in the northwest, the northern mountains (the most northeastern section of the Andes) extending in a broad east-west arc from the Colombian border along the Caribbean Coast, the savannas of the Orinoco River Basin in central Venezuela, and the Guyana highlands in the southeast.

The 1999 Constitution changed the name of the Republic of Venezuela to the Bolivarian Republic of Venezuela. The nation is composed of 20 federal states and a federal district, which contains the capital of Caracas. The country has an area of 352,144 square miles and approximately 85 percent of the national population lives in urban areas in the northern portion of the country, near the Caribbean Coast. Almost half of Venezuela's land area lies south of the Orinoco River, which contains only 5 percent of the total population.

According to the National Statistics Institute, the nation's total population on January 31, 2007, was

Venezuela

Religion	Followers in 1970	Followers in 2010	% of Population	Annual % growth 2000–2010	Followers in 2025	Followers in 2050
Christians	10,317,000	27,443,000	94.5	1.82	32,857,000	38,717,000
Roman Catholics	9,775,000	24,870,000	85.6	1.32	28,721,000	32,716,000
Protestants	148,000	1,300,000	4.5	4.04	2,200,000	3,300,000
Independents	131,000	976,000	3.4	2.47	1,500,000	2,200,000
Agnostics	49,000	667,000	2.3	2.53	1,300,000	1,800,000
Spiritists	100,000	305,000	1.1	1.84	370,000	440,000
Ethnoreligionists	200,000	205,000	0.7	1.84	230,000	260,000
Baha'is	24,900	170,000	0.6	1.84	250,000	350,000
Muslims	500	95,000	0.3	1.84	150,000	200,000
Atheists	10,000	60,000	0.2	2.23	85,000	115,000
Jews	12,000	57,000	0.2	1.84	72,000	85,000
Buddhists	2,000	36,000	0.1	1.84	50,000	70,000
Chinese folk	5,000	5,900	0.0	1.84	7,000	9,000
New religionists	500	1,200	0.0	1.84	2,000	3,000
Total population	**10,721,000**	**29,045,000**	**100.0**	**1.84**	**35,373,000**	**42,049,000**

27,750,163 inhabitants. About 60 percent of the population are *mestizo* (mixed races: Caucasian, African, and Amerindian), 29 percent Caucasian (mostly Spanish, Italian, German, and Portuguese), 8 percent Afro-Venezuelan, 1 percent Asian-Middle Eastern (Chinese, Japanese, Vietnamese, Korean, and Middle Easterners), and 2 percent Amerindian. The national and official language is Spanish, although 31 indigenous languages are spoken. Immigrant communities and their descendants commonly use their own native languages.

The Venezuelan people have a combination of ethnic heritages. The Amerindians, Spanish colonists, and Africans were joined by European groups and others from neighboring countries of South America during waves of immigration in the 20th century. There are various communities of Eastern Europeans. Some Venezuelans trace their ancestry to 10,000 expatriates from the southern United States who arrived after the Civil War (1865). The multiracial/ethnic combination is evident in Venezuelan culture: food, music, clothing, holidays, and the *mestizaje* identity.

Immigration since World War II has not only increased the spectrum of Christian denominations in the country, but also brought many of the world's religions to Venezuela. The 1961 Constitution guaranteed freedom of religion to all faiths; church and state are separate, although the majority of people still refer to themselves as Roman Catholic.

According to government estimates in 2006, 76 of the population was Roman Catholic, 29 percent was non-Roman Catholic Christians (includes Eastern Orthodox, Protestant, and other marginal Christian groups, such as Mormons and Jehovah's Witnesses), and the remaining 1 percent were "other religions" or claimed no religious affiliation. However, the Evangelical Council of Venezuela estimated that evangelical Protestants constituted approximately 10 percent of the population.

In 2008, the Constitution provided for freedom of religion, on the condition that its practice does not violate public morality, decency, or public order; and other laws and policies contributed to the generally free practice of religion. The government generally respected religious freedom in practice; however, there were some efforts by the Chávez government, motivated by political reasons, to limit the influence of religious groups in certain geographic, social and political areas.

The government continues to prohibit foreign missionary groups from working in indigenous areas. In 2005, the Ministry of Interior rescinded permission for the New Tribes Mission (NTM) to conduct its social programs among indigenous tribes; NTM appealed to the Supreme Court, and the case is still pending. The NTM withdrew more than 100 missionaries from indigenous areas in compliance with the government's order. In 2005, the Church of Jesus Christ of Latter-day Saints (Mormons) withdrew 219 missionaries, citing difficulties in obtaining religious visas from the government. Some Mormon missionaries working with indigenous peoples were expelled from those areas, while the others departed voluntarily.

The territory known today as Venezuela was inhabited by an array of Amerindian groups in prehistoric times. The Carib (including the Tamaques, Maquiritares, and Arecunas) settled along the Caribbean Coast, while other Native American groups, mainly Arawaks, settled in the mountains and in the Orinoco River basin of the interior.

The coast of Venezuela was discovered by Christopher Columbus (1451–1506) during his third voyage to the New World, on August 1, 1498. Its name, meaning "Little Venice," was given by reason of the fact that Alonso de Ojeda, who first explored the coast in 1499, found a small aboriginal village built on stilts in the region of Lake Maracaibo. Modified into Venezuela, the name afterward served to designate the whole territory of the captaincy general. Spanish settlements were established on the Caribbean Coast at Cumaná in 1520 and Santa Ana de Coro in 1527. The Spanish conquest was complete by 1600. By the end of the first century of Spanish rule, about half of the Amerindian tribes that existed previously in Venezuela had become extinct.

The Spanish settled and began to build an agricultural colony based on cacao (chocolate) production, for which they later imported slaves from Africa. Since then Venezuela has developed a regularly organized society with peculiar ethnic characteristics and a distinctive national culture. Venezuela was Spain's most

VENEZUELA

Map labels: Punto Fijo, Riecito, Caracas, La Guaira, Guiria, Cabimas, Ciudad Guayana, Curiapo, Cabruta, Caicara, Ciudad Piar, Guasipati, Bochinche, El Amparo, Ciudad Piar, El Dorado, Tumeremo, El Jobal, La Paragua, Canaima, Venezuela, San Juan de Manapiare, Santa Elena de Uairen, San Fernando de Atabapo, Esmeralda

N

successful agricultural colony, first with cacao production and export, and then, toward the end of the 18th century, with coffee.

As a result of the racial mixtures, Venezuelan society from its very beginnings displayed a more homogeneous ethnic makeup than most other Latin American colonies. The large group of freedmen worked mostly as manual laborers in the emerging cities or lived as peasants on small plots of land. Blacks, mulattos, and mestizos occupied the lower rungs on the social ladder, but they still enjoyed a number of rights and guarantees provided by Spanish law and customs.

The colony of Venezuela was under the administration of governors and captains general during the 17th and 18th centuries. In 1718, Spanish colonial authorities organized the Viceroyalty of New Granada, with Venezuela as its easternmost region under a captaincy general.

Much of the movement for the independence of northern part of South America from Spain originated in Venezuela. The battles for independence were fought between 1749 and 1830, during which Simón Bolívar became a national hero and built his dream of Gran Colombia (from what is today Ecuador, Colombia, Panama, northern Peru and Venezuela). An independent New Granada (Colombia, Ecuador, and Venezuela) finally emerged in 1819 as the Republic of Gran Colombia. The War of Independence finally ended with the Battle of Carabobo, won by the Liberator Simón Bolívar in 1821. When the Republic of Gran Colombia was dismembered, the Republic of Venezuela was established in 1830.

Thereafter, the country was ruled by an oligarchy under the leadership of an authoritarian leader (*caudillo*) well into the 20th century. The era of the caudillo began with 16 relatively peaceful and prosperous years under the rule of General José Antonio Páez (r. 1830–1835, 1839–1843). Using funds earned during the coffee-induced economic boom, he oversaw the building of fledgling social and economic infrastructures. Generally considered second only to Bolívar as a national hero, Páez (a mestizo) ruled in conjunction with the *criollo* elite (Venezuelan born of pure Spanish ancestry), which maintained its unity around the caudillo as long as coffee prices remained high.

In the 1840s, however, coffee prices plunged, and the oligarchy split into two factions: those who remained with Páez called themselves Conservatives, while his rivals called themselves Liberals. The Liberals first came to prominence in 1846 with Páez's surprising selection of General José Tadeo Monagas (1847–1851) as his successor. Two years later, Monagas ousted all the Conservatives from his government and sent Páez into exile, which precipitated a decade of dictatorial rule shared with his brother, José Gregorio. In 1857 they introduced a new Constitution in an obvious attempt to install a Monagas family dynasty. The regime was ousted the following year in a revolt that included elite members of both parties.

The elite factions failed to agree on a replacement for the Monagas, however, which produced 20 years of intermittent and chaotic civil war. Between 1858 and 1863, local caudillos engaged in a power struggle known as the Federal War, because the Liberals favored federalism. In the end, the Liberals triumphed and General Juan C. Falcón was named president. Central government authority was finally restored in 1870 under Falcón's chief aide, Antonio Guzmán Blanco (r. 1870–1887), who established a dictatorship that lasted for 20 years. During his term of office, strife and bloodshed continued, and Venezuela suffered from despotism such as the nation had not known until this time.

During the 20th century, Venezuela emerged as one of the wealthiest nations in South America because of the development of its petroleum industry in and around Lake Maracaibo, in the northwestern region, near the Colombian border. Since 1918, Dutch, British, and American companies have developed the rich oil fields found in several regions of the country. Many immigrants have assisted in the development of its industries.

This transformed the Venezuelan economy, and today this nation is the third largest producer in the Organization of the Petroleum Exporting Countries (OPEC), with particularly large reserves of heavy bitumen in the southeastern Orinoco River basin. The extra revenue meant that the road system could be developed to become the envy of South America, and Caracas and other central cities were virtually rebuilt.

The dependence on oil revenues has meant that other sectors such as agriculture and tourism have been underdeveloped and with the late 1970s' fall in oil prices inflation has risen somewhat from the previous 10 percent levels, as successive governments realized they must diversify the economy. The discovery of very rich iron ore deposits, as well as gold, diamonds, and nickel, has meant that the mining sector has been the most buoyant part of the economy since about 1984.

General Juan Vicente Gómez ruled the nation from 1908 to 1935, alternating between the posts of president and minister of war. Gómez justified his harsh dictatorship as the form of government (*caudillismo*) preferred by the predominantly mixed-race Venezuelans. The Gómez regime coincided with a protracted period favorable to Venezuelan exports, and the economy boomed.

Rómulo Ernesto Betancourt Bello (1908–1981), known as "The Father of Venezuelan Democracy," was president of Venezuela from 1945 to 1948 and again from 1959 to 1964, as well as leader of Acción Democrática, which became Venezuela's dominant political party in the 20th century. Betancourt became president in 1945 by means of a military coup d'état and, during his time in office, completed an impressive agenda. His accomplishments included the declaration of universal suffrage, the institution of social reforms, and securing half of the profits generated by foreign oil companies for Venezuela. His government worked closely with the International Refugee Organization to aid European refugees and displaced persons who could not or would not return home after World War II; his government assumed responsibility for the legal protection and resettlement of tens of thousands of refugees inside Venezuela.

Carlos Delgado Chalbaud became chairman of the military junta that governed Venezuela during 1948–1950. He was kidnapped and assassinated in November 1950, allegedly by his fellow junta member Marcos Pérez Jiménez, who began a brutal dictatorship that delayed the establishment of representative democracy in the nation until 1958. Since then, and continuing to the present, relatively free elections have been held every five years.

Hugo Rafael Chávez Frías (b. 1954), the current president of Venezuela, is the leader of the Bolivarian Revolution (named after the Liberator Simón Bolívar), which promotes a political doctrine of participatory democracy, socialism, and Latin American and Caribbean cooperation. He is also a strong critic of neoliberalism, globalization, and U.S. foreign policy. A career military officer, Chávez founded the left-wing Fifth Republic movement after orchestrating a failed 1992 coup d'état against President Carlos Andrés Pérez (r. 1989–1993, under Democratic Action).

Chávez's policies have evoked strong controversy in Venezuela and abroad, and have received everything from vehement criticism to enthusiastic support. The U.S. government under the George W. Bush adminis-

tration claimed that Chávez was a threat to democracy in Latin America; however, many other governments sympathize with his ideology and welcome his bilateral trade and reciprocal aid agreements. In 2005 and 2006, Chávez was named one of *Time* magazine's 100 most influential people.

The Roman Catholic Church   Catholicism was introduced to Venezuela by Franciscans and Dominicans in 1513. They created some of the first cocoa plantations and also taught the Amerindians the arts of domestic husbandry. The Jesuits operated within the vast savannas of the Orinoco River basin from 1628 until their expulsion in 1767. The Capuchins arrived in 1658 and over the next century spread out in the region around Caracas, where many of the settlements were founded by them.

The Diocese of Santa Ana de Coro was founded in Venezuela in 1531, which was transferred to the City of Santiago de León de Caracas and became the Diocese of Caracas in 1637; in November 1803 this diocese became the Archdiocese of Caracas, Santiago de Venezuela.

By 1662, the Catholic authorities had established five official zones for evangelization of the Amerindians: Llanos de Caracas, from the mouth of the Tuy River to Lake Maracaibo; Alto Orinoco Río Negro; Guyana, in the extreme eastern part of Venezuela; Trinidad; and Maracaibo. In 1734, the territory of Alto Orinoco was divided among the Capuchins, Franciscans, and Jesuits. Venezuela's independence from Spain was a disaster for the church, which had identified with the Spanish colonial leadership. The church suffered a great loss of property and mission stations during the drawn-out War of Independence.

Conflicts between the church and civil authorities occurred in the earliest period of the republic's existence. The first of these arose out of the refusal of the archbishop of Caracas to swear allegiance to the 1830 Constitution. This refusal, based on the absence of any explicit recognition of Catholicism as the state religion, resulted in the exile of the archbishop along with four bishops. Their exile lasted 16 months, after which the clerics (with the exception of the archbishop, who died in November 1831) returned in April 1832 upon reaching an understanding with the government.

Catholic church on Isla Margarita in Venezuela. Ninety-six percent of Venezuela's population is Roman Catholic. (iStockPhoto.com)

During the 1870s, President Antonio Guzmán Blanco poured out his wrath on the whole church and its more prized institutions, in an attempt to destroy the influence of the clergy and their criticism of his despotism. He expelled the last religious communities of nuns left in Venezuela and suppressed the seminaries, despoiling them of their possessions and destroying the budding revival of religious education in the country. He also destroyed churches, took possession of church-owned buildings, abolished revenues for the church, secularized the cemeteries, and defamed the clergy.

Finally, Guzmán decreed the total suppression of convents in the country and prohibited their future restoration. His attempt to establish a national church independent of the Vatican, however, was not popular among the Venezuelan citizens and he was forced to show some restraint. Nonetheless, during Guzmán's administration, civil marriage took precedence over the religious ceremony, the law being a constant source of demoralization among the Catholic faithful.

Guzmán's fall created a general reaction among the populace in favor of the church, which brought certain advantages for the clergy and for the advancement of the church. In 1886, the government itself invited the Sisters of Charity of St. Joseph of Tarbes to provide needed services in the nation's hospitals. Later the Sisters of Charity were able to establish educational and charitable centers in many cities, where they were joined by another congregation of Sisters of Charity, those of Saint Anne (Spanish). Other female religious orders were established to provide charitable work and catechistic instruction: the Little Sisters of the Poor of Maiquetia, the Servants of the Most Holy Sacrament, and the Franciscan Sisters.

In 1891, the government invited the Capuchin monks to work among the Amerindians in the Orinoco River basin, and they were allowed to establish residences in Caracas and Maracaibo. In 1894, the Salesians arrived and dedicated their efforts to the education of youth. The Augustinian Recollects arrived in 1899 to begin parochial work in the Archdiocese of Caracas and the dioceses of Guyana and Zulia. In 1903, also at the invitation of the government, the Sons of Mary Immaculate (French fathers) established themselves in Caracas, where they founded a college and provided needed assistance to the secular clergy. That same year, the Dominican fathers were allowed by the government to take possession of the Church of the Sacred Heart of Jesus in Caracas, and later engaged in teaching at the seminary of Caracas.

In 1910, the Archdiocese of Caracas administered 82 parishes, in addition to 22 affiliated churches and private chapels; it also operated 2 seminaries for training the local priesthood. At that time, there were only a total of 35 male religious and 242 sisters. The archbishop of Caracas, Monsignor Juan Bautista Castro, founded the Congregation of Servants of the Most Holy Sacrament in Caracas in 1911.

The Catholic Church adopted a conservative theological and social stance throughout the 19th and 20th centuries, and it had great difficulty in recruiting national priests and religious workers. For example, in 1969, only 19 percent of religious priests and 43 percent of female religious were native Venezuelans. Seventy-nine percent of the resident priests were born outside of Latin America and 2 percent were born in other Latin American countries. Forty-one percent of the resident nuns were born outside of Latin America and 16 percent were born in other Latin American countries.

During the 1960s and following years, diverse tensions and conflicts arose within the Venezuelan Catholic Church, which resulted from challenges posed by the Second Vatican Council (1962–1965), the General Conference of Latin American Bishops in Medellín in 1968, Latin American Liberation Theology, and the Catholic Charismatic Renewal.

These new movements polarized Catholic bishops, parish priests, religious workers, and the laity into various factions: *traditionalists,* who wanted the church to remain as it was prior to the reforms approved by the Second Vatican Council (late 1960s); *reformers,* who supported the church's modern stance; *progressives,* who sought to implement the new vision for "a preferential option for the poor" through social and political action aimed at transforming Venezuelan society and establishing social justice through peaceful democratic means; *radicals,* who adopted Liberation Theology, based on Marxist ideology, and advocated violent revolution by the people as a means of overthrowing the oligarchy and creating a socialist state that would serve the marginalized masses; and *charismatic agents* (priests, nuns, and lay members), who sought to transform the spiritual and communal life of Catholics by means of the power and gifts of the Holy Spirit (including the "baptism of the Holy Spirit and speaking in tongues").

Since the mid-1960s, the Venezuelan Catholic Church—influenced greatly by papal calls for a refocus of attention on the needs of the urban poor—has directed significant resources toward assisting the lower classes and empowering the laity in the local parishes.

The Catholic Charismatic Renewal (CCR) in Venezuela traces its origin to 1973, when the first Charismatic Conference was held at the Salesian retreat center in Los Teques, Miranda state, not far from downtown Caracas. Thereafter, the CCR became established and prospered in many locations throughout the country. In 1988, the CCR National Coordination Office was relocated from Maracaibo to Barquisimeto. In October of that year, 28 priests, 13 laypersons, and 5 bishops from Venezuela participated in the international Catholic Charismatic Renewal Conference held in Monterrey, Mexico. Leading this delegation were Monsignor Tulio Manuel Chirivella and Monsignor Carmen de Rúa, the national CCR advisor and the national CCR coordinator, respectively, in Venezuela. In April 1989, the National Day of Prayer was celebrated in Valencia, Carabobo state, with the participation of 10,000 people, under the leadership of a team of Catholic charismatic priests and nuns.

In the mid-1970s, the principal male religious orders in Venezuela were Augustinians, Benedictines, Capuchins, Claretins, Dominicans, Eudistas, French PP, Jesuits, Passionists, Paulists, Redemptorists, Salesias, Salle Brothers, Marists, and Brothers of Saint John of God. Female religious orders founded in Venezuela include Hermanitas de los Pobres, Franciscanas, Siervas del Santísimo Sacramento, Lourdistas, Agustinas, Dominicans, and Carmelitas.

In 1995, Monsignor Ignacio Antonio Velasco García (b. 1929) was appointed the archbishop of Caracas by Pope John Paul II. The current archbishop of Caracas (Santiago de Venezuela) is Cardinal Jorge Urosa Savino (appointed in 2005). The Venezuelan Episcopal Conference (CEV), composed of the nation's archbishops, bishops, and auxiliary personnel who meet periodically to manage church affairs, was first created in 1973.

The current CEV president is Monsignor Ubaldo Ramón Santana Sequera, the archbishop of Maracaibo. Presently, there are nine archdioceses in Venezuela: Barquisimeto, Caracas, Calabozo, Ciudad Bolívar, Coro, Cumaná, Maracaibo, Mérida, and Valencia. The Venezuelan Catholic Church administers 36 dioceses (including 4 Apostolic Vicariates) with a total of 1,256 parishes. In 2004, these jurisdictions were served by 1,493 diocesan and 1,064 religious priests (a total of 2,557) and assisted by 138 permanent deacons, 1,628 religious brothers, and 3,775 religious sisters.

Overall, there has been a decline in the number of priests and religious workers providing pastoral care and support services, which has weakened the church's ability to retain adherents in Venezuela since the mid-1970s. For example, the Archdiocese of Caracas reported the following statistics in 2006: 140 diocesan and 419 religious priests (down from 160 and 600, respectively, in 1976), 730 religious brothers (down from 757 in 1976), and 1,332 religious sisters (down from 1,500 in 1976).

The Protestant Movement Agents of the British and Foreign Bible Society (BFBS) were the first to attempt the introduction of Protestantism into Venezuela, but as with the rest of South America, there was a gap of more than a half-century between their first arrival (1819) and the entrance of permanent Protestant missionaries (1883). In the meantime, the Church of England established a chaplaincy to serve British nationals, beginning in 1832. That work, never large, would eventually be attached to the Church of the Province of the West Indies. In 1976, it became an independent diocese and then became affiliated with the Episcopal Church.

The first Lutheran pastor arrived in 1865 to minister among German and English expatriates, and a Protestant Council was formed in 1870 among foreign residents. In 1878, Messiah Methodist Church was established in Caracas, which later became affiliated with the Presbyterians. In 1886, American Bible Society agent Francisco Penzotti (an Italian Uruguayan) arrived in Caracas and established local depots for Bible distribution throughout the country.

Missionary work was begun in 1889 by representatives of the British and Canadian "Open Brethren" branches of the Christian Brethren. During the 1890s, several other Protestant missionaries arrived: the Christian and Missionary Alliance (1890), the Evangelical German Lutheran Church (1893), the Presbyterian Church in the U.S.A. (1897), the Hebron Institute and Missionary Association (1897), the Swedish Evangelical Free Church (1898), and the Evangelical Mission of South America (1899, which established a national church body, known as Asociación de Iglesias Evangélicas Libres de Venezuela [ADIEL]).

During the early 20th century (1900–1939), at least a dozen additional mission agencies arrived from Europe and North America: the Scandinavian Alliance Mission (1906, later renamed The Evangelical Alliance Mission [TEAM]); the first Pentecostal missionaries (1910, who later affiliated with the Assemblies of God in the U.S.A.); the Seventh-day Adventist Church (1910); the Orinoco River Mission (1915, which established a national church body, known as Asociación de Iglesias Evangélicas del Oriente [ASIGEO]); Bethel Pentecostal Assembly (1919); independent Pentecostal missionaries began church work in Barquisimeto (1919, which became part of the United World Mission in 1947); the Evangelical Free Church of North America (1920, which established Asociación de Iglesias Evangélicas Libres de Venezuela [ADIEL]); Baptist Mid-Missions (1924); independent Baptist missionaries began work in Carúpano (1926, which later became part of the Southern Baptist Convention); the Apostolic Missionary Evangelical Christian Church / Bethel Evangelical Church (1927, also known as Iglesias Nativas Venezolanas de Apure, founded by Arístides Díaz); and independent Pentecostal work in El Tocuyo (1929, which later became part of the United World Mission).

The Assemblies of God Foreign Mission board first arrived in Venezuela in 1940 and built on the pioneer work begun by Mr. and Mrs. Gottfried F. Bender and Hilda Meyrick in Barquisimeto (1910). The Reverend Irvin Olson founded a central church in Caracas that became known as the mother church of this denomination in Venezuela. However, a major schism occurred in 1957 that led to the founding of the Venezuela Evangelical Pentecostal Association, which also has become a large denomination. In addition, during the 1950s, the International Church of the Foursquare Gospel and the United Pentecostal Church International arrived and developed very successful missionary efforts. Pentecostalism has given birth to a host of national church bodies. By decades, the minimum number of Protestant denominations, national church associations and service agencies founded since 1940 were the following: 1940s (5), 1950s (15), 1960s (5), 1970s (8), 1980s (11), and 1990s (7).

In 1965, the total Protestant membership nationally was only 47,000 and, up to this time, the accumulative growth of the Protestant community was not very impressive. A generation later, in 2000, sociologist Timothy Steigenga estimated that the Protestant population of Venezuela was somewhere between 7 and 10 percent.

In 2005, the largest Protestant denominations were estimated to be the following: the Seventh-day Adventist Church (235 churches with 63,100 members), the International Trinitarian Light of the World Pentecostal Church (480 churches with 56,900 members), The Evangelical Alliance Mission–related churches (900 churches with 29,200 members), the Assemblies of God (315 churches with 25,200 members), the Southern Baptist Convention (245 churches with 20,800 members), the United Pentecostal Church (240 churches with 19,300 members), Ebenezer Pentecostal Churches (100 churches with 12,000 members), the International Church of the Foursquare Gospel (60 churches with 7,250 members), and Bethel Evangelical Church of Apure (55 churches with 5,500 members). All other denominations had fewer than 5,000 members each.

In 2009, more than 180 Protestant denominations, independent churches and service agencies were affiliated with the Evangelical Council of Venezuela (Consejo Evangélico de Venezuela [CEV]), founded in 1972, which in turn is associated with the World Evangelical Alliance. Many leaders of these associations are also members of the Latin American Confraternity of Evangelicals (CONELA). Groups affiliated with the ecumenical Latin American Council of Churches (CLAI) include the Anglican Episcopal Church, the Evangelical Lutheran Church, the Presbyterian Church of Venezuela, and the Venezuelan Pentecostal Evangelical Union. There are no Venezuelan-based churches that are members of the World Council of Churches, though the Latin American Council of Churches is affiliated.

Other Christian Traditions   Approximately 2 percent of the population is affiliated with "other religions," which includes the following traditions.

Eastern Orthodox and Independent Western Catholic   There are two kinds of Eastern Orthodox groups in Venezuela, those in communion with the Vatican and those that are not. The latter are represented by the Greek Orthodox Church (Greece), the Russian Orthodox Church Abroad (under Bishop Alexander in Los Angeles, California), the Orthodox Church in America (also Russian Orthodox but affiliated with the Archdiocese of Moscow), the Romanian Orthodox Church (Romania), the Armenian Apostolic Church (Lebanon),

the Byzantine Catholic Church (Mar Markus, Hungary), and the Orthodox Apostolic Catholic Church of Antioch (patriarch of Antioch in Damascus, Syria: Antiochian Orthodox Archdiocese of Mexico, Venezuela, and Central America–Caribbean). Those in communion with the Vatican are the Greek Melkite Apostolic Exarchate under Bishop Georges Kahhalé Zouhaïraty, established in Caracas in 1990; and the Syrian Catholic Apostolic Exarchate under Bishop Iwannis Louis Awad, established in 2001 in Maracay, Aragua state. In addition, the Apostolic Orthodox Old Catholic Church (founded by Monsignor Jorge Rodriguez, Chicago, Illinois) and the Reformed Catholic Church of Venezuela (under the jurisdiction of Bishop Leonardo Marín Saavedra of Ontario, Canada), with headquarters in Ciudad Ojeda, state of Zulia, are independent churches in the Western Catholic tradition that are not in communion with the Vatican.

Additional Christian Groups   These groups are considered "marginal" because each one rejects other branches of Christianity, usually claiming that their group is the only "true church." Because each of their doctrinal statements reject certain basic tenets of the Eastern Orthodox, Western Roman, and Protestant traditions, these groups are considered outside the mainstreams of Christianity. The Watch Tower Bible and Tract Society of New York (known as Jehovah's Witnesses) began work in Venezuela in 1936, and in 2005 reported 1,297 congregations with 98,785 members. The Church of Jesus Christ of Latter-day Saints (known as Mormons, Salt Lake City, Utah) entered Venezuela in 1966; in 2001, this church reported 210 wards and branches with a total of 89,484 members. The Universal Church of the Kingdom of God (also known as Strong Prayer to the Holy Spirit—Stop Suffering!), in 2004, reported 81 worship centers in Venezuela.

Also, the following organizations are reported to have work in Venezuela: The Children of God (now called The Family International, headquartered in Florida), the Light of the World Church (Guadalajara, Mexico), Mita Congregation (Puerto Rico), The Voice of the Cornerstone (Puerto Rico), Growing in Grace International Ministries (Miami, Florida), the Philadelphia Church of God (Oklahoma), and the Church of Christ, Scientist (Boston, Massachusetts).

Additional Religious Traditions Immigration since World War II not only increased the spectrum of Christianity in Venezuela, but also brought many of the world's religions as part of the immigrants' cultural heritage.

Buddhism Chinese immigrants first introduced Buddhism into Venezuela, although a large portion of the Chinese community is Roman Catholic. Later, Westernized Buddhist groups were founded, including International Zen Association (with headquarters in Paris, France) and Friends of Western Buddhism (FWBO, London); as well as Asian Buddhist groups: Soka Gakkai International (Japan), Soto Zen School (Japan), and Karma Thegsum Choling—Diamond Way (Tibet).

Hinduism A few Hindu-origin groups exist in Venezuela, including the International Society for Krishna Consciousness (ISKON, Florida), Swami Sivananda School of Yoga (affiliated with the Divine Life Society), Sri Chaitanya Saraswat Mandal (India), Sri Rupanuga Sridhar Ashram (India), International Sri Sathya Sai Baba (India), Transcendental Meditation, now organized as the Global Country of World Peace (Lebanon), Gaudiya Vaishnava Society (California), and Grace Essence Fellowship (United States).

Sant Mat Sant Mat includes the Divine Light Mission now known as Elan Vital (India) and the Movement for Spiritual Inner Awareness (MSIA, California).

Islam There are approximately 125,000 Muslims in Venezuela today, predominantly citizens of Lebanese, Syrian, and Palestinian descent, who mainly reside in Nueva Esparta state, Margarita Island, and the Caracas metropolitan area. The Al-Ibrahim mosque in Caracas is reportedly the largest in Latin America. It was constructed with funds from the Ibrahim bin Abdul Aziz Al-Ibrahim Foundation under the planning of world-renowned architect Oscar Bracho.

Other notable mosques and Islamic organizations include Isla Margarita-Caribe La Comunidad Islámica Venezolana, Centro Islámico de Venezuela, Mezquita al-Rauda in Maracaibo, Asociación Honorable Mezquita de Jerusalén in Valencia, Centro Islámico de Maiquetía in Vargas, and Asociación Benéfica Islámica in Bolívar.

Baha'i Faith In January 1953, the Baha'i community of Caracas began with 17 adults in Caracas, plus a few more believers in the interior of the country. During the period 1960–1961 three other Local Assemblies were formed (Sucre district de Caracas, Maracay, and Barquisimeto), which made possible the election of the First National Spiritual Assembly in Venezuela, in April 1961. During the period 1963–1964 many Amerindians joined the Baha'i community, which reported 1,218 Baha'is in 1965, of which 1,001 were members of Indigenous tribes. In 2000, there existed a National Baha'i Institute, a Moral Education Institute, a strong and growing youth movement, a solid and stable community of believers (more than 20,000), an Office of Foreign Affairs dedicated to the peace process, and 90 Local Assemblies.

Judaism Currently, more than 35,000 Jews live in Venezuela, with more than half in the Caracas metropolitan area. The majority of Jews are members of the middle and upper classes, which are divided almost equally between Ashkenazim and Sephardim. Most of the country's 16 synagogues are Orthodox: The Israelite Union of Caracas represents the Ashkenazi tradition and the Israelite Association of Venezuela represents the Sephardic tradition. There is one Conservative synagogue (Congregation Shalom, founded in 1990) and one Messianic synagogue (Bet El Shadai Congregation).

Animists—Native Americans or Amerindians According to the 2000 Venezuelan national census, there were 511,784 Amerindians (about 2 percent of the total population), mainly concentrated in the states of Amazonas (61.4 percent), Delta Amacuro (26.6 percent), and Zulia (10.6 percent). About 84 percent spoke Native indigenous languages and less than 50 percent also spoke Spanish. The major linguistic groups are Arawakan, Caribe, and independent (without any known linguistic affiliation to other groups). Although many of the Amerindians are nominal Roman Catholics and practice "popular Catholicism," most are also practitioners of Native American Spirituality (animism).

Animists—Afro-Americans   Present among, but not limited to, Afro-Venezuelans are a variety of animistic groups that combine African-derived belief systems with Roman Catholicism in the Latin American and Caribbean regions: Umbanda, Quimbanda, Santería, the Maria Lionza cult, and Myalism-Obeah. The Aboriginal Cult of Maria Lionza is a relatively new religion (since the 15th century) that draws on elements of Native Amerindian religion, African beliefs and practices, and Roman Catholicism.

Animists—Latin American Popular Religiosity (influenced by Roman Catholicism)   All Latin American countries, including Venezuela, have a variety of Virgin Mary and Christ Child cults that emerged as Roman Catholicism blended with existing Amerindian and African-derived belief systems to form a syncretistic "popular religiosity." Examples of these are the Cult of Our Lady of Coromoto, the Cult of the Virgin Mary of the Mystical Rose, and the Cult of the Nino Jesús in Capaya, Barlovento, Miranda state.

Western Esoteric-Occult Orders   Present in Venezuela today are various groups that represent the traditional magic of ancient Western Europe that came to Latin America as part of the Spanish Conquest in the form of witchcraft (magicians, diviners, healers, witches, and shamans), as well as groups that represent the ritual or ceremonial magic tradition: the Traditional Martinista Order (France), the Hermetic Order of the Golden Dawn (England and France), Freemasonry (Scottish and French rites: Grand Lodge of the Republic of Venezuela and R.L. La Esperanza No. 7, founded in the 1850s), the Ancient and Mystical Order Rosae Crucis (AMORC, United States), and the Ancient Rosicrucian Fraternity (Germany).

The neo-Pagan tradition is represented by Wicca, and the Satanist tradition by various secret societies that worship the biblical Lucifer. In 2007, the civil authorities reported that "practitioners of black magic cults" were stealing bones from the local cemeteries for use in Satanic and Santeria rituals, although the *babalaos* (Santeria priests) denied they use witchcraft ("black magic") and human bones in their rituals; rather, their ceremonies utilize "white magic" to cure sickness and help believers resolve personal and family problems and attain success in school and on the job.

Other occult orders (founded in Latin America) present in Venezuela are the Grand Universal Fraternity (known as GFU, founded in Venezuela in 1948 by Serge Justinien Raynaud, known internationally as "Dr. Serge Raynaud de la Ferrière," Ashram No. 1, El Limón, Maracay, State of Aragua) and Red-GFU (Venezuela, 1971, by José Manual Estrada), the Christian Gnostic movement (various groups inspired by the writings and teaching of Víctor Manuel Gómez Rodríguez, known as "Grand Master Samael Aun Weor," of Colombia), and the New Acropolis Cultural Association (Buenos Aires, Argentina, 1957).

Psychic-Spiritualist-New Age Traditions   The Psychic-Spiritualist Family is represented by the following: Spiritual Magnetic School of the Universal Commune (founded by Joaquín Trincado Mateo); the CIMA Movement of Spiritist Culture (Movimiento de Cultura Espírita [CIMA]) was founded in 1958 by David Grossvater (1911–1974) as Centro de Investigaciones Metapsíquicas y Afines (CIMA) in the city of Maracay, State of Aragua (affiliated with the Confederación Espírita Panamericana-CEPA, founded in Buenos Aires, Argentina, in 1946); and the Grand Cacique Murachi Portal Spiritual Center. Also present is The Theosophical Society (United States); the I AM—Ascended Master-related Sol Ray movement/St. Germain Grand Fraternity (founded in Venezuela by Connie Méndez in 1945); and the New Thought Development Foundation (Puerto Rico, 1987). The UFO Family is represented by the Raelian movement (founded in 1973 in France by Claude Vorilhon, known as Rael). The New Age Family includes the following groups: the Church of Scientology, or Dianetics (United States), Universal Life—The Inner Religion (Germany), the Unification Church of Rev. Moon (Korea), the International Society of Ascension (Canada), Ishaya Techniques (Colombia), and the Silvan Method or Silva Mind Control (Texas, founded by José Silva).

Clifton L. Holland

See also: Aboriginal Cult of Maria Lionza; Ancient and Mystical Order Rosae Crucis; Armenian Apostolic

Church (See of the Great House of Cilicia); Assemblies of God; Augustinians; Baha'i Faith; Benedictines; Capuchins; Christian and Missionary Alliance; Christian Brethren; Church of Christ, Scientist; Church of England; Church of Jesus Christ of Latter-day Saints; Church of Scientology; Dominicans; Elan Vital/Divine Light Mission; Episcopal Church; Evangelical Free Church of America; Family International, The; Franciscans; Freemasonry; Global Country of World Peace; Greek Orthodox Patriarchate of Antioch and All the East; International Church of the Foursquare Gospel; International Society for Krishna Consciousness; International Zen Association; Jehovah's Witnesses; Jesuits; Latin American Council of Churches; Light of the World Church; Melkite Catholic Church; Movement of Spiritual Inner Awareness; Orthodox Church in America; Philadelphia Church of God; Roman Catholic Church; Russian Orthodox Church Outside of Russia; Salesians; Santeria; Seventh-day Adventist Church; Soka Gakkai International; Soto Zen Buddhism; Southern Baptist Convention; Spiritism; Unification Movement; United Pentecostal Church International; Universal Church of the Kingdom of God; Wiccan Religion; World Council of Churches; World Evangelical Alliance.

References

Ayerra, Jacinto. *Los Protestantes en Venezuela: quiénes son, qué hacen.* Caracas: Ediciones Tripode, 1980.

Bauswein, Jean-Jacques, and Lukas Vischer, eds. *The Reformed Family Worldwide: A Survey of Reformed Churches, Theological Schools and International Organizations.* Grand Rapids, MI: William B. Eerdmans Publishing Company, 1999.

Brierly, Peter. *World Churches Handbook.* London: Christian Research, 1997.

Burgess, Stanley M., ed. "Venezuela." In the *International Dictionary of Pentecostal and Charismatic Movements.* Grand Rapids, MI: Zondervan, 2001–2002.

Catholic Hierarchy website at: http://www.catholic-hierarchy.org/country/sc1.html

http://www.catholic-hierarchy.org/diocese/dcsdv.html

Herring, Hubert, and Helen Baldwin Herring. *A History of Latin America, from the Beginnings to the Present.* 3rd ed. New York: Alfred A. Knopf, 1968.

Holland, Clifton L. "A Chronology of Protestant Beginnings in Venezuela: 1819–1995." http://www.prolades.com/cra/regions/sam/ven/ven-chron.pdf.

Holland, Clifton L. *Directory of Religious Groups in Venezuela, 2006.* http://www.prolades.com/cra/regions/sam/ven/ven-dir2006.pdf.

Kraul, Chris. "Not even the dead are safe in Caracas: A ghoulish crime wave in Venezuela supplies a black magic cult stoked by faith and politics." *Los Angeles Times* (September 5, 2007). http://articles.latimes.com/2007/sep/05/world/fg-blackmagic5.

Lewis, M. Paul, ed. *Ethnologue: Languages of the World.* 16th ed. Dallas, TX: SIL International, 2009. http://www.ethnologue.com/.

Navarro, Nicolás. "Venezuela." In *The Catholic Encyclopedia.* Vol. 4. New York: Robert Appleton Company, 1912. http://www.newadvent.org/cathen/15327a.htm.

Orozco, José. "Latin America: Evangelical Christianity moves the masses—A report from Venezuela." *ReligionScope* (December 8, 2004). http://www.religion.info/english/articles/article_121.shtml

PROLADES-RITA database. "Religion and Ethnic Diversity in Venezuela." http://www.prolades.com/cra/regions/sam/ven/ven-rd.htm.

Secretariado General de la CLAR. *Estudio sociográfico de los religiosos y las religiosas en América Latina.* Bogota, Colombia: Secretariado General de la CLAR (Confederación Latinoamericana de Religiosos), 1971.

Steigenga, Timothy, and David Smilde. "Contradiction Without Paradox: Evangelical Political Culture in the 1998 Venezuela Elections." *Latin American Politics & Society* 46, no. 1 (2004): 75–102.

U.S. Department of State. *International Religious Freedom Report, 2008: Venezuela.* http://www.state.gov/g/drl/rls/irf/2008/108543.htm.

Weber, Linda J., and Dotsy Welliver, eds. *Mission Handbook of U.S. and Canadian Christian Ministries Overseas (2007–2009)*. Wheaton, IL: Evangelism and Missions Information Service, 2007.

Vernal Equinox

See Spring Equinox.

■ Vietnam

Vietnam, a Southeast Asian country, shares borders with China, Laos, and Cambodia, while its long coastline touches the Gulf of Thailand, the Gulf of Tonkin, and the South China Sea. It includes 127,244 square miles of territory in which its 86,968,000 citizens reside.

At first sight Vietnam seems to be a manifestation of the synthesis of the *tam giao,* or three great teachings—Buddhism, Confucianism, and Daoism—that one finds in China, but Vietnam has also been open to the religious concepts of its Southeast Asian neighbors; consequently the influence of Indian and, more recently, Islamic world conceptions has also had an effect. Most recent of all, decades of French colonialism, and the American presence in the south, have made Vietnam a crucible where East and West have been forced to meet. Nevertheless, the prevailing characteristics and attitudes of the Vietnamese people have remained the backbone onto which foreign religious ideas have been grafted. Certainly during the 20th century the nation continued to respond in its own unique way to the challenge of foreign influence. Thus the

Worshippers in a temple of Cao Dai in south Vietnam. (Valery Shanin/Dreamstime.com)

Vietnam

Ha Giang
Lao Cai Cao Bang•
Lai Chau•
Tuyen Quang•Lang Son
Yen Bai• •Thai Nguyen
Son La• Viet Tri• •Bac Giang
Hoa Binh• ★ Hanoi
• Ha Dong•Haiphong•Hong Gai
Nam Dinh•
Ninh Binh• •Thai Binh
Thanh Hoa•
•Ky Son
Dien Chau
Vinh•
Ha Tinh•
•Ron
•Dong Hoi
Quang Tri•
Hue•
•Da Nang
Tam Ky•
Quang Ngai• •
•Dac To
•Kon Tum
Pleiku• •
•Qui Nhon
V i e t n a m •Tuy Hoa
•Buon Ma Thuot
Ninh Hoa•
•Nha Trang
•Da Lat
•Loc Ninh Dak Nong •Cam Ranh
•Phan Rang-Thap Cham
Tay Ninh•
Thu Dau Mot• •Bien Hoa •Phan Thiet
Tan An• •Ho Chi Minh City
Long Xuyen• Sa Dec• •Vung Tau
Rach Gia• Can Tho• •Ben Tre
• Soc Trang •Tra Vinh
Ca Mau Bac Lieu•

Vietnam

Religion	Followers in 1970	Followers in 2010	% of Population	Annual % growth 2000–2010	Followers in 2025	Followers in 2050
Buddhists	26,404,000	44,383,000	48.9	1.45	49,827,000	54,099,000
Agnostics	4,200,000	11,500,000	12.7	1.19	14,400,000	17,000,000
New religionists	4,500,000	10,040,000	11.1	1.45	11,800,000	13,300,000
Ethnoreligionists	1,960,000	9,380,000	10.3	1.52	11,000,000	12,400,000
Christians	3,264,000	7,796,000	8.6	1.87	10,574,000	13,571,000
Roman Catholics	2,899,000	6,250,000	6.9	1.73	8,500,000	11,000,000
Protestants	161,000	1,150,000	1.3	2.12	1,550,000	1,950,000
Independents	37,700	615,000	0.7	3.04	770,000	900,000
Atheists	1,080,000	6,240,000	6.9	1.45	7,000,000	7,600,000
Chinese folk	900,000	890,000	1.0	1.46	1,000,000	1,100,000
Baha'is	200,000	400,000	0.4	1.45	500,000	600,000
Muslims	390,000	160,000	0.2	1.46	180,000	200,000
Hindus	0	55,600	0.1	1.46	75,000	100,000
Shintoists	0	200	0.0	1.47	400	700
Daoists	0	170	0.0	1.47	300	500
Total population	**42,898,000**	**90,845,000**	**100.0**	**1.46**	**106,357,000**	**119,971,000**

Vietnamese characteristics of accommodation and development are strongly reflected in the rise of a number of new religious movements that developed in this period.

The origin of the Vietnamese people is explained in a now famous myth attributed to the pre-occupation Hung kings (although the earliest source for this myth is dated to the 14th century CE). This "original" dynasty attributed their ancestry to a primordial sea-dragon, Lac Long Quan. He swam into the rivers of Vietnam, subduing demonic forces as he went. He brought wet-rice cultivation and married the earth-goddess Au Co. From this union 100 children were born from eggs, half of which returned to the sea, the other half remaining on the land to become Vietnam's first rulers. This myth underlines a conceptualization of the natural world as a realm inhabited by spirits associated with prominent features of the landscape and other awe-inspiring phenomena. Much the same way that *kami* inhabit the Shinto conceptualization of the land in Japan (one example being the Great King of Mount Tan-vien. Tan-vien was also the first of the Hung kings).

Tracing the religious life of Vietnam before Chinese occupation is a dangerous job, as writing technology came late to the area. Certainly ancestor worship was an ever-present religious phenomenon. The Chinese, who occupied the nascent nation, invaded in 111 BCE and were not fully repelled until the late 10th century CE. It would seem that this 1,000-year occupation saw the adaptation of the Chinese social (and religious) model in Vietnam, but this is not necessarily the full story. It was during this period that the cult of national heroes began to develop. Foremost among these heroes, fighting for *nghia*, or national justice, against rapacious northern overlords, were the Trung sisters, who led a revolt against the Chinese in the first century CE.

Pre–Common Era Buddhist-designed pots (some possibly as early as the second century BCE) suggest that Vietnam was a vital route for the spread of Buddhism into China. Luy Lau, established around the second century CE, at the center of China's Giao Chi Province, near present-day Hanoi, was a significant center for the early dissemination of Buddhism. At Luy Lau Buddhist texts and deities were translated into accessible local conceptualizations. It was here that the early Buddhist scholar Mau Tu wrote a Buddhist treatise known in Vietnam as "Ly Hoac Luan."

According to one Vietnamese hagiographical source, the "Thien Uyen Tap Anh," in 580 BCE an Indian monk named Vinitaruci arrived in Giao Chau to preach Mahayana Buddhism. What is true is that from a very early stage Buddhism became subject to a process of domestication in Vietnam that helped its inclusion into the prevailing Sino-Vietnamese social model. One example is the translation of Buddhist personalities into deities who were understood to possess power over the climate. Other Buddhas possessed the sort of magical powers that local deities were thought to have. Over these early centuries Buddhism began to coalesce into a sophisticated religio-philosophical system, with a number of schools being established by Vietnamese and Chinese monks.

When Chinese occupation was brought to an end in 949 CE, Buddhist advisors were intimately involved in the establishment of the Vietnamese court, which, like China's, had at its center a king (*vu'o'ng*) who held a similar place to the Son of Heaven. Prominent monks were given the honorific title of Quoc Su, or Tutor of the State, and worked closely with the court. In this way Buddhism of the Mahayana strain was forever linked with Vietnamese nationalism, and many kings of the following dynasties were intimately associated with the Buddhist cause.

During the Ly (1010–1225) and Tran (1225–1400) dynasties, Thien Buddhism, known as Chan in China and Zen in Japan, became a sort of official ideology in the country now referred to as Dai Viet, or Great Viet. King Tran Thai Tong (1218–1277) composed a Buddhist treatise, the "Khoa Hu Luc," or "Discourse on Emptiness." Notably, in 1299 King Tran Nhan Tong (1258–1308) retired and became a Buddhist monk. He launched a local school of Thien, known as Truc Lam, or Bamboo Forest. Today, Buddhism remains the major tradition of this nation of 80-odd million.

The rise of the Le dynasty (1428–1788) led to the increasing influence of Confucian scholars at court. It has been argued by Taylor that to maintain independence, Vietnam adapted the Chinese social model more completely after independence in order to demonstrate to China the civility of the Vietnamese people. The adaptation of Chinese concepts reached its apotheosis at the start of the Nguyen dynasty (1802–1945), when the court adopted Confucian-based Ming dynasty law codes.

In the meantime, Daoism largely remained a marginal part of Vietnam's tam giao tradition, disseminated in popular novels from the Ming dynasty on, and since Chinese occupation an ongoing but shadowy philosophical influence. It was never fully institutionalized in major monasteries and temples as it was in China.

From independence the nation, which had until then been based around the Red River delta, began its southward movement, or Nam Tien, along the eastern part of the Indochinese peninsula, conquering and displacing the more Indianized Cham peoples as they went. These peoples were strongly influenced by Theravadan strains of Buddhism and Hindu ideas, which maintained an on-going influence in the south despite the eventual subjugation of the Cham. As Europeans began to appear in the 16th century, Vietnam, already too big to administer from Hanoi, started to bifurcate. Jesuit Alexandre de Rhodes (1591–1660) Romanized the Vietnamese language, undercutting the grip on communication held by Confucian-trained scholars and further undermining the state. The nation was reunified only in 1802 under the last dynasty, the Nguyen. The new national government, based in Hue, quickly became unsettled by the continued growth of Catholicism. Introduced firstly by the Portuguese and then the French, the tensions created between missionaries and nationalists proved a very convenient cause that eventually allowed Napoleon III to add Vietnam to the Second Empire. Continued European religious influence has resulted in Vietnam possessing the largest Catholic community in Southeast Asia outside of the Philippines.

The French also brought a number of Esoteric traditions with them, including Freemasonry and Theosophy, and in particular a vogue for séance and Spiritism which, when linked with the traditional practices of Chinese-style divination, gave rise in 1926 to the syncretic faith of Caodaism. It was also during the Nguyen dynasty that Buddhism, increasingly controlled by the court throughout the later dynasties, continued its general decline. It was revived only in certain millenarian forms such as the Buu Son Ky Huong movement of the 1850s. This brand of Buddhism eventually gave rise to the often militant and puritanical Hoa Hao Buddhism from 1939.

In response to the mistreatment of non-Catholics by the Ngo Dinh Diem regime (1954–1963) mainstream Buddhism underwent a remarkable resurgence and the Unified Buddhist Church brought together many Buddhist groups of both Mahayana and Theravadan strains. The monk Thich Nhat Hanh began his campaign to promote "Engaged Buddhism," a form of the religion more closely connected to social justice issues. After 1975, when Communist forces overran the South, there was a systematic attempt to control religious activity by Communist authorities. This included the establishment of "management committees" designed to ally all religious activity to the direction of the state. A great number of religiously minded Vietnamese were interned in "education camps" for months, sometimes years. Both the actuality and the threat of persecution led many to flee the nation. Today these Vietnamese comprise a diaspora that has taken their various religious traditions around the world.

Although international reports on religious freedom in Vietnam continue to express concern since the government's policy of "Doi Moi" began in 1986, there has been a significant increase in religious activity, from ancestor worship to informal séances with child and female mediums. There has also been a new awareness of the heritage of Cham peoples and other indigenous movements in their contribution to the spiritual life of the nation.

The main characteristics of the religious life of Vietnam have been of accommodation and adaptability. Many have referred to Vietnam as a crossroad of various socio-religious influences; however, we must be wary of ignoring the legacy that the Vietnamese themselves have made to internal religious developments which, after the events of 1975, are having a increasing influence on the world.

Christopher H. Hartney

See also: Ancestors; Caodaism; Hoa Hao Buddhism; Mahayana Buddhism; Shinto; Theravada Buddhism; Unified Buddhist Church.

References

Cadière, Leopold. *Croyances et pratiques religieuses des Vietnamiens.* 3 vols. Hanoi: Publications de l'Ecole Française d'Extreme-Orient, 1955, 1957.

Giap, Tran Van. *Le Bouddhisme en Annam des origines au XIIIème siècle*, 1932.

Taylor, Keith Weller. *The Birth of Vietnam.* Berkeley: University of California Press, 1983.

Taylor, Philip, ed. *Modernity and Re-enchantment: Religion in Post-revolutionary Vietnam.* Singapore: Institute of South Asian Studies, 2007.

Violence, Religious

The events of 9/11 shocked many because it was impossible to deny that religion seemed to be at the heart of this attack. Many have assumed that religion is about peace, but they were awakened on September 11, 2001, to the sight of people throwing themselves off burning towers that, only minutes later, toppled to the ground. For some, the hope that religion is only about peace was extinguished in those flames, but the question remains: does religion cause violence? In what ways is religion related to violence? Early French, English, and German thinkers of the Enlightenment portrayed religion as a form of superstition, and indeed the reason for the destruction of a third of the European population in the 16th century. David Hume (1711–1776) was convinced that religion did damage to the human character, and many European intellectuals in the 19th century called for its replacement. Marx called religion an opiate of the people, which kept them in chains. In the 20th century theorists of religion became more sanguine about religion—thinking of it as a form of the sacred (Mircea Eliade), or of meaning (Clifford Geertz), or a term of exchange with the gods (Rodney Stark), or a moral orientation to life (Christian Smith), or an ever-evolving organism with multiple socio-cultural dimensions (Ninian Smart). And while there is no generally accepted definition of religion, scholars have recently begun to conjecture about whether or not religion is the cause of violence.

Recent Explanations of Religious Violence Hector Avalos's *Fighting Words: The Origins of Religious Violence* (2005) does a comprehensive job of outlining the traditional explanations of religious violence. We will not review all of these here because Avalos's own hypothesis for religious violence is worth examining more specifically since it tends to give the best illustration of how some important contemporary thinkers explain religious violence: (1) Most violence is due to scarce resources, real or perceived. Whenever people

Fires still burn amid the rubble and debris of the World Trade Center in New York City in the area known as Ground Zero, two days after the 9/11 terrorist attacks. (U.S. Department of Defense)

perceive that there is not enough of something they value, conflict may ensue to maintain or acquire that resource. This can range from love in a family, to oil, on a global scale. (2) When religion causes violence, it often does so because it has created new scarce resources.

Avalos follows recent economic and socio-biological explanations in proposing that social reality is, at its base, a conflict over scarce resources. When resources are plenty and fair distribution occurs, tensions decrease; when resources are scarce or distribution is unfair, conflicts arise and violence ensues. For the sociobiologist Richard Dawkins, religion is a cultural maladaption; in other words, rather than benefiting the survival of genes, it leads to their extinction (Dawkins 1976). At one point in our history, religion may have increased our rates of survival, but in the modern world, religion seems to lead to our destruction. Avalos is sympathetic to this perspective but moves his explana-

tion toward the economic model. Most fundamentally, humans are resource managers and the lack thereof produces conflict and, frequently, violence.

For Avalos, religion becomes particularly problematic because religion has "created" a scarce resource. In other words the "goods" of religion, its resources, are manufactured. Whether the good is a miracle, eternal life, mystical experience, healing, or communion with force, power, or god, all of these resources are ephemeral, non-empirical, and, thus, non-existent. What is clearly most troubling for Avalos is that religions not only create resources but make them scarce to control individuals and groups, which by definition creates conflict: "If any acts of violence caused by actual scarcities are judged as immoral, then acts of violence caused by resources that are not actually scarce should be judged as even more immoral . . . any act of violence predicated on the acquisition or loss of nonexistent entity is always immoral and needless because bodily well-being or life is being traded for a nonexistent gain" (Avalos 2005, 29).

For Avalos, religion is, by definition, trafficking in nonexistent resources. Religion is, thus, a morbid fantasy to say the least, or at most, a useless waste of time. He claims that religions are "prone" to violence; some have a greater capacity for it than other cultural forms. Religions use various forms of manipulation of nonexistent goods to maneuver believers, including access to the divine will, claims to sacred space, group privileging, and, finally, exclusivist soteriology (study in matters of salvation). In other words, religions use a kind of shell game that keeps people believing that god(s), spirit(s), and forces will show them how to live, give them a place of their own, set them apart as special, and promise them rewards that no one else can gain.

But is it a plausible explanation? Avalos makes a clear argument that scarcity in general tends to create tension and violence within and between humans. In agreement, it seems that religions create symbolic and social boundaries that engender individual and group identity and, in doing so, act both to include and to exclude. Religions' "extra reasons," according to Steve Bruce, are powerful markers of identity that shape behavior, promise rewards, and mobilize social action. These extra reasons correlate to Bruce Lincoln's short-hand theory of religion—that religions make "exceptional claims" that mark common demands with a divine self-evidence.

So far, so good, but don't many cultural processes create boundaries that both include and exclude? It would seem that, yes, other cultural variables, such as class, race, and nationalism, establish similar boundaries and create scarce resources, but in fact, we would not say that any one of these mechanisms is a unique cause of violence. Perhaps the most reasonable perspective is to argue that all cultural elements can be used for good and ill, some to create identity and a flourishing human community and some to tear down humanity, to dehumanize the other for the sake of one's own sense of well-being. Religion is not unique in this pattern.

The Causes of Religious Violence   Yet, it is still worth asking: what is it about religion that, in fact, causes some to do damage to others in its name? A part of the answer is that religion relates to a critical feature of human nature. Human beings tend to embody and express a deep social desire for freedom and self-expression related to what they consider as ultimate. In this sense, we can define religion as a socially constructed desire and passion for the ultimate. We mean by this, an affective longing for something that is not simply a rational choice conceived of as a correct decision, but a deeply felt sense and passion for something that is a sustained preference, often developed and nurtured over years. It is social because language itself is developed in a group setting that embodies a moral order, often involving a religion that shapes preference, values, and behavior (Smith 2003). This affective social desire is often conceived of as a core sense of freedom—a deep and sustained desire for self-determination and liberty from want and oppression. In thinking about religion, one can see how religion is both an instrument of this desire and, perhaps, a facilitator of this aspiration. Like any definition, there are problems; one could argue that it is too vague, that it could include too many kinds of human activities, whether having to do with sexuality, family, sports, or nationalism, and of course, this is true. But it also makes the point that religion is a subjective and slippery intention, which, nonetheless, perseveres through time and circumstance, even as it changes in form and expression. This helps to explain both the power of religion and why it has not disappeared from the modern world.

Many scholars assumed that the process of secularization would cause religion to either disappear altogether or, at least, to sink into the inner compartments of the human heart, but, in light of 9/11, in light of the insurgent power of Christianity in Latin America and Africa and China, of Islam in the Middle East, and of Buddhism in Southeast Asia, these predictions have been revised. Religion acts as a source of deep joy, purpose, and meaning and not just in the personal lives of individuals across the globe but as a part of their political expressions. When religion becomes political, as we know it has in many places—the United States, the Islamic Republic of Iran, Sri Lanka, Israel, and the list could expand—it touches on aspects of conflict and violence that are very much a part of the human condition.

Religion creates symbolic and social boundaries. Often it creates moral binaries that are less than conducive to modern pluralism and peace between diverse groups. To some extent, the unique claims that religions make are the source of their genius and their staying power. People share an identity in these claims that bring them social solidarity, again a powerful sense of human security. But these exclusive claims create moral and cultural binaries—not only in the religions of the West but also in the religions of Asia. These binaries then form the basis of social conflict and, occasionally, of violence that are a part of all religions. At times, religion appears to be the very source of violence. Jessica Stern, in her book *Terror in the Name of God* (2004), interviewed a number of religious militants, many of whom had planned and committed acts of violence. During these interviews, it became clear to her that religion supported and even facilitated some of their most violent fantasies and human actions. As Stern argues: "[Religion] is terribly seductive in its ability to soothe and explain, but it is also dangerous. Converts such as the one I visited as a child (a Christian saint) make good people better, but they don't necessarily make bad people good. They might even make bad people worse" (2004, xxvii).

In the recent edited volume, titled *Belief and Bloodshed: Religion and Violence across Time and Tradition* (2007), we argued that there is nothing new in religious violence. Religious groups and leaders have turned to violence throughout history and in all the major religious traditions of the world. Religion creates moral exemplars that love and forgive as well as moral disasters that seek to annihilate any in their path. Religion seems to be a knife with which deep social desires are cut, some toward the good and some, frankly, toward evil.

Despite many of the predictions that religion would disappear in modern life, religion perseveres as a potent "technology" by which humans create their personal and social identities. Religion is one way humans express a deep social desire for the ultimate that has moved some to nonviolence, in figures like Gandhi and Martin Luther King Jr., and others to violence, in events such as the crusades and in the events of 9/11. What we do know is that religion has great power to mobilize and move people in both directions.

James Wellman

See also: Secularization.

References

Avalos, Hector. *Fight Words: The Origins of Religious Violence.* Amherst, NY: Prometheus Books, 2005.

Dawkins, Richard. *The Selfish Gene.* New York: Oxford University Press, 1976.

Lincoln, Bruce. *Holy Terrors: Thinking about Religion after September 11.* Chicago: University of Chicago Press, 2003.

Smith, Christian. *Moral, Believing Animals: Human Personhood and Culture.* Oxford: Oxford University Press, 2003.

Stern, Jessica. *Terror in the Name of God: Why Religious Militants Kill.* New York: Harper Perennial, 2004.

Wellman, James K., Jr., ed. *Belief and Bloodshed: Religion and Violence across Time and Tradition.* Lanham, Md.: Rowman & Littlefield, 2007.

Vipassana International Academy

The globally spread meditational movement of *vipassana* has its roots in the revival of Theravada Buddhism in the late 19th century. Reformers reinterpreted Buddhist tradition afresh, stressing rational aspects of the *dhamma* (Pali: Buddhist teachings). They emphasized meditation, lay participation, and texts, and underscored the possibility of reaching final liberation, *nibbana* (Pali) or *nirvana* (Sanskrit), in this life. This contrasted with traditional Buddhism, with its centrality on dhamma teachings by monks and devotional practices such as chanting Pali verses and reciting formulaic lists, intended as means for accumulating merit (Pali: *punna*) toward a better next life. The instructing of people, both ordained and laity, in meditational practices by monks was new and decisive, inasmuch as the practice of meditation had not traditionally constituted an option for lay Buddhists; furthermore, the tradition of meditation had been lost for centuries among the *sangha* (Buddhist order), at least among the village- and town-dwelling monks. In addition, since the mid-20th century, laymen have taught meditation, an activity traditionally the prerogative of monks only.

The Vipassana International Academy (VIA) constitutes an independent organization developed from one of the two most important Burmese lineages of meditational practice inaugurated by eminent Theravada monks in the early 20th century. The relevant lineage for VIA originates with Ledi Sayadaw (1846–1923) and was made widely known by his grand-disciple U Ba Khin (1899–1971), a layman and former state official (he was head of three government departments). Satya Narayan Goenka, an Indian born in Burma in 1924, a highly successful businessman, and the founder of the VIA, started meditation practice with U Ba Khin in 1955. Having received authorization to teach in 1969, Goenka settled in western India that same year, one of his aims being to "bring back" the dhamma to its land of origin.

In 1976, Goenka established the Vipassana International Academy at Dhammagiri in Igatpuri, 84 miles northeast of Mumbai (Bombay). The present-day academy is situated on a 20-hectare plot with a golden pagoda, 4 meditation halls, and 300 small meditation cells. The organization runs some 20 10-day courses a year, some of which are at times visited by as many as 500 participants. Students must adhere to a code of discipline, including the observation of so-called noble silence for the whole period, and a strict timetable starting at 4:00 a.m., with some 10 hours of meditation practice, Pali recitations, and a discourse by the teacher or a video lecture. Goenka has developed a systematic schedule of courses with introductory, advanced, and specialized levels. All other meditational practices and neighboring vipassana approaches are banned, so as to teach the "pure" dhamma.

The term "vipassana" derives from the Pali root *dis,* meaning "to see." Vipassana is understood to be a way of seeing or gaining an insight into reality, as understood in Theravada terms. Goenka and other modern vipassana teachers base their teachings primarily on the canonical Satipatthana sutta (Discourse on the Foundations of Mindfulness) and the classic meditation manual Visuddhimagga (Path of Purification) by Buddhaghosa. Closely related to vipassana, or insight meditation, is the concept of *sati,* mindfulness or awareness. Vipassana is developed through the practice of sati. To generate vipassana or insight, the meditator develops mindfulness of each of the four foundations of mindfulness (body, feelings or sensations, states of mind, and the mental objects). The Satipatthana sutta prescribes specific ways to meditate on each of these four foundations, beginning with the instruction on how to develop mindfulness of the body by focusing attention on the process of breathing. Vipassana is directed toward recognizing the "three marks of existence": in the arising and disappearing of breath, feelings, thoughts, and other objects, the meditator experiences the "truths" of impermanence (*anicca*), no-self (*anatta*), and unsatisfactoriness or suffering (*dukkha*). In Goenka's courses and in his own vocabulary, as well as that of U Ba Khin, this approach has come to be called "body sweeping"—that is, the focusing of mindfulness on each part of the body, "bit by bit, part by part," as Goenka stresses.

Attached to the VIA is the Vipassana Research Institute. It pursues studies on early Buddhist texts and has compiled the texts of the Pali canon with its commentaries on a CD-ROM (*Chattha Sangayana Tipitaka*), launched for free in 1997. Also in 1997, the foundation stone for a huge hall, taking the form of a 300-foot-high stupa and providing room for 10,000 people, was laid in Bombay. In 2009, Vipassana courses were being taught at some 55 Vipassana centers and numerous other localities in India and Nepal. Courses are also held in Indian prisons, with much success. Since the late 1970s, because of a growing number of non-Indian students and visits abroad by Goenka, this sweeping approach has spread to numerous Asian and Western countries, with some 50 centers globally and many places where 10-day courses are held.

Vipassana International Academy
Dramma Giri
Igatpuri 422 403
District Nasik
Maharashtra
India
http://www.dhamma.org

Vipassana Meditation Centre
Dhamma Dhara
386 Colrain-Shelburne Rd.
Shelburne Falls, MA 01370
http://www.dhara.dhamma.org

Martin Baumann

See also: Meditation; Theravada Buddhism.

References

Goenka, S. N. *The Art of Living: Vipassana Meditation.* Shelburne Falls, MA: Vipassana Meditation Center, [1980].

Goenka, S. N. *For the Benefit of Many: Talks and Answers to Questions from Vipassana Students 1983-2000.* Igatpuri: Vipassana Research Institute, 2005.

Goenka, S. N. *The Gracious Flow of Dharma.* Igatpuri: Vipassana Research Institute, 1994.

Guidelines for Practicing Vipassana Meditation as Taught by S. N. Goenka and His Assistant Teachers. Shelburne Falls, MA: Vipassana Meditation Center, n.d.

Hart, William. *The Art of Living Vipassana Meditation as Taught by S. N. Goenka.* San Francisco: Harper and Row, 1987, 1993.

Neubert, Frank. "Ritualdiskurs, Ritualkritik und Meditationspraxis: Das Beispiel von Vipassana nach S.N. Goenka im 'Westen.'" *Numen* 55 (2008): 411–439.

Sharf, Robert H. "Buddhist Modernism and the Rhetoric of Meditative Experience." *Numen* 42 (1995): 228–283.

Virasaivism

Virasaivism, also known as Lingayatism, is the religious system of the Virasaivas (heroic Saivites) or Lingayatas (those who have sought refuge in the *linga*); it is a variety of reformed Saivite Hinduism that rejects the traditional hierarchic structure of society by a radical emphasis on the worth of the individual as opposed to the traditional prominence of the social collectives known as castes. Besides having had a revolutionizing socio-political influence, Virasaivism has been the source of inspiration for a remarkable body of religious, mainly mystical, literature from the 12th century down to the present.

Virasaivism assumed an organized form in the late 12th century CE under the leadership of Basava (Basavanna, Basavesvara), in what is today the northern part of Karnataka state in India. The community is at present roughly estimated to have approximately 12 million members. Certain characteristics set Virasaivism apart from orthodox Brahminical Hinduism, of which the most striking are the rejection of the orthodox social order with its hierarchical system of *varnas* and *jatis* (castes); the notion of valid scripture; the concept of priesthood; the equal position accorded women; and the welcoming attitude toward religious conversion.

Basava (who lived around 1160 CE and should be considered the main organizer of the movement, rather than its founder) was born in an orthodox Brahmin Saivite family and thus by birth enjoyed a certain social prestige and privileges. He rose to a ministerial position at the court of the local king and became the royal treasurer, and thereby he gained a still higher social status. However, his attitude toward his ritual status in society was affected by his disgust at what he considered a formal, mechanically ritual religiosity of his religious community that had lost most of its meaning because genuine, individually felt devotion to god, which he thought to be the basis of the religion, had largely disappeared from public practice. His own profound devotion to and humility before Siva, who is the spiritual essence of the entire cosmos, made him reject the traditional high status that he had received by birth. He rejected the sacred thread that is the traditional insignia of his high caste and declared Allama Prabhu, a senior mystic of ritually low birth, to be his personal religious teacher. Around these two persons, the Virasaiva community took shape.

In this form of Hinduism the Vedas hold no place of special authority, and the main scriptures are the Saiva *agamas* and, particularly, a special genre of literature written in the Kannada language known as *vacanas,* or "sayings." These are relatively short prose-poems of often stunning literary beauty. Basava, Allama, Akka Mahadevi, and others have written many hundreds of them.

Virasaivism began as a religious community that was open to all individuals who accepted its tenets, and many vacanas express the gratitude of converts who thus found religious fulfillment and at the same time were freed from traditional social stigmas of birth, as is characteristic of orthodox Hinduism. The ritual hold of the Brahmin castes over the laity was broken by each devotee's possessing a personal linga, or symbolic image of Siva, and thereby becoming independent of ritual specialists. Although there is a quasi-Brahminical priestly section of such specialists in the community, these people have no special authority vis-à-vis the others. Still today Virasaivism openly welcomes religious conversion, regardless of ethnic, social, or national background.

The philosophical aspect of Virasaivism is known as *saktivisishtadvaita,* or "modified monism of energy," a form of monism in which ultimately everything is an emanation of Siva. The spiritual goal of the adherents is to merge with God via a six-staged path, the description of which is known as *shatsthalasiddhanta,* "the doctrine of six stages."

The primary strength of Virasaivism is in Karnataka state in India. Being the largest single religious community in Karnataka, the Virasaivas hold a position of considerable social, cultural, and political importance. In certain parts of the state, their social prestige is higher than that of the Brahmins, who form the traditionally highest castes in orthodox Hinduism.

In 1995, His Holiness Shri Siddharama Mahaswamiji, the head of Naganur Shri Rudraximath, founded the Central Research Library of Lingayat Studies.

Central Research Library of Lingayat Studies,
Nagnoor Shri Rudraximath, Sivabasava Nagar,
Belgaum 590 010, Karnataka,
India

Robert J. Zydenbos

References

Chekki, Dan A. *Religion and Social System of the Virasaiva Community.* Westport: Greenwood Press, 1997.

Glasbrenner, E.-M. "Religiöse Erfahrung im Bild. Eine religionsästhetische Betrachtung zeitgenössischer Virasaivakunst." In *Religiöse Erfahrung II. Interkulturelle Perspektiven,* edited by G. Haeffner. Stuttgart: Kohlhammer, 2007.

Ramanujan, A. K. *Speaking of Siva.* Harmondsworth: Penguin, 1973.

Zvelebil, K.V . *The Lord of the Meeting Rivers. Devotional Poems of Basavanna.* Delhi: Motilal Banarsidass, 1984.

Zydenbos, R. J. "Virasaivism, Caste, Revolution, et cetera." *Journal of the American Oriental Society* 117, no. 3 (1997).

■ Virgin Islands of the United States

The U.S. Virgin Islands are located on the northeastern edge of the Caribbean Sea east of Puerto Rico. The islands are the western part of a larger archipelago, the other half of which are British territory. The U.S. Virgin Islands include 3 main islands—St. Thomas, St. Croix, and St. John—and some 50 smaller islands, mostly uninhabited, with a total land area of 134 square miles. By 2008, the population approached 110,000.

Virgin Islands of the United States

Religion	Followers in 1970	Followers in 2010	% of Population	Annual % growth 2000–2010	Followers in 2025	Followers in 2050
Christians	62,900	105,000	94.7	0.10	99,200	73,600
Protestants	22,500	40,000	36.0	0.36	39,000	29,000
Roman Catholics	18,900	29,800	26.8	0.00	28,300	20,000
Anglicans	9,700	14,400	13.0	0.28	14,000	11,000
Agnostics	600	4,000	3.6	2.12	5,500	6,000
Baha'is	300	730	0.7	0.14	850	900
Hindus	0	480	0.4	0.17	600	650
Jews	200	360	0.3	0.17	360	360
Atheists	0	200	0.2	0.10	300	400
Muslims	0	120	0.1	0.17	150	180
Total population	**64,000**	**111,000**	**100.0**	**0.16**	**107,000**	**82,100**

Historic church in Charlotte Amalie, town on St. Thomas island, U.S. Virgin Islands, 2009. (Ramunas Bruzas/Dreamstime .com)

The islands were originally settled by Carib and Arawak people, all of whom were eventually killed by the Spanish. Christopher Columbus first landed in 1493. Denmark took control of the western Virgin Islands in the 18th century. They introduced sugarcane and cotton as well as slavery. In 1917 the United States paid $25 million for the islands. The Danes had previously established a local legislature, and U.S. officials built on it to create a system of local rule. Residents have U.S. citizenship and may vote in national elections. They have turned away from moves for independence or statehood. The great majority of residents are the descendants of Africans, though almost 40 percent have come to the islands from other Caribbean isles.

The Roman Catholic Church was originally established in the 17th century. Today it includes approximately one-third of the residents, and a diocese is headquartered on St. Thomas. It is a suffragan diocese to the Archdiocese of Washington, D.C.

During the years of Danish rule, a variety of churches entered, beginning with the Lutheran Church of Denmark. Lutherans are now a part of the Evangelical Lutheran Church in America. The Church of England spread through the islands in the 18th century, and by the middle of the 19th century approximately one-third of the residents were Anglicans. In 1916 this work was transferred to the Episcopal Church.

St. Thomas would play an important role in the modern Protestant missionary enterprise, which began with the Moravian mission to the slaves in 1732. From here, the Moravians would spread around the Caribbean and around the world. The Moravian work has been incorporated in the Moravian Church, Eastern West Indies Province. Methodists came to the Virgin

VIRGIN ISLANDS OF THE UNITED STATES

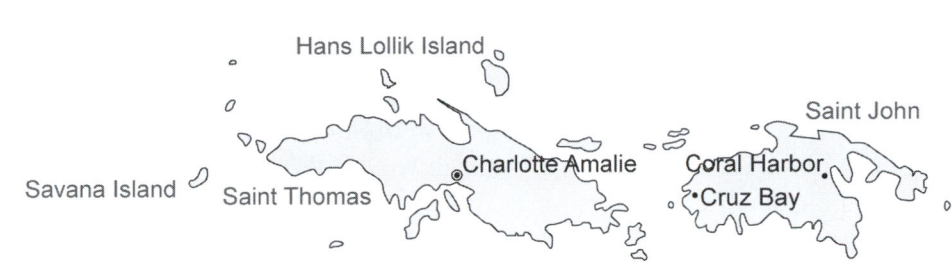

Virgin Islands of the United States

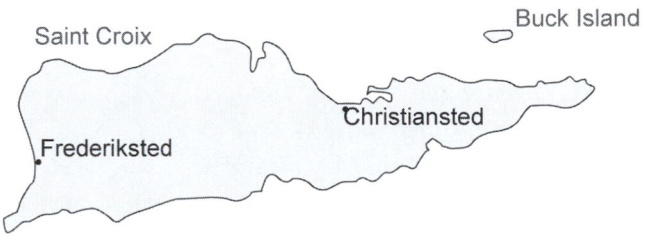

Islands in 1891. That work has now been merged into the Methodist Church in the Caribbean and the Americas, headquartered in Jamaica.

Throughout the 20th century a number of American churches opened congregations in the islands, but because of their relatively small size, most have only one or a few congregations. The Seventh-day Adventist Church has risen above the rest, and Pentecostals have split their support among the Assemblies of God, the Church of God of Prophecy, the Church of God (Cleveland, Tennessee), and the Damascus Christian Church, the latter a Spanish-speaking organization.

The Jewish community in the Virgin Islands dates to the 17th century. Today there are some 350 Jews, about half of whom are active in the synagogue, which is located on St. Thomas. In 1983 the members of the synagogue celebrated their 150th anniversary. There are also several spiritual assemblies of the Baha'i Faith, and fewer than 100 Muslims.

J. Gordon Melton

See also: Assemblies of God; Church of England; Church of God of Prophecy; Episcopal Church; Methodist Church in the Caribbean and the Americas; Moravian Church, Eastern West Indies Province; Roman Catholic Church; Seventh-day Adventist Church.

References

Baa, E. "Religious Development." In *Fifty Years: Commemorating the Fiftieth Anniversary of the Transfer of the Virgin Islands from Denmark to the United States of America, March 31, 1967,* edited by E. Downing. Charlotte Amaile, USVI: Friends of Denmark Society, 1967.

Chapman, W., and W. Taylor. *Historic Churches of the Virgin Islands.* St. Croix: Saint Croix Landmarks Society, 1986.

Cohen, Judah M. *Through the Sands of Time: A History of the Jewish Community of St. Thomas, U.S. Virgin Islands.* Waltham, MA: Brandeis, 2003.

Dookan, Isaac. *History of the Virgin Islands.* Kingston, Jamaica: University Press of the West Indies, 2000.

Frederick Evangelical Lutheran Church, 325th Anniversary, 1666–1991: Celebrate Our Past, Challenge the Future. St. Thomas: Frederick Evangelical Lutheran Church, 1991.

Hall, Neville A. T., and B. W. Higman. *Slave Society in the Danish West Indies: St Thomas, St John and St Croix.* Kingston, Jamaica: University Press of the West Indies, 1994.

Maynard, G. O. *A History of the Moravian Church: Eastern West Indies Province.* Port of Spain, Trinidad: Yuille's Printerie, 1968.

Vishwa Hindu Parishad

The Vishwa Hindu Parishad (Assembly of All Hindus) is an organization with a superdenominational structure. Its declared goal is to become the representative of a united Hinduism, an ambition with obvious political implications. The Vishwa Hindu Parishad (VHP) stresses the meaning of *hindutva*—Hindu lifestyle—as a central characteristic of the intended new order of Indian society. The concept of the VHP is based on the conviction that Hinduism possesses all principles needed for the organization and governing of society, as well as the structuring of the economy. Therefore the aims and programmatical actions of the VHP are habitually characterized as "political Hinduism."

In the middle of the 1990s, the VHP had about 1.6 million members worldwide, the majority of whom lived in India. However, there exist branches of the VHP in the United States, in Canada, as well as in several European, African, and East Asian countries. The non-Indian branches operate relatively independently from the head office, but normally they are organized in a kind of net structure in the various countries. The U.S. branch, for example, was founded in 1973 and has since organized various national meetings with members from about 100 U.S. cities, the most recent as of this writing having been in Austin, Texas, in 1999.

The VHP was founded in Bombay on August 29, 1964, the mythological birthday of God Krishna (Janmashtami). Some 150 leaders of different Hindu sects participated. The founding of the VHP as a forum of a united Hinduism was initiated by Swami Chinmayananda (1916–1993), who became the first president of the organization, and Shivram Shankar Apte, a high-ranking official of the Rashtriya Svayamsevak Sangh

Members of Durga Vahini, the women's wing of Hindu nationalist group Vishwa Hindu Parishad (VHP), participate in a self-defense training for women at Akhnoor, India, July 16, 2009. (AP/Wide World Photos)

(the national volunteers' organization), who functioned as secretary general.

The VHP is a lay organization with a relatively small number of full-time workers. A high degree of voluntary engagement by the members guarantees the efficiency of the activities, and the members' activities are declared a religious duty. The Organization Department, which is subdivided into the Central Board of Trustees, the Central Advisory Board, and the Central Executive Committee, constitutes the central administrative unit of the VHP.

The VHP's ambition as all-Hindu representative is expressed by the Religious Parliament (Dharma Samsad), a forum constituted by 1,008 *sadhus*, religious leaders, from different Hindu sects and denominations.

These sadhus function as transmitters and legitimists of the instructions and directives of the Organization Department. The practical work is done by 17 sub-departments that are responsible for different issues—for example, propaganda and publicity, finance, security, educational programs, mission, and so forth.

Dharmo rakshati rakshitah is the slogan of the VHP; it is translated as: "If you protect the Dharma, he will protect you." This motto expresses the conviction that Indian society suffers because the Dharma is not sufficiently observed nowadays. In the eyes of the VHP, a revitalization of the Dharma would regain the glorious strength of the Indian society. A basic prerequisite for this objective is the unification of the heterogeneous Hindu sects and denominations. With that goal in mind, the VHP has repeatedly formulated Hindu catechisms and catalogues of religious behavior, which are said to be authoritative for all Hindus.

In the 1960s and 1970s, the VHP concentrated on the development of its organizational structure. In addition, there were from the beginning two major fields of activity: several service projects, mainly among outcasts and tribals, and programs of reconversion. In both projects the VHP applied a strongly polemical tone against the Christian churches. Later, in the 1980s, there was an increase of activism, now directed against the alleged threat of a foreign Muslim influence in India. From the several actions against that threat, the most important—which received a negative press worldwide—was the Ramajanmabhoomi campaign for the liberation of Rama's birthplace. That crusade, initiated in 1984, pursued the aim of regaining the Babri-mosque in Ayodhya for the Hindus. This mosque was purportedly built in the 16th century on the ruins of a Rama temple. On December 6, 1992, the efforts culminated in an uncontrolled outburst of the fanaticized Hindu crowd that finally razed the mosque. As a result, several bloody altercations between Hindus and Muslims all over India arose, in which more than 300 people lost their lives. Following the Ayodhya incident the government banned the VHP, but in June 1995 it was legalized again.

Vishwa Hindu Parishad
Sankat Mochan Ashram
Sector 6

Ramakrishna Puram
New Delhi–110 022
India

VHP of America
PO Box 611
Iselin, NJ 08830
http://www.vhp-america.org/

Matthias Dech

See also: Hinduism; Janmashtami.

References

Basu, Tapan, et al. *Khaki Shorts and Saffron Flags: A Critique of the Hindu Right*. New Delhi: Orient Longman, 1993.

Dech, Matthias. "Hindus und Hindutum in Deutschland." Ph.D. diss., University of Marburg, 1998.

Hellman, Eva. "Political Hinduism. The Challenge of the Vishwa Hindu Parishad." Ph.D. diss., University of Uppsala, 1993.

Van der Veer, Peter. "Hindu Nationalism and the Discourse of Modernity: The Vishwa Hindu Parishad." In *Accounting for Fundamentalism*, edited by M. E. Marty. Chicago: University of Chicago Press, 1994.

Vlad Tepes (1431–1476), whose real name was Vlad III or Vlad Dracula, was a ruler of Wallachia known for his cruelty. (Getty Images)

Vlad Tepes

ca. 1431–ca. 1476

Vlad Tepes (or Vlad the Impaler), the obscure ruler of a small kingdom, Walachia, now a part of the modern state of Romania, has been rediscovered as a significant figure in 15th- and even 16th-century religious history. Though he ruled Wallachia a mere eight years (1456–1462), in that short time he was able to establish a reputation for cruelty in the process of suppressing the feudal lords and establishing a centralized nation. Today, Romanians see him as a founder of modern Romania. During most of his years on the throne, he also carried on an innovative, guerrilla-like war against the overwhelming forces of the Ottoman Empire, his actions contributing significantly to delaying the advance of the Muslim armies into Hungary. In the 20th century, as his political career was being rediscovered, his historical importance was overshadowed by the name he assumed as the son of Vlad II Dracul, which was adopted as the title of a horror novel by Irish writer Bram Stoker (1847–1912), Dracula, Son of the Dragon.

Vlad was the illegitimate son of Vlad II. In 1430, Vlad Dracula had been assigned the task of protecting the border at the Transylvanian town of Sighisoara. Here, Vlad was born as his father's second son toward the end of 1430 or beginning of 1431. Shortly after his son's birth, Vlad II traveled to Nuremberg, where he joined the Order of The Dragon (in Romanian Dracul), an alliance of Christian (both Roman Catholic and Eastern Orthodox) rulers. The Order was founded by Sigismund (1368–1437), the Holy Roman Emperor, as a means of defending Christianity whose major enemy at the time was seen as the Muslims who were invading.

In 1436, Vlad Dracul secured the Walachian throne and moved to Tirgoviste, the capital. The following year, Sigismund died, and Vlad Dracul signed a treaty with the Turks that allowed them to pass through Walachia and attack Hungary. Unfortunately for him, the Catholic Hungarians were able to drive the Turks back and in the process drove Vlad Dracul from his throne. He then turned to the Turks for help and they assisted him in the regaining of Walachia. As a guarantee of good faith toward his new allies, he allowed two of his sons, including Vlad, to be held at the sultan's court. In the meantime, Vlad Dracul's continuing efforts to play the Hungarians off against the Turks led to his defeat and death (along with his eldest son Mircea) in 1447.

Vlad, the son of Vlad Dracul, initially tried to take the throne in 1448, but could hold it only a matter of months. He then took refuge first in Moldavia, a neighboring Eastern Orthodox country. A powerful ruler was then on the Hungarian throne, John Hundayi (1400–1456). Only after Hundayi's death in 1456 was Vlad finally able to return to Walachia and begin his reign. In Tirgoviste, he had to contend with the power traditionally exercised by the feudal lords, the boyars. Frustrated with establishing his authority, he invited them to an Easter feast in 1459, at the close of which he arrested them, killed many of them, and forced the more able-bodied to march the 75 miles to Poenari, where over the next months they were forced to build a manor house on the top of a mountain overlooking the Arges River. The boyars' land was turned over to people who had supported and were now beholden to him.

Vlad next moved against the German cities that guarded the passes and hence controlled the trade between Walachia and Transylvania. Unable to obtain new trade agreements, he attacked the cities and impaled those individuals who had opposed him. He earned the hatred of the German communities of Transylvania and the nickname Tepes, or Impaler.

The major problem for Vlad now became the Muslim forces encamped along the Danube south and east of Bucharest. In 1461, he launched an effort to drive them out of what he considered to be his territory. In one bold move, he attempted to capture the sultan in his tent. The sultan gathered his forces and invaded Walachia with the goal of defeating Vlad. Vlad fought an effective hit-and-run retreat, killing many and taking prisoners. In the end, as the army approached Tirgoviste, Vlad created a forest of impaled Turkish soldiers and fled the city for his mountain retreat in Poenari. Deeply affected by what Vlad had done, the

sultan quit the chase, but sent his Romanian allies to finish him off. They surrounded the manor at Poenari, but before taking it, Vlad escaped north into Transylvania.

Vlad was placed under house arrest by the Hungarian king, Matthias Corvinus (1443–1490), but eventually emerged as the best candidate to retake the Walachian throne. In the meantime, he converted from his Romanian Orthodox Church faith to Roman Catholicism and married one of Corvinus's daughters, and in 1475 again became the ruler of Walachia. He would now join the battles against the Turks in Serbia.

His last attempt to rule Walachia would be cut short just a year after he returned. He was killed by an assassin at some point late in 1476. His head was taken back to the sultan for display as a trophy and his body reputedly taken to the Orthodox monastery at Snagov for burial, though that fact is highly contested.

In the generation after Vlad, the Ottoman rulers turned their attention elsewhere in their quest to expand their empire and thus it would be 1521 before Belgrade, Serbia, fell and the Hungarians defeated at the Battle of Mohacs in 1526. The fall of Hungary opened the way to Vienna, the final obstacle blocking access to Western Europe. The Ottomans were finally stopped in 1529 at the gates of Vienna, when the Catholics diverted their attention from the growing Reformation movement in Germany and Switzerland to concentrate their forces to prevent any further European expansion by the Ottoman Empire.

In the 1970s, the life of Prince Vlad Dracula was conflated with the fictional account of Count Dracula, the anti-hero of Bram Stoker's novel. In novels and movies, Prince Vlad and Count Dracula were identified with each other, and the confusion was used to create tourism in Romania, in spite of efforts by Romanian historians to counter the popular myths.

J. Gordon Melton

See also: Roman Catholic Church; Romanian Orthodox Church.

References

Florescu, Radu, and Raymond T. McNally. *Dracula: A Biography of Vlad the Impaler, 1431–1476.* New York: Hawthorn Books, 1973.

McNally, Raymond T., and Radu Florescu. *In Search of Dracula.* New York: Galahad Books, 1972.

Miller, Elizabeth. *Dracula: Sense & Nonsense.* Westcliffe-on-Sea: Desert Island Books, 2000.

Nandris, Grigore. "The Historical Dracula: The Theme of His Legend in the Western and in the Eastern Literature of Europe." *Comparative Literature Studies* 3, no. 4 (1966): 367–396.

Treptow, Kurt W. *Vlad III Dracula: The Life and Times of the Historical Dracula.* Iasi, Romania: Center for Romanian Studies, 2000.

Vodou

Vodou is a religion that blends a variety of traditional African (mainly Fon, Yoruba, and Kongo) and Catholic elements. Although decidedly more akin in its forms of ritual and belief to African traditional religion than to Catholicism, Vodou is not an African religion but a product of the Haitian experience. This experience began in the injustices and brutality of plantation slavery in the French colony of Saint-Domingue (1697–1804), followed by two centuries of general political oppression, environmental decay, and stifling poverty. Vodou therefore is a religion born of displacement, suffering, and the negotiation thereof.

Since emerging in a French colony that prohibited its practice, Vodou has always represented a formidable force of political resistance; indeed, its contribution to the success of the Haitian Revolution has been stressed by numerous writers. With the most dynamic early Vodou communities springing up in settlements of escaped slaves from diverse African ethnic groups, since its very inception the religion has demonstrated significant variety. Certain traditions are primarily ancestor cults, while others focus on particular spirits brought from West Africa or others revealed in the New World. Because of the clandestine and variegated nature of colonial-era Vodou, moreover, the religion has no founder, no unifying doctrine, and no formal organizational network. None of these, nor a Vodou scripture, have ever developed.

Slaves brought to the colony were baptized Catholic upon arrival and given minimal religious instruction by Dominicans, Capuchins, and Jesuits. Syncretism thus immediately resulted, as slaves identified Catholic saints as new manifestations of African spirits, and adopted crosses, holy water, and incense as powerful religious trinkets to be used in conjunction with the amulets they reconstructed from African religious memory. The Catholic "pantheon"—with its single high creator, God, the Virgin Mary, and host of the dead (the saints) who intervene in the world of the living—lent itself quite fluently to assimilation with the traditional African community of spiritual beings. African religion, likewise, has a single distant creator God (called Bondyè in Vodou) and numerous spirits and ancestors, who, much like the Catholic saints, are perceived as accessible and with whom the greatest amount of human/divine commerce transpires.

Spirit possession and divination are the main forms of communication with the dead (*lemò*) and the spirits (*lwa yo*) in Vodou and together form its ritual focus. Put simply, when our relationship with lemò or lwa yo is in harmony, life is full and pleasurable; when this relationship is discordant, sickness, some other hardship, or even death may result. Upon the occurrence of such misfortune, ritual specialists (female: *manbo*; male: *oungan*) are consulted. Either through divination or the orchestration of ceremonies aiming to provoke spirit possession (which most often take place in temples [*ounfò*], family burial compounds, or public cemeteries), the manbo or oungan effects communication with the lemò or lwa yo in order to discover the cause of the illness or discord and to determine a means of re-establishing harmony or effecting healing. Both the maintenance and the reconstitution of this harmony rely primarily on sacrifice in various forms, while healing often involves herbalism and ritual baths.

Vodou remains popular among the vast majority of Haiti's peasantry (which composes 70 percent of the national population) and is today the religion of choice for a smaller majority of the nation's urban population. Most practitioners also consider themselves faithful Catholics and see no contradiction in this. The religion has spread internationally mainly through massive emigration, as roughly one million Haitians have settled in the neighboring Dominican Republic and more than a million more in urban centers of North America, mainly New York, Montreal, Miami, and Boston. With most of Haiti's estimated 8 million inhabitants, a smaller majority of the more than 2 million Haitians abroad, and an insignificant yet growing number of *blan* (non-Haitian) converts practicing the religion in some form, the worldwide number of Vodou practitioners may be roughly estimated at between 8 and 10 million.

Terry Rey

See also: Ancestors; Capuchins; Dominicans; Jesuits; Mary, Blessed Virgin; Roman Catholic Church; Saints.

References
Desmangles, Leslie G. *The Faces of the Gods: Vodou and Roman Catholicism.* Chapel Hill: University of North Carolina Press, 1992.

Laguette, Michael S. *Voodoo and Politics in Haiti.* New York: St. Martin's Press, 1989.

Olmós, Marguerite Fernandez, and Lizabeth Paravisini Gebert, eds. *Sacred Possessions: Vodou, Santeria, Obeah, and the Caribbean.* New Brunswick, NJ: Rutgers University Press, 1997.

VRINDA/The Vrindavan Institute for Vaisnava Culture and Studies

VRINDA/The Vrindavan Institute for Vaisnava Culture and Studies, one of several groups to grow out of the International Society for Krishna Consciousness (ISKCON), was founded by Srila Bhakti Aloka Paramadvaiti Maharaja (b. 1954). Swami Paramadvaiti originally joined ISKCON in 1971 in Düsseldorf, Germany, and he rose to a position of leadership as a temple president. He was sent to South America by Swami Prabhupada (1896–1977), ISKCON's founder, where, in 1984, he created both the ISEV (Instituto Superior de Estudios Vedicos) and VRINDA (The Vrindavan Institute for Vaisnava Culture and Studies). By this time he had come into a relationship with Srila Sridhar Maharaja (d. 2004), a Vaisnava guru (one of Prabhupada's god brothers) to whom some ISKCON leaders turned

following Prabhupada's death. He took his *sannyas* vows (the renounced life) from Sridhar Maharaja.

VRINDA established centers (ashrams, farms, cultural centers, schools, and so forth) in Colombia, Chile, Brazil, Ecuador, Argentina, and Peru, and then spread to Central and North America and Europe (Germany, Bulgaria, Hungary, and Switzerland). In 1990, VRINDA was established in India, and a World Center opened in Vrinda Kunja. Also in Vrindavan, VRINDA opened the first Gaudiya Vaisnava Bookstore to distribute books from all of the groups in the Krishna Consciousness tradition, both classical texts as well as those produced by contemporary teachers. VRINDA has also committed itself to translating and publishing books in a variety of languages, especially German and Spanish.

VRINDA supports an expansive website, including the text of several books by Swami Paramadvaiti. It is a member of the World Vaisnava Association.

VRINDA
4138 NW 23 Rd. Ave.
Miami, FL 33142

Vrinda Kunja
Bhut Galli 169, Gopeshwara Road
Vrindavan, Mathura UP
281121
India
http://www.vrindavan.org/

J. Gordon Melton

See also: International Society for Krishna Consciousness; World Vaisnava Association.

References
Paramadvaiti, B. A., Swami. *My Life.* http://www.vrindavan.org/bap/01/01.html. Accessed April 24, 2009.

Paramadvaiti, B. A., Swami. *Our Family the Gaudiya Math.* http://www.vrindavan.org/English/Books/GMconded.html. Accessed April 24, 2009.

VRINDA. http://www.vrindavan.org/. Accessed April 24, 2009.

Wahhabi Islam

The Wahhabi movement was launched in the 1740s by its founder, Mohammad ibn Abd-al-Wahhab (ca. 1703–1791), as an attempt to purify and vivify Islam, especially in the Arabian Peninsula. Al-Wahhab was especially critical of the different Sufi brotherhoods, which he saw as having fallen into heresy. He took inspiration from the Hanbalite School of Sunni Islam and its more literalistic approach to the interpretation of the Koran, the Muslim holy book, and the *hadith,* the sayings of and traditions concerning the Prophet Muhammad. He tended to criticize the other Sunni schools as too accommodationist to the presence of the Sufis in their midst.

At the time that Wahhab began preaching, Arabia was part of the Ottoman Empire, which was dominated by the Hanafite School of Islam, of which Al-Wahhab was critical. He was able to gather an initial following by preaching to the pilgrims who annually flocked to Mecca. His efforts might have died out had they not become tied to the aspirations of the Saud family, which in the late 1800s began an effort to take central and eastern Arabia from the Ottomans. They were initially successful. They captured Mecca in 1806 and began to move into Iraq. The Ottoman caliph reacted, and in two campaigns, in 1812–1813 and 1816–1818, squelched the Saud family and the Wahhabi cause. The Saud family put together a coalition of Arab tribes and, in the 20th century, with the fall of the Ottoman Empire, was finally able to reconquer the peninsula. The kingdom of Saudi Arabia was proclaimed in 1932, with the Koran named its guiding authority and the head of the Saud family the country's king and absolute monarch.

The Wahhabi movement was institutionalized in the family of Abd al-Aziz ibn Sa'ud, the first king, who placed his many sons and grandsons in positions of power. The Wahhabi movement also is manifest in the Committee for Encouraging Virtue and Preventing Vice, and with the *mutawwah* (religious authorities), who enforce public conformity to Islamic law, especially on issues of dress and attention to daily times of prayer. They receive support from the majority of Saudis who adhere to the Hanbalite School.

The Wahhabi perspective exists as the most conservative and traditionalist of the spectrum within Sunni Islam. Wahhabis are opposed to ostentatious worship, and Wahhabi mosques tend to be simply furnished and lack minarets (towers from which the people are called to prayer). They have opposed any efforts toward religious pluralism in the Islamic world, especially the efforts of Christian missionaries. They have also advocated traditional roles for women, which in the most austere form allows only very narrow roles for females in the home.

Through the activities of the wealthy Saud family, the Wahhabi movement has exerted influence globally and has been notably present in the Muslim World League, headquartered in Mecca. It is also seen as the direct inspiration for a variety of traditionalist Islamist movements, such as the Muslim Brotherhood in Egypt, the Jamaat-e-Islam Party in Pakistan, and the Taliban in Afghanistan. Its influence has reached beyond Sunni Islam to affect Shia Islam through such movements as the Palestinian Hezbollah and the forces undergirding the Iranian revolution in 1979. It gained strength by denying those forces internal to the international Muslim community that sought to respond to modern intellectual currents (including criticisms of traditional

The 16th century Amiriya Madrasa, a religious school that was built by the Sultan Amir bin Abdul Wahhab in 1504, is seen in Radaa city, near the Yemeni capital Sanaa. (Corbis)

Muslim practices such as polygamy), as well as the insults felt from European intervention in Muslim societies. In the 20th century it most strongly opposed the secularizing tendencies represented in liberal Islam, Marxism, and the permeation of the world by Western culture. Wahhabi and Wahhabi-related groups have consistently argued for the development of Islamic states in which the *sharia* (Islamic law) is the law of the land. The Wahhabi perspective is also dominant in the Arabian state of Qatar.

Since the days of Abd-al-Wahhab, the Wahhabis have encountered opposition in the larger Muslim world and from many in the other schools of Sunni Islam, many of whom have written of it as if it were a heretical Muslim sect. In the West, Wahhabis have been seen as part of the larger world of "Islamic fundamentalism," a term rejected by most Muslim scholars, even those who might otherwise oppose the Wahhabi

perspective, preferring in its stead terms such as "Islamic revivalism" and "Islamic activism."

J. Gordon Melton

See also: Abd al-Aziz ibn Sa'ud; Hanafite School of Islam; Hanbalite School of Islam; Jamaat-e-Islam; Mecca; Muslim Brotherhood; Muslim World League; Shia Islam; Taliban.

References

Abu-Hakima, Ahmad M. *History of Eastern Arabia, 1750–1800: The Rise and Development of Bahrain, Kuwait, and Wahhabi Saudi Arabia.* Troy, MI: International Book Centre, 1988.

Al-Yassini, A. *Religion and State in the Kingdom of Saudi Arabia.* Boulder, CO: Westview, 1985.

Sabini, John. *Armies in the Sand: The Struggle for Mecca and Medina (the Egyptian Wahhabi War in the 19th Century).* New York: Thames and Hudson, 1981.

Wenner, Manfred W. "The Arabian Peninsula and the Islamic 'Revival.'" In *Islam in the Contemporary World,* edited by Cyriac K. Pullapilly. Notre Dame, IN: Cross Roads, 1980.

Wake Island

Wake Island is one of three islands in an isolated Pacific atoll that includes the nearby islands of Wilkes and Peale. The United States occupied the atoll in 1898 during the war with Spain, and has since kept Wake as a military base. It currently has some 1,600 residents, almost totally armed forces personnel. It is used as a business center, stopover point for trans-Pacific flights, and a missile-testing base.

Religious services on Wake are conducted by Roman Catholic and Protestant/Free church chaplains as needed, and there are no permanent congregations. The Roman Catholic Church considers Wake a part of its Diocese of Agana (Guam).

J. Gordon Melton

See also: Free Churches; Roman Catholic Church.

Reference
Barrett, David, ed. *The Encyclopedia of World Christianity.* 2nd ed. New York: Oxford University Press, 2001.

Waldensian Church

The Waldensian Church is the oldest pre-Reformation Protestant body still in existence, and it prides itself on the title *mater reformationis* (mother of the Reformation). In terms of its origins, disentangling fact from fiction is not always easy. Its founder was Waldo or Valdesius (not originally "Peter Waldo," the name "Peter" being added several centuries after his death in order to claim that, like the early church, the Waldensian Church had also been first led by an apostolic figure known as Peter). Waldo was a wealthy merchant in Lyons, France, who around 1170 underwent a conversion experience centered on his desire to live a life of poverty and to preach the gospel. He died around 1206. Notwithstanding the hostility of the Catholic hierarchy, the separation from Rome of Waldo's Poor of Lyons movement (only later known as Waldensians) did not initially seem to be entirely inevitable. One of the Poor of Lyons groups, led by Durandus of Osca, reconciled itself with Pope Innocent III (1160–1216) in the year 1208. Other groups remained in the margins of the Roman Catholic Church, breaking with Rome only gradually. In the 13th and 14th centuries, Waldensian ideas spread from France and Italy into Austria, Germany, Bohemia, Poland, and Hungary, largely through independent local groups quite different from each other and with no common leadership. It is even questioned whether the firmly established "Waldensian" groups active in France and Italy in the 15th century could really claim an undisputed genealogy going back to Waldo himself.

In 1532, with the Synod of Chanforan, the Waldensians of southern France and the Italian valleys of Piedmont joined the (Calvinist) Reformed Church. According to some historians, this was a crucial breach in their continuity with Waldo, while others claim some degree of continuity. In the 17th century, Waldensians endured terrible persecution during Europe's religious wars, particularly in 1655 and 1686. An armed resistance failed, and the community, now reduced to some 3,000 members entrenched in the Piedmont valleys, escaped to Protestant Switzerland. In 1689, however, they returned to Piedmont with a spectacular and epic march. They managed to obtain some measure of tolerance, although within a ghetto. Waldensians received help from European, particularly British, Protestants, and in the 19th century the Piedmont valleys entered a period of religious revival. Finally, in 1848, the Waldensians were granted religious freedom, with full civil and political rights, by the king of Sardinia, Charles Albert (1798–1849).

During Italy's Risorgimento, the conflict between its newly created national state and the Roman Catholic Church gave the Waldensians the opportunity to embark on a nationwide missionary effort among those dissatisfied with the Church of Rome. Not much was achieved in term of converts, however, although a Waldensian presence was established in most Italian cities. Following another difficult period during the

Fascist regime, the Waldensian Church was granted a new level of legal recognition after World War II, and in 1984 it entered into a Concordat with the Italian government, amended in 1993, allowing it inter alia to share in the national church tax. In 1975, Italian Waldensians and the Evangelical Methodist Church of Italy entered into an "integration agreement," which was not technically a merger. The two churches, under the name Union of Waldensian and Methodist Churches, are governed by the same executive body (the Waldensian Table), while also maintaining their own separate forms of organization.

Each local assembly in the Waldensian Church is led by elected elders and appoints delegates to the yearly church synod, which in turn elects the seven members of the Table, the governing body chaired by a Table chair (*moderatore*). The title of pastor is conferred upon men and women entrusted with the preaching ministry. There are at present 40,000 Waldensians, 25,000 in Italy and 15,000 in Uruguay and Argentina, where Waldensian immigrants settled in the 19th century.

After the Synod of Chanforan, the theology became Reformed-Presbyterian, and Waldensians share the general doctrines of the Reformed churches.

Waldensian Church
Via Firenze 38
00184 Rome
Italy
http://www.chiesavaldese.org
Massimo Introvigne and PierLuigi Zoccatelli

See also: Evangelical Methodist Church of Italy; Roman Catholic Church.

References

Hugon, Augusto-Armand. *Storia dei Valdesi II: Dall'adesione alla Riforma all'Emancipazione (1532–1848)*. Torino, Italy: Claudiana, 1989.

Molnar, Amedeo. *Storia dei Valdesi I: Dalle origini all'adesione alla Riforma (1176–1532)*. Torino, Italy: Claudiana, 1989.

Vinay, Valdo. *Storia dei Valdesi III: Dal movimento evangelico italiano al movimento ecumenico (1848–1978)*. Torino, Italy: Claudiana, 1990.

■ Wallis et Futuna Islands

Wallis et Futuna is a French South Pacific Island territory consisting of the Wallis, Futuna, and Afori islands. They are north of Fiji and west of Samoa. A French possession through the 19th century, the Wallis et Futuna Islands were named a protectorate in 1887 and an overseas territory in 1961. The current population of 15,000 (2008) resides on the mere 106 square miles of land.

The Roman Catholic Church is the only organized religion on the islands. It was first established in 1836 by a Marist priest. The Diocese of Wallis et Futuna was established in 1966. In 1974 the bishop, a Frenchman, withdrew and turned the diocese over to his auxiliary, a priest who had been elevated from among the

The Wallis & Futuna Islands

Religion	Followers in 1970	Followers in 2010	% of Population	Annual % growth 2000–2010	Followers in 2025	Followers in 2050
Christians	8,700	15,200	97.3	0.18	16,500	16,200
Roman Catholics	8,400	14,900	95.3	0.04	16,100	15,700
Protestants	0	120	0.8	6.58	180	250
Marginals	0	160	1.0	14.87	300	400
Ethnoreligionists	0	180	1.2	0.23	200	200
Baha'is	100	140	0.9	0.17	180	300
Agnostics	0	90	0.6	21.18	140	240
Atheists	0	10	0.1	0.00	10	20
Total population	**8,800**	**15,600**	**100.0**	**0.24**	**17,000**	**17,000**

WALLIS ET FUTUNA ISLANDS

PACIFIC
OCEAN

Wallis
Islands

Futuna
Islands

Taval

Toloke

Flua

Valsei

Nuku

Leava

Futuna

Horn Islands

Poi

Mala'e

Taoa

Ono

Kolia

Vele

PACIFIC OCEAN

Alofitai

Alofi

Nukuloa

Nukuteatea

PACIFIC
OCEAN

Vallala

Alele

Mala'e

Liku

Ahoa

Uvea

★ **Mata'utu**

Ha'afuasia

Tepa

WALLIS
ISLANDS

Mala'etoll

Halalo

Utufua

Nukuatea

Faioa

N

Polynesian people who constitute the primary citizens of the islands. An indigenous episcopal leadership has been present ever since. The bishop serves as an auxiliary to the archbishop of Noumea (Kanaky) and participates in the larger Episcopal Conference of the Pacific, headquartered in Fiji.

Over the course of the 20th century, an aggressive policy of Christianizing the islands has largely displaced the pre-Christian indigenous religion.

J. Gordon Melton

See also: Roman Catholic Church.

References

Aldrich, Robert. *France and the South Pacific Since 1940*. Honolulu: University of Hawaii Press, 1994.

Barrett, David, ed. *The Encyclopedia of World Christianity*. 2nd ed. New York: Oxford University Press, 2001.

Fischer, Steven Robert. *A History of the Pacific Islands*. London: Palgrave Macmillan, 2002.

Wang Chongyang

ca. 1123–1170

Wang Chongyang (or Yangqun, Wang Zhe) was the founder of Quanzhen Daoism, one of the two main surviving schools of Daoism. He is remembered for discovering a way to fruitfully integrate Daoism with Buddhist and neo-Confucianist perspectives, while the movement he founded incorporated many local Chinese deities into the hierarchy of Daoist gods.

Wang was originally a member of the literati during the Jin dynasty (1115–1234), which ruled northern China. This was a period of sudden political dislocation, with the passing of the Song dynasty (960–1279) in the north and the advent of a new dynasty ruled by foreigners. Wang had retired to a solitary life in the mountains when he had several meetings with such legendary immortals as Lu Dongbin, during which time he was pressed to start a new tradition of teaching. He finally evolved a highly syncretic mixture of teachings, practices, and morality seemingly well-suited to the times.

Wang's Quanzhen, or Complete Perfection, Daoist sect put greatest emphasis on self-cultivation and less emphasis on the intricate visualization exercises, elaborate rituals, and talismanic magic that had dominated earlier schools. For Wang, the primary goal was to refine the body's energies through the practices of inner alchemy (*neidan*). Wang called his meditative practice *jing zuo*, "quiet sitting," a term probably picked up from Chan Buddhism. From neo-Confucianism, he also borrowed an emphasis on the virtue of filial piety and some ascetic practices. The latter included the ab-staining from sex, alcohol, and strong vegetables. He and the small group of close followers lived a rather rustic lifestyle.

When Wang died, he had only about 15 followers. It would be due to his successors passing on Wang's approach that the Quenzhen sect of Daoism grew into such an important force in Chinese religion.

Edward A. Irons

See also: Alchemy, Daoist; Daoism; Meditation; Quanzhen Daoism; Zhengyi Daoism.

References

Bartholomew P.M. Tsui. *Taoist Tradition and Change: The Story of the Complete Perfection Sect in Hong Kong*. Hong Kong: Christian Study Centre on Chinese Religion and Culture, 1991.

Kohn, Levia, ed. *Daoism Handbook*. 2 vols. Leiden: Brill, 2000.

Warith Deen Mohammad, Ministry of

In 1975, following the death of his father Elijah Muhammad (1897–1975), Wallace Muhammad (1933–2008) was appointed leader of the Nation of Islam, or Black Muslim movement. Wallace, or Warith as he later became known, rapidly transformed the Nation's belief system: he eliminated the urgent apocalyptic message from his father's prophecies, and moved the organization closer to a more orthodox form of Islam. In 1992 Warith Deen Mohammad became the first Muslim cleric to lead prayers in the U.S. Senate.

The Nation of Islam originated in 1930 in Detroit, Michigan. Its founder, Wallace Fard, preached a combination of Islam and Black Nationalism. The doctrine was compelling, particularly in an urban environment in which large numbers of recently arrived southern blacks hoped to better their lives. The Great Depression magnified their economic marginalization and white prejudice, dashing the hopes of many. These individuals made a receptive audience for Fard's message. Within three years, the Nation developed a substantial following. Notably, it was supported by a well-organized administrative structure that included a security force

Imam Wahy Deen Sharif, standing center, spiritual leader of the Masjid Warith Deen mosque in Irvington, New Jersey, speaks in Washington Park in Newark during afternoon prayers, June 18, 2004. (AP/Wide World Photos)

and a school, as well as training classes for women on how to be good wives and mothers.

Fard disappeared in the early 1930s, but his appointed successor, Elijah Muhammad, developed the movement's doctrine, and further strengthened its membership core. Muhammad taught that Fard was actually Allah incarnate, and that black Americans were his Chosen People. Muhammad identified white Americans as "white devils," and he prophesied that white America would fall in 1965–1966. In preparation for that time, he emphasized economic self-sufficiency, and the Nation undertook a variety of business enterprises.

Muhammad also required the Muslims to adhere to a strict moral code, and he emphasized physical and mental purity. He outlined strict dietary regulations, and members of the Nation were forbidden to smoke, take drugs, or gamble. In addition, he encouraged pride in the black race.

Inter-racial marriages were forbidden, and many new members took the surname "X," to symbolize that black Americans could never know their real origins, and to suggest their potential but as yet unrealized power. In the late 1940s, Malcolm Little (1925–1965) converted to the Nation of Islam. Malcolm X, as he became known, soon rose to become one of the Nation's most prominent ministers and recruiters. In the early 1960s, however, Malcolm became disenchanted with Elijah Muhammad's moral guidance (believing that he had fathered several children outside his marriage); he was in turn censured by Muhammad for commenting that President John F. Kennedy's assassination was simply "the chickens [coming] home to roost." As a result, Malcolm was expelled from the Nation. Soon afterward he undertook a pilgrimage to Mecca (the Hajj), and returned to the United States as a convert to traditional, orthodox Islam. He was assassinated on February 21, 1965.

Elijah Muhammad led the Nation until his death in 1975. He appointed his son Wallace as his successor, a move that surprised many. Wallace had a turbulent history within the Nation. He was strongly influenced by Malcolm X, criticized his father's interpretation of Islam as early as 1961, and was twice expelled from the Nation during the 1960s. Nevertheless, the majority of Muslims followed him when he completely reinterpreted the movement's doctrine. Within six months he had removed the urgent apocalyptic message from Elijah's prophecies, and within the next year he initiated even more radical changes. In March 1976 he declared that his father was no longer to be interpreted as the "last Messenger of Allah," and in October he announced that the Nation was to become the World Community of al-Islam in the West (WCIW), and that people of all races were welcome to join it.

One notable Muslim did not accept these changes: Louis Farrakhan. He left the group in 1978 and "resurrected" the Nation of Islam, with its original doctrine. For the most part, however, the Muslims accepted the new direction that Wallace chose for the movement. This relatively easy transformation was the result of two factors. First, evidence suggests that in his declining years, Elijah Muhammad exhibited moderation in his language and political views. Second, Elijah's strict doctrine and calls for education and economic self-sufficiency had the unintended consequence of raising the Nation's membership among the middle class. Radical views were no longer as appealing as they once had been.

Wallace's successful redirection of the movement continued during the 1970s and 1980s. In 1980 the WCIW became the American Muslim Mission, and its publication became the *American Muslim Journal;* in addition, Wallace announced that he would now be known as Warith Deen Mohammad. In 1985, Warith decentralized the movement completely, and the network of people and the centers associated with him have been described simply as the Ministry of Warith Deen Mohammad. Its publication became the *Muslim Journal.* This move toward the mainstream was perhaps most clearly evidenced in 1992, when Warith became the first Muslim cleric to lead prayers in the U.S. Senate.

Wallace's relationship with Minister Louis Farrakhan and the Nation of Islam was a difficult one for most of the 1980s. During the 1990s, however, the two groups moved toward reconciliation. In February 2000, at Minister Farrakhan's request, Imam Muhammad spoke at the Nation of Islam's annual meeting. The two leaders embraced and called for the unity of all Muslims. Imam Warith Deen Mohammad died on September 8, 2008.

Like the Nation of Islam, Warith Deen Mohammad's movement has never published its membership numbers. The movement continues to publish the *Muslim Journal,* which can be found at http://www.muslim journal.net. Warith Deen Muhammad's ministry is located at http://www.wdmministry.com and www.wdm events.org.

Ministry of W. Deen Mohammed
PO Box 1061
Calumet City, IL 60409

Martha Lee

See also: Nation of Islam.

References

Curtis, Edward E. *Black Muslim Religion in the Nation of Islam, 1960–1975.* Chapel Hill: University of North Carolina Press, 2006.

Gardell, Mattias. *In the Name of Elijah Muhammad, Louis Farrakhan and the Nation of Islam.* Durham: Duke University Press, 1996.

Lee, Martha. *The Nation of Islam: An American Millenarian Movement.* Syracuse: Syracuse University Press, 1996.

Muhammad, Elijah. *Message to the Blackman in America.* Chicago: Muhammad Mosque of Islam No. 2, 1965.

Way International, The

The Way International, Inc., an international fundamentalist Christian fellowship, was founded in 1942 as a radio ministry under the name of Vesper Chimes by Victor Paul Wierwille (1916–1985), then a minister in the Evangelical and Reformed Church (now an integral part of the United Church of Christ). It assumed its present name in 1974, after being known successively as the Chimes Hour (beginning in 1944), the

Chimes Hour Youth Caravan (1947), and The Way, Inc. (1955).

Wierwille had decided to enter the ministry while a student at Mission House College. He later earned a B.D. at Mission House Seminary, in Minnesota, and did graduate work at the University of Chicago and Princeton Theological Seminary, earning an M.Th. in 1941. He was ordained in 1942 and became pastor of the Evangelical and Reformed Church at Paine, Ohio, from which he moved to Van Wert, Ohio, two years later, to become pastor of St. Peter's Evangelical and Reformed Church. During his stay in Van Wert he became an avid student of the Bible, concentrating upon the doctrine of the Holy Spirit. In 1948 he was awarded a Ph.D. by the Pikes Peak Bible College and Seminary, an unaccredited school in Manitou Springs, Colorado.

In 1951, Wierwille received God's Holy Spirit and spoke in tongues for the first time, the basic Pentecostal experience. Out of his subsequent Bible study he developed a course in Christian living that he called the Power for Abundant Living (PFAL) class. He first offered the class in 1953. The following year he began to study Aramaic, under the influence of biblical scholar George M. Lamsa, and began to develop the unique perspective on biblical doctrine that has become identified with the movement that grew up around him. In 1957 he left the Evangelical and Reformed Church, and henceforth devoted himself full-time to his own ministry. That ministry had been chartered as The Way, Inc., in 1955 (later changed to The Way International in 1975). He led The Way until his retirement in 1983. He established the headquarters of The Way at the Wierwille family farm outside New Knoxville, Ohio.

The Way grew steadily through the 1950s, but growth slowed in the 1960s. Then it suddenly experienced spectacular growth in the 1970s, as the ministry identified with the national Jesus People Revival that moved among the Baby Boom generation, which was just coming of age. The Way expanded its facilities at New Knoxville, which hosted the first national Rock of Ages Festival, an annual gathering of Way members, in 1971.

Wierwille established The Way Corps, a four-year leadership training program, and in 1974 he purchased the former Emporia College in Emporia, Kansas, which he transformed into the corps headquarters as The Way College. The Word Over the World (WOW) Ambassador program, initiated by Wierwille in 1971, began to send young Way members across the country for a year of witnessing activity.

Wierwille was succeeded as president of The Way by L. Craig Martindale (b. 1948) in 1983, at the 40th anniversary of The Way's founding. Martindale had joined The Way while in college, and he became involved full-time after his graduation. He led The Way through the 1990s but was forced to resign in 2000, when he was accused of some extramarital sexual relationships.

The beliefs of The Way are summarized in an 11-point doctrinal statement. It rejects the Trinitarian orthodoxy of most Western Christianity and denies the divinity of Jesus; Wierwille's opinion on this controversial point is the subject of his book *Jesus Christ Is Not God* (1975). Although believing in the divine conception of Jesus by God, The Way teaches that Jesus is the Son of God but not God the Son. The Way also believes in receiving the fullness of God's Holy Spirit, believed to be the power of God, not the third person of a Trinity. This view has traditionally been termed Arianism, considered a heresy since the condemnation of its early exponent, Arius, by the Council of Nicaea in 325.

The Way also teaches a form of biblical interpretation known as dispensationalism, a view that divides Bible history into successive periods during which God developed a different relationship with humanity. Wierwille followed a version of dispensationalism known as ultradispensationalism. Most dispensationalists believe that a new dispensation began at Easter, when Christ was resurrected from the dead, and that we currently live in the dispensation of grace that was initiated at that time. Ultradispensationalists believe that between Easter and the emergence of the New Testament church at Pentecost there was a period of transition whose story is largely told in the book of Acts. This period is identified with the institution of John the Baptist's water baptism. In the succeeding dispensation of grace, the baptism of the Spirit replaces John's baptism.

Ultradispensationalists regard the Old Testament, the four Gospels, and the epistles of Hebrews and James as representative of pre-Pentecost dispensations. The book of Acts is a transitional document. Paul's epistles, especially his later letters, are seen by ultradispensationalism as the prime documents of the dispensation of grace. The Way believes in one baptism, that of the Holy Spirit, and rejects water baptism.

The Way, like most scholars, believes that Aramaic was the language spoken by Jesus, but in addition it believes Aramaic to be the language in which the New Testament was originally written, contrary to almost all scholars, who believe it was written in Greek. This view is based on the work of George M. Lamsa, especially his *Holy Bible from Ancient Eastern Manuscripts* (1959), and the books of independent Indian bishop K. C. Pillai, *The Orientalisms of the Bible* and *Light through an Eastern Window*.

The Way's basic teachings are presented in the 12-session course, the Power for Abundant Living (PFAL). New members take the course and upon graduation may continue to attend "twig" fellowships. Those who wish to become more involved in The Way's work may attend The Way College, join The Way Corps, or become a WOW Ambassador for one year.

The Way International's organization is based on the model of a tree. At the root are the five educational and administrative centers that serve the organization as international headquarters, located at New Knoxville, Ohio; The Way College of Emporia at Emporia, Kansas; The Way College of Biblical Research, Indiana Campus, at Rome, Indiana; Camp Gunnison (The Way Family Ranch at Gunnison, Colorado); and Lead Outdoor Academy at Tinnie, New Mexico. Various national organizations are identified as trunks, and state and provincial organizations as limbs. Organizations serving cities and towns are branches. The small fellowship gatherings in a person's home, most analogous to a congregation, are called twigs. Individual members are likened to leaves. The ministry as a whole is administered by a board of trustees that appoints the cabinet overseeing the headquarters complex, as well as the staff of the other root locations.

In 1983, at the time that leadership was shifted to Craig Martindale, The Way reported 2,657 twigs in the United States, with approximately 30,000 people involved. Each twig gathering averaged approximately 10 members. The Rock of Ages Festival, held that year, hosted more than 17,000 people. Also, PFAL classes were conducted abroad in a number of countries, primarily Zaire (now the Democratic Republic of the Congo), Chile, Argentina, Venezuela, and Colombia. Shortly after that transfer of leadership, The Way was hit with significant internal controversy that only grew following Wierwille's death in 1985. Membership also declined in reaction to continuing criticism of the organization as a cult.

Soon after the emergence of The Way International in the 1970s, various groups began to attack it and its founder. Christian counter-cult organizations opposed it because of its non-Trinitarian theology. Secular anti-cult organizations accused it of brainwashing its members and attempted to deprogram members. Then, after Wierwille's death, charges of improprieties by Wierwille and several of his close associates resulted in the defection by several prominent Way leaders, a few of whom established rival groups. As a result The Way lost considerable support, although it had seemed to recover somewhat by the 1990s, when attendance at the annual Rock of Ages Festival began to return to its former level. Much of that gain was lost in the light of revelations concerning Martindale at the end of the 1990s. There are a number of Internet sites devoted to criticism of The Way International, posted primarily by those who disagree with its theological stance.

The Way International
Box 328
New Knoxville, OH 45871

James R. Lewis

See also: Fundamentalism; Pentecostalism; United Church of Christ

References

Martindale, L. Craig. *The Rise and Expansion of the Christian Church in the First Century.* New Knoxville, OH: American Christian, 1993.

Morton, Douglas V., and John P. Juedes. *The Integrity and Accuracy of The Way's Word.* St. Louis, MO: Personal Freedom Outreach, 1980.

Wierwille, Dorothea Kipp. *Victor Paul Wierwille: Born Again to Serve.* New Knoxville, OH: American Christian, 1996.

Wierwille, Victor Paul. *Jesus Christ Is Not God.* New Knoxville, OH: American Christian, 1975.

Wierwille, Victor Paul. *Power for Abundant Living.* New Knoxville, OH: American Christian, 1972.

Wesak

Early Buddhist sources (apart from the sutras) suggest that Gautama Buddha's birthday, day of enlightenment, and paranirvana or death) all occurred on the same day of the year. That day, designated Wesak (Vesak), is the night of the full moon of the Hindu month of Vaisakha (usually in May on the Common Era calendar). Through the centuries, Wesak was primarily an event commemorated by Theravada Buddhists, for whom its celebration emerged as the most important festival of the year. Originally a time to remember the birth and death of Buddha, it evolved primarily into a celebration of his enlightenment. In the 20th century, Wesak has been adopted as a favorite celebration within the Mahayana and Vajrayana Buddhist traditions, especially in the West.

The observance of Wesak usually includes both a formal and an informal aspect. The local temple or monastery will take the lead in the formal part of the celebration, which will include a procession by the monks, the presentation of an offering, and the chanting of sutras. In more recent times, the ceremony might also include a presentation on some aspect of the Buddha's teachings followed by the bathing of a statue of the Buddha. The Buddha's birth is usually acknowledged in the evening of the full moon with a *vaisakha puja* (sacramental offering).

Lay leaders take the lead in the more informal aspect of Wesak, which will occur over several days.

A devotee praying in front of a Buddha statue. (Kaikai/Dreamstime.com)

Gathering will include liberal amounts of food and drink, various artistic and cultural programming, and even academic discussions of Buddhist history and theology. This more informal program will usually begin immediately after the more formal rituals.

As Buddhism has become a recognized part of the global religious community and as the Buddhist diaspora have taken Buddhist to countries around the world, Wesak has acquired new functions. It is now a popular time for interaction between Buddhists of different sectarian and ethnic backgrounds, and a place to showcase the dialogue between Buddhists and their non-Buddhist neighbors. These functions have attained a high level of importance in the West, where Buddhists often exist as a religious minority.

Wesak is an official holiday in Hong Kong, Singapore, Thailand, Myanmar, Malaysia, Indonesia, India, and (since 1888) in Sri Lanka. In Tibet, February 8 is recognized as Paranirvana Day, a day to acknowledge the passing of Gautama Buddha. Wesak was accepted as the official Buddhist holiday by the United Nations in 1998. In Korea, Wesak is known as the Festival of the Lanterns. Along with the more familiar rituals conducted at Buddhist temples around the world, the Koreans decorate their temples and related structures with paper lanterns, covered with Buddhist symbols and inscribed with wishes for a long life. These lanterns will also be featured in parades through the street. The festival was designated as a Korean national holiday in 1975.

In the 20th century, several Western Esoteric groups have made an interesting appropriation of Wesak. In particular, theosophical teacher Alice A. Bailey (1880–1949) added three holidays that she saw as particularly relevant to the quest for spiritual enlightenment to the calendar of the Arcane School that she founded —Easter (full moon in April), the Day of Goodwill (full moon in June), and Wesak (full moon in May). In the 1970s, as Bailey's thought was integrated into the New Age movement, the celebration of Wesak as a ceremonial occasion spread far beyond the Arcane School and the several groups that had originated from it.

Edward A. Irons

See also: Bailey, Alice Ann; New Age Movement.

References

Bailey, Alice A. "The Wesak Festival." http://www .lucistrust.org/meetings/wesak2.shtml. Accessed September 15, 2005.

Ganeri, Aneri. *Buddhist Festivals Through the Year.* London: Watts Group, 2003.

Ganeri, Aneri. *Wesak.* London: Heinemann Educational Books, 2002.

Snelling, John. *Buddhist Festivals.* Vero Beach, FL: Rourke Enterprises, 1987.

Turpie, David. "Wesak and the Re-Creation of Buddhist Tradition." http://www.mrsp.mcgill.ca/ reports/html/Wesak/#111. Accessed September 15, 2005.

Wesley, John

1703–1791

John Wesley, a priest in the Church of England, founded the Methodist movement in the 1740s. The Methodists would expand across the Atlantic during his long life and in the 19th century from their bases in England and the United States to become a global community.

John Wesley was born June 17, 1703, in the rectory at Epworth, England. He was the 15th of 19 children born to Samuel and Susannah Wesley. Samuel was an Anglican priest and an accomplished musician. Susannah was a Puritan, remembered for her dedication to the education of her children. Both John and his brother and hymn writer Charles Wesley (1707–1788), with whom much of his life would be intertwined, attended Oxford University.

The seriousness with which John pursued a religious quest was shown at Oxford, where he assumed leadership of an informal organization of students originally called together by his older brother and dubbed the Holy Club. After graduation and ordination, both he and Charles accepted an invitation of James Oglethorpe (1696–1785) to help build the religious life of his new colony of Georgia. On the voyage to America, John had his first encounter with members of the Moravian Church, whose Bishop August Spangenburg (1704–1792) pressed him on his personal religious life. That encounter bore fruit upon Wesley's return to England, where he encountered other Moravians, most

Portrait of Methodist leader John Wesley (1703–1791). (Hayward Cirker and Blanche Cirker, eds., *Dictionary of American Portraits*. New York: Dover Publications, Inc., 1967)

notably Peter Böhler (1712–1775), and attended informal services at several lay-led religious societies in London. At one such society meeting on Aldersgate Street on May 24, 1738, he had a religious awakening, what he termed a "heart-warming experience," which is generally seen as a founding event of the Methodist movement.

Wesley eventually broke with the Moravians over several issues the following year, and the first Wesley-led "Methodist" religious societies began to take shape. Members of the societies were invited into smaller intimate groups called classes.

Another Oxford classmate, George Whitefield, had a pilgrimage not unlike that of Wesley. He had taken a parish church, but had become a roving evangelist. While Wesley had been setting up work in London, Whitefield had been preaching in Bristol. Before leaving for a preaching tour of America, he turned his Bris-

tol work over to Wesley. Bristol became the first site to which Methodism expanded outside of London. The movement, however, expanded throughout England and into Scotland and Ireland over the next decades, and as the movement spread, Wesley traveled throughout the British Isles periodically visiting the many Wesleyan societies.

Wesley regularly preached two or three times a day, and kept a daily journal of his activity. In addition, he wrote numerous books and created abridged editions of hundreds of others to educate the lay preachers that had emerged to assist him in leading the movement. Most prominent among his writings was a set of sermons that covered the basic teachings of Methodism and became an essential statement of its doctrinal position. In 1744, he began to hold conferences of the preachers at which he would answer their questions, the published minutes of their conferences becoming the major guide for the developing movement. Among the unique themes that Wesley developed was the need for Christians to lead a life of growing in grace and aiming at a separation from sin and toward becoming perfected in love.

Methodism evolved as a revitalization movement within the Church of England. In the 1760s the first classes and societies were organized in the American colonies. Wesley commissioned a number of preachers to travel through the colonies and build the movement; however, as the American Revolution began, all but one of those preachers, Francis Asbury (1745–1816), would return to their homeland. The success of the Revolution presented Wesley with a hard decision—what to do with the American Methodists. Unable to convince the Anglican authorities to assume responsibility for them, he assumed the office of a bishop and "set aside" two men, Thomas Coke (1747–1814) and Richard Whatcoat, as Methodist "superintendents" and assigned them the task of setting up American Methodism as an independent movement. At a conference held at Barrett's Chapel in Delaware, they oversaw the consecration of Asbury as the first American Methodist bishop and the organization of the independent Methodist Episcopal Church (now the United Methodist Church).

In England, Wesley's movement had followed a unique path. Following both his Anglican and Puritan roots, Wesley kept the movement officially within the established church, though it increasingly became a rival denomination. Wesley also adhered to the theology of Jacob Arminius (1560–1609), who had rejected the predestination so emphasized by John Calvin (1509–1564). Wesley preached a doctrine of the free grace of God immediately available to any who would turn and accept it. Only after his death would the Wesleyan movement finally reorganize as a separate church throughout the British Isles. Meanwhile, he and George Whitefield had parted company over the latter's Calvinism, and Whitefield went on to develop a form of Methodism that would later merge into the Presbyterian Church.

Wesley itinerated throughout the British Isles for some four decades, and during that time delivered more than 40,000 sermons (many of his sermons being repeated many times to different audiences). He remained active until close to the end of his life on March 2, 1791 in London. Among his last actions was the penning of a letter to William Wilberforce (1759–1833) supportive of his work to end slavery.

J. Gordon Melton

See also: Arminius, Jacob; Calvin, John; Calvinism; Church of England; Epworth; United Methodist Church.

References

Since his death, there have been several attempts to collect and issue Wesley's writings as a set. The most recent began in 1976 by Abingdon Press. To date some 20 volumes have been issued.

Baker, Frank. *John Wesley and the Church of England*. Nashville: Abingdon Press, 1970.

Collins, Kenneth J. *A Real Christian: The Life of John Wesley*. Nashville: Abingdon Press, 2000.

Green, V. H. H. *John Wesley*. London and New York: University Press of America, 1987.

Heitzenrater, Richard P. *The Elusive Mr. Wesley*. 2nd ed. Nashville: Abingdon Press, 2003.

Oden, Thomas C. *John Wesley's Scriptural Christianity: A Plain Exposition of His Teaching on Christian Doctrine*. Grand Rapids, MI: Zondervan, 1994.

Wesley, John. *The Heart of John Wesley's Journal*. Ed. by Percy Parker. Peabody, MA: Hendrickson Publishers, 2008.

Wesley, John. *John Wesley's Sermons: An Anthology*. Ed. by Albert C. Outler et al. Nashville: Abingdon Press, 1991.

Wesleyan Church

The Wesleyan Church, one of the leading products of the Holiness movement in the 19th century in the United States, was founded in 1968 by the merger of two older Holiness churches, the Wesleyan Methodist Church and the Pilgrim Holiness Church. The Wesleyan Methodist Church originated in the abolitionist wing of the Methodist Episcopal Church (now a constituent part of the United Methodist Church) in the 1840s. As the decade began, the church was divided into three factions; the largest groups were opposed to slavery but thought that it should be eradicated gradually over a period of time. On one side were many, primarily from the South, who tolerated or were even favorably disposed toward slavery. On the other side were the abolitionists, who demanded the immediate end to slavery.

As the debate became more intense, in 1843 a number of ministers and approximately 6,000 laymen withdrew from the Methodist Episcopal Church and formed the Wesleyan Methodist Church. Among their leaders were the Reverends Orange Scott (1800–1847), La Roy Sunderland (1805–1885), and L. C. Matlock. The new church not only took a strong position against slavery but also condemned the use of tobacco and alcohol, opposed membership in secret societies, and advocated modest dress. The church decided against reinstituting the episcopacy, and instead chose to be led by a president elected by the members. Over the next decades the church was also drawn into the Holiness movement and its search for congregations of sanctified believers. The Wesleyan tradition had held out the possibility of every believer's becoming sanctified or perfect in love, as a work of grace on the soul by an act of the Holy Spirit. A renewed emphasis on sanctification spread throughout U.S. Methodist churches in the years after the Civil War.

The Pilgrim Holiness Church, merged into the Holiness movement, was losing favor in the Methodist Episcopal Church, which at the end of the 19th century attempted to distance itself from the understanding of sanctification that had become normative within the Holiness movement. In 1897 two former Methodist ministers who had resigned from the church, Martin Wells Knapp (1853–1901) and Seth Cook Rees (1854–1933), founded the International Holiness Union and Prayer League in Cincinnati, Ohio. Emphasis was on holiness, spiritual healing, evangelism, and the Second Coming of Christ. As it grew the union evolved, and in 1922 it took the name Pilgrim Holiness Church. Through the 1920s, several other groups with similar origins merged into the new church.

Following the merger of the two churches in 1968, a modified episcopal government was established. The general superintendents (bishops) constitute the Board of General Superintendents. There are two legislative bodies, the North American General Conference and the Philippine General Conference, and all of the units of the church, including the work in more than 40 countries of the world, are attached to one of these two governing bodies. The International Center of the church was moved from Marion, Indiana, to Indianapolis in 1987.

In 2005 the Wesleyan Church reported 116,151 members in the United States and 5,927 in Canada. Internationally, in 2008, it reported some 400,000 adherents in 4,000 churches and missions in 80 countries. The church supports several colleges, universities, and seminaries. The church is a member of the Christian Holiness Partnership, World Methodist Council, and the National Association of Evangelicals, through which it is related to the World Evangelical Fellowship.

Wesleyan Church World Headquarters
13300 Olio Road
Fishers, IN 46037
http://www.wesleyan.org

J. Gordon Melton

See also: Christian Holiness Partnership; Holiness Movement; United Methodist Church; World Evangelical Fellowship; World Methodist Council.

References

McLeister, Ira Ford, and Roy S. Nicolson. *History of the Wesleyan Methodist Church*. Marion, IN: Wesley, 1959.

Thomas, Paul Westphal, and Paul William Thomas. *The Days of Our Pilgrimage: The History of the Pilgrim Holiness Church*. Marion, IN: Wesley, 1976.

Western Buddhist Order, Friends of the

The Friends of the Western Buddhist Order (FWBO) organization was founded in London by an Englishman, Sangharakshita (Dennis Lingwood, b. 1925), in 1967. A year later the Western Buddhist Order came into being, composed of both women and men. The FWBO seeks to give Buddhism a modern, up-to-date shape, fitting Western sensibilities. The FWBO is not aligned to a specific Buddhist tradition in Asia, but rather strives to create a Western form of Buddhist interpretation, practice, and organizational form.

The FWBO uses the texts and teachings of various Buddhist developments and traditions. Basic to the FWBO is its reference to the spirit of the original teaching, as Sangharakshita calls it. This "original teaching" and the "spirit" are to be brought to light again, to be reawakened. To that end, Western art and literature—among others, William Blake, Johann Wolfgang von Goethe, and Friedrich Nietzsche—are also introduced as so-called bridges to an understanding of the *dharma* (Buddhist teachings). This eclectic intra-Buddhist and interphilosophical approach also applies to the practices favored. Common are Buddhist meditation exercises from the Theravada tradition, especially those of the "mindfulness of breathing" (Pali: *anapanasati*) and the "cultivation of loving-kindness" (*metta bhavana*), but techniques from Zen and Tibetan traditions (such as visualization practices) are also used. Members regularly take part in *pujas* (worship) that include chanting, bowing, and prostration.

The authoritative and organizational focal point of the movement is the Western Buddhist Order. Order members are ordained in a ceremony, taking specific precepts, the title Dharmachari or Dharmacharini (male or female, Dharma-farer), and a religious name in Sanskrit or Pali. Order members might be single or married, live in celibacy and have full-time employment. Many, although not all, Order members live together in residential communities. Such communities, most often single-sex, are usually found near a center of the FWBO. The centers are visited by interested people and "friends"—that is, members of the FWBO. At the centers, Order members offer regular programs, including meditation classes, public talks, study on Buddhist themes and texts, and "bodywork" such as t'ai chi, yoga, and massage. In addition to the communities and the Buddhist centers, the FWBO has founded Right Livelihood cooperatives, such as vegetarian restaurants, whole food shops, or the successful wholesale and retail gift business Windhorse Trading in Cambridge, England. The movement's three pillars —communities, centers, and cooperatives—aim to change the local as well as the overall Western society, and to bring about a "New Society."

Founded in Britain in the late 1960s, a decade later, the FWBO began to gain a foothold in other European countries and overseas. An especially strong branch exists in western India, where Sangharakshita had supported Buddhist leader Babasaheb Ambedkar's conversion movement during the mid-1950s. Apart from Europe and India, FWBO institutions exist in Australia, New Zealand, Malaysia, Sri Lanka, and Nepal, and throughout North and South America. In Britain the movement has founded some 30 centers and 35 local groups (as of 1997), having grown to become one of Britain's principal Buddhist organizations. Globally, there are about 55 city centers, 15 retreat centers, and numerous local groups and cooperatives. In late 2000 the Order had approximately 900 members; the number of supporters and "friends" is estimated to be about 100,000, the vast majority of them being Buddhists in India. The FWBO publishes several journals, among them *Dharma Life,* and it has a prolific book-publishing house (Windhorse Publications).

During the 1990s, Sangharakshita started handing on responsibilities to senior Order members. Sangharakshita authorized these members to conduct ordinations and to take spiritual leadership. The selected members collectively compose the Preceptors College Council (19 persons), based in Birmingham, England.

A core group of this council, five men and three women, form the College of Public Preceptors. From this a chairman is elected to take the leadership of the order and thus of the entire movement. Although in the future the chairman is to be elected by the whole college and council for a term of five years (re-electable), the first chairman was chosen by Sangharakshita in the autumn of 2000. The movement's founder appointed senior member Dharmachari Subhuti (Alex Kennedy), who authored a prominent book about the FWBO and Sangharakshita.

Friends of the Western Buddhist Order
Communications Office
12 Park Rd.
Moseley, Birmingham B13 8AB
UK
http://www.fwbo.org/

Martin Baumann

See also: Ambedkar Buddhism; Theravada Buddhism; Tibetan Buddhism; Zen Buddhism.

References

Batchelor, Stephen. *The Awakening of the West: The Encounter of Buddhism and Western Culture.* Berkeley: Parallax, 1994.

Baumann, Martin. "Work as Dharma Practice: Right Livelihood Cooperatives of the FWBO." In *Engaged Buddhism in the West,* edited by Christopher S. Queen, 372–393. Boston: Wisdom, 2000.

Bluck, Robert. *British Buddhism Teachings, Practice and Development.* Abingdon: Routledge, 2006.

Sangharakshita. *The Rainbow Road.* Birmingham: Windhorse, 1997.

Sangharakshita: A New Voice in the Buddhist Tradition. Birmingham: Windhorse, 1994.

Subhuti, Dharmachari. *Buddhism for Today: A Portrait of a New Buddhist Movement.* Glasgow: Windhorse, 1988.

◆ Western Esoteric Tradition

"Esoteric" (Greek: *esoteros*) is a comparative term, meaning "more inward," in contrast to "exoteric"

(Greek: *exoteros*), which means "more outward." This usage, rooted in the terminology of Greek philosophy, presupposes a duality of insiders and outsiders. The defining characteristics of the esotericist are identification with the inside group, and consequent access to special or secret knowledge.

A prejudice in favor of classical Greece tends to date the Western Esoteric tradition from Pythagoras (sixth century BCE) and to root it in his travels in Egypt and Babylon. However, the legendary visit to Pythagoras of Abaris, a priest of Apollo from Hyperborea, points to an existing esoteric tradition in Northern Europe. The achievements in mathematics and astronomy of megalithic culture (fifth to second millennia BCE) bear witness to a technically educated elite, and almost certainly to a concomitant spiritual science. A residue of this prehistoric tradition survives in Celtic and Germanic myth and legend, and in what little is known of the Druids and other Pagan schools of the north.

The school of Pythagoras, which is much better documented, was divided into auditors (*akousmatikoi*) and students (*mathematikoi*). The auditors, seated outside the veil that hid the master as he spoke, received unexplained, dogmatic precepts, while the students were initiated into the reasons and realities behind these teachings. As the Greek name for the esoteric group suggests, one of their chief disciplines was mathematics. The same was true of Plato's Academy (fourth century BCE), whose portal bore the inscription "Let none ignorant of geometry enter."

Plato's teachings, following Pythagorean tradition, had an exterior side devoted to ethical questions and the education of the rational mind. That is their better-known aspect, immortalized in the Socratic dialogues. The esoteric side, in which Plato's debt to the earlier school is more evident, combined a science of number with a science of the soul. Platonic mathematics embodied insights, revolutionary for their time, into cosmology, harmony, and the invariable laws of the natural world. It is more difficult to reconstruct the Platonic science of the soul, because this was predicated on concepts and experiences that transcended verbal and logical expression.

However, there is little doubt that the inmost circles of Pythagoreans and Platonists alike were con-

Portrait of Plato, one of the most influential philosophers of the Western world (fifth and fourth centuries BCE). (Library of Congress)

cerned with matters classified today as mystical and occult. Their ultimate purpose was to prepare the student for death and its aftermath. In this respect they resembled the initiations of the Eleusinian and other mysteries, but with the difference that the philosophers sought not just a life-changing experience but also understanding.

The first centuries BCE and CE saw an international revival of interest in Pythagorean and Platonic philosophy that left its mark in the writings of Cicero, Ovid, and Virgil. Some of the prime movers were Cicero's friend Nigidius Figulus, a Roman neo-Pythagorean; Philo of Alexandria, who tried to reconcile the Greek philosophies with his native Judaism; the traveling magus Apollonius of Tyana; and the scholarly Plutarch, a priest of Apollo at Delphi.

Simultaneously there came the mystery religions from Egypt and the East, with their message of personal relationship with a savior god or goddess. The most widespread was Mithraism, which traveled with the Roman army to the outermost bounds of the empire. Mithraism as a whole was an esoteric cult that successfully guarded its secrets from outsiders. Within it, as in most esoteric groups, there was a further sifting of members as they progressed, through initiations, into ever more inward circles.

The philosophical revival, combined with the mysteries, was the soil out of which grew the great neo-Platonic movement of the third to sixth centuries CE, with its centers in Alexandria (Ammonius Saccas, Plotinus), Syria (Porphyry, Iamblichus), Rome (the later Plotinus, Porphyry), Carthage (Apuleius), and Athens (Proclus, Damascius). This was also the time during which Christianity rose to become the official religion of the Roman Empire.

The neo-Platonists at first ignored Christianity, as they had ignored Judaism, as being irrelevant to their interests. The exoteric society of which they constituted, by their own reckoning, the esoteric elite, was one of tolerant polytheism. Given their philosophic keys, they could easily discover the metaphysical and cosmological realities concealed in the Greco-Roman mythology and in everyday religious practice. The neo-Platonists were thoroughly in favor of the latter, being well aware of how much the established temple cults contributed to private piety and public order.

During the later period of the Roman Empire, they supported the convergence of cults toward a solar monotheism.

The new savior-religion of Christianity, originally an offshoot of Judaism, borrowed eclectically from the solar cult, from Gnosticism, and from the Egyptian and Mithraic mysteries. To an outsider, its most striking aspects were the solidarity of its followers and their contempt for all other religions. Spreading at first among the lowest classes, then among patrician women, it became a political force in proportion to the weakening of the empire. In the process it discarded most of its founder's teachings, as being too unworldly and disruptive of the social fabric, and built a powerful hierarchy of its own. After it achieved primacy as the empire's official religion (325), it set to work to liquidate its competitors.

After the failure of Emperor Julian to reinstitute the worship of the old gods (360–363), Greco-Roman Paganism was doomed, along with its esoteric academies and mystery schools. The closing of the Athenian Academy in 529 marked the end of a millennium-long tradition.

Esotericism lived on despite Christianity, not because of it. Primitive Christianity was essentially a way of love and renunciation, indifferent to profane learning and the natural sciences, and suspicious of any attempt to find salvation outside the church. The esoteric path, in contrast, is one of knowledge, or gnosis. Those for whom the science of the cosmos and the science of the soul were a consuming passion adapted the Christian framework for their own purposes. (The same happened with the Sufis in the Muslim world.) An example is the extraordinary figure known as Pseudo-Dionysius the Areopagite (seventh century). His mapping of the angelic hierarchy and its earthly parallel in the hierarchy of the church is a typically esoteric exercise, drawing on the doctrine of correspondences, in which heaven and Earth reflect one another. His "negative theology," similar to the higher metaphysical flights of Plotinus, bypasses all the dogmatic assertions that the "positive" theologians argued over.

There is little doubt that Dionysius was also an accomplished mystic, but esotericism is not the same as mysticism. The mystic, driven by love and emotion, yearns for union with God—an experience which, unexamined, can lead to delusion or fanaticism. The seeker after esoteric knowledge wants the transformative gnosis that reveals the true nature of himself, the world, and the divine. In a prescientific age, when illiteracy and superstition were the norm, this path of knowledge began with mathematics and natural science, logic, and the analysis of language. For this reason, Aristotle was nearly as important a contributor to it as Plato.

During the centuries after Dionysius, neo-Platonism continued to attract Christians unfulfilled by religious observance alone. The School of Chartres (11th to 13th centuries), inspired by Plato's Pythagorean dialogue *Timaeus* and by the encyclopedic work of Boethius, revived the sciences of number. Their lasting memorial is the Gothic cathedral, a triumph of geometry and the constructive imagination. The technical knowledge that went into this was the jealously guarded property of the master-masons, who came in time to constitute an esoteric brotherhood of their own.

The pointed arch that is the basis of Gothic architecture had appeared long before in the Arab world, where, too, the works of Aristotle, the Platonists, and the Greek scientists were studied in translation. Among other ancient sciences that passed through the Arabs to Christian Europe was alchemy, or the "Hermetic art." For four centuries and more, alchemy served as the principal nexus of the Western Esoteric tradition. It provided a cover under which one could pursue an esoteric path, in a more or less conscious way. There was nothing in it to disturb Christian orthodoxy: even the ambition to make gold could be excused by a wish to help the poor. When practiced at the physical level, it gave a plenitude of insights into organic and inorganic nature. When the alchemist became more identified with the work, it began to operate its transmutations simultaneously on the human subject. In some cases, laboratory work was entirely omitted, and the alchemical processes were carried out through active imagination alone. Then mercury, sulphur, salt, and so forth were allegories of states of mind and soul that were explored and manipulated in the cause of transformative knowledge.

The traditional secrecy of esotericism also applied to alchemy, in which the essential points were conveyed by word of mouth from master to pupil. For instance, no one ever stated outright what their First Matter was, or their Secret Fire. Moreover, just as Pythagorean cosmology included information such as heliocentrism, which remained unknown to the world in general for 2,000 years, so alchemy probably included some secrets about the natural world that have yet to be rediscovered. In both cases, esotericists act as the scientific preceptors of humanity, but only when the time is ripe. Until then, their ideas would be met with mockery or suppression.

The science of the soul that is the other side of esoteric training was even more alien to the majority and to their exoteric guardians—in earlier times, the church; in later ones, scientific materialism. For instance, all the neo-Platonists followed Pythagoras in embracing the doctrine of reincarnation. Exactly what they understood by that—what it is that they supposed to reincarnate—is a complex question. But certainly they did not envisage the after-death state of the soul as the Christians did: as an eternity of heaven, or else of hell. Nor could any philosophic mind take seriously the cult of relics, the trade in indulgences, the prayers to saints, and all the other apparatus that hinged on this belief concerning the afterlife. As for the idea of the New Testament, and even more the Old, as infallible works of divine inspiration, the Catholic Church did well to leave their improprieties and self-contradictions in the decent obscurity of Latin.

The existence of esoteric groups during the Middle Ages is beyond doubt, but largely beyond our historical grasp. Symptoms of their existence appear, as mentioned, in the Masonic guilds; also in the Courts of Love in southern France; in the Sicilian court of Emperor Frederick II; in the Knights Templar; and in Dante. But it is in the nature of esotericism not to advertise itself, nor to admit potentially unworthy and indiscreet persons to its secrets. The science of "how man makes himself immortal" (Dante's words) was transmitted along the thinnest of threads.

During the 15th century, the rediscovery and translation of Greek texts, especially the neo-Platonists and the Corpus Hermeticum, led to a renaissance of classical Pagan philosophy. The Byzantine philosopher George Gemistus Plethon planted the idea that divine wisdom was inherent in all religions, and that an "ancient theology" or a "perennial philosophy" had existed since the earliest ages, of which Christianity was the latest (if the most perfect) manifestation. The Roman Academy of Pomponio Leto went so far in its revival of antiquity that it was dissolved by papal order and its members imprisoned. Marsilio Ficino, head of the Florentine Academy, re-created the Orphic invocations and practiced astrological magic; his younger colleague Pico della Mirandola added Jewish Kabbalah to the mixture.

Early in the 16th century, Henry Cornelius Agrippa compiled an encyclopedia of natural, astrological, and Kabbalistic magic that has yet to be superseded. Neo-Platonic ideas permeated the arts of painting, sculpture, and architecture with an alternative mythology to that of Christianity.

All of these developments hinted at the possibility of an initiatic path existing outside the church, but they were soon extinguished. The climate of controversy and religious wars following the Reformation made it dangerous enough to be the wrong sort of Christian, let alone Pagan. Alchemy alone survived as a visible and acceptable witness to an Esoteric tradition.

In the 17th and 18th centuries, the two components of traditional Esotericism parted company. The science of the cosmos and of number became secularized in the Scientific Revolution, while the science of the soul found a new home in Protestant mysticism, invigorated by the example of Jacob Boehme (1575–1624). This "Theosophy" took for granted the Christian revelation contained in the Bible, but, like alchemy, regarded the Book of Nature as a parallel revelation in which the divine mind could be penetrated. Leaning to piety and mysticism rather than to philosophy, the Boehmians (or Behmenists) were the chief if not the only Esoteric tradition through the Age of Reason. Another candidate for the title is Freemasonry, especially in its more Theosophical, magical, and alchemical offshoots.

Although the majority of lodges were fraternal and political in intent, they offered a haven for discreet meetings and transmissions, while their symbolism had evident links with the ancient mysteries. Some of them, such as those frequented by the young Emanuel Swedenborg (1688–1772), gave access to Jewish esoteric teachings, notably those on sexual magic. With good reason, the church was suspicious of Freemasonry in all its varieties.

The Romantic era was a time of philosophical ferment comparable to the Roman Empire period and to the 15th century. Once again, European Esoteric traditions (Boehmian Theosophy, Freemasonry) met with extra-European influences, now coming from Persia, India, and China. Christianity, much weakened politically and discredited in the minds of many intellectuals, no longer served as the unquestioned substratum of belief. The first stages of Esotericism became freely accessible: the opportunity to study and cultivate, not merely to save, one's own soul; the opening of the world of the imagination through poetry and music; communion with a living nature.

However, no philosophical academies existed to carry the aspirant further, and the end-point was often a pantheistic mysticism.

The Romantic attitude also made itself felt as an alternative current to the natural sciences, deprecated today because of its unacceptable metaphysics (that is,

because it is not based on the materialistic assumption). Some examples are the medical practices of Franz Anton Mesmer (1734–1815); the theories of metamorphosis and of color espoused by Goethe (1749–1832); the homeopathy of Samuel Hahnemann (1755–1843); the universal science based on the doctrine of correspondences of Lorenz Oken (1779–1851); and the experiments of the later Mesmerists with animal magnetism and altered states of consciousness. The connection of these with Esoteric philosophy is obvious. Even more so is that of the Psychical Research Society, whose chief object was to settle the question of the soul's survival. Until World War I, some major figures in the natural sciences (for example, William Barrett, William Crookes, Oliver Lodge, Charles Richet, and Johann Zöllner) were dedicated to such research.

Both of these tendencies—the concordance of Western with Eastern traditions, and the pursuit of a nonmaterialistic science—met in the Theosophical Society. Founded in 1875 by Helena P. Blavatsky (1831–1891) and Henry S. Olcott (1832–1907), with a large contribution from the medium Emma Hardinge Britten (1823–1899), the Society was at first devoted to practical research into occultism. The 1880s saw the emergence of a rival group, the Hermetic Brotherhood of Luxor, largely based on the teachings of the American medium Pascal B. Randolph (1825–1875). Its influence was out of all proportion to its modest operation, which was not through personal contact or ritual but through a correspondence course in self-initiation. In the same decade the Theosophical Society founded an Esoteric Section, which still exists but whose activities have never been revealed. A little later, the Hermetic Order of the Golden Dawn provided more glamorous opportunities for ceremonial magic and initiatic ritual. Its vocabulary was Hermetic, Kabbalistic, Rosicrucian, and Enochian (that is, based on the "angelic conversations" of John Dee). Later offshoots of the Golden Dawn, notably those led by Dion Fortune (1891–1946) and Gareth Knight, were more Christocentric, as was the Anthroposophy of Rudolf Steiner (1861–1925).

The Western attraction to Eastern philosophies and to practices such as meditation and yoga was the most visible Esoteric phenomenon of the 20th century, comparable again to the influx of the Oriental mystery-religions (including Christianity) into the Roman Empire. Buddhism, first in its Japanese (Zen) then in its Tibetan form, provided a popular alternative religion to many former Christians and Jews. Toward the end of the century, the residue of all these tendencies—alternative science, occultism, Orientalism—congealed in the New Age movement.

At this point it is impossible to define a single Western Esoteric tradition. Some Christian Esotericists imagine an initiatic lineage going back to the secret teachings of Jesus himself, but the evidence, to an outsider, is nonexistent. Rather, the repeated impulses toward a "more inward" path seem to have led outside the Christianity of the churches, and the more so when the goal is knowledge of self and cosmos rather than mystical union. The fundamental teaching of Christianity is love, and its basis in the Gospels is anti-hierarchical and anti-individualistic. If in practice it has consistently violated those principles, they still remain as a powerful personal and social ideal, with their own virtues and rewards. To choose the Esoteric path is essentially to prefer self-perfection or self-realization to these ideals, which is why the Christian churches, unlike Hinduism, Buddhism, or Greco-Roman paganism, have never had a comfortable relationship with their Gnostic and Esoteric members.

Joscelyn Godwin

See also: Agrippa von Nettesheim, Heinrich Cornelius; Anthroposophical Society; Hermetic Order of the Golden Dawn; New Age Movement; Steiner, Rudolf; Swedenborg, Emanuel; Theosophical Society (America).

References

Faivre, Antoine. *Access to Modern Esotericism.* Albany: State University of New York Press, 1994.

Faivre, Antoine. *Theosophy, Imagination, Tradition: Studies in Western Esotericism.* Albany: State University of New York Press, 2000.

Faivre, Antoine, and Jacob Needleman, eds. *Modern Esoteric Spirituality.* New York: Crossroad, 1992.

Godwin, Joscelyn. *Mystery Religions in the Ancient World.* London: Thames and Hudson, 1981.

Godwin, Joscelyn. *The Theosophical Enlightenment.* Albany: State University of New York Press, 1994.

Godwin, Joscelyn, Christian Chanel, and John Patrick Deveney, eds. *The Hermetic Brotherhood of Luxor: Historical and Initiatic Documents of an Order of Practical Occultism.* York Beach, ME: Samuel Weiser, 1995.

Hanegraaff, Wouter J. *New Age Religion and Western Culture: Esotericism in the Mirror of Secular Thought.* Leiden: Brill, 1996.

Introvigne, Massimo. *Il cappello del mago: I nuovi movimenti magici, dallo spiritismo al satanismo.* Milano: Sugar Co., 1990.

Melton, J. Gordon, ed. *Encyclopedia of Occultism and Parapsychology.* 2 vols. Detroit: Gale Group, 2001.

Thomas, Keith. *Religion and the Decline of Magic.* New York: Charles Scribner's Sons, 1971.

Western Sahara

See Sahara.

White Brotherhood

The White Brotherhood, an occult order founded at the end of the 19th century, was formed in Bulgaria by Peter Konstantinov Deunov (1864–1944), better known by his spiritual name, Beinsa Douno. As a member of the Bulgarian Orthodox Church, Douno had considered becoming a monk. Instead, he became a schoolteacher. He later moved to the United States to attend seminary. He finally received one degree in religion and another in medicine. In the United States he had encountered the Rosicrucians and was also conscious of the Bogomils, an ancient Esoteric group from his own land. His first book, *Science and Education*, appeared in 1896. After returning to Bulgaria, he entered a period of seclusion and, in 1897, reported an initiatory experience during which he felt the Spirit of God descending upon him. When he finally reappeared to take students, he was recognized as having attained his masterhood. In what would be the first of regular annual meetings in August 1900, he created the White Brotherhood. His first three students were the only

Members of an international religious movement called the White Brotherhood perform their ritual dance, Panevritmia, as part of their New Year celebration on Rila Mountain, about 75 miles south of the Bulgarian capital Sofia, August 18, 2007. (AP/Wide World Photos)

members. The teachings became the basis for a series of books by Douno.

Douno traveled widely, and the organization developed a following throughout Bulgaria through its first decade. In 1914 he declared the advent of the new age of Aquarius and relocated to Sofia, the capital. Because it was wartime, his activities came under official scrutiny, and signs of tension with authorities appeared. In August 1915, the annual meeting was disrupted and Douno was expelled from the town in which it was held. In 1917 the Holy Synod of the Bulgarian Orthodox Church pressured the authorities to have the Brotherhood expelled from Sofia. Finally in 1922, in response to Douno's opening a School of the Great White Brotherhood in Sofia, the church excommunicated Douno and many of his followers. Various further attempts to suppress the movement included the arrest of members and the disruption of meetings.

In spite of its critics, however, the movement persisted. In 1926 a new headquarters complex, including a publishing center, was erected at Izfreva, near Sofia.

Douno's teachings included the practice of paneurhythmy, a set of exercises set to music. First introduced in 1934, the exercises were integral to the work when it opened its first group in Paris (1936), Latvia, and Estonia. Further spread of the movement was stopped, first by World War II, and then by the changes in the political situation following the war. Douno's death in 1944 occurred only a few weeks after the Soviet army took control of his homeland.

Not really understanding the drastic nature of postwar political changes, the Brotherhood reorganized in 1945 under a council and continued as it had prior to the war. Only three years later, their headquarters property was nationalized (and then leveled in 1970). Realizing now that they existed in a new, hostile environment, Brotherhood leaders took steps to preserve Douno's writings, an important move, as in 1957 the government confiscated all of Douno's books. Meanwhile, Douno's work had spread to Western Europe and the United States. His writings were translated and published. At the same time, Omraam Mikhael Aivanhov, whom in 1938 Douno had sent to take charge of the work in Paris, founded his own movement to perpetuate Douno's teachings as he understood and interpreted them. Aivanhov's work continues as the Universal Great Brotherhood.

Douno saw the White Brotherhood as embodying the true spirituality of Christianity and making a modern transmission of the eternal religion of Christ. The White Brotherhood thus continues the mystical Church of St. John, as opposed to the official church, the Church of St. Peter. Suppressed in the lands controlled by the Soviet Union, the White Brotherhood had only a few followers in the West. It was again allowed to hold meetings in the 1970s, and then in the 1990s it revived in Bulgaria as political changes brought a new level of religious freedom. It was officially recognized in November 1990, and a periodical was reinstituted the following year. The rebuilding of the White Brotherhood community and educational center in Sofia began in 1995.

Today the Brotherhood exists as a vital international organization. Douno's Bulgarian followers have translated a number of his works into English and other Western languages, the first of which translations appeared in the 1960s.

Society White Brotherhood, Bulgaria
c/o Chairman: Andrey Griva
Vitoshki ezera Street 48
Sofia 1334
Bulgaria
http://www.beinsadouno.org/old/in_en.htm

J. Gordon Melton

See also: Bulgarian Orthodox Church; Universal Great Brotherhood.

References

Douno, Beinsa. *The Master Speaks: The Word of the Great White Brotherhood*. Los Angeles: Sunrise, 1970.

Douno, Beinsa. *Paneurhythmy: Supreme Cosmic Rhythm*. Sofia, Bulgaria: Bialo Bratstvo Publishers, 2004.

Douno, Beinsa. *Reminiscences: Talks with the Master*. Los Angeles: Sunrise, 1968.

Douno, Beinsa. *The Teachings of Beinsa Douno: Pearls of Love*. Glasgow: Beyond the Rising Sun, n.d.

White Fathers

The White Fathers (officially the Society of Missionaries of Africa), as the name implies, has been one of the more important organizations assisting the spread of the Roman Catholic Church in the modern world, especially on the continent of Africa. The order was founded in 1868 by Charles M. Lavigerie (1825–1892), then the archbishop of Algiers. Algeria was at the time a French colony. The occasion for the founding was a typhoid epidemic in Algiers, and the first assignment of the members was the care of children and youth orphaned by the illness. The order subsequently gained oversight of various missionary centers in the country. They adapted a habit designed from the clothing commonly worn in North Africa.

In 1878, Lavigerie submitted a plan to evangelize Central Africa to Rome. It was approved, and he was appointed the apostolic delegate for equatorial Africa. The first group headed for Tanganyika (now Tanzania) and established work in the western part of the country and in Uganda. They were joined by new personnel annually. Twenty-two missionaries who were killed in the late 19th century in Uganda were canonized in 1964. The work spread to the Congo and the Sudan (1894), and in the early 20th century to Guinea, Mali, Upper Volta (Burkina Faso), and Ghana. In the years since World War II, they have also accepted work assignments in Nigeria and Mozambique.

The final approval of the White Fathers' constitution occurred in 1908. Members take an oath of dedication to the establishment of the Roman Catholic Church on the African continent. Only with the approval of the pope may they work outside of Africa. In 1880 the pope requested that they assume responsibility for opening a seminary in Jerusalem for the training of the clergy of the Melkite Catholic Church. To date, that has been their only work outside of Africa, except for centers in the West, where members are recruited and trained. Such centers are found in the United States, for example, at Franklin, Pennsylvania (novitiate); Onchiota, New York (seminary); and Washington, D.C. (headquarters). The work of the White Fathers is divided into provinces, the first of which were designated in 1936.

Lavigerie also founded a second order, the missionary Society of Our Lady of Africa, a female society popularly known as the White Sisters. It took special responsibility for improving the spiritual and material life of African women. Like their male counterparts, the White Sisters have spread across Africa, where they currently manage more than 150 houses. They also maintain a presence in Europe and the United States where administration, recruitment, and training occur.

White Fathers
Via della Nocetta 111
Roma 00164
Italy
http://www.thewhitefathers.org.uk/home_pg.shtml
(White Fathers, United Kingdom)

J. Gordon Melton

See also: Melkite Catholic Church; Roman Catholic Church; Saints.

References

De Arteche, J. *The Cardinal of Africa: Charles Lavigerie, Founder of the White Fathers.* London: Catholic Book Club, 1964.

Kittler, Glen D. *The White Fathers: A Chronicle of Nearly a Hundred Years of Saintly Heroism in Africa.* London: W. H. Allen, 1957.

Matheson, Elizabeth Mary. *African Apostles.* Staten Island, NY: Alba House, 1963.

Shorter, Aylward. *Cross And Flag in Africa: The "White Fathers During" during the Colonial Scramble (1892–1914).* Maryknoll, NY: Orbis Books, 2006.

White Plum Asanga

The White Plum Asanga is an organization designed to promote unity and maintain harmonious relationships among the Dharma successors of Japanese Buddhist teacher Taizan Maezumi Daiosho (1931–1995), the founder of the Zen Center of Los Angeles. Maezumi Roshi originally received Dharma transmission from Hakujun Kuroda, Roshi in 1955, but additionally received *inka* (approval as a teacher) from Koryu Osaka, Roshi, and Hakuun Yasutani Roshi. The members of the Asanga also look to Baian Hakujun Daiosho as the "honorary" founder of the White Plum Asanga. He headed the Supreme Court of the main Soto Zen group in Japan and was one of the leading figures of Japanese Zen.

The Asanga promotes communication and provides a forum for conflict resolution among members, as well as other Buddhist schools and traditions. Many of those who hold their lineage from Maezumi Roshi are currently leaders of otherwise independent autonomous Zen centers and associations. The White Plum Asanga extends voting membership to all who received *shiho* (Dharma lineage) from Maezumi Roshi, who trained 12 Dharma successors: Bernard Tetsugen Glassman, Dennis Genpo Merzel, Charlotte Joko Beck, Jan Chozen Bays, John Daido Loori, Gerry Shishin Wick, John Tesshin Sanderson, Alfred Jitsudo Ancheta, Charles Tenshin Fletcher, Susan Myoyu Andersen, Nicolee Jikyo Miller, and William Nyogen Yeo.

By the time Maezumi Roshi died in 1995, his students had in turn passed the Dharma lineage to nine second-generation teachers. Since then, many more have received the lineage and have spread it across North America to Europe and South America. By 2009, some 82 Zen teachers were part of the White Plume Sangha.

Bernard Glassman, one of the original founding members of the Zen center of Los Angeles, was a leading force in the formation of the White Plume Asanga, and then in 1996 led in the formation of the Soto Zen Buddhist Association, which has brought the teachers of the Maezumi Roshi lineage into fellowship with teachers of other Soto Zen lineages in the West. Shortly before his death, Maezumi Roshi gave inka to his senior disciple Tetsugen Glassman, Roshi. In this context, inka is considered an approval above and beyond Dharma transmission (shilo). It is granted only to someone considered to be an enlightened successor of the Buddha. Glassman later transmitted inka to

Genpo Merzel, Roshi head of the Big Mind Western Zen Center (and associated zendos) in Salt Lake City. He has passed inka to John Daido Loori, Zen Mountain Monastery in Mount Tremper, New York. Genpo Merzel, Roshi is currently the president of the White Plum Sangha (2008).

White Plum Asanga
Zen Mountain Monastery
PO Box 197
South Plank Rd.
Mt. Tremper, NY 12457
http://www.mro.org/zmm/white-plum.shtml

J. Gordon Melton

See also: Soto Zen Buddhism; Zen Buddhism.

References

Ford, James Ismael. *Zen Master Who?: A Guide to the People and Stories of Zen*. Ithaca, NY: Wisdom Publications, 2006.

Maezumi, Hakuyu Taizan, and Bernard Glassman. *On Zen Practice: Body, Breath, Mind*. Ithaca, NY: Wisdom Publications, 2002.

White, Ellen G.

1827–1915

Ellen Gould Harmon White was a prophetess, a health reformer, and, with her husband, the co-founder of the Seventh-day Adventist Church (SDA). She emerged in the 1850s among the disappointed followers of William Miller who had accepted the idea of Jesus returning in 1843–1844.

Ellen was born on November 26, 1827, in Gorham, Maine. When she was nine years old, she was accidentally hit in the head with a rock that left her unconscious for three weeks. She was henceforth unable to attend school and attempting to read always made her dizzy.

She was raised in a Methodist family, and in 1842 in her mid-teens experienced a conversion and joined the church. Her spiritual awakening occurred just as the movement built around William Miller's predictions concerning Christ's imminent return was reaching a fever pitch across the United States. Ellen's parents identified with the movement, and in 1843 the Methodists disfellowshipped them. They then lived through the Great Disappointment, when Christ did not return in 1844.

As Ellen passed into adulthood, she became one of several people who tried to rally the Adventist community. While others were revising Miller's calculations and setting new dates, she reinterpreted the events of 1844, proclaiming to the audiences that she addressed that Christ really had returned in 1844, only not as expected. Rather than come to Earth visibly, he had moved into the heavenly sanctuary, which he was now cleansing (Daniel 8:14). As soon as that task was completed, he would appear visibly.

As she was rethinking Miller's prophecies, Ellen met James White (1821–1881), and in 1846 they were married. They encountered some Seventh-day Baptists, who convinced them of the correctness of Sabbath worship, and they in turn introduced Sabbatarianism to the larger Adventist community. Sabbatarianism proved a first step for some Adventists to develop a new appreciation for Jewish law and culture. Over the next decades some would begin to follow the Jewish feast cycle, adopt Jewish dietary rules, and even begin using Jewish names for the Creator and his Son. White would become interested in diet reform and would develop a famous sanatorium close to church headquarters set up in Battle Creek, Michigan, 1851.

Through the 1860s, Adventism would remain a fluid movement as individual Adventists would decide about key issues concerning such matters as the new dates for Christ's return proposed by different leaders. White injected herself into the process with her advocacy of Sabbath worship and then her emergence as a visionary and prophetess. James White was a publisher and created a periodical through which Ellen's views, visions, and prophecies could be quickly disseminated and/or turned into pamphlets and books.

By the end of the 1850s, the following that had coalesced around the Whites began to be referred to as the Seventh-day Adventist Church, which was formally organized in 1863. The long-lived Ellen would lead the church over the next half century. During this time, she wrote 25 books and some 200 shorter works.

White died on July 16, 1915, in St. Helena, California. She was revered as a biblical interpreter and a prophet/visionary. Her prophetic works are still considered authoritative within the church though a spectrum of opinion exists as to just how the visionary material is to be used. The church she created had a missionary zeal that grew out of its belief in the approaching end of the present era. That zeal had carried it into more than 200 countries as the 21st century began.

A controversy concerning White's prophecies surfaced in the late 1970s following the publication of a book by then church member Ronald L. Numbers that suggested a variety of purely mundane explanations for the supposed supernatural experiences underlying the prophecies. He subsequently left the church and has remained a sympathetic critic. Meanwhile, a number of volumes appeared defending White.

J. Gordon Melton

See also: Great Disappointment; Methodism; Sabbatarianism; Seventh-day Adventist Church.

References

Nichol, Francis D. *Ellen G. White and Her Critics.* Takoma Park, MD: Review and Herald Publishing Association, 1951.

Numbers, Ronald L., *Prophetess of Health: A Study of Ellen G. White.* New York: Harper & Row, 1976; Rev. ed.: Knoxville: University of Tennessee Press, 1992.

White, Ellen G., *Early Writings of Ellen G. White.* 1882. Washington, DC: Review and Herald Publishing Association, 1945.

White, Ellen G ., *The Great Controversy Between Christ and Satan.* 1911. Mountain View, CA: Pacific Press Publishing Association, 1950.

White, Ellen G, *Life Sketches of Ellen G. White.* 1915. Mountain View, CA: Pacific Press Publishing Association, 1943.

Wiccan Religion

The Wiccan religion is a worldwide nature religion with roots in the ancient past and contemporary times. Also known as Wicca, the Old Religion, the Craft, and Witchcraft, it incorporates revivals, adaptations, and continuations of ancient folkways, symbology, and spiritual practices from old Pagan Europe and the classical civilizations of Greece, Rome, Egypt, and Mesopotamia. These include the ritual kindling of bonfires; celebrations of transition points in the cycles of nature; ecstatic dance and trance; use of intuitive perception and imaginal intention (magic); and developing and sustaining spiritual relationships with animals, plants, places, ancestors, and other forms of the Divine. In the 20th century, several major influences converged to shape the Wiccan religion into its 21st-century form. These include the writings and teachings of Gerald B. Gardner (1884–1964) and Doreen Valiente (1922–1999), which emerged in 1950s England and were taken to the United States in 1962 by Raymond Buckland (b. 1934); the back-to-nature counterculture movement of the 1960s United States; and the rise of feminist spirituality worldwide in the 1970s, inspired by the works of Merlin Stone (b. 1931), Z. Budapest (b. 1940), Margot Adler (b. 1946), Marion Weinstein (b. 1939), Starhawk (b. 1951), and others. In the late 20th century, the Wiccan religion and related forms of contemporary Paganism grew exponentially both in number of practitioners and in diversity of forms, not only throughout the United States, Canada, and Europe but also in many other parts of the world, such as Australia, New Zealand, South Africa, Brazil, and Japan. Contributing to this growth has been the emergence of multi-tradition and international gatherings, networking periodicals, and information exchange through the Internet.

Although the word "Wicca" is sometimes used as a synonym for Gardnerian Wicca and forms directly derived from it, increasingly it is more typically used to include the wider range of Wiccan paths that now exists. Some practitioners call themselves "witches," but others have abandoned that appellation because of its history of diverse and contradictory connotations. The Wiccan religion does not involve devil worship or malevolent practices. Across the many forms of the Wiccan religion, some commonalties are widespread, such as the spiritual practice of celebrating the new and full moons and the cycle of sun and seasons. The spiritual calendar, called the Wheel of the Year, consists of eight sabbats, or sacred festival times—the solstices and equinoxes and the midpoints between. These seasonal midpoints or cross quarters are also known as the Celtic Fire Festivals; they are Samhain (in mid-fall), Imbolc (winter), Beltane (spring), and Lughnassad (summer).

Also widespread are Wiccan spiritual principles, which include the following: (1) honor the Divine, understanding It as immanent and transcendent, as well as both multifaceted and as a united, interconnected whole; (2) live life with consideration of others as well as oneself, endeavoring to be of service and to do no harm; and (3) celebrate and attune to nature and nature's rhythms, understanding this as central to Divine understanding and worship. Wiccans across traditions also cultivate virtues, including integrity, honesty, reliability, responsibility, balance, perseverance, empathy, kindness, compassion, knowledge, service, and freedom. In addition, Wiccans seek to live with balance and moderation, such as balancing intellect and intuition in cognitive processing; work and rest in daily life; time with others and time alone. Furthermore, Wiccans seek to cultivate good communication and healthy relationships with family, friends, community, and the greater Circle of Life of All Nature.

"The Divine" is a gender-neutral term that can be used to refer to what is known in other religions as "God" (Christianity, Judaism), "Allah" (Islam), "Dao" (Daoism), and "Great Spirit" (Native American religions). Since the Divine is viewed in many Wiccan traditions as both immanent (indwelling) and as transcendent (beyond the limits of humanness), Wiccan spiritual philosophy is pantheistic. In that the Divine is viewed as a Great Unity, spiritual philosophy has a monotheistic dimension. The Divine is also viewed as multifaceted. In many traditions, the Divine is honored as both Mother Goddess and Father God, as well as Their Unity, also known as the "Great Mystery." In addition, The Goddess and The God have many sacred forms or aspects, such as the Triple Goddess in the forms of Maiden, Mother, and Crone, and the Dual God, symbolically represented by the sacred Oak (waxing Sun) and sacred Holly (waning Sun). The Divine also is acknowledged as manifest through the five elements of nature (earth, air, fire, water, and spirit). As with most other nature religions, spiritual philosophy also is animistic, in that The Divine takes the form of a spiritual dimension not only within living humans

(higher power or inner self) but also within ancestors, animals, plants, places, and all things. Attunement to and communion with nature are central to spiritual philosophy and practice. Humans are viewed as part of nature, not as dominators or as owners of nature.

The predominant ritual and social space arrangement for Wiccans is the circle. As in ancient times, the circle represents many concepts, including wholeness, balance, the cycles of nature, continuity, partnership, and interconnectedness. The circle is used by individuals in personal rituals as well as by groups for rituals and festivals. The circle facilitates shared experience and encourages participation.

Although classified by some as a new religious movement because it gained visibility and growth in the 20th century, Wicca and related forms of contemporary Paganism do not fit neatly into the profile of the majority of new religious movements. Wicca is very decentralized, and thus it differs from those many new religions that typically center around the authority and teachings of a particular charismatic religious leader. The Wiccan religion and contemporary Paganism are nature-centered and with an emphasis on direct personal experience rather than being of "the book" or adhering to a specific, detailed, structured worldview, as revealed to a prophet or teacher. Wicca and Paganism are best grouped with other nature religions, sometimes called primal or oral religions, which encompass animistic worldviews, shamanic spiritual practices, and celebrations of the cycles of nature. The Wiccan community overlaps with the related traditions of Goddess Spirituality and Druidism.

Selena Fox

See also: Druidism; Fall Equinox; Gardnerian Wicca; Goddess Spirituality; Pantheism; Spring Equinox; Summer Solstice; Winter Solstice; Witchcraft.

References

Adler, Margot. *Drawing Down the Moon.* Boston: Beacon, 1997.

Berger, Helen, Evan A. Leach, and Leigh S. Shaffer. *Voices from the Pagan Census: A National Survey of Witches and Neo-Pagans in the United States.* Colombia: University of South Carolina Press, 2003.

Buckland, Raymond. *Buckland's Complete Book of Witchcraft.* St. Paul, MN: Llewellyn, 1997.

Clifton, Chas. *Witchcraft Today.* 3 vols. St. Paul, MN: Llewellyn, 1992–1994.

Crowley, Vivienne. *Wicca: A Comprehensive Guide to the Old Religion in the Modern World.* Lanham, MD: Element Books, 2003.

Cunningham, Scott. *Wicca: A Guide for the Solitary Practitioner.* St. Paul, MN: Llewellyn, 1988.

Curott, Phyllis. *Witchcrafting: A Spiritual Guide to Making Magic.* New York: Broadway, 2001.

Fox, Selena, Dennis Carpenter, and Theresa Berrie. *Circle Guide to Pagan Groups.* Mt. Horeb, WI: Circle, 2001.

Guiley, Rosemary Ellen. *The Encyclopedia of Witches and Witchcraft.* New York: Checkmark/Facts on File, 1999.

Melton, J. Gordon, and Isotta Poggi. *Magic, Witchcraft and Paganism in America: A Bibliography.* New York: Garland, 1992.

Pike, Sarah. *New Age and Neopagan Religions in America.* New York: Columbia University Press, 2006.

Starhawk. *The Spiral Dance.* Rev. ed. San Francisco: Harper and Row, 1999.

Valiente, Doreen. *The Rebirth of Witchcraft.* London: Robert Hale, 1989.

Winter Solstice

The shortest day of the year, Winter Solstice was among the earliest astronomical phenomena observed by human cultures that observed the sky and related it to the weather and agricultural seasons. In the Northern Hemisphere, if one observes the rising Sun in the fall, it appears to rise a little bit farther south day by day until it reaches a point in the last half of December where the southern drift stops. After what appears to be a pause, it begins to rise bit by bit farther north each day. In the Southern Hemisphere, the drift is exactly opposite. The Winter Solstice is the point at which the drift stops and pauses before starting in the opposite direction.

The Julian calendar, adopted in 45 BCE, established December 25 as the Winter Solstice throughout the Roman Empire. That calendar was officially adopted by the Christian church in 324 as the calendar of Christianity. Christmas, the celebration of the birth of Jesus Christ, was set on the 25th of December. In the meantime, the Winter Solstice gradually drifted due to small inaccuracy in the Julian calendar.

In 1582 Pope Gregory XIII (r. 1572–1585) made the changes in the calendar to account for the problem in the Julian calendar. The Gregorian revisions mean the northern Winter Solstice occurs around December 21.

In ancient Rome, the Winter Solstice was associated with the deity Saturn, the god of agriculture and the harvest. He was also believed to have had oversight of a mythological Golden Age. Rome's Winter Solstice festival was the Saturnalia, held in his honor. Originally held on December 17, it was gradually expanded as Rome prospered to a week-long event during which time war would not be declared, slaves and masters swapped status, prisoners would not be executed, and people gave gifts. In general, people forgot their problems and enjoyed life. The Romans also tended to conflate Saturn with the deity Cronus, the god associated with calendars, seasons, and harvests.

Though no date for the birth of Jesus is given in the New Testament, biblical scholars have frequently noted that events described in the Gospels in association with Christ's birth, such as shepherds being in the outdoors in the evening, do not support a winter event. Many have suggested that the dating of Christ's birth was affected by the attempt to supplant the Saturnalia with Christmas. Christmas more directly supplanted the Sol Invictus festival, which was added to the calendar in Rome in the later centuries of the empire and was celebrated on December 25. Attributes of the sun-god were later applied directly to Jesus.

The Winter Solstice was celebrated in most ancient cultures, especially in temperate zones. For some it was the middle of winter and for some the beginning. It would be a time when one batch of wine would have finally fermented and when some animals would be slaughtered in order to save for human consumption the food the animals would consume. Most of these celebrations were supplanted by the holy days of the larger world religions either by absorption or force.

Nahuatl indigenous women in San Andres make offerings during a winter solstice celebration to mark the start of winter in the Northern Hemisphere. (AP/Wide World Photos)

In the modern West, the emergence of neo-Paganism, a large movement inspired by ancient Pagan practice and belief, has signaled a return of the Winter Solstice. Neo-Pagans, including their largest segment, the Wiccans, annually celebrate Yule on the Winter Solstice, and make note of the many practices of ancient Pagans that have been adopted by Christians—Yule logs, Christmas trees, and carol singing.

At the same time, as religious pluralism has increased in predominantly Christian lands, Christmas has developed a prominent secular element and other religions have emphasized holidays that also occur in close proximity to it. That new emphasis, along with the commercial aspects of Christmas gift giving and the close proximity of New Year's Day the week after Christmas, has contributed to the defining of a winter holiday season in Western society. In this regard, com-munities of Unbelief, especially Humanists, have revived the Winter Solstice as an occasion for celebration, and American Humanists have proposed Human Light Day (December 23) as a day to celebrate humanity and the production of culture with events that include art, music, dancing, storytelling, and candle light events, and social outreach through developing social awareness, helping the needy, and community involvement. As least one new holiday, Kwanzaa, was created to allow people (in this case African Americans) who did not want to observe Christmas to have a holiday to celebrate during the winter holiday season.

J. Gordon Melton

See also: Calendars, Religious; Christmas; Common Era Calendar; Hanukkah; Humanism; Summer Solstice.

References

DeChant, Dell. *The Sacred Santa: Religious Dimensions of Consumer Culture*. Cleveland, OH: Pilgrim Press, 2002.

Matthews, John. *The Winter Solstice: The Sacred Traditions of Christmas*. Wheaton, IL: Quest Books, 2003.

Ratsch, Christian, and Claudia Müller-Ebeling. *Pagan Christmas: The Plants, Spirits, and Rituals at the Origins of Yuletide*. Rochester, VT: Inner Traditions, 2006.

Wisconsin Evangelical Lutheran Synod

The Wisconsin Evangelical Lutheran Synod, one of the more conservative Lutheran bodies, began with the arrival of German-speaking immigrants in the American Midwest in the 1840s. They appealed to their homeland for ministerial oversight, and several mission societies (Berlin, Basel) responded. An original Wisconsin Synod was organized in 1850 with John Muelhaeser (1803–1867), pastor of the Salem Evangelical Lutheran Church in Milwaukee, Wisconsin, as its first president. Increasingly over the years, the Synod moved toward an emphasis upon doctrinal conservatism and became aligned with the Lutheran Church–Missouri Synod.

A similar beginning also occurred in Minnesota, under the leadership of Christian Frederick Heyer (1793–1873), formerly a missionary in India, and Eric Norelius (1833–1916), a Swedish Lutheran pastor. A third such effort arose in 1840 in Michigan, where a synod was organized by Stephan Koehler and Christoph Eberhardt. The Michigan Synod eventually affiliated with the General Synod, the large Lutheran body that became the core of the Lutheran unity movement in America that is now embodied in the Evangelical Lutheran Church in America. In 1968 it withdrew, however, a move reflective of its growing conservatism.

In 1872 the Wisconsin and Missouri synods formed the Synodical Conference, an association of conservative Lutheran synods. Eventually the Michigan and Minnesota synods also joined. In 1892 the Wisconsin, Michigan, and Minnesota synods federated to form the Evangelical Joint Synod of Wisconsin, Minnesota, and Michigan. A more formal merger occurred in 1917 with the formation of the Evangelical Lutheran Joint Synod of Wisconsin and Other States. That body changed its name to Wisconsin Evangelical Lutheran Synod in 1959.

The Wisconsin Synod represents the most conservative extreme of Lutheranism in North America. It withdrew from its association with the Missouri Synod through the Synodical Conference in 1963. It follows the unaltered Augsburg Confession and holds to the position that it cannot adopt formal relations with other churches unless full doctrinal agreement is reached. This position has kept the church out of ecumenical bodies, though it has relations with a similar conservative Confessional Lutheran Church in Finland, Sweden, and Norway.

Through the 20th century the church built a world mission program, beginning with evangelism among the Apache people in Arizona, and currently it has affiliated congregations in Puerto Rico, Mexico, Colombia, Zambia, Malawi, Taiwan, Hong Kong, and Indonesia. It also supports missionaries in India, Nigeria, and Cameroon.

The Wisconsin Evangelical Lutheran Church in 2006 reported 395,947 members in the United States (and an additional 30,000 members in other countries) in 1,285 churches. It sponsors two colleges and a seminary in the United States.

Wisconsin Evangelical Lutheran Church
2929 N. Mayfair Rd.
Milwaukee, WI 53222
http://www.wels.net/

J. Gordon Melton

See also: Evangelical Lutheran Church in America; Lutheran Church–Missouri Synod.

References

Continuing in the Word. Milwaukee, WI: Northwestern, [1951].

Fredrich, Edward C. *The Wisconsin Synod Lutherans: A History of the Single Synod, Federation & Merger*. Milwaukee, WI: Northwestern Publishing House, 1992.

Koehler, John Philip. *The History of the Wisconsin Synod*. La Crosse, WI: Faith-Life The Protestant Conference, 1981.

Witchcraft

Witchcraft is a term that has been used to describe a broad range of real and fictional practices. "Witchcraft" (with a capital "W") is commonly used to describe the religion of Witchcraft as practiced mainly in Western countries in the last half century, and "witchcraft" (with a lower case "w") to describe beliefs and practices of many indigenous cultures where witchcraft is a label for describing painful experiences and malicious individuals.

Witchcraft is a new religious movement that began in England in the 1940s and has spread worldwide in subsequent decades (Luhrmann 1987; Hutton 1999; Salomonsen 2002). It is particularly strong in the United Kingdom, Canada, and the United States, but has practitioners in many countries, although it tends to be most common in industrialized countries. The early growth of Witchcraft was primarily through personal friendships and networks—similar to the growth of other new religious movements. However, in the mid-1990s there was an explosion of information about Witchcraft available on the Internet, through introductory books found in mainstream bookstores, and displayed in popular movies and television programs. This led to a rapid growth of interest in Witchcraft among young people (Berger and Ezzy 2007). The new generation of younger Witches have often learned about Witchcraft from books or the Internet and are much more likely to practice on their own than the older generation.

Contemporary Witchcraft is generally understood to be part of the more general Pagan revival. Other contemporary Pagan religions include Druidry, Heathenry, and various reconstructionist movements such as those reconstructing classical Greek religious practice. Witchcraft itself divides into a number of "denominations." These include Gardnerian and Alexandrian Wicca, feminist Witchcraft (which is closely related to Goddess Spirituality), and solitary practitioners.

Beliefs about the history of European witchcraft played an important role in the development of the new religious movement of Witchcraft. Margaret Murray (1921) published *The Witch Cult in Western Europe*, in which she argued that "victims of the early modern witch trials have been practitioners of a surviving pagan

Sonja Kulmitzer, a self-described witch who runs the School of Witchcraft, uses a pendulum over a map to find energy lines, October 22, 2002, in the garden of her witch school in Klagenfurt, Austria. (AP/Wide World Photos)

religion" (Hutton 1999, 195). Further, she asserted that the worship of the horned god of the greenwood in modern England was a continuation of the worship of Pan that she traced back through Europe to the Near East. Pan "had been the focus of worship for the witches, and the origins of the figure of the Christian Devil" (Hutton 1999,196). Hutton is scathing of Murray's scholarship, arguing that she quoted very selectively and ignored evidence that contradicted her thesis.

Murray's thesis was apparently supported by various academic works, including Carlo Ginzburg's (1991), which suggested that there was a "core of truth" to the Murray thesis. Ginzburg's work, however, demonstrates that witchcraft beliefs can be traced to indigenous European practices of shamanism and spirit-travel. This is not quite the same as Murray's argument that medieval and early modern Europeans were practicing the rites of a secret religion of Witchcraft with links back to classical times. Witches do appear in classical Greek and Latin literature as powerful women, although their representations in this tradition are almost entirely as fictional figures (Ogden 2002).

The idea that millions of women died in the early modern witch trials was also important to the development of feminist Witchcraft (Starhawk 1979). Starhawk saw contemporary Witchcraft as a reclaiming of feminine power and spirituality that was brutally persecuted during the witchcraft trials. There has been considerable recent research on the early modern witch trials. This research has dismantled some of the earlier claims that millions of women died. "It has been established beyond any reasonable doubt that there was no long-lasting or wide-ranging persecution of witches in early modern Europe . . . only a tiny percentage of people suspected by their neighbours of witchcraft were executed as a result, and mass arrests only occurred in very exceptional circumstances" (Hutton 1999, 379).

Forster in a 1976 article describes the term "witchdoctor" as an "outmoded" synonym for a shaman or healer that was used in the early anthropological literature about Africa. This usage probably reflected the general disrespect that many early anthropologists held for indigenous religious and healing practice. "Witch," in this sense, held similar derogatory overtones to that used by the Catholic Inquisition to describe medieval witches. Similar uses of the term "witchcraft" are found among American indigenous peoples, where witchcraft refers to "the aggressive use of supernatural techniques" (Carrasco 1989, 3)

The term "witchcraft" continues to be used in many African, and other indigenous, cultures to describe malevolent practices, often understood to be associated with supernatural means of acquiring illicit wealth or power. Accusations of witchcraft are often linked to political struggles for power such as local elections and debates over changing gender relations (Englund 1996). For example, Gescheiere and Nymnjoh (1998) describe accusations of "zombie witchcraft" associated with recently acquired wealth and urban-rural tensions in Cameroon. New technology, Western culture, and Christianity have been integrated into witchcraft beliefs and practices and it continues to thrive as a term used to describe and denigrate parties with opposed political interests.

In South Africa many people with AIDS interpret their suffering as a product of witchcraft. Ashforth (2002, 123) emphasizes that within the South African cultural context this is not a form of irrationality or superstition, but "entirely plausible." The consequence of this "witchcraft paradigm" for the explanation of AIDS is important to understand in order to develop informed public policy responses that address the role of traditional healers, and the silence and public accusations that may be associated with it.

In classical Greek culture the term "witch" was used to describe those who practiced magical spells, such as that to return a wandering lover. In Latin literature, accusations of witchcraft followed similar lines to those of Africa and other indigenous cultures, where it was associated with struggles for power and images of malicious old wealthy women in Roman society (Stratton 2007). Murray (2007, 284) makes a similar argument that the charge of "witchcraft" was used by Jewish rabbis in the first and second centuries who were "attempting to establish their authority" and who found "aspects of women's religious culture" threatening.

This situation is very different in contemporary Western Witchcraft. Although it has its share of evil and malicious individuals, there is no evidence that Witches are any more or less likely to be involved in illegal activities. Their rituals are typically positive and for healing. Berger and Ezzy (2007) argue that among the young Witches they interviewed, Witchcraft probably has a similar positive effect on self-esteem and a similar reduction in delinquent activities to that observed among young people participating in other religious groups.

Contemporary Witchcraft is a religion of practice. Belief is a secondary concern (Harvey 1997). The focus of Witchcraft practices is the celebration of nature, particularly through celebrating the changing seasons. Practitioners of Witchcraft participate in regular shared rituals, such as the festivals of the wheel of the year and full moon rites. The members of one group, however, may vary in their beliefs from those who think deities are real beings, to those who see them as symbols of the self, to participants who see them as symbolic representations of nature and might call themselves "atheist" Pagans. The term "Wicca" is sometimes reserved for those who have been initiated into an established tradition, with "Witchcraft" used as a more general term. However, many people who have not been initiated into an established tradition also call themselves practitioners of "Wicca," and the two terms are often used interchangeably.

The rituals of the wheel of the year follow the seasons of the sun and consist of eight major festivals approximately 6 weeks apart (Hutton 1999). Samhain or Halloween (generally celebrated around October 31 to November 2) is a festival celebrating the dark of the year when those who have died are remembered and honored. The Winter Solstice or Midwinter or Yule (December 19–23) celebrates the rebirth of the Sun. Imbolc or Candlemas (February 1–2) celebrates the growing of the year. The Vernal Equinox or Ostara (March 19–23) celebrates the beginning of spring. Beltane or May Day (May 1) is a major festival of spring, often celebrated with bonfires and maypole dancing. Midsummer or Litha (June 19–23) celebrates the Summer Solstice. Lammas or Lughnasadh (August 1–2) celebrates the first harvest. The Autumnal Equinox or Mabon (September 19–23) is a time of celebration of the year past and anticipation of the coming winter.

In the Southern Hemisphere the dates of the festivals are usually switched to match the seasons—for example, midwinter is in June and midsummer in December. However this is not always the case, particularly among Witches influenced by ceremonial magic, who may continue to follow the Northern Hemisphere wheel (Hume 1997). The situation is even more confusing for those in equatorial areas, who may adapt or develop a set of seasonal festivals based on local seasons.

Witchcraft rituals may be practiced by solitary practitioners, in small groups of approximately a dozen people (sometimes referred to as covens), and at larger festivals with participants numbering 100 or more (these tend to be annual events). Participants will typically stand in a circle and remain standing for the duration of the rite. A ritual usually begins with a circle casting, in which the four directions of East, North, West, and South are honored. The circle is cast following the apparent movement of the Sun (counterclockwise in the Southern Hemisphere, clockwise in the north). The presiding priestess will "seal" the circle by walking around it with a sacred knife (*athame*) chanting an invocation. The ritual itself will depend on the festival and the particular tradition of the group. It may include a ritual drama in which a Greek myth (such as Persephone's descent into the underworld and return) is acted out. It may include ritual chanting and dancing. Women's and men's roles are not hierarchically differentiated in Witchcraft. While some traditions do privilege women (Dianic Wicca only has female members), most Witches celebrate the different roles of males and females, but do not consider one to be privileged over the other.

Greenwood (2000) and Berger and Ezzy (2007) have argued that the magic practiced by Witches is mostly about self-development. While Witches may engage in magical practices designed to physically change the world around them, the magic of Witches is much more likely to involve rituals to improve a person's self-esteem, to deal with poor body image, or to encourage success in relationships. Healing spells for an ill friend and rituals to heal ecological harm are also common.

In summary, the term "witchcraft" has been, and continues to be, used in indigenous cultures and in classical Roman, Greek and rabbinical writing, to describe malicious individuals and practices, often associated with political power struggles. Contemporary Western Witchcraft, in contrast, is a new religious movement that focuses on developing a greater awareness of nature, has established rituals and practices, and is widely accepted as a legitimate religion in many Western countries.

Douglas Ezzy

See also: Fall Equinox; Gardnerian Wicca; Goddess Spirituality; Spring Equinox; Summer Solstice; Wiccan Religion; Winter Solstice.

References

Berger, Helen A., and Douglas Ezzy. *Teenage Witchcraft: Magical Youth and the Search for the Self.* New Brunswick, NJ: Rutgers University Press, 2007.

Carrasco, David. "Introduction." In *Witchcraft and Sorcery of the American Native Peoples*, edited by Deward E. Walker, 1–11. Moscow: University of Idaho Press, 1989.

Englund, H. "Witchcraft, Modernity and the Person." *Critique of Anthropology* 16, no. 3 (1996): 257–279.

Forster, G. "Disease Etiologies in Non-Western Medical Systems." *American Anthropologist* 78, no. 4 (1976): 773–782.

Geschiere, P., and F. Nymnjoh. "Witchcraft as an Issue in the Politics of Belonging." *African Studies Review* 41, no. 3 (1998): 69–91.

Ginzburg, Carlo. *Ecstasies: Deciphering the Witches' Sabbath*. Trans. by R. Rosenthal. London: Hutchinson, 1991.

Greenwood, Susan. *Magic, Witchcraft and the Otherworld*. Oxford: Berg, 2000.

Harvey, Graham. *Listening People, Speaking Earth: Contemporary Paganism*. London: C. Hurst and Co., 1997.

Hume, Lynne. *Witchcraft and Paganism in Australia*. Melbourne: Melbourne University Press, 1997.

Hutton, Ronald. *The Triumph of the Moon: A History of Modern Pagan Witchcraft*. Oxford: Oxford University Press, 1999.

Luhrmann, T. M. *Persuasions of the Witch's Craft*. Oxford: Blackwell, 1987.

Murray, Margaret. *The Witch Cult in Western Europe*. Oxford: Clarendon Press, 1921.

Murray, Michele. "The Magical Female in Graeco-Roman Rabbinic Literature." *Religion and Theology* 14, nos. 3–4 (2007): 284–309.

Ogden, Daniel. *Magic, Witchcraft and Ghost in the Greek and Roman Worlds*. Oxford: Oxford University Press, 2002.

Salomonsen, Jone. *Enchanted Feminism*. New York: Routledge, 2002.

Starhawk. *The Spiral Dance*. San Francisco: Harper and Row, 1979.

Stratton, Kimberly B. *Naming the Witch: Magic, Ideology, and Stereotype in the Ancient World*. New York: Columbia University Press, 2007.

Women, Status and Role of

As humanity moved out of localized ethnic-based societies, developed written languages, and created the civilized societies with their specialized roles, hierarchical and patriarchal structures became pronounced. Women were restricted to roles defined initially by their gender uniqueness, the bearing of children, and their role as wife, mother, and homemaker. Religiously they had a variety of functions as priestess, healer, seeress, and magical practitioner. These roles have survived and still operate in many of the indigenous religions worldwide.

Both modernity and urbanization contributed to the roles of women in religion through the establishment of hierarchies that regulate women's sexuality and relationships to men and each other, roles within the family, participation in religious traditions and worship, and the opportunity for formally recognized religious leadership roles (that required some form of ordination). Contention often lies within varying interpretation of religious texts upon which doctrine is based. It is clear, however, that women's roles at one time were not restricted in religious traditions as they were prior to the changes brought by the contemporary feminist movements. The roles of women in religion have been impacted by locale and history.

Hinduism Women's roles in Hinduism began to shift approximately 800 BCE in the early Vedic period. Prior to this shift, women were religious leaders and participated actively in sacred rituals and rites. As social hierarchies emerged, women were restricted to domestic roles of service and obedience to their husbands and families. It is important to note that other aspects of Indian culture, such as social caste, stage of life, family association, and age contributed to the diversity of experiences of women. Women could also draw on the images and stories of the many goddesses in the Hindu sacred literature.

Near 400 CE women became increasingly involved in their participation in religious activities once again. Women saints played important roles as religious figures in women's lives and roles within devotional activities. With the onset of the modern period (1700 CE through the present) cultural traditions that dictated women's roles, such as sati, the ban on remarriage of widows, child marriage, and the dowry were made illegal. As social justice movements continue to progress, women's roles in Indian culture and Hinduism will continue to shift.

A demand for women's rights emerged in India along with the general demand for both secular and religious reforms in the late 19th century, with the strongest progress noticeable in Bengal and Maharashtra. Annie Besant (1847–1933), the leader of the Theosophical Society, contributed to this movement with a program to found schools for girls throughout the country. By the mid-20th century, a small number of women guru-saints (such as Sri Anandamayi Ma, 1896–1982) had emerged, and following independence in 1947, their number multiplied exponentially. As Hinduism moved to become a global religion several women have assumed roles as the leader of new international Hindu spiritual movements: Shree Maa (b. 1950), Amritanandamayi Ma (b. 1953), Sri Mataji Niemala Devi (b. 1923), Swami Chidvilasananda (b. 1955), Shivananda Radha (1911–1995), Sri Daya Mata (SRF) (b. 1914), Ma Jaya Sati Bhagavati (b. 1940), and Mother Meera (b. 1960).

Buddhism   Buddhism was founded primarily as a monastic movement. Mahaprajapati, the stepmother of Siddhartha Gautama known as the Buddha (563–483 BCE), sought and acquired permission to become a nun although the Buddhist monks and Buddha himself resisted women's participation in the monastic movement in the early years of the Buddhist tradition. Upon granting Mahaprajapati permission, Buddha essentially asserted that women could achieve enlightenment. While Buddha added eight restrictive rules that women were required to follow to maintain their subordinate relationships to the monks, the monks also received restrictive orders that disabled their ability to abuse their authority. Subsequently, women's status was elevated and the recognition of their spiritual, if not their social, equality was acknowledged.

As in other modern religious traditions, women faced a variety of subordinating structures. In Theravada societies, the contemporary struggle for women's rights has found a focus in the revival of women's monastic orders. In Mahayana and Vajrayana tradition, women have been able to draw upon the stories of women saints in previous centuries and the female bodhisattvas, such as Guan Yin and Mahasthamaprapta. While full ordination for women is currently available in Chinese, Korean, and Vietnamese Buddhism, through a monastic lineage called Dharmaguptaka, not until 2007 did His Holiness the 14th Dalai Lama announce full support for the establishment of full ordination for women in the Tibetan tradition.

In North America in the 1970s, women protested their subordination in the emerging movement (which had in some cases led to abuse). Their organization led to marked changes in the temples and supported the emergence of a spectrum of leaders who followed in the footsteps of the pioneer leaders in Zen Buddhism, Ruth Fuller Everett Sasaki (1893–1967) and Jiyu-Kennett Roshi (1924–1996).

Judaism   While women's primary responsibilities traditionally lie within the household and family relationships, in Judaism, women also are viewed as separate but equal to men. Women have traditionally held the right to purchase, own, and sell property and establish contracts and participate in business ventures. Women also possess the right to choose their marriages and neither spousal beating nor mistreatment has ever been condoned in Judaism. Women's role within the synagogue is limited and this is due to the observance of the separation of women and men. Prayer and devotional activities are performed with women and men separated. Women are not required to attend religious services and are restricted from participating in many portions of the services they do attend. Although men are obligated to perform more commandments than women, there are three mitzvoth, or commandments, reserved specifically for women: *nerot,* which is candle lighting; *challah,* which refers to separation of a portion of the dough; and *niddah,* which entails a ritual immersion upon the conclusion of a woman's menstrual period.

In the 20th century, Judaism struggled with the issue of ordination of women. Above and beyond the tradition limiting the rabbinate to males, questions

Buddhist nuns wearing pink robes worship in Myanmar, 2007. (iStockPhoto.com)

arose concerning women's ability to lead a congregation and meet various elements of the law (*mitzvah*) which male youth agree to follow at their bar mitzvah ceremony. Both the Reform and Conservative Jewish movements have dealt with these questions and beginning in 1972 (Reform) and 1984 (Conservative) welcome women to the rabbinate. The orthodox still oppose such ordinations.

Christianity   Historically, there were a number of women that held power in the Christian tradition. Many served as missionaries to carry Jesus Christ's message to outlying villages with the intent of converting individuals and communities to Christianity. Despite social justice movements and proponents asserting that Christ's vision encompassed equality for humankind, women have been viewed as submissive to men in the Christian tradition. Women's status has been related to the interpretation of Eve as the temptress who offered Adam the apple in the Garden of Eden. This act, subsequently, caused the fall of civilization into the hands of Lucifer.

Women were pushed aside as the hierarchy developed, especially as the church came out of its period as a clandestine religion in the fourth century. Shortly thereafter, a new role for women developed as Christian monasticism developed and women's orders, led by women, were authorized along with those led by men. As the orders developed, they offered an array of new possibilities (including occupations) for women, in spite of their being held in a somewhat secondary role relative to the expansive men's orders. Women's orders were largely abandoned by Protestants.

In the 19th century, Christian women began to challenge the traditional interpretations of the Bible, which had blocked their progress in the secular world and limited their leadership possibilities within the various churches. A new debate on women's leadership was opened in the 19th-century Holiness movement led by such people as Methodists Phoebe Palmer

(1807–1874) and Frances Willard (1839–1898). Such movements as the Salvation Army pioneered the ordination of women. The openness to the ordination of women passed to the Pentecostal moment which saw itself as the fulfillment of the prophecies of Acts 2, which included the promise that "your sons and daughters shall prophesy" (Acts 2:17). Further openings were found as Lutherans, Anglicans, and Methodists created a new deaconess movement (a Protestant form of the ordered life).

Through the 20th century, a small number of women were ordained in various denominations, often to serve specific missions for which no one else was available, and a movement slowly emerged to admit women to holy order and then in the episcopally led churches, to the bishopric. Leadership in this endeavor came for such diverse bodies as the United Church of Canada, the Anglicans in Hong Kong, the American Methodists, and the Swedish Lutherans.

Today, most of the larger Protestant churches welcome women to all levels of leadership, with some prominent exceptions among the more conservative, including the Southern Baptist Convention and several of the Anglican churches. The Church of England has yet to elect a woman as bishop, though it has passed enabling legislation. Both the Roman Catholics and Eastern Orthodox churches have closed debate on the issue for the time being. However, the debates pertaining to the interpretations of religious texts relative to women is ongoing and many scholars have elected to highlight important women in the Bible, while also researching the root of the translations of the original texts to clarify meaning.

While many Christian churches and denominations assert full equality for women and men in the church, women continue to be restricted from opportunities for ordination and various lay leadership positions in the majority of churches. Social movements directed at effecting change in women's ecclesiastical privileges, roles, and rights continue to shape and reform traditions over time.

Islam   The status and role of women in Islam, the Muslim religion, instigates heated debate. The status and role of women is based on the historical understanding of women being equated with slaves and being

Women wearing burqas, Afghanistan. (iStockPhoto.com)

viewed as property. It is at this point where contention in interpretation of religious texts becomes paramount. While the Koran, the primary Muslim text, confers the responsibility for women to men, what this responsibility is and what it entails is often challenged. While strides have been made in modernity to liberate women from the status of property, little movement has actually occurred regarding women's rights in countries where Islam is dominant. A lively debate on the status and role of women is ongoing in the West.

Women's traditional dress of complete veiling in Muslim culture has been a target for many Western feminists. It has also become the subject of widespread public debate in both Europe and North America, with several countries passing legislation against veiling in a variety of circumstances from attendance at public school or driving an automobile. At the same time, within the cultural context, many women in Muslim culture adhere to and uphold the veiling, viewing this as a form of protection and integrity as it is situated within their cultural context.

Within Islam, responsibility for the household falls in the women's domain and is upheld by doctrine. Women's sexuality is highly restricted while men are able to practice polygamy (though most men are monogamous). Women who engage in sexual activity outside of marriage risk being stoned to death as punishment, although there are many social movements aimed to discourage this. Women's roles and status within the Muslim culture continue to be restrictive of women's independence.

Western Esotericism   The Esoteric tradition, drawing on Gnostic, Hermetic, and alchemical themes, emerged anew in the 17th century. It did not challenge the dominant concepts of the status and role of women at the time and its primary 18th-century manifestation, Freemasonry, became known as a "men's club." Its tendency to see men and women as polar opposites (right-left, light-dark) tended to leave women as the embodiment of the negative side of the pole. This was amply demonstrated in the emerging ceremonial magic tradition in the 19th century, which tended to reduce women to the role of simply another magical tool (vividly seen in the writings of Aleister Crowley).

At the same time, the more popularized forms of the Esoteric tradition in the 19th century became allies of the women's movement. Spiritualism was founded by women and most of its mediums were female. Theosophy, Christian Science, and the New Thought movement were also founded by women (Helena P. Blavatsky, Mary Baker Eddy, and Emma Curtis Hopkins) and all employed women in important leadership positions. Spiritualist Victoria Woodhull became the first woman to run for president on a third-party ticket. Through the 20th century, women were as likely as men to found Esoteric movements or head its various centers. The larger Esoteric world would provide a nurturing context for the contemporary revival of Pagan women's Spirituality.

Women's Spirituality   While religion has often aligned with those social structures that have contributed to women's oppression, many women find religion to be empowering. They find a sense of community and spiritual solace within their traditions. As religions change in response to women's movements, many women also find opportunities for leadership and service and support for activities aimed at social justice. Reinterpretation of texts, reshaping of rituals, rights and religious myths, and a revaluing of ecology and the feminine in the sacred are just a few ways women have participated in religion. Women and men have also elected to form new religions that honor the sacred in ways that uphold equality for everyone. Wicca, neo-Paganism, and Goddess spiritualities are a few of the paths that women and men have elected as solutions to celebrate the sacred while honoring the equality and dignity of humankind. Many of these religions are pantheistic and panentheistic to encompass an immanent sense of unity with the cosmos while including or rejecting the notion of a transcendent source of the sacred, as well.

Wendy Mason

See also: Besant, Annie; Crowley, Aleister; Eddy, Mary Baker; Freemasonry; Holiness Movement; Methodism; Mother Meera, Disciples of; Pentecostalism; Sahaja Yoga; Salvation Army; Self-Realization Fellowship; Siddha Yoga; Western Esoteric Tradition; Zen Buddhism.

References

Aune, Kristin, et al. *Women and Religion in the West.* Aldershot: Ashgate, 2008.

Awde, Nicholas. *Women In Islam: An Anthology From the Qur'an and Hadiths.* New York: Hippocrene Books, 2005.

Berzin, Alexander. "A Summary Report of the 2007 International Congress on the Women's Role in the Sangha: Bhikshuni Vinaya and Ordination Lineages." University of Hamburg, Hamburg, Germany, 18–20 July 2007.

Biale, Rachel. *Women and Jewish Law: The Essential Texts, Their History, and Their Relevance for Today.* New York: Schocken Publishers, 1995.

Goodwin, Allison. "Right Views, Red Rust, and White Bones. The Eight Garudhammas and Buddhist Teachings on Female Inferiority Reexamined in Light of Psychological and Social Research." Paper presented at the Conference on Gender and Religion in Taiwan, 2007.

Greenberg, Blu. *On Women & Judaism.* Philadelphia: Jewish Publication Society of America, 1981.

Gross, Rita. *Feminism and Religion.* Boston: Beacon Press, 1996.

Heath, Jennifer, ed. *The Veil: Writers on Its History, Lore, and Politics*. Berkeley: University of California Press, 2008.

Jones, Connie, and James D. Ryan. *Encyclopedia of Hinduism*. New York: Checkmark Books, 2008.

Malone, Mary T. *Women and Christianity: The First Thousand Years*. Maryknoll, NY: Orbis Books, 2001.

Malone, Mary T. *Women & Christianity: From 1000 to the Reformation*. Maryknoll, NY: Orbis Books, 2002.

Malone, Mary T. *Women & Christianity: From the Reformation to the 21st Century*. Maryknoll, NY: Orbis Books, 2003.

Nadall, Pamela, and Jonathan Sarna. *Women and American Judaism: Historical Perspectives*. Waltham, MA: Brandeis University Press, 2001.

Pike, Sarah. *New Age and Neopagan Religions in America*. New York: Columbia University Press, 2004.

Sharma, Arvind, and Katherine K. Young, eds. *Women and World Religions*. Upper Saddle River, NJ: Prentice Hall, 2002.

Won Buddhism

Won Buddhism (Won Pulgyo) is one of the most successful of Korea's new religions. The essence of its message is that it "provides hope to the world by providing balance between spiritual and material life." The religion calls the human mind the "mind-field" and seeks to teach people to attain sagehood by cultivating their "original minds." The purpose of the mindfulness teaching provided by Won Buddhism is to provide "personality instruction" to adherents so that they might enrich their lives in the material world by appropriately cultivating their minds spiritually through study, training, and activities in the material world. The religion has established missionary and community outreach programs throughout Korea and in several countries in Europe, Asia, and the United States, and it has translated its primary scriptural text into 20 major world languages.

Won Buddhism was founded in 1916 by Pak Chungbin (1891–1943), who is better known by his literary name, Sot'aesan. Sot'aesan was aware of the three traditional religions of East Asia—Confucianism, Daoism, and Buddhism—yet he felt that his enlightenment experience was independent of any tradition. Nevertheless, upon further inquiry he realized that all of the ancient sages had known that to which he had awakened, and, after reading the Diamond Sutra, he declared that the vehicle of Buddhism was the best for elucidating his vision of ultimate truth, the true understanding of the Dharmakaya Buddha (the body or law of the teaching).

Studies on Won Buddhism are based on The Canon of Won Buddhism (Won Pulgyo kyojon), which contains two books: the Principle Book (Chongjon), composed by Sot'aesan, and the Records (Taejong-gyong), a chronicle of his sayings and doings. The next important book of the tradition is the Religious Discourses of Master Chongsan (Chongsan Chongsa Pobo), the words of Sot'aesan's successor, Song Kyu (1900–1962), the first prime master of Won Buddhism. These books express the religious vision articulated by these two leaders. Sot'aesan represented his enlightened vision of ultimate reality in a perfect circle, known as the One-Circle-Figure (Irwonsang), which he equated to the concept of Dharmakaya of conventional Buddhism.

No images of Buddha are found in Won Buddhist temples; instead, "four graces" are viewed as the incarnations of the Dharmakaya Buddha: Heaven and Earth, Parents, Brethren (fellow creatures), and Law (religious, moral, and civil). Won Buddhism rejects the traditional concept of deliverance or liberation from the world as nihilistic; instead, it tries to realize a paradise on earth by helping people to develop their own abilities, wisdom, education, and altruism. The path to achieving the ideal of enlightenment as expressed in the One-Circle-Figure is the "Threefold Learning." In conventional Buddhism these three are known by the Sanskrit terms *samadhi* (meditation), *prajna* (wisdom), and *sila* (morality).

Sot'aesan recasts these in modern language as the "cultivation of spirit," "study of facts and principles," and "choice of conduct." Religious practice in Won

Buddhism consists of worship of the One-Circle-Figure in the place of images of Buddha, recitation of the name of the Buddha Amitabha, seated meditation, repentance and prayer, and scripture study. Won Buddhism operates a number of branch temples and other organizational establishments primarily in Japan and the United States. One such institution is Wonkwang University, which has a College of Won Buddhist Studies in which Won Buddhist priests, educators, and other leaders are educated in both undergraduate and graduate programs. Religious tracts and philosophical treatises are published by the faculty and research institute of the university, usually in Korean, although Won Buddhist scholars also publish in Western languages in a journal called *Won Buddhism*. As of 2003, the religion operated 15 dioceses, 550 temples, and 180 organizations in Korea and 5 dioceses, 51 temples, and 9 organizations outside of Korea that served a membership that was reaching approximately 1.4 million members.

Won Pulgyo
Sinyong-dong 344-2
Iri-si, Cholla Pukto, 570-754
Republic of Korea
http://www.wonbuddhism.info

Richard D. McBride II

See also: Korean Buddhism; Meditation; Pure Land Buddhism.

References

Chung Bong-Kil. *The Sacred Books of Won Buddhism*. Classics of East Asian Buddhism, vol. 6. Honolulu: University of Hawaii Press, 2002.

Chung, Bongkil. "Won Buddhism: The Historical Context of Sot'aesan's Reformation of Buddhism for the Modern World." In *Buddhism in the Modern World: Adaptations of an Ancient Tradition*, edited by Steven Heine and Charles S. Prebish. New York: Oxford University Press, 2003.

Park Kwangsoo. *The Won Buddhism (Wonbulgyo) of Sot'aesan: A Twentieth Century Religious Movement in Korea*. San Francisco: International Scholars, 1997.

Wonhyo

617–686

Wonhyo, a Buddhist lay practitioner, partnered with the monk Uisang to effectively establish Buddhism across Korea some two centuries after its original transmission in the fifth century. Wonhyo's work was partially aided by the unification process that saw the three kingdoms of Silla, Koguryo, and Paekche brought together into the United Kingdom of Silla, a disruptive process that took most of the 660s to complete.

Wonhyo was born in 617 into a noble family and grew up near Sorabal, the capital of the Silla Kingdom in the southern portion of the Korean peninsula. He turned to serious spirituality as a youth and made the decision to become a Buddhist monk at the age of 15. Following his ordination, he transformed his home into a Buddhist temple. He would remain a monk for the next three decades.

At one point, he decided it was necessary for him to go to China to study in some of the famous temples there. He was accompanied by his younger colleague Uisang (625–702). In 650, the pair left to travel from Koguryo (the northern Korean kingdom) to China to study, but were mistaken as spies and arrested at the border. They returned home and 11 years later tried again. This time they planned to sail from a port city in Paekche. As they made their way, they were caught in a rainstorm. They took refuge in an underground shelter for the night and discovered on awakening that they were in an old tomb. Before the rain ceased, Wonhyo had an intense spiritual experience that led to an enlightenment of sorts, in which he concluded the world was made of mind alone. When the mind is stilled, the differences in the world cease to matter. A tomb and a temple are all the same. With this realization, he felt that he had lost any reason to continue on to China.

Abandoning his career as a monk in 661, he would spend the next decade in contemplation of his insight and writing some 80 works expanding upon it. Then beginning in 676 he would devote a decade to popularizing Buddhism among the masses. His most famous book, the *Commentary on the Awakening of Faith in Mahayana*, explained his insight on the mind. In his *Treatise on Ten Approaches to Reconciliation of the*

Doctrinal Controversy, he turned to the problem of the divisions among a still minority faith on the Korean peninsula. He affirmed that all religious positions have at least some validity but emphasized that the different perspectives will find their reconciliation in the experience of the One Mind beyond all distinctions.

While articulating a mystical philosophy that could lead to inactivity, Wonhyo also refused to move in that direction. Rather, he remained active himself and called upon his students and audiences to demonstrate their concern for all sentient beings. As human life was relatively short, he argued that the years should not be wasted. Our efforts should be made to assist others in their appropriation of Buddhist truth.

Wonhyo finally passed away at a cave temple near Kyongju, Korea, in 686. His emphasis on unifying Korean Buddhism meant that he did not organize a new school, and in the short term his contribution seemed unfulfilled. However, his student Uisang did accomplish much toward both introducing Hwaom Buddhism to Korea and successfully using it to unify most of the Buddhists, still a minority faith in the country. Through the next century Buddhism continued to grow and with further growth came new divisions. As Korean Buddhists struggled with their own divisions, along with the pressure of both hostile rulers and foreign invaders, Wonhyo was rediscovered and his value recognized. At the end of the 11th century he was named the "National Preceptor of Harmonizing Controversies."

Edward A. Irons

See also: Korean Buddhism; Uisang.

References

Lancaster, Lewis R., and C. S. Yu, eds. *Assimilation of Buddhism in Korea: Religious Minority and Innovation in the Silla Dynasty*. Berkeley, CA: Asian Humanities Press, 1991.

McGreal, Ian P., ed. *Great Thinkers of the Eastern World*. New York: HarperCollins, 1995.

Word of Life Church

The Word of Life Church (Kale Heywet) grew out of the efforts initiated by the Sudan Interior Mission (SIM) in 1927. The Mission had begun in 1893 with a vision to evangelize the Sudan, but it was slowed by the African climate, which led to the deaths of two of the founders and the retreat from Africa by the third. Eventually work would be established in several African nations other than the Sudan (Nigeria and Niger) before the Sudan was reached.

In the 1920s the Presbyterians established a mission in Ethiopia. Among its leaders was Dr. Thomas A. Lambie, who founded the Presbyterian hospital in Addis Ababa in 1923. Several years later he began an independent Abyssinian Frontiers Mission, which in 1927 merged with the Sudan Interior Mission. The mission grew slowly and had fewer than 100 baptized converts over the next decade. After the Italians occupied the country, foreign missionaries were kicked out (which became the occasion of SIM missionaries finally establishing work in the Sudan). When they returned in 1941, they discovered that the church had expanded dramatically. There were 20,000 members in some 100 congregations.

The church continued to grow, reaching 100,000 members by 1960 and 500,000 by 1974, by which time it had taken the name Kale Heywet (Word of Life) Church. This progress is attributed to its being a truly indigenous church that has developed its own missionary society, which has targeted the different peoples of Ethiopia. The church has also developed a literacy program for the poverty-stricken country, and in the 1990s it cooperated with the Baptist General Conference in developing a program of famine relief.

The church follows a conservative evangelical Christianity. As the new century begins, it had more than 2 million members. It has developed an extensive educational system and a medical ministry.

J. Gordon Melton

See also: Evangelicalism.

References

Fuller, Harold. "Serving in Mission: Linking Hands around the Globe." http://images.sim.org/pdfs/history/whfuller-sim-history.pdf. Accessed April 24, 2009.

Kane, J. Herbert. *A Global View of Christian Missions*. Grand Rapids, MI: Baker, 1971.

World Alliance of Reformed Churches

The World Alliance of Reformed Churches was formed in 1970 in Nairobi, Kenya, by the merger of the Alliance of the Reformed Churches throughout the World Holding the Presbyterian Order and the International Congregational Council. The Alliance of Reformed Churches was founded in 1875 in London, England, as an association of Reformed and Presbyterian church leaders. It was designed to facilitate cooperation and common action, especially in the mission field. The fellowship gradually grew to include members from the European continent. In 1946 the Alliance, originally headquartered in Edinburgh, Scotland, moved to Geneva, Switzerland, in anticipation of the formation of the World Council of Churches (WCC). It self-consciously decided to make no moves that could be just as easily accomplished through the WCC.

The International Congregational Council was founded in 1892 for purposes similar to those of the Reformed Alliance. In the ecumenical atmosphere during the years following the formation of the WCC, the mutual affirmation of a Reformed theological perspective drew the two organizations together.

The Alliance carries out theological dialogues, promotes programs of mutual cooperation between member churches, and sponsors a program of publications led by its periodical, *The Reformed World*. It has a history of witnessing against racism and in the promotion of human rights. In the 1980s it experienced particular concern over the apartheid policies of South Africa and the role of some Reformed churches' support of it. In 1982 the Alliance suspended the membership of two South African Reformed bodies until they brought their policies in line with the alliance's antiapartheid stance. One church left the Alliance, the other remained in association and was received back into full membership in 1997.

In 2008, the Alliance reported a membership of 214 churches scattered in 107 countries with an inclusive membership of 75 million people. In 2008, it focused attention on the 500th anniversary of the birth of John Calvin (1509–1564), the founder of the Reformed Christian tradition.

The World Alliance of Reformed Churches and the Reformed Ecumenical Council decided to form a new ecumenical organization to be known as the World Communion of Reformed Churches. The merger took place in June 2010. The Council has, in the past, provided a more conservative alternative to the Alliance.

World Alliance of Reformed Churches
150 route de Ferney
PO Box 2100
1211 Geneva 2
Switzerland
http://warc.jalb.de/warcajsp/side.jsp?news
    _id=2&part2_id=19&navi=8

J. Gordon Melton

See also: Calvin, John; Congregationalism; Reformed Ecumenical Council; Reformed/Presbyterian Tradition.

References

Bauswein, Jean-Jacques, and Lukas Vischner, eds. *The Reformed Family Worldwide: A Survey of Reformed Churches, Theological Schools, and International Organizations*. Grand Rapids, MI: William B. Eerdmans Publishing Company, 1999.

The Legacy of John Calvin: Some Actions for the Church in the 21st Century. Geneva: WARC/ John Knox International Reformed Center, 2008.

World Brotherhood Union Mevlana Supreme Foundation

The World Brotherhood Union Mevlana Supreme Foundation was founded in Istanbul, Turkey, in 1986 to teach the channeled work of the Celestial Totality (a ranked hierarchy similar to the Great White Brotherhood of the Theosophical tradition). Mevlana, the foundation's founder, who is called the pen of the Golden Age, is responsible for channeling the organization's sacred scriptures, particularly the *Knowledge Book*. Mevlana, through what her group calls "reverse transfer" (this organization's term for reincarnation), has returned to the Earth in order to serve the divine purpose of the World Brotherhood Union (WBU). The WBU purports the *Knowledge Book* to contain the spiritual manifesto essential for personal and planetary transformation in the new millennium. The years from 2000 to 2005 are noted as foundational years, heralding a future Golden Age in which everyone attains Universal Consciousness. The WBU teaches that two UFOs are stationed above the Earth to monitor and police the activities of the people of the planet. Should human behavior err beyond the parameters set by the WBU a galactic military force based on the UFOs will intercede to reshape the destructive behavior according to the Divine Plan. They believe their plan to be based on goodwill, self-sacrifice, capacity, and consciousness.

The WBU proselytizes in people's homes. A group leader who receives special spiritual messages calls six friends who meet at her home and write down, date, and sign her unique messages, which are given to another six, and so forth. The WBU claims to unite feminist and egalitarian principles and teaches that the Earth is the only planet in the solar system on which discrimination between the sexes exists. Paradoxically, the specific messages to Mevlana are sent by Mustafa Molla and a Captain Riviere. Mohammed Mustafa is the messenger of Allah, and Kurtairce is the Savior or Jesus figure; both dwell with Buddha in the Celestial Totality—while touting equality, the ruling aristocracy is male.

By acknowledging the Koran as one of a number of sacred texts and Mohammed as a messenger of this particular sacred text, the WBU courts an Islamic population. However, the WBU should not be considered an Islamic revitalization movement, as it has only a cursory link with Islam. It has received its major inspiration from Theosophy and the Western Esoteric tradition, which it has synthesized with a unique Turkish twist. Thus the WBU integrates Theosophy with beliefs about UFOs and flying saucers in a concerted attempt to wed science and religion in a sophisticated, technological way. Because of the secrecy of this group, no accurate data exist for the number of its adherents.

World Brotherhood Union Mevlana Supreme
    Foundation
Catalcesme Baggat Caddesi Ahmet Cevdet Pasa
    Sokak
No. 1/6
81110 Bostanci-Kadikoy
Istanbul

Turkey
http://www.dkb-mevlana.org.tr

Gail M. Harley and J. Gordon Melton

See also: Reincarnation; Theosophical Society (Adyar); UFO Religions; Western Esoteric Tradition.

Reference

Harley, Gail M. "From Turbans to the Tarot: Radical Religious Trends in Modern Turkey." Unpublished paper, 1998. Copy in files of the American Religions Collection, Davidson Library, University of California–Santa Barbara.

World Buddhist Sangha Council

The World Buddhist Sangha Council (WBSC) was founded in 1966 as an expression of the international Buddhist Sangha (community). Delegates from Ceylon, Vietnam, Malaysia, Republic of China, Hong Kong, Nepal, Cambodia, Korea, Pakistan, India, Singapore, Thailand, England, and Laos, along with a special delegation representing the Dalai Lama, assembled at Colombo, Sri Lanka, May 8–11, 1966, to adopt the original constitution.

Within Buddhism, *Sangha* refers to two distinct phenomena, the *Savaka-Sangha*, or the community of (noble) disciples (the larger community of all believers), and, more narrowly, the *Bhikkhu-Sangha*, or the community of Bhikkhus (monks). This latter grouping, especially prominent in Theravada Buddhist groups, is also referred to as the *Sammati-Sangha*, or the conventional Sangha. The World Buddhist Sangha Council is organized around the Sangha in the more narrow sense of that term, as an association of Buddhist monks and clergy. In Theravada thinking, monks serve as the core and leading part of the larger Buddhist lay community. They attempt to lead exemplary and noble lives and thus exercise influence on the people in treading the Noble Eightfold Path. The Bhikkhu-Sangha also serves as the center for training both those who join it and the lay community.

The WBSC gathers in a general conference or assembly at five-year intervals. The assembly selects an executive council that meets annually to carry on the assembly's business between the larger meetings. As the new century begins, the executive council includes some 149 members drawn from all the major schools of Buddhism. The Most Venerable Wu Ming of the Republic of China (Taiwan) and the Most Venerable Kok Kwong of Hong Kong have been named the "lifelong honorable president" and vice president, respectively.

The WBSC has its headquarters in Taiwan. WBSC members come not only from the traditionally Buddhist countries but also from Buddhist communities around the world, especially North America and Europe.

The Council has taken stands on a variety of social issues, beginning with the Vietnam War. In more recent years it has encouraged the development of Buddhist education, especially for leadership training. It has argued for a consensus Buddhism representative of mainline Theravada and Mahayana Buddhist traditions. This perspective was noted in a 1995 declaration that stated that "fanatic elements are to be found even in the modern world who proclaim that they are the living Buddhas. Therefore, we solemnly declare that these wrong views expressed by certain elements of the Buddhist community will not be approved by the WBSC. The Buddha once admonished the disciples that even though they have cultivated the stage of obtaining supernormal power, they should not perform miracles leading to the misunderstanding of the path shown by the Buddha. In this context, we, the WBSC, appeal to the world not to be misled by such modern elements in the name of Buddhism. We hereby declare that the whole members of the Sangha should abide by and uphold the authentic teachings of the Buddha for the betterment of mankind."

This stance can be seen as posing opposition to adherents of Vajrayana Buddhism (especially Tibetan Buddhists), who recognize various leaders as a living Buddha, or Rinpoche, but would equally apply to the leader of the controversial groups such as Falun Gong, whose leader, Li Hongzhi, is seen as a Living Buddha.

The Council draws its strength from Sri Lanka, Vietnam, and Taiwan, and the Chinese diaspora across Southeast Asia and from Chinese, Vietnamese, and Asian Theravada groups in the West.

World Buddhist Sangha Council
6 Shaoshing Street N.
Taipei
Taiwan 100
http://www.wbsc886.org/Enlish/E-index2/E-index.
    html

Edward A. Irons

See also: Falun Gong; Mahayana Buddhism; Theravada Buddhism; Tibetan Buddhism.

Reference

Payutto, Ajahn Prayudh. "Sangha: The Ideal World Community. "http://www.saigon.com/~anson/ebud/ebdha062.htm. Accessed October 1, 2001.

World Communion of Reformed Churches

The World Communion of Reformed Churches is a new organization designed to represent Christian churches of the Protestant Reformed tradition, still in process of formation as of 2009. The Communion began with a proposal initiated in 2005 by the Reformed Ecumenical Council, which represented a number of the more conservative Reformed denominations, to merge its work into the much larger World Alliance of Reformed Churches. The Council dates to 1946 and its membership had been built around a common allegiance to the traditional Reformed confessional statements. The Alliance dates to 1975 and the formation of the Alliance of the Reformed Churches Throughout the World Holding to the Presbyterian System. In 1970, it merged with the International Congregational Council, Congregational churches, being Reformed in theology, merely disagreeing on the matter of polity. Over the years, churches have evolved in their discernment of those issues that are most important relative to cooperative action and fellowship, and those that are of lesser significance.

Following the initial overture of the Council, the Alliance made a counterproposal. Rather than simply absorbing the Council, it suggested that both bodies dissolve and their member groups then form a new ecumenical organization in which all would be new and equal participants. That idea was welcomed by all and acted upon. A draft constitution was sent out for consideration in October 2008 and a proposed inaugural gathering of the new communion was held in Grand Rapids, Michigan, in June 2010.

The new communion is the home of some 257 denominations worldwide. It has established an Internet presence at http://reformedchurches.org/.

J. Gordon Melton

See also: Congregationalism; Reformed Ecumenical Council; World Alliance of Reformed Churches.

Reference

Van Beek, Huibert. *A Handbook of Churches and Councils: Profiles of Ecumenical Relationships.* Geneva: World Council of Churches, 2006.

World Conference on Religion and Peace

The World Conference on Religion and Peace (WCRP) is an international organization that attempts to bring religious resources and religious leadership to bear in interfaith attempts to create world peace. WCRP dates to the Cuban Missile Crisis of 1962, during which time the United States and the Soviet Union stood on the brink of war. At that time, Dr. Dana McLean Greeley (1908–1986), a leader with the Unitarian-Universalist Association, called together Rabbi Maurice N. Eisendrath (1902–1973), Methodist Bishop John Wesley Lord (1902–1989), and Roman Catholic Bishop John Wright (1909–1979). Their informal meeting led to an initial conference on religion and peace in 1964 in New York City and a national Inter-Religious Conference on World Peace in Washington, D.C. Following that conference two representatives of the national conference made a world tour to assess the global situation and build a network of interested leaders.

The first World Conference on Religion and Peace met at Kyoto, Japan, in 1970. The WCRP was formally established at that time. In 1973, WCRP was granted consultative status with the Economic and Social Council of the United Nations. In the subsequent quarter-century of its existence, WCRP has created a variety of programs and responses to the changing world situation and shifting global hotspots. In 1970 it created the WCRP International Coordinating Committee for Women. A decade-long concern for children caught in war led to its sponsorship of the 1995 religious participation in the UN's study entitled "The Impact of Armed Conflict on Children."

The program is carried out through regional councils in Europe, Asia, and Africa, as well as chapters in some 40 countries. World assemblies are held every five years. The most recent met in Kyoto, Japan, in 2006. Members committed themselves to confront violence around the world and in their own country and continue their efforts toward world peace.

World Conference on Religion and Peace
777 UN Plaza
9th Floor
New York, NY 10017
http://www.wcrp.org/

J. Gordon Melton

References

Arinze, Cardinal Francis. *Religions for Peace: A Call for Solidarity to the Religions of the World.* Garden City, NY: Doubleday, 2002.

Braybrook, Marcus. *Inter-Faith Organizations, 1893–1979: An Historical Directory.* New York: Edwin Mellen, 1980.

Jack, Homer. *WCRP: A History of the World Conference on Religion and Peace.* New York: World Conference on Religion and Peace, 1993.

World Conference on Religion and Peace. *Religions for Peace: Action for Common Living.* Maryknoll, NY: Orbis, 2000.

World Congress of Faiths

The World Congress of Faiths, one of the oldest interfaith organizations in existence as the 21st century began, traces its beginning to the 1893 World Parliament of Religions and the series of interfaith conferences and organizations inspired by it. Especially important was the Religions of the Empire Conference, held in London in 1924, which brought to the fore Francis Younghusband (1863–1942). As a young

Indian-born British explorer Sir Francis Edward Young-husband (1863–1942) founded the World Congress of Faiths. (Getty Images)

man he had developed a mystical view of religion and come to believe that the Divine Spirit is latent in all people—that they are children of the same Father, and that people should nurture and develop the Divine Flame. His conclusions were confirmed in a vivid religious experience he had in Tibet in 1903.

Out of his experience, Younghusband began to work for a congress of faiths at which he could share his vision of the unity of religions. He helped to plan the Religions of the Empire Conference, chaired a committee of the Society for the Study of Religions that grew out of it, and later spoke at the World Fellowship of Faiths Conference in 1933 in Chicago. From the Chicago conference, he returned to London and in 1934 established the British National Council of the World Fellowship of Faiths. He also proposed a Congress of Faiths, which convened in London in 1936, notable for its allowing actual discussion between the participants, and not just the giving of lectures. In spite of Younghusband's own beliefs, the Congress reached the opinion that the desirable end of its activity was the spread of understanding and a sense of unity between different religious communions.

Following the Congress a continuing committee was set up as the World Congress of Faiths (Continuation Movement). Subsequent conferences were held in 1937, 1938, and 1939. Then its work was curtailed by World War II. Younghusband died in 1942. The Congress moved forward through the succeeding decades, largely on the shoulders of a few people dedicated to interfaith activity and often in the face of many Christians who felt that interfaith commitments called into question the truth claims of Christianity. In 1949 a journal, *World Faiths* (now *World Faiths Encounter*), was begun, currently the oldest interfaith periodical in circulation. During the last decades of the 20th century, the successes of the Congress were in large part the result of the long tenure of its general director, Marcus Braybrooke, an Anglican priest who also served as editor for *World Faiths*. In 2004, the archbishop of Canterbury awarded Braybrooke an honorary doctorate for his "contribution to the development of inter-religious co-operation and understanding throughout the world."

In 1993, in cooperation with the International Association for Religious Freedom and Westminster College, Oxford, the World Congress was able to put together an endowment for the International Interfaith Centre, inaugurated in Oxford on December 6, 1993. In part inspired by the centennial of the World's Parliament of Religions, and a perception of an increasing amount and variety of interfaith activity around the world, leaders of the congress came to believe that a need existed for an international interfaith center that was informed about interfaith work globally and could offer encouragement to continuing interfaith understanding and cooperation.

World Congress of Faiths
c/o London Inter Faith Centre
125 Salusbury Rd.
London, NW6 6RG
UK
http://www.worldfaiths.org/

International Interfaith Centre
http://www.interfaith-center.org/

J. Gordon Melton

See also: Council for a Parliament of the World's
Religions; International Association for Religious
Freedom.

References
Braybrooke, Marcus. *Beacons of the Light: 100 Holy
People Who Have Shaped the History of Human-
ity*. Oxford: O Books, 2009.
Braybrooke, Marcus. *A Heart for the World: A
Program to Transform the World Based on Non-
violence and Compassion*. Oxford: O Books,
2006.
Braybrooke, Marcus. *Inter-Faith Organizations,
1893–1979: An Historical Directory*. New York:
Edwin Mellen, 1980.
Braybrooke, Marcus. *Wider Vision: A History of the
World Congress of Faiths*. Oxford: Oneworld,
1996.

World Convention of Churches of Christ

The World Convention of Churches of Christ grew out
of an attempt to revive the fellowship that had been
broken between the various segments of the Restoration movement that had begun around the revivalistic
efforts on the American frontier of Barton Stone (1772–
1844), Thomas Campbell (1763–1854), Alexander
Campbell (1788–1866), Walter Scott (1796–1861), and
others during the first decades of the 19th century. Most
of the leaders had formerly been ministers in Presbyterian and Baptist churches. As the movement grew
over the century, it also developed some differences,
primarily concerning the development of structures
serving the larger community of congregations. One
wing of the movement remains fiercely congregational,
and rejects any structures tending toward denominational structures. These differences led to the formation of three separate fellowships: the Christian Church
(Disciples of Christ), the Christian Churches and
Churches of Christ, and the Churches of Christ (Non-
instrumental).

In spite of their differences, the three bodies share
a number of agreed-upon principles, 10 of which stand
out: (1) a concern for Christian unity, (2) a commitment to evangelism and mission, (3) an emphasis on
the centrality of the New Testament, (4) a simple
Confession of Faith, (5) believer's baptism, (6) weekly
Communion, (7) a biblical name, (8) congregational autonomy, (9) lay leadership, and (10) diversity/freedom/
liberty.

An initial attempt to bridge the divisive forces in
the Restoration movement culminated in the first meeting of the World Convention of Churches of Christ
in 1930. With an interruption due to World War II, the
Convention has met regularly every five years, and
more recently every four years. The Convention unites
congregations in 168 countries that have their heritage
in the 19th-century Restoration movement. The Convention is primarily for fellowship, the tradition being
opposed to pan-congregational structures.

World Convention of Churches of Christ
1279 Brentwood Highlands Drive
Nashville, TN 37211
http://users.aol.com/worldconv/

J. Gordon Melton

See also: Christian Church (Disciples of Christ);
Christian Churches and Churches of Christ; Churches
of Christ (Non-instrumental).

References
Foster, Douglas A., et al., eds. *The Encyclopedia of
the Stone-Campbell Movement*. Grand Rapids,
MI: William B. Eerdmans Publishing Company,
2004.
World Convention of Churches of Christ. http://users
.aol.com/worldconv/. Accessed April 24, 2009.

World Council of Biblical Churches

The World Council of Biblical Churches is an international association of separatist fundamentalist
Christian denominations. It was organized in 1987,
originally taking the name Council of Bible Believing
Churches International, following the break between
the American Council of Christian Churches (ACCC)

and the International Council of Christian Churches (ICCC). In the 1930s, the more conservative wing of U.S. Protestantism, known as Fundamentalists, split into two factions. One, the evangelicals, agreed to work with conservative colleagues who remained within the larger liberal Protestant church bodies. The other faction, the Fundamentalists, demanded that their colleagues completely renounce and separate from the larger Protestant groups, which they believed had become apostate. Under the leadership of Presbyterian minister Carl McIntire (1906–2002), the Fundamentalists founded the ACCC.

In 1948, occasioned by the founding of the World Council of Churches, McIntire called together conservative church leaders from around the world to form the ICCC. From 1948 to 1969 the two organizations worked together, but then in 1969, the ACCC removed McIntire from its board. In the ensuing controversy, the ICCC sided with McIntire, and the two organizations discontinued their relationship.

For the next few years, the ACCC operated without an international affiliate, but in 1987 it led in the founding of the Council of Bible Believing Churches International. The Council sees itself primarily as an issue-oriented body designed to address with a united voice the primary topics facing Fundamentalist Christians globally.

As a Fundamentalist organization, the Council affirms the infallibility and inerrancy of the Bible and the importance of complete separation from heresy and apostasy. The World Council of Churches and its member churches are viewed as heretical organizations. The Council also opposes all accommodation to "Romanism, Ecumenism, Materialism, Communism," and any other movement or group that teaches anything contrary to sound doctrine.

Members of the Council cannot be associated in any manner with the World Council of Churches or any of its affiliates; the World Evangelical Alliance or any of its affiliates; or the ICCC or any of its affiliates. The Council also opposes the modern Pentecostal/Charismatic movement. Between gatherings, the World Council of Biblical Churches is headed by an executive committee consisting of representatives from each member body. It shares headquarters space with the American Council of Christian Churches.

World Council of Biblical Churches
625 E. 4th St.
PO Box 5455
Bethlehem, PA 18015

J. Gordon Melton

See also: Fundamentalism; International Council of Christina Churches; World Council of Churches; World Evangelical Alliance.

Reference

Falwell, Jerry. *The Fundamentalist Phenomenon.* Garden City, NY: Doubleday, 1981.

World Council of Churches

The World Council of Churches (WCC) is the primary organizational expression of the 20th-century ecumenical movement within the Christian community. Beginning in the 19th century and continuing through the first half of the 20th, Protestant Christian leaders from around the world voiced their concern that the splintering of the Protestant movement into hundreds of denominations was a scandal to the church. They called for new organized expressions of Christian unity. Such expressions began with agreements to stop direct competition on the mission field, and it grew into major conferences that focused issues around broad areas of Faith and Order (theological and ecclesiastical issues) and of Life and Work (the mission and activity of the church in the world).

Three important organizations operated through the early 20th century: the Universal Christian Council of Life and Work, the Continuation Committee of the World Conference on Faith and Order, and the International Missionary Movement. In 1933 prominent U.S. theologian William Adams Brown suggested to Archbishop William Temple of the Church of England that these three organizations enter into conversations with the World Alliance for International Friendship and the Student Christian Movement about a common future. From conversations initiated by Temple, a proposal to form a World Council of Churches was promulgated in 1937. Work on the constitution began the next year.

Slowed by World War II, the Council was not inaugurated until 1948, when delegates from a variety of their presence known in their dissent from the thrust of various Council activities centered on theological and liturgical innovation and involvement in controversial social programs. In the late 1990s, several of the more conservative Orthodox churches resigned from the Council, and others have threatened to resign.

The work of the World Council is carried out through the meetings of its general assembly and a program centered on the international headquarters in Switzerland. There are four internal administrative groupings, with a focus upon Issues and Themes; Relationships; Communication; and Finance, Services, and Administration. None operate as self-contained entities, working instead in an interdependent relationship with all the others. The Council has specialized in dialogue, which it promotes at all levels. The work of the Council is extended by the efforts of a variety of regional, national, and local church councils, as well as the efforts of structures that promote dialogue and cooperation within a single Christian family, such as the World Methodist Council and the Anglican Communion. The World Alliance of Reformed Churches, the Ecumenical Patriarchate, and the Lutheran World Federation have their offices in the same building that houses the World Council.

Nobel peace laureates Archbishop Desmond Tutu of South Africa, right, and Adolfo Perez Esquivel of Argentina light candles during a march by the 9th Assembly of the World Council of Churches in Porto Alegre, Brazil, on February 21, 2006. (AP/Wide World Photos)

As of 2009, the World Council of Churches included more than 349 member churches based in some 110 countries representing over 560 million Christians. Membership runs the spectrum of Christian belief and practice from quite liberal and socially engaged churches to more conservative and evangelistically oriented. It includes most of the large international Protestant and Orthodox churches. Originally founded as a largely European and North American organization, currently the majority of WCC membership is from churches based in Africa, Asia, the Caribbean, Latin America, the Middle East, and the Pacific. Internationally, the work of the Council is made effective by its various regional councils such as the All Africa Council of Churches, the Middle East Council of Churches, the Caribbean Council of Churches, the Latin American Council of Churches, and the Pacific Conference of Churches. National councils affiliated with the World Council also operate in most countries. In most of the regional and national councils, the Roman Catholic Church is also intimately involved.

Protestant and Orthodox bodies gathered in Amsterdam. Its formation was opposed by a small group of the more Fundamentalist churches, which that same year formed the International Council of Christian Churches (ICCC). The ICCC should not be confused with the World Council.

The World Council has served as a fellowship of most of the larger Protestant and Orthodox Christian churches in the world. During the decades of its existence, it has assisted the process by which its North American and European members have granted autonomy to former mission churches around the world, and the Council's membership has grown considerably as it has welcomed these churches into its midst. Through the 1990s, the Orthodox churches have made

The Council has a special status for affiliated regional and national councils of churches, and for the organizations representing the various world Christian communions. Its Internet sites contain the Internet addresses of its member churches and affiliated organizations.

The Council describes itself as "a fellowship of churches that confess the Lord Jesus Christ as God and Savior according to the scriptures and therefore seek to fulfill together their common calling to the glory of the one God, Father, Son and Holy Spirit." This wording has been accepted as a bridge to the Council's primary function of bringing Christians of different persuasions into dialogue. It provides a basis for agreement without making the arena so narrow as to exclude churches that do not affirm particular items of traditional orthodox Christianity. Because of its relative openness, it has been accused by more conservative believers of being open to liberal and heretical views, and, increasingly, conservative churches have refused to participate in its programs. The primary alternative to the World Council of Churches has been provided by the World Evangelical Alliance, which, through the 1980s and 1990s, has established a set of regional and national councils of conservative churches and missionary agencies that parallels that of the WCC.

Most of the churches of the Anglican, Lutheran, Reformed/Presbyterian, Congregationalist, Methodist, and Orthodox traditions are members, while a relatively small number of Baptist, Holiness, and Pentecostal bodies are related. Although the Roman Catholic Church (RCC) is not a member, there are close links with it. The WCC/RCC joint working group meets annually, and the WCC Faith and Order Commission includes Roman Catholics who are members with full voting rights. The Council has built cordial relationships with the Pontifical Council for Promoting Christian Unity, the primary structure growing out of the Second Vatican Council to conduct ecumenical dialogue by the Roman Catholic Church. The Council conducts dialogue with leaders of the other major religious traditions through its Office for Inter-religious Relations.

World Council of Churches
PO Box 2100

150 route de Ferney
CH-1211
Geneva 2
Switzerland
http://www.wcc-coe.org

J. Gordon Melton

See also: All Africa Conference of Churches; Caribbean Conference of Churches; Ecumenical Patriarchate/Patriarchate of Constantinople; International Council of Christian Churches; Latin American Council of Churches; Lutheran World Federation; Middle East Council of Churches; Pacific Conference of Churches; Roman Catholic Church; World Alliance of Reformed Churches; World Evangelical Alliance; World Methodist Council.

References

Kinnamon, Michael, and Brian Cope, eds. *The Ecumenical Movement: An Anthology of Key Texts and Voices.* Geneva: World Council of Churches, 1997.

Raiser, Conrad. *To Be the Church: Challenges and Hopes for a New Millennium.* Geneva: World Council of Churches, 1997.

Van Beek, Huibert. *A Handbook of Churches and Councils: Profiles of Ecumenical Relationships.* Geneva: World Council of Churches, 2006.

Van der Bent, Ans J., ed. *Handbook of Member Churches: World Council of Churches.* Geneva: World Council of Churches, 1982.

Yearbook. Geneva: World Council of Churches, issued annually.

World Evangelical Alliance

What is now known as the World Evangelical Alliance developed among the new generation of Protestant and Free church evangelical Christians following World War II, but it traces its organizational identity to the Evangelical Alliance that formed in England in 1846. The Alliance was an early expression of the Christian ecumenical movement, an organizational expression of Christian unity. The original gathering, held in London, brought together representatives of some 52 denominations from Europe and North America. The delegates had responded to a number of calls for such an alliance that had been issued by Christian leaders for several decades.

The initial organization was seen as an association of individual Christians, rather than a confederation of churches. A doctrinal statement emphasizing both the authority of the scriptures and the need for individual interpretation was adopted, along with statements on the Trinity, human depravity, and salvation through Jesus Christ. The development of a strong international organization foundered on the question of slavery, still a fact of life in the United States. Thus power was passed to a series of national alliances, the first established in England, Canada, Germany, and Sweden. Indian and Turkish chapters were opened in 1849 and 1855, respectively. No U.S. branch was formed until 1867, after the Civil War had settled the slavery issue.

The European branches of the Alliance have continued active. However, the U.S. branch became inactive at the beginning of the 20th century, and its corporation was formally dissolved in 1944 and its assets turned over to the Federal Council of Churches (now the national Council of Churches in the U.S.A.). Work in America had fallen victim to the Fundamentalist-Modernist controversy. Out of the controversy, in the early 1940s the more forward-looking among the conservative evangelicals organized the National Association of Evangelicals.

In the years following World War II, evangelical leaders began again to look for some kind of international cooperation. Initial contacts resulted in the calling of a meeting to be held at Woudschiten, near Zeist, in The Netherlands, August 5–11, 1951, at which time the World Evangelical Fellowship (WEF) was created. A brief doctrinal statement was adopted and three purposes accepted. The WEF would direct its activities to the furtherance of the gospel, the defense and confirmation of the gospel, and fellowship in the gospel. An initial outreach tour was conducted by several WEF leaders to determine needs within the global evangelical community. Within the first year, six national evangelical fellowships had affiliated with WEF—Ceylon (Sri Lanka), Cyprus, Great Britain, India, Japan, and the United States. Six more—Singapore, Hawaii, Switzerland, Germany, France, and Holland—joined at the first meeting in 1952.

The WEF subsequently grew into a worldwide network of more than 120 national/regional evangelical church alliances, 104 organizational ministries, and 6 specialized ministries. In 2001, the WEF voted to change its name to World Evangelical Alliance. It is headed by an international executive council, whose members are drawn from every region of the world. It operates through seven regional bodies that in turn coordinate the activity of national bodies in their region. The World Evangelical Alliance serves those more conservative evangelical Christians who do not identify with the World Council of Churches, whose stance they consider too liberal.

In 2009, the Alliance coordinated a network of churches in 128 nations, each nation having formed a national evangelical alliance, and of some 100 international organizations. Together the member churches and organization represent more than 420 million people.

World Evangelical Alliance
13351 Commerce Parkway, Ste. 1153
Richmond, BC
V6V 2X7
Canada
http://www.worldevangelical.org/

J. Gordon Melton

See also: Evangelicalism; Fundamentalism; World Council of Churches.

References

Fuller, W. Harold. *People of the Mandate*. Carlisle, UK: Paternoster; Grand Rapids, MI: Baker, 1996.

Howard, David M. *The Dream That Would Not Die: The Birth and Growth of the World Evangelical Fellowship, 1846–1986*. Exeter, UK: Paternoster, 1986.

Klauber, Martin, and Scott M. Manetsch, eds. *The Great Commission: Evangelicals and the History of World Missions*. Nashville: Broadman & Holman Books, 2008.

World Fellowship of Buddhists

The World Fellowship of Buddhists (WFB) is an international organization, founded on May 25, 1950, and

The Dalai Lama, right, presents a Buddhist image to Kaiko Kanto, General Secretary of the All-Japan Buddhist Association, in October 1978, at the Zojoji Temple in Tokyo during the 12th conference of the World Fellowship of Buddhists. (AP/Wide World Photos)

inaugurated at its first general conference in Colombo (Sri Lanka) that same year. This was probably the first time in the history of Buddhism that representatives from nearly every school of Buddhism in the Theravada, Mahayana, and Tibetan traditions gathered to share their mutual understanding and Buddhist activities. The WFB is the best known Buddhist organization recognized by the state and the *sangha* around the world.

According to the WFB constitution, the general conference is to be held once in every two years. The president holds office for a term of four years, and his or her country is the place of the organization's headquarters. Accordingly, the first WFB headquarters was in Colombo. The respected scholar Dr. G. P. Malalasekera (1899–1973) was the WFB's first president, from 1950 to 1958. In the time of the WFB's second president, Hon. U. Chan Htoon (from 1958 to 1961), the

headquarters was in Burma. Afterward, all WFB presidents have been Thais, and thus the headquarters is permanently situated in Bangkok, as adopted at the WFB ninth general conference in 1969.

The WFB has the following aims and objectives: (1) to promote among the members strict observance and practice of the teachings of the Buddha; (2) to secure unity, solidarity, and brotherhood among Buddhists; (3) to propagate the teachings of the Buddha; (4) to organize and carry on activities in the field of social, educational, cultural, and humanitarian services; and (5) to work for securing peace and harmony among men and happiness for all beings, and to collaborate with other organizations working for the same ends.

Inasmuch as the WFB organization is composed of different Buddhist denominations, all members learn to accept each other's beliefs, worship, and practices. In the first WFB conference, some significant resolutions were adopted. The Dharmacakra (Wheel of the Law), with eight spokes representing the Noble Eightfold Path, was adopted as the international Buddhist symbol, and the six-color Buddhist flag, at that time in use in Sri Lanka, was adopted as the international Buddhist flag. The term "Hinayana" in all contexts was replaced by the term "Theravada." In the historical context, there was a stage when the Mahayanists, as a derogatory remark, called some of the earlier Buddhists followers of the lesser vehicle (Hinayana) while they believed that they were following the greater vehicle (Mahayana).

The WFB is a traditional rather than a controversial organization. According to its constitution, it refrains from involving itself directly or indirectly in any political activity. Currently, its patrons include, among others, the supreme patriarch of Thailand, the head of the Sri Lankan Sangha, the king of Thailand, the king of Nepal, and the president of the republic of India.

The organization is led by an elected president and the Office Bearers (15 vice presidents, 9 chairpersons of standing committees, an honorary secretary-general, an honorary deputy secretary-general, an honorary assistant secretary-general, and an honorary treasurer). According to the WFB, the duties and responsibilities of standing committees are particularly important and beneficial to all people. For example, the Standing Committee of Publication, Publicity, Education, Culture, and Art can work for the knowledge and peace of Buddhists and non-Buddhists, as can the Humanitarian Services Committee.

Nowadays, missions and activities of the WFB are carried on through its 147 regional centers in 37 countries in Asia, Europe, Africa, and North America (including Hawaii). It maintains Formal Consultative Relations with the United Nations Educational, Scientific and Cultural Organization (UNESCO) as a Category B nongovernmental organization, to represent the Buddhist point of view on matters relating to education, culture, and communication in UNESCO conferences and meetings. It has also been recognized as a nongovernmental organization (Category I), cooperating with the United Nations in the domains of peace, human rights, and development. The WFB has proposed to UNESCO that the Vesakh Day be recognized as the International Day. The proposition was well approved.

At present, the Vesakh Day is considered by all WFB members as the World Meditation Day that contributes to World Peace.

The true number of members within the WFB is unknown. It covers all Buddhists who join activities of regional centers around the world. The number of delegates and observers who join each WFB general conference is approximately 500.

The World Fellowship of Buddhists
616 Benjasiri Park
Soi Medhinivet
Off Soi Sukhumvit 24
Sukhumvit Road
Bangkok 10110
Thailand
http: //www.wfb-hq.org

Pataraporn Sirikanchana

See Also: Buddhism.

References
Guruge, Ananda W. P. "The Buddha's Contribution to Humanity and World Peace: Keynote Address." *Journal of the World Buddhist University*, vol. 4, no. 1 (2007): 8–30.
Miyabara, Sunao. *A History of the World Fellowship of Buddhists 2493 B.E. (1950) to 2533 B.E. (1990)*. Bangkok: Darnsuttha Press Co., Ltd., 1994.
Sirikanchana, Pataraporn. *A Guide to Buddhist Monasteries and Meditation Centres in Thailand*. Bangkok: The Printing House of Thammasat University, 2004.
World Fellowship of Buddhists. *Record of Proceedings: The 23rd General Conference of the World Fellowship of Buddhists (WFB); The 14th General Conference of the World Fellowship of Buddhist Youth (WFB Y); The 6th Meeting of the World Buddhist University (WBU) Council*. Bangkok: The Printing House of Thammasat University, 2008.

World Methodist Council

Formed in 1951, the World Methodist Council (WMC) continues the intra-Methodist cooperative activity that

Participants of the World Methodist Council float balloons symbolizing peace on the Korean peninsula during a prayer meeting in Paju, near the inter-Korean border, July 23, 2006. (Getty Images)

began in 1881 with the first Ecumenical Methodist Conference that assembled in London. Attendees at the first conference represented primarily the various North American and British organizations into which the Methodist movement had splintered through the 19th century. The ecumenical conferences continued to meet every decade until the 1941 meeting was stopped by World War II. The desire to reunite the several churches into which both the British and Americans had split and the wish of American and British Methodists to keep fraternal relations strong fueled the meetings through the middle of the 20th century.

Significant changes in world Methodism led to the Council's creation. The larger American churches participated in a series of mergers (1939, 1946, and 1968) that led to the creation of the United Methodist Church; similar mergers in England led to the present Methodist Church. The constituent bodies of both churches had

created a far-flung international missionary endeavor, and following World War II they began the process by which most of the missions were transformed into autonomous church bodies. This process was recognized in 1951 with the change of name of the Ecumenical Conference to the World Methodist Conference, and the establishment of a permanent secretariat.

In 1953 the Council's permanent headquarters was established at the Methodist campground at Lake Junaluska, North Carolina. Elmer T. Clark (1886–1966), the Council's first secretary for the Western Hemisphere, took the lead in the construction of the headquarters building and organized the following WMC conferences at Lake Junaluska (1956) and Oslo, Norway (1961). The conferences have continued to meet at five-year intervals.

The program of the WMC includes efforts to support Methodist education, strengthen family life in the various cultures, sponsor worldwide evangelism programs, develop worship and liturgical life in the churches, sponsor youth work, promote Methodist publishing worldwide, and provide an annual program of world exchange of clergy and laity. Through the quinquennial Oxford Institute of Methodist Theological Studies (where the Wesley brothers, George Whitefield, and others met in the earliest Methodist gatherings), WMC facilitates scholarly studies and timely theological reflection.

Between meetings, the work of the Council is entrusted to an executive committee and an executive staff headed by the general secretary. At the 2001 meeting, the general secretary, Joe Hale, who had held the post for 25 years, retired and was succeeded by the Reverend George Freeman. The Geneva office is currently led by the Reverend Denis Dutton, past bishop of the Methodist Church of Malaysia. The current chairperson of the World Methodist Council is His Eminence Sunday Mbang of the Methodist Church Nigeria. He succeeded Frances Werner Alguire, the first female chairperson. Churches from 108 countries are members of the Council.

World Methodist Council
545 N. Lakeshore Dr.
Lake Junaluska, NC 28745

J. Gordon Melton

See also: Methodist Church, Nigeria; Methodist Church of Malaysia; United Methodist Church; Wesley, John.

References

Harmon, Nolan B. *Encyclopedia of World Methodism.* 2 vols. Nashville: United Methodist Publishing House, 1974.

World Methodist Council. Handbook of Information, 2002–2006. Lake Junaluska, NC: World Methodist Council, 2006.

World Muslim Congress

The World Muslim Congress (Motamar Al-Alam Al-Islami), the oldest of the several organizations aimed at bringing unity to the Muslim global community, was founded in 1926 at a gathering of Muslim leaders hosted by King Abd al-Aziz ibn Sa'ud of Saudi Arabia. At a second gathering, held in Jerusalem in 1931, a constitution with the necessary rule and regulations was adopted for an organization that could promote solidarity among Muslims and cooperation on a global scale. Alhaj Aminul Husseini, the grand mufti of Palestine, was elected as one of the presidents. In the 1930s the idea of the congress fell by the wayside, but it was revived in the wake of the founding of the nation of Pakistan in 1947. A revived World Muslim Congress met at Karachi, Pakistan, in 1949. Those who gathered sought to unite Muslims against the newly independent India, from which Pakistan had broken away, and the newly formed nation of Israel.

At a second meeting, in 1951, the revived organization began to take shape, and permanent headquarters were established in Karachi. Alhaj Aminul Husseini continued as the organization's president. Proposals were accepted for the development of a World Muslim News Agency and the founding of a bank for the development of the Muslim community internationally.

Of the several Islamic cooperative organizations, such as the Muslim World League, the World Muslim Congress has been the least defined by the political concerns of the Muslim community. This has not, however, kept it from speaking out on various issues of particular concern for Muslims, such as the persecution of Muslims in minority situations, the struggles of Muslims in the Middle East, and, most recently, expressions of solidarity with the Muslims of Bosnia. However, it has shown a particular interest in the religious expression of Islam, and its leaders have attempted to represent Islam in numerous interfaith conferences.

The Congress periodically sponsors international conferences, the most recent of which met in Pakistan in 2000. Dr. Abdullah Bin Omar Nasseef of Saudi Arabia currently serves as president. Mir Nawaz Khan Marwat, the assistant secretary general, is in charge of the office in Karachi. Its work is carried out through a number of regional offices that range from Beijing, China, to South Africa and London. North American offices are located in Miami, Florida.

In 1987, the Congress received the Niwano Peace Prize from Japan, and the following year, Dr. Inamullah Khan, then the secretary general of the Modern World Muslim Congress, was awarded the Templeton Prize for progress in religion.

The Congress enjoys consultative status with the United Nations through its Economic and Social Council and UNICEF, and observer status with the Organization of the Islamic Conference.

World Muslim Congress
9-A, Block-7, Gulshan-e-Iqbal
PO Box 5030
University Rd.
Karachi-74000
Pakistan
http://www.motamaralalamalislami.org/

J. Gordon Melton

See also: Abd al-Aziz ibn Sa'ud; Islam; Muslim World League.

Reference

Burdett, Anita L. P. *Islamic Movements in the Arab World, 1913–1966.* 4 vols. Slough, UK: Archive.

World Plan Executive Council

See Global Country of World Peace.

World Reformed Fellowship

The World Reformed Fellowship was formed in October 2000 by the merger of two ecumenical associations operating among conservative churches of the Reformed tradition: the World Fellowship of Reformed Churches (WFRC) and the International Reformed Fellowship (IRF). The World Fellowship of Reformed Churches, formed in 1992, brought together the National Presbyterian Church of Mexico, the Presbyterian Church of Brazil, and the Presbyterian Church of America. The World Evangelical Fellowship (WEF) was a catalyst for the formation of the World Fellowship as it existed under the WEF umbrella, and it held its meetings in conjunction with WEF assemblies. The organization considered the situation of evangelical churches in the Reformed tradition in the Western Hemisphere. Among the affiliated Spanish-speaking churches, 14 formed the Confraternidad Latinoamericana de Iglesias Reformadas, which initiated several missionary consultations concerning Latin America.

The International Reformed Fellowship was formed in 1992 in Pasadena, California, and was in its early years notable for the strong participation of Korean Presbyterian churches. Like the WFRC, the IRF assumed a conservative theological stance and opposed the contemporary theological trends it saw embedded in the World Council of Churches and the associated World Alliance of Reformed Churches.

The new fellowship found agreement in adherence to the Westminster Confession of Faith, the formative document of the Presbyterian tradition, and in contemporary standards accepted by many conservative evangelicals concerning the authority of scripture, affirming the Bible's infallibility and inerrancy. The 23 original member churches were drawn from 23 countries. In 2009, the fellowship reported 42 member churches from around the world; in addition there are a number of organizations and local churches that have affiliated.

World Reformed Fellowship
430 Montier Road
Glenside, PA 19038
http://www.wrfnet.org/

J. Gordon Melton

See also: Reformed Ecumenical Council; World Alliance of Reformed Churches; World Council of Churches.

Reference

Green, Bill. "Is There a Need for a Reformed Fellowship?" http://www.reformedmissions.org/fellowship.htm. Accessed July 30, 2001.

World Religion Day

World Religion Day, observed worldwide on the third Sunday of January each year, is a Baha'i-inspired idea that has taken on a life of its own. In 2009, for instance, the Halifax (Nova Scotia) Regional Municipality in Canada celebrated its sixth annual World Religion Day in the Cathedral of All Saints, in recognition of which the mayor and councilors of the Halifax Regional Municipality issued a proclamation. In 2007, at the World Religion Day event hosted by the Entebbe Municipal Council of Entebbe, Uganda (situated on the northern shores of Lake Victoria, Africa's largest lake), participating religious leaders signed a joint declaration to establish the Entebbe Inter-Faith Coalition. The signatories pledged to use "the unifying power of religion to instill in the hearts and minds of all people of faith the fundamental facts and spiritual standards that have been laid down by our Creator to bring them together as members of one family."

As these examples illustrate, World Religion Day is now observed internationally, its American Baha'i origins notwithstanding. The history of World Religion Day dates back to 1949, when the National Spiritual Assembly of the Baha'is of the United States (the national Baha'i governing council) instituted an annual World Religion Day "to be observed publicly by the Baha'i Communities wherever possible throughout the United States." Then as now, the third Sunday of January each year was designated for this celebration. The first World Religion Day event took place on January 15, 1950, and was observed by Baha'i communities across the United States.

The Baha'i Faith, among the younger of the independent world religions, emphasizes unity in the human community, and the inauguration of World Religion

Day could be seen simply as a natural expression of the Baha'i focus on the unity of religions, races, and nations. However, interfaith association was not the exclusive, nor even the primary original purpose of World Religion Day. In 1968, the Universal House of Justice, the international Baha'i governing body established in 1963, wrote: "Your letter of September 30, with the suggestion that 'there should be one day in the year in which all of the religions should agree' is a happy thought, and one which persons of good will throughout the world might well hail. However, this is not the underlying concept of World Religion Day, which is a celebration of the need for and the coming of a world religion for mankind, the Baha'i Faith itself. Although there have been many ways of expressing the meaning of this celebration in Baha'i communities in the United States, the Day was not meant primarily to provide a platform for all religions and their emergent ecumenical ideas. In practice, there is no harm in the Baha'i communities' inviting the persons of other religions to share their platforms on this Day, providing the universality of the Baha'i Faith as the fulfillment of the hopes of mankind for a universal religion are clearly brought forth" (*Lights of Guidance*, no. 1710).

While proclaiming the Baha'i Faith as the advent of a "universal religion" for humankind remains a constant among Baha'i sponsors of World Religion Day, the emphasis has slowly shifted over time. In a sample press release for Baha'i communities to use as a model, the following statement is made: "Baha'is celebrate the day by hosting discussions, conferences, and other events which foster understanding and communication between the followers of all religions. The purpose of World Religion Day is to call attention to the harmony of spiritual principles and the oneness of the world's religions and to emphasize that world religion is the motivating force for world unity." The wording of this model press release was likely based on a 2002 story on World Religion Day, published by the Baha'i World News Service.

In April 2002, the Universal House of Justice issued a letter addressed "To the World's Religious Leaders," in which interfaith dialogue is highly regarded. However, the letter states that the initiatives of the interfaith movement of the 20th century—as the progeny of the historic World's Columbian Exposition's

World's Parliament of Religions (Chicago, 1893) did, in fact, "lack both intellectual coherence and spiritual commitment." For its part, "the Baha'i community has been a vigorous promoter of interfaith activities from the time of their inception" and will continue to assist, valuing the "cherished associations" that these activities create. The letter stresses the paramount importance of the universally recognizing that "religion is one" as a unific truth that can effectively dispel religious prejudice: "We owe it to our partners in this common effort, however, to state clearly our conviction that interfaith discourse, if it is to contribute meaningfully to healing the ills that afflict a desperate humanity, must now address honestly . . . the implications of the overarching truth . . . that God is one and that, beyond all diversity of cultural expression and human interpretation, religion is likewise one."

While neither the Universal House of Justice nor the National Spiritual Assembly of the Baha'is of the United States currently plays an active role in promoting World Religion Day events, the Baha'i International Community (an official organ of the Universal House of Justice) has consistently reported on such events, with obvious appreciation.

The process of World Religion Day taking on a life of its own has been punctuated by several notable events. On January 20, 2007, in Brazzaville, the Republic of the Congo became the second country to issue a postage stamp for World Religion Day. Featuring a globe surrounded by the symbols of 11 religions, the stamp bears a French superscription which, translated, reads: "God is the source of all religions." Following a World Religion Day program that drew more than 250 participants from 8 faith-communities, agents were present to sell both the stamps and first-day covers. In 1985, Sri Lanka had become the first country to issue a World Religion Day stamp.

The purpose of World Religion Day today is to highlight the essential harmony of the world's religions; to foster their trans-confessional affinity through interfaith ecumenism; and to promote the idea and ideal of world unity, in which the world's religions can play a potentially significant role. This generalization is based on observations of how World Religion Day is celebrated in events that are sponsored by organizations that are not Baha'i, whether in concert with local

Baha'i sponsorship or entirely independent of it. (In most cases, the Baha'is continue to play a vital role in the orchestration and success of these events.) The day is celebrated with interfaith dialogue, conferences, and other events that advance not only mutual understanding (or what scholars call "spiritual literacy"), but recognition, respect, and reciprocity among the followers of all religions who join together in celebrating World Religion Day.

Where observed, World Religion Day events typically do not attract representatives and participants from *all* local faith communities, primarily for religious reasons. As such, World Religion Day provides an insightful social barometer of the extent to which various religious groups are willing to formally associate with each other. While World Religion Day events are still sponsored and co-sponsored by local members of the Baha'i Faith worldwide, an increasing number of World Religion Day events are independently organized by interfaith or multi-faith coalitions. For instance, in Tralee, Ireland, the local World Religion Day observance was organized by the Kerry Diocesan Justice, Peace and Creation Committee, a Member Organisation of Pax Christi International in Ireland. In 2009 the third annual observance of World Religion Day in Greensboro, North Carolina, was organized by FaithAction and the Piedmont Interfaith Council. Also in 2009, World Religion Day was celebrated by Vadamalayan Hospitals and Vadamalayan Institute of Paramedical Sciences, in which a quiz competition was held to mark the occasion.

In certain cases, civic governments, both national and local, have tended to recognize the positive social value of World Religion Day events, perhaps more than the non-participating religious communities themselves, taken together, have been willing to admit. In 2004, for instance, the House of Representatives of the General Assembly of the Commonwealth of Kentucky proclaimed January 17–18, 2004, as "World Religion Weekend" and went on to "urge the Commonwealth's citizens to participate in the observance of World Religion Weekend." In 2007, the Republic of Ghana's Secretariat organized a symposium themed "The Unity of the Faiths" on World Religion Day on Sunday, February 18, 2007. In January 2008, the City Council of Duncan, British Columbia (Canada) proclaimed January 20, 2008, as World Religion Day. In a 2009 World Religion Day event in Australia, Parliamentary Secretary for Multicultural Affairs and Settlement Services Laurie Ferguson declared, on behalf of the government of Australia: "Interfaith dialogue plays an important role in increasing understanding of our nation's religious and cultural diversity and bringing Australians closer together. The Australian Government supports interfaith dialogue at the highest levels." Many World Religion Day Events are associated with mayoral or municipal proclamations.

World Religion Day is self-perpetuating, thanks to the initiatives of progressive individuals and institutions who share a vision of religious confraternity. It is an inspired idea, with widespread appeal and remarkable longevity.

Christopher Buck

See also: Baha'i Faith.

References

Baha'i Computer and Communications Association (BCCA). "World Religion Day" ("Sample Press Release"). http://www.bcca.org/orgs/usnsa/samples.html. Accessed September 30, 2009.

Baha'i International Community. "Congo Republic issues stamp for World Religion Day." *One Country* 18, no. 4 (January–March 2007).

Lights of Guidance: A Baha'i Reference File. Comp. by Helen Hornby. 6th ed. New Delhi, India: Baha'i Publishing Trust, 1999.

National Spiritual Assembly of the Baha'is of the United States. "World Religion Day." *Baha'i News,* no. 226 (December 1949): 5.

Parliamentary Secretary for Multicultural Affairs and Settlement Services. "World Religion Day 2009." http://www.minister.immi.gov.au/parlsec/media/media-releases/2009/lf09002.htm.

Universal House of Justice. "To the World's Religious Leaders," 2002.

Universal House of Justice. Letter dated October 22, 1968, to a Local Spiritual Assembly. *Lights of Guidance*, no. 1710.

World Religion Day Program (Lal Fernando, Director-General). http://www.worldreligionday.org.

World Sephardic Federation

The Sephardic Jewish community traces its origins to the Iberian Peninsula (Spain and Portugal), where a Jewish presence can be traced to the third century BCE during the days of imperial Rome. The community grew following the scattering of Jews from Palestine as a result of the destruction of the temple in 70 CE. Over the next centuries Christianity came to power in the region and Jews became subject to an increasing number of repressive and discriminatory measures. Then in 711, Arab Muslim forces invaded southern Spain and quickly overran the peninsula.

Islam would control the territory for the next centuries. In the eighth century, at the time that the Umayyad dynasty was replaced by the Abbasid dynasty in the Middle East, a member of the Umayyad family escaped to the western Mediterranean. His arrival in Spain became the occasion of the setting up of a new Umayyad dynasty in Spain and the independence of Spain from the formerly united Arab Muslim empire.

Under Muslim rule, the Jews of Spain enjoyed the protection of the Arab rulers as a people of the book, though the separation of Spain from the larger empire would mean that the Jews in Spain would be somewhat isolated from large segments of the developing Jewish community, especially as it grew in Germany and in the Christian-dominated lands farther to the east. Meanwhile in Spain, Jews participated in the high culture developed in Muslim Spain. Jewish philosophers and scientists would arise, and the community would enjoy the leadership of learned theologians and jurists. The height of Jewish life in Spain could be said to have occurred in the 12th century, during the time that Moses ben Mamon (more popularly known as Maimonides or Rambam) lived (1135–1205). Maimonides wrote three important Jewish texts, though he is best remembered for his third volume, *The Guide of the Perplexed* (1190), which synthesized Jewish thought with Aristotelian philosophy. He also developed a widely quoted summary of Orthodox Jewish belief. Maimonides' writings circulated widely and not only provoked a reaction from other segments of the Jewish community but also caused many Christians to respond to his thought. In Paris, the Dominicans burned his writings in a public ceremony.

Within Spain, one group of Jews, largely in reaction to Maimonides, created a circle of mystics who in turn began to produce texts partially inspired by neo-Platonism and the Jewish mystical text, the Zohar. This movement would have an effect upon the development of the Hassidic community in other parts of the Jewish world.

Shortly after Maimonides's death, Christian partisans in Iberia, never completely pacified, began a reconquest of the land. Over the next two centuries, various kingdoms were established, and the Jewish community entered a new era of discrimination and persecution. In the kingdom of Aragon intense efforts to convert the Jews to Christianity were pursued. The height of reaction to the Jewish presence came in Castile and Aragon in 1391, when violence broke out and over a period of several months many Jews were massacred. A significant number of conversions to Christianity were noted over the following decades. The conversions decimated the Jewish community in many urban areas and by the end of the 15th century, as modern Spain was being created, led to a call for the complete expulsion of the remaining followers of the Jewish faith. At the same time a reaction against the Jewish Christians set in, and beginning in 1449 they were denied government positions.

In 1480 the Inquisition was established in Spain, with the specific task of rooting out any heresies among Jewish and Muslims converts. For the Jews, it meant scrutiny for tendencies among Jewish Christians to continue practicing Judaism after their conversion, and the beginning of the legends of the Conversos (aka Marranos), the secret Jews who though outwardly operating as Christians, in their private and family lives continued to practice Judaism and pass it along to their children.

The emergence of the modern state of Spain—with the conquest of the remaining territory held by Muslims in the south and the union of the states of Castile and Navarre—culminated in the orders of 1491 (Portugal) and 1492 (Spain) for the complete expulsion of the Jews from the Iberian Peninsula. The great majority of the Jews who left at this time found their way to Muslim territory and established centers for the perpetuation of Sephardic traditions throughout the Ottoman Empire and across North Africa. Here they would

Indian Sephardic Jews place their hands to their faces as they take part in prayers at a synagogue in Aizawl, India, 2004. (AFP/Getty Images)

enjoy a new era of prosperity, and a number of outstanding scholars and political leaders would emerge. Some of these communities would quietly flourish until the late 20th century, when they would be decimated by the immigration of their members to Israel and to a lesser extent Western Europe and North America.

A smaller number moved to Holland and the other European countries. In Holland they were allowed to live somewhat peacefully, and Amsterdam became the new center of the Sephardic community. A smaller number of the expelled Jews relocated to the Americas. There is reason to believe that among the sailors who served with Christopher Columbus in his first voyage to the New World in 1492 were several Jews; a number of Portuguese Jews/Marranos relocated to Brazil. Some fled to Holland, possibly the most tolerant country of the era, where a new Jewish intelligent-

sia would develop. Possibly the most famous Dutch Jew is philosopher Baruch Spinoza (1632–1677).

In the early 1600s, the Netherlands attacked Brazil and established themselves in Recife. Jewish settlers emerged out of the population to found the first openly Jewish community in the Americas, Kahal Kodesh, the Holy Congregation. Unfortunately for them, Recife returned to Portuguese control in 1654. As a result, the members of the community were redistributed to Curacao in the Dutch West Indies, Surinam, and two North American locations, the Dutch colony of New Amsterdam (now New York) and the recently established Rhode Island colony. In the mid-1750s, Sephardic Jews organized the first Jewish community in Canada, in Halifax. A more permanent congregation, Shearith Israel, was later organized in Quebec. From Surinam and Curacao, the Sephardic community has spread across Latin America and now constitutes 15 to 20 percent of the whole. The beginnings of Judaism in both North and South America resulted from the Sephardic diaspora.

In the early 19th century, as German Jews began to arrive in force, many with Reformist tendencies, the German (Ashkenazi) and Sephardic Jews tended to go their separate ways. A small Sephardic presence remained, as first the Germans and then the Eastern Europeans came to dominate the Jewish community. Beginning in 1885, Sephardic life was established anew by the migration of Jews reacting to the decline of the Ottoman Empire. The mostly poor immigrants had difficulty integrating with the more affluent American Sephardic community.

In the meantime, in 1655, Oliver Cromwell found cause to admit the first Jews to England after their expulsion in the 13th century. Abraham Israel Carvajal (ca. 1590–1659) and his two sons received residency rights. As others arrived, Cromwell authorized a cemetery (but no public worship), the event from which the modern London Jewish community dates its existence. Cromwell saw the Jews as a vital source of information on England's perennial rival—Spain.

By the end of the 17th century, the Sephardic community was widely distributed across North Africa and the Middle East (the lands of the Ottoman Empire) and in scattered centers in the Americas and Europe. They resided in relative peace through the mid-20th century but were radically affected by the establishment of the nation of Israel and the growing enmity between Muslims and Jews in general over the Palestinian question. Through the last half of the 20th century, many of the old Sephardic Jewish communities in predominantly Muslim lands relocated to Israel, where they now form the largest segment of the Jewish community as a whole. (The Sephardic communities in the Balkans were largely destroyed by the Holocaust.) In 1984 a Sephardic party was founded in Israel, which through the 1990s became one of the largest political parties in the country.

In 1925, U.S. Sephardic Jews took the lead in founding the World Sephardic Federation in an attempt to build a cooperative network that could participate in the development of global Jewry. It became a strong supporter of the Zionist cause. At one level, the Sephardic community is integrated into the larger world

of Orthodox Judaism, and its synagogues are part of the several Orthodox Jewish congregation associations. At another level, Sephardic leaders have worked to keep Sephardic distinctives alive. In 1928, they founded a Union of Sephardic Congregations in New York.

The American Sephardic Federation, founded in 1951, is the World Sephardic Federation's strongest national affiliate. The European Sephardic community has a focus through the Institut Sépharade Européen. There are numerous Internet sites representative of the Sephardic community.

World Sephardic Federation
13 Rue Marignac
Geneva 1206
Switzerland
http://www.jafi.org.il/wsf/

American Sephardic Federation
15 W. 16th St.
6th Floor
New York, NY 10011
http://www.americansephardifederation.org/

J. Gordon Melton

See also: Hasidism; Orthodox Judaism.

References

Cohen, Martin A., and Abraham J. Peck, eds. *Sephardim in the Americas: Studies in Culture and History*. Tuscaloosa: University of Alabama Press, 1993.

Stillman, Norman A. *The Jews of Arab Lands in Modern Times*. Philadelphia: Jewish Publication Society of America, 1991.

Zohar, Zion. *Sephardic and Mizrahi Jewry: From the Golden Age of Spain to Modern Times*. New York: New York University Press, 2005.

World Vaisnava Association

The World Vaisnava Association (WVA) was founded in 1994 by a spectrum of leaders (*arcaryas* and *sannyasis*) representing organizations that had grown from the Gaudiya Math. The Gaudiya Math had emerged at the beginning of the 20th century as the leading voice in the revival of the monotheistic devotional form of

Vaisnava associated with Shri Chaitanya Mahaprabhu (ca. 1486–1533). In the last generation, beginning with the work of Srila A. C. Bhaktivedanta Prabhupada (1896–1977), the founder of the International Society for Krishna Consciousness (ISKCON), the devotional form of Vaisnavism spread from Bengal, India, around the world.

In the years following Prabhupada's death, ISKCON experienced a number of schisms over issues of guru leadership. Members asked whether the gurus who succeeded Prabhupada should be venerated in the same manner that he had been. Other gurus had problems with the governing body that assumed headship over the international movement. A few turned to teachers (gurus) associated with the Gaudiya Math for new leadership. ISKCON split into a number of competing organizations, several of which grew into large international groups.

Initially, several former ISKCON leaders met in Vrindavan with B. V. Tripurari Swami, B. G. Narasingha Swami, and B. A. Paramadvaiti to discuss the possibility of founding a new organization as an expression of the unity of the flourishing global movement that had emerged from the Gaudiya Math. The group met again in 1993 and made several decisions. First, they agreed to approach Srila B. P. Puri Maharaj, then 97 years old, the most senior Vaisnava then alive, who agreed to become the first president of the proposed organization. They also decided to invite the leadership from all the different related groups to participate as founders of what would become the World Vaisnava Association.

An initial edition of the *World Vaisnava Association Newsletter* was issued in February 1994 and distributed to all the ISKCON-related groups. It invited suggestions and participation in a founding meeting that was held in November 1994. Some 120 people were present, and 28 arcaryas and sannyasis became founding members. The Association was seen as a revival of the Visva Vaisnava Raj Sabha, originally founded by Srila Jiva Goswami in the 19th century.

In promoting the unity of the various member organizations, WVA seeks to help others understand what it thinks of as the real Hinduism Sanatan Dharma, its theism, and its answers to the problems of contemporary society. It seeks to motivate the leaders and adherents of the member organizations in their propagation of Vaisnavism and to promote the circulation of Vaisnava literature. It was agreed that the organization would seek to build respect and fraternal relations between the various member organizations and would not in any way compete with any of them. In that regard, WVA would not create any ashrams, nor facilitate the guru-disciple relationship.

Founding members of the association included: Chaitanya Math, the Gaudiya Vaisnava Society, Sri Chaitanya Math, ISEV (Il Instituto Superior de Estudios Vedicos), ISKCON, Gaudiya Sangha, Sri Caitanya Gaudiya Math, Vedanta Samiti, Sri Caitanya Bhakti Gemeinschaft, VRINDA, the Bhaktivedanta Ashram, the Hungarian Vaisnava Association, the Sri Sri Radha Govindaji Trust, the Gaudiya Mission, the Bhaktivedanta Institute, the Sri Krishna Chaitanya Mission, Gopinath Gaudiya Math, and Mantra Meditation Hawaii.

Any organization in the Chaitanya tradition may associate with the WVA. While primarily formed and energized by the Western Chaitanya disciples, those organizations that broke away from the International Society for Krishna Consciousness, the Association has been able to integrate Indian leadership into its life. All three of the Association's presidents, Srila B.P. Puri Maharaj, Srila Nayananandana Das Babaji, and the current president, Srila Bhakti B. Tirtha Maharaj, are Indians. The organization publishes the *WVA Journal*.

World Vaisnava Association
No. 154 Gopeswar Road
Mohala, Vrindaban
U.P. Dist.
Mathura Pin 281 121
India
http://www.wva-vvrs.org/

J. Gordon Melton

See also: Gaudiya Math; International Society for Krishna Consciousness; Vaishnavism.

References

Paramadvaiti, B. A., Swami. *Our Family the Gaudiya Math*. http://www.vrindavan.org/English/Books/GMconded.html. Accessed October 1, 2001.

World Vaisnava Association. http://www.wva-vvrs
.org/. Accessed October 1, 2001.

World Zoroastrian Organization

In the 1970s, some British Zoroastrians began to argue publicly for the creation of a worldwide Zoroastrian association that could assist the survival of the Zoroastrian community, which in every country of its existence is a minority and hence vulnerable to changing political climates. Unable to enlist the backing of the leadership in India and Iran, and spurred by the problems encountered by members of the faith in East Africa and fears for the situation in Iran following the Islamic Revolution, British Zoroastrians assembled a set of concerned leaders from around the globe to form the World Zoroastrian Association (WZO). The WZO grew out of a network put together as the result of several world Zoroastrian congresses that had been held through the 1970s and 1980s.

Within the London community, questions had arisen over the allowance of non-Zoroastrians to attend worship (an increasing problem in pluralistic London), the plight of children of mixed marriages, and the double use of the term "Zoroastrian" to indicate an ethnic Parsee as well as a practitioner of Zoroastrianism. In 1983 the World Zarathushtrian Trust Fund was established to support the WZO.

The WZO has found its strongest support in North America, among the member associations of the Federation of Zoroastrian Associations of North America, founded in 1987. It has not received the support of many of the Zoroastrians in India, where the WZO is seen as challenging older communal structures. The WZO is also perceived as representing the less traditional segment of the international Zoroastrian community, symbolized in 1993 by its acceptance of the children of mixed marriages into the Zoroastrian fellowship. Traditional Zoroastrians reject mixed marriages and make no provision for the conversion of non-Zoroastrians. They also have strict rules about the admittance of non-Zoroastrians into the most sacred space where important rituals are performed. The more traditionalist community members in the United Kingdom have withdrawn their support from the world organization.

The WZO is headed by a 37-member board with international representation, and a British-based executive committee. The organization has made it its job to intervene with governments on behalf of Zoroastrians; provide support for adherents living in poverty; assist the strengthening of Zoroastrian youth in the faith; and sponsor conferences, seminars, and research on Zoroastrianism.

The World Zoroastrian Organisation Trust
WZO Senior Citizen Centre,
Pinjar Street,
Malesar,
Navsari 396 445
India

World Zoroastrian Association
135 Tennison Rd., South Norwood
London SE25 5NF
United Kingdom
http://www.w-z-o.org/

J. Gordon Melton

See also: Zoroastrianism.

Reference

Hinnells, John R. *Zoroastrians in Britain*. Oxford: Clarendon, 1996.

Worldwide Church of God

The Worldwide Church of God (WCOG) officially changed its name in 2009 to Grace Communion International, thus severing its last link with the past. Today it is a fairly mainstream conservative evangelical church, which bears almost no resemblance to the church founded in 1934 by Herbert W. Armstrong (1892–1986) and run by him for half a century until his death. Much of the description here concentrates on the "historical" Worldwide church, whose background and summary of beliefs are essential to understanding the majority of the church's numerous splinter groups.

The Worldwide Church of God shared common roots with the Seventh-day Adventist movement. When with the encouragement of Ellen G. White (1827–1915) a large group of Sabbatarian Adventist assemblies agreed to take the name Seventh-day Adventist

Church at a conference in Battle Creek, Michigan, in 1860, a much smaller dissenting group split away under the name Church of God Seventh Day. Armstrong, a failed advertising executive, joined a congregation of one branch of this church in 1929, was ordained a minister in 1931, and was associated with the church until it removed his preaching credentials in 1937. In 1934 he started a small radio ministry (later to be called *The World Tomorrow*) and published the first mimeographed copy of *The Plain Truth* magazine, the two main activities by which the church reached out to non-members. His church was called the Radio Church of God until changing to the Worldwide Church of God in 1968.

The church was Sabbatarian and millenarian. It laid a strong emphasis not just on the Seventh-day Sabbath but also on holding the seven Jewish Holy Days and obeying Jewish dietary laws. It taught the literal (and soon-to-come) millennium, in which Christ would rule in peace on Earth for 1,000 years, with true believers (that is, members of the church) being rulers under Christ. It had a strong emphasis on biblical prophecy, and held a particular version of British Israelism, in which mentions of the subtribes of Ephraim and Manasseh in the Bible refer specifically to the present-day nations of Britain and the United States, respectively. Armstrong and other preachers and writers in his church examined political, military, and moral world affairs to prove that these are the end times. The church also taught that God is a family, currently with two members, the Father and the Son, but that true believers will become part of the God-family.

Throughout its history the WCOG met with much hostility from mainstream Christians and from anti-cultists, not only for its radical theological teachings but also for its insistence on two full tithes of gross income, and in some years a third tithe, and for its strict top-down governance, which allegedly led to much abuse of authority.

Until Armstrong's death the most traumatic period for the Worldwide Church of God was the decade of the 1970s. Many members believed from Armstrong's teaching that the end times would begin around 1972, and that Christ would return by 1975 (there was even a booklet entitled *1975 in Prophecy*); when that did not occur, some disillusioned members left. Doctrinal changes on the date of Pentecost and a reversal of the church's formerly strict ruling against remarriage after divorce caused a number of members to leave in 1974, some to found splinter churches. In 1977, Armstrong married a divorcée 46 years younger than himself, much to the disapproval of his son and heir-apparent, Garner Ted Armstrong (1930–2003). The younger Armstrong was involved in sexual scandals early in the decade and was suspended from preaching for some months; on his return he liberalized some of his father's teachings until, in 1978, his father banished him from the church. Garner Ted Armstrong founded his own Church of God, International. In 1979, in response to allegations by former members of financial impropriety by Herbert W. Armstrong and the church's lawyer, Stanley Rader, the state of California placed the church in receivership for a time. In 1980 a former senior member published a book that detailed the authoritarian nature of the church, and also alleged that Armstrong had had sexual relations with one of his own daughters many years earlier.

The church recovered from all of these trials. At its height it had a baptized membership of very nearly 100,000, and its flagship magazine, *The Plain Truth*, had a worldwide circulation of more than 6 million.

A week before his death Armstrong appointed the church's administrative officer, Joseph W. Tkach (1927–1995), as his successor. Initially Tkach followed Armstrong's teachings and practices, but soon (strongly encouraged by his son Joseph Tkach Jr. [b. 1951], who became pastor general on his father's death) he withdrew all of Armstrong's books and booklets and began changing doctrines. Ministers who disagreed with the changes either resigned or were fired for refusing to teach them. In 1989 Gerald Flurry left to found the Philadelphia Church of God; in 1982 longstanding senior evangelist Roderick C. Meredith left to found the Global Church of God (see Living Church of God); and in 1995 a large group of ministers left to found the United Church of God. This last was in reaction to Joseph W. Tkach's Christmas Eve 1994 sermon, in which he formally renounced most of Armstrong's teachings and declared that the Worldwide Church of God was now effectively a standard evangelical Protestant church that "by tradition" worshipped on Saturday. Many of the offshoot groups had splits of their own; there are currently more than 400 separate offshoot groups, though many are minuscule.

With a massive drop in members and with tithing now voluntary rather than mandatory, the church's income plummeted. It laid off many of its staff, sold buildings, and had to close Ambassador University (formerly Ambassador College), which Armstrong had established in 1947 to train the church's members as ministers. In 2004 it sold its prestigious headquarters complex in Pasadena, California.

The Worldwide Church of God is now mainstream Trinitarian, has little emphasis on end-time prophecy, and has completely abandoned any belief in British Israelism. It celebrates Christmas and Easter, formerly condemned as Pagan festivals. The church's leaders encouraged congregations to hold services on Sundays instead of Saturdays, though that move has met with resistance from some of the membership, with some individual churches still meeting on Saturday.

In the United States, the WCOG was accepted as a member of the National Association of Evangelicals in May 1997, and in the United Kingdom it was accepted in the equivalent Evangelical Alliance in July 2000. Through these it is related to the World Evangelical Alliance.

By 2009 the church claimed a membership of 42,000, in 900 congregations worldwide. It no longer publishes its former flagship magazine *The Plain Truth*, which has been replaced by *Christian Odyssey*. The U.S *The Plain Truth* is now a cover-price magazine published by Plain Truth Ministries, founded in 1996 by one of the architects of the doctrinal changes in WCOG, Greg Albrecht, but officially unconnected with WCOG. The U.K .*The Plain Truth*, a completely separate non-denominational magazine, is still free, as all of WCOG's publications had formerly been, and is supported by donations.

In April 2009 the Worldwide Church of God in the USA made the final break with the past by changing its name to Grace Communion International. However, it still owns the copyright in the old name, and both individual U.S. congregations and non-U.S. national churches are free to continue calling themselves Worldwide Church of God.

Worldwide Church of God/Grace Communion
    International
PO Box 5005
Glendora, CA, 91740-0730
www.wcg.org

David V. Barrett

See also: British Israelism; Evangelicalism; Living Church of God; Philadelphia Church of God; Sabbatarianism; Seventh-day Adventist Church; United Church of God; White, Ellen G.; World Evangelical Alliance.

References

Armstrong, Herbert W. *Autobiography*. 2 vols. Pasadena, CA: Worldwide Church of God, 1986, 1987.

Barrett, David V. *The New Believers*. London: Cassell, 2001.

Hopkins, Joseph. *The Armstrong Empire: A Look at the Worldwide Church of God*. Grand Rapids, MI: William B. Eerdmans Publishing Company, 1974.

Nichols, Larry, and George Mather. *Discovering the Plain Truth: How the Worldwide Church of God Encountered the Gospel of Grace*. Downers Grove, IL: InterVarsity, 1998.

Robinson, David. *Herbert Armstrong's Tangled Web*. Tulsa, OK: John Hadden, 1980.

Tkach, Joseph. *Transformed by Truth*. Sisters, OR: Multnomah, 1997.

Wu Tai Shan

Wu Tai Shan (or in Chinese, Wenshu Pusa) is one of four mountains especially sacred to Chinese Buddhists. The four are scattered around the country, and Wu Tai Shan, located in Shanxi Province between Taiyuan and Beijing, is the mountain to the north. The sacred area of Wu Tai Shan is focused on five peaks with relatively flat tops, hence its name, which means "Five Terrace Mountain."

Wu Tai was originally a Daoist mountain and participated in the conception of mountains as pillars that held heaven in place above the Earth. It was also home

Tourists climb to a temple on Wu Tai Shan, one of four sacred mountains in China. (Carmentianya/Dreamstime.com)

to various Daoist deities. The mountain, however, began to participate in the first transmission of Buddhism to China and as early as the reign of the Emperor Ming Di (58–75 CE) a first Buddhist temple was built there. It seems to have been the result of the settlement of an Indian Buddhist monk on the mountain. During the next centuries more than 100 temples and monasteries appeared, and by the middle of the sixth century there were more than 200. Buddhism flourished until the reign of Emperor Wuzong, who in 845 turned on the Buddhist community and closed down temples and monasteries throughout his empire and forced hundreds of thousands of the Buddhist monks and nuns back into a secular life. Most of the temples now found on Wu Tai date to the post-Wuzong period though there are a few notable exceptions including the Nan Chan Si temple, the oldest surviving wooden temple in China, built in 782.

The mountain is sacred to the bodhisattva Manjushri, who is believed to reside there. Reportedly, the same Indian monk who settled there in the first century had a vision of Manjushri, the first of many that would be reported over the centuries. In the seventh century, the Korean monk Chajang visited Wu Tai. He reported meeting a local monk who gave him several relics of Manjushri and instructed him to return to his home. A short time later he had a vision in which he was told that the monk was in fact Manjushri and that upon his return to Korea home he must build a temple to the bodhisattva, which he did.

During the time of Kublai Khan (r. 1260–1294), and his descendants, Tibetan Buddhism was favored, and Vajrayana monasteries began to develop at Wu Tai Shan. Ten of these monasteries are still active.

Today, there are 48 Chinese Buddhist temples on Wu Tai, plus the 10 Tibetan lamaseries. Most were built relatively close to Taihuai, the town in the middle of the five peaks. Because of its relatively isolated location, the temples on Wu Tai suffered little damage during the Cultural Revolution and the area around Taihuai retains much of the religious aura of pre-revolutionary China.

J. Gordon Melton

See also: Chajang; Emei Shan; Jiu-Hua Shan; Monasticism; Putuo Shan; Tibetan Buddhism.

References

Nanquin, Susan, and Chün-Fang Yü, eds. *Pilgrims and Sacred Sites in China.* Berkeley: University of California Press, 1992.

Shunxun, Nan, and Beverly Foit-Albert. *China's Sacred Sites*. Honesdale, PA: Himalayan Institute Press, 2007.

Steinhardt, Nancy Shatzman. *Chinese Traditional Architecture*. New York: China Institute in America, China House Gallery, 1984.

Y

■ Yemen

Yemen is the southernmost country on the Arabian Peninsula. Its western border faces the Red Sea and its southern the Gulf of Aden. On the north and east it shares borders with Saudi Arabia and Oman. Much of its 204,000 square miles of territory is desert, and most of its 23,000,000 people (2008) live near the coastline.

Yemen has been inhabited at least since the end of the second millennium BCE, and a sophisticated civilization, the kingdom of Saba, or Sheba, developed there. It was based upon trade in spices, and over the next 1,000 years its cities became popular stops for caravans from both east and west. As sea trade between the Mediterranean area and India emerged, Yemen prospered even more.

Early in the Christian era, Yemen developed a special relationship with Ethiopia, which it faced across the Red Sea. Ethiopia conquered Yemen in 525 and remained in control for half a century until driven out by the Persians in 570. Yemen became a prize for different would-be conquerors for the next 300 years. Then in the seventh century, the leadership of the country converted to Islam, and within a generation Islam became the religion of the people. As the capital of the Islamic world moved to Damascus and then to Baghdad, Yemen was left somewhat isolated from the centers of both political and religious life.

In 897 a stable dynasty, the Yadyi, was established in the northern part of the country. A series of dynasties arose and fell in the south. For a time in the 16th and 17th centuries, the Ottoman Empire attempted to establish hegemony in the region. The British first made

Yemen

Religion	Followers in 1970	Followers in 2010	% of Population	Annual % growth 2000–2010	Followers in 2025	Followers in 2050
Muslims	6,380,000	24,248,000	99.1	3.02	36,148,000	57,223,000
Hindus	4,000	155,000	0.6	3.02	300,000	600,000
Christians	2,100	41,300	0.2	2.92	60,500	87,700
Orthodox	0	11,000	0.0	1.09	15,000	20,000
Independents	1,400	12,000	0.0	4.14	20,000	35,000
Protestants	290	7,500	0.0	3.62	10,000	12,000
Agnostics	1,800	22,000	0.1	3.32	45,000	80,000
Atheists	400	4,800	0.0	3.02	8,000	10,000
Jews	1,300	1,300	0.0	3.02	1,300	1,300
Baha'is	300	1,300	0.0	3.00	2,000	4,000
Zoroastrians	600	1,000	0.0	1.61	1,000	1,000
Jains	0	250	0.0	3.06	500	800
Buddhists	0	150	0.0	3.04	300	600
Sikhs	100	130	0.0	3.04	200	300
Total population	**6,391,000**	**24,475,000**	**100.0**	**3.02**	**36,567,000**	**58,009,000**

View of the colorful and intricate skyline of San'a, the capital of Yemen and one of the oldest continuously inhabited sites in the world. (Zanskar/Dreamstime.com)

their presence felt in 1618, when they established the headquarters of the East Indies Company at the city of Mukha. Then in 1839, they took control from Mukha through the Strait of Bab al Mandeb along the coast to Aden (the best port in the region). In response, the Turkish army moved into North Yemen. The opening of the Suez Canal in 1870 gave Aden new importance, and Great Britain moved to establish its control of the coast all the way to Oman, a process not completed until 1934.

In 1911 the Imam Yahya Ad-din began to reassert the rights of the Yadyi dynasty, which had survived though subservient to the Turks. It soon displaced the Turks, challenged Saudi influences on its northern border, and put pressure on the British over Aden. During the rest of the century, the struggle to unite Yemen as an independent country led to various wars, border re-alignments, and even the involvement of the country

in the short-lived United Arab Republic (1958–1961). In 1967 a Socialist republic was declared in South Yemen, and in 1969 the British were forced out. The merger of North and South Yemen was delayed by the continued meddling of Saudi Arabia and other Arab nations that had interests in the north, but it was finally accomplished in 1990. Through the 1990s, the population increased dramatically as a result of the expulsions of Yemenis from Saudi Arabia and the return of Yemenis from Africa.

The Islamization of Yemen has been one of the more determinative factors in its history. The first mosques to be built in Yemen, reportedly erected by some men sent by the Prophet Muhammad himself, were in San'a al-Janad and near Wadi Zabid. These mosques may still be visited today. The country was also affected by the division of the Muslim community into Sunni and Shia. The Shias, the backbone of

YEMEN

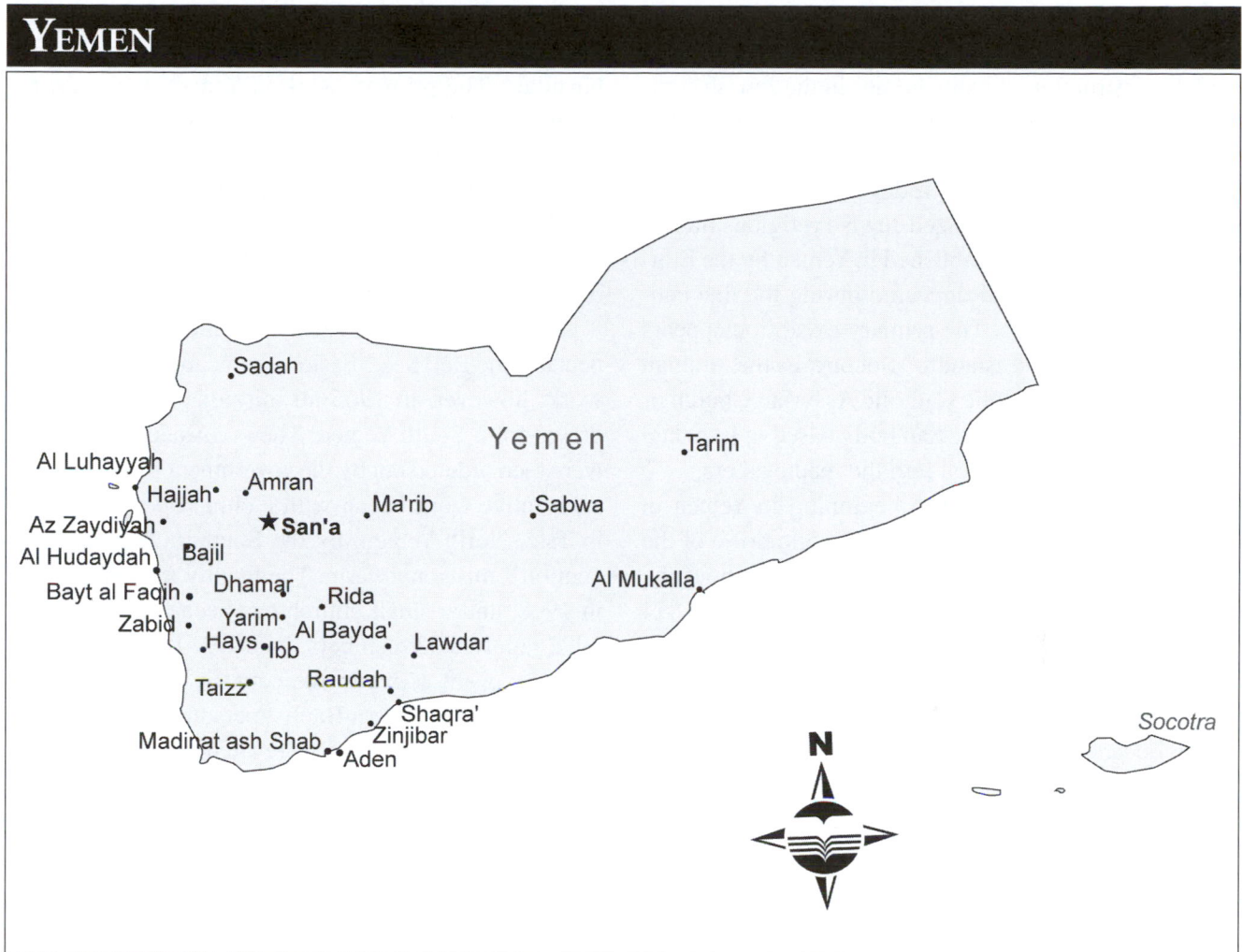

the former Yadyi dynasty, are the majority in the northern part of the country, while the south is dominated by followers of the Sunni Shafaiite School. There is also a measurable Ismaili community and an even smaller number of followers of the Ahmadiyya Muslim movement, a 19th-century revivalist movement.

Islam is considered the established religion of Yemen, and Islamic law is the basis of all legislation. Non-Muslim religions are not permitted to proselytize, and Yemeni Muslims are not permitted to convert to another faith. Although the government has taken steps to present an open face to the West, it has been opposed by some Muslim groups, such as the Aden-Abyan Islamic Army, a militant movement opposed to Western presence in the Middle East. In 1990 the leader of the army was sentenced to death for his kidnapping of 20 Western tourists in the country.

Judaism had been present in Yemen for many centuries; but then at the beginning of the fifth century CE, a group of Yemenis, the Himyarites, decided to convert to the Jewish faith. It took control of South Yemen and established Judaism as the official religion. The Himyarites also moved to suppress Christianity, which had come into the country from Ethiopia. The Ethiopians reacted, and Himyarite rule was short-lived. In 525 the Ethiopians overran the Himyarite kingdom.

Through the succeeding centuries the Jews in Yemen lived quietly, though they were frequently the target of oppression and conversionist activity, and they created a unique Jewish community. In the mid-20th century it numbered upward of 50,000 people. Through the early 20th century, new anti-Jewish forces began to operate. In 1922, Yemen revived an ancient Muslim law that demanded the forced conversion to Islam of all Jews under the age of 12. In 1947, Aden was the scene of anti-Jewish riots that cost 82 Jews their lives and the destruction of many homes in the Jewish community. Continued pressure on the community led to the 1950 immigration of almost the entire community to the new state of Israel. Today almost no Jews are left, and there is no organized Jewish religious life.

Christianity was established in Yemen by the Ethiopians but gradually disappeared during the first centuries of Muslim rule. The primary exception appears to have been on the island of Socotra in the Arabian Sea, where the Apostolic Catholic Assyrian Church of the East (a Nestorian Christian body based in Iraq) had a bishopric that lasted well into the medieval era.

Christianity made a new beginning in Yemen in the 19th century, when a Roman Catholic priest of the Servite Order settled in Aden. Work throughout the Arabian Peninsula had grown to the point that in 1854 a prefecture was created. It became a vicariate in 1888 and remained in Aden until 1974, when it was transferred to Abu Dhabi, where it remains. Catholic work in the decades after World War II has been primarily among expatriates, the number of whom radically declined after the British were driven out of Aden. However, in 1973 the North Yemen government invited the Missionaries of Charity (headed by Mother Teresa) to come to Hodeida and take charge of a home for the aged. That became the first of a variety of charitable and medical projects supported and managed by various Roman Catholic orders and missionary agencies. At the same time South Yemen nationalized the schools, and all but two Roman Catholic missionaries (except for two priests) were expelled. The Roman Catholic Church retains a minuscule presence in Yemen, but no proselytizing is allowed.

Protestant presence in Yemen goes back to 1885, when Ion Keith-Falconer, a Scottish nobleman, settled in Aden with a vision of spreading Christianity across Arabia. He died two years later, unable to adapt to the climate. The Church of Scotland adopted his mission, but more important, two students at the seminary of the Reformed Church in America at New Brunswick, New Jersey, were inspired to take the deceased missionary's place. James Cantine and Samuel M. Zwemer organized the American Arabian Mission and then left to attend language school in Beirut. Their work was greatly assisted by the adoption of their mission by the Reformed Church, which supplied funds for several hospitals. The primary work in Yemen, however, remained the single original mission in Aden and the hospital subsequently opened by the Church of Scotland.

The Scottish work united with the Danish Mission in 1961, and the church in Aden became known as the Church of South Yemen, almost the only congregation of Yemeni nationals in the country.

Beginning in the 1960s, several other groups, especially the Red Sea Mission Team, attempted to open work; however, in 1965 all missionaries were withdrawn from South Yemen. They returned in 1968 but were then ordered out by the government in 1973. More substantive work began with a clinic opened in 1964 in Taiz, North Yemen, by the Southern Baptist Convention's missionary arm. The facility moved to Jubia in 1968, and a small church has been formed that in 1992 reported 92 members. By 1972, 15 medical missionaries were active in the country. Today there are more than 30 Southern Baptist personnel in Yemen.

Although Protestants were attempting to establish work, the Anglicans had begun worship services led by chaplains with the forces that captured Aden in 1839. An Anglican parish was established in Aden and has continued to the present under the jurisdiction of the far-flung Diocese of Cyprus and the Gulf of the Episcopal Church in Jerusalem and the Middle East.

In addition, Yemen has a very small Baha'i Faith community and a few practicing Hindus (from India and Pakistan).

J. Gordon Melton

See also: Ahmadiyya Movement in Islam; Apostolic Catholic Assyrian Church of the East; Baha'i Faith; Church of Scotland; Episcopal Church in Jerusalem and the Middle East; Ismaili Islam; Missionaries of Charity; Reformed Church in America; Roman Catholic Church; Shafiite School of Islam; Southern Baptist Convention; Zwemer, Samuel Marinus.

References

Ahroni, Reuben. *Jewish Emigration from the Yemen 1951–98: Carpet Without Magic*. London: RoutledgeCurzon, 2001.

Burman, R., ed. *The Jews of Aden*. London: London Museum of Jewish Life, 1991.

Dresch, Paul. *A History of Modern Yemen.* Cambridge: Cambridge University Press, 2001.

Horner, N. A. "Present-day Christianity in the Gulf States of the Arabian Peninsula." *Occasional Bulletin of Missionary Research* 2 (April 1978): 53–63.

Meissner, J. R. "Tribes at the Core: Legitimacy, Structure, and Power in Zaydi Yemen." Ph.D. diss., Columbia University, 1987.

Pridham, B. R., ed. *Economy, Society and Culture in Contemporary Yemen.* London: Croom Helm Centre for Arab Gulf Studies, University of Exeter, 1985.

Al-Rasheed, Madawi, and Robert Vitalis, eds. *Counter-Narratives: History, Contemporary Society, and Politics in Saudi Arabia and Yemen.* London: Palgrave Macmillan, 2004.

Yezidis

The Yezidis are a small religious group of approximately 600,000 Kurmanji-speaking people, who are geographically dispersed in several areas of Kurdistan and the Caucasus. They constitute a minority in a two-fold meaning: first, as Kurds they represent an often persecuted ethnic minority within their countries of origin; second, as followers of Yezidism they are a religious minority within the Muslim majority, having often (wrongly) been denounced as "devil-worshippers." The largest Yezidi communities live in Northern Iraq (about 500,000) and the main sanctuary of the Yezidis, the shrine of Sheykh 'Adi, is situated in the Valley of Lalish just north of Mosul.

Yezidis played an influential part in Kurdish tribal confederations under the Ottoman Empire. Successive religious persecutions, however, drove waves of emigrants into the Caucasus, particularly Armenia and Georgia (40,000), but also Azerbaijan and Russia. In Syria live about 5,000 Yezidi, while most of the approximately 10,000 Yezidis of Eastern Turkey have fled during the 1980s, mainly to Germany, where there is a community of at least 35,000 people at present. Maybe 50 families live in the United States and Canada, having come after the First Gulf War in 1992. As they had cooperated with the Americans, they had to fear reprisals after it was decided to keep Saddam Hussein (1937–2006) in office.

Yezidism developed out of the Muslim 'Adawiyya Order of the Sufi Sheykh 'Adi ibn Musafir (ca. 1073–1162), who was born in Lebanon and studied in Baghdad. When he settled at Lalish, in the Hakkari Mountains, he drew many followers from the local Kurdish population as well as from outside Kurdistan. Being childless, Sheykh 'Adi was succeeded after his death by a nephew, whose descendants continued to lead the movement for more than a century. Under Sheykh Hasan b. 'Adi (d. 1254), his great-grandnephew, the Order seems to have deviated from acceptable Islamic norms by regarding Sheykh 'Adi as the sole source of religious authority. As many similarities with the cults of the Ahl-e Haqq and Alevis suggest, Yezidi tradition also incorporated pre-Islamic, presumably Western Iranian or Kurdish beliefs and observances. Its followers subsequently were regarded as non-Muslims and "devil-worshippers." Ever since, persecutions and attacks by their Muslim neighbours have marked Yezidi history.

One of the essential characteristics of Yezidi tradition is its non-literate nature—its holy texts have been orally transmitted over the generations, especially so as literacy was formerly forbidden to Yezidis. The body of religious texts is mainly constituted by the so-called *qewls,* sacred hymns in Kurmanji, which are chanted by trained bards (*qewwal*) on religious occasions (for a selection of these in English, see Kreyenbroek 1995; Kreyenbroek/Rashow 2005) and the two sacred books of the Yezidis, the *Kitaba Jilwe* (Arabic: "Book of Revelation") and the *Meshef Resh* (Kurdish: "The Black Book") (both translated in Guest 1993). Although these books most probably were not written before the 19th century, they seem to represent a genuine tradition, containing the essential teachings of the founders of the faith as they were once laid down in written texts of the same name.

The oral tradition prevented the development of a doctrinal body, making Yezidi tradition a belief-system in a very loose sense, with many variations in practice between individuals and the scattered communities. To generalize, the Yezidis venerate a God called Khode (a *deus otiosus*) and seven Holy Beings or Angels (*khas*), to whom God has entrusted the worldly affairs.

The leader of the Angels is the Peacock Angel (Kurdish: Tawusi Melek, hereafter Melek Tawus), who is responsible for all that happens in the world, whether good or bad, which may have promoted his identification with the Satan of other religions (although Yezidis are forbidden to use this name). The Yezidis believe in reincarnation, whereby the quality of a person's future life depends on his or her behavior in the previous one.

Being a Yezidi is a matter of birth, not belief—one cannot become a Yezidi. Personal convictions may result from membership of the community, but cannot lead to it. Participation in festivals, observance of some prohibitions, and formal obedience to religious authorities are essential elements of religious life, more so than individual verbal prayer. If Yezidis pray, they usually do so facing the Sun in the morning and evening. Wednesday is the holy day of the Yezidis.

Besides the veneration of Melek Tawus, the most conspicuous markers of Yezidi identity are their caste system and their strict rule of endogamy, as well as a number of prohibitions. Yezidi society is separated into two basic endogamous classes or castes, the laymen or commoners, called *mirid,* and the priestly castes. The community is led by both the mir of sheykhan, who is traditionally regarded as the vice-regent of Sheykh 'Adi (and also of Melek Tawus), and the Baba Sheykh ("Father Sheykh"), the leader of the sheykhs and thus the spiritual leader of the faith (although recent developments in Iraq as well as the process of migration have limited their influence to some extent). The clergy is divided further into several castes or titles, among which the sheykh and the pir are the most important. Each Yezidi—including the sheykhs and pirs themselves —must have a sheykh or pir, who acts as a spiritual guide for him or her. The sheykh participates on behalf of his mirid in the performance of religious rites, such as those of birth, circumcision, baptism, marriage, and death. For this, the commoners pay him a certain sum of money each year. Prohibitions regarding purity in both spiritual and physical matters include marriage with non-Yezidis (which results in exclusion from the community) and polluting the "elements" by spitting, cutting or shaving one's facial hair, wearing blue clothes, eating certain types of food (for example, lettuce, fish, pumpkin, broad beans, cabbage), as well as using words connected with the devil.

The last decades have seen the continuing migration of Yezidis to Europe, particularly Germany, where a "diasporization" of the Yezidi community can be observed (Ackermann 2004). Against the background of a widespread fear that the Yezidi identity might disappear in the course of migration, the religious authorities have called for the collection of all relevant oral traditions, to forge a written scripture, and to reform some of the taboos. Free from religious persecution and having become simultaneously more urban and literate, Yezidi intellectuals (among them many mirid) try to reconstruct and represent their religion through the publication of journals, the creation of websites, and the cooperation with academics, according to the conditions of a modern, culturally complex society. At the moment it seems that these attempts will eventually result in the transformation of Yezidi tradition from an orthopraxy to a more orthodox scriptural religion—a Yezidism—where differing local traditions become homogenized into a more binding diasporic identity.

The diaspora will become even more important as the situation of the Yezidis in their traditional heartland, Northern Iraq, seems to become increasingly problematic. Radical Muslims once more label the Yezidis "devil-worshippers" that should be persecuted and even killed. Following a short period of relief after the downfall of Saddam Hussein (r. 1979–2003), a rising number of attacks on the Yezidi community has been reported, culminating in the terrible terrorist bombing attacks of August 14, 2007, which completely destroyed two Yezidi villages in the Sinjar region, killing more than 300 people. Again, Yezidis have become a most vulnerable minority.

Andreas Ackerman and J. Gordon Melton

See also: Reincarnation, Sufism.

References

Ackermann, Andreas. "A Double Minority: Notes on the Emerging Yezidi Diaspora." In *Diaspora, Identity and Religion: New Directions in Theory and Research*, edited by Waltraud Kokot, Khachig Tölölyan and Carolin Alfonso, 156–160. London and New York: Routledge, 2004.

Allison, Christine. *The Yezidi Oral Tradition in Iraqi Kurdistan*. Richmond: Curzon Press, 2001.

Guest, John S. *Survival Among the Kurds. A History of the Yezidis*. London and New York: Kegan Paul International, 1993.

Kreyenbroek, Philip G. *Yezidism—Its Background, Observances and Textual Traditions*. Texts and Studies in Religion, 62. Lewiston, Queenston, and Lampeter: Edwin Mellen Press, 1995.

Kreyenbroek, Philip G., and Khalil Jindy Rashow. *God and Sheikh Adi Are Perfect. Sacred Poems and Religious Narratives from the Yezidi Tradition*. Wiesbaden: Harrassowitz, 2005.

Yoga

Yoga, a term from the Sanskrit that means both "yoke" and "union," refers to a tradition of belief and practice that originated on the Indian subcontinent that has as its core intention the uniting of the individual self with ultimate reality variously understood as the true self, an impersonal absolute, or a personal deity. In common parlance, the word is used to refer to three primary aspects of the larger yoga tradition. First, it designates the philosophical system derived from the teachings of Patanjali, considered the founder of yoga and the author of a book, the Yoga Sutras. The path of yoga is considered one of the six great philosophical traditions of India. Second, yoga refers to a set of disciplined practices followed by those who accept the yoga philosophical system as a means of attaining *moksha* (or salvation). Traditionally, the philosophical teachings and the practice are combined, each supporting the other. Third, in the modern West (though originating in India), yoga may be used to refer just to the physical exercises known as *hatha* yoga. In the contemporary West, largely as a result of yoga being introduced into the New Age movement, a number of Western teachers have integrated one or more aspects of yoga into what is otherwise a Western Esoteric system. An adept practitioner of yoga is called a yogi.

History of Yoga No consensus has developed over the origins of yoga. Archaeological evidence of its ancient practice has been traced to figurines showing people in a meditative posture. These figurines, found in the Indus River valley, have been dated to 3000 BCE.

In Hinduism, "sadhu" is a common term for a mystic, an ascetic, a yogi (practitioner of yoga), and/or wandering monks. The sadhu is dedicated to achieving the fourth and final Hindu goal of life, *moksha* (liberation), through meditation and contemplation of Brahman. (iStockPhoto.com)

Yoga also is present in the later hymns of the Hindu holy texts, the Upanishads (600–500 BCE), the last phase of the Vedic writings (1000–800 BCE), and the religious philosophy derived from them, Vedanta (100 BCE). Yoga is also mentioned in the classic Indian epic, the Mahabharata (ca. 400 BCE–400 CE), especially the most famous segment of the epic, the Bhagavad Gita. Thus, by the time of the writing of the Yoga Sutras, which systematized the teachings, yoga had been widely discussed in Indian culture.

Patanjali is rightly remembered for his work of assembling and ordering the dispersed information on yoga; however, little is known about him. Most scholars assume that the Yoga Sutras were compiled in three stages, suggesting multiple authorship. The original Patanjali may have been a grammarian who lived in the second century BCE. He seems to have authored the first part of the sutras, three books of the sutras as known today. The second part, the final book of sutras, was added at a later date, possibly by a second person who wished his work would stand beside and be identified with the original. The third part is an early commentary written by Vyasa. Most later commentaries rely on Vyasa's authoritative work.

Vyasa is a legendary Hindu figure who is also identified with the writing of a number of Hindu holy texts, including the Mahabharata and many of the Puranas. Authorship of the Mahabharata and the commentary on the Yoga Sutras was certainly by two different individuals. Information on the Vyasa who authored the original Yoga Sutras commentary is lacking.

Patanjali defined the purpose of yoga as knowledge of the true self and outlined the eight steps leading to a direct experience of the true self—*yamas, niyamas, asanas, pranayana, pratyahara, dharana, dhyana,* and *samadhi*. The yamas and niyamas are the major moral dos and don'ts. The asanas, originally understood to be meditative postures, have come to be seen as the many postures for conditioning the body practiced as hatha yoga. Once the asanas are mastered, the student moves on to the disciplines of breathing, concentration, and meditation that culminate in an experience of union with the ultimate (samadhi). Over the years, the number of basic yogic disciplines has multiplied, and the relative merits of each are still hotly debated by various yogis. Patanjali's approach has been integrated into a variety of different Hindu groups, as well as non-Hindu schools of thought.

The modern Western appropriation of yoga begins with the discovery of Hinduism by Western scholars in the 19th century. Even as the West was being informed of Hindu ideas, a few Westerners began to practice yoga, albeit in an abbreviated form. In the 19th century, Western translations of essential yoga texts, the Yoga Sutras and the Vashita Yoga, appeared. The appropriation of the Bhagavad Gita into the mysticism of the Transcendentalists of New England in the middle of the century and the subsequent arrival of the first In-

dian guru (spiritual teacher) in 1882 in the person of Protap Chunder Mozoomdar (1840–1905), serve as markers for the rise of Hinduism in North America.

The first book that circulated in the West that both explained and advocated the practice of a form of yoga was *Nature's Finer Forces* by Rama Prasad, a treatise on pranayama (yogic breathing) that was published by the Theosophical Society (Adyar) in 1890. It was compiled from articles previous published serially in *The Theosophist*. The Theosophical Society was becoming the major conduit of Eastern teachings, both Buddhist and Hindu, to the West. Included among its yoga texts, the Society published a commentary on the Yoga Sutras by co-founder William Q. Judge (1851–1896) and a set of lectures on yoga by its then president Annie Besant (1847–1933) in 1908.

The first concerted effort to introduce the West to the broad range of yoga thinking began with Swami Vivikananda (1863–1902), the founder of the Vedanta Society. Vivekananda initially came to America to attend the Parliament of the World's Religions held in Chicago in 1893. After the Parliament, he stayed in the country and toured North America. Yoga proved to be among the more popular subjects upon which he lectured, and he subsequently wrote a series of books on the various branches of yoga—*karma, bhakti, jnana,* and *raja*. Missing was a work on hatha yoga, which Vedantists tended to ignore. One of Vivekanandas's associates, Swami Abhedananda (1866–1939), would later become head of the New York Vedanta Society and author four books on yoga.

The introduction of yoga in the late 19th century created an audience upon which a variety of Indian teachers would build through the first half of the new century. Among these, Baba Bharati Premanand, a bhakti yogi from Bengal, arrived on the West Coast to introduce devotional yoga directed toward the deity Krishna (later reintroduced by the International Society for Krishna Consciousness, aka the Hare Krishna movement). He would establish temples in Los Angeles and New York and though he stayed in America for only a few years, his following remained visible into the 1990s.

Along with the various Indian teachers who came to America, a small number of Americans emerged as yoga teachers, possibly the most notable being William

Walker Atkinson (1862–1932). He was an attorney who went through a personal crisis from which he emerged as teacher of New Thought metaphysics. He would author a number of popular books espousing New Thought, though he never identified with any of the various New Thought denominations. Then in 1902, he began to publish books on yoga under the pseudonym of Yogi Ramacharaka, with only a small number of people knowing his true identity. Many Indians accepted him as another Indian teacher. These books were kept in print into the 1970s by the Yogi Publication Company, and have more recently entered into the public domain and remain in print from a variety of reprint publishing houses. Though he authored very popular texts, Atkinson did not found a Hindu center or group.

About the same time that Atkinson settled in Chicago, Pierre Bernard emerged as a most controversial teacher in New York. He is credited with introducing America to Tantrism and the *kundalini* yoga that is integral to it. Tantra has a much more positive attitude toward the human body and sexuality than do the more traditional and somewhat ascetic teachings associated with yoga. Eventually, Bernard moved his center from New York City to Long Island and would become an important resident of Nyack, New York, where he was best known as the president of one of the local banks. Bernard's nephew, Theos Bernard (1908–1947), would attend Columbia University, where he wrote a master's thesis on hatha yoga, later published as *Hatha Yoga: The Report of a Personal Experience* (1945)

In England, the introduction of hatha yoga was partially facilitated by Aleister Crowley, who authored *Book 4* (1913), a text on Patanjali's eight-step path. He would subsequently introduce hatha yoga to the members of the Ordo Templi Orientis, the ceremonial magic group he later came to head. One of Crowley's students, J. F. C. Fuller, would author *Yoga* (1925), a textbook on the subject.

During the 1920s, the U.S. government passed additional restrictions against immigration from Asia, including India, and following a 1926 court decision, it even revoked the citizenship of some Indian Americans. Just before the passing of the new immigration law in 1924, however, two important teachers entered the country. Besudeb Bhattacharya and Mukunda Lal

Ghose. Both were better known by their respective religious names, Pundit Acharya and Swami Paramahansa Yogananda (1893–1952). Acharya began as a dramatist and published several plays under his given name before assuming the role of yoga teacher in the 1920s. He founded the Temple of Yoga, the Yoga Research Institute, and Prana Press (which published his many books) in New York City and later in Nyack, New York.

Yogananda, who far eclipsed Acharya and the other Hindu teachers in the West during the first half of the century, came to the United States in 1920 to attend a Unitarian-sponsored interfaith conference in Boston. He stayed to establish the Yogoda Sat-sang (later known as the Self-Realization Fellowship) and to teach *kriya* yoga (a system for awakening the kundalini, the latent power believed to reside at the base of the spine). Most important, Yogananda developed a correspondence course and a ministerial training course, both of which could be accessed through the mail, which served to spread the organization he led far beyond the center he established in Southern California in 1925. Toward the end of his life, Yogananda authored his *Autobiography*, now a classic statement of Westernized Hinduism. His successors continued to build his movement throughout the Western world.

The last of the significant Hindu teachers to come to America in the first wave of gurus to arrive before the 1924 immigration law was Shri Yogendra (1897–1989). Yogendra had founded the Yoga Institute, the first modern facility dedicated to the revival of yoga (especially hatha yoga) and the study of it scientifically, in Bombay in 1918. In 1919, Yogendra came to the United States, where he would work with physicians at the Life Extension Institute in New York City and the Bloomingdale Hospital at White Plains, New York. He also founded the Yogashrama, the Yoga Institute of America, to facilitate his teaching yoga to Americans. He also authored a booklet, *Lost Science of Five Thousand Years*, written for a Western scientifically oriented audience. Through the ashram, he came into contact with some of the leading spokespersons of the natural healing movement, including Benedict Lust (1872–1945), Bernarr MacFadden (1868–1955), and John Harvey Kellogg (1852–1943).

Yogendra attracted a popular response that included the rich and famous. He is said to have initiated more than 3,000 people in the practice of yoga and introduced its practice into naturopathy and other drugless forms of healing. He returned to India in 1922 with plans for later visits, but was blocked by America's Asian Exclusion policies.

In 1924, the small institute he had formed earlier was superseded by the Yoga Institute of India, which with the backing of J. G. Gune (1883–1966) would become the major point of dissemination for an understanding of yoga as a scientific discipline. A number of Westerners would find their way to the Institute. Gune would take the name Swami Kuvalayananda and later train Vijayendra Pratap, who later moved to Philadelphia and found the Swami Kuvalayananda Yoga (SKY) Foundation.

The growth of Eastern religion in general and the practice of yoga in particular were stymied by the Asian Exclusion Act, which became law in the United States in 1924. Those Indian teachers who were outside the country at the time of its passing could not return and American seekers had access to those few gurus who had earlier decided to settle in America (such as Yogananda and Acharya). Yoga would be spread during this period by the few Hindu organizations, the Theosophical Society (among whose members Ernest Wood [1863–1965] was a popularizer of yoga), and Americans who took it upon themselves to get trained as yoga teachers.

In spite of the ban on teachers from India, a number of books on yoga would appear between the two World Wars. Prominent among these books were L. Adam's Beck's *A Beginner's Book of Yoga* (1927), F. Yeats-Brown's *The Eight Steps to Yoga* (1933), Claude Bragdon's *An Introduction to Yoga* (1933), and Kovoor Behanan's *Yoga: A Scientific Evaluation* (1937). These volumes prepared the way for the watershed books of Theos Bernard (1908–1947).

Bernard was raised in a Hindu environment and as a youth traveled to India, where he studied at Yogendra's yoga institute. He then attended Columbia University, in New York, where he wrote his master's thesis on yoga. It proved a popular introductory text complete with pictures of the basic postures (asanas) for hatha yoga and instructions on a method to awaken the kundalini energy. He followed with two additional books, *Hindu Philosophy* (1947) and *Land of a Thou-*

sand Buddhas (1950). The last book was published posthumously. Bernard was killed in Tibet during the Chinese invasion of Tibet.

Europe became open to yoga practice especially in the years after World War II. Beginning in the mid-1940s, Hindu and yoga centers would be opened in England, Sweden, Holland, and Switzerland. British teachers Wilfred A. Clark, publisher of the *Wheel of British Yoga*, and Sir Paul Dukes became nationally known as advocates of yoga. Indian gurus began to make their way to the West, their travel facilitated by laws governing movement through the British Commonwealth. Meanwhile, Chinese-born Westerner Michael Volin launched the practice of yoga in Australia. He studied yoga in the 1930s in the Chinese center opened by Indra Devi (1899–2002), who had studied in Bombay while acting in Indian films.

Devi moved to the United States at the beginning of the 1950s and opened a yoga center in Los Angeles. She also introduced yoga to the emerging health spa movement through the center founded by Edmond Bordeaux Skekely (1905–1979) in Tecate, Mexico. She authored two early yoga texts, *Forever Young, Forever Healthy* (1953) and *Yoga for Americans* (1950).

An almost faddish interest in yoga emerged in the 1950s. These books generally followed Yogendra's lead in arguing for the scientific (as opposed to religious) nature of yoga, emphasizing the health values in the practice of hatha yoga, and identifying the practice with famous people and their success. Following Indian independence, Indian teachers found additional opportunities to travel the world and disseminate their teachings throughout the West. Among the new Indian teachers who found himself able to immigrate to the United States and settle there was Yogi Gupta, a disciple of Swami Sivananda Saraswati (1887–1963), one of the most prominent of the 20th-century yoga teachers and founder of the Divine Life Society. From his center in New York, Yogi Gupta published two popular texts, *Yoga and Long Life* (1958) and *Yoga and Yogic Powers* (1960).

Among the early Indian teachers in Canada was Swami Vishniu Devananda (1927–1993), also like Yogi Gupta a disciple of Swami Sivananda. Previous to his move to Canada, he was a senior instructor at Sivananda's Yoga Vedanta Forest Academy in Rishikesh.

After settling in Canada in 1959, he published the *Complete Illustrated Book of Yoga*, which subsequently became one of the most popular yoga texts in the English-speaking world. From his headquarters in Quebec, he founded centers across North America.

Possibly the most popular teacher of hatha yoga in North America in the last half of the 20th century was Richard Hittleman (1927–1991), who had initially discovered yoga in the 1930s. He sought out several yoga instructors and gradually developed his own variation of hatha yoga that he termed the "Yoga for Health" system. In 1957 he opened a center in Florida but soon moved to California where he developed the *Yoga for Health* television show that first appeared in 1961. Over the next two decades he wrote more than 15 books and issued several long-playing records on yoga. He introduced hundreds of thousands of people to the practice of yoga.

Hittleman exemplified the late-20th-century Western separation of hatha yoga from the larger yoga system advocated by Patanjali. Hittleman offered hatha yoga as a discipline that someone of any religion (or no religion) could adopt. At the same time, hatha yoga served as an introduction to Hindu philosophy and the broader teachings of the yoga tradition. Most of Hittleman's books concentrated upon hatha yoga as an exercise technique, but he also ventured into the religious aspects of yoga in books such as *Yoga Philosophy and Meditation* (1964), the *Guide to Yoga Meditation* (1969), and *Yoga: The 8 Steps to Health and Peace* (1975). It would appear that the spread of yoga in the 1950s and 1960s was one reason that Hinduism spread so quickly in the 1970s and 1980s.

The change of the immigration law in 1965, which placed immigration from the countries of southern and southeast Asia on the same quotas as Western Europe, would lead to tens of thousands of Indians migrating to the United States annually. The change was heralded by the arrival of a few new Indian teachers, some of whom, like Rammurti Mishra (1923–1993), came in because of their special skills, in this case as a professor at the New York University Post-Graduate Medical College. While teaching, he used his leisure time to speak on Hinduism and yoga and in 1958 he founded the Yoga Society of New York, which soon developed centers in Manhattan and Monroe, New York (near

Syracuse). In 1959 he published his yoga text, *Fundaments of Yoga*.

Once the immigration law changed, a growing number of Indian teachers came to the United States, among the first being Swami Satchidananda (1914–2002), another student of Sivananda. He taught Sivananda's system under the label "integral yoga" but quickly specialized in hatha yoga. His text, *Integral Hatha Yoga*, rivaled that of Swami Vishnu Divananda.

Arriving for a visit the same year as Satchidananda, B. K. S. Iyengar (b. 1918) had studied yoga with Swami Krishnamacharya (1888–1989), the same guru who taught Indra Devi. He had developed his own system for teaching yoga and it proved equally popular to that offered by the students of Sivananda. His book *Light on Yoga* (1966) emerged as the single most popular textbook for the training of yoga teachers, even though Iyengar remained headquartered in India and only visited North America sporadically.

Yoga expanded rapidly through the 1970s. By the beginning of the decade major yoga centers had been created by Swami Yogananda, Ramurti Mishna, Iyengar, and the students of Sivananda. During the decade, the many emerging yoga teachers would organize the first professional associations, of which the California Yoga Teachers Association proved the most important. It published the *Yoga Journal,* the first newsstand magazine on yoga. Iyengar's students organized the Institute for Yoga Teacher Education, while Vishnu Devananda and Satchidananda offered teacher certification through their centers in Montreal and Virginia, respectively. New teachers emerging through the decade included Swami Rama (1925–1996) of the International Institute of Yoga Science and Philosophy; Yogi Amrit Desai, founder of the Kripalu Yoga Ashram; and Swami Kriyananda, who had left the Self-Realization Fellowship to found the Ananda Church of Self Realization.

The Yogi Tradition   In India, yoga is seen as one of the six classical schools of philosophy. It encompasses a worldview and in practice involves a system by which the soul, the true essence of the individual, can reach samadhi, which is variously described as pure concentration, a consciousness of pure detachment from the world in which the soul abides in its own essence alone.

Ultimately, samadhi is the supreme indescribable mystic experience. As various forms of yoga practice have been disseminated, yoga has been incorporated in a number of variant philosophical systems, and many have attempted to describe the experience or event of samadhi.

B. K. S. Iyenger describes yoga as the union of the soul with God and the experience of samadhi as a state in which the body and senses are at rest while the faculties of the mind and reason are alert, but beyond mere consciousness. S. K. Majumdar notes that in samadha, the yogi discovers his or her true identity as transcendent spirit and perceives the basic unity of existence. Thus, yoga might be described as a process to reach samadhi and the ultimate truth it offers.

The yoga sutras of Patanjali describe an eight-step *sadhana* (or path) to reach samadhi. This path is often called *ashanga* yoga, or the yoga of eight arms. The first two steps, *yama* (ethical disciplines) and *niyama* (rule of conduct), set the lifestyle of the yogi. The five commandments of yama include allegiance to *ahimsa* (nonviolence), *satya* (truth), *astaya* (non-stealing), *brahmacharya* (continence), and *aparigratia* (non-coveting). From ahimsa comes a respect for life that finds expression in a respect for animals and vegetarianism. From the virtue of the brahmacharya comes the preference for, if not insistence on, in the celibate life. Niyama includes the virtues of *saucha* (purity), *santosa* (contentment), *tapas* (austerity), *svadhyaya* (study of the self), and *Isvara pranidhana* (dedication to the Lord).

The third step in yoga is asana, or posture. The asanas are the exercises which have, in the West, been isolated from the yoga sadhana and turned into a system of physical exercise as hatha yoga. The asanas were originally developed over the centuries and passed from teacher to student. In the 20th century the asanas became the subject of numerous books and scientific speculation, and several yoga teachers have developed their own variations based upon what they deem the essential aspect of the performance of the yoga postures. Thus, various schools of yoga, such as those headed by Iyengar, Mishna, Baba Hari Das, and Hittleman, have distinguished themselves from the others. Among the most unique new yoga systems is that of Bikram Choudhury which is generally practiced in a room heated to 105° F with a humidity of 40 percent.

Pranayana, the fourth step of yoga, has, like asanas, frequently been isolated from the sadhana and taught as a physical psychological discipline. It is often taught in connection with hatha yoga, though by no means always. Pranayana is breath control. The student is taught the basics of inhalation, exhalation, and the retention of breath. *Prana* (breath) is the individual's portion of *Pramatma* (universal; spirit), which is conceived of as a subtle vital energy. Proper breathing enlivens the body as it enhances the flow of prana (as subtle vibrant energies) through the body. Pranayana and its accompanying understanding of vital energies flowing through the body have become the basis for a number of forms of psychic healing that are based on the transference of prana from one person to another.

The practice of pranayana leads directly to *pratyahara,* or sense control, the fifth step on the path. In yoga, the mind is pictured as a chariot hitched to two powerful horses prana and *vasana.* Vasana is a collective term for the bodily desires from hunger to sex. If prana is in control, all is well. If vasana is in control, the yogi is scattered and blocked in the past, which requires him or her to follow a single-minded course. Hence, along with pranayana, the yogi needs to work on sense control. This work might include, on the positive side, a healthy dose of bhakti, devotional service in a temple, to remind the yogi of the attractiveness of the divine. It will also include a soul-searching examination of the dominant sensual desires and a philosophical assessment of their limited value and ultimate uselessness. The yogi will attempt to detach himself or herself from the sensual desires.

After conditioning the body, taking control of the breath, and suppressing the desires, the yogi is ready for the next steps: *Dharana* (concentration), and *dhyana* (meditation). In dharana the yogi learns to fix the mind on a single object and to concentrate on it to the exclusion of all other thoughts. The ability to concentrate leads directly to dhyana, in which the flow of concentration is uninterrupted. Dhyana then leads to samadhi.

In addition to the practice of the eight-limbed path, the yogi also has access to a variety of yoga disciplines, which may enhance or substitute for the eight traditional steps. Some yoga practices may be used with or in addition to the eight-limbed approach, such as *japa* yoga, the use of mantras (or words of power) or bhakti (devotional service to the divine). Other practices, such as *surat shabd* yoga, the yoga of the sound current, are generally practices apart from the traditional eight-limbed approach.

Of special interest is kundalini yoga. The literature on the eight-limbed yoga mentions kundalini, the latent power believed by students of Tantrism to lie as a latent force at the base of the spine. The practice of kundalini yoga is supposed to arouse the kundalini energy (often pictured as a coiled cobra) and free it to rise up the spinal column and bring enlightenment as it reaches the crown of the head. Kundalini yoga teaches methods that focus on the arousal of the kundalini, methods that usually include an intense form of pranayana. Some gurus offer what is termed *shaktipat* (*shakti* being another name for kundalini) by which they use their own power to awaken the kundalini in others.

J. Gordon Melton

See also: Besant, Annie; Crowley, Aleister; Divine Life Society; Hinduism; Integral Yoga International; International Society for Krishna Consciousness; Meditation; New Age Movement; Ordo Templi Orientis; Self-Realization Fellowship; Sivananda Saraswati, Swami; Tantrism; Theosophical Society (Adyar); Vegetarianism; Western Esoteric Tradition.

References

Alter, Joseph S. *Yoga in Modern India: The Body between Science and Philosophy*. Princeton, NJ: Princeton University Press, 2004.

Behanan, Kovoor T. *Yoga: A Scientific Evaluation*. 1937; rpt.: New York: Dover Publications, 1960.

Bernard, Theos. *Hatha Yoga: The Report of a Personal Experience*. New York: Columbia University Press, 1945.

Choudhury, Bikram. *Bikram's Beginning Yoga Class*. Los Angeles: J. P. Tarcher, 2000.

Day, Harvey. *Yoga Illustrated Dictionary*. New York: Barnes & Noble, 1971.

DeMichelis, Elizabeth. *A History of Modern Yoga—Patanjali and Western Esotericism*. New York: Continuum, 2005.

Devy, Indra. *Forever Young, Forever Healthy*. New York: Prentice-Hall, 1953.

Feuerstein, Georg. *The Yoga Tradition: Its History, Literature, Philosophy and Practice*. Prescott, AZ: Hohm Press, 1998.

Hittleman, Richard. *Guide to Yoga Meditation*. New York: Bantam Books, 1969.

Iyengar, B. K. S. *Light on Yoga*. New York: Schocken Books, 1966.

Mishna, Rammurti. *Fundamentals of Yoga*. New York: Lancer Books, 1969.

Samuel, Geoffrey. *The Origins of Yoga and Tantra*. Cambridge: Cambridge University Press, 2008.

Satchidananda, Swami. *Integral Yoga Hatha*. New York: Holt, Rinehart and Winston, 1970.

Vishnu Devananda, Swami. *The Complete Illustrated Book of Yoga*. New York: Pocket Books, 1960.

Yogi Tradition

The Yogi tradition is among Hinduism's oldest living traditions. The tradition has no separate modern-day form, as it permeates all of Hinduism. Essentially, as individuals desire to know the Ultimate, or Brahman, they are inspired to seek out Brahman. Yoga is the name given to a spectrum of ways to search for and come to know God.

The "Father of Yoga" was Patanjali (ca. second century BCE), the author of multiple discourses—that is, the Yoga Sutras that contain the knowledge about knowing God through yoga. Patanjali is considered the first yogi, in the strictest sense, though yoga itself derives from the Harappan civilization (2300 BCE). Among the Harappan archaeological sites in Mohenjo Dharo, an ancient statue of a man in a yoga posture was uncovered.

A yogi (or yogini, for a female) lives a life of asceticism. Many Hindus turn to the life of a yogi in the end stages of life in order to gain release from the cycle of reincarnation after their death. A yogi may undergo rigorous training in some form of yoga in order to achieve the deep level of concentration necessary for true yoga. The number of bodily postures (*asanas*) for hatha yoga is in the thousands, with some masters claiming to know them all. Asanas go from simple leg raises to seemingly impossible contortions.

A yogi may have one or more pupils that he or she will instruct in the ways of yoga, or he or she may be completely alone. This habit of teaching is central to Hinduism. There is no modern organization for the yogi tradition because it is a tradition that is incorporated into all forms of Hinduism.

The yogi will meditate until the ultimate goal is achieved. When the yogi sees all beings—friends, enemies, animals, plants, and everything else—as one, the yogi has broken the chain of illusion (*maya*). No more are there illusory distinctions and classes. No longer does logic or common sense seem real to the yogi. When the yogi sees all things as one, the yogi is ready to die, and after death to actually become one with Brahman, the Ultimate Reality.

Hatha yoga, the proto-yoga exercises (postures) that serve as a precursor to the practice of the other forms of yoga (*karma, raja, bhakti,* and *jnana*), had largely disappeared from India by the beginning of the 19th century. It was revived in that century by Yogi Madhavdas (ca. 1798–1921), who operated out of an ashram in Gizrat in western India, and Shyam Sundar Goswami of Calcutta. Madhavdas's student, Shri Yogendra (1897–1989), who built a center in Myambai (Bombay), was a major force in spreading hatha yoga to the West in the early 20th century.

Kumar Jairamdas

See also: Asceticism; Patanjali; Yoga.

References

Aranya, Hariharananda. *Yoga Philosophy of Patanjali.* Trans. by P. N. Mukerji. Calcutta: University of Calcutta, 1977.

Basham, A. L. *The Origins and Development of Classical Hinduism.* New York: Oxford University Press, 1989.

Desikachar, T. K. V. *Religiousness in Yoga.* New York: University Press of America, 1980.

Jarrell, Howard R. *International Yoga Bibliography, 1950–1980.* Metuchen, NJ: Scarecrow, 1981.

Stone, Michael, and Richard Freeman. *The Inner Tradition of Yoga: A Guide to Yoga Philosophy for the Contemporary Practitioner.* Boston: Shambhala, 2008.

Yoido Full Gospel Church

The Yoido Full Gospel Church (Assemblies of God) was founded by Paul David Yonggi Cho in 1958 in an old U.S. Army tent located in a slum area of Seoul, Korea. Forty years later it was acclaimed the largest Christian congregation in the world, with some 730,000 members. The story of Cho and the Yoido church is to a great degree the story of Christianity in Korea since World War II.

Cho was born in 1936 in the District of Uljin near the southern port city of Pusan. He was raised in a Buddhist home in a nation under Japanese occupation. By the time he was 16, Cho was dying of tuberculosis when a young Christian girl told him of Jesus Christ and his healing power. After a miraculous healing in 1955, Cho became a Christian and joined the newly formed Assemblies of God.

The Korean Pentecostal movement began in 1928, when the first Pentecostal missionary from the United States, Mary Rumsey, arrived in Korea. After ordaining her first pastor, Sung San Park, in 1938, she organized the Chosun Pentecostal Church and Mission Center. She later organized five more churches before being expelled from Korea by the Japanese. After the devastation caused by the Korean War, Rumsey turned her churches over to the American Assemblies of God in 1952. The mission soon organized a Bible school in Seoul, where one of the first students was Yonggi Cho.

With the help of U.S. Army chaplains, Cho learned English and became an interpreter for visiting American evangelists. One of his heroes was the healing evangelist Oral Roberts. Cho patterned much of his ministry on Roberts's teachings and evangelistic methods.

In 1962, Cho built a new sanctuary that seated 1,500 persons, but this soon overflowed with crowds seeking salvation and healing. By 1964 the church claimed 2,000 members. Exhausted by his labors, Cho began to organize his church into "cells" that met in homes. These cells provided pastoral care for the exploding congregation. By 1985 there were more than 50,000 such cells, mostly led by women.

Stories of miraculous healings spread over the city, attracting ever-larger crowds. By 1973, with 23,000 members, Cho began construction of a huge new church on Yoido Island, near the site of the new South Korean parliament building. In 1973 the 10,000-seat sanctuary was completed in time to host the Pentecostal World Conference. The growth of the church skyrocketed. By 1979 membership passed the 100,000 mark. In the following years there were periods in which 10,000 new members were added to the church each month. By 1994 the membership had reached the 700,000 mark and the church made plans to be the first congregation to reach the 1,000,000 mark. The membership peaked about 1995, however, with 730,000 members. Slower growth resulted from the organization of new daughter congregations from the Yoido membership.

By 1990, Cho had led in a rebuilding program that saw his sanctuary enlarged to seat 22,000 persons. By this time he led seven Sunday services with more than 30,000 in attendance in each service through the use of additional auditoriums and closed-circuit television. It was claimed that Cho spoke face to face each week to more people than any other person on Earth.

Beyond his local church, Cho became well known as the author of several books on cell groups and church growth. These included his autobiographical *Fourth Dimension* (1979) and *Successful Home Cell Groups* (1981). In 1989 he founded a daily newspaper called the *Kook Min Daily News,* which quickly reached a million subscribers. In this newspaper as well as in his books and sermons, Cho expounded his "Fivefold Message of the Gospel," which included Salvation, the Holy Spirit, Divine Healing, Blessings, and the Second Coming of Jesus. By the end of the century, Cho was probably the best-known Korean Christian leader in the world. His congregation was widely recognized as the largest Christian local church in history.

Yoido Full Gospel Church
PO Box 7
Seoul 150-600
Korea
http://www.yfgc.org/

Vinson Synan

See also: Assemblies of God; Pentecostal World Fellowship.

References

Cho, Paul (David) Yonggi. *The Holy Spirit, My Senior Partner: Understanding the Holy Spirit and His Gifts.* Mary's Lake, FL: Charisma House, 1996.

Cho, Paul (David) Yonggi. *Prayer: Key to Revival.* Waco, TX: Word, 1984.

Vinson, Synan. "The International Ministry of Dr. David Yonggi Cho." In *The Holy Spirit and the Church: A Collection of Scholarly Papers in Celebration of the 40th Anniversary of Dr. Yonggi Cho's Ministry.* Seoul: Privately printed, 1998.

Wilson, D. J. "Paul Yonggi Cho." In *Dictionary of Pentecostal and Charismatic Movements,* edited by Stanley Burgess, Garry McGee, and Patrick Alexander, 161–162. Grand Rapids, MI: Zondervan, 1988.

Yom HaShoah

Yom HaShoah (Holocaust Remembrance Day) is a Jewish commemoration day dedicated to the remembrance of the Holocaust, the destruction of some 6 million Jews that began with the rise to power of the National Socialist Party (the Nazis) in Germany in the 1930s and reached its zenith in the last years of World War II with the development of the gas chambers in the several death camps, most notably Auschwitz in Poland. *Shoah* is a Hebrew word meaning "catastrophe" or "utter destruction."

Yom HaShoah is held on the 27th of Nissan (which occurs in late April or early May on the Common Era calendar) and is an official holiday in Israel. In 2005, the United Nations designated January 27 as the international Holocaust Memorial Day, and that date is acknowledged in most of the countries of the European Union. Neither day is recognized in the United States, but the Jewish community and many in the Christian community hold a commemoration on or near Nissan 27.

As a relatively new day of commemoration, not only has no date been agreed upon by all, but there is no set ritual. Many will light candles, often 6 candles symbolic of the 6 million who died, though much more

Holocaust survivors light candles during the Annual Gathering of Remembrance, April 23, 2006, in New York. The annual event is held on the Sunday closest to Yom HaShoah, Holocaust Remembrance Day. (AP/Wide World Photos)

emphasis is placed upon holding some form of commemoration rather than the form that the observance will take. In Israel, a siren will sound, at which point everyone stops any activity in which they are engaged. Integral to the day is the retelling the stories of what people experienced. The United Kingdom first celebrated a Holocaust Remembrance Day in 2001, the year following the opening of a permanent Holocaust Exhibition at the Imperial War Museum.

In 1994, following the release of *Schindler's List* (1993), director Steven Spielberg formed the Survivors of the Shoah Visual History Foundation (now the USC Shoah Foundation Institute for Visual History and Education) to record and preserve video testimonies of survivors of the Holocaust. The Foundation concentrated on documenting the stories of Jewish survivors, but also interviews other victims including homosex-

uals, Jehovah's Witnesses, Gypsies, and a variety of others who had knowledge of the events. By the end of the 1990s, the archive (since 2006 housed at the University of Southern California) included some 52,000 video testimonies offered by people from 56 different countries.

The Holocaust began with a campaign of anti-Semitism by the Nazis and accompanying acts of violence and destruction. Once Adolf Hitler came to power, plans were put in place to eradicate various segments of the population including homosexuals and Gypsies, but most notably the Jews. In the end, the Nazis adopted a policy, termed the "Final Solution," that looked toward the complete annihilation of the Jews from all of Europe. Systematically, Jews were confined to over-crowded ghettos, then sent to concentration camps, and as additional countries were overrun, sent to death camps. By the time the Nazi regime was brought down, two-thirds of Europe's Jews had been killed.

J. Gordon Melton

See also: Common Era Calendar; Jehovah's Witnesses; Judaism.

References

Berman, Judith E. *Holocaust Remembrance in Australian Jewish Communities*. Perth: University of Western Australia Press, 2002.

Cargas, Harry James. *A Holocaust Commemoration for Days of Remembrance: For Communities, Churches, Centers and for Home Use*. Philadelphia: Holocaust Remembrance Foundation, 1982.

Hornstein, Shelley, and Florence Jacobowitz. *Image and Remembrance: Representation and the Holocaust*. Bloomington: Indiana University Press, 2002.

Miller, Marjorie. "Britain Devotes a Day to Holocaust Victims." *Los Angeles Times*, January 27, 2001.

Smith, Lyn. *Remembering: Voices of the Holocaust: A New History in the Words of the Men and Women Who Survived*. New York: Basic Books, 2007.

A Jewish man observing kaparot, an ancient and mystical custom connected to the Jewish Day of Atonement, Yom Kippur. (Yehuda Bernstein/Dreamstime.com)

Yom Kippur

Yom Kippur (the Day of Atonement), possibly the single most observed holy day in the Jewish year, is one of two Jewish holidays not related to a specific historical event in Jewish memory (as are, for example, Passover or Purim). Like Rosh Hashanah, it is related primarily to the commandment of God for an annual act of atonement. It occurs on the 10th day of the month of Tishri in the Jewish calendar and follows more than a month of preparation that began on the first day of Elul, the previous month. During the month of Elul, one begins to think about the issues of self-reflection, repentance, and atonement for one's failings, and begins to bring one's consciousness and behavior into a repentant mode. This preparation leads to Rosh Hashanah, the Day of the Shofar Blast or the Jewish New Year, which kicks off the High Holy Days. The High Holy Days are seen as a time of concentrated self-reflection and repentance, and for special acts of charity and forgiveness. Following Rosh Hashanah, the Days of Awe lead to the Day of Atonement in which God seals his judgment for the coming year.

The observance of Yom Kippur is mandated in Leviticus 23:26-32: "And the LORD spoke unto Moses, saying: Howbeit on the tenth day of this seventh month is the day of atonement; there shall be a holy convocation unto you, and ye shall afflict your souls; and ye shall bring an offering made by fire unto the LORD. And ye shall do no manner of work in that same day; for it is a day of atonement, to make atonement for you before the LORD your God. For whatsoever soul it be that shall not be afflicted in that same day, he shall be cut off from his people. And whatsoever soul it be that doeth any manner of work in that same day, that soul will I destroy from among his people. Ye shall do no manner of work; it is a statute for ever throughout your generations in all your dwellings. It shall be unto you a sabbath of solemn rest, and ye shall afflict your souls; in the ninth day of the month at even, from even unto even, shall ye keep your sabbath."

On Rosh Hashanah, believers think of God writing a judgment upon them relative to their behavior and motivations over the previous year. The succeeding Days of Awe are a time to reflect upon the past year, seek forgiveness, and make amends. The Day of Atonement represents one last chance to change the judgment of God in one's favor before the day ends, and God seals his judgment for the coming year. That judgment heralds one's prosperity, happiness, and even life or death for the coming year.

Yom Kippur is observed as a Sabbath. One refrains from all work. It is also a day of fasting with no food or drink beginning shortly before sunset and continuing for the next 25 hours. Additional restrictions punctuating the uniqueness of the day include refraining from washing and bathing, not using cosmetics products such as deodorants, wearing shoes made of something other than leather (like canvas sneakers), and of course, refraining from sexual relations. Many people will dress in white.

Most of Yom Kippur is spent in communal prayer in the synagogue, there being five services; the first one at sundown on the eve of Yom Kippur begins the start of the fast; the last ends at nightfall the next day, and concludes the fast with the *shofar* (ram's horn) sounded in a final long blast. Part of the Yom Kippur liturgy is a lengthy and broadly worded confession of the sins of the community, with an emphasis on sins that were detrimental to one's neighbor, including acts of both omission and commission.

Yom Kippur is a public holiday in Israel. Radio and television stations cease broadcasting; airports and other public transportation shut down; and all businesses, including restaurants, close. In Israel, even many who consider themselves irreligious Jews fast and avoid using prohibited transportation and communication systems. Soldiers seek leave to be with their families for the day.

In 1973, well aware of Israel's vulnerability on this, the most sacred day in the Jewish calendar, Egypt and Syria attacked Israel. As radios, which had been silent, began calling up the reserves and soldiers left their prayers to return to their units, Israel retreated before the advancing Egyptian and Syrian armies. However, within a few days, Israel recovered and fought the war to a point that victory seemed imminent before a cease-fire went into effect.

By 2008, 63 percent of the Israeli public said they planned to fast on Yom Kippur, the great majority for religious reasons. Those who did not intend to fast (a third of the Israeli public) did not plan to observe openly the traditional observance of the holy day.

J. Gordon Melton

See also: Days of Awe; Judaism; Rosh Hashannah.

References

Cohen, Jeffrey M. *1,001 Questions and Answers on Rosh HaShanah and Yom Kippur*. New York: Jason Aronson, 1997.

Eckstein, Yecheil. *What You Should Know About Jews and Judaism*. Waco, TX: Word Books, 1984.

Greenberg, Irving. *The Jewish Way: Living the Holidays*. New York: Jason Aronson, 1998.

Posner, Raphael, Uri Kaploun, and Sherman Cohen, eds. *Jewish Liturgy: Prayer and Synagogue Service through the Ages*. New York: Leon Amiel Publisher; Jerusalem: Keter Publishing House, 1975.

Schauss, Hayyim. *The Jewish Festivals: A Guide to Their History and Observance*. New York: Schocken, 1996.

"63% of Israeli Jews plan to fast on Yom Kippur." Ynet News. http://www.ynetnews.com/articles/0,7340,L-3606942,00.html. Accessed June 15, 2009.

Yoruban Religion/Spirituality

The Yoruban people of Nigeria emerged out of prehistory with the founding of Ife, a city in southwestern Nigeria, which has been their center for a millennium. Yoruban towns are traditionally headed by a chief (*oba*) who is invested with authority by the chief in Ife. Although they are an agricultural people, everyday life is

A family gives an offering to Yemanja, the Yoruban sea goddess, during a religious celebration in Montevideo, February 2, 2007. West African slaves brought their Yoruban beliefs to the Americas, where they have spread throughout many countries. (AP/Wide World Photos)

centered in the villages that are placed in the center of the local farmland.

The Yorubans divide the cosmos into Orun, the sky, and Aiye, the Earth. In the sky dwells Olorun, the High God, a number of associated deities (the Orissa), and the ancestors. Olorun is seen as somewhat remote and difficult to approach; hence he is not the object of shrines, rituals, or prayers. He is seen as the source of all and the creator of the first 16 human beings. However, it is Orisa-nla who is credited with creating the Earth and transferring the first humans to their new home. It is also believed that Orisa-nla began his acts of creation at Ife. Hence Ife is the center of all religious and spiritual power. Other locations have power as derived from Ife. (An alternate story suggests that Orisa-nla messed up his work and that Odunuwa had to redo it.)

Orisa-nla and Odunuwa are but two of the Orissa. Others include Ogun, the god of metals, and Esu, generally associated with divination. Also important to the Yoruban system are the ancestors. Outstanding ancestors are seen as residing in the abode of the Orissa and are venerated with their own shrines and rituals. Some ancestors are recognized for their role in Yoruban history and are recognized above their association with a single family. Some have attained status for the nation as divine beings, including Sango, Orisa-oko, and Ayelala, virtually identical to the Orissa. Both the Orissa and the ancestors are sources of power.

The role of the various religious functionaries in Yoruban society is to mediate between the people and the Orissa and ancestors. Each of the deities has priests. Some priests (*aworo*) are diviners (*babalawo*) who are consulted on the questions of life. Other priests attend the shrines of various deities. Yorubans believe that deities possess various people, called the *elegun*, who operate as a medium through whom the deities communicate. There are also healers, the *oloogun*, and the masked dancers (*egungun*), whose traditional masks are seen as possessors of power.

There are between 5 and 10 million Yorubans, most of whom reside in western Nigeria. There is a great variety in the practice associated with the widespread Yoruban system, not only in Nigeria and neighboring countries but also in its New World incarnations in Cuba and Brazil (where it developed an overlay of Christianity and is known variously as Santeria or Macumba). Both Christianity and Islam have come into Yoruban lands, resulting in a situation in which syncretistic religions have emerged. Among the primary groups to arise in reaction to Christianity are the various Aladura churches, which exist along a spectrum between orthodox Protestant Christianity and traditional Yoruban religion. The Church of the Lord, Aladura is a member of the World Council of Churches. Others, such as the Aladura and Eternal Sacred Order of the Cherubim and Seraphim, have incorporated elements of possession practices from the traditional practice.

Yoruban religious leaders in the West have made themselves available to interpret the faith of their coreligionists in Africa. Prominent organizations include the Ife Foundation of North (http://www.ifafoundation .org/), the Iglesia Lukumi Babalu Aye (http://home .earthlink.net/~clba/index.htm), and the African Theological Archministry centers on the Oyotunji African Yoruban Village at Shelton, South Carolina.

J. Gordon Melton

See also: Aladura Churches; Ancestors; Church of the Lord; Santeria; World Council of Churches.

References

Curry, Mary Cuthrell. *Making the Gods in New York: The Yoruba Religion in the African American Community*. New York: Garland, 1997.

Edwards, Gary, and John Mason. *Black God—Orisa Studies in the New World*. Brooklyn,

NY: Yoruba Theological Archministry, 1985.

Ìdòwú, E. Bólájí. *Olódùmaré: God in Yorùbá Belief*. New York: Wazobia, 1994.

Lawson, E. Thomas. *Religions of Africa*. San Francisco: HarperSanFrancisco, 1985.

Young Buddhist Association of Malaysia

The Young Buddhist Association of Malaysia (YBAM) was established on July 29, 1970, in Kuala Lumpur. The YBAM is a nonprofit religious organization that espouses a nonsectarian approach toward all Buddhist traditions.

The objectives of the YBAM are the following: (1) to be the national organization of all Buddhist youths in Malaysia; (2) to encourage, foster, and develop the practice of the teachings of the Buddha among youths; (3) to coordinate the religious, social, and recreational activities of Buddhist youths through its member organizations; (4) to provide leadership training for Buddhist youths; and (5) to further all other interests of Buddhist youths as may be decided upon at a National Council meeting. The YBAM carries out its activities through the following committees: (1) Dharma Propagation, (2) Education, (3) Publication, (4) Welfare, (5) Culture, (6) Training, (7) Buddhist Graduates and Buddhist Undergraduates, (8) Government Affairs and External Relations, (9) International Affairs, and (10) Finance.

Its core activities are based on Dharma propagation, education, culture, and welfare. The YBAM organizes Dharma propagation activities by inviting Buddhist scholars, both locally and overseas, to give teachings on Buddhism through public lectures, seminars, study camps, and conferences. In 1996 the Dharma Propagators Training Program was launched to train Dharma speakers. It also publishes an English journal, *Eastern Horizon,* three times a year, and a quarterly Chinese journal, *Buddhist Digest,* in addition to other Buddhist literature. In the area of education, it has produced a Buddhist syllabus for the primary schools and is preparing the syllabus for the secondary schools.

Inasmuch as Malaysia is a plural society, YBAM ensures that cultural programs representing Buddhist values are incorporated into the local Buddhist community. In 1994 it launched the organ donation campaign to educate the public on the importance of donating organs after death. In 1980 the YBAM launched its first Six-Year Plan (1980–1986) to ensure that programs are well strategized and in line with its national objectives. A formal planning process also allows it to monitor the success of its implemented programs. During the latest Six-Year Plan (1998–2003), a Quality Management System was launched to ensure that programs achieve quality standards.

Membership in the YBAM comprises ordinary membership and associate membership. Ordinary members are Buddhist organizations with youth members, while associate members are individuals. As of January 1, 2001, there were a total of 250 ordinary members and more than 2,000 individual members. In 2009, it reported 270 member organisations engaged in propagating the Dharma and training youth.

YBAM is a member of the Malaysian Youth Council, and it is affiliated to the World Fellowship of Buddhist Youth (WFBY). It hosted the WFBY's 13th General Conference in 2002 in Kuala Lumpur. The YBAM operates a full-time secretariat based at its headquarters.

Young Buddhist Association of Malaysia
10 Jalan SS 2/75
47300 Petaling Jaya
Selangor
Malaysia
http://www.ybam.org.my/

Benny Liow Woon Khin

See also: World Fellowship of Buddhists.

References

YBAM 10th Anniversary Souvenir Magazine. Penang, 1980.

YBAM 15th Anniversary Souvenir Magazine. Penang, 1987.

"YBAM 15th National Council Biennial Report." Petaling Jaya, 2000.

YBAM National Council Handbook. Petaling Jaya, 2000.

Young Israel

The movement Young Israel grew out of an effort to reach out to the Orthodox youth, who were alienated from the Yiddish-speaking Orthodox worship that dominated within the immigrant communities of the Lower East Side of Manhattan. The founders of Young Israel, among them Jewish Theological Seminary Professors Mordecai Kaplan (who later founded the Reconstructionist movement) and Israel Friedlander, sought to bridge the Old World and New by creating an Americanized Orthodox synagogue for the immigrants' English-speaking children.

The first Young Israel congregation was established in 1915. Its sermons were in English; there was no charge for synagogue honors; and it included components of a community center to reach out to its intended audience.

Over time new Young Israel congregations emerged —today the movement claims 25,000 families as members. As these synagogues developed, they discovered that their approach differed in degree from that of other Orthodox groups. For example Young Israel set minimum standards for the partition separating men and women in worship, while other Orthodox bodies did not. Hence it remained a separate organization. Over the next decades, as the youth with whom the movement began grew to adulthood, Young Israel emerged as a powerful representative of Orthodoxy.

The movement incorporated in 1926. During the 1930s it spread across the United States and into Canada. By the beginning of World War II, there were 35 affiliated synagogues. After the establishment of the State of Israel, the American Friends of Young Israel was founded to establish centers in the new country. Today (2009) there are some 150 affiliated synagogues in the United States and 50 in Israel.

Young Israel, at its beginning, represented the liberal end of the spectrum of Orthodox Judaism. Yet, it steadily became more traditionalist through the 20th century, advocating punctilious Sabbath observance.

National Council of Young Israel
111 John Street, Ste. 450
New York, NY 10038

Young Israel
PO Box 7306
Jerusalem 91371
Israel
http://www.youngisrael.org/

J. Gordon Melton

See also: Conservative Judaism; Orthodox Judaism;
Reform Judaism.

References

Rosenthal, Gilbert S. *Contemporary Judaism:
Patterns of Survival*. New York: Human Sciences,
1986.

"Young Israel—Movement to Synagogue." In *The
Jewish Directory and Almanac,* edited by Ivan L.
Tillem. New York: Pacific, 1984.

Young Men's Buddhist Association

The Colombo Young Men's Buddhist Association
(YMBA), known in Sinhala as Taruna Bauddha Sami-
tiya, was founded on January 8, 1898. Many other
similar Buddhist societies emerged as a result of the
religious revival that began among Buddhists in Sri
Lanka in the late 19th century. The Colombo YMBA's
motto teaches that a life in which morality is well
combined with wisdom brings one victory (*sila pan-
nanato jayam*). One of the aims of the YMBAs was "to
advance the moral, cultural, physical and social welfare of Buddhists." As a lay Buddhist movement, its
strength and prestige increased with the spread of its
branches in local areas in the first half of the 20th century. YMBAs were invented to increase the knowledge
in *dhamma*, to hold discussions on Buddha's teachings, and to help people to organize life in accordance
with Buddhist doctrines (according to the dominant
Theravada Buddhism in Sri Lanka). When YMBA grew
in strength, it was assigned to organize the Dhamma
schools (*daham pasal*) that have become a characteristic feature of Buddhist education in modern Sri Lanka.
Until the Sri Lankan government took over its functions
in 1961, YMBA had established a national network of
Buddhist Sunday schools for which they provided
printed texts and other educational resources.

In organizing the Dhamma schools, YMBA has
made a distinctive contribution. On December 20, 1919,
Sir D. B. Jayathilaka (1868–1944) chaired a gathering
of Buddhist organizations held at Ananda College (f.
1895). In that assembly, YMBA was asked to hold
Dhamma examinations. In the first Dhamma school
examination, held in 1920, 374 male and female students from 27 Dhamma schools participated. Although
its success encouraged YMBA to hold exams every
year, it also introduced Bauddhacarya examination for
teachers of the Dhamma schools in 1926, in which 12
teachers took part. During the time of *Buddha Jayanti*
(1956), the interest in Dhamma schools developed
steadily. Students could attend the Dhamma schools
until the age of 23, and in one class students studied
for 2 years. Although four to five books were assigned
for each class, students were also expected to finish the
study of texts such as the *Abhidharmarthasangraha*.

Although the Dhamma examinations, held at five
levels, were open to any person interested in the study
of Theravada Buddhism, candidates who were over
the age of 25 were permitted to take diploma examinations without taking the prior ones. The examinations
were held on the fourth Sunday of June at centers
in Sri Lanka and abroad, and candidates were able
to apply through Dhamma schools. The examination
contained two papers, testing students' knowledge of
Dhamma and Abhidhamma. Further, in the 1980s, the
Colombo YMBA was asked to produce the Dhamma
schoolbooks that were published and distributed free
of charge by the Ministry of Buddhist Affairs.

In addition, since 1902, the Colombo YMBA has
continuously published an English periodical, *The Buddhist,* which was originally published by the Colombo
Theosophical Society, beginning in 1888.

To meet the expectations of lay Buddhists, local
YMBAs scattered around the country organize a variety of activities to enhance the learning experience of
the laity. For instance, since its founding in 1944, the
YMBA in Balapitiya has provided religious instruction on Buddhism by sponsoring preaching sessions
by famous Buddhist preachers, such as the Venerable
Hinatiyana Dhammaloka (1900–1981).

Most YMBAs across the island nation support
observing the precepts on special days, the practice of

meditation, holding Dhamma discussions, the distribution of printed sermons, the celebration of Vesak, providing facilities for the sick, sponsoring sports activities, creating library facilities, and promoting the education of local children through financial support and guidance.

Colombo Young Men's Buddhist Association
70 D.S. Senanayake Mawatha
Colombo 8
Sri Lanka
http://www.ymba-colombo.org/index.htm

Mahinda Deegalle

See also: Theravada Buddhism.

References

Bechert, Heinz. *Buddhismus: Staat und Gesellschaft in den Landern des Theravada Buddhismus.* 3 vols. Wiesbaden: O. Harrassowitz, 1966–1973.

Bond, George. *The Buddhist Revival in Sri Lanka: Religious Tradition, Reinterpretation and Response.* Columbia: University of South Carolina Press, 1988.

Gombrich, Richard F. *Theravada Buddhism: A Social History from Ancient Benares to Modern Colombo.* London: Routledge and Kegan Paul, 1988.

Gombrich, Richard F., and Gananath Obeyesekere. *Buddhism Transformed: Religious Change in Sri Lanka.* Princeton, NJ: Princeton University Press, 1988.

Valitota: Balapitiya Taruna Bauddha Samitiye Rajata Jayantiya. Ed. by D. D. M. Seneviratna et al. Colombo: Anula Mudranalaya, 1971.

Z

■ Zambia

Zambia, in the heart of Central Africa, is a landlocked country surrounded by the Democratic Republic of the Congo, Angola, Namibia, Zimbabwe, Mozambique, Malawi, and Tanzania. Some 11,700,000 people (2008) reside on its 286,000 square miles of territory. More than 70 languages are spoken by the various Native people who make up 98 percent of Zambia's population.

Over the centuries, what is now Zambia was settled by various Bantu peoples who attempted to make a place for themselves in the several river valleys and along the lakes that constitute its border with neighboring countries. Modern history begins with the initial trek of Portuguese explorers attempting to find a land route tying together Mozambique and Angola. They were frustrated first by the Sotos, who moved

into the Congo when driven out of their lands to the south, and then by the British, who moved into the area from South Africa. The British both coveted the mineral resources of the region and wanted to build their own land route across Africa (from South Africa to Egypt).

The British–South Africa Company kept control of what became known as Northern Rhodesia (named for Cecil Rhodes) through the 19th century, and the British government assumed direct hegemony only in 1924. The oppressive conditions in the mines became the catalyst to unite people in the effort to gain independence. In 1953 the British moved Zambia into a federation with Southern Rhodesia (Zimbabwe) and Nyasaland (Malawi). Kenneth Naunda led the forces boycotting an election that would institutionalize European domination of the federated states. The struggle would be fought openly over the next decade, but

Zambia

Religion	Followers in 1970	Followers in 2010	% of Population	Annual % growth 2000–2010	Followers in 2025	Followers in 2050
Christians	2,772,000	10,775,000	85.3	1.95	14,496,000	20,653,000
Protestants	296,000	4,180,000	33.1	2.78	5,500,000	7,700,000
Roman Catholics	923,000	3,890,000	30.8	3.24	5,300,000	7,400,000
Independents	391,000	1,800,000	14.3	1.57	2,600,000	3,750,000
Ethnoreligionists	1,451,000	1,411,000	11.2	1.52	1,366,000	1,200,000
Baha'is	10,300	250,000	2.0	1.89	400,000	600,000
Muslims	13,000	135,000	1.1	1.89	180,000	250,000
Agnostics	10,000	22,400	0.2	1.89	50,000	90,000
Hindus	7,700	17,200	0.1	1.89	25,000	40,000
Atheists	0	8,800	0.1	1.89	13,000	20,000
Buddhists	0	4,200	0.0	1.90	7,000	12,000
Jews	800	1,600	0.0	1.89	2,000	3,000
Total population	**4,265,000**	**12,625,000**	**100.0**	**1.89**	**16,539,000**	**22,868,000**

ZAMBIA

after Naunda's United National Independence Party won the 1964 elections, independence immediately followed.

Naunda survived Zambia's isolation from its neighbors with an economy built on copper mining, and saw the situation reverse when the other countries gained their independence. He led the country until 1991, when a multiparty system was adopted and Frederick Chiluba was elected to succeed him.

Traditional religions have had a rich history since the coming of the Europeans. The religions that were developed by the various Bantu groups held in common the belief in a supreme being, variously called Mulungu or Lesa, the veneration of one's ancestors, and the practice of magic. In reaction to the presence of whites, a variety of movements have developed, drawing adherents from multiple peoples; new movements have come in from neighboring countries, especially the Mahamba movement from Angola and the Mashave movement from lands to the south. Most of these movements have in common an emphasis on spiritual healing or spirit possession. Somewhat different has been the Mchape movement from Malawi, which aims to counter witchcraft—that is, malevolent magic.

The first Christians in Zambia were Portuguese Catholics who entered the region in the late 1700s. The first permanent missionary station, however, was opened in 1885 by the Paris Mission affiliated with the

Reformed Church of France. The London Missionary Society, the Church of Scotland's (Presbyterian) missionaries, and the British Methodists arrived within a few years. Each of these missions grew into churches, which finally merged in 1965 to form the United Church of Zambia, the largest church in the country. Kenneth Naunda was himself a Presbyterian. Other early churches with a sizable following include the Reformed Church in Zambia (started from South Africa), the Christian Brethren, the Seventh-day Adventist Church, and the African Methodist Episcopal Church. Representatives of the Church of England arrived in Zambia in 1909 and built their church primarily among white settlers. Zambian Anglicans are now part of the Church of the Province of Central Africa.

The Roman Catholic Church finally established permanent work in 1891 through the efforts of the White Fathers. They were later provided assistance by the Franciscans, Capuchins, and Jesuits. The church grew steadily through the 20th century, and the first bishop was established in Lusaka in 1959. The first African bishop was consecrated in 1963.

The Jehovah's Witnesses entered Zambia in 1911 and soon spread among the Native population. At their height as many as a fourth of the population were affiliated, and 15 to 20 percent remain aligned. Their growth has come in the face of periodic attempts by the government to suppress them, the most recent being in the late 1960s, when the new independent government banished all foreign leadership and tried (unsuccessfully) to destroy the movement. Today the Witnesses claim some 375,000 adherents. Their influence is extended through several large independent Witness groups. Of these, the independent Watchtower group is most interesting, as it has built its work around four cooperative villages. The New Apostolic Church, a German-based 19th-century millennial group, came to Zambia in 1915 and, like the Witnesses, has had spectacular success.

Zambia has been a center of new African Indigenous Churches, especially in the years since the country's independence. Among the most important is the Lumpa, or Visible Salvation, Church founded by Alice Lenshina (1920–1978) in 1954. It still has an active following counted in the tens of thousands, though it was officially banned in 1965. Also functioning is the Mutima Walowa Wa Mukumbi (Sweet Heart of the Clouds), founded in 1951 by Emilio Mulolani Chishimba (b. ca. 1921). The majority of the more than 100 independent churches known to exist in the country have come into Zambia from neighboring countries, though most have only small followings.

At least three ecumenical councils now operate in Zambia. The more liberal churches, those associated with the World Council of Churches, have remained in the Christian Council of Zambia, originally founded in 1945. The more conservative evangelical groups compose the Evangelical Fellowship of Zambia, associated with the World Evangelical Alliance. Many of the independent churches have banded together in the Association of Independent Churches.

Zambia has attracted only a small representative sampling of the world's religions. There is a small Jewish community of less than 50 resident members in Lusaka who support the Lusaka Hebrew Congregation. A larger Muslim community is focused upon Asian expatriates residing in Lusaka and several other urban centers. Similar is Hinduism, also brought to Zambia from India, but having little appeal to the population at large. Following a distinct course is the Baha'i Faith, which has enjoyed some success since the 1960s among various Zambian peoples.

J. Gordon Melton

See also: African Methodist Episcopal Church; Baha'i Faith; Capuchins; Christian Brethren; Church of England; Church of Scotland; Church of the Province of Central Africa; Franciscans; Jehovah's Witnesses; Jesuits; London Missionary Society; Mutima Walowa Wa Mukumbi; New Apostolic Church; Paris Mission; Reformed Church in Zambia; Reformed Church of France; Roman Catholic Church; Seventh-day Adventist Church; United Church of Zambia; White Fathers; World Council of Churches; World Evangelical Alliance.

References

Banda, Alick. *Church-State Relations in Zambia: A Policy Proposal*. New York: Peter Lang Publishing, 2004.

Cross, S. "The Watchtower Movement in South Central Africa." Ph.D. diss., Oxford University, 1973.

Hinfelaar, Hugo F. *Bemba-Speaking Women of Zambia in a Century of Religious Change, 1892–1992*. Leiden: Brill, 1997.

Hinfelaar, Hugo F. *History of the Catholic Church in Zambia 1895–1995*. Sarasota, FL: Bookworld Services, 2004.

Macmillan, Hugh. *Zion in Africa: The Jews of Zambia*. London: I. B. Tauris, 1999.

Roberts, A. D. "The Lumpa Church of Alice Lenshina." In *Protest and Power in Black Africa*, edited by R. Rotberg and A. Mazrui. New York: Oxford University Press, 1970.

Rotberg, R. *Christian Missionaries and the Creation of Northern Rhodesia*. Princeton, NJ: Princeton University Press, 1965.

Zaydites

Most Shia Muslims trace the lineage of their leadership, the imams, through al-Husayn's surviving son, Ali, better known as Zayn al-Abidin (d. 714), and his son, Muhammad al-Baqir (d. ca. 732). However, between their time in office, the Shia community had to face the challenge posed by the elder son of Zayn al-Abidin, Zayd b. Ali (d. 740), who had been named the new Shia imam ahead of al-Baqir.

Zayd came to his office as the understanding of the imam as guide of the community was being elevated. Zayd rejected this trend and the ascription of any divine or supernatural elements to the imam's authority. As his opinions became known, the majority of the Shiite leadership rejected him, and moved to substitute al-Baqir in his place. The Shias came to consider Zayd as never having been the imam. His small following survived, however, and in the ninth century they were able to establish hegemony in two countries, Tabaristan (south of the Caspian Sea) and Yemen. The former Zaydi state came to an end in 928, was re-established in 964, but declined in the 12th century. Most of the Zaydis were absorbed into the larger Shiite community.

Yemen, as a Zaydi state, was founded in 890. Zaydi supremacy was challenged in the years after the fall of the Fatimid dynasty in Egypt as Ismaili Islam grew strong in the region, but in spite of the attacks from the Ismailis, the Yemeni state retained its independence. Then in 1539, it was incorporated into the Ottoman Empire (based in the Hanafite School of Sunni Islam). Their rule lasted only until 1595, when the Zaydis revolted; they drove the Ottomans out in 1635. Yemen retained its independence for more than two centuries, but in 1872 the Ottomans once again took over the region. As the Ottomans declined, Yemen received independence (albeit with strong British influence) as World War I progressed.

The Zaydites disagree with the Shiites on the issues of the imamate (the same issue that split Sunnis and Shias). They did retain the office of the imam, though he was chosen on merit, military skill often being more important than any spiritual or intellectual qualifications. There are reports of two rivals for the imam's office fighting to the death to demonstrate their higher qualifications.

The Zaydite community has been dramatically affected by events since 1949. In 1949 there was an attempt to overthrow the government by coup. Although Imam Yahya was killed, the coup did not succeed. His successors remained in power until 1962, when a secular coup was successful in deposing the imam and establishing the Yemen Arab Republic (superseded in 1990 by the People's Democratic Republic of Yemen). Since that time, the office of the imam has remained vacant.

The Zaydites have no separate headquarters, though it is the official religion of Yemen. There is a Ministry of Awqaf (endowments) and Religious Guidance in the government at the national level. Most of the world's 8 million Zaydites reside in Yemen, but they may now be found scattered around the globe.

J. Gordon Melton

See also: Hanafite School of Islam; Ismaili Islam.

Reference

Yann, Richard. *Shi'ite Islam*. Oxford: Blackwell, 1995.

Zen Buddhism

Zen Buddhism is a branch of Mahayana Buddhism. According to legend, the Buddha established the foun-

Statue of Buddha, Thailand. (Margouillat/Dreamstime.com)

dations of Zen Buddhism during a discourse on Vulture Peak in which he held up a flower. Only Mahakashyapa understood this message, becoming the first Indian patriarch in the Zen Buddhist lineage. Legend continues that an Indian monk named Bodhidharma transmitted this new form of Buddhism to China around 500 CE. Bodhidharma's teachings mixed with Daoism to form a new school of Mahayana Buddhism, called Chan. Chan is the Chinese pronunciation of the Sanskrit word *dhyana*, which means "meditation." In Japan, Chan became known as Zen, which is the Japanese pronunciation of Chan. The two main schools of Japanese Zen Buddhism, Rinzai and Soto, were introduced into Japan from China in the 12th and 13th centuries, respectively. Both schools adapted to Japanese culture, while still retaining elements of their Chinese roots.

The aim of Zen Buddhism is to achieve enlightenment. The essential nature of Zen is often summarized as follows: a special transmission outside the scriptures; no dependence upon words and letters; direct pointing at the human heart; seeing into one's nature and the realization of Buddhahood.

Zen claims to differ from other Buddhist schools in its emphasis on seated meditation. In contrast with his contemporaries, Bodhidharma de-emphasized the existing focus on priestly ritual and the endless chanting of the sutras or Buddhist scriptures. Although other Buddhist schools often balance meditation with other religious practices such as intellectual analysis of doctrines or devotional practices, Zen considers those practices useless in attaining enlightenment. The core of Zen practice is seated meditation, called *zazen*. Meditation practices differ in different schools: generally, Soto Zen teaches *shikantaza*, and Rinzai Zen teaches *koan* practice. Shikantaza (nothing but sitting) involves sitting, in a state of alert attention that is free of thoughts. Koans are paradoxical questions, phrases, or stories that cannot be solved using intellectual reasoning, such as "What is the sound of one hand clapping?"

Like other Buddhist traditions, Zen Buddhism has begun to develop in Western countries in the last 100 years. In 1893, Shaku Soyen attended the Chicago World's Parliament of Religions, becoming the first Zen master to visit the United States. In the early 1900s a few Rinzai priests moved to the United States, and in 1930 one of these established the first Zen center in the United States in New York, the Buddhist Society of America. Works on Zen by authors such as D. T. Suzuki had an important role in contributing to an understanding of Zen at an intellectual and philosophical level in both the United States and Europe. Interest in the practice of Zen came later, beginning with the influence of the Beat generation in the 1950s and increasing in the 1960s with the arrival of Japanese teachers coming to teach and establish centers in Europe and the United States.

The vast majority of Zen practitioners outside of Japan are converts. There are now indigenous Zen teachers from a variety of lineages leading Zen groups in countries as diverse as the United States, Canada, the United Kingdom, France, Germany, Poland, Spain, Sweden, Switzerland, Australia, New Zealand, Argentina, Brazil, India, and the Philippines. As Zen has developed it has been recontextualized to suit Western cultures. Major changes include an emphasis on lay practice, equality for women, the application of democratic principles, an emphasis on ethics, and secularization and the linkage to some sciences, particularly psychology and psychotherapy.

Zen Buddhism has an extensive presence on the Internet, a good starting point being the Zen Buddhism Virtual Library at http://www.ciolek.com/WWWVL-Zen.html. It includes a directory of groups and centers internationally.

Michelle Barker

See also: Bodhidharma; Mahayana Buddhism; Meditation; Rinzai (Japan), Lin-Chi (China), Imje (Korea), Lam-Te (Vietnam); Soto Zen Buddhism.

References
Dumoulin, Heinrich. *Zen Buddhism: A History*. Wisdom, 2005.
Kapleau, Philip. *The Three Pillars of Zen*. Rev. ed. New York: Anchor, 1989.
Rommeluère, Éric. *Guide du Zen*. Paris: Livre de poche, 1997.
Shunryu Suzuki. *Zen Mind, Beginner's Mind*. Shambhala Library, 2006.

Zhang Daoling

Zhang Daoling (Zhang Ling; second century CE) established Daoism as a unique religious movement. Until that point Daoist philosophers had created a philosophical school of Daoism, but no institutional framework in which to develop a religion and, eventually, a functioning state.

According to tradition Zhang was a hermit living in the mountains of western Sichuan. In 142 he experienced a vision from Taishang Laojun (Laozi). Taishang Laojun announced he was withdrawing the Mandate of Heaven from the current ruling dynasty, the Han, and giving it to Zhang. Zhang was given the title of *tianshi* (heavenly master) and powers to combat demons. He had become Laozi's spokesperson.

Zhang quickly established the Wudoumi (five pecks of rice) sect, so named because each follower was levied a tax of five pecks of rice. The movement passed under the control of Zhang's son and grandchildren and created a new state in Sichuan. While the state did not last long as a political entity, the Heavenly Master lineage established by Zhang has continued into the modern period. Daoist priests who receive ordination through this lineage are still widely accepted as orthodox.

Edward A. Irons

See also: Daoism.

References
Miller, James. *Daoism: A Short Introduction*. Oxford: Oneworld, 2003.
Robinet, Isabelle. *Taoism: Growth of a Religion*. Trans. by Phyllis Brooks. Stanford, CA: Stanford University Press, 1997.
Thompson, Laurence G. *Chinese Religion: An Introduction*. Belmont, CA: Wadsworth, 1996.

Zhengyi Daoism

The Zhengyi represent the second group of legitimate Daoists active today (the other being Quanzhen). They are sometimes called Tianshi Daoists because they claim to trace their lineage back to the Heavenly Masters of the Han dynasty (Daoism), though scholars doubt the continuity. The Zhang family of Jiangxi Province, unknown before the ninth century, took on the mantle of the Zhang family of Sichuan Province of the second century and received imperial recognition. Thus the Zhengyi (Orthodox Unity) Order of Longhushan (Dragon Tiger Mountain) was created. That is still their headquarters in mainland China.

In 1304 the Yuan emperor appointed the Celestial Master to supervise the registers of other sects, and many folded into the Zhengyi. The Zhengyi was the dominant school during the Ming, and many of the Zhang family married into the imperial family.

Early Western accounts of Zhengyi called the hereditary Celestial Master "the Daoist Pope." In 1949 the 63rd Celestial Master moved to Taiwan, where the 64th lives today. (That is the 64th counting from Zhang Daoling, though the lineage is verifiable only through the 23rd, dating to the middle of the Tang.) Today approximately 20 percent of Daoists on the mainland are Zhengyi, concentrated mainly in southeast China. Taiwan (where many southeast Chinese immigrated after the Communist takeover) is predominantly Zhengyi. In Beijing, Zhengyi was represented by Dongyue miao

Daoist priest Dong Zhiguang, right, performs a ceremony at Qingyanggong, or Green Ram Palace, in Chengdu, China, 2005. (AFP/Getty Images)

(Eastern Peak Temple), built during the Yuan dynasty, now a museum.

Zhengyi ordination is passed down from father to son within individual families, or through master-disciple as legitimated through adoption. Priests work out of their homes, where they maintain an altar. They provide ritual services on demand or according to the calendar to community members, who are not necessarily Daoist. Zhengyi is sometimes seen as "folk Daoism," though that is a misnomer.

Major rituals include *jiao* (communal sacrifice), which harmonizes the entire community with the cosmos. Used to commemorate a special event, the jiao includes a celebratory offering of flowers, fruit, and incense. The *zhai* are rituals of repentance in which the priests inside the temple fast on behalf of the com-

munity. Paradoxically, in the modern Daoist temple, zhai refers to the special community banquet (vegetarian dishes prepared to look and taste like meat) that follows.

Both jiao and zhai are commonly performed in conjunction with each other as part of an entire series of rituals held during a multiday festival. Other Zhengyi rituals include the *gongde* (requiem service), healing, and exorcisms. These rites incorporate many layers of previous ritual going back 2,000 years in Daoist history.

The division of labor in a traditional Zhengyi ritual is complicated. Priests nicknamed "black hats" perform classical rites inside the temple, to which the public is not admitted. "Red hats" (called *fangshi*, a Han dynasty term meaning "ritual master") orally describe what is going on to the masses thronged outside the temple. Also, significant local variation has developed over time, depending on family lineage.

Important fieldwork on Zhengyi Daoist ritual has been done in Taiwan, in particular by scholars who have been initiated as Zhengyi priests, notably Kristofer Schipper and Michael Saso. Besides these scholar-practitioners, there are few true Zhengyi Daoists in the Western world. One attempt to re-create a Zhengyi ritual community in the West is Orthodox Daoism in America (ODA). Founded by the Euro-American Liu Ming (born Charles Belyea), the ODA accepts serious students interested in investiture (text completion) or ordination. Liu Ming also lectures to the public. The ODA publishes a quarterly newsletter, *Frost Bell,* which explains Zhengyi Daoism to a Western audience.

Longhushan Tainshi Association
Longhushan
Jiangxi 335411
People's Republic of China

Elijah Siegler

See also: Daoism; Quanzhen Daoism; Vegetarianism.

References

Dean, Kenneth. *Taoist Ritual and Popular Cults of Southeast China.* Princeton, NJ: Princeton University Press, 1993.

Kohn, Livia. *Daoism Handbook.* 2 vols. Leiden: Brill, 2000.

Saso, Michael. *Taoism and the Rite of Cosmic Renewal.* Pullman: Washington State University Press, 1973.

Zhi Yi

538–597

Zhi Yi (Chih Yi) established the Tian Tai School of Chinese Buddhism, a movement whose effects are still seen throughout East Asian Buddhist practice. Born in the region of the modern city of Nanjing, in central China, Zhi Yi came from a wealthy family and received a classical education. As a monk he learned from Hui Si (515–576), who emphasized the central-

ity of the Lotus Sutra. Later Tian Tai teachings put the Lotus Sutra as the key text in Buddhism because it contains the Buddha's essential teachings. Other schools and texts are then criticized for being incomplete in perspective.

Zhi Yi's major ideas are found in the *Mohe Zhiguan,* a dense text composed of notes from Zhi Yi's lectures and recorded by Guang Ding (561–632), his major disciple. Zhi Yi enumerated his teachings by using a categorization schema called the *panjiao* to rank and distinguish different teachings. Zhi Yi also gave meditation and practice great emphasis. His *zhiguan* (cessation of consciousness) techniques are still widely practiced.

Today, Zhi Yi is best remembered as the first Chinese Buddhist to present a complete and systematic classification of the Buddhist sutra and their teachings, in large part to explain the seemingly contradictory ideas moving through the larger Mahayana Buddhist community. He is also seen as among the first group of Buddhists to break from their Indian tradition and propose a truly Chinese form of Buddhism that in many ways left the Theravada texts behind.

Edward A. Irons

See also: Hui Si; Mahayana Buddhism; Meditation; Theravada Buddhism; Tian Tai/Tendai Buddhism.

Reference

"Chih-I." In *The A to Z of Buddhism,* edited by Charles S. Prebisch. Lanham, MD: Scarecrow Press, 2001.

Zhong Gong

Zhong Gong, founded in 1988, is one of the most popular of the qigong groups operating in the People's Republic of China. By the end of the 1990s it was estimated to have tens of millions of followers. However, in 1999, in the wake of the government's crackdown on the Falun Gong, it also was singled out for repressive measures.

Zhong Gong, the China Health Care and Wisdom Enhancement Gong, was founded by Zhang Hongbao (1955–2005) during the heyday of government support for qigong. He taught a traditional form of qigong, emphasizing the use of exercises and meditation as a means of stimulating *qi* energy. Such energy, once properly flowing through the body, would bring health and enhance mental functioning. Zhong Gong operated independently of the officially sanctioned National Qigong Association, and it speedily spread across the country. In spite of its independent stance, it was favorably mentioned in the official press. Its training school in Shaanxi Province had more than 2,000 students. Reportedly, no lesser a personage than the country's president, Jiang Zemin, had sought out a Zhong Gong master to treat his arthritis and back pain.

Through the 1990s, the group had some minor run-ins with the authorities. Its independent ways became known, but no ideological elements appeared to contradict government authority (as was the case with Falun Gong). However, in December 1999, police abruptly closed the Zhang Gong training facility in Shaanxi. Then in January 2000, a Zhong Gong leader in Zhejiang Province was sentenced to two years for the Chinese equivalent of practicing medicine without a license, a changed evaluation of the group that potentially placed all qigong groups at risk. The government has charged that following qigong has been accompanied with admonitions to stop seeing medical doctors.

China declared Zhong Gong an illegal organization, and subsequently moved to confiscate its assets as well as those of the Unicorn Group, a commercial enterprise in which many members had an interest. Leaders were arrested and an arrest warrant was issued for Zhang Hongbao. He fled to U.S. territory, entering Guam illegally. He applied for political asylum, which was refused, but he was granted protective resident status in 2001. Unfortunately, five years later, while still involved in a variety of legal actions, he was killed in an automobile accident.

Zhong Gong continued. Though at one point larger than Falun Gong, it never attracted much attention and its cause received little media attention. It has all but disappeared in mainland China and never developed a significant following in the Chinese diaspora.

J. Gordon Melton

See also: Falun Gong; Qigong.

References

Eckholm, Erik. "China Imprisons a Leader of Healing-by-Meditation Society." *New York Times,* January 20, 2000.

Lee, Richard E. *Scientific Investigations in Chinese Qigong.* San Clemente, CA: China Healthways Institute, 1999.

Peisheng, Wang, and Chen Guanhua. *Relax and Calming Qigong.* Hong Kong: Peace, 1986.

"Zhang Hongbao in Blast Furnace: A Documentary on How the Outstanding Spiritual Leader Transformed to a Political Leader." http://www.tianhuaculture.net/eng/b1.html. Accessed July 1, 2009.

Zhou Dunyi

1017–1073

Zhou Dunyi (Shou Lianxi, Chou Lien-his) was a key figure in the establishment of neo-Confucianism, a broad-based intellectual movement that transformed Chinese thinking in the later part of the 10th century CE. While Zhu Xi is the most famous thinker in this movement, Zhou Dunyi helped create the field itself. Zhu Xi in fact considered Zhou to be a Confucian sage on the same level as Mencius and Confucius.

Zhou was a minor official during the Song dynasty (969–1279). He did not reach the highest degree possible (*jinshi*), and his greatest influence was as a teacher. Among his students were the two Cheng brothers, Cheng Hao and Cheng Yi, important neo-Confucian figures in their own right. In addition Zhou authored two main texts, *Explanation of the Diagram of the Supreme Ultimate* (*Taiji tushuo*) and *Penetrating the Classic of Changes* (*Tongshu*). With these he set the major themes of neo-Confucian metaphysics. He explained the universe through a complete scheme starting from ultimate nothingness (*wuji*) through to the Supreme Ultimate (*taiji*), along the way generating the five phases (*wuxing*) of water, fire, wood, metal, and earth and other mixtures of yin and yang energies. He also emphasized that sagehood and humanity, Confucian virtues, are expressions of *qi*. It is clear Zhou was intimate with Daoism and Buddhism, and probably did not see the need to separate these ideas from

Confucian concepts. By bringing in the cosmological dimension, which Confucianism had previously lacked, he opened the door for a major revival of Confucian energy.

Edward A. Irons

See also: Confucius; Daoism; Mencius.

References

Chang, Carson. *The Development of New-Confucian Thought*. New York: Bookman Associates, 1957.

McGreal, Ian P. R. *Great Thinkers of the Eastern World*. New York: HarperCollins, 1995.

Zhuangzi

475–221 BCE

Zhuangzi (born Zhuang Zhou, also sometimes written as Chuang Tzu; fourth century BCE) was a bureaucrat and Daoist philosopher in the Warring States period of early Chinese history. Born in the city of Meng in the state of Song, in contemporary Honan, he had been an official and had a family. He had been well tutored by a Prince Changsang (other details unknown) and he himself had a group of disciples. Little else is known of his history.

Zhuangzi is the second major figure in Daoism, after Laozi (b. ca. 571 BCE), and as such is comparable to Mencius (ca. 372–289 BCE) and his relationship with Confucius. However Zhuangzi did not know Laozi, nor does it appear he considered himself to be a disciple. Zhuangzi was an iconoclastic observer of nature and the social order. He criticized the governments and leaders, and was equally unhappy with philosophical and political ideas then current. This led him to denounce the penal system in China. In addition his writing style has been consistently admired throughout China's long history. Indeed, in his writings Zhuangzi coined more than 100 new terms.

Edward A. Irons

See also: Confucius; Daoism; Laozi; Mencius.

References

Hamill, Sam, and J. P. Seaton, trans. *The Essential Chuang Tzu*. Boston: Shambhala, 1998.

McGreal, Ian, OP., ed. *Great Thinkers of the Eastern World*. New York: HarperCollins, 1995.

Mair, Victor. "The Zhuangzi and Its Impact." In *Daoism Handbook,* edited by Livia Kohn, 30–52. Leiden and Koln: Brill, 2000.

Wu, Chung. *The Wisdom of Zhuang Zi on Daoism.* New York: Peter Lang, 2008.

■ Zimbabwe

The modern nation of Zimbabwe (formerly the British colony of South Rhodesia), proclaimed in 1980, is a landlocked southern African nation surrounded by Zambia, Botswana, South Africa, and Mozambique. Its 11,350,000 people reside on 149,300 square miles of territory.

Zimbabwe traces its history to the arrival of Bantu miners who came to work the extensive iron ore deposits around the fifth century CE. They also worked the copper and tin deposits they found. Today, the Shona Bantu make up more than 80 percent of the Zimbabwean population. The Zimbabwean Bantu society created one of the highest medieval cultures in Africa, symbolized by the 10th-century walled city of Zimbabwe, from which the contemporary nation takes its name.

The Shona Bantu were divided into a number of subgroups. The Karanga people who built Zimbabwe extended their rule into present-day Mozambique and Malawi, and they traded their metal with the Asian market. The Karanga were displaced in the 15th century by the Rotsi, who continued their Asian trade until the Portuguese disruption of East African coastal life in the 16th century.

In 1834 the Zulus came into the area and pushed the Rotsi northward and westward. Zulu hegemony prevailed in southeastern Zimbabwe. In 1889 a representative of the British South African Company (headed by Cecil Rhodes) negotiated rights to exploit the mineral resources of the Zulu-controlled part of the country. The British founded the town of Salisbury (now Harare), and over the course of the next years they created a situation to legitimize their takeover of the Shona Bantu land (1895).

Zimbabwe

Religion	Followers in 1970	Followers in 2010	% of Population	Annual % growth 2000–2010	Followers in 2025	Followers in 2050
Christians	2,716,000	9,512,000	69.1	1.00	12,265,000	15,571,000
Independents	672,000	5,930,000	43.1	1.74	7,250,000	9,000,000
Protestants	730,000	2,450,000	17.8	3.41	3,300,000	4,200,000
Roman Catholics	557,000	1,382,000	10.0	2.27	1,900,000	2,500,000
Ethnoreligionists	2,408,000	3,905,000	28.4	0.09	3,269,000	2,972,000
Agnostics	8,000	140,000	1.0	0.72	180,000	250,000
Muslims	50,000	100,000	0.7	0.72	120,000	145,000
Baha'is	9,700	44,000	0.3	0.72	60,000	80,000
Atheists	1,000	21,700	0.2	0.72	25,000	30,000
Hindus	3,600	20,500	0.1	0.72	30,000	40,000
Jews	5,200	13,000	0.1	0.72	15,000	16,000
New religionists	1,200	1,800	0.0	0.72	2,500	4,000
Buddhists	0	1,000	0.0	0.71	1,800	3,000
Spiritists	300	660	0.0	0.72	800	1,200
Total population	**5,203,000**	**13,760,000**	**100.0**	**0.72**	**15,969,000**	**19,112,000**

In the 1960s, the white-led government resisted attempts to transfer power to the African majority, and in 1965 independence was proclaimed. The Ian Smith government held on for more than a decade, but the process of transferring power began in 1979 with the election of Abel Muzorewa (b. 1925), a bishop in the United Methodist Church, as president. He changed the name of the country to Zimbabwe-Rhodesia, but his government fell the next year; in new elections, the Zimbabwe African National Union led by Robert Mugabe was swept into power. Mugabe was able to reconcile with his main political rival later in the decade, and the merged Patriotic Front of the Zimbabwean African National Union has subsequently remained the primary political organization in the country. Mugabe remains in power after having faced several elections through the 1990s to the present (2010). He has faced growing opposition to his long rule and was, in 2008, forced to share power with the major dissenting party.

Zimbabwe has one of the most diverse religious communities of any nation in Africa. Some 30 percent of the population continues to follow traditional African religions, with some of the smaller groups not a part of the Bantu being among the most resistant to the various new religious traditions that entered in the nineteenth century. The Shona people worship a supreme being known as Mwari. In Shona thought, unlike that of most traditionalists in nearby countries, the supreme being provides ongoing contact through a variety of intermediaries (similar to mediums in Western Esoteric traditions) between God and his human children. Religious functionaries become possessed by Mwari, various ancestor spirits, and the lion spirits, the spirits of chiefs who ruled in Zimbabwe in ancient times. Various mediumlike functionaries serve as leaders of different movements among the various subdivisions of the Shona.

Christianity was brought into the area in the 16th century, the Portuguese having made contact with the Shona in 1561. However, no permanent Christian community was established. Then in 1859, the London Missionary Society (Congregationalists from England) made contact with the Zulu chief and were granted permission to open a mission station. The LMS would dominate Protestant effort in Zimbabwe until the end of the 1880s.

The Roman Catholic Church returned in 1879 and established early centers in Salisbury and Bulawayo. It established itself within the white community in the country, but steadily in the last half of the 20th century it found support among native Zimbabweans. The first African bishop was consecrated in 1973, during the years of the Smith government. To the present the church has not produced a sufficient number of black

Rabbi Ambros Makuwaza conducts a Rosh Hashanah service on September 14, 1996, at Rusape's Jewish Tabernacle, 70 kilometers (105 miles) east of Harare, Zimbabwe. (AP/Wide World Photos)

priests, and the majority of the priests remain foreign born. The church is supported by four indigenous female religious orders, among which the largest part of the church's African leadership is found.

A new day for Zimbabwean Christianity began in 1888, when the British government, having asserted some hegemony in the region, gave the Church of England–related Universities Mission to Central Africa a grant of land, and work was subsequently initiated among both the Shona and Zulu peoples. The Diocese of Rhodesia was erected in 1891. The work was incorporated into the Church of the Province of Central Africa, created in 1955.

British Methodists arrived in 1890, and their American cousins six years later. The former had substantial support among Zimbabweans of British background, while the latter was a totally African church (apart from the small number of missionaries) from the beginning. The British work grew into what is today the Methodist Church in Zimbabwe. The American work remains attached to the United Methodist Church as its Zimbabwe Conference. Abel Muzorewa (b. 1925), the first African bishop, was consecrated in 1968. In 1992 the United Methodists founded Africa University.

The Salvation Army came to Rhodesia in 1891, and now it has one of its largest followings among the Shona. Other Protestant churches with substantial followings include the Seventh-day Adventist Church (1894), Churches of Christ (1896), the African Methodist Episcopal Church (1900), the Evangelical Lu-

ZIMBABWE

theran Church in Zimbabwe (1903), and the New Apostolic Church (1910). Baptist work began in 1917 but was largely related to the white community. The Southern Baptist Convention directed its concern to Zimbabwe after World War II, and in 1950 it picked up the support of an independent Baptist missionary couple who had been working in the country since 1930. With added support from the United States, the mission grew rapidly and matured in 1963 into the Baptist Convention of Zimbabwe.

In the early 20th century, the first of the African Initiated Churches appeared, and several—such as the African Apostolic Church of Johane Marange, the Mai Chaza Church, and the Zimbabwe Assemblies of God Africa—are among the largest Christian bodies in the country. The Zionist and Apostolic churches from South Africa have also garnered a significant following, and the Zion Christian Church is now larger than the Roman Catholic Church. The Zionist and Apostolic churches have grown into a large body in the years since the country's independence.

The various Christian churches in Zimbabwe are associated in several ecumenical organizations. The Zimbabwe Council of Churches, with its roots in the Southern Rhodesia Missionary Council, founded in 1903, is affiliated with the World Council of Churches.

The Evangelical Fellowship of Zimbabwe is affiliated with the World Evangelical Alliance. A spectrum of the African Initiated Churches came together in 1972 to found the African Indigenous Churches Conference.

Also representing the larger Christian world are the Church of Jesus Christ of Latter-day Saints (which arrived in 1950) and the Jehovah's Witnesses (ca. 1910). In the 20th century, Zimbabwe became home to a spectrum of the world's major religious traditions. Daniel Montage Kisch, a Jew, arrived in Zimbabwe in 1869 and became an advisor to King Lobengula, the Zulu ruler. In the 1880s, Jewish immigrants from Eastern Europe (primarily from Lithuania and Russia) began to arrive. They were joined by German Jewish immigrants in the 1930s, and British and South African Jews in the decades after World War II. The contemporary community of some 10,000 Jews has its center in the Zimbabwe Jewish Board of Deputies and the two synagogues in Harare and Bulawayo.

Zimbabwe is also home to one of the African groups that claim a relationship to the larger community. The Lemba people identify themselves as Jews culturally, following a set of traditional cultural and ritual practices that signify to them their Hebrew ancestry. Although their status as Jews is a matter of debate, in 1996 a set of studies began to appear that provided scientific support to their claims of Hebrew ancestry.

The small Muslim community grew 10fold (from 8,000 to 80,000) during the last quarter of the 20th century, primarily because of the immigration of Muslims from neighboring Malawi and Mozambique. Most are Sunnis of the Shafaiite School. There is a Hindu community based in the Indian community, and the Baha'i Faith has experienced considerable growth, in large part at the expense of the Muslims and Hindus.

Zimbabwe has provided a welcoming environment for many of the new religious groups from around the world, and today one can find centers of the Ancient and Mystical Order Rosae Crucis, the Church of Scientology, the International Society for Krishna Consciousness, and the Unification Movement. Buddhism is represented by Soka Gakkai International, and there is a single Tibetan Buddhist center in Harare.

J. Gordon Melton

See also: African Apostolic Church of Johane Marange; African Methodist Episcopal Church; Ancient and Mystical Order Rosae Crucis; Baha'i Faith; Church of England; Church of Jesus Christ of Latter-day Saints; Church of Scientology; Church of the Province of Central Africa; Churches of Christ; Evangelical Lutheran Church in Zimbabwe; Great Zimbabwe; International Society for Krishna Consciousness; Jehovah's Witnesses; Lemba; London Missionary Society; Mai Chaza Church/City of Jehovah; Methodist Church in Zimbabwe; New Apostolic Church; Salvation Army; Seventh-day Adventist Church; Shafiite School of Islam; Soka Gakkai International; Southern Baptist Convention; Unification Movement; United Methodist Church; World Council of Churches; World Evangelical Alliance; Zimbabwe Assemblies of God Africa; Zion Christian Church; Zionist and Apostolic Churches; Zulu Religion.

References

Antsen, Hilde. *The Battle of the Mind: International New Media Elements of the New Religious Political Right in Zimbabwe*. Oslo: University of Oslo, 1997.

Daneel, M. L. *Zionism and Faith Healing in Rhodesia: Aspects of African Independent Churches*. The Hague: Mouton, 1970.

Ellison, Kudzayi Madenyika. *Zimbabwe: The Betrayal of a Noble Nation*. AuthorHouse, 2006.

Ezeani, George B. *The Church and State in Zimbabwe*. Kent, UK: Veritas Lumen, 1998.

Hall, Martin, and Rebecca Stefoff. *Great Zimbabwe*. New York: Oxford University Press, 2006.

Hallencreutz, C. F., and A. Mayo, eds. *Church and State in Zimbabwe*. Vol. 3, *Christianity South of the Zambesi*. Gweru, Zimbabwe: Mambo, 1988.

Mandivebga, E. C. *Islam in Zimbabwe*. Gweru, Zimbabwe: Mambo, 1983.

Owomoyela , Oyekan. *Culture and Customs in Zimbabwe*. Westport, CT: Greenwood Press, 2002.

Ranger, Terence O. *Voices from the Rocks: Nature, Culture & History in the Matopos Hills of Zimbabwe*. Bloomington: Indiana University Press, 1999.

Shoko, Tabona. *Karanga Indigenous Religion in Zimbabwe*. Aldershot, Hampshire, UK: Ashgate Publishing, 2007.

Welch, P. *Church and Settler in Colonial Zimbabwe: A Study in the History of the Anglican Diocese of Mashonaland/Southern Rhodesia, 1890–1925*. Leiden: Brill, 2008.

Zvobgo, C. J. M. *History of Christian Missions in Zimbabwe*. Gweru, Zimbabwe: Mambo, 1996.

Zimbabwe Assemblies of God Africa

One of the largest denominations in Zimbabwe is the Zimbabwe Assemblies of God Africa (popularly called ZAOGA), a newer Pentecostal church with roots in South African Pentecostalism, the Apostolic Faith Mission of South Africa (AFM). ZAOGA commenced in urban areas of Zimbabwe and is led by Archbishop Ezekiel Handinawangu Guti. In 1959, Guti and a group of young African pastors were expelled from the AFM after a disagreement with white missionaries. The group joined the South African Assemblies of God of Nicholas Bhengu, but separated from there in 1967 to form the Assemblies of God, Africa (later the ZAOGA). Guti went to the independent Pentecostal Christ for the Nations Institute in Dallas, Texas, in 1971, and he too received financial and other resources from the United States. But Guti, like many leaders of the new Pentecostalism in Africa, resists any attempts to identify his church with the "religious right" of the United States or to be controlled by what are considered "neocolonial" interests. In a very pertinent development in 1986, leaders of 12 of the largest Pentecostal churches in Zimbabwe, including Guti, wrote a fierce rebuttal to a right-wing attack on the Zimbabwean state by a North American Charismatic preacher.

Since 1986, ZAOGA has also had churches in Britain. Zimbabwean ZAOGA missionaries went to South Africa to plant churches there in 1989, and the church also has branches, called Forward in Faith Ministries International, in 17 other African countries. ZAOGA is now organized as a fully fledged denomination with headquarters complex and administrative structures in Harare, headed by Guti. By 1999, ZAOGA had an estimated 600,000 affiliated members, which made it the third largest denomination in Zimbabwe after the African Apostolic Church of Johane Marange and the Roman Catholic Church, with more than 10 percent of the Christians in the country. ZAOGA itself claimed to be the largest, with one and a half million members in 1995. Although the figure is disputed, it remains one of the largest and most prominent churches in Zimbabwe. Guti's leadership style and expensive overseas trips were contentious issues in the late 1990s, as were the lifestyles of some of his more powerful pastors. ZAOGA has already experienced various splits, resulting in several new and vigorous Pentecostal churches in Zimbabwe.

13 A Powell Rd.
Waterfalls, Harare
Zimbabwe

Allan H. Anderson

See also: African Apostolic Church of Johane Marange; Apostolic Faith Mission of South Africa; Pentecostalism; Roman Catholic Church.

References

Anderson, Allan H. *African Reformation: African Initiated Christianity in the Twentieth Century*. Trenton, NJ: Africa World Press, 2001.

Maxwell, David. *African Gifts of the Spirit*. Athens, OH: Ohio University Press, 2007.

Maxwell, David. "'Delivered from the Spirit of Poverty': Pentecostalism, Prosperity and Modernity in Zimbabwe." *Journal of Religion in Africa* 28, no. 3 (1998): 350–373.

Zion Christian Church (South Africa, Zimbabwe)

The Zion Christian Church (ZCC), not a typical Zionist church but now the largest denomination in South Africa, was founded by Engenas (Ignatius) Lekganyane (ca. 1880–1948). ZCC tradition says that in about 1910, the official year of the commencement of the church, Lekganyane was praying when he received a revelation through a whirlwind that he would found

Members of the Zion Christian Church, the largest church in South Africa, gather for afternoon prayers in Moria, northern Transvaal, April 2, 1994. (AP/Wide World Photos)

a large church. In about 1916, Elias Mahlangu founded the Zion Apostolic Church of South Africa (ZAC), and Lekganyane was ordained and emerged as leader of a ZAC congregation in his home village. Mahlangu began to promote customs among ZAC members that Lekganyane objected to, such as wearing white robes, growing a beard, and taking off shoes before services —practices found in many Zionist and Apostolic churches today but not allowed in the ZCC. Lekganyane's break with the ZAC came in 1920, when he went to Lesotho and joined Edward (Lion) Motaung's Zion Apostolic Faith Mission (ZAFM), where he was ordained bishop. Differences emerged, and at about the end of 1924, Lekganyane founded the Zion Christian Church.

In 1930, Lekganyane bought a farm near Pietersburg that became the church headquarters, Moria, to which Zionists flock today. In keeping with Zion City near Chicago and other African Zions, Lekganyane established a mecca for pilgrimage, a center of ritual power. In 1935 the ZCC membership was about 2,000, but by 1942, when the church was at last officially registered, there were 55 congregations and 27,487 members, having spread to Zimbabwe, Botswana, and the Northern Cape Province. A year later, the ZCC membership was more than 40,000. Lekganyane died in 1948, and a leadership struggle ensued between his sons Edward and Joseph. It was not clear whom Engenas had appointed as successor, and the brothers formed two separate churches in 1949. The followers of Joseph, the minority faction, are now St. Engenas Zion Christian Church and use the emblem of a dove, and are now led by Joseph's son Engenas. The majority of ZCC people followed Edward in the Zion Christian Church. There is very little difference between the two in beliefs and practices.

Under Edward Legkanyane (1925–1967) the ZCC continued to grow, so that by 1954 the membership was some 80,000, probably the biggest AIC in southern Africa at that time. Edward was a very effective leader, and after his premature death in 1967, his son Barnabas, the present bishop (b. 1954), succeeded him, although a superintendent governed the church until 1975, Barnabas's 21st birthday. Since being registered with the government in 1942, the ZCC has enjoyed the favor of the ruling regime. Edward Lekganyane invited the government to the annual Easter conference in 1965, during apartheid's worst years. Barnabas also invited the regime, beginning in 1980. In the much-publicized event at the 75th anniversary celebration at Easter 1985, President P. W. Botha was given the Freedom of Moria. After this event, ZCC members in Soweto were subject to a spate of violent attacks, as the visit reinforced the suspicion that the ZCC was a supporter of the status quo. Nevertheless, the ZCC has emerged from the fear of an oppressive regime to play a role in the radical changes since 1990. There were an estimated 4 to 6 million members of the ZCC in 2009, one of the largest AICs in the continent.

The ZCC is also the most significant Zionist church in Zimbabwe, and it has existed separately from the South African ZCC. Samuel Mutendi (ca. 1898–1976) had a series of dreams in 1919 revealing that he would start an African church. He was baptized by Engenas Lekganyane in Pretoria in 1923 and commissioned as the ZAFM's missionary to Zimbabwe. In 1925, Lekganyane called Mutendi and other Zionist leaders to Pretoria, where the ZCC was organized. Mutendi was the only Zimbabwean leader to join the new church, and Lekganyane ordained him a minister. Mutendi modeled the new Zimbabwean church on the ZCC in South Africa, and he remained loyal to Lekganyane until his death in 1948. Thereafter, the two ZCC churches had less contact, and although Edward Lekganyane managed to visit Mutendi in 1953, the ZCC in Zimbabwe became fully autonomous. It had 13 minor schisms between 1929 and 1961, but the most serious schism occurred after Mutendi's death in 1976. A succession struggle between his sons Ruben and Nehemiah resulted in two separate ZCC churches: Ruben with the smaller faction of some 50,000 members by 2000, and Nehemiah, who had received the support of most of the senior ministers, with more than 200,000.

Zion Christian Church
Zion City Moria
PO Boyne
nr Pietersburg
South Africa

Allan H. Anderson

See also: Zionist and Apostolic Churches.

References

Anderson, Allan H. "The Lekganyanes and Prophecy in the Zion Christian Church." *Journal of Religion in Africa* 29, no. 3 (August 1999): 285–312.

Anderson, Allan H. *Zion and Pentecost: The Spirituality and Experience of Pentecostal and Zionist/Apostolic Churches in South Africa.* Pretoria: University of South Africa Press, 2000.

Daneel, M. L. *Old and New in Southern Shona Independent Churches.* 2 vols. The Hague: Mouton, 1971, 1974.

Zion Christian Church. The ZCC Messenger (Johannesburg). Various issues.

Zionism

Zionism is the doctrine that the Jews deserve to have their own national home, and the location is normally taken to be Palestine, their ancestral home. The doctrine can take a secular form, where it is linked up with any national group and their claim to a national home. It can take a religious shape, where God is said to have promised the land to the Jews, and so they are entitled to claim it, since God created the world and everything belongs to him. The link between the doctrine and the state of Israel has made it very controversial, given the hostility that many have to the state, while others see anti-Zionism as nothing more than a modern form of anti-Semitism.

Zionism has a variety of forms, but there are two main Jewish doctrines, one secular and one religious. The creator of the modern Zionist movement, Theodor Herzl (1860–1904), was a secular Viennese journalist who it is said was impressed by the Dreyfus Affair in thinking that the Jews had no long-term future in Europe. They required a national home, and in the 19th century many nationalities such as the Italians, the Greeks, the Germans, and so on campaigned for and won a national home of some kind. It was in line with this desire that Zionism was established, and for Herzl that home did not have to be in Palestine; he was prepared to countenance anywhere available, even seriously considering part of Uganda when this was proposed by the British. His book *Altneuland* argued that once the Jews had their own country they would be able to lead normal lives and would be regarded as a normal community by the Gentile world.

Religious Zionism is the doctrine that the land of Israel was promised to the Jews by God, as recounted in the Torah, and so they have a right to live there, and indeed a duty to settle the land. Israel should be a Jewish state not just in the sense of having a Jewish majority, but also in that its character is Jewish. This means that Jewish religious law should be the law of the state (for Jews at least) and the state should be infused with Jewish values based on Torah observance. Some religious Zionists see the settling of the land as an important stage in the messianic future of the world, a view that is shared by some Christian Zionists who see the return of the Jews to Israel as a preliminary to the Second Coming of Jesus, and this has led them to support Israel against its enemies. On the other hand, some religious Jews are totally opposed to Zionism, seeing it as pre-empting God's decision as to when to send the Messiah and lead the Jews back to Israel. Secular Jews also have opposed Zionism, seeing it sometimes as a narrow form of nationalism and viewing a national home for the Jews as a poor alternative to integration in the countries with Gentile majorities.

For most Israelis Zionism is an abstract notion that has little to do with their life in the land in which they have been born and live, and like most people they think they have a right to live where they do, although some Israelis reject the Zionist idea that there should be something exclusively Jewish about the country, arguing that a state in which both Jews and Gentiles could live as equals would be preferable to the existing situation. Most Israelis are secular, although the religious Jewish community is rapidly growing in numbers

and so influence, and they accept the Herzl view of Zionism, where Israel is seen as the national home of the Jews as a people, but not necessarily with any requirement to institute a religious lifestyle for its Jewish citizens.

Zionism has been pilloried by its enemies as racist and as a particularly evil idea, and Israel as an especially problematic country. The fact that it is the only state with a non-Muslim majority in the Middle East has perhaps had something to do with this, since the Muslim states around it do like Israel recognize a major religion in the state, in their case Islam. They are not generally so well-disposed toward the religious minorities in their states, unlike Israel, and have ever since Zionism became effective in their region opposed it violently. They do not on the whole have as strong democratic values as Israel either, and it is difficult to see why Zionism has aroused such universal ire apart from the fact that it stands in the way of a total Islamicization of the Middle East. On the other hand, opponents of Zionism sometimes argue that it was the creation of Israel that has led to all the present-day problems in the Middle East, including the expulsion of the Jews from the Arab world and the growing hostility between Islam and the other two Abrahamic religions. Regarding Israel as a pariah state is an appropriate reaction to Zionism since the doctrine is close to apartheid in giving preferential treatment to one racial group over others, according to its detractors.

Oliver Leaman

See also: Judaism.

References

Herf, Jeffrey, ed. *Anti-Semitism and Anti-Zionism in Historical Perspective*. London: Routledge, 2006.

Laquer, Walter. *The History of Zionism*. London: Weidenfeld and Nicolson, 2003.

Whaley, J. *Theodor Herzl and the Origins of Zionism*. Ed. by Richie Robertson and Edward Timms. Edinburgh: Edinburgh University Press, 1997.

Zionist and Apostolic Churches

The beginnings of African Zionist and Apostolic churches in southern Africa are found in Zion City, near Chicago, where a Christian theocracy created in 1896 by healer John A. Dowie of the Christian Catholic Church (since 1997 known as the Christ Community Church of Zion) emphasized divine healing and triune baptism by immersion. This church was established in Johannesburg in 1895. It was joined in 1903 by Pieter L. le Roux, a Dutch Reformed missionary, with three African evangelists (Daniel Nkonyane, Muneli Ngobesi, and Fred Lutuli) and 400 preachers and converts in the eastern Transvaal (now Mpumalanga). In 1904, Dowie sent Daniel Bryant to South Africa as overseer. He baptized 141 Zion believers in the river near le Roux's church. This group of "Zionists," the great majority being Zulus, grew within a year to 5,000. In 1908 a team of North American Pentecostal missionaries arrived in Johannesburg and used the Zion church building there for services. Le Roux joined their Apostolic Faith Mission, but his African fellow workers remained Zionists while embracing the new Pentecostal doctrine.

One of the Zion leaders, Daniel Nkonyane, seceded from the AFM in about 1910, forming the Christian Catholic Apostolic Holy Spirit Church in Zion, having already obtained and paid for a "three hundred acre" building site, which became a prototype for many African "Zion Cities" to come. In 1917, Elias Mahlangu founded the Zion Apostolic Church of South Africa. From Mahlangu's church, Edward Motaung (Lion) seceded in 1920 to form the Zion Apostolic Faith Mission (ZAFM), and Engenas Lekganyane's Zion Christian Church seceded from the ZAFM in 1925. Paul Mabiletsa, another founding Zion leader, commenced the Apostolic Church in Zion in 1920, and J. C. Phillips, a Malawian, commenced the Holy Catholic Apostolic Church in Zion.

In theology, there are no significant differences between African Zion and Apostolic churches on the one hand and the Pentecostal churches on the other, but in practices the differences are considerable. A Zionist becomes a Christian through baptism by triune immersion in water, which usually must take place in running water—that is, in a river often called "Jordan." There is an emphasis on divine healing, although the methods of obtaining this healing differ. Whereas most Pentecostals practice laying on of hands or prayer for the sick, this will usually be accompanied in Zion and Apostolic churches by the use of symbolic objects such as blessed water, ropes, staffs, papers, ash, and so on. Prophecy and speaking in tongues are also practiced in most Zion and Apostolic churches. There are strong regulations for members, and many churches do not allow alcohol, tobacco, medicines, or eating pork. The attitude to traditional religious practices in Zion and Apostolic churches is generally ambivalent, particularly when it comes to ancestors, and some of these churches allow polygyny. For the outsider, the biggest distinguishing feature is the almost universal use of uniform clothing, usually white robes with colored belts and sashes and other markings, or, in the case of the ZCC, khaki uniforms and green and gold colors. These churches do not have many church buildings and often meet in the open air.

In Zimbabwe, Zionist and Apostolic churches arriving from about 1921 through migrant laborers returning from South Africa soon eclipsed other AICs in size and influence. The first Zionist church was the Christian Apostolic Church in Zion, planted in Matabeleland by migrants from Mabiletsa's church in South Africa. David Masuka joined the Zion Apostolic Church of South Africa (ZAC) of Elias Mahlangu in 1921, when he was working in Pietersburg, and he returned to be minister for the church in Zimbabwe in 1923. The *ndaza* (sacred cord) Zionists wear white or multicolored robes tied with cords, and the ZAC of Masuka was one of the first of these among the Mashona. Like many other Zionist churches, the ZAC experienced schism from 1930 onward, starting with the Sabbath Zion Church, the Zion Protestant Church, the Zion Apostolic City, and several other schisms retaining the name Zion Apostolic Church. In contrast, the ZAFM under the flexible and highly respected Andreas Shoko, one of the first Zionist leaders, managed to avoid any further serious schisms after Mutendi left the church with Lekganyane to form the ZCC.

Allan H. Anderson

See also: Apostolic Faith Mission; Christ Community Church of Zion/Christian Catholic Church; Zion Christian Church.

References

Anderson, Allan H. *Zion and Pentecost: The Spirituality and Experience of Pentecostal and Zionist/*

Apostolic Churches in South Africa. Pretoria: University of South Africa Press, 2000.

Daneel, M. L. *Old and New in Southern Shona Independent Churches.* 2 vols. The Hague: Mouton, 1971, 1974.

Sundkler, B. G. M. *Zulu Zion and Some Swazi Zionists.* London: Oxford University Press, 1976.

◆ Zoroastrianism

Zoroastrianism, the ancient religion of Persia (Iran), is most known in the West from the biblical story told of the Magi visiting the child Jesus (Matthew 2). The wise men known for their searching the heavens for signs were Zoroastrians who would take note of a new star. In ancient Persia, large pyramidal structures called ziggurats were erected from which the Zoroastrian priests could make their astronomical/astrological observations.

Zoroastrianism is named for Zarathustra (or Zoroaster). Little is known about Zarathustra, including the years in which he lived. The best estimate is that he came from that area of modern Kazakhstan east of the Volga River from which the Iranian people originated. It is believed that he influenced a tribal chief named Vishtaspa in his favor, and that his faith was then carried among the Iranians when they moved into northeastern Iran around the 12th century BCE. Zarathustra may have lived as early as the 17th century BCE. From that base, Zoroastrianism spread among the Medes and Persians in western Iran.

During the reign of Cyrus the Great (559–530 BCE), an empire was created that extended from Turkey to Afghanistan. Under Cyrus, Zoroastrianism moved from its pre-historical to its historical phase, when Cyrus made it the empire's state religion. By this time the ziggurats were in place, as were the Magi, originally the priestly class from the Medes. The life of Zoroastrianism was completely disrupted during the conquests of Alexander the Great. Among other actions in subduing the land, Alexander burned Persepolis, the capital, and in the process destroyed many Zoroastrian records and writings. In the process of spreading Hellenistic culture, his successors suppressed Zoroastrianism until a new Persian Empire was finally created toward the end of the second century BCE. The Parthian Empire (ca. 129–224) re-established the primacy of Zoroastrianism, which it enjoyed through successive regimes until the coming of the Arabs and Islam in the seventh century CE. For the next centuries Zoroastrianism would battle Islam for the hearts of the people, and by the 10th century it had become not only the state religion but also the dominant religion practiced across the Persian lands.

The dislodging of the Zoroastrian leaders from the Persian court became the motivation for some to begin the migration to what was perceived as a less hostile land, and early in the eighth century migrations to western India began. They became the nucleus of the Parsee (or Persian) Zoroastrian community, which from India has now spread to Africa and the West.

Zarathustra preached a dualistic understanding of the universe. In it, two forces fight for the hearts of humans. Ahura Mazda, the eternal God, is wise, good, and just, but unfortunately, not omnipotent. There also exists a second entity, Angra Mainyu, like Ahura Mazda uncreated, but the embodiment of evil. In order to defeat Angra Mainyu, Ahura Mazda created the world, which exists as a battleground between the good and the bad. To assist him in the creative act, he called upon his Holy Spirit and evoked the Holy Immortals, all emanations of the one God. His emanations are, however, properly seen as divine and, as such, objects of veneration and even worship. Each of these seven emanations represents a high value, such as truth, health, or power. Zoroastrians should invite these Holy Immortals into their lives and make these qualities/values their own.

In the cosmic battle, Angra Mainyu brought evil spirits to oppose the Holy Immortals, some pictured as gods of war. They brought death into the world. The good spirit countered evil by bringing more life into existence to replace those who had died. Individual are called through their life to align with good or evil and will be judged at the end by which choices they made.

Humans have an important role in the cosmic battle. Collectively, they have the power to align with good and become the decisive force in the ultimate triumph of goodness. Then, at the end of earthly life,

Carved representation of Ahura Mazda from the Royal Audience Hall of Darius I (548 BCE–486 BCE) at Persepolis, Achaemenid dynasty. (Jupiterimages)

each person will be judged; those who were more good than bad will go to a heavenly existence, and the others are destined for hell and punishment. Although the dominant form of Zoroastrianism looked for the gradual triumph of good over evil and the eventual destruction of the evil order, a second form of understanding the end times, an apocalyptic system, also developed. In that second presentation, evil would gradually win, with an accompanying increase in chaos, natural disasters, and social ills. The inevitable growth of evil would at the last moment be halted by the appearance of a Saoshyant, a Savior figure who will appear out of the family of Zarathustra to lead a final battle of good people triumphing over the evil one. The dead will then be resurrected and the final judgment will take place. At that time the evil will be destroyed and the good purged of the remaining evil they possess. The good will enjoy eternal life. The correlation of this form of Zoroastrianism with later Christian perspectives is obvious.

The Zoroastrian cosmology is derived from its scripture, the Avesta, a volume of approximately 1,000 pages. The oldest part of it consists of the Gathas, the hymns of Zarathustra, which are written in an ancient dialect known as Old Avestan. The original collection of the Avesta, known to have existed in the ninth century (two centuries after the Muslim takeover of Persia), included some 21 books. Much of the text was lost in subsequent years, the present text being the result.

In addition to the Avesta, Zoroastrians recognize a second level of holy writings that were written and compiled in the centuries of the Sassanian Persian Empire (third to seventh centuries CE). They are distinguished by being written in a later Persian dialect called Pahlavi. These texts include commentaries on the Gathas and summaries of the lost Avesta texts. Although the Pahlavi texts have an important role, the Avesta remains the primary sacred text.

Leadership in the Zoroastrian community is supplied by the priests, identified by their all-white clothing, a symbol of the high value placed on purity and cleanliness in Zoroastrian culture. They oversee the temples, at the center of which are the ever-burning fires, symbols of righteousness. Fire is a key reality in Zoroastrian life and culture. It symbolizes light and ties the believer to the heavens through the fiery lightning bolt—and acknowledges the importance that fire has had in the daily life of individuals, at least in pre-technological cultures. The Gathas speak of fire as the creation of Ahura Mazda and set fire as the superior symbol of divinity, as opposed to the idols, which it replaced. The primary fire is the Atash Bahram, which is created with special rituals of consecration and remains burning brightly in the primary hall of a temple. Lesser fires, the Atash-I-Aduran and the Dadgah, are used for minor rituals and as the center of space used for daily prayers.

Youth are initiated into the faith by passing through a simple ceremony that begins with learning a set of prayers. On the day of the ceremony, they engage in some purification rituals and don a sacred shirt. Performing ablution rituals will be a standard beginning to all sacred acts in the future. The heart of the rather brief ceremony is the reception of the sacred cord, called a *kusti*, from a priest. The cord is wrapped three times around the waist over the shirt, and then tied with a simple knot. The ceremony is like a wedding, a moment for general celebration by friends and relatives. The full member of the faith is expected to engage in prayer five times daily (similar to Muslim practice) before a fire. During the prayers, the kusti is untied and retied.

Among the important rituals to which Zoroastrians must periodically give attention are funerals. Rituals are designed to deal with the uncleanliness of the body of the deceased and to assist the soul on its way. Traditionally, the body is placed on a high tower and its flesh devoured by vultures and the bones bleached by the Sun. Today, cremation is more common, especially in the West. The funeral is then directed toward the soul, which is believed to linger close by for three days. The funeral is done the day after the death, but the priests continue the rituals for the deceased for the next several days. The family joins in important good-bye activities on the fourth day. Commemoration of the deceased will continue monthly for the next year and then annually for the next 30 years at the annual ceremony for the dead. The day may be celebrated in the temple or in people's homes.

The annual acknowledgment of the deceased is just one holy day ritualized by Zoroastrians. The most important are the seven obligatory holy days that acknowledge the one God Ahura Mazda and the six Holy Immortals, No Ruz, or "New Day" (which celebrates the beginning of the year according to the Zoroastrian calendar), and the six *gahambars,* or days of obligation. Celebration of the gahambars is largely limited to the Iranian Zoroastrians today, among whom they are occasions for five-day festivals. Like other major religious communities, the Zoroastrians have their own calendar that has to be reconciled with the common solar calendar now used by the international community.

The movement of Zoroastrians to India beginning in the ninth century created two somewhat separated communities. Given their poverty and existence in a more-or-less hostile climate, there was little contact between them over the next centuries, and each community developed its own distinctive customs while trying to preserve its community and faith. Some changes came to the communities as they began to interact with the British in the 18th and 19th centuries. The rise of British power in India preceded the emergence of the Parsees as a well-to-do trading community. In the 18th century they had developed trading centers in the Orient (the history of which continues in the small Parsee community still found in Hong Kong).

As the British entered East Africa, Zoroastrians relocated to Zanzibar, Mombasa, and Nairobi, from where they expanded inland. By the mid-20th century, though remaining a somewhat separatist community culturally and religiously, they became prosperous, with members assuming leading roles in the business community and the professions. As decolonization proceeded, the Parsees were among the Asians who were viewed as having secured their position because of colonial advantages, and pressure came to bear on many to leave—especially during the regime of Idi Amin in Uganda. Rather than return to India, many Parsees relocated to the West. The largest community has emerged in London and its immediate environs, but scatted communities have also appeared across the United States and Canada, and more recently in Australia.

Meanwhile in India, the Parsee community had tended to shift from Gujarat southward toward Mumbai and into what is now Pakistan. The largest communities currently are in Mumbai and Karachi. In both countries, Parsees have become prominent business leaders and on occasion have appeared in important political posts.

The Zoroastrian community in Iran almost disappeared at the end of the 19th century, but through the 20th century it experienced a revival, growing fivefold. Zoroastrians have enjoyed guarantees of religious freedom articulated in the 1906 Constitution of Iran, and toleration under the post-1979 changes wrought by the Islamic revolution. They are expected to observe Islamic codes of public conduct. They are represented at the Majlis (Parliament) and serve in the armed forces. Furthermore, many members of these religions fought side by side with Moslem Iranians in the Constitutional Uprising of the late 19th century that finally resulted in the Constitution of 1906.

A visit by a group of Parsee priests to Iran in the late 1990s found that in spite of the revival, much was still lacking in the Iranian Zoroastrian community. The religion is, to put it bluntly, in shambles. There was no place where the major ritual ceremonies could be performed. None of the priests were holding the *barashoom*, the purification ceremony necessary to perform the "inner" rituals, which can be done only by a priest in the sacred space in the temple. There are fire temples in several cities, but some did not have the fires burning. The priests are largely uneducated, and many do not wear their priestly garb. Many laypeople do not wear the sacred shirt and cord. Although discouraged somewhat by what they had observed, the delegation held out hope for the continued revival and rebuilding of the Iranian community with assistance from India and the West.

Currently, Zoroastrians may be seen as divided into two primary communities, one based in Iran and the other in India, with both communities represented by diaspora communities in Africa and the West. The communities are further divided by what might be seen as traditionalist and modernist wings. The latter group has adapted to life in urban centers and the modern West. Traditionalists adhere with more strictness to older rituals and prayer life, and pay attention to the laws of purity relative to women in their menstrual cycle and the bodies of the dead (traditionally there were people set apart as unclean whose job was to handle corpses). They eschew cremation and demand disposal of corpses by carrion birds and the sun. They do not sanction marriage outside the faith, and do not engage in attempts to convert others to Zoroastrianism.

In the West several organizations have arisen to serve the Zoroastrian community. In 1980 an international group of Zoroastrian leaders founded the World Zoroastrian Organization, based in London, out of an expressed desire especially among diaspora Zoroastrians for an international structure to protect, unite, and sustain what is a very small community, almost invisible in the pluralistic West. In North America, where many Parsees migrated after 1965, a number of local Zoroastrian associations were established. In 1987 a number of these associations came together to create the Federation of Zoroastrian Associations of North America. Many of these associations, representative of the more modernist trends in the Western Zoroastrian community, also support the World Zoroastrian Organization. There are several local associations of Iranian Zoroastrians in North America, primarily along the Canadian and U.S. west coasts.

As early as 1962, a World Zoroastrian Congress was held in Tehran, Iran. Successive congresses have been held irregularly, the ninth meeting having been in Dubai in 2009.

J. Gordon Melton

See also: World Zoroastrian Organization.

References

Boyce, Mary. *A History of Zoroastrianism.* 3 vols. Leiden: Brill, 1975, 1982, 1991.

Boyce, Mary. *Zoroastrians: Their Religious Beliefs and Practices.* London: Routledge, 2001.

Geldner, K. *Avesta: The Sacred Books of the Parsis.* 3 vols. Stuttgart, Germany: Kohlhammer, 1986.

Hinnells, John R. *Zoroastrians in Britain.* Oxford: Clarendon, 1996.

Kriwaczek, Paul. *In Search of Zarathustra: Across Iran and Central Asia to Find the World's First Prophet.* New York: Vintage, 2004.

Nigosian, S. A. *The Zoroastrian Faith: Tradition and Modern Research*. Montreal: McGill-Queen's University Press, 1993.

Writer, R. *Contemporary Zoroastrians: An Unstructured Nation*. Lanham, MD: University Press of America, 1994.

Zulu Religion

The Zulu people are one of the Bantu groups that migrated into what is now South Africa at some unknown point in the last two millennia. They date their own origin myth from a chief named Malandela, who had a son named Zulu who became the head of his own clan. He brought his clan to the Mfolosi Valley, north of the Thuleka River in present-day Natal. The Zulu people then entered into history with the emergence generations later of Shaka (1785–1828). A remarkable leader, Shaka reorganized the Zulus and turned them into a notable military force. His kingdom eventually covered some 11,000 square miles of territory. The British attacked the Zulu kingdom in 1879, captured the chief, Cetshwayo, and sent him into exile. In 1897, Zulu land was annexed and passed to the newly created Union of South Africa. The Zulu were pushed into a small "reserve" while most of their land was settled by whites.

The Zulu trace their ancestry to Inkosi Yezulu, the Sky God, also known as Umvelingqangi. The male Sky God and his female counterpart, Earth, brought forth the people, Abuntu, though the exact process of creation is not clear. Also important to the Zulu are the ancestral spirits, especially those of outstanding chiefs, local village headmen, and men, in that order. The departed souls of the ancestors are known collectively as the *amalozi* or *amathinga*, and are pictured as residing in the earth but still having an active role in the life of their present progeny.

Various ritual figures are designated to assist the process of relating positively to the spirit world. At each village, the headman (*umnumzane*) serves as both secular and religious leader. He serves as priest, focusing the devotion of his people to the ancestors, and he symbolizes the chief's ancestors to the people. He is present at almost all ritual occasions. Diviners, most often women, deal with human problems by using their divinatory skills to find the cause of the problem. They work hand-in-hand with an herbalist (usually a man) who prescribes the cure once the problem is found. Herbalists are usually specialists in either medicine (*izinyanga zemithi*) or healing (*izinyanga zokwelapha*). Zulu medicine today is a mixture of traditional healing practices and Western medicine. Finally, attention to the ritual chores is completed by the *izinyanya zezula*, a specialist in relating to the sky, a function that evolved in part because of the thunderstorms that are important in local weather.

Less formally active in Zulu religion are the sorcerers, often herbalists who also have a knowledge of magic, though anyone may be a sorcerer. The sorcerer uses magic to redress a grievance. Finally, there is the witch, a person, usually believed to be female, who is thought to be living a concealed existence in the village. The witch is one who uses magic for evil and inappropriate ends. The witch is judged to be present by the manifest evil consequences of her actions.

Ritual activity for the Zulu happens most frequently in the circular villages called *kraals,* typically built on the side of a hill with the entrance facing down the slope. In the center of the kraal are the very important cattle herds. On the west side, at the highest point in the kraal, is the home of the headman, and adjacent to his house is the *umsamo*, the most important ritual center for the community. The umsamo is the place for communing with the ancestors. The surrounding hills of Zulu land (those unoccupied by kraals) provide the sites for special rituals, including those that invoke the Sky God.

Most Zulu ritual is about power (*amandla*), its use (and misuse). Power is derived from the Sky God, the ancestors, and medicine. Ritual connects with the source of the power that sustains life and creates order. Witches, of course, pervert the power.

Today's 4 million (some estimate as many as 6 million) Zulu live across South Africa, but they are concentrated in Kwazulu, the name of the old reserve. The royal house originally established by Shaka still exists, and the Zulu nation's current king is Zwelithini Goodwill KaCyprian Bhekuzulu. At various points in the 20th century, the Zulu king was an important voice challenging South Africa's racial policies.

Christian missions were first established among the Zulu in the 19th century, and today many Zulu mix life as a member of a Christian church with traditional rituals and varying levels of belief. Out of the conflict between Christianity and traditional beliefs have come some new African Initiated Churches, the Nazareth (Nazarite) Baptist Church being the most prominent.

J. Gordon Melton

See also: Ancestors; Nazareth (Nazarite) Baptist Church; Witchcraft.

References

Berglund, Axel-Ivar. *Zulu Thought-patterns and Symbolism.* London: C. Hurst, 1976.

Hexham, Irving. *Texts on Zulu Religion: Traditional Zulu Ideas About God.* Lewiston, NY: Edwin Mellen Press, 1988.

Lawson, E. Thomas. *Religions of Africa.* San Francisco: HarperSanFrancisco, 1985.

Von Kapff, Uli. *Zulu: People of Heaven.* Cape Town: Holiday Africa, 1997.

"Zulu Information and Links." http://www.zulupage .co.za/index-ien.html, Accessed November 1, 2001.

Zwemer, Samuel Marinus

1867–1952

Samuel Marinus Zwemer was a pioneer Protestant missionary in the Middle East, author, and missiologist scholar. He opened the first Protestant churches in several Middle Eastern countries and finished his career as a prominent theorist of the Christian missionary enterprise.

Zwemer was born April 12, 1867, in Vriesland, Michigan. He graduated from Hope College (A.B, 1887) and New Brunswick Theological Seminary (M.A., 1890). Following graduation he was ordained as a minister in the Reformed Church in America by the Pella (Iowa) Classis.

Before his graduation, Zwemer joined fellow student James Cantine in a decision to become missionaries. They had been inspired by bicycle racing champion Ion Keith-Falconer (1856–1887), who had left his affluent life to master Arabic and open a small mission in Aden, Yemen. He died of malaria soon after he settled into his work. The pair decided to concentrate their efforts on the Middle East and become missionaries to the Islamic world. They were initially unable to find any agency willing to sponsor them, and as a result founded a new independent organization, the American Arabian Mission. Only in the mid-1890s, after they had launched their work, did the Reformed Church agree to sponsor the Mission.

Zwemer began his career in 1890 in Beirut, where he began to master Arabic and then moved on to Aden, where he found that the Church of Scotland had assumed sponsorship of the Keith-Falconer mission. It accepted Zwemer's assumption of the late missionary's position. Among his first tasks was the formation of a hospital. Within a few years the Reformed Church added its resources, enabling Zwemer to open additional hospitals in Bahrain, Kuwait, Muscat (Oman), and Basrah (Iraq). Operating in an atmosphere where direct proselytization was prohibited, maintaining the hospitals and operating associated bookrooms from which Bibles and Christian literature could be distributed became the main job of the Mission.

In Iraq in 1896, Zwemer met Anglican missionary Amy Elizabeth Wilkes. They were wed shortly thereafter and made their home in Bahrain. Zwemer wrote his first book, *Arabia: Cradle of Islam,* in 1900. In 1911 he would become the founding editor of *The Moslem World,* a quarterly journal that filled a significant information gap for English-speaking scholars. He would continue his editing task for 37 years. In 1913, Zwemer moved his headquarters to Egypt, where he remained until 1929.

When he returned to the United States in 1929, Zwemer was acknowledged by all as the foremost authority on the Christian missionary enterprise in the Muslim world. He accepted a position as the professor of history of religions and Christian missions at Princeton Theological Seminary. He remained at Princeton for the next decade, during which time he wrote the bulk of his more than 50 books he produced during his career. He retired in 1939. He lived in New York City, where he remained active in writing, editing and teaching for another decade. He died in New York City on April 2, 1952, still dealing with the problem of how Christians could effectively evangelize within the Muslim context.

J. Gordon Melton

See also: Reformed Church in America.

References

Wilson, J. Christy. *Apostle to Islam: A Biography of Samuel M. Zwemer*. Grand Rapids, MI: Baker Book House, 1952.

Zwemer, Samuel M. *Across the World of Islam.* New York: Fleming H. Revell Company, 1939.

Zwemer, Samuel M. *Arabia: The Cradle of Islam.* New York: Fleming H. Revell, 1900.

Zwemer, Samuel M. *The Cross Above the Crescent: The Validity, Necessity and Urgency of Missions to Moslems.* Grand Rapids, MI: Zondervan, 1941.

Zwemer, Samuel M. *Evangelism Today: Message Not Method.* New York: Fleming H. Revell, 1944.

Zwemer, Samuel M. *The Influence of Animism on Islam: An Account of Popular Superstitions.* New York: The Macmillan Company, 1920.

Index